THE

EXPOSITOR'S

BIBLE

COMMENTARY

REVISED EDITION

Daniel ~ Malachi

Tremper Longman III & David E. Garland

General Editors

ZONDERVAN.com/
AUTHORTRACKER
follow your favorite authors

ZONDERVAN

The Expositor's Bible Commentary: Daniel-Malachi

Daniel — Copyright © 2008 by Andrew E. Hill
Hosea — Copyright © 2008 by M. Daniel Carroll R. (Rodas)
Joel — Copyright © 2008 by Richard D. Patterson
Amos and Micah — Copyright © 2008 by Thomas E. McComiskey and Tremper Longman III
Obadiah, Nahum, and Habakkuk — Copyright © 2008 by Carl E. Armerding
Jonah — Copyright © 2008 by John H. Walton
Zephaniah — Copyright © 2008 by Larry L. Walker
Haggai and Malachi — Copyright © 2008 by Eugene H. Merrill
Zechariah — Copyright © 2008 by Kenneth L. Barker

Requests for information should be addressed to:
Zondervan, *Grand Rapids, Michigan 49530*

IBSN 978-0-310-26893-2 (hardcover)

Printed in the United States of America

13 14 15 16 17 18 19 /DCI/ 25 24 23 22 21 20 19 18 17 16 15 14 13 12 11 10 9 8 7 6 5 4 3

CONTENTS

CONTRIBUTORS TO VOLUME EIGHT

Daniel: **Andrew E. Hill** (PhD, University of Michigan) is professor of Old Testament studies at Wheaton College in Wheaton, Illinois. He is the coauthor with John Walton of *A Survey of the Old Testament* and the author of *Malachi* in the Anchor Bible commentary series.

Hosea: **M. Daniel Carroll R. (Rodas)** (PhD, University of Sheffield) is Distinguished Professor of Old Testament at Denver Seminary in Colorado and adjunct professor at El Seminario Teológico Centroamericano in Guatemala City, Guatemala. He has published *Contexts for Amos: Prophetic Poetics in Latin American Perspective* (T. & T. Clark) and *Amos — the Prophet and His Oracles: Research on the Book of Amos* (Westminster John Knox), and regularly writes for Spanish and English language journals.

Joel: **Richard D. Patterson** (PhD, University of California, Los Angeles) is distinguished professor emeritus of Liberty University. He has written well over 100 articles for major publishers and periodicals and served as associate editor of Zondervan's *New International Dictionary of Old Testament Theology and Exegesis*.

Amos and Micah: The late **Thomas E. McComiskey** was professor of Old Testament and Semitic languages and director of the PhD program at Trinity Evangelical Divinity School.

Obadiah, Nahum, and Habakkuk: **Carl E. Armerding** (PhD, Brandeis University) is professor emeritus of Old Testament at Regent College.

Jonah: **John H. Walton** (PhD, Hebrew Union College) is professor of Old Testament at Wheaton College Graduate School. He is the author or coauthor of several books, including *Chronological and Background Charts of the Old Testament*; *Ancient Israelite Literature in Its Cultural Context*; *Covenant: God's Purpose, God's Plan*; and *A Survey of the Old Testament*.

Zephaniah: **Larry L. Walker** (PhD, Dropsie College for Hebrew and Cognate Learning) was professor of Old Testament at Southwestern Theological Seminary and Mid-America Theological Seminary. He has been an active member of the Committee on Bible Translation, which produced the NIV and TNIV.

Haggai and Malachi: **Eugene H. Merrill** (PhD, Columbia University) is distinguished professor of Old Testament studies at Dallas Theological Seminary.

Zechariah: **Kenneth L. Barker** (PhD, Dropsie College for Hebrew and Cognate Learning) is an author, lecturer, biblical scholar, and the general editor of *The NIV Study Bible*.

General editor: **Tremper Longman III** (PhD, Yale University) is Robert H. Gundry professor of biblical studies at Westmont College in Santa Barbara, California.

General editor: **David E. Garland** (PhD, Southern Baptist Theological Seminary) is associate dean of academic affairs and William M. Hinson professor of Christian Scriptures at George W. Truett Seminary, Baylor University, in Waco, Texas.

PREFACE

Frank Gaebelein wrote the following in the preface to the original Expositor's Bible Commentary (which first appeared in 1979): "The title of this work defines its purpose. Written primarily by expositors for expositors, it aims to provide preachers, teachers, and students of the Bible with a new and comprehensive commentary on the books of the Old and New Testaments." Those volumes achieved that purpose admirably. The original EBC was exceptionally well received and had an enormous impact on the life of the church. It has served as the mainstay of countless pastors and students who could not afford an extensive library on each book of the Bible but who wanted solid guidance from scholars committed to the authority of the Holy Scriptures.

Gaebelein also wrote, "A commentary that will continue to be useful through the years should handle contemporary trends in biblical studies in such a way as to avoid becoming outdated when critical fashions change." This revision continues the EBC's exalted purpose and stands on the shoulders of the expositors of the first edition, but it seeks to maintain the usefulness of the commentary by interacting with new discoveries and academic discussions. While the primary goal of this commentary is to elucidate the text and not to provide a guide to the scholarly literature about the text, the commentators critically engage recent academic discussion and provide updated bibliographies so that pastors, teachers, and students can keep abreast of modern scholarship.

Some of the commentaries in the EBC have been revised by the original author or in conjunction with a younger colleague. In other cases, scholars have been commissioned to offer fresh commentaries because the original author had passed on or wanted to pass on the baton to the next generation of evangelical scholars. Today, with commentaries on a single book of the Old and New Testaments often extending into multiple volumes, the need for a comprehensive yet succinct commentary that guides one to the gist of the text's meaning is even more pressing. The new EBC seeks to fill this need.

The theological stance of this commentary series remains unchanged: the authors are committed to the divine inspiration, complete trustworthiness, and full authority of the Bible. The commentators have demonstrated proficiency in the biblical book that is their specialty, as well as commitment to the church and the pastoral dimension of biblical interpretation. They also represent the geographical and confessional diversity that characterized the first contributors.

The commentaries adhere to the same chief principle of grammatico-historical interpretation that drove the first edition. In the foreword to the inaugural issue of the journal *New Testament Studies* in 1954, Matthew Black warned that "the danger in the present is that theology, with its head too high in the clouds, may end by falling into the pit of an unhistorical and uncritical dogmatism. Into any new theological undertaking must be brought all that was best in the old ideal of sound learning, scrupulous attention to philology, text and history." The dangers that Black warned against over fifty years ago have not vanished. Indeed, new dangers arise in a secular, consumerist culture that finds it more acceptable to use God's name in exclamations than in prayer and that encourages insipid theologies that hang in the wind and shift to tickle the ears and to meet the latest fancy. Only a solid biblical foundation can fend off these fads.

The Bible was not written for our information but for our transformation. It is not a quarry to find stones with which to batter others but to find the rock on which to build the church. It does not invite us simply to speak of God but to hear God and to confess that his Son, Jesus Christ, is Lord to the glory of God the Father (Php 2:10). It also calls us to obey his commandments (Mt 28:20). It is not a self-interpreting text, however. Interpretation of the Holy Scriptures requires sound learning and regard for history, language, and text. Exegetes must interpret not only the primary documents but all that has a bearing, direct or indirect, on the grammar and syntax, historical context, transmission, and translation of these writings.

The translation used in this commentary remains the New International Version (North American edition), but all of the commentators work from the original languages (Hebrew and Greek) and draw on other translations when deemed useful. The format is also very similar to the original EBC, while the design is extensively updated with a view to enhanced ease of use for the reader. Each commentary section begins with an introduction (printed in a single-column format) that provides the reader with the background necessary to understand the Bible book. Almost all introductions include a short bibliography and an outline. The Bible text is divided into primary units that are often explained in an "Overview" section that precedes commentary on specific verses. The complete text of the New International Version is provided for quick reference, and an extensive "Commentary" section (printed in a double-column format) follows the reproducing of the text. When the Hebrew or Greek text is cited in the commentary section, a phonetic system of transliteration and translation is used. The "Notes" section (printed in a single-column format) provides a specialized discussion of key words or concepts, as well as helpful resource information. The original languages and their transliterations will appear in this section. Finally, on occasion, expanded thoughts can be found in a "Reflections" section (printed in a double-column format) that follows the Notes section.

One additional feature is worth mentioning. Throughout this volume, wherever specific biblical words are discussed, the Goodrick-Kohlenberger (GK) numbers have been added. These numbers, which appear in the *Strongest NIV Exhaustive Concordance* and other reference tools, are based on the numbering system developed by Edward Goodrick and John Kohlenberger III and provide a system similar but superior to the Strong's numbering system.

The editors wish to thank all of the contributors for their hard work and commitment to this project. We also deeply appreciate the labor and skill of the staff at Zondervan. It is a joy to work with them—in particular Jack Kuhatschek, Stan Gundry, Katya Covrett, Dirk Buursma, and Verlyn Verbrugge. In addition, we acknowledge with thanks the work of Connie Gundry Tappy as copy editor.

We all fervently desire that these commentaries will result not only in a deeper intellectual grasp of the Word of God but also in hearts that more profoundly love and obey the God who reveals himself to us in its pages.

David E. Garland, associate dean for academic affairs and
William M. Hinson professor of Christian Scriptures, George W.
Truett Theological Seminary at Baylor University

Tremper Longman III, Robert H. Gundry professor of biblical
studies, Westmont College

ABBREVIATIONS

Bible Texts, Versions, Etc.

ASV	American Standard Version	NET	New English Translation (www.netbible.com)
AT	*The Complete Bible: An American Translation* (NT: E. J. Goodspeed)	NIV	New International Version
Barclay	*The New Testament, A New Translation*	NJB	New Jerusalem Bible
		NJPS	New Jewish Publication Society
Beck	*New Testament in Language of Today*	NKJV	New King James Version
		NLT	New Living Translation
BHS	*Biblia Hebraica Stuttgartensia*	Norlie	*New Testament in Modern English*
CEV	Contemporary English Version	NRSV	New Revised Standard Version
CSB	Christian Standard Bible	Phillips	*New Testament in Modern English*, J. B. Phillips
ESV	English Standard Version		
GNB	Good News Bible (see also TEV)	REB	Revised English Bible
GWT	God's Word Translation	Rieu	*Penguin Bible*
JB	Jerusalem Bible	RSV	Revised Standard Version
KJV	King James Version	RV	Revised Version
Knox	*Holy Bible: A Translation from the Latin Vulgate*	TCNT	Twentieth Century New Testament
MLB	Modern Language Bible	TEV	Today's English Version
Moffatt	*A New Translation of the Bible,* James Moffatt	TNIV	Today's New International Version
Montgomery	*Centenary Translation of the New Testament in Modern English*	TNK	Tanak (Jewish translation of the Hebrew Bible)
NA27	*Novum Testamentum Graece,* Nestle-Aland, 27th ed.	UBS4	*The Greek New Testament,* United Bible Societies, 4th ed.
NAB	New American Bible	Weymouth	*New Testament in Modern Speech,* R. F. Weymouth
NASB	New American Standard Bible		
NCV	New Century Version	Williams	*The New Testament in the Language of the People,* C. B. Williams
NEB	New English Bible		

Old Testament, New Testament, Apocrypha

Ge	Genesis	Dt	Deuteronomy
Ex	Exodus	Jos	Joshua
Lev	Leviticus	Jdg	Judges
Nu	Numbers	Ru	Ruth

1–2Sa	1–2 Samuel	Ac	Acts
1–2 Kgdms	1–2 Kingdoms (LXX)	Ro	Romans
1–2Ki	1–2 Kings	1–2Co	1–2 Corinthians
3–4 Kgdms	3–4 Kingdoms (LXX)	Gal	Galatians
1–2Ch	1–2 Chronicles	Eph	Ephesians
Ezr	Ezra	Php	Philippians
Ne	Nehemiah	Col	Colossians
Est	Esther	1–2Th	1–2 Thessalonians
Job	Job	1–2Ti	1–2 Timothy
Ps/Pss	Psalm/Psalms	Tit	Titus
Pr	Proverbs	Phm	Philemon
Ecc	Ecclesiastes	Heb	Hebrews
SS	Song of Songs	Jas	James
Isa	Isaiah	1–2Pe	1–2 Peter
Jer	Jeremiah	1–2–3Jn	1–2–3 John
La	Lamentations	Jude	Jude
Eze	Ezekiel	Rev	Revelation
Da	Daniel	Add Esth	Additions to Esther
Hos	Hosea	Add Dan	Additions to Daniel
Joel	Joel	Bar	Baruch
Am	Amos	Bel	Bel and the Dragon
Ob	Obadiah	Ep Jer	Epistle of Jeremiah
Jnh	Jonah	1–2 Esd	1–2 Esdras
Mic	Micah	1–2 Macc	1–2 Maccabees
Na	Nahum	3–4 Macc	3–4 Maccabees
Hab	Habakkuk	Jdt	Judith
Zep	Zephaniah	Pr Azar	Prayer of Azariah
Hag	Haggai	Pr Man	Prayer of Manasseh
Zec	Zechariah	Ps 151	Psalm 151
Mal	Malachi	Sir	Sirach/Ecclesiasticus
Mt	Matthew	Sus	Susanna
Mk	Mark	Tob	Tobit
Lk	Luke	Wis	Wisdom of Solomon
Jn	John		

Dead Sea Scrolls and Related Texts

CD	Cairo Genizah copy of the *Damascus Document*	1QapGen	*Genesis Apocryphon* (texts from Qumran)
DSS	Dead Sea Scrolls		

1QH	*Hôdāyōt* or *Thanksgiving Hymns* (texts from Qumran)	4Q44 (4QDt^q)	Deuteronomy (texts from Qumran)
1QIsa	Isaiah (texts from Qumran)	4Q174	*Florilegium* (texts from Qumran)
1QM	*Milḥāmāh* or *War Scroll* (texts from Qumran)	4Q252	*Commentary on Genesis A*, formerly *Patriarchal Blessings* (texts from Qumran)
1QpHab	Pesher Habakkuk (texts from Qumran)		
1QS	*Serek hayyaḥad* or *Rule of the Community* (texts from Qumran)	4Q394	*Miqṣat Maʿaśê ha-Torah^a* (texts from Qumran)
1QSa	*Rule of the Congregation* (texts from Qumran)	4Q400	*Songs of the Sabbath Sacrifice* (texts from Qumran)
1QpMic	*Pesher Micah* (text from Qumran)	4Q502	*Ritual of Marriage* (texts from Qumran)
4QpNa	*Pesher Nahum* (texts from Qumran)	4Q521	*Messianic Apocalypse* (texts from Qumran)
4QpPs	*Pesher Psalms* (texts from Qumran)	4Q525	*Beatitudes* (texts from Qumran)
		11QPs^a	*Psalms Scroll^a*
4QQoh^{a,b}	Qoheleth (Ecclesiastes)	11Q13	*Melchizedek* (texts from Qumran)

Other Ancient Texts

Abraham	*On the Life of Abraham* (Philo)	*Ascen. Isa.*	*Ascension of Isaiah*
Ad.	*Adelphi* (Terence)	*As. Mos.*	*Assumption of Moses*
Aeth.	*Aethiopica* (Heliodorus)	*Att.*	*Epistulae ad Atticum* (Cicero)
Ag.	*Agamemnon* (Aeschylus)	*b. ʿAbod. Zar.*	*ʿAbodah Zarah* (Babylonian Talmud)
Ag. Ap.	*Against Apion* (Josephus)		
Agr.	*De Lege agraria* (Cicero)	*2–4 Bar.*	*2–4 Baruch*
Alc.	*Alcibiades* (Plutarch)	*b. B. Bat.*	*Bava Batra* (Babylonian Talmud)
Alex.	*Alexander the False Prophet* (Lucian)	*b. Ber.*	*Berakhot* (Babylonian Talmud)
		b. Ketub.	*Ketubbot* (Babylonian Talmud)
Amic.	*De amicitia* (Cicero)	*b. Meg.*	*Megillah* (Babylonian Talmud)
An.	*De anima* (Tertullian)	*b. Ned.*	*Nedarim* (Babylonian Talmud)
Anab.	*Anabasis* (Xenophon)	*b. Pesaḥ.*	*Pesaḥim* (Babylonian Talmud)
Ann.	*Annales* (Tacitus)	*b. Roš Haš.*	*Roš Haššanah* (Babylonian Talmud)
Ant.	*Antigone* (Sophocles)		
Ant.	*Jewish Antiquities* (Josephus)	*b. Šabb.*	*Šabbat* (Babylonian Talmud)
Ant. rom.	*Antiquitates romanae* (Dionysius of Halicarnassus)	*b. Sanh.*	*Sanhedrin* (Babylonian Talmud)
		b. Šebu.	*Šebuʾot* (Babylonian Talmud)
1 Apol.	*First Apology* (Justin Martyr)	*b. Soṭah*	*Soṭah* (Babylonian Talmud)
Apol.	*Apologia* (Plato, Tertullian)	*b. Taʿan.*	*Taʿanit* (Babylonian Talmud)
Apos. Con.	*Apostolic Constitutions*	*b. Yebam.*	*Yebamot* (Babylonian Talmud)

Bapt.	*De baptismo* (Tertullian)	*Ep. Tra.*	*Epistulae ad Trajanum* (Pliny)
Barn.	*Barnabas*	*Eth. nic.*	*Ethica nichomachea* (Aristotle)
Ben.	*De beneficiis* (Seneca)	*Exod. Rab.*	*Exodus Rabbah*
Bibl.	*Bibliotheca* (Photius)	*Fam.*	*Epistulae ad familiares* (Cicero)
Bibl. hist.	*Bibliotheca historica* (Diodorus Siculus)	*Fid. Grat.*	*De fide ad Gratianum* (Ambrose)
		Flacc.	*In Flaccum* (Philo)
Bride	*Advice to the Bride and Groom* (Plutarch)	*Flight*	*On Flight and Finding* (Philo)
		Fr. Prov.	*Fragmenta in Proverbia* (Hippolytus)
Cels.	*Contra Celsum* (Origen)	*Gen. Rab.*	*Genesis Rabbah*
Cic.	*Cicero* (Plutarch)	*Geogr.*	*Geographica* (Strabo)
Claud.	*Divus Claudius* (Suetonius)	*Gorg.*	*Gorgias* (Plato)
1–2 Clem.	*1–2 Clement*	*Haer.*	*Adversus Haereses* (Irenaeus)
Comm. Dan.	*Commentarium in Danielem* (Hippolytus)	*Heir*	*Who Is the Heir?* (Philo)
		Hell.	*Hellenica* (Xenophon)
Comm. Jo.	*Commentarii in evangelium Joannis* (Origen)	*Hist.*	*Historicus* (Polybius, Cassius Dio, Thucydides)
Comm. Matt.	*Commentarium in evangelium Matthaei* (Origen)	*Hist.*	*Historiae* (Herodotus, Tacitus)
		Hist. eccl.	*History of the Church* (Eusebius)
Corrept.	*De correptione et gratia* (Augustine)	*Hist. Rome*	*The History of Rome* (Livy)
Cyr.	*Cyropaedia* (Xenophon)	*Hom. Acts*	*Homilies on Acts* (John Chrysostom)
Decal.	*De decalogo* (Philo)	*Hom. Col.*	*Homilies on Colossians* (John Chrysostom)
Decl.	*Declamationes* (Quintilian)		
Def. orac.	*De defectu oraculorum* (Plutarch)	*Hom. Jo.*	*Homilies on John* (John Chrysostom)
Deipn.	*Deipnosophistae* (Athenaeus)		
Deut. Rab.	*Deuteronomy Rabbah*	*Hom. Josh.*	*Homilies on Joshua* (Origen)
Dial.	*Dialogus cum Tryphone* (Justin Martyr)	*Hom. Phil.*	*Homilies on Philippians* (John Chrysostom)
Diatr.	*Diatribai* (Epictetus)	*Hom. Rom.*	*Homilies on Romans* (John Chrysostom)
Did.	*Didache*		
Disc.	*Discourses* (Epictetus)	*Hom. 1 Tim.*	*Homilies on 1 Timothy* (John Chrysostom)
Doctr. chr.	*De doctrina christiana* (Augustine)		
Dom.	*Domitianus* (Suetonius)	*Hom. 2 Tim.*	*Homilies on 2 Timothy* (John Chrysostom)
Ebr.	*De ebrietate* (Philo)		
E Delph.	*De E apud Delphos* (Plutarch)	*Hom. Tit.*	*Homilies on Titus* (John Chrysostom)
1–2 En.	*1–2 Enoch*		
Ench.	*Enchiridion* (Epictetus)	*Hypoth.*	*Hypothetica* (Philo)
Ep.	*Epistulae morales* (Seneca)	*Inst.*	*Institutio oratoria* (Quintilian)
Eph.	*To the Ephesians* (Ignatius)	*Jos. Asen.*	*Joseph and Aseneth*
Epist.	*Epistulae* (Jerome, Pliny, Hippocrates)	*Joseph*	*On the Life of Joseph* (Philo)

Jub.	*Jubilees*	*Pesiq. Rab.*	*Pesiqta Rabbati*
J.W.	*Jewish War* (Josephus)	*Pesiq. Rab Kah.*	*Pesiqta of Rab Kahana*
L.A.E.	*Life of Adam and Eve*	*Phaed.*	*Phaedo* (Plato)
Leg.	*Legum allegoriae* (Philo)	*Phil.*	*To the Philippians* (Polycarp)
Legat.	*Legatio ad Gaium* (Philo)	*Phld.*	*To the Philadelphians* (Ignatius)
Let. Aris.	*Letter of Aristeas*	*Phorm.*	*Phormio* (Terence)
Lev. Rab.	*Leviticus Rabbah*	*Planc.*	*Pro Plancio* (Cicero)
Liv. Pro.	*Lives of the Prophets*	*Plant.*	*De plantatione* (Philo)
m. ʾAbot	*ʾAbot* (Mishnah)	*Pol.*	*Politica* (Aristotle)
m. Bek.	*Bekhorot* (Mishnah)	*Pol.*	*To Polycarp* (Ignatius)
m. Ber.	*Berakot* (Mishnah)	*Posterity*	*On the Posterity of Cain* (Origen)
m. Bik.	*Bikkurim* (Mishnah)	*Praescr.*	*De praescriptione haereticorum* (Tertullian)
m. Giṭ.	*Giṭṭin* (Mishnah)		
m. Mak.	*Makkot* (Mishnah)	*Princ.*	*De principiis* (Origen)
m. Mid.	*Middot* (Mishnah)	*Prom.*	*Prometheus vinctus* (Aeschylus)
m. Naz.	*Nazir* (Mishnah)	*Pss. Sol.*	*Psalms of Solomon*
m. Ned.	*Nedarim* (Mishnah)	*Pud.*	*De pudicitia* (Tertullian)
m. Nid.	*Niddah* (Mishnah)	*Pyth.*	*Pythionikai* (Pindar)
m. Pesaḥ	*Pesaḥim* (Mishnah)	*Pyth. orac.*	*De Pythiae oraculis* (Plutarch)
m. Šabb.	*Šabbat* (Mishnah)	*Quaest. conv.*	*Quaestionum convivialum libri IX* (Plutarch)
m. Sanh.	*Sanhedrin* (Mishnah)		
m. Taʿan.	*Taʿanit* (Mishnah)	*Quint. fratr.*	*Epistulae ad Quintum fratrem* (Cicero)
m. Tamid	*Tamid* (Mishnah)		
m. Ṭehar.	*Ṭeharot* (Mishnah)	*Rab. Perd.*	*Pro Rabirio Perduellionis Reo* (Cicero)
Magn.	*To the Magnesians* (Ignatius)		
Mand.	*Mandate* (Shepherd of Hermas)	*Resp.*	*Respublica* (Plato)
Marc.	*Adversus Marcionem* (Tertullian)	*Rewards*	*On Rewards and Punishments* (Philo)
Mem.	*Memorabilia* (Xenophon)		
Midr. Ps.	*Midrash on Psalms*	*Rhet.*	*Rhetorica* (Aristotle)
Migr.	*De migratione Abrahami* (Philo)	*Rhet.*	*Volumina rhetorica* (Philodemus)
Mor.	*Moralia* (Plutarch)	*Rom.*	*To the Romans* (Ignatius)
Moses	*On the Life of Moses* (Philo)	*Rosc. com.*	*Pro Roscio comoedo* (Cicero)
Nat.	*Naturalis historia* (Pliny)	*Sacrifices*	*On the Sacrifices of Cain and Abel* (Philo)
Num. Rab.	*Numbers Rabbah*		
Onir.	*Onirocritica* (Artemidorus)	*Sat.*	*Satirae* (Horace, Juvenal)
Or.	*Orationes* (Demosthenes)	*Sera*	*De sera numinis vindicta* (Plutarch)
Or.	*Orationes* (Dio Chrysostom)	*Serm.*	*Sermones* (Augustine)
Paed.	*Paedagogus* (Clement of Alexandria)	*Sib. Or.*	*Sibylline Oracles*
		Sim.	*Similitudes* (Shepherd of Hermas)
Peregr.	*The Passing of Peregrinus* (Lucian)	*Smyrn.*	*To the Smyrnaeans* (Ignatius)

Somn.	*De somniis* (Philo)	*T. Levi*	*Testament of Levi*
Spec.	*De specialibus legibus* (Philo)	*T. Mos.*	*Testament of Moses*
Stat.	*Ad populum Antiochenum de statuis* (John Chrysostom)	*T. Naph.*	*Testament of Naphtali*
		Trall.	*To the Trallians* (Ignatius)
Strom.	*Stromata* (Clement of Alexandria)	*T. Reu.*	*Testament of Reuben*
T. Ash.	*Testament of Asher*	*Tusc.*	*Tusculanae disputationes* (Cicero)
T. Dan	*Testament of Dan*	*Verr.*	*In Verrem* (Cicero)
T. Gad	*Testament of Gad*	*Virt.*	*De virtutibus* (Philo)
Tg. Neof.	*Targum Neofiti*	*Vis.*	*Visions* (Shepherd of Hermas)
Tg. Onq.	*Targum Onqelos*	*Vit. Apoll.*	*Vita Apollonii* (Philostratus)
Tg. Ps.-J.	*Targum Pseudo-Jonathan*	*Vit. beat.*	*De vita beata* (Seneca)
Theaet.	*Theaetetus* (Plato)	*Vit. soph.*	*Vitae sophistarum* (Philostratus)
t. Ḥul.	*Ḥullin* (Tosefta)	*y. ʿAbod. Zar.*	*ʿAbodah Zarah* (Jerusalem Talmud)
t. Sanh.	*Sanhedrin* (Tosefta)		
T. Jos.	*Testament of Joseph*	*y. Ḥag.*	*Ḥagigah* (Jerusalem Talmud)
T. Jud.	*Testament of Judah*	*y. Šabb.*	*Šabbat* (Jerusalem Talmud)

Journals, Periodicals, Reference Works, Series

AASOR	Annual of the American Schools of Oriental Research	ANF	*Ante-Nicene Fathers*
		AnOr	Analecta orientalia
AB	Anchor Bible	*ANRW*	*Aufstieg und Niedergang der römischen Welt*
ABD	*Anchor Bible Dictionary*		
ABR	*Australian Biblical Review*	ASORMS	American Schools of Oriental Research Monograph Series
ABRL	Anchor Bible Reference Library		
ABW	*Archaeology in the Biblical World*	*ASTI*	*Annual of the Swedish Theological Institute*
ACCS	Ancient Christian Commentary on Scripture		
		AThR	*Anglican Theological Review*
ACNT	Augsburg Commentaries on the New Testament	AUSDDS	Andrews University Seminary Doctoral Dissertation Series
AEL	*Ancient Egyptian Literature*	*AUSS*	*Andrews University Seminary Studies*
AJBI	*Annual of the Japanese Biblical Institute*		
		BA	*Biblical Archaeologist*
AJSL	*American Journal of Semitic Languages and Literature*	BAGD	Bauer, Arndt, Gingrich, and Danker (2d ed.). *Greek-English Lexicon of the New Testament and Other Early Christian Literature*
AnBib	Analecta biblica		
ANEP	*The Ancient Near East in Pictures Relating to the Old Testament*		
		BAR	*Biblical Archaeology Review*
ANET	*Ancient Near Eastern Texts Relating to the Old Testament*	*BASOR*	*Bulletin of the American Schools of Oriental Research*

BBCOT	*Bible Background Commentary on the Old Testament*	RT	*The Bible Translator*
BBR	*Bulletin for Biblical Research*	BTB	*Biblical Theology Bulletin*
BDAG	Bauer, Danker, Arndt, and Gingrich (3d ed.). *Greek-English Lexicon of the New Testament and Other Early Christian Literature*	BZ	*Biblische Zeitschrift*
		BZAW	Beihefte zur Zeitschrift für die alttestamentliche Wissenschaft
		BZNW	Beihefte zur Zeitschrift für die neutestamentliche Wissenschaft
BDB	Brown, Driver, and Briggs. *A Hebrew and English Lexicon of the Old Testament*	CAD	*Assyrian Dictionary of the Oriental Institute of the University of Chicago*
BDF	Blass, Debrunner, and Funk. *A Greek Grammar of the New Testament and Other Early Christian Literature*	CAH	Cambridge Ancient History
		CahRB	Cahiers de la Revue biblique
		CBC	Cambridge Bible Commentary
		CBQ	*Catholic Biblical Quarterly*
BEB	*Baker Encyclopedia of the Bible*	CGTC	Cambridge Greek Testament Commentary
BECNT	Baker Exegetical Commentary on the New Testament	CH	*Church History*
Ber	*Berytus*	ChrT	*Christianity Today*
BETL	Bibliotheca ephemeridum theologicarum lovaniensium	CIG	*Corpus inscriptionum graecarum*
		CIL	*Corpus inscriptionum latinarum*
BGU	*Aegyptische Urkunden aus den Königlichen Staatlichen Museen zu Berlin, Griechische Urkunden*	CJT	*Canadian Journal of Theology*
		ConBNT	Coniectanea biblica: New Testament Series
BI	*Biblical Illustrator*	ConBOT	Coniectanea biblica: Old Testament Series
Bib	*Biblica*		
BibInt	*Biblical Interpretation*	COS	*The Context of Scripture*
BibOr	Biblica et orientalia	CTJ	*Calvin Theological Journal*
BibS(N)	Biblische Studien (Neukirchen)	CTM	*Concordia Theological Monthly*
Bijdr	*Bijdragen: Tijdschrit voor filosofie en theologie*	CTQ	*Concordia Theological Quarterly*
		CTR	*Criswell Theological Review*
BJRL	*Bulletin of the John Rylands University Library of Manchester*	DDD	*Dictionary of Deities and Demons in the Bible*
BJS	Brown Judaic Studies	DJD	Discoveries in the Judean Desert
BKAT	Biblischer Kommentar, Altes Testament	DRev	*Downside Review*
		DukeDivR	*Duke Divinity Review*
BLW	*Babylonian Wisdom Literature*	EA	El-Amarna tablets
BR	*Biblical Research*	EBC	*Expositor's Bible Commentary*
BRev	*Bible Review*	ECC	Eerdmans Critical Commentary
BSac	*Bibliotheca sacra*	EcR	*Ecumenical Review*
BST	The Bible Speaks Today	EDNT	*Exegetical Dictionary of the New Testament*

EgT	*Eglise et théologie*	*HeyJ*	*Heythrop Journal*
EGT	Expositor's Greek Testament	HNT	Handbuch zum Neuen Testament
ErIsr	*Eretz-Israel*	HNTC	Harper's New Testament
ESCJ	Etudes sur le christianisme et le		Commentaries
	judaisme (Studies in Christianity	*Hor*	*Horizons*
	and Judaism)	*HS*	*Hebrew Studies*
EstBib	*Estudios bíblicos*	HSM	Harvard Semitic Monographs
ETS	Evangelical Theological Society	HSS	Harvard Semitic Studies
EuroJTh	*European Journal of Theology*	HTKNT	Herders theologischer Kommen-
EvQ	*Evangelical Quarterly*		tar zum Neuen Testament
EvT	*Evangelische Theologie*	*HTR*	*Harvard Theological Review*
ExAud	*Ex auditu*	HTS	Harvard Theological Studies
Exeg	*Exegetica*	*HUCA*	*Hebrew Union College Annual*
ExpTim	*Expository Times*	IB	*Interpreter's Bible*
FF	Foundations and Facets	IBC	Interpretation: A Bible Com-
FOTL	Forms of Old Testament		mentary for Teaching and
	Literature		Preaching
FRLANT	Forschungen zur Religion und	*IBHS*	*Introduction to Biblical Hebrew*
	Literatur des Alten und Neuen		*and Syntax*, by B. Waltke and
	Testaments		M. O'Connor
GBS	Guides to Biblical Scholarship	*IBS*	*Irish Biblical Studies*
GKC	*Genesius' Hebrew Grammar*	ICC	International Critical
GNS	*Good News Studies*		Commentary
GR	*Greece and Rome*	*IDB*	*Interpreter's Dictionary of the Bible*
Grammar	*A Grammar of the Greek New*	*IDBSup*	*Interpreter's Dictionary of the Bible:*
	Testament; in the Light of Historical		*Supplement*
	Research (A. T. Robertson)	*IJT*	*Indian Journal of Theology*
GRBS	*Greek, Roman, and Byzantine*	*Int*	*Interpretation*
	Studies	Interpretation	Interpretation: A Bible Com-
GTJ	*Grace Theological Journal*		mentary for Teaching and
HALAT	Koehler, Baumgartner, and		Preaching
	Stamm. *Hebräisches und aramäisches*	*ISBE*	*International Standard Bible Ency-*
	Lexicon zum Alten Testament		*clopedia*, 2d ed.
HALOT	Koehler, Baumgartner, and	ITC	International Theological
	Stamm. *The Hebrew and Aramaic*		Commentary
	Lexicon of the Old Testament	IVPNTC	IVP New Testament
HAR	*Hebrew Annual Review*		Commentary
HBD	*HarperCollins Bible Dictionary*	*JAAR*	*Journal of the American Academy of*
HBT	*Horizons in Biblical Theology*		*Religion*
Herm	Hermeneia commentary series	JAARSup	JAAR Supplement Series

JANESCU	*Journal of the Ancient Near Eastern Society at Columbia University*	LCC	Library of Christian Classics
JAOS	*Journal of the American Oriental Society*	LCL	Loeb Classical Library
		LEC	Library of Early Christianity
JBL	*Journal of Biblical Literature*	*LS*	*Louvain Studies*
JBMW	*Journal for Biblical Manhood and Womanhood*	LSJ	Liddell, Scott, and Jones. *A Greek-English Lexicon*
JCS	*Journal for Cuneiform Studies*	MM	Moulton and Milligan. *The Vocabulary of the Greek Testament*
Jeev	*Jeevadhara*	NAC	New American Commentary
JETS	*Journal of the Evangelical Theological Society*	*NBD*	*New Bible Dictionary*, 2d ed.
JNES	*Journal of Near Eastern Studies*	NCBC	New Century Bible Commentary
JNSL	*Journal of Northwest Semitic Languages*	*Neot*	*Neotestamentica*
		NewDocs	*New Documents Illustrating Early Christianity*
JPOS	*Journal of the Palestine Oriental Society*	*NIB*	*New Interpreter's Bible*
JPS	Jewish Publication Society	NIBC	New International Biblical Commentary
JQR	*Jewish Quarterly Review*	NICNT	New International Commentary on the New Testament
JRS	*Journal of Roman Studies*		
JRT	*Journal of Religious Thought*	NICOT	New International Commentary on the Old Testament
JSNT	*Journal for the Study of the New Testament*		
JSNTSup	JSNT Supplement Series	*NIDNTT*	*New International Dictionary of New Testament Theology*
JSOT	*Journal for the Study of the Old Testament*	*NIDOTTE*	*New International Dictionary of Old Testament Theology and Exegesis*
JSOTSup	JSOT Supplement Series	NIGTC	New International Greek Testament Commentary
JSP	*Journal for the Study of the Pseudepigrapha*	NIVAC	NIV Application Commentary
JSS	*Journal of Semitic Studies*	NIVSB	Zondervan NIV Study Bible
JTC	*Journal for Theology and the Church*	*Notes*	*Notes on Translation*
JTS	*Journal of Theological Studies*	*NovT*	*Novum Testamentum*
K&D	Keil and Delitzsch, *Biblical Commentary on the Old Testament*	NovTSup	Novum Testamentum Supplements
		NPNF	*Nicene and Post-Nicene Fathers*
KEK	Kritisch-exegetischer Kommentar über das Neue Testament	NTC	New Testament Commentary (Baker)
KTU	*Die keilalphabetischen Texte aus Ugarit*	NTD	Das Neue Testament Deutsch
		NTG	New Testament Guides
L&N	Louw and Nida. *Greek-English Lexicon of the New Testament: Based on Semantic Domains*	*NTS*	*New Testament Studies*
		NTT	New Testament Theology

NTTS	New Testament Tools and Studies	SBLABS	Society of Biblical Literature Archaeology and Biblical Studies
OBO	*Orbis biblicus et orientalis*	SBLDS	Society of Biblical Literature Dissertation Series
OBT	Overtures to Biblical Theology		
OJRS	*Ohio Journal of Religious Studies*	*SBLSP*	*Society of Biblical Literature Seminar Papers*
OLA	Orientalia lovaniensia analecta		
Or	*Orientalia* (NS)	SBLMS	Society of Biblical Literature Monograph Series
OTE	*Old Testament Essays*		
OTG	Old Testament Guides	SBLSymS	Society of Biblical Literature Symposium Series
OTL	Old Testament Library		
OTS	Old Testament Studies	SBLWAW	Society of Biblical Literature Writings from the Ancient World
OtSt	*Oudtestamentische Studiën*		
Parab	*Parabola*	*SBT*	*Studies in Biblical Theology*
PEGLMBS	*Proceedings, Eastern Great Lakes and Midwest Bible Societies*	*ScEccl*	*Sciences ecclésiastiques*
		ScEs	*Science et esprit*
PEQ	*Palestine Exploration Quarterly*	ScrHier	Scripta hierosolymitana
PG	Patrologia graeca	*SE*	*Studia evangelica*
PL	Patrologia latina	*SEÅ*	*Svensk exegetisk årsbok*
PNTC	Pillar New Testament Commentary	SEG	Supplementum epigraphicum graecum
Presb	*Presbyterion*	*Sem*	*Semitica*
PresR	*Presbyterian Review*	SHANE	Studies in the History of the Ancient Near East
PRSt	*Perspectives in Religious Studies*		
PTMS	Pittsburgh Theological Monograph Series	SJLA	Studies in Judaism of Late Antiquity
PTR	*Princeton Theological Review*	*SJT*	*Scottish Journal of Theology*
RB	*Revue biblique*	SNT	Studien zum Neuen Testament
RBibLit	*Review of Biblical Literature*	SNTSMS	Society for New Testament Studies Monograph Series
RefJ	*Reformed Journal*		
RelSRev	*Religious Studies Review*	SNTSU	Studien zum Neuen Testament und seiner Umwelt
ResQ	*Restoration Quarterly*		
RevExp	*Review and Expositor*	SP	Sacra Pagina
RevScRel	*Revue des sciences religieuses*	*SR*	*Studies in Religion*
RHPR	*Revue d'histoire et de philosophie religieuses*	*ST*	*Studia theologica*
		Str-B	Strack, H. L., and P. Billerbeck, *Kommentar zum Neuen Testament aus Talmud und Midrasch*
RHR	*Revue de l'histoire des religions*		
RTR	*Reformed Theological Review*		
SAA	State Archives of Assyria	*StudBT*	*Studia biblica et theologica*
SAAS	State Archives of Assyria Studies	SUNT	Studien zur Umwelt des Neuen Testaments
SBB	Stuttgarter biblische Beiträge		
SBJT	*Southern Baptist Journal of Theology*		

SVF	*Stoicorum veterum fragmenta*	*TynBul*	*Tyndale Bulletin*
SwJT	*Southwestern Journal of Theology*	*TZ*	*Theologische Zeitschrift*
TA	*Tel Aviv*	*UBD*	*Unger's Bible Dictionary*
TBT	*The Bible Today*	*UF*	*Ugarit-Forschungen*
TDNT	Kittel and Friedrich. *Theological Dictionary of the New Testament*	*UT*	*Ugaritic Textbook*
TDOT	Botterweck and Ringgren. *Theological Dictionary of the Old Testament*	*VE*	*Vox evangelica*
		VT	*Vetus Testamentum*
		VTSup	Supplements to Vetus Testamentum
Text	*Textus*	*WAW*	Writings from the Ancient World
TF	*Theologische Forschung*	*WBC*	Word Biblical Commentary
ThT	*Theologisch tijdschrift*	*WBE*	*Wycliffe Bible Encyclopedia*
THAT	*Theologisches Handwörterbuch zum Alten Testament*	*WMANT*	Wissenschaftliche Monographien zum Alten und Neuen Testament
Them	*Themelios*	*WW*	*Word and World*
ThEv	*Theologia Evangelica*	*WTJ*	*Westminster Theological Journal*
THKNT	Theologischer Handkommentar zum Neuen Testament	*WW*	*Word and World*
ThT	*Theologisch tijdschrift*	WUNT	Wissenschaftliche Untersuchungen zum Neuen Testament
ThTo	*Theology Today*	*YCS*	*Yale Classical Studies*
TJ	*Trinity Journal*	*YNER*	*Yale Near Eastern Researches*
TLNT	*Theological Lexicon of the New Testament*	*ZAW*	*Zeitschrift für die alttestamentliche Wissenschaft*
TLOT	*Theological Lexicon of the Old Testament*	*ZDPV*	*Zeitschrift des deutschen Palästina-Vereins*
TNTC	Tyndale New Testament Commentaries	*ZNW*	*Zeitschrift für die neutestamentliche Wissenschaft und die Kunde der älterern Kirche*
TOTC	Tyndale Old Testament Commentaries		
TQ	*Theologische Quartalschrift*	*ZPEB*	*Zondervan Pictorial Encyclopedia of the Bible*
TS	*Theological Studies*	*ZWT*	*Zeitschrift für wissenschaftliche Theologie*
TWOT	*Theological Wordbook of the Old Testament*		

General

AD	*anno Domini* (in the year of [our] Lord)	Arab.	Arabic
		Aram.	Aramaic
Akkad.	Akkadian	BC	before Christ

ca.	*circa* (around, about, approximately)	MS(S)	manuscript(s)
		MT	Masoretic Text of the OT
cf.	*confer*, compare	n(n).	note(s)
ch(s).	chapter(s)	n.d.	no date
d.	died	NS	New Series
diss.	dissertation	NT	New Testament
ed(s).	editor(s), edited by, edition	OT	Old Testament
e.g.	*exempli gratia*, for example	p(p).	page(s)
esp.	especially	par.	parallel (indicates textual parallels)
et al.	*et alii*, and others		
EV	English versions of the Bible	para.	paragraph
f(f).	and the following one(s)	repr.	reprinted
fig.	figuratively	rev.	revised
frg.	fragment	Samar.	Samaritan Pentateuch
Gk.	Greek	s.v.	*sub verbo*, under the word
GK	Goodrick & Kohlenberger numbering system	Syr.	Syriac
		Tg.	Targum
Heb.	Hebrew	TR	Textus Receptus (Greek text of the KJV translation)
ibid.	*ibidem*, in the same place		
i.e.	*id est*, that is	trans.	translator, translated by
Lat.	Latin	v(v).	verse(s)
lit.	literally	vs.	versus
LXX	Septuagint (the Greek OT)	Vul.	Vulgate

DANIEL

ANDREW E. HILL

Introduction

1. **Historical Background**

2. **Authorship and Date**

3. **Structure and Unity**

4. **Place of Composition, Audience, and Purpose**

5. **Social Setting**

6. **Literary Form**

7. **Theological Emphases**

8. **Text and Versions**

9. **Languages**

10. **Canonicity (and the Additions)**

11. **Daniel and the New Testament**

12. **Special Problems**

13. **Bibliography**

14. **Outline**

The book of Daniel is one of the most contested books in OT scholarship. Issues of historical and chronological accuracy, literary genre and biblical interpretation, and the nature of OT prophecy continue to stir debate among scholars.

The book is an enigma — written in two languages (Aramaic and Hebrew), composed of two genres (narrative and visionary literature), narrated in two voices (third-person court stories and first-person visions embedded in third-person narrative), and organized in a two-part structure (stories, chs. 1–6; visions, chs. 7–12). Quite naturally, these features have led to two rather distinct understandings of the book.

Interestingly, the interpretive alternatives have so polarized the scholarship on Daniel that some recent commentators have resorted to incorporating materials typically associated with the critical introduction of biblical books (e.g., authorship, date, structure, genre, etc.) as an epilogue or appendix to the analysis of the text of Daniel in an effort to focus attention on the message and theology of the book.[1] Some even suggest that whether the stories of Daniel are history or fiction and whether the visions are actual prophecies or historical reports after the fact make little difference to the exegesis of the book.[2] There is some

---

1. See, e.g., J. E. Goldingay, *Daniel* (WBC 30; Dallas: Word, 1989); E. C. Lucas, *Daniel* (Apollos Old Testament Commentary 2; Downers Grove, Ill.: InterVarsity Press, 2002).

2. See, e.g., Goldingay, *Daniel*, xl; cf. J. G. Baldwin, *Daniel* (TOTC 21; Downers Grove, Ill.: InterVarsity Press, 1978), 499.

truth in such a statement, since in the end each reader understands the book of Daniel on the basis of what the text says. Yet the reader's assumptions about the nature of divine revelation, the dynamics of the historical process, and the character of literary genres deeply color the theology derived from any study of the biblical documents. At what point, if any, are the original audience of Daniel's message and today's audience of this preserved tradition "children of a lesser God" if the stories of Daniel are fiction and the visions of Daniel are not prophecy?

The conventional labels "traditional" and "mainline" are the tags employed for the two basic interpretive views of the book of Daniel. The "traditional" or conservative approach typically understands the book as a sixth-century BC composition, while the "mainline" or critical approach typically considers the book largely a second-century BC work. According to Collins, the last gasp of the "fundamentalist" reading of Daniel was the work of Robert D. Wilson (although he notes conservative scholars continue to fight "rear-guard" actions in defense of the book's reliability).[3]

Collins further confidently asserts that in academic circles the fundamentalist view of Daniel was defeated at the beginning of the twentieth century. Today the triumph of the critical understanding of Daniel is widely recognized.[4] This does not mean, however, that voices championing the traditional view of Daniel ceased, as the scholarship of the likes of E. J. Young, J. G. Baldwin, K. A. Kitchen, and D. J. Wiseman attest. The history of biblical scholarship reveals that "post-mortems" are rarely final, and such may be the case with Daniel.

Naturally, these rubrics are not necessarily meant to reflect any particular "theological camp" with respect to a "view" of Scripture or prejudge any certain ideological posture regarding the realm of the supernatural. As Longman has recognized, "faithful interpreters find themselves on two sides of the debate."[5] And further, Lucas reminds us that "on both sides of the argument there are those who see their conclusions as compatible with acceptance of the inspiration and authority of Scripture."[6] In the end, "let God be true, and every human being a liar" (Ro 3:4).

1. HISTORICAL BACKGROUND

The book of Daniel contains nine date formulas (1:1, 21; 2:1; 5:30; 7:1; 8:1; 9:1; 10:1, [cf. v.21]; 11:1). The earliest formula refers to the third year of the reign of King Jehoiakim (i.e., 605 BC) and reports the first Babylonian invasion of Judah by King Nebuchadnezzar (1:1).[7] This means Daniel was among the first of the Hebrews taken captive by the Babylonians and deported to Mesopotamia, a fact that has significance for his later prayer (cf. 9:2–3). The latest date formula places Daniel in the Persian royal court during the third year of the Persian king Cyrus (537 or 536 BC; 10:1). This means the historical setting for Daniel

---

3. J. J. Collins, "Current Issues in the Study of Daniel," in *The Book of Daniel*, ed. J. J. Collins and P. W. Flint (Leiden: Brill, 2002), 1:1–2.

4. Cf. B. S. Childs, *Introduction to the Old Testament as Scripture* (Philadelphia: Fortress, 1979), 612.

5. T. Longman III, *Daniel* (NIVAC; Grand Rapids: Zondervan, 1999), 2.

6. Lucas, *Daniel*, 309.

7. On the Babylonian advance against the Egyptians see J. Bright, *A History of Israel*, 4th ed. (Louisville: Westminster John Knox, 2000), 326–27; I. Provan, V. P. Long, and T. Longman III, *A Biblical History of Israel* (Louisville: Westminster John Knox, 2003), 279–80.

is the Babylonian exile in the royal courts of Babylonian, Median, and Persian kings between 605 and 536 BC. The dated portions of Daniel may be outlined as follows:

1:1 — third year, King Jehoiakim of Judah, 605 BC
1:21 — first year, King Cyrus of Persia, 539 BC
2:1 — second year, King Nebuchadnezzar of Babylonia, 604 or 603 BC
5:30 — last year, King Belshazzar of Babylonia/first year, Darius the Mede, 539 BC
7:1 — first year, King Belshazzar of Babylonia, ca. 553 BC
8:1 — third year, King Belshazzar of Babylonia, ca. 551 BC
9:1 — first year, Darius the Mede, 539 BC
10:1 — third year, King Cyrus of Persia, 537 or 536 BC

King Josiah of Judah died in battle near Megiddo in 609 BC (2Ki 23:30). Perhaps obligations to the Babylonians motivated his attempt to intercept the Egyptian forces of Pharaoh Neco en route to Carchemish (23:29).[8] Josiah was the last reformer and "good" king of Judah, and his death precipitated the rapid decline of the southern Hebrew monarchy. The last twenty-plus years of the Judahite monarchy saw four kings ascend to the throne. Two of these kings, Jehoahaz (609 BC) and Jehoiachin (597 BC), each ruled for but three months (23:31–34; 24:8–17). The other two were puppet kings of the superpowers competing for control of the land bridge of Syro-Palestine.

Eliakim/Jehoiakim (609–597 BC) was installed by Pharaoh Neco of Egypt (2Ki 23:34). He later surrendered to King Nebuchadnezzar of Babylonia but rebelled three years later (ca. 603 BC; 24:1–7). Nebuchadnezzar was unable to resume his military campaigns in Syro-Palestine until 598 BC but then moved swiftly to punish the disloyal vassal. By the time Nebuchadnezzar reached Jerusalem, Jehoiakim had died and Jehoiachin succeeded him as king of Judah (24:8). As a result of the second Babylonian invasion of Judah, King Jehoiachin was deposed and exiled along with ten thousand citizens of Jerusalem (including Ezekiel; cf. 2Ki 24:10–17; Eze 1:1–2).

Mattaniah/Zedekiah was installed by King Nebuchadnezzar as a puppet king of Babylonia after the exile of Jehoiachin (2Ki 24:17). Zedekiah foolishly rebelled against the Babylonian overlord and allied Judah with Pharaoh Hophra of Egypt in 589 BC. The third Babylonian invasion of Judah was swift and decisive. Nebuchadnezzar surrounded Jerusalem in 588 BC, and after a lengthy siege the city was sacked, Yahweh's temple was destroyed, and Davidic kingship in Judah ceased (24:18–25:21).[9]

2. AUTHORSHIP AND DATE

For centuries traditional Jewish and Christian scholarship ascribed the book of Daniel to the sixth-century BC Hebrew courtier of the same name employed in the service of King Nebuchadnezzar of Babylonia (Da 1:3). Daniel was among the first Hebrews taken captive from Judah and was conscripted into the civil service corps of the Babylonian government (1:6). Internal evidence in the second half of the book (the visions of chs. 7–12) is usually cited in support of this view. This includes the first-person reporting

---

8. See Provan, Long, and Longman, *A Biblical History of Israel*, 276–77.
9. See ibid., 279–85; Bright, *A History of Israel*, 324–31.

(of personal memoirs or journal accounts [?]; cf. 7:2–28; 8:1–27; 9:1–27; 10:2–12:4; 12:5–13) and the angelic command to Daniel himself to "seal up the book."[10] The court stories of the first half of the book (chs. 1–6) are written in the third person (except the first-person report of Nebuchadnezzar's dream about a tree; 4:4–18). Yet the presumed eyewitness detail of these accounts is considered indirect evidence of Daniel's authorship of this section of the book as well.[11] Lastly, proponents of the traditional view for the authorship and date of the book of Daniel appeal to the testimony of Jesus, who credits the prophet Daniel with the authorship of the prophecy concerning "the abomination that causes desolation" (Mt 24:15; Mk 13:14).

Biblical scholarship of the late nineteenth and early twentieth century challenged the traditional understanding of the origin of the book of Daniel. The views of Porphyry (AD 233–304), a Neoplationist philosopher, are frequently cited as precursors of the critical assessment of this book.[12] As an early dissenting voice in the scholarship on Daniel, Porphyry questioned the historicity of the figure of Daniel and dismissed the idea of prophecy in Daniel. Instead, he argued that Daniel was written by a Palestinian Jew living at the time of Antiochus IV Epiphanes, who related the past but did not foretell the future.[13]

Such analysis represents the dominant view of the book of Daniel today. A number of historical, literary, theological, and canonical trajectories have converged to shape this understanding of the book. Primary among them was the perceived inferiority of postexilic prophecy and apocalyptic literature when compared to preexilic prophecy according to the canons of nineteenth-century literary criticism.[14] The traditional view of Daniel was further eroded by the Enlightenment's antisupernaturalist assumptions of biblical scholarship rooted in the elevation of reason over revelation—thus dismissing a priori such categories as "miracle" and "predictive prophecy" in the biblical record.[15]

Today the discussion extends beyond the issue of *vaticinium ex eventu* (or "prophecy after the fact") to the nature and character of the apocalyptic genre that comprises portions of Daniel. Collins states that the "issue is not 'a dogmatic rejection of predictive prophecy' as conservatives like to assert, but a calculation of probability" (since for him the weight of the literary, linguistic, historical, and textual evidence points to a second-century BC date for Daniel).[16] One feature of apocalyptic literature—pseudonymity (ascribing a writing to someone other than its actual author)—is of particular importance. Pseudonymity was a known literary practice in the ancient world, particularly in the Hellenistic age. Despite the fact that such a literary device is rarer in our own culture, Goldingay cautions that we should not "infer that God could not use it in another culture."[17]

---

10. T. Longman III and R. B. Dillard, *Introduction to the Old Testament*, 2nd ed. (Grand Rapids: Zondervan, 2006), 373–75.

11. S. R. Miller, *Daniel* (NAC 18; Nashville: Broadman & Holman, 1994), 26–27.

12. See, e.g., J. J. Collins, "Daniel," *ABD*, 2:30.

13. As cited in J. Braverman, *Jerome's Commentary of Daniel* (CBQMS 7; Washington, D.C.: Catholic Biblical Association of America, 1978), 116. Jerome parts company with Porphyry at this juncture in Daniel 11:21 since Jerome believed "all these things are spoken prophetically of the AntiChrist who is to arise at the end of time."

14. See Baldwin, *Daniel*, 14; on the history of the interpretation of Daniel, see Goldingay, *Daniel*, xxv–xxxviii.

15. So E. Krentz, *The Historical-Critical Method* (Philadelphia: Fortress, 1975), 30.

16. J. J. Collins, *The Apocalyptic Imagination*, 2nd ed. (Grand Rapids: Eerdmans, 1998), 88.

17. Goldingay, *Daniel*, xl.

As a result, mainline scholars now consider the book of Daniel the product of one or more unknown Jewish pseudepigraphers writing shortly after the Maccabean crisis (ca. 160 BC).[18] In fact, some scholars date the final compilation of the book to shortly before 163 BC since the person(s) responsible for the book erroneously place Antiochus's death in Palestine, not Syria (as recorded in Polybius, *Histories* 33.9). This critical approach to the book also assumes that the anonymous author(s) incorporated the court stories about Daniel (chs. 1–6) in the book since these earlier materials were already circulating in a relatively fixed form.[19] Beyond this, a growing number of biblical scholars who might be categorized broadly as conservative or evangelical in persuasion adhere to this view.[20]

In summary, the book of Daniel is a blend of third-person report and first-person memoir, divided into a narrative section (chs. 1–6) and an apocalyptic section (chs. 7–12). The internal evidence demands that only the first-person visions of the second half of the book be ascribed directly to Daniel.[21] And in some cases even these visions are framed by third-person introductions (e.g., 7:1; 9:1; 10:1). Given this two-part (or bifid) structure, it seems likely that the book represents an anthology or edited collection of selections of Daniel's personal journal or memoirs and adaptations of more formal chronicles documenting his service in the Babylonian royal court. The book was probably composed in the Babylonian Diaspora by Daniel, or more likely by associates who outlived him, sometime after 536 BC (the last date formula in the book; 10:1) and before 515 BC (since the composition makes no reference to the rebuilding of the second temple in Jerusalem). This places the current study in what Collins calls "an ongoing tradition of conservative scholarship that holds to the exilic date."[22]

3. STRUCTURE AND UNITY

Two basic methods for determining structure have been applied to the book of Daniel. One is based on the two languages utilized in the composition of the book. For example, while acknowledging the bifid structure of the book on the basis of genre, Wood states that "the employment of two languages points to an equally valid division, which has to do with the people concerned, rather than with literary criteria."[23] The organization of the content of Daniel as determined by the language patterns of the book may be outlined as follows:[24]

"Preface" (in Hebrew) for the Jews, ch. 1

Messages (in Aramaic) to the Gentile nations, chs. 2–7

Prophecies (in Hebrew) to the Jews about the kingdom of God, chs. 8–12

---

18. Cf. Collins, "Current Issues in the Study of Daniel," 1:2.
19. See, e.g., Collins, "Daniel," *ABD*, 2:30–31.
20. E.g., Goldingay, *Daniel*, xxxix–xl; Lucas, *Daniel*, 309.
21. So Longman and Dillard, *Introduction to the Old Testament*, 373.
22. Collins, *The Apocalyptic Imagination*, 88.
23. L. J. Wood, *A Commentary on Daniel* (Grand Rapids: Zondervan, 1973), 18.
24. Ibid., 18–19; cf. Miller, *Daniel*, 51.

This approach to the structure of Daniel assumes a bilingual audience for the book and that chs. 2–7 were in some way made available to the Gentile public. The widely recognized chiastic arrangement of the Aramaic section of the book (see below) is often cited in support of a language-based approach to the structure of Daniel.[25]

A a dream about four world kingdoms replaced by a fifth (2:4b–49)
  B three friends in the fiery furnace (3:1–30)
    C Daniel interprets a dream for Nebuchadnezzar (4:1–47)
    C' Daniel interprets the handwriting on the wall for Belshazzar (5:1–31)
  B' Daniel in the lions' den (6:1–28)
A' a vision about four world kingdoms replaced by a fifth (7:1–28)

More commonly, the literary structure of Daniel is determined by appealing to the two types of literature found in the book: the court stories of Daniel composed in a narrative genre (chs. 1–6) and the visions of Daniel composed in an apocalyptic genre (chs. 7–12). Beyond this, the two halves of the book each share a chronological scheme that sequences Babylonian, Median, and Persian rulers.

Redditt goes so far as to identify a "plot" in the book of Daniel that extends from the Babylonian invasion of Judah and the beginning of the Hebrew exile to the fall of the "fourth kingdom" and establishment of the kingdom of God. He identifies the plot shape as essentially "comedic" in that the events of the story line turn out "happily" or for the good rather than tragically for the Hebrews.[26]

The traditional approach to Daniel understands the book as a literary unity composed by Daniel himself or compiled by associates who outlived him sometime during the last quarter of the sixth century BC (see Authorship and Date). Beckwith has summarized:

> The book of Daniel gives every appearance of being a unity. Its material is carefully organized, with six chapters of narrative chronologically arranged ... followed by six chapters of visions, again chronologically arranged. The two halves are connected ... by the close parallels between the dream of ch. 2 and the vision of ch. 7, and by the continuance of the Aramaic language from Dan. 2:4–7:28, though the book begins and ends in Hebrew.[27]

H. H. Rowley espoused the early critical view that Daniel was the product of a single author of the Maccabean era (see Place of Composition, Audience, and Purpose).[28] More recent critical scholarship considers the book of Daniel a diverse collection of materials put together in several stages over the course of two or three centuries. Redditt is representative of the contemporary critical approach, theorizing that the book of Daniel underwent three recensions: the first edition of the book (R_1 = chs. 4–6) was compiled by the "wise teachers" either before or after they moved to Jerusalem from Babylonia (a date is unspecified); the second edition of the book (R_2 = chs. 2–7, along with ch. 1 as an introduction) was published

---

25. See, e.g., P. L. Redditt, *Daniel* (NCBC; Sheffield: Sheffield Academic Press, 1999), 27.
26. Ibid., 34.
27. R. Beckwith, *The Old Testament Canon of the New Testament Church* (Grand Rapids: Eerdmans, 1985), 416, n. 76.
28. H. H. Rowley, "The Unity of the Book of Daniel," in *The Servant of the Lord and Other Essays*, 2nd ed. (Oxford: Blackwell, 1965), 264–67.

sometime between 169 and 167 BC; and the third edition of the book (R_3 = chs. 8–9, 10–12) was published before the death of Antiochus IV Ephiphanes and the cleansing of the second temple in 164 BC (with the exception of 12:5–12, which was added shortly after the rededication of the temple).[29] Naturally the later Greek Additions to Daniel constitute yet another edition of the book. This study adheres to the traditional approach, namely, assuming the book is a literary unity compiled sometime during the last quarter of the sixth century BC by associates who outlived Daniel.

4. PLACE OF COMPOSITION, AUDIENCE, AND PURPOSE

Scholars adhering to a sixth century BC date for the entirety of Daniel assume a Babylonian provenance best accounts for the Aramaic core of book[30] and the convincing (albeit subtle) unity of the book.[31] In addition, the Persian loanwords for administrative terms and officers suggest a final form for the book when Persian rule in Mesopotamia was firmly established.[32] The apparent misunderstanding of these terms by the later Greek translators of the versions of the LXX further substantiates a pre-Hellenistic date for the book.[33] Thus the primary audience of the book of Daniel was the Hebrew population of the Babylonian Diaspora. The book was both theological instruction in the faithfulness of God to his covenantal people and an exhortation to the Hebrew captives to imitate the faithfulness, wisdom, and piety of Daniel and his three friends.[34]

Rowley championed the view that Daniel was the product of a single author of Maccabean times (who may have borrowed and reworked earlier traditions).[35] Thus the primary audience of the book was the Jewish population of second-century BC Palestine suffering intense persecution under Seleucid rule. Daniel may be considered a sort of "Hasidic manifesto" composed and circulated in order "to urge and encourage the faithful Jews to remain steadfast in the practice of the religion of their fathers during the brutal persecution of Antiochus IV Epiphanes."[36] The weight of the linguistic data (i.e., both the Aramaic of Daniel and the Persian loanwords included in the book) and the textual evidence (i.e., the Prayer of Nabonidus and the Qumran documents) now suggest that chs. 1–6 may have had a lengthy prehistory.[37] This makes the position of holding to a single author of Maccabean times less tenable, although it is still espoused (with variations) by Porteous and Hartman and Di Lella.[38]

---

29. Redditt, *Daniel*, 33–34.

30. See, e.g., Miller, *Daniel*, 30–32.

31. See, e.g., R. S. Wallace, *The Lord Is King: The Message of Daniel* (BST; Downers Grove, Ill.: InterVarsity Press, 1979), 20–22.

32. Cf. K. A. Kitchen, "The Aramaic of Daniel," in *Notes on Some Problems in The Book of Daniel*, ed. D. J. Wiseman et al. (London: Tyndale, 1965), 35–44; see J. J. Collins, *Daniel* (Herm.; Minneapolis: Fortress, 1993), 18–120, in his discussion of "Foreign Words" in response to Kitchen.

33. See Kitchen, "The Aramaic of Daniel," 42–43; cf. Collins (*Daniel*, 19), who notes this only weighs against the theory that the entire book of Daniel originated in the second century BC.

34. Wallace, *The Lord Is King*, 16.

35. Rowley, "The Unity of the Book of Daniel," 264–67.

36. L. F. Hartman and A. Di Lella, *The Book of Daniel* (AB 23; New York: Doubleday, 1978), 43.

37. So Collins, "Daniel," *ABD*, 2:33.

38. N. W. Porteous, *Daniel* (OTL; Philadelphia: Westminster, 1965), 20; Hartman and Di Lella, *The Book of Daniel*, 16.

Today most critical scholars recognize that the court stories of chs. 1–6 ("tales" or "legends," as categorized form-critically by Collins)[39] may have circulated independently during the Hellenistic era. Thus the court stories about Daniel reflect the setting of the Mesopotamian Jewish Diaspora and were intended to encourage the Jews to resist compromising their religion. The stories also teach that Jews might advance in the Gentile world while remaining faithful to Yahweh.[40]

The visions of Daniel (chs. 7–12) are determined to presuppose a Jewish audience in second-century BC Jerusalem since the setting of the visions is the persecution of the Jews by Antiochus IV Epiphanes (168–164 BC).[41] The purpose of the visions is not so much a call to arms in revolt against the Seleucid oppressors as a call to ethical living in adherence to the law of Moses in the face of persecution.[42] The visions assure the Jews of God's final victory over evil and the nations doing the bidding of the Evil One, but with the recognition that martyrdom is a reality and deliverance will only come later with the resurrection of the dead.[43]

5. SOCIAL SETTING

The traditional understanding of the social setting of Daniel accepts the prima facie report that the Jewish Diaspora of the Babylonian and early Persian periods is the backdrop of the book. The conditions for the Hebrews in exile were far from ideal, but they provided a "comfortable" setting for getting on with life (Jer 29:5–7), some freedom of movement (Eze 8:1; 14:1), and permitted advancement for Jews faithful to Yahweh in a somewhat "tolerant" Gentile world (Da 1:6–17). Hence the primary audience of the book was the Hebrew population of the Babylonian captivity. The book was both a theological treatise on God's faithfulness to his covenantal people and his sovereign rule of the nations (1:1–5). In addition, the document was an exhortation to the displaced Hebrews to imitate the faithfulness, wisdom, and piety of Daniel and his three friends while awaiting the inbreaking of God's heavenly kingdom (2:44–45).

Collins flatly states that the social setting of the book of Daniel is difficult to reconstruct because the book is pseudepigraphic, "so the explicit setting in the Babylonian exile is known to be fictional."[44] A majority of critical scholars assign the so-called "court tales" (chs. 1–6) to unknown authors or editors living in Syro-Palestine during the Hellenistic era. The favorable treatment of the Jews, including opportunities for advancement under Gentile rule, may reflect the more benign rule of early Seleucid kings such as Seleucus I Nicator (312–280 BC) and Antiochus III (222–187 BC). Redditt extends this back to early Greek and later Persian periods.[45] It is possible the composers of the court stories even worked in the service of these foreign kings.[46]

---

39. J. J. Collins, *Daniel with an Introduction to Apocalyptic Literature* (FOTL 20; Grand Rapids: Eerdmans, 1984), 42–43.

40. Collins, "Daniel," *ABD*, 2:30.

41. Cf. R. Anderson, *Daniel: Signs and Wonders* (ITC; Grand Rapids: Eerdmans, 1984), xiii.

42. On Daniel as wisdom literature, cf. Collins, "Daniel," *ABD*, 2:35; L. L. Grabbe, "A Dan(iel) for All Seasons," in *The Book of Daniel*, ed. J. J. Collins and P. W. Flint (Leiden: Brill, 2002), 230.

43. Collins, "Daniel," *ABD*, 2:35; also Porteous, *Daniel*, 20.

44. Collins, "Current Issues in the Study of Daniel," 1:9.

45. Redditt, *Daniel*, 5–6.

46. See, e.g., Collins, "Current Issues in the Study of Daniel," 1:10.

By contrast, the visions of Daniel (chs. 7–12) are understood to reflect the persecution of the Jews by Antiochus IV Epiphanes during the Maccabean era.[47] Thus the visions were a type of "resistance literature," calling the Jews to ethical living in adherence to the law of Moses in the face of Seleucid persecution. Some scholars connect this resistance movement with the Hasidim.[48] In fact, Towner identifies this group as containing the likely authors and audience of Daniel.[49] The Hasidim were scribes and teachers of the Mosaic law but were also militant supporters of the Maccabees (cf. 1 Macc 2:42; 7:12–13; 2 Macc 14:6).[50] Collins, however, finds no evidence of such militancy in the book of Daniel.[51]

Still others have connected the visions with the wisdom teachings of the *maśkilîm*. The *maśkilîm* were expert teachers, schooled in the ways of wisdom broadly defined.[52] Their duties included instructing the common people in the ways of wisdom that lead to righteousness, especially in times of crisis (Da 11:33–35). Daniel and his friends are connected to this learned guild (1:3–5, 18–20), and the association of the visions in Daniel with a highly educated intellectual elite or "upper class" seems a better fit with the social context of the Maccabean era. This helps explain the "passive" resistance encouraged by the "wise teachers" (many of whom themselves will be martyred during the times of persecution; 11:33–34). Collins rightly discounts the supposed ties between the *maśkilîm* and the Hasidim proposed by some scholars such as Lacocque.[53]

Smith-Christopher takes an even more extreme stance, suggesting that the court tales are also the product of a later period reflecting the circumstances of Gentile oppression of the Jews. He categorizes the court stories (at least chs. 2 and 4) as "oppositional literature," the subversive dreams of the disenfranchised. Rationale offered in support of the Daniel tales as a "folklore of resistance" includes the notion that the dream reports portray the Babylonian kings as arrogant buffoons.[54] The point of the court stories is to "re-negotiate" Jewish identity in the periods from 587 to 163 BC by inculcating the subversive strategy that wisdom is a greater force than power or wealth for ensuring the survival of the minority culture.

Thus Smith-Christopher concludes, "the Daniel tales teach that knowledge of Jewish identity as the people of Yahweh's light and wisdom is the key not only to survival, but also to the eventual defeat of the Imperial rule of 'the nations' on earth."[55] Despite this elaborate socio-literary reconstruction, Collins

---

47. Ibid., 5–6; C. L. Seow, *Daniel* (Wycliffe Bible Commentary; Louisville: Westminster John Knox, 2003), 6–7.

48. A. Lacocque, *Daniel in His Time (Studies on Personalities of the Old Testament)* (Columbia: Univ. of South Carolina Press, 1988), 27–28.

49. W. S. Towner, *Daniel* (Interpretation. Atlanta: John Knox, 1984), 7.

50. R. Albretz, "The Social Setting of the Aramaic and Hebrew Book of Daniel," in *The Book of Daniel*, ed. J. J. Collins and P. W. Flint (Leiden: Brill, 2002), 1:200–202.

51. Collins, "Current Issues in the Study of Daniel," 1:10; see also P. R. Davies, *Daniel* (OTG; Sheffield: Sheffield Academic Press, 1985), 122.

52. Collins, *Daniel*, 66.

53. Collins, "Current Issues in the Study of Daniel," 1:10; Lacocque, *Daniel in His Time*, 29–30.

54. D. L. Smith-Christopher, "The Book of Daniel," *NIB*, 7:57; idem, "Prayers and Dreams: Power and Diaspora Identities in the Social Setting of the Daniel Tales," in *The Book of Daniel*, ed. J. J. Collins and P. W. Flint (Leiden: Brill, 2002), 1:285–86; see also H. I. Avalos, "The Comedic Function of the Enumerations of the Officials and Instruments in Daniel 3," *CBQ* 53 (1991): 580–88.

55. Smith-Christopher, "Prayers and Dreams," 1:289.

reminds that the attitude toward Gentile rule in the two halves of Daniel is still very different: the court stories allow "for the viability of Gentile rule in the present," while "the visions portray Gentile rule as utterly unacceptable."[56]

6. LITERARY FORM

The book of Daniel is composed in two literary genres and predominantly narrated in two voices (with the first-person voice typically embedded in third-person narration). In literary form, the first half of the book (chs. 1–6) is largely third-person narrative, and the second half (chs. 7–12) essentially first-person visionary or apocalyptic prophecy. Numerous subgenres within these broad literary categories are often identified. For example, according to Goldingay Daniel consists of such types of material as romance, legend, myth, midrash, court tale, vision, quasi-prophecy, and apocalyptic.[57] Despite this consensus recognizing both narrative and visionary literature in Daniel, there remains considerable debate in biblical scholarship as to exactly what is meant by these form-critical designations.

There is general agreement that Daniel 1–6 is "story" by way of literary form. A story is defined as "a narrative which creates interest by arousing tension or suspense and resolving it."[58] The chapters concerning Daniel and his friends are usually labeled "court stories," since they comprise a series of narratives about the experiences of Hebrew captives in a foreign royal court.[59] Comparisons between Daniel and the stories of Joseph in Pharaoh's court (e.g., Ge 41–47) and Esther in Xerxes' court (e.g., Est 2–6) are commonly drawn as illustrative of the court-narrative subgenre (e.g., Lacocque, 1979: 26).[60]

Scholars dating Daniel to the Maccabean era prefer the rubric "court tale" for these narratives since they do not recognize this subgenre as reporting history. Instead, the court tales are considered fictive since they adhere to stereotypical literary patterns characteristic of folklore and legendary literature.[61] In addition, they introduce "marvelous" or miraculous elements, another indicator of the ahistorical nature of the Daniel court tales for the mainline scholar.[62]

The court stories of Daniel are often further subdivided into court stories of conflict and court stories of contest. The stereotypical plot of the "court conflict" tells the story of a hero figure living in a state of prosperity and suddenly endangered by a conspiracy. The hero eventually gains release and is elevated to a position of honor as a result of the virtue or wisdom demonstrated through the trial (e.g., chs. 3, 6). The stereotypical plot of the "court contest" tells of a person of lower status who is called on by a person of higher status to answer a difficult question or solve an acute problem. The person of higher status poses the problem that has baffled others, and the person of lower status solves the puzzle and is rewarded (e.g., ch. 2).[63]

---

56. Collins, "Current Issues in the Study of Daniel," 1:11–12.
57. Goldingay, *Daniel*, 6–7, 320–22.
58. Collins, *Daniel with an Introduction to Apocalyptic Literature*, 41.
59. Seow, *Daniel*, 9,
60. See, e.g., A. Lacocque, *The Book of Daniel* (Atlanta: John Knox, 1979), 26; W. L. Humphreys, "A Life-Style for Diaspora: A Study of the Tales of Esther and Daniel," *JBL* 92 (1973): 211–23.
61. Collins, *Daniel with an Introduction to Apocalyptic Literature*, 41.
62. E.g., Smith-Christopher, "The Book of Daniel"; Gowan, *Daniel*, 24–28.
63. For these two types of court stories, see Collins, *Daniel with an Introduction to Apocalyptic Literature*, 119.

Those espousing the traditional view of Daniel naturally emphasize the court stories of Daniel 1–6 as a reliable reporting of history, a recounting of actual events situated in the Jewish Diaspora of the Babylonian and Persian periods.[64] Although important, it is not enough simply to affirm the didactic function of the stories as ethical instruction for Diaspora Jews living under foreign oppression.[65] Nor is it adequate to speak only of the historical intentions of Daniel as "fictive" literature;[66] rather, the traditional view of Daniel upholds the historical knowledge of the writer of the book and "still finds a sixth-century date defensible."[67]

All biblical scholars agree on the genre shift from court narrative (chs. 1–6) to apocalyptic vision or prophecy in second half of Daniel (chs. 7–12). The origin and nature of Jewish apocalyptic literature, however, remain a matter of debate. The roots of biblical apocalyptic may be traced to the Hebrew prophetic tradition.[68] Daniel not only knew the writings of the earlier Hebrew prophets (cf. 9:2), but he also shared their theological understanding of Yahweh as the Lord of history (see Theological Emphases).

In addition, it is apparent that Hebrew wisdom tradition influenced the development of biblical apocalyptic. Like the practical or utilitarian wisdom of Proverbs, the book of Daniel shares an emphasis on ethical behavior and prudence and tact in leadership.[69] This book is considered "mantic wisdom" rather than "proverbial wisdom" since Daniel's wisdom is revelatory and is attached to dreams and visions, not empirical observation.[70]

According to Collins,[71] at issue in identifying a text (or group of texts) as apocalyptic is whether or not these texts "share a significant cluster of traits that distinguish them from other works." Numerous literary, temporal, and eschatological elements comprising the genre of biblical apocalyptic have been identified, including: symbolism, dualism, pseudonymity, persecution of the righteous, cosmic transformation, resurrection from the dead, and *ex eventu* prophecy.[72] Collins distills the essence of the apocalyptic genre to three characteristics: narrative framework, mediated revelation, and eschatological content.[73]

Despite the diagnostic analysis of biblical and extrabiblical documents according to a shared "cluster of traits," there is no consensus on what constitutes the genre of apocalyptic literature as distinct from biblical prophecy. Beyond this, sorting out the difference(s) between an "apocalypse" (as a literary genre) and "apocalyptic eschatology" (as a theological perspective in biblical prophetic literature) proves equally

---

64. Cf. Miller, *Daniel*, 26–28; Baldwin, *Daniel*, 19–29.

65. Cf. Gowan, *Daniel*, 38–39.

66. E.g., Towner, *Daniel*, 4–6; Frederick J. Murphy, "Introduction to Apocalyptic Literature," *NIB*, 7:2.

67. Longman, *Daniel*, 24; cf. Baldwin, *Daniel*, 29, 46.

68. Longman and Dillard, *Introduction to the Old Testament*, 388–89.

69. Cf. Wallace, *The Lord Is King*, 27–29.

70. Collins, "Daniel," *ABD*, 2:35.

71. Collins, *The Apocalyptic Imagination*, 4.

72. Cf. Collins, *Daniel with an Introduction to Apocalyptic Literature*, 6–23. On the characteristics of apocalyptic literature, see D. Aune, *Revelation* (WBC 52a; Dallas: Word, 1997), lxxvii–xc; J. J. Collins, ed., *Apocalypse: Towards the Morphology of a Genre* (Semeia 14; Missoula, Mont.: Scholars, 1979); L. Morris, *Apocalyptic* (Grand Rapids: Eerdmans, 1972).

73. Collins, *Daniel with an Introduction to Apocalyptic Literature*, 4.

difficult. Finally, according to Lucas, "apocalypticism" as a sociopolitical and religious movement must be distinguished from the apocalypse and apocalyptic eschatology in the analysis of so-called apocalyptic literature.[74]

Based on the presence of the foregoing shared cluster of characteristics common to apocalyptic prophecy, the book of Daniel is identified as an apocalypse.[75] Daniel is further classified as an "historical" apocalypse (i.e., characterized by visions and an interest in the development of history), in contrast to the "otherworldly journey" type of apocalypse (i.e., marked by the heavenly ascent of a hero figure and an interest in cosmological speculation). According to the grid published by the SBL Genres Project, Daniel shares seven traits with other historical apocalypses, such as the extrabiblical books of *2 Baruch*, *4 Esdras*, and *Jubilees*. The seven apocalyptic elements discerned in Daniel include: recollection of the past, *ex eventu* prophecy, persecution, eschatological upheavals, judgment of the wicked, judgment of otherworldly beings, cosmic transformation, and resurrection.[76]

Typically, apocalypses are considered "crisis literature," tractates composed during times of oppression and persecution of the people of God by foreign powers. According to Murphy, two crises in the second temple period led to the production of apocalypses: the persecution by Antiochus IV Epiphanes beginning in 167 BC, and the Roman sacking of Jerusalem in AD 70.[77] By definition, apocalypses differ from prophetic texts in their heavy use of symbolic visions, pseudonymity, the periodization of history, and *ex eventu* prophecy.[78] The idea of resurrection from the dead (12:3) — one of the book's major contributions to Jewish and Christian theology — is also regarded as a key trait of the genre of apocalypse and a signal of a late date for the document.[79]

It should be noted, however, that Daniel is the only OT canonical book included in the catalog of Jewish intertestamental documents determined apocalypses by the SBL Genres Project. Yet Collins insists that the inclusion of Daniel in the Hebrew canon "does not negate the fact that its closest literary relationships are with noncanonical Jewish writings of the Hellenistic age."[80] Adherents to the traditional understanding of Daniel admit the Seleucid period parallels but protest the equation of apocalyptic with a late date for Daniel, since protoapocalyptic texts have a long history in the ancient Near East.[81]

Others are less rigid in defining the differences between apocalyptic and prophecy and recognize that genres "are fluid literary characterizations that have overlapping boundaries."[82] For example, Niditch traces the development of the form of the symbolic visions in Daniel (especially chs. 7–8) in stages to similar literary types in the earlier Hebrew prophets (e.g., the visions of Am 7–8 and especially Zec 1–6).[83]

---

74. Lucas, *Daniel*, 310.

75. So Collins, *The Apocalyptic Imagination*, 5, 7.

76. Ibid., 7.

77. Murphy, "Introduction to Apocalyptic Literature," 6–7.

78. So Smith-Christopher, "The Book of Daniel," 4.

79. Collins, "Daniel," *ABD*, 2:35.

80. Collins, "Current Issues in the Study of Daniel," 5.

81. Cf. Longman and Dillard, *Introduction to the Old Testament*, 389.

82. Ibid., 386.

83. S. Niditch, *The Symbolic Vision in Biblical Tradition* (HSN 30; Chico, Calif.: Scholars, 1983), 186–88, 243–48.

Appropriately understood, genre identification provides a larger context for the study of biblical and extrabiblical documents than many critical scholars are willing to admit. Serious study of intertestamental apocalyptic literature must take into consideration the other biblical examples of so-called "proto-apocalyptic" literature such as Isaiah 24−27, Ezekiel 36−39, Joel 2, Zechariah, and the relationship of Daniel in the OT and the book of Revelation in the NT.

One case study serves to illustrate the point of the interrelationship of the prophetic and apocalyptic genres in the OT. Collins has identified a cluster of eight apocalyptic traits (including *ex eventu* prophecy) in the book of Daniel that place the book in the category of second-century BC apocalypses as noted above.[84] Yet analysis of the visions of Zechariah 1−6 by the same criteria shows that this series of early postexilic prophetic revelations also contains seven apocalyptic traits or eschatological elements. This list contains seven of the twelve apocalyptic traits or eschatological elements (apart from *ex eventu* prophecy) cataloged by Collins: mediated revelation (Zec 1:9), recollection of the past (1:18−21), persecution (2:8), other eschatological upheavals (4:7), judgment of the wicked (1:21), judgment of other worldly beings (5:5), and cosmic transformation (1:16−18; 2:5).

Beyond this, analysis of so-called "Second Zechariah" (Zec 9−14) yields similar results in that these eschatological oracles contain six of the diagnostic apocalyptic traits used to categorize the (presumably) late genre of apocalypse. Here the list of eschatological elements (following Collins' order) includes: recollection of the past (Zec 12:10), persecution (13:7), other eschatological upheavals (14:6, 12), judgment of the wicked (9:1−8; 14:12), judgment of other worldly beings (13:2), and cosmic transformation (14:6−9).[85] Clearly, the distinctions between the later genre of the apocalypse and the proto-apocalyptic genre of the earlier Hebrew prophets are less dramatic than many critical studies of Daniel acknowledge.

Mention must be made of Daniel and the issue of predictive prophecy since *ex eventu* prophecy is one of the twelve assumed traits of the genre of apocalypse identified by Collins. The visions of Daniel focus on the time of Antiochus IV Epiphanes, prompting Collins to ask why a Hebrew prophet of the sixth century BC would have such preoccupation with events of the second century BC.[86] Goldingay concurs, arguing that such far-reaching detailed prediction of the future is not consistent with the portrayal of God elsewhere in the Bible.[87] The so-called "Akkadian Prophecies" are often cited as a parallel

---

84. Collins, *The Apocalyptic Imagination*, 7. Collins' complete list of twelve features characterizing the genre of apocalypse includes: cosmogony, primordial events, recollection of the past, *ex eventu* prophecy, persecution, other eschatological upheavals, judgment/destruction of the wicked, judgment/destruction of the world, judgment/destruction of otherworldly beings, cosmic transformation, resurrection, and others forms of afterlife.

85. Two independent studies employing differing methodologies place Zechariah 9−14 in the first half of the fifth century BC. See A. E. Hill, *Malachi* (AB 25D; New York: Doubleday, 1998), 80−84, 395−400 (utilizing a linguistic methodology); and C. L. Meyers and E. M. Meyers, *Zechariah 9−14* (AB 24C; New York: Doubleday, 1993), 22−31 (utilizing archaeological and social scientific methodologies).

86. Collins, *Daniel*, 26.

87. J. E. Goldingay, "The Book of Daniel: Three Issues," *Themelios* 3 (1977): 45.

literary form since these texts, for the most part, appear to have been written after many of the events they describe.[88]

Adherents to the traditional understanding of Daniel counter that such prediction serves both to reinforce the message of God's sovereignty central to the book and provide encouragement and assurance to the people of God who must endure the impending persecution.[89] Rather than an inconsistency in the biblical portrayal of God, such foreknowledge is basic to his divine character and one of the attributes that distinguishes him as the true God over all false deities (cf. Isa 41:22; 45:21; 46:10). Neither should the fact that Daniel represents an unusual or even unique narrative in the OT discount its credibility given the many other "one-time" experiences recorded in the Bible (e.g., Moses' encounter with God in the burning bush, the story of Jonah and the great fish, Hosea's marriage to the prostitute Gomer, etc.). Finally, there are numerous examples of God's forecasting of coming events (e.g., Joseph's dreams, Ge 37; Zechariah's visions, Zec 1:7–6:8) or warning the righteous of impending peril (e.g., the Magi, Mt 2:12; Mary and Joseph, Mt 2:19, 22). Certainly this is in keeping with his character as a God consistently depicted as merciful and compassionate (Ex 34:6; Dt 4:31; Pss 86:16; 103:8).

In the end, mainline biblical scholarship desires to assess the book of Daniel on the "balance of probabilities."[90] Depending on one's assumptions about the character of God, the nature of biblical revelation, and the development of biblical literary genres, the "balance of probability" may be understood in different ways.[91] Certainly, lumping Daniel with the late Jewish apocalypses is one option—but not the only option. Given the foregoing analysis of Zechariah 1–6 and 9–14, it is possible to place Daniel on a continuum of "proto-apocalyptic literature emerging from the early post-exilic period of Hebrew history."[92]

Such a conclusion is reinforced by the fact that the apocalyptic portions of Daniel (chs. 7–12) continue the themes found in the court stories of chs. 1–6.[93] Moreover, it is recognized that only Daniel 10–12 fits the definition of the apocalypse genre well. In addition, Daniel is a "child of prophecy,"[94] so it is only natural to look for the origins of biblical apocalyptic in the prophetic tradition of the OT.[95] Lucas's cautious summary statement is insightful:

---

88. Cf. Lucas, *Daniel*, 269–72; Goldingay, *Daniel*, 282. The texts cited in this collection typically include: the Marduk Prophecy, the Shulgi Prophecy, the Dynastic Prophecy, the Uruk Prophecy, and Text A (cf. Lucas notes that Text B and LBAT 1543 are also similar to this group). See A. K. Grayson and W. G. Lambert, "Akkadian Prophecies," *JCS* 18 (1964): 7–30; A. K. Grayson, *Babylonian Historical-Literary Texts* (Toronto: Univ. of Toronto Press, 1975); H. Hunger and S. A. Kaufman, "A New Akkadian Prophecy Text," *JAOS* 95 (1975): 371–75; W. G. Lambert, *The Background of Jewish Apocalyptic* (London: Athlone, 1978); T. Longman, "The Marduk Prophecy," *COS*, 1:480–81; idem, "The Dynastic Prophecy," *COS*, 1:481–82. Compare M. Nissinen, *Prophets and Prophecy in the Ancient Near East* (WAW 12; Atlanta: SBL, 2003).

89. E.g., Baldwin, *Daniel*, 66–67; Miller, *Daniel*, 47.

90. Collins, *The Apocalyptic Imagination*, 87–88; Lucas, *Daniel*, 309.

91. Wallace, *The Lord Is King*, 23–27.

92. Cf. Collins, *The Apocalyptic Imagination*, 23–25, who admits postexilic prophecy as one matrix for biblical apocalyptic.

93. Cf. Wallace, *The Lord Is King*, 20–22; Longman and Dillard, *Introduction to the Old Testament*, 392–93.

94. E.g., Lucas, *Daniel*, 310–11.

95. Cf. Longman and Dillard, *Introduction to the Old Testament*, 389.

It seems that Daniel does lie somewhere on a line of development between the later Hebrew prophets and the Jewish apocalypses and, on balance Daniel appears to be closer in form and content to the apocalypses. Exactly what this means in terms of the date of the final form of the book is hard to judge, since the line of development may not have been straight, and the rate of development was probably not uniform.[96]

7. THEOLOGICAL EMPHASES

The book of Daniel presents a "theology of history." Theology is understood as the portrayal of the person and work of God as revealed in the Bible. History is considered the chronological record of significant events affecting a nation or institution (and often including an explanation of their causes). In one sense, God is always both "cause" and "effect" in biblical history since he "acts" in history so that Israel and the nations might know that he is the Lord (e.g., Eze 5:5, 13). The specific historical referent here is the nation of Israel as the people of God and the Hebrew institutions of Yahweh's temple and the Davidic monarchy.

Naturally this study of history spills over to include other nations since biblical Israel existed in a particular time and space continuum (cf. Dt 7:6–8). Beyond this, the destinies of Israel and all other people groups are entwined because God chose one nation to bless all nations (Ge 12:1–3). Daniel's "theology of history" is summarized in Nebuchadnezzar's confession that God lives forever, his dominion is eternal, he rules the powers of heaven and the peoples of the earth, and nothing can prevent him from accomplishing his purposes in the world (Da 4:3, 34–35).

A theology of history was essential for the Israelites exiled in Babylonia because they suffered from "an intense condition of theological shock."[97] The four pillars of divine promise that undergirded Israel's confidence in Yahweh have been identified as: the irrevocability of God's (Sinaitic) covenant with Israel, Yahweh's ownership of the land of Canaan, Yahweh's eternal covenant with David, and Yahweh's residence in Jerusalem.[98] How were the captive Hebrews to understand the reality that Jerusalem had been sacked, Yahweh's temple razed, the Davidic dynasty terminated, and a substantial population of Israelites deported to Babylonia?

The several distinct components comprising Daniel's theology of history may be outlined as follows:

- God is sovereign over his creation as the God of gods and Lord of kings (2:47), and he determines the destiny of nations (1:2), dispenses knowledge and understanding (1:17), possesses all power and wisdom (2:20), appoints and deposes kings (2:21), reveals deep and hidden things—including the future (2:22; 7:17–18; 8:19; 10:14)—exercises eternal dominion (4:3; 7:14), controls the fate of individuals (5:23), performs signs and wonders and rescues and saves (3:28–29; 6:27), and keeps his covenant of love (9:4). Davies summarizes that as the God of history Yahweh *knows* all, *controls* all, and *rescues*.[99]

---

96. Lucas, *Daniel*, 311.
97. D. I. Block, "Ezekiel, Theology of," *NIDOTTE*, 4:616.
98. Ibid.
99. Davies, *Daniel*, 86.

- The people of God living under his sovereign rule must trust in his control, accept responsibility for their actions, and look to the future in hope. Prayer is the vehicle for this hopeful outlook and the catalyst for change. Daniel's example and message assure the Hebrews that despite the fact that the Jerusalem temple—Yahweh's house of prayer—is destroyed, he still hears and answers prayer. Prayer to Yahweh may or may not bring deliverance (as the testimony of Daniel's three friends acknowledges; 3:16–18). That is not the point, however, but rather the posture of faithfulness toward God in the face of trial, whether that posture results in deliverance or martyrdom. It is through prayer that Israel maintains covenantal relationship with God (1Ki 8:30), and prayer is one means by which order is recovered out of chaos (1Ki 8:34, 36, 39, 43, 45, 50; cf. Jas 5:16).

- God's people living under his sovereign rule must discern that not all suffering is retributive based on the blessings and curses of covenantal relationship with Yahweh (cf. Dt 28). Daniel warns God's people of times of persecution and oppression ahead inflicted by the nations ruling over Israel (Da 7:25; 8:24; 11:16, 24). Unlike the divine judgment of the Babylonian exile, they need to know that this suffering is not necessarily punishment for sin but divine discipline for purification (11:35). Daniel makes it clear that this "time of distress" is temporary (11:32) and that the true people of God will persevere and experience deliverance (12:1). Death itself proves to be no barrier to God's sovereignty or faithfulness, as the promise of resurrection will bring vindication to the righteous who die as a result of the persecution (12:2–3).

- God's people living under his sovereign rule must recognize that a series of empires must rise and fall and that an interim period of "waiting" must elapse before the kingdom of God breaks into history (12:4, 9–13). This means God's promises for Israel's restoration after the exile, as forecast by Jeremiah (e.g., Jer 31:31–34) and Ezekiel (e.g., Eze 34:23–25; 37:24–25), have not failed but will be delayed until God's purposes are accomplished through the historical process of the rise and fall of nations. This ability to make known to his people such things pertaining to the future is both a mark of God's omniscience and an act of his grace (cf. Isa 41:21–22; 44:26–27).

8. TEXT AND VERSIONS

Overall, the Hebrew and Aramaic of Daniel as represented in the Masoretic Test (MT) have been well preserved—a conclusion supported by the evidence of the LXX and other ancient versions. Montgomery has noted that the MT of Daniel contains an unusual amount of variation both in the Kethib and Qere and in the variant readings of the manuscripts.[100] Generally speaking, the Qumran fragments of Daniel support the MT and offer testimony to the faithful transmission of the text over the centuries. Baldwin has commented that the range of individual variants found in the Qumran manuscripts suggest that when these texts were written the Qumran community had no standardized "canonical" text.[101] We have no Aramaic Targum of the book of Daniel.[102]

---

100. J. A. Montgomery, *The Book of Daniel* (ICC; Edinburgh: T. & T. Clark, 1927), 12.

101. Baldwin, *Daniel*, 44–45.

102. See the discussions of the Hebrew text and ancient versions of Daniel in Collins, *Daniel*, 2–24; Hartman and Di Lella, *The Book of Daniel*, 72–84; Lucas, *Daniel*, 19–22; and Montgomery, *The Book of Daniel*, 11–57.

According to Lucas, the primary witnesses to the original Hebrew and Aramaic text of Daniel beyond the MT are the Qumran manuscripts, the Greek versions, the Latin Vulgate, and the Syriac Peshitta.[103]

The Qumran evidence is especially important for the study of Daniel since it attests the changes from Hebrew to Aramaic and back at 2:4b and 8:1. Further, the prayers of the Additions to Daniel in the ancient Greek version of the book are not contained in the text of ch. 3 in the Qumran manuscripts.[104] Collins summarizes by saying that "on the whole, the Qumran discoveries provide powerful evidence of the antiquity of the textual tradition of the MT."[105]

The textual history of the Greek versions of Daniel is complex, and little consensus has emerged in the scholarly debate. Two distinct textual traditions of Daniel have been preserved: the Old Greek (or LXX) and the Greek version of Theodotion. The relationship between the two Greek versions remains a puzzle. Both of the Greek textual traditions include the Additions to Daniel. Di Lella concludes that the Greek forms of the text of Daniel are valuable to study for their own sake quite apart from their relationship to parent text(s) since they represent an early interpretation of the book.[106]

Jerome translated the book of Daniel into Latin between AD 389 and 392. His Latin Vulgate version was based on the Hebrew and Aramaic text, but he was clearly aware of the earlier versions through the Hexapla. The Old Latin version, which predates Jerome's Vulgate, is known only from patristic citations and a few fragmentary manuscripts.[107]

The Old Syriac or Peshitta is a translation of the Bible dating to the third century AD and has been preserved in three versions (the Peshitta, the Syro-Hexapla, and the revision of Jacob of Edessa). There is some question as to exactly when the OT was translated into Syriac and whether or not the translation was made by non-Christian Jews or Jewish Christians. The Peshitta was translated from the Hebrew and Aramaic text but also shows dependency on the Greek version of Theodotion.[108]

9. LANGUAGES

The book of Daniel is written in two languages, Hebrew (1–2:4a; 8–12) and Aramaic (2:4b–7:28). Daniel shares with the book of Ezra this feature of composition in dual languages; Ezra includes portions of four chapters written in Aramaic (4:8–6:18; 7:12–26). Beyond this, only two other verses in the OT contain Aramaic (Ge 31:47; Jer 10:11).

Aramaic is a west-Semitic language closely related to Hebrew and is associated with the Arameans, who lived in northwestern Mesopotamia. Aramaic has a long history of usage in the biblical world, attested by inscriptions written in the Old Aramaic dialect dating back to the ninth century BC. Imperial Aramaic

---

103. Lucas, *Daniel*, 21.

104. Ibid., 19.

105. Collins, *Daniel*, 3; cf. P. W. Flint, "The Daniel Tradition at Qumran," in *The Book of Daniel*, ed. J. J. Collins and P. W. Flint (Leiden: Brill, 2002), 2:329–67.

106. A. A. Di Lella, "The Textual History of Septuagint-Daniel and Theodotion-Daniel," in *The Book of Daniel*, ed. J. J. Collins and P. W. Flint (Leiden: Brill, 2002), 2:604–5.

107. See Montgomery, *The Book of Daniel*, 29–32.

108. See K. D. Jenner, "Syriac Daniel," in *The Book of Daniel*, ed. J. J. Collins and P. W. Flint (Leiden: Brill, 2002), 2:608–37; R. A. Taylor, *The Peshitta of Daniel* (Peshitta Institute Monograph 7; Leiden: Brill, 1994).

became the dominant language of the ancient Near East, supplanting Akkadian as the lingua franca of the region during the Neo-Assyrian Empire (ca. 1100–600 BC) and the Neo-Babylonian Empire (ca. 600–540 BC). Aramaic reached its zenith as the official language of the Persian Empire (ca. 500–300 BC) but was then replaced by Greek as the lingua franca of the Hellenistic era.

Speculation persists as to why portions of Daniel were written in Aramaic. According to Archer, the subject matter of chs. 2–7 pertained directly to the citizenry of Babylonia and Persia.[109] Hence the material was composed in Aramaic and perhaps made available to the Gentile public in some way. Others have suggested the entire book was originally composed in Aramaic but later portions were translated into Hebrew to ensure the book's canonicity.[110] Others consider the Aramaic section of Daniel a literary device on the part of the narrator for the purpose of lending authenticity to the dialogue.[111]

The reason for the shift from Hebrew to Aramaic and then back to Hebrew in the book of Daniel remains an open question. Maier's proposal is as plausible as any of the several options offered by biblical interpreters. He suggests that Daniel 1:1–2:4a may reflect notes taken from the (Hebrew) journal of Daniel in his youth, while 2:4b–7:28 is based on more official Aramaic documents of the Babylonian royal archives. Daniel reverts to the Hebrew language of his youth in chs. 8–12—perhaps an indication of his more marginal status in the royal circles at this juncture in his career. The angelic command to "seal ... the scroll" (12:4) prevented him (or anyone else) from rewriting the entire book in a single language.[112]

Scholars on both sides of the debate concerning the date of writing for the book of Daniel have marshaled impressive catalogs of linguistic and lexical data comparing the Aramaic of Daniel with other Aramaic documents, all in an effort to connect the Aramaic of Daniel with an earlier or later dialect of the language, depending on the predilection of the proponent assembling the data for an early or late date for the book.[113] It is clear that the Aramaic portions of Daniel belong to the official or imperial Aramaic utilized between 700 and 200 BC. It appears distinct from the Aramaic used at Qumran, a later Middle Aramaic dialect in use between 200 BC and AD 200. There seems to be a growing consensus that Baldwin is correct in her observation that "the date of Daniel cannot be decided on linguistic grounds."[114]

10. CANONICITY (AND THE ADDITIONS)

Two issues have emerged in the scholarly debate related to the canonicity of the book of Daniel. The first concerns that of Daniel's position in the arrangement of books in the Hebrew Bible as represented by the MT. There Daniel is grouped among the Writings, being placed after the book of Esther and before the books of Ezra-Nehemiah and Chronicles. Presumably, an emphasis on the court stories of the first half of

---

109. G. L. Archer, "Daniel," *EBC*, 7:6.

110. Hartman and Di Lella, *The Book of Daniel*, 14.

111. See discussion in Longman and Dillard, *Introduction to the Old Testament*, 389.

112. G. Maier, *Der Prophet Daniel* (Wuppertaler Studienbibel; Wuppertal: R. Brockhaus, 1982), 98–100.

113. Cf. Kitchen, "The Aramaic of Daniel," 31–79; Collins, *Daniel*, 12–23.

114. Baldwin, *Daniel*, 35; cf. Lucas, *Daniel*, 308: "The evidence of the [Greek] loan-words is now seen to be quite indecisive with regard to dating. The character of the Hebrew and Aramaic could support a date in the fifth or fourth century for the extant written form of the book, but does not demand a second-century date."

the book (chs. 1–6) made it a logical parallel to the book of Esther as complementary stories about the experience of Jewish displacement during the exile.[115] The LXX or Greek version of the OT and other ancient versions included Daniel as the last of the four books of the so-called Major Prophets (along with Isaiah, Jeremiah, and Ezekiel).[116] It is assumed that the affinities of Daniel's visions (chs. 7–12) with the book of Ezekiel made Daniel's association with the Hebrew Prophets a logical one.[117] The English Bible follows the convention of the Greek OT (LXX) in placing Daniel in the collection of the Major Prophets.

Generally, the collection of books known as the Writings (*Ketubim* or Hagiographa) is considered the latest addition to the canon of the Hebrew Bible (completed sometime between the second century BC and AD 90).[118] Critical scholars infer that Daniel's inclusion in the "third canon" (or Writings) of the Hebrew Bible was further evidence of a later (i.e., Maccabean era) date for the composition of the book.[119] The omission of Daniel in the hymn honoring the faithful ancestors of the Israelites in Ben Sira is often cited as supporting evidence for this view.[120] In addition, the literary device of pseudepigraphy is seen as a link connecting Daniel with Ecclesiastes and the Song of Solomon in the collection of the Writings.[121]

The rebuttal by proponents of the traditional view to the argument that the placement of Daniel in the Hebrew Bible signals a late date for the book is multifaceted.

1. Daniel was a governmental official and not formally a member of the prophetic corps, as were Isaiah, Hosea, and Jeremiah.[122]

2. It is apparent that the canonical order of the books in the Latter Prophets (Isaiah through Malachi) and the Writings (Psalms through Chronicles) in the Hebrew Bible was not as fixed as the order of the books in the Torah (Genesis through Deuteronomy) and the Former Prophets (Joshua through Kings). For instance, Josephus (*Ag. Ap.* 1:1–5) does not include Daniel in the collection of the Writings.

3. The rationale for the ordering of the four historical books in the Writings (Daniel, Esther, Ezra–Nehemiah, Chronicles) is chronological (based on the evidence of the *baraitas* [i.e., independent collections of Jewish teaching and commentary never incorporated into the Mishnah]).[123]

4. Finally, conservative scholars cite the existence of Daniel in its full form in the LXX and Qumran scrolls fragments as an indication that the book had been distributed and accepted over a wide geographical area prior to the time of Antiochus IV Epiphanes.[124]

---

115. So Seow, *Daniel*, 2.

116. Cf. Baldwin, *Daniel*, 71.

117. So Seow, *Daniel*, 2.

118. Cf. Beckwith, *The Old Testament Canon*, 138–53.

119. Ibid., 355.

120. Cf. A. Jeffery, "The Book of Daniel, Introduction and Exegesis," *IB*, 6:349.

121. D. N. Freedman, "Canon of the Old Testament," *IDBSup*, 133.

122. Miller, *Daniel*, 25.

123. Cf. Beckwith, *The Old Testament Canon*, 157, 160.

124. E.g., W. S. LaSor, D. A. Hubbard, and F. W. Bush, *Old Testament Survey*, 2nd ed. (Grand Rapids: Eerdmans, 1996), 574.

The differences between the Hebrew and Greek texts of Daniel are not restricted to placement in the canon. The Greek version of Daniel contains three extra chapters of material: the Prayer of Azariah and the Hymn of the Three Young Men (inserted after 3:23); the story of Susanna (inserted before ch. 1 in some Greek versions and after ch. 12 in others); and the story of Bel and the Dragon (placed at the end of the book).[125]

The Prayer of Azariah and the Hymn of the Three Young Men is the only one of the Additions to Daniel that directly supplements the canonical book of Daniel. The document purports to record the prayer of Azariah (or Abednego) after he and his two friends were bound and thrown into a blazing furnace for refusing to worship the golden image erected by King Nebuchadnezzar (3:12, 21–23). The Hymn of the Three Young Men is the song of praise sung by the three Hebrews while they walked about in the furnace.

The story of Susanna is considered one of the finest short stories in world literature. It recounts the tale of how a young "hero" named Daniel rescues the "heroine" Susanna from false charges of adultery levied against her by two lecherous Jewish elders.

The stories of Bel and the Dragon combine two popular tales in which Daniel destroys the idol Bel and kills the Dragon, worshiped as a "living god" by the Babylonians. Both stories mock the false worship of the pagans and expose the folly of idolatry.

The Additions to Daniel belong to the collection of Jewish writings dating from the intertestamental period of Judaism known in the Protestant church as the Apocrypha. These fourteen (or fifteen, depending on enumeration) books were composed in Hebrew, Greek, and Aramaic during the intertestamental period of Judaism (ca. 200 BC to AD 100). The books have been preserved in Greek, Latin, Ethiopic, Coptic, Arabic, Syriac, and Armenian. The Apocrypha contains six different genres of literature: didactic, religious, historical, prophetic (epistolary and apocalyptic), and legendary writings.

The books of the Apocrypha were never incorporated into the canon of the Hebrew Bible. They were added one by one to later editions of the Greek versions of the OT. The early Christian church appealed to these additional Jewish documents in its preaching and teaching, to the point where the Synod of Hippo (AD 393) authorized the use of the Apocrypha as canon. The books of the Apocrypha were rejected as canon by the Protestant Reformers but affirmed by the Catholic Church at the Council of Trent (AD 1546) as part of the Roman Counter-Reformation.[126]

11. DANIEL AND THE NEW TESTAMENT

The NT makes direct appeal to the book of Daniel in only five instances (the citation of Da 7:13 in Mt 24:30; 26:64; Mk 13:26; 14:62; Lk 21:27 in reference to the sign of the coming of the "son of man").[127] Beyond this, allusions to the book of Daniel indexed in the major editions of the Greek NT number in the

---

125. See D. A. deSilva, *Introducing the Apocrypha* (Grand Rapids: Baker, 2002), 222–43.

126. On the history of the canonical status of the OT Apocrypha, see ibid., 26–41.

127. According to the Scripture Index of the Nestle-Aland *Novum Testamentum Graece* (26th ed.), 66–67. The 27th edition of *Novum Testamentum Graece* (796–98) includes citations to Daniel 3:6 [Mt 13:42, 50]; Daniel 9:27 [Mt 4:5; 24:15; Mk 13:14]; Daniel 11:31 [Mt 24:15; Mk 13:14]; Daniel 12:11 [Mk 13:14]; Maier (*Der Prophet Daniel*, 63) agrees with these.

hundreds.[128] The identification of such intertextual relationships between Daniel and the NT are dependent, in part, on one's definition of what constitutes a NT allusion to an OT precursor text and the degree of imagination biblical scholars apply to the NT text in isolating such allusions.

Numerous NT allusions to the book of Daniel have been identified as a result of the comparative analysis of the two Testaments. For example, Jesus' reference to the time of "great distress" before the second advent of the Messiah echoes the "distress" Daniel foresees in the end times (Mt 24:21; cf. Da 12:1). Paul appears to associate the "man of lawlessness" who exalts himself "over everything that is called God" (2Th 2:3–4) with the "king" described by Daniel who "speaks against the Most High" (Da 7:24–25). The ledger of the OT faithful in the book of Hebrews preserves the tradition of Daniel's deliverance from the lions' den (Heb 11:33; cf. Da 6:21). Additionally, James's blessing of those who have "persevered" in the face of suffering (Jas 5:11) may be linked to Daniel's blessing of those who "wait" until the end (Da 12:12).

Daniel's influence on the NT is most prominent in the book of Revelation. For instance, more than fifty-five percent of the "Index of Quotations" citations in the UBS Greek NT are to the book of Revelation, while forty-two percent of the citations in the Nestle-Aland index are to the book of Revelation. Specific examples include the vision of a terrifying beast with seven heads and ten horns (Rev 12:3; cf. Da 7:7), the reference to the "beast" or "little horn" that speaks boastfully (Rev 13:5; cf. Da 7:8), the description of the Ancient of Days (Rev 1:14; cf. Da 7:9), the vision of the thrones of judgment (Rev 20:4; cf. Da 7:9), and the report of the casting down of the starry host of heaven to earth (Rev 12:4; cf. Da 8:10).[129]

Evans summarizes that the book of Daniel is important to the NT in terms of Christology, especially Jesus' understanding of the kingdom of God, his suffering and his rule as Son of Man, the coregency of his disciples, and the day of judgment.[130] The discussion of specific examples of intertextuality between the NT and Daniel is taken up in the commentary where pertinent.

12. SPECIAL PROBLEMS

The critical study of Daniel has raised numerous questions related to the book's understanding of certain aspects of ancient Near Eastern chronology and history, as well as the use of select vocabulary items. Beyond this, the inclusion of the apocalyptic literary genre and Daniel's place in the Hebrew canon are typically cited as further difficulties complicating the study of the book (see Literary Form, as well as Canonicity, above). The catalog of special problems associated with the book of Daniel includes, but is not necessarily restricted to:

- the report of the siege of Jerusalem in the third year of King Jehoiakim (1.3)
- the use of the term "Chaldean" for a guild of astrologers (2:2, 4–5)
- the use of the Aramaic language in the book (2:4b–7:28)

---

128. E.g., the Scripture Index of the United Bible Societies' *Greek New Testament* (4th ed.) lists more than 130 allusions to Daniel in the NT, while the tables in the Nestle-Aland *Novum Testamentum Graece* (27th ed.) list more than two hundred allusions to Daniel in the NT.

129. See G. K. Beale, "The Influence of Daniel on the Structure and Theology of John's Apocalypse," *JETS* 27 (1984): 413–23.

130. C. A. Evans, "Daniel in the New Testament: Visions of God's Kingdom," in *The Book of Daniel*, ed. J. J. Collins and P. W. Flint (Leiden: Brill, 2002), 2:526; see also the discussion in Collins, *Daniel*, 90–113.

- the use of Greek loanwords for musical instruments (3:5)
- the account of King Nebuchadnezzar's "madness" (ch. 4)
- the reference to Belshazzar as "king" (5:1)
- the reference to Darius the Mede (5:30)
- the reference to Darius son of Xerxes (9:1)

These issues are addressed in the commentary as appropriate.

13. BIBLIOGRAPHY

Anderson, Robert A. *Daniel: Signs and Wonders.* International Theological Commentary. Grand Rapids: Eerdmans, 1984.

Archer, G. L. "Daniel." Pages 3–157 in *The Expositor's Bible Commentary.* Vol. 7. Edited by F. E. Gaebelein. Grand Rapids: Zondervan, 1985.

Baldwin, Joyce G. *Daniel.* Tyndale Old Testament Commentaries 21. Downers Grove, Ill.: InterVarsity Press, 1978.

Collins, John J. *Daniel: with an Introduction to Apocalyptic Literature.* Forms of the Old Testament Literature 20. Grand Rapids: Eerdmans, 1984.

———. *Daniel.* Hermeneia. Minneapolis: Fortress, 1993.

Davies, P. R. *Daniel.* Old Testament Guides. Sheffield: Sheffield Academic Press, 1985.

Fewell, D. N. *Circle of Sovereignty: Plotting Politics in the Book of Daniel.* Journal for the Study of the Old Testament Supplement Series 72. Sheffield: Sheffield Academic Press, 1988.

Goldingay, John E. *Daniel.* Word Biblical Commentary 30. Dallas: Word, 1989.

Gowan, Donald E. *Daniel.* Abingdon Old Testament Commentaries 20. Nashville: Abingdon, 2001.

Hartman, Louis F., and Alexander A. Di Lella. *The Book of Daniel.* Anchor Bible 23. New York: Doubleday, 1978.

Heaton, E. *Daniel.* Torch Bible Commentaries. London: SCM, 1956.

Humphreys, W. L. "A Life-style for Diaspora." *Journal of Biblical Literature* 92 (1973): 211–23.

Keil, C. F., and F. Delitzsch. *Commentary on the Old Testament: Ezekiel, Daniel.* Vol. 9. Repr., Grand Rapids: Eerdmans, 1975.

Kraemer, R. S. "Women in Daniel." Pages 340–44 in *Women in Scripture.* Edited by C. Meyers. Grand Rapids: Eerdmans, 2000.

Lacocque, Andre. *The Book of Daniel.* Translated by D. Pellauer. Atlanta: John Knox, 1979.

Longman, Tremper. *Daniel.* NIV Application Commentary. Grand Rapids: Zondervan, 1999.

Lucas, E. C. *Daniel.* Apollos Old Testament Commentary. Downers Grove, Ill.: InterVarsity Press, 2002.

Miller, Stephen R. *Daniel.* New American Commentary 18. Nashville: Broadman & Holman, 1994.

Montgomery, J. A. *The Book of Daniel.* International Critical Commentary. Edinburgh: T. & T. Clark, 1927.

Porteous, Norman W. *Daniel.* Old Testament Library. Philadelphia: Westminster, 1965.

Redditt, P. L. *Daniel.* New Century Bible Commentary. Sheffield: Sheffield Academic Press, 1999.

Russell, D. S. *Daniel.* Daily Study Bible. Philadelphia: Westminster, 1981.

Seow, C. L. *Daniel.* Wycliffe Bible Commentary. Louisville: Westminster John Knox, 2003.

Smith-Christopher, Daniel L. "The Book of Daniel." Pages 19–152 in *The New Interpreter's Bible.* Vol. 7. Edited by L. E. Keck. Nashville: Abingdon, 1996.

Towner, W. Sibley. *Daniel.* Interpretation. Atlanta: John Knox, 1984.

Wallace, Ronald S. *The Lord Is King: The Message of Daniel.* The Bible Speaks Today. Downers Grove, Ill.: InterVarsity Press, 1979.

Wills, L. M. *The Jew in the Court of the Foreign King.* Harvard Dissertations in Religion 26. Minneapolis: Fortress, 1990.

Wiseman, Donald J. *Notes on Some Problems in the Book of Daniel.* London: Tyndale, 1965.

———. *Nebuchadrezzar and Babylon.* Oxford: Oxford University Press, 1985.

Wood, L. J. *A Commentary on Daniel.* Grand Rapids: Zondervan, 1973.

Young, E. J. *The Prophecy of Daniel: A Commentary.* Grand Rapids: Eerdmans, 1949.

14. OUTLINE

I. Stories about Daniel (1:1–6:28)

  A. Daniel and the Three Friends in Nebuchadnezzar's Court (1:1–21)

    1. Historical Introduction (1:1–2)

    2. The Main Characters (1:3–7)

    3. The Plot (1:8–17)

    4. Foreshadow of the Outcome (1:18–21)

  B. Nebuchadnezzar's Dream of the Statue (2:1–49)

    1. A Troubling Dream for the King and a Crisis for the Wise Men (2:1–13)

    2. Daniel's Intervention and God's Intervention (2:14–23)

    3. Daniel Describes the Content of the King's Dream (2:24–35)

    4. Daniel Interprets the King's Dream (2:36–45)

    5. The King's Response to Daniel's Interpretation (2:46–49)

  C. The Golden Image and the Fiery Furnace (3:1–30)

    1. Nebuchadnezzar's Golden Image (3:1–7)

    2. The Three Hebrews Accused (3:8–12)

    3. The Three Hebrews Stand Trial before Nebuchadnezzar (3:13–18)

    4. The Three Hebrews Sentenced (3:19–23)

    5. The Three Hebrews Delivered (3:24–27)

    6. Nebuchadnezzar's Proclamation (3:28–30)

  D. Nebuchadnezzar's Dream of the Tree (4:1–37)

    1. Nebuchadnezzar's Proclamation and Doxology (4:1–3 [3:31–33])

    2. The Report of the King's Dream (4:4–18 [4:1–15])

    3. The Interpretation of the Dream (4:19–27 [4:16–24])

    4. The Fulfillment of the Dream (4:28–33 [4:25–30])

    5. Conclusion and Doxology (4:34–37 [4:31–34])

  E. Belshazzar's Feast and the Writing on the Wall (5:1–31 [5:1–6:1])

    1. Belshazzar's Great Banquet (5:1–9)

    2. The Queen Introduces Daniel (5:10–12)

    3. Belshazzar Summons Daniel (5:13–16)

    4. Daniel Explains the Handwriting on the Wall (5:17–28)

    5. Conclusion (5:29–31 [5:29–6:1])

  F. The Lion's Den (6:1–28 [6:2–29])

    1. Daniel's Success (6:1–3 [6:2–4])

    2. The Conspiracy against Daniel (6:4–9 [6:5–10])

    3. Daniel Accused and Condemned (6:10–18 [6:11–19])

    4. Daniel's Deliverance (6:19–24 [6:20–25])

    5. Darius's Letter of Proclamation and Doxology (6:25–28 [6:26–29])

Text and Exposition

I. STORIES ABOUT DANIEL (1:1–6:28)

A. Daniel and the Three Friends in Nebuchadnezzar's Court (1:1–21)

OVERVIEW

The opening chapter of Daniel introduces the "court stories" section of the book (chs. 1–6). These stories are narrative episodes told in the third person and relate the exploits of Daniel and his three companions during their captivity in Babylon. The content of ch. 1 may be outlined in four units: the first (vv.1–2) provides the setting of the book of Daniel (the royal court of King Nebuchadnezzar of Babylonia and his successors; v.1), and the central theological theme of the book (God's sovereignty, as "the Lord delivered" Jehoiakim to the Babylonians; v.2); the second (vv.3–7) introduces the main

characters, or protagonists, of the narratives—the Hebrew captives Daniel, Hananiah, Mishael, and Azariah; the third (vv.8–17) offers clues as to the key elements of the "plot" of the book as a narrative, especially nonconformity to the dominant culture (v.8), the testing of faith in God (v.12), and divine provision (v.17); the final literary unit (vv.18–21) foreshadows the outcome of the court stories of the first half of the book—the success and longevity of the four Hebrew captives as officials in the royal court of Babylon.

1. Historical Introduction (1:1–2)

¹In the third year of the reign of Jehoiakim king of Judah, Nebuchadnezzar king of Babylon came to Jerusalem and besieged it. ²And the Lord delivered Jehoiakim king of Judah into his hand, along with some of the articles from the temple of God. These he carried off to the temple of his god in Babylonia and put in the treasure house of his god.

COMMENTARY

1 King Jehoiakim (609–597 BC) was installed as a "puppet king" by Pharaoh Neco of Egypt after the death of King Josiah (cf. 2Ki 23:30, 34). The third year of Jehoiakim's reign dates Nebuchadnezzar's siege of Jerusalem and Daniel's subsequent captivity

to 605 BC. This date accords with the accession-year method characteristic of the Babylonian system for computing regnal years (i.e., reckoning a king's first full year of kingship to commence on the New Year's Day after his accession to the throne, or 608

BC for Jehoiakim; cf. Wiseman, *Nebuchadrezzar and Babylon*, 16–18). Critics point to the chronological discrepancy in the biblical reporting of the date of the event in that Jeremiah synchronizes the first year of Nebuchadnezzar's reign with the fourth year of King Jehoiakim's reign (Jer 25:1, 9; cf. Porteous, 25–26). Yet if one assumes that Jeremiah is based on a nonaccession-year method of reckoning regnal years (more common to Egyptian and Syro-Palestinian practice), the difficulty fades and the dates are readily harmonized (cf. Longman and Dillard, 376–77).

Beyond this, critics dispute the historical veracity of Daniel's report of a Babylonian siege of Jerusalem in 605 BC because there is no record of such an incursion into Palestine at that time (cf. Redditt, 43). There is, however, indirect evidence for a Babylonian campaign in Palestine in 605 BC. Josephus (*Ag. Ap.* 1:19) cites a Babylonian priest-historian named Berossus, who recorded that Nebuchadnezzar was engaged in campaigns in Egypt, Syria, and Phoenicia at the time his father died (cf. Wiseman, *Nebuchadrezzar and Babylon*, 15). Further, a cuneiform tablet published in 1956 indicates that Nebuchadnezzar "conquered the whole area of the Hatti-country" shortly after the battle of Carchemish in 605 BC. The geographical term "Hatti" would have included the whole of Syria and Palestine at this time period (cf. Miller, 57; see also Donald J. Wiseman, *Chronicles of the Chaldean Kings* [London: Trustees of the British Museum, 1961], 69).

The siege of Jerusalem in 605 BC, then, was the first of three major invasions of Palestine by Babylonians (although there is no reference to armed conflict in vv. 1–2, and the verb "besieged" [Heb. *ṣwr*] may suggest more threat than substance, as evidenced in Goldingay's [3] translation "blockaded"; cf. Wood, 30, who comments that "likely only token resistance was made, with the Judeans recognizing the wisdom of peaceful capitulation").

The second incursion occurred at the end of Jehoiakim's reign in 598 BC, when King Nebuchadnezzar was finally in a position to move against the disloyal Judean vassal (Jehoiakim had rebelled earlier against Babylonia ca. 603 BC; cf. 2Ki 24:1–7). By the time Nebuchadnezzar reached Jerusalem, Jehoiakim had died and Jehoiachin his son was king of Judah (2Ki 24:8). As a result of this invasion of Judah, King Jehoiachin was deposed and exiled along with ten thousand citizens of Jerusalem (including Ezekiel; 2Ki 24:10–17; cf. Eze 1:1–2).

The third Babylonian invasion of Judah was swift and decisive. Nebuchadnezzar surrounded Jerusalem in 588 BC and after a lengthy siege, the city was sacked, Yahweh's temple was plundered and destroyed, and Davidic kingship in Judah ceased (2Ki 24:18–25:21).

Nebuchadnezzar II was the eldest son of Nabopolassar and is considered one of the greatest kings of ancient times. He ruled the Babylonian Empire from 605–562 BC—an empire that stretched across the ancient Near East from Elam in the east to Egypt in the west. Miller, 56, notes that the writer of Daniel refers proleptically to Nebuchadnezzar as "king of Babylon," since he was actually crowned king some two or three months after the siege of Jerusalem.

The city of Babylon lay on the Euphrates River, some fifty miles south of modern Baghdad in Iraq. It reached the height of its splendor as the capital of the Chaldean or Neo-Babylonian Empire because of the extensive building activities of Nabopolassar and Nebuchadnezzar. The storied Hanging Gardens of Babylon were counted among the "wonders" of the ancient world. The prophet Jeremiah predicted the overthrow of Babylon as divine retribution for her evil deeds (Jer 25:12–14; cf. Isaiah's prophecy in Isa 13:2–22 against the city of Babylon during the Assyrian period). In the NT,

Babylon symbolizes the decadence and wickedness of Rome (cf. 1Pe 5:13; Rev 14:8).

2 From the outset of the book, the record clearly indicates that Nebuchadnezzar's success is not entirely his own doing. The Lord "delivered" (cf. NASB, "gave") Jehoiakim into the hands of King Nebuchadnezzar in that he permitted the Babylonian subjugation of Judah. (See *NIDOTTE*, 3:206, on the use of the Heb. verb *nātan* ["to give"] to connote "hand over in judgment.") This introductory statement reveals the unifying theme for the whole book: God's sovereign rule of human history. God's judgment of the divided kingdoms of Israel and Judah was not capricious or arbitrary. The threat of divine punishment, including exile from the land of the Abrahamic promise, was embedded in the blessings and curses of the Mosaic covenant (cf. Lev 18:24–30; 26; Dt 28). Owing to God's covenantal faithfulness, he was extremely patient and longsuffering with his people Israel, warning them through his prophets over centuries of the dire consequences of habitual covenantal disobedience (cf. Ne 9:29–32). Daniel was not oblivious to all this, as attested by his prayer for his people (Da 9:4–11).

Placing objects plundered from the temples of vanquished enemies as trophies of war in the temple(s) of the gods of the victors was common practice in the biblical world (e.g., 1Sa 5:2). The act symbolized the supremacy of the deities of the conquering nation over the gods of the peoples and nations subjugated by the imperialist armies (cf. *BBCOT*, 287). The articles or vessels from the Jerusalem temple confiscated by Nebuchadnezzar are not itemized. It is possible these articles were given as tribute to Nebuchadnezzar in order to lift the siege against the city (after the earlier example of the payments made by kings Ahaz and Hezekiah to the Assyrians; cf. 2Ki 16:8; 18:15). The temple treasury cache may have included gold and silver ceremonial cups and utensils displayed to the envoy

of the Babylonian king Merodach-Baladan by King Hezekiah a century earlier (cf. 2Ki 20:12–13). The prophet Isaiah rebuked Hezekiah's pride and predicted his treasures would be plundered and carried off to Babylon (Isa 39:6; cf. the prohibition in Dt 17:17 against stockpiling wealth given to the Hebrew kings in anticipation of an Israelite monarchy).

Later, King Belshazzar paraded these gold and silver goblets before his nobles at a great feast, precipitating the episode of the writing on the wall and the demise of his kingship (Da 5:1–2, 25–31). Finally, some of these implements may have been part of the larger inventory of temple treasure plundered by the Babylonians that King Cyrus of Persia restored to the Hebrews and that were relocated in Judah when the exiles returned to the land under the leadership of Sheshbazzar (Ezr 1:7–11). All this serves as a reminder that everything under heaven belongs to God and that he providentially oversees what belongs to him—whether his people Israel or drinking bowls from his temple (cf. Job 41:11).

The historical setting laid out in the opening verses is also important to the theology of exile developed in the book of Daniel. It is clear from Daniel's prayer in ch. 9 that he is aware of Jeremiah's prophecies projecting a Babylonian exile lasting some seventy years (Da 9:2; cf. Jer 25:12; 29:10). The date formulas in books of subsequent prophets of the exile, such as Jeremiah (e.g., Jer 52:31) and Ezekiel (e.g., Eze 1:2), serve as "covenantal time-clocks" of sorts as they track the chronological progression of God's judgment against his people for their sin of idolatry in anticipation of the restoration of Israel to the land of covenantal promise (Jer 44:3–6; cf. Lev 18:24–30). Elements of Daniel's "theology of exile" developed in later sections of the commentary include: the value of prayer for Hebrews in the Diaspora, the role obedience and faithfulness to God play in the success of the Hebrews in the Diaspora, and insights into the nature and character of divine justice and human suffering in the light of the persecution experienced by Israel during and after the Babylonian exile.

More significant for the Hebrews was the crisis in theology created by the historical setting of the Babylonian exile. The Israelites, the people of Yahweh, lost possession of their land, had their temple razed, and had the office of kingship eradicated in one fell swoop to the marauding hordes of King Nebuchadnezzar and the gods of Babylonia. As Wallace, 31, observes, the Hebrews needed a new theology. God's people needed a "Diaspora theology" addressing the problem of how to live as a minority group in an alien majority culture sometimes hostile, sometimes friendly; how were they to "fit in without being swallowed up?" The remainder of ch. 1 and the rest of the court stories take up the challenge of answering this very question.

NOTES

1 The form of the name נְבֻכַדְנֶאצַּר (*nᵉbûkadneʾṣṣar*, "Nebuchadnezzar") given in Daniel is also found in 2 Kings, Chronicles, Ezra, Nehemiah, and Esther. The alternative spelling נְבֻכַדְרֶאצַּר (*nᵉbûkadreʾṣṣar*, "Nebuchadrezzar") appears in Jeremiah (except ch. 28) and Ezekiel. According to Wiseman (*Nebuchadrezzar and Babylon*, 2–3), there is no need to assume that the name Nebuchadnezzar reflects an Aramaic pronunciation shift from *r* to *n* since an Aramaic tablet dated to Nebuchadrezzar's thirty-fourth year spells the name with *n* after the (dental) *d*. The name probably means "O Nabu, protect my offspring" (so Wiseman, ibid., 3). Nabu was the son of Marduk and the god of wisdom in the Babylonian pantheon.

2 The phrase "in Babylonia" is literally a reference to "the land of Shinar" (cf. NIV note), a name for the whole of Mesopotamia found elsewhere in a handful of OT passages (Ge 10:10; 11:2; 14:1, 9; Jos 7:21; Isa 11:11; Zec 5:11). Daniel is the one exception in the OT where Shinar is used more restrictively to mean Babylonia. Shinar was the site of the tower of Babel (Ge 11:1–9), and according to Baldwin, 78, the reference is a deliberate archaism, since it "was synonymous with opposition to God; it was the place where wickedness was at home (Zec 5:11) and uprightness could expect opposition."

The phrase "his god" (אֱלֹהָיו, *ʾĕlōhāw*) is a plural form, "his gods" (Archer, 32, observes that the Babylonians were polytheists). The writer may be making a subtle theological statement about "religious pluralism" in the ancient world, as the first divine name used is "Lord" in v.2—אֲדֹנָי, *ʾᵃdōnāy*, meaning God was "owner" or "sovereign ruler" for the Hebrews. The next divine epithet is "God" (הָאֱלֹהִים, *hāʾĕlōhîm*), including the definite article (see Miller, 58). This designation for God by the Hebrews is often understood as a plural of majesty (cf. *NIDOTTE*, 1:405). The final reference to deity is this citation to the treasure house of "his god," i.e., Nabu, the patron deity of Nebuchadnezzar (see Notes on v.1). The divine names "Lord" and "God" may serve as foils emphasizing the supremacy of the one Hebrew God over the many "non-gods" of the Babylonian pantheon.

2. The Main Characters (1:3–7)

³Then the king ordered Ashpenaz, chief of his court officials, to bring in some of the Israelites from the royal family and the nobility — ⁴young men without any physical

defect, handsome, showing aptitude for every kind of learning, well informed, quick to understand, and qualified to serve in the king's palace. He was to teach them the language and literature of the Babylonians. [5]The king assigned them a daily amount of food and wine from the king's table. They were to be trained for three years, and after that they were to enter the king's service.

[6]Among these were some from Judah: Daniel, Hananiah, Mishael and Azariah. [7]The chief official gave them new names: to Daniel, the name Belteshazzar; to Hananiah, Shadrach; to Mishael, Meshach; and to Azariah, Abednego.

COMMENTARY

3–7 This unit introduces the protagonists of the story line of the book of Daniel. Four young men taken captive from Judah are identified by name as among those Israelites belonging to the royal family and Hebrew nobility deported to Babylonia (v.3). All four bore theophoric names (v.6) associating them with the God of the Israelites: "Daniel" ("God is my judge"), "Hananiah" ("Yah[weh] has been gracious"), "Mishael" ("Who is/what is God?"), and "Azariah" ("Yah[weh] has helped").

The name "Ashpenaz" (v.3) is an attested proper name in Aramaic known from an incantation bowl dating to ca. 600 BC (cf. Collins, *Daniel*, 134). The name is associated with "lodging" in some manner and may mean "innkeeper." His title, "chief of [the] court officials," indicates a position of oversight vested with some degree of royal authority (since he was in a position to make a decision concerning Daniel's request concerning food rations without appealing to a superior; v.8). Ashpenaz probably served both as a type of chamberlain overseeing the accommodations (i.e., "room and board") for the captives and headmaster in terms of supervising the education of the captive foreign youth and approving them for "graduation" into the civil service corps upon completion of their prescribed period of training.

The policy of incorporating capable foreign captives in the civil service corps as officials of the king was widespread in the ancient world (cf. *BBCOT*, 730). Such practice had the benefit of depleting the leadership ranks in subjugated territories as well as harnessing that administrative potential in civil service to the ruling nation. Wiseman (*Nebuchadrezzar and Babylon*, 81) has suggested that in Babylonian practice such "diplomatic hostages" were sometimes educated for eventual return to their homeland as loyal supporters of the Babylonian regime. This training or education was essentially a programmatic indoctrination of the captives in the worldview of a conquering nation (see Lucas, 53). The reprogramming included studies in the language and literature of the host nation (v.4), a special diet, and training in royal protocol (v.5). The goal or desired outcome was reorientation of the exiled individual in the thoughts, beliefs, and practices of the suzerain nation.

Typically, this reorientation included a change of name symbolic of the loyalty of the subject to a new king, his nation, and his gods. Accordingly, Daniel and his three friends became (v.7): "Belteshazzar" ("Bel [i.e., Marduk, the supreme god of the Babylonian pantheon] protects his life"), "Shadrach" (perhaps "command of Aku" [i.e., the

Sumerian moon-god] or "I am fearful of Aku"), "Meshach" (perhaps "Who is what [the god] Aku is?"), and "Abednego" ("servant of the shining one" or "servant of Neg[b]o" [i.e., Nabu, son of Marduk and patron deity of the scribal guild]; cf. Goldingay, 18, on naming and renaming in the OT).

Two things stand out in the passage: the exceptional qualifications of the young men chosen for the civil service training and the extensive nature and duration of that diplomatic training. Concerning the former, it is likely that Daniel and his friends were teenagers when they were taken captive from Judah and exiled to Babylonia, the presumption on the part of the Babylonians being that young boys generally would be more teachable and would be in a position to give more years of fruitful service to the state. Natural good looks and physical prowess were commonly associated with leadership in the biblical world (cf. 1Sa 9:2; 16:18). The three expressions referring to intellectual capabilities (v.4, "aptitude for ... learning, well informed, quick to understand") should probably be regarded as synonyms for "gifted learners" rather than signifying distinctive aspects of the human intelligence (cf. Miller, 61). The cumulative effect of the triad simply stresses the emphasis King Nebuchadnezzar placed on inherent intellectual ability.

According to Wiseman (*Nebuchadrezzar and Babylon*, 86), Babylon prided itself on being the "city of wisdom," a title that earlier belonged to Assur as the capital of Assyria. The schools of King Nebuchadnezzar's day would have continued to copy "sign lists ... word lists, paradigms and extracts of legal terminology ... religious documents of all kinds ... fables, and omens of various categories including those about devils and evil spirits ... as well as texts of possible historical interest." The language of the Babylonians (v.4) would have been the Akkadian dialect known as Neo-Babylonian. Beyond this, Daniel and his friends would have known several other languages, including Hebrew, Aramaic, and probably Persian.

Akkadian was a cuneiform writing system made up of wedge-shaped characters, commonly etched on clay tablets. The language was cumbersome and required learning hundreds of symbols, many with multiple syllabic values. Collins (*Daniel*, 140) has observed that length of Babylonian education varied depending on the specialization of the student (in some cases from ten to eighteen years). He further comments that the three-year instructional program for Daniel and his friends seems "unrealistically short for anyone who had no previous training in Akkadian letters." Those who have studied the Akkadian language might be inclined to agree!

Mastery of Akkadian was accomplished by copying simple exercises set forth by an instructor, then advancing to the copying of important literary texts, and finally to the composition of original documents of various sorts. As Baldwin, 80, notes, to study Babylonian literature was "to enter a completely alien thought-world." This Mesopotamian worldview was polytheistic in nature, superstitious in character, and pluralistic in practice. Lucas (*Daniel*, 53) summarizes that "the learning process intended for these Judean exiles was thus one of induction into the thought-world and culture of Babylonia." This makes all the more remarkable the fact that Daniel and his friends were able to devote themselves to the study of Babylonian language and literature without compromising their faith in Yahweh and their Hebrew worldview. Baldwin, 80, aptly reflects, "evidently the work of Jeremiah, Zephaniah, and Habakkuk had not been in vain." Likewise, the Christian church needs individuals of faith who are "students" of the "language and literature" of modern culture both for the sake of effective gospel outreach (cf. Ac 17:22–28) and for discerning the spirits in terms of maintaining sound doctrine (cf. 1 Jn 4:1).

NOTES

3 The title רַב סָרִיס (*rab sārîs*), "chief of the court officials," uses the Akkadian loan-phrase *rab-sārîs*, literally, "chief eunuch" (cf. Baldwin, 79). The expression occurs elsewhere as a designation for the "chief officer" of the king of Assyria (2Ki 18:17; cf. Jer 39:3, 13; understood in the NASB as a proper noun, "Rab-saris"). The use of castrated males as royal officials, since eunuchs were considered more loyal and trustworthy servants, is best attested during the Persian period (cf. Collins, *Daniel*, 134). The text of Daniel does not imply that the four Hebrew captives were made eunuchs. According to Collins (ibid., 135), the notion that Daniel and his three companions were eunuchs as reported in rabbinic literature goes beyond the text. In fact Potiphar, a סָרִיס (*sārîs*, "official"), was a married man (Ge 39:1, 7).

4 The NIV renders the Hebrew כַּשְׂדִּים (*kaśdîm*, "Chaldeans") as "Babylonians." From Assyrian royal inscriptions, the Chaldeans (Akk. *kaldu/kašdu*; Aram. כַּשְׂדָּי, *kaśdāy*) are known to have inhabited the lowlands south of Babylon and north of Persia as early as the ninth century BC. The OT regularly equates the Chaldeans with the people of Babylonia in general, although the Babylonians did not identify themselves in this way (e.g., Isa 13:19; Jer 24:5; Eze 1:3; cf. Ezr 5:12). Some scholars suggest that the word designates a special guild or priestly class of wise men (e.g., Collins, *Daniel*, 138; Goldingay, 16). It seems more likely that the term *kaśdîm* as used in the context of v.4 (i.e., "the language and literature of …"; cf. "all kinds of literature and learning" in v.17) refers more generally to the Chaldeans or Babylonians (as in Da 5:30; 9:1) and hence to the larger body of knowledge known and studied in Babylon.

5 The Hebrew phrase פַּת־בַּג הַמֶּלֶךְ (*pat-bag hammelek*, lit., "fine-food of the king") is an unusual OT expression found only in Daniel 1:5 and 11:26, rendered "food … from the king's table" (cf. NASB's "the king's choice food"). According to Baldwin, 81, the term is derived from Old Persian and refers to "honorific gifts from the royal table." Similar gifts of "delicacies" from the royal table are mentioned in Genesis 43:34 and 2 Samuel 11:8.

7 The only other reference to Daniel's Babylonian name occurs in 4:8, where context suggests that the name "Belteshazzar" is a theophoric name related to the Babylonian god Bel or Marduk. The name "Belteshazzar" may be a shortened from of the Akkadian [*Bēl*]-*balāṭsu-uṣur* ("[Bel] protect his life"; cf. Miller, 65) or *Bēlet-šar-uṣur* ("Lady, protect the king," in reference to the consort of Bel; cf. Baldwin, 81; Lucas, 53).

3. The Plot (1:8–17)

> **8**But Daniel resolved not to defile himself with the royal food and wine, and he asked the chief official for permission not to defile himself this way. **9**Now God had caused the official to show favor and sympathy to Daniel, **10**but the official told Daniel, "I am afraid of my lord the king, who has assigned your food and drink. Why should he see you looking worse than the other young men your age? The king would then have my head because of you."

¹¹Daniel then said to the guard whom the chief official had appointed over Daniel, Hananiah, Mishael and Azariah, ¹²"Please test your servants for ten days: Give us nothing but vegetables to eat and water to drink. ¹³Then compare our appearance with that of the young men who eat the royal food, and treat your servants in accordance with what you see." ¹⁴So he agreed to this and tested them for ten days.

¹⁵At the end of the ten days they looked healthier and better nourished than any of the young men who ate the royal food. ¹⁶So the guard took away their choice food and the wine they were to drink and gave them vegetables instead.

¹⁷To these four young men God gave knowledge and understanding of all kinds of literature and learning. And Daniel could understand visions and dreams of all kinds.

COMMENTARY

8–17 The plotline of a story unfolds in the arrangement of events recorded in the narrative. The basic ingredient of a good story plot is conflict moving toward resolution. The opening scene of Daniel reports such conflict. The conflict for Daniel and his three friends is an ideological or moral conflict dilemma. This type of conflict usually occurs within the protagonist(s) of the story and generally focuses on issues of worldview and ultimately "good" versus "evil." Specifically, the issue here is the royal food and wine that Daniel and his friends were required to eat and drink (v.8). The rejection of the royal food by Daniel and his friends foreshadows further episodes of conflict as the story of the Hebrew captives progresses, conflicts with other characters (e.g., the Babylonian wise men; 3:8–12; 6:1–5), and physical danger in the form of execution by fire (3:11) and exposure to wild beasts (6:7).

The expression Daniel "resolved" (v.8) is an idiom expressing a deliberate act of the will motivated by a deep-seated personal conviction (Heb. *śîm* + *lēb*, "to set the heart"; cf. NASB's "Daniel made up his mind"). The word "defile" (Heb. *gāʾal*) occurs fewer than a dozen times in the OT and

may refer to moral or ceremonial impurity (e.g., Isa 59:3; Mal 1:7, 12). Wallace, 42–43, observes that Daniel believed "faith in God and the forgiveness of God had made him clean"—clean from the idolatry and moral pollution of the surrounding world. To eat the king's food would compromise God's forgiveness and draw him back into the very same "world" from which he had been cleansed.

The royal food rations posed a problem for Daniel and his friends for several possible reasons. First, the law of Moses prohibited the obedient Hebrews from eating certain types of food, and there was no assurance that such fare would be left off the menu (cf. Lev 11; Dt 12:23–25; 14). Yet the Mosaic dietary restrictions do not include wine, also rejected by Daniel and his friends.

Second, the royal food rations would have probably been associated with idol worship in some way (either by the food's having been offered to idols or blessed by idolatrous priests). Yet Daniel and his friends do not refuse all the royal food rations (as though only meat and drink but not "vegetables" were dedicated to the Babylonian gods). On both counts the royal food would have been regarded as ritually unclean on theological grounds, and hence the eating of such food would constitute an act of disobedience against Yahweh and his commands.

Beyond this, it is possible that Daniel simply interpreted the eating of the royal food rations as a formal demonstration of allegiance to the Babylonian king. Baldwin, 83, and Felwell, 40, suggest that Daniel's motivation for rejecting the king's menu was political in the sense that eating the royal provisions was tantamount to accepting the lordship of the Babylonian king, whereas Daniel and his friends owed loyalty to Yahweh alone as their "king" (cf. 3:17–18; on the issue of cultural assimilation see *BBCOT*, 731). But again, Daniel and his friends do agree to certain provisions of royal food, thus weakening the argument of political allegiance to King Nebuchadnezzar by virtue of the "meal custom" of the biblical world. Longman, 53, suggests that the food-rations test was essentially a means by which Daniel and his friends might demonstrate that their healthy physical appearance (and hence their intellectual gifts) was the miraculous work of their God—not King Nebuchadnezzar's palace food or the Babylonian pantheon. As J. H. Sims ("Daniel," in *A Complete Literary Guide to the Bible*, ed. L. Ryken and T. Longman [Grand Rapids: Zondervan, 1993], 333–34) points out, whatever the motivation for rejecting the royal food rations, the greater issue theologically is that of divine nurture versus human nurture—on whom or what will the Hebrews rely for sustenance in their captivity?

The question of conformity to the surrounding culture was of paramount concern for the Diaspora Hebrews. To what degree, if any, should the displaced Israelites make accommodation to the surrounding dominant culture? What place was there for the Hebrew distinctives of religious monotheism and ethical absolutism based on the law of Moses in the religious pluralism and moral relativism of the Gentile superpowers? Rather than react in open defiance of the king's decree, Daniel and

his friends arranged a compromise with Ashpenaz and his appointed guardian (vv.10–14). The alternative to eating the king's food was a "rations test," with the Hebrew captives to be fed a diet of vegetables and water (v.12), against the control group of those young men eating the royal provisions (v.13). Goldingay, 20, interprets the "ten-day" testing period pragmatically as a standard round number of days that would not arouse the suspicion of Ashpenaz's superiors and yet be long enough for the effects of the test to be observed.

The example of nonconformity by Daniel and his friends became a model for the Israelite response to Gentile culture in later Judaism. For example, the characters of both Judith and Tobit are portrayed as pious Jews who observe strict adherence to the Mosaic law in the books of the apocryphal OT literature that bear their names. Separation from Gentile culture was an important component in an emerging "Diaspora theology" for the Hebrews during the intertestamental period. By the time of the NT, the Jewish worldview was tainted with attitudes of particularism, exclusivism, and superiority in reaction to the influences of Hellenism.

This "Judaism against Gentile culture" paradigm made Jesus' apparent laxity toward the Mosaic law and his accommodation to Gentile culture difficult to interpret and accept. The church, as the counterculture agent of God's kingdom in the world, has no less difficulty in discerning and practicing what Jesus meant when he instructed his followers that though they were in the world, they were not to be of the world (Jn 17:14–18; see the discussion of the Christian's interface with culture employing Niebuhr's classic Christ and culture paradigms in Longman, 62–69).

In the process we learn that God's providential rule of history is not restricted to nations and kings, as God caused Ashpenaz, the chief official, "to show favor and sympathy to Daniel" (v.9).

The passage is reminiscent of Joseph, who "found favor" in Potiphar's eyes (Ge 39:4), and Esther, who "pleased [Hegai] and won his favor" during her preparations for the royal beauty contest (Est 2:9). The repetition of the verb "gave" (Heb. *nātan*; GK 5989) echoes God's deliverance of King Jehoiakim to the Babylonians (v.2). The NIV's "God had caused" (v.9) fails to convey the full theological freight of the original (cf. NASB, "Now God granted Daniel favor and compassion ..."). Literally, "God *gave* Daniel for favor and mercies before the chief official." Even as God *gave* Jehoiakim to the Babylonians for judgment, God *gave* Daniel to Ashpenaz for grace.

This language of divine intervention is in keeping with the theme of Daniel established in the opening verses, namely God's sovereignty. As Seow, 27, notes, "the sovereignty of God is thus affirmed; the theological paradox of judgment and grace is maintained ... God is the narrator's 'lord' ... God is at work and ever providing." In fact, God's testing and providing are key themes of the OT and justify his name as "Yahweh Yir'eh" or "Jehovah Jireh" ("The LORD Will Provide," Ge 22:14).

The four Hebrews passed the rations test, actually emerging "healthier and better nourished" than their counterparts, whose diet consisted of the royal food (v.15). For the third time in the chapter we read that God "gave" (Heb. *nātan*; v.17). In this instance, as a result of their resolve not to defile themselves with the royal food, God granted Daniel and his friends "knowledge and understanding" (v.17a). The term "knowledge" (Heb. *maddā'*) implies academic learning (cf. v.4, "quick to understand"), and the word "understanding" (Heb. *haśkēl*) suggests both "aptitude for learning" (cf. v.4) and insight with respect to prudence or sound judgment.

In other words, the food rations episode offers practical commentary of sorts on Proverbs 1:7a: "the fear of the LORD is the beginning of knowledge" (cf. Ps 111:10). Baldwin, 84, has summarized that even small acts of faith and self-discipline, when undertaken out of loyalty to godly principle, set "God's servants in the line of his approval and blessing. In this way actions attest faith, and character is strengthened to face more difficult situations." (But see Goldingay, 20, who denies the cause-and-effect relationship between faithfulness and reward.) The added statement in v.17b that Daniel received a special divine endowment to understand or interpret visions and dreams foreshadows those "more difficult situations" he will face in the key role he plays as interpreter of dreams and seer of visions in the rest of the book.

NOTE

12 The meaning of the word rendered "vegetables" (Heb. זֵרֹעִים, *zērō'îm*), is somewhat uncertain. (On the alternative spelling *zērō'nîm* in v.16, see Collins, *Daniel*, 144.) The term is connected to the Heb. זֶרַע (*zera'*, "seeds") in some way, perhaps signifying a type of porridge made from ground grain (cf. *BBCOT*, 731).

4. Foreshadow of the Outcome (1:18–21)

[18]At the end of the time set by the king to bring them in, the chief official presented them to Nebuchadnezzar. [19]The king talked with them, and he found none equal to Daniel,

Hananiah, Mishael and Azariah; so they entered the king's service. ²⁰In every matter of wisdom and understanding about which the king questioned them, he found them ten times better than all the magicians and enchanters in his whole kingdom. ²¹And Daniel remained there until the first year of King Cyrus.

COMMENTARY

18–21 The conclusion of the first court story is a fortuitous one for Daniel and his three friends. After their three-year program of study in the "arts and sciences" of Babylonia, the Hebrews appear before King Nebuchadnezzar for an interview and subsequent appointment to posts of civil service (v.18). All four pass their oral examination with "honors" and are deemed by the king to be superior to all the other wise men of the kingdom in "wisdom and understanding" (v.20). The expression "ten times better" is a common idiom in the OT for expressing hyperbole in dialogue (e.g., Ge 31:41; Nu 14:22; Ne 4:12).

Induction into the civil-service corps of the king meant candidates had to be "qualified to serve in the king's palace" (v.4). Once the qualifications of the four Hebrews were certified, they "entered the king's service" or received administrative appointments as civil servants (v.19). The same word (lit., "stand," ʿāmad) is used in both statements to express the idea of entering the king's service. To "stand" before the king is an idiom for serving the king (cf. 1Ki 10:8; 12:8) and connotes both loyalty to the crown and adherence to royal protocol and etiquette (cf. Miller, 61).

The purpose of the final section of the first court story is twofold. First, we learn that there is a difference between learning as an "acquired skill" and wisdom as a divine gift (v.20; cf. v.17). Daniel and his friends learned the secret lore of the Babylonian magicians and priests, but they clearly understood

the God of Israel to be the source of all knowledge and wisdom (cf. 2:20). The rest of the court stories of Daniel give testimony to the four Hebrew captives' reliance on God as the fountainhead of knowledge and wisdom, unlike their Babylonian counterparts, who relied on occultic arts and all the gods and demons associated with Babylonian religion (e.g., 2:20–23, 28; 4:18, 24; 5:12). Much like Joseph, who served Pharaoh in Egypt, Daniel and his friends recognized that it is God in heaven who reveals mysteries to his faithful servants (2:28; cf. Ge 40:8; 41:16).

Russell, 32, sums up the outcome of the king's examination of the Hebrew apprentices by noting that "even in this highly skilled field [i.e., Babylonian 'arts and sciences'] Daniel and his friends were so obviously better than them all! By the goodness of God they could beat the Babylonian experts at their own game. The secrets of Babylon were no secrets to Yahweh who made them known to whomsoever he willed." The experience of Daniel and his friends anticipates the instruction of the apostle Paul about the "only wise God" (Ro 16:27) and his son Jesus the Messiah, who is the "wisdom from God" for the Christian (1Co 1:30).

Second, the chronological notice in v.21—attached as an addendum to the opening court story explaining how Daniel and his friends came to be royal officials in Babylonia under King Nebuchadnezzar—attests to the "staying power" of Daniel (cf. Wallace, 47–48). The first year of King

Cyrus of Persia is dated to 539 or 538 BC, depending on the source consulted. This means Daniel held an administrative post in the royal court of Babylon for more than sixty years, and his time spent in Babylonian captivity was nearly seventy years (given his deportation in 605 BC; cf. 1:1). Earlier the prophet Jeremiah had predicted that the Hebrew captivity would cover seven decades (Jer 25:11–12; 29:10). The reference to the accession year of Cyrus to the throne of Babylon probably marked the end of this enforced exile of the Hebrews by the Babylonians (so Goldingay, 27; Lucas, 56).

In reality, Daniel's longevity testified both to God's sovereignty over the nations and his faithfulness to his people Israel. Even as Daniel outlasted the kings of the Babylonian Empire, so God's people were sustained in captivity and eventually permitted to return to their homeland of covenantal promise (2Ch 36:22–23; Ezr 1:1–4). Likewise, the presence of the Israelite named Daniel in the royal court of seven Babylonian monarchs and the first king of Persia was a tangible reminder that God is the one who sets up kings and deposes them (Da 2:21).

NOTE

20 The conjunctive phrase "wisdom and understanding" is more precisely a construct-genitive in the MT, "wisdom of understanding." Although unmarked, the NIV and NASB read the LXX and Syriac versions at this point. The term חָכְמָה (*ḥokmâ*, "wisdom"; GK 2683) refers to a matrix of qualities including aptitude, technical skill, intuitive good sense, and experience—demonstrated, for example, in navigating a ship in open waters or crafting fine art from metal, wood, or precious stones (Pr 8:12–14; cf. *NIDOTTE*, 2:130–34). The word בִּינָה (*bînâ*, "understanding"; GK 1069) means to discern, distinguish, or differentiate, perceive or have insight, comprehend; with respect to Hebrew wisdom literature, it denotes "problem-solving" ability (Pr 1:6; cf. *NIDOTTE*, 1:652–53). In either case, the construction calls attention to the idea of wisdom as "applied knowledge"—that is, Daniel and his friends had "agile" minds and were adept at problem solving as a result of the critical-thinking skills garnered through rigorous academic training coupled with the insight and sound judgment instilled by their fear of Yahweh.

The term חַרְטֹם (*ḥarṭōm*, "magician") is used of the soothsayer-priest of Egypt (cf. Ge 41:8, 24; Ex 7:11, 22), and it may be an Egyptian loanword in Hebrew. The magician was a mantic skilled in the occultic arts, including astrology, sorcery, exorcism, performing signs and wonders, and various forms of mechanical divination such as hydromancy (the mixing of liquids in a divining cup; cf. Ge 44:5), haruspicy (the study of animal entrails), hepatoscopy (the analysis of animal livers; cf. Eze 21:21), augury (the tracking of the behavior of sacred animals; cf. 2Ki 21:6), and oneiromancy (the interpretation of dreams; cf. Ge 40:8; Dt 13:1). Technically, the magicians were wise men or scholars who functioned literally as "engravers" or "scribes" by meticulously recording such things as astrological phenomena to inform the process of royal decision-making (see Miller, 72; Wiseman, *Nebuchadrezzar and Babylon*, 88–89).

The word אַשָּׁף (*ʾaššāp*, "enchanter"; "conjurers," NASB) occurs only in 1:20; 2:2 in the OT. The term is derived from the Akkadian word *āšipu*, an "incantation priest" (cf. Hartman and Di Lella, 131). The enchanter or conjurer belonged to a priestly class skilled in communication with the spirit world (including the realm of the dead) by means of magic spells and incantations. These and other classes of priests specializing in the occultic arts (cf. 2:2) had prominent roles as advisers to the king in the royal courts of the ancient world (see Miller, 72–73).

B. Nebuchadnezzar's Dream of the Statue (2:1–49)

OVERVIEW

The second chapter of Daniel continues the court-stories section of the book (chs. 1–6). It forms part of a distinct literary unit within the book that includes chs. 2–7. Lucas, 69, has outlined the chiastic structure of the section as follows:

A Dream about four earthly kingdoms and
   God's kingdom (ch. 2)
   B Story about Jews being faithful in the
      face of death (ch. 3)
      C Story about royal hubris that is
         humbled (ch. 4)
      C' Story about royal hubris that is
         humbled (ch. 5)
   B' Story about a Jew who is faithful in the
      face of death (ch. 6)
A' Vision about four earthly kingdoms and
   God's kingdom (ch. 7)

The plot of the story in ch. 2 may be outlined in five scenes: the king's troubling dream and the resulting crisis for the royal wise men (vv.1–13); Daniel's intervention followed by God's intervention (vv.14–23); Daniel's description of the contents of the king's dream (vv.24–35); Daniel's interpretation of the king's dream (vv.36–45); and the king's response to Daniel's interpretation (vv.46–49).

The literary unity of this chapter has for several reasons been disputed by some biblical scholars (e.g., Davies, 45–46; Anderson, 14–15). For example, the Aramaic section of the book begins in 2:4b, after the king has reported his disturbing dream to the royal advisers. The chapter combines

a number of diverse literary subgenres according to form critics, including court tale, dream report, legend, aretalogy, doxology, and midrash (so Goldingay, 36). Instances of repetitiveness in the account (e.g., vv.28–30) and the lack of continuity with other portions of Daniel are sometimes cited as evidence of editorial activity (e.g., the fact that the king needs an introduction to Daniel after previously interviewing him after the completion of his educational training, cf. 1:18). In fact, Fewell, 62, suggests that this tension in the biblical text compromises the narrator's reliability as an accurate storyteller. Yet Goldingay, 44, observes that such repetitiveness and discontinuity "may as likely be the responsibility of the author as a redactor."

In the end it is best to read the chapter completely as it stands—a court story of contest featuring a dream report (cf. Humphreys, 219, though he denies the historicity of the story and labels it a "tale"). The story plot is one of contest, and it plays out at two different levels of understanding. On the human level the contest to interpret the king's dream pits the king himself against his corps of royal advisers. Once Daniel is drawn into the story, he becomes a rival to the other royal advisers in responding to the king's demand for an "answer" to his dream.

On a spiritual level the contest sets Yahweh of Israel, the true God, against the pantheon of gods represented in the idolatry of Babylonian religion. A related aspect of this cosmic dimension of the contest to interpret the king's dream is the ultimate source of knowledge and wisdom—the God of the Hebrews or the occultic lore of the Babylonian wise men (cf. 2:21–23). On this count Seow, 35, observes that the narrative of 2:1–49 echoes those poems of Isaiah 40–55 that highlight the wisdom and foreknowledge of Israel's God over against the idols of the nations (e.g., Isa 41:21–29; 45:19; 46:9–10; 47:13–14; 48:5–6, 16). In fact, it is Yahweh

> who foils the signs of false prophets
> > and makes fools of diviners,
> who overthrows the learning of the wise
> > and turns it into nonsense,
> who carries out the words of his servants
> > and fulfills the predictions of his messengers.
> > > (Isa 44:25–26)

Numerous parallels have been drawn between Daniel's experience in Nebuchadnezzar's court and Joseph's in Pharaoh's court (Ge 41). In each case a Hebrew servant of God interprets a king's dream that has puzzled the royal advisers and as a result is elevated to a place of prominence in the kingdom. The form-critical scholar attributes this to the shared folklore pattern of the success story of a wise courtier, "in which a lower-class hero solves a problem for a higher-class person and is rewarded for doing so" (Redditt, 50). Others ascribe the similarities to the rule of a sovereign God in history in cultures where special emphasis is placed on dreams and the interpretation of them. According to Goldingay, 36, Daniel, like Joseph, is "a model of Israelite wisdom (v.14) and a model of Israelite piety, in his prayer (v.18), his vision (v.19), his praise (vv.19–23), his witness, (vv.27–28), his self-effacement (v.30), his conviction (v.45); the fruit of his work is not merely rewards and promotions (v.48) but obeisance and recognition of his God (vv.46–47)."

Daniel's godly living in the Babylonian exile served as an example for Jews living in a foreign culture in the literature of the later Jewish Diaspora (e.g., Tobit, Judith; cf. Longman, 62–69, on the application of Daniel's example to the relationship between faith and culture for the contemporary Christian). But Humphreys, 221, correctly observes that in ch. 2 "the God of Daniel is the central figure and not the courtier."

1. A Troubling Dream for the King and a Crisis for the Wise Men (2:1–13)

[1]In the second year of his reign, Nebuchadnezzar had dreams; his mind was troubled and he could not sleep. [2]So the king summoned the magicians, enchanters, sorcerers and astrologers to tell him what he had dreamed. When they came in and stood before the king, [3]he said to them, "I have had a dream that troubles me and I want to know what it means.'"

[4]Then the astrologers answered the king in Aramaic, "O king, live forever! Tell your servants the dream, and we will interpret it."

[5]The king replied to the astrologers, "This is what I have firmly decided: If you do not tell me what my dream was and interpret it, I will have you cut into pieces and your houses turned into piles of rubble. [6]But if you tell me the dream and explain it, you will receive from me gifts and rewards and great honor. So tell me the dream and interpret it for me."

⁷Once more they replied, "Let the king tell his servants the dream, and we will interpret it."

⁸Then the king answered, "I am certain that you are trying to gain time, because you realize that this is what I have firmly decided: ⁹If you do not tell me the dream, there is just one penalty for you. You have conspired to tell me misleading and wicked things, hoping the situation will change. So then, tell me the dream, and I will know that you can interpret it for me."

¹⁰The astrologers answered the king, "There is not a man on earth who can do what the king asks! No king, however great and mighty, has ever asked such a thing of any magician or enchanter or astrologer. ¹¹What the king asks is too difficult. No one can reveal it to the king except the gods, and they do not live among men."

¹²This made the king so angry and furious that he ordered the execution of all the wise men of Babylon. ¹³So the decree was issued to put the wise men to death, and men were sent to look for Daniel and his friends to put them to death.

COMMENTARY

1 The date formula sets the story in the second year of the Babylonian king Nebuchadnezzar (ca. 604 BC). A close reading of Daniel reveals that Daniel's training in the wisdom guild lasted for three years (1:5). Yet the court story relating the dream of the king includes Daniel among the "condemned" wise men as though he has already graduated and received his appointment as a member of the royal advisers (2:14). While a definitive answer to the chronological conundrum remains elusive, plausible harmonizations have been constructed offering possible solutions to the problem. For example, Wood, 48–50, places the event within Daniel's three-year apprenticeship (thus explaining why Nebuchadnezzar needs an introduction to Daniel; cf. Fewell, 55). Young, 56, however, prefers to understand the three years of training as including "partial years" and thus reconciles the internal chronology of chs. 1 and 2 according to the following chart:

Year of *Daniel's Training*	Reign of *Nebuchadnezzar*
first year	year of accession
second year	first year
third year	second year

As in the case of 1:1, the date formula here serves simply to set the stage for the narrative. Specifically, the scene unfolds in the royal court of Nebuchadnezzar in Babylon. More important, the date formula is a feature of ancient historiography and serves to mark the king's dream as an actual event within the time-space continuum of ancient history.

2–3 The text uses the term "wise men" (v.12) as an umbrella term used to designate the cadre of royal advisers serving in the Babylonian court. These men are "professionals" trained in the literature and lore of the Babylonians—especially divination and other magical arts. The wise men represent several different learned guilds or classes of priest-scholars, including "magicians, enchanters [conjurers, NASB], sorcerers and astrologers [Chaldeans, NASB]."

These and other classes of priests specializing in the occultic arts had prominent roles in the royal courts of the ancient world as advisers to the king (see Miller, 72–73, 78–79; *BBCOT*, 732). Collectively these experts "were the political consultants, trend spotters, and religious gurus of the day" (Longman, 77). Generally speaking, the OT condemns these classes of priest-scholars and the specialized occultic art(s) practiced by the adherents of each guild (e.g., Ex 22:18; Dt 18:10–11; cf. Lucas, 69–70; Smith-Christopher, 50).

This distinguished group of wise men has been assembled because King Nebuchadnezzar has had a troublesome dream (v.3; cf. the more literal rendering of the NASB, "my spirit is anxious to understand the dream"). In the ancient world, dreams were considered a significant medium of insight for the future, and Babylonian religion especially encouraged the seeking of such portents through dreams and unusual circumstances of everyday life. The success of a king and the welfare of his kingdom were often dependent on the correct interpretation of an unusual dream or some bizarre natural event. Longman, 77, observes that it is in dreams and the interpretation of dreams "that Babylonian religion and Daniel's faith come closest, and perhaps that is why God chose to speak to Nebuchadnezzar in this way.... After all, God had spoken through dreams in the past (e.g., Gen 28:10–22; 1Kgs 3:5), but not through other means of divination so popular in Babylonia." Naturally, this similarity by no means discounts the profound difference between prophecy as the product of divine initiation and revelation, and divination, which is the result of human initiation or manipulation (cf. Longman, 77).

4 The response of the astrologers to the king marks the beginning of the Aramaic section of this book (2:4b–7:28). The NIV interprets the word "Aramaic" (Heb. *ʾᵃrāmît*) so as to give the impression that the astrologers speak to the king in Aramaic. It would be only logical for the wise men to communicate in a language common to all, since the wise men are a racially and ethnically diverse group. Miller, 80, prefers to understand the phrase "in Aramaic" as a parenthetical notation identifying the shift in the text to the written language of Aramaic. Still others consider the word a gloss based on the manuscripts found at Qumran (e.g., Hartman and Di Lella, 138). On the composition of Daniel in two languages, Hebrew and Aramaic, see Languages in the Introduction.

The acclamation "O king, live forever" (v.4a) is standard court etiquette. According to Baldwin, 87, the expression has a long history in the royal circles of the ancient world and reflects the association of the king with both the god(s) and the community he rules. The address was apparently part of Hebrew royal protocol as well (cf. 1Ki 1:31).

The astrologers speak for the group of wise men (v.4b), perhaps because the interpretation of dreams is their special domain of expertise (cf. *BBCOT*, 732). They are confident of reaching an understanding of the dream's meaning both because of their training in the mantic arts and also because they have access to dream manuals that documented historical dreams and their aftermath, explained the significance of dream patterns, and decoded the various dream symbols (cf. Baldwin, 87; Wiseman, *Nebuchadrezzar and Babylon*, 92–93).

5–9 The threat of punishment or the promise of reward is a characteristic feature of the court contest (cf. Goldingay, 36). The dismemberment of enemies ("have you cut into pieces," v.5) has parallels in the annals of the ancient Near East (Montgomery, 146; cf. Ezr 6:11). The brutal practice is in keeping

10–13 Three times the king has asked his wise men the content and interpretation of his dream (vv.3, 5–6, 8–9). Finally the astrologers (who speak for the group throughout the scene) admit defeat. The task lies beyond the capabilities of mortals (v.10a); the king's answer requires revelation from the gods, and they do not cohabit with humanity (v.11b). Beyond this, there is no precedent for such a request from any king previous to Nebuchadnezzar—implying the king is both unrealistic and unfair (vv.10b–11a). This response infuriates the king, and he decrees the execution of all the wise men of Babylon (v.12).

The king's fury with his sages may be explained on two counts. First, their accusation of unfairness impugns the king's sense of justice (a royal epithet for Mesopotamian kings) and hence is construed as an act of insubordination. More telling is the self-indictment of the royal advisers since, as Miller, 83, has recognized, they have admitted that only "the gods knew the dream, [so] whoever revealed the dream must be in touch with gods." This is exactly what the professions of magician, enchanter, sorcerer, and astrologer claim as their exclusive domain—communication with the spiritual world. Without thinking, the wise men have more or less confessed to the king that they are charlatans—deserving of death for deceiving the king!

The indirect response of the diviners to the king sets the stage for Daniel, since he and his three friends face the same death sentence decreed for all the wise men of Babylon—despite the fact that they are unaware of the consultation Nebuchadnezzar held with his royal advisers (v.13).

with the cruelty of the Babylonians reported elsewhere in this book (i.e., execution by incineration and exposure to wild beasts; cf. 3:15; 6:7).

The king makes an impossible demand of the wise men—they must first describe the content of the king's dream and then interpret it (vv.5, 9). The king's request is so unreasonable that it fails to register fully with the wise men, thus prompting them to repeat their standard exchange with him almost automatically (i.e., "let the king tell his servants the dream and we will interpret it"; vv.4, 7). Baldwin, 87–88, attributes Nebuchadnezzar's extraordinary challenge to the fact the he has forgotten the details of the dream. It is more likely that the king does remember the dream, and as Lucas, 70, observes, his concern stems from the need for a reliable interpretation.

This would especially be the case if A. L. Oppenheim ("The Interpretation of Dreams in the Ancient Near East," *Transactions of the American Philosophical Society* 46 [1956]: 219) is correct in his understanding that for the Babylonians "the telling of the dream content removes the influence it has on the person who experienced it" (suggesting that Nebuchadnezzar assumes a "worst-case scenario" for the implications of his dream). Yet the king's lapse of memory fails to account for his lethal rage (v.12) in reaction to the wise men's appeal to relate the contents of the dream so they might interpret it (so Longman, 77). The tone and context of v.8 implies that the king fears manipulation at the hands of the diviners—and not without good reason (cf. Lucas, 70–71, on King Sennacherib's separation of the royal diviners into groups to reduce collusion among the experts).

NOTES

2–3 Oppenheim, 238, links the word for "magician" (חַרְטֹם, *ḥarṭōm*) to the dream interpreters of the Assyrian royal court. The term as used in Daniel seems to identify those skilled more broadly in the occultic arts, including divination, sorcery, exorcism, astrology, and the like (see Notes on 1:20).

The "enchanter" or conjurer (אַשָּׁף, ʾaššāp) belonged to a priestly class adept at communication with the spirit world, including the realm of the dead (see Notes on 1:20).

The term for "sorcerer" (מְכַשֵּׁפָה, mᵉkaššēpâ) is associated with the Akkadian word kašāpu and connotes those skilled in charms and incantations. The sorcerer engaged in the magical arts and witchcraft involving the use of spells, incantations, amulets, charms, and other specialized rituals to manipulate natural powers and to influence circumstances, events, people, and the gods—whether for good or evil (cf. *NIDOTTE*, 2:735–38).

The last category of wise men, the "astrologers," translates the Hebrew word כַּשְׂדִּים (kaśdîm; GK 4169; Aram. כַּשְׂדָּי, kaśdāy; Akk. kaldu/kašdu, or "Chaldeans" [so NASB]). The term may be understood in two ways in Daniel: either to refer to the Babylonian people generally in an ethnic sense (see Notes on 1:4), or (in a more restricted sense) to delineate a special class of Babylonian priest-scholar. In this context the kaśdîm are clearly part of the cohort of royal advisers serving King Nebuchadnezzar. No doubt their expertise includes but is not restricted to astrology, as evidenced by the use of the term elsewhere in Daniel (e.g., 2:5, 10; 4:7; 5:7, 11). (For an extensive treatment of the terms related to the mantic arts as presented in the OT, see *NIDOTTE*, 3:945–51.)

13 Lacocque, 35, suggests that the massacre of the royal wise men has already begun when Daniel intervenes (cf. Wood, 55). It is more likely that Miller, 84, is correct in understanding the force of the participle as conveying "imminent action" (i.e., the wise men are about to be executed). The assertion of Montgomery, 149–50, that the execution of the wise men would have been a "formal execution under the proper officials and in the appointed place" supports the idea that the executions have not yet begun.

2. Daniel's Intervention and God's Intervention (2:14–23)

¹⁴When Arioch, the commander of the king's guard, had gone out to put to death the wise men of Babylon, Daniel spoke to him with wisdom and tact. ¹⁵He asked the king's officer, "Why did the king issue such a harsh decree?" Arioch then explained the matter to Daniel. ¹⁶At this, Daniel went in to the king and asked for time, so that he might interpret the dream for him.

¹⁷Then Daniel returned to his house and explained the matter to his friends Hananiah, Mishael and Azariah. ¹⁸He urged them to plead for mercy from the God of heaven concerning this mystery, so that he and his friends might not be executed with the rest of the wise men of Babylon. ¹⁹During the night the mystery was revealed to Daniel in a vision. Then Daniel praised the God of heaven ²⁰and said:

"Praise be to the name of God for ever and ever;
    wisdom and power are his.
²¹ He changes times and seasons;
    he sets up kings and deposes them.
He gives wisdom to the wise
    and knowledge to the discerning.

> ²²He reveals deep and hidden things;
>   he knows what lies in darkness,
>   and light dwells with him.
> ²³I thank and praise you, O God of my fathers:
>   You have given me wisdom and power,
>   you have made known to me what we asked of you,
>   you have made known to us the dream of the king."

COMMENTARY

14–16 The second scene of the court story recounts the problem of interpreting the king's dream and reports Daniel's intervention on behalf of the condemned wise men (including himself!) and God's subsequent intervention on behalf of Daniel. Anderson, 14, considers this section of the narrative (vv. 13–23) as secondary, since it may be omitted without causing any interruption in the story, given the smooth transition from v.12 to v.24. He fails to appreciate, however, the importance of the absence of Daniel and his friends during the king's first interview with the wise men as part of the narrator's literary technique (cf. Lucas, 71–72). More significant is the role Daniel's doxology (vv.20–23) plays as a theological touchstone underscoring the foil between the silence of the Babylonian gods of heaven (v.11) and the God of heaven, who reveals deep and hidden things (vv.18, 22).

Arioch is apparently in the process of rounding up the king's wise men from various locations in the palace complex for formal sentencing and then mass execution. Daniel's boldness in speaking to the king's royal guard was witnessed earlier in the food-rations episode (1:11–12). In addition to boldness, the narrative indicates that Daniel speaks with "wisdom and tact" ("discretion and discernment," NASB, v.14). According to Wood, 56, Daniel acts "wisely and in good taste," befitting the gravity of the situation. His question about the king's harsh decree ("urgent," NASB, v.15) indicates that Daniel and his friends have not been party to the initial encounter between the king and his royal advisers. Daniel displays similar boldness in approaching the king, no doubt through the mediation of Arioch (though this is unspecified).

Interestingly, Daniel asks the king for time to seek an interpretation for the dream (v.16), when previously the king accused the wise men of stall tactics (v.8). Daniel is most persuasive with the king, but we are given no details as to the exchange between Daniel and Nebuchadnezzar. We can only assume that Daniel's request for a stay of execution of the wise men is granted because he assures the king that "his God, Yahweh, could reveal the dream and its interpretation to him within a reasonable interval" (Miller, 85). Clearly, God continues to bestow favor on the Hebrew captive Daniel in his encounters with his Babylonian overlords (cf. Seow, 40). As a wise man Daniel has great power (Pr 24:5a), and thus he is able to appease the king's wrath (Pr 16:14). Goldingay, 55, sums up by saying that Daniel "embodies both the experiential wisdom of a statesman and the revelatory wisdom of a seer."

17–19 Upon receiving the king's approval for a period of time to seek an interpretation of the king's dream, Daniel immediately enlists the aid of his three companions (v.17). He exhorts them to "plead for mercy" ("request compassion," NASB, v.18a). Daniel and his friends know that Yahweh is a God of compassion (Ex 34:6), and they know from the accounts of Joseph's experience in Egypt that God alone reveals the meanings of dreams (Ge 40:8; 41:16). Thus they have good cause to believe in the power of urgent petition in prayer to God.

The eventual goal or outcome of this petition is the deliverance of Daniel and his friends from the chief executioner and the royal decree that has placed all the Babylonian wise men on "death row" (v.18c). Not coincidentally, these elements of prayer and faith in the God of heaven, who both rules the nations and reveals mysteries, later become standard "equipment" in the "survival kit" for Jews of the Diaspora seeking deliverance from the persecution and suffering of Gentile oppression (cf. Tob 3:11, 16; 8:4; Jth 4:13; 8:31; 11:17).

The epithet "the God of heaven" is used four times in ch. 2 (vv.18–19, 37, 44) and may be a shortened form of the title for God found in the context of oath-taking in Genesis 24:3, "the God of heaven and the God of earth" (cf. 24:7, "the God of heaven," and "the LORD, God Most High, Creator of heaven and earth," Ge 14:22). The expression "the God of heaven" is recognized as a divine title characteristic of the postexilic period and appears frequently in Ezra and Nehemiah (e.g., Ezr 1:2; Ne 1:4; see the discussions in Russell, 44; Lucas, 72). The name speaks to God's transcendence and supremacy over all that is temporal and earthbound. This is why he knows the deep and hidden things and what lies in darkness (v.22).

20–23 Daniel's natural and immediate response to God's revelation is praise. His doxology or hymn of descriptive praise celebrates the reality that God is God. According to Russell, 44, the hymn is probably an original composition by Daniel appropriate to the setting but in keeping with Israel's hymnic tradition (cf. Seow, 41). The specific attributes of God's character extolled include his wisdom and power (v.20), sovereignty (v.21), grace and compassion evidenced in his willingness to share this knowledge with his servants (v.22), and mercy in hearing and responding to their prayers (v.23).

Daniel's name is associated with the gift of wisdom throughout the book. Yet Russell, 40, notes that this wisdom "is not just technical know-how or professional skill or academic learning or native ability. It is penetrating insight, God-given and God-inspired, that sees meaning in mysteries and light in darkness because it knows God is there and that God is in control." Daniel fully recognizes this "wisdom" is not his own but instead a gracious gift bestowed by the God of wisdom (vv.20–21). The NT's exhortation to petition God for wisdom indicates that he still imparts this divine gift to those who seek it (Jas 1:5).

Daniel's doxology is especially important for the Hebrews of the Babylonian captivity for its affirmation of God's sovereign rule of the nations, the efficacy of prayer offered to the God of power and wisdom, and the reminder of continuity they share within the covenantal promises made to Israel by the God of their ancestors (v.23; on Daniel's hymn see Russell, 43–46).

NOTES

14 The meaning of the name "Arioch" is uncertain, though the king of Ellasar (an unknown region, perhaps of southern Mesopotamia) from a much earlier time period bears the same name (Ge 14:1). In Judith 1:6 the name "Arioch" is ascribed to the king of the Elymeans. His title as "commander of the king's guard" is better understood as "chief of the royal executioners" (see discussion of the Aram. word טַבָּח, *ṭabbaḥ*, in Collins [*Daniel*, 158]; Miller, 84).

The word for "wisdom" (Aram. עֵטָה, *ʿēṭâ*; GK 10539) is related to a root word meaning "to counsel" and "means that which is the cause or product of good counsel" (Wood, 56). The Aramaic word טְעֵם (*ṭeʿēm*, "tact" [NIV], or "discretion" [NASB]) literally means "taste" and "speaks of *appropriateness, suitability*" (Wood, 56).

15 Montgomery, 156, contends that in this context the Aramaic word חֲצַף (*ḥṣp*, "harsh"; GK 10280) should be understood as "urgent" or "hasty" (so NRSV; or possibly "peremptory"; cf. Collins, *Daniel*, 158; Hartman and Di Lella, 135). Since the root *ḥṣp* denotes "harshness" or "stiffness," Miller, 84–85, prefers the translation "harsh" (cf. Goldingay, 31, "severe") and argues that the translation "hasty" is derived from the use of *ḥṣp* in 3:22.

18 Specifically, Daniel urges his friends to invoke "the God of heaven" with the intent to bring resolution to the "mystery" of the king's dream (v.18b). The Aramaic word רָז (*rāz*, "mystery"; GK 10661) is a Persian loanword meaning "secret" and is a key term in ch. 2 (occurring eight times; vv.18–19, 27–30, 47[2x]). When used with the verb גְּלָה (*glh*, "to reveal," v.19; GK 10144), the expression becomes almost a technical term for divine revelation required for matters beyond human comprehension (cf. Lucas, 72). Redditt, 55, notes that the secrets revealed by God have implications for the "days to come" (v.28), infusing the word "mystery" with eschatological overtones in ch. 2.

20 The word "wisdom," חָכְמָה (*ḥokmâ*; GK 10266), speaks of knowledge and the capacity for proper decision-making (Wood, 60). The term also denotes skill (both innate talent and learned expertise) and experience that reflects maturity (cf. *NIDOTTE*, 2:130–34). As it relates to God, wisdom is a divine attribute (Job 9:4; Ro 16:27) and a means by which his presence and activity in the world are demonstrated (Pr 3:19–20; Eph 3:10). Daniel understands that wisdom is God's domain, and he may graciously grant wisdom to his servants who seek the gift in prayer (v.23; Job 12:13).

3. Daniel Describes the Content of the King's Dream (2:24–35)

²⁴Then Daniel went to Arioch, whom the king had appointed to execute the wise men of Babylon, and said to him, "Do not execute the wise men of Babylon. Take me to the king, and I will interpret his dream for him."

²⁵Arioch took Daniel to the king at once and said, "I have found a man among the exiles from Judah who can tell the king what his dream means."

²⁶The king asked Daniel (also called Belteshazzar), "Are you able to tell me what I saw in my dream and interpret it?"

²⁷Daniel replied, "No wise man, enchanter, magician or diviner can explain to the king the mystery he has asked about, ²⁸but there is a God in heaven who reveals mysteries. He has shown King Nebuchadnezzar what will happen in days to come. Your dream and the visions that passed through your mind as you lay on your bed are these:

²⁹"As you were lying there, O king, your mind turned to things to come, and the revealer of mysteries showed you what is going to happen. ³⁰As for me, this mystery has been revealed to me, not because I have greater wisdom than other living men, but so that you, O king, may know the interpretation and that you may understand what went through your mind.

³¹"You looked, O king, and there before you stood a large statue — an enormous, dazzling statue, awesome in appearance. ³²The head of the statue was made of pure gold, its chest and arms of silver, its belly and thighs of bronze, ³³its legs of iron, its feet partly of iron and partly of baked clay. ³⁴While you were watching, a rock was cut out, but not by human hands. It struck the statue on its feet of iron and clay and smashed them. ³⁵Then the iron, the clay, the bronze, the silver and the gold were broken to pieces at the same time and became like chaff on a threshing floor in the summer. The wind swept them away without leaving a trace. But the rock that struck the statue became a huge mountain and filled the whole earth.

COMMENTARY

24–28 The parenthetical reference to Daniel's Babylonian name, Belteshazzar, links this court story with ch. 1 (1:7). Lucas, 72, has identified two functions for this section of the narrative (vv.24–28). First, these verses advance the plot of the story by increasing the tension and expectation on the part of the audience awaiting the content and interpretation of the dream. Second, they emphasize the supremacy of the God of the Hebrews over the Babylonian gods. Daniel reports with confidence to Arioch, the chief executioner, that he can interpret the king's dream and thus bring about the stay of execution negotiated with Nebuchadnezzar earlier (v.16).

Longman, 79, has observed that Daniel's injunction to Arioch not to execute the wise men of Babylon (v.24) is an example of love for one's enemies mandated in the OT (Ex 23:4–5) and advocated by Jesus (Lk 6:27). Arioch seems to claim credit for finding someone to interpret the king's dream (v.25), though Porteous, 43, suggests his self-important haste and enthusiasm for presenting Daniel to the king may have stemmed from the fact that he is now

spared the task of carrying out his grim assignment of executing all the royal wise men.

Arioch secures an audience for Daniel with the king, (v.25), and in keeping with royal protocol Daniel does not speak until the king has addressed him (v.26). The king's question is tinged with incredulity. Unlike Arioch, Daniel does not mention himself in his response to the king's question. In fact, Miller, 89, states that his initial statement may seem rather discouraging since the content and the interpretation of the dream lie beyond the divining arts of the several classes of royal advisers (v.27a). Daniel acknowledges his understanding as supernatural insight obtained by direct revelation and attributes his knowledge concerning the king's dream to a "God in heaven who reveals mysteries" (v.27b; confirming the royal sages' observation that such revelation could only come from "the gods," 2:11).

Explicit in Daniel's testimony is the superiority of God's wisdom over all the accumulated lore and learning of the "magical arts" practiced by the king's wise men. Implicit in Daniel's confession is the supremacy of Yahweh of the Hebrews over the gods of the Babylonian pantheon worshiped by the royal wise men. The king learns that his dream has both immediate and future ramifications.

29–35 Daniel not only interprets the king's dream but also recalls its occurrence by rehearsing for the king his troubled mind as he lay in his bed on the night of his dream (v.28). Beyond this, Daniel makes it clear that this divine communication was expressly intended for the king (v.29). And it is only in the reiteration of this fact that Daniel humbly mentions himself as a "player" in the unfolding drama of Nebuchadnezzar's dream (v.30). Daniel discloses that the king saw an image of human likeness of enormous proportion and frightening luminosity. The term used here signifies that the image was a statue (Aram. ṣᵉlēm), not an idol. According to Seow, 43, the word is used for images erected to represent the presence of gods and kings.

The awesomeness of the statue in the king's dream was due both to its extraordinary size and dazzling brilliance (v.31). The statue had an identifiable human form, but it is unclear initially whether it represented a god or a human king. The statue was most unusual in its composition, cast in four different metals. The head was made of gold, the chest and arms were made of silver, the belly and thighs were made of bronze, the legs were made of iron, and the feet were made of an amalgam of iron and clay (v.32–33). The various metals suggest a combination of preciousness and strength in inverted emphasis as the statue is viewed from head to feet. That is, as one moves down the sequence of metals in the statue, its splendor dissipates (from gold to iron and clay) but its hardness increases (from gold to iron).

No doubt, more frightening for the king was his vision of the obliteration and disintegration of the statue by a rock that marvelously transformed into a gigantic mountain that filled the entire earth (vv.34–35). All this was accomplished without any human intervention (v.34a). The reference to the rock that was cut, "but not by human hands," probably means "that it originates by divine will and power" (Seow, 44; cf. 8:25; Job 34:20 for similar expressions). The stone struck the statue at its weakest point, the feet made of iron and clay at its base, and the entire image was broken to pieces. The disintegration of the statue like chaff blown away by the wind (v.35) recalls the prophecy of Isaiah in which the nations who oppressed Israel are reduced to chaff and blown away by the wind (Isa 41:15–16).

The motif of the mountain that fills the entire earth echoes the vision of Isaiah in which the "mountain of the LORD's temple" (i.e., Mount Zion and Jerusalem) will be glorified among the nations (Isa 2:2–4; Mic 4:1–2; cf. Lacocque, 49, 124). For an elaboration of the temple motif in Daniel 2, see G. K. Beale, *The Temple and the Church's Mission* (New Studies in Biblical Theology 17; Grand Rapids: Baker, 2004), 144–53.

NOTES

27 The list of royal advisers given here differs slightly from the earlier delineation of the several guilds skilled in the occultic arts of ancient Babylonia (vv.2–3). The Aramaic term for "wise man" or sage, חַכִּים (ḥakkîm; GK 10265; Heb. חָכָם, ḥākām), derives from the root word meaning "to be wise, wisdom" in the OT (see Notes on v.20). The word refers generally to those individuals who possess both physical skill (related to "arts and crafts") and intellectual knowledge; in this context it denotes a class or guild trained formally in the "wisdom tradition" of the age (cf. *NIDOTTE*, 2:132–33). The "enchanter" (אָשַׁף, ʾaššāp) and the "magician" (חַרְטֹם, *ḥarṭōm*) are discussed above (see the Notes on vv.2–3). The Aramaic term "diviners" (גָּזְרִין, *gāzᵉrîn*) appears for the first time (cf. 4:4; 5:7, 11). The root word, גזר (*gzr*), means "to cut," a term that refers generally to "fate determiners" (cf. Collins, *Daniel*, 161).

28 The expression "days to come" (v.28) is deliberately vague and "refers not strictly to the end of the world, but rather to what will happen 'one day,' a goal for history some time 'in the future'" (Baldwin, 91). Contrast the more sweeping understanding of the expression by Archer, 47–48, signifying all the events subsequent to Nebuchadnezzar's lifetime and including the establishment of the fifth kingdom (= the millennial age).

4. Daniel Interprets the King's Dream (2:36–45)

> [36]"This was the dream, and now we will interpret it to the king. [37]You, O king, are the king of kings. The God of heaven has given you dominion and power and might and glory; [38]in your hands he has placed mankind and the beasts of the field and the birds of the air. Wherever they live, he has made you ruler over them all. You are that head of gold.
>
> [39]"After you, another kingdom will rise, inferior to yours. Next, a third kingdom, one of bronze, will rule over the whole earth. [40]Finally, there will be a fourth kingdom, strong as iron—for iron breaks and smashes everything—and as iron breaks things to pieces, so it will crush and break all the others. [41]Just as you saw that the feet and toes were partly of baked clay and partly of iron, so this will be a divided kingdom; yet it will have some of the strength of iron in it, even as you saw iron mixed with clay. [42]As the toes were partly iron and partly clay, so this kingdom will be partly strong and partly brittle. [43]And just as you saw the iron mixed with baked clay, so the people will be a mixture and will not remain united, any more than iron mixes with clay.
>
> [44]"In the time of those kings, the God of heaven will set up a kingdom that will never be destroyed, nor will it be left to another people. It will crush all those kingdoms and bring them to an end, but it will itself endure forever. [45]This is the meaning of the vision of the rock cut out of a mountain, but not by human hands—a rock that broke the iron, the bronze, the clay, the silver and the gold to pieces.
>
> "The great God has shown the king what will take place in the future. The dream is true and the interpretation is trustworthy."

COMMENTARY

36–45 Redditt, 59, notes that Nebuchadnezzar's dream ends as ominously as it began; meanwhile, the audience is still waiting in suspense for some understanding of the significance of the colossal statue. Daniel proceeds to interpret the king's dream, thus fulfilling the second half of the monarch's demand to relate both the content and the meaning of the dream (v.6).

Daniel's statement "we will interpret" may be a veiled reference to the God of heaven, who has made the dream and its interpretation known to Daniel (so Miller, 92). Daniel's choice to leave God unnamed here is in keeping with his earlier reference to God as the "revealer of mysteries" (v.29). It is clear from v.28, however, that Daniel infers his own God, the God of Israel and the God of heaven. It is also possible that Daniel's "editorial we" may be an inclusive reference to his three fellow Hebrew captives, since they too prayed fervently for God's revelation in the matter of the king's dream (vv.17–18). This may account for the report at the end of the story of their elevation to administrative appointments within the province of Babylon (v.49).

Daniel's interpretation of the dream suggests that the statue represents a human king, since Nebuchadnezzar is identified as the "head of gold" (v.38). Seow, 44, understands Daniel's address to Nebuchadnezzar as "king ... the king of kings" (v.37) as a summary of the substance of his interpretation of the dream. The statue represents human kingship bestowed by an even greater king—Daniel's "God of gods and Lord of kings" (v.47). This is a lesson Nebuchadnezzar will relearn as a result of his dream about a tree in ch. 4. King Nebuchadnezzar and Babylonia are given preeminence in Daniel's

interpretation, but only as "a microcosm of the true power, an earthly reflex of a greater power that is the source of 'the kingdom [or, better, 'kingship'], the power, the might, and the glory'" (Seow, 44). King David understood this reality (1Ch 29:10–13), as did the apostle Paul (cf. 1Ti 6:15).

The rest of Daniel's interpretation of the statue in the king's dream outlines a succession of kingdoms rising and falling subsequent to the Babylonian Empire (vv.39–43). The second kingdom, the arms and chest of silver, will prove inferior to Babylonia (v.39a). The third kingdom, the belly and thighs of bronze, will be distinctive for its worldwide rule (v.39b). The fourth kingdom, the legs of iron and the feet of iron and clay, will be singularly ruthless and destructive—yet it will be a divided kingdom mixing strength and weakness (vv.40–43).

Beyond the identification of the head of gold as the Babylonian Empire, there is no interpretive consensus as to the identity of the remaining three kingdoms described in Daniel's understanding of the dream. Two basic approaches have emerged in the scholarly debate: the Greek view (with variation) and the Roman view. The chart below outlines the patterns of historical identification of the corresponding body parts of the statue:

	Roman View	*Greek View 1*	*Greek View 2*
Head of Gold	Nebuchadnezzar (Babylonian Empire)	Babylonian Empire	Babylonian Empire
Chest/Arms of Silver	Medo-Persian Empire	Median Kingdom	Medo-Persian Empire
Belly/Thighs of Brass	Greek Empire	Persian Empire	Alexander's Kingdom
Legs of Iron/Clay	Roman Empire	Greek Empire	Alexander's Feet of Iron (plus successors)

Generally, conservative scholars hold the Roman view (supported by the NT; see below), while mainline scholars tend to opt for one of the Greek views. The issue of predictive prophecy versus *ex*

eventu prophecy is the fault line (see the Introduction: Authorship, and Literary Form). Yet the interpretive situation is not clearly represented by this kind of reductionism. Not all mainline scholars hold to one of the Greek views, and there are scattered examples of recent evangelical scholarship's forwarding of arguments for the Greek views.

Beyond this, disagreement persists as to the interpretation of certain details, such as the blend of iron and clay in the statue's feet as representing mixed marriages of some sort (e.g., political marriages between the Seleucids and Ptolemies; cf. Collins, *Daniel*, 170) or the significance of the ten toes of the statue (e.g., Miller, 97–99, equates the "toes" with ten kingdoms). (See on the "interpretive confusion" surrounding the analysis of Da 2 the helpful discussion in Longman, 81–82.)

Beyond the immediate historical situation of the Babylonian Empire, the revelation of the dream and its interpretation in ch. 2 is not intended as a precise schematic of world history. As Longman, 82, writes, Daniel's point is "something more general, but also more grand: God is sovereign, he is in control despite present conditions." This is in keeping with the tenor of Daniel's doxology, as kingship belongs to God and "he sets up kings and deposes them" (v.21). Moreover, Daniel's audience only needs to know that a series of kingdoms will rise and fall before God's kingdom breaks into history. Such information serves to allay any fears that God's promises about Israel's restoration after the Babylonian exile have failed (see Theological Emphases in the Introduction).

Mainline scholars, especially those associating Daniel with later Jewish apocalypticism, detect the influence of Persian Zoroastrianism in the four-empire scheme in the dream of the statue in ch. 2

and the vision of the four beasts in ch. 7 (e.g., Collins, *Daniel*, 163). Lucas, 75–76, finds the Persian thesis weak and sees the formative influence on the imagery of Daniel 2 in Greek literature, especially Hesiod's myth of the four ages represented by the same metals of declining value (gold, silver, bronze, iron; cf. Porteous, 44–45; Lacocque, 48; *BBCOT*, 733–34). Quite apart from the speculation about possible Persian or Greek influence on the imagery of the dream narrative, the simple fact remains that history knows of four major Near Eastern/Mediterranean empires intervening between Daniel and the incarnation of Jesus of Nazareth. (See the discussion of the visions of chs. 7 and 8, since they elaborate the theme of successive world empires as a prelude to the kingdom of God.)

Daniel concludes his interpretation of the king's dream by announcing that a fifth kingdom will emerge during the rule of the fourth kingdom represented by the legs of iron and feet of an iron-clay mix (v.44). Like the first of the four kingdoms of the statue, this kingdom is identified by name—the kingdom of the God of heaven (v.44a). Unlike the four successive empires represented by the statue of a human king, this kingdom is completed unrelated to the statue symbolizing earthly kingship (i.e., "the rock cut out of a mountain, but not by human hands"; v.45a). God's kingdom will crush and obliterate all earthly kingdoms (vv.35, 44a). It will be an eternal kingdom built on the ruins of failed human kingship (v.44b), and it will be universal—filling the whole earth (v.35).

REFLECTION

John the Baptist announced that the kingdom of God was near (Mt 3:2), and Jesus claimed to have inaugurated the kingdom of God in his earthly ministry of teaching and healing (Mt 4:23; 12:28;

Mk 9:1; Lk 9:1–2). Thus the NT supports the identification of the fourth kingdom (made of iron) as the Roman Empire. What's more, Jesus clearly stated that his kingdom was entirely other—not of this world (Jn 18:36). But more important than the historical identification of the regimes alluded to in the king's statue-dream is the message of this court story for Daniel's audience. Seow, 47, keenly observes that hope for the Hebrew exiles lay in their divine election and the fact that they were heirs of God's promises to Abraham—the rock from which they were cut (Isa 51:1–2).

In addition, two more timeless principles may be extracted from the interpretation of the statue-dream. First, human kingdoms are transient, but God's kingdom is eternal—so we set proper priorities (Mt 6:33) and we "invest" wisely (Mt 6:20; cf. Longman, 82–83). Second, the declining value of the successive metals in the composition of the statue speaks of the increasing "inferiority" of the successive earthly empires (v.39). There is a degenerative principle inherent in the cumulative impact of sin upon humanity, yet humanity deceives itself with delusions of progress and advancement (cf. Ro 1:22; see Porteous, 45–46, who acknowledges the degenerative principle but regards it as secondary). This explains the numerous biblical admonitions to beware of sins of pride and arrogance (Pr 16:18; Jas 4:6), and the equally numerous biblical exhortations to contrition and humility (Isa 57:15; Mt 11:29). Jesus' message still has currency: "The kingdom of God is near. Repent and believe the good news!" (Mk 1:15).

5. The King's Response to Daniel's Interpretation (2:46–49)

> ⁴⁶Then King Nebuchadnezzar fell prostrate before Daniel and paid him honor and ordered that an offering and incense be presented to him. ⁴⁷The king said to Daniel, "Surely your God is the God of gods and the Lord of kings and a revealer of mysteries, for you were able to reveal this mystery."
>
> ⁴⁸Then the king placed Daniel in a high position and lavished many gifts on him. He made him ruler over the entire province of Babylon and placed him in charge of all its wise men. ⁴⁹Moreover, at Daniel's request the king appointed Shadrach, Meshach and Abednego administrators over the province of Babylon, while Daniel himself remained at the royal court.

COMMENTARY

46–49 The narrative concludes with Nebuchadnezzar's paying homage to Daniel (v.46), offering tribute to Daniel's God as the "God of gods" (v.47), and appointing Daniel to an administrative post over the province of Babylon (v.48). It should also be noted that Daniel did not forget his friends, and at Daniel's request they, too, were given administrative appointments by the king in the province of Babylon (v.49).

The report of the worship offered to Daniel by the Babylonian king has raised numerous questions for biblical commentators. Was the king indeed worshiping Daniel in his prostration and presentation of ritual offerings? Why would Daniel accept such worship? As a result, some interpret the silence of the text about Daniel's response as tacit rejection of Nebuchadnezzar's worship since in the context Daniel repeatedly gives God the glory and credit for the interpretation of the dream (cf. Miller, 103). Others admit the embarrassment of the report and understand Daniel's acquiescence as tantamount to the acceptance of worship—revealing the humor of the narrator (so Porteous, 51) or the "humanness" of Daniel (cf. Anderson, 26). Redditt, 61, sees the king's response of worship offered to Daniel as clear evidence that he failed to comprehend what had really transpired, thus casting aspersion on his confession in v.47.

Lucas, 77, contends that the king's response is understandable in that he treats Daniel as the representative of the deity. Goldingay, 61, agrees, noting that "to experience God at work leads to an awareness of who God is ... he offers the only possible response, an acknowledgement of the revealer—God and his agent." Furthermore, Longman, 83, reminds us that vv.46 and 47 must be read together: "Daniel is honored because of what his God has done, not because of what he has done." Lastly, Russell, 57, calls us to enter the spirit of the story, since "as a representative of God's faithful people Daniel sees in the king's obeisance a fulfillment of the promise of Scripture 'that kings shall see and arise: princes, and they shall bow down to you, and lick the dust of your feet' (Isa 49:7, 23)."

Smith-Christopher, 56, isolates in this last section of the story of the king's dream a theme that recurs in the subsequent court stories of Daniel (and to a lesser degree in the court stories of Joseph and Esther), namely, "the transformation of the king." Nebuchadnezzar's transformation is seen in his confession that Daniel's God is supreme among all the deities and overlord of all earthly kings (v.47). His mini-doxology draws attention to the theological import of ch. 2—the sovereignty, power, and wisdom of God as "the revealer of mysteries" (vv.22, 48). The king's confession provides evidence of his "transformation" in that "to acknowledge God as Master among kings is to qualify the meaning of his own kingship in a revolutionary way, as to acknowledge him as God among gods is radically to qualify the ascription of divinity to other deities" (Goldingay, 61). The king's testimony lauding Daniel's God, however, does not mean he has "converted" to the religion of the Hebrews. "As a polytheist he can always add another god to the deities he worships" (Baldwin, 95).

The king is lavish in his rewarding of Daniel, in keeping with his earlier promise of rewarding the one who could reveal the dream and its meaning (v.6). Daniel receives royal gifts and is appointed "ruler over the entire province of Babylon," as well as chief among the wise men (v.48). Daniel's promotion sets up a rivalry with the other wise men that will surface in the later court stories. Daniel is stationed in Babylon as a member of the royal cabinet ("remained at the royal court"; v.49). At Daniel's request his three fellow Hebrew captives are given administrative posts that move them out of Babylon as "subordinate officers" in the provincial districts (cf. Montgomery, 183); alternatively, Lacocque, 54–55, understands that Daniel relinquishes his political charges for the sake of his friends. The references to Shadrach, Meshach, and Abednego set the stage for the next court story in Daniel—the account of the image of gold and the fiery furnace (ch. 3).

NOTES

46 Nebuchadnezzar's prostration before Daniel is more than just the reversal of royal protocol (i.e., a Gentile king bowing before a Hebrew sage as though he were a royal figure). Hartman and Di Lella, 150, note that "one cannot evade the difficulty by supposing that the 'worship' (סְגִד, sᵉgid) was merely civic homage: the words 'sacrifice' (מִנְחָה, *minḥâ*) and 'incense' (נִיחֹחַ, *nîḥôaḥ*, literally, 'pleasant-smelling offerings') are strictly religious terms, borrowed in fact from the Hebrew ritual vocabulary."

48 As ruler over the province of Babylon, Daniel would have the role of supervisor of the various prefects of the administrative districts of the province. His position as "chief prefect" (NASB) over the wise men designates a position of high rank, though the Aramaic term itself, סְגַן (*s̆egan*), is an Assyrian loanword signifying royal officials of various rank.

49 Literally Daniel remains, תְּרַע מַלְכָּא (*t̆eraʿ malkāʾ*, "on call") at the "king's gate" since "the 'king's gate' is where the king's retainers wait to be summoned to duty" (Seow, 49; cf. Est 2:19, 21; 3:2–3).

C. The Golden Image and the Fiery Furnace (3:1–30)

OVERVIEW

Daniel 3 continues the "court stories" section of the book (chs. 1–6). It forms part of a distinct literary unit within the book that includes chs. 2–7 (see Overview to 2:1–49). Goldingay, 68, regards the story as midrash (or stylized rabbinic interpretation) of Isaiah 41:1–3 composed during the Antiochene period. Collins (*Daniel*, 193) challenges the midrashic approach to the story since there is no explicit reference to the Isaianic text and "the story hardly exemplifies 'walking through' fire." Porteous, 55, labels the narrative a martyr story, but the miraculous deliverance of the heroes from death seems to overturn the basic motif of this form-critical approach to literary genre (see Redditt, 65, on the story as "wisdom court legend" and Hartman and Di Lella, 160, on the story as "witness literature"; cf. Smith-Christopher, 66–67). The narrative is best understood, from a literary perspective, as a court story of conflict given the fact that "here the Judeans encounter the animosity of their enemies in a way that they have not yet experienced" (Longman, 97; cf. Lucas, 86).

The fantastic details of the court story (e.g., the size of the golden image, the intense heat of the furnace) and the element of the miraculous (i.e.,

the preservation of the three Hebrews in the midst of roaring flames of the furnace) have prompted a majority of biblical interpreters to view the story metaphorically rather than historically (e.g., Anderson, 27–29; Gowan, 62–63; Towner, 48). Yet Baldwin, 100, points out that the Colossus of Rhodes stood seventy cubits high (ten cubits taller than Nebuchadnezzar's statue or stele) and that both the OT (e.g., Isa 40:19; 41:7) and the Greek historian Herodotus refer to the practice of overlaying images with gold plating. For Smith-Christopher, 62, the issue of whether or not Nebuchadnezzar ever erected such a statue is beside the point. "The point was that he could—he could amass that much gold; he could assemble the leaders; he could demand obedience and threaten horrible punishment—and this is the plausibility (i.e., a political plausibility) that the stories of Daniel are based on."

The plot of the story in ch. 3 may be outlined in seven scenes. According to Lucas, 86, the chiastic structure of the narrative calls attention to the words spoken by Shadrach, Meshach, and Abednego to Nebuchadnezzar. They are the only words uttered by these Hebrew civil servants of the king and are thus marked as the key scene in the story.

The structure of the story identified by Lucas may be outlined as follows:

A Nebuchadnezzar's decree to worship the golden image (vv.1–7)

  B The Jews accused (vv.8–12)

    C The Jews threatened (vv.13–15)

      D The Jews confess their faith (vv.16–18)

    C' The Jews punished (vv.19–23)

  B' The Jews vindicated (vv.24–27)

A' Nebuchadnezzar's decree honoring the Jews and their God (vv.28–30)

Lucas, 87, has observed that from the literary perspective of characterization, Nebuchadnezzar is the only "full-fledged" character in the story. That is, he is the one who speaks, acts, shows emotion, and initiates the action of the story. By contrast, Shadrach, Meshach, and Abednego are "type characters" in the story, even a "composite type character" since they speak and act as one (cf. Lucas, 96). In fact, in this chapter Towner, 47, sees Nebuchadnezzar as moving "toward the model of a persecuting tyrant," though he admits it is an open question whether or not the king should be viewed as a "persecuting *divinized* tyrant" since it is unclear whether the statue of gold was an image of a god or the king himself. This question notwithstanding, recent commentators have mined effectively Nebuchadnezzar's despotism for contemporary application to issues of political power, oppression, colonialism, and ethnic hatred (e.g., Anderson, 28–29; Smith-Christopher, 65–66; Gowan, 71–73).

The court story of the golden statue shares features with ch. 6 in that both are stories of conflict with heroes put in peril because of professional jealousy but finally delivered through divine intervention. Other literary features in the golden-statue narrative include what Towner, 47–48, calls "the

amazing redundancy ... and constant repetition" of the story (perhaps a stylistic device to heighten tension as well as entertain?), the propensity for lists (e.g., the repeated lists of Babylonian officials, vv.2–3, 26; the repeated lists of musical instruments, vv.5, 7, 10, 15), and the comedic impact of the humorous tone set by the narrator's use of irony and repetition (cf. Towner, 48; Lucas, 87; Goldingay, 67–68).

The setting for the conflict is the plain of Dura, located a few miles south of the city of Babylon (v.1). The event precipitating the conflict was King Nebuchadnezzar's decision to erect a golden image and issue a decree that on threat of death, all of his subjects must fall down and worship the image of gold (vv.5–6). The plot of the story hinges on the accusation against the three Hebrews, Shadrach, Meshach, and Abednego, by fellow astrologers for their failure to bow down and worship the golden image set up by the king (vv.8–12). The Babylonian astrologers appear to have been motivated both by professional jealousy and ethnic prejudice, given their statement; "but there are some Jews whom you have set over the affairs of the province of Babylon" (v.12).

The three Hebrew courtiers remain stalwart in their conviction to worship God alone, confessing faith in God whether or not they are spared death in the king's furnace (vv.16–18). In a fit of rage Nebuchadnezzar has the three Hebrews thrown into the blazing oven, only to witness their miraculous deliverance (vv.24–27). As a result the king praises the God of Shadrach, Meshach, and Abednego and promotes his civil servants within the ranks of the provincial officials (vv.28–30).

Most commentators agree that above all else the court story of the golden image and the fiery furnace is a polemic against idolatry (e.g., Russell, 60–61). The court story is also an exhortation to the Hebrews in exile to remain loyal in their worship of Yahweh, even at the risk of martyrdom by those who would seek to impose idolatrous worship on them. The deliverance of the three Hebrew sages demonstrates that God has both the will and the power to intervene and rescue his faithful servants—a theological reality attested by Nebuchadnezzar himself (v.28; cf. Towner, 57)!

The Roman Catholic and Orthodox editions of Daniel insert two additions to ch. 3: after v.23, the Prayer of Azariah (3:24–45) and then the Song of the Three Young Men (3:46–90). The conclusion of the story as known in the Hebrew Bible (3:24–30) then follows the two additions (3:91–97). The Prayer of Azariah includes confession of sin (after the pattern of Da 9), an acknowledgment of God's justice, and a plea for deliverance. The Song of the Three Young Men begins with a description of the furnace (3:46–50), transitions to a liturgical hymn extolling the glory and power of God (3:51–56), and concludes with a liturgical exhortation to all creation to join in praising the Lord (3:57–90). On these Additions to Daniel see the Introduction.

1. Nebuchadnezzar's Golden Image (3:1–7)

[1]King Nebuchadnezzar made an image of gold, ninety feet high and nine feet wide, and set it up on the plain of Dura in the province of Babylon. [2]He then summoned the satraps, prefects, governors, advisers, treasurers, judges, magistrates and all the other provincial officials to come to the dedication of the image he had set up. [3]So the satraps, prefects, governors, advisers, treasurers, judges, magistrates and all the other provincial officials assembled for the dedication of the image that King Nebuchadnezzar had set up, and they stood before it.

[4]Then the herald loudly proclaimed, "This is what you are commanded to do, O peoples, nations and men of every language: [5]As soon as you hear the sound of the horn, flute, zither, lyre, harp, pipes and all kinds of music, you must fall down and worship the image of gold that King Nebuchadnezzar has set up. [6]Whoever does not fall down and worship will immediately be thrown into a blazing furnace."

[7]Therefore, as soon as they heard the sound of the horn, flute, zither, lyre, harp and all kinds of music, all the peoples, nations and men of every language fell down and worshiped the image of gold that King Nebuchadnezzar had set up.

COMMENTARY

1–7 No time frame is assigned to this episode, but most likely the event occurs early in Nebuchadnezzar's reign as a test of loyalty to the new administration (cf. Miller, 107). The date given for the incident in the LXX (the eighteenth year of Nebu-chadnezzar's reign) is borrowed from Jeremiah 52:29 as a possible rationale for the unusual royal ceremony (cf. Porteous, 57). The story features Daniel's three friends, Shadrach, Meshach, and Abednego, with no mention of Daniel himself. Daniel's absence at the

"Festival of the New Babylon" may be explained by the reference to his role as an adviser in the royal court (2:49). Either Daniel has relinquished his administrative authority for the profit of his friends (so Lacocque, 55), or his duties are of such a highly specialized nature that he is required to remain at the royal palace (so Miller, 108).

At issue in the story is a giant image erected by Nebuchadnezzar (v.1) and his subsequent decree that all of his royal subjects must bow down and worship the image (vv.6, 11). The term "image" (Aram. ṣᵉlēm) simply refers to a statue or stela of some sort. The extreme height (ninety feet) and narrow width (nine feet) of the image suggests the form of an obelisk or totem pole (e.g., Porteous, 57; see *BBCOT*, 734). Commentators debate whether the image represents the king or a deity of the Babylonian pantheon (cf. Goldingay, 70). Wallace, 64, rightly points out that the matter is left intentionally vague. The statue could represent whatever anyone wants it to symbolize, whether the spirit of Babylon, the king himself, one of the traditional deities (e.g., Marduk according to Wiseman, *Nebuchadrezzar and Babylon*, 109), or even a syncretistic focal point for the various religions of Nebuchadnezzar's realm. The fact that the statue is overlaid with gold may indicate that Nebuchadnezzar has been influenced by Daniel's interpretation of the king's statue-dream identifying him as the "head of gold" (2:28; cf. Young, 84).

The "plain of Dura" (v.1) may have been a site near the city wall (since the Akk. *duru* refers to a "walled place"; cf. Wiseman, *Nebuchadrezzar and Babylon*, 111), but more traditionally the location has been identified with Tulul Dura ("tells of Dura") some sixteen miles south of Babylon (cf. Miller, 111). Seven classes of state officials are named (vv.2–3), presumably rank-ordered in terms of importance (cf. Miller, 111; see Notes). These administrators represent the many peoples, nations, and languages of the king's wide domain. The lesser officials and civil servants are addressed collectively in the umbrella phrase "all the other provincial officials" (v.2). Goldingay, 70, has noted that "in many cultures, music draws attention to state and religious processions and ceremonials."

Six types of musical instruments are specifically mentioned as examples of the array of instruments comprising the royal band (v.5; see Notes). None of the instruments named were used in Hebrew worship, and most are designated by loanwords from other languages. Rhetorically, the repetition of the musical component of the event (vv.5, 7, 10, 15) attests the grandiose nature and cosmopolitan character of the ceremony (cf. Porteous, 57; Wallace, 64; Miller, 114). Theologically, the repetition of the foreign terms for the musical instruments "imply a double judgment on the alien, pagan nature of the [idolatrous] ceremony Nebuchadnezzar is inaugurating" (Goldingay, 70).

Ceremonies marking the installation of statues or the dedication of buildings are well documented in the ancient world (cf. Montgomery, 197–98). This ceremony probably included the taking of a loyalty oath as Nebuchadnezzar solidified his rule over the vast Babylonian Empire (cf. *BBCOT*, 735). The word "dedication" (vv.2–3; Heb. ḥᵃnukkâ; GK 10273) means to inaugurate or put into use for the first time (and implies some ongoing function for the object so dedicated; cf. *TDOT*, 5:19–23). The same term is used in the OT for the dedication of the altar (Nu 7:10–11), the temple (1Ki 8:63), and the rebuilt wall of Jerusalem (Ne 12:27; cf. Seow, 53). "Hanukkah" is the name applied to the Feast of Rededication of the temple after its cleansing by Judas Maccabeus (1 Macc 4:56, 59). Later the NT records that Jesus was in the temple during the Feast of Dedication or Hanukkah (Jn 10:22).

The role of the herald (v.4) as public crier and messenger or courier is known in the biblical world (e.g., Est 3:13; cf. Collins, *Daniel*, 183); according to Wiseman (*Nebuchadrezzar and Babylon*, 111), "the use of the herald for public proclamations was a long-standing Babylonian tradition." The king's decree is probably announced to the assembly in the Aramaic language, the *lingua franca* of Nebuchadnezzar's empire (so Miller, 113). Burning (v.6) is a well-attested penalty for the punishment of criminals throughout the Babylonian, Persian, and Greek periods (cf. Jer 29:22; see Goldingay, 70; Collins, *Daniel*, 185–86). Nebuchadnezzar's "blazing furnace" (v.6) may have been a beehive-type oven or kiln with an opening at the top (into which the men were thrown) and a door at the side (permitting a view to the inside of the furnace; cf. Hartman and Di Lella, 161), or a tunnel-shaped brick furnace (so Baldwin, 103). While such details lend authenticity to narrative, the story itself has little to do with "the Festival of the New Babylon" (see Wallace, 63–64) and everything to do with idolatry and apostasy—the very cause of the Hebrews' exile to Babylonia (see Russell, 59–61; cf. Dt 29:25–28).

NOTES

2 Seven classes of officials are assembled for the dedication of Nebuchadnezzar's gigantic golden image. These royal administrators represent the people of the Babylonian Empire and presumably are listed in order of importance. Two of the seven titles are of Akkadian origin, while the other five terms are of Persian origin. According to Lucas, 89, since none of the titles are Greek, "the form in which we have this story comes from the Persian period."

The Aramaic term "satraps" (אֲחַשְׁדַּרְפְּנַיָּא, ⁾aḥašdarpᵉnayyā⁾) is a loanword from the Persian *hšatra-pāvan*, meaning "protectors of the kingdom." These officials were in charge of the largest divisions of the empire. The Aramaic term "prefects" (סְגְנַיָּא, signayyā⁾) is a loanword from Akkadian (*šaknu*), and these high-ranking officials were directly responsible to the satraps. The Aramaic word for "governors" (פַּחֲוָתָא, paḥᵃwātā⁾) is a loanword from Akkadian (*pihātu, pahātu*), and these rulers were heads of regions or provinces within the larger satrapies. The Aramaic word אֲדַרְגָּזְרַיָּא (⁾ᵃdargāzᵉrayyā⁾) is from the Old Persian (*handarza-kara*) and signifies "advisers" ("counselors," NASB). The Aramaic word for "treasurers" (גְּדָבְרַיָּא, gᵉdābᵉrayyā⁾ or gizbārayya [cf. Ezr 7:21]) is probably derived from the Persian *ganzabara*. The Aramaic word for "judges" (דְּתָבְרַיָּא, dᵉtābᵉrayyā⁾, from the Persian *dātabara*) means literally "law bearers." The Aramaic word for "magistrates" (תִּפְתָּיֵא, tiptāyē⁾) is probably derived from the Persian *tayu-pata* ("police magistrate"; so Hartman and Di Lella, 157). See the discussions in Hartman and Di Lella, 156–57; Miller, 111–12.

4 The Aramaic word for "herald" (כָּרוֹזָא, kārôzā⁾) is often understood as a loanword from the Greek (*kēryx*; cf. Montgomery, 202; Lacocque, 57). More recent scholarship associates the term with the Old Persian ʿrausa (e.g., Hartman and Di Lella, 157). In either case, the derivation of the terms has long been disputed and is inconclusive as evidence for the dating of the book of Daniel (cf. Collins, *Daniel*, 183).

5 The names of the musical instruments belong to a technical vocabulary, and most are foreign terms used in secular contexts. At least three of the instruments are loanwords from Greek. The Aramaic word for "lyre" (קִיתְרוֹס, qîtᵉrôs) is derived from the Greek *kithara* (which gives rise to the English words "zither" and "guitar"; cf. Hartman and Di Lella, 157). The Aramaic term for "harp" (פְּסַנְתֵּרִין, p^{e}santērîn) is derived from the Greek word *psaltērion*. The term usually rendered "pipes" (or "bagpipe," NASB), סוּמְפֹּנְיָה (sûm^{e}pōnyâ), is derived from the Greek word *symphōnia* (lit., "accompanying sound"; cf. Collins, *Daniel*, 184; Goldingay, 65 [n.5.f.], who notes the word may refer to a double-flute, drums, or bagpipes).

The "horn" (Heb./Aram. קֶרֶן, *qeren*) is widely attested as a musical instrument in the biblical world. The "flute" (Aram. מַשְׁרוֹקִי, *maśrôqî*) is related to the root word *š^{e}raq*, meaning "to hiss, whistle" (cf. Miller, 113). The "zither" (or "trigon," NASB; Aram. סַבְּכָא, *śabb^{e}kā'*) was a triangular instrument with four strings and is probably of non-Semitic origin (cf. Hartman and Di Lella, 157). See J. Braun, *Music in Ancient Israel/Palestine* (Grand Rapids: Eerdmans, 2002), 32–35.

The word "worship" (Heb./Aram. סגד, *sgd*; GK 6032/10504) occurs four times in Isaiah (Isa 44:15, 17, 19; 46:6), "always in conjunction with [the word חוה] *ḥwh*, always of false worship; it reinforces the idea of obeisance" (*NIDOTTE*, 3:222). The root word *sgd* in the Aramaic of Daniel 2:46; 3:5–28 is used "instead of, and as an equivalent of, [the word] *ḥwh*" (*NIDOTTE*, 3:222). The repetition of the root word *sgd* in Daniel 3:5–28 highlights true worship versus false worship as the key theme of the chapter.

2. The Three Hebrews Accused (3:8–12)

> [8]At this time some astrologers came forward and denounced the Jews. [9]They said to King Nebuchadnezzar, "O king, live forever! [10]You have issued a decree, O king, that everyone who hears the sound of the horn, flute, zither, lyre, harp, pipes and all kinds of music must fall down and worship the image of gold, [11]and that whoever does not fall down and worship will be thrown into a blazing furnace. [12]But there are some Jews whom you have set over the affairs of the province of Babylon — Shadrach, Meshach and Abednego — who pay no attention to you, O king. They neither serve your gods nor worship the image of gold you have set up."

COMMENTARY

8–12 The heart of a good story is gripping conflict moving toward resolution. In this episode of the court stories of Daniel the conflict centers on what Wallace, 65, calls "the miracle of resistance." The gist of the story is the refusal of three Jewish nonconformists to bow in worship before the towering image erected by King Nebuchadnezzar on the plain of Dura (v.12). The "plot" conflict for Shadrach, Meshach, and Abednego occurs at multiple levels in the story, including character conflict in the form of rivals who bring accusations against them before the king (v.9), the spiritual and moral issue of participating in false worship (v.10), and physical conflict since their disobedience to the king's decree puts them under the threat of death by incineration (v.11).

Apparently the king does not see the three rebels left standing at the sound of the musical fanfare signaling the worship of the golden image, given the throng of royal officials at the event. The failure of the Hebrews to bow upon command, however, is duly reported to the king by fellow astrologers ("Chaldeans," NASB; v.8). The ambiguity of the term "astrologer" (NIV) or "Chaldean" (NASB; Heb. *kaśdîm*; Aram. *kaśdāy*) has been noted (see Notes on 1:4.). The accusers are either Babylonian officials generally or members of a special guild of diviners or priestly class of wise men. It seems likely that the more technical understanding of the term as a reference to the professional guild of royal astrologers should be read in this context.

These rival astrologers come forward, have a formal audience with the king, and "denounce" the Hebrews ("brought charges," NASB; v.8). Russell, 65, notes that the word "denounce" is an idiom (Heb. *ʾākal* + Aram. *qᵉraṣ* = "slander, backbite") that literally means "ate their pieces, or as we might say, they made mincemeat out of them!"

The astrologers are careful to observe protocol in the customary address, "O king, live forever!" (v.9), perhaps insinuating that their Hebrew counterparts also violate royal protocol, since later they address Nebuchadnezzar by name but not by title (cf. v.16). The astrologers also politely remind the king of his own edict with obvious intention—the destruction of these Hebrew rivals (v.10). These "worship police" have two motives: ethnic or racial distrust (if not hatred) given the references to the "Jews" (vv.9, 12), and professional jealousy given the reference to the status of the three Hebrews as rulers over the affairs of the province of Babylon (v.12; cf. Seow, 54, who observes that the Chaldean diviners are provoked both by professional jealousy and xenophobia).

The behavior of Shadrach, Meshach, and Abednego is both an act of treason (since they do not serve the king's gods, v.12) and insubordination (since they refuse to obey the king's edict and bow to the golden image, v.12). The display of such disloyalty is deserving of death. Though the rival astrologers do not ask for the execution of three Hebrews, the request is implicit in their reminder to the king of the consequences for failure to comply with his decree (v.11).

Russell, 65, comments, "informers and the totalitarian state go hand in hand." But the role of the accusers may be less sinister, since self-interest tends to dictate behavior in politics—whether ancient or modern. As Porteous, 59, notes, the accusation made by the accusers is not a false one, "since the men had undoubtedly refused to conform to the king's order, but it was definitely malicious." The rival astrologers may have had hope of some personal advantage in their display of zeal for the honor of King Nebuchadnezzar. In either case, the accusation of the three Hebrews by their Babylonian counterparts "highlights the dilemma of the Diaspora Jew who wished to get involved in the social and political life of a pagan city" (Lucas, 90).

3. The Three Hebrews Stand Trial before Nebuchadnezzar (3:13–18)

[13]Furious with rage, Nebuchadnezzar summoned Shadrach, Meshach and Abednego. So these men were brought before the king, [14]and Nebuchadnezzar said to them, "Is it true, Shadrach, Meshach and Abednego, that you do not serve my gods or worship the image of gold I have set up? [15]Now when you hear the sound of the horn, flute, zither, lyre, harp,

pipes and all kinds of music, if you are ready to fall down and worship the image I made, very good. But if you do not worship it, you will be thrown immediately into a blazing furnace. Then what god will be able to rescue you from my hand?"

[16]Shadrach, Meshach and Abednego replied to the king, "O Nebuchadnezzar, we do not need to defend ourselves before you in this matter. [17]If we are thrown into the blazing furnace, the God we serve is able to save us from it, and he will rescue us from your hand, O king. [18]But even if he does not, we want you to know, O king, that we will not serve your gods or worship the image of gold you have set up."

COMMENTARY

13–18 The astrologers' charge against the three Hebrews incites the king's rage (v.13). The NIV's "furious with rage" renders the hendiadys "in fury [Aram. *regaz*] and rage [Aram. *ḥemâ*]" (cf. NASB's "in rage and anger"). Previously, the king's rage had been directed against these same royal astrologers because they were unable to interpret his dream (2:12). Now these courtiers have managed to turn Nebuchadnezzar's anger toward their Hebrew counterparts, with little thought that it was a Hebrew who earlier spared their lives (2:24).

Shadrach, Meshach, and Abednego are summoned to appear before the king, who queries them, almost in disbelief, on the veracity of the accusation against them; but he waits for no reply (vv.13–14). The king actually parrots the charge of the accusers, indicating the deep impact the report of open defiance has on him (v.14; cf. v.12). To his credit, Nebuchadnezzar does not simply act on the testimony of the accusers. Instead, he offers the three Hebrews another opportunity to obey the decree and bow down in worship before the golden image (v.15). The reason for the king's leniency is unclear, though time and money have been invested in these civil servants and they have proven useful to the king on an earlier occasion (cf. 2:17, 49).

The king offers to repeat the same ritual of musical fanfare leading to prostration in worship before the image (v.15). By means of this test he will determine the guilt or innocence and ultimately the fate of his three servants, Shadrach, Meshach, and Abednego. Compliance with the king's edict ensures survival and presumably ongoing service as provincial officials. Disobedience carries the same threat of punishment previously announced in the royal decree—execution by incineration in the crematory oven (cf. vv.6, 11).

A new twist is added to the confrontation with the king's postscript, "Then what god will be able to rescue you from my hand?" (v.15). Montgomery, 208, notes that the construction of the king's statement is emphatic (lit., "What [at all] god is there?"). The question implies that the image represents a Babylonian deity of some sort. It also suggests that Nebuchadnezzar assumes he possesses absolute authority—that he alone is sovereign in this situation. The king's rhetorical question echoes the challenge brought by the envoys of the Assyrian king Sennacherib against King Hezekiah of Judah and the city of Jerusalem: "Has the god of any nation ever delivered his land from the hand of the king of Assyria?" (2Ki 18:33; cf. Isa 36:18). As

Russell, 66, observes, the temptation to be like God is as old as Eden (cf. Ge 3:5).

The NIV's rendering "we do not need to defend ourselves before you" is interpretive (v.16; cf. NASB, "we do not need to give you an answer"). The text says nothing about presenting a defense before the king. Literally, the verse indicates that there is no need "to give back" or "to return" (Aram. *twb*) to the king on the matter. That is, the young men "feel no compunction to give a comeback, as it were, regarding 'this matter,' namely, the theological challenge raised by Nebuchadnezzar" (Seow, 56).

Lacocque, 63, understands the response of the young men as discourteous, even arrogant (since they address Nebuchadnezzar by name, but not by title). For him the demands of the genre of martyr story require the courageous stand of God's faithful in the face of persecution. Yet the title "O king" is found in the subsequent speech of the three Hebrews addressing Nebuchadnezzar (cf. vv.17–18). Instead, according to Miller, 119, the response of the three men is not a proud reply but a "firm reply" spoken out of deep conviction concerning their faith in God and their understanding of true worship. Seow, 56, confirms this when he comments: "Rather, Shadrach, Meshach, and Abednego do not feel compelled to respond to the king's taunt at all. Courage is not really the issue, for a 'comeback' is simply not theirs to give."

The conditional clauses in vv.17–18 make for difficulty in translation. Some ancient versions simply ignore the conditionality of the confession of the three Hebrews and render the verse as a creedal affirmation of divine deliverance (e.g., LXX and Vulgate; cf. Lucas, 90). According to Seow, 56–57, modern translations ignore the "if, if not" point-counterpoint structure of vv.15 and 17–18 "to circumvent the implied conditionality of God's being and power." Thus the NIV reads, "the God we

serve is able to save us ..." (v.17; cf. NASB, "If it be so, our God whom we serve is able to deliver us ..."). More literally the clause reads, "if he is able, the God we serve ..." (cf. NJB).

Likewise, the verbal form (Aram. *yᵉšêzib*) in the latter part of the verse carries the force of a future tense ("he will deliver us") or a modal force ("he may deliver us"). As Miller, 119, has observed, the modal force of the verb ("he may rescue us") better fits the context of the passage: "Although no doubt existed in the minds of Shadrach, Meshach, and Abednego about the ability of God to deliver them, they humbly accepted the fact the God does not always choose to intervene miraculously in human circumstances." The conditional response by the three Hebrews is a rhetorical refocusing of Nebuchadnezzar's challenge away from themselves and their submission to the king's edict to whether or not God is present and willing to deliver his servants. Seow, 57, aptly summarizes:

> ... by structuring the dialogue in this point-counterpoint fashion, the narrator indicates that the decisive issue at hand is really not the courage of the Jews.... Rather, the critical question is the presence and power of God: inasmuch as a God exists who is able, it is entirely up to God to deliver, if that be the divine will.

Quite apart from the interpretation of v.17, commentators generally agree "that the point being made here is that the youth's primary reason for standing firm is not their confidence that God will deliver them, but their adherence to the first two commandments of the Decalogue. They will not honour any god other than the God of Israel, and they will not worship any idol" (Lucas, 91). Thus the response of the three Hebrews to Nebuchadnezzar is both a confident statement of faith in the God of Israel and a solemn declaration of independence from royal authority. Their bold expression of civil disobedience to the law of the king is not without consequences (cf. Smith-Christopher, 64). Like the apostles of Jesus later in the NT era, Shadrach, Meshach, and Abednego accept full responsibility for their decision to defy human authority and obey God (cf. Ac 4:19–20; 5:29).

4. The Three Hebrews Sentenced (3:19–23)

¹⁹Then Nebuchadnezzar was furious with Shadrach, Meshach and Abednego, and his attitude toward them changed. He ordered the furnace heated seven times hotter than usual ²⁰and commanded some of the strongest soldiers in his army to tie up Shadrach, Meshach and Abednego and throw them into the blazing furnace. ²¹So these men, wearing their robes, trousers, turbans and other clothes, were bound and thrown into the blazing furnace. ²²The king's command was so urgent and the furnace so hot that the flames of the fire killed the soldiers who took up Shadrach, Meshach and Abednego, ²³and these three men, firmly tied, fell into the blazing furnace.

COMMENTARY

19–23 For the second time in this court story the king is "furious," or more literally "filled with wrath" (NASB; cf. v.13). The three Hebrews experience firsthand that "a king's wrath is a messenger of death" (Pr 16:14). The NIV interprets the altering of the king's facial expression toward Shadrach, Meshach, and Abednego (so NASB) as a change in attitude toward his three Hebrew provincial officials. This change of countenance may suggest some previous affinity for the young men, but then again, it may simply mean that the king has lost his calm demeanor, "dropped his kingly control and fell into a rage so that his very visage was contorted" (so Russell, 68; cf. Smith-Christopher, 64 on the king's "hysterical rage").

Every precaution is taken to prevent the escape of the resisters so as to make them a public example of those who defy the decree of the king. The heating of the oven "seven times hotter than usual"

(v.19) is a proverbial expression or an "idiomatic way of saying 'as hot as possible'" (Hartman and Di Lella, 162; cf. Baldwin, 105). The cohort of handpicked "strong men" from the army is probably as much a public show of power as it is a precaution against the escape of the insurgents. Likewise, the binding of the prisoners is symbolic of royal authority as well as standard procedure to facilitate the job of the executioners (cf. Smith-Christopher, 64; Collins, *Daniel*, 188).

Goldingay, 71, remarks that the king is so eager to implement the death sentence that the executioners are not even permitted time to strip the prisoners. The curious nature of the clothing worn by the three Hebrews has generated much scholarly discussion. It seems likely that the garments were ceremonial dress worn over their ordinary clothes (so Porteous, 60). Collins (*Daniel*, 188–89) concludes that the first two garments in the list (Aram.

sarbāl = "robe, mantle, shirt"?; and Aram *paṭṭîš* = "coat" or "trousers"?) cover the upper body and the legs (yet these are interchanged in the NASB's "trousers … coats"), while the third term certainly refers to a hat or some other type of head-covering (Aram. *karbᵉlâ*). The final term of the series (Heb. *lᵉbûš*) is understood as an inclusive term for clothing. Naturally, the detailed reference to the peculiar garments of Shadrach, Meshach, and Abednego only serves to heighten the extraordinary nature of their deliverance, since even their clothing ends up unsinged by the fire (v.28).

The king's urgency to execute the insubordinate Hebrews by incineration means that the military guards are unable to take the necessary precautions to protect themselves from the intense heat of the blazing furnace (v.22). Perhaps as a sign of what's to come, the three bound Hebrews are not thrown into the fire in compliance with the king's command (v.23); rather, they fall through the opening at the top of the furnace into its roaring flames. According to Lucas, 92, in "court tales" the tormentors often suffer the same torture they plan or inflict on their victims (e.g., 6:24; Est 7:9 10). As Porteous, 60, observes, however, "it is scarcely adequate poetic justice that the executioners are killed by the heat instead of the informers." This may be why the Greek Additions to Daniel known as the Song of the Three Young Men (along with the Prayer of Azariah), which are inserted at this point in the narrative, report that the flames of the furnace leap out some seventy-five feet and burn some of the Chaldeans (or rival astrologers; 3:48 LXX).

Commentators are quick to point out the mixture of "mockery and miracle" in the narrative of Nebuchadnezzar's golden image and the blazing furnace as evidence of the legendary character of the court story (e.g., Russell, 69; cf. Porteous, 60, on the element of "caricature" in the story). Yet the report of the "absurdity of the king's rage" (Smith-Christopher, 64), which results in the death of his own executioners, only reinforces the truth that "a quick-tempered man does foolish things" (Pr 14:17). All the more reason why "the One enthroned in heaven laughs" at the plotting of the kings of the earth (Ps 2:4).

5. The Three Hebrews Delivered (3:24–27)

²⁴Then King Nebuchadnezzar leaped to his feet in amazement and asked his advisers, "Weren't there three men that we tied up and threw into the fire?"

They replied, "Certainly, O king."

²⁵He said, "Look! I see four men walking around in the fire, unbound and unharmed, and the fourth looks like a son of the gods."

²⁶Nebuchadnezzar then approached the opening of the blazing furnace and shouted, "Shadrach, Meshach and Abednego, servants of the Most High God, come out! Come here!"

So Shadrach, Meshach and Abednego came out of the fire, ²⁷and the satraps, prefects, governors and royal advisers crowded around them. They saw that the fire had not harmed their bodies, nor was a hair of their heads singed; their robes were not scorched, and there was no smell of fire on them.

COMMENTARY

24–27 King Nebuchadnezzar expects to witness the incineration of three insubordinate provincial officials. Rather than seeing three men burned to death in the roaring flames of the furnace, the king observes four men alive in the midst of the fire (v.24). His startled response to the sight is captured with verbs of immediate action, as he "leaped to his feet in amazement" (or "he was astounded and stood up in haste" [NASB], v.24).

In his bewilderment the Babylonian monarch requests and receives verification of simple math—yes, three bound men were tossed into the crematory oven. How is it that the king counts four men, unbound at that, in the flames of the furnace (v.25)? What's more, it appears that only Nebuchadnezzar beholds this bizarre apparition (cf. Lucas, 92; Seow, 58). In a way this is fitting, since earlier he is the one who raises the challenge to the three Hebrews as to what god could possible rescue them from his authority (v.15).

Incredibly, not only are the men unharmed, they are actually walking around in the fire. The king even describes the fourth man as "a son of the gods" (v.25). According to Montgomery, 214, the expression "is given language entirely genuine to Aramaic Paganism" (rather than terms borrowed from Babylonian mythology or Greek ideology). The phrase indicates the king understands the fourth figure in the furnace to be a divine being—a member of the class of gods (not an angel as Lacocque, 65, and Porteous, 60, suggest). "For a polytheist like Nebuchadnezzar, this would mean [the divine being was] a member of the pantheon" (Lucas, 92).

The extraordinary turn of events prompts the king to act as his own agent—having lost all sense of his royal station. In an almost humorous scene, the king invites his prisoners by name to come out of the blazing furnace (v.25), into which he has them thrown only moments earlier! Presumably the kiln has a door at ground level in addition to the hole in the top of the structure. Nebuchadnezzar identifies them as "servants of the Most High God" (v.26). Whether fully conscious of the fact or not, the king tacitly recognizes what lies at the heart of the episode concerning the image and the furnace—the defiance of the Hebrews in submitting to the royal edict to bow to the golden image is due precisely to their status as servants of the God of Israel. The title "Most High God" occurs in Genesis 14:18–24, where it is used both by Melchizedek (a Canaanite priest-king) and Abram. The epithet is often used for God by non-Hebrews (cf. Baldwin, 106); "for a pagan it would mean the highest among many gods" (Lucas, 93).

Upon emerging from the fire, Shadrach, Mesach, and Abednego are examined by the other ranking officials present at the ceremony (v.27). These civil servants of Nebuchadnezzar are witnesses to the miraculous deliverance of the three servants of the Most High God as they are not harmed, singed, or scorched by the fire (cf. Miller, 124, on the more literal meaning of each of these terms). In fact, there is not even the faintest trace of the smell of fire on them!

The Greek version expands the narrative at this point and explains how an angel descends into the furnace in response to Azariah's prayer, drives out the flames, and causes a cool damp breeze to blow, thus preserving the lives of the three Hebrew faithful (3:49–50, LXX). The comments of Seow, 59, are insightful at this point. He notes that the Aramaic text "preserves the mystery and wonder of divine presence in the furnace" contrary to the expanded Greek version. Beyond this he observes that the narrator clearly states that the four individuals are not walking in the furnace but amid the fire. Thus the text does not indicate that the three men are rescued *from* the fire. "Rather, the story is that they are with a divine being *in the midst* of the fire. They encounter divine presence in the middle of the fire." Typical of the ironic twist often found in the biblical narrative, the fire, an instrument of death for the Babylonian king, is a source of life for the three Hebrews, since fire is one symbol of divine presence for the God of Israel (Ex 3:2; 13:21; Dt 4:11–12; Ps 18:8).

6. Nebuchadnezzar's Proclamation (3:28–30)

²⁸Then Nebuchadnezzar said, "Praise be to the God of Shadrach, Meshach and Abednego, who has sent his angel and rescued his servants! They trusted in him and defied the king's command and were willing to give up their lives rather than serve or worship any god except their own God. ²⁹Therefore I decree that the people of any nation or language who say anything against the God of Shadrach, Meshach and Abednego be cut into pieces and their houses be turned into piles of rubble, for no other god can save in this way."

³⁰Then the king promoted Shadrach, Meshach and Abednego in the province of Babylon.

COMMENTARY

28–30 Goldingay, 75, comments that the deliverance of the three Hebrews from Nebuchadnezzar's crematory furnace is but one of three climaxes to the court story. The second is his praise of the God of Shadrach, Meshach, and Abednego and his decree legitimizing the religion of the Hebrews in his realm. The third climax is his promotion of the three young men within the ranks of provincial officials of Babylon (v.30).

The king's blessing or doxology echoes his earlier praise of Daniel's God (2:47) and anticipates the later proclamation by King Darius lauding the God of Daniel (6:26–27). The doxology is a brief descriptive praise psalm that pronounces a blessing and then offers rationale for the statement (cf. Collins [*Daniel*, 191], though he rejects the authenticity of the three blessings of the God of Israel by foreign kings).

Nebuchadnezzar credits the rescue of the three Hebrews to an "angel" (GK 10417; Heb. *malʾāk*; NIV, NASB). Since the expression "a son of the gods" (v.25) identifies a divine being, the word "angel" here is better understood as a "divine messenger" or "divine agent" (cf. Miller, 125; Collins, *Daniel*, 191). The king's statement also juxtaposes the defiance of the three Israelites with their "trust" in God (v.28). The rejection of idolatry and trust in Yahweh is basic to Israel's covenantal relationship with God (Ps 31:6, 14; Isa 26:3–4; Jer 17:5, 7). Here the story of the three men in the blazing furnace bears out the truth of the wisdom tradition that says, "whoever trusts in the LORD is kept safe" (Pr 29:25).

The NIV's "then the king promoted ..." (v.30) is somewhat interpretive. Literally, the king "caused Shadrach, Meshach, and Abednego to prosper"

(NASB; cf. "showered favours," NJB). At the very least, the three Hebrews receive material goods as rewards for their staunch conviction in their God and his ability to deliver them.

In another example of dramatic irony, the representatives of the peoples of the world as a whole are assembled, not to bow before a golden image, "but to witness how God himself may act when people bow before him alone" (Goldingay, 75). By royal decree King Nebuchadnezzar formally recognizes the God of Israel and the religion of the Hebrews as a legitimate religious ideology in his vast kingdom (v.29). The king himself is probably not a "convert" to the religion of Israel, as Russell, 70, admits. Yet he does offer royal protection to those who are (or may become) worshipers of the God of Shadrach, Meshach, and Abednego as a result of their miraculous deliverance. Those who violate the king's decree are subject to the same punishment (i.e., "cut into pieces and their houses ... turned into piles of rubble") as that threatened against the astrologers for their failure to interpret his dream (2:5).

Two facts about the episode impress the Babylonian king: the willingness of the three Hebrews to die rather than compromise their religious integrity, and the firsthand experience of seeing that "no other god ... is able to deliver in this way" (NASB; v.29). Both facts point to theological truths that cross the Old and New Testaments. First, whether implicit in Abraham's willingness to sacrifice Isaac (Ge 22; cf. Heb 11:17–19) or explicit in Paul's exhortation to the Colossian church (Col 3:3), the righteous know that they have died and their life is hidden with Christ in God. Second, the Bible emphatically declares that there is no other God apart from Yahweh of Israel (Isa 43:10–13; 45:5–6, 14, 18, 21–22; Jude 25).

The court story of ch. 2 portrays a God who can reveal the mysteries of heaven, while the court story of ch. 3 shows that there is a God who miraculously intervenes in individual and national life (cf. Goldingay, 75). Both portrayals of Israel's God are important, lest the Babylonians assume that their conquest of Judah meant their gods were greater than the God of the Hebrews. By miraculously delivering his three servants from incineration in the king's furnace (along with the other miracles in the book of Daniel), "Yahweh made it clear to Nebuchadnezzar (who blatantly challenged Yahweh's power by his actions in this incident) and to the entire world that Judah's defeat was not because their God did not exist or was anemic" (Miller, 126).

D. Nebuchadnezzar's Dream of the Tree (4:1–37 [3:31–4:34])

OVERVIEW

Daniel 4 continues the "court stories" section of the book (chs. 1–6). For a discussion of this larger literary context within the book of Daniel, see comments on 2:1–13 and 3:1–7.

Goldingay, 82, detects in the story elements of court contest tale, legend, and aretalogy (i.e., the promotion of traditions concerning the mighty deeds or virtues of a god or hero figure), although these features are less prominent here than in ch. 2. The dominant literary form of this passage is that of dream report, including an introduction, report of the dream, interpretation, and fulfillment of the dream. According to Goldingay, the first-person point of view maintained through much of the narrative is natural to the dream report (cf. Longman, 118). Collins (*Daniel with an Introduction to Apocalyptic Literature*, 61) identifies several subsidiary literary forms in Daniel 4, including doxology (v.3), tale of court contest (vv.4–8), and symbolic vision (vv.9–16). He classifies the overall genre of this chapter, however, as that of "epistle" (as opposed to "letter") since the correspondence is a public proclamation. Lucas, 103, summarizes by noting that the author of the story has taken the form of the basic "tale of court contest" genre and modified it by inserting a dream report and then presents the entire narrative in the form of a royal letter "in order to give it a note of special authority."

The account reports the Babylonian king's second dream and his third miraculous encounter with the God of Israel. The contents of ch. 4 may be outlined as follows: Nebuchadnezzar's proclamation and doxology (vv.1–3); the report of the king's dream (vv.4–18); the interpretation of the dream (vv.19–27), the fulfillment of the dream (vv.28–33), conclusion and doxology (vv.34–37). Redditt, 75–76, adapts Shea's chiastically structured outline of ch. 4 and offers a more comprehensive schematic of the narrative:

Prologue. Proclamation. Doxology 1 (4:1–3)
   Dream reception by the king (4:4–6)
   Instructions: King to Daniel (4:7–9)
   Dream recital: King to Daniel (4:10–17)
   Dialogue: King and Daniel (4:18–19)
   Dream interpretation: Daniel to the king
      (4:20–26)
   Instructions: Daniel to the king (4:27)
   Dream fulfillment upon the king (4:28–33)
Epilogue. Restoration. Doxology 2 (4:34–37)

Older biblical scholarship questioned the unity of the chapter on the basis of the shifts in the narrative from first person to third person and back again (e.g., Montgomery, 223). More recently Goldingay, 82, has countered that the alternation between the first-person and third-person voice in the narrative is "dramatically appropriate," while Hartman and Di Lella, 174, have observed the importance of the third-person voice as a literary device to demonstrate the king's incapacity to give an account of what happened to him while he was out of his mind. (On the first-person voice of the story, see Lucas, 103, and Longman, 118.) The story of Nebuchadnezzar's second dream is undated, but some scholars suggest that the episode occurs near the close of his reign, since there is peace throughout the realm (v.4) and his great building projects appear to stand complete (v.30; cf. Miller, 127).

The plot of the fourth court story has parallels to ch. 2 in that King Nebuchadnezzar has a troubling dream and appeals to the royal magicians for an interpretation—but to no avail. Like ch. 2, the story makes use of suspense to heighten audience interest (see Lucas, 102; cf. Russell, 73). For example, tension mounts because of the delay caused by the search for an interpreter of the dream (vv.6–7). Daniel then enters the scene at the opportune moment (v.8), although his task is made easier since this time the king remembers his dream and seeks only an interpretation. Finally, Daniel's reluctant interpretation and admonition (vv.19–27) raises the question of King Nebuchadnezzar's response: Will he be alarmed (v.19)?

The gist of Daniel's interpretation of the dream about a great tree is the threat of divine judgment directed at Nebuchadnezzar's pride and a call to repentance (vv.24–27; cf. Longman, 122, who states "the moral of the story is the last word: 'Those who walk in pride he is able to humble'"). The dream was fulfilled twelve months later when the king was afflicted with a bizarre mental illness causing him to abandon the throne and behave like an animal in the wild (v.33). Only when the king "raised [his] eyes toward heaven" (v.34) was he healed of his insanity and restored to the throne of Babylonia (v.36). Nebuchadnezzar "published" his experiences as testimony to the power, glory, and justice of the God of Israel as the King of Heaven (v.37).

According to Baldwin, 107, "the king tells the story against himself to explain how he came to capitulate to the God of the captives he had brought from Judea." Porteous, 65, has noted that the theme of ch. 4 is summed up in declaration that the Most High is sovereign over the kingdoms of the earth and that he gives them to whomever he desires (v.25). The doxologies forming an envelope for the royal epistle (vv.3, 37) highlight God's sovereignty and confirm this general observation. Towner, 59, goes further by condensing the narrative into a "story about two sovereignties ... juxtaposing the strength and power of the greatest of all human sovereigns ... with the strength and power of the Most High." For him the story pitting the kingdom of Babylon against the kingdom of heaven pivots on the term "grow strong" (Aram. *tqp*; vv.11, 20, 22; cf. v.3).

The account of King Nebuchadnezzar's rebuke, madness or illness, exile, and restoration has several extrabiblical parallels (cf. Goldingay, 83–84). These include a story of Nebuchadnezzar's madness or possession written by the Greek historian Megasthenes (ca. 300 BC?) as reported in Eusebius; a fragmentary cuneiform text that makes reference to a mental disorder that afflicted Nebuchadnezzar; the story of a similar divine chastisement, illness, and humiliation in the wisdom literature known as "The Babylonian Job"; and the reference to a malady from which Nebuchadnezzar died as mentioned by the Jewish historian Josephus (cf. Goldingay, 83–84; Lucas, 106–7).

In addition, a second series of nonbiblical sources concerns Nabonidus, the last king of the Neo-Babylonian dynasty. According to these accounts Nabonidus was led by a dream to abdicate the throne and spend ten years living in the oasis village of Tema in Arabia. Conflicting inscriptions report that Nabonidus was exiled as punishment for his neglect of Marduk and other deities of the Babylonian pantheon. The "Prayer of Nabonidus" among the finds of the Dead Sea Scrolls has fueled a growing consensus that Nabonidus's absence from the Babylonian throne actually lies behind the story of Nebuchadnezzar's madness in Daniel 4 (cf. Lucas, 106; Smith-Christopher, 72). In this (fragmentary) document, Nabonidus testifies to being afflicted by God with a physical ailment for seven years in Tema. Despite praying to his gods, he receives healing only after a Jewish exorcist admonishes him to honor the name of God Most High (cf. Goldingay, 84).

Scholars have held a wide variety of views on the relationship between these various biblical and nonbiblical sources and the historical traditions they represent. Lucas, 107, is even more guarded, acknowledging that the literary relationship between the extrabiblical stories and Daniel 4 is complex but unclear, and he warns that some caution is necessary before assuming stories about Nabonidus were transferred to Nebuchadnezzar, since little is known from Babylonian sources about the last thirty years of Nebuchadnezzar's life. Longman, 117, concludes that the surface similarities of these stories "are overwhelmed by the differences ... it seems more reasonable to believe, if we follow the sixth-century BC dating for Daniel, that they were written not before but in light of the story of Daniel 4."

The variance between the versification of the Aramaic and English versions of the text of ch. 4 has been noted in brackets. (On the history of the chapter division see Lucas, 107–8.) For a discussion of the differences between the Greek versions and the Aramaic text of Daniel 4, see Montgomery, 247–49; Lucas, 104–5; Smith-Christopher, 72; and the "Critical Notes" in Lacocque, 69–89.

1. Nebuchadnezzar's Proclamation and Doxology (4:1–3 [3:31–33])

> [1]King Nebuchadnezzar,
> To the peoples, nations and men of every language, who live in all the world:
> May you prosper greatly!
> [2]It is my pleasure to tell you about the miraculous signs and wonders that the Most High God has performed for me.
>
> [3]How great are his signs,
> how mighty his wonders!
> His kingdom is an eternal kingdom;
> his dominion endures from generation to generation.

COMMENTARY

1–3 These opening verses are cast in the form of a royal letter, or more properly an epistle since the content of the letter is intended for public consumption (cf. Collins, *Daniel: with an Introduction to Apocalyptic Literature*, 61). Baldwin, 107, correctly observes that the king's proclamation is not an edict, for no law is enacted. Goldingay, 82, considers the introductory verses of the chapter a type of "royal encyclical." The format of the address identifying author and audience, along with a salutation, is the standard epistolary formula in Aramaic letters from the postexilic period (cf. Seow, 64–65). The form of a royal letter gives the content a special degree of authority, used in this remarkable case "to testify to a higher authority than the human king" (Goldingay, 82).

Nebuchadnezzar's appeal to a "universal audience" is typical of both Assyrian and Babylonian claims to rule the entire world (cf. Miller, 129). The reference to "peoples, nations and men of every language" (v.1a) previously occurred in the message of the king's herald to the assembly gathered before the great statue on the plain of Dura (3:4).

The new element introduced in the royal letter is the addendum "who live in all the world" (v.1b). The expression is clearly hyperbole for the entire realm of King Nebuchadnezzar, yet commentators have noted "subtexts" in the author's terms, such as "world (e.g., v.1), "land" (e.g., v.10), "earth" (e.g., v.11), and "heaven" (e.g., vv.11–12). For instance, Lucas, 102, has suggested the pair of antithetical terms (i.e., "earth" and "heaven") conveys a double meaning emphasizing both the extent of Nebuchadnezzar's rule and the depth of his humiliation. Seow, 65, understands the juxtaposition of the terms throughout the chapter as a spotlight on the issue of earthly power (the power of Nebuchadnezzar) and heavenly power (the power of God; cf. Goldingay, 87, who concurs that the central concern of ch. 4 is the kingship of Nebuchadnezzar and the kingship of the Most High God).

The salutation "may you prosper greatly" (v.1c) is typical of Aramaic letters, and according to Baldwin, 110, the formula was in use internationally. This expression (lit., "may your peace abound" [NASB]) reappears in 6:25. Collins (*Daniel*, 221) states that such a greeting invariably included the word "peace" (Aram. $\check{s}^e l\bar{a}m$), and it may have influenced the salutations found in 1 Peter 1:2 and 2 Peter 1:2. On the epithet "Most High God," see comments on 3:24–27.

The phrase "signs and wonders" (Aram. $\bar{o}t$ + $t^e m\hat{a}$) recalls the devastating plagues God brought against the Egyptians as "signs and wonders" (Heb. $\bar{o}t$ + $m\hat{o}p\bar{e}t$) in delivering the Hebrews from their slavery in Egypt (e.g., Ex 7:3; Dt 6:22). For Collins (*Daniel*, 221), the word pair betrays the Jewish authorship of the story. The reference here is to those signs and wonders witnessed by King Nebuchadnezzar himself (namely, the interpretation of his dream by Daniel and the deliverance of the three Hebrews in the blazing furnace), not the signs and wonders associated with the event of the Hebrew exodus from Egypt. According to Seow, 65, this is the "ostensible purpose" of the royal communiqué. Theologically, the report of divine "signs and wonders" makes the point that God is still in the business of performing miracles for his people—the Hebrew community in exile needed this assurance.

The king's doxology (v.3) anticipates the doxology at the close of the narrative (v.34), and the two combine to underscore the central teaching of the court story—the eternal dominion of the God of Israel. For Porteous, 67, the doxology is reminiscent of Psalm 145:13, though Baldwin, 110, states that nothing in the poetry of v.3 demands knowledge of the Psalms or other Scriptures, since Marduk was regarded in similar terms in the Babylonian creation epic. Collins (*Daniel*, 222) thinks otherwise, but whether or not the doxology of v.3 is biblically inspired, commentators do agree that "the use of such a doxology in the introduction of a royal proclamation is compatible with neo-Babylonian and especially Persian practice." Remarkably, Nebuchadnezzar's imperial message begins and ends in praise of the eternal sovereignty of the God of Israel (cf. Smith-Christopher, 72, on the Aram. term $\check{s}\bar{a}lt\bar{a}n$ ["sovereignty"] in Daniel 1–6). His "public confession" of Yahweh's eternal dominion serves as a testimonial to the admonition in Psalm 2:10–11:

> Therefore, you kings, be wise;
>   be warned, you rulers of the earth.
> Serve the LORD with fear
>   and rejoice with trembling.

2. The Report of the King's Dream (4:4–18 [4:1–15])

⁴I, Nebuchadnezzar, was at home in my palace, contented and prosperous. ⁵I had a dream that made me afraid. As I was lying in my bed, the images and visions that passed through my mind terrified me. ⁶So I commanded that all the wise men of Babylon be brought before me to interpret the dream for me. ⁷When the magicians, enchanters, astrologers and diviners came, I told them the dream, but they could not interpret it for me. ⁸Finally, Daniel came into my presence and I told him the dream. (He is called Belteshazzar, after the name of my god, and the spirit of the holy gods is in him.)

⁹I said, "Belteshazzar, chief of the magicians, I know that the spirit of the holy gods is in you, and no mystery is too difficult for you. Here is my dream; interpret it for me. ¹⁰These are the visions I saw while lying in my bed: I looked, and there before me stood a tree in

the middle of the land. Its height was enormous. ¹¹The tree grew large and strong and its top touched the sky; it was visible to the ends of the earth. ¹²Its leaves were beautiful, its fruit abundant, and on it was food for all. Under it the beasts of the field found shelter, and the birds of the air lived in its branches; from it every creature was fed.

¹³"In the visions I saw while lying in my bed, I looked, and there before me was a messenger, a holy one, coming down from heaven. ¹⁴He called in a loud voice:'Cut down the tree and trim off its branches; strip off its leaves and scatter its fruit. Let the animals flee from under it and the birds from its branches. ¹⁵But let the stump and its roots, bound with iron and bronze, remain in the ground, in the grass of the field.

"'Let him be drenched with the dew of heaven, and let him live with the animals among the plants of the earth. ¹⁶Let his mind be changed from that of a man and let him be given the mind of an animal, till seven times pass by for him.

¹⁷"'The decision is announced by messengers, the holy ones declare the verdict, so that the living may know that the Most High is sovereign over the kingdoms of men and gives them to anyone he wishes and sets over them the lowliest of men.'

¹⁸"This is the dream that I, King Nebuchadnezzar, had. Now, Belteshazzar, tell me what it means, for none of the wise men in my kingdom can interpret it for me. But you can, because the spirit of the holy gods is in you."

COMMENTARY

4–18 The king's dream report or recital consists of the circumstances of the dream (vv.4–5), the interpreter of the dream (vv.6–9), the contents of the dream (vv.10–17), and the request of the dreamer (v.18). The king's dream is set against the backdrop of peace and prosperity throughout the Babylonian Empire (v.4). The king found himself at home in the royal palace, "contented" (or "at ease" [so NASB], or "at rest"; Aram. šᵉlēh) and "prosperous" (or "flourishing" [NASB], "luxuriant"; Aram. raᶜⁿan). The synonymous terms convey the idea that King Nebuchadnezzar was "thriving" (Lucas, 108), since "his opposition (including the Egyptians) had been subdued, and there was no serious threat to his authority" (Miller, 130; cf. Wood, 103, who suggests a difference in meaning between the two phrases). The circumstances of the dream,

especially the word "prosperous" or "luxuriant," prepares readers for the tree image that follows.

In the ancient world, "the dreams of kings cannot be other than portentous" (Porteous, 67). The report of the terrifying visions and images the king saw while lying on his bed drastically alters his circumstances (v.5). His carefree existence has been shattered by a troubling dream. The mood of contentment induced by the ease and luxury of a realm at peace has been replaced by one of fear and terror since the meaning of the enigmatic dream for the rule of Nebuchadnezzar is unknown.

The search for an interpreter of the dream among the king's royal advisors—namely, the magicians, enchanters, astrologers, and diviners (v.7)—has similarities to the dream report of ch. 2 (see Notes on 2:2–3). As Lucas, 114, observes, however, the "court contest" of ch. 4 "is in reality a case of 'no contest.'" Towner, 61, comments that the issue is not the failure of the king's royal advisers satisfactorily to interpret the dream, nor is it Daniel's success in solving the king's problem. The heart of the matter is the methodology employed to unravel "mysteries" and reveal the "mind of God (or the gods)" (cf. A. Wolters, "Untying the King's Knots: Physiology and Wordplay in Daniel 5," *JBL* 110 [1991]: 117–22). Or as Porteous, 67, states, "the idea is once again to throw into relief the bankruptcy of Babylonian wisdom." Unlike the Babylonian magicians, who depended on the interpretation of dreams and omens by means of a scholarly enterprise that required thorough knowledge of a large corpus of omen literature assembled over centuries, Daniel's ability to interpret the king's dreams was not based on professional skill but instead flowed "from his personal relationship with God, from whom he gains insight directly" (Lucas, 114).

What Seow, 66, describes as the "careless posture" of the king suddenly shifts to one of alarmed frenzy. The royal advisers in immediate proximity are summoned but proved incapable of interpreting Nebuchadnezzar's dream—either because of impotence or out of fear (if they realize the meaning of the dream but lack the courage to relay it to the king; so Baldwin, 111). Towner, 61, raises the question as to why Daniel is not brought before the king immediately as "chief of the magicians" (v.9). The story line offers no explanation for his belated appearance on the scene (and the LXX omits vv.6a–10, "evidently in an attempt to solve the difficulty of Daniel's late arrival"; cf. Miller, 131, n. 16). Most likely, Daniel was not in the palace at the time of the event since he was attending to other duties as "chief of the magicians."

Three times in this section of the narrative King Nebuchadnezzar identifies Daniel as one who has "the spirit of the holy gods" in him (vv.8–9, 18). Montgomery, 225–26, Wood, 106, and Goldingay, 78, 87 prefer to translate the expression in the singular (i.e., "the s/Spirit of the holy g/God" or "the spirit of holy deity"). Porteous, 67, has observed that although the word "gods" is plural (Aram. *ʾelāhîn*), it is not necessarily a polytheistic expression, since "even paganism was becoming familiar with the concept of a supreme deity." Yet the larger context of Daniel would suggest that the phrase "is most naturally taken in a polytheistic sense" (Lucas, 109).

Beyond this, Baldwin, 111, has observed that the plural adjective "holy" (Aram. *qaddîšîn*) supports this understanding of the difficult expression as well. Quite apart from the polytheistic or monotheistic implications of the expression, the king recognizes that Daniel's extraordinary insight into the meaning of mysterious dreams and visions is due to something not inherent in Daniel but beyond himself—an endowment of a divine spirit that enables him to reveal what is known only to the "gods" (or to God; cf. 2:11). On the name Belteshazzar (v.8), see Notes on 1:7.

Nebuchadnezzar's dream recital breaks naturally into two sections: an optimistic scene (vv.10–12) followed by a more pessimistic one (vv.13–17). The dream opens with a vision of an enormous tree that is unrivaled in its size, strength, dominance, beauty, and beneficence because of its abundant growth. Seow, 67, observes that the tree appears to be of a "cosmic nature" and that the terms used in v.11 for its greatness (Aram. *rbh*) and strength (Aram. *tqp*) mirror those used in praise of the Most High God in the introductory doxology ("*great* ... signs" and "*mighty* ... wonders," v.3; on the concept of the "world tree," see *BBCOT*, 736).

The second part of the dream reveals that the tree is not cosmic but an earthly one—as indicated by the descent of the holy messenger from heaven (v.13). The heavenly messenger orders the destruction of the tree (v.14) but decrees that a stump will remain, albeit bound with bands of iron and bronze (v.15a). The dream scenario concludes with the stump drenched with dew and "living" among the plants and animals of the earth (v.15b). This situation will persist for "seven times," and in the process the stump will forfeit the mind of a human being for that of an animal (v.16). Finally, as an epilogue to the dream sequence, the heavenly messengers proclaim that all sovereignty over human kingdoms belongs to the Most High (v.17).

Commentators (e.g., Russell, 74–75; Redditt, 80) have noted the similarities between the king's dream of a tree in Daniel 4 and Ezekiel's allegory of a great tree representing the nation of Egypt (Eze 31:3–14; cf. Hos 14:5–8). Porteous, 67, among others, argues that the Ezekiel passage is actually the source of Nebuchadnezzar's dream. Others have drawn attention to the image of the stump as a symbol of hope and a new beginning (e.g., Lucas,

111). Still others see the movement in the dream from heaven to earth as reminiscent of the story of God's destruction of the Tower of Babel erected by arrogant human beings (Ge 11). Several difficult elements surface in the dream recital that complicate the interpretation of the dream and, no doubt, frighten the king given their abnormality. Among the puzzling and unnatural features of the dream are the identity of the heavenly messenger (vv.13, 17), the reference to fetters of iron and bronze (v.15), and the shift in imagery from tree to human to animal (vv.15–16).

The king's confidence in Daniel's ability to interpret the dream (v.18) stems from both his previous experience with the Hebrew captives' unraveling of his dream of the giant statue (ch. 2) and the recognition that Daniel is uniquely endowed with some sort of divine spirit that permits him to penetrate the mysterious interface of the human psyche and divine revelation with respect to dreams and visions (vv.8–9, 18).

NOTES

13 The "messenger" (Aram. עִיר, *îr*; GK 10541), or "angelic watcher" (NASB), refers to a celestial being since the creature descends from heaven and is identified as a "holy one" (Aram. קַדִּישׁ, *qaddîš*). The word occurs only in 4:13, 17, 23 in the OT and is one of several terms for heavenly beings found in Daniel (cf. 3:28; 7:16; 10:13). Goldingay, 88, describes the beings as "supernatural watchmen" who by analogy to the watchmen of an earthly king serve as "the eyes and ears" of God and see to it that his will is put into effect throughout the earth (cf. 2Ch 16:9; Zec 1:10; 4:10). According to Baldwin, 112, the idea of heavenly beings whose task is to keep watch over the earth probably originated in Babylon (cf. Eze 1:17–18).

The "angelic watchers" are widely attested in later Jewish literature of the Hellenistic and Roman eras. Perhaps the best-known example is the "Book of the Watchers" in *1 Enoch* 1–36 (speaking of fallen angels). Elsewhere the term refers to righteous or good angels who watch and never sleep (cf. *Jub* 4:15; *1En* 20:1; 39:12–13; 71:7). These "watchers" who never sleep are reminiscent of God, who unceasingly keeps watch over Israel (Ps 121:4). Lucas, 110, notes that "the class of heavenly beings known as 'Watchers' may have been conceived as those whose activities reflected this particular divine concern to look after and protect human beings." See Porteous, 68; Collins, *Daniel*, 224–26; *BBCOT*, 736.

15 According to some Babylonian documents, "dew" (Aram./Heb. טַל, *ṭal*) fell from the stars and could bring either sickness or healing to those it covered (cf. *BBCOT*, 736).

16 The East Semitic cognate (Akk. *šanû*) of the Aramaic verb שְׁנָה (*šnh*), rendered "let his mind be changed," is sometimes used for mental derangement (cf. *CAD*, 17:405). On lycanthropy and boanthropy see Miller, 134; Lucas, 111–12; *BBCOT*, 736.

3. The Interpretation of the Dream (4:19–27 [4:16–24])

¹⁹Then Daniel (also called Belteshazzar) was greatly perplexed for a time, and his thoughts terrified him. So the king said, "Belteshazzar, do not let the dream or its meaning alarm you."

Belteshazzar answered, "My lord, if only the dream applied to your enemies and its meaning to your adversaries! ²⁰The tree you saw, which grew large and strong, with its top touching the sky, visible to the whole earth, ²¹with beautiful leaves and abundant fruit, providing food for all, giving shelter to the beasts of the field, and having nesting places in its branches for the birds of the air — ²²you, O king, are that tree! You have become great and strong; your greatness has grown until it reaches the sky, and your dominion extends to distant parts of the earth.

²³"You, O king, saw a messenger, a holy one, coming down from heaven and saying, 'Cut down the tree and destroy it, but leave the stump, bound with iron and bronze, in the grass of the field, while its roots remain in the ground. Let him be drenched with the dew of heaven; let him live like the wild animals, until seven times pass by for him.'

²⁴"This is the interpretation, O king, and this is the decree the Most High has issued against my lord the king: ²⁵You will be driven away from people and will live with the wild animals; you will eat grass like cattle and be drenched with the dew of heaven. Seven times will pass by for you until you acknowledge that the Most High is sovereign over the kingdoms of men and gives them to anyone he wishes. ²⁶The command to leave the stump of the tree with its roots means that your kingdom will be restored to you when you acknowledge that Heaven rules. ²⁷Therefore, O king, be pleased to accept my advice: Renounce your sins by doing what is right, and your wickedness by being kind to the oppressed. It may be that then your prosperity will continue."

COMMENTARY

19–27 Unlike the interpretation of the king's earlier dream (ch. 2), there is apparently no significant interval of time between Nebuchadnezzar's dream and Daniel's interpretation. Previously Daniel had required time for prayer in order to seek the revelation of the matter from God (cf. 2:17–19).

Here Daniel seems to have nearly immediate understanding of the meaning of the king's dream of the great tree.

Daniel is visibly shaken by what he hears and understands about the king's dream. He is "greatly perplexed" and "terrified" for a time, not because the meaning of the dream escapes him (v.19a); rather, his alarm stems from the implications of the meaning of the dream for the king, the Babylonian Empire, the fate of the Hebrews in captivity, and perhaps even his own fate as "chief of the magicians" for Nebuchadnezzar. The verb "greatly perplexed" (Aram. *šmm*) is better rendered "astounded" or "shocked" (cf. NASB's "appalled"). Baldwin, 113, comments that Daniel is silent for a time because he is "*dumbfounded* and *dismayed* at the embarrassing message he had to give" to the king (cf. NEB).

Only the encouragement of the king prompts Daniel to reveal the meaning of the dream to his overlord (v.19b). Essentially the king's conciliatory admonition mitigates Daniel's responsibility for the content of his interpretation — even if the meaning of the dream bodes ill for the monarch. Baldwin, 113, senses the exchange suggests a warmth of relationship between the king and his Hebrew adviser.

Daniel interprets the two parts of the dream of the great tree in sequence. The first scene of the king's dream is recounted (vv.20–21), and the interpretation is a hopeful one for Nebuchadnezzar. He is identified as the great tree, and the dominion of his kingdom spreads from the center to the ends of the earth (v.22). As Goldingay, 89, recognizes, Daniel's interpretation of the dream presupposes Babylon's position as the world power of the day — a fact established previously in Nebuchadnezzar's dream of the gigantic statue (2:36–38).

The second scene of the king's dream is faithfully recounted by his chief magician (v.23). Daniel's explanation of the symbolism, however, is most disturbing because the interpretation comes as a decree from the Most High "against" King Nebuchadnezzar (v.24). This, no doubt, accounts for Daniel's initial astonishment and fright at the revelation of the meaning of the dream (v.19a) — and the negative omen is something Nebuchadnezzar has probably anticipated, given his urging of Daniel to proceed with divulging the tidings come what may (v.19b).

Daniel identifies the king himself as the stump of the tree cut off according to the announcement of the heavenly messenger. The fact that the king is "driven away" from his people (v.25a) suggests that the ruler is ousted or deposed in some fashion by other members of the royal court as a result of his incompetence to govern (cf. Goldingay, 79: "you are going to be led away from human society"). The king will live among the "wild animals" (v.25b), although the phrase is better rendered more literally as "animals of the field" (cf. NASB, "beasts of the field"). The image then is one of a domesticated animal tethered and grazing in the open fields. The king's food will consist of "grass" (v.25d), although Miller, 137, observes that the "royal diet" may have been more varied, since the term for grass (Aram. *ᶜᵃśab*) includes herbs and vegetables. The expression "drenched with dew of heaven" (v.25c) means that the king will not come inside at night and sleep like a human being but will remain overnight in the open fields and thus be wet with dew in the mornings.

Nebuchadnezzar's delusion that he was an animal like an ox or a bull is a form of mental illness (cf. v.16, "let his mind be changed"), and the condition is known medically as lycanthropy or more precisely boanthropy. The king will remain in this condition for "seven times" — perhaps seven seasons or even seven years (see Notes on v.25). Daniel does offer the king the assurance that he will be restored to power, the meaning of the remaining "stump of the tree with its roots" (v.26a). Nebuchadnezzar's restoration to the throne of Babylonia, however, is contingent on his confession that God alone is sovereign (v.26b). Only acknowledging the reality that "Heaven rules" (v.26c) will release the king from his disease.

Daniel's interpretation of the dream of the great tree ends with instructions to the king to renounce his sin by engaging in works of mercy and social justice (v.27; see the discussion of "righteousness" [Aram. ṣidqâ] in Lucas, 113; Collins, *Daniel*, 230). Earlier the king gave instructions to Daniel at the end of his dream recital (v.18); now the roles are reversed. Daniel's bold summons to the king to repent from his sin is reminiscent of the ministry of the OT prophets, who challenged Hebrew kings and people alike (often upon threat of their very lives) to repent from their sin and instead practice righteousness (e.g., 2Sa 12:7–14; 2Ki 17:13; Isa 1:16–18; cf. Wallace, 81–82). The verb "renounce"

(Aram. *prq*; GK 10596) literally means to "break off" (cf. NASB's "break away now from your sins"), and the imagery is that of breaking a yoke from the neck (Miller, 138, n. 38; cf. Anderson, 46–47, who takes issue with Hartman's and Di Lella's, 170, translation, "atone for your sins by good deeds," as a misunderstanding of the Jewish doctrine of salvation).

Daniel's admonition to do right and show kindness to the poor contrasts starkly with the carefree, indulgent lifestyle of the king portrayed at the beginning of the narrative (v.4). Apparently, Daniel understands that the king's obedience to God's word is a tangible way to confess that "Heaven rules" (v.26). According to Miller, 139, Daniel's call to repentance "held out to the king the genuine possibility of foregoing this judgment, demonstrating God's willingness to forgive" (but cf. Towner, 63, who sees only a "faint glimmer of hope" being offered to the king).

NOTES

25 The cryptic "seven times" (vv.16, 25; cf. v.34) specified as the duration of King Nebuchadnezzar's madness (some form of monomania) refers to "seven periods of time" (NASB) of unknown length (whether days, weeks, months, change of seasons, or years). The LXX, along with other ancient Jewish sources (e.g., Josephus, *Ant.* 10.10.6), interpret the "seven times" as "seven years" (cf. Collins, *Daniel*, 231; Miller, 134–35; *BBCOT*, 736). The seven periods of time may simply be a symbolic cipher rather than an indicator of any specific length of time (see Longman, 120, n. 13).

26 The Aram. expression שְׁמַיָּא (šᵉmayyāʾ, "Heaven rules") is the only instance in the OT of the word "heaven" used as a periphrasis for God. Collins (*Daniel*, 229–30) notes that this usage is common in the Hellenistic and Roman periods, including in intertestamental Jewish literature (e.g., 1 Macc 3:18–19; 4:10), rabbinic literature (e.g., *m.* ʾAbot 1:3, 11), and the NT (e.g., Lk 15:18, 21).

4. The Fulfillment of the Dream (4:28–33 [4:25–30])

²⁸All this happened to King Nebuchadnezzar. ²⁹Twelve months later, as the king was walking on the roof of the royal palace of Babylon, ³⁰he said, "Is not this the great Babylon I have built as the royal residence, by my mighty power and for the glory of my majesty?"

³¹The words were still on his lips when a voice came from heaven, "This is what is decreed for you, King Nebuchadnezzar: Your royal authority has been taken from you. ³²You will be driven away from people and will live with the wild animals; you will eat grass like cattle. Seven times will pass by for you until you acknowledge that the Most High is sovereign over the kingdoms of men and gives them to anyone he wishes." ³³Immediately what had been said about Nebuchadnezzar was fulfilled. He was driven away from people and ate grass like cattle. His body was drenched with the dew of heaven until his hair grew like the feathers of an eagle and his nails like the claws of a bird.

COMMENTARY

28–33 Regrettably for the king, Daniel's instructions went unheeded. (Whether Nebuchadnezzar was frightened into temporary compliance or continued arrogantly in his sinful ways is unclear [cf. Longman, 121].) The final section of the narrative recounts the fulfillment of the dream in the life of Nebuchadnezzar (vv. 28–33). The opening verse of the section (v. 28) reports the realization of the dream summarily—as a matter of fact. In a way the statement is anticlimactic to the plot of the story, for the emphasis implicitly has shifted from the pathetic madness of the boastful Babylonian king to the Most High, who is faithful to his word—attested by the "voice from heaven" (v. 31; cf. Redditt, 83).

The lapse of an entire year between the dream and its fulfillment is testimony to the patient, long-suffering nature of God (v. 29). Redditt, 83, comments, "God granted Nebuchadnezzar that much time to repent and change his behavior toward both God and Israel." Nonetheless, the horrible and humiliating predictions of Daniel's interpretation of the king's dream are realized. The narrative is careful to report that Nebuchadnezzar brings disaster on himself since "a great outburst of pride on the part of the Babylonian monarch became the

catalyst for the dream's fulfillment" (Miller, 139). Three times the king uses the first-person pronoun in his boastful musings over his architectural achievements in Babylon (v. 30; see Miller, 139–41, on Nebuchadnezzar's record as a prolific builder). Beyond this, Nebuchadnezzar applies the words "mighty power … glory … majesty" to his own rule (v. 30). Typically these terms are reserved for the God of Israel—the Most High—and he bestows them on human rulers as he wills (2:37; cf. Ex 15:6–7; Isa 35:2; 48:11).

A mysterious voice from heaven pronounces divine judgment on Nebuchadnezzar by repeating the last portion of the announcement made by the heavenly messenger in the king's dream (v. 31; cf. vv. 13–16). It is unclear whether this voice from heaven speaking to Nebuchadnezzar is God or one of the heavenly messengers (vv. 13, 17). What is clear is that Nebuchadnezzar's "royal authority" (or "sovereignty," NASB; Aram. *malkû*) has been forfeited until such time as he testifies that the Most High is sovereign over human kingdoms (v. 32; cf. v. 25). Sovereignty in the realm of human kingdoms is the prerogative of the Sovereign God, who enthrones and deposes human rulers—the lesson of the king's statue dream (2:21). In contrast to the year-long window of opportunity for repentance, the fulfillment of the dream is immediate (while "the words were still on his lips," v.31a). The divine punishment inflicted on Nebuchadnezzar serves as an ominous reminder that God's judgment is certain and sometimes swift (cf. Dt 28:20; Pr 6:15; Isa 47:11; Na 1:3; although for Gowan, 78–79, the sudden reversal of fortune is simply a literary device typical of the so-called "*hybris*-texts" in the OT).

The narrative reports that Nebuchadnezzar's hair grew like "the feathers of an eagle" and that his nails were like "the claws of a bird" (v.33b). Archer, 66, explains that the king's hair became "matted and coarse" from lack of care and came to look like feathers (although the picture could be one simply of long hair that looked like the tail feathers of a bird). Naturally, uncut fingernails and toenails will eventually grow hooked, much like a bird's claws. As Goldingay, 90, notes, however, the point of the story is theological, not medical. The real issue is the temporary transformation of the greatest king of that day into a subhuman creature as a result of divine judgment for the sin of pride (cf. Miller, 142). Baldwin, 115, summarizes that "the pathetic condition of the erstwhile king, disheveled and unkempt among the animals, brings to an end the account in the third person." Yet Nebuchadnezzar's story illustrates the wisdom of the book of Proverbs at two important points: first, the wise person listens to advice and accepts instruction (Pr 12:15; 19:20); second, pride often leads to disgrace and even destruction (Pr 11:2; 16:18; 29:23; cf. Jas 4:6).

NOTE

30 Collins (*Daniel*, 230) points out that the boastful title "Babylon the great" (so NASB; cf. NIV's "the great Babylon") occurs as a negative symbol for Rome in Revelation 14:8; 16:19; 18:2.

5. Conclusion and Doxology (4:34–37 [4:31–34])

³⁴At the end of that time, I, Nebuchadnezzar, raised my eyes toward heaven, and my sanity was restored. Then I praised the Most High; I honored and glorified him who lives forever.

His dominion is an eternal dominion;
    his kingdom endures from generation to generation.
³⁵All the peoples of the earth
    are regarded as nothing.
He does as he pleases
    with the powers of heaven
    and the peoples of the earth.
No one can hold back his hand
    or say to him: "What have you done?"

> ³⁶At the same time that my sanity was restored, my honor and splendor were returned to me for the glory of my kingdom. My advisers and nobles sought me out, and I was restored to my throne and became even greater than before. ³⁷Now I, Nebuchadnezzar, praise and exalt and glorify the King of heaven, because everything he does is right and all his ways are just. And those who walk in pride he is able to humble.

COMMENTARY

34–37 The conclusion of the fourth court story returns to first-person narrative, as King Nebuchadnezzar resumes his personal testimony of events associated with his dream of the great tree. The story not only recycles back to its beginning by way of the narrator's voice, but also to its theme as the king recapitulates his doxology lauding the Most High God and published in the form of a royal letter (vv.34c–35; cf. vv.2–3). Porteous, 73, comments that Nebuchadnezzar's praise "of Daniel's God is more generous than what he had to say of the God of the three confessors [ch. 3]. This time he had not only witnessed the power of God, he had felt it in his own person." Critics of the historicity of Daniel remind us that "extant Babylonian records say nothing of Nebuchadnezzar's losing control of or vacating his throne for a significant period of time" (Redditt, 85; cf. Gowan, 84). But the argument from silence is just that—inconclusive for want of evidence.

The phrase "at the end of that time" (v.34a) simply refers cryptically to the period of "seven times" stipulated for the duration of Nebuchadnezzar's madness (cf. vv.16, 25). The king's "sanity" or "reason" (NASB) was restored, but not automatically. The expression "I ... raised my eyes toward heaven" suggests seeking God's aid (so Goldingay, 90), even a simple act of repentance (cf. Seow, 72; Russell, 82). The restoration of Nebuchadnezzar's sanity (and subsequently his honor and splendor; v.36) is testimony to God's grace (cf. Miller, 143) and a reminder that the book of Daniel teaches that such "transformation is possible" (Smith-Christopher, 77). The king's experience has taught him that the Most High is sovereign over human kingdoms (vv.17, 25), thus demonstrating "the point which animates the narrative" (Towner, 64; cf. Russell, 82).

Nebuchadnezzar's doxological confession is the longest of such testimonials in the book of Daniel. Smith-Christopher, 76, has isolated three important themes in the king's confession: (1) the perpetual or eternal sovereignty of God as his kingdom or dominion endures from generation to generation (v.34c; cf. 3b); (2) God's rule extends to all the earth; and (3) no one has the power or ability to question the work of God. Nebuchadnezzar's declarations about God are in keeping with OT teaching about the nature and character Yahweh of Israel (e.g., Pss 115:3; 145:13; Isa 14:27; 40:17; cf. Baldwin, 115).

The full restoration of King Nebuchadnezzar both to physical health and his position of royal authority on the throne of Babylonia (being accorded even greater honor and splendor than before; v.36) is a reminder that God honors those who honor him (1Sa 2:30; 1Ch 29:12). The king's reference to his "advisers and nobles," who seek him out, speaks to his formal reinstallation as king of Babylonia (v.36b). The king's praise of God as the "King of heaven"(v.37) is a unique epithet for God in the OT, and the repetition of the term "heaven" echoes what Baldwin, 116, has observed as a "catch-word" in ch. 4 (vv.13, 20, 26, 34, 37). Ironically, Nebuchadnezzar confesses that God does what is right and that his ways are just (v.37)—essentially the instructions Daniel gave the king in his summons to repentance (v.27).

Goldingay (97) summarizes ch. 4 by citing King Nebuchadnezzar as an example—"a warning of how not to be led astray by power and achievement, a model of how to respond to chastisement and humiliation ... [and] a promise that earthly authorities are in the hand of God, not merely for their judgment, but for his glory." And though

Nebuchadnezzar's formal acknowledgment of God's power and justice may fall short of penitence and true faith (so Baldwin, 116; cf. Gowan, 83, "Nebuchadnezzar is not 'converted'"), the king is also an example of another important biblical principle, namely, that "God opposes the proud but gives grace to the humble" (Jas 4:6; 1Pe 5:5; cf. Pr 3:34). Nebuchadnezzar has learned the lesson of humility tragically but confessed the truth of the proverb with conviction given the aftermath of his personal experience (v.37c). In fact, his confession encapsulates the basic message of the Bible: assume a posture of humility before the Most High God (cf. Isa 57:15; Mic 6:8; Mt 18:4; 23:12; Php 2:8).

E. Belshazzar's Feast and the Writing on the Wall (5:1–31 [5:1–6:1])

OVERVIEW

The fifth chapter of Daniel continues the "court stories" section of the book (chs. 1–6). For a discussion of this larger literary context within Daniel, see comments on 2:1–13 and 3:1–7.

The literary form of this story is "straightforward narrative" (Collins, *Daniel: with an Introduction to Apocalyptic Literature*, 67) and the subgenre is generally recognized as that of "court tale of contest" (ibid.; Towner, 68). Lucas, 123, reminds us that the classic elements of the tale of court contest include a king's being confronted with an unresolved problem, the king's resident advisers failing to resolve the problem, the hero figure being called and succeeding in resolving the problem, and his elevation (or restoration) to a high position.

Not surprisingly, Goldingay, 102–3, considers ch. 5 a "prophetic legend," a blending of court-contest tale, legend, and midrash (cf. Collins, *Daniel: with an Introduction to Apocalyptic Literature*, 67–68, who

identifies similar subordinate literary forms in ch. 5, including legend, indictment speech, and pesher). A "legend" is a narrative "concerned with the wonderful and aimed at edification" (ibid., 111). In this case "the marvelous" is the handwriting on the wall (v.5). A "midrash" is a stylized rabbinic interpretation emphasizing the application or relevance of a biblical text for a later generation. (Goldingay, 103, identifies two examples of midrash—the attack on idolatry and the scorning of the Babylonian sages.) A "pesher" is an allegorical understanding of a mysterious form of revelation, such as a dream, vision, or (in this case) the cryptic writing on the wall. An "indictment speech" is a formal speech-act, "which both formulates an accusation and declares a sentence [of judgment]" (Collins, *Daniel: with an Introduction to Apocalyptic Literature*, 111).

The rubric of "court-contest tale" may prove helpful as a literary category for classifying the genres of biblical literature, but it tends to be pejorative with respect to the historicity of the biblical narrative. While this study appreciates the contribution of form criticism to biblical studies, it rejects the prejudgment of biblical texts as "ahistorical" on the basis of genre classification. On the genres of Daniel, see "Literary Form" in the introduction.

The story of Belshazzar's feast begins abruptly, introducing a new character to the book and offering no chronological notice or transitional introduction. Despite the sudden shift in the narrative from the reign of Nebuchadnezzar to the reign of Belshazzar, Redditt, 87, rightly notes that the bridge between chs. 4 and 5 is the theme of the doxology concluding ch. 4: "and those who walk in pride, he is able to humble" (4:37).

The story itself features two main characters, King Belshazzar and Daniel, and is dominated by three speeches (of the queen, vv.10–12; Belshazzar, vv.13–16; and Daniel, vv.17–28). The setting of the story is the royal palace in Babylon and a bacchanal feast prepared by Belshazzar for his nobles (vv.1–4). A significant event in the orgiastic revelry is the profaning of Hebrew drinking vessels plundered from Solomon's temple in Jerusalem by Nebuchadnezzar (vv.2–4). The plot of the story hinges on the interpretation of an inscription written by a detached human hand that suddenly appears on the wall of King Belshazzar's banquet hall (vv.5–6). The king's royal advisers (once again) prove incompetent and are unable to decipher the meaning of the encoded message (vv.7–9).

A key pivotal point in the story is the speech of the "queen" (vv.10–12), who introduces, or better reintroduces, Daniel, since he is apparently a forgotten figure in the royal court (v.11). The king heeds the queen's advice and summons Daniel, requests an explanation of the writing, and promises him wealth and position upon success (vv.13–16). Daniel interprets the cryptic Aramaic writing on the wall and in so doing pronounces the doom of Belshazzar and the end of the Babylonian Empire (vv.17–28). Belshazzar keeps his word and promotes Daniel to "third" in the kingdom (v.29). Later that same night, Belshazzar is assassinated by the Median/Persian invaders—and the kingdom of Babylonia passes to "Darius the Mede" (vv.30–31).

Apart from the three speeches, there are few internal markers suggesting literary structure. The following outline reflects the standard approach to this chapter: Belshazzar's great banquet (vv.1–9), the queen's speech (vv.10–12), Belshazzar's speech (vv.13–16), Daniel's speech (17–28), and the conclusion (vv.29–31). The first unit, the banquet scene, may be subdivided into two pericopes: the report of the feast (vv.1–4) and the report of the writing on the wall (vv.5–9). Both Lucas, 124, and D. Dorsey (*The Literary Structure of the Old Testament* [Grand Rapids: Baker, 1999], 261) offer differing (and somewhat forced) chiastically structured outlines of ch. 5.

The story of Belshazzar's feast is set within the context of the fall of the Babylonian Empire in 539 BC, more than two decades after the death of Nebuchadnezzar in 562 BC. According to the Greek historians Herodotus and Xenophon, the Persians dug a trench around the city of Babylon and temporarily diverted the Euphrates River. The Persian army entered under the walls of the city by means of the riverbed, swiftly moved to the palace, and killed the drunken guards and the (unnamed) king (cf. Seow, 76).

Porteous, 77, admits that the book of Daniel may contain genuine reminiscences of historical fact and authentic information about Mesopotamian customs, but he concludes, "this is not history but story-telling for the communication of religious truth." Redditt, 2–3, notes several historical problems in ch. 5, such as the report of the "marvelous" handwriting on the wall (v.5), the identity of the "queen" (v.10), the discrepancy as to whether the kingdom passes on to the Medes and Persians or the Medes (vv.28, 30–31), and the identity of "Darius the Mede" (v.31).

Conservative scholars committed to the historicity of the book of Daniel are quick to enumerate the thirty-seven archival texts dating to the first fourteen years of the reign of Nabonidus attesting Belshazzar's coregency (e.g., Miller, 147–48). Beyond this, since Belshazzar was virtually forgotten to history within a few decades after Babylon's fall (e.g., Herodotus knows nothing of Belshazzar), Baldwin, 23, asserts "there is important evidence here for a contemporary witness" (see her discussion of "King Belshazzar," 21–23). The "apologetic jousting" between conservative scholars and their critical or mainline counterparts on the "historical problems" of ch. 5 are addressed in the pertinent sections of the commentary and notes below. See also "Literary Form" and "Special Problems" in the Introduction.

1. Belshazzar's Great Banquet (5:1–9)

¹King Belshazzar gave a great banquet for a thousand of his nobles and drank wine with them. ²While Belshazzar was drinking his wine, he gave orders to bring in the gold and silver goblets that Nebuchadnezzar his father had taken from the temple in Jerusalem, so that the king and his nobles, his wives and his concubines might drink from them. ³So they brought in the gold goblets that had been taken from the temple of God in Jerusalem, and the king and his nobles, his wives and his concubines drank from them. ⁴As they drank the wine, they praised the gods of gold and silver, of bronze, iron, wood and stone.

⁵Suddenly the fingers of a human hand appeared and wrote on the plaster of the wall, near the lampstand in the royal palace. The king watched the hand as it wrote. ⁶His face turned pale and he was so frightened that his knees knocked together and his legs gave way.

⁷The king called out for the enchanters, astrologers and diviners to be brought and said to these wise men of Babylon, "Whoever reads this writing and tells me what it means will be clothed in purple and have a gold chain placed around his neck, and he will be made the third highest ruler in the kingdom."

⁸Then all the king's wise men came in, but they could not read the writing or tell the king what it meant. ⁹So King Belshazzar became even more terrified and his face grew more pale. His nobles were baffled.

COMMENTARY

1–4 The setting of the story is a great banquet hosted by King Belshazzar of Babylon for a thousand of his nobles (v.1). Belshazzar, whose name means "O Bel, protect the king" (cf. Collins, *Daniel*, 243), was known only from scriptural references until archaeological discoveries of the nineteenth century verified the biblical record. According to the Nabonidus Chronicle and other Neo-Babylonian archival documents, Belshazzar was the son of Nabonidus (cf. Baldwin, 21–23; Miller, 147–48). He was the "grandson" or third-generation descendant of Nebuchadnezzar only loosely understood, since Nabonidus was a contemporary of Neriglissar but not a direct descendant of Nebuchadnezzar. He usurped the throne from Labashi-Marduk, Neriglissar's son (cf. *ABD*, 4:973; Goldingay, 108). Nabonidus ruled the Babylonian Empire from 556 BC until the fall of the empire to Cyrus and the Persians in 539 BC. Belshazzar was a coregent or deputy ruling in Babylon for more than half of Nabonidus's seventeen-year reign, given the latter's ten-year hiatus in Tema in northwestern Arabia (cf. Seow, 76). According to K. Kitchen (*On the Reliability of the Old Testament* [Grand Rapids: Eerdmans, 2003], 73–74), "without actually having the title of king in official usage, Belshazzar enjoyed the powers ... his father had in practice."

The opening scene is "one of ostentatious opulence" (Seow, 78). Belshazzars's banquet is similar to the feast hosted by the Persian king Xerxes described in the book of Esther (Est 1:2–5). Such royal revelry is widely attested in Persian times, and Porteous, 78, comments, "it is not unlikely that Babylonian practices were similar." Whether or not the feast was orgiastic and cultic is open to question, but Towner, 72, is correct when he states that the scene portrayed "is intended to be a revolting picture."

The occasion of the extravagant banquet is also uncertain. Miller, 151–52, has aptly summarized the various proposals: a morale building in the light of the incursion of the Medes and Persians into Babylonian territory; the coronation of Belshazzar as king of Babylon, given the news of the recent defeat of Nabonidus by Cyrus at Sippar some fifty miles to the north; or some association with one of the Babylonian annual religious festivals, per-haps the Akitu festival observed each fall season (cf. Redditt, 89–90). The story of Belshazzar's feast records the downfall of the Babylonian Empire, so the implied date of the banquet (cf. vv.30–31) "was the fifteenth day of the seventh month of the seventeenth year of the reign of King Nabonidus, that is, the night before the Persians entered Babylon in October 539."

King Belshazzar is drinking wine "with" (NIV) his nobles, or better, "in the presence of the thousand" (NASB). The preposition "with" (Aram. *qābēl*) normally means "before," and Miller, 151, suggests that is significant here since customarily the king was hidden from the view of his guests at such state banquets. Seow, 78, understands this to mean that the king "is showing off" and that the presence of the harem women at the banquet "suggests debauchery" (cf. Kraemer, 340–41). The expression "while ... drinking his wine" is generally taken to mean that the king acts under the influence of alcohol and that his action is "flagrantly sacrilegious" (Collins, *Daniel*, 245; cf. Hartman and Di Lella, 187; Miller, 152).

In any case, the king's revelry results in his reckless gesture to lead his guests in (what the Hebrew would deem) the blasphemy of drinking from the gold and silver goblets looted from the Jerusalem temple sacked by Nebuchadnezzar. Baldwin, 120, assumes that the king is intoxicated, for "superstition alone would normally guard a man from putting sacred vessels to a common use." Lucas, 138, speculates that in calling for the temple vessels from Jerusalem "Belshazzar may have been deliberately 'going one better' than his 'father.'" Porteous, 78, sums up that whether the occasion is sacred or secular, "there was the invoking of the idol gods, and so the sacrilege of drinking from sacred vessels was increased by associating them with heathen worship." Thus the power and sovereignty of the God of Israel and the Hebrew exiles are "blatantly called into question" (Seow, 78). The stage is set for God's dramatic response to Belshazzar's rash impiety.

5−9 The raucous crowd does not have to wait long for God to "crash the party," as the narrator indicates an act of divine intervention occurs "suddenly" at the height of Belshazzar's blasphemy (v.5). Collins (*Daniel*, 246) regards the immediacy of the response as evidence of the folkloric genre of the tale. Sudden judgment is not out of character in God's dealings with humanity (cf. Zep 1:18), but the righteous need not fear the sudden disaster that overtakes the wicked (Pr 3:25). The king's impious revelry (v.4) is interrupted by the apparition of a disembodied hand writing a message on the plastered wall of the banquet hall (v.5a).

Lacocque, 95, interprets the event as a "sign, not a marvel," since natural laws are not violated and the king's vision "may be explained by his drunkenness or his having become delirious" (cf. Baldwin, 124, on the "natural means" by which God produces divine messages). Montgomery, 264, rightly counters, "the phenomenon of the writing Hand is of course meant as a miracle." The expression "the king watched the hand as it wrote" (v.5b) refers more literally to "the palm of the hand" (perhaps "the back of the hand" from the wrist to the fingertips [so Seow, 79; Goldingay, 101, n. 6b; cf. NASB]; or the palm of the "severed hand" itself, assuming the king sees the writing from a frontal view; cf. Collins, *Daniel*, 246; Hartman and Di Lella, 184; Miller, 155).

The mysterious writing appears on the wall "near the lampstand" (or "opposite the lampstand," NASB). The narrative suggests this is the only source of light for the large banquet hall, but Baldwin, 121, notes that the word "lampstand" (Aram. *nebraštāʾ*) may have been unusual, for the word is otherwise unknown (cf. *BBCOT*, 738). Seow, 78−79, contends that the reference to the lampstand does more than merely locate the scene. Either the hand

is seen "because of the lampstand" since the light of the lamp illuminates the writing hand, or (and for Seow more likely), the hand appears "before the lampstand," thus casting a shadow against the wall on which the king sees an unattached hand writing a message.

The text implies that only the king sees the writing hand ("the king watched"; v.5b), but also that the inscription on the wall is later visible to others (cf. Seow, 79, though Anderson, 54, and Lucas, 129, disagree). Given the analogy of Nebuchadnezzar's singular experience of viewing the four figures in the blazing furnace (3:25), it seems likely that only Belshazzar sees the writing hand (since the message is directed to him as king). On the archaeology of the royal palaces in ancient Babyon, see Baldwin, 120−21; Miller, 155.

The king's terror at the eerie sight cannot be internalized. His face turns pale (lit., "the king's splendor [of face] changed"; v.6a; cf. Miller, 156). He is frightened (v.6b) or "his thoughts alarmed him" (NASB), meaning the king is bewildered. Beyond the emotional and psychological distress he experiences, the king's body also reels from the shock of seeing the disembodied writing hand. First, "his hip joints went slack" (NASB; v.6c), and then his "knees began knocking together" (NASB; v.6d). The expression "his hip joints went slack" (lit., "the knots of his loins were loosed"; cf. Lucas, 130, meaning either the king collapsed or he lost control of his bowels [cf. Seow, 79; Reddit, 92]) may involve wordplay with v.12, since Daniel has the ability "to loosen knots" (lit. trans. of Aram. *qṭr*; i.e., to "solve difficult problems"). Seow, 79, comments that "this portrayal of fear is as vivid and comical as any in the Bible" (cf. A. Wolters, "Untying the King's Knots: Physiology and Wordplay in Daniel 5," *JBL* 110 [1991]: 117−22).

The NIV weakly translates the king's call for help from his royal advisers (v.7), omitting the phrase "with strength" (cf. NASB's "called aloud"). The sense of the participial form of the verb "to call" (Aram. *qr*) and the emphatic complement indicate the king "kept on screaming" for his sages (cf. Miller, 156; Seow, 79). The "enchanters, astrologers and diviners" are dutifully presented to the king (v.7a; on these guilds or classifications of royal, see comments and notes for 1:20 and 2:2). According to Baldwin, 121, the reward Belshazzar offers for deciphering the message inscribed on the wall is based on terms that appeal to him: "the right to wear royal purple, a gold chain of office and the status of third ruler in the kingdom" (see also the discussion in Smith-Christopher, 82).

All the king's wise men fail to fulfill the king's charge; they can neither read the inscription nor explain its meaning (v.8; cf. Miller, 159, who suggests they may have understood the words but the isolated words convey no intelligible meaning).

What makes the words of the (Aramaic) inscription unreadable as well as unintelligible is unclear since there is no indication they were written in code (cf. Miller, 158–59; Redditt, 98–99, on the Jewish tradition that the letters were written vertically instead of horizontally). Goldingay, 109, offers several possible explanations (including the use of ideograms, or an unusual script of cuneiform writing, or even the use of abbreviations), but in the end he concludes: "but most straightforwardly the story envisages them written as unpointed consonants: being able to read out unpointed text is partly dependent on actually understanding it, and Daniel later reads the words out one way and interprets them another." Of course, speculation as to the reasons for the wise men's inability to interpret the inscription is "pointless"—the incompetence of the royal advisers only compounds his personal distress and befuddles his nobles (v.9).

NOTES

1 The Aramaic form of the name Belshazzar, בֵּלְשַׁאצַּר, *bēlšaʾṣṣar*, is based on the Akkadian *bēl-šar-uṣur* ("O Bel, protect the king"). The Greek form of the name, *Baltasar*, is further removed from the Akkadian original. Goldingay, 100, and Lucas, 120, among others, suggest the Aramaic rendering is a bit anomalous, since one might expect *bēlšarʾeṣer* by analogy to *nērgal šarʿeṣer* in Jeremiah 39:3, 13 (for the Akkadian *nērgal-šar-uṣur*). An alternative spelling, בֵּלְאשַׁצַּר, *bēlʾšaṣṣar*, is found in Daniel 5:30; 7:1; 8:1.

2–3 King Solomon commissioned Huram, a skilled artisan from Tyre, to craft the gold and silver vessels for Yahweh's temple (cf. 1Ki 7:40–50). Lucas, 128, notes that the fate of the vessels looted from Solomon's temple by Nebuchadnezzar was an issue in Jeremiah's time. Jeremiah rebuffed the priests and false prophets who declared that within two years God would return Jehoiachin to the throne of Judah and the temple vessels to the "Lord's house" (Jer 27:16; 28:3; cf. Isa 52:11). These implements were among the treasures plundered from the temple and royal palace during Nebuchadnezzar's second invasion of Judah in 598 BC (cf. 2Ki 24:12–13). According to the inventory lists of Ezra, 5,400 gold and silver vessels (including dishes, pans, and bowls) taken earlier by Nebuchadnezzar were returned to the Jews by King Cyrus and accompanied the first wave of Hebrew expatriates back to Jerusalem after the Babylonian exile (cf. Ezr 1:7–10).

5 Lacocque, 96, compares the "fingers of a human hand" to the finger of God as a symbol of the power of God responsible for the plagues against the Egyptians (Ex 8:19) or the finger that wrote the tablets of the law for Moses (31:18). Collins (*Daniel*, 246) aptly counters that the finger is not visible on those occasions and that "the failure to identify the writer is a deliberate artistic device."

7 Belshazzar's reward of promotion to the rank of third in the kingdom for deciphering the inscription is variously understood to mean: third in rank behind King Belshazzar and the queen mother (so Smith-Christopher, 82; cf. Montgomery, 254, 257), or third in rank behind Nabonidus and Belshazzar (so Longman, 139). Jewish interpreters (e.g., Rashi and Ibn Ezra) took the expression to mean rule over a third of the empire (cf. Redditt, 92). Others equate the Aramaic word תַּלְתִּי (*taltî*, "third") with the Akkadian *šalšu* and the Hebrew שָׁלִישׁ, *šālîš*, which may denote a high-ranking official or military officer of some kind (cf. Lucas, 121; Redditt, 92), or even a triumvir (i.e., one equal in rank with two others; cf. Wood, 138), based on the later reference to "three administrators" in 6:2 (so Hartman and Di Lella, 184; Collins, *Daniel*, 247). Miller, 158, is confident that "the third highest ruler in the kingdom" (NIV) most accurately conveys the meaning of the term, but Seow, 79, soberly summarizes that "with our present knowledge the problem remains insoluble."

2. The Queen Introduces Daniel (5:10−12)

COMMENTARY

[10]The queen, hearing the voices of the king and his nobles, came into the banquet hall. "O king, live forever!" she said. "Don't be alarmed! Don't look so pale! [11]There is a man in your kingdom who has the spirit of the holy gods in him. In the time of your father he was found to have insight and intelligence and wisdom like that of the gods. King Nebuchadnezzar your father — your father the king, I say — appointed him chief of the magicians, enchanters, astrologers and diviners. [12]This man Daniel, whom the king called Belteshazzar, was found to have a keen mind and knowledge and understanding, and also the ability to interpret dreams, explain riddles and solve difficult problems. Call for Daniel, and he will tell you what the writing means."

10−12 The queen enters the banquet hall upon hearing the commotion caused by the mysterious writing on the wall (v.10; although the Old Greek has Belshazzar summoning the queen into the room; cf. Collins, *Daniel*, 237). The "queen" is unnamed. Since Belshazzar's wives and concubines are present at the banquet (v.3), and the queen is free to enter the king's presence unbidden, she is probably the "queen mother" (so Lucas, 130; cf.

Kraemer, 341−42). The importance of the queen mother in the royal courts of the ancient Near East is widely attested (cf. Goldingay, 109; Collins, *Daniel*, 248; on the queen mother in ancient Israel, see Susan Ackerman, "The Queen Mother and the Cult in Ancient Israel," in *Women in the Hebrew Bible*, ed. A. Bach [New York: Routledge, 1999], 179−94). As Lacocque, 97, notes, the queen plays a role similar to that of Arioch (ch. 2), an agent who brings Daniel to the attention of the king. Yet she is integral to the narrative because it is her initiative that brings resolution to the "plot conflict" of the story—albeit unhappily for King Belshazzar and the Babylonians.

Those scholars interpreting "father" rigidly to mean that Belshazzar was the "son" of Nebuchadnezzar (v.2) identify the "queen" or "queen mother" as Nitocris, the widow of King Nebuchadnezzar (e.g., Lacocque, 97; Collins, *Daniel*, 248; Redditt, 93; but see Miller, 160, who suggests Nitocris may have been the wife of Nabonidus). Neo-Babylonian archival documents indicate that Belshazzar was the son of Nabonidus, making him the "grandson" or "descendant" of Nebuchadnezzar (see comments on v.2). Baldwin, 121–22, is probably correct in identifying the "queen mother" as the wife of Nabonidus (and probably a daughter of Nebuchadnezzar; so Miller, 160) and the mother of Belshazzar. The fact that the formal queen mother (i.e., the mother of Nabonidus) died in the ninth year of her son's reign, according to the Nabonidus Chronicle, lends support to this identification (cf. Longman, 139).

Kraemer, 342, suggests that, apart from the queen's identity, her "absence from the banquet, and thus her implicit abstinence from the impious activity, align her with Daniel and remove any taint from her recommendation." The queen's acclamation of long life for the king (v.10a)—standard court etiquette (see comment on 2:4)—is tinged with irony since Belshazzar is doomed to die that very night. The queen mother is portrayed as a decisive and sagacious woman in her response to the king's dilemma, but not without feminine instincts for compassion, as her twofold admonition to allay the king's fears attests (v.10b).

As queen mother (whether wife or daughter of King Nebuchadnezzar), her memory extends beyond that of King Belshazzar, so she has recollections of Daniel and his role as a royal adviser in previous administrations. Often overlooked is the fact that women were the keepers of family stories in the biblical world, and the queen admirably fills that role here (cf. Carol L. Meyers, "Of Drums and Damsels: Women's Performance in Ancient Israel," *BA* 54 (1991): 22–23; idem, "The Family in Ancient Israel," in *Families in Ancient Israel*, ed. L. G. Perdue et al. [Louisville: Westminster John Knox, 1997], 31–32).

This literary unit features the foil contrasting the king's fright ("alarm" that causes him to turn "pale"; v.10) and Daniel's exceptional abilities (vv.11–12). There is almost a hint of sarcastic indictment in the queen's declaration, "there is a man in your kingdom"—a wise king should know his own "people resources." The queen's recognition that Daniel was endowed with "the spirit of holy gods" recalls Nebuchadnezzar's threefold declaration of the same (see the comments on 4:8–9, 18; cf. Porteous, 80, who suggests the queen repeats the very words she heard Nebuchadnezzar use of Daniel). Likewise, her litany in praise of Daniel's "insight and intelligence and wisdom" (v.11b) echoes those (divinely granted) aptitudes that characterized his early days as an apprentice in the service of King Nebuchadnezzar (see comments on 1:4, 17).

The queen's reference to Daniel's role as a former "chief of magicians" (v.11c) indicates that Daniel had been demoted (always the prerogative of the new regime with respect to "holdover" civil servants), had retired (as he would have been eighty years old or even older at this time), and had been forgotten by the king given the size of the city of Babylon and the number of civil servants on the king's payroll. Or perhaps "the liquor could have clouded his memory" (so Miller, 161; cf. Lucas, 130, on the various reasons why the queen must intervene before Daniel is summoned to the king).

Finally, in addition to twice referring to Daniel by his Hebrew name, the queen mentions that the man in question was renamed Belteshazzar by King Nebuchadnezzar. Smith-Christopher, 82, suggests the queen casts aspersion on Daniel in her reference to his name change, perhaps to remind the king of Daniel's status as an exile. The similarity of the king's name, Belshazzar, to Daniel's Babylonian name, Belteshazzar, may have necessitated the queen's identification of Daniel by the use of his two names simply for clarification. Whether known by his Hebrew or Babylonian name, Daniel's repu-

tation as one who possessed wisdom of a supernatural quality meant he could "interpret dreams, explain riddles and solve difficult problems" (v.12a; cf. Lucas, 130–31). For this reason the queen has the utmost confidence in his ability to explain the riddle of the handwriting on the wall (v.12b). The queen's directive to the king is (a third-person) form of a command ("let Daniel now be summoned," NASB), so Belshazzar had no choice but to summon Daniel (cf. Seow, 81).

NOTE

11–12 Goldingay, 109–10, observes that the skills the queen attributes to Daniel "relate directly to the interpretation of a portent." He comments further that "insight" suggests illumination from God (cf. NASB's "illumination"); "insight" (or "intelligence," NIV) indicates Daniel both possesses intellect and knows, by God's gift, how to use it; and "wisdom" identifies in Daniel the "supernatural intuition of an interpreter of dreams or omens."

3. Belshazzar Summons Daniel (5:13–16)

¹³So Daniel was brought before the king, and the king said to him, "Are you Daniel, one of the exiles my father the king brought from Judah? ¹⁴I have heard that the spirit of the gods is in you and that you have insight, intelligence and outstanding wisdom. ¹⁵The wise men and enchanters were brought before me to read this writing and tell me what it means, but they could not explain it. ¹⁶Now I have heard that you are able to give interpretations and to solve difficult problems. If you can read this writing and tell me what it means, you will be clothed in purple and have a gold chain placed around your neck, and you will be made the third highest ruler in the kingdom."

COMMENTARY

13–16 According to Porteous, 80, Belshazzar essentially "treated Daniel with the greatest courtesy" (cf. Hartman and Di Lella, 189; Towner, 74). Lucas, 131, concurs, observing that "from the view of a Diaspora Jew, it presents the welcome picture of

a pagan king's recognizing the unique abilities of a Jewish courtier." Felwell, 127, however, argues rather convincingly that Belshazzar's speech is "a complex mixture of skepticism, challenge, desperation, and resentment rather than a 'friendly welcome.'"

The king's interview with Daniel follows the "script" for court stories in that Belshazzar first repeats the queen's speech recommending Daniel (v.14), then he rehearses the failure of the other wise men to explain the mysterious writing (v.15), and finally he reiterates his offer to promote the one who deciphers the cryptic inscription (v.16). As Lucas, 131, notes, such repetition is expected in the genre of court contest since it "serves to build up Daniel's reputation and emphasize the extent of his success."

Two things stand out in the king's speech here. First, in the dramatic "standing before the king" scene, the first question Belshazzar poses to Daniel concerns his status as a Jewish exile—this despite the queen mother's accolades for Daniel (v.13a). Interestingly, Belshazzar also addresses Daniel by his Hebrew name, perhaps to avoid confusion with his own (so Young, 123). More likely is the assessment of Smith-Christopher, 82, that the king begins his interrogation of Daniel "with a reminder of his station as a prisoner of war." Felwell, 122–23, suggests Belshazzar's query indicates that Daniel is not an unknown figure to him, and his knowledge about Daniel goes beyond the queen's biography. Lucas, 131, interprets the king's comment as a slight and argues that it "favors the view that Belshazzar is to be seen as having deliberately ignored Daniel when seeking sages to read and interpret the writing."

Second, Belshazzar's omission of the adjective "holy" in his description of the divine source of Daniel's wisdom (v.14) may have significance in view of the king's corrupt character. It is possible that "the king may have been fearful of Daniel's interpretation since this man worshiped the God whom Belshazzar had just blasphemed" (Miller, 161). Felwell, 126–27, suggests the tone and content of the king's speech is symptomatic of a much deeper psychological problem, namely, Belshazzar's personal insecurities and his resentment of his (grand)father Nebuchadnezzar's power and success. Lucas, 138, discerns that Nebuchadnezzar's pride had a quality of arrogance because of his great achievements, whereas Belshazzar's pride is marked by insolence because of his lack of achievements. Daniel reminds the king of all that his (grand)father was and all that he is not.

Belshazzar needs an explanation for an apparition that has terrified him. The king may suspect the message is a negative pronouncement (so Lacocque, 101)—"he does not want to know bad news, but not knowing is worse.… He is desperate, he is vulnerable, and he resents having to depend upon Daniel, the man who most represents his [grand]father's power and success" (Felwell, 127). This helps explain Daniel's rather undiplomatic (and uncharacteristic) disdain for the king's gifts after successfully interpreting the enigmatic graffiti on the wall of the royal banquet hall (v.17); "the problem for Daniel is the person offering the reward. Daniel's refusal is designed to offend" (Felwell, 127, though she erroneously attributes Daniel's motivation to his pride rather than his humility).

4. Daniel Explains the Handwriting on the Wall (5:17–28)

¹⁷Then Daniel answered the king, "You may keep your gifts for yourself and give your rewards to someone else. Nevertheless, I will read the writing for the king and tell him what it means.

¹⁸"O king, the Most High God gave your father Nebuchadnezzar sovereignty and greatness and glory and splendor. ¹⁹Because of the high position he gave him, all the peoples and nations and men of every language dreaded and feared him. Those the king wanted to put to death, he put to death; those he wanted to spare, he spared; those he wanted to promote, he promoted; and those he wanted to humble, he humbled. ²⁰But when his heart became arrogant and hardened with pride, he was deposed from his royal throne and stripped of his glory. ²¹He was driven away from people and given the mind of an animal; he lived with the wild donkeys and ate grass like cattle; and his body was drenched with the dew of heaven, until he acknowledged that the Most High God is sovereign over the kingdoms of men and sets over them anyone he wishes.

²²"But you his son, O Belshazzar, have not humbled yourself, though you knew all this. ²³Instead, you have set yourself up against the Lord of heaven. You had the goblets from his temple brought to you, and you and your nobles, your wives and your concubines drank wine from them. You praised the gods of silver and gold, of bronze, iron, wood and stone, which cannot see or hear or understand. But you did not honor the God who holds in his hand your life and all your ways. ²⁴Therefore he sent the hand that wrote the inscription.

²⁵"This is the inscription that was written:

MENE, MENE, TEKEL, PARSIN

²⁶"This is what these words mean:

Mene: God has numbered the days of your reign and brought it to an end.

²⁷*Tekel*: You have been weighed on the scales and found wanting.

²⁸*Peres*: Your kingdom is divided and given to the Medes and Persians."

COMMENTARY

17 Daniel's speech in response to the king's request for an explanation of the mysterious handwriting on the palace wall may be outlined in three units: his refusal of the king's gifts (v.17), his indictment of Belshazzar (vv.18−24), and his decipherment of the inscription (vv.25−28). The repetition of the independent pronoun "you" (Aram. *ʿantᵉ*; vv.18 [omitted from NIV], 21) quite naturally divides Daniel's indictment of the king into two parts: his recollection of God's dealings with Nebuchadnezzar (vv.18−21) and his rebuke of Belshazzar (vv.22−24).

Unlike the queen (v.10), Daniel offers the king no salutation following royal protocol upon his summons before the king. Moreover, his initial response to Belshazzar is rather curt and ungracious. Seow, 81, goes so far as to say Daniel's comment "sounds somewhat disingenuous, for he had accepted rewards before (2:48) and at the end of this episode, he does accept the reward after all (5:29)." Lucas, 131, reminds us, however, that Daniel's rejection of the king's rewards are more understandable if Belshazzar's greeting is viewed as a put down. More importantly, Daniel must establish the fact that he cannot be bribed—his message must remain independent of any price the king attempts to set.

18–24 Daniel begins his indictment of King Belshazzar with the rehearsal of God's humiliation of King Nebuchadnezzar for his sin of pride (vv.18–21). Nebuchadnezzar had claimed a position of absolute freedom and power that typically the OT reserves for God alone (cf. Seow, 82). For this reason God afflicted Nebuchadnezzar with a mental illness (boanthropy), and the king was deposed, stripped of his glory (v.20), and driven away to live like an animal for a time (v.21). As a result Nebuchadnezzar learned that God had granted kingship to him (v.18) and that ultimately the Most High God is sovereign over all earthly kingdoms (v.21). (See the discussion of ch. 4.)

Daniel rebukes Belshazzar for his pride on two accounts. First, the king has learned nothing from the example of Nebuchadnezzar despite his awareness of the episode (v.22). Second, Belshazzar has "exalted" (NASB) himself against the Lord of heaven in his arrogant act of desecrating the drinking vessels from the Jerusalem temple (v.23a). God holds Belshazzar equally culpable for the sin of pride—perhaps even more so, since his sacrilege is combined with blatant idolatry (v.23b; cf. Miller, 163). Thus the handwriting on the wall of the banquet hall is God's response to the proud heart and profane actions of the Babylonian king (v.24). Naturally, Daniel's indictment of Belshazzar sets the judgmental tone and portends the apocalyptic content of the divine message encrypted in the supernatural inscription.

The epithet "Lord of heaven" (v.23) is synonymous with "Most High God" (v.18) in the sense of God's sovereign rule over human affairs. The title also serves to emphasize the spiritual contrast between the true God and the earthly nature of the idolatrous gods made of silver, gold, bronze, iron, wood, and stone (v.23). This name for God also has implications for the nature of God as a "living God" and for the spiritual or heavenly source behind the message on the wall. Some of the most biting satire of the Bible is found in the OT prophets' denunciation of those who worship humanly fabricated gods made of wood, stone, and precious metals (cf. Isa 40:18–20; 44:9–20; Hab 2:18–20; cf. Ps 115:2–8).

Daniel exposes both Belshazzar's ignorance and foolishness for his failure to "honor" the God who holds his "life" (or "life-breath," NASB) in his hand (v.23) by worshiping "lifeless" objects made with human hands. The prophet Jeremiah recognized as much when he acknowledged that a person's life is not one's own and that individuals do not direct their own steps (Jer 10:23). The "ways" (v.23; Aram. ᵊʾrah; GK 10068) of a person refers to the destiny of an individual, "the course of life that someone follows, which is seen as plotted and controlled by God—without implying that it is predetermined in such a way as to make human decision-making illusory" (Goldingay, 110). The concept is prominent in OT wisdom literature (Job 8:13; 22:28; 24:23; Pr 3:6; 4:18; 20:24), as is the idea that God holds a person's breath or life in his hand (cf. Job 12:10; 34:14–15; Ps 104:29).

25–28 Daniel identifies the hand that wrote the message as an agent of God, thus confirming the divine source of the message (v.24; cf. Seow, 82, on the idea of hypostasis [the extension of divine presence through some entity that represents the deity] in the biblical world). Collins (*Daniel*, 250) states, "the fact that the message was written conveys a sense of finality, even of determinism."

The inscription itself contained but four words: "MENE, MENE, TEKEL, PARSIN." Presumably the inscription was written in (unpointed) Aramaic; that is, the words were composed of consonants only. (The NIV omits the conjunc-tion "*û*" ["and"] in "*ûparsîn*"; cf. Archer, 74, on the Aramaic script.) Thus several different meanings for the inscription are possible, depending on the vowels supplied by the interpreter. Certain textual problems in the inscription have been identified as well: (1) the omission of the second *m^enē^{>}* in some of the ancient versions (e.g., Old Greek and Vulgate), leading Montgomery, 262, Lacocque, 100, 102, and Collins (*Daniel*, 250) to declare the three-word inscription original because of an error of dittography in the MT; (2) the inversion of the words *t^eqēl* and *parsîn* in the Old Greek version (cf. Redditt, 98); and (3) the plural form *parsîn* (v.25) considered by some as secondary, replac-ing the original *p^erēs* found in Daniel's interpre-tation (v.28; e.g. Hartman and Di Lella, 183; yet Lacocque, 102–3, deems it original). We concur with Goldingay, 102, and Lucas, 132, on retaining the MT as the original reading of v.25.

Daniel reads the four words of the inscription as noun forms (v.25): *m^enē^{>}* (Aram. "mina"), *m^enē^{>}* (= a "mina"), *t^eqēl* (Aram. "shekel"), and *parsîn* (Aram. *p^erēs*; pl. *parsîn* = "half-pieces"). He takes the roots of the nouns, however, and reinterprets them as verbs (passive participles; vv.26–28): *m^enē^{>}* ("numbered"), *m^enē^{>}* ("numbered"), *t^eqēl* ("weighed"), and *p^erēs* ("divided"). This form of wordplay is an interpre-tive method evidenced later in the Qumran com-munity (cf. Lucas, 133). The perfect form of the verbs (i.e., "has numbered," "have been weighed") indicates that the matter has been decided—the outcome is certain. Finally, he applies the mean-ing of the riddle directly to King Belshazzar ("your reign," "you," "your kingdom"; vv.26–28).

God himself has "numbered" the days of Bels-hazzar's life and closed the books on his reign (v.26; Miller, 165, understands the repetition of *m^enē^{>}* as emphasis on the certainty of the fulfillment of the divine decision).

The idea of God's "weighing" a person's motives and actions in a balance scale (v.27) is found in Hebrew wisdom tradition (e.g., Pr 16:2; 21:2; 24:12; cf. *BBCOT*, 738). The "weighing of souls" on a balance scale before Osiris, god of the underworld, is a common motif in ancient Egyptian religion (e.g., the heart of the deceased is weighed against the feather of truth in a scene from the *Book of the Dead*). Specifically, Belshazzar has been "found wanting" for his failure to humble himself and acknowledge the Most High God as sovereign over human kingdoms, and for his idolatrous profanation of the vessels looted from Yahweh's temple in Jeru-salem (vv.22–23; cf. Miller, 165, who understands this more generally as "deficient in moral worth").

Finally, his kingdom is "divided" and given to others—namely the Medes and the Persians (v.28). Daniel does not mean that the Babylonian Empire will be divided between the two conquering nations, but "rather that Belshazzar's dynasty will be broken and his authority will pass on to others" (Goldingay, 111; cf. Miller, 165).

Note too that the words *parsîn* (v.25) and *p^erēs* (v.28) may also be another form of wordplay on the name "Persian," since the Persians succeeded the Babylonians as the Mesopotamian "superpower" of the biblical world (cf. Miller, 166). Seow, 84, detects per-haps one final subtle form of wordplay in the inscrip-tion: if the words are read as weights and *parsîn* refers to two half-shekels, then the total weights counted in the message add up to "sixty-two"—the age of Darius the Mede (v.31), Belshazzar's successor!

For a discussion of scholarly renderings of the inscription different from that of the interpretation given by Daniel (e.g., the metaphorical approach explaining the terms as monetary weights or mea-sures and applying them to a successive Babylonian king-list), see Goldingay, 110–11, Miller, 165 (esp. n. 92), Collins (*Daniel*, 250–52), Lucas, 132–34, and Redditt, 98–99.

5. Conclusion (5:29–31 [5:29–6:1])

²⁹Then at Belshazzar's command, Daniel was clothed in purple, a gold chain was placed around his neck, and he was proclaimed the third highest ruler in the kingdom.
³⁰That very night Belshazzar, king of the Babylonians, was slain, ³¹and Darius the Mede took over the kingdom, at the age of sixty-two.

COMMENTARY

29–31 King Belshazzar rewards Daniel according to the dictates of his earlier pronouncement concerning the decipherment of the mysterious inscription (v.29; cf. v.7). The king must save face by not breaking a promise in front of his nobles (cf. Lucas, 134). As for his part, Daniel inexplicably accepts the king's gifts after having refused them earlier (v.17; cf. Lucas, 134, who states that Collins [*Daniel*, 252] "sidesteps the problems by seeing here a traditional motif of the tale of court contest"). The gifts are bestowed on Daniel at the king's command (v.29), making them irrefutable in one sense.

Moreover, Daniel is now free to accept the king's gifts since they are no longer "bribes" that could influence his message. Besides all this, the gifts are essentially meaningless given the imminent collapse of the Babylonian Empire. Miller, 166, has noted that Belshazzar makes no (recorded) acknowledgment of the greatness of Daniel's God (unlike Nebuchadnezzar in the previous court stories of chs. 3 and 4), but simply "conferring the promised gifts upon Yahweh's representative ... itself was an indication of Yahweh's reality and power" (cf. Seow, 83, who notes that Belshazzar has learned nothing from the experience of his predecessor).

According to the narrator of the court story, Daniel's interpretation of the cryptic inscription written on the wall of the royal palace by the supernatural hand is fulfilled "that very night" with the assassination of Belshazzar (v.30). Seow, 84, in his insightful summary of ch. 5, observes that all the events of the story occur on a single night. Moreover, Belshazzar is slain on the very night he has committed the sacrilege with the drinking vessels plundered from Yahweh's Jerusalem temple. The story begins with a reference to the "Chaldean king" Nebuchadnezzar, who looted Solomon's temple and was responsible for the Jewish exile in Babylonia. The story ends with a reference to the "Chaldean king" Belshazzar, whose kingdom is literally "received" (so NASB) by the Medes and Persians. Finally, the passive voice is used to report the execution of Belshazzar, and the fall of Babylonia to the Persians is narrated in nonmilitary terms. What else may one conclude from this pointed evidence other than "in context, one can only see Belshazzar's demise as an event according to the will of the sovereign God whom he dared to defy" (Seow, 84).

Persian and Greek historical sources report several traditions concerning the fall of Babylon (cf. *BBCOT*, 738). None of the extrabiblical documents mention Belshazzar by name as the king slain when the Median/Persian armies took the city. The sources do tend to agree that Babylon fell without a battle (see the discussions in Miller, 166–69; Collins, *Daniel*, 29–33, 252–53; Hartman and Di Lella, 191; Goldingay, 106–8; Lucas, 126–27).

The reference to Darius the Mede (v.31 [6:1]) is one of the several historical problems of this biblical book. Generally for critical commentators the character is simply a literary fiction appropriate to the genre of court-contest tale (e.g., Hartman and Di Lella, 36; Lacocque, 106, 109; Montgomery, 65; Porteous, 83). Redditt, 100, concedes that Darius the Mede is a composite drawn from various sources, not just the creation of the author (namely, the conflation of the historical King Darius I of Persia and the text of Jeremiah 51:11 stating that God stirred up the Medes to defeat the Babylonians; cf. Collins, *Daniel*, 253).

Those commentators seeking to harmonize the biblical record of Daniel with ancient Near Eastern history have posed any number of possible identifications for Darius the Mede, such as Cyaxares II, Cyrus, Ugbaru, Gubaru, Cambyses, Darius, and Darius II. Conservative scholars tend to line up in one of two camps: either Darius the Mede is Gubaru (or Gobryas), who was appointed governor of Babylon by Cyrus after the city was conquered by the Persians (e.g., Archer, Wood); or Darius the Mede is a title for Cyrus the Great (e.g., Baldwin; see the discussions in Miller, 171–77; Lucas, 134–37). Yet it must be admitted that "none of those nominated ... is ever called Darius the Mede in extant literature from that time" (Redditt, 100). For now, the identity of "Darius the Mede" remains a puzzle.

F. The Lions' Den (6:1–28 [6:2–29])

OVERVIEW

Daniel 6 completes the "court stories" section of the book (chs. 1–6) and concludes what Felwell, 15–16, calls a "story of stories" about God's sovereignty. For a discussion of this larger literary context within the book of Daniel, see comments on 2:1–13 and 3:1–7.

The literary form of the story is typically identified as a tale of court conflict (e.g., Goldingay, 122). Collins (*Daniel: with an Introduction to Apocalyptic Literature*, 71) construes the character of the tale to be that of "legend" because of numerous features, especially the miraculous preservation of Daniel and the virtual conversion of the pagan king (see the comments on 5:1–9 on the form-critical definition of "legend"). Lucas, 145–47, has observed that the stories of the three Hebrews in the furnace (ch. 3) and Daniel in the lions' den (ch. 6) have several words and phrases in common, suggesting these two chapters were intentionally composed as a literary pair. See "Literary Form" in the introduction and the discussion of the genre of "story of court conflict" in the comments on 3:1–7.

Collins (*Daniel: with an Introduction to Apocalyptic Literature*, 71) equates the plot of the story with the folkloric plot typical of the "disgrace and rehabilitation of a minister of state." In Daniel, the two stories of court conflict share the same formal elements:

- jealous colleagues who accuse the recalcitrant Jews of defying the king's authority and insist that the king follow through on the death sentence he has decreed for the perpetrators
- a king who capitulates to the demands of his courtiers and orders the execution of the defiant civil servants (meanwhile ensuring there is no possibility of escape)

- a reference to the possibility of divine deliverance that is realized when God sends a messenger to preserve his chosen one(s) unharmed through the ordeal
- the reversal of the action as the king releases the Jews wrongly accused and executes their malicious detractors
- a concluding doxology in praise of the God of Israel

Lucas, 145, however, calls attention to major differences between the two stories of conflict, especially the facts that the accusers in ch. 6 are other political officials (not the sages as in ch. 3), an element of conspiracy is present in ch. 6 (whereas the action in ch. 3 seems to be "opportunistic"), and Darius hears of Daniel's deliverance in ch. 6, whereas Nebuchadnezzar witnesses the deliverance of the three Hebrews (ch. 3).

Since the story type is known from different cultures, critical scholars speculate as to the dating of the pericope (cf. Redditt, 102: "the only issues here are when people in the Diaspora began to tell the story and when its hero became Daniel"). Hartman and Di Lella, 197, place the story broadly within the Persian period on the basis of Persian loanwords. For Porteous, 88, the story "comes alive" as literature for the Jews during the persecution under the Seleucid king Antiochus IV Epiphanes in the second century

BC (cf. Redditt, 102). Baldwin, 127, represents the conservative approach by noting, "old [i.e., early Persian period], authentic stories would have provided comfort to sufferers of later generations far more convincingly than a book of new parables."

The plot of the story may be outlined in five major scenes: the report of Daniel's success (vv. 1–3), the conspiracy against Daniel (vv. 4–9), Daniel accused and condemned (vv. 10–18), Daniel's deliverance (vv. 19–24), and Darius's letter of proclamation and doxology (vv. 25–28). Unlike the court stories in chs. 3 and 5, the story in ch. 6 contains less reported speech by the main characters. Instead, the straightforward narrative is "carried along by the repeated use of the conjunction … 'then'" (Aram. *ᵉdayin*, vv. 4–7, 12–17, 19–20, 22–23, 26 [MT]; Lucas, 146). The repetition and wordplay in the story underscore certain of its points, notably, the foil of obedience to God's law or the civil law (vv. 5, 8) and the virtue of a daily prayer ritual (vv. 5, 11; i.e., Daniel's conspirators can "find" nothing against him until they "find" him praying). For Collins (*Daniel: with an Introduction to Apocalyptic Literature*, 71), a major goal of the story "is to evoke wonder: 'that in all my royal dominion men tremble with fear before the God of Daniel' (v. 27)."

Goldingay, 124, following Towner, 79, has outlined the contents of the chapter in a chiastic pattern:

A Introduction: Daniel's success (vv. 1–3)
   B Darius's edict and Daniel's response (vv. 4–10)
      C Daniel's opponents plot his death (vv. 11–15)
         D Darius hopes for Daniel's deliverance (vv. 16–18)
         D' Darius witnesses Daniel's deliverance (vv. 19–23)
      C' Daniel's opponents sentenced to death (vv. 24)
   B' Darius's edict and doxology (vv. 25–27)
A' Conclusion: Daniel's success (v. 28)

Lucas, 146, has noted that the chiastic structure of the story highlights Daniel's deliverance and

God's role as the agent of that deliverance — doing what Darius can only hope for. Yet the outline is somewhat artificial in that the report of Darius's publishing of his decree (v.9) more naturally concludes the unit containing the conspiracy against Daniel (vv.4–9; cf. Baldwin, 127; Miller, 179; Seow, 88). The repetition of the conjunction "then" (Aram. *ʾedayin*) in each of vv.12–17 permits the division of the pericope describing the condemnation of Daniel (vv.10–18) at numerous points (e.g., v.13 [Seow, 90]; v.14 [Baldwin, 129]; v.15 [Lucas, 151]; v.17 [Porteous, 90]). Finally, Darius's edict and doxology (B/B') are loosely related at best.

The story features Daniel as the protagonist (v.2), with Darius (v.1) playing a central role as a supporting character, while the unnamed "administrators and satraps" (v.3) are the chief antagonists (cf. Towner, 80, who identifies the protagonists of the story as the hundred-plus administrators and satraps [including Daniel]). The setting of the story is the Persian period and continues the narrative of ch. 5 by "illustrating how Daniel continues to function during the reigns of the Median and Persian kings who succeed Belshazzar" (Goldingay, 126).

By way of literary context, the doxology published as an edict by Darius (vv.25–27) "sums up the confessions of the pagan rulers in the preceding stories" and emphasizes the theme of the court stories, namely, God's sovereignty. The last verse of ch. 6 echoes 1:21, the testimony of Daniel's longevity as a civil servant in the royal courts of the Babylonians and Persians. Daniel is a living example of God's power to sustain (and even prosper) his people through the "dislocation" of the Babylonian exile. Finally, the court stories are instructional for the Diaspora Jews since they reveal that the Hebrew in exile "is defined by his religion and its outward observance, not by language, personal name, or profession ... these stories convey both security and insecurity; political success and martyrdom are equally possible" (Davies, 55).

The shared motifs of Daniel in the lions' den and a pagan king's doxology praising Daniel's God has led some to see a relationship between ch. 6 and the deuterocanonical story of Bel and the Serpent belonging to the Additions to Daniel (e.g., Wills, 134–38). Collins (*Daniel*, 264) downplays the connections and suggests that the lions'-den motif is an older tradition that circulated independently and then was developed later in different ways. The story of Bel and the Serpent, however, is a polemic against idolatry, not a story of court conflict. Lucas, 147, is probably correct in his speculation that the lions'-den motif was borrowed from the canonical story and included in the story about Bel and the Serpent, "which seems a more contrived story, especially with the transportation of Habakkuk to feed Daniel in the lion's den."

For discussions of the divergences from the MT in the Greek versions of ch. 6, see Lacocque, 108–21 [Critical Notes sections]); Collins (*Daniel*, 262–64); Lucas, 147–48).

1. Daniel's Success (6:1–3 [6:2–4])

[1]It pleased Darius to appoint 120 satraps to rule throughout the kingdom, [2]with three administrators over them, one of whom was Daniel. The satraps were made accountable to them so that the king might not suffer loss. [3]Now Daniel so distinguished himself among the administrators and the satraps by his exceptional qualities that the king planned to set him over the whole kingdom.

COMMENTARY

1–3 [2–4] Historical problems abound in ch. 6 to the extent that Porteous, 88–89, comments, "the author of our book is not concerned about historical accuracy." For instance, as noted in ch. 5, the identity of "Darius the Mede" (v.1) is in question (see the survey of opinions in Miller, 171–73). In addition, the "three administrators" appointed by Darius as overseers of the satraps (v.2) are unknown royal offices in the extant Persian documents (cf. Redditt, 104). Beyond this, there is no mention of Daniel himself as a high-ranking Persian bureaucrat in any extrabiblical documents.

The problems are not insurmountable, however, and conservative scholars have offered plausible solutions to explain perceived historical difficulties and harmonize seemingly conflicting data. Darius the Mede has been equated with Cyrus the Great, understanding the conjunction ("and") in v.28 explicatively or epexegetically: "Daniel prospered during the reign of Darius, namely, the reign of Cyrus the Persian" (e.g., Baldwin, 132; cf. Miller, 176, on a similar example from 1Ch 5:26 with the Assyrian king Pul or Tiglath-pileser). Others suggest Darius the Mede was a "king" or "governor" of Babylon appointed by Cyrus, perhaps the official named Gubaru (or Ugbaru if they are the same person?) in neo-Babylonian documents (cf. Miller, 173). Still others note that both "Cyrus" and "Darius" were titles, and kings in the ancient world often bore more than one name or title (cf. Wiseman, *Notes on Some Problems*, 16).

The number of satrapies or administrative districts within the Persian Empire varied according to time period and historical source (anywhere from twenty to twenty-nine; cf. Miller, 177). The text of Daniel 6, though, mentions satraps—not satrapies. The word "satrap" (Aram. *ʾaḥašdarpan*) means "protector of the kingdom," and the term was used loosely (by Greek historians) to refer to various royally appointed officials (cf. Montgomery, 269). Thus the figures of 120 (6:1) and 127 (Est 1:1) "refer to smaller divisions within the empire than those which the term 'satrapy' would apply when used in its strictest sense" (Lucas, 148; cf. Seow, 88, who notes that the term is used of governmental officials in Daniel 3:2–3 even before the Persians came to power).

Greek historians refer to the Persian kings' seven counselors or princes, but there is no known parallel to the three "administrators" or "commissioners" (NASB) in the Persian government. As is the case with any argument from silence, absence of evidence is not evidence of absence. Perhaps further archaeological discovery will shed new light on this aspect of Persian royal administration. Daniel is named as one of the three chief administrators (v.2), a supervisory role of some sort in the context of the narrative (cf. Redditt, 104). Some scholars have connected Daniel's role among the three with his promotion for interpreting the writing on the wall (e.g., Collins, *Daniel*, 265; Hartman and Di Lella, 198; see comment on 5:29). But Lucas, 148, comments that this is unlikely, since "that was a different office under a different king in a different empire" (cf. Redditt, 104, who also sees no clear connection between the two passages).

Unlike the Babylonian king Belshazzar, Darius the Mede is portrayed as a friend of Daniel (so Redditt, 104); but like the other kings in the court stories of Daniel, Darius is not above being duped by advisers. The satraps reported directly to their designated administrative overseers, and presumably the three chief administrators reported directly to the king. This organizational hierarchy was designed to prevent the king from suffering loss (v.2). Baldwin, 128, understands this to mean "loss of territory" because of uprisings and "loss of taxation" because of graft.

How Darius came to know of Daniel is never mentioned, though stories of his role in deciphering the cryptic message given to Belshazzar concerning the fall of Babylonia to Persia no doubt circulated widely. As was the case at every stage in his long diplomatic career, Daniel's distinguished service was attributed to his "exceptional qualities" (NIV; v.3). More literally, the narrator states that Daniel "possessed an extraordinary spirit" (NASB). Presumably this recognized his endowment with a "divine spirit" (as in 4:8, 18; 5:12; cf. Seow, 89), not just affirmed his exceptional abilities. Daniel's success is the main point of the introductory verses, since Darius considers elevating the Hebrew civil servant to an unspecified position of supremacy in the kingdom (v.3). The king's intention stirs up professional (or ethnic?) jealousy among Daniel's colleagues, and this becomes the point of conflict in the story.

2. The Conspiracy against Daniel (6:4–9 [6:5–10])

⁴At this, the administrators and the satraps tried to find grounds for charges against Daniel in his conduct of government affairs, but they were unable to do so. They could find no corruption in him, because he was trustworthy and neither corrupt nor negligent. ⁵Finally these men said, "We will never find any basis for charges against this man Daniel unless it has something to do with the law of his God."

⁶So the administrators and the satraps went as a group to the king and said: "O King Darius, live forever! ⁷The royal administrators, prefects, satraps, advisers and governors have all agreed that the king should issue an edict and enforce the decree that anyone who prays to any god or man during the next thirty days, except to you, O king, shall be thrown into the lions' den. ⁸Now, O king, issue the decree and put it in writing so that it cannot be altered — in accordance with the laws of the Medes and Persians, which cannot be repealed." ⁹So King Darius put the decree in writing.

COMMENTARY

4–9 The king incites the jealousy of Daniel's colleagues because he "planned" (or more literally was "inclined" [v.3; Aram. ᶜšt; Redditt, 105; Lucas, 143]) to elevate Daniel to a place of supremacy in the kingdom. Implicitly, Darius bases his promotion of Daniel on his flawless character and professional abilities. These qualities are made explicit in the narrator's commentary on the failure of Daniel's detractors to "find" any grounds on which to bring charges against him. Specifically we are told that Daniel is honest, trustworthy, and reliable (v.4). In short, his impeccable record as a civil servant places him beyond indictment (v.5a).

Once aroused, the jealousy of Daniel's rivals festers until an alternative "solution" emerges. Whether for purposes of political self-preservation or ethnic cleansing, Daniel's critics become conspirators, and they hatch a plot to "find" another way to bring charges against the Hebrew diplomat. The collaborators in the conspiracy include the other two administrators or commissioners (v.4) and an unspecified number of the 120 satraps (probably a "handful" according to Miller, 179; but cf. Wills, 137–38, who assumes all the satraps are involved in the scheme and wonders how the lions' pit can hold such a crowd [cf. v.24]).

Since the conspirators can find no fault in Daniel's professional conduct, their assault against Daniel must shift to the personal sphere — namely, "something to do with the law of his God" (v.5b). According to Russell, 100, the word "law" (Aram. *dāt*; GK 10186) is the Aramaic equivalent of the Hebrew "Torah" or the revealed law of God. In context the phrase "law of his God" refers to the practice of law-keeping or "religion." The conspirators attempt to trap Daniel "in respect of private religious observances which, if performed without proper state authority, were indictable offenses and punishable by the laws of the land" (Russell, 100). Gowan, 96, considers the two words "law" and "petition" (Aram. *bᶜh*, "seek, request"; GK 10114) as key words in the narrative because "they point to the tension that runs through the story ... [that is] whose law must Daniel obey given his daily practice of prayer — the law of the Medes and Persians or the law of the living God (vv.20, 26)?"

The administrators and satraps go "as a group to the king" to set the trap for "religious" Daniel (v.6). The NIV's translation is weak here, as the verb (Aram. *rᵉgaš*; GK 10656) suggests both collusion (cf. NASB's "came by agreement") and agitation — "the implication is that these government officials are conspiring to agitate" (Seow, 89; "conspired and came," NRSV). Towner, 81, offers a vivid word picture when he says the word conveys some sense of "swarming." Baldwin, 128, has observed that "the writer is not claiming that Daniel was sinless, but only that he was law-abiding, and that his first allegiance was to his God." It is upon this question of loyalty or allegiance that Daniel's enemies seek to topple him "from the king's good graces" (Miller, 179).

The test matches Daniel's unquestioned loyalty to the state against his loyalty to God in an attempt to show "how his devotion to his job might be compromised when it is pitted against commitment to his religion" (Seow, 89; cf. Wallace, 114–15, on the "law-and-order trap"). The recommendation to the king is made all the more persuasive by the exaggerated claim that "all" the subordinate officials, from royal administrator, prefect, satrap, adviser, to governor, have endorsed the proposed edict (v.7; on these classes or ranks of officials, see Notes on 3:2).

The governmental officials have conspired and swarmed to the king for the purpose of encouraging the monarch to enact a law that will entrap Daniel (vv.7–9). Beyond this, they have presumed to specify the exact dictates of the law (no one may pray "to any god or man during the next thirty days, except to ... [the] king"; v.7b) and the commensurate punishment for violation (execution by exposure to wild beasts, i.e., a pit of lions; v.7c). In so doing, as Seow, 90, notes, they go beyond the astrologers and other royal advisers, who merely tattled on the three Hebrew insubordinates and left King Nebuchadnezzar to deal with the case as he saw fit (cf. 3:8–12).

What's more, the law is contradictory in that it is enacted for thirty days and yet is said to be irrevocable (v.8). Miller, 180, following Montgomery, 270, and others, understands that the decree to pray to the king alludes to the role of the priests through whom petitions were mediated to the gods — "thus Darius was to be the only priestly mediator during this period." There is no extant record of the use of wild-animal pits for the execution of criminals in the ancient Near East, prompting Redditt, 107, to comment that both the law and the punishment are exceptional.

This ploy by the conspirators is obviously designed to play on the king's pride — "to boost his ego and give expression to his new authority" (Baldwin, 128). The narrative reports the episode by ascribing a sense of urgency among the petition-ers, who seek the immediate issuing of the decree in writing (v.8). Presumably they fear the king may see through their devious scheme if given time for thoughtful reflection on the matter. The idea of the immutability of "the law of the Medes and Persians," also mentioned in Esther (Est 1:19; 8:8), has been challenged by some biblical scholars (e.g., Collins, *Daniel*, 267–68; Gowan, 98; Redditt, 107). Lacocque, 113, finds supporting evidence in the Roman histo-rian Diodorus Siculus for the accuracy of Daniel's statement. (Compare *BBCOT*, 739, Miller, 181, and Lucas, 150, who emphasizes the need to distinguish between Persian "law" and "custom.")

Thus, gullible Darius gets hoodwinked into compliance with the requests of Daniel's conspira-tors and posthaste puts the decree in writing (v.9). Goldingay, 131, speculates that Darius is either a "victim of his own vanity" or enamored with the idea of "quasi-divine authority," given the advan-tages it held for his leadership of the state. Porteous, 90, is probably correct to remark that Darius has the document drafted by royal scribes and then affixes his seal to authorize it (v.9).

NOTE

7 Persian kings were not inclined to self-deification (cf. *BBCOT*, 739), so some scholars suggest that the background for Darius's edict is some sort of "intramural" religious squabble between the advocates of a pure Zoroastrianism and those who favor a more syncretistic religion (e.g., the Magi; cf. J. H. Walton, "The Decree of Darius the Mede in Daniel 6," *JETS* 31 [1988]: 282–85; Gowan, 97–98). Such specula-tion assumes what is known about Zoroastrianism from the later Achaemenid period applies to the early history of the religion. Beyond that, there is the problem of "how early," given the uncertainty as to the identity of Darius the Mede. Historically, "religion" in the biblical world was frequently used to manipu-late kings for the sake of personal or professional advantage—with or without the pretense of some "ideo-logical" issue that must be addressed for the sake of social stability in the kingdom.

The Aramaic word גֹּב (*gōb*; translated lions' "den," NIV, NASB), refers to a "pit" (cf. Lucas, 150). The pit envisaged here seems to be an underground, cavern-like cavity (Daniel has to be "lifted" out; vv.22–23) with two entrances: a ramp down which the animals might enter and a small opening in the roof for feed-ing purposes (cf. Baldwin, 130).

3. Daniel Accused and Condemned (6:10–18 [6:11–19])

¹⁰Now when Daniel learned that the decree had been published, he went home to his upstairs room where the windows opened toward Jerusalem. Three times a day he got down on his knees and prayed, giving thanks to his God, just as he had done before. ¹¹Then these men went as a group and found Daniel praying and asking God for help. ¹²So they went to the king and spoke to him about his royal decree: "Did you not publish a decree that during the next thirty days anyone who prays to any god or man except to you, O king, would be thrown into the lions' den?"

The king answered, "The decree stands — in accordance with the laws of the Medes and Persians, which cannot be repealed."

[13]Then they said to the king, "Daniel, who is one of the exiles from Judah, pays no attention to you, O king, or to the decree you put in writing. He still prays three times a day." [14]When the king heard this, he was greatly distressed; he was determined to rescue Daniel and made every effort until sundown to save him.

[15]Then the men went as a group to the king and said to him, "Remember, O king, that according to the law of the Medes and Persians no decree or edict that the king issues can be changed."

[16]So the king gave the order, and they brought Daniel and threw him into the lions' den. The king said to Daniel, "May your God, whom you serve continually, rescue you!"

[17]A stone was brought and placed over the mouth of the den, and the king sealed it with his own signet ring and with the rings of his nobles, so that Daniel's situation might not be changed. [18]Then the king returned to his palace and spent the night without eating and without any entertainment being brought to him. And he could not sleep.

COMMENTARY

10–13 No doubt when Daniel learns "that the decree had been published" (v.10a) he knows it is directed primarily against him. Yet he is not dissuaded from maintaining his daily discipline of prayer (v.10b). Naturally, Daniel's enemies count on his being resolute in this matter of his "personal religion," and they plant themselves outside Daniel's home waiting to catch him in the act of defying the king's edict by praying to "another god" (v.11). Miller, 183, rightly implies that despite the gravity of the situation, there is a humorous side to this scene of the story — "dignified" governmental officials spying on Daniel.

Once they have garnered the necessary evidence against Daniel, the conspirators come "in a throng" (so Collins, *Daniel*, 269; see the discussion of the Aram. r^{e}gaš in v.6) to verify (by trapping the king in his own testimony; so Seow, 91) that the edict and the requisite punishment for its violation are still in force (v.12). Then the officials bring formal charges against Daniel for breaking the king's edict by praying to his own God three times a day (v.13). The accusation leveled against Daniel echoes the charge levied against Daniel's three Hebrew colleagues in that it insinuates that this act of insubordination makes Daniel a dangerous subversive, "who pays no attention to you" (v.13; cf. 3:12), and thus a threat to the stability of the kingdom.

The direction of Daniel's prayer (facing the Jerusalem temple; v.10) is based on the injunctions mentioned in Solomon's prayer at the dedication of the temple (i.e., "pray toward this place"; 1Ki 8:35, 38, 44, 48). The custom of praying three times a day probably stems from the psalmist who cried out to God evening, morning, and midday (Ps 55:17), perhaps an indication that this had become a traditional pattern of prayer by the time of Daniel. Many different prayer postures are mentioned in the OT, and while particular postures and gestures are not commanded, they are always conditioned by the mood, content, and circumstance of the prayer. Kneeling is the posture in which a person is the most "defenseless," and in prayer it is a symbol of dependence, humility, and contrition before God.

Porteous, 90, comments that Daniel is not "flaunting his religion" by immediately retiring to his home to pray, but rather "a man like Daniel was not prepared to lower his flag when trouble threatened." Daniel learned early on in his experience as a Hebrew exile in Babylon to entrust crisis situations to God in prayer, and as an octogenarian he is not going to abandon that resource now (cf. 2:18).

Daniel's custom is to pray and give thanks to his God (v.10). Goldingay, 131, sees two major aspects of prayer in the report, that of intercession (perhaps for the government in which he served and for exiled Israel) and confession (in the sense that Daniel offers "thanksgiving" because he knows God hears and answers prayer). Beyond this, Daniel asks God for help (v.11) or seeks mercy (Aram. *hnn*, "to show favor, grace"; GK 10274) "in contravention of the law against petitioning anyone other than the king" (Seow, 91). It is also possible that Daniel is praying for other Jews who might be targeted by the king's edict, since he well understands that he belongs to the Hebrew covenantal community (cf. 9:5 and the repetition of the first-person plural "we"). As in his previous tests of loyalty (e.g., 1:8), Daniel remains true to God despite the high personal risk. The confession of the three Hebrews before Nebuchadnezzar in the episode of the blazing furnace could be Daniel's confession as well (3:16–18). Like the apostles of Jesus several centuries later, Daniel knows he "must obey God rather than men" (Ac 5:29).

14–18 The indictment of Daniel "greatly distressed" the king (v.14a), though Goldingay (121, n.15a, 132) contends the more natural understanding of the word (Aram. *bᵊʾēš*) is "displeased." The reason or source for the king's distress or displeasure is unspecified, but he may have been angry with Daniel for ignoring his edict, or upset that Daniel is now under a charge of sedition. More likely, he is distressed by the plot concocted by Daniel's conspirators and his own naiveté in being duped by subordinates. Darius spends the daylight hours seeking to rescue or "deliver" (NASB) Daniel, but no information is given as to what options may have been open to the king (v.14b). Miller, 184, deduces that Daniel must have been observed praying at midday, so the king has only the afternoon to secure Daniel's release, and Seow, 92, suggests that an investigation or formal trial may have been among the options that Darius might pursue in an effort to stay Daniel's execution. The king's diligence in seeking to rescue Daniel ("he was determined ... and made every effort"; v.14) is commendable and indicates Daniel is well liked by Darius (even his "favorite" according to Seow, 92; cf. v.3).

The attempt by Darius to rescue Daniel unsettles the conspirators, for they come "thronging" or "swarming" back to the king for a third time (v.15). Even as these enemies of Daniel presume to know the content of Daniel's prayer(s), they now presume to instruct the king on "law enforcement." For the third time in the story, reference is made to the irrevocable law of the Medes and Persians (v.15b; cf. vv.8, 12). The law is the law, and the king has no choice but to order Daniel's execution (v.16). Interestingly, the king complies with his own law in having Daniel thrown into the lions' pit (v.16a) but then violates his own edict by invoking the name of Daniel's God in his petition that his choice servant be delivered (v.16b).

The scene reveals how jealousy breeds hatred and that the real issue for Daniel's rivals is removing him permanently from any position of authority (cf. Baldwin, 130: "the tyrants would not permit the king to play for time" but pressure the king to carry out the death sentence that very day). One wonders whether Darius, in his affirmation of Daniel's loyal service to his Hebrew God (v.16b), understands any direct relationship between that and his honesty, integrity, reliability, and competence as a civil servant in the royal bureaucracy.

Daniel's fate is sealed, literally by a stone barrier placed over the opening of the lions' pit and then by seal impressions from the signet rings of Darius and his nobles (v.17). The two acts serve to heighten the foreshadowing of Darius's petition in v.16 for the divine deliverance of Daniel because human intervention is now impossible—the situation cannot be changed (v.17b). Seow, 93, observes that the double sealing of the stone (v.17) "ensures that neither side will be able to rig the outcome of Daniel's trial in the pit" (since the king and Daniel's friends are unable to rescue him, and the nobles will be unable to kill him if somehow the lions do not).

The king's distress over Daniel's predicament—one Darius himself has created by issuing the edict—induces such anxiety that he is unable to eat ("fasting," NASB). Goldingay (121, n. 19a) and Lucas, 144, consider this normal deprivation of food but not religious fasting (though the king's failure to eat is interpreted by some as "fasting and praying"; cf. Miller, 186; Smith-Christopher, 93). Neither does the king seek enjoyment in any forms of royal entertainment (or "diversions"; so Russell, 105), nor does he sleep the night (lit., "his sleep fled from him," NASB; v.18). The king's self-denial and misery are perhaps another sign of the depth of feeling he has for Daniel (cf. Pr 14:35, "a king delights in a wise servant"; 22:11, "he who loves a pure heart and whose speech is gracious will have the king for a friend").

NOTES

10 The "upstairs room" of Daniel's house may indicate his high status (cf. Goldingay, 129; Miller, 182). According to J. J. Slotki (*Ezra–Nehemiah–Daniel* [London: Soncino, 1951], 49), "this was not an attic but a room on the flat roof of the house. These rooms were, and still are, common in the East, being used as private apartments to which one retired when wishing to be undisturbed. They usually had latticed windows which allowed free circulation of air."

17 The "signet ring" was an engraved stone set on a ring or inscribed stone worn as a ring or on a chain cord around the neck (cf. Redditt, 110). Each person's seal was carved with distinctive symbols (usually some combination of pictures and words), making the signet the equivalent of one's personal mark or "signature." Miller, 185–86, suggests that "soft clay was attached to the chains draped over the stone, and the king and his nobles made their personal marks (seals) by pressing their rings to the clay. After the clay hardened, the chains could not be removed without breaking the seal." The door of Bel's temple is sealed with the king's signet ring in the story of Bel and the Serpent in the Additions to Daniel (14:14).

18 There is no agreement on the forms of "entertainment" (NIV, NASB) King Darius shuns while keeping vigil during Daniel's night in the lions' pit because the meaning of the Aramaic דַּחֲוָן (*dah⁺wān*) is unknown (so Lucas, 144). Special food, musicians, dancing girls, and concubines are among the suggested royal "diversions" the king rejects because of his distress over Daniel's fate (see Montgomery, 277–78).

4. Daniel's Deliverance (6:19–24 [6:20–25])

> [19]At the first light of dawn, the king got up and hurried to the lions' den. [20]When he came near the den, he called to Daniel in an anguished voice, "Daniel, servant of the living God, has your God, whom you serve continually, been able to rescue you from the lions?"
>
> [21]Daniel answered, "O king, live forever! [22]My God sent his angel, and he shut the mouths of the lions. They have not hurt me, because I was found innocent in his sight. Nor have I ever done any wrong before you, O king."
>
> [23]The king was overjoyed and gave orders to lift Daniel out of the den. And when Daniel was lifted from the den, no wound was found on him, because he had trusted in his God.
>
> [24]At the king's command, the men who had falsely accused Daniel were brought in and thrown into the lions' den, along with their wives and children. And before they reached the floor of the den, the lions overpowered them and crushed all their bones.

COMMENTARY

19–24 The king's anxiety over Daniel's fate is captured in three expressions: "at first light of dawn" ("at dawn, at the break of day," NASB; v.19a; cf. Hartman and Di Lella, 196), "the king … hurried" ("went in haste," NASB; v.19b), and "he called … in an anguished voice" ("he cried out with a troubled voice," NASB; v.20a). Lacocque, 118, wonders whether the king's hasty return to the lions' pit early the next morning should be viewed in the light of the Babylonian custom that the victim would be pardoned if he were tortured and had not died by the following day. Miller, 186, interprets the subsequent events to "indicate that this must have been the practice involved here."

Darius identifies Daniel as a "servant of the living God" (v.20b). This epithet for God is often used in the OT for the God of Israel as the true God (Jer 10:10; 23:36; cf. Seow, 93). Goldingay, 133, states that "this rich OT title for God suggests not merely that God is alive rather than dead, but that he is active and powerful, awesome and almighty, involved in bringing judgment and blessing." The

repetition of Daniel as one who serves God continually (v.20; cf. v.16) accents the constancy of his character and anticipates the rationale for his vindication as one "innocent" before God (v.22). Reddit, 110, appropriately summarizes, "the martyr story was broken; God turned out to be the 'living God' as Darius had hoped (v.16)." Seow, 93, surmises that Darius's acknowledgment of Daniel's deity as the "living God" is tantamount to a confession of faith, albeit a tentative one (cf. Miller, 186–87).

Ironically, Daniel greets the king with the same address, "O king, live forever" (v.21), as that proffered earlier by his accusers (v.6). They had "swarmed" to the king seeking Daniel's death; but hauntingly, Daniel's formal response to the king's question provides dramatic testimony that their nemesis still lives (cf. Lacocque, 117, on the LXX's "O king, I am alive"). This is the only time in the book of Daniel that a Hebrew addresses a foreign king with the salutation "live forever." According to Seow, 93, given the reference to the "living God" in the context, "the phrase serves to link and to subsume the life of the king to the will of the God from whom life derives and on whom life depends" (cf. Goldingay, 133: "Daniel's prayer that Darius may do so [i.e., 'live forever'] both honors and relativizes Darius's kingship by the interweaving of references to the living God with those to the living king").

Daniel's vindication is acknowledged at two levels. First, he is found "innocent" before God (v.22a); and second, his survival of the lion-pit ordeal proves he is guiltless of any wrongdoing before the king ("I have committed no crime," NASB; v.22b). According to Lucas, 144, the word "innocent" (Aram. *zākû*) is a legal term signifying formal acquittal, probably borrowed from Akkadian (cf. *CAD*, 21:23-25). Redditt, 111, notes that technically Daniel "was guilty of breaking the king's law, but was not disloyal to the king in so doing." The narrator reports both the king's joy at discovering Daniel has survived the ordeal (v.23a) and the reason for it—"he had trusted in his God" (v.23b; on the "ordeal" in the biblical world see Longman, 163). The verbal root for "trust" (Aram./Heb. *ʾmn*; GK 586. 10041) means to "have faith, to believe" in theological contexts in the sense of "standing fast" (cf. *THAT*, 1:142). Wood, 173, deduces that "the mention of trust at this point suggests that after their inspection, the examiners came to recognize this trust as having accounted for the miracle."

The agent of Daniel's deliverance was an "angel" of God (v.22). Naturally, scholarly speculation abounds as to the identity of this being who shut the mouths of lions, apparently visible to Daniel. Whether Daniel's divine rescuer was a member of the angelic host (so Hartman and Di Lella, 200) or "the angel of the LORD" himself (so Miller, 187) is not the point; rather, the text means to convey that the "angel" is "nothing other than the very presence of God, as the LXX has well understood" (Lacocque, 118; cf. the LXX's "God ... closed the lions' mouths"). The moral of the story is not the deliverance of the righteous from the "jaws" of death, but "the fulfilling of God's purpose" (Goldingay, 134). Seow, 94, observes that much like Daniel's three friends, Daniel, too, experiences the divine presence in the midst of trial—thus suggesting "that God knows what transpires on earth and God does respond whenever God wills."

The king's retributive act of throwing those who had "maliciously accused" (NASB; v.24) Daniel into the lions' pit is one of the more gruesome passages of the Bible, as these conspirators are ripped apart by the wild beasts before they reach "the floor of the den" (v.24b). The execution of the wives and children of Daniel's defamers as accomplices in the conspiracy strikes the modern reader as cruel and unjust. Yet Collins (*Daniel*, 271) observes that such practice "follows the ancient custom of corporate responsibility, rather than the ideal of individual responsibility" (cf. Jos 7; see discussion in Longman, 163-64). Baldwin, 131, comments that the Bible simply records the event "as a fact, without either approval or disapproval."

The miracle of Daniel's emergence from the lions' pit without "wound" (NIV) or "injury" (NASB) is rooted in the original creation mandate giving humanity dominion over the animal kingdom (Ge 1:26). According to the Hebrew prophets, harmony between humanity and the animals and within the animal kingdom itself will be restored in the eschaton (Isa 11:6; 65:25; Eze 34:25; Hos 2:18). Baldwin, 131, projects that "in the man of God [i.e., Daniel] the powers of the world to come have broken in, in anticipation of what will be when the king comes to reign." This may explain, in part, the inclusion of summary statements of both stories of court conflict from Daniel (the three Hebrews and the blazing furnace in ch. 3 and Daniel and the lions' pit in ch. 6) in the so-called "honor roll of OT faith" found in Hebrews 11:33–34. Daniel and his three friends are among those of the great cloud of OT witnesses who point to "Jesus, the author and perfecter of our faith" (Heb 12:2).

NOTE

24 Goldingay, 129, and Redditt, 111, among other commentators, erroneously assume the other two administrators and all 120 of the satraps are party to the conspiracy against Daniel, raising the question of logistics with respect to the number of individuals thrown into the lions' pit and the reasonable size of such a pit. Nowhere does the text explicitly cite "all" these officials as coconspirators, and logic would suggest that the contention of Young, 138, that "the plot was the work of a few men," better represents the reality of the situation.

5. Darius's Letter of Proclamation and Doxology (6:25–28 [6:26–29])

25Then King Darius wrote to all the peoples, nations and men of every language throughout the land:
"May you prosper greatly!
26"I issue a decree that in every part of my kingdom people must fear and reverence the God of Daniel.

"For he is the living God
    and he endures forever;
his kingdom will not be destroyed,
    his dominion will never end.
27 He rescues and he saves;
    he performs signs and wonders
    in the heavens and on the earth.
He has rescued Daniel
    from the power of the lions."

28So Daniel prospered during the reign of Darius and the reign of Cyrus the Persian.

COMMENTARY

25–27 Like his predecessor King Nebuchadnezzar (see comments on 4:1–3), King Darius writes a royal letter (v.25a), or "epistle," since publication is intended for a "universal audience" (i.e., the peoples of his vast realm; cf. Collins, *Daniel: with an Introduction to Apocalyptic Literature*, 61, 72). The letter is Darius's personal confession of his own experience with Daniel's God, Darius having witnessed Daniel's miraculous deliverance from the lions' pit. According to Goldingay, 129, whether or not King Darius "converted" to the Hebrew religion is not the point; rather, it is his confession acknowledging the living, eternal, saving, and active power of Daniel's God—an affirmation desperately needed by the Hebrews enduring the dark days of Babylonian exile (cf. Porteous, 92).

Both royal epistles offer the same greeting or salutation, "may you prosper greatly" (v.25b; see comments on 4:1–3). The formal proclamation of Darius here (vv.26–27) contains the additional literary forms of decree, commanding the subjects of his kingdom to respect the God of Daniel (v.26a). Both "encyclicals" (as Seow, 95, labels them) conclude with a doxology in praise of the God of the Hebrews (vv.26b–27). The hymnic language of the doxology justifies the poetic format of the king's decree in the more recent English translations.

The decree of Darius that his subjects must hold "the God of Daniel" in awe is stated more positively than the decree of Nebuchadnezzar that threatened dismemberment to anyone who defamed "the God of Shadrach, Meshach, and Abednego" (3:29). To "fear" (lit., "tremble," Aram. *zûaʿ*) and "reverence" (lit., "fear," Aram. *dᵉḥal*) God mean to both "respect Him and recognize that they could be hurt by Him, Darius thus admitting that this God's power extended far beyond the boundaries of Judah" (Wood, 175). The decree of Darius serves two purposes: first, it gives official sanction to the God of the Hebrews as a legitimate and even superior deity to the gods of the Babylonian pantheon; and second, it rescinds the "irrevocable" edict that Darius had earlier published forbidding petition to anyone but the king (cf. Redditt, 112). How ironic, as Seow, 95, observes, that "now the king himself publicizes to the world the reversal of his supposedly unchangeable edict, for God has brought about the change."

The doxology of Darius repeats the epithet "the living God" (v.26b; cf. v.20), whereas Nebuchad-

nezzar makes reference to the Most High God (4:2). The reference to God as "the living God" not only contrasts Yahweh with the lifeless gods of the nations (e.g., Jer 16:18; Hab 2:19) but also calls attention to his capacity to preserve life as a God who saves and rescues his followers (v.27a). The doxology of Darius extols the eternality of God and the indestructibility of his kingdom, echoing the affirmation of Nebuchadnezzar (4:3). Like Nebuchadnezzar, Darius also testifies to God's ability to perform "signs and wonders" (v.27a; see comments on 4:1–3). Lastly, God's power to perform signs and wonders is applied specifically to his rescue of Daniel "from the power of the lions" (v.27b).

Both royal epistles make the same claim—God alone is sovereign, and "he does as he pleases with the powers of heaven and the peoples of the earth" (4:35; cf. Seow, 95). Perhaps for the Hebrews in Babylonian captivity the testimony by a pagan king to God's power to perform signs and wonders and deliver his people stirred thoughts of the "signs and wonders" associated with the exodus from Egypt and the possibility of a "second exodus" (cf. Lucas, 153).

28 Baldwin, 132, observes that the chapter ends with "an enigmatic note connecting the reign of Darius with that of Cyrus," understanding that the conjunction "and" (NIV, NASB) actually conveys the explicative force of "namely" or "that is" (i.e., "during the reign of Darius, *namely*, Cyrus the Persian"). Thus the writer explains to the reader that the two names, "Darius" and "Cyrus," belong to the same person. Given the current state of scholarship on the book of Daniel, this solution is as plausible as any of the attempts to identify the "King Darius" mentioned in ch. 6. The approach has merit in that it unifies the court-stories section of the book by forming an envelope construction with the reference to Cyrus in 1:21 (cf. Lucas, 153).

NOTES

26 Lucas, 145, notes that Qumran documents (4QDan[b]) support the more difficult reading "a living God" also found in the LXX(θ). This suggests that Darius's decree merely elevates Yahweh, as God of the Hebrews, to the status of other "living gods" (i.e., his own Babylonian pantheon?).

II. DANIEL'S VISIONS (7:1–12:13)

A. The Four Beasts (7:1–28)

OVERVIEW

Daniel's dream of the four beasts rising out of the sea described in ch. 7 begins the "visions" or "apocalyptic" section of the book (chs. 7–12). The chapter also completes the Aramaic portion of the book, the messages to the Gentile nations (2:4–7:28). This unit of the narrative of Daniel's experience as a captive in Babylon ends as it began, with a vision of four world kingdoms that come to an end and then are replaced by a fifth (cf. Seow, 99–100, on the similarities and differences between chs. 2 and 7). The widely recognized chiastic arrangement of the Aramaic passages of the book demonstrates the inverted structure of the messages to the Gentile nations (see "Structure and Unity" in the introduction):

A A dream about four world kingdoms
   replaced by a fifth (2:4b–49)
  B Three friends in the fiery furnace
     (3:1–30)
    C Daniel interprets a dream for Nebu-
       chadnezzar (4:1–37)
    C' Daniel interprets the handwriting on
       the wall for Belshazzar (5:1–31)
  B' Daniel in the lions' den (6:1–28)
A' A vision about four world kingdoms
   replaced by a fifth (7:1–28)

Commentators are unanimous in their assessment of the importance of Daniel 7 as both a transitional and pivotal chapter in the book (e.g., Seow, 99). The chapter is transitional in terms of the literary architecture of the book because it marks the shift from the narrative genre of court story (chs. 1–6) to the apocalyptic genre of vision (chs. 7–12; cf. Towner, 91). Longman has summarized the themes of chs. 7–12 under six headings: (1) human evil is horrible; (2) a specific time of deliverance (for the Jews from oppression) is announced; (3) repentance leads to deliverance; (4) a cosmic war stands behind human conflict; (5) judgment is certain for those who resist God and oppress his people; and (6) equally true is the fact that God's people will experience new life. The "visions" half of the book also denotes the change in genre and point-of-view from "report" in the third-person voice to that of "diary" or "personal journal" in the first-person voice. Last, the transitional nature of ch. 7 is observed in its relationship to chs. 2–6 as part of the Aramaic portion of the book and in its relationship to chs. 8–12 by way of the subject matter (cf. Collins, *Daniel: with an Introduction to Apocalyptic Literature*, 80).

The chapter is also pivotal in terms of audience since the message of the visions is directed toward the Hebrews, especially the group known as the *maśkîlîm* (or those "wise"; cf. 11:33, 35; 12:3, 10), rather than the Gentile nations (cf. Seow, 99). The setting of the visions moves from an emphasis on Daniel in the foreign setting of Babylon "to the fate of Jerusalem and the community living there" (Redditt, 115). Beyond this, the topic or subject matter of the eternal kingdom of the Ancient of Days is developed specifically with a view toward "the saints of the Most High" (v.22). The chapter also introduces the notoriously difficult "son of man" figure in the OT (vv.13–14). In addition, ch. 7 (and the visions section of the book) is important because of its place in the development of proto-apocalyptic prophetic literature in the OT and its influence on later Jewish apocalyptic literature. Finally, ch. 7 is pivotal for the role it plays in the issue of predictive prophecy (versus *ex eventu* prophecy) in the OT.

The literary form of ch. 7 is symbolic vision account encapsulated in a dream report (so Lucas, 163). Collins (*Daniel: with an Introduction to Apocalyptic Literature*, 78) identifies the additional subgenres of "throne vision" (vv.9–10), "description of judgment scene" (vv.11–15), and (characteristic of critical scholarship on Daniel) "*ex eventu* prophecy" with reference to Antiochus IV Epiphanes (vv.23–25). The basic structure of the chapter is widely recognized and may be outlined as follows:

1. Introduction (v.1)
2. Dream Report (vv.2–14)
3. Interpretation of the Dream in Two Parts (vv.15–27)
4. Four Kingdoms (vv.15–18)
5. Fourth Beast (vv.19–27)
6. Conclusion (v.28)

According to Lucas, 165, the structure of the chapter "makes clear what it is that the author wants to emphasize." The dream report (vv.2–14)

is a palistrophe (i.e., a chiastic literary device that inverts or counterbalances key themes hinging on one fundamental teaching or idea), and the throne scene (vv.9–11) stands at the center of the vision report of the four beasts. "Human kings may seem to be free to rampage at will, but there is a throne in heaven and One on it to whom they are ultimately subject" (Lucas, 165). Goldingay, 154, notes that the lengthy opening formula (v.11a) serves to highlight the announcement of divine judgment of the "little horn" (v.11b). The poetic form of vv.13–14 at the close of the palistrophic vision report (vv.2–14) accents the establishment of the everlasting kingdom as "the climax of the vision" (Lucas, 165). Finally, the repetition of the judgment of the "little horn" and the establishment of the everlasting kingdom in the interpretation of the dream (vv.26–27) reiterate the climax of Daniel's symbolic vision.

Biblical scholars still debate the historical validity of Daniel's vision of the four beasts as reported in the date formula of the introduction (v.1). Conservative scholars accept the report as an account of an authentic vision experienced by Daniel set at the beginning of the coregency of Nabonidus and Belshazzar (ca. 553 BC; e.g., Miller, 194). Baldwin, 138, courageously rejects the "literary device" approach and avers, "we shall treat them [i.e., the visions] as direct revelations from God to Daniel." By contrast, critical scholars tend to regard the dream or vision reports as simply a literary device employed by a later writer. For example, Goldingay, 157, discounts ch. 7 as "an actual predictive vision from the sixth century" and instead identifies the pericope as "a quasi-predictive vision deriving from the period on which it focuses" (i.e., the actions of Antiochus IV Epiphanes in mid-167 BC). Redditt, 116, and Gowan, 105, are representative of more recent critical scholarship assigning the setting and date of ch. 7 to the action of Antiochus IV Epiphanes against Jerusalem in 167 BC.

Like Porteous, 96, some critical scholars still struggle with the literary integrity or unity of ch. 7 (see the discussion in Collins, *Daniel*, 277–80; cf. Redditt's three-redactor hypothesis, 114–16). Lucas, 167, is more cautious. He typifies a growing trend for appreciation of the literary artistry of the Bible and notes that "there is less willingness than there used to be to assume that repetition, variation, and unevenness are evidence of more than one hand at work. These features can often be explained as deliberate rhetorical features" (cf. Smith-Christopher, 100, who admits only vv.21–22 as a possible later addition to ch. 7, "if any"; and Seow, who takes a "final form" literary approach and omits any discussion of the unity of ch. 7). On the textual issues in Daniel 7, including a discussion of the variances between the Hebrew MT and the Greek LXX, see Lacocque, 135–37, 149–51; Goldingay, 143–46; and Lucas, 160–63.

Daniel's vision consisted of a series of animals rising out of a churning sea (vv.2–3). The first three beasts (vv.3–6) are well-known creatures of the animal kingdom in the biblical world (albeit each with some unusual variation in appearance): a lion (with eagle's wings and human feet), a bear (with ribs in its mouth), and a leopard (with four heads and four wings). Esoteric symbolism is typically listed as one of the characteristic features of the genre of apocalyptic literature (cf. Collins, *Daniel*, 54–56; see "Literary Form" in the introduction). Considerable ink has been spilled in attempts to identify the source or sources behind the image of Daniel's vision in ch. 7. Among the "usual suspects" in the lineup are the Babylonian creation myths (especially the *Enuma Elish*) and Canaanite mythology (especially the Baal and Yamm cycle; see the summaries in Collins, *Daniel*, 280–94; Lucas, 167–76; J. H. Walton, "The Anzu Myth as Relevant Background for Daniel 7?" in *The Book of Daniel*, ed. J. J. Collins and P. W. Flint [Leiden: Brill, 2002], 1:69–89).

Russell, 115, cautions against seeing any wholesale dependence of Daniel's account on the sources of Babylonian mythology or reading into it the "meanings and nuances" of the Babylonian creation stories. He goes on to say that "the writer is taking over the stock-in-trade of symbolic imagery handed down in those religious circles in which he moved, using them to convey a message relevant to his own day affirming the victory of God over evil forces ranged against him and his faithful people." Walton ("The Anzu Myth," 88) concurs, at least to the extent that the imagery of Daniel's vision represents "an informed and articulate literary mosaic whose author has assimilated and mastered a wide spectrum of literary traditions in order to transform them to his own theological will and purpose."

According to Towner, 94, although the beasts of the animal allegory may have had their origin in the myths of the ancient Near East, they have been stripped of their mythic character and "have become arbitrary symbols for a succession of historical kingdoms." Russell, 115–16, equates those kingdoms not with the malevolent powers associated with the Babylonian creation epics but rather with "those brute forces of evil which become only too evident in the unfolding of history—kings and rulers who tyrannise the people of God, empires and kingdoms which terrify for a time but whose 'doom is writ.'"

Naturally, the extensive symbolism in Daniel's vision gives rise to multiple interpretations of the imagery. For example, critical scholars tend to identify the kingdoms represented by the four animals of Daniel's vision as Babylonia, Media, Persia, and Greece (e.g., Redditt, 119; Porteous, 105–6), while conservative or traditional scholars equate the animals with Babylonia, Media-Persia, Greece, and Rome (e.g., Baldwin, 147; Miller, 198–203). Likewise, the "little horn" (v.8) is variously viewed as a reference to the Seleucid king Antiochus IV Epiphanes (e.g., Lacocque, 141; Collins, *Daniel*, 299) or the Antichrist (e.g., Archer, 87; Young, 150). Finally, the figure of the "son of man" is considered alternately as the archangel Michael (e.g., Collins, *Daniel*, 310); the angel Gabriel; a lesser, unnamed angel; a Davidic king; a priestly figure; the nation of Israel; and so on (see the discussion in Collins, *Daniel*, 304–10; Redditt, 127; see the next section on "Understanding Visionary Literature").

Understanding Visionary Literature. Biblical proto-apocalyptic literature and its later offshoot, intertestamental Jewish apocalyptic literature, are visionary genres given to interpretation of current events and prediction of future events in symbols, ciphers, and codes—usually by means of angelic mediation (e.g., 7:16; 8:16). As such they represent subcategories of the genre of prophecy in the larger scheme of hermeneutics or biblical interpretation. Apocalyptic literature is "crisis" literature, typically conveying specific messages to particular groups of people caught up in dire situations. Several basic questions are helpful in interpreting visionary literature in the Bible: Who is addressed? By whom? When? In what setting? For what reason? What is the relationship of the passage under investigation to the rest of the Bible?

Visionary literature announces an end to the way things are and opens up alternative possibilities to the audience as a result of God's impending intervention in human affairs. Three types of messages are usually associated with the visionary literature of the Bible: (1) a message of encouragement to the oppressed; (2) a warning to the oppressor; and (3) a call to faith for those wavering between God's truth and human "wisdom."

Visionary literature portrays settings, characters, and events in ways different from ordinary reality. While the visions *depict* literal events, the symbolic descriptions do not necessarily *represent* the events literally. Leland Ryken (*How To Read the Bible as Literature* [Grand Rapids: Zondervan, 1984], 165–74) offers helpful guidelines for reading and understanding visionary literature:

- Be ready for the reversal of the ordinary.
- Be prepared to use your imagination to picture a world that transcends earthly reality.
- Be prepared for a series of diverse, self-contained units that tend to be kaleidoscopic in nature (instead of looking for a smooth flow of narrative).
- Seek to identify the historical event or theological reality in salvation history represented by the symbolism in the passage; to do so, observe the obvious, grasp the total scene, and do not press every detail of the vision for hidden meaning.
- Read widely in visionary literature (both biblical visionary literature and extrabiblical fantasy literature).
- Recognize the element of mystery and the supernatural quality of the Bible (and be willing humbly to admit that an exact understanding of a given vision may be beyond us).

Finally, visionary literature in the Bible has given rise to four major interpretive approaches to the understanding of the time-orientation of the divine revelation. The *preterist* approach views all the events described in the visions as past. By contrast, the *futurist* sees the events portrayed in the visions as yet come. The *historicist* appeals to the visions to trace the ideological or theological development of an age or an era (e.g., the history of Israel or the church age). The *idealist* understands the vision as a symbolic representation of the timeless conflict between good and evil (see W. W. Klein, C. L. Blomberg, and R. L. Hubbard, *Introduction to Biblical Interpretation* [Dallas: Word, 1993],

292–312, 369–74). The commentary below offers brief summaries of the both the *preterist* and the *futurist* understandings of Daniel's visions where appropriate.

1. Introduction (7:1)

> ¹In the first year of Belshazzar king of Babylon, Daniel had a dream, and visions passed through his mind as he was lying on his bed. He wrote down the substance of his dream.

COMMENTARY

1 The date formula locates Daniel's vision of the animals rising out of the sea to the first year of King Belshazzar's reign (v.1a). Belshazzar's first year would have been the initial year of the coregency he exercised in Babylon during the decade his father Nabonidus spent in Tema (Arabia; see comments on 5:1–4). Neo-Babylonian documents indicate that Nabonidus, during the third year of his reign, entrusted the kingship to his son Belshazzar (cf. Miller, 194). His rule commenced about 556 BC, meaning his third year would date approximately to 553 BC (cf. Baldwin, 138, who places the date at 552/551 BC).

Daniel's experience (v.1) is described both as a dream (Aram. *ḥēlem*) and as visions (Aram. *ḥᵉzû*) passing through his mind. According to Redditt, 117, the difference between dreams and visions is clear, since "dreams typically come while one is asleep, while visions come while one is in a state of altered consciousness." The fact that Daniel is "lying on his bed" (but apparently not asleep) suggests his experience has the character of a vision (cf. Lucas, 177). Daniel is also a participant in what he sees by speaking with a member of the heavenly court—another characteristic of the visionary-type experience. Daniel's two subsequent experiences relate to the reception of divine revelation are described as visions (8:1; 10:1).

Verse 1 also records that Daniel "wrote down the substance of his dream." The precedent of writing down such revelations is established in the earlier Hebrew prophets (e.g., Isa 8:1; Jer 30:2; Eze 43:11). The documentation of prophetic dreams, visions, and oracles made the prophecies more concrete and facilitated their dissemination to the intended audience. Beyond this, as Goldingay, 160, observes, putting the revelation in writing "made prophecy, prophet, and God open to vindication: the written word was fixed and could be tested by events."

NOTE

1–2 A "vision" (Aram./Heb. חזה, *ḥzh*; GK 10256) sometimes entails "the experience of seeing images in a revelatory dream" (J. A. Naudé, " חזה," *NIDOTTE*, 2:58). The visual manifestation of the vision was designed to complement the revelation of the divine word, enabling the "seer" to proclaim God's message with authority. The primary emphasis in the revelatory vision, however, "was on the revelation of the divine word" (ibid.). The seeing of a vision was a divine gift granted by God to his chosen messengers. The word "vision" is often associated with the OT prophets (e.g., Jer 14:14; 23:16; La 2:9; Mic 3:6), although Daniel himself is not designated a "prophet" (Heb. נָבִיא, *nābîʾ*).

2. Dream Report (7:2–14)

²Daniel said: "In my vision at night I looked, and there before me were the four winds of heaven churning up the great sea. ³Four great beasts, each different from the others, came up out of the sea.

⁴"The first was like a lion, and it had the wings of an eagle. I watched until its wings were torn off and it was lifted from the ground so that it stood on two feet like a man, and the heart of a man was given to it.

⁵"And there before me was a second beast, which looked like a bear. It was raised up on one of its sides, and it had three ribs in its mouth between its teeth. It was told, 'Get up and eat your fill of flesh!'

⁶"After that, I looked, and there before me was another beast, one that looked like a leopard. And on its back it had four wings like those of a bird. This beast had four heads, and it was given authority to rule.

⁷"After that, in my vision at night I looked, and there before me was a fourth beast — terrifying and frightening and very powerful. It had large iron teeth; it crushed and devoured its victims and trampled underfoot whatever was left. It was different from all the former beasts, and it had ten horns.

⁸"While I was thinking about the horns, there before me was another horn, a little one, which came up among them; and three of the first horns were uprooted before it. This horn had eyes like the eyes of a man and a mouth that spoke boastfully.

⁹"As I looked,

"thrones were set in place,
  and the Ancient of Days took his seat.
His clothing was as white as snow;
  the hair of his head was white like wool.
His throne was flaming with fire,
  and its wheels were all ablaze.
¹⁰A river of fire was flowing,
  coming out from before him.
Thousands upon thousands attended him;
  ten thousand times ten thousand stood before him.
The court was seated,
  and the books were opened.

¹¹"Then I continued to watch because of the boastful words the horn was speaking. I kept looking until the beast was slain and its body destroyed and thrown into the blazing fire. ¹²(The other beasts had been stripped of their authority, but were allowed to live for a period of time.)

¹³"In my vision at night I looked, and there before me was one like a son of man, coming with the clouds of heaven. He approached the Ancient of Days and was led into his presence. ¹⁴He was given authority, glory and sovereign power; all peoples, nations and men of every language worshiped him. His dominion is an everlasting dominion that will not pass away, and his kingdom is one that will never be destroyed.

COMMENTARY

2−8 By recording his vision (v.1), Daniel invites the reader to be a spectator and observe the action as it unfolds before him. The shift to the first-person voice distinguishes the visions portion of the book from the court stories and gives one the impression that Daniel shares excerpts from his personal journal. Daniel is standing on a promontory over looking the Mediterranean Sea with a storm brewing upon the waters (v.2). The "four winds" are the winds from the four compass points: north, east, south, and west (cf. Jer 49:36; Eze 37:9). The "great sea" is no doubt the Mediterranean Sea (cf. Eze 47:10, 15). The emergence of "four beasts" (v.3), unnatural animal figures, from the churning waters brings an "other-worldly" dimension to the vision. As Goldingay, 184, notes, "the collocation of supernatural winds, agitated sea, and huge animals suggests more than an ordinary storm in the Mediterranean."

The cosmic nature of Daniel's vision is widely recognized, given the shift in scene back and forth from earth to heaven. Beyond this, numerous attempts have been made to link the imagery of Daniel's vision with the mythological literature and iconography of the ancient Near East. For example, some commentators connect the animal imagery with Mesopotamian astrological geography (e.g., Lacocque, 157; Porteous, 122). Others associate the animal imagery of Daniel's vision with Babylonian birth omens, since the creatures are "deformed" animals in some sense as hybrids of different types of animals (cf. the discussion in Lucas, 170−71). The picture of "beasts rising out of the sea" is typically connected with the Babylonian creation myth, *Enuma Elish*, in which the gods bring order out of chaos (cf. Seow, 102), or the Canaanite mythology that pits Baal against Yam (e.g., cf. the discussion in Lucas, 169−70). Likewise the background for the imagery of the throne scene in the vision has been tied to the Baal cycle of Ugaritic mythology (e.g., Lacocque, 129−30).

Hartman and Di Lella, 212, caution, however, that "there is no need to look for any direct borrowing from ancient mythological literature ... our author could have easily derived his idea of monsters coming up out the sea from the Bible." Furthermore, as Goldingay, 152−53, observes, tracing the development of the ideas or motifs of Daniel's vision to ancient Near Eastern parallels "does not in itself explain their significance ... the sea and animals stand here not for otherworldly cosmic or cosmogonic chaos forces but for historical ones."

The first great animal is "like a lion" with the "wings of an eagle" (v.4). The winged-lion (v.4a) was a familiar motif in Babylonian art, and the lion and eagle as symbols of speed and strength are still widely recognized. According to Goldingay, 186, "the first animal represents a large, powerful, and expansionist nation, a mortal threat to smaller peoples." The winged lion is widely recognized as a symbol for the Babylonian Empire, a parallel to the head of gold in the earlier statue dream of King Nebuchadnezzar (2:38; cf. Redditt, 120; Gowan, 106; Miller, 197). The removal of the lion's wings and his human characteristics may be an allusion to God's rebuke and subsequent restoration of King Nebuchadnezzar (ch. 4; cf. Seow, 103, on the reversal of imagery in the two passages [chs. 2 and 7] and the possible rescision of God's decision to contain the arrogant Nebuchadnezzar). Given the obscure nature of some of the symbolic descriptions of the four beasts, Russell, 116, appropriately cautions that interpretation "should not be unduly pressed." Futurist interpretations of the animal images in ch. 7 sometimes equate the winged lion, transformed into a two-legged creature endowed with a human heart, with the United Kingdom or the United States (assuming the "heart" symbolizes democracy in some fashion; v.4b; cf. Russell, 116, on the use of animal symbols for nations in modern times).

The second beast looks "like a bear," although it is "raised up on one of its sides, and it had three ribs in its mouth" (v.5). The creature is given permission to rise up and eat its fill ("Arise, devour much meat!" NASB). The bear is characterized by its voracious appetite and depicted as raised on one side, perhaps to pounce on its prey (so Baldwin, 139), or simply standing on its hind legs as a show of strength (so Hartman and Di Lella, 205). Goldingay, 186, observes that the bear is huge, ungainly, and fearsome—but normally not a predator. He concludes that since the creature is encouraged to gorge its appetite, "the greedy expansionism of nations can evidently have a place within the purpose of God."

Daniel later learns that the beasts represent earthly kingdoms (v.17), and the bear is variously interpreted as the kingdom of Media (cf. Lacocque, 140; Seow, 103–4) or as the composite Medo-Persian Empire (cf. Young, 145; Wood, 182–83). Miller, 198, based on the vision of the ram with two horns (one larger than the other) in ch. 8, prefers to interpret the image of the bear as the composite empire of Medo-Persia. This explains why the bear is raised up on one side (representing two kingdoms, with the higher side symbolizing Persia, which rose to a position of dominance in the alliance). The three ribs in the mouth of the animal may simply represent "the insatiable nature of the beast" (Young, 145), the military prowess of the kingdom generally, or the three major conquests of the Medo-Persian Empire (Lydia 546 BC; Babylonia, 539 BC; Egypt, 525 BC; see Archer, 86). Futurist interpretations of the animal images in ch. 7 often equated the bear with the former Soviet Union and now equate it with the nation of Russia.

The third animal rising out of the churning sea looks like a leopard, but it has four wings and four heads (v.6). The temporal expression "after that" (v.6a) suggests the kingdoms represented by the beasts of Daniel's vision do not arise simultaneously but follow each other in sequence. Goldingay, 186, describes the third creature as "another fearsome predator whose natural speed is enhanced by an unusual capacity to see and swoop in any direction." Baldwin, 140, reminds us that "like the other two beasts it is subject to an unnamed higher power. It does not achieve dominion by its own abilities" (i.e., "it was given authority to rule"; v.6d). The symbol of the leopard is variously understood historically as a reference to the Persian Empire (Redditt, 121;

Seow, 104) or the empire of Alexander the Great and Greece (Archer, 86; Miller, 199–200 [with the four heads understood as a reference to the Diadochi, the four generals who divided up Alexander's empire upon his death]). Futurist interpretations of the animal images in ch. 7 sometimes equate the leopard with some type of coalition of modern-day nations (given the four heads), whether Asian, Arab, or European states.

The fourth beast rising out of the churning sea is an unnamed animal, and its only identifying features are "iron teeth" and "ten horns" (v.7). The animal is not compared with other known creatures, thus adding to the mystery about it and suggesting that "it is an even less earthly creature that its predecessors" (Lucas, 180). The defining feature of this creature is the fact that it is "different from all the former beasts" (v.7d). The first three beasts (the lion, bear, and leopard) are all dangerous predators, but more significantly they are all described as hybrid or mutant creatures. As such they represent evil, malignant human kingdoms, and the imagery was especially repulsive to Jewish sensibilities, given God's unique and separate creation of animals according to their "kind" (cf. Ge 1:24–25) and the ritual impurity associated with the mixing of "kinds" in the Mosaic law (cf. Lev 11; see Longman, 183; Seow, 102).

The fourth beast, however, is especially characterized as "terrifying and frightening and very powerful" (v.7a). According to Seow, 105, this difference of species in the fourth animal of the vision makes it all the more terrifying, as "the beast is a new kind of terror—something for which there is no known analogy or antecedent." Unlike the other three creatures, this beast seems to have asserted its independence from the Almighty as the source of dominion and power in its ability wantonly to "crush" and "devour" and "trample" its victims (v.7c).

The fourth beast or kingdom is described as having "ten horns" (v.7d), but even as Daniel watches the vision unfold, an eleventh horn, one "little horn," arises and uproots three of the original ten horns (v.8a). Beyond this, the small horn is personified as one with human eyes and a boastful mouth (v.8b). The "horn" (Aram./Heb. *qeren*; GK 10641) is a metaphor for power and kingship in the OT (so Seow, 105; cf. M. L. Brown, "קֶרֶן," *NIDOTTE*, 3:990–92). Montgomery, 291, has noted that these human features of eyes and a mouth are the most expressive traits of the individual person, and they "interpret the little horn as an individual." Lucas, 180–81, further observes that a person's eyes and speech often reveal character (cf. the "haughty eyes" and "lying tongue" heading the list of the six things that the Lord hates; Pr 6:16–19). Although no particular bent of character is explicitly attributed to the small horn, the description seems to anticipate the arrogance, irreverence, and wickedness of this little horn (vv.23–25).

The historicist interpretation alternatively understands the fourth kingdom as the Macedonian Empire inaugurated by Alexander the Great (e.g., Towner, 95–96; Lucas, 188) or as the Roman Empire (e.g., Baldwin, 147). The reference to the "little horn" is considered an allusion to the Seleucid king Antiochus IV Epiphanes (e.g., Lacocque, 122–23; Wallace, 130). Those favoring this view appeal to the wider context of the book of Daniel for support, since the references to the "little horn" seem consistently to depict Antiochus Epiphanes (cf. Collins, *Daniel*, 299, 320–21; Redditt, 122–23). Those identifying the fourth kingdom as the Roman Empire contend the parallels to Nebuchadnezzar's statue dream (ch. 2) are more appropriate to this interpretation since the first advent of Jesus the Messiah during the Roman Empire marks the inbreaking of God's kingdom in human history (e.g., Archer, 47–48, 87; cf. 2:44). In addition, the vision of the ram and the goat in ch. 8 seems further to explain the identity of the second and third creatures of Daniel's vision in ch. 7 (e.g., Baldwin, 161–62; cf. summary of the Roman period interpretation in J. H. Walton, "The Four Kingdoms of Daniel," *JETS* 29 [1986]: 28).

The futurist interpretation equates the little horn with the Antichrist figure and considers the fourth beast symbolic of the Roman Empire (e.g., Wood, 188). Thus, the fourth beast or final kingdom of Daniel's vision represents the empire of the Antichrist, a ten-nation federation emanating from the old Roman Empire (e.g., Miller, 202; cf. Longman's critique of this view, 190, rejecting the identification of four specific evil empires and preferring instead to regard the four kingdoms as symbolic of the course of history from the Babylonian exile to the climax of history). See comments on vv.23–25.

9–10 As Daniel's vision continues, the scene shifts from the monstrous beasts emerging from the churning sea to the heavenly realm (or "mythic space" for Collins [*Daniel*, 303]) and the throne room of God (vv.9–10; but Goldingay, 164, argues that the judgment scene takes place on earth; cf. Gowan, 106–7). The language and style of the account shifts as well, from prose to short phrases presented in poetic parallelism (cf. Lucas, 165, 181] on arguments for the originality of the section). Seow, 106, suggests that the shift from prose in the first scene of the vision to poetry in the second may be rhetorical, "reflecting a shift from the prosaic realities of earthly experience to the sublime encounter of the heavenly court."

Much scholarly attention has been given to the multiple "thrones" in the heavenly court (v.9), since the Hebrews recognized only one deity—Yahweh (cf. the discussion in Collins, *Daniel*, 299–302). The context provides rationale for plural "thrones," since God is seated on his throne (v.9a) and the "one like a son of man" (v.13) is given an ever-

lasting kingdom—and presumably a throne (v.14). The NT reflects this understanding of the thrones in the heavenly court in the description of Jesus as the "Son of Man sitting at the right hand of the Mighty One" (Mt 26:64; Mk 14:62; cf. Lk 22:69). Redditt, 125, observes that nothing is said about the occupants of the other thrones, and they may have remained empty; "or the writer may have employed a plural form though only one throne was intended." In either case, Anderson's comment is cogent, 82: "there was one throne of judgment and only one, as there was one Judge and only one."

In the OT the divine title "Ancient of Days" for God is unique to Daniel 7 (7:9, 13, 22). Literally the epithet (Aram. ʿattîq yômîn) means "advanced with regard to days" (cf. Lacocque, 135, "The-One-Who-Endures"), and similar descriptions of God may be found in later intertestamental Jewish literature (cf. *1En* 46:1–2; 47:3; 98:2). The expression is an idiom for the eternality of God and in context contrasts the eternal God and his eternal kingdom with all temporary earthly kingdoms.

The white garments (v.9b) symbolize both God's splendor and his purity (so Gowan, 107; cf. Ps 51:7; Isa 1:18). The white hair like "wool" (v.9b) also speaks to God's majesty and splendor as well as to his experience and "old age" (so Lacocque, 143; cf. Rev 1:14). Towner, 98, comments that the color white emphasized here depicts God as "a wise and honorable judge." The origin of the "aged-deity" motif is typically traced to Ugarit and the descriptions of El as the "patriarch" of the Canaanite pantheon (e.g., *BBCOT*, 741; Collins, *Daniel*, 301–2; Seow, 107–8). One wonders to what extent such background informs Daniel's imagery, since the larger context of the court stories and the visions of the book are Yahweh's supremacy over the Babylonian pantheon and his sovereignty over all earthly kingdoms (cf. Smith-Christopher, 103).

Fire is commonly associated with theophanies in the OT (e.g., Moses at the burning bush [Ex 3:2] and the Israelites at Mount Sinai [19:18]). Daniel's vision of the throne of flaming fire and its fiery wheels (v.9c) is reminiscent of Ezekiel's vision of God's throne resting atop a majestic carriage (Eze 1; cf. *1En* 14:15–23). The reference to the "river of fire" (v.10a) is unique to Daniel in the OT and has it closest parallel in the fire that goes out before God and consumes his enemies (perhaps lightning? cf. Ps 97:3). Fire not only "represents an awe-inspiring supernatural force" (Gowan, 107) but is also a symbol of God's judgment, destroying everything in its path (Isa 66:15–16; Jer 21:12; Eze 21:31; cf. Lucas, 182, who comments on the "dangerous splendor" of fire and its association with divine judgment). On occasion God's fire is a symbol of his holiness, which purifies everything in its presence (cf. Isa 1:25; Jer 6:29; Mal 3:2).

The other (rare) OT visions of the heavenly court also feature angelic attendants around the divine throne (e.g., 1Ki 22:19–22; Job 1; Isa 6; cf. Collins [*Daniel*, 301, 303] on parallels to the divine-council motif). Daniel sees thousands upon thousands of (angelic) beings attending God (v.10b). Towner, 99, notes that the numbers multiplied by ten to the seventh power emphasize the cosmic nature of the scene and "present Yahweh in the grandest setting possible" (cf. Rev 5:11–12).

Some scholars contend that the "books" of the throne vision (v.10c) are analogous to the Babylonian Tablets of Fate (e.g., Lacocque, 144). Lucas, 182, rightly rejects the parallel and states, "more to the point is the practice of record-keeping in ANE courts" (e.g., Ezr 4:15; Est 6:1). What is clear is that although no trial is described and no judgment is pronounced, "the opened books are records that become the basis for judgment" (Gowan, 107). The "books" Daniel sees opened are no doubt akin to the scroll or book of remembrance mentioned in Malachi 3:16, a comprehensive divine ledger containing the names and ongoing accounts of the words and deeds of all humanity (cf. Hartman and Di Lella, 218). The records of such a book (or books) serve as the basis for God's winnowing of the righteous and the wicked (cf. Mal 3:18).

11–12 The vision reverts back to the fourth terrible beast, as Daniel's attention is drawn to the arrogant speech of the boastful "little horn" (v.11). Lucas, 183, observes that the return to prose and the lengthy introduction formula in v.11a serve to highlight the fate of the fourth kingdom. The immediate context suggests that the slaying and destruction of the fourth beast by fire is the sentence of judgment passed by the heavenly court. Miller, 206, is probably correct in assuming that Daniel is riveted to the actions of the fourth beast because he is shocked at its insolence and arrogance and is waiting to see what will happen to this creature described as "boastful" (Aram. *mālal* + *rab*; vv.9, 11). Presumably, the boastful speech deprecating the Ancient of Days is one of the reasons for the condemnation of the beast by the heavenly court.

The burning of a corpse in the OT was a punishment reserved for those guilty of particularly heinous crimes (cf. Lev 20:14; 21:9; Jos 7:25). Although two different words are used for "fire" in the section (Aram. *nûr*, v.9; *ʾeššāʾ*, v.11), the point is the utter destruction of the fourth beast or earthly kingdom and its arrogant ruler. (But some connect the fire of v.11c with the eternal torment of hell; e.g., Miller, 206.)

The parenthetical reference to the other three beasts or kingdoms is enigmatic (v.12). Though stripped of their authority or power to rule, they persist to exist in some form for a time. Miller, 206, suggests this may imply that these kingdoms continue to exert some cultural influence or perhaps regain some form of independence short of dominance. Porteous, 109–10, speculates that these kingdoms are among the nations who become vassals to the saints of the Most High. Lucas, 183, more appropriately calls attention to two theological truths set forth here: first, God's judgment is just — since the fourth beast is "different" (v.7) from the others it receives the punishment it deserves; second, God has promised that Israel will rule over her former oppressors and the nations will serve her — as 7:14, 27 indicate (cf. Heaton, 181–82).

13–14 After the destruction of the fourth beast or kingdom, a humanlike figure appears in Daniel's vision (v.13). The introductory formula ("in my vision at night I looked," v.13a) echoes the formula introducing the vision (v.2a) and forms an envelope for the literary unit (vv.2–14). The construction serves to underscore the importance of the final scene as the climax of Daniel's vision. The humanlike figure is described as one like "a son of man" (v.13b). The expression "son of man" (Aram. *bar ᵉnāš*) is idiomatic for a human being (cf. the ninety-plus references to Ezekiel as "son of man" [Heb. *ben ᵓādām*], denoting his prophetic role as representative Israelite and ultimately a human being; Eze 2:1, 3; etc.).

According to Baldwin, 142, "the effect of the idiom is to intensify the quality in question, so that 'son of man' lays stress on the humanity of the person (Ps 146:3)." Collins (*Daniel*, 305) states that "*like a son of man*" in v.13 "is best understood as indicating the mode of perception proper to a vision, so that 'like a son of man' means 'a human figure seen in a vision,' where the figure may or may not represent something other than a human being." Baldwin, 143, further notes that "he is like a human being, just as the beasts were 'like' a lion or a bear ... the one who comes with the clouds is like a human being in the sense that he is what every human being should be if he is true to type, that is, one who is made in the image of God."

Clouds are frequently connected with theophanies in the OT (e.g., the Sinai event; Ex 16:10;

19:9; cf. Lev 16:2; Dt 1:33; 1Ki 8:10; Isa 19:1). Typically, the motif of God as "riding clouds" is discussed against its ancient Near Eastern background, especially descriptions of the Canaanite storm-god Baal as a "rider of clouds" (cf. Collins [*Daniel*, 286–94], who contends that Canaanite myths provide the most adequate background for understanding the motifs of Daniel 7). Lucas, 173–76, acknowledges possible connections between Canaanite mythology and the imagery of the throne scene in Daniel 7, yet he concludes, "it is used in Daniel to express a distinctively Jewish understanding of Yahweh's rule and purposes." One still wonders, especially in view of the second-century BC date assigned to Daniel by critical scholars, about the influence of Canaanite mythology on literature more than ten centuries removed from the fact. Beyond this, Gowan, 105, admits that no "son of man" tradition has been found outside Daniel 7, indicating a distinctiveness for the biblical record apart from Canaanite mythology.

Longman, 198, affirms that the "clouds" (v.13b) "signal the divine status of this human-like figure" (cf. Miller, 208). The "son of man" figure approaches the Ancient of Days and is led into his presence, presumably following the conventions of "entrance protocol" (v.13c). Daniel then witnesses the investiture of this one like a human being with absolute power and supreme authority as sovereign over all humanity (v.14). The Ancient of Days grants the "son of man" figure authority, glory, and sovereign power so that the nations worship him (v.14a). In contrast to the human kingdoms swept away by divine judgment, the "son of man" figure receives an eternal and indestructible kingdom (v.14b).

Daniel's throne-scene vision affirms the truths set forth in the statue-dream of Nebuchadnezzar that God alone is sovereign and that he will establish an eternal kingdom (cf. 2:20–22). Seow, 109, draws parallels between the "rock cut ... not by human hands" (2:34, 44–45) with the "son of man" figure, since both represent the "divine response to the threat of domination by pernicious earthly powers." Longman, 188, summarizes that Daniel's vision is more than a description of the realms of human evil and divine judgment, since "it also narrates a conflict between the two, with a certain and clear conclusion."

Commentators are not content to leave the figure of "one like a human being" as merely a symbol of God's rule breaking into human history. Following the interpretive analogy of the four beasts representing human kingdoms, it is assumed that the "son of man" figure must have some historical referent as well. This has led to numerous attempts to identify this figure. The list of potential candidates put forth by scholars includes a Davidic king, a priestly figure, the high priest, the angel Michael, the angel Gabriel, the nation of Israel, the righteous remnant of Israel, the angelic host, or even the Messiah (cf. Baldwin, 148–54; Redditt, 127). According to Lucas, 185, the earliest interpretations of the "son of man" figure were individualistic and messianic, but such is not the case today.

Since the NT associates the "son of man" figure with Jesus as "the Son of Man," traditional Christian scholarship has determined that "only one person may be properly identified as the "son of man," and that person is Jesus Christ" (Miller, 209; cf. Young, 293–94). Redditt, 127, remarks, however, that Daniel 7:14 does not use the "son of man" figure as the technical title "the Son of Man," and NT Christology does not determine the meaning of the reference in Daniel (cf. Goldingay, 190–93). At the very least, the "son of man" in Daniel 7 "is not only king but God, though, as is characteristic of apocalyptic style, this is conveyed in veiled terms" (Baldwin, 154).

NOTE

12 Archer, 91, notes that the expression "for a period of time" combines two Aramaic words for time, זְמַן (z^eman; GK 10232) and עִדָּן (ʿiddān; GK 10530). The first refers to an appropriate time for something to happen or an appointed time (i.e., "event" time), while the latter refers to time as duration or as the interval between set points of measurement (i.e., "clock" time). The LXX's rendering of Daniel 7:12 bears this out, employing καιρός (kairos; "time as opportunity for event") for z^eman and χρόνος (chronos; "time as the interval of time between two points of measurement") for ʿiddān. According to Archer, as used here the expression "probably implies 'up to the appointed length of time and to the appointed moment of time' when the four beasts (or kingdoms) will have lived out their various periods of supremacy and come to the time appointed for their destruction" (cf. NASB's "an appointed period of time"). Lucas, 162, however, explains the expression simply as a hendiadys.

3. Interpretation of the Dream (7:15–27)

> [15]"I, Daniel, was troubled in spirit, and the visions that passed through my mind disturbed me. [16]I approached one of those standing there and asked him the true meaning of all this.

"So he told me and gave me the interpretation of these things: [17]'The four great beasts are four kingdoms that will rise from the earth. [18]But the saints of the Most High will receive the kingdom and will possess it forever — yes, for ever and ever.'

[19]"Then I wanted to know the true meaning of the fourth beast, which was different from all the others and most terrifying, with its iron teeth and bronze claws — the beast that crushed and devoured its victims and trampled underfoot whatever was left. [20]I also wanted to know about the ten horns on its head and about the other horn that came up, before which three of them fell — the horn that looked more imposing than the others and that had eyes and a mouth that spoke boastfully. [21]As I watched, this horn was waging war against the saints and defeating them, [22]until the Ancient of Days came and pronounced judgment in favor of the saints of the Most High, and the time came when they possessed the kingdom.

[23]"He gave me this explanation: 'The fourth beast is a fourth kingdom that will appear on earth. It will be different from all the other kingdoms and will devour the whole earth, trampling it down and crushing it. [24]The ten horns are ten kings who will come from this kingdom. After them another king will arise, different from the earlier ones; he will subdue three kings. [25]He will speak against the Most High and oppress his saints and try to change the set times and the laws. The saints will be handed over to him for a time, times and half a time.

[26]"'But the court will sit, and his power will be taken away and completely destroyed forever. [27]Then the sovereignty, power and greatness of the kingdoms under the whole heaven will be handed over to the saints, the people of the Most High. His kingdom will be an everlasting kingdom, and all rulers will worship and obey him.'

COMMENTARY

15–18 The interpretation of Daniel's dream is given in two parts. The first part (vv. 15–18) reports Daniel's distress over the experience of his vision (v. 15) and his need for an interpreter of the strange images he has seen (v. 16). The vision has scared Daniel both because he does not fully understand it (Redditt, 129) and because he is an empathetic visionary—"one who shares the terror of the world that is being judged" (Seow, 109). The same type of physical, psychological, and emotional reaction to the experience of divine revelation is recorded elsewhere in the book (e.g., 8:17; 9:20;

10:7, 15–16). Baldwin, 143, reminds us that "the personal cost of receiving divine revelation is never underestimated in the Old Testament."

Daniel saw "thousands" of angelic attendants around the throne of God in his vision of the heavenly realm after witnessing the beasts rising out of the sea (v. 10). Presumably, "one of those standing there" (v. 16), whom Daniel approaches for help in understanding the meaning of his vision, is one of these angelic attendants (cf. Russell, 129). The prophet Zechariah received similar aid from an unnamed angelic interpreter (cf. Zec 1:9; 2:3).

Later Daniel will receive help from an angel named Gabriel in the interpretation of another vision (8:16; 9:21), prompting Miller, 211, to speculate that Gabriel may be represented here as well.

The interpreting angel offers a simple summary of the entire vision: the beasts are kingdoms or human governments that will rise from the earth (v.17), but God will conquer all these kingdoms and his saints will receive an eternal kingdom (v.18). Although the conflict associated with the rise and fall of these human kingdoms is inescapable, the outcome is certain. The emphatic repetition of "forever—yes, for ever and ever" (v.18) is a superlative expression and indicates "continued possession" (Young, 158; cf. Redditt, 130). Smith-Christopher, 104, represents the critical view that contends Daniel's interest in the fourth beast or kingdom is due to the fact that "it was the beast with which they are currently contending." The traditional view, however, explains Daniel's interest in the fourth beast (a kingdom yet to arise in the future) as justifiable concern for the implications of the rule of the terrible fourth beast for the people of Israel (cf. Wallace, 135; Baldwin, 145). Futurist interpreters of ch. 7 struggle to reconcile the "eternal kingdom" of v.18 with the "millennial kingdom" of the NT (Rev 20:1–6; cf. Wood, 197; Miller, 211).

19–27 Daniel has received a general explanation of the meaning of the four beasts from the interpreting angel, but he expresses further curiosity about the fourth beast, the most terrible of all the animal figures (vv.19–22). The repetition of the original vision (vv.19–20; cf. vv.7–8) has its parallel in the recitation of the contents of the dreams in chs. 2 and 4. Daniel's recounting of the vision to the interpreting angel reveals additional details about the fourth terrible beast, including its "bronze claws" (v.19) and specific actions of the "little horn" (v.20). Beyond this, Daniel sees the "little horn" waging war against the saints and defeating them (v.21).

This scene continues until "the Ancient of Days" (see v.9) intervenes and pronounces judgment in favor of the saints of the Most High (v.22a). The success of the "little horn" against the saints ends abruptly, at which time they take possession of the kingdom (v.22b). Redditt, 131, observes that Daniel reports no battle, only the word of divine judgment by which the "little horn" is defeated and the saints are awarded the kingdom (v.22). According to Baldwin, 145, Daniel's vision continues even while he queries the interpreting angel about the meaning of the fourth beast. The reference to the "little horn" prevailing over the saints (v.21) foreshadows the fuller account of the conflict presented in Daniel's vision of the ram and the goat (8:24). The point of its brief mention here seems to be one of assurance for Daniel that the downfall of the saints of the Most High will be temporary.

23–25 At this point in Daniel's vision, the interpreting angel proceeds to explain the meaning of the fourth terrible beast (vv.23–25). Like the other animals of Daniel's vision, the fourth beast is an earthly kingdom that will arise (presumably after the other three kingdoms; v.23a). Emphasis is placed on two features of this kingdom: first, it is "different" from all the other kingdoms; second, it wreaks destruction over the whole earth. Gowan, 106, sees the "difference" between the fourth kingdom and the previous three as lying in its origin, since it (Greece) represents a European rather than an Asiatic empire. Goldingay, 186–87, links the "difference" between the fourth beast and the previous three to the immediate context and observes that the fourth kingdom is likened to no animal species; it is portrayed as explicitly fearsome and destructive—the chief difference being that this kingdom is "more bellicose" than its predecessors. Baldwin, 146, agrees, noting that the verbs "trampling" (Aram. *dwš*) and "crushing" (Aram. *dqq*; v.23) "imply wanton destruction."

The ten horns on the head of the beast (vv.7, 20) represent ten kings who will rule over this kingdom or empire since it "devours" the whole earth (v.23). It is unclear whether these ten kings rule in succession, since three of the ten are subdued by an "eleventh" king (perhaps suggesting the three rule simultaneously, v.24b). The "little horn" (v.8) or "other horn" (v.20) represents an "eleventh" king (v.24), who is described as "different" from the previous kings and who will subdue three kings (v.24bc). This difference is explained by the following verse — the "eleventh" king is marked by his arrogance and godlessness (v.25).

The four characteristics marking the rule of this "eleventh" king are summarized by Baldwin, 146: speaking against or blaspheming the Most High (v.25a); oppressing the saints of the Most High or long, drawn-out persecution ("wear down the saints" or "wear out" like a garment, NASB; v.25b; cf. Miller, 214); attempting to change the "set times" or implement a new table of religious festivals (v.25c; cf. Redditt, 131, who identifies the "sacred seasons" [NRSV] as the Sabbath and annual festivals); and attempting to change the laws or impose a new morality (v.25d; this assumes that the word "laws" [NIV, though the Aram. *dāt* is singular] refers to the Mosaic code; cf. Goldingay, 146, n. 25.b-b, who understands "times and law" as a type of hendiadys meaning "times set by decree").

The saints of the Most High will be handed over to this blasphemous king for a specified amount of time, namely, "a time, times, and half a time" (v.25e). The expression is generally taken to mean a period of three and a half years (so Collins, *Daniel*, 322; cf. Redditt, 131, who notes the word "time" [Aram. ʿ*iddān*] can mean "year" on the basis of 8:14 and 9:27 but that word is less precise than the word *šᵉnâ*, meaning "year"). Some commentators relate

the three-and-a-half years to the period between the desecration of the temple by Antiochus IV Epiphanes (15 Chislev in year 145 of the Seleucid era, or December 6, 167 BC) and its purification by Judas Maccabeus (25 Chislev in year 148 of the Seleucid era, or December 14, 164 BC) — a time span of three years and eight days (e.g., Hartman and Di Lella, 215–16). Yet Lucas, 194, prefers to understand the numbers symbolically, since three "as half of the perfect number, seven ... denotes a short period of evil."

As discussed above, the fourth beast or kingdom of Daniel's vision is variously interpreted as Macedonia or Greece (continued under the Ptolemies and Seleucids) or the Roman Empire. Those interpreting the fourth beast as the kingdom of Greece tend to agree that Antiochus IV, son of Antiochus III and brother of Seleucus IV, is the "little horn" who oppresses the people of God (vv.8, 20, 24–25). These scholars disagree, however, on the identification of the "ten horns" or "ten kings" associated with the fourth beast (vv.7, 20, 24). Hartman and Di Lella, 216–17, view the "ten kings" as contemporaries of Antiochus IV (cf. Lucas, 193, for alternative suggestions concerning the identity of the "ten kings"). Others identify the "ten kings" as ten successive rulers from Alexander the Great to Seleucus IV (e.g., Goldingay, 180).

The "three horns" that were uprooted (vv.8, 20, 24) are interpreted as Seleucus IV and his two sons (so Collins, *Daniel*, 321), though there is no direct historical evidence linking Antiochus IV to the assassination of Seleucus IV (cf. Lucas, 193). In this interpretation, the "eyes" of the "little horn" (v.20) allude to his covetousness for the Seleucid throne, and its arrogant mouth (vv.8, 20, 25) refers to "the infamous blasphemy of his self-designation as 'God Manifest' [i.e., Epiphanes]" (Seow, 111).

Those scholars interpreting the fourth beast of Daniel's vision as the Roman Empire equate the "little horn" with an "antichrist" figure who will rule over some form of a "revived" Roman Empire (cf. Young, 160–62; Wood, 200–203; Miller, 213–16). The futurist interpretation recognizes that the kingdom of God did not come in its fullness after the death of Antiochus IV (unless one opts for the establishment of the Hasmonean dynasty as a partial fulfillment of Da 7; cf. Gowan, 114–15). Likewise, the kingdom of God did not come in its fullness during the Roman Empire of the first century AD (although the first advent of Jesus the Messiah clearly inaugurated the kingdom of God; cf. Mk 1:14–15). Thus, the futurist interpretation contends, "since the Lord's return puts an end to the rule of these horns (vv.13–14), the ten kings must reign at the end of the present age" (Miller, 213).

Typically, Daniel's vision of the fourth beast, with its ten horns, is compared to the ten-horned confederacy led by a beast described in Revelation 13 and 17. The two groups of ten horns are understood to symbolize the same empire, and the little horn and the beast are regarded as merely "different figures for the same evil leader, the Antichrist" (Miller, 216). Longman, 190, 198, acknowledges that this approach has much to commend it "in the light of later, fuller biblical revelation."

26–27 The dominion of the little horn ends almost as quickly as it began, as its power is taken away and it is completely destroyed (v.26). Goldingay, 181, reminds us that the death and destruction of the fourth creature (v.11) is directly linked to the vanquishing of the authority of the king symbolized by the beast's small horn. The reference to the "court" (v.26) harkens back to the throne room scene (vv.9–11), in which God presides as the Judge of the earth (cf. Pss 82:8; 94:2; 96:13) and the heavenly court of angelic beings sits (or stands) before him (cf. 1Ki 22:19; Jer 23:18, 22).

The kingdom of God, the Most High, will take the place of the fourth creature or earthly king-dom destroyed by the judgment pronounced by the heavenly court (v.27a). This divine kingdom will be universal and eternal (v.27b). Human authorities and kingdoms will still exist in some form, but they will worship and obey God (v.27c; cf. Isa 60:6–9; Zec 14:16). Here Daniel's vision of the four creatures and Nebuchadnezzar's statue dream are in concord—after a series of earthly kingdoms God will demonstrate his absolute sovereignty by establishing an eternal and universal kingdom (cf. 2:44).

Baldwin, 146, correctly recognizes that v.27 is an interpretation of v.14 and that there is some relationship between "the saints, the people of the Most High" (v.27a; cf. NASB, "the people of the saints of the Highest One") and the "son of man" (v.14). The word for "saints" (lit., "holy ones"; Aram. *qaddîšîn*; GK 10620) is unusual, and elsewhere in Daniel it refers to angelic beings (cf. 4:13, 17, 23). Three possible meanings of the expression have emerged in the scholarly debate: "holy ones" may refer to the company of celestial beings or angels; it may refer to the faithful element among the people of Israel as the people of God; or it may refer to both angels and human beings assimilated into a community of "saints" to whom God will give his kingdom (see the discussions in Russell, 130–32; Goldingay, 181–82).

Russell, 131, admits that the NT takes up the same theme "where there is no doubt about the identity of 'the saints': they are Christ's people, the Church." Goldingay, 182, eschews Daniel 7 as "messianic eschatology." Yet in light of the NT it is difficult not to side with those interpreters who connect Daniel's vision concerning the "son of man," who receives a "kingdom" from the Most High (v.14) and who shares his dominion in some fashion with the "holy ones" (v.27), with Jesus the Messiah (cf. Wallace, 125–28; Miller, 216–17).

Finally, Smith-Christopher, 105–6, cautions against an overzealous reading of the "reversal of fortune motif" (i.e., the saints who were delivered over to persecution by the rulers of earthly kingdoms [v.25] are subsequently given the kingdom of God [v.27]) that results in a vengeful tone, lest we forget that God's final rule will be one of peace and healing for the nations (cf. Eze 47:12; Rev 22:2). Note that Jesus inaugurated the kingdom by teaching peace and healing all manner of diseases (Mt 4:23; Jn 14:27; 16:33; cf. Lk 1:79; 2:14).

NOTES

18 The expression "the saints of the Most High" is difficult, since one would normally expect the singular form of the divine name, Aramaic עֶלְיוֹן (ʿelyôn, "Most High"), instead of the plural form עֶלְיוֹנִין (ʿelyônîn; cf. Lucas, 162–63). Montgomery, 308, explained the plural form as a "plural of majesty" and recognized the construction as a Hebraism in Aramaic (so Lacocque, 149). Collins (*Daniel*, 312) argues for the traditional translation of the construct chain as well, suggesting the plural is "a plural of manifestations" (cf. his discussion of "Holy Ones," 313–17). Goldingay, 146, 177–78, considers the plural divine epithet a second plural form in the construct chain used when the entire expression is plural and indeterminate, and he renders the expression adjectivally or epexegetically as "holy ones on high," in reference to celestial beings rather than earthly ones. See the discussion of the word "saints" (Aram. קַדִּישִׁין [qaddîšîn], in the comments on vv.26–27).

25 The combination of verbs סבר (sbr, "to strive") and שנה (šnh, "to change") in the clause "to change the set times and the laws" suggests that the king's initiatives to implement these changes to the Hebrew calendar and law failed or were only partially successful (cf. Miller, 214). Baldwin, 146, reminds us that the passive form of the Aramaic verb יהב (yhb ("be handed over")) indicates that one greater than this "little horn" is in control.

4. Conclusion (7:28)

28 "This is the end of the matter. I, Daniel, was deeply troubled by my thoughts, and my face turned pale, but I kept the matter to myself."

COMMENTARY

28 The closing formula has parallels in Ecclesiastes 12:13 and Jeremiah 51:64. The expression closes the account of the vision in ch. 7 as the counterpart to the report of Daniel's recording of the vision in v.1b (cf. Heaton, 190, who posited that the closing formula once marked the end of the book of Daniel). Smith-Christopher, 106, states that experiencing such a vision would naturally be exhausting, but he finds Daniel's alarm puzzling since the vision is somewhat positive as far as God's people are concerned. He wonders whether "the experience of seeing such a vision of holiness and power itself, though positive, gives rise to fearful awe." Seow, 113, notes that Daniel is already disturbed and terrified by the visions while in his dream state (cf. v.15). He speculates that Daniel's troubled spirit is due either to the enormity of the evil threat to God's people presented by the images of the vision (especially the "little horn"; vv.7–8), or to there being no clear indication of when the oppression of the holy ones of the Most High will end (Seow, 113).

Most commentators agree with Lucas, 194, in understanding the report of Daniel's perplexity over the vision as an encouragement to the audience (or reader) to expect more to come in order to clarify the meaning of the vision (cf. Porteous, 117; Lacocque, 155). Since Daniel has written down the vision (v.1), Seow suggests that he keeps the matter to himself (v.28c) in the sense "that he did not lose sight of it; he kept on pondering it."

B. The Ram and the Goat (8:1–27)

OVERVIEW

The Aramaic section of Daniel opened and closed with a preview of world history, a series of four earthly kingdoms replaced by a fifth heavenly kingdom (2:4–49 and 7:1–28; see comments on 7:1). Daniel's second vision (ch. 8) not only marks the resumption of the Hebrew portion of the book, but it also signals a narrowing of the focus of God's revelation to his servant. In contrast to the earlier pattern of four distinct animals used to represent four realms or kingdoms, the vision of ch. 8 features only two animal figures symbolizing but two earthly empires. The setting of the vision shifts as well, presumably from Babylon (7:1) to Susa (8:2). The date formula (v.1) sets the vision during the third year of King Belshazzar (ca. 551 or 550 BC), which means the events of ch. 8 actually precede the events recorded in ch. 5 of the book.

Baldwin, 155, has observed that 550 BC was a significant year in ancient Mesopotamia, for in that year Cyrus broke free from his alliance to Astyages the Mede and established the joint kingdom of the Medes and Persians. This is the same Cyrus whom Isaiah the prophet identified as "the LORD's anointed" (cf. Isa 45:1) and who would serve God's

purposes in restoring his captive people Israel to their homeland from Babylonian exile (Ezra 1:1–4). Daniel's last vision occurred during the reign of Cyrus the Great, king of Persia (cf. 10:1).

The literary form of ch. 8 is symbolic vision report (Lucas, 208). In fact, the word "vision" occurs six times in the passage (vv.1, 2 [2x], 13, 15, 26). Similarly to ch. 7, ch. 8 employs several introductory formulas to mark transitions in the narrative, including the lengthy visionary formula used to introduce the ram and the goat (vv.3, 5), and the "I, Daniel" formula (i.e., the proper name reinforced by the first-person pronoun) found at the beginning of the vision (v.1), the beginning of the interpretation of the vision (v.15), and the end of the vision (v.27; cf. Goldingay, 204–5). The structure of ch. 8 is also similar to that of ch. 7, but here there is only a single interpretation of the vision instead of a two-stage explanation. A new feature is the formal introduction or the "epiphany" of the interpreter of the vision (vv.15–18). Both Goldingay, 205–6, and Lucas, 209–10, highlight repeated words and phrases that unify the different sections of the pericope and set the tone for the chapter—namely, "power and conflict."

As a follow-up to the disturbing contents of Daniel's previous vision (ch. 7, especially the persecution of the saints of the Most High, v.25), the vision of ch. 8 addresses the question of "how long" the rebellious "little horn" will oppress the people of God (vv.13–14). The contents of the vision may be outlined: introduction (vv.1–2), symbolic vision (vv.3–14), appearance of the interpreter (vv.15–19), message of the interpreter (vv.20–26), and conclusion (v.27).

1. Introduction (8:1–2)

¹In the third year of King Belshazzar's reign, I, Daniel, had a vision, after the one that had already appeared to me. ²In my vision I saw myself in the citadel of Susa in the province of Elam; in the vision I was beside the Ulai Canal.

COMMENTARY

1 Belshazzar was the son of Nabonidus, who ruled Babylonia from ca. 556–539 BC. Belshazzar ruled as coregent or deputy for more than half of Nabonidus's seventeen-year reign, given the latter's ten-year hiatus in Tema in northwestern Arabia (see comments on 5:1–4.)

In the OT the word "vision" (Heb. *ḥāzôn*; GK 2606) is associated with receiving revelation from God (e.g., Isa 1:1; Na 1:1). The term refers both to the experience of the thing(s) seen (i.e., the images of the vision itself) and the effects of the vision on the seer (cf. the report in v.27 indicating Daniel was exhausted and ill after the vision). According to Redditt, 117, "the difference between dreams and visions is clear: dreams typically come while one is asleep, while visions come while one is in a state of altered consciousness." It is also possible for the seer to be transported to another geographical location during the experience of a vision (as Daniel is transported from Babylon to Susa in Elam, v.2; cf. Eze 8:2–3). Lacocque, 158, understands the expression "a vision appeared" (Heb. *ḥāzôn nirʾâ*) to signify both a visual and an auditory experience for the seer (cf. vv.13, 16).

The repetition of verbs of "seeing" (vv.1, 3–5, 7) "conveys something of the involvement of the seer's consciousness as he oriented himself first to the fact that he was receiving a vision, then to his geographical surroundings, and finally to the particular image presented to his gaze" (Baldwin, 155). The expression "after the one that had already appeared to me" (v.1; i.e., the vision of ch. 7) indicates the sequencing of God's revelation to Daniel, but no indication is given as to the time of day of Daniel's vision—only that he is in a "deep sleep" (v.18).

2 The introduction further specifies that the setting for this vision is the citadel of Susa in the province of Elam in the proximity of the Ulai Canal (v.2). The city of Susa (Heb. *šûšan*, but called "Susa" by the Greeks) was situated some 220 miles east of Babylon and 150 miles north of the Persian Gulf. Susa was the capital of Elam at the time of Daniel's vision and became a Persian royal city, used by Persian kings as a winter residence. King Darius I made Susa the administrative capital of the Persian Empire in 521 BC. The term "citadel" (Heb. *bîrâ*) may refer to a temple (e.g., 1Ch 29:1, 19), a fortress within a city (sometimes situated on an acropolis; cf. Ne 2:8), or a city itself as a "fortress-city." Goldingay, 196, notes that the word is used in apposition to Susa, thus denoting Susa as a fortress-city (cf. Ne 1:1; Est 1:2).

The province of Elam, later known as Susiana, was the region northeast of the lower Tigris River (now located in modern-day Iran). The city of Susa bordered the Ulai Canal, an artificial river nearly a thousand feet wide, on the northeast. According to Baldwin, 156, the name was given later to the Abi-diz waterway to the east of Susa down which Alexander sailed his fleet.

2. Vision Report (8:3–14)

³I looked up, and there before me was a ram with two horns, standing beside the canal, and the horns were long. One of the horns was longer than the other but grew up later. ⁴I watched the ram as he charged toward the west and the north and the south. No animal could stand against him, and none could rescue from his power. He did as he pleased and became great.

⁵As I was thinking about this, suddenly a goat with a prominent horn between his eyes came from the west, crossing the whole earth without touching the ground. ⁶He came toward the two-horned ram I had seen standing beside the canal and charged at him in great rage. ⁷I saw him attack the ram furiously, striking the ram and shattering his two horns. The ram was powerless to stand against him; the goat knocked him to the ground and trampled on him, and none could rescue the ram from his power. ⁸The goat became very great, but at the height of his power his large horn was broken off, and in its place four prominent horns grew up toward the four winds of heaven.

⁹Out of one of them came another horn, which started small but grew in power to the south and to the east and toward the Beautiful Land. ¹⁰It grew until it reached the host of the heavens, and it threw some of the starry host down to the earth and trampled on them. ¹¹It set itself up to be as great as the Prince of the host; it took away the daily sacrifice from him, and the place of his sanctuary was brought low. ¹²Because of rebellion, the host ⌞of the saints⌟ and the daily sacrifice were given over to it. It prospered in everything it did, and truth was thrown to the ground.

¹³Then I heard a holy one speaking, and another holy one said to him, "How long will it take for the vision to be fulfilled — the vision concerning the daily sacrifice, the rebellion that causes desolation, and the surrender of the sanctuary and of the host that will be trampled underfoot?"

¹⁴He said to me, "It will take 2,300 evenings and mornings; then the sanctuary will be reconsecrated."

COMMENTARY

3–4 The first image Daniel sees in his vision is a ram (v.3). Unlike the unclean hybrid animals that emerged from the sea in Daniel's dream (ch. 7), the ram is considered a clean animal according to the Hebrew ritual purity laws (cf. Ex 29:1). The only unusual feature of the ram is the unevenness in the length of its horns. The ram's power is irresistible, and it charges at will in three directions—west, north, and south (v.4a). Unrestrained, the ram does as it pleases and "became great" (v.4b). Goldingay, 209, notes that there is nothing inherently wrong with doing great things, but when "become great" (Heb. *higdîl*) is used of human beings "it tends to suggest arrogance…or at least achievement at someone else's expense." Since leaders are sometimes symbolized by animals in the OT (e.g., rams and goats; cf. Eze 34:17), there is already something ominous about this ram even before Daniel hears the vision's interpretation.

5–8 The second image Daniel sees in his vision is that of a goat with a prominent horn between its eyes (v.5a). The goat appears suddenly from the west and is notable for its swift movement, "crossing the whole earth without touching the ground" (v.5b). The goat charges and attacks the ram as it stands by the canal, breaking off its two horns, knocking it to the ground, and then trampling over it (vv.6–7). The rage of the goat and the fury of the attack are details Daniel notes as he watches the action unfold before him. Even as there was no one to rescue the helpless from the power of the ram (v.4), so there is no one to rescue the ram from the power of the goat (v.7d). The goat becomes greater than the ram (Heb. *higdîl ʿad mᵉʾōd*, "magnified himself exceedingly," NASB), but at the zenith of its power the goat's large horn is broken off (v.8a). As Daniel watches, four "prominent horns" grow up in its place and spread themselves toward the

"four winds of heaven" or the four primary points of the compass (v.8b).

9–12 This is not the end of the vision, however, as another horn grows out of one of the four horns now on the goat (v.9a). This horn begins small but grows "in power," encroaching to the south, to the east, and toward the "Beautiful Land" (Heb. *haṣṣebî*; v.9b). Ezekiel calls the land of Israel "the most beautiful of all lands" (Heb. *ṣebî*), "a land flowing with milk and honey" (Eze 20:6, 15). The horn continues to grow until it reaches the heavens, "and it threw some of the starry host down to the earth and trampled on them" (v.10).

The "starry host" is the panoply of stars in the heavens (Lucas, 215; cf. Dt 17:3). According to Baldwin, 157, "the little horn, in reaching for the stars, is claiming equality with God" (cf. Goldingay, 210); but she goes on to say that the reference to the stars could allude to rival earthly rulers whose kingdoms fall as the little horn grows in power. Miller, 226, understands the "starry host" as a symbolic representation of the Hebrews in Palestine who are persecuted by Antiochus IV. Collins (*Daniel*, 333) admits the expression is difficult but sees the "starry host" as a mythic-realistic symbol for the angels or their visual representations. What does seem clear is that the phrase "starry host" points in some fashion "to the transcendent dimension of the conflict between Antiochus and the Jews" (Lucas, 215).

This horn continues to exalt itself as though it is the "Prince of the host" (v.11a). The "Prince of the host" may refer to the high priest or the priesthood generally, since priests officiated at the daily sacrificial ritual in the Jerusalem temple (cf. Goldingay, 209–11). Most recent commentators, however, understand the "Prince of the host" to refer to God himself as "LORD of hosts" (cf. Lucas, 216). The horn has the power to halt the daily sacrifice at the Prince's sanctuary; thus he "brings low" the sanctuary by interrupting the daily worship that takes place there (v.11b). The phrase "daily sacrifices" (Heb. *hattāmîd*, "regular sacrifice," NASB) is a technical expression for the daily morning and evening sacrifices prescribed in the Mosaic law (Ex 29:38–42), and by this "one word the whole sacrificial system is implied" (Baldwin, 157).

The opening phrase of v.12, "because of rebellion" ("on account of transgression," NASB), is obscure (cf. Miller, 226; Lucas, 206). The word "rebellion" or "transgression" (Heb. *pāšaʿ*) suggests that the horn's tyrannical rule over God's people is divine retribution for Israel's (unspecified) sin. If so, it helps explain the placement of Daniel's prayer of confession immediately after the vision of the ram and the goat (although the date formula places the event a dozen years or so after the vision; cf. 9:1).

No doubt disturbing for Daniel is the idea that the horn "prospered in everything it did" (v.12b). But as Seow, 124, reminds us, the passive verb in the clause "[the host ... and the daily sacrifice] were given" (v.12a; Heb. *ntn* [niphal]) "is a circumlocution for divine agency." As in the case with the passive verbal construction seen previously in 7:25, someone greater than the "little horn" is in control (cf. Baldwin, 146). Daniel also learns that during the trampling of the Beautiful Land by the renegade horn, "truth was thrown to the ground" ("it will fling truth to the ground," NASB; v.12c) — probably a reference to the Torah, the law of Moses (cf. Lucas, 217).

13–14 Lucas, 217, notes that these verses provide a "heavenly" perspective on the events described in the vision, much like throne room scene in the previous vision (cf. 7:9–10). Daniel overhears (presumably) the end of a conversation between two heavenly beings (v.13). The "holy one" (Heb. *qādôš*) is an angelic being similar to the "holy one" (Aram. *qaddîš*) in 4:13, 23 (cf. Collins, *Daniel*, 335; see also

Notes on 4:13). The prophet Zechariah has a similar experience of listening in on an angelic conversation (cf. Zec 2:3–8). Lacocque, 163, understands the expression as an "angelized Saint," erroneously equating the "holy one" with the "host" (Heb. *ṣābāʾ*) or army of Israel in v.12.

The question posed by the heavenly messenger is not "why?" but "how long?" This question is a feature of the lament psalm and is echoed at times in the OT prophets (e.g., Isa 6:11; Jer 12:4; Zec 1:12; cf. Collins, *Daniel*, 326). Lucas, 218, finds a parallel between the question in Daniel 8:13 and Zechariah 1:12, since both are a call for God's mercy on Jerusalem (cf. Porteous, 126). Baldwin, 158, interprets the angelic conversation as a word of encouragement, for it "presupposes that God is limiting the triumph of evil." The remainder of v.13 summarizes the preceding account of the events associated with the "small horn" (vv.9–12), though as Baldwin, 158, observes, the "trampling of the host and the sanctuary" (v.13b) adds further detail to the narrative.

Curiously, the angel answers directly to Daniel ("He said to me"; v.14). Logic might expect the answer to be directed to the other angelic being (cf. the ancient versions, "He said to *him*"; see Montgomery, 342; Collins, *Daniel*, 326). Either "the seer is asking the same question" as the other angelic being, or the answering angel anticipates a similar query from Daniel (Baldwin, 158).

The answer to the question of "how long?" is given in relationship to the termination of the daily sacrifices mentioned previously (v.11). The "2300 evenings and mornings" (v.14) compute to 1150 days when the total number is divided by the twice-daily sacrifices, offered each evening and morning. (The evening to morning rhythm of time for the Hebrews is based on the creation account pattern of "evening and morning" constituting a "day" [Ge 1:5].) The length of time indicated for the "prospering" of the small horn of the vision is just shy of three and a half years (thirty-eight months and ten days, though the Greek and Latin versions calculate the "evening–morning" idiom as two thousand three hundred days). The verbal form rendered "reconsecrated" is unique to v.14 (Heb. *ṣdq* [Niphal]). Collins (*Daniel*, 336) translates it "set right," and "the versions give the clearer paraphrase, 'cleansed.'" Goldingay, 210, summarizes the vision by commenting that the "army, sanctuary, and truth are all portrayed as victims of the goat's charging and butting."

NOTE

11–12 Montgomery, 335, comments that vv.11–12 "constitute *crescendo* the most difficult short passage of the book." Heaton, 194, describes the same two verses as "the most puzzling of the whole book." Lucas, 216, goes on to note, "there are problems with gender concord, verbal tenses and general syntax … not to mention debate about the intended referents" (see his discussion, 206; cf. Goldingay, 197–98, notes 11.a–11.d-d and 12.a-a–12.b-b).

3. Interpretation of the Vision (8:15–26)

a. Appearance of the interpreting angel (8:15–18)

> [15]While I, Daniel, was watching the vision and trying to understand it, there before me stood one who looked like a man. [16]And I heard a man's voice from the Ulai calling, "Gabriel, tell this man the meaning of the vision."
> [17]As he came near the place where I was standing, I was terrified and fell prostrate. "Son of man," he said to me, "understand that the vision concerns the time of the end."
> [18]While he was speaking to me, I was in a deep sleep, with my face to the ground. Then he touched me and raised me to my feet.

COMMENTARY

15–18 It is unclear whether Daniel has returned to a state of consciousness after the vision of the ram and the goat. The first-person report suggests that the seer has awakened, since the narrative indicates he is in the process of reflecting on the vision and "trying to understand it" (v.15a). Either way, Baldwin, 158, states, "he was soon back in a visionary state and saw before him a man-like figure." The figure who interrupts Daniel's thought process is described as "one who looked like a man" (v.15b). The term "man" (Heb. *geber*) may mean "young man" or "strong man," "a rather macho word for a male … but comes to denote a man who is strong in and because of his relationship to God" (Goldingay, 214). Miller, 231, says the word "describes a 'mighty' being in human form," but he misconstrues the figure as God himself rather than an angelic being.

The human voice that speaks to Daniel from the waters (or above the waters) of the Ulai Canal (cf. v.2; see Miller, 231, on "from the Ulai") is usually identified as the voice of God introducing the angel Gabriel to the seer (v.16a; cf. Goldingay, 214; Lucas, 219). Collins (*Daniel*, 336), however, contends that the "human voice" (Heb. *qôl-ʾādām*) represents an "angelic voice" (cf. Redditt, 141: "the speaker is either God or one of the two holy ones"). The intervention of the celestial being anticipates Daniel's as-yet unasked question, "What does the vision mean?" (v.16b).

Commentators acknowledge the clear wordplay between the phrase for the figure who "looks like a man" (Heb. *kᵉmarʾēh-gāber*) and the name "Gabriel" (Heb. *gabrîʾēl*). The name Gabriel is usually understood to mean "man of God" (e.g., Hartman and Di Lella, 227), but Collins (*Daniel*, 336) prefers the meaning "God is my hero/warrior." Only in Daniel in the OT are angels named (Gabriel in 8:16; 9:21; Michael in 10:13, 21; 12:1). Both names are attested in the list of archangels in the Jewish pseudepigraphical book of *1 Enoch*—another reason critical scholars date the book of Daniel to the later intertestamental period of Judaism.

Daniel's response to the approach of the interpreting angel is one of terror and change of posture, from standing erect to prostration (v.17a). Such a reaction is not atypical of angelic epiphanies and theophanies in recognition of other-worldly majesty (e.g., Jos 5:14; Eze 1:28). The angel Gabriel addresses Daniel as "son of man" (Heb. *ben-ʾādām*; v.17b). The phrase means "a mere mortal" and "emphasizes Daniel's weakness and mortality" (Miller, 231; cf. Redditt, 142). Daniel's prostration at the theophany and his address as a "son of man" link his experience with that of the prophet Ezekiel (cf. Eze 1:28; 2:1, 3; 3:23). Goldingay, 216, recognizes that the phrase "the time of the end" (v.17b) "is a more allusive expression." Certainly the expression refers to the end of the persecution of Israel by the "small horn" of the vision in answer to the question posed earlier in v.13 (cf. Baldwin, 159; Seow, 127). Beyond this, Goldingay, 216, suggests that the phrase also hints at "*the* End ... the end of an era ... the closing scene of this history of Israel and the nations ... and the moment of final judgment."

Daniel's prostration before the interpreting angel produces the effect of a "deep sleep" (v.18). The verb (Heb. *rdm*; GK 8101) depicts a trancelike state of unconsciousness, or "a coma-like state of deep sleep brought about by supernatural agency" (Goldingay, 214−15; cf. Ge 2:21; 15:12). Ezekiel is empowered by "the spirit" to stand and receive his divine commission after falling prostrate during his experience of a theophany (Eze 2:2). Here, the angelic touch produces a similar effect. Lacocque, 169, describes this as a "miraculous touch" and notes that it is repeated in Daniel 10:10, 16, 18. Redditt, 142, comments, "the point is either that he [i.e., the interpreting angel] brought Daniel out of his trance, or that he simply stood Daniel on his feet to hear what Gabriel had to say." In either case, the seer has been readied to receive the interpretation of the vision.

b. Message of the interpreting angel (8:19−26)

¹⁹He said:"I am going to tell you what will happen later in the time of wrath, because the vision concerns the appointed time of the end. ²⁰The two-horned ram that you saw

represents the kings of Media and Persia. ²¹The shaggy goat is the king of Greece, and the large horn between his eyes is the first king. ²²The four horns that replaced the one that was broken off represent four kingdoms that will emerge from his nation but will not have the same power.

²³"In the latter part of their reign, when rebels have become completely wicked, a stern-faced king, a master of intrigue, will arise. ²⁴He will become very strong, but not by his own power. He will cause astounding devastation and will succeed in whatever he does. He will destroy the mighty men and the holy people. ²⁵He will cause deceit to prosper, and he will consider himself superior. When they feel secure, he will destroy many and take his stand against the Prince of princes. Yet he will be destroyed, but not by human power.

²⁶"The vision of the evenings and mornings that has been given you is true, but seal up the vision, for it concerns the distant future."

COMMENTARY

19 Gabriel, the interpreting angel, begins his message to Daniel by setting the interpretation of the vision in the context of two somewhat ambiguous temporal references. The first, "later in the time of wrath" (Heb. *bᵉʾaḥᵃrît hazzāʿam*) specifies when the events of the vision will occur. This expression is a time span of unspecified duration. The word "wrath" (Heb. *zᶜm*) means "indignation" (cf. NASB's "the final period of the indignation"). According to Lacocque, 170, the term, with the exception of its use in Hosea 7:16, "always designates the wrath of God." For Baldwin, 159, "*the indignation* is the sentence of God, which must eventually fall on those who rebel against him and fail to repent" (including his own people, the Hebrews).

The "time of wrath" likely refers to the period of Hebrew history from the Babylonian exile onward, that era covered by the rise and fall of the four kingdoms described in the statue dream of ch. 2 and the vision of animals arising out of the sea in ch. 7 (cf. Lucas, 220). The qualifier "later" refers to the Seleucid persecution of the Hebrews

by Antiochus IV Epiphanes as indicated in the interpretation of the vision of the shaggy goat in vv. 23–25 (see below).

The second temporal expression, "the appointed time of the end" (Heb. *lᵉmôʿēd qēṣ*) is parallel to the phrase "the time of the end" used earlier by the interpreting angel (v. 17; see the commentary above). The idea behind the phrase "the end" (Heb. *qēṣ*; GK 7891) is a punctiliar moment in time, the end of the kingdom of Anitiochus IV and hence his persecution of the Hebrews, and the reconsecration of the Jerusalem temple (v. 14). The fact that this is "the *appointed time* of the end" emphasizes that "the 'time' has been set ... by the Lord of history" (Miller, 233), underscoring God's sovereignty over the historical process. "The important point scored in this talk of the wrath of God is that God is still in charge, not human powers, despite signs to the contrary" (Seow, 128–29).

Lucas, 219–20, correctly ties Daniel's vision of the ram and goat to the teaching of the visions of Zechariah (especially the first three visions; cf. Zec 1:7–2:13) that indicate "the 'ongoing' [divine] wrath is not seen as a continuing, deserved punishment for Israel's sins, but rather as the harsh treatment of Israel by the nations into whose power God has delivered her." The import of Daniel's vision of the ram and the goat for a later generation of Hebrews suffering at the hands of the Seleucid "madman" Antiochus IV is twofold: first, God is indeed in control of the historical situation in which his people find themselves; second, not all suffering and persecution experienced by the people of God is retributive.

20–22 Unlike the previous vision (ch. 7), the interpreting angel explicitly identifies the referents of the animal symbols. Daniel is told that the ram with two horns represents the kings of the one Medo-Persian Empire (v.20). Animals are sometimes used to symbolize leaders in the OT (e.g., "rams and goats" depict people of power and influence who were oppressing the poor in Judah; Eze 34:17). The ram and the goat were both "clean" animals according to the OT food laws, in contrast to the "unclean" hybrid animals used to portray "predator nations" in ch. 7 (cf. Dt 14:3–6). Goldingay, 208, notes that the ram was readily identifiable as a symbol for Persia, since in the zodiac Persia was under Aries, the ram.

Daniel learns that the "shaggy goat" (v.21) with one large horn "between its eyes" (or on "the front of its head"; so Baldwin, 159) represents the first king of Greece. Alexander the Great is universally identified as this Greek ruler. The four horns that sprout from the broken horn are four lesser kingdoms that emerge from the short-lived Greek Empire (v.22). These four kingdoms are widely recognized as "mini-empires" carved out of Alexander's empire by his four generals: Macedonia and Greece ruled by Cassander; Thrace and Asia Minor ruled by Lysimachus; northern Syria, Mesopotamia, and the other eastern regions ruled by Seleucus; and southern Syria, Palestine, and Egypt ruled by Ptolemy.

23–25 This passage is the core of the vision and the purpose for the revelation given to Daniel. Conservative scholars view this historical summary interpreting Daniel's vision as necessary disclosure enabling the Hebrews to prepare for a future crisis—a time of severe persecution (cf. Miller, 234). Mainline scholars consider the vision of ch. 8 an *ex eventu* prophecy, dating the writing of the account to 167–165 BC (Redditt, 135; cf. Collins [*Daniel*, 343], who places the writing of ch. 8 to shortly after the desecration of the Jerusalem temple by Antiochus). In either case, commentators agree that the vision refers to the later Seleucid king known as Antiochus IV Epiphanes.

Antiochus rose to power in 175 BC and died in 163 BC. He wrested Palestine from the Ptolemies in 167 BC and desecrated the Jerusalem temple (cf. 1 Macc 1), thus prompting the Maccabean revolt and the eventual reconsecration and dedication of the Jewish temple in 164 BC (cf. 1 Macc 2, 4). The "latter part of their reign" (v.23a) refers to a period near the end of the era of the four kings who succeed Alexander the Great and carve up his empire into quadrants (cf. v.22). Baldwin, 160, notes that this telescoping of history is common to apocalyptic literature, since the focus is on "what is significant."

Antiochus is described as a "stern-faced" king (NIV; v.23c). The expression (Heb. ʿaz pānîm) may be better rendered "defiant, shameless" or "insolent" (so NASB), though Baldwin, 160, is content to recognize that this king is both "hard" and "insolent." Russell, 159, comments, "he is a man with an insolent face ('of bold countenance'), the kind of face that one associates with a brazen prostitute (cf. Pr 7:13)." He is also depicted as a "master of intrigue" (Heb. mēbîn ḥîdôt, lit., "an interpreter of riddles"; v.23d). Goldingay, 218, equates the expression with "problem solving" as a necessary attribute for a king (cf. 1Ki 10:1). In this context the expression is better understood as "a man given to double-talk and double-dealing" (Russell, 159; cf. Porteous, 129). Seow, 131, cautions that these formulaic descriptions of character traits are sufficiently vague so as to refer to Antiochus or any foreign ruler.

This insolent and treacherous king increases in strength by means of military conquest (cf. v.9, "the horn grew in power to the south and to the east and toward the Beautiful Land"). This may refer to the campaigns of Antiochus against Egypt in 169–68 BC, Parthia in 166 BC, and Israel in 165 BC (cf. Hartman and Di Lella, 235–36). The explanatory clause "but not by his own power" (v.24a) indicates that this king "succeeds only by the permission of God" (Collins, *Daniel*, 340; cf. Lacocque, 165, 171), though some suggest Antiochus was empowered by Satan (e.g., Miller, 234).

The destructive power of this king is aimed at "the mighty men" and "the holy people" (v.24c). The "mighty men" (Heb. ʿ*ṣûmîm*) are probably other rivals to the Seleucid throne whom Antiochus "liquidated" along the way on his rise to power (cf. Russell, 160; Seow, 131; though Miller, 235, applies the term to the kings, nobles, and champion warriors of other nations killed by Antiochus and his armies). The title "holy people" (Heb. ʿ*am-qᵉdōšîm*, "people of the saints") refers to Israel, the people of God (cf. Baldwin, 160; Miller, 235).

Porteous, 129, aptly interprets the difficult expression "he will cause deceit to prosper" to mean "that the king's mind is always busy hatching plots which he carries through to a great measure of success." The reference to this king's destruction of many "when they feel secure" (v.25b) adds the traits of cunning and treachery to his despicable character profile (cf. Russell, 160; Miller, 235, who connect the verse to the deceitful attack of Jerusalem in 167 BC by Apollonius, Antiochus's tribute collector; see 1 Macc 1:29–32). Antiochus's

delusions of grandeur will include equating himself with the gods (or God), as evidenced by his self-proclaimed title, "Epiphanes," or "god-manifest." His arrogance drives him to stand against "the Prince of princes," no doubt a reference to God himself (cf. Goldingay, 218).

Specifically, Antiochus did indeed take his stand against God when he exalted himself as a god, abolished the worship of Yahweh in the Jerusalem temple, plundered the temple of its treasures, set up a statue of Zeus on the temple altar, and offered profane sacrifices there (cf. Hartman and Di Lella, 236). Antiochus will meet the same fate as all those "kings of the earth" who set themselves up against "the One enthroned in heaven" (Ps 2:2, 4). Finally, the angelic interpreter reveals to Daniel that this insolent and imperialistic king will himself be destroyed, "but not by human power" (v.25c). According to conflicting historical traditions, Antiochus did not die from an act of violence; rather, he "self-destructed" either as a result of some hideous disease, a fit of insanity, or a bout of depression resulting from his defeat at Elymais in Persia (cf. Russell, 160; Miller, 236).

26 The interpreting angel's final words to Daniel confirm the veracity of the vision. The angel refers to Daniel's entire visionary experience as "the vision of the evenings and mornings" (v.26a). Presumably this feature of the vision is singled out because "it told the exact length of the persecution period, information that would be of great interest to those suffering this ordeal" (Miller, 236).

The command to "seal up" the vision (v.26b) is due to the fact that "it concerns the distant future" (v.26c) and implies that the vision has been written down (cf. 7:1). The verb "to seal" (Heb. *stm*; GK 6258) may simply mean to close up in the sense of preserving and keeping it safe until the time when it is needed (cf. Goldingay, 218). The term may also denote keeping the interpretation of the vision "secret" (so NASB), given its relevance to the distant rather than the immediate future (cf. Collins, *Daniel*, 341–42). The verb "close up" (Heb. *stm*) is coupled with the verb "seal up" (Heb. *ḥtm*; GK 3159) in 12:4, 9 in the sense that Daniel is instructed to "close up and seal" the scroll or book of his visions both for the purposes of safeguarding them for the future and keeping them secret until the time of the generation for whom they were intended. Lucas, 221, notes here that on at least one occasion Ezekiel's contemporaries dismissed what he said because his vision concerned "the distant future" (Eze 12:27).

For critical scholars the angel's instruction to "seal up" the vision is simply a literary convention of pseudepigraphy, declaring the "secrecy of the book" for the intervening period after the fact to emphasize the point that "something foretold long ago seems to be coming to fulfillment" (Collins, *Daniel*, 342; cf. Goldingay, 218–19). Scholars adhering to the traditional or face-value reading of the passage counter that the angelic affirmation of the "truth" of the prophecy rings hollow for the audience receiving a "prophetic" message about persecution while already in the midst of the persecution (cf. Miller, 236).

NOTES

24 The phrase "not by his own power" is omitted from the LXX and other ancient versions and is treated by many commentators as a gloss (a later scribal insertion) in the MT (e.g., Smith-Christopher, 116; Collins [*Daniel*, 340], who explains the phrase as a corruption from v.22). Goldingay, 195, 199, note 24.a–a, acknowledges the phrase as a gloss (either accidental or intentional as a negative evaluation of Antiochus) but understands it to refer back to v.22 in the sense that this kingdom will have strength, "but without its strength" in reference to the strength of its predecessor (i.e., Alexander's empire).

Others identify "the holy people" with the angelic host, "since it builds the crescendo toward the confrontation with the prince of the host and is in accordance with the references to the holy ones (v.13) and to the heavenly host (v.10) earlier in this chapter" (Collins, *Daniel*, 341). Seow, 131, understands the expression "holy people" to include both the angelic host and the Jews. Gowan, 122, equates the expression "the people of the holy ones," along with the terms "the mighty" (v.24) and "the many" (v.25), with the Jews. Hartman and Di Lella, 223, transpose the phrase "the holy people" from the end of v.24 to the beginning of v.25 ("His cunning will be against the holy people").

26 According to Baldwin, 160–61, the Hebrew verb סתם (*stm*, "to stop up, hide"; GK 6258) has the idea "of making unrecognizable to the enemy access-points and wells; applied to a book it is not strictly 'seal' but rather 'guard from use' and therefore from misuse."

4. Conclusion (8:27)

> [27]I, Daniel, was exhausted and lay ill for several days. Then I got up and went about the king's business. I was appalled by the vision; it was beyond understanding.

COMMENTARY

27 The conclusion reports the physiological and psychological effects of the vision on Daniel. The experience has left him exhausted, precipitating an unspecified illness. The fact that Daniel is "quite old" at this time (cf. Miller, 236) only partially explains the vision's effect on him. Goldingay, 222, comments that "awareness of where history is going puts you in a complicated position ... you may ... be awed and troubled, by having been put in touch with heavenly realities."

Such is Daniel's case, and he admits as much when he states, "I was appalled by the vision" (v.27c). The verb "appalled" or "astounded" (NASB; Heb. *šmm*) is rendered "dismayed" in the NRSV (cf. Collins, *Daniel*, 328). Despite the fact that Daniel receives an interpretation of the vision (vv.20–26), it is still "beyond understanding" (v.27d). Part of Daniel's astonishment or dismay is due to the fact that the

vision has spoken to the "distant future" and that he is required to "seal up the vision" (v.26; see comments on vv.15–26). As Seow, 132, notes, "to be instructed that human actions on earth can have consequences beyond the mundane world—that violence on earth can somehow be violence against heaven—is frightening and sobering."

Perhaps more disconcerting, however, is the implication of the vision for the Hebrew people. Both the dream of the creatures rising out of the sea and the vision of the ram and goat bode ill for God's people (v.24; cf. 7:21, 25). Similar to the dream of the creatures rising out of the sea (ch. 7), questions related to the enormity of the threat to the Hebrews, and its duration no doubt troubles Daniel (cf. Seow, 113). The two experiences leave a similar mark on the seer (cf. 7:28) and anticipate Daniel's prayer for his people in ch. 9.

NOTE

27 The word translated "exhausted" (Heb. נִהְיֵיתִי, *nihyêtî*) is problematic and is typically understood as a passive form of the verbal root הָיָה (*hyh*, "to be"), meaning "stricken" (Lucas, 203), "overcome" (NRSV), or even "pass out, faint" (Lacocque, 167). Goldingay, 195, 200, renders the Heb. construction נִהְיֵיתִי וְנֶחֱלֵיתִי (*nihyêtî wᵉneḥᵉlêtî*) idiomatically: "fell ill." Collins (*Daniel*, 328), however, relates the form to the Hebrew root הוה (*hwh*, "to come to ruin") and reads, "I, Daniel, was undone and sick for many days."

C. The Seventy Years and Seventy "Sevens" (9:1–27)

OVERVIEW

Daniel 9 begins with a date formula or a chronological notice, as in 1:1; 2:1; 7:1; 8:1; and 10:1. The date formula, "the first year of Darius," places the events of ch. 9 between 539 and 538 BC—some eleven or twelve years after the vision of ch. 8.

The historical setting of ch. 9 is the first year of the Persian Empire established by Cyrus the Great, as Mesopotamia transitioned from Babylonian to Persian rule. It is assumed the name Darius is a title or alternative name for Cyrus the Mede (5:31), but both the names "Darius" and "Xerxes" in the date formula pose problems (see comments on v.1).

The literary setting of ch. 9 is the visions or "apocalyptic" section of Daniel (ch. 7–12). The "visions" half of the book denotes a change in genre and point-of-view from "report" in the third-person voice to that of "diary" or "personal journal" in the first-person voice. This chapter stands out from the rest of Daniel for several reasons. First, as Seow, 135–36, notes, the point of departure for the account is neither a threat posed by an oppressive regime (as in chs. 1, 3, 6) nor a dream or vision by one of the main characters of the narrative (as in chs. 2, 4–5, 7–8, 10–12). Rather, "the story begins with reflections on what is 'in the books,' a reference to certain prophecies of the prophet Jeremiah" (cf. Collins, *Daniel*, 347). The chapter is also distinctive because of the recitation of Daniel's lengthy prayer of confession and supplication (vv.4–19). In addition, Baldwin, 162, observes that this is the first time in the book that Daniel's initiative occasions an event of divine revelation.

Collins (*Daniel: with an Introduction to Apocalyptic Literature*, 91) identifies three main genres in ch. 9: prayer (vv.3–19), (angelic) epiphany (v.21b), and angelic discourse (vv.22–27). Goldingay, 231, rather clumsily identifies the literary form of ch. 9 as a report of an angelically mediated revelation to a seer (akin to those of ancient Near Eastern oracular dreams). Both Collins and Goldingay agree that the angelic discourse is a type of expository or exegetical "midrash" based on the precursor text of Jeremiah 25:11–12 (cf. v.2). Miller, 239, somewhat simplistically equates Daniel's "vision" (Heb. *maʾeh*; v.23) with "prophetic revelation" after the manner of the "visions" (Heb. *ḥāzôn*) of Obadiah (Ob 1), Nahum (Nah 1:1), and Habakkuk (Hab 2:2). Towner, 127, calls this chapter a "meditation," since "it revolves around a 'perception' which Daniel experienced

(v.2) about the meaning of the seventy years" of exile forecast by Jeremiah (Jer 25:11–14).

Lucas's designation, 231, of "epiphany vision" (in contrast to "symbolic vision") is more helpful. He identifies a six-part form for an epiphany vision and notes that it is unique to Daniel in the OT (ch. 9, 10–12). The form of the epiphany vision may be outlined as follows (see Lucas, 35):

1. Circumstances (vv.1–2)
2. Supplication (vv.3–19)
3. Appearance of nessenger (vv.20–21)
4. Word of assurance (vv.22–23)
5. Revelation (vv.24–27)
6. Charge to seer (omitted; cf. 12:4)

The basic structure of ch. 9 is marked by the narrative framework: first in the date formula and occasion of the revelatory event (vv.1–2); second, in the introduction to the prayer of confession (vv.3–4a); and finally in the narrative introducing the occasion of the angel Gabriel's revelation to Daniel (vv.20–21a). Broadly understood, the chapter may be outlined in three units: the historical introduction (vv.1–2), Daniel's prayer of confession (vv.3–19), the revelation given to Daniel by the angel Gabriel (vv.20–27).

The immediate purpose of ch. 9 is to assure the persecuted Hebrews of the Babylonian Diaspora that the time of exile is almost over; the seventy years of Jeremiah's prophecy are about to be fulfilled (v.2). Beyond this, ch. 9 serves as further commentary on the question posed in the vision of ch. 8: "how long" will the rebellious "little horn" oppress the people of God (8:13)? Daniel's epiphany vision assures the Hebrews that the future time of trial and persecution has definite chronological boundaries by locating "the time of wrath" (8:19) within an overview of history (cf. Collins, *Daniel: with an Introduction to Apocalyptic Literature*, 93).

1. Introduction (9:1–2)

¹In the first year of Darius son of Xerxes (a Mede by descent), who was made ruler over the Babylonian kingdom — ²in the first year of his reign, I, Daniel, understood from the Scriptures, according to the word of the Lord given to Jeremiah the prophet, that the desolation of Jerusalem would last seventy years.

COMMENTARY

1 The reference to "Darius son of Xerxes" is problematic. Previously Daniel has equated "Darius the Mede" with Cyrus II (the Great) as the first king of the Medo-Persian Empire and successor to the Babylonian hegemony (6:1 [5:31]; cf. 6:28). Critical scholars contend that the mention of Darius is a historical blunder, since Xerxes was the son Darius I, not his father (e.g., Davies, 27; Anderson, 64–65). As such, the verse is offered as further evidence in support of the idea that "Darius the Mede" is an invented personage, simply a literary fiction (e.g., Hartman and Di Lella, 240; Collins, *Daniel*, 348). Lacocque, 109–10, suggests that the biblical writer confounded the two seizures of Babylon, the one by Cyrus in 539 BC and the other by Darius in 529 BC, and then created a third ruler (i.e., Darius the Mede) out of the confusion to solve the dilemma. He thus categorizes the biblical author with the Greek historians who "constantly confused Persian and Median names and events" (Lacocque, 110).

Conservative scholars recognize that the name "Xerxes/Ahasuerus" (Heb. *ʾhašwērôš*) is generally regarded as the Hebrew transliteration of the Persian name *khashavārshā*, understood by the Greeks as Xerxes. The only Darius known from the time period is Darius I, the son of Cyrus II the Great and the father of Xerxes, king of Persia from 486–465 BC. Earlier in the court stories, Daniel apparently equated Darius the Mede with Cyrus II (the Great; cf. 6:1, 28). Cyrus the Great was of Median descent in that his mother was Mandane, daughter of Astyages, king of the Medes (cf. Wiseman, *Notes on Some Problems*, 13). Cyrus the Great was the son of Cambyses I, king of Anshan, and historical records indicate he would have been about sixty-two years of age in 539–538 BC (ibid., 14–15). As a result, Wiseman considers the name Xerxes (or Ahasuerus) an Achaemenid royal title or dynastic throne name applied to Cyrus II the Great. Following Lucas, 235, if one is looking for a historical rather than a literary explanation of the name Xerxes (or Ahasuerus) in Daniel 9:1, "Wiseman's seems the more plausible suggestion" (see comments on 6:1, 28).

Quite apart from the identification of the enigmatic "Darius the Mede," the first year of the king's overseeing of the Medo-Persian Empire after the conquest of the Babylonians is dated to 539–538 BC.

2 Many critical scholars consider the phrase "in the first year of his reign" (v.2a) a secondary addition—"a gloss to explain, in shorter form, the preceding cumbersome expression" (Hartman and Di Lella, 241; cf. Collins, *Daniel*, 344). Yet Lucas, 235, regards the repetition as original and even essential to the context, since it places emphasis on "the fact that this was an appropriate time for Jewish exiles to take note of Jeremiah's words" concerning the seventy years of exile (cf. Anderson, 104–5; Redditt, 152, who also consider the repetition as "noteworthy"). It is possible that Daniel (or the narrator of his visions) understands Jeremiah's prophecy concerning the defeat of the Babylonians by "kings of the Medes" (Jer 51:28) to now be fulfilled, perhaps paving the way for the return of the Hebrew exiles (cf. Gowan, 128). At the very least, the transition from the Babylonian Empire to the Persian Empire affords an opportunity for reflection on the seventy years of exile predicted by Jeremiah (so Seow, 138; cf. Jer 25:11–12; 29:10).

The expression "the Scriptures" (v.2b) is interpretive. The phrase (Heb. *bassepārîm*) means literally "the scrolls" or "the books" (NASB). Baldwin, 164, among others, considered the expression a technical term from some portion of the OT Scriptures (i.e., the books of the Prophets, the second segment of the later Hebrew canon), recognized as an authoritative collection of religious writings by the Hebrews (cf. Lucas, 235). Naturally the reference to the book or scroll of Jeremiah indicates that this document was among the prophetic books considered "canonical" at the time of Daniel (cf. Anderson, 105; Collins, *Daniel*, 348). It is possible, however, that the reference to "the writings" refers more specifically to the two letters (Heb. *sēper*) Jeremiah sent to the Hebrew exiles in Babylonia that mention the seventy years of captivity (Jer 29:1, 10, 25;

cf. G. H. Wilson, "The Prayer in Daniel 9: Reflection on Jeremiah 29," *JSOT* 48 [1990]: 93; Redditt, 152; Seow, 138–39).

The "seventy years" of Jerusalem's "desolation" (v.2c) may be a round number used symbolically to represent a normal human life span, a lifetime (so Lucas, 235; cf. Ps 90:10; Isa 23:15). Attempts to interpret Jeremiah's seventy years of exile (cf. Jer 25:12; 29:10) in a strictly chronological fashion must reckon from set dates determined to begin the captivity (whether Judah's submission to Babylonia in 605 BC, Nebuchadnezzar's invasion of Jerusalem in 597 BC, or the fall of Jerusalem in 587 BC) and to end it (whether the fall of Babylonia in 539 BC, the initial wave of Jewish repatriation of Judah in 538 BC, or the dedication of the second temple in 517 BC).

The third set of dates, tied to the destruction and rebuilding of the Jerusalem temple, span an exact seventy-year time period. The context of Daniel's prayer in ch. 9 (as well as the context of Jer 25:12) suggests that the fall of Babylon marks the end of the Hebrew exile. This means the seventy-year captivity is a round number for the sixty-six years counted from the submission of Judah to Babylonia (and Daniel's own captivity, 605 BC) to the fall of Babylonia and the decree of Cyrus (539 BC; cf. the discussions in Goldingay, 239; Lucas, 235–36).

NOTES

1 The passive expression "was made ruler" is the only example of the Hophal form of the verb מלך, *mlk*, in the OT. While others emend the text and read a Hiphil form of the verb (e.g., Montgomery, 360–61; Lacocque, 175), Wood, 232, comments that "the passive form of the verb fits the history involved" (though he incorrectly understood that Darius was made ruler by Cyrus). If Darius is a throne-name applied to Cyrus (II) the Great (see comment on v.1), then the passive form of the verb does indeed fit the history, but it calls attention to God's rule of human history in setting up kings and deposing them (2:21; see discussion in Lucas, 227).

2 The word בִּינֹתִי, *bînōtî*, is an anomalous form for the Qal stem of the verbal root בִּין, *byn*, prompting some commentators to regard the term as a shortened form of the Hiphil stem (e.g., Hartman and Di Lella, 241; Goldingay, 226) and translate it "considered" rather than "understood" (so NIV). The Qal form of the MT is preferred, and the word expresses the idea of observing ("observed," NASB; cf. Collins, *Daniel*, 344) or perceiving ("perceived," NRSV; cf. Wood, 232) — something as a result of reading or study.

2. Daniel's Prayer (9:3 – 19)

³So I turned to the Lord God and pleaded with him in prayer and petition, in fasting, and in sackcloth and ashes.

⁴I prayed to the LORD my God and confessed:

"O Lord, the great and awesome God, who keeps his covenant of love with all who love him and obey his commands, ⁵we have sinned and done wrong. We have been wicked and have rebelled; we have turned away from your commands and laws. ⁶We have not listened to your servants the prophets, who spoke in your name to our kings, our princes and our fathers, and to all the people of the land.

⁷"Lord, you are righteous, but this day we are covered with shame — the men of Judah and people of Jerusalem and all Israel, both near and far, in all the countries where you have scattered us because of our unfaithfulness to you. ⁸O LORD, we and our kings, our princes and our fathers are covered with shame because we have sinned against you. ⁹The Lord our God is merciful and forgiving, even though we have rebelled against him; ¹⁰we have not obeyed the LORD our God or kept the laws he gave us through his servants the prophets. ¹¹All Israel has transgressed your law and turned away, refusing to obey you.

"Therefore the curses and sworn judgments written in the Law of Moses, the servant of God, have been poured out on us, because we have sinned against you. ¹²You have fulfilled the words spoken against us and against our rulers by bringing upon us great disaster. Under the whole heaven nothing has ever been done like what has been done to Jerusalem. ¹³Just as it is written in the Law of Moses, all this disaster has come upon us, yet we have not sought the favor of the LORD our God by turning from our sins and giving attention to your truth. ¹⁴The LORD did not hesitate to bring the disaster upon us, for the LORD our God is righteous in everything he does; yet we have not obeyed him.

¹⁵"Now, O Lord our God, who brought your people out of Egypt with a mighty hand and who made for yourself a name that endures to this day, we have sinned, we have done wrong. ¹⁶O Lord, in keeping with all your righteous acts, turn away your anger and your wrath from Jerusalem, your city, your holy hill. Our sins and the iniquities of our fathers have made Jerusalem and your people an object of scorn to all those around us.

¹⁷"Now, our God, hear the prayers and petitions of your servant. For your sake, O Lord, look with favor on your desolate sanctuary. ¹⁸Give ear, O God, and hear; open your eyes

and see the desolation of the city that bears your Name. We do not make requests of you because we are righteous, but because of your great mercy. ¹⁹O Lord, listen! O Lord, forgive! O Lord, hear and act! For your sake, O my God, do not delay, because your city and your people bear your Name."

COMMENTARY

3–4a Daniel's preparations for prayer demonstrate both his humility and the depth of his pathos for the people of Israel. Daniel turns to Lord God (v.3a; lit., "gave his face" in prayer; NASB, "gave my attention"). The idiom alludes to the practice of facing Jerusalem when a Hebrew prays (see comments on 6:10; cf. 1Ki 8:35). The idiom may also imply that Daniel is determined "to look to God in prayer until the Lord gave him an answer" (Miller, 242; cf. Wood, 234).

Next we learn that Daniel "pleaded with [God] in prayer and petition" (v.3b). The verb "pleaded" (Heb. bqš; GK 1335) more literally means "to seek" (so NASB), and some commentators suggest that Daniel is seeking divine revelation (e.g., Montgomery, 361; Heaton, 205). More generally, this word in the OT prophets means to turn to God in humility and repentance as a demonstration of dependence and covenantal loyalty (cf. C. Chhetri, "בקש," *NIDOTTE*, 1:724–25). Lucas, 236, has noted that the verb bqš in 9:3 echoes the call to "seek" God with a whole heart in Jeremiah 29:13, the very passage Daniel reflects upon with regard to Jeremiah's prophecy concerning the seventy years of exile (cf. Jer 29:10–14). Porteous, 136, grants the possibility that the construction "seek to pray" (Heb. bqš + tᵉpillâ) conveys the idea of "praying earnestly." The word for "prayer" (Heb. tᵉpillâ) means "intercession," and the term translated "petition" (Heb. taḥᵃnûnîm; "supplications," NASB) means "entreaty for mercy" (cf. Wood, 234).

The combined ritual acts of fasting and donning sackcloth and ashes (v.3c) were a sign of mourning and repentance in the OT (cf. Ne 9:1; Est 4:1–4; Jnh 3:6). The discipline of fasting is sometimes a part of the preparation process for receiving revelation from God (cf. Ex 34:28; Dt 9:9). Here the two acts of mourning and seeking revelation merge as Daniel prays "to comprehend God's purpose in the destruction of Jerusalem" (Lucas, 236). According to Wood, 234, all three actions (fasting, wearing a coarse sackcloth garment, and sprinkling ashes on one's head) demonstrate the degree of the burden Daniel carries for his people and are "customary for the day when genuine contriteness of heart was felt."

The object or recipient of Daniel's prayer is "the Lord God" (v.3a). The divine name "Lord" (Heb. ᵃdōnāy) means "master, overlord," indicating Daniel's subservience to his God. The name "God" (Heb. ᵉlōhîm) is a reference to God in the abstract, conveying the idea of God's majesty and power as Creator and the universal God. Daniel actually addresses God by his personal and covenantal name "Lord" or "Yahweh" (Heb. yhwh; v.4a) as he begins his prayer. This name serves to remind one of Daniel's role as a member of the Hebrew covenantal community and calls attention to God's obligations to his people Israel as covenant-maker. Finally, Daniel understands his prayer as a "confession" (Heb. ydh, Hithpael) in that he readily identifies with his Hebrew people, penitently acknowledges his guilt, and confesses his sins against Yahweh along with theirs.

4b–19 Many commentators consider Daniel's prayer of confession a secondary insertion since it seems to interrupt the logical flow of thought and action from Daniel's preparation for prayer (vv.1–4a) and the divine revelation he receives while praying (vv.20–27; e.g., Hartman and Di Lella, 245–46). Redditt, 153, observes that since the rituals of self-abnegation were appropriate both to seeking divine revelation and demonstrating contrition, it afforded the author an "opportunity to insert the prayer."

Others, however, defend the authenticity of the prayer and the literary unity of ch. 9 by suggesting the author incorporates some form of a preexisting prayer of confession, "a set prayer—a liturgical prayer" into the narrative (so Seow, 141; cf.; Collins, *Daniel*, 347; Lucas, 233–34). Still others contend that the prayer has been composed by the author of ch. 9 (e.g., Porteous, 135–37; Goldingay, 236–37). In any case, this helps explain why the language of the prayer flows smoothly, is full of "traditional phrases," and lacks the Aramaisms of the rest of the chapter (cf. Collins, *Daniel*, 347). Smith-Christopher, 122, offers an interesting perspective on the importance of the prayer in the structure of the chapter by suggesting a direct relationship between the prayer and the appearance of the angelic figure. According to him, fasting is an essential aspect of communal prayers of deliverance, and "these prayers are part of an exilic tradition of calling God to spiritual warfare."

The literary form of the prayer is usually identified as that of communal confession (note the use of the first-person plural pronouns; vv.5–7, etc.), perhaps an adaptation of the community lament (cf. Goldingay, 234–35). The prayer develops the theme of Israel's sin and breach of Yahweh's covenant in a somewhat chiastic structure around the affirmation of God's mercy—the principal point of the prayer (for other structural features of the prayer, including the use of the word "now [Heb. *ʿattâ*; v.15] to mark the transition from confession to an appeal for mercy, see Lucas, 231–32).

Towner, 129, describes Daniel's prayer (and the entire chapter) as "a meditation of Scripture upon earlier Scripture" (since more than eighty-five percent of the texts falls "within quotation marks"). According to Montgomery, 361–68, the bulk of Daniel's prayer consists of language found in other liturgical prayers (especially 1Ki 8; Ezr 9; Ne 1; 9; Jer 26; 32; 44; note that his analysis assumes a critical understanding of the date of Daniel, whereas traditional scholarship considers Ezr 9 and Ne 1 and 9 dependent on Da 9). As a result, Heaton, 206, considers the prayer (especially vv.4–14) "a splendid catena of Old Testament fragments."

The prayer reflects the theology of Deuteronomy, a theology rooted in the covenantal relationship established by Yahweh with the nation of Israel at Mount Sinai (cf. Ex 19–24; Longman, 219, 231–34). Yahweh's covenant with Israel was regulated by stipulations designed to instill holiness in God's people in imitation of his own holy character. Blessings or curses were applied to Israel as Yahweh's vassal contingent on their obedience to the stipulations of his covenant. The prayer begins with an ascription of praise to God (v.4b), followed by a confession of sin (vv.5–10) that is expanded into an acknowledgment of God's just punishment (vv.11–14), and finally a concluding plea for God's mercy (vv.15–19).

4b Daniel addresses his prayer to the "Lord" (Heb. *ʾadōnāy*), a return to the divine name utilized previously in v.3 (see comments on vv.3–4a). The invocation praising "the great and awesome God" is a typical characterization of the Hebrew deity in the OT (cf. Dt 7:21; Ne 1:5). Seow, 142, comments that "the prayer begins by assuming God's power to deliver and God's sovereignty over the whole universe. The 'great and awesome God' is at once an immanent God who saves and a transcendent God who rules the cosmos."

Daniel also declares that God is one who "keeps his covenant of love" (lit., "the covenant"; Heb. bᵉrît; GK 1382) and "the lovingkindness" (Heb. ḥesed; GK 2876; cf. NASB, "his covenant and lovingkindness"). The term "covenant" signifies a ritually ratified agreement or treaty that establishes a relationship between two parties (cf. G. J. Mcconville, "בְּרִית," NIDOTTE, 1:747–48). The use of the definite article ("the covenant") may mean Daniel has in mind the Abrahamic covenant, since it included the promise of the land to Abraham's descendants (so Miller, 244; cf. Ge 12:1–3). Yet Wood, 235, correctly recognizes that the use of the word "covenant" in the context of Daniel's situation may be used as an umbrella term for Yahweh's covenantal tradition with Israel (i.e., the covenants with Abraham, Israel at Mount Sinai, and David).

The word "love" or "lovingkindness" (NASB) is used as an expression of "a relationship of mutual loyalty and faithfulness" between the parties bound by a covenant (Lucas, 237). Daniel affirms that God has fulfilled his covenantal obligations. But Yahweh's ḥesed or covenantal love is contingent on Israel's loving obedience in response to his commands (Heb. miṣwôt), since they express his will for his people. The final clause of v.4b echoes the Decalogue, in which Yahweh promises to show "love to a thousand generations of those who love me and keep my commandments" (Ex 20:6; Dt 5:10). The context both in the Pentateuch and Daniel's prayer "makes clear that what is called for is not so much an emotional as a moral commitment" (Lucas, 237).

5–11a Daniel's confession begins with an admission of corporate guilt, piling up five synonymous terms for sin in "liturgical style" (i.e., "sinned…done wrong…been wicked…rebelled… turned away"; cf. Towner, 131). Seow, 143, observes that these general expressions for sin are repeated throughout the prayer (vv.9–11, 13–16; see Lucas, 237, for a discussion of the five Hebrew terms used for sin in the prayer). The language (i.e., the repetition of the first three terms for sin) and setting (i.e., foreign captivity) of v.5 have parallels to Solomon's temple-dedication prayer (cf. 1Ki 8:47).

The acknowledgment that Israel has not listened to God's prophets echoes Jeremiah's indictment of the people prior to the Babylonian exile (cf. Jer 25:4; 29:19, the very passages alluded to in v.2). The emphasis placed on the role of the prophets (v.6a) means that people were without excuse—God had provided ample warning and time for repentance (cf. Jer 29:19; cf. Ne 9:26, 34). The reference to "our kings, our princes and our fathers, and … all the people" (v.6b) indicates all strata of Hebrew society have been equally guilty of breaking Yahweh's covenant (so Porteous, 137).

The stark contrast between the covenantal faithfulness of God and the covenantal betrayal of Israel is manifest in the foils of the personal pronouns used in vv.7–8 ("you" [God] vs. "us" [Israel]) and the terms "righteous" (Heb. ṣᵉdāqâ; GK 7407) and "shame" (Heb. bōšet; GK 1425) applied to God and Israel respectively. Both Goldingay, 241–42, and Lucas, 238, agree on the forensic connotations of the word "righteous" in this context; if the setting were a court of law, God "is in the right" (so Goldingay) and "justice is on his side" (so Lucas). Consequently, Israel's shame or disgrace is deserved. The reason for Israel's shame and scattering is explained by their "unfaithfulness" (Heb. maʿal; GK 5085/5086; v.7b)—a form of treachery linked "with encroachment on the holy by violating an oath" (Lucas, 238). The clause "all the countries where you have scattered us" (v.7b) repeats Jeremiah 16:15; 23:3; 32:37, further connecting Daniel's meditation and prayer with the prophet Jeremiah (cf. v.2).

Daniel concludes the formal confession of sin by testifying that God is "merciful and forgiving" (v.9). The words for "merciful" (Heb. *raḥªmîm*; "compassion," NASB) and "forgiving" (Heb. *sᵉliḥôt*) are both plural. These plurals are intensive and have the effect of "emphasizing God's great and manifold 'mercies' and his abundant forgiveness" (Miller, 246). Yahweh remains who he is, the faithful, merciful, and forgiving God of Israel's covenant. By contrast, Israel has rebelled (Heb. *mārad*) against God, perhaps an allusion to the Hebrews' postexodus wilderness experience (cf. Nu 14:9) and tragically the all-too-characteristic posture of his people (cf. Dt 31:27; Ps 78:8; Jer 5:23). As Seow, 143, summarizes, "hope, if any, can come only on account of God's steadfast love" (cf. La 3:22). The repetition of Israel's disobedience (vv.10–11a) completes the chiasmus with v.4b in this section of the prayer.

11b–14 Daniel's prayer moves from communal confession to theological reflection on God's justice (vv.11b–14). The "curses and sworn judgments" (v.11b) are the covenantal curses recorded in Leviticus 26:27–45 and Deuteronomy 28:15–68. Miller, 247, notes that the words for "curses" and "sworn judgments" are singular and may even be translated "the curse, *even* the sworn judgment," indicating the particular curse for breach of the Sinaitic covenant (Dt 28:20; cf. Towner, 133). This is confirmed by references to the documentation of Yahweh's covenant with Israel found in the "Law of Moses" (vv.11b, 13).

The twofold appeal to the "written … Law of Moses" (v.11b, 13) also implies "that the experience of judgment had confirmed the authority of the Mosaic writings because their words had come to pass" (Baldwin, 166). The verb "poured out" (Heb. *ntk*; GK 5988) is equated with God's wrath (cf. 2Ch 12:7; Jer 7:20; Eze 22:22) and depicts Yahweh as "the guarantor of the covenant, and the pouring out of the curse is described more personally as his keeping his verbal undertaking" (Lucas, 239).

Daniel affirms that God is faithful to the word of his covenant, whether for blessing or cursing, and that his punishment of Israel is just (v.12). The expression "the words spoken against us" (v.12a) alludes to the ministry of the prophets mentioned previously (vv.6, 10). The assumption is that "the prophets teach orally what Moses teaches in writing" (Goldingay, 245). The prophets of Yahweh did not cause the exile, but heeding their warnings may have prevented it (cf. Towner, 133–34). All Israel, people and rulers alike, were guilty before God (v.12a).

The "great disaster" (v.12b) brought by God against Israel was the destruction of Jerusalem and the subsequent Babylonian captivity (though critical scholars understand that the historical experience of the exile has been "recontextualized" for the Jews of the second century BC suffering at the hands of Antiochus IV Epiphanes; e.g., Seow, 142–43). Surely other cities and temples had been razed and other nations had been taken into exile, but "the destruction of Jerusalem was in a category apart from the destruction of any other city because in no other had the Lord deigned to dwell" (Baldwin, 166).

This makes the failure of God's people to turn to him in repentance and renewed obedience all the more remarkable (v.13). The expression "did not hesitate" (Heb. *šqd*; v.14a) means "to watch over" in the sense that God "had kept the disaster ready … in case Israel did not repent" (Miller, 248; cf. NASB's "the LORD has kept the calamity in store"). A summary of Daniel's earlier prayer of confession frames his meditation on God's justice, as he recognizes the "great disaster" that befell Israel was a result of their sin (v.11b) and disobedience (v.14c).

15–19 The adverb "now" (Heb. *ʿattâ*) marks the transition from confession to supplication or petition in Daniel's prayer (v.15). Daniel invokes God by the name "Lord" six times in the passage (vv.15, 16, 17, 19 [3x]; see comments on vv.3–4a). The name means "master, overlord," indicating

Daniel's (and Israel's) subservience to God as the suzerain of the Sinaitic covenant (since the context is the exodus from Egypt). Daniel appeals to the God who acted on behalf of Israel to deliver them from slavery in Egypt and thus to fulfill covenantal promises made earlier to Abraham (cf. Ge 12:1–3).

That act of redemption, a demonstration of divine grace that revealed aspects of Yahweh's character, left an indelible imprint on the collective memory of Israel (cf. Porteous, 138). The renown that God gained in delivering Israel from Egypt becomes the basis for Daniel's petition for the Lord to act in behalf of Israel again for the sake of his reputation (vv.17, 19). The pronouns "our God" and "your people" (v.15a) emphasize the relationship God still has with his covenantal people. Lucas, 239, has noted the lexical parallels between v.15a and Deuteronomy 6:21 and 9:26, and between v.15b and Jeremiah 32:20 and Nehemiah 9:10.

Daniel's plea to the Lord divides neatly into two sections. First, he asks God to "turn away" his anger and wrath (v.16) and to "look with favor" upon his ruined temple (v.17). The expression "turn away" (Heb. *šwb*; GK 8740) is used in the sense of relenting from or revoking his punishment of Israel for their sin. The call for God to "look with favor" or let his "face shine" (so NASB) on his desolate sanctuary echoes the Aaronic blessing (Nu 6:25).

Next, Daniel begs God to take note of "the desolation of the city" that bears his name (v.18) and to hear his prayer and act quickly to remedy the situation (v.19). The reference to Jerusalem as "the city that bears your [God's] name" (v.18) denotes the city as that one place of worship where God established

his name (Dt 12:5)—the "joy of the whole earth" (Ps 48:2). The phrase "your servant" (v.17) is an expression of humility and submission, "appropriate before 'the great and awesome God' for whose mercy Daniel was appealing" (Miller, 249). The suppliant's summons to God to "give ear ... hear; open your eyes" echoes a similar plea in Solomon's temple-dedication prayer (cf. 1Ki 8:28–29).

Daniel's appeal is also grounded in two essential spiritual realities. The first is the character of the Lord himself, a God known for his "righteous acts" (v.16a) and "great mercy" (v.18). Yahweh revealed himself as "the compassionate and gracious God, slow to anger, abounding in love" from the earliest days of the exodus from Egypt (Ex 34:6).

The second basis is God's reputation before "all those" who surround Israel (v.16) because Daniel reminds the Lord that his people, his temple, and his city are now the objects of scorn (vv.16b, 18). Much like Moses before him, Daniel pleads with God not to afford the surrounding nations any opportunity to doubt the power or goodness of Israel's God because of their sin (cf. Ex 32:9–14). Here Baldwin, 167, comments, "The fact that God's name has been dishonoured by the disciplinary measures his people have forced Him to take make the appeal to Him to vindicate His righteousness a powerful plea." Porteous, 139, summarizes that Daniel's "final appeal is based, not on anything of merit in the lives of those who pray, but solely on God's great mercy." For this reason, he and others (e.g., Montgomery, 368; Heaton, 209) agree that the prayer is aptly described as the OT *kyrie eleison*—"Lord, have mercy."

NOTES

15 The "mighty hand" motif echoes the narrative of the exodus from Egypt (cf. Ex 15:6), a victory image borrowed from Egyptian pharonic iconography and applied to Yahweh by the Hebrews since he was the victor in the cosmic battle against the gods of the Egyptians (Ex 12:12; 18:11; cf. *BBCOT*, 90–91).

18 Miller, 249, notes that the Hebrew expression "give ear" (נטה, *nṭh*, + אזן, *'ōzen*, lit., "turn the ear" or "bend the ear") is a word picture of "a person bending the ear in order to hear more clearly."

3. The Revelation (9:20–27)

> ²⁰While I was speaking and praying, confessing my sin and the sin of my people Israel and making my request to the Lᴏʀᴅ my God for his holy hill — ²¹while I was still in prayer, Gabriel, the man I had seen in the earlier vision, came to me in swift flight about the time of the evening sacrifice. ²²He instructed me and said to me, "Daniel, I have now come to give you insight and understanding. ²³As soon as you began to pray, an answer was given, which I have come to tell you, for you are highly esteemed. Therefore, consider the message and understand the vision:
>
> ²⁴"Seventy 'sevens' are decreed for your people and your holy city to finish transgression, to put an end to sin, to atone for wickedness, to bring in everlasting righteousness, to seal up vision and prophecy and to anoint the most holy.
>
> ²⁵"Know and understand this: From the issuing of the decree to restore and rebuild Jerusalem until the Anointed One, the ruler, comes, there will be seven 'sevens,' and sixty-two 'sevens.' It will be rebuilt with streets and a trench, but in times of trouble. ²⁶After the sixty-two 'sevens,' the Anointed One will be cut off and will have nothing. The people of the ruler who will come will destroy the city and the sanctuary. The end will come like a flood: War will continue until the end, and desolations have been decreed. ²⁷He will confirm a covenant with many for one 'seven.' In the middle of the 'seven' he will put an end to sacrifice and offering. And on a wing ⌊of the temple⌋ he will set up an abomination that causes desolation, until the end that is decreed is poured out on him."

COMMENTARY

20–23 The answer to Daniel's prayer comes while he is still in the act of praying (v.20), and the repetition of that fact emphasizes God's grace in the timing of his response to Daniel's supplication (v.21). The opening verse (v.20) serves as a summary of Daniel's supplication and connects the revelation he receives with the prayer of penitence by repeating the words for "praying" (Heb. *pll*) and "confessing" (Heb. *ydh*) used earlier (cf. v.4). Daniel's reference to "my sin and the sin of my people" (v.20) indicates that he both considers himself a guilty party before Yahweh and a representative for the people. The repeated reference to God's "holy hill" (v.20; cf. v.16) suggests Daniel's primary concern is the "desolate sanctuary" of Yahweh in Jerusalem (cf. v.17).

Gabriel (v.21a) was the interpreting angel in Daniel's earlier vision of the ram and the goat (see comments on 8:16). Lucas, 240, is probably correct to identify the unnamed interpreter of Daniel's vision of strange creatures rising out of the sea with Gabriel as well (cf. 7:16). The phrase "in swift flight" is difficult (v.21c). The word rendered "flight" may be connected to the verbal root ʿwp ("to fly"; so NIV, NRSV) but is more logically associated with the verbal root yʿp, meaning "to be weary, faint" (cf. NASB's "in my extreme weariness"). The latter understanding better fits the context since Daniel has been engaged in an extended period of prayer and fasting, quite apart from the description of Gabriel in the form of a man (v.21b; cf. the discussions in Collins, *Daniel*, 351–52; Miller, 250–51). The "evening sacrifice" (v.21d) was offered in the late afternoon, perhaps at twilight (cf. Ex 29:39), and was probably the appointed time for Daniel's evening of prayer (cf. 6:10). Later, Ezra offered his prayer of confession to God at the time of the evening sacrifice (Ezr 9:4–5).

As in the case of the vision of the ram and the goat (8:16), Gabriel is sent to "instruct" Daniel, in the sense of imparting "insight and understanding." "Insight" (Heb. *śākal*; GK 8505) and "understanding" (Heb. *bînâ*; GK 1069) were divine gifts (see comments on 1:17), and they place Daniel among the company of the wise who instruct those suffering persecution (11:33) and who will "enjoy the brightness of the coming resurrection victory (12:3)" (Towner, 141). Baldwin, 167, has observed, "one of the most important contributions of the book of Daniel is its new insistence on the link between faith and intelligence." Lucas's comment, 241, is helpful here as he notes that "the point was not that Daniel did not understand the meaning of Jeremiah's prophecy, but that it had a reference beyond its most obvious reference to the ending of the Babylonian exile." Daniel learns that God's answer to his prayer was granted as soon as he began to pray (v.23a), not because his prayer was superfluous (so B. W. Jones, "The Prayer in Daniel IX," *VT* 18 [1968]: 493) but because "God is eager to respond to his servants when they come to him on behalf of his people in need" (Goldingay, 255).

Daniel is "highly esteemed" (v.23b; cf. 10:19) or "greatly beloved" (NRSV), presumably because he is a man of humble faith and contrition and is given to prayer (cf. Ps 51:17; Isa 57:15). This notice provides the rationale for "the high favor bestowed on Daniel in being selected to receive this important information" (Wood, 246). Gabriel charges Daniel to "consider the message and understand the vision" (v.23c). Goldingay (228, n. 23.d-d) understands the expression as a double hendiadys ("give careful heed to the revelatory word"; cf. Collins, *Daniel*, 352). Wood, 246–47, however, relates the word "vision" (Heb. *marʾeh*) to the appearance of Gabriel and paraphrases: "Consider the word I am about to give you and understand all concerned in connection with my appearance to you."

24 Baldwin, 163, considers Daniel 9:24–27 "the most difficult text in the book," and Miller, 252, regards this next section as "four of the most controversial verses in the Bible." Such comments only serve to lend support to the often-quoted remark of Montgomery, 400, that "the history of the exegesis of the 70 Weeks of Daniel is the Dismal Swamp of O.T. criticism."

Daniel learns from the angelic messenger Gabriel that "seventy sevens" are decreed for the people of Israel and their holy city, Jerusalem (v.24a), since Daniel has prayed both for the people and the city of God. It is generally understood that the "seventy sevens" represent seventy weeks or heptads of years by analogy to the "seven weeks of years" associated with the Year of Jubilee (cf. Lev 25:8). The verb "are decreed" (Heb. *ḥtk*; GK 3155; Niphal, lit., "to cut off" in the sense of "determine, ordain") is unique to Daniel 9:24 in the OT and "the thought is that God had cut off these 490 years from the rest of history through which to accomplish the deliverances needed for Israel" (Wood, 248).

Six distinct purposes or goals are outlined for accomplishment during this extended period of time: "to finish transgression, to put an end to sin, to atone for wickedness, to bring in everlasting righteousness, to seal up vision and prophecy and to anoint the most holy" (v.24b). Baldwin, 168, has observed that the six verbs divide neatly into two sets of three: the first three address (negatively) the grounds on which God forgives human sin (in response to Daniel's prayer), and the second three focus (positively) on the fulfillment of God's righteous purposes in human history.

The first objective achieved during the heptad of years is to "finish transgression" (Heb. *peša*ᶜ; v.24a). The historicist interpreter notes that the word for "transgression" is definite and that previously "the transgression" was associated with the attack on Jerusalem and desecration of the temple by Antiochus IV in 167 BC (cf. 8:13; e.g., Seow, 147). Others equate "the transgression" with Israel's rebellion against God and subsequent exile in Babylonia, finally ending with the overthrow of Antiochus (cf. Russell, 184). Futurist interpreters understand the reference to "transgression" as a term for "sin in general" (so Baldwin, 168) that will not end until the second coming and eternal reign of Jesus Christ (so Miller, 260).

Similarly, historicist interpretation ties the second objective of the heptad of years ("to put an end to sin"; v.24b) to the desecration of the Jerusalem temple, since that is the context for the use of the expression, "to put an end" (Heb. *ḥātēm*), in the only other place it occurs in Daniel (cf. 8:23). By contrast, futurist interpretation connects putting an end to sin with God's kingdom and the end of human history (e.g., Baldwin, 168; Miller, 260).

The third objective of the heptad of years is "to atone for wickedness" (v.24c). The verb "atone" (Heb. *kpr*; GK 4105) is used for making atonement or reconciliation, especially by the blood sacrifices of animals offered by Levitical priests (cf. Lev 1; 3–4). The word is "associated with the removal,

and so the forgiveness of sin" (Lucas, 241). The word for "wickedness" or "iniquity" (so NASB; Heb. ᶜ*āwôn*; GK 6411) is a comprehensive term for wrongdoing in the OT (often understood as an umbrella term for "rebellion" [Heb. *pšᶜ*] and "sin" [Heb. *ḥṭᵓ*]; cf. A. Luc, " עָוֹן ," *NIDOTTE*, 3:351). The context of Daniel's prayer, including the verbal links between the prayer and the divine response in vv.20–27, suggest the object of the atonement is Israel's wickedness.

Although Collins (*Daniel*, 354) and Goldingay, 259, understand the referent to be the sinful acts of Antiochus IV Epiphanes, Porteous, 141, correctly recognizes that the writer intends to imply that both the wickedness of Antiochus and of Israel are at issue. More generally, Baldwin, 169, comments that God is announcing that he has "found a way of forgiving sin without being untrue to His own righteousness. This assurance was what the prayer [i.e., Daniel's prayer in ch. 9] had been feeling after; it was the great longing expressed in the Old Testament as a whole." Miller, 260, sees the definitive fulfillment of the atonement for humanity's wickedness in the redemptive work of Jesus Christ on the cross of Calvary.

The fourth of goal of the heptad of years is "to bring in everlasting righteousness" (v.24d). The word "righteousness" (Heb. *ṣdq*; GK 7406) means "justice, correctness, rightness, vindication," and bringing in righteousness suggests "causing right to be acknowledged" (Goldingay, 259; see also comments on *ṣdq* at vv.5–11a). The objective echoes references to the righteousness or justice of God in Daniel's prayer (vv.7, 14, 16, 18). Baldwin, 169, acknowledges that righteousness is the attribute of God alone and that theologically "it is a short step to justification by faith (Rom 3:25, 26), a truth grasped also by Zechariah (Zech 3:4)." The historicist applies this righteousness to "the restoration of the temple's rightness—its legitimacy—after the transgression" (Seow, 147). Heaton, 212, summarizes for the futurists that "everlasting righteousness ... is a compendious and unique description of the nature of the coming Kingdom."

The fifth objective of the heptad of years is to "seal up vision and prophecy" (v.24e). The "sealing" of the prophetic vision (Heb. *ḥtm*) involves formally closing a document for preservation by rolling up the scroll and affixing a personal stamp or seal to the bundle. More important, to "seal" a document in the ancient world was to authenticate it with one's own engraved stamp, a type of signature (cf. Baldwin, 169; Lucas, 242). Alternatively, Towner, 141, argues that "sealing vision and prophecy refers to the fictional setting of Daniel. When the supposedly long-hidden message is found, taken out of its time capsule, as it were, the seal is broken and the text is found to be extraordinarily descriptive of the present moment."

The last objective of the heptad of years is "to anoint the most holy" (v.24f). The verb "anoint" (Heb. *mšḥ* indicates the smearing or pouring of oil over a person or object as an act of consecration for religious purposes (cf. J. N. Oswalt, "משח," *NIDOTTE*, 2:1123–25). The immediate reference of the final clause is most likely the rededication of the Jerusalem temple, the "Most Holy Place" (Heb. *qōdeš qādāšîm*) for the Hebrews of Daniel's day (so Lucas, 242; cf. Montgomery, 376; Wood, 250). Numerous other interpretations of this anointing have been suggested, such as the ministry of Jesus Christ as Messiah (e.g., Young, 201; cf. Isa 61:1), the church as God's spiritual temple (e.g., K&D, 349), and the inner sanctuary of Ezekiel's "millennial temple" (e.g., Archer, 113; Miller, 262). Baldwin's, 169, comment on the contextual ambiguity of the expression "to anoint the most holy" is pertinent: "In 539 BC concern was centered on the holy place in Jerusalem, and the rededication of the Temple was not excluded, but the Lord's anointed

was ultimately to be a man ... the subject of 'vision and prophet.'"

25–27 In the verses that follow, the angel Gabriel proceeds to outline more specifically how and when these six objectives (v.24) will be accomplished. He does this by addressing figures and events associated with three distinct time periods within the seventy sevens or weeks of years (i.e., 490 years) decreed for Israel and the city of Jerusalem: a period of seven sevens (or forty-nine years), a period of sixty-two sevens (or 434 years), and a final one-week period (or seven years). The first two periods are tied closely to two main events: the rebuilding of Jerusalem and the appearance of an unnamed "anointed" one (v.25a). Daniel also learns from the angelic messenger that the city of Jerusalem will be rebuilt, including "streets and a trench," but during troubled times (v.25b).

We are not told how Daniel himself understood all this (cf. 8:27), but the initial statement of Gabriel's revelation poses several problems for the modern interpreter. For instance, to which "decree to restore and rebuild Jerusalem" (v.25a) does the angel refer? Lucas, 242–43, notes seven possibilities: Jeremiah's prophecy about the seventy years of Babylonian exile (Jer 25:12; 605 BC), Jeremiah's prophecies of Israel's restoration (Jer 30:18–22; 31:38–40; 587 BC), Gabriel's words to Daniel (Da 9:24–27; 539 BC), the decree of Cyrus (Ezr 1:1–4; 539 BC), the decree of Darius (Ezr 6:1–12; 521 BC), the decree of Artaxerxes I to Ezra (Ezr 7:12–26; 458 BC), and the charge of Artaxerxes I given to Nehemiah (Ne 2:7–9; 445 BC). According to some scholars the referent of the "decree" (Heb. *dābār*, "word") is more logically associated with the words of Jeremiah's oracles (note the similarities between Jer 29:10 and Da 9:25; cf. Collins, *Daniel*, 354–55).

Beyond this, the decrees of Cyrus and Darius refer only to the rebuilding of the Jerusalem temple.

The decree of Artaxerxes to Ezra does not mention any rebuilding initiatives. In fact, apart from Jeremiah's promises of restoration for Jerusalem after the exile, only the decree of Artaxerxes to Nehemiah makes reference to the rebuilding of Jerusalem. The identity of the "Anointed One" who is predicted to come is a mystery, since that figure is unnamed (v.25a). The meaning of the terms "Anointed One" (Heb. *māšiaḥ*) and "ruler" (Heb. *nāgîd*) applied to this unnamed figure also raise questions. Finally, what is meant by the unique OT word "trench" or "moat" (so NASB; Heb. *ḥārûṣ*) around the city of Jerusalem, whether a literal trench designed to increase the exterior height of the city walls (e.g., Hartman and Di Lella, 244), or a "wall" of some sort (e.g. A. Jeffery, "The Book of Daniel, Introduction and Exegesis," *IB*, 6:496)?

Gabriel's message to Daniel concerning the seventy weeks further specifies that "after the sixty-two sevens, the Anointed One will be cut off" (v.26a). Moreover, the city of Jerusalem and its temple will be destroyed by "the people of the ruler who will come" (v.26b). Finally, the "end will come like a flood," and it will include war and desolation (v.26c).

Again, the angel's cryptic revelation raises numerous questions for the biblical interpreter. First, what is the extent of the time lapse indicated by the adverb "after" (Heb. *ʾaḥarê*), and how is the period of sixty-two sevens related to the first period of seven sevens (i.e., are they each sequential from a common *terminus a quo* or sequential with respect to each other)?

Next, is the "Anointed One" of v.26 to be equated with the "Anointed One" of v.25, and what does it mean for an "Anointed One" to be "cut off" (cf. Lucas, 244)? The verb "cut off" (Heb. *krt*) is generally understood to mean "killed" (so NLT) or "put to death" (so NJB; cf. E. Carpenter, "כרת," *NIDOTTE*, 2:729–30; Baldwin, 171), but in

reference to whom—the postexilic leader Zerubbabel (an option listed but rejected by Porteous, 142), the Hellenistic era priest Onias III (e.g., Collins, *Daniel*, 356), or Jesus the Messiah based on NT teaching (e.g., Miller, 268)?

Third, who are "the people of the ruler who will come" (v.26b)—the Seleucids under Antiochus IV (e.g., Lucas, 244), the Romans under Titus (e.g., Baldwin, 171), or the future "antichrist" figure (e.g., Miller, 268–69)?

Last of all, what is meant by the repeated formula "the end" (v.26c)—the end of the sixty-two sevens, or the sixty-nine sevens, or the seventy sevens, or even the end of the age?

The final installment of Gabriel's message to Daniel concerning the seventy sevens makes reference to a "covenant with many for one seven" (v.27) made by the ruler who is to come (v.26). Midway through this last seven—the third and final period of the seventy sevens—the ruler will "put an end to sacrifice and offering," presumably in reference to the Jerusalem temple (v.27b). Further, "he will set up an abomination that causes desolation" on one wing of the temple (v.27c) until "a complete destruction ... is poured out on the one who makes desolate" (NASB; v.27d).

Regrettably, the end of Gabriel's message to Daniel brings no end to the interpretive difficulties associated with the passage. For example, "historicist" interpreters tend to equate the "covenant" (Heb. *bᵉrît*) confirmed with many with the alliance made between Antiochus IV Epiphanes and the Hellenizing Jews of Jerusalem (e.g., Collins, *Daniel*, 357; cf. 1 Macc 1:11). But Goldingay, 262, cautions that this covenant could refer to the covenant between God and Israel mentioned in Daniel 9:4; 11:22, 28, 30, 32. By contrast, "futurist" interpreters understand the "one seven" (v.27a) to refer to the last years of human history prior to the second coming of Jesus the Messiah and associate the "firm covenant" (NASB) with policies established by the antichrist figure (e.g., Miller, 269–70).

Additional questions arise, especially concerning the identity of "the many" (Heb. *rabbîm*) with whom the covenant is made and the relationship between this alliance and the cessation of temple sacrifices (whether the Hellenized and apostate Jews [so Heaton, 215] or the believing Jews [so Archer, 111]). The word "abomination" (Heb. *šiqqûṣ*; GK 9199) is frequently used of idolatry and "implies something filthy and loathsome of which people should be ashamed" (Baldwin, 172; cf. 1Ki 11:7; Jer 4:1; 7:30; 13:27). Goldingay, 262, summarizes that "the worship prescribed by the Torah will

cease and be replaced by a repellent alternative." The question of the exact nature of this desolating abomination still remains, as well as its correlation to the "abomination that causes desolation" cited in Daniel 11:31; 12:11.

Finally, one thing is certain: Quite apart from the identity of the ruler who brings war, desolation, and sacrilege to the Jews and Jerusalem, his doom is sure, since it has been decreed by God (v.27d). War and desolation (v.26) will overwhelm Jerusalem in fulfillment of Isaiah's prophecy (cf. Isa 10:22–23), but only for a God-ordained, limited period of time. The desolation "is determined, not endless ... within the gloom are gleams of light" (Goldingay, 263).

NOTES

24 Lucas, 232, has noted that two prophetic surveys of history found in *1 Enoch* have some affinity with Daniel 9:24–27 in that they also divide history into distinct "weeks" or periods of time (though he finds no evidence of any literary dependence between *1 Enoch* and the book of Daniel; cf. "The Animal Apocalypse" in *1 Enoch* 85–90 and "The Apocalypse of Weeks" in *1 Enoch* 91:11–17; 93:1–10).

26 The NASB's "its end" more correctly represents the MT's קִצּוֹ (*qiṣṣô*; cf. NIV's "the end"). The logical antecedent is the city of Jerusalem and its temple (cf. Wood, 256), though Collins (*Daniel*, 346) translates "his end" and associates the construction with the eventual downfall of the coming ruler who will destroy Jerusalem and its temple.

27 Baldwin, 171, calls attention to the expression "make a firm covenant" (NASB) since the Hebrew verb גבר (*gbr*, Hiphil, "be strong") is unusual and "has the implication of forcing an agreement by means of superior strength."

The phrase "on a wing of the temple" is difficult, and the NIV follows the Old Greek and Latin readings (cf. NASB's "on the wing of abominations"). The MT is not unintelligible, and Wood's, 261, rendering is as plausible as any: "even unto the overspreading of abominations of desolation" (see the discussions in Goldingay, 230; Lucas, 230).

REFLECTION

Several views of Daniel's "seventy sevens" (v.24a), or seventy weeks of years, have emerged in Jewish and Christian interpretation of the book of Daniel. (See the helpful distillations of these views in Montgomery, 390–401; Baldwin, 172–78; Miller, 252–57; Lucas, 245–48.) Lucas, 244, conveniently sorts the Christian interpretations into two categories: the "messianic" approach, which understands the seventy weeks of years as fulfilled in the life and ministry of Jesus the Messiah (based on the NT interpretation of Daniel's message; cf. Baldwin, 174–75); and the "Antiochene" approach, which relates the message of Daniel exclusively to the known history of the Hebrew Babylonian captivity, the restoration of Jerusalem during the Persian period, and the persecution of the Jews by Antiochus IV Epiphanes during the Hellenistic era. This approach emphasizes "the absence of any clear interest in a messianic figure elsewhere in Daniel" (Lucas, 246; cf. Porteous, 141–42). Beyond this, the interpretive approach of each camp may be further subdivided into those adhering to a literal chronological understanding of Daniel's "seventy weeks" of years and those espousing a schematic or symbolic approach to the numbers and time periods of the revelation given to Daniel by the angel Gabriel.

The messianic interpretation of 9:24–27 has a long tradition in the church, first appearing in Christian exegesis toward the end of the second century AD (cf. Collins, *Daniel*, 355). The messianic approach may be summarized as follows (recognizing that both so-called "premillennial" and "amillennial" interpreters may be included under this umbrella rubric):

(1) The 490 years are understood literally and extend from the command to rebuild Jerusalem after the Babylonian exile to the second advent of Jesus the Messiah at the end of human history as we know it. Typically this command to rebuild Jerusalem is connected to either of two decrees made by the Persian king Artaxerxes I (i.e., to Ezra in 458 BC or Nehemiah in 445 BC). The end of the first set of seven weeks, or forty-nine years, coincides with the completion of the work of Ezra and Nehemiah in restoring Jerusalem (either 409 BC

or 396 BC). The next set of sevens, the sixty-two sevens or 434 years, extends sequentially from the end of the set of seven sevens to the first advent of Jesus the Messiah (either his baptism about AD 26 or his triumphal entry into Jerusalem before his passion in AD 32 or 33).

For some, the final week of years, or the seventieth seven, is fulfilled in the first Jewish war (AD 67–73), when the Roman general Titus sacked Jerusalem and destroyed the Jewish temple "midweek" in AD 70 (cf. v.27). For others, the final week of seven years is associated with events connected to the second advent of Jesus the Messiah based on Daniel 11:36–45 and NT teaching found in Matthew 24 and Revelation 6–18. Thus a great gulf of time intervenes between the end of the sixty-ninth week and the beginning (or middle) of the seventieth week (depending on the interpreter's understanding of the length of the "great tribulation" [whether three and one-half years (so Miller, 271–72) or seven years (so Wood, 260; cf. Da 12:7; Rev 12:14; 13:5). The final seven-year period will conclude with the second coming of Jesus the Messiah, thus bringing about the deliverance of modern-day Israel, the destruction of the Antichrist, and the inauguration of the kingdom of God (cf. Mt 24; Rev 18–19; see the discussions in Wood, 255–63; Baldwin, 176–77; Miller, 257; Lucas, 246).

(2) It is frequently noted that the number "seven" in the OT is often symbolically associated with ideas of completeness, totality, and perfection (cf. P. P. Jenson, "שֶׁבַע," *NIDOTTE*, 4:34). Likewise, the number six is sometimes used to represent the antithesis of perfection (cf. P. P. Jenson, "שֵׁשׁ," *NIDOTTE*, 4:258). Thus "a span of seventy weeks represents a complete period [of time], the one needed to bring in the perfect kingdom" (Lucas, 248). Young, 201, represents those messianic interpreters who regard Daniel's "seventy sevens" as

symbolic periods of time culminating in the advent of Jesus the Messiah in the first century AD during the Roman occupation of Palestine.

Keil and Delitzsch, 399–401, and Baldwin, 176–78, are among those messianic interpreters who understand the numbers of Daniel's "seventy sevens" symbolically rather than as literal chronology, in reference to the second advent of Jesus the Messiah. Keil and Delitzsch, 400, view the entire "seventy sevens" of Daniel's message as a "symbolical measure of time" that culminates in the second coming of Jesus the Messiah at the end of the eschaton. Baldwin, 177, however, considers the first sixty-nine sevens of Daniel's message to have commenced with the decree of Cyrus (538 BC) and concluded with the first advent of Jesus the Messiah. For her, Daniel's final seven, or seventieth week of years, spans the interval between the first and second advents of Jesus the Messiah.

The Antiochene interpretation (or the "historical interpretation" for Baldwin, 172–73) may be summarized as follows:

(1) The 490 years are understood literally and extend from 605 BC to the rededication of the Jerusalem temple (164 BC; so Montgomery, 394) or the death of Antiochus IV Epiphanes (163 BC; so Hartman and Di Lella, 250). The *terminus a quo* of 605 BC is determined by interpreting "the issuing of the decree to restore Jerusalem" (v.25) as an allusion to Jeremiah's prophecy delivered in 605 BC concerning the seventy years of Babylonian captivity for the Hebrews (Jer 25:1, 11; cf. Towner, 143, who admits Jeremiah's oracle does not speak directly to the rebuilding of the city of Jerusalem). The interval between 605 BC and 163 BC considers only about 440 years of Hebrew history, leaving fifty years unaccounted for. The discrepancy is typically attributed to "a chronological miscalculation on the part of the writer" (so Montgomery, 393), since "the historical memory which the Jews

retained of the period in question was very dim as regards facts" (so Porteous, 141; cf. Towner, 142; Lacocque, 178).

Specifically, the three sets of weeks of years are interpreted as follows. The first set of "seven sevens," or forty-nine years, refers to the interval of time between the fall of Jerusalem (587 BC) and the decree of the Persian King Cyrus to restore and rebuild Jerusalem (538 BC). The second set of weeks of years (i.e., the sixty-two sevens, or 434 years) is usually understood to extend from the installation of Joshua as high priest or Zerubbabel as governor in the Jerusalem restoration community in 538 BC (in fulfillment of the coming of the "Anointed One"; v.25) to the death of the High Priest Onias III in 171 BC (in fulfillment of the "cutting off" of the Anointed One; v.26). This calculation falls short of accounting for the duration of the sixty-two sevens (434 years) by sixty-five years (cf. Lacocque, 178, who traces the *terminus a quo* for the time period of the sixty-two sevens (434 years) to the "decree" of Jeremiah 25:11 pronounced in 605 BC). The third set of years, the final week of (seven) years, is ascribed to the persecution of the Jews by Antiochus IV from 170–163 BC (see Russell, 187–92).

(2) Goldingay, 257–58, is among those Antiochene interpreters affirming the 490 years of Daniel's "seventy sevens" not chronologically but symbolically as chronography—"a stylized scheme of history used to interpret historical data rather than arising from them" (257).

Quite apart from the interpretive details of Gabriel's message to Daniel concerning the "seventy sevens" (vv.24–27), one thing is certain: the NT indicates that the message of seventy weeks of years had significance for times well beyond the persecution of the Jews by Antiochus IV Epiphanes (cf. Mt 24:15; Mk 13:14; Rev 11:2; 13:5). Wallace, 166, correctly observes that in Daniel 9:24–27 "we think of Jesus" because "within the sphere of salvation history, coming events cast their shadow before. In the shape of earlier and smaller events, we can discern patterns that are going to be manifested in the final events."

Furthermore, whether the 490 years of Daniel's seventy weeks are understood literally or symbolically, and whether or not they represent an "apocalyptic report" of current events related to the persecution of the Jews by Antiochus IV Epiphanes or the prognostication of the advent(s) of Jesus the Messiah, the message of ch. 9 is consistent with the theological teaching of the book of Daniel. First, prayer is vital to the life of faith in God for the Hebrews of the "Diaspora" (cf. Russell, 171–74).

Second, God is the sovereign ruler of human history (cf. Wallace, 162–65). Third, repentance is the essential prerequisite for reconciliation with God (cf. Longman, 239–43). Fourth, God is faithful to his covenantal promises to deliver and restore his people (Goldingay, 234).

The natural and logical response by the people of faith to the God who orchestrates the redemption of fallen creation and humanity through the historical process is worship. Biblical commentators, however, seem more concerned with solving the puzzle of Daniel's "seventy sevens" than calling the people of faith to worship the God who revealed this remarkable message through Gabriel.

D. The Vision of Israel's Future (10:1–12:13)

OVERVIEW

Daniel's final vision begins with a date formula or a chronological notice, as is the case in 1:1; 2:1; 7:1; 8:1; and 9:1. The date formula, "the third year of Cyrus king of Persia" (10:1a), places the events of chs. 10–12 in 536 BC, or approximately three years after the vision of ch. 9. Miller, 276, has noted that each of the four visions of chs. 7–12 is dated, and they appear in two groups: the first and third year of King Belshazzar of Babylonia, and the first and third year of King Cyrus of Persia. If Daniel was conscripted into the Babylonian civil service in 606 or 605 BC, then the third year of Cyrus marks the end of the seventy years of (Babylonian) captivity predicted by Jeremiah (cf. Jer 25:11–12; 29:10).

In addition, the repatriation of Jerusalem had begun two years earlier, and a fledgling effort to rebuild the temple of Yahweh was initiated (Ezr 3:1–3; cf. 3:8). Seow, 155, remarks that even "the prophecies of Isaiah 40–55 should have been fulfilled" since Judah's "hard service had been completed" (Isa 40:2). Yet a cursory reading of the postexilic prophets Haggai, Zechariah, and Malachi indicate that the restoration community in Jerusalem experienced at best only a partial fulfillment of earlier prophetic oracles promising God's blessing.

The literary setting of ch. 9 is the visions or "apocalyptic" section of Daniel (ch. 7–12). The "visions" half of the book denotes a change in genre and point of view from "report" in the third-person voice to that of "diary" or "personal journal" in the first-person voice. According to Towner, 147, a number of features demonstrate the decisive importance of this panel at the end of the book of Daniel: the third-person narrative of the opening verse (10:1), the sheer size of the literary unit (the largest pericope of the book), and the extensive trials the seer must undergo in preparation to receive the vision.

The number of characters participating in the final apocalyptic narrative is difficult to ascertain. The narrator of the story delivers only one verse (10:1). Daniel (10:2) is one of two primary characters (v.2) in the account and the only one to see the vision (though other "men" were with him at the time, cf. 10:7). Much of the prologue (10:1–19) and epilogue (12:5–13) of the vision report is first-person narrative by Daniel himself. The other key figure in the story is the unnamed "man dressed in linen" (10:5), presumably an angelic interlocutor. Given the larger context of the visions section of the book, the "man dressed in linen" is likely the angel Gabriel, who appeared to Daniel and revealed the "seventy sevens" (9:21; cf. Towner, 149–50). God is mentioned as the one who has heard and responded to Daniel's prayer (10:12). Cryptic references are made to the "prince of the kingdom of Persia" (10:13, NASB) and the prince of Greece (10:21). Lastly, another angel named Michael is mentioned as one who brought aid to the man in linen in his struggle with the "prince of the Persian kingdom" (10:13, NIV).

Collins (*Daniel: with an Introduction to Apocalyptic Literature*, 91) identifies the bulk of Daniel's final vision (10:1–12:4) as a complete "historical apocalypse" in the form of an "epiphany" and an "angelic discourse." He construes the epilogue (12:5–13) as a "revelatory dialogue" (ibid., 101). The vision has affinities with Ezekiel's chariot vision (Eze 1; 8–10) and is echoed in Revelation 1:13–15. Goldingay, 281–82, describes the literary form of the book's concluding section as "vision report" (10:1–19), "audition" (10:20–12:4, with the content of the revelation embedded in the audition), and "closing address" (12:5–13). Lucas, 231, designates the literary form of the entire unit as "epiphany vision" (in contrast to "symbolic vision")—a helpful expression. He identifies a six-part form for the epiphany vision and notes that it is unique to Daniel in the

OT (chs. 9; 10–12; see Overview to ch. 9). The form of the epiphany vision may be outlined as follows (see Lucas, 35):

1. Circumstances (10:1)
2. Supplication (10:2–3)
3. Appearance of messenger (10:4–9)
4. Word of Assurance (10:10–11:1)
5. Revelation (11:2–12:3)
6. Charge to seer (12:4)

Most biblical scholars recognize in the last three chapters of the book a broad, tripartite structure consisting of a prologue (10:1–19), a vision report (10:20–12:4), and an epilogue (12:5–13). Beyond this, internal markers delineate subsections of the larger literary structure. For instance, the date formula and third-person voice distinguish 10:1 as the introduction to the section. Likewise, the date formula in 10:4 identifies a new literary unit. Typically in biblical narrative, the adverb "behold" (NASB; Heb. [w^e]$hinn\bar{e}h$) introduces a new scene (cf. 10:10; 12:5). The adverb "now" (Heb. [w^e]$^c att\hat{a}$) also commonly functions as a section marker (cf. 11:2). The narrative of ch. 11 may be outlined on the basis of the kings mentioned: four kings of Persia (v.2), the mighty king (vv.3–4), a series of northern and southern kings (vv.5–19), the king of v.20, and the contemptible king (vv.21–45). Finally, the return to first-person speech by Daniel demarcates the epilogue to the vision (cf. 12:5).

Critical scholars question the literary unity of chs. 10–12, considering it "disordered" (so Porteous, 115) or "jumbled" as a result of incompetent editorial redaction (so Hartman and Di Lella, 285). Alternatively, Goldingay, 292, and Lucas, 267–68, observe both thoughtful chiastic structure and the rhetorical use of repetition in the section indicating literary design within the pericope (the "idiosyncratic Hebrew influenced by Aramaic" notwithstanding; cf. Goldingay, 288). Goldingay,

284–85, has described chs. 10–12 as "situational midrash," or an exposition addressing a contemporary problem shaped by an appeal to earlier OT Scriptures. These precursor texts include Isaiah 10:22 23; 28:15–22; 40:1–11; Ezekiel 1–3; 7:14–27; 9–10; and Zechariah 1:9; 4:4–5, 13; 6:4 (see the discussions in Goldingay, 284–85; Lucas, 268–69).

1. Introduction (10:1)

[1]In the third year of Cyrus king of Persia, a revelation was given to Daniel (who was called Belteshazzar). Its message was true and it concerned a great war. The understanding of the message came to him in a vision.

COMMENTARY

1 The opening verse summarizes the contents of the final vision (chs. 10–12) by introducing the section as a "revelation" (v.1a), affirming its reliability ("its message [is] true"; v.1b), summarizing its content ("a great war"; v.1c), and stating the fact that Daniel's understanding of the message "came to him in a vision" (v.1d). The word for "revelation" (Heb. *glh*; GK 1655) means to "uncover" in the sense of revealing a secret (for the complete idiom, cf. NASB's "a message [Heb. *dābār*, "word"] was revealed"). The expression serves to summarize the predictive information given to Daniel through the heavenly messenger and recorded in 10:20–12:4 (cf. Wood, 265). The form of Daniel's revelation is a "vision" (Heb. *marʾeh*), in which the "auditive aspect is predominant over the visual element. It is revelation by word instead of picture" (J. A. Naudé, "ראה," *NIDOTTE*, 3:1012; cf. "vision" [Aram./Heb. *ḥzh*] in the Notes on 7:1–2). The third-person narration of the introduction calls attention to the importance of the revelation to follow (cf. Lucas, 265).

As noted in the Overview, the date formula places Daniel's final vision in the third year of King Cyrus of Persia, or 536 BC. Goldingay, 14–15, has noted that the date formulae in Daniel cluster in the first three years of a king, perhaps affirming "God's Lordship at key transition points in history ('first' or 'third' can be merely concrete ways of saying 'at the beginning' or 'not long after the beginning')." The final vision of the book occurs three years after the revelation of the "seventy weeks of years" (ch. 9). If Daniel was conscripted into the Babylonian civil service in 606 or 605 BC, then the third year of Cyrus marks the end of the seventy years of (Babylonian) captivity predicted by Jeremiah (cf. Jer 25:11–12; 29:10).

King Cyrus entered the city of Babylon in October of 539 BC, thus establishing Persian control of the former Babylonian Empire. His edict, issued in March of 538 BC, permitted people groups taken captive by the Babylonians to repatriate their homelands (including the Hebrews, although they are not mentioned on the famous clay barrel known as the Cyrus Cylinder). Within a year, Babylonian Jews returned to Jerusalem under the leadership of Sheshbazzar (Ezr 1:1–4, 11) and rebuilt the sacrificial altar (3:1–3). The foundation for the second temple was laid in April of 536 BC (3:8), but the meager rebuilding project was soon abandoned because of the opposition of "local enemies" of the Jews (4:1, 24).

Despite the hopeful beginnings, the restoration community of postexilic Jerusalem was still under Persian control, and the mood of the people was one of cynicism and despair—as the prophets Haggai and Zechariah discovered. Seow, 154, has observed, "as one learns from the preceding chap-ter [ch. 9], the desolation is not over. Even in the restoration period and beyond, the Jews remained a captive people, and Daniel's name, Belteshazzar [v.1], is a reminder of that fact." This initial disappointment associated with the early stages of Israel's restoration from the exile is countered by the promise of complete restoration after the "time of distress" (12:1−3).

2. *Prologue (10:2−19)*

OVERVIEW

The vision report (10:2−19) serves as a prologue to the revelation Daniel receives from the angelic messenger (10:20−12:4). This prologue includes an account of Daniel's fasting (and implied supplication; vv.2−3), a vision report rehearsing the angelic epiphany (vv.4−9), and an explanatory address by the angel coupled with a report of the angel's strengthening Daniel in his weakness (vv.10−19).

²At that time I, Daniel, mourned for three weeks. ³I ate no choice food; no meat or wine touched my lips; and I used no lotions at all until the three weeks were over.

⁴On the twenty-fourth day of the first month, as I was standing on the bank of the great river, the Tigris, ⁵I looked up and there before me was a man dressed in linen, with a belt of the finest gold around his waist. ⁶His body was like chrysolite, his face like lightning, his eyes like flaming torches, his arms and legs like the gleam of burnished bronze, and his voice like the sound of a multitude.

⁷I, Daniel, was the only one who saw the vision; the men with me did not see it, but such terror overwhelmed them that they fled and hid themselves. ⁸So I was left alone, gazing at this great vision; I had no strength left, my face turned deathly pale and I was helpless. ⁹Then I heard him speaking, and as I listened to him, I fell into a deep sleep, my face to the ground.

¹⁰A hand touched me and set me trembling on my hands and knees. ¹¹He said, "Daniel, you who are highly esteemed, consider carefully the words I am about to speak to you, and stand up, for I have now been sent to you." And when he said this to me, I stood up trembling.

¹²Then he continued, "Do not be afraid, Daniel. Since the first day that you set your mind to gain understanding and to humble yourself before your God, your words were heard, and I have come in response to them. ¹³But the prince of the Persian kingdom

resisted me twenty-one days. Then Michael, one of the chief princes, came to help me, because I was detained there with the king of Persia. [14]Now I have come to explain to you what will happen to your people in the future, for the vision concerns a time yet to come."

[15]While he was saying this to me, I bowed with my face toward the ground and was speechless. [16]Then one who looked like a man touched my lips, and I opened my mouth and began to speak. I said to the one standing before me, "I am overcome with anguish because of the vision, my lord, and I am helpless. [17]How can I, your servant, talk with you, my lord? My strength is gone and I can hardly breathe."

[18]Again the one who looked like a man touched me and gave me strength. [19]"Do not be afraid, O man highly esteemed," he said. "Peace! Be strong now; be strong."

When he spoke to me, I was strengthened and said, "Speak, my lord, since you have given me strength."

COMMENTARY

2–3 The expression "at that time" (v.2) connects the account of Daniel's fasting to the third year of King Cyrus (536 BC) cited in v.1. In later apocalyptic literature fasting is a means of preparation for receiving revelation (e.g., 2 Esd 5:13; *2Ba* 9:1; 12:5; 20:5–6). A strict fast entails the complete abstinence from all food and drink. Daniel abstains from "choice food" ("tasty food," NASB; Heb. *lehem h*ª*mudôt*), meat, and wine (v.3). The "choice food" is probably a reference to royal fare that Daniel was entitled to as a courtier. Nothing is said, however, about whether or not Daniel sustains himself during the fast with "coarse" or "simple" foods and water.

In addition to a restricted diet, Daniel also abstains from anointing himself with "lotions" ("ointment," NASB) for the duration of the fast (v.3). The anointing with oil (Heb. *swk*) most likely means that Daniel "neglected the usual niceties of personal grooming, such as fragrant oil on his hair or body" (Archer, 122). The three-week duration of the fast is significant but not unusual, since in certain circumstances fasting extended over forty days (e.g., Ex 34:28; 1Ki 19:8; cf. Lacocque, 205,

on the literal expression "three weeks [i.e., sevens] of days" as a way to prevent confusion with the "weeks of years" from ch. 9).

We may also assume that fervent prayer is part of this ordeal (cf. 10:12). Daniel refers to his entire experience as one of "mourning" (Heb. *ᵓbl*, Hitpael, "to observe mourning rites"; v.2). The word is used to describe mourning for the dead (Ge 37:34), mourning over sin (Ezr 10:6), and mourning over national calamity (e.g., Babylonian exile; Eze 7:12). The participial form of the term expresses both the ongoing state of mourning and the depth of Daniel's concern, presumably his regret over the plight of the people in Jerusalem that Nehemiah mourns some years later (Ne 1:4).

4–9 The date formula ("twenty-fourth day of the first month"; v.4) indicates that Daniel's fast overlaps the feasts of Passover and Unleavened Bread (cf. Lev 23:5). Lucas, 274, notes that Daniel's self-denial during his fast would have included the festal anointing with oil symbolizing joy and gladness, associated with Hebrew festivals (cf. Ecc 9:7–8).

Daniel is physically present along the banks of the Tigris River when the vision of the heavenly messenger overtakes him (v.4). The reason for his presence here is unclear (whether "official business" [so Archer, 123] or seeking seclusion and quiet as part of his fasting regimen [so Miller, 280]; yet there are others with Daniel [see v.7]). The Euphrates and the Tigris (the easternmost of the two great rivers of Mesopotamia) flow from the southern slopes of the Taurus mountains in Turkish Armenia to the Persian Gulf. The Tigris is also mentioned as one of the branches of the river flowing out of the garden of Eden (Ge 2:14).

The expression "looked up" ("lifted my eyes," NASB; v.5) is used elsewhere in the OT to describe the beginning of a visionary experience (cf. Zec 1:18; 2:1; 5:1). The idiom "lifted my eyes and looked" (NASB) suggests a complex process that occurs while one is engrossed in thought, only to have that thought interrupted by something that draws attention upward, and at that very moment the experience of the vision begins. The interjection that follows, "and behold" (NASB; Heb. *hinnēh*; omitted from the NIV]) conveys both the unexpected nature of the experience and the excitement it generates (cf. Miller, 280).

The "man dressed in linen" whom Daniel sees in his vision (v.5) is unidentified. Linen garments were traditional dress for the Hebrew priests (e.g., Ex 28:5, 39, 42). In this case, the linen raiment is also the dress of a heavenly being, as in Ezekiel's vision of the angelic scribe clothed in linen (Eze 9:2-3, 11; 10:2, 6-7). The NT also describes angels "as beings clothed in bright linen, a sign of holiness" (Seow, 156; e.g., Rev 15:6; cf. Mk 16:5). Numerous scholarly suggestions have been forwarded as to the identity of the radiant heavenly being of Daniel's vision. Montgomery, 420, concludes it is simplest to equate the being with the angel Gabriel, who previously appeared to Daniel in the revelations of

chs. 8 (v.16) and 9 (v.21). Lacocque, 206, rejects this identification because Daniel is not affected in the same way by Gabriel's appearance in the encounter described in 9:21 (yet Daniel reacts in terror to the approach of Gabriel in 8:16-17). Wood, 268, prefers to view the man of Daniel's vision as another high-ranking angel, "perhaps of parallel importance with Gabriel and Michael."

Miller, 282, is among those interpreters who prefer to see two personages in the narrative, identifying the theophany of the man dressed in linen with God himself (vv.5-6) and the "hand" in v.10 as the interpreting angel (cf. Longman, 250). More specifically, he equates this being with some preincarnate manifestation of the second Person of the Godhead, given the similarities of the appearance of the man in Daniel's vision to the description of Jesus Christ in Revelation 1:12-16. (But it is unlikely that God or some manifestation of Jesus Christ preincarnate would require the assistance of a mere angel.) In the end, it seems best to identify the man in the vision as an angelic being—either Gabriel or another angel of similar heavenly stature and purpose. The waterfront location of vision and the references to chrysolite, lightning, flaming torches, body parts gleaming like burnished bronze, and the voice like a multitude (v.6) all have their parallels in Ezekiel's vision of God's throne and his description of the living creatures attending the Lord (Eze 1:1, 7, 13-16, 24).

Seow, 157, correctly points out that the redundancy of the Hebrew texts emphatically indicates that Daniel alone sees the vision (lit., "I saw—I, Daniel"; v.7a). The solitary nature of Daniel's experience is underscored by the report that the men with him flee the vicinity in terror although they do not actually see the vision (v.7b). It is unclear what causes Daniel's companions to flee the scene terror-stricken, but much like those men with Saul on the Damascus road who froze dumbfounded because they heard the sounds of Saul's vision (cf. Ac 9:1-7), Daniel's friends also feel, sense, or hear something that causes great alarm. The "aloneness" of the individual experiencing the vision is not unusual given other revelatory experiences recorded in the OT (e.g., Ge 15:9-16; 32:24-30).

Daniel is riveted by "the great vision" (v.8a), and he is overcome to the point of immobilization by wonderment and fear (v.8b). His response is much like those to his previous revelations, where he "was deeply troubled ... and turned pale" (7:28), and "was exhausted and lay ill for several days" (8:27). Daniel's physical reaction to the vision is no doubt compounded by his state of weakness because of his three-week fast but is also in keeping with the reports of human responses to other OT theophanies (whether trembling with fear, like the people of Israel at Mount Sinai [Ex 20:18], or falling face down before the glory of the Lord, like Ezekiel [Eze 1:28]). At the sound of the voice of the angelic messenger Daniel falls into a trance ("deep sleep"; v.9a; on the Heb. rdm see comments on 8:18). The account echoes Daniel's previous encounter with Gabriel, when he "was terrified and fell prostrate" (8:17). Seow, 158, comments (almost humorously) that despite his swoon, Daniel manages "to remain in a posture of worship, his 'face to the ground'" (v.9b).

10-19 The opening verses (vv.10-11) reporting the angel's strengthening of Daniel in his weakness after the vision (vv.10-19) share similarities with the "strengthening report" in 8:18 in that in each case the heavenly messenger touches Daniel and raises him to his feet (v.10). Unlike the revelatory event in 8:17-18, where Daniel was immediately raised to his feet, the unnamed angel here restores Daniel's equilibrium and upright posture in stages. First, Daniel is helped to his hands and knees from his prostrate position (v.10a), and then he is enabled to stand upright in the angel's presence (v.11a).

In each case, Daniel is still "trembling" from the effects of the ordeal of his three-week fast coupled with the overpowering encounter with an angelic being.

The initial encounter between the angelic being and Daniel in the strengthening report also has affinities with the previous vision, in which he received the revelation concerning the "seventy sevens" (ch. 9). There Daniel was greeted as one "highly esteemed" (see comments on 9:23.). Here Daniel is affirmed as one "highly esteemed" (Heb. ḥᵃmudôt). Lacocque, 208, and Goldingay, 291, miss the point in associating Daniel's restoration by the angelic being with stages of movement from an animal-like state to that of a human being. The angel is simply fulfilling his role as "a ministering spirit" in extending the mercy and grace of God to one of his faithful servants—Daniel (cf. Heb 1:14). As a result, Daniel is now in a position to receive the heavenly messenger's revelation concerning the troubling vision he has just seen and heard.

Once Daniel is restored to some measure of strength, the angel assures him that his tardiness in coming to Daniel is not due to any reluctance on God's part to respond to fervent prayer (v.12). The words of assurance, "do not be afraid" (v.12a), are used elsewhere to introduce epiphanies (e.g., Ge 15:1; Jdg 6:23; Lk 1:13, 30; cf. Seow, 158). Daniel need not be alarmed, for God has already shown him favor in responding to his petition (cf. Wood, 272), and he has learned from his previous revelations that God rules history and looks after the welfare of his people Israel. Instead, Daniel learns that the heavenly messenger's three-week delay was due to resistance from "the prince of the Persian kingdom" (v.13a).

This "prince" (Heb. śar) probably refers to a patron evil angel exercising some sort of influence over the Persian Empire on behalf of Satan (cf. Seow, 159). The exact nature of the resistance experienced by the heavenly messenger during his journey to visit Daniel is unspecified (the Heb. idiom ʿmd + ngd in v.13 simply means "to stand before" or "opposite"; cf. Wood, 273, who notes that the phrase "need not mean an antagonistic withstanding," but in view of the angel's further words in verse twenty ... it clearly means that here"). Miller, 285, suggests that this demonic spirit whose activities have been assigned to Persia may have been Satan himself; hence the need for assistance from an angel of Michael's rank and prowess.

The reality of evil angels is attested explicitly by the biblical references to angels that sinned (2Pe 2:4; Jude 6) and implicitly by the biblical acknowledgment of "elect angels" (cf. 1Ti 5:21). Elsewhere in the Bible, connections are made between idolatry and demons (cf. Dt 32:17; Ps 106:37–38; 1Co 10:20). The idea that events on earth are affected by heavenly involvement is seen in the angelic forces that come to the aid of Israel (e.g., Dt 33:1–2; Jdg 5:19–20; 2Ki 6:17; cf. Lucas, 276). The notion in the biblical world that nations are under the care of either gods or angels may be seen in the Rabshakeh's taunt to the defenders of Jerusalem (2Ki 18:33–35; cf. Lucas, 276) and perhaps in God's assigning of "territorial lots" to the gods or angels (Dt 32:8–9 [see NIV note]; cf. Seow, 159). No doubt, this type of angelic conflict in the heavenly spheres is one aspect of the "spiritual warfare" that Paul describes in the NT (cf. Eph 6:11–12). The heavenly messenger's audition with Daniel (10:20–12:4) indicates that his presence marks but a temporary lull in the spiritual conflict with the demon princes of Persia and Greece (cf. v.20; see Longman, 253–56).

Michael, "one of the chief princes," is dispatched to assist the unnamed angel who has been detained in the Persian realm with the king of Persia (v.13b). This is the first time Michael, whose name means "Who is like God?" appears in the OT. The title "one of the chief princes" (v.13a) identifies Michael as an angelic being of high rank and one of the leading "commanders" of the angelic host. Seow, 159, comments that this title is probably an equivalent for "archangel." The NT also identifies Michael's rank as that of archangel (i.e., "first" or "chief angel"; Jude 9). According to *1 Enoch*, Michael, like Gabriel, is one of the seven archangels (*1 En* 20:5). He functions as the heavenly protector or guardian for the nation of Israel (cf. 12:1).

The purpose of the heavenly messenger's appearance is finally divulged after the detailed explanation of his delay in coming to Daniel—he will "explain" ("give you an understanding," NASB; Heb. *byn*, Hiphil) the meaning of the vision in fulfillment of Daniel's desire to understand the revelation (v.12). The vision concerns "the future" ("latter days," NASB; v.14). The expression "latter days" (Heb. *bᵉʾaḥᵃrît hayyāmîm*) refers not to the end of history but to "a decisive turning point in history" (Lucas, 277). The messenger's emphasis on "your people" (v.14) is especially important for Daniel since throughout his long tenure as a civil servant in the courts of Mesopotamian kings, his constant concern was his people, that is, God's people—the people of Israel (cf. 9:19).

Despite being strengthened by the heavenly messenger (vv.10–11), Daniel is still frightened ("overcome with anguish because of the vision," v.16b) and in a severely weakened physical condition (his "strength is gone" and he "can hardly breathe," v.17). In fact, Daniel's first utterance after his initial recovery of speech "is an outright admission of his debility in the face of the anguish of his vision" (Seow, 162). Once again the angel touches Daniel—first his lips to enable his speech (v.16a) and then his body to restore physical strength (v.18).

Daniel's experience of being touched on the lips calls to mind the throne vision of Isaiah, in which his lips were touched by a live coal from the altar held by an angelic being (Isa 6:6–7). Unlike Isaiah's situation, the need here is strength, not cleansing. Lucas, 277, comments that this duplication of the earlier acts of restorative touch by the angel "emphasizes the awesomeness of the experience." The second round of supernatural ministrations by the angelic being also speaks to the significance of Daniel's vision and the revelation he is about to receive, as the lengthy audition with the heavenly messenger attests. Lucas, 277, and Seow, 158, 162, among others, question whether it is the same being who touches Daniel three times (vv.10, 16, 18), given the ambiguity of the language in the passage. There is reason to assume that it is the same heavenly being who is strengthening Daniel by touching him—the ambiguity of the text is simply a reflection of Daniel's confusion and weakness during the experience. Miller, 287, reminds us that Daniel's use of the title "my lord" (Heb. *ʾǎdōnî*; v.16b) is not an indication of deity but an address of respect carrying the force of "sir" or "master" in English.

The interpreting angel reiterates his previous admonition to Daniel not to be afraid and the affirmation that Daniel is "highly esteemed" (v.19a). The greeting of "peace" (v.19b) is not so much a salutation (see the address of the letters in 4:1 [3:31] and 6:25 [26] in the commentary) but an assuring "statement of fact … 'you are safe'" (Hartman and Di Lella, 265). Daniel need not fear his present situation, for the angel's "concern was for the prophet's well-being" (Miller, 288). The emphatic repetition of the angel's exhortation to Daniel to "be strong" (v.19a) echoes the Lord's exhortation to Joshua (Jos 1:9). Seow, 162, has observed that "various forms of the verb 'be strong' [Heb. *ḥzq*] appear four times in verse 19, thus offering a powerful counterpoint to Daniel's loss of energy and spirit in verse 17." After hearing these words Daniel is sufficiently strengthened to receive the message from the interpreting angel (v.19b).

NOTES

6 The exact identification of the gemstone (Heb.) תַּרְשִׁישׁ (*taršîš*; "chrysolite," NIV; "beryl," NASB) is uncertain. According to Lucas, 259, some yellowish-colored stone such as topaz is probably intended rather than beryl, which is green (cf. Eze 1:16, where the wheels of God's chariot gleam like "chrysolite").

8 The expression "deathly pale" (Heb. לְמַשְׁחִית, *lᵉmašḥît*) is derived from the same root word as מִשְׁחַת (*mišḥat*) in Isaiah 52:14, where the term is used to describe the "disfigured" appearance of God's servant.

3. The Angel's Revelation (10:20–12:4)

OVERVIEW

The issue of *vaticinium ex eventu* (i.e., "prophecy after the fact") as a feature of apocalyptic literature has already been addressed in the introduction (see "Literary Form"). The problems associated with the analysis of the genre of *ex eventu* prophecy are perhaps most acute in chs. 10–12 because of the detailed reporting of the "chronological unfolding of history between the fourth and second centuries

[BC]" (Lacocque, 214). Goldingay, 282, understands Daniel's final vision as a form of "quasi-prophecy" that combines "quasi-prediction" (i.e., extensive rehearsal of events before the writer's day in the guise of prophecy) with a more limited "actual prophecy" of events still to come. Lacocque, 214, describes the literature of ch. 11 as "an enigmatic form designed to establish the fiction of a prophecy *ante eventum*, and also perhaps to maintain a prudently esoteric manner."

The so-called Akkadian Prophecies (especially The Dynastic Prophecy) are often cited as examples of the genre of "prophetic surveys of history," offering parallels from ancient Near Eastern literature to backward-looking history framed as prophecy in the apocalyptic visions of Daniel 8 and 11 (cf. Goldingay, 282; Lucas, 269–72). Literary definitions and ancient Near Eastern parallels aside, the scholars who regard chs. 10–12 as *ex eventu* prophecy written in the second century BC typically understand the purpose of this last section of the book as an exhortation to Jews to adopt "a certain form of behavior, namely, resistance to Seleucid/reformist pressures" (Goldingay, 285).

Baldwin, 182–85, finds the arguments for *ex eventu* prophecy in ch. 11 unconvincing for several reasons. First, critical scholars present the genre of prophetic survey of history as a widely accepted and readily recognized literary convention that deceived no one (cf. Porteous, 156). Yet there are no examples of this literary form in the OT outside the book of Daniel. Furthermore, the ancient Near Eastern examples of *ex eventu* prophecy offered as parallels assume an uncommonly sophisticated literacy among the Hebrews comprising the audience of Daniel. Second, the literary presentation of "revelation" that is in reality not revelation at all seems disingenuous on the part of a biblical author seeking to encourage an oppressed and persecuted Jewish audience. Third, the omniscience of God

that enables him to reveal the future as a character trait distinguishing him from the false gods of the biblical world rings hollow if his seers can only report past history as "quasi-prediction" (cf. Isa 41:22, 26; 43:12; 44:7). All this leads Baldwin, 184–85, to conclude:

> With regard to prophecy as foretelling, the church has lost its nerve. An earthbound, rationalistic humanism has so invaded Christian thinking as to tinge with faint ridicule all claims to see in the Bible anything more than the vaguest of references to future events. Human thought, enthroned, has judged a chapter such as Daniel 11 to be history written after the event, whereas God enthroned … may surely claim with justification to "announce of old the things to come" (Isa 44:7).

Longman, 272, concurs with Baldwin on the difficulty of ch. 11 but also treats the unit as "forward-looking prophecy": "In order to build up the reader's confidence that God controls history and that he is sovereign over the future, the reader must believe that the prophecy is precisely that." This study concurs with Baldwin and Longman in acknowledging ch. 11 as predictive prophecy, humbly recognizing that each of the two views are not without their problems. Finally, we must acknowledge the difficulties in sorting out what Baldwin, 184, refers to as "the baffling historical allusions" of ch. 11, especially the possible transition from Antiochus IV to a future king—perhaps even an antichrist figure in 11:36–45.

This section of the vision containing the angel's revelation may be broadly outlined as follows: further dialogue with the revealing angel (10:20–11:1), revelation concerning Persia (11:2), revelation concerning Greece (11:3–4), revelation concerning Egypt and Syria (11:5–20), revelation concerning Antiochus IV Epiphanes (11:21–35), and further revelation concerning "the king who exalts himself" (11:36–12:4). Unlike Daniel's previous visions, the content of this revelation lies in the audition or discourse of the celestial messenger. In this instance, the vision is preparatory for the revelation or message of the revealing angel rather than conveying the actual content of God's revelation to Daniel.

The English versions agree with the MT and LXX in placing the chapter division at 11:1, presumably because the date formula is similar to the headings of the previous chapters (cf. 7:1; 8:1; 9:1; 10:1; see Miller, 289). The emphatic adverbial construction "Now then" (Heb. *hinnēh-ʿôd*) clearly marks the beginning of a new paragraph, and certain English versions include 11:1 in the paragraph beginning at 10:20 (e.g., NIV, NLT, NRSV; contra NASB).

a. Further dialogue with the revealing angel (10:20–11:1)

²⁰So he said, "Do you know why I have come to you? Soon I will return to fight against the prince of Persia, and when I go, the prince of Greece will come; ²¹but first I will tell you what is written in the Book of Truth. (No one supports me against them except Michael, your prince.

¹And in the first year of Darius the Mede, I took my stand to support and protect him.)

COMMENTARY

20 Critical scholars tend to regard 10:20–11:1 as disordered and muddled, so they reorder the verses (cf. Lacocque, 212). Others, however, have noted in the literary unit a chiastic structure that "serves to emphasize the importance of the message that is about to be delivered" (Lucas, 277; cf. Goldingay, 292). The angel's opening question to Daniel: "Do you know why I have come to you?" (10:20a) is rhetorical in view of the statement of purpose made previously (10:14). According to Lucas, 277, the rhetorical question has two purposes: first, it reveals that the heavenly messenger is in a hurry to return to the heavenly conflict from which he came, indicating the importance of the message he delivers; and second, it foreshadows the contents of the revelation since the message addresses the time period of the Persian and Greek hegemony over Judah.

Hartman and Di Lella, 265, 285, find the Hebrew text of 10:20b–21 jumbled and confusing and so emend v.20b to read: "I must now go back to fight against the prince of Persia, and when he departs...." Montgomery, 418, acknowledges that this understanding is plausible, suggesting that "the parallel vbs. [i.e., the verbs 'go' and 'come'] may be best taken as expressing the exit of the angel after his success over Persia and the introit of the Prince of Greece, for whose coming the angel has prepared." Or put more simply, as soon as the conflict with the Prince of Persia ends, another conflict with the Prince of Greece begins.

The heavenly messenger relates that he only reports what is already "written in the Book of Truth" ("the writing of truth," NASB; 10:21a). The figurative reference to such a divine scroll "aptly conveys God's control and knowledge of past, present and future" (Baldwin, 182). The "Book of Truth" should not be equated with the "books" mentioned previously in conjunction with Daniel's vision of the beasts rising out of the sea (see comments on 7:9–10). Presumably this "Book of Truth" contains the course of history for the nations and the Hebrews as God's people, a portion of which is about to be revealed to Daniel. Lucas, 278, finds parallels to the "Book of Truth" in the "heavenly tablets" revealed to Enoch (*1En* 93:1–2) and the Babylonian Tablets of Destiny, which recorded the events of the coming year (cf. *BBCOT*, 746).

21 The parenthetical statement concerning Michael's role in cosmic conflict with the (spirit) princes of Persia and Greece (10:21b) explains the revealing angel's hasty manner and underscores the urgency of the hour and the importance of the message Daniel is about to receive. As Goldingay, 292, observes, the effect of the statement is "to tie the delivering of the earthly message and the reality of the heavenly conflicts closely together … [thus indicating] its delivery [i.e., the message] was worth the turning of the messenger's attention away from such crucial conflicts." No doubt encouraging to Daniel is the knowledge that "even though the enemies of Israel seem to have supernatural powers on their side, the people of Israel, too, have their supernatural protectors, most notably Michael" (Seow, 168).

Collins (*Daniel*, 374–76) and Goldingay, 292–93, interpret the conflict between Persia or Greece and Israel as a political, not a religious one. (Yet Haman's plot to annihilate the Jews, hatched

during the reign of the Persian king Xerxes, challenges this assumption at a number of levels, including the role of "evil angels" in motivating such a conspiracy against the people of God.) Baldwin, 182, comments that "the conflict will be such as to cause doubt as to whether God's people can survive, and the vision is intended to give unshakeable assurance that, desperate as the situation will be, God is so fully in control as to be able to disclose the sequence of events before they happen."

11:1 Some commentators are troubled by the date formula in 11:1a, which mentions the first year of the reign of Darius or Cyrus the Mede, because Daniel's vision is set in the third year of the Persian king Cyrus (10:1). According to Seow, 168, the reference makes sense because the problem addressed in this section of the book, namely, the ongoing experience of exile and desolation for the Hebrews, "is precisely the issue Daniel considered during the first year of the reign of Darius the Mede (9:1)." Furthermore, Lucas, 278, observes that the date formula of 11:1a functions to identify the heavenly interpreter, in all likelihood the angel Gabriel (cf. 9:1). Baldwin, 182, connects the work of the revealing angel in allying himself with the angel Michael (11:1b) during the first year of Cyrus's reign with the downfall of the Babylonian Empire and the decree of the Persian king permitting captive Hebrews to return to Jerusalem (cf. Lucas, 278; Lacocque, 212, prefers to understand 11:1b in the durative sense that Gabriel has been standing near Michael to strengthen and support him "since the first year of Darius the Mede").

NOTES

20 The proper name יָוָן (*yāwān*, "Greece") refers to the Greek kingdom of Alexander the Great in 10:20 and 11:2 (contra those espousing an *ex eventu* interpretation of chs. 10–12; e.g., Montgomery, 423, and

Lucas, 260, who identify Greece with the "Seleucid Empire"). Compare Collins (*Daniel*, 377), who questions whether or not there was "any Jewish memory" of Xerxes' campaign against Greece when Daniel's final vision was composed (i.e., mid-second century BC).

b. Concerning Persia (11:2)

> [2]"Now then, I tell you the truth: Three more kings will appear in Persia, and then a fourth, who will be far richer than all the others. When he has gained power by his wealth, he will stir up everyone against the kingdom of Greece.

COMMENTARY

2 Quite apart from how remarkable the interpretation of the vision may seem, the celestial being indicates that his message is the "truth" (v.2a). The repetition of the word "truth" (Heb. *ʾemet*) no doubt authenticates the revelation by connecting it to the "Book of Truth" mentioned previously (10:21). There is some confusion among biblical interpreters as to the number of kings reckoned in the vision—either a "fourth" king (v.2b) in a series beginning with Cyrus, or a fourth king in sequence after the reign of Cyrus the Great (cf. Lucas, 278–79). The most straightforward reading is to understand that the interpreting angel refers to four Persian kings in sequence after Cyrus, during whose reign the vision is dated (10:1).

Assuming the first three Persian kings succeeding Cyrus the Great refer to Cambyses (530–522 BC), the usurper Smerdis (pseudo-Smerdis or Gaumata, 522 BC), and Darius I Hystaspes (522–486 BC), the fourth king identified is Xerxes (or Ahasuerus; 486–465 BC). The description of a king who is powerful, wealthy, and wages war against the Greeks (v.2b) fits nicely with the reign of King Xerxes, especially in the massive military campaign he launched in 481/480 BC against the Greeks in

an effort to avenge the earlier defeat of his father (Darius I) by the Greeks at Marathon (490 BC). Although the Persians sacked Athens and burned the Parthenon, the Greeks defeated Xerxes and repulsed the Persians in a land battle at Thermopylae in 480 BC and naval battle at Salamis in 479 BC (see Miller, 291).

Other biblical interpreters suggest that the use of "three ... then a fourth" (v.2) is a Hebrew idiom that telescopes the exact number of Persian kings into a stylized history simply to indicate that a totality of monarchs will rise and fall—"denoting the Achemenids as a whole" (Goldingay, 295); "but the point is made that Persian wealth will eventually invite attack from all, even the kingdom of Greece" (Baldwin, 185; cf. Seow, 169–70). The fact that two hundred years of Persian history are compressed into a single verse is due primarily to the intent of Daniel's original query concerning the fate of the Hebrew people (cf. 10:14). The message of the revealing angel gives prominence to the kingdoms of the Ptolemies (the "kings of the south") and the Seleucids (the "kings of the north") because their political and military interplay directly affects the history of Israel (11:5–20).

NOTE

2 Baldwin's instruction, 184, here is helpful as she encourages the student of the Bible to have "at hand a secular history of the period to give a perspective wider than that of the chapter in question," given the many baffling allusions to ancient history (cf. Archer, 134−35, n. 9, for a list of the principal ancient sources of historical information for this time period).

c. Concerning Greece (11:3−4)

> [3]Then a mighty king will appear, who will rule with great power and do as he pleases. [4]After he has appeared, his empire will be broken up and parceled out toward the four winds of heaven. It will not go to his descendants, nor will it have the power he exercised, because his empire will be uprooted and given to others.

COMMENTARY

3−4 There is little doubt that the "mighty king" who appears (v.3a) is a reference to the Macedonian king Alexander the Great. Alexander came to power in 336 BC and subsequently embarked on an unprecedented military campaign to the east. Within a decade he marched from Turkey to India, gaining control of the largest empire the world had yet known. Yet at the height of his power Alexander died abruptly in 323 BC without a viable heir to his throne. Hence his empire was "broken up and parceled out toward the four winds of heaven" (v.4a). The reference to the parceling out of Alexander's empire in quarters was realized in the four "mini-empires" carved out of his kingdom by his four generals: Macedonia and Greece ruled by Cassander; Thrace and Asia Minor ruled by Lysimachus; northern Syria, Mesopotamia, and the other eastern regions ruled by Seleucus; and southern Syria, Palestine, and Egypt ruled by Ptolemy.

The revelation of Daniel's final vision repeats elements of the earlier vision of the four great beasts that arise out of the churning sea, in this case the leopard with four heads (7:6). The uprooting of Alexander's empire and its division into quadrants (v.4b) recalls the breaking of the single horn of the goat and its regrowth "toward the four winds of heaven" in Daniel's vision of the ram and the goat (8:8; see comments; cf. Collins, *Daniel*, 377−78; Lucas, 279−80).

d. Concerning Egypt and Syria (11:5−20)

> [5]"The king of the South will become strong, but one of his commanders will become even stronger than he and will rule his own kingdom with great power. [6]After some years,

they will become allies. The daughter of the king of the South will go to the king of the North to make an alliance, but she will not retain her power, and he and his power will not last. In those days she will be handed over, together with her royal escort and her father and the one who supported her.

⁷"One from her family line will arise to take her place. He will attack the forces of the king of the North and enter his fortress; he will fight against them and be victorious. ⁸He will also seize their gods, their metal images and their valuable articles of silver and gold and carry them off to Egypt. For some years he will leave the king of the North alone. ⁹Then the king of the North will invade the realm of the king of the South but will retreat to his own country. ¹⁰His sons will prepare for war and assemble a great army, which will sweep on like an irresistible flood and carry the battle as far as his fortress.

¹¹"Then the king of the South will march out in a rage and fight against the king of the North, who will raise a large army, but it will be defeated. ¹²When the army is carried off, the king of the South will be filled with pride and will slaughter many thousands, yet he will not remain triumphant. ¹³For the king of the North will muster another army, larger than the first; and after several years, he will advance with a huge army fully equipped.

¹⁴"In those times many will rise against the king of the South. The violent men among your own people will rebel in fulfillment of the vision, but without success. ¹⁵Then the king of the North will come and build up siege ramps and will capture a fortified city. The forces of the South will be powerless to resist; even their best troops will not have the strength to stand. ¹⁶The invader will do as he pleases; no one will be able to stand against him. He will establish himself in the Beautiful Land and will have the power to destroy it. ¹⁷He will determine to come with the might of his entire kingdom and will make an alliance with the king of the South. And he will give him a daughter in marriage in order to overthrow the kingdom, but his plans will not succeed or help him. ¹⁸Then he will turn his attention to the coastlands and will take many of them, but a commander will put an end to his insolence and will turn his insolence back upon him. ¹⁹After this, he will turn back toward the fortresses of his own country but will stumble and fall, to be seen no more.

²⁰"His successor will send out a tax collector to maintain the royal splendor. In a few years, however, he will be destroyed, yet not in anger or in battle.

COMMENTARY

5-6 It is generally agreed that the citations to the "king of the South" (v 5) and the "king of the North" (v.6) refer to the rulers of the Ptolemaic dynasty in Egypt and the Seleucid dynasty of Syria and western Mesopotamia. These were the two most powerful of the Hellenistic kingdoms emerging from Alexander's divided empire. These two kingdoms vied for control of the land bridge connecting Africa and Asia, since it meant both economic and military advantage for that kingdom able to establish its authority over the land of Palestine. Naturally, the political and military energies expended by the Ptolemies and the Seleucids on controlling this key piece of real estate in the ancient Near East had a direct impact on the Jews living in Palestine.

The "king of the South" (v.5a) refers to the founder of the Ptolemaic dynasty, Ptolemy I Soter, who ruled from 323–285 BC. He seized rule over Egypt upon the death of Alexander the Great in 323 BC. The reference to "one of his commanders" (v.5b) alludes to Seleucus I Nicator, who upon Alexander's death initially claimed the throne of Babylonia. He was soon driven from power, however, by Antigonus, who governed Asia Minor. As a result, Seleucus fled to Egypt and became one of Ptolemy's generals. Seleucus eventually regained control of Babylonia when he and Ptolemy I defeated Antigonus at the battle of Gaza in 312 BC, and he ruled as founder of the Seleucid dynasty from 311–280 BC. He later gained control of Asia Minor when Antigonus was defeated and killed by the Diadochi (or successors of Alexander) at the battle of Ipsus in 301 BC, thus making the Seleucid realm the largest of the four successor kingdoms of Alexander's empire.

The marriage alliance mentioned in v.6 is probably a reference to a treaty sealed between the Ptolemies and Seleucids by means of the marriage of Berenice (daughter of Ptolemy II Philadelphus [285–246 BC]) and Antiochus II Theos (261–246 BC [grandson of Seleucus I]) around 250 BC (cf. Kraemer, 342–43). The agreement included the provision that only the sons of Berenice could succeed Antiochus to the throne.

After Ptolemy's death, however, Antiochus divorced Berenice and remarried his former wife and half-sister, Laodice, whom he had previously divorced for the purpose of entering into the marriage alliance with the Ptolemies. Subsequently,

Laodice murdered Antiochus, Berenice, their infant son, and several of the Egyptian attendants in the service of Berenice. This purging of the royal household ensured the succession of Laodice's son, Seleucus II. Berenice's father died in the same year, thus rounding out the fulfillment of the prediction that the power of the alliance created by marriage would not last (v.6b) and the Egyptian bride, her attendants, and even her father would "be handed over" (i.e., to death; v.6c).

7–9 The reference to "one from her family" (v.7a) is probably an allusion to Ptolemy III Euergetes (246–221 BC). He was the brother of Berenice and succeeded his father Ptolemy II in 246 BC. He waged a successful sea and land campaign against the Seleucid Empire, overrunning much of Syria and avenging his sister Berenice's death by executing Laodice (v.7b). According to tradition, among the booty plundered by Ptolemy III were images of Egyptian deities carried away by the Persian King Cambyses in 525 BC (which eventually ended up in the possession of the Greeks; v.8a). According to Collins (*Daniel*, 378), Ptolemy III was given the name "Euergetes" (or "benefactor") by his people because he had returned the images of the Egyptian gods to their homeland (cf. Hartman and Di Lella, 290). There was a lull in the conflict between the two kingdoms from 244–242 BC (v.8b). Seleucus II mounted a counter-invasion of Egypt in 242 BC but was eventually forced to withdraw his troops from the region (v.9).

10–13 Towner, 156, comments that the next section (vv.10–19) refers "to the extraordinarily confusing events of the reign of the greatest of all Seleucid monarchs, Antiochus III (223–187 BC)." Seleucus III Ceraunus (226–223 BC) and Antiochus III are "the sons" of Seleucus II who waged war against the Ptolemies, even to the "fortress" of Ptolemy III in southern Palestine at Raphia (v.10). The next passage (vv.11–13) distills two campaigns waged against Egypt by Antiochus III. In the first, Antiochus was defeated at Raphia by Ptolemy in 217 BC (v.11). As a result, Ptolemy was able to regain control of Palestine and southern Syria (besides inflicting heavy casualties on the Seleucids (some 17,000 of 68,000 troops; v.12a).

Yet Ptolemy would "not remain triumphant" (v.12b), for he failed to press his advantage and made peace with Antiochus and the Seleucids (cf. Lucas, 281). Fourteen years later, after extending Seleucid rule into Asia Minor and eastern central Asia, Antiochus again mustered his forces to invade Egypt (v.13). He defeated Scopas (the Aetolian mercenary commander of the army) and the Egyptians at Banias (or Panias, near one of the sources of the Jordan River) in 200 BC, and the control of Judea now passed from the Ptolemies to the Seleucids. The turn of events in the royal family of the Ptolemies at this time no doubt precipitated the actions of Antiochus against Egypt. In 204 BC, Ptolemy IV Philopator (221–204 BC) and his queen died mysteriously (following unrest in Egypt that began as early as 207 BC). Ptolemy V Epiphanes (204–181 BC) was only a boy six years of age when he succeeded his father to the throne of Egypt. Antiochus was able to exploit the political upheaval and low morale among the Egyptians to military advantage.

14–19 The military campaign of Antiochus III against Egypt was but an omen of further aggression against the Ptolemies by many who would "rise up against the king of the South" (v.14a). Collins (*Daniel*, 379), citing Jerome, lists the "many" who rebelled against the Ptolemies, including those outlying provinces subjected to Egyptian rule, sedition in Egypt itself, and the pact made between Philip King of Macedon and Antiochus the Great. The identification of the "violent men among your own people" who led an unsuccessful rebellion against Egyptian rule is unclear (v.14b), although the Jewish historian Josephus reports that pro-Seleucid

and pro-Ptolemaic Jewish factions vied for power in Jerusalem at the time (*Ant.* 12.3.3–4; see the discussion in Collins, *Daniel*, 379–80).

According to Montgomery, 439, the siege of a "fortified city" (v.15) alluded to the siege of Gaza by Antiochus III in 201 BC. More recent commentators agree that the flow of the narrative points to Antiochus's successful siege of Sidon; he captured the city in 198 BC (cf. Collins, *Daniel*, 380; Lucas, 282). Scopas, the commander of the Egyptian forces in Palestine, retreated to Sidon after the defeat at Banias, and the mention of "their best troops" (v.15b) probably refers to Scopas's Aeolian mercenaries (cf. Lucas, 282).

This invader will do "as he pleases" (v.16a) — an expression applied previously to Alexander the Great (v.3) and subsequently to the king who exalts himself (v.36). After the surrender of Scopas and the Egyptians at Sidon in 198 BC, because of famine resulting from the lengthy siege of the city, Antiochus the Great gained control of all Palestine — including Judah and Jerusalem. Palestine is identified as the "Beautiful Land" in Daniel's vision of the ram and the goat (see comments on 8:9; cf. 11:41). Palestine remained within the Seleucid sphere of influence until the Maccabean revolt in 165 BC.

In a move to protect himself against the growing menace of Rome, Antiochus the Great made an alliance with Ptolemy V (v.17a), sealing it with the marriage of Antiochus's daughter Cleopatra to Ptolemy V in 193 BC at Raphia (after a four-year betrothal). Antiochus apparently hoped to "overthrow the kingdom" of the Ptolemies from within by means of the marriage pact (v.17b), but "whatever hopes he had of furthering his designs against Egypt through her proved false. She became staunchly loyal to her husband, even encouraging an alliance between Egypt and Rome against her father" (Lucas, 282; Kraemer, 343–44).

Ignoring his treaty with the Ptolemies, Antiochus the Great turned "his attention to the coastlands" (v.18a). This verse alludes to Antiochus's campaign in Asia Minor, overrunning Egyptian held territories along the coast and capturing numerous Greek islands as well. The waning power of Philip V of Macedon permitted Antiochus to threaten Greece itself, despite warnings from Rome against such a move. Antiochus invaded Greece in 192 BC but was defeated by the Romans at Thermopylae in 191 BC.

The Romans, having crushed the Seleucids at the battle of Magnesia, drove Antiochus's army back to the east of the Taurus Mountains in 190 BC. The "commander who put an end to his insolence" (v.18b) was the Roman general Lucius Scipio. According to Lucas, 282, "Antiochus was forced to accept humiliating peace terms at the Treaty of Apamea in 189 BC. He became a vassal to Rome, and had to send twenty hostages to Rome (including his son, the future Antiochus IV) and pay a huge indemnity." Antiochus retreated to Syria and "the fortresses of his own country" (v.19a). In 187 BC he was assassinated while attempting to sack the temple of Bel at Elymais in order to secure money to pay tribute to Rome (cf. Collins, *Daniel*, 381) — thus the reference that he "will stumble and fall, to be seen no more" (v.19b).

20 Towner, 157, comments that "the brief and undistinguished reign of the son of Antiochus, Seleucus IV Philopater (187–175 BC), is dismissed in verse 20." Antiochus the Great had two sons. Seleucus IV succeeded his father on the throne; his brother Antiochus was held hostage in Rome. The reference to the "tax collector" (v.20a) is probably a reference to Heliodorus, the finance minister of Seleucus (cf. 2 Macc 3 on Heliodorus's attempt to confiscate the monies in the treasury of the Jerusalem temple). Collins (*Daniel*, 381) summarizes that the reign of Seleucus IV "was dominated by financial exigency, because of the tribute to Rome." Seleucus was assassinated in 175 BC in a plot hatched by Heliodorus (possibly in a conspiracy including Antiochus, who had been released from prison in Rome). The report that Seleucus died "not in anger or in battle" (v.20b) may indicate the king died in disgrace, since he was not killed fighting valiantly on the battlefield (cf. Montgomery, 445).

NOTE

7 The MT reads כַּנּוֹ (*konnô*, "his place"); cf. NASB's "in his place." Archer (134, n. 7) prefers this, understanding "his place" as "in his own capital down in Egypt."

e. Concerning Antiochus IV Epiphanes (11:21–35)

21"He will be succeeded by a contemptible person who has not been given the honor of royalty. He will invade the kingdom when its people feel secure, and he will seize it through intrigue. 22Then an overwhelming army will be swept away before him; both it and a prince of the covenant will be destroyed. 23After coming to an agreement with him, he will act deceitfully, and with only a few people he will rise to power. 24When the richest provinces feel secure, he will invade them and will achieve what neither his fathers nor his forefathers did. He will distribute plunder, loot and wealth among his followers. He will plot the overthrow of fortresses — but only for a time.

²⁵"With a large army he will stir up his strength and courage against the king of the South. The king of the South will wage war with a large and very powerful army, but he will not be able to stand because of the plots devised against him. ²⁶Those who eat from the king's provisions will try to destroy him; his army will be swept away, and many will fall in battle. ²⁷The two kings, with their hearts bent on evil, will sit at the same table and lie to each other, but to no avail, because an end will still come at the appointed time. ²⁸The king of the North will return to his own country with great wealth, but his heart will be set against the holy covenant. He will take action against it and then return to his own country.

²⁹"At the appointed time he will invade the South again, but this time the outcome will be different from what it was before. ³⁰Ships of the western coastlands will oppose him, and he will lose heart. Then he will turn back and vent his fury against the holy covenant. He will return and show favor to those who forsake the holy covenant.

³¹"His armed forces will rise up to desecrate the temple fortress and will abolish the daily sacrifice. Then they will set up the abomination that causes desolation. ³²With flattery he will corrupt those who have violated the covenant, but the people who know their God will firmly resist him.

³³"Those who are wise will instruct many, though for a time they will fall by the sword or be burned or captured or plundered. ³⁴When they fall, they will receive a little help, and many who are not sincere will join them. ³⁵Some of the wise will stumble, so that they may be refined, purified and made spotless until the time of the end, for it will still come at the appointed time.

COMMENTARY

21–24 The revealing angel's audition sets the stage for the summary of the reign of Antiochus IV Epiphanes. Lucas, 283, notes that this has been foreshadowed in various ways in the preceding visions (e.g., 8:23–25) and that "he encapsulates a more intensive form of the bad traits and deeds of his predecessors." The "contemptible person" who succeeds Seleucus IV Philopator is generally understood as a reference to his younger brother, Antiochus IV Epiphanes (175–164 BC). This Seleucid king was "contemptible" from the Jewish standpoint because he "severely persecuted the Jews, massacring thousands, and rep-

resented one of the greatest threats to Yahweh worship in all of Israel's history" (Miller, 298).

Antiochus IV was not "given the honor of royalty" (v.21a) but rather usurped it, seizing the throne "through intrigue" (v.21b). Lucas, 282, summarizes that just prior to his death, Seleucus IV sent his son, Demetrius, to Rome as a "hostage replacement" for Antiochus IV. Seleucus was murdered while Antiochus was en route to Syria. Heliodorus (see comments on v.20) then seized the throne, ostensibly acting as regent for the legal heir, Demetrius. Antiochus arrived in Syria with an army conscripted with the help of Eumenes of Pergamum, forcing the flight of Heliodorus. Antiochus claimed the throne of the Seleucid Empire, nominally as regent for his older nephew Demetrius (now a political hostage in Rome), with his younger nephew (also named Antiochus) as coregent. This younger nephew Antiochus was murdered in 170 BC, and Antiochus IV usurped the throne by means of the fiction of claiming to act as regent for the exiled Demetrius.

Commentators differ on their understanding of the section that follows (vv.22–24). Some view the reference to "an overwhelming army" that will "be swept away" (v.22a) as an allusion to the invasion of Palestine by Ptolemy VI Philometor (181–146 BC) in an attempt to regain territories previously lost to the Seleucids (e.g., Miller, 299). The reference to "a prince of the covenant" (v.22b) is applied to Ptolemy VI as a betrayer of the treaty he had made with Antiochus IV, thus enabling him to regain the Egyptian throne usurped by his brother Ptolemy VII Euergetes II.

More recently, biblical commentators equate the Jewish high priest Onias III with "a prince of the covenant," since typically the expression "the king of the South" is used to identify the Ptolemies. Onias opposed the influence of Hellenism in Judea and was murdered by Menelaus in 171 BC in league with Jason (the brother of Onias), who had bribed Antiochus with the promise of supporting a policy of Hellenization in Jerusalem if he were appointed high priest (cf. Lucas, 284). Verses 23–24 are considered a summary of either his dealings with Jason and Judea (e.g., Lucas, 284) or more generally his policy toward Egypt and Judea (e.g., Miller, 299; though Collins [*Daniel*, 382] considers v.23 a flashback to Antiochus's alliance with Pergamum permitting him to seize the Seleucid throne with a small force.

25–28 These verses allude to Antiochus's first invasion of Egypt in 169 BC and the victory of the Seleucids over Ptolemy VI, "the king of the South" (v.25a; perhaps the same event described earlier in v.22; cf. Towner, 158). According to 1 Maccabees 1:17, the "large army" of Antiochus included chariots, elephants, cavalry, and a fleet, in addition to footsoldiers. Despite amassing a large counter-force (v.25b), Ptolemy's army was routed and the Egyptian king "fled in terror, leaving behind many casualties" (1 Macc 1:18). The "plots devised" against Ptolemy leading to his defeat (v.25c) included both sedition within Egypt itself on the part of disloyal subjects, and unwise counsel from royal advisers (cf. Miller, 300).

As a result, Antiochus "captured the fortified cities of Egypt and plundered the entire land" (1 Macc 1:19). Seow, 178, and others attribute the portrayal of Antiochus IV as the aggressor in the conflict to "the anti-Seleucid bias" of the narrator. In reality, it appears that Antiochus was responding to a military campaign launched by the Egyptians in 170 BC in an effort to regain control of Palestine (cf. Porteous, 166; Goldingay, 300–301).

The reference to "those who eat from the king's provisions" (v.26a) probably alludes to two Egyptian courtiers, Eulaeus and Lenaeus. Royal power in Egypt passed to them after the death in 169 BC of Cleopatra, who had been acting as regent for her underaged son Ptolemy VI (cf. Lucas, 285). Presumably the attempt to "destroy him" (v.26a) refers first to their unwise advice in encouraging Ptolemy to wage war against Antiochus in a bid to regain control of Palestine, and second to their counsel to him to flee to Samothrace after the Egyptian defeat near Pelusium (leading to his subsequent capture by Antiochus). The Egyptian army was "swept away" (v.26b) in the sense that the Egyptian forces were thoroughly routed. Antiochus invaded Egypt, advancing to Memphis and even laying siege to Alexandria (cf. Seow, 178–79).

With Ptolemy VI now a prisoner of Antiochus, his brother Ptolemy VII Euergetes II Physcon was installed as king of Egypt by powerful nobles of Alexandria. At this turn of events, Antiochus shifted his efforts to "diplomacy" in an attempt to gain further control over Egypt (cf. 1 Macc 1:16–19). The "two kings" (v.27a) mentioned are the captive Ptolemy VI and Antiochus. Antiochus sought an alliance with Ptolemy VI, under the guise of uniting with him in the common cause of restoring Philometor to power, "so that he could have a puppet that he could manipulate" (Seow, 178). Both were "bent on evil" (v.27b) in that each sought the alliance for the sake of double-crossing the other in their lust for power and wealth.

Seow, 179, notes that "the diplomatic niceties at the Memphis summit are recognized as the farce that they were"—two kings sitting at the same table and lying to each other (v.27c). Hartman and Di Lella, 296–97, comment that the biblical author severely indicts both kings in this exchange of lies because in "the grossness of their treachery ... each was guilty of violating a solemn principle of ancient Near Eastern ethics, plotting evil against a table companion (cf. Ps 41:9–10; John 13:18)." The Memphis treaty will be to "no avail" ("will not succeed," NASB) in that neither party will be able to gain an advantage through deceitful diplomacy. That the "end will still come at the appointed time" (v.27d) indicates the demise of Antiochus lay in the future, beyond the events of his first Egyptian invasion. Furthermore, the phrase "appointed time" serves to remind Daniel and his audience that God is still in control and "that there is a deeper (divine) purpose behind the events of history" (Lucas, 285). Montgomery, 454, aptly connects the phrase "appointed time" (v.27d) with the parallel expression, "but only for a time" (v.24d), placing "ultimate doom in the counsels of God."

Antiochus IV ("the king of the North") returned to Syria with "great wealth" (v.28a) as a result of his victory over Ptolemy VI and the Egyptians. The phrase "his heart will be set against the holy covenant" (v.28b) describes both the venting of his anger in frustration at the setback in his failed siege of Alexandria and also some deeper hatred of the Jews—almost a demonic malignancy directed against God and his people. The expression "holy covenant" (v.28b) is an umbrella term encompassing the people of God's holy covenant, the Jews, and their land of Judah—"all things religious in Israel" (especially the Jerusalem temple, cf. Wood, 299). Seow, 179, comments that after withdrawing his forces from the failed siege of Alexandria, Antiochus set "his heart on an easier target—the Jews."

There is some confusion in the historical sources concerning the activity of Antiochus in Judah after his first Egyptian campaign. Lucas, 285, contends that the looting of the Jerusalem temple and the murder of many Jews (cf. 1 Macc 1:20–24) by Antiochus after his first Egyptian campaign is better associated with events connected with his attack on Jerusalem after his failed second campaign against the Egyptians two years later (cf. 1 Macc 1:29–40). He finds no motive for Antiochus's action against the Jews on his return through Palestine in 169 BC and assumes the conflation of the account of the first attack against Jerusalem (1 Macc 1:20–28) with the second attack against Jerusalem (1 Macc 1:29–40), as understood in 2 Maccabees 5, is more in keeping with the facts of the matter (cf. Lucas, 285).

Miller, 300, and Porteous, 167, however, are convinced that Antiochus vented his rage against the Jews in the aftermath of both of his Egyptian campaigns, first in 169 BC after the failed siege of Alexandria, and then again two years later in 167 BC after his second campaign ended in defeat at the hands of the Ptolemies. Antiochus's reputation as "the madman" meant he needed no motive for his wanton cruelty against the Jews. In keeping with Daniel's forecast of future events, it seems likely that Antiochus "took action" (v.28c) against Jerusalem after each Egyptian campaign (cf. v.30–32). On the first occasion, Antiochus personally plundered the Jerusalem temple and butchered many among the Jewish citizenry, while on the second occasion he acted through his emissary Apollonius (cf. Goldingay, 301).

29–30 Antiochus invaded "the South again" (v.29a) two years later (167 BC), but this time his Egyptian campaign was unsuccessful (v.29b). The Ptolemy brothers Philometor and Euergetes had reconciled, undoing the results of Antiochus's first invasion of Egypt. The "ships of the western coastlands" ("Kittim," NASB [v.30a], the Heb. *kittîm* is derived from Citium on Cyprus, and the term constituting a Hebrew convention for "islands" and "maritime countries" [cf. Collins, *Daniel*, 384]) refer to the Roman fleet sent to Alexandria at the request of the Ptolemy brothers. The invader will "lose heart" (v.30b), a reference to Antiochus's intimidation and humiliation by the Roman envoy Popilius Laenas, forcing the Seleucid withdrawal from Egypt (cf. Collins, *Daniel*, 384).

Tragically, Antiochus vented his humiliation by the Romans in Egypt in the form of "fury" or persecution against the Jews (the people of the "holy covenant," v.30b). Some see an allusion to Numbers 24:24 ("ships will come from the shores of Kittim; they will subdue Asshur") in the "ships of Kittim," with Rome opposing the Seleucids as the "new Assyria" (cf. Baldwin, 194). Antiochus's showing of "favor to those who forsake the holy covenant" probably refers to the treachery of Antiochus's envoy Apollonius, who feigned coming to Jerusalem in peace, only to attack the Jews on the Sabbath and plunder the city (cf. 1 Macc 1:29–40; 2 Macc 5:24–26). Not only did the general Apollonius massacre the Jews, but he also rewarded those Jewish traitors who supported his policies of forced Hellenization (e.g., Menelaus, who had outbid his brother Jason for the office of high priest; cf. 2 Macc 4).

It is likely that Jason's revolt against Menelaus, triggered by the rumor that Antiochus had been killed in Egypt, took place at this time as well. Jason returned to Jerusalem in rebellion against Menelaus and the Tobiad family (2 Macc 5:5–10; cf. Lucas, 286). Assuming the city of Jerusalem was in revolt, Antiochus exploited the situation as a pretext to attack Jerusalem and restore control on his return from defeat in Egypt in 167 BC. The repetition of the phrase "the appointed time" (v.29a; cf. vv.24, 27) is another reminder to Daniel's audience that the sovereign God, who "sets up kings and deposes them," is still in control of history and the destiny of Israel.

31–32 The "temple fortress" (v.31a) was either the temple complex itself, which functioned secondarily as a military citadel at this time (so Montgomery, 457), or an adjacent structure on the temple mount that served as a garrison and armory (cf. Goldingay, 302). This temple citadel was rebuilt and fortified and became the base of operations for Antiochus's forces in quelling the "revolt" in Jerusalem (cf 1 Macc 1:29–35). The citadel was called the Akra, and "for a period of twenty-five years the Akra stood as a loathsome symbol of pagan domination" (Hartman and Di Lella, 299; cf. 1 Macc 3:45; 14:36).

Later in 167 BC Antiochus issued an edict decreeing the forced Hellenism of the Jews in Judea and outlawing all Jewish religious practices, such as circumcision, possessing the Hebrew Scriptures, observance of Sabbath and feast days, and the daily morning and evening sacrifices (all on threat of death; cf. 1 Macc 1:50, 63). The paganization of the Hebrew temple culminated in the institution of imperial cult worship in Jerusalem and the erection of an altar or idol dedicated to Zeus in the temple on 15 Chislev (December) 167 BC (cf. 1 Macc 1:54–61; 2 Macc 6:2; see also comments on 9:27). This "abomination that causes desolation," or desecrating sacrilege, rendered the temple unfit for Hebrew worship because of the violation of Mosaic purity and tradition associated with worship at the temple (cf. Ex 20:3–4, 22–26; 1Ki 8).

Within three years the temple was an abandoned structure, overgrown with weeds like a vacant lot (cf. 1 Macc 4:36–40). In addition, pagan altars were set up across Judah on which swine and other animals judged "unclean" by Jewish food laws were offered (1 Macc 1:47). Presumably the same kinds of profane sacrifices were offered at the Jerusalem temple as well (cf. 1 Macc 1:54, 59). The desecration of the Jerusalem temple by Antiochus prefigured a later "abomination" to be erected in the Jerusalem temple, as predicted by Jesus in his Olivet discourse (cf. Mt 24:15).

The Jews of Jerusalem divided into two camps in response to Antiochus's temple desecration and his attendant persecution of those adhering to their ancestral religious rituals and practices. One group is identified as those who have "violated the covenant" (v.32a), corrupted by Antiochus's "flattery" (mentioned previously as "those who forsake the holy covenant," v.30c). The "forsakers" (Heb. *rš'*, "act culpably, make oneself guilty"; GK 8399) of the covenant are those who have already "acted wickedly" with respect to God's law as codified in the Mosaic covenant (suggested by the participial form of the verb; cf. Wood, 301). The word typically connotes the "wicked acts" of disobedience or general unfaithfulness to the stipulations of God's covenant with Israel enacted at Sinai, but implicit in this disloyalty is false worship in violation of the command not to worship idols (Ex 20:3–4; cf. 9:5; 1Ki 8:47; Ne 9:33; 2Ch 22:3).

The reference to "flattery" ("smooth words," NASB; Heb. *ḥālāq*, "smooth, smoothness") probably alludes to the enticing promises made by Antiochus to bestow honor and wealth on those Jews who join in the support of his pagan policies (cf. 1 Macc 2:18; 2 Macc 7:24). The book of 1 Macca-

bees reports that many Jews abandoned the law of Moses at this time and joined in the pagan worship and evil deeds promoted by Antiochus's officers (1 Macc 1:51–52; 2:15).

The second group of Jews are those who "firmly resist" Antiochus because they "know their God" (v.32b). These Jews remained loyal to God by persisting in their obedience to the law of Moses and refusing to compromise the Mosaic covenant by engaging in false worship (cf. 1 Macc 2:16). Since the larger context of the Hebrew resistance to the policies of Antiochus forcing Hellenism on the Jews included martyrdom (vv.33–35), Lucas, 287, comments that the reference to those who resist "is best taken as including all forms of resistance to Antiochus's edict, whether it took the form of passive resistance (1 Macc 1:29–38) or of armed revolt (1 Macc 1:42–48)." These faithful Jews faced persecution and the threat of death on two fronts: the military forces of the Seleucid Hellenists occupying Judah, and the turncoat Jews who forced the faithful Israelites to hide in whatever refuge they could find (1 Macc 1:53).

33–35 The final passage of the section alludes to the persecution of the Jews by Antiochus IV in the aftermath of his failed second Egyptian campaign (vv.33–35). As Baldwin, 195, iterates, these verses highlight the polarization between those who are seduced by "flattery" (v.32a) and those "who know their God" (v.32b), since "persecution eliminates the waverers." The expression "those who are wise" (v.33a) refers to those Jews who remain faithful to Yahweh's covenant despite the atrocities committed against them by their Seleucid oppressors (i.e., those with "spiritual discernment," according to Miller, 302). These "wise" (Heb. *maśkîlîm*) Jews will also teach or instruct (Heb. *byn*) many others during the time of the Seleucid persecution (v.33a).

Goldingay, 303, describes the wise or discerning Jews as the "conservative leaders who possess the wisdom which consists in awed submission to Yahweh, that understanding which has reflected deeply on his ways in history, and that insight which perceives how his cause will ultimately triumph." Presumably, this comprised the instruction the wise shared with others, along with their modeling of obedience to the stipulations of the Mosaic law. The fact that some "will fall" (v.33b) indicates the Jews faithful to Yahweh's covenant risk capture, torture, and even martyrdom, whether death by the sword or by burning (v.33c; cf. Heb 11:34–35).

The revealing angel goes on to indicate that those who fall "will receive a little help" (v.34a). Seow, 181, comments that two responses to the persecution of Antiochus were available to the Jews: a more passive resistance, as reflected in the example of the "wise"; and an active resistance, exemplified among the "zealous" or "devout Jews" (Heb. *ḥᵃsîdîm*) described in 1 Maccabees 2:42. The enigmatic allusion "help" may refer to the Maccabean freedom fighters, who rose up actively to resist the forced Hellenism of Seleucid rule by means of guerilla warfare (e.g., Baldwin, 196–97; cf. 1 Macc 3). The rest of the verse ("many will join them in hypocrisy," NASB; v.34b) may allude to the harsh actions the Maccabees took against those Jews who complied with the edict of Antiochus, thus leading "some to join them out of fear rather than out of principle" (Lucas, 287; cf. 1 Macc 2:44–47; 3:5–8).

The Antiochene persecution leading to the capture, imprisonment, and even martyrdom of some of the "wise" Jews has the effect of refining and purifying them—making them "spotless" (v.35a). Their suffering is not viewed as divine judgment in punishment for sin, but rather as "a means of testing and purifying their commitment" (Lucas, 287). Hartman and Di Lella, 300–301, understand the suffering in a communal sense as the purification of the Israelite nation and the vindication of the worship of Yahweh. It seems more likely that Collins (*Daniel*, 386) is correct to view the test of suffering in more individualistic terms as "purification [that] bespeaks an interest in individual salvation as distinct from (though not opposed to) the deliverance of the nation."

No doubt the Antiochene persecution also had the effect of further purging the faithful Jews by winnowing out the insincere (so Goldingay, 303). Yet "the death of the martyrs is not vicarious. They are the ones who are purified," and they have their primary effect on the community by their instruction (Collins, *Daniel*, 386). For the third time in this section (v.35c; cf. vv.24–27), the revealing angel indicates that the period of suffering the Jews must endure as a result of the persecution of Antiochus is an interim one. There is an "appointed time" for its end (v.35c)—yet another reminder of God's sovereign control of human history and Israel's destiny (see comment on v.27d).

f. Concerning the king who exalts himself (11:36–45)

OVERVIEW

Both conservative and critical biblical scholars agree that 11:2–35 summarizes events associated with the reign of the Seleucid king Antiochus IV

Epiphanes. Granted, the two camps take differing approaches to the literature, whether predictive prophecy or *ex eventu* apocalyptic prophecy.

Assumptions concerning the possibility of divine revelation in the form of predictive prophecy, however, cause a marked divergence in the assessment of 11:36–45 by the two interpretive schools.

Typically, critical scholarship today regards vv.36–39—a recapitulation of the offenses of Antiochus—as a summary judgment against his character and policies (e.g., Seow, 182; Lucas, 289). Goldingay, 304, considers the unit a "quasi-prophecy" based on known historical facts. Despite acknowledgment that the content of the passage is difficult to harmonize with what historical resources report concerning the life of Antiochus, scholars adhering to this interpretation tend to dismiss the discrepancies as "polemical exaggeration" on the part of the author (e.g., Collins, *Daniel*, 386; cf. Lucas, 290).

According to Collins (*Daniel*, 388), beginning with v.40, "modern scholarship marks the shift from *ex eventu* prophecy to real (and erroneous) prediction" (cf. Towner, 165, who quips that at the point at which the seer actually begins to look into the future, "he gets it all muddled"). Goldingay, 305, concurs, admitting that although vv.40–45 cannot be correlated to the known events of Antiochus's life, "it is not the nature of biblical prophecy to give a literal account of events before they take place." Many of the "modern" scholars assume vv.36–45 continue the narrative of vv.21–35, since there are no grammatical markers hinting at a transition of any sort, and they presuppose that the passage "imaginatively" looks forward to the downfall of Antiochus IV—the king of the North (e.g., Towner, 163–65; Hartman and Di Lella, 303; Goldingay, 305; Lucas, 292–93; Seow, 184–86).

Other historical figures have also been cited as the possible fulfillment of Daniel's prophecy about the king who will "exalt and magnify himself," such as the general Pompey, who brought Roman control to Palestine in 63 BC (cf. Goldingay, 305);

Herod the Great (cf. Miller, 305, n. 82); the Roman general Titus, who sacked Jerusalem in AD 70; and the Roman king Constantine the Great (cf. Anderson, 140–41). Calvin is among those commentators understanding vv.36–45 to refer to the fourth empire (or Rome) of Daniel's vision of the beasts rising out of the sea, rather than to any particular individual (cf. Miller, 305, n. 82).

Since the time of Jerome, some Christian interpreters have seen an "antichrist" figure in vv.36–45 (cf. Lucas, 292). The interpretation is based on Daniel's description of the "little horn" (7:8), "another horn" (8:9), and "the ruler who will come" (9:26) in his previous visions, as well as NT teaching concerning "the man of lawlessness" (2Th 2:3–12), the "antichrist" (1Jn 2:18), and the "beast" (Rev 11–20; cf. Miller, 306). The extreme difficulties inherent in understanding the text of Daniel at this point must be recognized and the need to proceed with humility and charity acknowledged (agreeing with Longman, 280; cf. Archer, 144, on the difference of opinion even among conservative interpreters on the meaning of vv.36–45).

The chief problem in assigning an eschatological meaning to the passage is that, unlike the earlier portion of the chapter (e.g., vv.2, 7, 20–21), there is no clear grammatical marker or transitional language indicating a shift of subject between v.35 and v.36 or between v.39 and v.40 (cf. Goldingay, 305; Longman, 281). Yet the tendency of biblical prophecy to "telescope" future events (or the idea that "the more distant event appears to merge with the nearer so as to become indistinguishable from it" (Baldwin, 202) has already been noted in Daniel (cf. 7:23–25). Thus Longman, 282, concludes that in vv.36–45 "we see references to Antiochus Epiphanes taking on larger than life characteristics, which we, living in the light of the New Testament, might describe as anticipatory of a figure called the Antichrist."

Baldwin's summary assessment, 199, moves the discussion in the proper direction when she states that "although the chapter [i.e., Da 11] finds its first fulfillment in the character and reign of Antiochus IV, the matter does not stop there." I am inclined to agree. Quite apart from whether vv.36–45 address some historical personage beyond the reign of Antiochus or the antichrist figure of the end of the age, it seems quite clear "that the divine intention [of vv.36–45] may have been much broader" (Longman, 281). In addition to acknowledging the larger context's teaching about resurrection from the dead (12:1–3), Longman, 281, goes on to cite several signals for assigning an "eschatological meaning" to vv.36–45, such as the "cosmic" language of the verses, the reference to "the time of the end" (v.40), and the fact that "verses 40–45

simply do not work when applied to the life and death of Antiochus Epiphanes."

Furthermore, Wood, 304–5, observes that any further treatment of Antiochus IV is unexpected, since his story (at least with respect to the persecution of the Jews) has been completed, and the designation "the king" (v.36a) has not been applied to Antiochus at any time in the preceding narrative. Naturally, this position is not without its detractors, as Hartman and Di Lella, 303, dismiss the view as "exegetically witless and religiously worthless." Anderson, 141, states that the view "now has minimal appeal beyond the circle of some sects." Such polemics notwithstanding, the commentary below addresses both the historicist and futurist interpretations of vv.36–45 (and sides with Baldwin, 199–203, and Longman, 282–83, on the merits of assigning an eschatological meaning to the pericope).

---

[36]"The king will do as he pleases. He will exalt and magnify himself above every god and will say unheard-of things against the God of gods. He will be successful until the time of wrath is completed, for what has been determined must take place. [37]He will show no regard for the gods of his fathers or for the one desired by women, nor will he regard any god, but will exalt himself above them all. [38]Instead of them, he will honor a god of fortresses; a god unknown to his fathers he will honor with gold and silver, with precious stones and costly gifts. [39]He will attack the mightiest fortresses with the help of a foreign god and will greatly honor those who acknowledge him. He will make them rulers over many people and will distribute the land at a price.

[40]"At the time of the end the king of the South will engage him in battle, and the king of the North will storm out against him with chariots and cavalry and a great fleet of ships. He will invade many countries and sweep through them like a flood. [41]He will also invade the Beautiful Land. Many countries will fall, but Edom, Moab and the leaders of Ammon will be delivered from his hand. [42]He will extend his power over many countries; Egypt will not escape. [43]He will gain control of the treasures of gold and silver and all the riches of Egypt, with the Libyans and Nubians in submission. [44]But reports from the east and the north will alarm him, and he will set out in a great rage to destroy and annihilate many. [45]He will pitch his royal tents between the seas at the beautiful holy mountain. Yet he will come to his end, and no one will help him.

COMMENTARY

36-39 The king who "will do as he pleases" (v.36a) is depicted as an autocrat with no regard for humanity or God. Seow, 182, notes that in this he is hardly a unique figure, since Daniel has characterized other rulers in the same way (cf. 8:4; 11:3). This boastful "little horn" or "other horn" was introduced earlier (in Daniel's vision of the beasts rising out of the sea) as one who opposed God and his people (cf. 7:8, 20). The verbs "exalt" and "magnify" are normally reserved for God or those who impiously challenge God in the OT, and Lucas, 289, finds echoes of Isaiah's oracle against the pride of the king of Assyria in the passage (cf. Isa 10:12–15).

The phrase "unheard-of things" ("monstrous things," NASB; v.36c) has a word in common with the description of the "astounding devastation" wrought by the "stern-faced king" (cf. 8:24). The term (Heb. *pl*; Niphal) is found forty-three times in the OT and is used exclusively in reference to the "wonderful works" of God in creation and salvation—except in the two cases where Daniel applies the word to the boasting of Antiochus IV Epiphanes. This, coupled with the fact that the word for "God/god(s)" (Heb. ʾᵉlôah/ʾᵉlōhîm) occurs eight times in vv.36–39, thus emphasizing the profane character of the ruler, indicates that the "boasting" of this arrogant king is "nothing short of blasphemy" (Seow, 182).

The historicist interpreter points to the expansion of the inscriptions on the coins minted by Antiochus IV Epiphanes from the simple "of King Antiochus" to "of King Antiochus, God Manifest, Victory Bringer" as tangible evidence confirming his identification as the impious king described in vv.36–39. The futurist interpreter views the sacrilegious character and policies of Antiochus IV Epiphanes as but a pale foreshadowing of the "atheism" and "shocking blasphemy" of the antichrist

figure (Miller, 306; cf. Baldwin, 197). The "time of wrath" is generally understood to refer to the wrath of God, whether a brief time of divine judgment or an "age" of divine wrath (cf. Lucas, 219–20). The historicist equates the "time of wrath" (v.36d) with the "end" of Antiochus's reign of terror against the Jews (e.g., Collins, *Daniel*, 386), while the futurist understands "the time of wrath" as divine judgment poured out on the earth at the end of the age—even the "great tribulation" (e.g., Wood, 306–7; Miller, 307).

The rest of the section (vv.37–39) fills out more completely the profane character and sacrilegious policies of the boastful ruler. The impiety of the king, who exalts himself above the God of gods, includes irreverence for his own gods (v.37a). Typically this is viewed as the preference Antiochus showed for Zeus over the god Apollo, the patron deity of the Seleucids (e.g., Seow, 183). The reference to "the one desired by women" (v.37b) is usually considered an allusion to the fertility cult of Tammuz (cf. Eze 8:14), a deity with a long history in the ancient Near East (cf. Smith-Christopher, 146; Kraemer, 344). Futurist interpreters counter that there is no historical evidence indicating any opposition by Antiochus to the Tammuz cult (e.g., Archer, 144; cf. Lucas, 290, who admits problems with the historicist interpretation and appeals to the writer's "polemical exaggeration" at this point in the narrative). Instead they see an indirect reference to the rejection of Messiah by the antichrist figure in his contempt for the desire of Jewish women to be the mother of Messiah (so Miller, 307), or more generally as the disregard of the antichrist figure for the feminine traits of grace, mercy, and kindness (so Wood, 306). The verse concludes with a reemphasis on the self-exaltation and godlessness of the king who will do as he pleases (v.37c).

The god whom this boastful king honors is a "god of fortresses" (v.38a). Several suggestions have been made identifying this "god" with one of the numerous fortresses established by Antiochus IV Epiphanes: the god Jupiter Capitolinus, to whom Antiochus erected a great statue at Antioch; the god Zeus, based on an inscription found at Scythopolis; and the Jerusalem citadel, or Akra, where Antiochus profaned the temple precinct by erecting an image of Zeus (cf. Lucas, 290). Since the term "fortresses" (Heb. *māʿuzzîm*) is plural, the reference may not be to one particular "fortress deity" as much as to the idea that this godless ruler worships only military might, and the "god of fortresses" simply symbolizes his own tyrannical rule over his kingdom. The homage paid to the "god of fortresses" in the form of offerings of gold, silver, and precious stones (v.38b) may be little more than a reference to booty plundered during the military campaigns of Antiochus and stockpiled in his fortress treasuries—a metaphor for the "worship" of his ill-gotten wealth.

The beginning clause of the final verse of the section (v.39a) is difficult. Literally, the text indicates that "he [i.e., the boastful king] will act for [or deal with] mighty fortresses" (cf. NRSV, "he shall deal with the strongest fortresses"). The NIV interprets the verb "act" (Heb. *ʿśh*) as military aggression and translates it as "attack" (cf. NASB, "take action against"). Seow, 184, is among those commentators who emend the Hebrew text and read, "and he shall act for those who fortify the fortresses, people of a foreign god." In either case, the verse calls attention to the "crafty manipulation of religion" by the godless king (Seow, 184). Those who support the king's rule (perhaps those apostate to their own religion; cf. Smith-Christopher, 147) are rewarded accordingly by placement in positions of authority (v.39b).

There is some question as to whether the allotments of land confiscated from the conquered peoples are given as a "reward" for loyalty to the king's allies (so Porteous, 169) or are sold for a "price" to the highest bidder (so Seow, 184; Redditt, 187). The historicist relates this verse to the Tobiads of Jerusalem, favored by Antiochus because of their support for his polices promoting Hellenism among the Jews (e.g., Goldingay, 305). The futurist considers the verse a vague reference to the rewards of political leadership and territorial allotments the antichrist figure will grant to those in league with him (e.g., Miller, 308).

40–45 As noted above, the final section (vv.40–45), which reveals the angel's audition with Daniel, is fraught with difficulties. The historicist interpreter must acknowledge that the details of these verses "are not in accord with historical records" (Seow, 185). The "embarrassing inaccuracy" of the "daring preview of the future" (ibid.) is excused on two counts: first, the biblical writer is assumed to engage in "polemical exaggeration" (so Collins, *Daniel*, 386); and second, biblical prophecy is defined in such a way as to exclude the fulfillment of predictions down to the precise details (so Goldingay, 305). Yet the futurist who views the passage as a projection to the distant future concerning the antichrist figure must admit that there are no lexical or grammatical hints of such a transition in the passage. Beyond this, "the narrator expects the difficult situation to continue for just a little while longer" (Seow, 184).

For the historicist, the "time of the end" (v.40a) coincides with the end of the reign of Antiochus IV Epiphanes and hence the end of the persecution of the Jews (Redditt, 187), already anticipated in vv.27 and 35 (see comments above). The futurist equates "the time of the end" with the eschaton and the wars waged by the antichrist figure (cf. Wood, 308; Miller, 309). The historicist assumes that the "him" of v.40a and "the king of the North" are the same person (e.g., Goldingay, 305), while some futurists identify "the king of the North" with the antichrist figure's heading a coalition centered in central Asia (so Miller, 309), and other futurists view "him" as the antichrist figure being's attacked on two fronts by "the king of the South" and "the king of the North" (so Wood, 308).

The passage forecasts a great battle between "the king of the South" and "the king of the North," presumably geopolitical confederations representing the modern-day regions of "Egypt" and "Mesopotamia" respectively (v.40b). There are no historical records reporting any further battles between the Ptolemies and Seleucids during the reign of Antiochus IV Epiphanes. The account also places emphasis on the wide-ranging arsenal of the king of the North, including "chariots and cavalry and a great fleet of ships" (v.40c). The identity of this "king of the North" aside, he is able to marshal a massive army and invade and sweep "like a flood" through many (unspecified) countries (v.40d).

The invading force of "the king of the North" will sweep over the "Beautiful Land" (v.41a), a designation for Palestine or the land of Israel—previously in Daniel, the people of God (cf. v.16). Curiously, the trans-Jordanian states of Edom, Moab, and Ammon will be delivered ("rescued," NASB) from the attack of the invader (v.41b). Smith-Christopher, 147, speculates that these nations "once again conspire with the aggressor against the Jewish people." The futurist interpreter assumes that Daniel alludes to some kind of confederation of modern states as occupying the territories of these archaic biblical kingdoms (cf. Miller, 311). In addition, the futurist approach associates the invasion of Israel by the Antichrist with the prophecies of Ezekiel, Joel, Zechariah, and Revelation concerning the city of Jerusalem (e.g., Archer, 148; Wood, 312–14; Miller, 312; cf. Eze 39:2–29; Joel 3:2–16; Zec 12:2–9; 13:8–9; 14:1–21; Rev 19:19–20). The "boastful king" will extend his rule into the far reaches of North Africa, including Egypt, Libya, and Nubia (vv.42–43).

Disturbing "reports" from the east and the north will cause "the king of the North" to abandon his campaign against "Egypt" and turn back to counter the threats against his "homeland" or other "special interests" (v.44a). The rumors elicit "great rage" in the king, such that his intent is "to destroy [Heb. *šmd*] and annihilate [Heb. *ḥrm*] many" (v.44b). The "boastful king" will pitch camp between the "seas" (i.e., the Mediterranean Sea and the Dead Sea) and "the beautiful holy mountain" (i.e., the temple mount of Jerusalem; v.45a). There the "boastful king" will "come to his end," though his specific fate is unspecified (v.45b). All the "favors" doled out to those who supported his tyrannical rule will prove to be of no avail, as the "boastful king" will meet his end with no allies "to help him" (v.45b; cf. v.39).

Lucas, 290–91, summarizes four different versions of the death of Antiochus IV Epiphanes, all of which report his death as occurring in Persia, not Palestine. Miller, 311–12, equates vv.44–45 with the final battle of the eschaton—Armaggedon (cf. Rev 16:16)—and he associates the forces of the North and the East that attack the army of the antichrist figure with the great armies described in Ezekiel 38–39 and Revelation 9:13–19 (cf. Wood, 312–14). Naturally, futurist interpreters continue to theorize as to the confederations of nations involved in the catastrophic end of human history, given the ever-changing geopolitical landscape of Africa and Asia. Whether "the king of the North" refers to Antiochus, the antichrist figure, or even some other intervening historical personage, Goldingay's comment, 305, on the symbolism of the passage is appropriate: "this final battle takes place, as it must ... at the center of the world, at the place where the Scriptures had therefore long expected the final conflict; it signifies the end of this apparently unassailable earthly power. He schemes against an unsuspecting and vulnerable people but finds himself God's victim."

NOTE

45 The phrase "royal tents" translates the Hebrew אָהֳלֵי אַפַּדְנוֹ (*ʾāhŏley ʾappadnô*, "tents of his pavilion"). The term אַפֶּדֶן (*ʾappeden*) is a Persian loanword for "palace" (cf. Collins, *Daniel*, 389). The context suggests a "portable palace," that is, a cluster of tents forming a "royal pavilion" (NASB).

The preposition לְ (*lᵉ*, "to, for") in the phrase לְהַר־צְבִי־קֹדֶשׁ (*lᵉhar-ṣᵉbî-qōdeš*) may be translated "at" (so the NIV's "between the seas at the beautiful holy mountain") or as a conjunction, "and" (so the NASB's "between the seas and the beautiful Holy Mountain"). Collins (*Daniel*, 389) considers "seas" (Heb. יַמִּים, *yammîm*) a poetic plural for the Mediterranean Sea. Goldingay, 280, prefers reading the preposition לְ as "and" since the reference of "at" is unclear.

g. Concerning Michael the great prince (12:1–4)

> [1]"At that time Michael, the great prince who protects your people, will arise. There will be a time of distress such as has not happened from the beginning of nations until then. But at that time your people—everyone whose name is found written in the book—will be delivered. [2]Multitudes who sleep in the dust of the earth will awake: some to everlasting life, others to shame and everlasting contempt. [3]Those who are wise will shine like the brightness of the heavens, and those who lead many to righteousness, like the stars for ever and ever. [4]But you, Daniel, close up and seal the words of the scroll until the time of the end. Many will go here and there to increase knowledge."

COMMENTARY

1 The phrase "at that time" (v.1a) links this section to the previous chapter, specifically, "the time of the end," when the kings of the South and the North engage in battle (11:40). The reference to the archangel Michael also connects 12:1–4 with chs. 10–11, since he was first introduced in 10:13 and named again in 10:21. Michael is described as a "great prince" (Heb. *śar gādôl*) and protector (Heb. *ʿmd*; "the Hebrew text here suggests one who stands up 'over' or 'beside' or 'for' the people" [Seow, 186]), or guardian angel of the nation of Israel—"essentially a fighter" (Baldwin, 1203). Seow, 186, observes that the entire historical overview of 11:2–45 is framed by the presence of Michael and that he is

"subliminally present throughout that historical recitation," since we were told that he is involved in the fight against the supernatural patrons of the world empires of Persia and Greece (10:21). He apparently functions in the dual roles of celestial commander of the heavenly host standing as guardian over the people of Israel, as well as the chief angel who stands in the divine council and represents his people Israel before God.

The historicist interpreter understands this unparalleled "time of distress" (v.1b) as the enormity of the persecution of the Jews by Antiochus IV (e.g., Lucas, 294; Redditt, 190). The futurist interpreter equates this "time of distress" with the "great tribulation," the cataclysmic wrath of God poured out against unbelieving Israel and the entire world at the end of the age just before the second coming of Jesus Christ (e.g., Miller, 314–15; cf. Rev 6–16). The revealing angel promises deliverance for "everyone whose name is found written in the book" (v.1c). This book or scroll is to be distinguished from the "Book of Truth" that the revealing angel unveils to Daniel (10:21), and from the "books" of past deeds that provide the basis for God's judgment of individual and nations (7:10). The figurative reference to "the book" is usually equated with "the book of life," in which all the saints are enrolled (cf. Ex 32:33; Ps 69:28; Mal 3:16; Php 4:3; Rev 3:5; 20:12).

Goldingay, 306, understands this book as "a list of those who belong to God's people, the citizen list of the true Jerusalem" (cf. Miller, 315–16, who roots the idea of the book in the practice of village record-keeping of worthy residents who enjoyed the blessings of community membership). Baldwin, 203, comments that "though he [i.e., Michael] is great, he does not prevent them [i.e., God's people] from enduring the suffering, rather he delivers them in the midst of it." Most significant, no doubt for Daniel, is the revelation that God's people Israel will indeed be delivered or escape ("be rescued," NASB; Heb. *mlt*). Understood in the context, the term suggests some of the Jews will be kept safe through the "time of distress," while those who perish during the intense period of persecution will be rewarded with the "deliverance" of resurrection from the dead (v.2).

2 That those "who sleep in the dust of the earth will awake" (v.2a) is generally understood to describe some sort of bodily resurrection from the dead. Even Collins (*Daniel*, 391–92) admits that "there is virtually unanimous agreement among modern scholars that Daniel is referring to the actual resurrection of individuals from the dead, because of the

explicit language of everlasting life." The extent to which the Hebrews had any understanding of life after death during OT times is a topic of considerable debate. The minimalist position denies any hope of afterlife among the Hebrews in OT times. The maximalist view reads a full-orbed doctrine of afterlife into the OT on the basis of the NT report that Abraham believed God could raise Isaac from the dead if necessary (Heb 11:19).

It seems best to understand the doctrine of resurrection from the dead as one of those theological concepts that develops progressively through the history of God's revelation from the OT to the NT. Lucas, 302, identifies several strands of thought in the OT that "move toward some kind of meaningful existence beyond death." These strands include the strong belief of the psalmist that a deep relationship with God does not end at death (Pss 16:9–11; 49:15; 73:23–26), the language of the national restoration of Israel after the judgment of God (especially in the Prophets; cf. Eze 37:12–13; Hos 6:2), and Job's reference to the existence of a "redeemer" who will establish his innocence after his death (cf. Job 19:23–27). According to Lucas, 303, "all three strands contribute something to the belief in resurrection that finds its expression in Dan 12:1–3" (cf. Miller, 316–18, for a less cautious approach to the OT teaching concerning afterlife—an approach rooted in Lacocque's assertion, 235–36, that "the faith 'in resurrection, immortality, and eternal life' is very old in Israel").

Yet the text poses many problems for biblical interpreters. This is the first and only unambiguous reference to resurrection from the dead in the OT, although the concept is not entirely foreign to Hebrew thought, given the statement by Isaiah that "your dead will live" (Isa 26:19), and both the prophets Elijah and Elisha were miracle workers who brought individuals back to life (cf. 1Ki 17:19–23; 2Ki 4:32–35). Seow, 187, notes that the text does not speak of the resurrection of all humanity but only of "many of those who sleep" (v.2, NASB). Who then are the many, and when do they awake from their sleep? Again, according to Seow, 187, the context suggests the "time of the end" in the sense of the end of the persecution of the Jews experienced during the reign of Antiochus IV (cf. 11:40; 12:1). Furthermore, is "sleep in the dust" (v.2b) a reference to soul sleep in Sheol or the underworld, like that experienced by Samuel the prophet (cf. 1Sa 28:15)?

All these "loose ends" in the writer's language prompt Towner, 187, to regard the passage as a divine "judgment scene in which the righteous dead receive in death the peace and the joy which were denied them in life and in which, conversely, the oppressors receive the contempt which is their due but which life never meted out to them." Alternatively, Seow, 187, understands the verse as "a metaphor for the restoration of the people of Israel after a time of destruction ... using the imagery of resurrection to convey hope in the revival of the Jewish people after a history of suffering and death." Lucas, 294, however, finds this position untenable given the references to "everlasting life" and "everlasting contempt."

Finally, futurist interpreters contend that the word "many" (Heb. rabbîm) may have the force of "all" (cf. Baldwin, 204; Lucas, 294–95), and they consider the word "sleep" (v.2b) a figure of speech for physical death (cf. Miller, 316). Hence, they argue that Daniel's reference to resurrection from the dead to either eternal life or eternal shame is associated with the resurrection of the righteous dead after the great tribulation and before the millennial reign of Jesus Christ, and the resurrection of the wicked dead for divine judgment after the millennial rule of Jesus the Messiah (Rev 20:4–6, 11–15; cf. Wood, 318–19; Miller, 316–18).

Naturally, it is impossible to construct a complete doctrine of any theological truth based on a single verse of the Bible. Yet, following Longman, 284, "we can confidently affirm that it [i.e., Da 12:2] celebrates the vindication that will come both in reward for which the righteous are destined and in the punishment for which the wicked ... are reserved."

3 The righteous are described as "wise" (Heb. maśkilîm; v.3a). The parallel expression, "those who lead many to righteousness" (v.3b), further describes "those who are wise" (cf. Baldwin, 205). The "wise" were introduced previously as those who "will instruct many" (11:33). These wise or righteous Jews are similar to the "righteous servant" of Isaiah who will "justify many" by his knowledge (Isa 53:11). Collins (Daniel, 393) outlines the two different views on how the "wise" make "many" righteous: either by their propitiatory death as martyrs (cf. Lacocque, 230) or by their teaching, meaning "instruction rather than martyrdom is the means of justification." Clearly the latter understanding is more likely given the context of chs. 10–12, but more important is Baldwin's observation, 205, that "there is only one source of righteousness—God himself" (cf. Da 9:7, 14). No doubt Daniel and those belonging to his group (or the teachers among them) are included among "those who are wise" (cf. Longman, 284).

As in the case with "the wise" (v.3a) and "those who lead many to righteousness" (v.3b), the phrases "like the brightness of the heavens" (v.3a) and "like the stars" (v.3b) should be understood as parallel synonymous expressions (cf. Miller, 319). Collins (Daniel, 393) connects the exaltation of the wise with the exaltation of the servant who acts wisely; "he will be raised and lifted up and highly exalted" (Isa 52:13). Lucas, 295, finds an allusion to the motif of the wise shining like celestial bodies in "dew of light" mentioned in connection with those who will rise from the dead in Isaiah's "little apocalypse" (Isa 26:19).

Both Lacocque, 244–45, and Collins (Daniel, 393–94) take the promise to mean that the wise will become angels in the next life, based on the influence of Hellenistic beliefs and later intertestamental apocalyptic literature (e.g., *1En* 104:2–6). Goldingay, 308, and Longman, 284, however, caution against pressing the language of an obvious metaphor too literally. Seow, 188–89, aptly calls attention to the reversal of destiny between the humiliation of those who attempt to ascend to the stars (cf. 8:10; 11:36–37) and the vindication of those who act wisely (v.3).

4 The revealing angel charges Daniel to "close up" ("conceal," NASB; Heb. *stm)* the scroll—an instruction intended to ensure the safekeeping of the document more than keeping it secret (cf. Lucas, 221; see also comments on 8:26). The command to "seal the words of the scroll" has "the double sense of authenticating and of preserving intact ... kept from general knowledge [since] they were not yet relevant" (Baldwin, 206; on "the time of the end," see comments on 11:40; 12:9).

Verse 4b is obscure, primarily because it is unclear whether the statement indicates what will happen when the sealed scroll is opened, or the cryptic remark refers to what takes place during the interim before mystery is revealed (cf. Seow, 189). Lucas, 296, suggests that the verse alludes to the "famine of hearing the words of the LORD" (Am 8:11) and likens the sealed scroll to Isaiah's metaphorical use of a sealed scroll to depict the spiritual blindness of those willfully in rebellion against God—thus prompting him to conclude that it may "take the Antiochene crisis to make people ready to listen to the teaching of the wise." By contrast, Seow, 189–90, prefers to read v.4b as the aftermath of the opening of the scroll and the revelation of Daniel's vision when the knowledge of God will indeed increase—"a dramatic reversal of the gloomy vision of Amos 8."

NOTE

3 The expression יַזְהִרוּ כְּזֹהַר (*yazhirû kᵉzōhar*) is a cognate accusative construction in Hebrew from the root זהר (*zhr*, "to shine"). Montgomery, 471, attempts to capture the idiom, translating: "And the Wise shall shine like the sheen of the sky" (cf. NASB's "shine brightly like the brightness").

4. Epilogue (12:5–13)

OVERVIEW

This epilogue returns to the setting of the final vision (vv.5–7) and includes a request posed by Daniel for further information concerning his vision (v.8). The interpreting angel informs Daniel, however, that no additional revelation will be given (vv.9–12) because the "words are closed up and sealed" (v.9). This section closes with a word of assurance to Daniel that he too will share in the resurrection to receive his "allotted inheritance"

(v.13). Some scholars consider this final section of the book as an appendix or later gloss (esp. vv.11–12; cf. Towner, 170). Porteous, 171, counters, "These verses [vv.5–13] form an epilogue to the book rather than a late addition to it." Longman, 285, further notes, "It is fitting, now that the message of prophecy has been delivered, to return to the scene and characters described in 10:4–21."

⁵Then I, Daniel, looked, and there before me stood two others, one on this bank of the river and one on the opposite bank. ⁶One of them said to the man clothed in linen, who was above the waters of the river, "How long will it be before these astonishing things are fulfilled?"

⁷The man clothed in linen, who was above the waters of the river, lifted his right hand and his left hand toward heaven, and I heard him swear by him who lives forever, saying, "It will be for a time, times and half a time. When the power of the holy people has been finally broken, all these things will be completed."

⁸I heard, but I did not understand. So I asked, "My lord, what will the outcome of all this be?"

⁹He replied, "Go your way, Daniel, because the words are closed up and sealed until the time of the end. ¹⁰Many will be purified, made spotless and refined, but the wicked will continue to be wicked. None of the wicked will understand, but those who are wise will understand.

¹¹"From the time that the daily sacrifice is abolished and the abomination that causes desolation is set up, there will be 1,290 days. ¹²Blessed is the one who waits for and reaches the end of the 1,335 days.

¹³"As for you, go your way till the end. You will rest, and then at the end of the days you will rise to receive your allotted inheritance."

COMMENTARY

5–7 Daniel's final vision ends where it began, along the banks of the Tigris River (v.5; cf. 10:4). The flashback to the river scene reveals that four distinct characters participate in the conclusion of the vision report: Daniel, two unnamed figures, and the man clothed in linen (vv.5–6). Gowan, 154, has noted the similarities between 12:5–8 and 8:13–14, including the riverbank setting, the portrayal of Daniel in the role of one overhearing a conversation between unnamed celestial beings raising the question of "How long?" and the report that Daniel eventually joins in the conversation. The two unnamed figures, one on each side of the river, are presumably heavenly beings, one of whom has served as Daniel's interpreting angel (vv.5–6). Miller, 322, assumes the one angelic being

accompanying Daniel is Gabriel, who is named as the interpreting angel in the previous visions (8:16; 9:21). The ambiguities associated with the identification of the third figure—that is, whether the man clothed in linen above the waters (v.7) is an angelic or divine being—remain.

The oath sworn by the man clothed in linen (v.7) attests both the truthfulness of the testimony given and the certainty of the promise that all these things will be accomplished within the specified time period of three and a half years (v.7c). The raising of the hand as part of a ritual of oath taking was a customary practice in the biblical world and acknowledged God as witness (e.g., Ge 14:22; Nu 14:30; Dt 32:40; Ne 9:15; cf. Rev 10:5–6). The lifting of both hands in swearing an oath is unusual (v.7b), since in the Bible this is typically a gesture of prayer or entreaty (cf. Ne 8:6; Ps 141:2; 1 Ti 2:8). It is presumably an especially emphatic gesture (so Collins, *Daniel*, 399; Miller, 323) and serves "as the more complete guarantee of the truth that is about to be affirmed" (Baldwin, 207). The third-person appeal to "him who lives forever" is a reference to God himself and is reminiscent of the language of Deuteronomy 32:40, the one place where God speaks of himself in this manner ("as surely as I live forever," v.40b).

Given the importance of "witnesses" in legal proceedings and oath taking in the Mosaic law, it is interesting to note that there are two angelic beings in the scene (e.g., Dt 17:6; 19:15; Jos 24:22; cf. Porteous, 171). Also intriguing are the possible associations of the two unnamed angelic beings with known divine council motifs in the ancient Near East, including the sending of heavenly messengers in pairs and the procession of the deity flanked by two angelic retainers (cf. *ABD*, 2:214–17). As Longman, 285, observes, however, the uncertainties associated with the identification of the figure in linen "make the scene a bit murky, but this ambiguity does not affect the interpretation."

8 Although Daniel heard the exchange between the angelic being on the riverbank and the man clothed in linen above the waters of the river, he confesses a lack of understanding (v.8a). This prompts a further question from Daniel to the interpreting angel as to "the outcome" of the vision (v.8b). The import of Daniel's question evades biblical commentators. Lucas, 297, citing Jerome, takes the question to mean: "What will come after these things?" Collins (*Daniel*, 400) explains that Daniel is merely asking for further information, since "the 'end' in Daniel is never the utter cessation of history, so something will happen even after the resurrection."

The last word Daniel overhears in the conversation between the celestial beings is that all these things will be completed after the "power of the holy people has been finally broken" (v.7b). The likely identity of the "holy people" is the people of Israel. Throughout the book Daniel's concern has been the plight of God's people, Israel. Given this fact, Wood's observation, 325, that the nature, character, and severity of the events that will bring this period of Hebrew history to an end seems more in keeping with the meaning of the seer's question as to the "outcome" of the vision.

Finally, there is a certain irony in Daniel's question, since the book begins with his receiving from God the ability to "understand" (Heb. *byn*) "visions and dreams of all kinds" (1:17). Yet the book ends with Daniel perplexed and confessing that he does not fully understand what he has seen and heard (v.8a)—perhaps an important reminder that "wisdom and power" belong to God, that he alone "knows what lies in darkness," and that he alone dispenses this knowledge to the wise among humanity (2:20–21).

9–12 In response to his question concerning the "outcome" of the vision (v.8), Daniel learns that no more revelation will be given (vv.9–12). The instruction given by the interpreting angel to Daniel to "go your way" (v.9a) should not be construed as a rebuke; rather, Daniel is encouraged to return to his post in the administration of King Cyrus and resume his duties as a civil servant. Previously Daniel was charged to "close up and seal the words of the scroll" (12:4; see comments). Now the heavenly messenger reminds Daniel that the vision is "closed up and sealed" (v.9c). That the scroll of the vision is "closed up" (Heb. *stm*, "hide, keep secret"; GK 6258) signifies both that the revelation is completed and that its record is safely preserved for the future, "much as a present is kept a treasured secret until the day for presentation arrives" (Baldwin, 206). The words reporting the vision are also "sealed" (Heb. *ḥtm*), indicating that the document is not only preserved and authenticated but also withheld until the appropriate time (cf. Goldingay, 309). Lucas, 297, adds, "because the vision is 'sealed,' true understanding is available only to 'the wise'" (cf. v.10b).

Full understanding of the vision is reserved "until the time of end" (v.9c). The phrase repeats what Daniel has already heard concerning the disclosure of the meaning of the vision (12:4). The context of the final vision (chs. 10–12) suggests that "the time of the end" refers to cessation of the distress and persecution that Israel will endure at the hands of the king "who will exalt himself above [every god]" (11:37; cf. 12:1). Historicists who interpret the visions of Daniel as *ex eventu* prophecy understand that "the end is not far away but imminent" (as a projected schedule is spelled out in vv.11–12; cf. Seow, 194). Specifically, the three-and-a-half-year time period (12:7, 11–12) forecast (for the end of the reign of Antiochus) is calculated from the desecration of the Jerusalem temple by Antiochus IV Epiphanes in 167 BC to the swirl of events surrounding the defeat of the Seleucids, the rededication of the temple, and the death of Antiochus (164–163 BC; cf. Towner, 170–71; Seow, 195). Futurists equate the "time of the end" with the final events of human history, especially "the great tribulation" of three-and-a-half years ushered in by the antichrist figure against the people of God and the world (e.g., Archer, 156; Wood, 327–28; Miller, 324–25; cf. Da 12:7, 11–12; Rev 11:2–3).

The interpreting angel recapitulates what has been said about "the wise" (Heb. *mśkl*) earlier in the vision (cf. 11:33–35; see comments). Seow, 193–94, however, notes a subtle difference in the two passages in that "some of the wise will stumble so that they may be refined, purified, and made spotless" (11:35) while they are instructing others (11:33). According to the epilogue, "many will be purified, made spotless, and refined" during the period of distress and persecution endured by the Hebrews (v.10). "The implication is that the suffering of the wise will not have been futile after all, for redemption will be extended to many—the many who will be led to righteousness (see 12:3)" (Seow, 194). Miller, 325, interprets "the wicked" to represent all humanity in the end times and views the verse as a proof text refuting postmillennial theology. Seow, 194, correctly observes that in the context "the wicked" refers to "the renegade Jews who abandoned the covenant" (cf. Wood, 326–27).

The lack of spiritual discernment as a mark of distinction between the righteous and the wicked is a familiar one in the OT. The psalmist recognized that in their pride the wicked entertain no thought of God (Ps 10:4), the prophet lamented that despite the grace shown to the wicked they do not learn righteousness (Isa 26:10), and the sage observed that the wicked are destroyed by their own evil (Pr 11:5). According to Lacocque, 249, "the wicked are confirmed in their wickedness" since, like the sea tossing up mire, they persist in doing evil (cf. Isa 57:20). More disturbing, perhaps, is the biblical pattern of the intensification of evil before it is finally defeated (cf. Da 7; Eze 38–39; Mt 24; Rev 12–17).

The interpreting angel finally returns to the question posed by one of the two celestial beings along the riverbank (v.6): "How long will it be before these astonishing things are fulfilled?" Although no further revelation will be forthcoming in response to Daniel's question about the outcome of the vision (v.8), he is privileged to hear the timetable for the fulfillment of the vision. Some critical scholars view the conclusion of Daniel (vv.11–13) as a later addition to the document, or more precisely "two successive glosses (v.11 and vv.12–13)" (Lacocque, 249; Towner, 170). Others consider the closing verses an integral part of the epilogue (vv.5–13) since they "carry the heart of the revelation of the epilogue" (Redditt, 199; cf. Porteous, 172).

As Baldwin, 209, has noted, "the answer is given in the number symbolism typical of the book." The numbers are enigmatic, as attested by the numerous interpretive approaches to the passage. Naturally, questions arise as to whether the numbers should be understood in a literal or symbolic sense and whether they reference an immediate time frame or some distant one. The interpretive problems are only complicated by the differing calendars in use during biblical times (lunar, solar, and luni-solar; cf. Lucas, 297–98). Lucas, 297, despairs that "no-one has been able to suggest a satisfactory explanation of the two time periods given in verses 11–12." Miller, 325, confidently asserts that the two verses provide "further details concerning history's final events," though he admits exact certainty as to the time of the events is impossible to determine. An overview of the essential categories for interpreting the 1290 days (v.11) and 1335 days (v.12) is presented below.

(1) For some scholars, the two time periods represent glosses in the form of "successive corrections" to the 1,150 days mentioned in Daniel's vision of the ram and the goat (8:14). According to this view, a later writer (or writers) attempted to extend the time period for the fulfillment of the prediction of the rededication of the Jerusalem temple when that event did not occur within the time frame originally expected (e.g., Montgomery, 477; Lacocque, 250; see discussion in Baldwin, 209). Yet Porteous, 172, questions "how urgent corrections, such as these would be, could have been added to a book that had just been issued."

(2) Those interpreting Daniel's visions as apocalyptic *ex eventu* prophecy attempt to relate the two sets of "days" to different pairs of key events during the reign of the Seleucid king Antiochus IV Epiphanes, especially his persecution of the Jews.

Typically, the two sets of "days" are understood literally as the number of days delimiting the persecution of the Jews by Antiochus. The three-and-a-half years of the Antiochene persecution (7:25; 12:7) are calculated (based on a solar calendar) from December 7, 167 BC (the desecration of the Jerusalem temple), to June 21, 163 BC (the collapse of the Antiochene dynasty), approximately 1,290 days (1,293 to be exact; v.11). The fulfillment of the second time period (the set of 1,335 days; v.12) is assigned to the anniversary of the public reading of the Torah (August 5, 163 BC), some forty-five days after the collapse of the dynasty of Antiochus (cf. Redditt, 195–197, who associates the *terminus ad quem* of the first set of 1,290 days with the summer solstice; Seow, 194–95).

Towner, 170, assumes that the significant pair of dates delineating the three and a half years of persecution cited in v.7 is the three-year period from Antiochus's desecration of the temple in 167 BC (December 7) and the rededication of the temple by Judas Maccabeus and his brothers in 164 BC (December 14), and he simply concludes that the biblical writer was in error (hence the need for a second glossator to update "the true facts in the matter").

Goldingay, 309–10, prefers to consider the two periods of days as an approximate time frame for the fulfillment of the question, "How long will the persecution last?" (v.8), which could be related to several different sets of events during the reign of Antiochus. For example, the *terminus a quo* might be the time of one of Antiochus's edicts, his capture of Jerusalem, the actual desecration of the Jerusalem temple, or even the full enforcement of the ban on the temple sacrificial ritual. Likewise, the *terminus ad quem* might be the string of Jewish victories scored by Judas Maccabeus, the rededication of the temple, the death of Antiochus, or other events associated with the collapse of the Antiochene dynasty.

(3) The two sets of "days" refer to time periods associated with events in the distant future, related to "the great tribulation," the rise of the antichrist figure, the persecution of God's people, the second advent of Jesus Christ and the defeat of the antichrist figure, and the establishment of the kingdom of God on earth. For example, Archer, 156, considers the three and a half years (or 1,260 days; v.7) as an approximate number for the length of the great tribulation, while the 1,290 days is the exact length of time of the persecution inflicted on the righteous by the Antichrist during the great tribulation. Wood, 327–29, prefers to ascribe the extra thirty days beyond the 1,260 days of the great tribulation to the time allotted for the time of divine judgment immediately after the second advent of Jesus Christ (cf. Mt 25:31–46; Rev 20:11–15). The additional forty-five days of the 1,335 day period (beyond the 1,290 days of the first time period) are accounted for in the time necessary for Christ to set up "the governmental machinery" necessary for carrying out his rule of an earthly millennial kingdom (Wood, 328–29; cf. Miller, 325–26).

(4) Lucas, 298, suggests that "the numbers may have some symbolic significance that is now lost to us."

Quite apart from the alternative interpretations of the sets of days, the gist of the passage for Daniel and his audience is that God knows and controls the future (cf. 2:20–21). Furthermore, the word of revelation concerning the two sets of periods of days serves as an exhortation to Daniel and his audience to persevere because the time of persecution and suffering has definite time limits and will end soon (cf. Lucas, 298). Finally, a blessing (Heb. ʾšr) is promised to those who "wait" (Heb. ḥkh) and endure through the 1,335 days. The blessing for the righteous is manifest in experiencing the deliverance of God through the time of persecution and in the assurance of God's faithfulness to his word as witnessed in the fulfillment of the account of Daniel's vision. The encouragement to wait may echo God's charge to Habakkuk to wait for the fulfillment of the revelation, even though it lingers (Hab 2:3), and implies a posture of expectant and hopeful obedience on the part of God's people during the interim.

13 Collins (*Daniel*, 401) notes that the book ends "appropriately with a promise of resurrection to Daniel himself" (v.13). The language referring to Daniel's "rest" and "rising" (v.13b) "picks up on the imagery of death and resurrection as sleep and awakening" found in 12:2. The hortatory charge to "go your way till the end" (v.13a) is not an admonition of rebuke, but rather an exhortation to the seer to persevere until his own death. Implicit in the exhortation is both the reality that at this time Daniel is an old man and not far from the end of his life, and that he has ably fulfilled his commission as God's servant. The word used for "allotted inheritance" (Heb. *gôrāl*; v.13b) signifies the "lot" cast to determine a decision or "that which falls to one by lot." Naturally, the Hebrews understood that God's will stood behind the outcome of lot-casting (Pr 16:33). Daniel is assured that his "destiny is clearly with that of the *maśkîlîm* [v.3], who rise to eternal life" (Collins, *Daniel*, 402).

As Longman, 287, notes, "by these words, God gives Daniel and all of his heirs the confidence to persist in the light of continuing persecution and trouble." There is a sense in which the epilogue of Daniel anticipates the later teaching of Jesus: "In this world you will have trouble. But take heart! I have overcome the world" (Jn 16:33). Daniel can "go his way," knowing that God's rule will ultimately triumph (Da 2:44; 7:27) and that God's people will be delivered—even those who do not live to see the final outcome, since they will experience resurrection from the dead (vv.2–3)!

HOSEA

M. DANIEL CARROLL R. (RODAS)

Introduction

1. HISTORICAL BACKGROUND

The book of Hosea provides little specific information of a personal nature about the prophet. He is from the northern kingdom (his hometown is not mentioned) and is said to be the son of Beeri (1:1), of whom nothing is known. The opening chapter describes his marriage to Gomer, but the meaning of these verses is debated. There is also a question as to whether the woman of ch. 3 is Gomer or someone else.

The sociopolitical setting for Hosea's ministry is equally difficult to pinpoint with precision. The superscription lists four Judean kings and Israel's Jeroboam II, a time span that potentially covers almost the entire eighth century BC. The conjunction of social injustice, political chaos, and looming military defeat, however, strongly suggests that Hosea began to prophesy in the latter part of Jeroboam's reign (ca. 790–753 BC). After this king's death the northern monarchy was plagued by a series of assassinations and coups. Within thirty years Israel was conquered by the Assyrians and its territory assimilated as a province of the empire.[1]

Jeroboam's son Zechariah was on the throne for only a short time before he was killed by Shallum, who in turn was eliminated by Menahem one month later (2Ki 15:8–16). Menahem's rule lasted a decade (752–742 BC). During this period Assyria regained prominence under Tiglath-pileser III (also known as Pul or Pulu; 745–727 BC) and began to reassert its presence to the west. The Bible records Menahem's paying tribute to Tiglath-pileser III in order to maintain his hold on the throne (2Ki 15:17–22).

Pekahiah, Menahem's son, succeeded him as king, but two years later he was killed by Pekah, one of his commanders (739 BC; 2Ki 15:23–26). In contrast to Menahem and Pekahiah, Pekah pursued an

---

1. For details, see S. H. Horn, rev. by P. K. McCarter Jr., in "The Divided Monarchy: The Kingdoms of Judah and Israel," in *Ancient Israel: From Abraham to the Roman Destruction of the Temple*, ed. H. Shanks (rev. ed.; Washington, D.C.: Biblical Archeology Society, 1999), 165–74; B. Becking, *The Fall of Samaria: An Historical and Archaeological Study* (SHANE 2; Leiden: Brill, 1992). The dates given for the Israelite kings follow E. R. Thiele, *The Mysterious Numbers of the Hebrew Kings* (rev. ed.; Grand Rapids: Zondervan, 1983).

anti-Assyrian policy. Along with Rezin of Aram-Damascus and other neighboring states, he formed a coalition to resist the empire's expansion. In what is now called the Syro-Ephraimite War (734–732 BC), they tried to force Ahaz, the king of Judah, to join the rebellion. He refused and, in fact, appealed to Tiglath-pileser III for help, in the process reducing the southern kingdom to the status of Assyrian vassalage (2Ki 16:5–10; 2Ch 28; cf. Isa 7–10). The Assyrian forces quickly crushed the coalition, and only Hoshea's assassination of Pekah spared Israel from annihilation (732 BC; 2Ki 15:29–30).

For several years a diminished Israel was subservient to the Assyrians, but eventually Hoshea too conspired against them. He stopped paying tribute and turned to Egypt for support. The nation's fate was sealed. The king of Assyria, Shalmaneser V, attacked Israel and besieged the capital city of Samaria for three years and took it in the summer of 722 BC. Thousands of Israelites were sent into exile, and peoples from different parts of the empire were brought in to take their place, thus exacerbating the syncretism of the region (2Ki 17:1–6, 24–41). Two years later rebellion flared up again, and Shalmaneser's successor Sargon II returned, defeated the rebels, and exiled even more of the population. The changing policies toward Assyria and the political intrigues of the last years of Israel's existence may well be represented in the descriptions of Hosea 5–7 and other passages scattered throughout the book.

In light of the fact that the superscription mentions Hezekiah, whose reign extended decades beyond Israel's defeat, the prophet may have witnessed his nation's fall. That his words survived Israel's demise suggests that his message (and maybe even Hosea himself) made its way to Judah, although it is impossible to know when. Whether his words were recorded in some written form before their appearance in the southern kingdom or were penned afterward remains speculation.

2. Authorship and Composition

Scholars disagree on how much of the book ascribed to Hosea actually comes from the hand of the prophet himself. It is often assumed that prophets, by definition, were strictly orators and did not write down their own words. According to this perspective, Hosea's words would have circulated in oral form for some time before being written down by a scribe or a circle of disciples; other material of various kinds would have been added to complete what today is our canonical text. Hypotheses differ as to how to distinguish the original from what is secondary and the time when these sections may have been included. Reconstructions range from traditional source theory to form and redaction criticism.[2]

Four kinds of material have been considered not to be original. First, all or at least some of the verses that mention Judah and the Davidic monarchy are said to be inauthentic. The reasoning is that since Hosea was from the northern kingdom, his message concentrated on Israel. The Judah passages, it is claimed, were inserted by a later hand in an attempt to apply the prophet's message to the south after the fall of Samaria.

---

2. For source theory, see W. R. Harper, *Amos and Hosea* (ICC; Edinburgh: T&T Clark, 1905), clviii–clxiii; for form criticism, H. W. Wolff, *Hosea* (Hermeneia; Philadelphia: Fortress, 1974), xxix–xxxii; for redaction criticism, G. I. Emmerson, *Hosea: An Israelite Prophet in Judean Perspective* (JSOTSup 28; Sheffield: Sheffield Academic Press, 1984); G. A. Yee, *Composition and Tradition in the Book of Hosea: A Redaction Critical Investigation* (SBLDS 102; Atlanta: Scholars, 1987).

Second, some scholars argue that the passages of future hope cannot be original (esp. 3:5; 11:8–11; 14:2–8). Hosea announced definitive judgment, so hints of national prosperity must have been added during the exilic or postexilic period in order to give subsequent generations the assurance that the Lord had not totally abandoned them.

Third, similarities between Hosea and Deuteronomy (e.g., the demand to worship only one God, the condemnation of idolatry, the election of Israel, and calls for repentance and covenantal love) suggest to some that editing of Hoseanic material was done by Deuteronomistic circles, which critical approaches date to the reforms of Josiah in the seventh century or later.

Finally, the closing verse (14:9) is deemed an addition from the wisdom tradition.

Nevertheless, it is possible to affirm that the book could have come substantially from the prophet Hosea. To begin with, recent studies on prophecy in the ancient world demonstrate that it was common practice to transcribe prophetic messages at the time of their promulgation or soon thereafter by a scribe (or, in some cases, by the prophet himself). In other words, the argument for a long process of oral transmission is more a modern hypothesis born of critical convictions than an accurate reflection of ancient religious realities.[3] At the same time, it is not possible to insist that Hosea wrote down his own words, except on the basis of Jewish and Christian tradition. (The book makes no so such claim.)

The case for a complicated process of composition is not compelling for other reasons. To begin with, a careful reading reveals that the references to Judah are often integral to the very structure of the passages where they appear. In addition, the entire book can be located reasonably within the sociopolitical and religious world of the second half of the eighth century. At that time, the political fortunes of Israel and Judah were inseparably connected, so it is not surprising that both nations are mentioned.

Moreover, the hope of a united people under a Davidic monarchy does not reflect the more developed Zion theology of the Judean eighth-century prophets Isaiah and Micah or of the exilic and postexilic prophets. The prophet recognizes that the future of the nation cannot lie with the corrupt government of the north. Hosea also is critical of the south (e.g., 5:5; 6:11), even as his contemporaries in Judah condemned Israel. His occasional expectations of a future stable government and time of peace are those of a more general hope grounded in historic Davidic promises.

The parallels with Deuteronomy are evident, but discussions of dependence or the direction of influence between the two books rely largely on decisions concerning the date of the composition of Deuteronomy and of the possible sources of its theological ideas. If the concepts are early — a fact increasingly recognized by critics — then this argument loses its force, irrespective of Deuteronomy's literary provenance.

Finally, the last verse of the book of Hosea echoes some of the prophet's characteristic vocabulary, making a denial of its authenticity problematic (see comments).

The work exhibits a complex literary coherence that points to a unity of composition. Diverse themes, vocabulary, and characterizations are repeated and interconnect its various parts in multiple ways, and it

---

3. A. R. Millard, "La prophétie et l'écriture: Israël, Aram, Assyrie," *RHR* 202/1 (1985): 125–45; M. deJong Ellis, "Observations on Mesopotamian Oracles and Prophetic Texts: Literary and Historiographic Considerations," *JCS* 41/2 (1989): 127–86; H. M. Barstad, "No Prophets? Recent Developments in Biblical Prophetic Research and Ancient Near Eastern Prophecy," *JSOT* 57 (1994): 39–60 (esp. 56–60).

is possible to trace a movement of thought that climaxes in the expectation of restoration and the closing exhortation of ch. 14. Redaction there may have been, but it is difficult to identify the editor's hand (apart from the superscription, 1:1).

Two trends in contemporary research deserve brief mention. Scholars have begun to probe the possibility of intentional organization in the creation of the Book of the Twelve (i.e., the Minor Prophets) as a single work. The fact that Hosea appears at the head of this corpus has led to hypotheses concerning its potential role in introducing key motifs that are consciously developed in the books that follow. These themes include, for instance, the day of Yahweh, the demand for the exclusive worship of the one true God, the call to return to Yahweh, and the love of God. Others argue that catchwords connect adjacent books, which may help explain why Joel (which does not have a historical superscription) is placed after Hosea (cf. Hos 14:4–9 with Joel 1:1–12).[4]

Another tendency in some scholarly circles has been to date the composition of the biblical books to the postexilic period. From this perspective Hosea, along with other prophetic texts, would have been penned by and for a literary elite in Persian Yehud. This book would have informed these literati about Israel's past, confirmed the fulfillment of God's warnings of judgment, and given them hope for an ideal future different from their present experience.[5] The content of the book makes perfect sense against its putative eighth-century setting, however, so this late dating is neither necessary nor probable.

3. STYLE AND IMAGERY

The Hebrew of Hosea is notoriously problematic. The presence of *hapax legomena* (words that appear only once in the OT), alternative verbal forms, and syntactical peculiarities complicate the task of translation.[6] The book's irregular structure, difficult imagery, and obscure historical allusions contribute to these difficulties. Comparison with the ancient versions, such as the LXX, reveals that they, too, wrestled with trying to understand the Hebrew text (apparently one very close to the MT) and were not always successful. An earlier generation of scholars believed that many of these problems were evidence of corruptions that had made their way into the process of transmission. Arguments for emendations were the order of the day.[7]

---

4. For different perspectives, see, e.g., J. Nogalski, *Literary Precursors to the Book of the Twelve* (BZAW 217; Berlin: de Gruyter, 1993), 21–24; J. Jeremias, "The Interrelationship between Amos and Hosea," in *Forming Prophetic Literature*, ed. J. W. Watts and P. R. House (JSOTSup 235; Sheffield: Sheffield Academic Press, 1996), 171–96; J. D. W. Watts, "A Frame for the Book of the Twelve: Hosea 1–3 and Malachi," in *Reading and Hearing the Book of the Twelve*, ed. J. D. Nogalski and M. A. Sweeney (SBLSymS 15; Atlanta: SBL, 2000), 209–17; L. J. Braaten, "God Sows: Hosea's Land Theme in the Book of the Twelve," in *Thematic Threads in the Book of the Twelve*, ed. P. L. Redditt and A. Schart (BZAW 325; Berlin: de Gruyter, 2003), 104–32.

5. E. Ben-Zvi, *Hosea* (FOTL 21; Grand Rapids: Eerdmans, 2005); J. W. Trotter, *Reading Hosea in Archaeminid Yehud* (JSOTSup 328; Sheffield: Sheffield Academic Press, 2001).

6. The many differences between the English versions are testimony to these challenges in translation. In order to inform the reader of this variety, the commentary often includes a list of versions with each translational option and in several instances explores issues more fully in the Notes.

7. E.g., Harper, *Amos and Hosea*, clxxi–clxxvii.

Today commentators are less prone to offer solutions based on conjecture and give more weight to the possibility that Hosea's language reflects idiosyncrasies of a northern dialect.[8]

The challenges in translation do not detract from the literary richness of the book and its powerful language, which so engages the reader. Unlike other prophetic texts that present biographical scenes (e.g., Isa 6–8, 36–39; Jer 18–21, 26–29, 32–43; Eze 1–3, 24; Am 7), Hosea nowhere portrays the prophet as speaking directly to the community or national leaders. Perhaps this was a literary work from the beginning instead of simply a compilation of orally delivered sermons. Variety in genres and literary devices abound. There are, among others, judgment speeches, oracles of salvation, woes, rhetorical questions, and wordplays. Themes and vocabulary are introduced and then taken up again later and elaborated. The result is a complex thematic and lexical unity more akin to a densely woven tapestry than to a logical treatise that unfolds in linear fashion.[9]

The imagery is diverse and emotionally charged (cf. 12:10).[10] On the one hand, Israel is represented by a battery of unflattering metaphors. The nation is an unfaithful wife (chs. 1–3), a stubborn heifer (4:16; 10:11), evaporating dew (6:4; 13:3), fleeting mist and smoke (6:4; 13:3), a hot oven (7:3–7), a burnt cake (7:8), a silly dove (7:11; 11:11), a foolish farmer (8:7), a useless vessel (8:8), a stray donkey (8:9), a worthless fruit tree (9:10, 16), a bad vine (10:1), a hapless twig (10:7), a disobedient child (11:1–4), and a childless woman (13:13). Not all is negative or hopeless, however. Someday Israel will be wooed by the Lord and their marital bonds renewed (2:14–20). Then the nation will be a beautiful flower and like a firmly rooted, bountiful tree (14:5–7).

Yahweh, too, is characterized in assorted metaphors, each of which reveals a different facet of the profound mystery of his person and character. Some reference judgment: he is a moth that will ruin the nation (5:12), a wild animal that devours (5:14–15; 13:8), a fowler who traps birds (7:12), and a farmer who yokes Israel, his ox (11:4). Yet Yahweh is not solely a stern judge: he is a forgiving and romantic husband (chs. 2–3), a loving parent (11:1–4; 14:3–4), a healing physician (14:4), fresh dew (14:5), and the source of all blessing (14:8).

These metaphors and similes are designed to strike the hearts and imaginations of God's people. Some shock, by exposing the ugliness and depth of sin and straightforwardly compelling repentance; others comfort and encourage the faithful to trust in the goodness of God and persevere through the coming judgment. It is important to emphasize that the overriding pictures of Yahweh and his people point to restoration. The book's final word is not one of an angry deity committed to destroying a sinful nation.

---

8. A. A. Macintosh, *A Critical and Exegetical Commentary on Hosea* (ICC; Edinburgh: T&T Clark, 1997), liii–lxi, lxxiv–lxxxiii, 585–93.

9. Note, e.g., G. Morris, *Prophecy, Poetry and Hosea* (JSOTSup 219; Sheffield: Sheffield Academic Press, 1996). Space limitations will not permit the citing of many of these literary features in the commentary.

10. Metaphor is a major topic of research on Hosea. Note, e.g., F. Landy, "In the Wilderness of Speech: Problems of Metaphor in Hosea," *BibInt* 31 (1995): 35–56; G. Eidevall, *Grapes in the Desert: Metaphors, Models, and Themes in Hosea 4–14* (ConBOT 43; Stockholm: Almquist & Wiksell, 1996); B. Oestreich, *Metaphors and Similes for Yahweh in Hosea 14:2–9 (1–8)* (Friedensauer Schriftenreihe: Theologie, 1; Frankfurt: Peter Lang, 1998). Also see below under "Feminist Approaches."

Above all else, Yahweh is a caring spouse, a patient parent, and a beneficent doctor, who rejoices in the renewal of his people.

4. RELIGION AND THEOLOGY IN HOSEA

The central message of Hosea is grounded in the fact that Israel has violated its relationship with Yahweh. Because the nation does not repent of its sins, it will suffer judgment. Nevertheless, the promise is that someday Israel will sincerely return to Yahweh and experience full restoration and blessing.

In that ancient social construction of reality that was Israel, religion—both popular and official—underpinned interpersonal, social, and political values. A distorted view of Yahweh and belief in other gods shapes how people think of life and death and the agricultural cycle, and it affects the decision making of the nation's leadership.[11] This religious world will not do for a country that claims Yahweh for its own; Yahweh will not tolerate this view of himself or this perverse society. The book censures the twisted understanding of Yahweh, the pursuit of other gods, and all the social and political deviation that follows. The religious life of Israel and its religious personnel—priests (5:1; 6:9; 10:5) and prophets (4:5; 9:7–9)[12]—stand condemned. The high places are to be destroyed (10:8); even the historic shrines at Bethel (e.g., 5:8; 10:5, 15; 12:4) and Gilgal (9:15; 12:11) will not avoid his wrath. Israel's festivals are rejected and the priesthood denounced (e.g., 2:11–13; 5:1–2, 6–7; 9:4–5).

The bond between Yahweh and Israel, although often problematic, was established centuries before with the patriarchs (12:3–7, 13–14) and solidified at the exodus (11:1; 12:9a; 13:4) and in the wilderness wanderings (2:14–15; 9:10; 12:9b; 13:5–6). It demanded a very different religious social construct. To continue on their self-destructive path will lead Israel to defeat and captivity—in a sense, taking it back to those oppressive days in Egypt (7:16; 8:13; 9:3, 6; 11:5). As mentioned earlier, the book employs a series of metaphors to portray this relationship between Yahweh and Israel. The most familiar is that of marriage. Israel is God's wayward wife, a reality reflected in the experience of the prophet Hosea with Gomer (chs. 1–3).

Marriage, however, is not the only familial description utilized by the prophet. Yahweh is the nation's parent—Israel's father and mother (11:1–4; 14:3–4[4–5]). The book abounds in the vocabulary of relationship, though much is of an ominous tone and deeply emotive. There is anger and profound disappointment at Israel's obstinate rebellion (e.g., 8:5; 12:14). The verb "to know" (*yādaʿ*, GK 3359) and its

---

11. M. D. Carroll R., "Reexamining Popular Religion: Issues of Definition and Sources. Insights from Interpretive Anthropology," in *Rethinking Contexts, Rereading Texts: Contributions from the Social Sciences to Biblical Interpretation*, ed. M. D. Carroll R. (JSOTSup 299; Sheffield: Sheffield Academic Press, 2000), 146–67. For the archaeological data, see O. Keel and C. Uehinger, *Gods, Goddesses, and Images of God in Ancient Israel* (Minneapolis: Fortress, 1998); M. S. Smith, *The Early History of God: Yahweh and the Other Deities in Ancient Israel* (2nd ed.; Grand Rapids: Eerdmans, 2002); R. S. Hess, *Israelite Religions: An Archaeological and Biblical Survey* (Grand Rapids: Baker, 2007). It is important to distinguish surveys of data from the hypothetical historical reconstruction of Israelite religion that a particular scholar might offer.

12. Wolff believes that the portrayal is always positive, so anything negative is considered an addition (*Hosea*, xxii–xxiii, 70–71 [regarding 4:5]). M. S. Odell interprets the references to prophets as negative ("Who Were the Prophets in Hosea?" *HBT* 18/1 [1996]: 78–95). The textual data are more complex, reflecting respect for the prophets of the past (6:5; 12:10[11], 13[14]) and disdain for those in the present, who lead the nation astray (4:5; 9:7–8).

derivative "knowledge" (*da'at*, GK 1981) are prominent. The people do not "know" Yahweh, his efforts in their behalf, or his demands (e.g., 2:8; 5:4; 13:4), so they perish for lack of "knowledge" (e.g., 4:6). One day, however, they will finally "know" him and enjoy his bounty (2:20|22|; 6:3; 8:2).

Another key word is "return" or "repent" (*šûb*; GK 8740). Israel refuses to turn truly to Yahweh (5:4; 6:1; 7:10; 11:5), but in the future the nation will come to him in sorrow for its sin (3:5; 12:6; 14:1–2). There also is a rich terminology of affection. The Lord longs to show compassion but cannot (*rāḥam*; 1:6–7; 2:4, 23; 14:3); he has loved Israel (*'āhab*; 3:1; 14:4), even though its love is twisted and misdirected (4:18; 9:1). He demands that the nation demonstrate loyal-love (*ḥesed*; GK 2876) to him through obedience to the law (4:1; 6:4; 10:12; 12:6).

In two instances the prophet uses the term "covenant" (*bᵉrît*; GK 1382) to describe this relationship between Yahweh and Israel (6:7; 8:1; with different referents at 2:18; 10:4; 12:1). Some scholars question whether a substantive covenantal idea could have existed in the eighth century,[13] but the centrality of that idea and the presence of related relational concepts throughout the book make it difficult to deny that the prophet bases much of what he communicates on it.[14] One finds, for example, indictments for ignoring the *tôrâ* of God (4:6; 8:1), appeals to the exodus, echoes of the Decalogue (4:2), and apparent allusions to the covenantal curses (such as punishment by the sword [7:16; 11:6; 13:16] and crop failure [2:3, 9, 12(14)]) and the blessings (e.g., abundance [2:18–22]) of Leviticus 26 and Deuteronomy 27–28.

The one to whom Israel is bound is sovereign over all. Yahweh is Lord over creation; he alone grants fertility to the nation's crops (e.g., 2:8, 18–22). He directs the movement of every nation and the superpowers. Yahweh can utilize other peoples for judgment (e.g., 10:6–10, 14–15; 11:6; 13:15–16), emphasizes the folly of entering into alliances with them (5:13; 7:11; 8:9; 9:3; 12:1), and exposes the limited power of empires (5:13; 14:3). The politics of Israel should be guided by a unique set of priorities and commitments. Its ruling elites and monarchy are fiercely criticized for their lack of ethics and for policies that manifest rebellion against God and that are, on occasion, associated with a cult that Yahweh abhors (e.g., 5:1–2, 10; 6:11–7:7; 8:4; 13:9–11). Sharp attacks on the monarchy have led some to wonder whether the prophet is against the very institution of kingship. This is too extreme a view. What is made clear is that the northern kingdom's king and government are illegitimate in God's sight. The hope is that someday Israel will be reunited with Judah under a Davidic king (1:11; 3:4–5).[15]

---

13. For a recent statement of this position, see S. L. McKenzie, *Covenant* (Understanding Biblical Themes; St. Louis: Chalice, 2000).

14. See, e.g., F. C. Fensham, "The Covenant-Idea in the Book of Hosea," *Studies on the Books of Hosea and Amos: Papers Read at the 7th and 8th Meetings of die O. T. Werkgemeenskap in Suid-Africa (1964–65)* (no publ. info, 1966), 35–49; W. Brueggemann, *Hosea: Tradition for Crisis* (Atlanta: John Knox, 1968); J. Day, "Pre-Deuteronomic Allusions to the Covenant in Hosea and Psalm LXXVIII," *VT* 36 (1986): 1–12; E. W. Nicholson, *God and His People: Covenant and Theology in the Old Testament* (Oxford: Clarendon, 1986), 179–87; D. Stuart, *Hosea–Jonah* (WBC 31; Waco, Tex.: Word, 1987), 6–8.

15. See Emmerson, *Hosea*, 105–13; A. Gelston, "Kingship in the Book of Hosea," *OtSt* 19 (1974): 71–85; P. Machinist, "Hosea and the Ambiguity of Kingship in Ancient Israel," in *Constituting the Community: Studies on the Polity of Ancient Israel in Honor of S. Dean McBride, Jr.*, ed. J. T. Strong and S. S. Tuell (Winona Lake, Ind.: Eisenbrauns, 2005), 153–81.

The unacceptable beliefs about Yahweh are exacerbated by the worship of other deities. The book of Hosea condemns the worship of *baʿal* (2:8[10]; 13:1) and the *bᵉʿālîm* (plural form; 2:13[15], 17[19]; 11:2). *Baʿal* (Baal) was the chief god of Canaan and Phoenicia.[16] The marriage of Ahab to the Sidonian princess Jezebel in the previous century provided official support to the *baʿal* cult (1Ki 16:31–33; 18:3, 19, 22) until its purging through the ministry of Elijah and Elisha and the slaughter of its priests by Jehu (1Ki 18; 2Ki 10). Scholars disagree as to whether references to the *bᵉʿālîm* are various local manifestations of the one god *baʿal* or whether the prophet is attacking several gods, but these two options are not mutually exclusive. Hosea could be hitting both at the more prominent god of Israel's neighbors as well as at other deities, whom he labels *bᵉʿālîm*.[17] Some suggest that at some of the shrines the goddess Asherah (or Astarte) was worshiped as well.[18]

Discussions of the religious world of Hosea often center on the possible existence of a fertility cult in relation to the worship of other deities (Hos 4:14; cf. Ge 38:21–22; Dt 23:17–18[18–19]). Earlier commentators uniformly contended that "cultic prostitution" was an integral element of these non-Yahwistic cults. According to this view, women offered themselves sexually to male worshipers at the sanctuaries as acts of imitative magic in order to secure fertility for crops, livestock, and human families. This interpretation can be traced back as far as the Greek historian Herodotus, but it is now questioned by many. Some scholars claim that there is no concrete evidence in the ancient Near East to associate women at worship centers with sacred prostitution; perhaps the image of infidelity is polemical language to describe the worship of other deities.[19]

Others believe that there was sexual activity at the high places but that it was not a formal part of the rituals themselves. Some women, it is said, engaged in this activity to acquire income for these cultic centers or to pay off religious vows.[20] Alternatively, prostitutes may have frequented these areas for clientele, or worship could have degenerated into sexual license because of the drinking that presumably accompanied the rituals. Nonetheless, a few studies do substantiate the existence of sacred prostitution in the ancient world, even though the notion of imitative magic has been generally discredited.[21] It is difficult to decide among these alternatives, but some sort of sexual activity is hard to deny in the light of 4:10–14.

---

16. Smith, *The Early History of God*, 65–107; J. Day, "Baal," *ABD*, 1:545–49; W. Herrmann, "Baal," *DDD*, 132–39.

17. J. A. Dearman, "Interpreting the Religious Polemics against Baal and the Baalim in the Book of Hosea," *OTE* 14 (2001): 9–25.

18. M.-T. Wacker, "Traces of the Goddess in the Book of Hosea," in *A Feminist Companion to the Latter Prophets*, ed. A. Brenner; Feminist Companion to the Bible 8; Sheffield: Sheffield Academic Press, 1995), 219–41; J. M. Hadley, *The Cult of Asherah in Ancient Israel and Judah: Evidence for a Hebrew Goddess* (University of Cambridge Oriental Publications 57; Cambridge: Cambridge Univ. Press, 2000), 75–83; W.G. Dever, *Did God Have a Wife? Archaeology and Folk Religion in Ancient Israel* (Grand Rapids: Eerdmans, 2005).

19. J. G. Westenholz, "Tamar, Qᵉdēšâ, Qadištu, and Sacred Prostitution in Mesopotamia," *HTR* 82 (1989): 245–65; P. A. Bird, "'To Play the Harlot': An Inquiry into an Old Testament Metaphor," in *Missing Persons and Mistaken Identities: Women and Gender in Ancient Israel*, ed. P. A. Bird (Minneapolis: Fortress, 1997), 219–36.

20. K. van der Toorn, "Prostitution [Cultic Prostitution]," *ABD*, 5:510–13.

21. W. G. Lambert, "Prostitution," in *Aussenseiter und Randgruppen: Beiträge zu einer Sozialgeschichte des alten Orients*, ed. V. Haas (Xenia 32; Konstanz: Universitätsverlag Konstanz, 1992), 127–57; J. Day, "Does the Old Testament Refer to Sacred Prostitution and Did It Actually Exist in Ancient Israel?" in *Biblical and Near Eastern Essays: Studies in Honour of Kevin J. Cathcart*, ed. C. McCarthy and J. F. Healey (JSOTSup 375; London: T&T Clark, 2004), 2–21.

Increasingly, scholars argue that in ancient Israel it was acceptable to worship Yahweh together with other deities until the appearance of Elijah and Elisha, the ministry of Hosea, and others of a so-called "Yahweh-alone" movement. Archaeological discoveries are making the scale of syncretism in Israel and Judah more evident, thus leading to diverse hypotheses about how monotheism might have developed. Nevertheless, faith in a single God was not a later innovation or the result of a long evolutionary process. The demand to have no other gods before Yahweh stands as the first of the commandments (Ex 20:1–3; Dt 5:6–7). The prophets contributed to the articulation and deepening of belief in Yahweh, and Hosea was part of that stream of powerful witnesses. The historic portrayal in the OT suggests that faith in the one true God was in constant tension with the worship of other deities from the entry into the Promised Land until the fall of Jerusalem.

5. FEMINIST APPROACHES

The book of Hosea has been a target of feminist critiques primarily because of the husband and wife imagery of the first three chapters. The descriptions there are interpreted as reflecting the actual treatment of wives by husbands in Israelite culture: female sexuality is considered to be evil; Gomer/Israel are publicly degraded, physically abused, and then cynically wooed back. The fact that Yahweh acts within the unequal power relationships of this patriarchal framework gives men divine sanction for the mistreatment of women—both then and today. For many feminists the problems generated by Hosea are not limited to inappropriate appropriations of the book; they argue that the prophetic text itself is irredeemably misogynist. Evangelical commentators are beginning to engage feminist arguments.[22]

In response to these feminist concerns, it must be stressed above all else that interpretations that lead to the exploitation of women should be universally condemned. At the same time, it is important to ask whether the biblical text is as morally bankrupt as some feminists insist. Four observations about the book's metaphors are apropos here (also see "Style and Imagery," above). First, parts of the book are clearly designed to shock through use of exaggerated imagery drawn from familial life and the animal world. To equate hyperbole with ancient social realities is to misread the intent of the text.

Second, it is clear that all metaphors have limitations and finally break down. For example, in Hosea Yahweh is portrayed as a moth, a wild beast, a farmer, a parent, morning dew, and a tree, as well as a husband. This wide repertoire of tropes serves to illuminate different things about God, each of which, however, can only be taken so far. A comprehensive picture of Yahweh requires a judicious appreciation of what each word picture can offer and discernment about when certain aspects of a metaphor just do not apply. For instance, does the fact that God is a moth mean that he is fragile and weak? By the same token, to keep pressing the marriage metaphor to what some today might conceive as its logical implications may exceed its purpose and design.

Third, metaphors can overlap with other imagery. A celebrated example is 2:3, 10, where Yahweh declares that he will strip Israel naked. The verse goes on to say, however, that this barrenness refers to drought. The dryness of the ground and the loss of foliage in a sense are like a woman exposed, but it does

---

22. E.g., D. A. Hubbard, *Hosea* (TOTC 22A; Downers Grove, Ill.: InterVarsity Press, 1989), 43–45; D. A. Garrett, *Hosea, Joel* (NAC 19A; Nashville: Broadman & Holman, 1997), 124–33.

not mean that men in fact publicly disrobed their wives. To argue that they did is to miss the point. It is precisely because such an action would be so far beyond the bounds of social behavior that the picture shakes the reader so deeply. Recent studies also postulate that the metaphors that on the surface portray violent behavior in ch. 2 actually refer to symbolic acts related to divorce and disinheritance or to complex socioeconomic tensions in the land.[23]

Fourth, metaphors must be read within their cultural framework. Some read the biblical text through the lens of certain modern Western ideals of gender relationships and sexual mores that are foreign to the OT's worldview and thus misunderstand and misrepresent what the text is trying to communicate. Even those sympathetic to feminist concerns point out this interpretive weakness.[24]

6. BIBLIOGRAPHY

Andersen, F. I., and D. N. Freedman. *Hosea.* Anchor Bible 24. Garden City, N.Y.: Doubleday, 1980.

Brenner, A., ed. *A Feminist Companion to the Latter Prophets.* The Feminist Companion to the Bible 8. Sheffield: Sheffield Academic Press, 1995.

Davies, G. I. *Hosea.* New Century Bible. Grand Rapids: Eerdmans, 1992.

Dever, W. G. *Did God Have a Wife? Archaeology and Folk Religion in Ancient Religion.* Grand Rapids: Eerdmans, 2005.

Emmerson, G. I. *Hosea: An Israelite Prophet in Judean Perspective.* Journal for the Study of the Old Testament Supplement Series 28. Sheffield: Sheffield Academic Press, 1984.

Garrett, D. A. *Hosea, Joel.* New American Commentary 19A. Nashville: Broadman & Holman, 1997.

Harper, W. R. *Amos and Hosea.* International Critical Commentary. Edinburgh: T&T Clark, 1905.

Hubbard, D. A. *Hosea.* Tyndale Old Testament Commentaries 22A. Downers Grove, Ill.: InterVarsity Press, 1989.

Kakkanattu, J. P. *God's Enduring Love in the Book of Hosea: A Synchronic and Diachronic Analysis of Hosea 11:1–11.* Forschungen zum Alten Testament 14. Tübingen: Mohr Siebeck, 2006.

Keil, C. F. *Commentary on the Old Testament.* Vol. 10. Grand Rapids: Eerdmans, 1977.

Kelle, B. E. *Hosea 2: Metaphor and Rhetoric in Historical Perspective.* Society of Biblical Literature Archaeology and Biblical Studies 20. Leiden: Brill, 2005.

Landy, F. *Hosea.* Readings: A New Biblical Commentary. Sheffield: Sheffield Academic Press, 1995.

McComiskey, T. E. "Hosea." In *The Minor Prophets: An Exegetical and Expositional Commentary.* Edited by T. E. McComiskey. Vol. 1. Grand Rapids: Baker, 1992.

Macintosh, A. A. *A Critical and Exegetical Commentary on Hosea.* International Critical Commentary. Edinburgh: T&T Clark, 1997.

Mays, J. L. *Hosea.* Old Testament Library. Philadelphia: Westminster, 1969.

Nielsen, K. *Yahweh as Prosecutor and Judge.* Journal for the Study of the Old Testament Supplement 9. Sheffield. Sheffield Academic Press, 1978.

Oestreich, B. *Metaphors and Similes for Yahweh in Hosea 14:2–9 (1–8).* Friedensauer Schriftenreihe: Theologie, 1. Frankfurt: Peter Lang, 1998.

Smith, M. S. *The Early History of God: Yahweh and the Other Deities in Ancient Israel.* 2nd ed. Grand Rapids: Eerdmans, 2002.

Stuart, D. *Hosea–Jonah.* Word Biblical Commentary 31. Waco, Tex.: Word, 1987.

Sweeney, M. A. *The Twelve Prophets.* Berit Olam. Collegeville, Minn.: Liturgical, 2000.

Wolff, H. W. *Hosea.* Hermeneia. Philadelphia: Fortress, 1974.

Yee, G. A. "Hosea." In *The New Interpreter's Bible.* Vol. 7. Nashville: Abingdon, 1996.

---

23. B. E. Kelle, *Hosea 2: Metaphor and Rhetoric in Historical Perspective* (SBLABS 20; Leiden: Brill, 2005), 47–79; A. A. Keefe, *Woman's Body and the Social Body in Hosea* (JSOTSup 33810; London: Sheffield Academic Press, 2001), 213–16.

24. Keefe, *Woman's Body and the Social Body in Hosea,* 140–61; cf. C. Myers, *Households and Holiness: The Religious Culture of Women* (Minneapolis: Fortress, 2005).

7. OUTLINE

I. Superscription (1:1)

II. The Marriage Relationship between Yahweh and Israel (1:2–3:5)

  A. The Marriage of Hosea to Gomer (1:2–2:1[3])

    1. The Command to Marry Gomer (1:2–3a)

    2. The Birth and Significance of the Three Children (1:3b–9)

    3. The Future Hope for the Nation (1:10–2:1[2:1–3])

  B. The Marriage between Yahweh and Israel (2:2–23[4–25])

    1. The Violation of the Marriage Bond between Israel and the Divine Judgment (2:2–15[4–17])

    2. The Reestablishment of the Marriage between Yahweh and Israel (2:16–23[18–25])

  C. The Restoration of Gomer and Israel (3:1–5)

III. The Announcement of Judgment and the Promise of Restoration, Part One (4:1–11:11)

  A. The Religious and Political Corruption of Israel (4:1–7:16)

    1. The Indictment of Israel (4:1–3)

    2. The Perversion of Worship (4:4–5:7)

      a. The failure of Israel as the priest of God (4:4–10a)

      b. The syncretism of Israel (4:10b–19)

      c. The blind arrogance of Israel (5:1–7)

    3. Political Chaos and Intrigue (5:8–7:16)

      a. Disastrous decisions in war (5:8–15)

      b. The unacceptable repentance of the people (6:1–6)

      c. Dangerous national politics (6:7–7:7)

      d. Senseless foreign policy (7:8–16)

  B. The Religious and Political Judgment of Israel (8:1–11:11)

    1. The Violation of the Covenant (8:1–9:9)

      a. The politics of rebellion (8:1–10)

      b. The religion of forgetfulness (8:11–14)

      c. The religion of fools (9:1–9)

    2. Metaphors of Rebellion and Judgment (9:10–11)

      a. Grapes in the wilderness (9:10–17)

      b. A "luxuriant"/destructive vine and plant (10:1–8)

      c. A trained heifer (10:9–15)

      d. A beloved child (11:1–11)

IV. The Announcement of Judgment and the Promise of Restoration, Part Two (11:12–14:9 [12:1–14:9])

  A. Lessons from History (11:12–13:16[12:1–14:1])

    1. The Indictment of Israel and Judah (11:12–12:2[12:1–3])

    2. The Positive Example of Jacob (12:3–14[4–15])

Text and Exposition

I. SUPERSCRIPTION (1:1)

¹The word of the Lord that came to Hosea son of Beeri during the reigns of Uzziah, Jotham, Ahaz and Hezekiah, kings of Judah, and during the reign of Jeroboam son of Jehoash king of Israel.

COMMENTARY

1 Like other prophetic books (with the exceptions of Joel and Obadiah), the book of Hosea begins with a notice that locates the prophet historically. Only the book of Amos, Hosea's contemporary, also includes names of kings of both the northern and southern kingdoms. (For more details, see "Historical Background" in the introduction.)

Although Hosea is not called a prophet, what is communicated is characterized as "the word of the Lord." (In fact, only later prophetic books have the word "prophet" in their superscriptions; see Hab 1:1; Hag 1:1; Zec 1:1). The prophet's name, *hôšēaʿ* (most properly "Hoshea"), is probably a shortened form of *hôšaʿyâ* (e.g., Ne 12:32; Jer 42:1; 43:2), which means "Yahweh has delivered" or "Yahweh, deliver!" (Hiphil perfect or imperative of the verb *yšʿ*).

Hosea's father's name is attested elsewhere (Ge 26:34) and can signify "my wellspring," but nothing about his background or place of origin is offered. The mention of Beeri, however, does distinguish Hosea from others of the same name, such as the Hoshea sent by Moses to explore the land (Nu 13:8) and the last of the Israelite kings (2Ki 15:30).

II. THE MARRIAGE RELATIONSHIP BETWEEN YAHWEH AND ISRAEL (1:2–3:5)

OVERVIEW

This first section of Hosea is the best-known part of the book. It presents the account of the prophet's marriage to Gomer and weaves an analogy between that relationship and the one between Yahweh and his people Israel. Discussions focus especially on whether the marriage between Hosea and Gomer actually took place and whether the story of that union extends through the full three chapters or is limited to chs. 1 and 2. These chapters have been the object of many feminist reflections (see "Feminist Approaches" in the introduction).

A. The Marriage of Hosea to Gomer (1:2–2:1[3])

1. The Command to Marry Gomer (1:2–3a)

²When the Lord began to speak through Hosea, the Lord said to him, "Go, take to yourself an adulterous wife and children of unfaithfulness, because the land is guilty of the vilest adultery in departing from the Lord." ³So he married Gomer daughter of Diblaim.

COMMENTARY

2 The opening line of this verse reveals that Hosea's marriage to Gomer occurs at the commencement of his prophetic ministry. He is commanded to "take a woman," a phrase used of marriage (Ge 4:19; 24:3, 67; 34:4; Jer 29:6). What kind of woman Yahweh tells Hosea to marry, however, has been the focus of much debate. Disagreement centers on the significance of the nominal construct ʾēšet zᵉnûnîm and hence its translation (cf. NASB, "a wife of harlotry"; NIV, "an adulterous wife"; NRSV, "a wife of whoredom").

The root *znh* (GK 2393) is a broad term for sexual impropriety, and context determines whether or not this misconduct occurs in violation of the bonds of marriage (G. H. Hall, "זנה," *NIDOTTE*, 1:1122–25). The word combination here is not the designation for a prostitute (*zônâ* or *ʾiššâ zônâ*; cf. Jos 2:1; Jdg 11:1; 1Ki 3:1; etc.). *Zᵉnûnîm* is an abstract plural that describes a character trait (cf. "woman of contention" in Pr 21:9; 27:15; GKC §128s–v). In other words, this is a promiscuous woman. Two questions divide commentators: Is what is referred to actual sexual behavior, and to what time period in this woman's life might this description apply?

Earlier commentators often took this label in a symbolic sense, as emblematic of the spiritual apostasy of the nation (cf. Tg.). This view was based on the conviction that God would never ask a prophet to marry an immodest woman (note Lev 21:7, 14). The figurative names of the children that follow in this chapter also could indicate symbolic intent. Today most scholars, while not denying the use elsewhere of the metaphor of infidelity to depict Israel's faithlessness to God, consider this phrase to be an indication of sexual misconduct. Some see it as proleptic, or anticipatory, of what happens after the marriage—that is, the woman was pure at the marriage but afterward turns to evil. (Note the NIV, "adulterous wife"; adultery by definition is inconstancy in marriage.) The historical analogy with the relationship of God and his people may further support the view that the woman's infidelity happens after the marriage, as Israel has been unfaithful after being redeemed by Yahweh at the exodus.

The most natural reading of the Hebrew, however, is that God asks Hosea to marry a woman of ill repute. The character trait depicts what she *is*, not what she *will become*. It is possible that her immorality is connected to her devotion to the *baˁal* cult, but that idea is not explicit in this text. (Wolff, 14–15, suggests that what is in view is a one-time initiatory rite of females before marriage, but there is no evidence of such a sacral act.)

If this interpretation is correct, then it follows that the children who are called "children of fornications" (the same descriptor; NIV, "children of unfaithfulness") in the next clause are those the woman already has at the time of her marriage to Hosea. The same divine command ("take") governs both objects; the prophet is to take her and adopt her offspring at the same time. These are not the children born after the marriage (vv.3b−9). What is uncertain is the precise meaning of the epithet in connection with the children. Perhaps the best option is to consider "of fornications" not as a characteristic genitive but rather as a genitive of source (i.e., they were born of illicit relationships).

This verse makes clear that the sexual looseness of the woman is a picture of the faithlessness of the nation toward Yahweh. The Hebrew construction is emphatic (infinitive absolute + imperfect of the same root, *znh*), and English translations reflect the weight of this expression: "guilty of the vilest adultery" (NIV), "commits flagrant harlotry" (NASB), and "commits great whoredom" (NRSV, ESV). The analogy with Israel, however, is not with its

history since the exodus but, instead, illustrates the condition of the nation in the prophet's day. Israel is playing the whore, but God in his justice and mercy still reaches out—an initiative visualized in Hosea's marriage to this promiscuous woman.

3a Hosea obeys Yahweh's directive, apparently without hesitation. There is no mention of his feelings or possible doubts, or of a courtship or betrothal period. He simply complies with what he is charged to do. For the first time the woman is named. She is Gomer, daughter of Diblaim (probably the name of her father, not a place). Gomer appears as the name of a man in Genesis 10:2−3 and later of a people (Eze 38:6). Although some have tried to ascertain a figurative meaning behind these two names, the text does not proffer any such significance (Macintosh, 11−13). Such is not the case in the following verses with the names given to the next three children to be born by Gomer.

2. The Birth and Significance of the Three Children (1:3b−9)

And [Gomer] conceived and bore him a son. ⁴Then the LORD said to Hosea, "Call him Jezreel, because I will soon punish the house of Jehu for the massacre at Jezreel, and I will put an end to the kingdom of Israel. ⁵In that day I will break Israel's bow in the Valley of Jezreel."

⁶Gomer conceived again and gave birth to a daughter. Then the LORD said to Hosea, "Call her Lo-Ruhamah, for I will no longer show love to the house of Israel, that I should at all forgive them. ⁷Yet I will show love to the house of Judah; and I will save them—not by bow, sword or battle, or by horses and horsemen, but by the LORD their God."

⁸After she had weaned Lo-Ruhamah, Gomer had another son. ⁹Then the LORD said, "Call him Lo-Ammi, for you are not my people, and I am not your God.

COMMENTARY

3b−4 The notice of marriage is followed by this announcement that Gomer bears to Hosea a son. This child is the first of three who are given

symbolic names—not the only instance of this phenomenon in the prophetic literature (cf. Isa 7:3; 8:3−4).

The name that Yahweh tells Hosea to give the child is "Jezreel." This name is derived from the verb *zrᶜ* in combination with the divine epithet *ʾēl* ("God") and means "God sows." While Jezreel was the name of a town in Judah (1Sa 25:43), the reference here surely is to the so-named valley or town in Israel, both of which were situated between Galilee and Samaria. While a number of unfortunate events in the nation's history had occurred there (e.g., the gathering against the Philistines [1Sa 29:1]; the injustice concerning Naboth's vineyard [1Ki 21]), this verse relates the name specifically to the massacre (*dāmîm*, lit., "bloods"; cf. GKC §124n; *HALOT*, 225) carried out at Jezreel in 2 Kings 9–10. There Jehu, a high-ranking officer, slew King Jehoram of Israel, King Ahaziah of Judah, and Queen Mother Jezebel; in Samaria he slaughtered the remaining descendents of Ahab and the ministers of *baᶜal*.

At first glance, this verse contradicts God's relatively positive verdict on Jehu's actions (2Ki 10:30). Why would Israel be penalized for what Yahweh apparently had approved a century earlier? If, however, one interprets the verb *pqd* (GK 7212) not as "punish" but as "visit," the translation then reads: "I *will bring* the bloodshed of Jezreel *upon* the house of Jehu" (cf. 2:13). That is, the monarchy of Hosea's day will suffer the same fate as that suffered by the house of Ahab and others. It will be eliminated violently by divine judgment.

5 Scholars have tried to identify the precise circumstances of the fulfillment of this prophecy of defeat. Options include the assassination of Zechariah by Shallum (2Ki 15:10–12; 752 BC), the disaster of the Syro-Ephraimite War (2Ki 15:27–31; 734–733 BC), and the definitive fall of the northern kingdom in 722 BC. The last of these possibilities fits best the harsh language of these two verses. At the same time, this prediction may be a general word of an imminent severe judgment and does not need to be taken as an explicit prediction

(with a particular date and agent) of the demise of the northern kingdom. The first-person verbs of vv.4–5 emphasize that the destruction ultimately comes from Yahweh's hand, but his instrument of judgment is not identified. After Israel's demise, it would be natural to see these words as a pointed prophecy with a specific fulfillment.

6 The second child that is born is a daughter. The text does not state that Hosea fathered her; the same is true of *Lōʾ-ᶜammî* in v.8. If Hosea is not the father, the severity of the names of these two children might find a trenchant and quite literal sense ("not-loved," "not my people"), instead of only symbolizing issues between Yahweh and Israel. The terseness of the verse, however, may simply be due to economy of language. The girl is given the name *Lōʾ-ruḥāmâ*, "Not Loved." This verb is a denominative from *reḥem*, "womb," and is used for God's affection for his people elsewhere (e.g., Ex 33:19; Mic 7:19).

The meaning of the phrase that follows is debated. The most natural translation is, "But I will surely forgive them" (adversative *kî*, GKC §163a; infinite absolute + imperfect of *nśʾ*). This same verb is used for forgiveness in 14:2. This translation appears blatantly to contradict the first half of the verse. The juxtaposition of judgment and mercy, though, characterizes the entire chapter (see vv.9–10; Garrett, 60–69). These words forcefully communicate that judgment has a purpose and is not Yahweh's final goal. In the end, mercy overrides wrath; restoration follows discipline and purification.

7 This verse continues the thought of the preceding clause (contra versions that begin the line with "yet" or "but"), expanding the promise of the gracious work of God to Judah. How this deliverance is *not* to be achieved is described in a list of five prepositional phrases. It will not come by bow, sword, battle, horses, or riders. (The first two refer to foot soldiers, the last two to chariots.) The salvation of Yahweh, in other words, will not come by warfare. Even as judgment will come by his direct intervention, so will future blessings.

More critical approaches believe that the mention of Judah is an interpolation designed to actualize the text for a later audience. This line, though, anticipates 1:11, where the prophetic hope encompasses both North and South, once more reunited under a Davidic king (cf. 3:5). This is the same expectation of Hosea's contemporary Amos, who also discredits the governing house of Israel and points to the reestablishment of a Davidic monarchy (Am 9:11). This discrediting does not mean that these prophets have a fully developed theology of Zion or that they idealize Judah. It does underscore their conviction that Israel's king and leadership are sinful in the eyes of God and that the ancient divine commitment to the house of David still holds sway.

8–9 The weaning period in the ancient world was done at up to three years of age (2 Macc 7:27; cf. 1Sa 1:23). After this time, Gomer bears another son. Once more it is not stated that Hosea is the father (see comment on v.6). Yahweh again tells the prophet to give a child a symbolic name, in this case *Lōʾ-ʿammî*, "Not My People." This is the most shocking of the three names, as it may be a reversal of the foundational covenantal declaration of Exodus 6:7 and Leviticus 26:12. Yahweh communicates as well that neither is he their God any longer. The audience (and the reader) is left to wonder how this severing of the relationship with Yahweh can be coordinated with the assurances of the preceding two verses. Clearly, then, this declaration is not irrevocable. What must unfold is when and how the renewal will be accomplished.

NOTES

6 Scholars and the versions attempt to nuance the last clause כִּי־נָשֹׂא אֶשָּׂא לָהֶם (*kî nāśōʾ ʾeśśāʾ lāhem*) in such a way as to remove the perceived incongruity with the beginning of the verse. Interpretive alternatives include taking the grammatical construction in a negative sense ("that I should at all forgive them"; NIV, NASB) or asserting that "I will no longer," from earlier in the verse, governs the clauses through v.7 ("I will no longer show compassion … forgive them … show compassion … save them"; NRSV; cf. Andersen and Freedman, 188–94). Others propose a different meaning for the verb נשׂא (*nśʾ*), translate it as "take away," and suggest that either the people will be taken into exile (McComiskey, 25; Macintosh, 21–22) or that God's compassion will be taken away (Wolff, 8, 20). Still others contend that there was a confusion of נשׂא (*nśʾ*) with נשׁא (*nšʾ*, "reject"; cf. Stuart, 31) or שׂנא (*śnʾ*, "hate"; BHS).

9 The last clause of v.9 reads literally, "and I will not be for you" or "I am not yours" ("I do not exist for you," NJB). The translation "I am not your God" is based on a slight emendation of the text (NIV, NRSV, NASB) but also follows logically (cf. 2:23). Some argue for "because I am not 'I will be' to you," as an allusion to Exodus 3:14 (e.g., Wolff, 21–22; Andersen and Freedman, 198–99; Stuart, 33–34).

3. The Future Hope for the Nation (1:10–2:1[2:1–3])

10"Yet the Israelites will be like the sand on the seashore, which cannot be measured or counted. In the place where it was said to them, 'You are not my people,' they will be called 'sons of the living God.' [11]The people of Judah and the people of Israel will be reunited, and they will appoint one leader and will come up out of the land, for great will be the day of Jezreel.

[2:1]"Say of your brothers, 'My people,' and of your sisters, 'My loved one.'

COMMENTARY

10 [2:1] This section expands the reversal of fortune first mentioned in v.7, but here this glorious future is not limited to Judah. Both North and South will experience the blessing of God. The language used to describe that future echoes the content of Israel's covenants.

First, the "sons of Israel" (lit.; i.e., the nation Israel; 3:1, 4–5; 4:1) will greatly increase in population. This prophetic word is welcome news after the announcement of the death and destruction foretold in vv.4–5. After the casualties of that defeat, Israel will be "like the sand on the seashore." This phrase recalls the assurances of progeny given to Abraham centuries before (Ge 22:17; cf. 32:12). As an idiom to depict innumerability, this phrase is not limited to the patriarchal narratives (e.g., Ge 41:49; Jos 11:4; 1Ki 4:20, 29), but its combination with other statements of hope based on other covenants indicates that it is likely an allusion to the Abrahamic promise.

Second, the annulment of the Mosaic formula in v.9 is overturned. The name "You are not my people" will change to "sons of the living God." The "place" is ambiguous. In the context, the most natural interpretation is to see it as a reference to Israel itself. The nation stood condemned, but it will not always be so. That place and that people can look forward to a renewed relationship with God.

11 [2:2] The third component of future reversal is the reunification of Judah and Israel under "one head" (NIV, "one leader"), a pointer to the

Davidic covenant (2Sa 7). Divided since 931 BC and in conflict intermittently over the years (and in Hosea's time in the Syro-Ephraimite War), the southern and northern kingdoms will again be reconciled (cf. Eze 37:15–28). There is no need to propose that the title "king" is deliberately avoided here, either because of a negative stance toward the monarchy of that day (although true) or because "king" could have eschatological connotations. It is used of David in 3:5, so the term "leader" may be simply a stylistic variation.

Scholars disagree on the meaning of "they will come up out of the land." Three principal options have been put forward (see Macintosh, 31–33). One is to understand this phrase as signifying the return from their place of exile. The term "the land," however, usually refers to the Promised Land of Israel. Another interpretation argues that "the land" denotes the underworld (e.g., Job 10:21–22; Isa 44:23); to come up from there, metaphorically, then depicts national "resurrection" or renewal. The best alternative, however, is to understand the verb *ʿlh* in the sense of "spring up" or "sprout" (Dt 29:23; cf. *HALOT*, 829). That is, Israel will be fruitful and prosper once more. This agricultural picture for national restoration reappears in ch. 2 and at the end of the book (2:21–23, 14:5–8) and fits the wordplay with "Jezreel" ("God plants").

In sum, the greatness of the "day of Jezreel" will be the glories of the time of national renewal. In accordance with the ancient promises, Israel will increase in number in the land, enjoy once again its relationship with God, live under the rule of a future Davidic king, and flourish by Yahweh's hand.

2:1 [3] The change in Israel's status is emphasized in this verse. What the people are to say (the Hebrew verb is in the plural) affirms the reversal and the revitalization of their association with Yahweh. These are not to be the words of God or of his prophet; the people themselves will confess to one another the truth of this new reality.

Has the fulfillment of this vision of the future already taken place? All agree that there was a measure of fulfillment in the sixth and fifth centuries BC, when many in exile returned to Palestine. Ezra and Nehemiah and the prophetic books Haggai, Zechariah, and Malachi describe the experiences and expectations, as well as the frustrations, of the returnees. It is clear that they looked ahead to something grander than what they had in the land under Persian rule (Hag 2; Zec 14). Were these promises then fulfilled with the coming of Jesus, the Son of David, and the establishment of the Christian church? New Testament authors relate this section of Hosea to the incorporation of the Gentiles into the new people of God (Ro 9:25–26; 1Pe 2:10).

Evangelical theological systems differ in their interpretation of these passages. Is the language of the prophet being utilized analogically to explain the breadth of God's people and as a type to reveal the workings of his grace, or do these verses claim that the geopolitical promises to Israel find their final realization in Jesus and in the church as the new Israel? Is there still a national future for believing ethnic Israel? The answers to these questions depend on whether the reader interprets these verses within an amillennial or a premillennial framework. While the former does not believe that these OT promises still await a literal fulfillment (although some amillennialists do relate them to the new heavens and earth of Rev 21–22), many premillennialists (especially dispensationalist premillennialists) do.

This verse forms an inclusio with 2:23 and so is a transition to what follows. The next section provides more details concerning the sin, judgment, and restoration of Israel.

B. The Marriage between Yahweh and Israel (2:2–23[4–25])

1. The Violation of the Marriage Bond between Israel and the Divine Judgment (2:2–15[4–17])

OVERVIEW

It is debated whether ch. 2 continues to combine a description of the relationship between the prophet and Gomer with Yahweh's indictment of Israel, or whether it deals solely with God's relationship with Israel. As details of Hosea's marriage are rather sparse, some commentators attempt to fill in hypothetical details of Gomer's actions by seeking analogies with Israel in this chapter. It is better, however, to interpret the chapter as God's words to the nation. In ch. 3 Yahweh again will turn to the prophet and command him to imitate the divine initiative in his own marriage. The following comments assume that the sin is fundamentally religious, not socioeconomic (see A. A. Keefe, *Woman's Body and the Social Body in Hosea* [JSOTSup 338; London: Sheffield Academic Press, 2001], 190–221) or political (see Kelle), even though the rest of the book makes it abundantly clear that Israel's religious beliefs and practices are intimately related to every dimension of national life.

This section begins with an accusation (vv.2–5), followed by the announcement of three consequences introduced by *lākēn*, "therefore" (vv.6–8, 9–13, 14–15). The first two of these pronounce punishment, but the last unexpectedly declares that God will turn in love to Israel his wife and woo her again. Once more, the text reveals that restoration, not judgment, is Yahweh's final word.

> 2 "Rebuke your mother, rebuke her,
>   for she is not my wife,
>   and I am not her husband.
> Let her remove the adulterous look from her face
>   and the unfaithfulness from between her breasts.
> 3 Otherwise I will strip her naked
>   and make her as bare as on the day she was born;
> I will make her like a desert,
>   turn her into a parched land,
>   and slay her with thirst.
> 4 I will not show my love to her children,
>   because they are the children of adultery.
> 5 Their mother has been unfaithful
>   and has conceived them in disgrace.
> She said, 'I will go after my lovers,
>   who give me my food and my water,
>   my wool and my linen, my oil and my drink.'
> 6 Therefore I will block her path with thornbushes;
>   I will wall her in so that she cannot find her way.
> 7 She will chase after her lovers but not catch them;
>   she will look for them but not find them.
> Then she will say,
>   'I will go back to my husband as at first,
>   for then I was better off than now.'
> 8 She has not acknowledged that I was the one
>   who gave her the grain, the new wine and oil,
> who lavished on her the silver and gold—
>   which they used for Baal.
>
> 9 "Therefore I will take away my grain when it ripens,
>   and my new wine when it is ready.
> I will take back my wool and my linen,
>   intended to cover her nakedness.

¹⁰So now I will expose her lewdness
    before the eyes of her lovers;
    no one will take her out of my hands.
¹¹I will stop all her celebrations:
    her yearly festivals, her New Moons,
    her Sabbath days—all her appointed feasts.
¹²I will ruin her vines and her fig trees,
    which she said were her pay from her lovers;
I will make them a thicket,
    and wild animals will devour them.
¹³I will punish her for the days
    she burned incense to the Baals;
she decked herself with rings and jewelry,
    and went after her lovers,
    but me she forgot,"
                       declares the Lᴏʀᴅ.

¹⁴"Therefore I am now going to allure her;
    I will lead her into the desert
    and speak tenderly to her.
¹⁵There I will give her back her vineyards,
    and will make the Valley of Achor a door of hope.
There she will sing as in the days of her youth,
    as in the day she came up out of Egypt.

COMMENTARY

2 [4] The verb *rîb* (GK 8189) appears twice in the opening clause. While it has been suggested that this term signals a formal covenantal lawsuit (Stuart, 45; Nielsen, 34–38), the meaning is more general here (cf. 4:1; 12:2). God, the divine husband, rhetorically commands individual citizens of Israel (the children) to repudiate or rebuke the nation as a whole (their mother). They are called to denounce the sin all around them, thereby affirming God's accusation and choosing covenantal loyalty over unfaithfulness to Yahweh.

The words "she is not my wife, and I am not her husband" echo the doubly negative statement of 1:9. Do they represent a legal divorce proceeding? This scenario is doubtful. There is no imaginary court scene, no call to witnesses, and no challenge to respond to the charges. The fact that Yahweh warns Israel in the next verse of potential punishment, later judges her, and then woos her reveals that the marriage relationship is still in place. This situation is a far cry from the most severe sentence for adultery in the law: death by stoning (Dt 22:22–24).

What must change is any appearance of infidelity. This charge is depicted graphically as the need to remove "her fornications from her face and her adulteries from between her breasts" (lit. trans.). The image is of a brazen woman, who flaunts her infidelity. Abstract plurals are used here and need be understood as references to jewelry (contrast 2:13; cf. Jer 4:30; SS 1:13).

3 [5] God threatens to strip Israel and leave it as helpless "as on the day she was born." Similar threats of exposing the nakedness of the nation appear in other prophets (Jer 13:22–27; Eze 16:37–39; cf. Na 3:4–5). Some claim that these words reflect, and therefore condone, violence of husbands against their wives in ancient Israel (e.g., R. J. Weems, *Battered Love: Marriage, Sex, and Violence in the Hebrew Prophets* [OBT; Minneapolis: Fortress, 1995], 45–49). But such an interpretation misses the intent of the verse. In extrabiblical literature this language is used in curses for violating treaty agreements (D. Hillers, *Treaty-Curses and the Old Testament Prophets* [BibOr 16; Rome: Pontifical Biblical Institute, 1964], 58–60), and this evidence is cited by those who see this verse as proof of cruel behavior. More pertinent, however, is that this imagery also is found in texts dealing with divorce or remarriage: the stripping and going out naked is symbolic of leaving behind one's property and economic status and not a literal punishment for adultery (P. Day, "Adulterous Jerusalem's Imagined Demise: Death of a Metaphor in Ezekiel XVI," *VT* 50 [2000]: 285–309; Kelle, 59–64). In other words, the background for this verse is not the supposed sexual violence of the time but ancient Near Eastern marital customs and legal procedures.

The next line clarifies the import of these words in this context. The "stripping" that Yahweh will perform is agricultural: the land will be laid waste from lack of water, one of the curses for failure to obey the covenantal obligations (Lev 26:19–20; Dt 28:22–24). Uncovering is a metaphor for arid barrenness, not the imitation of a hypothetical, abusive cultural practice.

4–5 [6–7] The language of v.4 recalls 1:2, 6. From the rhetorical device of challenging individual Israelites to reject the corrupt ways of the nation, Yahweh now moves to announce that all Israel stands condemned for being unfaithful. They believe that their sustenance comes from elsewhere. The "lovers" (v.5) are not foreign nations with which Israel may have had alliances and commercial agreements (contra Kelle, 112–22; cf. Tg.); rather, they are the *bᵉʿālîm*, those false gods that the people thought provided bounty—in flocks that would produce their wool and linen, and in crops that would give them oil and drink. (For textiles, oil, and beverages, see P. E. King and L. E. Stager, *Life in Ancient Israel* [Library of Ancient Israel; Louisville: Westminster John Knox, 2001], 146–62, 95–98, 101–3, respectively.) Verse 3 had made it clear that it is Yahweh who controls the rainfall. Here, his sovereignty over the very things for which Israel turned to other deities is further emphasized. The punishments that follow will continue to underscore his sovereignty.

6–8 [8–10] This pericope is the first of three "therefore" passages. The punishment is described as Yahweh's obstructing wayward Israel from going where it should not go—that is, on the well-worn paths leading to other gods. The language of being hemmed in is used elsewhere for the feeling that God constricts movement in an oppressive way (Job 19:8; Pr 15:19; La 3:7, 9; cf. Ps 139:5). Perhaps the picture, as elsewhere in the book, is that of an animal that tends to wander away from its home (cf. 4:16; 8:9).

The purpose is to drive Israel to confess its need to return to Yahweh. This is not a picture of remarriage after a supposed divorce, a scenario not envisioned in the law (Dt 24:1–4). For Israel these words will signal the dawning of an awareness of the futility of seeking other deities (contrast v.5) and thus anticipate future reconciliation with God.

The decision "to return" reappears in 3:5; 6:1; and 14:1. The key in each case is to determine whether these words are sincere and reveal a genuine change of heart. The verb "to know" (*yd*ᶜ; "acknowledge," NIV; GK 3359) is an important term that is used multiple times (e.g., 2:20; 5:4; 7:9; 13:4), as is the noun "knowledge" (4:1, 6; cf. 6:6, "acknowledgment," NIV). In a relational setting, such as this one, the root means more than simply intellectual awareness; it speaks of an engagement in right relationship, along with all that it entails. Yahweh desires that his people recognize his gracious hand in their behalf, that they move beyond willful ignorance to see that he has bestowed their material abundance (cf., e.g., Dt 7:13; 11:13–15). This book culminates with Israel's finally embracing this calling (14:1–3).

9–13 [11–15] Two issues stand out in this second "therefore" passage. The first one is the focus on agricultural disaster. The preceding passage said that Yahweh would prevent Israel from pursuing other gods, so that the people might recognize that he was the one supplying food and covering; now God says that he will take back what he has provided, spoil the trees, and allow wild animals to attack them. The removal of these goods is portrayed as stripping (cf. v.3). The new element is that this exposure will be executed before "her lovers," those other gods. They will witness the nation's misfortune, but they will be powerless to do anything about it. Their helplessness before this judgment of Yahweh exposes them as false (vv.9–10).

Second, this passage makes abundantly clear the connection between the nation's sin and religious beliefs and practice (vv.11–13). Israel continues to observe rituals dedicated to Yahweh. The list moves from the annual gatherings to the monthly New Moon festivals to the weekly Sabbath celebrations. The inventory closes with the summary phrase, "all her appointed feasts." Clearly, no aspect of their devotion stands outside divine condemnation. Israel's understanding of God is skewed, and every aspect of its worship of Yahweh is unacceptable. At the same time that the nation claims devotion to him, its religious activity includes offering sacrifices to other gods, her "lovers," on "the days of the *b*ᵉ*ālîm*" (lit., v.13; cf. "Religion and Theology in Hosea" in the introduction). Israel, in essence, has "forgotten" who God is and what he has done. The god they honor and call "Yahweh" is one of their own creation. The true God will tolerate neither self-serving religiosity nor hapless rival deities.

The passage closes with "declares the LORD" (*n*ᵉ*um yhwh*). This phrase provides an appropriate conclusion to the judgment section, because the third "therefore" passage unexpectedly shifts the tone and direction of God's words.

14–15 [16–17] This final "therefore" passage interrupts the series of declarations of judgment. It begins with "behold" (*hinnēh*; NASB, ESV) plus the personal pronoun "I." Whereas the reader anticipates that God will "forget" his people even as they have ignored him (v.13), Yahweh instead declares his intent to seduce (*pātâ* [GK 7331]; cf. Ex 22:16; Jdg 14:15) the nation and "speak to her heart" ("speak tenderly," NIV). At first glance, these words appear to conflict with what has gone before, but they reinforce the fundamental truth that divine wrath is not motivated by spite or revenge. Yahweh longs that his wife and he be reunited in love and devotion. These verses and the following section (vv.16–23) offer a glimpse into how the restoration promised in 1:10–2:1 will be accomplished.

Yahweh will lead Israel again into the wilderness (note the Excursus in Garrett, 88–91). The Pentateuchal accounts of the wanderings, however, do not conjure feelings of affection. To the contrary, in the wilderness Israel was a complaining, obstinate people (Ex 16–18; Nu 20–27; Dt 1–2; cf. Hos 9:10; 13:6). The wilderness also can symbolize a place of desolation and punishment (Eze 29:5). Here, however, Yahweh portrays the time in the desert as one that afforded him time alone with Israel, then completely reliant on his care (cf. Hos 13:5).

After the judgment everything will be reversed. Israel's vineyards will be restored (cf. vv.3, 9, 12); negative experiences will become opportunities for new life ("a door of hope"). Years before, during the conquest, Achan had taken what God had prohibited and was punished; in judgment the location was given the name the Valley of Achor (Jos 7:24–26; ʿākôr means "trouble"). Although a literal place, here it serves as a metaphor of a rebellious land, whose punishments will end and whose bounty will return (Macintosh, 74–75). In the future, the nation will "answer" properly to God's favor (ʿānâ; "sing," NIV; see vv.21–22), as it had done long ago at the exodus (Ex 15:1–21). Here is the first place where the theme of the exodus is mentioned in the book. In Hosea it can have either positive or negative connotations, depending on the context (see "Religion and Theology in Hosea" in the introduction).

NOTE

10[12] The *hapax legomenon* נַבְלוּת (*nablût*; "lewdness," NIV; GK 5578) has been taken as a reference to female genitalia (e.g., Wolff, 37; Garrett, 83; cf. J. A. Naudé, "נַבְלוּת," *NIDOTTE*, 3:15; *HALOT*, 664). For some feminists the term makes plain the voyeurism of the text; some go so far as to label this line an example of "prophetic pornography." The husband's actions are said to be cruel physical and psychological treatment of the wife that theologically could justify spousal abuse today (Yee, 225–27; cf. J. C. Exum, "The Ethics of Biblical Violence against Women," in *The Bible and Ethics: The Second Sheffield Colloquium*, ed. J. W. Rogerson, M. Davies, and M. D. Carroll R. [JSOTSup 207; Sheffield: Sheffield Academic Press, 1995], 248–71).

Does the term refer to a woman's pudenda? It comes from the root נבל (*nbl*). A *nābāl* is a fool, and נְבָלָה (*nᵉbālâ*), a variation of the word found here, means "senseless folly"—which can be sexual (e.g., Jdg 19:23; 2Sa 13:12), but is not exclusively so (e.g., Jos 7:15; 1Sa 25:25). It is better to interpret נַבְלוּת (*nablût*) to mean Israel's crass behavior, whose stupidity and shame are evident, even in front of the very gods from which it sought provision (Andersen and Freedman, 248–49; Macintosh, 59–61).

2. The Reestablishment of the Marriage between Yahweh and Israel (2:16–23[18–25])

OVERVIEW

As in the previous section, this passage can be divided structurally into three parts. Here, each is marked by "in that day" (vv.16, 18, 21). The first and last instances of the phrase are combined with "declares the LORD" (*nᵉʾum yhwh*). Unlike the case of these two occurrences, the second "in that day" in the Hebrew text does not appear at the start of the line. This variation suggests that the middle passage is set apart from the surrounding material. This section, in other words, exhibits a ring-like structure with its center and key revelation at vv.18–20.

¹⁶"In that day," declares the Lᴏʀᴅ,
  "you will call me 'my husband';
  you will no longer call me 'my master.'
¹⁷I will remove the names of the Baals from her lips;
  no longer will their names be invoked.
¹⁸In that day I will make a covenant for them
  with the beasts of the field and the birds of the air
  and the creatures that move along the ground.
Bow and sword and battle
  I will abolish from the land,
  so that all may lie down in safety.
¹⁹I will betroth you to me forever;
  I will betroth you in righteousness and justice,
  in love and compassion.
²⁰I will betroth you in faithfulness,
  and you will acknowledge the Lᴏʀᴅ.
²¹"In that day I will respond,"
  declares the Lᴏʀᴅ—
"I will respond to the skies,
  and they will respond to the earth;
²²and the earth will respond to the grain,
  the new wine and oil,
  and they will respond to Jezreel.
²³I will plant her for myself in the land;
  I will show my love to the one I called 'Not my loved one.'
I will say to those called 'Not my people,' 'You are my people';
  and they will say, 'You are my God.'"

COMMENTARY

16–17 [18–19] The first eschatological passage introduced by "in that day" carries on the marriage motif of the preceding lines by mentioning terms used for spouses. In ancient Israel wives could called their husbands either "my man" (ʾîšî; cf. v.7) or "my lord" (baʿᵉlî). Sometimes these terms are interchangeable (2Sa 11:26). Culturally, this use of the word baʿal was legitimate and without religious overtones. The wordplay, though, is obvious. Yahweh, as the nation's husband, does not want any form of baʿal to be on their lips for any reason. His marriage to Israel, and so their address to him, must be unique. Not only will Yahweh not be called baʿal, but neither will the names of the bᵉʿālîm be remembered (*zkr*, "invoked," NIV). These *b^ecālîm* are other deities or the various local manifestations of the god *ba^cal* (see comment on v.13).

18–20 [20–22] As mentioned earlier, this second unit is the center of the section and discloses two concepts. First, in the Hebrew the phrase "in that day" is prefaced by "and I will make a covenant for them." To which covenant does this declaration refer? Possibly, it is an initial inkling of the concept of the new covenant. Jeremiah, who draws some of his theological roots from Hosea, will develop that idea much further (Jer 31:31–34; cf. Isa 59:21; Eze 37:26). This action, though, is "for" (not "with") Israel but "with" the animal world, thereby indicating that more than likely the declaration is not a reference to the new covenant.

What is announced is that the nation will be the beneficiary of a new reality, where they will not suffer attacks from wild animals or enemies. Each of these dimensions is comprised of three items, suggesting completeness. The language about creation follows the order of Genesis 1:30. A rehabilitated relationship with nature is part of the hope of the messianic age (Isa 11:6–9; Eze 34:25), as is the elimination of warfare (e.g., Isa 2:4; Mic 4:3–4). Thus, this promise represents a reversal of the threats of 2:12 and 1:4–5 (cf. v.7), respectively (cf. Lev 26:14–33; Dt 28:25–26, 49–57).

The second part of this pericope returns to the marriage metaphor (vv.19–20). Three times Yahweh declares that he will betroth Israel, thus repeating the stylistic device of the previous line. This commitment preceded the wedding ceremony and signaled that the marriage agreement had been settled.

A list of five qualities follows: righteousness, justice, love, compassion, and faithfulness. Each of these qualities is preceded by the inseparable preposition *b^e*. Grammatically, this construction could mean that these qualities represent the bride price that Yahweh will pay for Israel (cf. 2Sa 3:14) or the attributes that will characterize this renewal of the marriage relationship. In both options, they are what God will bring to the marriage to guarantee its success. These qualities also are what he demands of Israel (4:1; 6:6; 10:12; 12:6). In other words, Yahweh will model what he expects from his people, yet in more glorious ways. This future restoration will be permanent, "forever," with the result that Israel will "know" Yahweh (contrast vv.8, 13).

21–23 [23–25] This final "in that day" passage uses the verb "answer" ("respond," NIV; cf. v.15) five times. This choice of verb is difficult to understand. Could God be answering a prayer or responding to a ritual? That the verb has the heavens, the earth, and agricultural products also as subjects implies that neither is a viable interpretation. It is best to take the term to mean a reaction to a situation (cf. 14:8). That is, the change in the relationship triggers a series of consequences in the created order. Abundance will be the byword "in that day." Only Yahweh can truly provide the cosmic bounty that some attributed to *ba^cal* (cf. Smith, 73–75).

"Jezreel" no longer will carry the ominous overtones of the prophet's firstborn son (1:3–5), but instead the hopeful connotations of the promises of 1:10–2:1(2:1–3). The nation will be "planted" (*zr^c*, the root for "Jezreel") back in the land. The agricultural and marital reversals are expressed by negating the impact of the meaning of the names of ch. 1. "No-Compassion" will experience divine care, and "Not-My-People" will be welcomed anew as the chosen ones of God. The nation, in turn, will call Yahweh "my God." For the fulfillment of these words, see the comments at 2:1.

NOTE

18[20] The opening words are literally, "I will cut a covenant." For the possible origin of this expression see *TDOT*, 2:259–61; cf. R. S. Hess, "The Slaughter of Animals in Genesis 15: Genesis 15:8–21 and its Ancient Near Eastern Context," in *He Swore an Oath: Biblical Themes from Genesis 12–50*, ed. R. S. Hess, P. E. Satterthwaite, and G. J. Wenham (Cambridge: Tyndale, 1993), 67–92.

C. The Restoration of Gomer and Israel (3:1–5)

¹The LORD said to me, "Go, show your love to your wife again, though she is loved by another and is an adulteress. Love her as the LORD loves the Israelites, though they turn to other gods and love the sacred raisin cakes."
²So I bought her for fifteen shekels of silver and about a homer and a lethek of barley.
³Then I told her, "You are to live with me many days; you must not be a prostitute or be intimate with any man, and I will live with you."
⁴For the Israelites will live many days without king or prince, without sacrifice or sacred stones, without ephod or idol. ⁵Afterward the Israelites will return and seek the LORD their God and David their king. They will come trembling to the LORD and to his blessings in the last days.

COMMENTARY

1 God now speaks to the prophet. What in 2:2–23 Yahweh has just declared he will do with Israel in order to restore that marriage is to be a model for what Hosea is to do with his wife. He, too, is to go to extraordinary lengths to reestablish the marital relationship. There is some debate about whether the woman of this passage, who is not named, is Gomer or someone else (e.g., Stuart, 64; G. I. Davies, *Hosea* (OTG; Sheffield: Sheffield Academic Press, 1993), 79–92). She is simply called "a woman" (contra NIV, "your wife") who has a lover. She is "an adulteress" whom Hosea is to "love." If Hosea were being told to marry again, the expected verb would be "take" (cf. 1:2–3). Noth-

ing requires the sudden appearance of another woman, and the description of her character and the mention of lovers remind the reader of the earlier chapters. More probably, she is Gomer. These verses, then, resume the account of ch. 1.

Raisin cakes were associated with some religious rituals (cf. Jer 7:18; 44:19), so the syncretism of Israel is reiterated.

2–3 In obedience to the divine demand, Hosea determines to redeem Gomer (for this difficult verbal form, see Macintosh, 99–101) from the situation in which she has found herself. Many questions surface. Has she reached a point parallel to what Israel eventually would come to and desires to return to her husband (cf. 2:7), or is Hosea's action totally self-initiated? The text does not say. The prophet pays in money (fifteen shekels of silver) and in kind (a homer and a lethek of barley). Even though it is not possible to be certain of the precise amounts of these goods (a homer may have been about six bushels, a lethek half a homer; cf. King and Stager, *Life in Ancient Israel*, 195–200), the total price is not large (e.g., the price for a female slave was thirty shekels; Ex 21:32).

Why the choice of the number fifteen? We cannot be sure. The fact that this is a combined payment also is curious. Is Hosea unable to give the full amount in cash? The reason for the need to pay for Gomer is in doubt as well. Is Hosea paying a second, supplemental bride price to bring her once again into his home? Does the sum represent a debt owed to her lover(s), or is this amount needed to release her from debt slavery to some creditor? Again, the text is silent.

Verse 3 is enigmatic, too. Apparently, Gomer is to live with Hosea for some sort of probationary period, whose length is not specified ("many days"). During that time she is to refrain from promiscuous behavior with other men. The prophet, it seems, also will abstain from sexual relations with her. She will not be a prisoner of her husband, however, forcefully quarantined from the outside world, as some feminists claim. The purpose is to chasten Gomer, but with the ultimate purpose of stabilizing the household and renewing their relationship, even as God promised he would do with Israel.

4–5 The parallel between the prophet's marriage and Yahweh's relationship with Israel is made patent by the repetition of "many days." Just as Gomer will be cut off from certain people and situations, so Israel will be deprived of its political institutions and cult (v.4). The nation will lose its monarchy ("king") and leadership ("prince"). Historically, this prediction finds fulfillment in the Assyrian inva-

sion and Israel's incorporation into the empire (see "Historical Background" in the introduction).

The judgment also will affect Israel's religion. Four religious aspects are listed. Some divide these into two pairs, the first component of which refers to orthodox elements (sacrifices, ephod) and the second to things devoted to other deities (sacred stones, idols). Several items, though, cannot be so easily categorized. "Sacrifices" are unacceptable to Yahweh apart from covenantal faithfulness (6:6; 8:13; 9:4) and are condemned if offered to another god (4:19; cf. the corresponding verb *zbḥ* in 4:13–14; 12:11). While the "ephod" was part of the high priest's garments (Ex 28:28–30), in which were stored the Urim and Thummim, it could be worn by one undeserving of that honor (1Sa 2:28) and used for wrongful ends (Jdg 18:14–20).

Jacob raised standing "stones" as a memorial (Ge 28:20–22), but elsewhere these pillars are roundly condemned for their association with idolatrous worship (Dt 16:22). "Idols" (lit., *tᵉrāpîm*) apparently were figurines connected to ancestor worship or used for divination (e.g., Ge 31:19, 31–35; Jdg 18:14–20; 1Sa 19:13–16; cf. T. J. Lewis, "Teraphim," *DDD*, 844–50). The composite nature of this list perhaps is a reflection of the religious chaos in Israel.

The end result of Israel's deprivation is that Israel will turn from its ways and come to God (v.5). "Afterward" God's people will come in awe ("trembling," NIV), in genuine contrition (cf. 11:10–11). Unlike in the present, Israel will seek Yahweh (*bqš*) and "in the last days" will "return" (*šûb*) to Yahweh. (Note 2:7 and 7:10, where both verbs are used.) What, therefore, will be taken away in judgment—the king and religious practices—will be the centerpieces of renewed national life. This state of affairs mirrors the renewed relationship, the covenant of peace, the betrothal, and the "responding" in the second half of ch. 2 (2:16–23). This verse concludes the expansion of the promises in 1:10–11.

NOTE

1 In the versions, the adverb עוֹד (ʿôd, "again") is related to God's speaking (NRSV, NJPS) or to the command to go love the woman (NJB, NASB, NIV, ESV). Either option is syntactically viable and can make sense in the context. There is no great difference in meaning.

III. THE ANNOUNCEMENT OF JUDGMENT AND THE PROMISE OF RESTORATION (4:1–11:11)

A. The Religious and Political Corruption of Israel (4:1–7:16)

OVERVIEW

The marriage metaphor and the corresponding experience of the prophet Hosea in the chs. 1–3 vividly portray the rebellion of Israel and the judgment and grace of God. The second major part of the book details the sins of Israel in the various spheres of national life. There is little hope offered in these chapters. They are an extended denunciation of Israel with announcements of divine punishment.

1. The Indictment of Israel (4:1–3)

OVERVIEW

These verses signal a new section in the book. The image of marriage that has dominated the opening chapters is no longer central, although it will resurface. The passage opens with the command to God's people to hear the word of Yahweh anew. Commentators disagree on whether 4:1–3 is the introduction to chs. 4–7, chs. 4–11, or the rest of the book. The closing phrase of ch. 11, "declares the LORD" (nᵉ ʾum yhwh; 11:11), could mark an inclusio with "hear this word" in 4:1. If so, then structurally the passage signals the beginning of the second major part of the book, which runs from chs. 4 to 11.

¹Hear the word of the LORD, you Israelites,
  because the LORD has a charge to bring
  against you who live in the land:
"There is no faithfulness, no love,
  no acknowledgment of God in the land.

> ² There is only cursing, lying and murder,
>   stealing and adultery;
> they break all bounds,
>   and bloodshed follows bloodshed.
> ³ Because of this the land mourns,
>   and all who live in it waste away;
> the beasts of the field and the birds of the air
>   and the fish of the sea are dying.

COMMENTARY

1 Yahweh brings an accusation against his people. As in 2:2 the root *rîb* is used (cf. 12:2), and as there, what follows is probably not a formal lawsuit (contra Nielsen, 32–34; Stuart, 73–75), since elements of a full lawsuit genre are lacking, such as the call to witnesses (cf. Mic 6:1–2). But there is no doubt that the accusation is an indictment for violating the covenantal relationship.

Three fundamental covenantal qualities are absent in the land. The first, *ʾᵉmet* (GK 622), is often translated as "faithfulness" and refers to constancy and integrity in word and deed (e.g., Ex 18:21; 1Sa 12:24). *Ḥesed* (NIV, "love"; GK 2876) is grounded in the bonds of a mutual relationship and therefore has been rendered as "loyalty" (NRSV) or "steadfast love" (ESV). It is exemplified consummately by God in his compassionate dealings with his people (e.g., Ex 34:6; Ps 36:7; cf. G. R. Clark, *The Word Ḥesed in the Hebrew Bible* [JSOTSup 157; Sheffield: Sheffield Academic Press, 1993]). The third quality is "knowledge" (*daᶜat*; GK 1981; NIV "acknowledgment") — not merely intellectual understanding, but a quality reflected in values and a lifestyle commensurate with the covenantal demands. The verbal root of this word (*ydᶜ*) appears twice in ch. 2 (2:8, 20).

2–3 A list of specific offenses illustrates these sins of omission. These charges correspond to the Ten Commandments (Ex 20:1–17; Dt 5:1–21; cf. Jer 7:9), although the order is not quite the same. All have sociopolitical implications that will become evident as the prophetic denunciation continues. The last part of the verse is problematic. The verb *prṣ* ("break out" or "abound") can be taken to be a descriptor of the impact of these five crimes (NJB, NRSV, NJPS) or as another, separate violation (NEB, NASB, NIV, NLT). If the latter, the number of sins adds up to a total of seven. Israel, in other words, commits "perfect sin" and so deserves comprehensive judgment.

Consequently, the nation will suffer great loss according to the covenantal curses (v.3; cf. Lev 26; Dt 28). In a sense, the blessings of the created order are turned on their head (cf. the word order with Ge 1:26, 28). The land will mourn as the nation experiences the ruin of the world as they know it: the end of its social construction of reality — that is, the ordering of its familial, social, and political life — and the devastation of its natural environment (cf. M. D. Carroll R., "The Prophetic Denunciation of Religion in Hosea 4–7," *CTR* 7 [1993]: 15–38 [22–24]).

2. The Perversion of Worship (4:4–5:7)

a. The failure of Israel as the priest of God (4:4–10a)

OVERVIEW

This passage is difficult to interpret. Most commentators maintain that the "priest" in v.4 and the accusations that follow are directed at a particular person or at the priesthood more broadly. The various changes in pronouns complicate the problem, and not a few emend the text. Notice the lexical echoes of vv.1–3: the root *rîb* (4:1, 4), "knowledge" (4:1, 6), and "abound" (4:2, 10). These connections suggest that these verses function to expand on that opening censure by providing more details of the sins of 4:1–2 (cf. McComiskey, 60–61; M. DeRoche, "Structure and Meaning in Hosea IV 4–10," *VT* 33 [1983]: 185–98; Carroll R., "The Prophetic Denunciation of Religion in Hosea 4–7," 24–28).

⁴"But let no man bring a charge,
    let no man accuse another,
for your people are like those
    who bring charges against a priest.
⁵You stumble day and night,
    and the prophets stumble with you.
So I will destroy your mother—
⁶   my people are destroyed from lack of knowledge.

"Because you have rejected knowledge,
    I also reject you as my priests;
because you have ignored the law of your God,
    I also will ignore your children.
⁷The more the priests increased,
    the more they sinned against me;
they exchanged their Glory for something disgraceful.
⁸They feed on the sins of my people
    and relish their wickedness.
⁹And it will be: Like people, like priests.
    I will punish both of them for their ways
    and repay them for their deeds.
¹⁰"They will eat but not have enough;
    they will engage in prostitution but not increase,
because they have deserted the LORD....

COMMENTARY

4–5a Unlike God, who has the authority and every justification to question his people, they have no moral basis to argue with anyone or to complain. In terms of its character, Israel is stubborn. The people are like "those who contend with a priest," meaning that they are unwilling to heed a true word that might come from Yahweh's representatives (cf. Dt 17:12–13; Am 2:11–12). So the people stumble in their sin (cf. 5:5; 14:1, 9), and in this stumbling they are joined by the very religious leaders, the prophets, who were to have been their guides and models (cf., e.g., Isa 3:2; 28:7; Jer 2:26; 23:9–40; Mic 3:5–8).

5b–6 The diatribe now finds expression in a series of alternating denunciations and announcements of punishment. The "mother" and "children" images bracket these lines and are a reminder of their interplay in 2:2, 5. The mother is Israel, and the children individual Israelites. The repetition of verbs in each pairing reveals that the judgment corresponds to the sin. As a consequence of persisting in rebellion against God, Israel will forfeit its privileged role as "priest" (singular in the Hebrew, contra NIV; NLT) to the nations (cf. Ex 19:5–6; Isa 61:6). Ironically, this people, who contend with the priests, will themselves be disqualified from that honor. Sadly, they have become like all the other peoples of the earth.

7–10 This passage continues the denunciation of 4:4–6; thus, the "increase" in v.7 refers to the prosperity of the nation, perhaps in terms of economic and military success (NASB, NRSV, ESV). Some, taking this section as condemning the priesthood, interpret it to mean the proliferation in the number of priests (NEB, NIV, NLT). As Israel flourished, its craving for sin also multiplied (vv.7–8); therefore, God will "change their glory into shame" (v.7, NASB). This loss of "glory" reinforces v.6, where Israel is debarred from its unique and favored position as priest to the world. "Glory" also may allude to the "increase" of which the nation is proud; now those achievements will be taken away (cf. 9:11).

The enigmatic proverbial saying "like people, like priest" communicates that the priests exhibit the same character as the nation and will endure a similar fate (v.9). This verse anticipates the attention that will be given to the religious leaders in the next chapter. Verse 10 returns to the metaphor for "forsaking" Yahweh as practicing harlotry (the verb *znh*). The ending of this verse (the infinitive construct *šᵉmōr* with the preposition *lᵉ*) is difficult. Most commentators and versions consider that the object of this verb is the first word (NEB, NRSV, NJPS) or the opening series of terms in v.11 (NIV, ESV). Verses 9–10 serve as a transition to the prophetic critique of Israel's religious practices in the next pericope.

NOTES

4 To align the translation with the interpretation that a priest or the priesthood is being singled out, commentators and versions change עַמְּךָ כִּמְרִיבֵי כֹהֵן (ʿammᵉkā kimrîbê kōhēn, "your people are like those who bring charges against a priest"; NIV, NASB; cf. Tg.), to עִמְּךָ רִיבִי הַכֹּהֵן (ʿimmᵉkā rîbî hakkōhēn, "for with you is my contention, O priest"; NEB, NRSV, NJPS, ESV, NLT).

7 Many emend אָמִיר (ʾāmîr, "I exchanged") to הֵמִירוּ (hēmîrû, "they exchanged," so that the nation, not God, is the subject of the verb (NJB, NIV, NRSV, NLT). In this way, the clause is made parallel to the preceding colon instead of its consequence. In rabbinic tradition this emendation is one of the eighteen *tiqqune sopherim* ("changes of the scribes"). See E. Würthwein, *The Text of the Old Testament* (rev. ed.; Grand Rapids: Eerdmans, 1995), 17–18.

b. The syncretism of Israel (4:10b–19)

> ...to give themselves [11]to prostitution,
> to old wine and new,
>   which take away the understanding [12]of my people.
> They consult a wooden idol
>   and are answered by a stick of wood.
> A spirit of prostitution leads them astray;
>   they are unfaithful to their God.
> [13]They sacrifice on the mountaintops
>   and burn offerings on the hills,
> under oak, poplar and terebinth,
>   where the shade is pleasant.
> Therefore your daughters turn to prostitution
>   and your daughters-in-law to adultery.
>
> [14]"I will not punish your daughters
>   when they turn to prostitution,
> nor your daughters-in-law
>   when they commit adultery,
> because the men themselves consort with harlots
>   and sacrifice with shrine prostitutes —
>   a people without understanding will come to ruin!
>
> [15]"Though you commit adultery, O Israel,
>   let not Judah become guilty.
>
> "Do not go to Gilgal;
>   do not go up to Beth Aven.
>   And do not swear, 'As surely as the LORD lives!'
> [16]The Israelites are stubborn,
>   like a stubborn heifer.
> How then can the LORD pasture them
>   like lambs in a meadow?
> [17]Ephraim is joined to idols;
>   leave him alone!

> [18] Even when their drinks are gone,
>   they continue their prostitution;
>   their rulers dearly love shameful ways.
> [19] A whirlwind will sweep them away,
>   and their sacrifices will bring them shame.

COMMENTARY

10b−12 Wherever one might begin the sentence (see comment on v.10), the end result is the same: worshiping other gods clouds the understanding of the people (lit., "take[s] away the heart"). Only a skewed view of the supernatural can lead them to inquire of a piece of wood for guidance. (The verb *š'l* with the preposition *bᵉ* is a technical phrase for seeking oracles [e.g., Jdg 1:1; 2Sa 2:1].) This harlotry (*zᵉnût*), this straying from God, is deeply rooted in their being; they are governed by a "spirit of prostitution" (*rûaḥ zᵉnûnîm*). This state explains why repentance will prove so challenging. Only after severe chastisement will the nation admit its guilt (14:1−3).

13−14 Rituals are performed at all sorts of shrines. Who is being worshiped is not specified, but the strong language makes it plain that whatever is being done is unacceptable. If these ceremonies are for Yahweh, their form and substance will not be tolerated. Perhaps *baʿal* or the *bᵉʿālîm* are in view. Others see in this passage an allusion to a tree cult (O. Keel, *Goddesses and Trees, New Moon and Yahweh: Ancient Near Eastern Art and the Hebrew Bible* [JSOTSup 261; Sheffield: Sheffield Academic Press, 1998], 49−57) or to the worship of Asherah, who could be represented by trees (M.-T. Wacker, "Traces of the Goddess in the Book of Hosea," in Brenner, ed., 219−41; Dever, 211−36).

As discussed in the introduction (see "Religion and Theology in Hosea"), scholars debate whether this scene portrays rites of sacred prostitution or refers to sexual intercourse to raise money for the cult or to pay off vows or to general debauchery, which may have been the result of heavy drinking at these worship sites. Clearly, sexual immorality is taking place. Whatever the correct interpretive option, this text reveals that, first, these illicit activities cut across gender and generational lines, and second, that the prophet holds the men most responsible for this deplorable state of affairs. This worship underscores the people's lack of discernment (cf. v.11) and will lead to their demise.

15 The verb *znh* ("commit adultery") again is used, thereby connecting this verse to the preceding lines. Judah appears for the first time since 1:7, 11. Although critical scholars argue that "Judah" is a gloss (e.g., Emmerson, 77−83), the southern kingdom is within the prophet's purview throughout the book (see "Authorship and Composition" in the introduction). The hope is that Israel's example will be an object lesson for Judah, so that the people might not repeat Israel's corruption and avoid similar punishment.

It is interesting to note that the condemnation of Israel's religious practices expands from a concentration on rural cultic centers to two historic

Yahwistic shrines, Gilgal and Bethel (ridiculed here as Beth Aven, "House of Nothingness"). In words reminiscent of Hosea's contemporary Amos (Am 5:5; 8:14), God will not abide his people's coming to these venerable sites of worship. (J. Jeremias believes that this comment is a later addition based on Amos material; cf. his "The Interrelationship between Amos and Hosea," in *Forming Prophetic Literature*, ed. J. W. Watts and P. R. House (JSOT-Sup 235; Sheffield: Sheffield Academic Press, 1996], 171–86.)

What are they doing that merits these harsh words? Surely the people celebrated rituals dedicated to Yahweh (though perhaps to other gods as well). What is made plain here is that proclaiming the correct name of God is not the only requirement for worship to be acceptable; more important is the content given that name. If the people believe in and praise a Yahweh of their own creation, whether he is confused with *baʿal* or is shaped by the reigning nationalistic ideology, he cannot be the true God and worship cannot be authentic. In sum, the religious world of ancient Israel is complex. One must appreciate that syncretism necessarily corrupts faith and distorts their understanding of the person and work of Yahweh.

16–18 Israel's waywardness is incorrigible. The nation is like a stubborn heifer and is inexorably drawn to its idols; it persists in dissipation and harlotry. While the precise context is difficult to identify, some cultic activity is in view.

The last part of the final line of v.18 literally says, "They dearly love the shame of their shields." On the basis of other passages, such as Psalm 47:9 and 89:18, some commentators interpret "shields" as a metaphor for Israel's rulers and take the term to be the subject of the verb (NASB, NIV, ESV; Keil, 84; Harper, 265; cf. Tg.). Others see the term as an allusion to a female goddess (G. I. Emmerson, "A Fertility Goddess in Hosea IV 17–19?" *VT* 24 [1974], 492–97). J. L. McLaughlin (*The Marzeaḥ in the Prophetic Literature: References and Allusions in Light of the Extra-Biblical Evidence* [VTSup 86; Leiden: Brill, 2001], 129–53) suggests that the setting is a *marzeaḥ* feast, with the goddess as the patron. It is possible, however, that the word refers to the shields connected with cultic centers (e.g., 1Ki 10:16–17). This interpretation is more in keeping with the context, that is, with the focus on religious practices and objects (Garrett, 138–39; Macintosh, 170–71). Israel is passionate about its religious life, twisted and mistaken as it is.

19 A "wind" (*rûaḥ*; GK 8120) confines Israel. This word is the same one translated "spirit" in v.12, but in contrast to those deeply controlling and destructive impulses that are driving the nation, here it denotes the unstoppable force of divine judgment (cf. 13:15). The people's misdirected sacrifices (4:13; cf. 2:11, 13) cannot secure bounty or protection; they bring only shame and suffering. These offerings will be exposed as useless before the sovereign person of Yahweh, his holy demands, and his powerful actions in history.

NOTE

18 Other interpretive options for מָגִנֶּיהָ (*māginneyhā*, "her shields") require slight textual changes. Common is the emendation to מִגְּאוֹנָם (*miggeʾônām*, "more than their pride [or 'glory']" (comparative מִן, *min*, plus גָּאוֹן, *gāʾôn*), which yields, "They love their shame more than their glory" (NJB, NEB, NRSV, NLT). Another suggestion is the modification to מְגִנָּה (*meginnâ*) or מְגִנִּים (*meginnîm*, "insolence"; Mays, 76; Wolff, 73; Stuart, 72; cf. LXX): "they love the shame of insolence."

c. The blind arrogance of Israel (5:1−7)

OVERVIEW

The entire nation was the target of 4:1−19. This next section resumes this denunciation of the people, but 5:1 also specifies two particular groups within Israel, the priests and the monarchs ("house of the king"). Some contend that "the Israelites" (lit., "house of Israel") refers to the country's leaders, but this is not the case. Elsewhere the phrase refers to the northern kingdom (1:4, 6; 6:10; 11:12; cf. "house of Judah" in 1:7; 5:12, 14), and there is no reason to seek an exception here. The numerous lexical parallels with 4:1−19 (and earlier chapters) reinforce this interpretation: "turned to prostitution" (v.3; 4:10−15, 18), "their deeds" (v.4; 4:9), "spirit of prostitution" (v.4; 4:12), "stumble" (v.5; 4:5), and "children" (v.7; 4:6). This passage reinforces that there is no lack of religious zeal in Israel, but it is unacceptable to Yahweh.

[1] "Hear this, you priests!
    Pay attention, you Israelites!
Listen, O royal house!
    This judgment is against you:
You have been a snare at Mizpah,
    a net spread out on Tabor.
[2] The rebels are deep in slaughter.
    I will discipline all of them.
[3] I know all about Ephraim;
    Israel is not hidden from me.
Ephraim, you have now turned to prostitution;
    Israel is corrupt.

[4] "Their deeds do not permit them
    to return to their God.
A spirit of prostitution is in their heart;
    they do not acknowledge the LORD.
[5] Israel's arrogance testifies against them;
    the Israelites, even Ephraim, stumble in their sin;
    Judah also stumbles with them.
[6] When they go with their flocks and herds
    to seek the LORD,
they will not find him;
    he has withdrawn himself from them.

> [7]They are unfaithful to the LORD;
>   they give birth to illegitimate children.
> Now their New Moon festivals
>   will devour them and their fields.

COMMENTARY

1–2 This new section begins with the same command as 4:1 ("hear"). There Yahweh was bringing an accusation; here he has a "judgment" against them. The imagery of trapping animals is fitting, as the activities of the people and its rulers are ensnaring and self-destructive. At our distance from the historical situation, it is impossible to be certain of the significance of the choice of Mizpah and Tabor. In the literary context, it is tempting to say that they are mentioned because both may have been cultic centers, but there is no textual evidence that such was the case in Hosea's time, when other sites, such as Gilgal and Bethel (4:15), were prominent centers of worship. Mizpah was a gathering place early in Israel's history (Jdg 20–21), a place of worship (1Sa 7:2–12), and one of the stops on Samuel's circuit (1Sa 7:15–16). Mount Tabor is located within the Jezreel valley in north-central Palestine.

Common emendations in v.2 (*šaḥᵃṭâ* to *šaḥat*, and *śēṭîm* to *šiṭṭîm*) add a third trap ("pit") and place name ("Shittim"), respectively, to this reproof (e.g., NJB, NRSV). Nevertheless, the line can be taken as it stands. Though grammatically difficult, v.2 conveys that the nation is sinking deeper into sin and will experience the discipline of God.

3 This verse returns to the metaphor of prostitution (the verb *znh*) of previous passages. There also is an interesting wordplay with v.4: God "knows" Israel, even as his people do *not* "know" him or what he has done in their behalf (v.4; cf. 2:8, 4:1, 6). The nation is "corrupt" or "unclean" (the root *ṭmʾ*), a technical term associated with cultic impurity (R. E. Averbeck, "טמא," *NIDOTTE*, 2:365–76). This statement is ironic: A people so fascinated with worship exclude themselves from that activity because what they practice is objectionable and defiling.

4–7 The people's religiosity is to no avail. All that they do and their spirit of whoredom (cf. 4:12) keep them from truly returning (or repenting, *šûb*; contrast 3:5) to God and from being able to know him (v.4). It does not matter that they bring animal sacrifices to the sanctuaries to seek a word from God (for *bqš* in connection with the cult, see *TDOT*, 2:236–39). Their rituals have produced the opposite effect: Yahweh distances himself from them (v.6). Rituals are no substitute for truth and character (cf. 6:6). In ch. 2 God had said he would put an end to their worship (2:11; cf. 3:4).

The blindness of Israel is reflected in its arrogance, which causes it—and Judah—to "stumble" (cf. 4:5; 14:1, 9) in its sin and precipitates its downfall (v.5; for Judah as a redactional gloss, see Emmerson, 65–68). Though the nation might believe that pilgrimages to the holy sites will gain favor before Yahweh and exhibit their faithfulness, in actuality they have betrayed him (v.7). Their improper celebrations (such as the New Moon festivals; cf. 2:13) are the reason for their judgment.

3. Political Chaos and Intrigue (5:8–7:16)

OVERVIEW

This long section shifts attention from the cult to the political sphere. Religion is not totally lost from view, however; it could not be in the ancient world. Conceptions of the divine were bound up closely with socioeconomic and political structures and with national ideologies. The universal conviction was that the gods established the parameters of society, legitimated thrones, and went to war to defend their territory and people. Scholars continue to investigate the complex relationship between religious beliefs and practices and the different dimensions of human reality in the nation-states and empires of Israel's world (e.g., L. K. Handy, *Among the Hosts of Heaven: The Syro-Palestinian Pantheon as Bureaucracy* [Winona Lake, Ind.: Eisenbrauns, 1994]; D. I. Block, *The Gods of the Nations: Studies in Ancient Near Eastern National Theology*, 2nd ed. (Grand Rapids: Baker, 2000]; N. K. Gottwald, *The Politics of Ancient Israel* [Library of Ancient Israel; Louisville: Westminster John Knox, 2001], 113–57).

The scholarly consensus is that the historical background for this section is the Syro-Ephraimite War, the events immediately preceding it, and its aftermath (2Ki 15–17; 2Ch 28; see "Historical Background" in the introduction). Some attempt to identify with precision the events alluded to in these passages by positing, for example, that 5:8–13 follows a strict chronological sequence within that conflict (e.g., Macintosh, 194–98). Nevertheless, a detailed historical reconstruction and its correlation with other epigraphic evidence have proven to be elusive, so it is advisable to be cautious in any attempt to detect specific referents. This commentary echoes the position that these years in general lie behind what is proclaimed in these oracles, but only occasionally will I propose possible historical connections. The primary concern will be the lessons that the prophet draws from those experiences.

a. Disastrous decisions in war (5:8–15)

8 "Sound the trumpet in Gibeah,
     the horn in Ramah.
  Raise the battle cry in Beth Aven;
     lead on, O Benjamin.
9 Ephraim will be laid waste
     on the day of reckoning.
  Among the tribes of Israel
     I proclaim what is certain.
10 Judah's leaders are like those
     who move boundary stones.

I will pour out my wrath on them
　　like a flood of water.
[11] Ephraim is oppressed,
　　trampled in judgment,
　　intent on pursuing idols.
[12] I am like a moth to Ephraim,
　　like rot to the people of Judah.

[13] "When Ephraim saw his sickness,
　　and Judah his sores,
　then Ephraim turned to Assyria,
　　and sent to the great king for help.
　But he is not able to cure you,
　　not able to heal your sores.
[14] For I will be like a lion to Ephraim,
　　like a great lion to Judah.
　I will tear them to pieces and go away;
　　I will carry them off, with no one to rescue them.
[15] Then I will go back to my place
　　until they admit their guilt.
　And they will seek my face;
　　in their misery they will earnestly seek me."

COMMENTARY

8 This section begins with a trumpet blast to prepare for war. The scene is of a watchman on a tower alerting his people of an approaching army (e.g., Jdg 3:27; 1Sa 13:3; Eze 33:3–6; Am 2:2). The three places—Gibeah, Ramah, and Bethel (for Beth-Aven as Bethel, see comment on 4:15)—were located within the territory of Benjamin, for many years a disputed border area between the northern and southern kingdoms.

Some commentators believe that there is a directional progression in the geographical locations of these towns that suggests a line of attack, coming from Judah. Such a raid may have taken place as a counteroffensive soon after the Syro-Ephraimite War in order to take advantage of Israel's vulnerability. If such were the case, Judah would be trying to take advantage of Israel's subjugation to the Assyrians as a vassal to the empire. While this scenario is a possibility, no record exists of such a foray. In addition, it is difficult to know whether this shout to arms is defensive and geared to rally these towns to brace themselves for an attack or, alternatively, is designed to encourage troops to press forward.

9–11 Doom awaits both Israel (vv.9, 11) and Judah (v.10). The meaning of the words against Judah is debated. The accusation regards moving boundary stones, which was strictly forbidden in the law (Dt 19:14; 27:17). Could this reference have been to Judah's incursion into the northern kingdom to extend its own borders, mentioned in the previous verse? Again, this possibility must remain at the level of conjecture and lacks firm textual support.

12–15 The divine judgment is described in a series of metaphors. Yahweh is compared to an ʿāš, which has been translated as "moth," "maggot," and "pus" (cf. *HALOT*, 895; Macintosh, 207), and to rāqāb, "rot" (v.12). Whatever the exact meaning of these terms (both appear in Job 13:28, but in reverse order), the picture is one of deterioration and perhaps disease. This motif continues into v.13 with the terms ḥ°lî ("sickness") and māzôr ("wound, sores"). These images all picture an incurable malady or fatal weakness. The metaphor for Israel and Judah as the mangled prey of Yahweh the lion emphasizes even more their helplessness and the terrible affliction that awaits them (vv.14–15; cf. 13:8; B. A. Strawn, *What Is Stronger than a Lion? Leonine Imagery and Metaphor in the Hebrew Bible and the Ancient Near East* [OBO 212; Göttingen: Vandenhoeck & Ruprecht, 2005]).

These diverse metaphors underscore the difference between the absolute sovereignty of God over against his people's failings and fate. The weight of this disparity is felt not only by the presence of the personal pronoun with the finite verb in v.14b, something not necessary in Hebrew, but also by its repetition (lit., "I, even I, will tear"). Another contrast is drawn between Yahweh and the most powerful human ruler at that time, the "great king," the king of Assyria. (In 2Ki 18:19 [par. Isa 36:13] he is called the "great king" [hammelek haggādôl], but that construction is not the same as the one here.)

Though mighty, he cannot cure his vassals' wounds, which Yahweh has inflicted (v.13).

Israel and Judah sought Assyrian help on different occasions. Israel under Menahem (738 BC; 2Ki 15:19–20) and later under the usurper Hoshea (732; 2Ki 17:3) paid tribute to appease the Assyrian Empire, while Ahaz, king of Judah, petitioned Tiglath-pileser III for assistance in the Syro-Ephraimite War and then presented himself before the Assyrian in Damascus (2Ki 16:1–18). If these political contracts are what underlie these lines in Hosea, then the prophet is not condemning a linear sequence of historic events but rather viewing these interconnected conflicts as a whole.

These petitions to Assyria for assistance are not just political decisions; they reflect theological convictions about the power and rule of God (cf. J. L. Sicre, *Profetismo en Israel* [Navarra: Verbo Divino, 1992], 369–75). Is Yahweh in fact in control of the nations of the earth? Is he able to act within history in tangible ways? In the end, these moves could not save the two nations from the lion's jaws and exposed Israel's truncated view of God. Their Yahweh is not the Yahweh of the prophet.

The image of the lion extends through the final two verses of the chapter. This text makes the important point that the goal of divine judgment is to effect a profound change in the heart of God's people. What Yahweh desires is that they come to him and admit their sin and guilt, so that their seeking might be genuine (cf. 3:5; contrast 5:6). Tragically, it will be out of their suffering that they will come to him earnestly.

NOTE

13 The meaning of מֶלֶךְ יָרֵב (melek yārēb; also at 10:6) is disputed. At least three options have been offered (cf. *HALOT*, 434). (1) Most commentators and versions render these words as "great king," taking them as the Hebrew equivalent to the Akkadian šarru(m) rabû(m) (e.g., Wolff, 104; Garrett, 154). This translation requires an emendation to either מֶלֶךְ רַב (melek rab) or מַלְכִי רָב (malkî rāb). If the latter, the *yod* is explained as a *yod-compaginis* that moved over from יֵרֵב (yrb). *Mlk rb* is a title that is found in the Sefire I inscription, B 7 (COS, 2:214). (2) יָרֵב (*Yārēb*) is a proper name, either of a place ("king of Yareb"; McComiskey, 85) or of the king himself ("King Yareb"; NASB; cf. LXX). (3) יָרֵב (*yārēb*) is a wordplay. It is identical to the Qal jussive of the root רִיב (*ryb*), so the meaning could be "a king who would contend [with you]" (cf. Jdg 6:32; the Gk. versions of Aquila, Symmachus, and Theodotion, and the Latin Vulgate).

b. The unacceptable repentance of the people (6:1−6)

OVERVIEW

The literary flow from the previous section through 6:6 appears to indicate an exchange between Yahweh and Israel: God's accusation and warning (5:8−15), the nation's answer (6:1−3), and the divine evaluation of that gesture (6:4−6). How do God's people react to the preceding announcement of judgment? Do they forsake their sin and come in penitence as Yahweh desired? Does he accept Israel's gesture?

> [1] "Come, let us return to the LORD.
>   He has torn us to pieces
>   but he will heal us;
> he has injured us
>   but he will bind up our wounds.
> [2] After two days he will revive us;
>   on the third day he will restore us,
>   that we may live in his presence.
> [3] Let us acknowledge the LORD;
>   let us press on to acknowledge him.
> As surely as the sun rises,
>   he will appear;
> he will come to us like the winter rains,
>   like the spring rains that water the earth."
>
> [4] "What can I do with you, Ephraim?
>   What can I do with you, Judah?
> Your love is like the morning mist,
>   like the early dew that disappears.
> [5] Therefore I cut you in pieces with my prophets,
>   I killed you with the words of my mouth;
>   my judgments flashed like lightning upon you.
> [6] For I desire mercy, not sacrifice,
>   and acknowledgment of God rather than burnt offerings.

COMMENTARY

1-3 The lexical connections between the opening verse of this chapter and the preceding passage establish that these lines are a response to that divine pronouncement. There is the recognition (v.1) of being mauled by Yahweh the lion (5:14) and that he can "heal" (contrast 5:13); there is as well a call to "return" to Yahweh even as he says he will "return" to his place ("I will go back," NIV; 5:15).

It is difficult to decide, however, whether these words are from the people or are the composition of someone else. The LXX (cf. Tg.) adds "saying" (*legontes*) to the end of 5:15, thus explicitly marking 6:1-3 as the nation's resolve to reply to God. If the words are from someone else, the options are that the prophet himself is speaking and exhorting the people to repentance or that this expression is one of remorse offered by a priest on their behalf, perhaps in the context of a liturgy of lament. While these alternatives are possible, nothing literarily signals that anyone but the nation is in view.

Is this turning to God genuine? At first glance, the impression is that the people have learned from their mistakes and troubles and are trying to move toward what he requires of them. The use of the verbs "return" (v.1) and "know" (v.3, an emphatic construction; cf. NJB, NRSV) lends credence to the likelihood that this response is worthy. Yahweh desired that his people "return" to him (12:6) and complained that they do not "know" him (2:8; 5:4; 11:3; cf. 4:1, 6). Is not this approach the resolution to these problems?

Yet to place these lines within the broader context of the book makes clear that in the final analysis the answer to this question must be "No." Israel's vain religiosity is precisely what prevents it from being able to "return" (5:4), and the nation's rebellious heart, reflected in foreign policy and political decisions, pushes it farther from repentance

(cf. 7:10, 16). The turning that God seeks still lies in the future, beyond the coming judgment (2:9; 14:1). Only then will the declared intention of returning, accompanied by an admission of guilt and restoration, be possible (14:2). The kind of knowing that Yahweh covets will have to wait until that time (2:20). This confession is vacuous (cf. 8:2). Interestingly, the book closes with the statement that only the wise and discerning can "know" ("understand," NIV) the prophet's message.

Another interpretive issue in this pericope is whether v.2 might be a prediction of or a typological allusion to the resurrection wrought by Jesus the Messiah. Might this be the reference behind the assertion in 1 Corinthians 15:4 that Christ arose on the third day "according to the Scriptures" (Lk 24:7; Garrett, 159; J. Day, "Resurrection Imagery from Baal to the Book of Daniel," in *Congress Volume Cambridge*, ed. J. A. Emerton [VTSup 61; Leiden: Brill, 1997], 125-33)?

Three observations are apropos. To begin with, the concept of coming to life as a picture of national renewal appears elsewhere in the OT—importantly within this very book (13:14), but most famously in the vision of the dry bones in Ezekiel 37:1-14 (cf. Dt 30:17-20; Am 5:1-6). The hope of individual resurrection was not unknown, though existing perhaps in rudimentary form (esp. Da 12:2), but this verse is speaking corporately and not of particular pious individuals (cf. P. S. Johnston, *Shades of Sheol: Death and the Afterlife in the Old Testament* [Downers Grove, Ill.: InterVarsity Press, 2002], 221-27). The expectation is for Israel to be made whole again after the attack of the divine lion.

Second, from the available evidence it seems that 6:2 did not become a proof text for resurrection until Tertullian (ca. 155-230 AD; cf. Wolff, 118).

Third, in the context the numerical sequence itself—"two/three"—is revealing. It is a way of expressing a short period of time. The n/n+1 combination (here n = 2) indicates a vague period of time (GKC §134s), while the numbers "two" and "three" themselves signify a short span (e.g., Isa 7:21; 17:6; 2Ki 20:5, 8). In other words, this sinful people presume that a favorable verdict from God will come in quick order—another sign that they appreciate neither the seriousness of their transgressions nor the uselessness of their religious activities. This blind audacity is confirmed in v.3. Israel takes for granted that its darkness will turn into light and that divine blessings will come as refreshing rains. Quite a bold denial of the drought foretold in 2:3!

4–5 Yahweh's reaction reflects his frustration at his people's sanctimonious verbiage (v.4). The rhetorical questions concerning both Israel and Judah demonstrate that these unacceptable attitudes and misconstrued ideas pervade both kingdoms; once again the prophet's vision is inclusive (cf. 11:8; for Judah as a later addition, see Emmerson, 70–74).

God mocks their words with an ironic twist: They fully expected that he would be to them like the rain (v.3), but their affections (*ḥesed*) toward him in reality are like the mist and dew, quickly gone and without substance (cf. 13:3; 14:5). They thought that God would "go forth" (*yṣʾ*; NIV, "come") like the winter rains (v.3); he declares that judgment will "go forth [*yṣʾ*] like the light" (v.5; NIV, "flash like lightning"). This simile communicates perhaps that God's judgment is as dependable as the day or that it will openly reveal their sin. Repeatedly in the past God spoke to them through the prophets (12:10, 13). They (and Hosea), unlike other prophets in the present (4:5; 9:7–8), spoke the truth to the people. Yahweh's words of warning went unheeded, so Israel is without excuse.

6 This is one of the best-known verses of the book and is cited in the NT (Mt 9:13; 12:7). The point is not that religious ritual is rejected in favor of what might be called an "ethical monotheism." Empty ritual is Yahweh's target. He desires to see those covenantal qualities that are absent in the land (cf. 4:1): loyal love (*ḥesed*) and knowledge (*daʿat*).

The context of chs. 4–7 reveals the breadth of the significance of these words. These qualities encompass personal morality, religious attitudes and commitments, and national and international politics. Yahweh's covenant with Israel takes in every sphere of the people's existence. What is demanded is constancy, not the passing show of *ḥesed* of 6:4. To believe in and follow Yahweh is to submit to his sovereign will in all of life. Fully acceptable worship values this comprehensive view of God and recognizes that rituals separated from complete obedience are intolerable. If worship does not generate virtuous living and just societal structures, it makes a mockery of Yahweh and is nothing but self-serving piety (also see Isa 1:10–2:5; Jer 7:1–11; Am 5:4–27; Mic 6:1–8; cf. M. D. Carroll R., "Can the Prophets Shed Light on Our Worship Wars?—How Amos Evaluates Religious Ritual," *Stone-Campbell Journal* 8/2 [2005]: 215–27).

NOTE

5 The last line has been variously understood. A literal reading yields either "Can judgments in your favor be a shining light?" (Macintosh, 231–33), or "And your judgments [as] light shall go forth" (Garrett, 160–61; cf. NASB, NKJV). Most commentators and versions follow the LXX (cf. Tg.) and emend מִשְׁפָּטֶיךָ אוֹר (*mišpāṭeykā ʾôr*) to מִשְׁפָּטִי כָאוֹר (*mišpāṭî kāʾôr*), "my judgment like light" (e.g., Andersen and

Freedman, 429; Davies, 168–69; cf. NJB, NIV, NRSV). This slight change in word division harmonizes this line with the first-person sequence of the preceding line and the next verse. In reality, the sense of these options ("the judgments upon you" or "my judgment") is similar. Israel's transgressions will be laid bare in judgment.

c. Dangerous national politics (6:7–7:7)

OVERVIEW

At this juncture the text directs its attention to social and political tensions within the nation of Israel itself. Because of the general historical setting of the Syro-Ephraimite conflict, it is tempting to relate these verses to events and developments within that time frame. Once again, the vagueness of the details makes such efforts a less-than-certain enterprise. What this section conveys quite clearly is the sordidness of the character and actions of the nation's leaders.

Several lexical connections link 6:8–11 to 5:1–7: the sin of dealing falsely (v.7; 5:7), the explicit condemnation of priests (v.9; 5:1), the mention of an historic sanctuary (v.9; 5:1), the defilement of Ephraim (i.e., Israel; v.10; 5:3), the recurrence of the harlotry metaphor (v.10; 5:4), and the juxtaposition of Ephraim (Israel) and Judah (vv.10–11a; 5:5). In other words, this section may serve to expand what is decried in that earlier passage. This repetition of vocabulary is very much Hoseanic in style. The text keeps returning to the same themes, even as it probes them more deeply throughout the book.

> [7] Like Adam, they have broken the covenant—
> they were unfaithful to me there.
> [8] Gilead is a city of wicked men,
> stained with footprints of blood.
> [9] As marauders lie in ambush for a man,
> so do bands of priests;
> they murder on the road to Shechem,
> committing shameful crimes.
> [10] I have seen a horrible thing
> in the house of Israel.
> There Ephraim is given to prostitution
> and Israel is defiled.
> [11] "Also for you, Judah,
> a harvest is appointed.
>
> "Whenever I would restore the fortunes of my people,

7:1 whenever I would heal Israel,
 the sins of Ephraim are exposed
  and the crimes of Samaria revealed.
 They practice deceit,
  thieves break into houses,
   bandits rob in the streets;
2 but they do not realize
  that I remember all their evil deeds.
 Their sins engulf them;
  they are always before me.

3 "They delight the king with their wickedness,
  the princes with their lies.
4 They are all adulterers,
  burning like an oven
 whose fire the baker need not stir
  from the kneading of the dough till it rises.
5 On the day of the festival of our king
  the princes become inflamed with wine,
  and he joins hands with the mockers.
6 Their hearts are like an oven;
  they approach him with intrigue.
 Their passion smolders all night;
  in the morning it blazes like a flaming fire.
7 All of them are hot as an oven;
  they devour their rulers.
 All their kings fall,
  and none of them calls on me.

COMMENTARY

7 The conceptual movement back to the political arena is complicated by the Hebrew k^e'ādām (lit., "like Adam"). Who or what is meant? An interpretation with a long history is that this is a personal name, an allusion to the first human, and that the breaking of the covenant refers to the disobedience in the garden of Eden (NASB, NIV, NLT, ESV; cf. Keil, 100; McComiskey, 95; idem,

The Covenants of Promise: A Theology of Old Testament Covenants [Grand Rapids: Baker, 1985], 213–16). A variation of this position is that this is a generic reference to humanity: "like humankind" (Harper, 288, cf. LXX). Either way, the meaning is that the Israel of the prophet's day has violated its relationship with Yahweh and in so doing is imitating an ancient pattern.

The locative "there" in the next clause, however, strongly suggests that Adam must refer to a place. A town of that name is mentioned in Joshua 3:16 (probably to be identified with the modern ed-Damiyeh at the mouth of the Jabbok River in Transjordan). Most scholars today understand it in this way and many emend the text to "in [or 'at'] Adam" (*beʾādām*; cf. NJB, NRSV; e.g., Wolff, 105; Macintosh, 236–37) or offer another place name, "Admah" (*beʾadmâ*; cf. NEB; Ge 19:29; Hos 11:8).

What occurred at Adam was a violation of "a covenant." The noun is anarthrous, so it can signify any kind of agreement. The option for the place name Adam and the political nature of the indictments in the following verses may indicate that this violation refers to human betrayal, not to a breach of covenant with Yahweh (cf. 10:4; 12:1). If so, it connotes that breaking accords among themselves and with others is a character trait (Garrett, 163). Something more specific may be in view, such as a particular act of treason committed by certain individuals (Macintosh 238–39; S. L. McKenzie, *Covenant* [Understanding Biblical Themes; St. Louis: Chalice, 2000], 22–23).

Several observations challenge this interpretation (Wolff, 121–22; Mays, 100–101). First, elsewhere in the OT the idiom *ʿābar berît*, "break covenant," always refers to the relationship between Yahweh and Israel (cf. *HALOT*, 779; e.g., Dt 17:2; Jos 7:15; Jdg 2:20; 2Ki 18:12). In fact, it reappears in 8:1, where there is no doubt that God's covenant is in view. That passage, along with this one, is important for substantiating the existence of the idea of covenant already in the eighth century (see "Religion and Theology in Hosea" in the introduction). The expression for violating human treaties is *pārar berît* (*prr* I, Hiphil; cf. *HALOT*, 974–75; e.g., 1Ki 15:19; Eze 17:15–19). Second, the next clause says that this activity is at heart a betrayal of God. Third, the proximity to vv.4–6 suggests that this violation is an example of the lack of *ḥesed* (cf. 4:1). The ethics of covenantal life required mutuality and compassion. Horizontal "loyal-love" is inseparable from vertical *ḥesed* toward Yahweh. The breaking of covenant with Yahweh is not limited to irresponsible rituals; it also involves the social and political spheres.

8–9 Here begin the details of that betrayal of covenant. Do these verses list three separate crimes, or are the misdeeds all interrelated? If these acts of violence allude to different incidents, then these verses vividly portray the chaos reigning in the country. It is probably better to see them, though, as episodes of a larger conspiracy. The hostilities at Gilead may refer to the revolt led by Pekah against Pekahiah in which fifty Gileadites participated (v.8; 2Ki 15:23–25). If the killings by groups of priests were part of that coup, then religious leaders were involved in the brutal insurgency (v.9). The text reveals neither the motivation for the priests' involvement nor the identity of the victims. Were the ones murdered targets from rival priestly circles or pilgrims who had contrary political loyalties, or is it that these priests were actively taking part in the battles of the putsch?

Whatever their actual role, those who were supposed to point the people to the God of life and model *ḥesed* and the knowledge of Yahweh are involved in intrigue; their god is tightly bound to an ideology and its agenda. This deplorable action is exacerbated because it occurs on the road to Shechem, a center of historical religious import since the time of the patriarchs (Dt 27; Jos 24), where major political events had taken place (e.g., 1Ki 12:1). Long ago Shechem had been the scene of infamous duplicity (Ge 34); treachery once more is rearing its ugly head.

10–11a The summary evaluation of the events and of the nation's leadership is expressed in three ways. It is all "a horrible thing" and "prostitution," and by it Israel (Ephraim) "is defiled" (v.10). The violence and sedition are called "prostitution" and a source of corruption, images used earlier for Israel's unacceptable rituals (cf. 5:3). Religious beliefs, in other words, cannot be neatly compartmentalized and separated from sociopolitical realities. Transgression of the covenant in any sphere is part of a larger tapestry of sin and idolatry and merits judgment.

Judgment also awaits Judah. Critical scholars assume that v.11a is a later gloss designed to make Hosea's words applicable to the southern kingdom (e.g., Wolff, 123; Macintosh, 247–50). There is no need to date it late, however. Hosea constantly has both nations in view, and this line is parallel in intent to the statement at 5:5. "Harvest" is used elsewhere as a description of a time of divine reckoning (Isa 18:5; Jer 51:33; Joel 3:13; cf. Hos 10:13).

6:11b–7:2 The text returns to a depiction of the state of affairs inside the nation. This passage may be a general description without any specific incidents in mind, but in the context the sense is that it continues the portrayal of the social and political violence of the events before and after the Syro-Ephraimite War.

Judgment is not what Yahweh desires. Whereas he wants to restore and heal "my people" (also called here Israel, Ephraim, and Samaria), what always is evident are its "sins" and "crimes." Three kinds of disobedient behavior give concrete expression to the accusation (7:1). They "practice deceit," "thieves break into houses," and "bandits rob"—words that recall the general indictment of 4:2 as well as the accusation of 6:7–9. Perhaps this disobedience is what is happening in the city of Samaria itself. The social fabric is disintegrating.

What compounds the sinfulness of what they do is their deluded thinking. They believe (lit., "say in their heart") that God does not take account of their transgression. As a consequence, they are entrapped in the snares of their evil, which Yahweh indeed does see (v.2)! If the protagonists are the

priests, then this blindness is even more ironic … and damning.

3–7 Earlier passages have alluded to international arrangements (5:8–13) and the violence beyond (6:7–10) and within the capital (7:1b–2). The scene now shifts to the royal palace. The plot line is not hard to follow (vv.3, 5, 7b). The passage depicts a conspiracy against the king, which involved a drunken feast and led to an assassination. Verse 7 says that "their rulers" (lit., "judges") and "all their kings" have fallen. These plurals suggest multiple deaths, circumstances that match the closing decades of the northern kingdom (see "Historical Background" in the introduction). If the referent is a single plot, then the best options are the coup by Pekah (in parallel with 6:7–11) or that by Hoshea.

The messy scenario is portrayed with the metaphor of a baker and his oven (vv.4, 6–7a). Professional bakers worked in the royal precincts (Ge 40–41; 1Sa 8:13). The image here is complex and has occasioned all manner of suggestions for textual changes to try to clarify the meaning of the symbolism or to coordinate it with the history of the time. Such technical discussions lie beyond the purview of this commentary. (For details, though with differing interpretations, see especially Wolff, Andersen and Freedman, and Macintosh.) The English versions for the most part are in agreement in their translations.

3, 5, 7b The persons involved in the plot are not identified. The continuity from 6:7 through 7:2 suggests that the incident resumes the description of the removal of Pekahiah by Pekah, in which priests were prominent among the schemers. The setting for their sedition is some sort of festivities; the carousing illustrates the low moral state of both the royal house and conspirators alike. The occasion for the joyful revelry was "the day of the festival of our king" (v.7), which could be the celebration of an unnamed festival, his birthday, or the anniversary of his coronation.

Whichever the case, the king and his officials participate in the partying that will be the scene of their demise. If the "he" of v.5 is the king and the translation "joins hands with the mockers" is correct, then the sad fact is that the warm hand of fellowship soon would turn into the cold kiss of death. The closing indictment is that these political machinations are carried on without regard for God. Again, if priests are major actors in the plot, the accusation is yet more serious. Those who are supposed to lead the people before God ignore Yahweh at a fateful moment in the nation's history.

4, 6–7a While the substance of the metaphor of the hot oven is transparent—the unrestrained passion of the conspirators—the details are harder to establish. In particular there is disagreement over the identity of the baker and the nature of his inactivity in v.4. It is possible that this is simply a figure of speech that highlights the character and emotions of the political moment with no intent of connecting the image with actual individuals. It seems more likely in the context of chs. 5–7, however, that real events and people lurk behind the words.

If this assumption is correct, the question then becomes: Is the baker a leader of the plotters who deliberately leaves the oven to smolder and returns when it has fired to fever pitch, or is he one (such as the king or another functionary) who should have controlled the fiery emotions of the court and out of naïveté or negligence allowed the violence to occur? Either reading can make sense of the passage. The flow of the larger section (5:8–7:16), which focuses on those actively engaged in sinful behavior, may imply that the better choice between these two interpretations is the first option.

Finally, mention should be made of the label given to these conspirators in v.4. They are called "adulterers." Though from a different root (*n*ʾ*p*) from "harlot" (*znh*), this metaphor reveals yet again that the whoredom of Israel is not only religious; it is also political.

NOTES

11 There is disagreement as to whether the second line ("when I restore the fortunes of my people") should be construed with the first line of this verse (NJB, NASB, ESV, NLT) or whether it should be considered with 7:1 (NEB, NIV, NRSV, NJPS). The MT unmistakably separates 6:11 from 7:1. If 6:11 is a single unit, what is its meaning? Keil, 103, understands the verse to mean that Judah also will need to be punished for the full restoration of God's people to take place. Stuart, 112–13, argues that 6:11–7:1a are a prediction of restoration that echoes 1:10–2:1; 2:14–23; and 3:4–5. He believes "harvest" is better taken in a positive sense and not as a metaphor for judgment (cf. Andersen and Freedman, 443–44). The conjunction "also" at the beginning of 6:11, however, indicates that the announcement about Judah is coupled with the negative content of v.10. The promise of renewal in v.11b conflicts with this coupling but coordinates well with 7:1a, so the option to divide the verse seems best.

7:6 Many commentators and most versions (cf. Syr., Tg.) emend אֹפֵהֶם (*ʾōpēhem*, "their baker") to אַפֵּהֶם (*ʾappᵉhem*, "their anger"). Several recent commentators choose to remain with the MT, as do I. The slumber of the baker in this verse matches the idleness in v.4 (Andersen and Freedman, 451; Hubbard, 135; McComiskey, 105; Macintosh, 263; cf. NJPS, NKJV).

d. Senseless foreign policy (7:8–16)

[8]"Ephraim mixes with the nations;
   Ephraim is a flat cake not turned over.
[9]Foreigners sap his strength,
   but he does not realize it.
His hair is sprinkled with gray,
   but he does not notice.
[10]Israel's arrogance testifies against him,
   but despite all this
he does not return to the Lord his God
   or search for him.

[11]"Ephraim is like a dove,
   easily deceived and senseless—
now calling to Egypt,
   now turning to Assyria.
[12]When they go, I will throw my net over them;
   I will pull them down like birds of the air.
When I hear them flocking together,
   I will catch them.
[13]Woe to them,
   because they have strayed from me!
Destruction to them,
   because they have rebelled against me!
I long to redeem them
   but they speak lies against me.
[14]They do not cry out to me from their hearts
   but wail upon their beds.
They gather together for grain and new wine
   but turn away from me.
[15]I trained them and strengthened them,
   but they plot evil against me.
[16]They do not turn to the Most High;
   they are like a faulty bow.
Their leaders will fall by the sword
   because of their insolent words.
For this they will be ridiculed
   in the land of Egypt.

COMMENTARY

8–10 This pericope continues the image of baking, but attention now turns to the bread (v.8). Ovens were made of clay and were round and cone-shaped. They had openings at floor level, through which the fire was lit and stoked, and an aperture at the top. When the fire was at the appropriate temperature, the bread was lowered into the cavity and pressed against the walls or laid on the coals. A loaf would need to be turned over periodically so it would not come out half-cooked. The image in v.9a could extend the bread metaphor still further. "Grey hair" could mean mold, thus reinforcing that the bread is inedible (Andersen and Freedman, 467–68; Hubbard, 139–40; Garrett, 170). But grey hair may also denote old age and decrepitude. The end result is the same—uselessness. Israel through its foreign policies has become worthless.

What follows are evaluations of Israel's character as demonstrated by its politics. Twice the text says that Israel "does not know" (v.9). What the leadership may have thought were astute strategies actually testify to their ignorance of the consequences of what they are doing. They are arrogant in setting the direction for the nation, and the refusal to "return to" (contrast 2:7; 3:4) or "seek after" Yahweh their God is a testimony to this foolish, self-destructive pride (v.10). The opening clause of v.10 repeats the words of 5:5. The same smugness of Israel on display in its religious practices is also a core quality of its politics.

11–12 The metaphor now changes from an oven to birds, "easily deceived" and "senseless" (NIV; lit., "without a heart"). Those in charge of foreign policy vacillate between the two superpowers, Assyria and Egypt. The mention of Assyria recalls 5:13 (see comments); the reference to Egypt may be to Hoshea's appeal in 723 BC, when he refused to pay tribute and revolted against the Assyrian Empire. The outcome was disastrous for Israel. What was left of Israel after the Syro-Ephraimite War was taken by Assyria in 722 BC and converted into a province (2Ki 17:3–6). That invasion marked the culmination of God's punishment of the North.

13–16 The last pericope in this section begins with a "woe," which is God's cry of frustration over his people. Yahweh's design has always been to redeem his people, but they rebuff his gracious gestures (v.13). In the past he fought for them, but they now do not seek his help (v.15). The list of verbs describing Israel's attitude and actions is extensive: they have strayed, rebelled, and spoken lies (v.13); the nation does not cry out to God but instead turns aside (v.14); they plot evil (v.15) and speak insolent words (v.16).

The howling and self-lacerations of v.14 probably allude to non-Yahwistic rituals that try to secure sustenance (cf. 2:5, 8), practices forbidden in Deuteronomy 14:1 and reviled in 1 Kings 18:28. Even in the worst of times, with sure defeat and exile before them, the nation and its leaders stubbornly refuse to respond to the merciful God of their history, the "Most High," who is sovereign over all nations. They refuse to admit their guilt (v.16). Their idolatry is all-encompassing and all-consuming. Whatever beliefs Israel may have concerning Yahweh are seriously distorted and have brought them death and disaster.

NOTES

8 The verb *balal* can have two nuances. It can refer to the literal mixing of ingredients (e.g., Lev 7:12); it is also the one used in the Tower of Babel narrative (Ge 11:7, 9), where it signifies confusion. In the first option, the sense is that Israel is getting involved—to its detriment—with other nations; in the second case, the idea would be that Israel is making senseless and incoherent (i.e., confused) policy decisions.

12 The phrase כְּשֵׁמַע לַעֲדָתָם (kᵉšēmaʿ laʿᵃdātām) in the last clause of this verse is difficult. A literal translation is, "when a report [comes] to their assembly" (NASB, NRSV, NKJV, ESV). This report might be the pronouncement of the prophets on their sin (Keil, 109) or diplomatic correspondence coming from another nation (McComiskey, 111–12; Garrett, 171; Macintosh, 276–78). The NEB and NIV have, "When I hear them flocking together," taking the meaning of the noun עֵדָה (ʿēdâ, "assembly") as similar to that in Judges 14:8, where it refers to a swarm (of bees). Here the referent would be a flock of birds, thus continuing the bird metaphor (Davies, 189). Others suggestions include changing לַעֲדָתָם (laʿᵃdātām) to עַל־רָעָתָם (ʿal-rāʿātām, "of their evil" [NJB, NLT]; cf. Wolff, 107; Stuart, 116, 122) or to עֵדוּתָם (ʿēdûtām, "of their treaties" [Andersen and Freedman, 471]).

14 The second line has יִתְגּוֹרָרוּ (yitgôrārû), a Hitpolel form of the root גור (perhaps gwr II, "stir up strife"; cf. *HALOT*, 184–85; Andersen and Freedman, 475), but commentators and versions emend the text. The NASB, NIV, and NKJV translate, "they gather together," apparently based on the root גדד II (gdd II; cf. *HALOT*, 177; Ps 94:21). Most opt for the root גדד I (gdd, "cut"; cf. *HALOT*, 177; NEB, NJB, NRSV, NLT, ESV; LXX; Macintosh, 280–83).

16 The opening phrase יָשׁוּבוּ לֹא עַל (yāšûbû lōʾ ʿāl) has garnered much discussion. If it were "they do not (re)turn," the word order of the first two words would be reversed (note NIV). What is it that Israel turns to? עַל (ʿal) can be understood as an epithet for a deity, a variant of אֵלִי (ʾēlî, "my God") or עֶלְיוֹן (ʿelyôn, "Most High"; cf. 11:7). The translation would be, "They return [but] not to the Most High," an allusion to Yahweh (NKJV, NLT; cf. NEB, NIV). Another option is to read לֹא עַל (lōʾ ʿāl) as "no-god" and interpret this phrase as an epithet for בַּעַל (baʿal; Andersen and Freedman, 477–78; Hubbard, 142; Garrett, 173; cf. לֹא אֵל, lōʾ ʾēl, Dt 32:21). If the term does not refer to a deity, then it could be, "They return to not what is above" (NASB, ESV; cf. McComiskey, 116; Macintosh, 285, 288–89). Proposed emendations include לְלֹא יוֹעִיל (lᵉlōʾ yôʿîl, "to what does not profit"; NJB, NRSV, NJPS; cf. Mays, 110), and לַבְּלִיַּעַל (labbᵉliyyaʿal, "to Belial") or לַבַּעַל (labbaʿal, "to Baʿal"; JB, RSV; cf. Harper, 307; Davies, 192).

B. The Religious and Political Judgment of Israel (8:1–11:11)

1. The Violation of the Covenant (8:1–9:9)

OVERVIEW

Consonant with the book's style, this section returns to earlier themes to reflect on them afresh from different angles. The targets of divine anger are the politics of the northern kingdom and the religion that sustains those policies. This section is full of metaphors and a variety of literary genres. Much of ch. 8 uses first-person language to express Yahweh's frustration and anger with his people. Once again, identifying the precise historical backdrop is difficult, though most relate the material to the Assyrian invasion of 733 BC and its aftermath. Where appropriate, the commentary will mention events to which the text possibly alludes.

a. The politics of rebellion (8:1–10)

1 "Put the trumpet to your lips!
    An eagle is over the house of the LORD
because the people have broken my covenant
    and rebelled against my law.
2 Israel cries out to me,
    'O our God, we acknowledge you!'
3 But Israel has rejected what is good;
    an enemy will pursue him.
4 They set up kings without my consent;
    they choose princes without my approval.
With their silver and gold
    they make idols for themselves
    to their own destruction.
5 Throw out your calf-idol, O Samaria!
    My anger burns against them.
How long will they be incapable of purity?
6   They are from Israel!
This calf — a craftsman has made it;
    it is not God.
It will be broken in pieces,
    that calf of Samaria.

7 "They sow the wind
    and reap the whirlwind.
The stalk has no head;
    it will produce no flour.
Were it to yield grain,
    foreigners would swallow it up.
8 Israel is swallowed up;
    now she is among the nations
    like a worthless thing.
9 For they have gone up to Assyria
    like a wild donkey wandering alone.
    Ephraim has sold herself to lovers.
10 Although they have sold themselves among the nations,
    I will now gather them together.
They will begin to waste away
    under the oppression of the mighty king.

COMMENTARY

1–3 This section begins with an exclamation to sound the trumpet (v.1). Perhaps the prophet is envisioned as the watchman of the nation (cf. 5:8; 9:8), who is to announce the impending judgment. God's instrument of chastisement will come like a bird of prey, swiftly and mercilessly (Dt 28:49; Jer 4:13; Hab 1:8). The term *nešer* is a broad term and can refer to a species of eagle (most English versions) or to a vulture (NEB, ESV). If the former is the sense, this may be a bit of an ironic ploy. Yahweh as an eagle for his people can be a positive image (Ex 19:4; Dt 32:10–11), but here there is no such comfort. It has been suggested that *nešer* be repointed as *naśśār* (G. I. Emmerson, "The Structure and Meaning of Hosea 8:1–3," *VT* 25 [1975]: 700–710; cf. JB), yielding "set the trumpet to your lips like a herald," but this change is unnecessary.

Commentators also disagree as to the meaning of the phrase "house of the LORD [Yahweh]." Many compare it to the ancient Near Eastern practice of using a proper name with "house" to designate a place (e.g., "the land of Bīt-Humria [Omri]" for Israel in Summary Inscription 4 of Tiglath-pileser III, *COS*, 2:288) and understand this to be a reference to the land of Israel. The more natural meaning, however, is that "house of the LORD" is a sanctuary dedicated to Yahweh (NEB; Davies, 195–96; Garrett, 181; cf. 9:4, 8, 15). Judgment will begin at the very center of the nation's distorted ideology, at the temple (cf. Am 9:1; 7:9–17). As previous chapters demonstrate and the rest of the book will echo, religion is at the service of the state. Yahweh will not tolerate such machinations or misconceived ideas as to his person and will.

The reason for the judgment is the violation of Yahweh's covenant and laws (for the covenant, see "Religion and Theology in Hosea" in the introduction). The rest of the chapter provides details of this rebellion. The people may cry out to God (v.2), but in truth they reject "what is good" (*ṭôb*; GK 3202)—probably his way and the benefits thereof (v.3; cf. Am 5:14–15; Mic 2:7; 3:2; 6:8)—so an (unidentified) enemy will pursue them. Some take *ṭôb* to mean the Good One, that is, Yahweh (Andersen and Freedman, 491; Stuart, 131).

4–6 These verses explain in what ways Israel has rejected the "good." To begin with, Israel has not sought Yahweh's designs in the choice of leadership (v.4a). These words may refer to the chaotic political situation within Israel either in the buildup to or right after the Assyrian invasion. This period was characterized by intrigue and violence (cf. 6:7–7:7).

Second, they have participated in idolatry. The people worship what their own hands have made, but "it is not God" (vv.4b, 6; cf. 7:16; Isa 40:18–20; 44:9–20; Jer 10:1–16; Hab 2:18–19). The plural "idols" (v.4b) suggests that idol worship was widespread, but there is one special target that triggers the wrath of God: the "calf of Samaria" (vv.5–6; cf. 10:5; 13:2). Israel has rejected "what is good," so he rejects their idol. God wonders "how long" it will be until Israel regains its senses and recovers its purity.

What was this "calf of Samaria"? "Samaria" most likely refers to the country of Israel, here identified by its capital city. The implication is that this calf is a most prominent image. The Deuteronomistic History relates that Jeroboam I set up calf images in Daniel and Bethel (1Ki 12:29–30; cf. 2Ki 10:29). The fact that the calf at Dan is not mentioned may indicate that it has already been destroyed (possibly by the Assyrians in 733 BC) or that at this time it was not as important as the one at Bethel.

Amos, the other eighth-century prophet to Israel, vehemently denounces this sanctuary as well (Am 4:4; 5:5–6; 7:10–17).

The calf/bull image was associated with Canaanite mythology (cf. O. Keel and C. Uehlinger, *Gods, Goddesses, and Images of God in Ancient Israel* [Minneapolis: Fortress, 1998], 191–95; Smith, 82–85; N. Wyatt, "Calf," *DDD*, 180–82). It was a symbol of strength and fertility, and a representation of this animal was often taken as a pedestal on which the deity stood. Here, however, it appears that Israel reveres the image as a god. Witness A. Mazar's celebrated archaeological find in northern Israel of a bronze calf figurine in 1981 ("The 'Bull Site': An Iron Age I Open Cult Place," *BASOR* 247 [1982]: 27–40).

7–10 This pericope combines proverbial sayings with powerful images. The nation is locked in a cycle of inescapable, self-destructive futility. Israel is a foolish farmer who yields disastrous results and loses what he has to others (v.7); it is a discarded and useless pot (v.8; cf. Jer 18), a wandering solitary donkey that lacks discernment, and a harlot who must hire clients (v.9).

Israel's imprudence is marked in its foreign affairs. It has "gone up" to Assyria (v.9; cf. 5:13; 7:11), perhaps an allusion to Menahem's tribute to Tiglath-pileser III in 738 BC (2Ki 15:19–20) or to that paid by Hoshea in 732/31 BC after his assassination of Pekah (17:3). In the end, Israel will succumb to the empire and be reduced to the status of a vassal (v.10). Tribute cannot guarantee safety; it is a weighty burden that will further weaken the nation (cf. 5:13; 7:9). The lack of faith in God and refusal to seek him in policy decisions will bring Israel to its knees. The greatest sovereign, Yahweh himself, will cause this doom by the hand of the invader.

NOTES

2 The syntax of this verse is awkward. The Hebrew literally reads, "To me they cry out: 'My God, we know you, Israel.'" Some make Israel the subject of the verb "cry out" (NIV, NLT, NJPS), but its placement in the line speaks against that view. The NRSV has "Israel" as the subject but also retains it in the quote. The LXX and the Peshitta omit "Israel," so some scholars believe the word to be a gloss (e.g., Wolff, 131; Davies, 198). It is best to interpret it as in apposition to "we" for emphasis (NJB, NASB, NRSV, ESV). A few emend to "God of Israel" (NEB, BHS; Andersen and Freedman, 490).

5 The subject of the transitive verb זָנַח (*zānaḥ*, "reject, cast out") of the first clause is ambiguous (cf. v.3). Grammatically, either "your calf" or an unnamed "he" could be the subject. When "calf" is taken as the subject, the verb is interpreted intransitively (NEB; Macintosh, 301–2) or revocalized as a passive (NRSV; Mays, 113). With the alternative ("he"), Yahweh is the implied subject (NASB, NJPS). Some repoint the verb as an imperative (NIV; Wolff, 132; LXX); others emend to the first person, again with Yahweh as the subject, to harmonize this clause with what follows (NJB, NLT, ESV; Davies, 201).

10 Some emend מַשָּׂא (*maśśāʾ*, "burden") as מְשֹׁחַ (*mᵉšōaḥ*, "anointing") for a translation that resonates with v.4a, in that judgment will bring a stop to Israel's choosing leaders apart from God (RSV, JB, NEB; cf. LXX). There is no need to emend the text, however, and this interpretation ill fits these verses; the focus is on foreign, not domestic, policies. S. M. Paul ("*mśʾ mlk śrym*—Hosea 8:8–10 and Ancient Near Eastern Royal Epithets" [ScrHier 31 (1986)]: 193–204) places the line against an Akkadian background.

b. The religion of forgetfulness (8:11–14)

¹¹ "Though Ephraim built many altars for sin offerings,
　　these have become altars for sinning.
¹² I wrote for them the many things of my law,
　　but they regarded them as something alien.
¹³ They offer sacrifices given to me
　　and they eat the meat,
　　but the LORD is not pleased with them.
　Now he will remember their wickedness
　　and punish their sins:
　　They will return to Egypt.
¹⁴ Israel has forgotten his Maker
　　and built palaces;
　Judah has fortified many towns.
　But I will send fire upon their cities
　　that will consume their fortresses."

COMMENTARY

11–13a This set of verses provides an appropriate close to this chapter. It summarizes the incongruities in Israel's religion, which is typified by much activity toward wrong ends and the refusal to attend to the will of the true God. With words similar to those in Amos, Hosea describes the multiplication of altars as so much sin. The redundancy of the line in v.11 mirrors literarily the repetitiveness of the rituals and the duplication of worship sites.

The ironic contradictions of Israelite faith continue in v.12, where the detailed revelation of God's will (lit., "the multitude of my instructions") is seen as a foreign thing, not as something precious to Israel and worthy of obedience! Their religion and its god(s) reflect personal and national commitments and desires, even as divine revelation has become strange to them. Not surprisingly, Yahweh takes no pleasure in their erroneous religiosity (v.13a; cf. 9:4).

13b–14 These rituals and hence Israel itself, far from being acceptable to Yahweh, "now" will bring judgment (v.13b). God will visit the consequences of their sin upon them. Their religion, so intertwined with politics, will be the cause of their exile. The statement that they will return to Egypt is probably metaphorical, not literal — that is, the nation will experience the reversal of the exodus (cf. Dt 28:68). Instead of living in freedom under the protective and beneficent eye of Yahweh, again they will be in bondage to an oppressive empire — in this case, Assyria (7:16; 9:3, 6; 11:5). Exile was one of the covenantal curses (Lev 26:33–39, 41; Dt 28:36–41, 63–64).

The interweaving of religious critique and foreign policy, which is a feature of much of ch. 8, is underscored in the last verse (v.14). Both the northern and southern kingdoms had strengthened their fortifications, but all that effort and expense will be to no avail before the mighty foe (v.14). Such misplaced trust is folly (cf. 10:13–15; 11:6; 14:3). God will send fire on the cities and fortresses of Israel and Judah by the hand of their enemy.

Fire is a descriptor for destruction in war, where cities often were put to the torch after they had been taken. This is the same language that Amos uses in its oracles against the nations (e.g., Am 1:4, 7, 10; cf. the view of Jeremias at Hos 4:15). Their transgression is that they have forgotten (*škḥ*; cf. 2:13; 4:6; 13:6) their Maker (cf. Isa 44:2; 51:13). Yahweh created them and entered into a relationship with this people at the exodus; he provided the laws that should have defined and organized their existence in every facet of life and sustained them for centuries. Yet, because their short memory and their skewed understanding, he will turn them over to this miserable fate.

Some critical scholars deem v.14 as secondary because of the mention of Judah (e.g., Harper, 324; Wolff, 136, 147; yet note Andersen and Freedman, 511–12). Nevertheless, as has been stated repeatedly, the pairing of Judah and Israel is common throughout the book (note 1:6–7; 1:11; 4:15; 5:5, 12–14; 6:4; 10:11; 11:12). Interpreters must remember that the historical setting is the eighth century, in which Israel and Judah were forced to engage the Assyrians. That both nations appear in the text coheres with the foreign policy interests of the chapter.

NOTE

13 The opening two words of the first line are problematic. הַבְהָבַי (*habhābay*), the term in construct with זִבְחֵי (*zibḥê*, "sacrifices"), is a *hapax legomenon*. One solution is to take it as a reduplicative noun from the root יהב (*yhb*, "give") and read something akin to "given to me" (NIV; cf. NEB, NJB, NJPS, ESV). Another option is to connect the word to the root אהב (*ʾhb*, "love"; cf. *HALOT*, 236) and understand that the sacrifices were offered in the same spirit as in Amos 4:5 (RSV, JB, NRSV, NLT; note the end of v.12 in the LXX).

c. The religion of fools (9:1–9)

> ¹Do not rejoice, O Israel;
>   do not be jubilant like the other nations.
> For you have been unfaithful to your God;
>   you love the wages of a prostitute
>   at every threshing floor.
> ²Threshing floors and winepresses will not feed the people;
>   the new wine will fail them.
> ³They will not remain in the LORD's land;
>   Ephraim will return to Egypt
>   and eat unclean food in Assyria.

⁴They will not pour out wine offerings to the LORD,
　nor will their sacrifices please him.
Such sacrifices will be to them like the bread of mourners;
　all who eat them will be unclean.
This food will be for themselves;
　it will not come into the temple of the LORD.

⁵What will you do on the day of your appointed feasts,
　on the festival days of the LORD?
⁶Even if they escape from destruction,
　Egypt will gather them,
　and Memphis will bury them.
Their treasures of silver will be taken over by briers,
　and thorns will overrun their tents.
⁷The days of punishment are coming,
　the days of reckoning are at hand.
　Let Israel know this.
Because your sins are so many
　and your hostility so great,
the prophet is considered a fool,
　the inspired man a maniac.
⁸The prophet, along with my God,
　is the watchman over Ephraim,
yet snares await him on all his paths,
　and hostility in the house of his God.
⁹They have sunk deep into corruption,
　as in the days of Gibeah.
God will remember their wickedness
　and punish them for their sins.

COMMENTARY

1–2 The judgment of God will turn Israel's religious world upside down. Joy is the natural response of agricultural people at seeing the abundance of their harvests (Lev 23:40; Dt 16:14), but Israel will have no cause to celebrate (v.1). In words reminiscent of previous chapters, the nation is censured for playing the harlot (*znh*; "for you have been unfaithful to your God," NIV, NLT) and loving the wages of a prostitute (2:5, 8, 12; 8:9–10). Israel has forsaken Yahweh as its provider and trusted in false gods. The sites (the threshing floors and vats) and symbols (the new wine) of blessings will no longer translate into the provisions they desire and need (v.2).

3 Israel's time in the "the LORD's land" has come to an end. The Lord of the land (Lev 25:23) is also the Lord of history and the ruler of the nations, and as such he decrees Israel's fate. Once again, Egypt serves as a metaphor for the banishment to Assyria that will take place (cf. 8:13b). Away from the Promised Land, Israel can only eat unclean food.

4–5 This unclean status means that it will be impossible for the people to offer libations and sacrifices suitable for Yahweh (v.4; cf. Jer 6:20; Mal 3:4). Whatever they bring will be like the bread of mourners, which by definition is defiled (Dt 26:14; Jer 16:5–7) and thus unfit for the temple of Yahweh.

The rhetorical question of v.5 follows naturally. If they are unable geographically and incapable sacramentally of offering what is acceptable to God, then what are the people to do on the "day of your appointed feasts" and for the "festival days of the LORD"? The first phrase probably applies to the various stipulated gatherings as a people before God (Lev 23); the latter phrase could be a synonym for the first or may mean the Feast of Booths (*Sukkôt*) that elsewhere is called the "feast of the LORD" (Jdg 21:19; Lev 23:39). That festival commemorated God's care in the wilderness and, at the same time, was a celebration of the grape and olive harvest.

Jeroboam I had established an alternative festival to *Sukkôt* one month later than what was prescribed in the law (1Ki 12:32). If the Feast of Booths indeed is what is meant here, on all counts Israel is disqualified. In exile it cannot bring what is required; because of sin, it has forfeited all rights to observe the provision of God; and, if the aberrant feast set up by Jeroboam is in view, its harvest festival is a de facto perversion of the original. Israel will no longer participate in the worship of Yahweh. In that ancient understanding of life and the world, the inability to continue the cult meant that the people will lose a fundamental part of their identity

and an integral part of their mission and reason for existence among the nations of the earth.

6–7a There will be no escaping the judgment of Yahweh (v.6). Whether the reference to escaping to Egypt is in relation to Israel's foreign policy efforts to seek aid against the Assyrian onslaught (cf. 7:11) or to the prospect that some may flee and seek asylum in Egypt, the end result is the same. That country, instead of being a refuge, will become a burial ground.

This is an interesting twist on the Egypt-as-exile motif. While Assyria is Egypt in the sense of being the new enslaver and place of banishment (8:13; 9:3), Egypt itself will take in Israelites, but only to inter them (Memphis, a prominent city on the Nile in Lower Egypt, was famous for its large cemetery). In line with this interpretation and with most commentators, it is better to understand the ruination of treasures and the desolation of tents as a synonym for the loss of precious possessions and not as indicating the abandonment of cultic items of non-Yahwistic worship, such as expensive idols and their shrines (as argued by Wolff, 156; Hubbard, 158; cf. 2:8; 8:4b; 13:2).

The time of punishment has come (v.7a). In a sense it began in 748 BC with Menahem's tribute to the Assyrian Empire, but military pressure and human suffering greatly increased after 733 BC as a consequence of the Syro-Ephraimite War and will culminate with the defeat of the nation in 722 BC. The logic of what is happening and of what is to come is something that Israel must admit ("Israel knows").

7b–8 The prophet, "the man of the spirit," is called a fool and a maniac (v.7b; cf. 2Ki 9:11). What is the meaning of these insulting words, and who is this prophet? Is this statement an assertion from the mouth of Hosea aimed at ridiculing Israel's deceiving and self-deceived prophets? Or does it voice Israel's admission that other prophets were misdirected and had led them down the path to destruction? Another possibility is that the statement is the nation's angry rejection of Hosea for his condemnation of their sin and his announcements of judgment.

A few commentators support the first (e.g., Keil, 122; cf. NEB, NKJV) and second interpretive options (e.g., M. S. Odell, "Who Were the Prophets in Hosea?" *HBT* 18 [1996], 83–87). Most adopt the last and consider the insult to be the people's mockery of the true prophet of God. Hosea is being scorned for an unpopular message (cf. Am 7:10–13; Jer 29:26–27; Wolff, 152; Stuart, 145–46; Hubbard, 155). Perhaps his marriage to Gomer qualified him as odd in their eyes as well (R. D. Nelson, "Priestly Purity and Prophetic Lunacy: Hosea 1:2–3 and 9:7," in *The Priests in the Prophets: The Portrayal of Priests, Prophets and Other Religious Specialists in the Latter Prophets*, ed. L. L. Grabbe and A. Ogden Bellis [JSOTSup 408; London: T&T Clark, 2004], 115–33).

Theoretically, each of the three alternatives could work. If these words are Hosea's, he, as the true spokesperson of Yahweh, is saying that the nation's prophets are a snare and generators of violence (v.8; cf. 6:5; 1Ki 22:22; Mic 2:11; 3:5; Jer 23:13–40; 29:24–28). In this case, "prophet" is taken in a collective sense to refer to those who are preaching

weal, not woe (S. A. Irvine presents the case for a particular opponent in "Enmity in the House of God [Hosea 7:7–9]," *JBL* 117 [1998]: 645–53). If this verse is the nation's assessment that their prophets have failed them, it may bear witness to internal debates within the nation as the end draws near.

Lastly, if the comment is Israel's negative comment about Hosea, it confirms the people in their sin. Hosea, the watchman of Israel (5:8; 8:1; cf. Jer 6:17; Eze 33:2, 6–7), whose ministry the nation sees as traitorous, is being forced to navigate the obstacles they place in his way and faces continual resentment (v.8). Even though "the house of his God" may refer to the land, it may also be the temple (cf. 8:1). In other words, the very place where this man of God should have found agreement with Yahweh's demands has become the site of his greatest opposition.

9 Israel has deteriorated to the level of the awful sins committed at Gibeah that are recounted in Judges 19–21. To believe that the nation is repeating those very same acts misses the point. The issue is that its violence and religious perversion merit judgment (cf. 10:9). This verse repeats part of 8:13, perhaps establishing an inclusio. That verse announces exile as God's punishment; the intervening passage has enlarged that theme and explained its consequences.

NOTES

1 As Israel is a masculine proper noun, the jussive is in the masculine singular (אַל־תִּשְׂמַח, *ʾal-tiśmaḥ*; "Let Israel not rejoice"). While the MT has only this one verb, many versions translate it and the adverbial phrase ("with exultation"; NASB) as two imperatives (e.g., "Do not rejoice … do not be jubilant," NIV). The verse continues with "you have played the whore" (NRSV), but interestingly with a second masculine singular verbal form, זָנִיתָ (*zānîtā*); a second masculine singular suffix also is applied to אֱלֹהֶיךָ (*ʾelōheykā*, "your God"). The use of the masculine gender might seem at cross-purposes with the metaphor of playing the harlot, but the masculine subject is consistent with the beginning of the verse (Israel). This apparent gender anomaly complicates the harlot imagery of the book. Here Israel, the male, is unfaithful and unchaste.

7 Grammatically, the clause יֵדְעוּ יִשְׂרָאֵל (*yēdᵉʿû yiśrāʾēl*) can be translated in a future ("Israel will know"; RSV, ESV), jussive ("let Israel know"; NASB, NJPS, NIV), or customary sense ("Israel knows"; NJB, NKJV). Some, believing the proper root to be רוע (*nwʿ*, "shout") instead of ידע (*ydʿ*, "know"), emend to יָרִעוּ יִשְׂרָאֵל (*yārîʿû yiśrāʾēl*) and translate as "Israel cries out" (JB, NRSV; cf. Wolff, 150, 156; Stuart, 140). With this change, the clause introduces the people's disparaging words about the prophets (and can be regarded as an ironic counterpart to 8:2). The NLT incorporates both the MT and the emendation. The LXX has κακωθήσεται, apparently understanding the verbal form as יֵרַעוּ (*yērāʿû*), a Niphal imperfect of the root רעע (*rʿʿ*, "suffer").

The awkwardness of the line is due in part to the absence of any syntactical indicators of speech. Those who hold that these words are Israel's perception claim that this statement is parenthetical or support the aforementioned textual change. Toward the same end, the NIV reverses the order of the last two Hebrew lines, thereby offering a transition to the allegation of the people, and adds "is considered."

8 The Hebrew of the first line of this verse literally reads, "A watchman of Ephraim [is] with my God," and the Masoretic punctuation connects "a prophet" with what follows. Many English versions ignore that punctuation (RSV, NRSV, NIV, NLT, ESV). The JB does, too, but its rendition is based as well on the emendation of אֱלֹהָי (*ʾᵉlōhāy*) to אֹהֶל (*ʾōhel*): "Ephraim watches the prophet's tent."

2. Metaphors of Rebellion and Judgment (9:10–11:11)

OVERVIEW

This section divides into four parts, each of which centers around a metaphor: grapes in the wilderness (9:10–17), a vine (10:1–8), a heifer (10:9–15), and a child (11:1–11). These passages all look back at what Israel had been and could have become but did not. These passages then declare divine judgment on the nation's sin. Another feature is the extensive use of first-person verbs, as Yahweh voices his disappointment. History is important as well. Several incidents of the past are cited as examples of the seed of rebellion that had fully sprouted in the prophet's day. The formula "declares the LORD" (*nᵉʾum-yhwh*) closes the section (11:11).

a. Grapes in the wilderness (9:10–17)

> ¹⁰ "When I found Israel,
>   it was like finding grapes in the desert;
> when I saw your fathers,
>   it was like seeing the early fruit on the fig tree.
> But when they came to Baal Peor,
>   they consecrated themselves to that shameful idol
>   and became as vile as the thing they loved.

> [11] Ephraim's glory will fly away like a bird —
>   no birth, no pregnancy, no conception.
> [12] Even if they rear children,
>   I will bereave them of every one.
> Woe to them
>   when I turn away from them!
>
> [13] I have seen Ephraim, like Tyre,
>   planted in a pleasant place.
> But Ephraim will bring out
>   their children to the slayer."
>
> [14] Give them, O Lord —
>   what will you give them?
> Give them wombs that miscarry
>   and breasts that are dry.
> [15] "Because of all their wickedness in Gilgal,
>   I hated them there.
> Because of their sinful deeds,
>   I will drive them out of my house.
> I will no longer love them;
>   all their leaders are rebellious.
> [16] Ephraim is blighted,
>   their root is withered,
>   they yield no fruit.
> Even if they bear children,
>   I will slay their cherished offspring."
>
> [17] My God will reject them
>   because they have not obeyed him;
>   they will be wanderers among the nations.

COMMENTARY

10 Yahweh recalls the beginning of his relationship with Israel. He found them in the wilderness, mentioned in ch. 2 as the place of their original courtship (2:14–15). He likens the people to grapes and ripe figs. Finding these in the arid regions of that part of the world brings joy (cf. Isa 28:4), but that pristine goodness soon turned to rebellion at Baal Peor in Moab (Nu 25; Ps 106:28–30). There they indulged in idolatry and sexual promiscuity with foreign women.

That sin had a profound effect on the character of the nation. In essence, they had dedicated themselves

275

to "shame" (*bōšet*) and become as "vile" (*šiqqûṣîm*) as the idol to which they had bowed down. "Shame" is connected to the worship of *baʿal* elsewhere (e.g., Jer 3:24–25; 11:13), as is "vile" to other deities (e.g., 2Ki 23:13; Jer 4:1; 7:30). The momentary satisfaction they experienced in that unexcused excess had made them repulsive in God's sight.

11–12 Accordingly, the nation's "glory" will depart, as a bird on the wing (v.11a). "Glory" may refer to Israel's wealth or its posterity, but it is better to interpret the term as a descriptor for Yahweh (cf. 1Sa 4:21–22; Eze 8). He who should have been their security and the object of their affections will leave and turn the nation over to a dreadful fate. The One who could give Israel life now decrees sterility (v.11b). This reversal is matched by the inverse order of the verbs for childbearing. The severity of these words is strengthened in v.12a, that God will remove any children that might survive the disaster. What should have been occasions for joy will be motives for mourning. Such is the result of divine abandonment (v.12b).

13 The sharp differences between the English versions testify to the difficulties in translating the first line of this verse. Several emendations have been suggested, but the MT is as viable an option as any other. The sense is that Israel, even as Tyre, had been placed in a favorable setting but had forfeited potential blessings because of its sinful behavior.

The challenge in the second line is interpretive, not linguistic or grammatical. Some commentators see a reference to child sacrifice, with the "slayer" as *baʿal* (Andersen and Freedman, 538; Garrett, 202; cf. Ps 106:36–39; cf. Tg.). However, others who believe that this abhorrent ritual was practiced in ancient Israel do not reference this passage (e.g., Smith, 171–81). The more natural reading is to relate the clause to the surrounding context, which heralds losses in war and the barrenness of the women. To lead their children to the slaughter,

therefore, means that their sin will result in their families' meeting death at the hands of the invader.

14 It is not uncommon to interpret this verse as the prophet's intercession on behalf of the people (as in Am 7:3, 5). That is, horrified by the scope of divine wrath, Hosea pleads for what he considers will cause the least suffering (cf. 2Sa 24:11–17): childlessness instead of the butchery of the battlefield (Wolff, 166–67; Mays, 134–35; Hubbard, 166–67). The prophet, though, has been strident throughout in his proclamation of doom. This verse is not a plea for mercy, but rather Hosea's affirmation of what Yahweh has decreed. The promise of Genesis 49:25 has been overturned (Harper, 339; Garrett, 202; D. Krause, "A Blessing Cursed: The Prophet's Prayer for Barren Womb and Dry Breasts in Hosea 9," in *Reading between Texts: Intertextuality and the Hebrew Bible*, ed. D. N. Fewell [Literary Currents in Biblical Interpretation; Louisville: Westminster John Knox, 1992], 191–202).

Andersen and Freedman, 539, propose a chiastic structure for 9:10–17, with this verse as its center and climax. If this suggestion is correct, the structure focuses attention on the prophet's response to God's will (irrespective of whether it is an entreaty or an endorsement).

15 The NIV adds "because of" to the opening clause and in that way suggests that something in Israel's past at Gilgal has triggered Yahweh's judgment in the present (cf. 9:9–10). Some commentators follow a similar tact, usually hypothesizing that this is an allusion to the inauguration of Saul's kingship there (1Sa 11:14–15; cf. Wolff, 167; Stuart, 153–54; Garrett, 203). This then would be a continuation of Hosea's attack against the monarchy (5:1–2, 10; 6:11–7:7; 8:4; 13:9–11) with an historical argument that the institution from the very beginning had been flawed and deserving of Yahweh's rejection. A number of English versions perhaps reflect this view with their translation,

"There I *began* to hate them" (e.g., NLT, ESV). The phrase "all their leaders" adds weight to this political interpretation.

Nonetheless, a literal reading of the Hebrew is "All their sin is at Gilgal." Gilgal is targeted as an unacceptable cultic center in several passages (4:15; 12:11)—a stance echoed in Amos (Am 4:4; 5:5). It was a symbol of all that has been wrong with the faith of Israel, and there the nation's misconstrued worldview finds religious authorization; so Yahweh will expel the people from the sanctuary ("my house"; cf. 8:1; 9:8). The words "I will no longer love them" serve as a reminder of the opening chapters, where Israel's religious practices were the primary sin ("I will no longer show love" in 1:6–7; 2:23). Politics are inseparable from the religious beliefs and behavior that Hosea condemns, but the emphasis at this juncture (and in ch. 9 in general) is on the cult (McComiskey, 154–55).

16 Israel is a sick plant, not the luxurious vine that God found and wanted to flourish (v.10). Calamity is communicated as a pun: Ephraim (ʾeprayim) cannot bear "fruit" (pᵉrî). This fruit is their children. Death, not new life, is in the offing (cf. vv.11–13).

17 This first of four parts closes with the prophetic distinction between the false Yahweh and other gods that the nation follows and the God of Hosea ("my God"). It also reviews earlier material. Disobedience has brought divine abandonment (vv.11–12) and rejection (v.15). Exile from the land "among the nations" as the curse for rebellion is Israel's future (v.3; cf. Lev 26:33, 38; Dt 28:64).

NOTE

13 The Hebrew of the second clause of the first line, which reads (lit.) "for/to Tyre [לְצוֹר, lᵉṣôr] planted in a meadow," is followed by most English versions (e.g., NASB, NJPS, NLT; Keil, 126; Garrett, 201; J. K. Kuan, "Hosea 9:13 and Josephus, *Antiquities* IX, 277–287," *PEQ* 123 [1991]: 104–8). An alternative is to relate צוֹר (ṣôr) to an Arabic word for a palm tree (NRSV, ESV; Hubbard, 166; Macintosh, 371–72), an interpretation that could allude to the patriarchal blessing of Genesis 49:22. Others follow the sense of the LXX (εἰς θήραν παρέστησαν τὰ τέκνα αὐτῶν: "has presented its children as prey"), which requires the emendation of צוֹר (ṣôr) to צַיִד I (ṣayid I; cf. *HALOT*, 1020), among other changes (RSV, JB, NEB; Wolff, 160–61).

b. A "luxuriant"/destructive vine and plant (10:1–8)

¹Israel was a spreading vine;
    he brought forth fruit for himself.
As his fruit increased,
    he built more altars;
as his land prospered,
    he adorned his sacred stones.
²Their heart is deceitful,
    and now they must bear their guilt.

The LORD will demolish their altars
　　and destroy their sacred stones.

[3] Then they will say, "We have no king
　　because we did not revere the LORD.
But even if we had a king,
　　what could he do for us?"
[4] They make many promises,
　　take false oaths
　　and make agreements;
therefore lawsuits spring up
　　like poisonous weeds in a plowed field.
[5] The people who live in Samaria fear
　　for the calf-idol of Beth Aven.
Its people will mourn over it,
　　and so will its idolatrous priests,
those who had rejoiced over its splendor,
　　because it is taken from them into exile.
[6] It will be carried to Assyria
　　as tribute for the great king.
Ephraim will be disgraced;
　　Israel will be ashamed of its wooden idols.
[7] Samaria and its king will float away
　　like a twig on the surface of the waters.
[8] The high places of wickedness will be destroyed —
　　it is the sin of Israel.
Thorns and thistles will grow up
　　and cover their altars.
Then they will say to the mountains, "Cover us!"
　　and to the hills, "Fall on us!"

COMMENTARY

1 This passage is structurally delimited in at least two ways. To start with, it both opens and ends with horticultural imagery. Second, these verses record what the nation purportedly says in response to divine judgment (vv.3, 8).

The vine is used as a metaphor for Israel elsewhere, most famously in Isaiah 5:1–7 (cf. Eze 15, 17; Jn 15). Here, as there, the vine is a disappointment — it yields "poisonous weeds" (v.4). This same pattern of divine frustration occurs in the grape illustration of 9:10–17, although in this passage there is not the contrast between the past and present. What is the state of this vine? Based on an Arabic cognate, most English versions translate *bôqēq* in a positive sense (e.g., "spreading," NIV; "luxuriant," NRSV; Wolff, 170; LXX). In the OT, however, the root *bqq* is uniformly negative and is best taken as something like "destructive" ("rank," NEB; note Na 2:2; Garrett, 206–7; Macintosh, 383–84; cf. *HALOT*, 150).

How is the vine destructive? Whatever benefits came to Israel have led to the proliferation of altars and sacred pillars—that is, to the cult that the prophet decries. Instead of appropriately responding to the One who actually provided for them, the people saw in their agricultural bounty a confirmation of their idolatrous belief in *ba'al* (or the *b'ālîm*; cf. 2:5–8).

2–3 Verse 2 begins by describing the nation's character. Their heart is "deceitful" (*ḥlq*). The term literally means "smooth" and is used figuratively for speech that is not to be trusted (e.g., Pr 5:3; 26:28; Eze 12:24; cf. *HALOT*, 322, *ḥlq* I), thus reinforcing the point of the previous verse that Israel is a false vine. It must pay the consequences of its guilt.

Both v.2 and v.3 declare that the time of judgment is "now." The coupling of religion and politics is made clear in this juxtaposition. With their prosperity the people constructed altars and pillars (v.1), but "now" those will be destroyed (v.2). "The LORD" is supplied by many versions. The Hebrew text has "he"; the presence of the pronoun is emphatic (see NJB).

The quotation in v.3 of what the people are saying "now" ("then," NIV) has been taken in several ways. One can interpret these words as Hosea's opinion of what the people will confess in the near future once they realize the error of their ways. It may be better to consider them as the continuation of the frustration expressed in 9:7b–8, as they

see their world collapse around them in the face of the invasion. There they voiced their anger at the true prophet of God; here they admit that their trust does not lie in Yahweh, and they denounce the haplessness of their king. The realia of their religion were being destroyed, and the political system that in large measure was based on all of them was failing. The closing verse of this section (v.8) is their ultimate cry of despair.

Although most English versions have "a king" in the last clause, the Hebrew reads "*the* king." The article may suggest that a specific ruler is in view, or that the monarchy in general is the target. If the former option is correct, then most likely the reference is to Hoshea and to his unwise decisions. It is also possible to understand "the king" to be the divine king, Yahweh, hereby expressing a consistent rejection of God (Andersen and Freedman, 553). I take less of a religious interpretation and more of a political perspective on this and the following verses.

4 This verse may be a continuation of the words of the exasperated people. In the context, the "promises," "oaths," and "agreements" are probably related to political policies. In line with this governmental focus, *mišpāṭ* (GK 5477) can be translated as "litigation" or "lawsuits" (NEB, NIV, NRSV); the social fabric is breaking down as the people harass one another. The complaint of the people is comprehensive; all these legal matters are seen as vacuous.

Most commentators, however, believe that *mišpāṭ* refers to "justice" in the sense of the right ordering of life in accordance with God's design (cf. 2:19; 12:6). This line would be similar to the words of Amos, who bemoans that justice in Israel had been turned into poison (Am 6:12; cf. 5:7). If this approach is correct, then the entire verse is read more naturally as the prophet's bitter critique of Israel. There also may be a double entendre. As in

Habakkuk 1:4, *mišpāṭ* can denote both legal rulings as well as the more general ethical attribute. In Hosea's mind, each in its own particularly negative way is burgeoning like a noxious weed, not like the vine God intended.

5–6 Attention turns to the religious implications of the nation's defeat. With the disaster that comes with the judgment, the inhabitants of Samaria will fear for the idol at Beth-Aven (v.5), or the "House of Iniquity," a contemptuous name for the cultic center of Bethel (cf. 4:15). The word translated "calf-idol" is in the plural—either an abstract (cf. GKC §122q, 124e–f; *IBHS* §7.4.2.) or an honorific plural (cf. GKC §124g–i; *IBHS* §7.4.3.). If the former, the meaning is the calf-cult (cf. 8:5; 13:2); if the latter, the expression may constitute mockery of the defeated god (the "*great* calf"), which will be powerless to protect Israel.

The people's dread is not the ritual lamentation for the death and return to life of *baʿal* (as argued by Wolff, 175; Stuart, 161, Garrett, 209–10); rather, it is distress about the fate of the idol (*HALOT*, 185, *gwr* III). "Indeed" (asseverative *kî*; JB, NJPS; cf. GKC §159ee), disillusioned people and the idol's priests (*kōmer*, a term reserved for those of non-Yahwistic cults; cf. 2Ki 23:5; Zep 1:4) will mourn the end of their religious world. The idol's "splendor"—that is, all the wealth of the sanctuary—will be taken away into exile (cf. 1Ki 14:26; Da 1:2). This turn of phrase is ironic: Israel's true glory, Yahweh, will leave them (9:11), even as the empty glory of its idols will be taken. The sovereign God is leaving of his own free will; the idols and all the religious paraphernalia are to be carted away.

The calf's destination is Assyria (v.6). It will be part of the tribute to be turned over to the great king of Assyria (for *melek yārēb*, see comment on 5:13), most likely as part of the invader's booty. (For spoliation of gods in war, see M. Cogan, *Imperialism and Religion: Assyria, Judah and Israel in the Eighth and Seventh Centuries B.C.E.* [Missoula, Mont.: Scholars, 1974], 22–41; B. Becking, *The Fall of Samaria: An Historical and Archaeological Study* [SHANE 2; Leiden: Brill, 1992], 31 [cf. Am 5:26].) The coming defeat will make Israel's disastrous plans ("its counsel"; cf. NIV note) a disgrace.

7 It is possible that the prediction of v.6 is expanded in this verse in that the "king" is the calf idol that will be swept away (Mays, 142; Andersen and Freedman, 558; Hubbard, 175). It is more consistent, however, to maintain that all the kings mentioned in this passage are human (vv.3, 6–7; cf. vv.13–15). In other words, Israel's king will also be deported. Historically, this prediction found fulfillment in the imprisonment of Hoshea by Shalmaneser V (2Ki 17:4).

The language of the metaphor is difficult. It usually is understood as "like a twig on the surface of the waters." The term *qeṣep* ("twig") is a *hapax legomenon* (*qeṣep* II; cf. *HALOT*, 1125). An alternative in the Targum, some ancient Greek versions, and the Vulgate is "foam" (NJPS; Andersen and Freedman, 558–59; Macintosh, 406–07). In this case, the word reflects the verb *qṣp*, "to be angry" or to "boil over with rage" (*qeṣep* I; cf. *HALOT*, 1124–25), with the thought that the monarchy will vanish as quickly as foam on the surface of the waters.

8 The passage closes with another announcement of the destruction of Israel's religious life. The "high places of wickedness" (some believe *ʾāwen*, "wickeness, iniquity," is shorthand for *bēt-ʾāwen*, or Bethel; cf. v.5a and NIV note) and the nation's unacceptable religious practices ("the sin of Israel") will be demolished. The "high places" (*bāmôt*) are cultic platforms that often had altars on them (J. A. Emerton, "The Biblical High Place in the Light of Recent Study," *PEQ* 129 [1997]: 116–32). Israel, that vine that had so much potential for good, is defective (v.1) and has brought forth weeds (v.4); now its infamous altars will be cursed with thorns and thistles (v.8; this vocabulary is drawn from Ge 3:18). Instead of the people's shouts of joy in ceremonies to other deities, with defeat will come the wretched call for an end to their misery (cf. Lk 23:30; Rev 6:16). Those words of anger and frustration (9:7b–8; 10:2–4) will change to cries of lament.

NOTE

6 The term עֶצָתוֹ (*ᶜᵃṣātô*) literally means "his counsel" (NASB, NJB, NJPS, NKJV; cf. *HALOT*, 866–67, ᶜṣh I). Based on Syriac and Arabic parallels, a few scholars translate it as "disobedience" (Stuart, 157, 162; עצה II, ᶜṣh II, *HALOT*, 867; cf. NEB). Others argue that the word is a feminine form of "tree" (cf. Jer 6:6; עצה III, ᶜṣh III; *HALOT*, 867) and a metonymy for a wooden idol (Andersen and Freedman, 558; Hubbard, 175; cf. NIV). Many English versions reflect the slight emendation of עֶצָתוֹ (*ᶜᵃṣātô*) to עַצַבּוֹ (*ᶜᵃṣabbô*, "his idol"; Mays, 138; *HALOT*, 865; cf. JB, NIV, NRSV, NLT, ESV).

c. A trained heifer (10:9–15)

> 9 "Since the days of Gibeah, you have sinned, O Israel,
>   and there you have remained.
> Did not war overtake
>   the evildoers in Gibeah?
> 10 When I please, I will punish them;
>   nations will be gathered against them
>   to put them in bonds for their double sin.
> 11 Ephraim is a trained heifer
>   that loves to thresh;
> so I will put a yoke
>   on her fair neck.
> I will drive Ephraim,
>   Judah must plow,
>   and Jacob must break up the ground.
> 12 Sow for yourselves righteousness,
>   reap the fruit of unfailing love,
> and break up your unplowed ground;
>   for it is time to seek the LORD,
> until he comes
>   and showers righteousness on you.
> 13 But you have planted wickedness,
>   you have reaped evil,
>   you have eaten the fruit of deception.

> Because you have depended on your own strength
>> and on your many warriors,
> ¹⁴the roar of battle will rise against your people,
>> so that all your fortresses will be devastated —
>> as Shalman devastated Beth Arbel on the day of battle,
>>> when mothers were dashed to the ground with their children.
> ¹⁵Thus will it happen to you, O Bethel,
>> because your wickedness is great.
> When that day dawns,
>> the king of Israel will be completely destroyed.

COMMENTARY

9–10 The offensive incident at Gibeah reappears (v.9; cf. 9:9). In the prophetic argument, the sins committed there (Jdg 19–21) were determinative for Israel's rebellious character. The syntax in the second half of the verse is awkward (specifically the use of the negative *lōʾ*). Even though an interrogative particle is lacking, the line could be taken as a rhetorical question (the English versions; cf. GKC §150a). It also could be an emphatic statement (asseverative *lōʾ*): "Surely war will overtake them in Gibeah" (Wolff, 178; Macintosh, 411). Both translations yield a similar sense: Sin (whether of the past or in the present) brings judgment. The punishment will come by the hand of the sovereign God, when he pleases (v.10). Once again, this punishment is described as an invasion. The referents for the double iniquity are impossible to identify.

11–13a The central metaphor of this section is that of Israel as a "trained heifer." The nation is likened to a healthy draft animal eager to plow the ground (v.11). In this picture, Yahweh is the farmer who yokes Israel and Judah, with the goal of sowing a proper relationship with him and its attendant ethical conduct (*ṣᵉdāqâ*) in order to enjoy the benefits of his unfailing love (*ḥesed*). This is God's desire for both kingdoms (for arguments that Judah is a later addition, see Emmerson, 83–86). That investment of righteousness will redound to them for their benefit (v.12). Instead, Israel is doing just the opposite: devoting itself to rebellion (v.13a).

13b–15 This passage focuses on one dimension of the nation's sin — its confidence in military power (v.13b; cf. Isa 31:1; Am 6:13). Because of its large armies, Israel trusts in its war policies (lit., "your way"; McComiskey, 180; Macintosh, 425). The result of that miscalculation will be horrendous devastation, and they will be no match for a mightier foe (v.14). The cruelty unleashed against women and children in warfare is mentioned many times in the OT, from the fear of Jacob about what his brother Esau might do (Ge 32:11) to the descriptions of the suffering in cities under siege (2Ki 6:24–31; La 2:19–21) and the indiscriminate killing at their fall (Jos 6:21; 1Sa 22:19; 2Ki 8:12).

As in v.10, the interpreter is confronted with a referent in v.14 that cannot be identified with certainty (Davies, 248–49; Macintosh, 429–30). The coming defeat is compared to the destruction of

Beth-Arbel by Shalman. Neither the place name nor the person is known to us. Many commentators believe that Shalman is a variant of Shalmaneser. The Assyrian Shalmaneser III (859–824 BC) may have attacked Israel during his campaign against Damascus in 838 BC. Shalmaneser V (726–722 BC) did come up against Hoshea (2Ki 17:3). A lesson to be learned from the past, not a contemporary event, more often than not is the means of persuasion and indictment in the book. Another option is that the referent is Salamanu, a king of Moab, who may have launched raids against Israel (cf. 2Ki 13:20; Am 2:1–3).

The final verse reunites religion and politics (v.15). The mention of Bethel and the king connect these verses to the first part of the chapter (vv.5–8 and vv.3, 7, respectively). Soon ("When that day dawns," NIV) that religious center of the nation and its political system together will meet their demise.

NOTES

10 At the beginning of the verse the MT has בְּאַוָּתִי (bᵉʾawwātî, "in my desire"), from the term אַוָּה (ʾawwâ; *HALOT*, 21; McComiskey, 172–73; Macintosh, 414; cf. NASB, NIV, NKJV, NJPS, ESV). Many commentators and English versions echo the LXX (ἦλθεν, "he came") and emend to בָּאתִי (bāʾtî, "I have come"), from בוא (bwʾ; Wolff, 178; Stuart, 166; cf. NEB, NRSV, NJB, NLT). Andersen and Freedman (565–66) propose בַּאֲתֹותִי (baʾᵃtôtî, "when I came"), the infinitive construct of אתה (ʾth; cf. *HALOT*, 102) plus the preposition בְּ (bᵉ).

Most English versions follow the Qere for עינתם (ʿyntm) in the second line to read "crimes" (cf. LXX). An alternative relates the word to מַעֲנָה (maʿᵃnâ, "furrow"; cf. *HALOT*, 615) and so continues the farming metaphor (Macintosh, 414–16; cf. NJPS, Tg.).

13b The most common meaning of דֶּרֶךְ (derek) is "way" (NASB, NJPS, NKJV, ESV). It also can be translated as "power," a fitting parallel to "your many warriors" of the next phrase (*HALOT*, 232; Hubbard, 183; Davies, 248; cf. NIV, NRSV, NLT). The LXX has "in your chariots" (ἐν τοῖς ἅρμασι), which is the equivalent of בְּרִכְבְּךָ (bᵉrikbᵉkā), an emendation followed by the RSV, NEB, NJB (Harper, 357; Wolff, 181, 187). A historical datum cited to buttress this view is that Israel was famed for its chariots (S. Dalley, "Foreign Chariotry and Calvary in the Armies of Tiglath-pileser III and Sargon II," *Iraq* 47 [1985]: 31–48).

d. A beloved child (11:1–11)

> ¹"When Israel was a child, I loved him,
>   and out of Egypt I called my son.
> ²But the more I called Israel,
>   the further they went from me.
> They sacrificed to the Baals
>   and they burned incense to images.

³It was I who taught Ephraim to walk,
  taking them by the arms;
but they did not realize
  it was I who healed them.

⁴I led them with cords of human kindness,
  with ties of love;
I lifted the yoke from their neck
  and bent down to feed them.
⁵"Will they not return to Egypt
  and will not Assyria rule over them
  because they refuse to repent?
⁶Swords will flash in their cities,
  will destroy the bars of their gates
  and put an end to their plans.
⁷My people are determined to turn from me.
  Even if they call to the Most High,
  he will by no means exalt them.

⁸"How can I give you up, Ephraim?
  How can I hand you over, Israel?
How can I treat you like Admah?
  How can I make you like Zeboiim?
My heart is changed within me;
  all my compassion is aroused.
⁹I will not carry out my fierce anger,
  nor will I turn and devastate Ephraim.
For I am God, and not man—
  the Holy One among you.
  I will not come in wrath.
¹⁰They will follow the Lord;
  he will roar like a lion.
When he roars,
  his children will come trembling from the west.
¹¹They will come trembling
  like birds from Egypt,
  like doves from Assyria.
I will settle them in their homes,"
  declares the Lord.

COMMENTARY

1 The metaphor for Israel now shifts from the farm to the family, with Yahweh as the father. The nation is called a "child" (*na⁽ar*) and "my son" (J. R. Melnyk, "When Israel Was a Child," in *History and Interpretation: Essays in Honour of John H. Hayes*, ed. M. P. Graham et al. [JSOTSup 173; Sheffield: Sheffield Academic Press, 1993], 245–59). Once again, an image goes back to Israel's early history (cf. 9:10; 10:1, 11). Here the reference is to the exodus (Ex 4:22–23; cf. Jer 3:19), when the special relationship between Yahweh and Israel began (12:9; 13:4). The two verbs "love" and "call" combine affection with election, so whatever happens to God's people affects him deeply.

Tragically, Israel is never said to love Yahweh; its affections have been directed to other deities (Kakkanattu, 33–40). This verse is evidence for the covenantal relationship between Israel and Yahweh (F. M. Cross, "Kinship and Covenant in Ancient Israel," in *From Epic to Canon: History and Literature in Ancient Israel*, ed. F. M. Cross [Baltimore: Johns Hopkins Univ. Press, 1998], 3–21). "Love" is central to Deuteronomy, where it also is connected with the liberation of Israel from Egypt (e.g., Dt 7:8–13).

Matthew 2:15 cites Hosea 11:1 as "fulfilled" in Jesus. How can this be, if the allusion in Hosea to the exodus is retrospective and not a prediction? The answer is that in the gospel of Matthew the life of Jesus recapitulates the history of Israel in many ways. For example, paralleling the movement from bondage to Sinai, Jesus comes out of Egypt (Mt 2), goes through the waters (of baptism; Mt 3), is tempted in the desert (forty days and nights; Mt 4), and then goes to a mountain to speak of the law (Mt 5–7). He is the true and ideal Israel. The prophet recognized that the exodus offered patterns: it was a symbol of exile (8:13; 9:3) as well as a type for future hope (11:10–11; cf. Isa 11:11–16; 51:9–11; Jer 23:7–8;

Mic 7:15). Matthew sees patterns in God's liberating initiative at the exodus, too; as God redeemed his people from Egypt long ago, he now was accomplishing a more glorious redemption through Jesus, the greater Son (C. Keener, *Matthew* [Grand Rapids: Eerdmans, 1999], 106–9; cf. Garrett, 220–22).

2 The Hebrew of the first line of this verse literally says, "They called to them; thus they went from them" (cf. Tg.). The lack of an identified subject and object makes understanding difficult. Many versions and commentators follow the LXX and change the verb to a first-person singular (e.g., NIV, NRSV; Stuart, 175). This offers more continuity with v.1. If the MT is maintained (my option), then those who called could be the prophets. God repeatedly sent the prophets to charge "them"—that is, his people—but Israel turned its back and "went away from them" (Keil, 137; McComiskey, 184). This interpretation agrees with other passages that deal with the role of the prophets in the history of the nation (6:5; 9:8; 12:10, 13). Others who accept the MT consider either the women at Baal Peor (Nu 25:1–3; Andersen and Freedman, 577–78; Hubbard, 187) or Israel (Garrett, 222–23; Macintosh, 440) as the ones calling and interpret the line in a different manner.

The second line is clear. Israel has persisted in faithlessness. Apostasy has reared its ugly head from the beginning (Ex 32; Nu 25), and the people continued sacrificing to the *b⁽ālîm* (4:13–14; 8:13) and burning incense to other images (2:13). The nation has been a disobedient son and now deserves punishment (cf. Dt 21:18–21). This metaphor is also employed by the prophet Isaiah (Isa 1:2–4; 30:1, 9).

3 The text returns to the image of Israel as a child (v.3), and the contrast with the preceding is emphatic (lit., "but I, I taught Ephraim"). Yahweh was committed to this people since early on. The call came at the exodus (v.1), and his guardianship manifested itself in the wilderness and continued through the centuries. He "healed" them, perhaps an allusion to sociopolitical protection, material provision, or spiritual forgiveness (Kakkanattu, 54–57). Sadly, Israel refused to acknowledge (once again the key verb *ydᶜ*) Yahweh's care.

4 The sense of gracious nurture continues. What is debated is whether the image shifts to an agricultural setting with the metaphor of Israel as an ox (cf. 4:16; 10:11) or whether the familial ambiance is maintained. If the former, the image is of Yahweh as the kind farmer, merciful in his yoking, using cords suitable for humans and lovingly providing for Israel (NASB, NIV, ESV; Stuart, 179; Macintosh, 445–49). I prefer the latter view (NEB, NJB, NRSV). The parent–child metaphor can be visualized either as a reference to God as a father who lifts up and carries the tired or frightened child (Dt 1:31) or as a picture of a loving mother guiding the little one in its very first steps (Yee, 277; H. Schüngel-Straumann, "God as Mother in Hosea 11," in Brenner, ed., 194–218). Perhaps it is better to use the label "parental" and avoid imposing gender categories on God (Kakkanattu, 57–63, 127–31). In any case, tenderness is the spirit of the verse.

5–6 The translation of the initial *lōʾ* is crucial for interpreting this verse. While it can be the negative particle "no, not" (NASB, NIV, ESV), it can also be taken as an asseverative (NEB, NRSV, NLT; Wolff, 192; Andersen and Freedman, 583–84): Israel will "surely" return to Egypt (i.e., go into exile; cf. 8:13; 9:3) and submit to the sovereignty of Assyria. There is a wordplay on the verb *šûb*: Israel will "return" to Egypt, because it has refused to "return" to God (5:4; 7:10, 16). This sin of rebellion means that the nation's cities will be destroyed. Whatever the political and military plans might have been, they will not succeed (v.6; cf. 10:6).

7 The indictment of the character of Israel continues. In spite of this coming disaster, Israel is committed to "turning" *from* Yahweh (*mᵉšûbâ*, from the root *šûb*), not to him in repentance. The last half of the verse is difficult but should be interpreted as consonant with the first part; therefore, it is best to take the meaning to be that even if the people do call to Yahweh, the "Most High" (for this meaning of *ᶜal*, see comment on 7:16), he will not come to their aid. It is too late to cry out; with their hardened heart any such plea will probably be hypocritical anyway (cf. 6:1–3). Judgment is well deserved and inescapable.

8–9 Yet the necessity of judgment does not mean that Yahweh has irrevocably set aside his people. The love God has had for them from the very beginning (v.1) stirs him now to lament with deep feelings of longing (v.8). This declaration is emphatic; it is repeated with synonyms (Ephraim, Israel), and the same structure is used to contrast this devotion to the judgment on Admah. Admah and Zeboiim were other cities of the plain destroyed with Sodom and Gomorrah (Dt 29:23). Their judgment, unlike Israel's, was total and final (cf. Isa 1:9). The emotive power of v.8 goes beyond the repeated exclamatory particle "how!" (*ʾêk*) to Yahweh's expressing that his "heart" is in turmoil (cf. La 1:20) and that "all my compassion is aroused" in its desire for Israel (NRSV, ESV; cf. Ge 43:30; 1Ki 3:26).

The next verse reiterates Yahweh's refusal to utterly destroy (*šḥt*) his people (v.9; cf. 13:9). His anger, though fierce (cf. 8:5), will not be given full reign. His is not the wrath of a human, who might seek revenge out of an extreme sense of betrayal. No, Yahweh is God. Judgment is not about exacting retribution; its ultimate aims are purification and restoration. The juxtaposition of vv.8–9 exemplifies the symbiotic connection between divine love and holiness, a theme that runs throughout the Scriptures and culminates in the cross of Christ.

The Holy One is active in the midst of his people. Yahweh is not a distant and disinterested god. Because of his foundational promises to Israel, Yahweh will not "come into a city" (NKJV; cf. LXX)—that is, the coming invasion will have its limits (Hubbard, 195−96; McComiskey, 192−93; Garrett, 228−29). Such restraint was not the case for Admah and Zeboiim.

10−11 These last verses anticipate the effect of God's grace on Israel, and they explicitly return to earlier material in the book. The metaphor for Yahweh shifts from the caring parent to a powerful lion. The setting also has changed. Whereas the prophetic word was predicting the coming of God's wrath in the form of an invasion and the subsequent exile to Assyria/Egypt, here that suffering is past; the people now return to the land.

In 5:14−15 the divine lion devoured the people in judgment (cf. 13:8). With that judgment over, Yahweh roars in regal power, and the nation will respond. Israel, once described as a silly dove that flitted to and fro between Egypt and Assyria, will come from their dispersion (7:11; cf. 9:3). The One who punished and sent them away will settle them in peace to begin life anew with him.

Thus, this long section (4:1−11:11) closes with words of hope, as did 1:2−3:5. Judgment is not the end; its goal of restoring the covenantal communion between God and his people will someday be achieved. The formula "declares the LORD" (*nᵉʾum yhwh*) signals the conclusion.

NOTES

4 The parent−child view opts for the translation, "I had lifted them up as an infant to my cheek," which is based on the emendation of עֹל (ʿōl, "yoke") to עוּל (ʿûl, "infant"). See Kakkanattu, 20−22.

9 Few English versions follow the MT's לֹא אָבוֹא בְּעִיר (lōʾ ʾābôʾ bᵉʿîr, "I will not enter into a city"). Most commentators and versions translate עִיר (ʿîr) as "anger" instead of "city" (עִיר II, ʿîr II; cf. HALOT, 822); thus בְּעִיר (bᵉʿîr) would mean "in anger" (Keil, 142; Wolff, 193; Davies, 264; cf. NASB, NJB, NIV, NRSV, ESV). The only other place in the OT where the term has this meaning is in Jeremiah 15:8. Some scholars emend the text in various ways with the verb בער (bᵉr, "to burn"): לֹא אֲבַעֵר (lōʾ ᵃbāʿēr, "I will not burn"); לֹא אָבוֹא לְבַעֵר (lōʾ ʾābôʾ lᵉbāʿēr, "I will not come to burn"); לֹא אוֹבֶה לְבָעֵר (lōʾ ʾôbeh lᵉbāʿēr, "I am not willing to burn"). For this option, see the JB (Mays, 151).

IV. THE ANNOUNCEMENT OF JUDGMENT AND THE PROMISE OF RESTORATION, PART TWO (11:12−14:8[12:1−14:9])

OVERVIEW

The last section of the book powerfully depicts the judgment that is coming and the blessings that will ultimately be enjoyed by God's people. Passages appeal to the traditions of Israel and use a wide range of images to express both divine wrath and love. The book climaxes with words of hope that underscore Yahweh's deepest yearnings. The final verse challenges the reader to learn from the prophetic message and the experiences of Israel.

A. Lessons from History (11:12–13:16[12:1–14:1])

1. The Indictment of Israel and Judah (11:12–12:2[12:1–3])

¹²Ephraim has surrounded me with lies,
  the house of Israel with deceit.
And Judah is unruly against God,
  even against the faithful Holy One.
^{12:1}Ephraim feeds on the wind;
  he pursues the east wind all day
  and multiplies lies and violence.
He makes a treaty with Assyria
  and sends olive oil to Egypt.
²The LORD has a charge to bring against Judah;
  he will punish Jacob according to his ways
  and repay him according to his deeds.

COMMENTARY

12 [12:1] Hosea 11:12–12:14 present an interpretive challenge. This section is full of ambiguity and tantalizing allusions; there are a number of wordplays, which strengthen its unity and connect it to other passages in the book (e.g., R. B. Coote, "Hosea xii," *VT* 21 (1971): 389–402; Landy, 145–55). Not surprisingly, there are many disagreements among commentators as to the meaning and tone of these verses.

The difficulties begin with 11:12. It is necessary to decide whether it belongs conceptually with ch. 11, whether the message of 11:11 extends through 12:1 (NEB, NRSV), or whether 11:12 more appropriately goes with what follows (e.g., NIV). This commentary concurs with the last option; 11:11 ends with "declares the LORD," closing the major section that stretches from 4:1 through that verse. Clearly, the MT reckoned 11:11 to be a conclusion, as it is followed by the paragraph marker *sāmek*.

Hosea 11:12–12:2 serves as a general introductory indictment for which the following verses provide details. These verses could communicate the words of either Yahweh or the prophet. The fact that 12:1–8 uses third-person references for God inclines me to the latter option, but the message remains the same: "Lies" (*kaḥaš*; 7:3; cf. 7:13) and "deceit" (*mirmâ*; 12:8) are the order of the day and in evidence everywhere ("have surrounded me").

The second half of the verse is an interpretive crux. Many argue that "Judah" is a gloss (e.g., Macintosh 473, 476), but eliminating the southern kingdom contradicts other passages that condemn both nations (5:5, 10, 12, 14; 6:4, 11; 8:14; 10:11). Much of the difficulty in understanding the verse lies in ascertaining the meaning of the phrase *rād ʿim*. The verb is from the root *rwd*, "to roam about freely" (GK 8113; *HALOT*, 1194). Some interpreters take a positive slant and believe that the intent, as in 1:7, is to contrast Judah's faithfulness with Israel's apostasy ("walks with," NRSV, ESV; Wolff, 210; McComiskey, 197–98; cf. Tg.). I take the verb in a negative sense ("is unruly against," NASB, NIV; Keil, 144–45; Stuart, 185; cf. Jer 2:31). The condemnation of Judah parallels that of Israel.

Another exegetical decision concerns the identity of the objects of the verb. The word ʾēl could refer to Yahweh or to the Canaanite high god; qᵉdôšîm can be translated as "the Holy One" (a plural of majesty; cf. GKC §124h; Pr 9:10; 30:3) or be taken as an allusion to other gods or the divine court of ʾēl ("the holy ones"; Andersen and Freedman, 603; Hubbard, 199–200). Both ʾēl and qādôš (singular form) are used of Yahweh in 11:9. Consistency compels me to see correspondence here as well. Judah has squirmed under the sovereignty of God, even as the northern kingdom is corrupt to the core.

12:1 [2] The previous verse struck at the religious rebellion of Israel. This verse, as is common in the book, weds that indictment with the condemnation of foreign policy. Israel sins by making alliances ("treaty"; lit., "covenant") with other nations and by not trusting Yahweh for guidance and protection (5:13; 7:11; 8:9). The vacillation between Assyria and Egypt likely refers to the policies of King Hoshea, who withheld tribute from Assyria during Shalmaneser V's reign and later appealed to Egypt for help against that empire (725 BC; cf. 2Ki 17:4). Israel was known as an exporter of oil, a commodity not grown in Egypt, so perhaps Hoshea negotiated with export goods. But Israel's foolishness is like trying to control the powerful eastern winds (the sirocco)—an impossible task. These decisions are grounded in "lies" and will increase "violence" (in the form of an invasion).

2 [3] A conjunction connects this verse with the preceding (lit., "and a rîb"). The charge that Yahweh brings follows from those sins. As at 2:2 and 4:1, the term rîb (GK 8190) does not indicate a formal covenantal lawsuit, even though some scholars argue to the contrary (Mays, 161–62; Stuart, 190). Even if the literary form is not present, the indictment is clear. God condemns his people for sin and decrees judgment.

Many scholars believe that a redactor supplanted "Israel" with "Judah" in order to apply the prophet's warning to a later time (Macintosh, 479–80; cf. JB). This emendation is uncalled for, however, especially if "Judah" in 11:12 is authentic. The passage is comprehensive in its criticism of both kingdoms, as expressed in an alternating pattern (Ephraim/Judah, 11:12; Ephraim/Judah, 12:1–2). Both nations will be punished "according to his deeds." (Note the similar vocabulary in 4:9.)

The choice of the eponym "Jacob" presents a fascinating literary ambiguity. It can represent either Israel (and thus be a fitting parallel to Judah) or both nations together (thus serving as an appropriate closing, wide-ranging term for all the people of God in 11:12–12:2). In other words, "Jacob" is, at once, particular and inclusive. The name also functions as a transition to the next passage, which repeatedly appeals to the patriarch.

NOTE

12[12:1] The LXX misunderstood רָד (rād) as from the root יָדַע (ydᶜ, "to know"): νῦν ἔγνω αὐτοὺς ὁ θεός ("now God knows them"; cf. RSV, JB). Another issue is the syntactical significance of נֶאֱמָן (neʾᵉmān, Niphal masculine singular participle of אָמַן, ʾmn). It can be construed as a finite verb with Judah as the subject ("is faithful to"; NJB, NRSV, NJPS, ESV) or in an adjectival sense in reference to God ("the faithful Holy One"; NASB, NIV, NKJV). The latter option is congruent with my interpretation.

2. The Positive Example of Jacob (12:3–14[4–15])

OVERVIEW

This passage contains several allusions to the Jacob traditions (Ge 25–35), although they are not in strict canonical sequence. Scholars disagree about whether they have a positive or negative intent in the prophetic argument. If Jacob is a negative example, then the nation must not imitate the scheming, stubborn patriarch (Wolff, 218; Hubbard, 205; M. Fishbane, *Biblical Interpretation in Ancient Israel* [Oxford: Clarendon, 1985], 376–78).

If the purpose is positive, then Jacob is an example worth emulating (Stuart, 190–91; McComiskey, 202–3; Sweeney, 120, 127–28; P. R. Ackroyd, "Hosea and Jacob," *VT* 13 [1963]: 245–59; E. K. Holt, *Prophesying the Past: The Use of Israel's History in the Book of Hosea* [JSOTSup 194; Sheffield: Sheffield Academic Press, 1995], 30–51). The language of the passage leads us to favor the more affirmative interpretation.

³ In the womb he grasped his brother's heel;
    as a man he struggled with God.
⁴ He struggled with the angel and overcame him;
    he wept and begged for his favor.
He found him at Bethel
    and talked with him there —
⁵ the Lord God Almighty,
    the Lord is his name of renown!
⁶ But you must return to your God;
    maintain love and justice,
    and wait for your God always.

⁷ The merchant uses dishonest scales;
    he loves to defraud.
⁸ Ephraim boasts,
    "I am very rich; I have become wealthy.
With all my wealth they will not find in me
    any iniquity or sin."

⁹ "I am the Lord your God,
    ᴸwho brought youᴶ out of Egypt;
I will make you live in tents again,
    as in the days of your appointed feasts.

¹⁰I spoke to the prophets,
  gave them many visions
  and told parables through them."

¹¹Is Gilead wicked?
  Its people are worthless!
  Do they sacrifice bulls in Gilgal?
  Their altars will be like piles of stones
    on a plowed field.
¹²Jacob fled to the country of Aram;
  Israel served to get a wife,
  and to pay for her he tended sheep.
¹³The LORD used a prophet to bring Israel up from Egypt,
  by a prophet he cared for him.
¹⁴But Ephraim has bitterly provoked him to anger;
  his Lord will leave upon him the guilt of his bloodshed
  and will repay him for his contempt.

COMMENTARY

3–4 [4–5] The incidents in the life of Jacob that are referred to, in order, are: his grasping the heel of Esau in the womb (Ge 25:26); the struggle at Penuel (32:22–32); weeping at seeing Esau (33:3–4, 8, 10, with some believing the weeping to be a Hoseanic expansion of the incident at the Jabbok in Ge 32 or a reference to a story unknown to us); and Jacob's encounter with God at Bethel (28:10–22, and possibly 35:6–15). The movement from Jacob's birth to the wrestling at the river's edge to the emotional reunion with Esau to the dream at Bethel has as its goal to trace the transformation in Jacob. At Bethel he met God and was changed. This event is the theological climax of the allusions, even though they break with the order of the Genesis narrative. The message is that the great, but flawed, patriarch became a broken man before God.

At least three textual issues in v.4b concerning the Bethel episode are worthy of mention. First, there is a change in subject from the patriarch to Yahweh: It is God who finds Jacob and speaks. Second, unlike other instances in the book, where Beth-Aven ("House of Iniquity"; 4:15; 5:8; 10:5) appears, the true name of the sanctuary is maintained, probably because Jacob's meeting with Yahweh is reckoned as good, in contrast to the religious activities there that are condemned in the book. Third, the suffix on ʿimmānû can be translated as a third-person singular ("with him"; NEB, NIV, NRSV) or as a first-person plural ("with us"; NASB, NJB, ESV). The latter possibility is significant. The text would be saying that, according to the principle of corporate identity, the present people of God were at that meeting with Yahweh centuries before and heard his voice. Thus the connection to Jacob is made more direct, and the lessons to be learned from these traditions become yet more unavoidable. It is difficult to know whether this ambiguity is deliberate.

5 [6] Fittingly, this verse follows the Bethel reference with a doxology to confront the people with the person of their God. The name "the LORD God Almighty" (NIV; or "the LORD God of hosts") does not appear in Genesis, but this epithet of power and sovereignty underscores that this confrontation is the point of the appeal to those ancient narratives. Amos, Hosea's contemporary, used the epithet repeatedly in his own condemnation of Israel (Am 3:13; 4:13; 5:14–16, 27; 6:8, 14; 9:5; cf. Isa 6:3, 5). Yahweh should not be forgotten. The chastised Jacob saw him and was transformed. Will Israel follow his example?

6 [7] The nation is addressed straightforwardly and emphatically. (Note the use of the personal pronoun "you" [NRSV, ESV].) The demand for "love" and "justice" echoes earlier passages (2:19; 4:1). A surprising twist concerns Israel's "turn/return" (*šûb*)—Hosea's term for repentance—to Yahweh. Its present impossibility has been patently obvious (5:4; 6:1; 7:10, 16; 11:7), but still there was hope of future penitence (3:5; 14:1–2). What is new is that this summons is coupled with the promise of divine assistance, which will enable Israel to do what it cannot (and will not) do on its own. Many English versions translate the preposition *bᵉ* as "to" ("to God" in NASB, NRSV, NIV), but it is more properly taken as *beth instrumenti*: Israel can return "with the help of" God (NJB, NEB, ESV; cf. GKC §119o, W–O §11.2.5d). With his help, fickle Israel can be changed into a steadfast people, willing to wait on him. This wording may be a reminder of the words spoken to Jacob in Genesis 28:15; if so, it brings literary closure to this Jacob series.

7–8 [8–9] The Israel of the prophet's era, however, has its eyes on material gain. Surely, this fact is one of the motivations for the political decisions that are leading the nation to its ruin. The merchant (lit., "Canaanite"; cf. *HALOT*, 485) uses scales "of deceit." "Deceit" (*mirmâ*) recalls 11:12;

that character trait is here given a concrete illustration. In an agricultural economy, where much commerce took place in local markets, dishonest scales had no place (cf. Pr 11:1; 20:23; Am 8:5; Mic 6:11). Instead of loving Yahweh, this economic class "loves to oppress" (cf. Isa 30:12; Am 4:1; Mic 2:2). Greed and the lust for fortune, no matter the human cost, drive the economically powerful. The denunciation of socioeconomic sin is not as prominent as in the other eighth-century prophets—Amos, Isaiah, and Micah. Hosea's attention focuses instead on foreign policy and syncretism. All these prophets, though, condemn the inseparableness of the public square and faith in Yahweh.

Pride toward others and contempt for the things of God permeate national life (v.8). What is said testifies to this arrogance. This verse is rich in wordplays. "I have *found* wealth" (lit.) and "they will not *find* in me" stand in stark contrast to "He [God] *found* him [Jacob] at Bethel" in v.4b. They believe that "wealth" (*ʾôn*) secures an escape from divine judgment on "iniquity" (*ʿāwōn*); *ʾôn* also appears in v.3, where it is translated with phrases such as "as a man" (NIV) or "in his maturity" (cf. *HALOT*, 22; NASB, NJB). This wordplay links back to the Jacob traditions cited earlier and underlines the disparity between what the patriarch became and what Israel is actually like.

9–10 [10–11] In response to the confident assertions of Israel, God proclaims (lit.), "I am Yahweh your God from the land of Egypt" (cf. NASB, NJB, NRSV, ESV). This statement is not a reference to the exodus (contra NIV, NLT; Garrett, 243; cf. Tg.); rather, it affirms that Yahweh has been their God from the beginning of their existence as a nation, since Egypt. He has been constant over the centuries. This line is repeated in 13:4.

God will strip the Israelites of their self-assurance by (figuratively) putting them back in the wilderness ("in tents"), where they suffered deprivation and had to depend on him for everything. The words (lit.) "as in the days of the feast" have been understood in several ways. Some interpret *mōʿēd* ("feast") more generically as "meeting" and see this phrase as a reference to God's first encounter with Israel in the desert (Wolff, 215); others emend to *mēʿād* ("of old"; NEB, NJPS; cf. Tg.). I assume the term's more common meaning, an appointed feast (not "feasts," contra NIV), probably the Feast of Tabernacles, which commemorated the people's sojourn in the desert (cf. 9:5; 2:11; Lev 23:33–44).

Because this festival celebrated the care of God and because in 2:14 and 9:10 the wilderness is a positive symbol, commentators see this statement as a promise to offset the negative tone of the preceding clause. That is, though there will be rough times ahead, God will not abandon Israel (McComiskey, 206; Macintosh, 500–501). More commensurate with the rest of this section, however, is that Yahweh decrees that the living conditions of that memorial feast now will typify their circumstances (Mays, 168; Stuart, 193–94).

To this allusion to the Feast of Tabernacles God adds the "prophets" (v.10). Yahweh had been their God "from Egypt," and the commissioning of prophets was the process by which his divine will had been made known (cf. 6:5; 9:7–8). Yahweh says that he spoke in parables through them (Piel of *dmh* I; cf. *HALOT*, 225)—perhaps explaining the difficulty in grasping Hosea's complex imagery and thought!

11 [12] Gilead (6:8) and Gilgal (4:15; 9:15) have appeared in earlier passages, where they are described as wicked places. The syntax of the Gilead and Gilgal clauses (an initial *ʾim*) can be reckoned as conditional (ESV), interrogative (NEB, NASB, NJB, NIV), or emphatic (JB, NRSV, NJPS). The last option seems best here (cf. GKC §149e; Hubbard, 209). Yahweh continues his diatribe against Israel. Their religion is rejected; its centers

are nothing but a heap of stones. Puns continue to be a central stylistic technique. Gilead (*gilʿād*), Gilgal (*gilgāl*), and stones (*gallîm*) comprise an example of the punning in this section.

12–13 [13–14] Jacob once more takes center stage. The interpretation of these two verses depends on how the tenor of the earlier appeals to tradition is understood. If Jacob's actions and his person are to be criticized, this reference to his flight to Aram and toil under Laban (Ge 27:42–45; 29:15–30) are further examples of disobedience and conniving. If the assessment of Jacob is more positive—the stance taken in this commentary—then these verses present another case of the patriarch's being molded in a constructive direction within a difficult situation. Out of his love for Rachel, he worked for years to secure her as his wife.

The repetition of the verb *šmr* joins v.12 ("he tended [sheep]") to v.13 ("he [Yahweh] cared for"). Once again, the view taken of the Jacob reference is determinative. If the patriarch stands as a negative lesson, the "prophet"—most likely Moses—serves to contrast his behavior with Yahweh's providential provision. My approach, however, likens the dedication of the humbled patriarch to God's care as instances of grace. Moses was the prophet par excellence (Dt 18:15–19). He was the first of the prophets sent to Israel over these many years (cf. v.10). Now Hosea is another in that line. Will the nation respond to Yahweh through this prophet? Can they be transformed as dramatically as Jacob and receive God's blessing?

14 [15] This verse makes it clear that there is no chance for change in Ephraim. The lessons from Jacob's life and other incidents of the past have no effect on Israel. It has "bitterly [*tamrûrîm*, abstract plural of intensity, GKC §124d] provoked" Yahweh (cf. Dt 4:25–26). To this transgression is added the sin of "contempt" (*ḥerpâ*), possibly disdain for the true God and his demands (NIV, NRSV, NJPS;

Stuart, 196; Davies, 284). These descriptions reveal how deeply rooted is rebellion in the heart of the people (cf. "a spirit of prostitution" in 4:12; 5:4). Their crimes bring bloodguilt (*dāmîm*, "bloods"; cf. *HALOT*, 225). That is, their sins are worthy of the death penalty (cf. Lev 20)—in this case, destruction in warfare, which will come at the hand of Israel's divine Master (*ʾᵃdōnāy*).

NOTES

3[4] The verb "grasp the heel" or "supplant" is a denominative from עָקֵב (*ʿāqēb*, "heel"; cf. *HALOT*, 872–73). It is a pun on the name Jacob (יַעֲקֹב, *yaʿᵃqōb*; Ge 25:26; 27:36). The verb in the next clause, "strive," is שָׂרָה (*śārâ*), which the Genesis account uses to explain the etiology of the name "Israel" (יִשְׂרָאֵל, *yiśrāʾēl*; Ge 32:28; *HALOT*, 1354).

10[11] There is a possible double entendre with the homonym roots דמה I (*dmh* I, "be like, resemble": "I told parables"; cf. *HALOT*, 225; e.g., NASB, NJB, NIV) and דמה III (*dmh* III, "destroy"; cf. *HALOT*, 225–26; NRSV), which appears in 4:6; 10:7, 15.

12–13[13–14] At first glance, the mixing of allusions and reproof appears confused. Some scholars suggest putting the chapter into what they consider a more logical order (e.g., Harper, 373–74). A literary appreciation recognizes a pattern of alternating tradition (vv.3–4, 9–10, 12–13) with exhortation or condemnation (vv.5–8, 11, 14).

14[15] As in 1:4, דָּמִים (*dāmîm*) also can mean "bloodshed" (*HALOT*, 224). If that is the case, then this verse is an indictment of violence (1:4; 4:2; 6:8–9) and not an expression of judgment (Hubbard, 221; cf. NJB). Many commentators understand חֶרְפָּה (*ḥerpâ*) to be the "reproach" or shame brought upon God because of Israel's rebellion, instead of the attitude of the nation toward him (Wolff, 217; Hubbard, 221; Macintosh, 514; cf. RSV, NASB).

3. The Grace of God at the Exodus and in the Wilderness (13:1–8)

¹When Ephraim spoke, men trembled;
    he was exalted in Israel.
    But he became guilty of Baal worship and died.
²Now they sin more and more;
    they make idols for themselves from their silver,
   cleverly fashioned images,
    all of them the work of craftsmen.
   It is said of these people,
    "They offer human sacrifice
    and kiss the calf-idols."
³Therefore they will be like the morning mist,
    like the early dew that disappears,

like chaff swirling from a threshing floor,
　　like smoke escaping through a window.

[4]"But I am the LORD your God,
　　⌊who brought you⌋ out of Egypt.
You shall acknowledge no God but me,
　　no Savior except me.
[5]I cared for you in the desert,
　　in the land of burning heat.
[6]When I fed them, they were satisfied;
　　when they were satisfied, they became proud;
　　then they forgot me.
[7]So I will come upon them like a lion,
　　like a leopard I will lurk by the path.
[8]Like a bear robbed of her cubs,
　　I will attack them and rip them open.
Like a lion I will devour them;
　　a wild animal will tear them apart.

COMMENTARY

1 This verse returns to the past. Ephraim quickly established itself as one of the most powerful tribes, and that standing became a political reality when the northern tribes separated themselves from Judah and Benjamin and established a separate kingdom (1Ki 12). Israel often was stronger than Judah, so its political and military preeminence might be the exaltation that is meant here. The word usually translated as "tremble" (*reṭēt*) in the English versions is a *hapax legomenon*. (For a survey of views, see Macintosh, 518–19.)

Jeroboam I exploited religion for political expediency and incurred guilt on Israel (1Ki 12–13). His actions marked the country's leadership and citizenry until the end (2Ki 17:22). Under Queen Jezebel the worship of *baʿal* gained official sanction and support. Israel's "death" was its judgments, most dramatically executed in the drought that led to the confrontation on Mount Carmel (1Ki 17–18) and in Jehu's bloody coup (2Ki 9–10).

2 The text abruptly shifts to the present ("and now"). Israel's unacceptable worship (and, consequently, national life) continues in the historic sin. Full certainty, though, concerning what is being condemned is complicated by textual difficulties in the last line.

First, Israel is reviled for making molten images (*massēkâ*) and idols (*ʿaṣabbîm*). The former term is used of the golden calf in the exodus–wilderness tradition (Ex 32:4, 8; Dt 9:16; cf. Lev 19:4; Ex 34:17); interestingly, "calves" appears at the end of this verse (cf. 8:5; 10:5). Hosea denounces the making of idols elsewhere (8:4, 6; 12:11). The accusation is made more emphatic by mentioning that these images, "all of them," are made with precious metals by craftsmen.

What follows has generated many conjectures (see Notes). Questions include: Who is speaking and to whom? What sacrifices are meant? It seems best to assume continuity with the preceding censure of idol worship. This logic yields the following sense: They (i.e., those who venerate idols) say of them (i.e., of the idols), "The men [or, people] who worship kiss calves." Kissing the image of the deity evidently was part of *ba'al* ritual (1Ki 19:18). What we have, then, is a quotation of the people that reveals their involvement in these activities (Macintosh, 522–24). As on other occasions when Hosea cites the words of others, their speech serves to condemn them (cf. 6:1–3; 9:7–8)—a tactic Amos also employs to good effect (Am 4:1; 6:13; 7:10–13, 16; 9:10).

Some see an allusion to human sacrifice here (cf. 9:13). The most obvious challenge with this view is to explain why such a heinous sin is cited in such an oblique manner and only in this passage. Child sacrifice (though the reference in this verse is to "men") is always roundly condemned (e.g., 2Ki 23:10; Jer 32:35; Eze 23:37; see Notes).

3 Because of its idolatry, the nation has no future. It will pass away. The ephemeral nature of Israel's existence is described using four metaphors: morning mist, dew, chaff, and smoke. The first two also appear in 6:4, where they portray the shallow commitment of Israel toward God. In 14:5 the metaphor of dew has a different connotation. There God's love is as refreshing as the dew. The chaff (e.g., Isa 17:13; 41:15) and smoke (Isa 51:6) are symbols of transitoriness.

4 The first line repeats 12:9 (see comments). In this context, it serves to contrast what has been said of Israel with Yahweh's constancy. He has always been with them, and he has always been the same. The fact that Yahweh alone has been Israel's God means that they should know that there is no other whom they should obey or to whom they must

turn. This conviction (and demand!) is foundational to the covenantal relationship and is fundamental to the Ten Commandments (Ex 20:2–3; Dt 5:6–7). The belief that Yahweh alone can save Israel has enormous implications for national foreign policy. Instead, political leaders are turning to Assyria and Egypt for help instead of trusting him (see esp. 14:3).

5–6 The opening line of v.5 contrasts Yahweh and Israel by the repetition of the verb "know" (RSV, NKJV, ESV). He "knew" them from the earliest and difficult days in the desert, an allusion to their election (cf. 9:10), and he shepherded them there (v.6a); Israel should have "known" that Yahweh was their gracious provider (v.4). This is the last occurrence of "to know," a key term throughout the book of Hosea (see "Religion and Theology in Hosea" in the introduction).

Ideally, Israel's and Yahweh's knowing would have mirrored and complemented each other. The proper response always and now at this crucial juncture in history should have been gratitude and devotion to the one true God. But provision brought pride and satisfaction self-reliance (v.6). This danger of arrogant forgetfulness is a recurring theme in Deuteronomy (e.g., Dt 6:10–12; 8:7–14; 31:20; 32:15–18).

7–8 If v.3 assembled four metaphors to describe how perilous was Israel's future, these two verses use five metaphors to underscore the power and ferociousness of Yahweh in his judgment. He will be like a lion (*šāḥal*; cf. 5:14–15), a leopard, a bear, a lion (*lābî'*), and a wild beast. These animals are the kinds that attacked flocks in the countryside. In other words, no longer the protective shepherd of v.6, Yahweh comes against his people. The verbs are equally robust: lurk, attack, tear open, devour, and mangle.

The violence of these images must surely have shocked the prophet's audience and stagger the modern reader. The goal of these images is to push God's people to come to grips with the awfulness of divine judgment. These characterizations round out the other kinds of metaphors in the book that stress his love and care. The aggression announced here will come in the form of the Assyrian invasion and the destruction of the nation. Similar beasts appear in Daniel 7:1–8 (cf. Rev 13:1–2).

NOTES

2 In the last line the MT has the construct "sacrifices of men." If one takes this construction as an objective genitive, then the reference is to human sacrifice (Wolff, 219, 225; Andersen and Freedman, 632; Hubbard, 215; cf. NEB, NIV, ESV). The alternative, and my choice, is that the construction is a subjective genitive: this is what people do (McComiskey, 214; Macintosh, 523; cf. NASB, NJPS, NIV note, NKJV). Another option is to repoint זֹבְחֵי (*zōbᵉḥê*, "sacrifices of") as זִבְחוּ (*zibḥû*), a masculine plural imperative (cf. LXX), thus breaking up the construct, and "men" now is placed with the following: "men kiss calves" (Davies, 287; Garrett, 248–50; cf. NJB, NRSV, NLT).

5 Many commentators (e.g., Wolff, 220; Mays, 175) and versions (e.g., NASB, NIV, NRSV; cf. LXX, Tg.) emend יְדַעְתִּיךָ (*yᵉdaᶜtîkā*, "I knew you") to רְעִיתִיךָ (*rᵉᶜîtîkā*, "I took care of you" or "shepherded you"). This change serves as a nice transition to the next verse but misses the wordplay with the verb "know" in v.4.

4. The Rise and Fall of the Monarchy (13:9–16[13:9–14:1])

9 "You are destroyed, O Israel,
  because you are against me, against your helper.
10 Where is your king, that he may save you?
  Where are your rulers in all your towns,
 of whom you said,
  'Give me a king and princes'?
11 So in my anger I gave you a king,
  and in my wrath I took him away.
12 The guilt of Ephraim is stored up,
  his sins are kept on record.
13 Pains as of a woman in childbirth come to him,
  but he is a child without wisdom;
 when the time arrives,
  he does not come to the opening of the womb.

14 "I will ransom them from the power of the grave;
  I will redeem them from death.

> Where, O death, are your plagues?
>> Where, O grave, is your destruction?
> "I will have no compassion,
> 15 even though he thrives among his brothers.
> An east wind from the LORD will come,
>> blowing in from the desert;
> his spring will fail
>> and his well dry up.
> His storehouse will be plundered
>> of all its treasures.
> 16 The people of Samaria must bear their guilt,
>> because they have rebelled against their God.
> They will fall by the sword;
>> their little ones will be dashed to the ground,
>> their pregnant women ripped open."

COMMENTARY

9 This passage condemns the disastrous politics of Israel. It opens by declaring that Yahweh will "destroy" the nation (for the verb *šḥt*, see 11:9). This idea goes hand in hand with the preceding depiction of him as a devouring animal. Israel has been "against me, against your helper" (NIV, ESV). It has defied the One who rescued them in the past, the only one in the present crisis who can reverse their fortunes. As Israel's "helper" (*ʿēzer*), Yahweh came to the people's aid in mighty ways, and this fact became a basis for supplication and celebration (Dt 33:7; Pss 115:9–11; 121:1–2; 124:8; cf. 1Sa 7:12). If he is spurned, there is now no one left in whom to trust.

10–11 The target of Yahweh's scorn is Israel's government, its king and officials (lit., "judges"; cf. 3:4–5; 5:1; 7:3–7, 16; 8:4; 9:15). Where are those who are supposed to "save" the people in "all your towns" (v.10)? Clearly, the answer to this sarcastic question must be, "Nowhere." God, not the nation's

incapable and weak leaders, is in control of history and the events unfolding before them. He alone is their Savior (v.4). A possible wordplay between "save" (the root *yšʿ*) and Hoshea (*hôšēaʿ*), Israel's last king, underscores this divine disdain.

The nation has continued to follow the pattern of choosing kings who do not please God. Their incredulous spirit is evident from the very birth of the monarchy. At that time, Yahweh gave them Saul (v.11; cf. 1Sa 8). Moreover, the northern kingdom began with a lack of faith and now will fall because of rebellion. The last decades of its existence were a sad spectacle of political chicanery and ambition, a debilitating series of assassinations and poor policy decisions. Hoshea was the last in that line. In his sovereign judgment, Yahweh will now terminate Israel's royal establishment.

12–13 The judgment on Israel is presented in two metaphors, neither of which is easy to decipher. The first apparently likens its "iniquity"

($^{ca}w\bar{o}n$) to something that is stored up until a future day (v. 12). The term "iniquity" can refer to a transgression, the guilt due for it, or the punishment it incurs (cf. *HALOT*, 800); the choice of its significance determines the trope's meaning. One option is that Israel treasures up its sin (Hubbard, 220) or, more concretely, its idols (Andersen and Freedman, 637–38). Another possibility, and the one preferred here, since it coincides with the tenor of the surrounding lines, is that Israel's punishment has been recorded and sealed as on a scroll; it is like a legal document that is preserved. God will not forget what Israel has done (8:13; 9:9); the penalty must be paid (Wolff, 227–28; Mays, 180).

The second metaphor refers to childbirth (v. 13). Interestingly, the labor pains are ascribed to the masculine Ephraim (the mixing of gender recalls 9:1). This vivid image is utilized by other prophets to portray the suffering of national defeat (e.g., Isa 26:17; Jer 4:31; Mic 4:9–10). How does the notion of an unwise son relate to the childbirth metaphor? And what is the meaning of the last line of the verse? As many commentators progress through the verse, they switch the comparison from a woman in labor to the fetus (the foolish child) who is not able, or willing, to be born (cf. 2Ki 19:3). That is, Israel is both mother and child (Mays, 180; Landy, 164–65).

A better interpretation, however, maintains continuity of reference. The picture throughout is of an agonizing birthing process that never comes to fruition. It is symbolic of the prolonged torment that awaits Israel (Macintosh, 543–45). The unwise son clause is a parenthetical statement that explains why: The nation, the son of Yahweh (cf. 11:1), does not exhibit the godly wisdom that would have generated proper moral behavior, religious discernment, and political prudence.

14 The two clauses of the opening line can be construed as statements or promises of divine redemption, with the next line possessing two rhetorical questions expressing that same pledge in the form of a taunt of death and Sheol (NIV, NJPS, NKJV; Garrett, 264; cf. LXX). God's plans cannot be thwarted by the destruction coming with the imminent war. The last line is an important reminder that the hope of national restoration does not eliminate the inevitability of judgment; rather, it assures Israel that punishment is neither Yahweh's final dealing with Israel nor the voiding of their covenantal relationship. The juxtaposition of judgment and promise is found elsewhere in the book (e.g., 1:4–2:1; 3:1–5).

Many scholars take the first two clauses as questions, syntactically constructed without an interrogative particle (cf. GKC §150a; e.g., NASB, NRSV, ESV). In this case, the tenor of the questions depends on how the rest of the verse is understood. If the message is taken as consistently negative, then what follows is a summons to death to wreak its havoc. The final sentence, "compassion is hidden from my eyes," would confirm that sentiment (NEB; Stuart, 207; Hubbard, 222). If, however, the questions expect a positive answer, the interpretation approximates the option stated above.

Another attractive option is that these sentences are four questions, all of which reveal the torment in the mind of God. He wrestles with his love for Israel and the necessity of judgment (cf. 6:4; 11:8). They are, in other words, questions without answers. In the end, however, Yahweh recognizes that wrath must come; compassion cannot void the judgment. The nation cannot evade ruin (Macintosh, 547–49; cf. Hubbard, 222).

In 1 Corinthians 15:54–55 Paul quotes this line in conjunction with Isaiah 25:8 (both with modifications). He declares that the resurrection of Jesus assures the resurrection of all believers (vv. 12–34) and signals God's victory over death. Believers enter eternal life now in faith (the already) and will rise in glory on the other side of the grave (the not yet). Death is mocked as a defeated enemy (cf. G. Fee, *The First Epistle to the Corinthians* (NICNT; Grand Rapids: Eerdmans, 1987], 803–5). That is, the averting of divine wrath that Hosea cannot hope for, the apostle can confidently proclaim because of the power of the empty tomb.

15 The next two verses emphasize how devastating God's judgment will be. It will be like the scorching east wind (cf. 12:1), a powerful wind from Yahweh himself. Though Israel may "flourish" (*yaprî* being a biform of the root *prh* and a

wordplay on Ephraim) like lush reeds (see Notes; cf. Ge 41:2–18), it will be laid waste and its treasures plundered.

16 [14:1] While v.15 pictures the invasion through metaphor, this verse graphically portrays the terrible horrors of the (Assyrian) invasion (cf. 7:16; 10:4). The rebelliousness of Israel has wrought an awful human cost. Such cruelty was common in ancient warfare (e.g., 2Ki 15:16; Am 1:13). The language of these two verses may reflect the covenantal curses of Leviticus 26 and Deuteronomy 28 (Stuart, 208).

NOTES

9 The MT has שִׁחֶתְךָ (*šihetkā*, "he destroyed you"; ESV). Common emendations include אֲשַׁחֶתְךָ (*ʾašahetkā*, "I will destroy you"; NRSV) and שִׁחַתִּיךָ (*šihattîkā*, "I have destroyed you"; Wolff, 220; cf. NEB). The NIV, NKJV, NJPS, and NLT offer תִּשָּׁחֵת (*tiššāhēt*) or נִשְׁחָתָ (*nišhattā*, "you are destroyed"). Others configure the word as a noun with the second-person singular suffix, "your destruction" (Macintosh, 535–36; cf. NASB). In the light of the questions that follow in v.10, some also emend כִּי־בִי (*kî-bî*, "because against me") to מִי (*mî*, "who"; Stuart, 200; cf. NRSV; LXX).

10 English versions and most commentators believe אֱהִי (*ʾehî*) is a dialectical variant of the interrogatives אֵי (*ʾê*) or אַיֵּה (*ʾayēh*; Wolff, 221; e.g., NASB, NRSV, NIV; cf. LXX). Some rabbinic commentators see it as an apocopated first-person singular imperfect of הָיָה (*hyh*, "to be"), by which Yahweh declares that he is the sovereign of Israel (Sweeney, 133; cf. NKJV). Elsewhere in the OT this form is always prefixed with the *waw*-consecutive (e.g., 13:7). It reappears twice in v.14.

14 For אֱהִי (*ʾehî*), see Notes on v.10. Here, a few take it as an interjectory particle, such as "alas" or "so much for you" (Andersen and Freedman, 639–40; Macintosh 537–38). As at v.10, some rabbinic commentators interpret אֱהִי (*ʾehî*) as a verbal form. The point would be that Yahweh himself is the source of the disaster that is coming on Israel (Yee, 291–92; Sweeney, 134; cf. NKJV; Vul.).

15 Many commentators and English versions emend אַחִים (*ʾahîm*, "brothers"; NIV, NJKV, NLT, ESV) to אַחוּ (*ʾāhû*, "reeds"; cf. *HALOT*, 30–31; Wolff, 220; e.g., NEB, NASB, NRSV).

B. The Call to Authentic Repentance (14:1–3[2–4])

¹Return, O Israel, to the LORD your God.
Your sins have been your downfall!

² Take words with you
    and return to the Lᴏʀᴅ.
Say to him:
    "Forgive all our sins
    and receive us graciously,
        that we may offer the fruit of our lips.
³ Assyria cannot save us;
    we will not mount war-horses.
We will never again say 'Our gods'
    to what our own hands have made,
    for in you the fatherless find compassion."

COMMENTARY

1 [2] The threat and descriptions of divine judgment conclude with the previous verse. This verse contains the final call for genuine repentance. Israel has "stumbled" (*kāšal*; 4:4; 5:5) in its sin—that is, it has experienced sin's consequences. They must come to "the Lᴏʀᴅ your God," a name combination used twice before in passages extolling his sovereignty (12:9; 13:4). The verb "return" is vital to the theological purposes of the book and appears four times in this chapter (vv. 1–2, 4, 7). Iniquity (*ʿāwōn*) had kept the nation from approaching Yahweh as it should have done (2:7; 5:4; 7:10, 16); the people must come on God's terms.

2 [3] At first glance this verse seems to echo 6:1–3, but there is a fundamental difference. In 5:15 Yahweh had sought a confession of sin from the people, but 6:1–3 reflects a misplaced confidence in the certainty of national restoration. Here again is repeated the importance of humble contrition and the admission of guilt (cf. 3:5; 12:6). "Words" refers to what follows (instead of certain vows or prayers): "Take away all iniquity [*ʿāwōn*]; accept what is good" (NIV, "Forgive all our sins, and receive us graciously"). The latter clause probably expresses the desire that Yahweh receive whatever is appropriate from them, anything that is pleasing to him (cf. 6:6; 8:3, 13).

The last line is difficult to translate. The Hebrew text literally says, "so that we may pay bulls, our lips." Some commentators and versions maintain the bull reference (*pārîm*; e.g., ESV; Macintosh, 561–65), but many make the slight change to "fruit" (*pᵉrî*; NASB, NIV, NRSV; Garrett, 271; cf. LXX). The emendation is not required. "Bulls" can be taken as an adverbial accusative ("as bulls" or "with bulls"; cf. NIV note; NJB and NJPS have "instead of bulls"), metaphorically meaning that what their lips will say is as valuable as a costly animal sacrifice.

3 [4] In the context of Hosea's day, national repentance was inseparable from political and military policy. Wrong views about Yahweh led to decisions that disallowed his sovereignty within the international realities of that time. One day, though, the agreements with Assyria will be recognized as futile (5:13; 7:11; 8:9; 12:1). Assyria will be their destroyer, not their helper (9:3; 10:6; 11:5)! Ultimately, military equipment will also be ineffectual (cf. 1:7). This realization may have come after the Syro-Ephraimite War or the defeat of 722 BC.

Israel will admit that the images that they had made were useless, their idolatry a folly (8:5–6; 13:1–2). In the future Israel will acknowledge its orphan status before its heavenly King and Father. He is compassionate (the root *rḥm*). This statement recalls the wordplay of Hosea's daughter's name: She who was called *Lōʾ-Ruḥāmâ* will receive the mercy of Yahweh (1:6; 2:1, 21, 23).

C. The Loving Response of Yahweh (14:4–8[5–9])

4"I will heal their waywardness
 and love them freely,
 for my anger has turned away from them.
5I will be like the dew to Israel;
 he will blossom like a lily.
 Like a cedar of Lebanon
 he will send down his roots;
6 his young shoots will grow.
 His splendor will be like an olive tree,
 his fragrance like a cedar of Lebanon.
7Men will dwell again in his shade.
 He will flourish like the grain.
 He will blossom like a vine,
 and his fame will be like the wine from Lebanon.
8O Ephraim, what more have I to do with idols?
 I will answer him and care for him.
 I am like a green pine tree;
 your fruitfulness comes from me."

COMMENTARY

4 [5] Receiving punishment from God is likened to being wounded or sick, conditions that only the divine Judge-Physician can heal (cf. 5:12–14; 13:7–8). This healing Yahweh promises to bring out of his great love for Israel. The reestablishment that the nation too cavalierly had assumed in its arrogant rebellion (6:1; cf. 6:11–7:1; 11:3) is grounded in his infinite grace (cf. Oestreich, 57–155). Love within a renewed relationship, not anger in judgment, is God's design for his people. There are two wordplays with the verb "return" (*šûb*): When they "return" to Yahweh (vv. 1–2), he will heal their "turning away" (*mᵉšûbâ*; often translated "apostasy" or "waywardness"; cf. 11:7) and his wrath "turns" from them.

5–7 [6–8] It is important to compare the imagery of this section with ch. 2. There Yahweh had said that he, not *baʿal* or the *bᵉʿālîm*, is the provider of all of their abundance. This truth is repeated but on a grander scale.

Yahweh is like the dew, a refreshing and enriching moisture in that dry region (v.5). This aspect of the image contrasts with 6:4 and 13:3, where the focus is on how quickly dew disappears (cf. Oestreich, 157–89). Now with God's blessing, in these verses Israel is likened to a blooming lily, a splendid olive tree, and a fruitful vine. The Hebrew describes roots that spread "like Lebanon" and speaks of a fragrance "like Lebanon." It is assumed that this elliptical phrase refers to the trees of that region's forests. Some versions supply the name of a tree, such as the cedar (NASB, NJB, NIV, NLT), for which Lebanon was famous (Ps 92:12; 104:16).

Dwelling in "his shade" in v.7 is a pastoral picture of the nation as living under blessing, enjoying abundance once again. Not all agree. Some argue that the reference is to Yahweh and emend "his shade" to "my shade" (NEB, NJB, ESV; Wolff, 232). The metaphor of Israel as a tree, however, is consistent with the passage up to this point. With this miraculous transformation achieved by God's good hand, the mention, or renown, of Israel will be something wonderful, like that of the fine wine of Lebanon. It will no longer be associated with bitter memories of sin and judgment.

Much of the metaphorical language of these verses is found in the Song of Songs: bloom (SS 6:11; 7:13), lily (2:1–2, 16; 5:13; 6:3), Lebanon (e.g., 4:8, 11), fragrance (e.g., 1:3, 12; 4:10–11), shade (2:3); vine (2:13; 6:11; 7:12); and wine (e.g., 1:2, 4; 4:10; 7:9). Hosea 14:5–7 also is poetry that vividly expresses Yahweh's love for his people.

8 [9] It is difficult to determine who is talking in this verse. Some envision an exchange between Israel (Ephraim) and Yahweh, with Israel speaking in the first and third line and Yahweh answering in the second and fourth lines (Macintosh, 576–77; cf. Tg.). Others consider the words "What more do I have to do with idols" a senseless statement if from the mouth of God and emend "I" to "he" (NJB, NEB; Mays, 184) or assume that the first line quotes Israel (NJPS, NKJV). Neither option is convincing.

Throughout this section "I" is Yahweh. He declares that he has had enough dealing with the idolatry of Israel; the nation in these verses comprehends this fact as well. Yahweh's promise to care for them continues (for the root ʿnh, "answer," see 2:21–22). He is the one true source of life. In an interesting final twist, Yahweh himself is depicted as a tree — the only place in the OT where the symbol of a tree is used for Yahweh (Oestreich, 191–225).

NOTES

7[8] It is possible to translate יֵשְׁבוּ יֹשְׁבֵי בְצִלּוֹ (*yāšubû yōšᵉbê bᵉṣillô*) as "the ones dwelling in his shade will return" and interpret the clause as an allusion to the future return from exile, as was the case in 11:11 (Stuart, 216; cf. NJB, NKJV, ESV; LXX). But it is better to consider שׁוּב (*šûb*) as an auxiliary verb expressing a repeated action (cf. *HALOT*, 1430; W–O §39.3.1b): "The ones dwelling in his shade will again flourish" (Macintosh, 573–74; cf. NASB) or "They will dwell again" (Wolff, 232; cf. NIV, NRSV).

8[9] On the basis of a slight emendation of אֲנִי עָנִיתִי וַאֲשׁוּרֶנּוּ (*ᵃnî ʿānîtî waᵃšûrennû*, "I will answer and take care of him") to אֲנִי עֲנָתוֹ וַאֲשֵׁרָתוֹ (*ᵃnî ʿᵃnātô waᵃšērātô*, "I am his Anat and his Asherah"), some scholars see evidence for the worship of Asherah. Compare J. Day, "Asherah in the Hebrew Bible and Northwest Semitic Literature," *JBL* 105 (1986): 385–408; W.G. Dever, *Did God Have a Wife? Archaeology and Folk Religion in Ancient Israel* (Grand Rapids: Eerdmans, 2005), 214–15. Less sanguine are Hadley, *The Cult of Asherah in Ancient Israel and Judah: Evidence for a Hebrew Goddess* (University of Cambridge Oriental Publications 57; Cambridge: Cambridge Univ. Press, 2000), 75–83; Smith, 135–36. There is no textual support for the change.

V. POSTSCRIPT: CHALLENGING QUESTIONS (14:9[10])

⁹Who is wise? He will realize these things.
   Who is discerning? He will understand them.
The ways of the LORD are right;
   the righteous walk in them,
   but the rebellious stumble in them.

COMMENTARY

9 [10] Many critics believe this epilogue is an exilic or postexilic addition. The vocabulary (e.g., "wise," "right," "walk"), the call to the wise (cf. Ps 107:43; Ec 8:1; Jer 9:12), and the contrast between them and sinners (e.g., Pr 10:29; 24:16) are all said to reflect wisdom themes and not prophetic material (G. T. Sheppard, *Wisdom as Hermeneutical Construct: A Study in the Sapientializing of the Old Testament* [BZAW 151; Berlin: de Gruyter, 1980], 129–36).

In addition to the questionable presuppositions that Israel's theological traditions were incapable of mutual influence and that wisdom material is by definition late, this view must admit the lexical connections between this verse and other passages. The verbs "know," "stumble" (4:5; 5:5; 14:1), and "transgress" (7:13; 8:1) are important to Hosea's message. If this verse was added, it obviously has been shaped to sound like his voice. In addition,

the wisdom theme of self-destructive thoughtlessness appears throughout the prophet's oracles (C. L. Seow, "Hosea 14:10 and the Foolish People Motif," *CBQ* 44 [1982]: 212–24).

Because the style does differ sharply from the rest of the book, the verse draws attention to itself. (This ending also is unique among the prophetic books.) The verse says that what has been proclaimed through complex literary techniques and rich imagery requires discernment and self-examination. The nation had failed this test over and over again and will suffer punishment. Has anything been learned through the prophet's oracles?

Israel—and now the reader—must choose between the "ways of the LORD" (cf., e.g., Dt 8:6; 10:12; 32:4), those covenantal guidelines expressed in these fourteen chapters, and the decisions and actions that bring divine judgment. Hosea has laid out the problems and challenges with their respective consequences for his time and place. This closing verse reveals that his message always will be relevant. All now are without excuse, but none without hope.

NOTE

9[10] The syntax of the two verbs of the opening line (simple *waw* + imperfect) has been construed in a jussive sense ("Whoever is wise, let him understand these things; [Whoever is] discerning, let him know them," Macintosh, 582; cf. NASB, NJB, NEB, ESV); as introducing a final clause ("Who is wise, that he may understand these things, prudent, that he may know them?" Garrett, 281; cf. GKC §166a; NRSV, NJPS); or as expressing a logical consequence ("Those who are wise understand these things; [those who are] discerning know them," McComiskey, 236; cf. NIV, NRSV).

JOEL

RICHARD D. PATTERSON

Introduction

1. BACKGROUND

Because Joel's prophecies are undated, matters of background must be gleaned from internal details. This commentary proceeds from the perspective of a preexilic setting for the book (see Date). Beginning in the eighth century BC, Israel and Judah experienced a period of unparalleled prosperity. Indeed, in the early half of that century the twin kingdoms acquired nearly the same territorial dimensions as in the days of the united monarchy (2Ki 14:23–15:7).

With the death of Jeroboam in the north in 752 BC and Uzziah in the south in 740 BC, however, dramatic change in the fortunes of God's people took place, for they became involved in the affairs of the expanding Neo-Assyrian Empire. Tiglath-pileser III (745–727 BC) fought two campaigns in the western Fertile Crescent (744–743; 734–732 BC), the second of which culminated in the capture of Aramean Damascus and the submission of both Israel and Judah to Assyria (2Ki 15:27–31; 16:7–9). This set the pattern for Assyro-Israelite relations in the rest of the eighth century.

Neither Hoshea in the north nor Ahaz in the south was to prove equal to the challenge. Hoshea's ill-advised attempt at freeing Israel from Assyrian control failed and resulted in the fall of Samaria and the kingdom itself in 722 BC. In the southern kingdom matters went from bad to worse. Not only did Judah's vassalage to Assyria continue throughout the days of Shalmaneser V (727–722 BC) and Sargon II (721–706 BC), but Ahaz himself proved to be a wicked king who led his people into shameful apostasy (2Ki 16:10–18; 2Ch 28:19–25).

With the accession of Hezekiah to the throne in the latter portion of the eighth century BC, however, Judah experienced a period of spiritual revival. His commendation as a man of unequaled trust in God and faithfulness to the Lord and the law (2Ki 18:5–6) reflects his reform efforts. The author of Chronicles gives extensive attention to his cleansing and rededication of the temple, together with the reconstituting of proper worship services (2Ch 29–31). Nevertheless, he was faced with the continuing menace of Assyria, culminating in invasion by the forces of King Sennacherib.[1]

The next century witnessed still further changes in the political situation. Although in the earlier part of the seventh century BC Assyrian forces ranged far abroad, from Persia on the east to Arabia and Egypt in the south, the reigns of Esarhaddon (681–668 BC) and Ashurbanipal (668–626 BC) were largely peaceful. This period is often designated the *Pax Assyriaca*, an era when the two kings were often able to turn their attention to building projects, religious pursuits, and the cultivation of artistic and literary matters.

In the closing days of Ashurbanipal, however, the Assyrian Empire began to weaken, so much so that fourteen years after his death in 626 BC Assyria itself fell prey to the rising power of the Chaldeans and the Neo-Babylonian Empire. In such an era God raised up the great writing prophets, men of deep spiritual concern. Their message, unlike that of their predecessors, was not limited to national affairs but also took in the entire international scene from their own time to the culmination of God's teleological program.

2. UNITY

Critical doubt as to the unity of Joel became standardized with the work of Duhm.[2] He denied that any of the apocalyptic sections were Joel's and regarded only the nonapocalyptic sections of chs. 1 and 2 as from him. Other scholars followed his reasoning, especially Bewer, who eliminated as insertions all references to the day of the Lord, the apocalyptic portions, and the historical problem of 3:4–8. To Joel were ascribed the nonapocalyptic sections of chs. 1 and 2, along with 2:28–31a; 3:2a; and 3:9–14a.

The denial of the unity of the book is based on supposed literary differences and on differences in thought or outlook. A careful look at the literary form of the book, however, reveals a consistency of style and vocabulary. Supposed differences in outlook cannot be proved. On the contrary, the author has a single unifying theme: the terrible locust plague is a harbinger of awesome things to come. "The day of the Lord," rather than betraying a different hand, serves to unite historical occurrences with spiritual lessons. Moreover, all the extant Hebrew manuscripts and the ancient versions attest to the unity of the book.

3. AUTHORSHIP

Little is known of the personal circumstances of the author, Joel ("Yahweh is God"), except that which can be gleaned internally from the book. The son of Pethuel (LXX, "Bathuel"), Joel lived and prophesied in Judah (though Pseudo-Epiphanius indicates that his original home was in Reuben). Thus, he often referred to Judah and Jerusalem (2:32; 3:1, 17–18, 20) and to their citizens (3:6, 8, 19), or to Zion (2:1, 15; 3:17, 21) and its children (2:23). He was thoroughly familiar with the temple and its ministry (1:9, 13–14, 16; 2:14, 17; 3:18) and was intimately acquainted with the geography and history of the land (1:2; 3:2–8, 12, 14, 18).

Joel was a man of vitality and spiritual maturity. A keen discerner of the times, he delivered God's message to the people of Judah in a vivid and impassioned style, with a precision and originality of thought that served as a veritable quarry out of which many subsequent prophetic building stones were to be hewn.

---

1. Scholars are divided on the question of whether Hezekiah faced a second invasion by Sennacherib after the well-known campaign of 701 BC. See the remarks of W. Shea, "Jerusalem under Siege," *BAR* 25/6 (1999): 36–44.
2. B. Duhm, "Anmerkungen zu den zwölf Propheten," *ZAW* 31 (1911): 1–43, 184–88.

4. DATE

The date of Joel has occupied the attention of many scholars and has produced varying results. No date is given in the book's heading, nor is any date stated explicitly within its body. Moreover, none of the great powers of the ancient Near East (Assyria, Babylon, or Persia) is singled out for discussion, thus further complicating the problem; therefore, conjectures for the date of its composition have ranged from the ninth century BC to the Maccabean period. The more prominent views may be roughly divided into preexilic and postexilic theories.

Three general positions have been advanced by those who assign a preexilic date to Joel. The early preexilic view holds to a ninth-century date. Advocates of this theory stress Joel's failure to mention a king and the prominence he gives to the priesthood and elders. They explain these facts as pointing to the time of the boy king Joash (835–796 BC), who began his rule through the regency of the high priest Jehoiada.

The late preexilic view takes a late seventh-century date. Kapelrud attempts to harmonize the literary forms and religious outlook of Joel with Jeremiah. According to him, all historical, lexical, and sociological data are inconclusive for precise dating of the book. He finds Joel highly receptive to the influence of Jeremiah; hence, Joel was probably Jeremiah's younger contemporary.[3]

Falling somewhere between these two positions is the mid-preexilic view. It attempts to give an historical setting for the oracles against the six foreign nations in ch. 3. Thus the mention of the Greeks and Sabeans as far-off peoples can be harmonized well with this era.

The eighth century was a great age of awakened commercial and colonial expansion for the Greeks. A broad area from the Black Sea to Italy was exposed to their commercial ventures. The Hebrew text at 3:5 may point to the Ionian Greeks rather than to the Greeks of the mainland or of the Aegean world. If so, the eighth century is again an ideal time, for this is the precise period when the Ionians seized the mainland trade routes of Asia Minor. In either case the evidence harmonizes well with this era when the Greeks entered into the commercial arena long dominated by the Phoenicians. Reference to the commercially minded Phoenicians and Greeks fits well with the renewed commercial interests of Uzziah's day.

While the era of the Sabeans' great kingdom was centered in the fifth century BC, studies have established Sabean commercial operations to a considerably earlier time.[4] Certainly Joel's viewing the Sabeans as a people "far off" does not necessitate a postexilic date. Since Arabs are known to have been in contact with the Philistines in Uzziah's day (2Ch 26:7), and since Uzziah reopened Ezion Geber and the port of Elath, thereby reestablishing contact with the Arabs to the south, an eighth-century reference to the Sabeans is not improbable.

As for the references to the other four nations, admittedly these may be viewed simply as stylized language condemning Israel's traditional foes. Yet the discussion concerning the Phoenicians and Philistines seems more than conventional language, for specific sins are enumerated. Further, the details enumerated here fit nicely the mid-preexilic position.

---

3. A. S. Kapelrud, *Joel Studies* (Uppsala: Almquist and Wiksells, 1948).

4. See, e.g., A. B. Lloyd, "Necho and the Red Sea," *Journal of Egyptian Archaeology* 63 (1977): 147–48.

Thus, after the campaign of Adad-nirari III (805 BC), Phoenicia and Philistia were not again faced with outside intervention till the western campaigns of Tiglath-pileser III in 743 BC and 732 BC; thereafter their destiny is linked with that of Assyria throughout the eighth and seventh centuries. Accordingly, between 805 and 743 the Philistines were free to harass their old enemies, necessitating a campaign against them in Uzziah's day (2Ch 26:6–7). In that age of great prosperity, the Phoenicians were again the leading merchants of the day (cf. Joel 3:4–7). The whole Mediterranean basin was exposed to their commercial leadership, thus resulting in the foundation of Carthage in the western Mediterranean. Both the Phoenician and Philistine city-states were to experience the conqueror's heel, however, for Sargon II was victorious over both in his westward sweep in 720 BC.

Although little can be gained through the mention of Egypt and Edom, it is of interest to note that Amos associated Edom with the Philistines (1:6) and the Tyrians (1:9) in the slave trade and condemned their oppression of the Israelites (1:11–12). Additionally, Uzziah had to subdue Edom (2Ki 14:7), a subjugation quickly lost after his time.

The internal emphases also reflect well the eighth century BC. To be noted here are the importance of agriculture (1:4–20; 2:18–27), the ease and debauchery of society (1:5; cf. Hos 4:11; 7:5, 14; Am 2:8; 6:1–7; see also the many references in Isaiah), the occurrence of the locust attack itself (cf. Am 4:9; 7:1–3), and the sheer formalism of the established religion of the day (2:12–13; cf. Am 5:21–24).

In contrast to those who arbitrarily ascribe a dependence of Joel on the other prophets, a survey of the data relative to literary dependence reveals that Joel faithfully reflects the prevailing events, attitudes, and literary themes of his contemporaries in the eighth century BC. An intensive examination of Joel shows dozens of instances of linguistic formulas and special lexical emphases Joel has in common with the other eighth-century prophets. Likewise, a comparison of Joel's use of theological terminology with that of these prophets reveals numerous places in every section of his prophecy where his viewpoint is in harmony with the prevailing message and outlook of that era.

The postexilic view places stress on several data. (1) Joel fails to mention a king by name or title but does bring up the responsibilities of elders and priests. (2) Joel fails to mention Israel while concentrating on Judah and the temple. (3) Joel alludes to the walls of Jerusalem, thus indicating a time after the rebuilding activities in Nehemiah's day. Moreover, the allusion to captive Israelites and the call to "all in the land" (1:14) points to the fact of a scattered people, some of whom have been regathered to the land. (4) The mention of the Greeks reflects a later time when their presence in Israelite affairs was more common. (5) The reference to angelic armies implies an apocalyptic tone characteristic of later thinking.

In evaluating these various positions on the dating of Joel one must freely admit that none of the data is so determinative as to provide absolute certainty for any of the theories. Some data, however, tend to argue against one or other of the views. Thus the failure to mention a king is so fragile that *both* the early preexilic and postexilic views cite it as evidence. Likewise, the mention of elders, put forward by both of these views, assumes arbitrarily that the elders are officials. Joel may simply be referring to older men. Similarly, the concentration on the priesthood, championed by advocates of both views, need not indicate any formal governmental leadership. Joel may be singling out such leaders to remind them of their spiritual duties.

The other evidence adduced by the proponents of the postexilic view is at best "questionable or ambiguous."[5] Thus, (1) Joel's failure to mention Israel may be explained as either pointing to a time after the fall of the northern kingdom or may be a matter of the prophet's concentration on his homeland in Judah. (2) The allusion to the walls of Jerusalem may just as easily point to a time before they were breached by the forces of Nebuchadnezzar II in 586 BC. (3) The reference to the Greeks as "far off" scarcely fits the picture of the postexilic period when Greek interaction with the Near East was very strong. (4) The mention of angelic armies is not necessarily supportive of a postexilic position—indeed, Joel's use of angelic armies yields no positive support for any date for the book.

In the light of all these considerations, one must freely admit that absolute certainty for the date of Joel is lacking. It is a small wonder, then, that proponents of each view can rightly point out weaknesses in the other views. Nevertheless, because the dating of a book does affect one's interpretation of the data, it is necessary to posit a date for Joel, however tentatively it must be held. Since the mid-preexilic view appears to offer some positive data toward the solution of the problem rather than relying primarily on what Joel does *not* say (*argumentum ad ignoratium*), as in some of the views, it is provisionally adopted here. My own preference is for a date in the mid to latter half of the eighth century BC.

5. OCCASION AND PURPOSE

A locust plague without parallel has descended on Judah and ruined all the crops. Not only is the basic economy of the country disrupted, but all levels of society are deeply affected. Worst of all, the agricultural loss threatens the continuance of the sacrificial offerings, the central feature of the religious ceremony.

In these catastrophic circumstances Joel sees God's judgment on Judah. Although God has abundantly blessed the Judah of Uzziah's day, the people have taken God and his blessings for granted. Faith has degenerated into an empty formalism and will soon degenerate into outright apostasy. Moreover, Judah's social practice is becoming one of moral decadence.

Under divine inspiration Joel tells the people that the locust plague is a warning of a greater judgment, which is imminent unless they repent and return to full fellowship with God. If they do, God will abundantly pardon them, restore the health of the land, and give them again the elements needed to offer the sacrifices. The ceremonial system was designed to express a heartfelt relationship with God. By their sin they have forfeited any right to religious ceremony. What is needed is a repentant heart that will allow ceremony and spiritual condition to coincide. The thought of further judgment leads Joel also to reveal God's intentions for eschatological times.

6. LITERARY FORM

Joel's literary style is rich and vivid, being distinguished by its clarity, flow of thought, and beauty of expression. The structure of Joel is readily discernable. Major sections are built around dominant types of prophetic genre. Thus in 1:2–20; 2:1–17; and 2:18–27 Joel develops his prophecy as instructional accounts. These are commonly introduced or permeated by imperatives (e.g., 1.2, 5–13, 14–18, 2.1–11, 12–14, 15–17). These chapters often take on a tone of lamentation expressing the need for personal and

---

5. D. A. Garrett, *Hosea, Joel* (NAC; Nashville: Broadman & Holman, 1997), 286.

communal repentance. The messages of the first chapter are climaxed by a warning of judgment (1:15–20) and those of the second by promises of divine intervention and restoration (2:18–27).

The eschatological portions are dominated by kingdom oracles in which announcements of judgment are coupled with promises of blessing (2:28–3:21). Here each major section is introduced by a formula expressing future time (2:28; 3:1, 18). Individual subsections may be initiated in a variety of ways, such as lawsuit (3:4), summons for war (3:9), and exclamatory declaration (3:14).

In Joel's utilization of heightened, even fantastic, imagery at times (e.g., 2:30–31; 3:15–16, 18), some have seen evidence of apocalyptic genre. It is difficult, however, to classify any of his prophecies as apocalyptic for two reasons. (1) Joel's perspective is that of his own people, and his chief focus is in the immediate area of the Near East. (2) The portions in question lack such characteristic apocalyptic features as a preoccupation with otherworldly activities, a divine messenger sent to instruct a human recipient of revelation, and a broadened, more intense universal outlook. All that can be safely affirmed is that Joel at times makes use of standard prophetic imagery and themes that will one day become prevalent in later apocalyptic. All the portions in question may best be termed as emerging or proto-apocalyptic.

Joel's genius and originality can be seen in his use of data and literary features. He has skillfully woven the events of history and his day into the fabric of his prophetic warnings and pronouncements. Special attention must be called to the two most characteristic literary devices Joel uses to give balance and unity to his prophecy: (1) simile and metaphor (1:6; 2:2–7, 9, 11, 20, 25; 3:13, 16) and (2) repetition and recapitulation, later sections often taking up the themes and images mentioned previously. Other figures of speech include: allegory (2:1–11), apostrophe (3:4, 11), hendiadys (1:16), hyperbole (3:12), merism (1:11; 2:23), paronomasia (1:15), personification (2:21–22), and rhetorical question (1:2, 16; 2:11, 14; 3:4).

The tone of this short prophecy may be defined as pastoral, with scenes from the agrarian world and the world of nature being woven into the fabric of the book. These are used to reinforce the need for spiritual correction. Thus the lost harvests occasioned by the sin of God's people (1:2–4, 10–12, 16–17) can yet be restored (2:19, 22–26). Moreover, a day when the nation's sins will necessitate God's harvest of judgment (3:12–13) is coming. When God's chastening work has been accomplished, however, the countryside will reflect the presence of Israel's delivering God (3:17–18, 21b).

7. THEOLOGICAL VALUES

A man of implicit faith in God, Joel imparts that reliance on the sufficiency of God and his prior claim on the believer's life in every section of the book. Only the leading characteristics of Joel's theological outlook can be sketched here.

Perhaps the basic tenet is that God sovereignly guides the affairs of earth's history toward his preconceived final goal (1:15; 2:1–4, 18, 20, 25–27, 28–32; 3:1–21). He alone is God (2:27). A God of grace and mercy (2:13, 17), of lovingkindness and patience (2:13), and of justice (1:15; 3:1–8, 12–13) and righteousness (2:23), he calls for true and vital worship on behalf of his followers (2:13), who have trusted him for salvation by grace through faith (2:32). While the formal worship services are an essential part of the Israelite's religious experience (1:9, 13–14, 16; 2:13–17, 26–27), mere externalism is insufficient before God (2:13, 18–19, 23, 26–27, 32; 3:21). Accordingly, the place of prayer and repentance is emphasized (1:13–14, 19–20; 2:12–13, 17, 19).

Joel teaches that when sin becomes the dominant condition of God's people, they must be judged (1:15; 2:1, 11–13). God may use natural disasters (ch. 1) or political means (2:1–11) to chastise his people. For a repentant people (2:12–13) there will be the blessing of restored fellowship (2:14, 19, 23) and also restored blessings in nature (2:23–27).

Joel's theology contributes greatly to the field of eschatology. Of central concern is God's role with regard to his people, Israel (1:6, 13–14; 2:12–14, 17, 18–20, 23–27; 3:1–3, 16–18, 20–21). While he may allow other nations to chastise Israel for her sins (2:11; 3:1–8, 19), God has reserved a remnant to himself (2:28–32). On them he will pour out his Spirit (2:28–29), to them he will manifest himself with marvelous signs (2:30–31), and he will regather and bring them to the Promised Land (2:32–3:1). He will gather for judgment those nations who have dealt so severely with his people (3:2, 12–13) and bring them to a great final battle near Jerusalem (vv.9–16). On that awesome day (v.15), he himself (v.16) will lead his people in triumph (vv.16–17), thereby ushering in unparalleled peace and prosperity (vv.17–18, 20–21).

Integral to all Joel's prophecy is his teaching about the day of the Lord (see comments on 2:32). By the skillful use of this term, which gives cohesion to his entire message, Joel demonstrates that God is sovereignly operative in all that comes to pass, directing all things to their appointed end.

8. CANONICITY AND TEXT

There are no serious problems as to the canonicity and text of Joel. The LXX, Peshitta, and Latin Vulgate versions diverge only slightly from the MT and from one another. The recently found portion of Joel from Wadi Murabbaʿat (notice that the twelve Minor Prophets are in the traditional order) stands in the tradition of the MT. The minor variations in 4QXII[c,e] and the additions to the text in the LXX found at 1:5, 8, 18; 2:12; 3:1 are of questionable value.[6] Supposed corruptions in the MT (1:7, 17–18; 2:11; 3:11) are of doubtful status.

9. BIBLIOGRAPHY

Garrett, D. A. *Hosea, Joel*. New American Commentary. Nashville: Broadman & Holman, 1997.

Hurowitz, V. A. "Joel's Locust Plague in Light of Sargon II's Hymn to Nanaya." *Journal of Biblical Literature* 112 (1993): 597–603.

Keil, C. F. *The Twelve Minor Prophets*. Keil and Delitzsch. 2 vols. Grand Rapids: Eerdmans, 1949.

Rendtorff, R. "Alas for the Day! The 'Day of the Lord' in the Book of the Twelve." Pages 186–97 in *God in the Fray*. Edited by T. Linafelt and T. K. Beal. Minneapolis: Fortress, 1988.

Rudolph, W. "Ein Beitrag zum hebräischen Lexicon aus dem Joelbuch." Pages 244–50 in *Hebräische Wortforschung*. Edited by G. W. Anderson et al. Leiden: Brill, 1967.

Stuart, D. *Hosea–Jonah*. Word Biblical Commentary. Waco, Tex.: Word, 1987.

---

6. For the text at Qumran, see Martin Abegg Jr., Peter Flint, and Eugene Ulrich, *The Dead Sea Scrolls Bible* (San Francisco: HarperSanFrancisco, 1999), 428–32.

10. OUTLINE

Text and Exposition

I. SUPERSCRIPTION (1:1)

¹The word of the Lᴏʀᴅ that came to Joel son of Pethuel.

COMMENTARY

1 As with Hosea, Micah, and Zephaniah, Joel begins his prophecy by identifying himself and his lineage. More importantly, he clearly declares the divine source of his prophecy and the resultant need for readers to heed his utterance. Since the message is God's, it is implicitly to be followed.

II. INSTRUCTIONS CONCERNING THE PRESENT CRISIS (1:2–20)

A. The Occasion: The Locust Plague (1:2–4)

²Hear this, you elders;
    listen, all who live in the land.
Has anything like this ever happened in your days
    or in the days of your forefathers?
³Tell it to your children,
    and let your children tell it to their children,
    and their children to the next generation.
⁴What the locust swarm has left
    the great locusts have eaten;
what the great locusts have left
    the young locusts have eaten;
what the young locusts have left
    other locusts have eaten.

COMMENTARY

2–4 Because Joel's prophecy is God's urgent message, he instructs his people—from the eldest citizen downward—to give careful attention to what he has to say. None can recall such an intense and devastating calamity as the locust plague that has fallen on them. For this reason Joel's message and instructions based on the locust plague are to be handed down successively to the generations that follow.

Several theories have tried to account for the four different Hebrew words for locusts that appear in v.4. Probably the point is that the various Hebrew words indicate various types of locusts as well as the intensity of the plague. There had been a successive series of locusts, perhaps over several years (cf. 2:25), that made a thorough devastation of the land—a destruction indicated rhetorically by four distinct names. That there were four successive invasions may bear some relationship to the concept of thorough judgment. (Notice the four kinds of punishment mentioned in Jer 15:3 and the four types of judgment in Eze 14:21.) Amos also mentioned the utter destruction left behind by a locust plague (Am 4:9), but he noted that there had been no turning to God by the people of the northern kingdom. Joel recognizes the seriousness of the situation. The locusts are God's army in judgment on Judah.

NOTES

4 The Akkadian hymn to the goddess Nanaya contains details about a locust plague during the reign of Sargon II (721–705 BC). Of particular interest is Hurowitz's observation (599) that "nearly every detail in this passage has either general or quite specific parallels in Joel's description of the locusts afflicting Judah." Hurowitz, 602, also points out that "the rare motifs shared by the Nanaya hymn and Joel (destroying, desiccating) are not found in other biblical or Akkadian accounts. The correlation is thus unique."

Although Hurowitz is rightly hesitant in assigning any direct correlation between the two texts, their dating and parallel material are at least worthy of more than passing notice. Hurowitz also calls attention to several letters dealing with locust infestation in the Sargon archives.

For reports of devastating locust attacks in many parts of the world, see the useful excursus in S. R. Driver, *The Books of Joel and Amos* (Cambridge: Cambridge Univ. Press, 1915), 84–92, and J. D. Whiting, "Jerusalem's Locust Plague," *National Geographic Magazine* 28 (1915): 511–50.

B. The Call for Personal Penitence (1:5–12)

> [5] Wake up, you drunkards, and weep!
>   Wail, all you drinkers of wine;
> wail because of the new wine,
>   for it has been snatched from your lips.
> [6] A nation has invaded my land,
>   powerful and without number;
> it has the teeth of a lion,
>   the fangs of a lioness.
> [7] It has laid waste my vines
>   and ruined my fig trees.

It has stripped off their bark
    and thrown it away,
      leaving their branches white.

⁸Mourn like a virgin in sackcloth
    grieving for the husband of her youth.
⁹Grain offerings and drink offerings
    are cut off from the house of the LORD.
The priests are in mourning,
    those who minister before the LORD.
¹⁰The fields are ruined,
    the ground is dried up;
the grain is destroyed,
    the new wine is dried up,
    the oil fails.
¹¹Despair, you farmers,
    wail, you vine growers;
grieve for the wheat and the barley,
    because the harvest of the field is destroyed.
¹²The vine is dried up
    and the fig tree is withered;
the pomegranate, the palm and the apple tree —
    all the trees of the field — are dried up.
Surely the joy of mankind
    is withered away.

COMMENTARY

5–7 With v.5 begins the first major section of Joel's prophecy. It is marked structurally by the characteristic use of an instructional genre (see "Literary Form" in the introduction). Thematically it reflects Joel's deep concern that the people of Judah understand the underlying reasons for the locust plague and its relation to the future purposes of God for his people. In the light of the present crisis, Joel calls the people to penitence. This unprecedented plague is nothing else but a display of God's judgment and a harbinger and dire warning of still further judgment; therefore, they should pray earnestly.

Joel tells the populace to awaken from their sleep of drunkenness (cf. Pr 23:35b). In so doing he calls attention not only to the debased nature of society but also to the people's insensitivity to their own condition, a moral decadence that if unchecked will bring national disaster. Times of ease too often result in dissipation. The first half of the eighth century BC was one of great economic prosperity for both Israel and Judah (see "Background" in the introduction), but also one of spiritual, moral, and social corruption. As in the northern kingdom, so in Judah mere outward formalism veiled an ever-deepening apostasy, which was to become openly nourished by Ahaz's state-sponsored religious reforms (2Ki 16:10–18).

The lavish splendor of the northern kingdom has been confirmed by archaeological excavations, particularly at Samaria and Megiddo. Many of the Samaria Ostraca deal with receipts of wine, oil, and barley. The presence of many pagan names on these receipts may indicate a loss of vital religion. The prophets in the northern kingdom decried the free flow of wine. Hosea complained that wine and fornication had led to spiritual harlotry throughout society (4:11–19; 7:13–14); even the king was addicted to debauchery (7:5). Amos also placed wine among the lists of social evils (2:6–8), calling it the mark of an indolent and selfish luxury that had choked out spiritual concern (6:6). Joel demonstrates that the southern kingdom is not much better off, despite its better spiritual heritage.

The fruit of the vine was not itself evil, for it could be a sign of God's blessing (cf. 2:23–24) and was to be used in that high expression of the joy of a life willingly poured out to God, the drink offering (cf. Lev 23:12–13; Nu 6:17). What these prophets condemn is the misuse of wine, which lead to drunkenness, debauchery, and the resultant loss of spiritual vitality. Isaiah and Micah also continued to denounce the wine-drinking habits of the people, complaining that this evil practice had infected every area of life and all levels of society and had led to gross spiritual failure (cf. Isa 5:11–12, 22; 22:13; 28:1, 7; 56:12; Mic 2:11).

Joel pleads with his hearers to weep and wail with uncontrolled grief concerning the sweet wine that has been cut off from their mouths. The locusts, here likened to a great nation with a powerful and invincible army, has stripped bare the vines and fruit trees

of the land. Joel amplifies his hearers' need to cry out by describing the voracious locusts as having teeth like those of a lion. The accuracy of Joel's description of the great cutting power of the locusts has often been recorded. Pliny (*Natural History* 1.2.12) reported that they could even gnaw through doors.

All the land lies waste before that hostile army. The vine and the fig tree, symbols of God's blessing on his people (cf. Hos 2:12; Am 4:9; Mic 4:4 with 1Ki 4:25; 2Ki 18:31; cf. also Ps 105:33; Isa 36:16; Jer 5:17; 8:13; Hag 2:19; Zec 3:10), lie stripped even of their bark. All this greatly alarms the prophet of the Lord. The conditions that necessitate the divine judgment must have grieved even more the Lord himself, who still views Judah as "my land" (v.6; cf. 2:18; 3:2; Hos 9:1–3).

8–10 Having emphasized the seriousness of the cutting off of the source of wine and the attendant economic crisis (vv.5–7; cf. vv.11–12), Joel reminds the people that there are greater issues at stake. Far worse is what the locust plague means to their spiritual lives. The very worship of God has been compromised. This should be a deeper cause of grief. They will no doubt howl over being deprived of their luxuries; far better would it be to imagine the consequences of the disaster from God's point of view.

Joel instructs the citizenry to mourn like an espoused virgin whose intended husband has been taken from her before the wedding. How great would be her tragedy and sorrow! So also the people of Judah and Jerusalem should weep over the loss of vital religious experience through the devastation of the land.

The loss of agricultural produce means the early cessation of the meal and drink offerings. Both were offered in connection with the daily burnt offerings (Ex 29:38–42; Lev 2; 6:14–18; 9:16–17; 23:18, 37; Nu 15:5; 28:3–8). These offerings spoke of the very heart of the believer's daily walk before

God: the burnt offering, of a complete dedication of life; the meal offering, of the believer's service that should naturally follow; and the drink offering, of the conscious joy in the heart of the believer whose life is poured out in consecrated service to God.

The observance of these offerings has degenerated into merely routine ritual (cf. Isa 1:11; Hos 6:6; Am 4:4–5; Mic 6:6–7). Still worse, the Israelites have made these times an occasion for drunkenness or even offered the sacrifices to pagan gods (Hos 2:5; Am 2:8). So, as God had warned, he has taken away the privilege of offering that which symbolized purity of devotion (Hos 2:9–13; 9:1–4). The cutting off of the sacrifices is a severe step of chastisement, but it should have been a warning to the people of their grave condition. The loss of opportunity even to offer the sacrifices should have symbolized to them their breaking of the terms of the covenantal bond between themselves and the Lord. Nothing could be more serious!

Joel continues the description of this tragedy by noting that the priests, the ministers of the Lord, are mourning; the once-productive fields are utterly laid waste (cf. Mic 2:4); and the very ground, the custodian of the elements necessary for the sacrifice, is dried up.

Grain (i.e., wheat after threshing and separation from the husk), wine (i.e., the freshly squeezed fruit of the vine), and oil (i.e., the fresh juice of the olive) were all chief products in Israel and considered objects of God's blessing (note esp. Nu 18:12; Dt 7:13; 11:14; 28:51; 2Ki 18:32; Jer 31:12; Joel 2:19; Hag 1:11). These blessings, however, could be withdrawn as punishment for the people's sins (Hos 2:8–13).

11–12 Joel closes the section by turning to the ones who are most directly affected—those who care for the yield. He calls on the farmers and keepers of the vineyard to "despair" (cf. Job 6:20 [NIV, "disappointed"]; Isa 1:29; 20:5) and to "wail" (cf. v.5). The words Joel uses signify an intense disappointment revealed in a terrified look and a cry of despair (cf. Am 5:16–17). They are to lament the loss of the products of the field (v.11) and of the vineyard and orchard (v.12).

The vine and fig tree are first singled out for notice. These were often used to symbolize the blessings of the relationship between God and Israel (see Ps 80:8–15; Isa 5:2–6; Jer 2:21; Mic 4:3–4; Zec 3:10; cf. Mt 21:18–21, 28–46). Joel also mentions the pomegranate, palm, and apple (or apricot) trees, all of which were not only important to the economy but were also symbols of spiritual nourishment and refreshment and of the resultant joy and fruitfulness of life in the trusting believer (cf. Dt 8:6–10; Ps 92:12; SS 2:3). All these trees, so vital to the economy and so expressive of Judah's relation to her God, are withered up. The full joy of life that should have been theirs as God's children has been put to open shame.

NOTES

6 The metaphor of locusts = nation/army anticipates Joel's development of the metaphor into a full-blown allegory in 2:1–11.

8 בַּעַל נְעוּרֶיהָ (ba‛al n‛‛ûreyhā, "the possession of her youth") is a picture of the state of betrothal where both bride-to-be and bridegroom-to-be were under the same restrictions as a husband and wife (cf. Dt 22:23–24; Mt 1:18–19).

9 The mention of the priests provides literary stitching to the following section (vv.13–18), where priests and their function are the focus of attention.

10 הוֹבִישׁ (*hôbîš*, "destroyed") could be from בּוֹשׁ (*bôš*, "to be ashamed" [GK 1017; cf. Lat. *confusum*], as in v.11). But more than likely it is from יָבֵשׁ (*yābēš*, "to dry up" [GK 3312], as in v.12; cf. LXX ἐξηράνθη, *exēranthē*, "was withered"]). Keil, 1:1–5, suggests that the form is written defectively where the root *bôš* is intended. If so, there is a conscious wordplay in vv.10–12, *bôš* being found in vv.11–12 (second instance) and *yābēš* in vv.10 and 12 (first instance).

11 Wheat and barley constitute a merism for all harvested grains. Both were staple food products, particularly for the poor of the land.

12 כִּי (*kî*) is asseverative here: "yea, surely" (cf. 2:1, 11). For details, see R. Gordis, "Asseverative Kaph in Ugaritic and Hebrew," *JAOS* 62 (1943): 76–78; M. Dahood, *Psalms III* (AB 17a; Garden City, N.Y.: Doubleday, 1970), 400–406.

C. The Call for Communal Lament (1:13–18)

> ¹³ Put on sackcloth, O priests, and mourn;
>   wail, you who minister before the altar.
> Come, spend the night in sackcloth,
>   you who minister before my God;
> for the grain offerings and drink offerings
>   are withheld from the house of your God.
> ¹⁴ Declare a holy fast;
>   call a sacred assembly.
> Summon the elders
>   and all who live in the land
> to the house of the LORD your God,
>   and cry out to the LORD.
>
> ¹⁵ Alas for that day!
>   For the day of the LORD is near;
>   it will come like destruction from the Almighty.
>
> ¹⁶ Has not the food been cut off
>   before our very eyes—
> joy and gladness
>   from the house of our God?
> ¹⁷ The seeds are shriveled
>   beneath the clods.
> The storehouses are in ruins,
>   the granaries have been broken down,
>   for the grain has dried up.
> ¹⁸ How the cattle moan!

The herds mill about
because they have no pasture;
    even the flocks of sheep are suffering.

COMMENTARY

13 Joel begins this section with a special plea to the priests. They are urged to gird themselves with sackcloth and to mourn and wail. The prophet has noted their sorrow (cf. vv.8–9). He now demonstrates the urgency of the situation by pleading with them to spend the whole night in their garments of sackcloth in deep contrition and penitence (cf. Est 4:1–4) because of the loss of the daily sacrifices, the implications of which they should know full well.

14–18 Because the locust plague warns of still further and more drastic judgment, Joel calls for a solemn assembly to meet for prayer. The priests are called on to convene the entire assembly of people at the temple for a solemn fast and a season of heartfelt prayer. The call for national fasting is an extraordinary event (Ne 9:1–3; Jer 36:9). But dreadful times call for decisive measures. It is to be a holy fast on the part of a solemn assembly. Led by the elders (cf. 1Ki 21:8–12), all are to come and cry to the Lord (cf. Eze 30:2–3).

Hosea lamented that the people of the northern kingdom did not cry to the Lord from the heart in their assemblies but instead gathered themselves together only for the sake of their grain and new wine (Hos 7:14). Joel's observation is the same. The prophet is concerned that the people give a fervent cry of repentance and call on God for forgiveness, lest greater judgment descend on them soon.

Joel then proceeds to the reasons for the repentant cry. He warns his hearers most strongly that all the available evidence points to the fact that the "day of the LORD" stands near at hand. Joel's use of this term here seems clearly related to the historical situation.

The locust plague is a dire warning that the day of the Lord's judgment for Judah is imminent.

Amos viewed the situation in similar terms. He reported that certain "prophets" were under a strange misconception. The day of the Lord was not to be one of vindication for Israel but instead was to signal its demise (Am 5:16–20). Like Joel, Amos warned of judgment because of sin and moral decay (3:1–5:13), a condition that necessitated thorough repentance (5:17). Likewise, Hosea's constant message was one of rebuke for Israel's spiritual and moral corruption and of warning of judgment for its spiritual infidelity and sins. Joel's message is in accord with this same picture of life found in the eighth century BC—a scene of spiritual bankruptcy, despite great political and economic assets.

Not only is the day of the Lord imminent, but it is also certain—"like destruction from the Almighty." The paronomasia is striking here, for the words "destruction" [*šod*] and "Almighty" [*šadday*] are from the same Hebrew root. The verb is also in an unusual position. One might paraphrase thus: "Like a shattering from Shaddai, it will surely come!"

In vv.16–18 Joel gives some added reasons for the call to assemble for penitence and prayer. Their need ought to have been obvious from the terrible conditions that are right before their eyes! In the second of several rhetorical questions Joel reminds them that their food supplies have been cut off so that there can be no feasts or offerings of gladness (the words being in emphatic order in the Hebrew sentence). Surely they can see it! Worst of all, it has affected the worship in the house of "our God."

Joel turns from the spiritual realm to the physical world. It, too, is in shambles. The unfructified grains lie shriveled under their hoes, the barns are desolate, and the granaries are trampled down. All the cattle are without pasturage and therefore groan agonizingly.

NOTES

15 For the day of the Lord, see comments on 2:28–31. Rendtorff perceptively suggests that because the day of the Lord theme is common to Joel, Amos, and Obadiah, the books of Joel and Obadiah were attached to Amos as a framing device.

Several etymologies have been proposed for the divine name אֵל שַׁדָּי (ʾēl šadday). The older view that derives the second word from a root *šdd* ("to devastate, overpower," GK 8720) is perhaps still as good as any. The text here—and in Isaiah 13:6—demands a relationship between *šadday* and *šdd*. The idea behind the root in Akkadian and in Hebrew appears to be that of impelling force—hence, the sovereign God being the Almighty (One). Accordingly, the Hebrew *ʾēl šadday* is at times translated in the LXX as *pantokratōr* (e.g., Job 5:8) and in the Latin Vulgate as *omnipotens* (e.g., Ge 17.1).

17 עָבַשׁ (*ʿābaš*), פְּרֻדֹת (*perudôt*), and מֶגְרָפָה (*megrāpâ*) are all *hapax legomena* (i.e., they appear only here in the MT). *ʿĀbaš* appears to be related to the Arabic word for "to shrivel up" (*ʿabisa*); *perudôt* is possibly related to the Syriac word for "grain" or "parted things" (*perdāʾ*), though the root bears several meanings in the various Semitic languages. Even a relation with the Egyptian word for "fruit, seed" (*prt*) is not impossible. *Megrāpâ* is probably related to the Arabic word for "shovel, rake" (*mijrafatun*), which comes from the Semitic root that means "to sweep away" (*grf*).

מַמְּגֻרֹת (*mammegurôt*, "barns") is another seeming *hapax legomenon*. However, the word is probably מְגוּרָה (*megurâ*), as in Haggai 2:19, the first mem being either a case of prefixed מִן (*min*; "from," i.e., a partitive use) or an instance of enclitic mem (i.e., to be read with the previous word), as H. D. Hummel ("Enclitic *Mem* in Early Northwest Semitic," *JBL* 76 [1957]: 95) has suggested.

18 The Hebrew verb נֶאֶנְחָה (*neʾenḥâ*, "moan") is related to the Akkadian *anāhu* ("produce a moaning sound"). נָבֹכוּ (*nābōkû*) is from בּוּך (*bûk*, "to wander aimlessly"). The cattle wander listlessly and frustratedly to and fro (NIV, "mill about") in search of food because there is no pasturage for them.

נֶאְשָׁמוּ (*neʾšammû*, "suffering") is probably Niphal from the verb *ʾāšam* ("suffer punishment"), not as mistakenly in the KJV from the verb *šāmam* ("be desolate"). All creation is seen as suffering the results of human sin (cf. Ge 3:17–18; Jer 12:4; Zep 1:2–3; Ro 8:19–22).

D. The Prophet's Examples (1:19–20)

> ¹⁹To you, O LORD, I call,
>   for fire has devoured the open pastures
>   and flames have burned up all the trees of the field.
> ²⁰Even the wild animals pant for you;
>   the streams of water have dried up
>   and fire has devoured the open pastures.

COMMENTARY

19–20 The first major section concludes with two examples of the need for seeking God in the present crisis: one from the prophet himself (v.19) and the other from the animal creation (v.20). Overcome with the realization of the extreme danger of the situation, Joel breaks forth in a cry to the Lord, who alone can forgive and deliver his people and all creation from this calamity and the still greater one that seems certain to follow. The prophet speaks of the loss of pasturage as well as of the trees. What the locusts have not destroyed, a severe summer's heat and drought have ruined.

Likewise, the beasts of the field pant for God. Perhaps Joel is intimating that they are more sensi-tive to the basic issues at hand than are God's own people (cf. Isa 1:3).

The conditions of the land are desperate. In the midst of seemingly unending prosperity, all the land has suffered an unprecedented locust invasion accompanied by a great drought, with the subsequent loss of all harvests. To Joel, God's message is plain. The barrenness of the land reflects the dryness and decay of the hearts of the people. Accordingly, God has judged them. Even the animal world seems to sense this. How much more should the people! If, however, the hearts of God's people remain unmoved and unrepentant, worse judgment looms ahead.

NOTES

20 עָרַג (ʿārag, "to pant, ascend"; GK 6864) occurs in the OT only here and twice in Psalm 42:1[2], where also the idea of "ascending" is probably to be understood. This rare word is related to the Ethiopic word for "to ascend" (ʿärägä). The full idea in the OT seems to be that of ascending with longing desire and strong impulse.

For the term "streams of water" (NIV; NASB, "water brooks"), see W. Leslau, "Observations on Semitic Cognates in Ugaritic," *Or* 37 (1961): 350, who calls it "the innermost part of a valley flowing with water." Thus, because all the water courses—to their very center—have dried up, the beasts of the field must ascend to the higher lands and reach out in longing desire to God their Provider.

III. WARNINGS CONCERNING THE COMING CONFLICT (2:1–27)

A. The Occasion: The "Locust Plague" (2:1–11)

> [1] Blow the trumpet in Zion;
>   sound the alarm on my holy hill.
> Let all who live in the land tremble,
>   for the day of the LORD is coming.
> It is close at hand—

2   a day of darkness and gloom,
        a day of clouds and blackness.
    Like dawn spreading across the mountains
        a large and mighty army comes,
    such as never was of old
        nor ever will be in ages to come.

³ Before them fire devours,
        behind them a flame blazes.
    Before them the land is like the garden of Eden,
        behind them, a desert waste —
    nothing escapes them.
⁴ They have the appearance of horses;
        they gallop along like cavalry.
⁵ With a noise like that of chariots
        they leap over the mountaintops,
    like a crackling fire consuming stubble,
        like a mighty army drawn up for battle.

⁶ At the sight of them, nations are in anguish;
        every face turns pale.
⁷ They charge like warriors;
        they scale walls like soldiers.
    They all march in line,
        not swerving from their course.
⁸ They do not jostle each other;
        each marches straight ahead.
    They plunge through defenses
        without breaking ranks.
⁹ They rush upon the city;
        they run along the wall.
    They climb into the houses;
        like thieves they enter through the windows.
¹⁰ Before them the earth shakes,
        the sky trembles,
    the sun and moon are darkened,
        and the stars no longer shine.
¹¹ The LORD thunders
        at the head of his army;
    his forces are beyond number,

> and mighty are those who obey his command.
> The day of the LORD is great;
>   it is dreadful.
> Who can endure it?

COMMENTARY

1–2 Several views have been forwarded as to the identification of the locusts of 2:1–11 and their relation to the locust plague of ch. 1. The position taken here is that with the picture of the historical locust plague that Joel has just experienced vividly before him, and with the warning of judgment firmly in mind (1:15), the prophet develops his metaphor of locusts being a nation/army into a full-blown allegory portraying the coming Assyrian forces. The appearance and martial activities of the locusts are analogous to those of a real army. In describing throughout the next verses that coming contingent of invaders, Joel maintains the double figure of the locusts and the invading armies: their arrival and appearance (vv.2b–5), and their operation and effectiveness (vv.6–9).

That the imminent historical situation is in view under a double figure is understood from several elements. For one thing, the ancient world abounded with examples of likening armies to locusts or vice versa. Indeed, the locust was a common figure of the armies of the Neo-Assyrian kings. The fitness of the image is further seen in Joel's account: in the darkening of the day (vv.2, 10), in the suddenness of the locusts' arrival (v.2), in their horselike appearance (v.4), in the orderliness of the/battle (vv.7–8), and in the ubiquitous nature of their devastation (vv.3, 9).

Moreover, both locusts and armies are known to be the instruments of God's chastening (e.g., Dt 28:38–39; 1Ki 8:35–39; Isa 45:1; Am 4:9). Yet, while similar terms are used in connection with both (cf. 1:2 with 2:1; 1:6 with 2:2, 5), the imagery goes beyond a literal locust plague in 2:1–11 (e.g., vv.3, 6, 10), especially as amplified in the details contained in the spiritual challenge based on this event in 2:12–27 (cf. particularly vv.17, 20, 26–27).

Thus, Joel pictures the invaders as spread out before the walls of the city and cries out, "Blow the trumpet ... sound the alarm!" The trumpet involved was the *šôpār*, the ceremonial horn. Made from a ram's horn, it was used from earliest times as a signal to battle (e.g., Jdg 3:27; 6:34) or (as here) a signal of imminent danger (e.g., Hos 5:8; 8:1; Am 3:6). The *šôpār* had both sacred and secular uses; its combination with "my holy hill" here stresses the spiritual basis of the war situation.

At the sound of the alarm all will tremble because of the fearfulness of the events that are to take place. It is "the day of the LORD"! That which was viewed as impending (1:15) is now seen as having arrived in all of its frightful consequences: the arrival of the enemy army. Accordingly, that "day" will be one of darkness and gloominess, of clouds and thick darkness (v.2a; cf. Am 5:18–20). With the suddenness of dawn spreading over the tops of the mountains, a mighty army has appeared, which in its terrible battle array casts its shadow over the entire face of the land. The unparalleled locust invasion of Joel's day is a harbinger of even direr times to come.

3–5 Verses 3–9 form the middle unit of 2:1–11. The section falls into two strophes, each introduced by similar phraseology: "before them" (v.3) and "at the sight of them" (v.6). Joel portrays the effect of the invaders' advance (v.3). That which had been a scene of beauty will become a picture of utter desolation. Nothing in the land will escape. Joel then describes the appearance of that enemy horde under three similes: a rumbling like that of chariots, a raging fire, and a well-trained military force. If the locust swarm can be thus described, how much more that coming human army!

6–9 Indeed that coming army, like the preceding locusts, will prove to be an unstoppable force. It is a small wonder that terror will grip the hearts of all the people. Joel's description turns to infantry movements. The attack of that mighty army is compared to the ubiquitous nature of a locust swarm. They perform as heroic warriors; keeping their appointed place of service without deviation, they climb the walls of the city, rush through its streets, and reach the innermost recesses of every place.

Verse 7 describes the onrush of the mighty men of war, first against, then over the walls. All the while each moves straightforward (cf. Jos 6:5), holding his rank and course. Having reiterated the unity and harmony of action among the soldiers, Joel next depicts (v.8) the invincibility of the invading soldiers as they unswervingly continue through the city's defenses.

Verse 9 describes the power and swiftness of their attack. As the locusts did, so the soldiers rush unrestrictedly to and fro through the city; they run along the tops of its walls; and they scale up the house walls and enter in at the open or latticed windows in search of their prey with the speed and daring of a thief in search of that which is not his.

10–11 The third strophe of vv.1–11 is stitched to the previous one by the opening "before them" (*lepānāyw*, v.10; cf. v.3 and *mippānāyw*, v.6). Verse 11 contains the phrase *lipnê ḥêlô* ("before his army"), thus providing further unity to the whole section (vv.1–11).

Joel brings the entire description to a close by explaining this army's sure success. Its leader is none other than the omnipotent and sovereign God himself. Utilizing epithets that were well-known to every Israelite since the days of the exodus experience, Joel depicts God as moving with great might before the enemy host, "his army." There are signs on earth (a great shaking) and in the heavens (the luminaries darkened). Before the advancing army the thunderstorm rages. The sight of that force ought to be enough to strike terror into human hearts. The accompanying signs of God's visible presence leading that powerful battle array will melt the stoniest of hearts. It is nothing else than the day of the Lord's judgment against his own. Who can endure his visitation?

NOTES

2 Of the four words used here for the idea of darkness, the first, third, and fourth were used to describe the scene when the children of Israel were encamped at Mount Sinai (Dt 4:11); the first and second portrayed the ninth plague against Egypt (Ex 10:21–22). Zephaniah repeated all four in his description of that future "day of the Lord" (Zep 1:15) as being one of impenetrable darkness.

4 That Sennacherib failed to take Jerusalem in his third campaign (the inevitable coup de grace was left to the Neo-Babylonian Nebuchadnezzar) does not minimize God's warning, delivered in stylized language. Sennacherib reported that he thoroughly devastated the land, though admitting that he failed to take Jerusalem. "He himself [i.e., Hezekiah], like a caged bird, I enclosed him in Jerusalem, his royal city" (*Assyrian Annals* 3.18–49, in R. Borger, *Babylonish-Assyrische Lesestücke* [Rome: Pontificum Institutum Biblicum, 1963], 3, table 46). The resemblance of locusts to horses has occasioned both the Italian (*cavalletta*, "little horse") and German (*Heupferd*, "hay horse") terms for locusts.

5 The Assyrian war chariot was a dreaded item. Sennacherib's own special war chariot was named *sāpinat raggi u ṣēni* ("The Vanquisher of the Wicked and Evil"; *Assyrian Annals* 6.8) and *sāpinat zāiri* ("The Vanquisher of the Enemy"; *Assyrian Annals* 5.70).

6 The word translated "anguish" is a strong one. It is used of the anguish of a woman in labor (Isa 13:8; 26:17; Mic 4:9–10), of the Canaanites who trembled before the Israelites (Dt 2:25), of the dread of the Egyptians before the Babylonian invasion (Eze 30:16), and of the fear of the Babylonians before the oncoming assault of the Medes and Persians (Jer 51:29). The terrifying aspects of the approach of the Assyrian army are often mentioned in the *Assyrian Annals*.

קִבְּצוּ פָארוּר (*qibbᵉṣû pāʾrûr*, "turns pale"; GK 6999) is a rare (only here and Na 2:10) and difficult phrase. Nearly every etymology for the Hebrew consonants involved in the word *pāʾrûr* has been conjectured. The translations used for this commentary have followed the lead of most modern expositors in deriving the word from the root *pʾr* ("to beautify, glorify"; GK 6995).

7 יְעַבְּטוּן (*yᵉᶜabbᵉṭûn*, "swerving"; GK 6293) has proven to be troublesome. Two possibilities commend themselves. (1) A. Guillaume, *Hebrew and Arabic Lexicography* (Leiden: E. J. Brill, 1965), 2:27, suggests a relation to the Arabic *ᶜabaṭa* ("to go off the middle of the road"). (2) Alternatively, the Hebrew word may be understood in the sense of "to hold to." Thus taking the Hebrew לֹא (*lōʾ*, "not") not as a negative but instead as the asseverative particle לֻא (*luʾ*, "yea, indeed"), the whole line would read, "And each marches on his own way; yea, they hold to their own paths." That *lōʾ* occurs in the next verse as the regular negative particle is no argument against its being an asseverative particle here; for in 2 Samuel 18:12 it occurs twice, once with asseverative emphasis and once as a negative. For an excellent discussion of the verb involved, see J. C. Greenfield, "Studies in Aramaic Lexicography I," *JAOS* 82 (1962): 295–96. On the problem of *lōʾ*, see D. Rudolf Meyer, *Hebräische Grammatik* (2 vols.; Berlin: de Gruyter, 1969), 2:173; B. Waltke and M. O'Connor, *Biblical Hebrew Syntax* (Winona Lake, Ind.: Eisenbrauns, 1990), 211.

8 The Hebrew word שֶׁלַח (*šelaḥ*, "defense"; GK 8939) poses still another knotty problem. While it occurs in six other places in the OT (2Ch 23:9–10; 32:5; Ne 4:17, 23; Job 33:18; 36:12), the exact meaning has eluded exegetes in all ages. Either some sort of weapon, a watercourse, or a defensive wall makes good sense here; perhaps the former is preferable in the light of the verbs that follow. For details see Stuart, 247–48; H. W. Wolff, *Joel and Amos* (Hermeneia; Philadelphia, Fortress, 1977), 38, 46.

10 For details relative to the phenomenal events connected with the day of the Lord, see comments on 2:28–32.

B. The Call for Personal Penitence (2:12–14)

¹²"Even now," declares the Lᴏʀᴅ,
　　"return to me with all your heart,
　　with fasting and weeping and mourning."

¹³ Rend your heart
　　and not your garments.

> Return to the Lord your God,
>   for he is gracious and compassionate,
> slow to anger and abounding in love,
>   and he relents from sending calamity.
> ¹⁴Who knows? He may turn and have pity
>   and leave behind a blessing —
> grain offerings and drink offerings
>   for the Lord your God.

COMMENTARY

12 In the light of the impending day of the Lord, Joel turns to admonish the people to pray. He first pleads with each Israelite to approach with a repentant heart the God of all mercy (vv.12–14). By means of the introductory phrase ("'Even now,' declares the Lord") Joel presents God's own deep concern for his people. Like his contemporaries, Joel emphasizes the need to turn to God in true repentance and in total reliance on the God of all mercies, to turn from their past iniquities and recognize that the repentant heart is the only soil in which the regenerated soul can grow.

13–14 Joel pleads with the people for broken and contrite hearts (cf. Ps 51:17). Rendtorff, 191, appropriately remarks, "One message is important: as far as Israel is concerned, the only way to survive is to repent and call on the name of the Lord." Important as outward conformity to formal worship might be, the condition of the heart is still more important to God (cf. Isa 1:11–17; 58:3b–12; Am 5:21–24; Mic 6:6–8). Although Joel does not dare to presume upon God's mercy, his firm belief in God's compassion causes him to suggest that God may well relent. The divine attributes mentioned here provide assurance that where genuine repentance takes place, God may well relent from sending the deserved punishment (cf. Ex 32:14; 2Sa 24:16; 2Pe 3:9).

NOTE

13 The classic expression of these divine attributes occurs in Exodus 34:6–7 (cf. Jnh 4:2; Na 1:3), while various combinations of them are found in several places in the OT.

C. The Call for Communal Lament (2:15–17)

> ¹⁵Blow the trumpet in Zion,
>   declare a holy fast,
>   call a sacred assembly.

¹⁶Gather the people,
    consecrate the assembly;
  bring together the elders,
    gather the children,
      those nursing at the breast.
  Let the bridegroom leave his room
    and the bride her chamber.
¹⁷Let the priests, who minister before the LORD,
    weep between the temple porch and the altar.
  Let them say, "Spare your people, O LORD.
    Do not make your inheritance an object of scorn,
    a byword among the nations.
  Why should they say among the peoples,
    'Where is their God?'"

COMMENTARY

15–17 Joel issues another call for a solemn assembly (cf. 1:14). Once again the *šōpār* is to sound (cf. 2:1), this time to convene the assembly in the light of the revealed invasion that stands so near. All are to come, from the elders with their wise counsel (cf. 1:14) to the youngest suckling. All must meet with God and listen to his commandments and act on them, as is their privilege and responsibility as members of the assembly. Even the newlyweds, who might otherwise be legitimately exempted from such duties (Dt 24:5), are to attend.

The priests are to be the first to experience repentance in their lives. Then they are to lead the people while standing between the vestibule on the eastern side of the temple (1Ki 6:3), which separated the inner or priests' court (1Ki 6:36) from the great court of the laity (2Ch 4:9) and the brazen altar of burnt offering that lay within the inner court. Their main business is to implore the God of all grace to spare his people, not only for their good, but, more important, so that his inheritance be not a reproach before the world or his name be brought into disrepute because of what they have done.

D. The Lord's Assurance (2:18–27)

¹⁸Then the LORD will be jealous for his land
    and take pity on his people.

¹⁹The LORD will reply to them:

"I am sending you grain, new wine and oil,
  enough to satisfy you fully;
never again will I make you
  an object of scorn to the nations.

20 "I will drive the northern army far from you,
  pushing it into a parched and barren land,
with its front columns going into the eastern sea
  and those in the rear into the western sea.
And its stench will go up;
  its smell will rise."

Surely he has done great things.
21   Be not afraid, O land;
  be glad and rejoice.
Surely the Lord has done great things.
22   Be not afraid, O wild animals,
  for the open pastures are becoming green.
The trees are bearing their fruit;
  the fig tree and the vine yield their riches.
23 Be glad, O people of Zion,
  rejoice in the Lord your God,
for he has given you
  the autumn rains in righteousness.
He sends you abundant showers,
  both autumn and spring rains, as before.
24 The threshing floors will be filled with grain;
  the vats will overflow with new wine and oil.
25 "I will repay you for the years the locusts have eaten —
  the great locust and the young locust,
  the other locusts and the locust swarm —
my great army that I sent among you.
26 You will have plenty to eat, until you are full,
  and you will praise the name of the Lord your God,
  who has worked wonders for you;
never again will my people be shamed.
27 Then you will know that I am in Israel,
  that I am the Lord your God,
  and that there is no other;
never again will my people be shamed.

COMMENTARY

18–19 The Masoretic pointing calls for a past action ("and the LORD was jealous and took pity"; cf. LXX; Vul.; Syr.; NRSV; NJB; REB). Viewed in this way, vv.18–27 can be understood as recalling an occasion when God's people did repent in the light of threatened danger and God did respond graciously to them. Such a scenario is broadly reminiscent of the events involved in Sennacherib's invasion of Judah and his unsuccessful siege of Jerusalem in 701 BC (2Ki 19).

The reading of the NIV and NASB, however, takes the unpointed form as a future promise (cf. KJV; NKJV; Theodotian's version of the LXX). According to this understanding, God promises to the repentant heart that his godly, jealous love (as a husband's for his wife) will move him to have pity on his people. His first promise is twofold: he will immediately restore all that has been lost in the locust plague so necessary for their daily lives physically (1:4, 11–12) and spiritually (1:9), and they will be fully satisfied (cf. Dt 6:10–11; 8:7–10; 11:13–15). His second promise is that they will no longer be a reproach among the nations.

20 As the third of his promises, God pledges that he will take away from the people "the northern army" (lit., "the northerner"), a term that has been understood variously. When the term is interpreted in the light of the context and structure of ch. 2, the most adequate view sees it as a metaphor referring to a foreign invader (i.e., the Assyrians) descending from the north. This prediction is built on the incident of the locust plague.

God promises through Joel that he will drive that enemy far away, if only the people will turn to him in genuine repentance. He will drive that army into a dry and desolate land, no doubt primarily the desert west of the Dead Sea and south and southeast of Judah.

A further reason for this turned-about condition, despite its being the Lord's army, will be that Assyria's haughty pride will cause it to leave its proper bounds (cf. Pss 35:26; 38:16; cf. also La 1:9), thus bragging and assuming that the great destruction it will effect will be its own doing (similarly, cf. Eze 35:13; Da 8:4, 8, 11; 11:36–37).

21–27 Joel continues to give God's response. Should the people truly repent, not only will God's promises of restoration, rest, and protection be theirs, but certain additional benefits will accrue. The message is one of comfort: "Be not afraid."

The first object of God's consoling words is the personified ground—that which has directly suffered so much. It is not to fear but to rejoice and be glad (cf. 1:16); for God himself, the one who truly does great things (2:20; cf. 1Sa 12:24; Ps 126:2–5), will undertake for it.

Next the personification is applied to beasts of the field (cf. 1:18–20). They will have an abundance of tender grass. Furthermore, the fig tree and the vine (cf. 1:7, 12), the symbols of Israel's restored relation with her sovereign Lord, will bear again in full strength. This thought leads Joel to the third and central object of divine solace: Israel herself (v.23). The people of Zion (i.e., all true Israelites; cf. Ps 149:2) are to rejoice and be glad in the Lord their God, for he will restore them in righteousness. He will send again the refreshing former and latter rains, thus speaking to them of his renewed care for his people.

The careful play on words in the Hebrew text has caused a great deal of discussion. The twice-occurring Hebrew word *môreh* may be translated "rains" (as in the NIV). It may also be translated "teacher" (NIV note); and with the *liṣdāqâ* (lit., "for righteousness") that follows, the first *môreh* has been understood by some to refer to God's righteous prophets or to the Messiah himself.

However, there is another alternative. One may take the first *môreh* (lit., *hammôreh*, i.e., with the definite article) in accordance with its basic construction as a participle rather than as a noun, and view the construction impersonally. The verse can then be translated thus: "For he [God] will give to you that which gives instruction in righteousness, that is, he will send down to you the early and latter rain, as before." Two reasons lead to this as the proper interpretation.

(1) A wordplay is clearly intended. The correct reading of the second *môreh* may actually be *yôreh*, as is read in some thirty-four manuscripts; this seems to be the proper word for "early rain" (cf. Dt 11:14). The wordplay is thus between *hammôreh*, "that which gives instruction," and *yôreh*, "early rain."

(2) The conjunction that follows *hammôreh* is to be understood pleonastically, "yea, for," or as an explicative, "that is." Thus, that which follows identifies that which gives instruction in righteousness, namely, the renewed sending of the early and latter rains.

The renewed rain thus becomes another outward symbol of an inward reality, a restored fellowship with God. Since the signs of the covenant—the offerings—had been cut off in God's judgment through the locust plague, repentance of heart will bring restoration of fellowship, hence restoration of the covenantal privileges. The rains will serve as the sign of God's forgiveness and provision, not only for their daily necessities, but also of the revitalized earth that will enable the forfeited right to offer sacrifices to be regained (cf. Dt 6:24–25; 2Ch 6:26–27; 7:14; Mal 3:3).

The "autumn rain" comes at the beginning of the rainy season in October–November; the "spring rain" is that of March–April. The arrival of these rains on proper schedule as in prior times will demonstrate the blessing of God on the heart that is now properly prepared before him (cf. Dt 11:13–17; Jer 5:24–25; Hos 6:1–3).

Joel next mentions God's supplying of the people's third need. Not only will he give renewed fellowship (v.23a) and renewed rain (v.23b) but also renewed provisions (vv.24–25). Their threshing floors will be filled with grain, their collecting vats will overflow with fresh wine and oil, and God will thoroughly restore to them the years the devastating plague has caused them to lose (cf. 1:4, 10, 17; 2:19). Whereas the locust plague brought famine, the people will now experience the full satisfaction of an abundance of food (cf. 2:19); therefore, they can praise God in the full knowledge of all that his revealed name signifies (cf. Ex 6:3; Dt 12:7; Pss 8:1–2; 66:8–15; 67:5–7; Am 5:8–9; 9:5–6).

The restored fellowship will be attested by God's renewed designation of them as "my people." They need never again "be humiliated," whether before the heathen (2:17) or the whole world (cf. Isa 29:22; 49:22–23; 54:4). No, never again! Best of all, his people will know experientially the abiding presence of God himself dwelling in their midst (cf. 2:17; 3:17, 21; Hos 11:9; cf. also Eze 48:35).

NOTES

23 The only other occurrence of מוֹרֶה (*môreh*) in the sense of "autumn and spring rains" is in a difficult text (Ps 84:6[7]) and is by no means certain. Rudolph also takes the term impersonally but points the preceding אֵת (*ʾet*), the mark of the definite direct object, as *ʾôt* ("sign") and translates the phrase, "the sign that points to salvation." The three common Hebrew words for rain appear together in Jeremiah 5:24: *gešem* ("rain"), *yôreh* ("[early] rain"), and *malqôš* ("latter rain").

24 The יֶקֶב (*yeqeb*, "wine vat"; i.e., the place in which the juice collected) is to be contrasted with the גַּת (*gat*, "vat" [cf. 3:13], i.e., the place where the fruit was trodden). The *yeqeb* was usually hewn out of rock and stood below the *gat*, to which it was connected by a channel.

25 As J. L. Crenshaw (*Joel* [AB; New York: Doubleday, 1995], 157) notes, the form of the Hebrew verb used here (*šālēm*; GK 8966) has legal overtones and "designates payment for losses incurred." With full repentance God promises full compensation for the earlier losses.

26 By שֵׁם (*šēm*, "name"; GK 9005) is intended the revealed character and reputation of God. The term came to be substituted for God himself (Da 9:18–19; Am 2:7; 9:12), became applied to Christ in the NT (e.g., Ac 4:12; 5:41; 3Jn 7), and was so used by the apostolic fathers.

IV. PREDICTIONS CONCERNING THE FUTURE CIRCUMSTANCES
(2:28–3:21 [3:1–4:21])

A. The Outpoured Spirit (2:28–32 [3:1–5])

28 "And afterward,
   I will pour out my Spirit on all people.
  Your sons and daughters will prophesy,
   your old men will dream dreams,
   your young men will see visions.
29 Even on my servants, both men and women,
   I will pour out my Spirit in those days.
30 I will show wonders in the heavens
   and on the earth,
   blood and fire and billows of smoke.
31 The sun will be turned to darkness
   and the moon to blood
   before the coming of the great and dreadful day of the Lord.
32 And everyone who calls
   on the name of the Lord will be saved;
  for on Mount Zion and in Jerusalem
   there will be deliverance,
   as the Lord has said,
  among the survivors
   whom the Lord calls.

COMMENTARY

28–32 [3:1–5] The introductory formula with which this section begins clearly places the events that follow it after those detailed in 2:1–27. Since the previous section dealt with the near future, it may be safely presumed that the events prophesied here lie still further ahead. Indeed, these chapters disclose the Lord's eschatological intentions (3, 4, MT). Two primary thoughts are included: the Lord's promise of personal provision in the lives of his own (2:28–32) and the prediction of his final triumph on behalf of his own at the culmination of the history of humankind (ch. 3).

The Lord first promises that he will pour out his Spirit in full abundance and complete refreshment. Hosea prophesied that the Lord must pour out his fury on an idolatrous Israel (5:10). Joel sees beyond this chastisement to a time in the distant future (cf. Eze 36:16–38) when, in a measure far more abundant than the promised rain (cf. 2:22–26), God will pour out his Holy Spirit in power. In those days (cf. Jer 33:15) that power will rest on all (i.e., human) flesh (cf. Isa 40:5–6; 66:23; Zec 2:12–13).

God's covenantal people are primarily in view. Joel goes on to point out that what the Lord intends is that his Holy Spirit will be poured out, not on selected individuals for a particular task but on all believers, young and old, male and female alike, regardless of their status. It will be a time of renewed spiritual activity: of prophesying, of dreams, and of visions (cf. Nu 12:6).

Accompanying the outpouring of the Holy Spirit in those days and as visible signs of his supernatural and overseeing intervention in human history, God will cause extraordinary phenomena to be seen in nature. Thus the totality of everyone's experience will be affected. Although the heavens are mentioned first, the order that follows is one of ascending emphasis, beginning with events on earth (blood, fire, and smoke) and moving to signs in the sky (the sun and moon).

Joel's depiction of the phenomenal events concerned with the day of the Lord is indebted to stock phraseology available since Israel's redemption out of Egypt at the time of the exodus event. Miraculous occurrences in the heavens (Ex 10:21–23; 14:19–20; cf. Ps 105:28) and on earth (Ex 19:16, 18; cf. Jdg 5:4–5; Ps 114:3–5; Hab 3:6) during the movement from Egypt to the Promised Land were seen as part of God's arsenal of weapons of judgment that will ultimately lead to the full blessing of his people.

Such occurrences were not only repeated in the course of Israel's subsequent history (Jos 10:9–15; Jdg 5:20–21) but also became standard imagery for the prophetic oracles of judgment (e.g., Isa 13:10, 13; Eze 32:7–8; Am 5:18–20). From there they passed on naturally into the graphically intense and more universalistic outlook of the emerging apocalyptic prophecies dealing with the end times (e.g., Isa 24:1–3, 19–20; 60:19–20; Zep 1:14–18; Zec 14:3–7). These in turn developed into the full-blown apocalyptic literature of the intertestamental and NT eras (e.g., *Apocalypse of Zephaniah* 12:1–8; Rev 6:8–9; 11:15–19; 14:19–20). Similar conclusions can be reached concerning Joel's use of blood, fire, and smoke—all well-known symbols of warfare and its attendant evils (e.g., Nu 21:28; Jdg 20:38–40; Isa 10:16; 28:11; Zec 11:1).

As I pointed out in the discussion at 1:15, the term "day of the LORD" deals with judgment. This is particularly true in the case of the enemies of Israel, whether Babylon (Isa 13:6, 9), Egypt (Jer 46:10; Eze 30:2–4), Edom (Ob 15), or all nations (Joel 3:14–15; Ob 15; Zep 1:14–18; Zec 14:3–15; Mal 4:5–6; cf. 1Th 5:2; 2Th 2:2; 2Pe 3:10). It can also be true for Israel-Judah (Isa 2:12–22; Eze

13:5; Joel 1:15; 2:1, 11; Am 5:18–20; Zep 1:7; Zec 14:1–2).

As to the time of judgment, it can be present (Joel 1:15), lie in the near future (Isa 2:12–22; 13:6, 9; Jer 46:10; Eze 13:5; Joel 2:1, 11; Am 5:18–20), be future-eschatological (Eze 30:2–3; Zep 1:7, 14–18; Mal 4:1–6), or be purely eschatological (Joel 3:14–15; Zec 14:1–21; 1Th 5:1–11; 2Th 2:2; 2Pe 3:10–13). So teachings concerning the judgment associated with that day can apply anywhere along the continuum that culminates in the final day of the Lord. With such an understanding believers are assured of God's sovereign control of the flow of history and his ultimate good intentions for them. Such knowledge should bring a continuing realization of the necessity of trust and godly living.

Theologically, the scope of these passages makes it clear that the eschatological day of the Lord is the culmination of God's judging and restoring process. It involves the time of great affliction for God's people (Da 12:1; Mt 24:15–28) and of earth's judgment (Isa 26:20–21; Rev 6; 8–11; 14:14–16:21), and it closes with the return of the Lord in glory (Rev 19:11–16) and the battle of Armageddon (Rev 16:16; 19:17–21; cf. Eze 38–39). Joel's use of the term, then, is in harmony with the totality of Scripture. By "the day of the LORD" is meant that time when God, for his glory and humanity's good, actively intervenes in human affairs in judgment against sinners and on behalf of his own people.

The day of the Lord also deals with deliverance for God's people and the hope of a final blessed state (Joel 2:31–32; 3:16–21; Zep 3:9–20; Zec 14:3; Mal 4:5–6). The eschatological prophecies dealing with these two themes are characteristic of OT kingdom oracles.

Thus in v.32 the second of the twin themes associated with kingdom oracles comes into full view.

Along with the outpouring of the Holy Spirit, there will be the outworking of salvation for those who truly trust God as their Redeemer. To "call on the name of the LORD" is to invoke his name in approaching him (cf. Ge 4:26; 12:8), but especially to call on him in believing faith (Pss 99:6; 145:18; Ro 10:13). For such a one there will be not only physical deliverance but also spiritual transformation and the blessedness of peace and prosperity. While salvation-deliverance will be the experience of the one who truly "calls on the name of the LORD" (cf. 2:26) in that day, it is God himself who will summon that remnant.

Before leaving this chapter, we must briefly examine the issue of the citation of these words by Peter in his famous address at Pentecost (Ac 2:17–21). While several theories have been advanced as to the relation between these two passages of Scripture, the position taken here attempts to strike a balance between the extreme views of a total fulfillment at Pentecost and the complete lack of any relationship.

Although the full context of Acts 2 does not exhaust the larger context of Joel 2:28–3:21, we can scarcely doubt that Peter viewed Joel's prophecy as applicable to Pentecost, for he plainly said that such was the case (Ac 2:16). Moreover, both his sermon and subsequent remarks are intimately intertwined with Joel's message (e.g., cf. Joel 2:30–31 with Ac 2:22–24; Joel 2:32 with Ac 2:38–40).

The precise applicability of Joel's prophecy to Pentecost can be gleaned from some of the Petrine interpretive changes and additions to Joel's text. Thus, under divine inspiration Peter added to Joel's words relative to the outpouring of the Holy Spirit *kai prophēteusousin* ("and they will prophesy"; cf. Joel 2:29 with Ac 2:18). The intent of Joel's prophecy was not only the restoration of prophecy but that such a gift was open to all classes of people. The Spirit-empowered words of the apostles on

Pentecost were, therefore, evidence of the accuracy of Joel's prediction. (They were also a direct fulfillment of Christ's promise to send the Holy Spirit [see Lk 24:49; Jn 14:16–18; 15:26–27; 16:7–15; Ac 1:4–5, 8; 2:33].)

Again, Peter affirmed that Joel's more general term *ʾaḥᵃrê-kēn* ("afterward") is to be understood as *en tais eschatais hēmerais* ("in the last days"; cf. Joel 2:28 with Ac 2:17). The NT writers made it clear that both Israel's future age and the church age are designated by the same terms: "the last [latter] days [times]" (1Ti 4:1; 2Ti 3:1–8; Heb 1:1–2; Jas 5:3; 1Pe 1:5, 20; 4:7; 2Pe 3:1–9; 1Jn 2:18; Jude 18). Accordingly, the point of Peter's remark in Acts 2:16 must be that Pentecost, as the initial day of that period known as "the last [latter] days," which will culminate in those events surrounding the return of Jesus the Messiah, partakes of the character of those final events and so is a herald and earnest of what surely must come. Pentecost, then, forms a corroborative pledge in the series of fulfillments that will culminate in the ultimate fulfillment of Joel's prophecy in the eschatological complex.

It must also be noted that the outpouring of the Spirit is an accompanying feature of that underlying basic divine promise given to Abraham and the patriarchs, ratified through David, reaffirmed in the terms of the new covenant, and guaranteed in the person and work of Jesus the Messiah (cf. Ge 12:1–3; 15; 17; 2Sa 7:11–29; Ps 89:3–4, 27–29; Jer 31:31–34; Ac 2:29–36; 26:6–7; Gal 3:5–14; Eph 1:10–14; Heb 6:13–20; 9:15).

Christ's prophetic promise was directly fulfilled; Joel's prophecy was fulfilled but not consummated. It awaits its ultimate fulfillment but was provisionally applicable to Pentecost and the age of the Spirit as the initial step in those last days that will culminate in the prophesied the day of the Lord.

NOTES

31 For the term "kingdom oracles" (see above), see "Prophecy in the Old Testament" (in *Dictionary of Biblical Imagery*; ed. by L. Ryken, J. C. Wilhoit, and T. Longman III; Downers Grove, Ill.: InterVarsity Press, 1998), 668–70.

32 For the concept of "fulfillment without consummation," see R. T. France, *Jesus and the Old Testament* (London: Tyndale, 1971), 160–62. The Hebrew nouns used here (*pᵉlêṭâ ... ubaśśᵉrîdîm*, "deliverance [NIV; "those who escape," NASB] ... survivors") often occur together to express a complete escape as opposed to a few survivors (Jer 44:18) or none at all (Jos 8:22; Jer 42:17).

B. The Coming Judgment (3[4]:1–8)

¹"In those days and at that time,
   when I restore the fortunes of Judah and Jerusalem,
²I will gather all nations
   and bring them down to the Valley of Jehoshaphat.

> There I will enter into judgment against them
>   concerning my inheritance, my people Israel,
> for they scattered my people among the nations
>   and divided up my land.
> ³They cast lots for my people
>   and traded boys for prostitutes;
> they sold girls for wine
>   that they might drink.

⁴"Now what have you against me, O Tyre and Sidon and all you regions of Philistia? Are you repaying me for something I have done? If you are paying me back, I will swiftly and speedily return on your own heads what you have done. ⁵For you took my silver and my gold and carried off my finest treasures to your temples. ⁶You sold the people of Judah and Jerusalem to the Greeks, that you might send them far from their homeland.

⁷"See, I am going to rouse them out of the places to which you sold them, and I will return on your own heads what you have done. ⁸I will sell your sons and daughters to the people of Judah, and they will sell them to the Sabeans, a nation far away." The LORD has spoken.

COMMENTARY

1−3 Chapter 2 ends with blessings and safety for the believer of the future. The third chapter begins with a warning of judgment. The basis of that judgment is stated first (vv.1−3); the sure execution of that judgment follows (vv.4−8).

In contrast to what has gone before, Joel now has a new and important announcement. In those future times (cf. 2:29) in which God deals kindly with his covenantal people (cf. Jer 33:15−18), he will gather all nations together (cf. Zep 3:8) and enter into judgment with them in the Valley of Jehoshaphat concerning the treatment of his own (cf. Ro 11:25−26).

The words "I restore the fortunes" lend themselves to two basic meanings: (1) The translation of the KJV—"I shall bring again the captivity"—is supported by the ancient versions (LXX, Syr) and by such texts as Deuteronomy 30:3; Jeremiah 29:14; 30:3; 33:7, 11, 26 [note]; and Zephaniah 3:20 (cf. Pss 14:7; 53:6). (2) The rendering adopted by the NIV and NASB appears to be appropriate also in Hosea 6:11 and Amos 9:14 (see NIV note). The latter idea includes the former and also involves the idea of Israel's renewed prosperity and felicity. Since the OT prophets appear to have used the term in this way (Jer 30:18; 31:23 note; 32:44), it seems to be the better understanding of the words involved.

Joel's words are those of assurance. Even in those dire times, the immutable God is still on the throne, directing all things to their appointed end (cf. Mic 4:11−12).

While several views exist as to the words of the Hebrew text of "The Valley of Jehoshaphat," one must conclude that the primary idea here has to do with a place where God enters into judgment with the nations, not a known valley, as the wordplay makes clear. For the word "Jehoshaphat" and the verb for judging (cf. also v.12) come from the same Hebrew root (*šāpaṭ*). Joel subsequently calls it "the valley of decision" (v.14).

A. S. Kapelrud (*Joel Studies* [Uppsala: Almquist and Wiksells, 1948]) is no doubt correct in pointing out that there was a valley tradition in Israel with regard to battles of judgment. Nothing could be more natural in the light of the topography of the land of Canaan. Jeremiah told of the "Valley of Ben [Son of] Hinnom" (Jer 7:30–34; 19:1–7), which became the "Valley of Slaughter." Isaiah spoke of the "Valley of Vision" in a message of judgment against Israel (Isa 22:1–13). Ezekiel (Eze 39:11) prophesied against the valley of the ʿōbĕrîm ("those who travel"), which will form the burial ground for the defeated northern foes and will become the "Valley of Hamon Gog."

Zechariah's valley (Zec 14:3–5), formed by a cataclysmic earthquake, is also connected with the Lord's judgment against the nations in a great battle. Although it is true that battles associated with valleys became a traditional motif, this need not necessarily mean that Joel's "valley" is a mere metaphor for a "battle between Yahweh and the nations" (Garrett, 379). For although wordplay was Joel's primary intention rather than a specific location, if Zechariah's prediction of an earthquake is not itself metaphorical, it may indicate that a literal valley near Jerusalem is intended. Whether or not such is the case, the memory of the great earthquake in Uzziah's time (Am 1:1) forms a vivid picture of what could occur in the last days (cf. Isa 29:6; Eze 38:19 with Joel 3:16; Zec 14:5).

God rehearses the charges against the heathen nations for which he will judge them. First, they have scattered his people among the nations. God in his infinite wisdom and divine perspective calls attention to the scattering of his own among the nations not only after the fall of Jerusalem, but also up to the end times through their continued dispersion and persecution. God himself, therefore, will bring his people back to his land (cf. Jer 50:17–26).

Second, though the people have divided God's land (cf. Am 7:17), he has not renounced his claim to his people or to his land.

Third, so cheaply were his people valued that the heathen cast lots for them and, even worse, sold a boy for a harlot's hire (so Peshitta) and a girl so that they might drink a flask of wine.

4–8 Joel goes on to record God's solemn promise of the sure execution of his judgment on the nations. He begins with God's question as to their purposes regarding himself. The districts of western Canaan, Tyre, and Sidon (well-known slave dealers in the ancient world) and the Philistine coast (often prophetically condemned with the Phoenicians) are singled out as the chief representatives of Judah's enemies. Theirs had been the most inhuman of all crimes—that of dealing in human merchandise. God warns them that if they now add insult to this injury by taking vengeance without cause against the Lord himself, they can be assured that God will most swiftly repay them in just kind.

The charges against the nations are detailed in vv.5–6. They have taken the silver and gold of God's people. The reference is probably to the continual plundering of their houses that were so handsomely furnished in this period of great prosperity. Again, they have taken Judah's valuables to their palaces (or temples). Furthermore, they have sold the children into the hands of the Greek slave-traders so as to send them far away from the borders of their homeland.

No doubt more than commercial gain has motivated these hostile neighbors. There appears to be the deeper design of systematically reducing the number of God's children from the land of their promised inheritance. As such these powers of Joel's day stand as representatives of that great socio-religio-political system that will oppose God's people in a future day (cf. Da 2:44–45; 7:9–14; 8:23–27; 11:36–45; 2Th 2:3–4; Rev 13; 14:8–11; 17–18).

God warns these enemies that for their oppression he will righteously repay them in kind (vv.7–8; cf. Isa 24:14–23; 2Th 1:6–8) while arousing his dispersed and captive people from the distant lands of their bondage. As he had warned them (v.4), he will give those slave-dealers a taste of their own medicine. Their people will in turn be sold into captivity by the children of Judah to the Sabeans, who will send them afar. D. A. Hubbard (*Joel and Amos* [TOTC]; Downers Grove, Ill.: InterVarsity Press, 1989], 76–77) observes, "Their penchant for caravan trading meant that slaves sold to them could ultimately be dispersed almost anywhere from the Indian Ocean to the East Coast of Africa."

Tyre and Sidon would soon know the invader's heel, for Esarhaddon (681–668 BC) overran Sidon and deported its citizens to various places in the Neo-Assyrian Empire. Tyre survived a similar fate by paying a huge tribute to the Assyrian king as well as to his successor Ashurbanipal (668–626 BC). With the decline of the Assyrians both cities revived but were quickly absorbed, first into the Neo-Babylonian and then the Persian empires. Although the Persians treated both cities well, Sidon was especially favored.

In 345 BC Sidon was captured by King Antiochus III, who sold its citizens into slavery. Alexander the Great subjugated Tyre in 331 BC, even capturing the island city. Sidon survived by submitting to the Greek conqueror. Both cities revived and became important centers in Greco-Roman times, although with varying political fortunes.

The Philistines were repeatedly subdued by Assyrian kings: Tiglath-pileser III in 734 BC, Sargon II in 720 BC and again in 713/12 BC, and Sennacherib in 701 BC. The Chaldean Nebuchadnezzar II brought them into the Neo-Babylonian Empire in 604 BC.

NOTES

2 For God's concern for his people and the land, see W. C. Kaiser Jr., "The Promised Land: A Biblical-Historical View," *BS* 138 (1981): 302–12. On the Valley of Jehoshaphat, see F. Merrill, *Haggai, Zechariah, Malachi* (Chicago: Moody Press, 1994), 348–49.

3 For the selling of captives to foreign people, see Genesis 37:36; Obadiah 11; Nahum 3:10. This practice was common among the ancients (see Thucydides, *Hist* 3.50) as the Jews themselves were to experience (1 Macc 3:41; 2 Macc 8:11, 25; Josephus, *Ant.* 12.298–99 [7.3]; idem., *J.W.* 6.414–19 [9.2]). Lamentably, it was a charge also brought against the Jews in the northern kingdom by Amos (Am 2:6).

For the casting of lots for captives, see Nahum 3:10 and Thucydides (*Hist.* 3.50). One is also reminded of the casting of lots for Messiah's garments (cf. Ps 22:18 with Mt 27:35).

4 The slave trading of the Phoenicians is described in Homer's *Odyssey* (15.403–84); see also Herodotus, *Persian Wars* 1.1; 2.54, 56. The sense of the Hebrew idiom here is that of the Akkadian *gimilla turru* ("to return an act in kind").

C. The Coming Warfare (3[4]:9–17)

⁹Proclaim this among the nations:
    Prepare for war!
  Rouse the warriors!
    Let all the fighting men draw near and attack.
¹⁰Beat your plowshares into swords
    and your pruning hooks into spears.
  Let the weakling say,
    "I am strong!"
¹¹Come quickly, all you nations from every side
    and assemble there.

  Bring down your warriors, O Lord!
¹²"Let the nations be roused;
    let them advance into the Valley of Jehoshaphat,
  for there I will sit
    to judge all the nations on every side.
¹³Swing the sickle,
    for the harvest is ripe.
  Come, trample the grapes,
    for the winepress is full
    and the vats overflow —
  so great is their wickedness!"

¹⁴Multitudes, multitudes
    in the valley of decision!
  For the day of the Lord is near
    in the valley of decision.
¹⁵The sun and moon will be darkened,
    and the stars no longer shine.
¹⁶The Lord will roar from Zion
    and thunder from Jerusalem;
    the earth and the sky will tremble.
  But the Lord will be a refuge for his people,
    a stronghold for the people of Israel.

¹⁷"Then you will know that I, the Lord your God,
    dwell in Zion, my holy hill.
  Jerusalem will be holy;
    never again will foreigners invade her.

COMMENTARY

9−12 In the light of the prophecy of certain judgment, a warning challenge is issued, constituting a call to judgment (vv.9−12) and announcing the cause and course of that judgment (vv.13−17).

The proclamation of the Lord's message is to be circulated among the nations (cf. Am 3:9−11). All the men of war are to assemble and prepare themselves in accordance with the proper spiritual rites before battle (cf. 1Sa 7:5−9), for in the final analysis theirs is to be the culmination of all holy warfare. The mighty men of battle are to be called up for duty (cf. 2:7). All segments of society and the economy are to be on a wartime footing. The basic agricultural tools are to be fashioned into weapons; weak and cowardly men are to count themselves as mighty men of war (v.10). The nations are soon to learn that the Lord, too, is mighty in battle (cf. Ex 15:3; Ps 24:8).

All the surrounding nations are next commanded to come quickly and gather themselves together (v.11; cf. Pss 2:1−2; 110:1−3, 5−6) to that great final struggle that will culminate earth's present history (cf. Isa 24:21−23; Zec 14:1−3; Rev 19:17−19). Overcome by emotion, in a vivid apostrophe Joel cries out for their destruction: "Bring down your warriors, O LORD!" The reference is to the angelic host (cf. Dt 33:2b−3; Pss 68:17; 103:19−20; Zec 14:5) of him who is the "Mighty God" (Isa 9:6). Whereas God's mighty ones were the Gentile armies in ch. 2, God is now against those forces.

The nations are instructed to deploy themselves in the Valley of Jehoshaphat (v.12; cf. v.2). The Lord had warned that he would enter into litigation with the enemies of his people (cf. v.2 with Isa 50:8); now he sits as judge to impose sentence on them (cf. Isa 28:5−6; Mt 25:31−46).

13−17 In two bold metaphors God is pictured as sending his reapers into the harvest field (cf. Rev 14:14−20) and to the winepress of judgment (Isa

63:3). For the nations are ripe for judgment; their wickedness is great and filled to overflowing.

Then the reader is taken to the scene of that awesome event. The confused and clamoring throng of nations and the tumultuous uproar and din of battle in this great day of reckoning are vividly portrayed (v.14). The valley named Jehoshaphat (3:2, 12), in accordance with its purpose of being the place of final accomplishment, is now called "the valley of decision."

The accompanying signs in the natural world are depicted (vv.15−16). That which was applicable to the local scene of impending battle in the day of the Assyrian invasion (2:10b) is now seen in all its final intensity. The Lord comes forth out of Zion as a roaring lion (cf. Am 1:2). Because the nations have roared insolently against God's people (Isa 5:25−30), the Lord will be as a lion roaring after its prey against the nations but in behalf of the returned remnant (cf. Hos 11:10−11 with Jer 25:30−33). Heaven and earth are pictured as trembling at his presence here among the nations (cf. Ps 29; Isa 29:6−8; 30:30−31; Zec 14:3−7; Rev 16:16−18).

But the very manifestation of his coming, so fearful for the unbelieving nations (cf. Rev 6:12−17), gives assurance of protection and strength for God's own (v.17; cf. Isa 26:20−21). As Israel learned of God's sovereign concern for his people through judgment (cf. Eze 6:7), now it will know of his eternal compassion through its deliverance. In contrast to the nations who will learn who God really is (cf. Eze 36:36−38), Israel will know the redeeming power and the continuous enjoyment of his glorious presence (cf. Isa 60:16; Eze 34:27−30; 36:11, 23, Joel 3:21) forever (Jer 31:33−34, Heb 8:10−11). Because the Lord himself is there (cf. 2:32; 3:21), Jerusalem will be everlastingly holy (cf. Isa 52:1; 60:14, 21; Zec 14:21; cf. also Rev 21:2).

NOTES

9 That the Phoenicians were not above duplicity and double-dealing in their business relations may be seen in Homer's *Odyssey* (14.290–97).

For the summons to enemies to come to a battle they cannot win, see Jeremiah 46:3–6, 9–10. For the regulations about holy warfare at Qumran, see Y. Yadin, *The Scroll of the War of the Sons of Light against the Sons of Darkness* (Oxford: Oxford Univ. Press, 1962), 141–228.

10 The mustering of all the populace for war is mentioned in the Ugaritic Kert Epic (see *Krt* A.2.85–105, 176–94, in *UT*, 250–51).

רֹמַח (*rōmaḥ*, "spear") may also be translated "lance" (cf. 1Ki 18:28). It may be related to the Egyptian word *mrḥ*, Coptic *mereḥ*, which is found also in Ugaritic. See W. Spiegelberg, *Koptisches Handwörterbuch* (Heidelberg: Carl Winters, 1921), 64. If so, it may be an example of consonantal metathesis for lexical differentiation, as in Ugaritic *mdl* = Semitic *lmd* (see J. C. Greenfield, "Ugaritic *mdl* and Its Cognates," *Bib* 45 [1964]: 527–34).

11 The Hebrew עוּשׁוּ (*ʿûšû*) is a *hapax legomenon*. Rudolph (in loc.) is probably correct in relating it to an Arabic root *ġšš* ("to hasten, hurry"). If so, the verb is probably to be taken with the following verb as hendiadys, i.e., "come quickly."

17 The juxtaposition of judgment and salvation oracles in an eschatological setting illustrates well a familiar prophetic blending in the kingdom oracles. For discussion, see R. D. Patterson, "Old Testament Prophecy," *A Complete Literary Guide to the Bible*, ed. by L. Ryken, and T. Longman III (Grand Rapids: Zondervan, 1993), 302–3. For the theological significance of Zion, see W. A. VanGemeren, "Psalms," *EBC*, 5:354–57.

D. The Land's Condition (3[4]:18–21)

> 18 "In that day the mountains will drip new wine,
>   and the hills will flow with milk;
>   all the ravines of Judah will run with water.
> A fountain will flow out of the LORD's house
>   and will water the valley of acacias.
> 19 But Egypt will be desolate,
>   Edom a desert waste,
>   because of violence done to the people of Judah,
>   in whose land they shed innocent blood.
> 20 Judah will be inhabited forever
>   and Jerusalem through all generations.
> 21 Their bloodguilt, which I have not pardoned,
>   I will pardon."
> The LORD dwells in Zion!

COMMENTARY

18–21 Joel now looks beyond the great battle. He concludes his prophecy by contrasting the judgment of the nations—typified by Israel's most protracted antagonist, Edom, and by its most persistent source of spiritual defeat, Egypt—with the blessings that will rest on the repentant, restored, and revitalized people of God.

In glowing and hyperbolic terms, Joel describes the great fertility of soil of the coming time. That which was cut off in the locust plague of Joel's day because of sin (1:5) will be commonplace in that era permeated by the presence of the Holy One (cf. 2:19–27; Isa 55:1). The formerly barren hills will flourish again with vegetation. The wadis, dried by the drought of God's judgment, will flow again, giving renewed vitality to the land as God pours out his blessing to people of renewed spiritual vitality (cf. Isa 30:25–26; Eze 34:13–14).

In Jerusalem a fountain will issue forth from the house of the Lord. Ezekiel (Eze 47:1–12) reported that it will terminate in the Dead Sea, transforming it from salt water to fresh water. Zechariah (Zec 14:8) spoke of a great flow of water from Jerusalem emptying into both the Dead Sea and the Mediterranean Sea.

Joel goes on to say that these waters will gush through the Wadi Shittim (NASB; see NIV note on v.18). The exact location of this place is uncertain and has occasioned many suggestions. Perhaps the best solution is to identify it with the Wadi-en-Nar, which flows out of the Kidron Valley to the Dead Sea. It is of interest to note that "Shittim" is also the plural form of the word for the acacia tree; acacia trees are known to grow along the banks of the Wadi-en-Nar.

Joel next contrasts the future condition of Judah and Jerusalem with that of Egypt and Edom, long-time adversaries of Israel. In contrast with their desolation, Judah and Jerusalem will be inhabited forever. All Judah's sins will be forgiven, and the Lord himself will abide in its midst forever.

Joel's last prophetic view is a picture of Israel's everlasting felicity. The reason for this state of unending happiness is apparent. The Lord himself will tabernacle in its midst in all of his glory (cf. 3:17; Zec 8:3–8). Based on the basic idea of the Hebrew root *škn*, Jewish theologians have spoken of the Lord's *shekinah* glory. Throughout the OT, from Sinai to Solomon's temple, "the *shekinah* glory" designates the active presence now of the invisible God, who transcends the universe he created. Because of the spiritual and moral decay that led to religious formalism and open idolatry, the *shekinah* glory left the temple and Jerusalem (Eze 10; 11:22–25). The prophets, however, looked forward to a future time when God will again redeem his people and dwell among a repentant, regenerated, and grateful people (Eze 43:1–12; 48:35; Zec 2:10–13).

The NT writers reveal that before that day God has had another "tabernacling" with humans. The unique Son became flesh, dwelling among people (Jn 1:14) as the promised Immanuel (Isa 7:14). Having redeemed a lost humankind through his death and resurrection and being ascended into heaven, he now dwells in his own, whom he has taken into union with himself (Eph 1:15–2:22; Col 1:15–22, 27; 2:9–10). As the triumphant Redeemer, he has given to the church, his body, gifts that it is to steward (Eph 4:8–10).

The destiny of believers is to enjoy God's presence forever (Rev 21:2–3). Yet even now they are to partake of that blessing through the indwelling Christ (Jn 17:20–22; Eph 1:3–14) and the Holy Spirit (Jn 16:7–14), who is the earnest of that eternal happiness and well-being that lies before them (2Co 1:22; Eph 1:14; 5:5), and they must let Christ's glory be seen through them (Gal 1:16).

May the reality of Christ be for Christians—as for the saints of Joel's prophecy—a conscious, ever-abiding presence that allows Christ's glory to be seen in the entirety of their lives!

NOTES

21 The first sentence of this verse is a notorious crux. Some (e.g., Leslie C. Allen, *The Books of Joel, Obadiah, Jonah and Micah* [Grand Rapids: Eerdmans, 1976], Keil, and Stuart) suggest that the denunciation refers to Egypt and Edom (cf. v.19). Similarly the LXX (cf. Peshitta) reads, "I will avenge their blood and will not acquit [them]." The NLT takes the sentence to be a statement referring to Judah and Jerusalem: "I will pardon my people's crimes, which I have not yet pardoned." In that scenario God's forgiveness of Judah and Jerusalem stands in contrast to the judgment of Egypt and Edom.

AMOS

THOMAS E. MCCOMISKEY AND TREMPER LONGMAN III

Introduction

1. BACKGROUND

In many ways the eighth century BC was unique in the history of Judah and Israel. It witnessed the toppling of the northern kingdom from the glory of economic prosperity and international influence to virtual subjugation by a foreign power (722 BC). It also witnessed the near collapse of Judah, averted only by the steadying hand of King Hezekiah, who could do no more than slow Judah's progress toward certain ruin.

At the same time, however, the eighth century witnessed the rise of one of the most potent moral forces the world has ever known—the writing prophets (besides Amos, there are Isaiah, Hosea, and Micah). These men, from widely separated backgrounds, shared an overwhelming conviction that God had called them. They had various styles of writing, but all wrote with the authority of the Almighty. They denounced the sins of their contemporaries and also looked far into the future as they spoke of deliverance for both Israelites and Gentiles.

The dawn of the eighth century brought new hope to Israel and Judah. Israel's subjugation to Damascus ended abruptly when the Assyrians under Adad-nirari III crushed Damascus in 802 BC. The internal difficulties that had plagued Judah also ended with Uzziah's accession to the throne (792–740 BC). He built up a powerful army and increased Judah's mercantile activities.

In the northern kingdom, Jeroboam II (793–753 BC) came to the throne roughly at the same time as Uzziah. Jeroboam restored much of the territory that had fallen to Damascus (2Ki 14:28).

The conquest of Damascus and the attendant quiescence of Assyria, coupled with the brilliant leadership of Uzziah and Jeroboam, brought Judah and Israel to heights of prominence second only to Solomon's golden age. The kingdoms prospered financially and at the same time expanded their borders. But as their economic well-being and national strength continued to foster their security, an internal decay was eating at their vitals. This decay was primarily moral, for it involved a basic violation of the covenant established by God at Mount Sinai.

The covenantal stipulations required loyalty to God and love toward humanity. Yet the idolatrous worship of their pagan neighbors had infiltrated the two kingdoms, thereby producing a strange syncretistic worship. While pagan high places dotted the countryside and idols stood within the cities, the people continued to trust in such Yahwistic concepts as the "day of the LORD" (5:18) and aspects of Levitical worship (4:4–5).

Not only did the people disobey by worshiping idols, but they also violated the social legislation of the covenant. Amos is particularly vehement in denouncing the lack of social concern in his time. Archaeology has illuminated this period through a number of discoveries. Excavations at Samaria, the capital of the northern kingdom, have yielded hundreds of ivory inlays attesting the luxury enjoyed by these people as described by Amos (6:4).[1]

The nature of Canaanite Baal worship, which so damaged the social structure of Israel and Judah, is now well known from the Ugaritic epic material. The cult of Baal was primarily a fertility cult, which likely involved sexual rituals. Violence also played a part in this religion. Anat, one of the most prominent goddesses of the Canaanite pantheon, is pictured in the Ugaritic epic material as a brutal warrior. In one passage she wades in blood, and beneath her roll the heads of her victims (*UT*, ʿnt, 2:5–31). The intrusion of similar observances into Israel and Judah could lead only to a rending of the social fabric. The ethical concerns of the law were no longer necessary in a cult that required only external ritual.

The erosion of Israel's social structure showed itself primarily in a cleavage between the rich and the poor. The improved economic situation in Israel led to an increase of the wealthy, who not only neglected the poor but also used them to increase their own wealth. The social concern inherent in the very structure of the law was forgotten. God's will, as it applied to the nation of Israel, was ignored; and this spurred the eighth-century prophets to action. Though their protest was largely ignored (2Ki 17:13–14), it contributed to the establishment of a believing remnant. The prophets preserved faith by assuring the people that God had not forsaken his promise. They saw emerging from their fallen society a kingdom different from any other, an ideal kingdom headed by the messianic King, whose rule would be completely just.

2. UNITY

Many scholars agree that the prophecy of Amos is, at least in essence, an authentic production of the man whose name it bears.[2] The consonance of Amos's message with the eighth-century milieu and his vividly forthright style of writing make it difficult to think otherwise.

Some, however, have seen the book as the end product of a structural development, with certain redactive intrusions. Weiser held that the oracles of chs. 1–6 and the section containing the visions existed

---

1. For a discussion of the ivories found at Samaria, see *The New Encyclopedia of Archaeological Excavations in the Holy Land*, ed. E. Stern (New York: Simon & Schuster, 1993), 4:1304–6. See also "Nimrud," in *Archaeology and Old Testament Study*, ed. D.W. Thomas (Oxford: Clarendon, 1967), 69–70.

2. S. Paul is a good example of a modern scholar outside evangelical circles who argues that the evidence "supports the integrity of the book" (*Amos* [Hermeneia; Minneapolis: Fortress, 1991], 6), though he also admits that "most studies of Amos seriously question the integrity of the book" (5). By contrast, J. Jeremias (*The Book of Amos* [OTL; Louisville: Westminster John Knox, 1995], 5–9) suggests a fairly complex redactional history, though he also shows great sensitivity to the meaning of the final form of the text.

separately for a time until they were united in exilic or postexilic times.[3] The redactor revealed the union of these sections in the superscription to the book (1:1), which cites both the words and the visions of Amos. Weiser dated the oracles after Amos's mission to the northern kingdom and held that the visions preceded that mission. Yet the evidence for such a view is purely speculative. There is no reason Amos or an amanuensis could not have arranged the prophecies in their present order.

The early date cited by Weiser for the vision section seems somewhat artificial in view of its direct connection with the encounter between Amos and Amaziah during the northern ministry (7:10–17). The prediction of the destruction of the northern kingdom and the house of Jeroboam, an important element in the vision section (7:9), appears to have been the direct cause of Amaziah's protest (7:10–11).

An examination of the oracle section and the vision section reveals similar concerns. Both predict God's punishment of the northern kingdom (3:13–15; cf. 7:7–9), both foresee the captivity (4:1–3; cf. 7:17; 9:4), and both set forth the same denunciation of Israel's social crimes (3:10; cf. 8:4–6).

Some scholars believe that the encounter at Bethel (7:10–17) is the product of another author, possibly an eyewitness.[4] Their major reason for this supposition is the use of the third person throughout 7:10–17. In other accounts that have a personal reference, the prophet Amos characteristically uses the first person (7:1–9; 8:1–2; 9:1). While it is possible that biblical authors reverted to the third person as a literary device, it seems unlikely that Amos would have used this device only in this brief segment of the prophecy.

The detailed nature of the report of the Bethel encounter, with its direct quotations, seems to point strongly to the possibility of its having been written by an eyewitness. This person could have been a disciple of Amos, or the prophet himself. The use of the third person may be an indication that Amos reported the account to a disciple, who recorded it. This scenario need not diminish the authenticity of the account, nor need it be regarded as strong evidence for a complex process of redaction.

Some critical scholars regard the oracles against Tyre (1:9–10), Edom (1:11–12), and Judah (2:4–5) as later intrusions because they seem to reflect conditions in the exilic period or because they are similar to exilic or postexilic prophetic oracles. Some scholars also deny the authenticity of these sections on internal literary grounds. The concluding formula "says the Lord," which ends the other oracles, is lacking in these three oracles. And the intrusive nature of the oracle against Tyre seems to be supported by the fact that the crime cited in it is like the one cited in the oracle against the Philistines, which immediately precedes it.

While it is true that similar oracles against Tyre and Edom exist in later books (La 4:21–22; Eze 27:13; Joel 3:6; Ob 10–12), this circumstance is not necessarily an indication of the origin of these two oracles in Amos. As for Edom, the Edomites showed their hostility against Israel early in Israel's history and continued it up to the destruction of Jerusalem (see comments on 1:11–12). It is this long hostility against Israel that is emphasized in the oracle against Edom.

The internal differences do not provide a compelling reason for positing a later date for the three oracles. S. Paul observes a stairlike pattern in the first six oracles, in which certain phrases are repeated, thus creating a unified whole—*hikrattî* ("I will destroy," lit., "cut off"; 1:5, 8); *gālût šᵉlēmâ* ("whole communities"; 1:6, 9);

---

3. A. Weiser and K. Elliger, *Das Buch der zwölf Kleinen Propheten* (4 vols.; Göttingen: Vandenhoeck & Ruprecht, 1949), 1:110–13; A. Weiser, *Die Profetie des Amos* (Giessen: Alfred Topelmann, 1929), 249ff.

4. This is the view of J. Mays, *Amos: A Commentary* (Philadelphia: Westminster, 1969).

ʾāḥ ("brotherhood, brother"; 1:9, 11); bitrûʿâ ("war cries"; 2:2).[5] He does not conclude that this pattern necessarily indicates that Amos wrote the disputed oracles. However, these oracles are so closely woven into the structure of this section that it is not unreasonable to assume Amos did write them. S. Paul also notes that a later writer would probably not accuse the people of Tyre of violating the covenant of brotherhood (1:9), since they remained loyal to the rebels during the invasion of Nebuchadnezzar.

The three disputed oracles possess the common concluding formula "consume the fortresses" (1:10, 12; 2:5), while the other oracles conclude with the words "says the Lord." Some scholars allege that this departure supports the intrusive nature of these oracles and points to the presence of another hand in the composition of the book.

The dating of literary forms based on criteria that allow no room for creativity on the part of the author is rigid and artificial. The vivid forthrightness and vigor of Amos's style certainly argues for originality on his part. Amos seemed to make a studied attempt to avoid the tedious repetition of certain literary formulas. The formula "says the Lord" (ʾāmar yhwh) is used with great frequency in the book, but on occasion Amos used the expression "declares the Lord" (nᵉʾum yhwh); cf. 2:11, 16; 3:10, 15; et al.). On the whole there appears to be no compelling reason for assigning these disputed oracles to a later time.

One of the most difficult critical questions relating to the book of Amos is the authenticity of its hymnic elements. These great doxologies, praising God in highly exalted language, occur at 4:13; 5:8–9; 9:5–6. Among the first to express doubt about the authenticity of the doxologies was B. Duhm.[6] Since then other scholars have questioned them. The doxologies have been assumed to be late additions for several reasons. They seem to interrupt the narrative flow and apparently do not logically fit the sequence of thought. They seem to reflect a sophisticated theology (i.e., the use of later language). Moreover, a similar doxology in the LXX's text of Hosea 13:4 seems to establish a precedent for such doxological insertions.

Several things may be said about these contentions. As for the interruption of the narrative flow of the book, only the doxology of 5:8–9 poses serious difficulties. The first doxology (4:13) occurs at the end of a logical section and provides an appropriate meditation on the nature of God. The last doxology (9:5–6) occurs in a section in which the prophet sets forth the inevitability of Israel's downfall. The hymn it includes describes God's judgment in vivid, cosmic terms and is in no sense conceptually intrusive.

The second doxology (5:8–9) does seem to interrupt the flow of Amos's condemnation of those who pervert justice. Yet it may have been included at this point because of the awesome confirmation it gives of the threat of destruction, while v.9 confirms Yahweh's ability to destroy the mighty. Intrusiveness is not necessarily an indication of lateness. The pericope at 6:9–10, for example, is clearly intrusive, differing from the surrounding context in content and literary style. But it contains several literary characteristics that are also peculiarities of Amos's style. For example, the second major clause of the pericope (the first line of v.10) contains several suffixes, all of them unreferred. That is, the referents are implicit, not stated. This phenomenon may be found in the suffix nû ("him") on ʾašîbennû (lit., "I will turn back him [NIV, 'my wrath']") in 1:3, 6, 9, 11, 13; 2:1, 4, 6, which also has no clearly stated referent.

5. S. Paul, "Amos 1:3–23: A Concatenous Literary Pattern," *JBL* 90 (1971): 397–403.

6. Bernard Duhm, *Die Zwölf Propheten in den Versmassen der Urschrift übersetzt* (Tübingen: J. C. B. Mohr, 1910); and "Anmerkungen zu den Zwölf Propheten; III. Buch Amos," *ZAW* 31 (1911): 81–93.

Amos 6:9–10 is also characterized by the quick succession of dependent clauses that may be observed elsewhere in undisputed portions of Amos (cf. the oracles of 1:1–2:16; cf. also 5:14–15; 6:1–7; 8:4–6). There is thus a strong likelihood that 6:9–10 was written by Amos. In the light of this, the argument that a pericope is late because it is conceptually or structurally intrusive must be tempered by a consideration of the author's style.

The sophisticated theology attributed to the doxologies relates mainly to the concept of Yahweh as the one who "creates" (*bōrēʾ*; 4:13), a concept that closely parallels the thought of the alleged Second Isaiah. Since critics place Second Isaiah in an exilic milieu, the consonance between it and the theology of the doxologies is assumed strongly to favor an exilic origin for the doxologies. But the sovereignty of Yahweh that Amos sees as extending to all nations and that is evident in the realm of nature (4:7–8) is difficult to comprehend apart from the role of Yahweh as creator.

While it is true that Yahweh is not called *bōrēʾ* in undisputed passages earlier than Second Isaiah, it must be noted that Isaiah 37:16 and Jeremiah 27:5 attribute that role of fashioner of the universe to Yahweh. The word *ʿāśâ* is used in these passages, not *bārāʾ*; but the idea that Yahweh is the architect of the universe is clearly there. Neither passage has escaped critical examination, however, and some scholars question the authenticity of both passages. In recent years the prose material of Jeremiah has been studied closely, and many modern scholars affirm the Jeremaic authorship of 27:5. Thus, it is possible that the concept of Yahweh as the maker of the universe existed much earlier than the late exilic or postexilic period.

The later language attributed to the doxologies consists mainly in the word "creates" and the expression "the LORD God Almighty is his name" (*yhwh ʾelōhê ṣebāʾôt šemô*).[7] Since the concept of creator was considered above, it is necessary to consider only the latter expression. The refrain "LORD Almighty is his name" occurs four times in the section of the book of Isaiah generally regarded as exilic (47:4; 48:2; 51:15; 54:5). For this reason many critics regard the expression itself as belonging to the period of the exile. But Amos uses similar expressions throughout the book (3:13; 5:14–16; 6:8, 14). It is, however, the occurrence of the word "name" in the doxological expression that provides the correspondence with the second half of Isaiah and hence allegedly warrants a later date. One should, however, be cautious about using such an approach. We have only a small amount of written material from this vast historical period, and it is difficult to make conclusive statements on such limited evidence. To confine a given expression to one historical period may be assuming too much. Moreover, one may wonder why "Second Isaiah" could not have depended on Amos.

A divine title containing the word "name" can be found in Exodus 15:3: "Yahweh is his name" (*yhwh šemô*). F. M. Cross and D. N. Freedman date this poem as "scarcely later than the twelfth century in its original form."[8] This date is based on philological evidence, not critical assumptions, and thus rests on objective data. The possibility that a divine title containing the word "name" existed in Israelite tradition long before Amos's time deserves careful consideration.

---

7. For a thorough discussion of this expression from a form-critical standpoint, see J. Crenshaw, *Hymnic Affirmation of Divine Justice: The Doxologies of Amos and Related Texts in the Old Testament* (Missoula, Mont.: Scholars, 1975), 75–114.

8. F. M. Cross and D. N. Freedman, "The Song of Miriam," *JNES* 14 (1955): 240.

Some scholars approach the issue of the doxologies' authenticity from the standpoint that words were used within narrow chronological limits; for example, they assert that the expression *yhwh ᵉlōhê ṣᵉbāᵓôt šᵉmô* was dominant in the period of the exile. This approach, however, can lead to dubious conclusions because of the limited amount of extant Hebrew material. It is best to allow the context to govern our understanding of the hymnic elements.[9]

The presence of a doxological statement in the LXX's text of Hosea 13:4, if not a witness to the original Hebrew text, may establish a precedent for such insertions. But this circumstance in itself is not proof that the doxologies in Amos are intrusive material.

Scholars differ widely regarding the doxologies. No conclusive evidence has been given as to their genre or origin. If one posits the role of creator for Yahweh in the time of Amos, there is no compelling reason the doxologies must be assigned to the late exilic period. If the doxological material is not original to Amos, it may well be that he drew on a common bank of prophetic material or quoted stanzas of familiar hymns.

As for the section dealing with the downfall of the Davidic monarchy (9:8–15), some scholars assume it was written after that event, since it shows a knowledge of the end of the Judahite monarchy, which did not come till much later.[10] But the Hebrew word *hannōpelet* (v.11) is a participle and may connote continuing action: "crumbling." It need not be translated "fallen," as in some versions (NIV, NASB, RSV, et al.). Amos is well aware of the progressive dissolution of both kingdoms. His prophetic spirit gives him a perspective others do not have. He sees the monarchy already toppling; but out of the rubble of its collapse, he sees a new and greater kingdom emerging. The theology of this section is consonant with eighth-century prophetic theology.

Some also argue that the distinction between the righteous and the wicked (9:8–10) is foreign to the thought of Amos because he predicts the doom of the entire nation.[11] But if Amos expects the entire destruction of the nation, one may wonder why he appeals for repentance (5:14). Micah, another eighth-century prophet, set forth a full-orbed doctrine of a redeemed remnant (Mic 4:6–7; 5:4, 7–9) in language as denunciatory as that of Amos (Mic 1:6–7; 2:4; cf. also Isa 6:13). Amos predicts the demise of the nation as a political entity; he does not teach that the whole house of Israel will come to an end.

Those who deny the authenticity of this section[12] also appeal to the fact that in Amos the promise of the restoration is not based on ethical response, something that goes counter to the prophet's strongly ethical message. But does not Amos 9:10 imply that only the righteous will inherit the kingdom because of the expulsion of sinners from it? To deny a message of hope in Amos removes him from the mainstream of eighth-century prophetic thought, where the concept of doom is often followed by hope (Isa 3:1–4:1;

---

9. Story says on this issue, "to analyze words, to determine place and time when words were in vogue, and to add together the sum total of these facts as the basis for interpretation, fails to do justice to the interpretative structure of text and context" (C. Story, "Amos—Prophet of Praise," *VT* 30 [1980]: 79).

10. Mays, *Amos: A Commentary*, 13–14; H. McKeating, *The Books of Amos, Hosea and Micah* (Cambridge: Cambridge Univ. Press, 1971), 70.

11. See, e.g., R. Cripps, *A Critical and Exegetical Commentary on the Book of Amos* (ICC; London: Macmillan, 1929), 67.

12. See, e.g., ibid., 72–73.

cf. 4:2–6; 8:16   22; cf. 9:1–7; Mic 2:1–11; cf. 2:12–13; 5:1; cf. 5:2–4; see also La 3, where the themes of judgment and hope are intertwined within the one chapter).

3. AUTHORSHIP

The superscription of the book (1:1) attributes the work to Amos. Little is known of him apart from the sketchy references in the superscription and the body of the prophecy, though even this much information is more than most of the other Minor Prophets supply for their authors. Amos lived and worked in Tekoa (1:1), a town ten miles south of Jerusalem (five miles from Bethlehem) in the Judean hill country. The town was situated on a height commanding a magnificent view of the rugged wilderness below and of distant landmarks such as the Mount of Olives to the north. The eastern slopes of the Judean hill country around Tekoa are mostly arid, rock-strewn wastes. The western slopes, however, provide some pastureland and shelter in caves for shepherds grazing their flocks.[13]

Amos was a shepherd (1:1) who also tended sycamore trees (7:14). Traditionally, as a shepherd and one who "took care" of sycamore trees, he was thought to be from the lower classes of society. These sycamore trees were not like the ones common in North America but were sycamore fig trees, which produced a fruit not as popular as the regular fig but still usable for food (1Ki 10:27; 1Ch 27:28; 2Ch 1:15; 9:27). The Hebrew word for "tend" refers to a process of cutting into the fig in order to quicken the ripening process.[14] Amos's natural surroundings apparently had a profound effect on him, as his book is full of references to them (1:2; 2:9; 3:4–5; 5:19–20, 24; 6:12; 7:1–6; 8:1; 9:3–15).

Above all, Amos was a prophet. The dark days in which he lived called for a man of sturdy moral fiber and fearlessness. Such a man was Amos. His character, molded in the harsh terrain of the wilderness of Tekoa, enabled him to stand before priests and people alike to proclaim the word God had given to him.

4. DATE

We may best place the prophetic activity of Amos in the latter half of the reign of Jeroboam II (793–753 BC). It would certainly have taken some time for the affluence during Jeroboam's reign to lead to the social decay so widespread when Amos carries out his mission to the northern kingdom.

Some scholars have placed Amos's prophetic ministry after 745 BC to allow for the rise of Assyria under Tiglath-pileser III.[15] But it is significant that Amos does not mention Assyria by name, though he does affirm that Israel will go into exile "beyond Damascus." The mood of careless confidence pervading the nation at the time of Amos seems best to fit the period before the incursions of Assyria into Syro-Palestine.

---

13. It is surprising that Amos, a man from a town in Judea, prophesied against the northern kingdom. However, theories that the Tekoa from which Amos came was an otherwise unknown site in the north (so S. N. Rosenbaum, *Amos of Israel: A New Interpretation* [Macon, Ga.: Mercer Univ. Press, 1990] are unnecessary.

14. O. Borowski, *Agriculture in Iron Age Israel* (Winona Lake, Ind.: Eisenbrauns, 1987). On the basis of the particular Hebrew word used for shepherd (*nōqēd* rather than *rōʾeh*) and Mesopotamian analogies, some have argued that Amos actually was a wealthy man. Against this view stands the comment that Amos tended the flock (7:15, in a section that some suspect is a secondary addition), implying that he was not managing a huge operation but rather was a simple shepherd.

15. See, e.g., Cripps, *Amos*, 734–41.

The phrase "two years before the earthquake" (1:1) limits the date of the prophecy to a narrow period of perhaps no more than a year, and probably much shorter than that. It is difficult to find an exact time in which Amos's mission would fit. Several possibilities may, however, be noted. Jotham, Uzziah's son, acceded to the regency of Judah when Uzziah was stricken with leprosy (ca. 750 BC). That 1:1 mentions only Uzziah and not Jotham may point to a time before Jotham's accession, thus supporting a date before 750 BC for the northern, oracular ministry of Amos. The earthquake referred to in 1:1 may have occurred around 760 BC, in accordance with the archaeological evidence unearthed at Hazor.[16]

In the light of these factors, it seems best to place the prophetic ministry of Amos sometime before 760 BC — a view consonant with the narrow scope of the superscription (1:1). Such a date positions Amos as "the first written prophetic text."[17]

5. THEOLOGICAL VALUES

The Doctrine of God

Central in Amos's teaching about God is his divine sovereignty. Yahweh is the God of history. He effects the migrations of peoples (9:7) and controls the orderly progression of natural phenomena (4:13; 5:8). He is in no way a mere automaton controlled by the religious rituals of his creatures. Yet within that sovereign domain, humankind has freedom to bow in submission to Yahweh or to reject him.

The Covenant

Amos is not dissimilar to most prophets in their functioning as "lawyers" of the covenant. The covenant took the form of a treaty between God and his vassal people Israel. The shape of the covenant may be seen in an account of a renewal of the covenant, as is evident in the book of Deuteronomy. After a rehearsal of the relationship between God and Israel up to the present (Dt 1–4), that book contains an extensive legal section (chs. 5–26), followed by blessings for obedience and punishments for disobedience (Dt 27–28).

Prophets such as Amos were called into action when Israel broke the covenant. They threatened God's people with the covenantal punishments if they did not repent. Stuart's commentary on Amos shows the connection between the judgment oracles and covenantal curses most extensively.[18] A number of these connections are highlighted in the commentary that follows.

The Doctrine of Election

Amos affirms the historical election of Israel (3:2). But he inveighs against the perverted concept of election popularly held in his day — that is, the irrevocable commitment of Yahweh to the nation. Their election alone did not guarantee national blessing, for the sovereign Lord had promised they would be his

---

16. Y. Yadin et al., *Hazor II: An Account of the Second Season of Excavations, 1956* (Jerusalem: Magnes, 1960), 24, 26, 36–37. See also *The New Encyclopedia of Archaeological Excavations in the Holy Land*, 2594–605.

17. M. Daniel Carroll R., *Amos — The Prophet and His Oracles* (Louisville: Westminster John Knox, 2002), 3.

18. D. Stuart, *Hosea–Jonah* (WBC; Nashville: Nelson, 1987).

"treasured possession" if they obeyed him and kept his covenant (Ex 19:5). Amos, more than any other prophet, urges the responsibility of elective privilege.

Eschatology

The unique contribution of Amos to the eschatology of the OT is his teaching about "the day of the LORD." He stresses that it will be a time when the Lord will judge all sin, even in his own people. The gloomy portrayal of that day in the prophecy of Amos reflects the fact that Amos's hearers are for the most part guilty of transgression. For them that day will hold no ray of light (5:18–20).

Another day is coming, however, when hope will shine with glorious promise (9:13–15). The Davidic promise will be realized in the restoration of David's kingdom, and Jews and Gentiles will be united in the kingdom of David's greater Son.

6. BIBLIOGRAPHY

Jeremias, J. *The Book of Amos*. Old Testament Library. Louisville, Ky.: Westminster John Knox, 1995.
Mays, J. *Amos: A Commentary*. Philadelphia: Westminster, 1969.
Niehaus, J. "Amos." Pages 315–49 in *The Minor Prophets: An Exegetical and Expository Commentary*. Vol. 1. Edited by T. E. McComiskey. Grand Rapids: Baker, 1992.
Paul, S. M. *Amos*. Hermeneia. Minneapolis: Fortress, 1991.
Stuart, D. *Hosea–Jonah*. Word Biblical Commentary. Nashville: Nelson, 1987.
Wolff, H. *Joel and Amos*. Translated by W. Janzen, D. McBridge Jr., and C. Muenchow. Philadelphia: Fortress, 1977.

7. OUTLINE

I. Superscription (1:1)

II. Introduction to the Prophecy (1:2)

III. The Prophetic Oracles (1:3–6:14)

    A. Oracles of Judgment against the Surrounding Nations (1:3–2:5)

        1. The Oracle against Syria (1:3–5)

        2. The Oracle against the Philistines (1:6–8)

        3. The Oracle against Tyre (1:9–10)

        4. The Oracle against Edom (1:11–12)

        5. The Oracle against Ammon (1:13–15)

        6. The Oracle against Moab (2:1–3)

        7. The Oracle against Judah (2:4–5)

    B. Oracles of Judgment against Israel (2:6–6:14)

        1. A Lesson from History (2:6–16)

        2. A Lesson based on Cause and Effect (3:1–12)

        3. An Oracle against the House of Jacob (3:13–15)

        4. The Pampered Women of Samaria (4:1–3)

        5. Sinful Worship (4:4–5)

        6. A Look to the Past (4:6–13)

        7. A Lament for Fallen Israel (5:1–3)

        8. Seeking True Values (5:4–17)

        9. The Day of the Lord (5:18–20)

        10. Unacceptable Worship (5:21–27)

        11. A Warning to the Complacent (6:1–7)

        12. Pride before a Fall (6:8–11)

        13. A Grim Paradox (6:12–14)

IV. The Prophetic Visions (7:1–9:15)

    A. The Vision of the Locusts, Fire, and the Plumb Line (7:1–9)

    B. A Historical Interlude (7:10–17)

    C. The Vision of the Summer Fruit (8:1–14)

    D. The Vision of the Lord Standing by the Altar (9:1–15)

        1. The Destruction of the Temple (9:1–6)

        2. Israel and the Other Nations (9:7)

        3. The Restoration of the Davidic Kingdom (9:8–12)

        4. The Blessings of the Restored Kingdom (9:13–15)

Text and Exposition

I. SUPERSCRIPTION (1:1)

¹The words of Amos, one of the shepherds of Tekoa — what he saw concerning Israel two years before the earthquake, when Uzziah was king of Judah and Jeroboam son of Jehoash was king of Israel.

COMMENTARY

1 Most prophetic books (Isa 1:1; Jer 1:1; Hos 1:1; Joel 1:1; Na 1:1) as well as some wisdom books (Pr 1:1; Ecc 1:1; SS 1:1) begin with a superscription that serves a similar function to a title page on a modern book. The superscription was likely added by an editor or later tradent; in Amos, it identifies the genre, the author, his occupation, and the time period in which he ministered.

The prophecy is introduced by the formula "the words of Amos." Frequently this expression is used for collections of sayings, as in the case of the prophecy of Jeremiah (Jer 1:1), various collections of proverbs (Pr 30:1; 31:1), and Ecclesiastes (Ecc 1:1). Here it connotes the collection of prophetic oracles spoken by Amos during his northern ministry.

Nōqēd, used here, is not the usual word for "shepherd." In 2 Kings 3:4, its use of Mesha, king of Moab, implies that he was a breeder and supplier of sheep. In Amos 7:14 the word *bôqēr* describes Amos's occupation. This word occurs only once in the OT, so that its precise meaning is difficult to determine. While *bôqēr* may have been a general term that denoted a herdsman of any type, its linguistic connection with *bāqār* ("cattle") suggests the possibility that Amos kept cattle as well

as sheep. The word *ṣōʾn* (7:15) connotes smaller animals, such as sheep and goats; thus it is likely that Amos was a breeder of various types of animals besides sheep.

That Amos describes himself in 7:15 as "tending the flock" (*mēʾaḥᵃrê haṣṣōʾn*) shows that he personally cared for the herds rather than being a wealthy animal breeder who left the care of the flocks to others. The use of *nōqēd* for the king of Moab does not demand the conclusion that Amos was a wealthy and powerful person. It may simply show that Amos was a supplier of small animals. In conclusion, Amos was probably neither a wealthy cattleman nor a poor shepherd, but a mid-level manager (P. C. Craigie, "Amos the *nōqēd* in Light of Ugaritic," *SR* 2 [1982]: 29–32).

Amos's character and ideals have been shaped by the wilderness. There is no evidence that he was part of a prophetic movement in Judah; he denied that possibility by affirming that he was "neither a prophet nor a prophet's son" (7:14). Undoubtedly his simple life in the Judean wilderness lead him to see more clearly the evils of city life that are less apparent to the affluent who live within the city walls, confined by their heartless greed.

The word "saw" (*ḥāzâ*) is in a relative clause logically dependent on "the words of Amos." *Ḥāzâ* is not the common word for "see." Although it is used in poetic literature as a synonym for "see," *ḥāzâ* has a more distinctive meaning and includes the idea of mental apprehension as well as visual observation. In other words, it lends itself well to the process of prophetic reception. Several nominal forms meaning "vision" are based on this root.

Ḥāzâ implies the words of Amos were perceived mentally — that is, by divine revelation — before being communicated orally or in writing. That "these words" do not have their ultimate origin in Amos is communicated by the phrase "he saw." Other prophets make the same point by stating that their collection contains "the word of the LORD" (Hos 1:1; Mic 1:1; et al.).

The prophetic word of Amos concerns "Israel." While "Israel" may have included both kingdoms (6:1; 9:14), it is best to take the term as referring to the northern kingdom. The numerous references to localities in the north as well as the encounter with Amaziah support this. The reference to Judah in 2:4 need not indicate that the prophecy is directed to Judah as well. The Judah oracle is simply one of seven dealing with the nations surrounding Israel and leading up to the classic denunciation of Israel in the eighth oracle.

Uzziah (or Azariah), king of Judah, reigned from 783–742 BC. He was an energetic king whose policies contributed to the resurgence of Judah in the eighth century. He rebuilt the city of Elath and strengthened the defenses of Jerusalem. Jeroboam II, king of Israel, reigned from 786–746 BC. He also was a vigorous leader. His greatest accomplishment was the expansion of Israelite territorial holdings into Transjordan (2Ki 14:23–29).

For comments on "two years before the earthquake," see "Date" in the introduction; on "Tekoa," see "Authorship" in the introduction.

NOTE

1 In Akkadian the cognate to the Hebrew נֹקֵד (*nōqēd*, "shepherd") is *nāqidu*. This word sometimes reflects a hierarchical value, with the *re'û* below the *nāqidu*. In some texts the *nāqidu* is described as working for the state administration and as being in charge of herds that were used for state and cultic functions. In Ugaritic the word *nqd* occurs in several lists with little descriptive context. However, in *UT* 62:55 the word occurs in the honorific title *rb nqdm* ("chief of the herdsmen"). The bearer of this title is also called *rb khnm* ("chief of the priests"), which attests to his role as a cultic functionary, though without implying that he is a priest (Paul, 34).

חָזָה (*ḥāzâ*, "see") is used mainly in the poetic and prophetic literature of the OT. It occurs only four times in the narrative material. In Exodus 18:21 it has the sense of active choice, that is, the act of selecting (*ḥāzâ*) involves a mental seeing of the qualities of the people chosen. In Exodus 24:11 *ḥāzâ* is used of the Israelite leaders who "saw God"; and in Numbers 24:4, 16 it is used of seeing a מַחֲזֶה (*maḥăzeh*, "vision"). The range of meaning in poetic and prophetic material involves apprehension of visions (Isa 1:1; Eze 12:27) as well as mental perception and understanding (Job 15:17; 34:32; Pr 24:32). The emphasis on mental apprehension makes this word suitable for describing the process by which the prophets understood their revelations.

II. INTRODUCTION TO THE PROPHECY (1:2)

²He said:

"The Lᴏʀᴅ roars from Zion
  and thunders from Jerusalem;
the pastures of the shepherds dry up,
  and the top of Carmel withers."

COMMENTARY

2 The name "Lᴏʀᴅ" (*yhwh*, "Yahweh") introduces the prophecy; its initial position in the sentence gives it a certain emphasis. In the events associated with the Exodus from Egypt, the name "Yahweh" was given its greatest revelational content. Moses' first impression of God's character as revealed in Yahweh was that of his inviolable holiness (Ex 3:5). The awesome phenomena accompanying Yahweh's appearance on Sinai (19:16–25) and the restrictions he placed on the people (19:10–15) enforced that concept. His mighty power, which delivered the Hebrew people from Egyptian bondage, manifested his sovereignty and redemptive concern.

The prophet introduces a shocking note in depicting Yahweh as roaring from Zion. Though "roar" (*šāʾag*) is frequently used in the OT of a lion's roar, it need not always carry this connotation (Job 37:4; Pss 38:8[9]; 74:4). In the Hebrew here, Amos's words are identical to those of Joel 3:16, where *šāʾag* occurs with no apparent reference to a lion's roar. The cosmic effects of the roar of the Lord in Joel may connote the crashing of thunder. In Job 37:4 *šāʾag* is used in this way. Nevertheless, the use of the same verb in Amos 3:8, where the Lord does roar like a lion, indicates that the lion metaphor may be intended here. Whether a cosmic

roar or a lion's roar, the image evokes a sense of God's impending judgment.

The parallel expression "thunders" (*yittēn qôlô*, lit., "gives his voice") appears in a number of passages depicting God's intervention in history. This intervention may involve personal deliverance (Ps 18:13[14]; cf. 18:6[7]) or deliverance on a national scale effected by awesome judgment (Ps 46:6–11). It may be manifested in the continuing processes of nature (Jer 10:13; 51:16) or presage a mighty act of God (Joel 2:11). In each instance there is some manifestation of God's power expressed in natural phenomena, most frequently in a violent thunderstorm.

The roar of the Lord in 1:2 is also accompanied by cosmic changes. Instead of a storm, however, in an ironic twist the prophet sees God's storm-like wrath causing a withering drought to destroy the green hills of Mount Carmel—a landmark of the northern kingdom. In this vivid way, Amos pictures the impending judgment of God on that kingdom. God's appearance as warrior is often accompanied by such convulsions in nature (Na 1:3–5).

The roar of the Lord also points to his divine intervention in history and presages his dire judgment on the nations dealt with in the subsequent oracles.

The roar of the Lord, however, need not always be seen as heralding judgment; for in Hosea 11:10−11 it points to the restoration of God's people.

Verse 2 forms an appropriate introduction to the entire prophecy; its scope need not be limited to the oracles of 1:3−3:8.

NOTE

2 Zion in parallel with Jerusalem shows that Amos understands God as roaring from that city. The origin of God's judgment is not his heavenly abode but the city of Jerusalem. This reflects the Israelite belief that God was resident in Jerusalem, specifically in the temple (Pss 20:2[3]; 48:2−3[3−4]; 135:21; Isa 31:9). This statement would no doubt anger the citizens of the northern kingdom, for it impugned the validity of their religious sites. That voice of the Lord from Jerusalem produced results in the northern kingdom (Carmel) parallels Amos's mission from Judah to Israel.

III. THE PROPHETIC ORACLES (1:3−6:14)

A. Oracles of Judgment against the Surrounding Nations (1:3−2:5)

OVERVIEW

A striking pattern runs through these oracles. The prophet began with the distant city of Damascus and, like a hawk circling its prey, moved in ever-tightening circles from one country to another, till at last he seizes upon Israel. One can imagine Amos's hearers approving the denunciation of these heathen nations. They can even applaud God's denunciation of Judah because of the deep-seated hostility between the two kingdoms that went as far back as the dissolution of the united kingdom after Solomon. But Amos plays no favorites; he swoops down on the unsuspecting Israelites too in the severest language and condemns them for their crimes.

1. The Oracle against Syria (1:3−5)

³This is what the LORD says:

"For three sins of Damascus,
   even for four, I will not turn back ⌐my wrath⌐.
Because she threshed Gilead
   with sledges having iron teeth,

> [4] I will send fire upon the house of Hazael
>   that will consume the fortresses of Ben-Hadad.
> [5] I will break down the gate of Damascus;
>   I will destroy the king who is in the Valley of Aven
> and the one who holds the scepter in Beth Eden.
>   The people of Aram will go into exile to Kir,"
>   says the LORD.

3 The Syrian capital of Damascus represented the entire nation of Aram (Syria) and was its center of culture and influence. From the time of Ahab until the dawn of the eighth century, hostilities erupted between Israel and Damascus. Particularly embarrassing was the incursion of Syria into Israelite territory during the reign of Jehu in the latter half of the ninth century (2Ki 10:32–33).

The numerical motif—here "for three sins ... even for four"—is common in Semitic literature. It occurs mainly in the Wisdom literature (e.g., Job 5:19; 33:29; Pr 6:16; 30:15–31; Ecc 11:2) but is also used by the prophet Micah (Mic 5:5–6). In some instances the sequence is evidently to be taken literally, with the final number equaling the number of elements cited by the author (e.g., Pr 6:16–19). In other cases it is more general and denotes an indefinite number (Mic 5:5–6). The latter usage seems to be intended in Amos 1:3, 6, 9, etc., for Amos cites only one crime of Damascus in this oracle. He has in mind, however, the whole history of Aramean provocation of Israel.

Some scholars have suggested that the masculine pronominal suffix *nû* ("him") on ʾăšîbennû (lit., "I will turn back him ['my wrath,' NIV]") refers to Assyria, which would not be turned back in its progress toward the ultimate conquest of Israel. But this interpretation is unlikely, for Assyria is not mentioned in the immediate context, and Amos never specifically speaks of it as the instrument of

God's wrath. A reference to Assyria in the oracle concerning Judah (2:4–5) would be inappropriate, since Judah fell to the Babylonians. The nearest possible referent of the suffix is *qôl* ("voice" in v.2; "thunders," NIV), the voice of the Lord that presages the impending judgment. If the suffix finds its referent in "voice," the implication is that the Lord will not cause his voice to return; in other words, the judgment it heralds is final.

This solution, however, encounters certain difficulties. The word *qôl* is not in the immediate context of ʾăšîbennû, thus making the suggestion somewhat tenuous. The concept of recalling one's voice is unattested in the OT. The absolute identification of God's voice with the threatened judgment is also foreign to the OT. The voice of the Lord can herald divine judgment, but it is never one and the same with it. In Jeremiah 25:30–31, for example, the roar of the Lord presages punishment by the sword. Also, the formula "This is what the LORD says" introduces a new logical unit that makes the possibility of a syntactical connection between *qôl* and *nû* questionable.

On the whole, it is best to see the suffix *nû* as referring to the judgment that is to come on each of these nations (so the NIV, which supplies "my wrath"). In this case the suffix would not have a syntactical referent but one implicit in the clause, for one naturally expects the phrase "for three sins of" to be followed by some reference to punishment.

The lack of reference to a specific punishment following the statement "for three sins of" creates a feeling of dreadful uncertainty at the outset of the oracle. Thus the attention of the hearers is riveted on the prophet's words as they wait for the explicit description of the judgment that comes in the last section of each oracle.

The crime that provokes the judgment against Damascus is that the people have threshed Gilead with iron threshing sledges. Gilead, an extensive region east of the Jordan River, was known for its rich forests (Jer 22:6-7) and the balm produced there (Jer 8:22). The richness of the area, coupled with its being a frontier region, made it the object of numerous attacks by the nearby countries of Ammon and Syria.

The incident Amos refers to here is most probably the one recorded in 2 Kings 13:1-9. There an incursion of the Syrians into Israel during the reign of Jehoahaz is described as making the army of Jehoahaz "like the dust at threshing time" (v.7). The metaphor Amos uses is that of a threshing sledge, an agricultural implement made of parallel boards fitted with sharp points of iron or stone. We do not, of course, need to understand the metaphor as a literal act in which the bodies of Israelites were torn apart by sledges. The use of the somewhat similar expression in 2 Kings 13:7 seems also to be metaphorical. The intensity of the metaphor, however, implies the most extreme decimation and may hint at especially cruel or inhumane treatment.

4 The judgment the Lord decrees for Syria is "fire upon the house of Hazael." Hazael ruled Syria from about 841-806 BC. His accession to that throne was revealed by the Lord to the prophet Elisha (2Ki 8:13). The Lord also revealed that Hazael would commit monstrous crimes against the Israelites (2Ki 8:12). When Hazael ascended the throne, he fought against Joram and Ahaziah at Ramoth Gilead, an encounter in which Joram was seriously wounded (2Ki 8:28-29).

"Ben-Hadad" ("son of Hadad [an ancient storm god]") is the name of two or possibly three kings of Syria. It may be a dynastic name. Ben-Hadad I, a contemporary of Baasha, king of Israel (906-883 BC), and Asa, king of Judah (908-867 BC), took large territorial holdings from Baasha (1Ki 15:20). Each of the kings named "Ben-Hadad" perpetrated continual hostilities against Israel. The name "Ben-Hadad" in Amos 1:4 may well stand for all the kings who bore that name; yet since only one Hazael is known, it may be that Amos has in mind only one of the kings named "Ben-Hadad"—likely the one who was the son of Hazael (2Ki 13:3). The names "Hazael" and "Ben-Hadad" then represent the long history of Syrian conflict and oppression.

The fire mentioned in v.4 is not a description of an isolated occurrence relating only to Damascus, for it appears in all but one of the oracles (only the oracle against Israel lacks it, 2:6-16). It is best understood as a metaphorical representation of God's judgment (cf. 7:4).

5 The destruction of Damascus will involve the breaking of "the gate of Damascus" (lit., "the bar of Damascus"). The gates of ancient cities were equipped with massive bars, sometimes of iron or bronze (1Ki 4:13). The breaking of the bar implies that the enemies had gained entrance to the city. A similar statement is made at Nahum 3:14 (see also Jer 51:30; La 2:9), passages deriving from ancient Near Eastern treaty curses (see D. Hillers, *Treaty-Curses and the Old Testament Prophets* [Rome: Pontifical Biblical Institute, 1964], 66-68).

The "Valley of Aven" (*biqʿat ʾāwen*) has not been positively identified. Since this valley was associated with Syria, it is likely that it is the plain between the Lebanon and Anti-Lebanon ranges, the most prominent landmark of its kind in the area of Damascus. Today this plain is called *Beqaʿa*. The LXX renders the name *ʾāwen* ("Aven") as *ʾōn*, thereby adopting a vocalic tradition that differs from that in the MT. The name *ʾōn* was the name of the ancient Egyptian city of Heliopolis, a city dedicated to the worship of the sun god Re. One of the most prominent cities in the *Beqaʿa* in ancient times was also called Heliopolis by the Greeks. It is the site of the modern city of Baalbek. While there is no solid evidence that the Aramean Heliopolis was also called *ʾōn*, it may in fact have been, particularly if there was interaction between Syria and Egypt before this time. The vocalic reading of the MT may be a deliberate distortion changing *ʾōn* to *ʾāwen* ("evil") to make a derogatory pun on the name. The same type of pun on the name "Bethel" may be found in Hosea 4:15; 5:8; 10:5, where Beth Aven ("house of wickedness") is substituted for Bethel ("house of God").

"Beth Eden" is also difficult to identify. It seems best, however, to identify it with the Bit-adini of the Akkadian texts. This Aramean city-state, located on the banks of the Euphrates River, was important in the time of Amos. It was conquered by the Assyrians in 855 BC and thus was not under Syrian control when Amos was carrying on his prophetic ministry. Amos, however, seemed to be referring to the past history of Syria. Since Bit-adini was a flourishing city of that country for many years, it is likely that this city is the one named by him.

The name "Beth Aven" may mean "house of evil" according to the MT tradition, and "Beth Eden" may mean "house of delight." Some commentators have understood these names as surrogates for Damascus, thus expressing the idolatrous practices associated with that city. If this understanding is correct, however, such a use would be unique in the oracles. All the other places cited are referred to by their proper names, not symbolic ones.

The identification of "Kir" is also difficult. Its mention with Elam in Isaiah 22:6 leads some (e.g., Paul, 55) to believe its location is near that country (western Iran). Amos later cites Kir as the place of the national origin of the Syrians (9:7) and predicts their return to that place. His prophecy was fulfilled when Tiglath-pileser took the people of Damascus captive and transported them to Kir (2Ki 16:9). The crimes attributed to Syria by Amos are of a social nature—crimes of unmitigated cruelty perpetrated on the Israelites in the numerous attacks waged by the Syrians.

NOTES

3 Not only did Israel lose much of the Transjordanian region to Syria during the reign of Jehu, but also Jehoahaz, Jehu's son (814–798 BC), was conquered by Hazael, who allowed him to retain only a token military force (2Ki 13:7).

Examples of the numerical motif in Ugaritic may be found in *UT* 8:2–3:51; III, 17–18; 52:19–20, 66–67; 128: II, 23–24. For a discussion of numerical sequence in the OT, see W. Roth, "The Numerical Sequence x / x + 1 in the Old Testament," *VT* 12 (1962): 300–311, and, more recently, W. G. E. Watson, *Classical Hebrew Poetry* (Sheffield: Sheffield Academic Press, 1984), 144–49. R. N. Whybray, in *Book of Proverbs: A Survey of Modern Study* (Leiden: Brill, 1995), 97–98, lists possible motivations behind the numerical-proverb form: (1) entertainment, (2) simple observation, (3) education, and (4) reflection.

While the feminine suffix seems more appropriate for expressing the abstract idea of punishment, the masculine was also used in this way, probably thus reflecting colloquial usage (cf. GKC, par. 135o). In

Amos's use of the suffix, the gender is not always precise. Note 4:1, where the masculine suffix הֶם (hem) on אֲדֹנֵיהֶם (ʾdōnêhem), "their husbands," has a feminine referent. In 4:12 we encounter another instance of a threat followed by an unspecified judgment (see comments).

Note that Stuart, 307, follows the LXX and the Targum, which supplies "pregnant women" as the object of the threshing sledges. However, he is influenced by a faulty view of meter to create a longer poetic line.

4 Ben-Hadad was the name of two or possibly three kings of Syria. Several scholars posit only two kings with this name because the biblical accounts in 1 Kings and 2 Chronicles are not precise in this regard (F. Bruce, *Israel and the Nations* [Grand Rapids: Eerdmans, 1963], 42–50). Since Ben-Hadad, the son of Hazael, figured prominently in the events surrounding the reign of Jehoahaz (814–798 BC), it is probable that Amos has this Ben-Hadad in mind. Many of Amos's hearers in Israel would recall the oppressions under Hazael and his son Ben-Hadad (2Ki 13:1–3).

5 For further discussion of the identification of Beth Eden with Bit-adini, see A. Malamat, "Amos 1:5 in the Light of the Til Barsip Inscriptions," *BASOR* 129 (February 1953): 25–26.

2. The Oracle against the Philistines (1:6–8)

⁶This is what the LORD says:

"For three sins of Gaza,
  even for four, I will not turn back ⸢my wrath⸣.
Because she took captive whole communities
  and sold them to Edom,
⁷I will send fire upon the walls of Gaza
  that will consume her fortresses.
⁸I will destroy the king of Ashdod
  and the one who holds the scepter in Ashkelon.
I will turn my hand against Ekron,
  till the last of the Philistines is dead,"
        says the Sovereign LORD.

COMMENTARY

6–8 The prophet next turns his attention to the Philistines. These perennial enemies of the Israelites were a non-Semitic people who may have had their national origin in the Aegean area, probably Crete, or whose migrations took them through that area. They occupied the coastal plain in southwestern Palestine and conducted numerous raids on the Israelites until their power was broken by King David. The Philistines lived in five cities (Ashdod, Ashkelon, Ekron, Gath, and Gaza; cf. Jos 13:3; 1Sa 6:16–17) on the coastal plain, each ruled by a separate lord.

Amos mentions four of the cities of the Philistine pentapolis in this oracle (Gath is excluded). It is suggested by some that the exclusion of this city reflects its destruction by Sargon in 711 BC; thus the oracle is viewed as a later insertion. But perhaps Gath never fully recovered from Uzziah's successful military campaign described in 2 Chronicles 26:6. Uzziah reigned from about 783–742 BC; a coregency with his father, Amaziah, lasted from about 783–769 BC. Uzziah's Philistine campaign may have taken place shortly after the death of Amaziah, for it is the first event to follow the historical summary in 26:1–5. It is likely that Uzziah's sacking of Gath occurred sometime in the period between Amaziah's death (767 BC) and Amos's ministry (760 BC). The destruction of the wall of the city would thus be well known to Amos's hearers and would lend a sense of authenticity to his message predicting the doom of the other cities of the pentapolis.

There is a difficulty, however, with the latter view, for Ashdod is cited in 2 Chronicles 26:6 along with Gath. Both cities were sacked by Uzziah in the Philistine wars. The view does not explain why Ashdod is cited by Amos in the oracle of 1:6–8 and Gath alone is omitted. Perhaps Gath had not recovered sufficiently to be included among the five cities of Philistia in the time of Amos. Others scholars have suggested that Gath is not cited in Amos 1:6–8 because of its peculiar ethnic structure. Kassis argues that Gath was a Canaanite city, "ruled by a Canaanite king who was a vassal of Philistine overlords" (H. Kassis, "Gath and the Structure of 'Philistine' Society," *JBL* 84 [1965]: 259–71).

Another possibility explaining Gath's omission is that it had never fully recovered from an attack by Hazael (2Ki 12:17) during the reign of Jehoash of Judah (835–796 BC). But the later campaign of Uzziah against Gath indicates that the Philistines had regained control of the city and had sufficient strength to be a threat to Judah.

We cannot be certain of the reason for the exclusion of Gath, but its omission is insufficient evidence to impugn the authenticity of this oracle. Gath is excluded from all the lists of the Philistine cities cited after Amos (Jer 25:20; Zep 2:4; Zec 9:5–6).

The Philistines are denounced for the crime of enslavement (v.6)—again, a social crime. Though the event referred to here cannot be identified, it probably consisted in a series of border raids in which slaves were secured and sold to the Edomites. Amos indicates that whole communities were taken in this way, thus underscoring the enormity of the crime. It is likely (though unprovable) that the crime was committed against Israelites. The punishment to be inflicted on the Philistines will be their absolute destruction (vv.7–8).

NOTES

6 S. Paul, 60, argues that the Hiphil of *sgr* means "to hand over to one stronger." Practically speaking, however, in this context the NIV's translation "sold" likely reflects what actually happened.

7–8 Gaza and Ashdod were conquered by Nebuchadnezzar (605–562 BC), who transported their kings to Babylon (*ANET*, 307–8). Ashkelon was conquered by Tiglath-pileser III in 734 BC. Later, in 701 BC, Sennacherib conquered the city and carried off the king of Ashkelon to Assyria. In later years the city was overrun by the Scythians, Chaldeans, and Persians. Esarhaddon and Ashurbanipal required tribute of Ekron (*ANET*, 291, 294), a city that continued to exist till the time of the Crusades.

3. The Oracle against Tyre (1:9–10)

⁹This is what the LORD says:

"For three sins of Tyre,
　　even for four, I will not turn back ⌞my wrath⌟.
Because she sold whole communities of captives to Edom,
　　disregarding a treaty of brotherhood,
¹⁰I will send fire upon the walls of Tyre
　　that will consume her fortresses."

COMMENTARY

9–10 So far Amos has moved from Damascus in the northeast to the Philistine territory in the southwest. He moved next to Tyre, to the north of Israel and southwest of Damascus; in other words, he moves closer to Israel than were Damascus and the Philistine cities. Tyre was the most important city of Phoenicia at that time.

The crime of Tyre also involves the enslavement of entire communities (v.9), but Amos also adds a reference to its "disregarding a treaty of brotherhood." The treaty (*bᵉrît*) that this slave commerce violated may refer to the pact made between Hiram, king of Tyre, and Solomon (1Ki 5:12; cf. "brother" in 1Ki 9:13). This relationship was strengthened further by the marriage of Jezebel, daughter of Ethbaal, king of the Sidonians, to King Ahab (1Ki 16:31).

While Jehu's purge of the family of Ahab (2Ki 10) interrupted the good relationship between the two states, Amos may be referring to the generally amicable relations that characterized these nations over their long histories.

Tyre's security, however, was only temporary (v.10). It came under Assyrian hegemony during the long period of that empire's dominance but emerged from Assyrian control to enter a period of power and affluence. Tyre was later besieged by the forces of Nebuchadnezzar and never fully recovered. The massive efforts required for its defense greatly weakened the city, and it entered a period of decline. In 332 BC Alexander besieged Tyre and conquered it.

NOTE

9 Homer referred to the Phoenician practice of slave trading in *Odyssey* 4.288ff.; 15.473ff. See also "Contest of Homer and Hesiod," in *Hesiod: The Homeric Hymns and Homerica*, trans. H. Evelyn-White (Cambridge: Harvard Univ. Press, 1950), 569. For "sold" (Hiphil of *sgr*), see Note at 1:6.

4. The Oracle against Edom (1:11–12)

¹¹This is what the LORD says:

"For three sins of Edom,
    even for four, I will not turn back ⌊my wrath⌋,
Because he pursued his brother with a sword,
    stifling all compassion,
because his anger raged continually
    and his fury flamed unchecked,
¹²I will send fire upon Teman
    that will consume the fortresses of Bozrah."

COMMENTARY

11 The extensive, mountainous region of Edom lay to the southeast of the southern tip of the Dead Sea, east of the Arabah. It was one of the three Transjordanian kingdoms that included Ammon and Moab. Edom's crime was that "he pursued his brother with a sword" and "his anger raged continually"—a reference to the longstanding animosity of Edom toward the Israelites.

"Edom" is another name for "Esau," the twin brother of Jacob. The Edomites and Israelites thus had close ethnic ties, reflected in the use of the word "brother" in reference to the Israelites (cf. Nu 20:14; Ob 12; cf. Dt 23:7, where the Israelites were commanded not to hate an Edomite, "for he is your brother"). The bitter relations between Jacob and Esau were perpetuated in the affairs of the two countries. In their wilderness journey the Israelites sought access to the King's Highway, which ran through Edom. But the Edomites refused them passage and even sent a military force to block them (Nu 20:14–21).

In 1 Samuel 14:47 the Edomites are mentioned as enemies of Saul. David placed military garrisons in Edom (2Sa 8:14), and an Edomite rebellion against Judah during the reign of Jehoram is recorded in 2 Kings 8:20–22. Their greatest act of hostility against Israel occurred during the sacking of Jerusalem by Nebuchadnezzar in 587 BC. At that time the Edomites gloated over the destruction of their enemies and hindered the fugitives' escape, while delivering many fleeing Judahites over to their conquerors (Ob 10–14).

12 For these crimes the cities of Teman and Bozrah will be destroyed. Teman was one of the largest cities of Edom, and Bozrah was a strong fortress city in the north of Edom. These cities represent the whole country. Both are denounced in several prophetic oracles (Isa 34:6; 63:1; Jer 49:13, 20; Eze 25:13; Ob 9).

Edom became a tributary to Tiglath-pileser III in 732 BC and was overrun by the Nabataeans later in its history. The crime of Edom was in many ways similar to that of the other nations Amos speaks against—violence against humanity. In this oracle the prophet emphasizes that the Edomites stifle "all compassion" (cf. the NT's warning against failure to show love toward one's "brother" [Jas 4:11; 1Jn 2:9]).

NOTE

11 Remnants of Edom's past glory may be seen today in the ruins of Petra (in modern-day Jordan), an ancient Edomite city. The ruins probably date from Nabataean times.

5. The Oracle against Ammon (1:13–15)

> ¹³This is what the LORD says:
>
> "For three sins of Ammon,
>   even for four, I will not turn back ⌊my wrath⌋.
> Because he ripped open the pregnant women of Gilead
>   in order to extend his borders,
> ¹⁴I will set fire to the walls of Rabbah
>   that will consume her fortresses
> amid war cries on the day of battle,
>   amid violent winds on a stormy day.
> ¹⁵Her king will go into exile,
>   he and his officials together,"
>   says the LORD.

COMMENTARY

13 Ammon lay northeast of the Dead Sea and due north of Moab. The area was dominated by a vast expanse of desert, though the valley of the upper Jabbok in the north of Ammon was fertile. The account in Genesis 19:30–38 attributes the national origin of the Ammonites and Moabites to an incestual relationship between Lot and his two daughters. Israel under Moses came into contact with the Ammonites as they journeyed toward the Promised Land. God told Israel not to bother the Ammonites (Dt 2:19), but the Ammonites tried to stop the Israelites from reaching their destination. Deuteronomy 23:3–6 names the Ammonites and Moabites as responsible for hiring Balaam in the thwarted attempt to curse the Israelites.

At the time of the settlement, the tribe of Gad was given "the territory of Jazer, all the towns of Gilead, and half the Ammonite country as far as Aroer, near Rabbah" (Jos 13:25). War plagued Ammon and Israel throughout their common history. To cite only the notorious examples, the judge Jephthah had to counter the Ammonites' attempt to push into territory claimed by Israel (Jdg 10–11); Saul fought the Ammonite king Nahash over the city of Jabesh Gilead (1Sa 11); Joab led the armies of Israel against the Ammonites, during which time David impregnated Bathsheba (2Sa 10–11); and the Chronicler records a battle between Jehoshaphat and the combined forces of the Ammonites and Moabites (2Ch 20).

The Ammonites frequently sought to enlarge their territory, sometimes with the help of the neighboring Moabites and Syrians. In the time of the judges, the Ammonites crossed the Jordan and went deep into Israelite territory (Jdg 10:6–9). Through the personal leadership of Saul, a serious threat to Israel by the Ammonites was quelled (1Sa 11:1–11). They were finally subdued in David's time (2Sa 12:26–31).

The crime of which Amos accuses the Ammonites is, like that of the other nations, a crime against humanity. The Ammonites "ripped open the pregnant women of Gilead." This violence evidently took place in one of their attempts to expand their territorial holdings at Israel's expense. While we do not know the particular circumstances of this monstrous crime, it may have occurred during the campaigns of Hazael against Israel toward the end of the ninth century BC (cf. 2Ki 8:12). At this time all Israel's territory in Transjordan fell into the hands of the Arameans. The Ammonites may have taken advantage of this opportunity to exploit Israel's weakness. Apparently it was a notorious event, and its mention would stir feelings of revulsion in Amos's hearers.

Gilead was a mountainous region east of the Jordan, in the tribal territories of Gad and the half-tribe of Manasseh. It is easy to understand how this fertile frontier region would suffer when Israel was attacked by her enemies to the east. Certainly the crime Amos accuses the Ammonites of goes far beyond necessary acts of war and is attributed to the Ammonites' insatiable desire for Israelite territory.

14 Rabbah was the capital of ancient Ammon. Today it is the site of the modern city of Amman. As its punishment Ammon is to be destroyed by fire, with the accompaniment of battle cries and "violent winds." The word translated "war cries" (*tᵉrûᶜâ*) may connote shouting for joy (Ezr 3:12), a trumpet signal (Nu 10:5), or the shout of battle (Jos 6:5). In this instance it is the shout of the enemy "on the day of battle," a sound that will terrify the people as the enemy rush to take the city.

The word "winds" (*saᶜar*) is used of a wind storm on three occasions (Ps 55:8[9]; Jnh 1:4, 12) but occurs most frequently as a metaphor of God's wrath (Ps 83:15[16]; Jer 23:19; 25:32; 30:23). Here, however, it need not connote a theophany. (Its parallel *tᵉrûᶜâ* ["war cries"] does not do so.) The word simply describes the great force with which the enemy will sweep over the city.

15 The king of Ammon will go into exile along with his officials. In an oracle against the Ammonites, Ezekiel berated them for rejoicing over the fall of Jerusalem (Eze 25:1–7). Yet their rejoicing will last only a little while; for they are to be caught up in the same turmoil that will affect Israel.

Ammon's dominion came to an end when Nebuchadnezzar sacked the city of Rabbah and took large numbers of its citizens captive. This opened the way for Arabian invaders to occupy their territory. The Ammonites passed from history for good.

NOTES

14 For a discussion of the possibility of a "Yahweh theophany" here, see Mays, 37–38.

15 In the parallel passage in Jeremiah 49:1–3 (30:17–20 LXX), the word מַלְכָּם (*malkām*, "their king," NIV margin) is rendered *milkōm* in the RSV. "Milcom" was the name of the national deity of the Ammonites. The NASB renders the word "Malcam" and the NIV "Molech." The LXX translates the word by Μελχομ (*Melchom*). The passage in Jeremiah shows dependence on Amos 1:13–15 (cf. Jer 49:3) but does not necessarily warrant reading "Milcom" in Amos 1:15. The use of the word שָׂרָיו (*śārāyw*, "his officials") in the parallel line of v.15 favors the reading "their king," not a reference to the Ammonite deity. Also, Jeremiah may have used a play on words in his oracle about Ammon, for in Jeremiah 49:3 the parallel line has כֹּהֲנָיו (*kōhᵃnāyw*, "his priests") in addition to *śārāyw*. Amos 1:15 has הוּא (*hûʾ*, "he") at that point.

6. The Oracle against Moab (2:1–3)

¹This is what the LORD says:

"For three sins of Moab,
　　even for four, I will not turn back ⌐my wrath⌐.
Because he burned, as if to lime,
　　the bones of Edom's king,
²I will send fire upon Moab
　　that will consume the fortresses of Kerioth.
Moab will go down in great tumult
　　amid war cries and the blast of the trumpet.
³I will destroy her ruler
　　and kill all her officials with him,"
　　　　　　　　says the LORD.

COMMENTARY

1 Moab lay to the east of the Dead Sea, between Ammon to the north and Edom to the south. The Wadi Arnon formed Moab's natural northern border, although the Moabites extended their territory north of the Arnon in times of national strength. The region of Moab, today occupied by the nation of Jordan, is a land of deep ravines and extensive plateaus.

The Bible paints the origin of the Moabites in dark colors. In Genesis 19, after the destruction of Sodom and Gomorrah and the death of Lot's wife, Lot's daughters got him drunk and had intercourse with him. The products of this act were two boys, named Ammon and Moab.

The Israelites camped in the plains of Moab before entering Canaan (Nu 22:1). The king of Moab, concerned over the strength of the Israelites, engaged Baalam, the enigmatic seer, to curse them (Nu 22:4–6). It was in the plains of Moab that the Moabite women seduced the Israelites to join in their idolatrous worship (Nu 25:1–3). As a result God excluded the Moabites from the assembly of Israel (Dt 23:3–4).

During a period of Israelite weakness in the time of the Judges, a coalition of Moabites, Ammonites, and Amalekites invaded Israel and subjugated them for eighteen years (Jdg 3:13–14). Antipathy between the Hebrews and Moabites developed further when the king of Moab would not permit the Hebrews to travel northward via the King's Highway (11:17).

Saul defeated the Moabites (1Sa 14:47), as did David (2Sa 8:2). During Solomon's reign Moab seems to have remained under Israelite dominion, for Solomon included Moabite women among his many wives (1Ki 11:1). But Mesha, king of Moab, rebelled against Israel after the death of Ahab (2Ki 1:1). Joram of Israel and Jehoshaphat of Judah, along with the king of Edom, made an abortive attempt to subdue them (2Ki 3). The Moabite Stone, one of the few Moabite language sources available to scholars, commemorates this event. Later on Hazael, an Aramean king, wrested from Jehu the disputed Moabite territory north of the Arnon (2Ki 10:32–33).

The crime with which Amos charges the Moabites is their burning of the bones of the king of Edom. While this act is not mentioned specifically in the OT, it may have taken place during the attempt of the coalition of the kings of Israel, Judah, and Edom to suppress the Moabite rebellion (2Ki 3; cf. Notes). The expression "burn the bones" (śārᵉpô ᶜaṣmôt) never refers to the burning of an individual as punishment for a crime. Except for two metaphorical uses where burning of bones connotes extreme suffering (Job 30:30; Ps 102:3[4]), the expression refers to the burning of the skeletal remains of a corpse (2Ki 23:20; cf. v.16; cf. also 1Ki 13:2; Eze 24:10) or the burning of the corpse itself (Amos 6:9–10). Thus the crime of Moab involves the desecration of the body of an Edomite king. How long after his death this happened is unknown.

2–3 The punishment of Moab is to be by fire that will consume Kerioth (v.2). Though Kerioth may be translated "cities," it is likely a proper noun referring to a major city in Moab (a city mentioned in Nu 32:37; Jos 13:19; 1Ch 6:76; Eze 25:9; Jer 48:23). This site is also mentioned in the Moabite Stone.

Amos used vivid language to describe the conflict that will end in the overthrow of Moab. One can almost hear the "war cries" and "the blast of the trumpet." Clearly the "fire" that will come on Moab symbolizes war.

Moab became subject to Tiglath-pileser III in 734 BC. Later, it was involved in a rebellion against Assyrian domination quelled by Sennacherib. During the period of Babylonian supremacy, Moab was forced to pay tribute to Babylon. The Moabites rebelled against Babylon shortly after 598 BC and, according to Josephus (*Ant.* 10.181–82 [9.7]), were conquered by Nebuchadnezzar, thus opening the way for Arabian tribes to occupy Moabite territory.

Highly significant is the fact that Amos here pronounces the punishment of Yahweh for a social crime involving a non-Israelite. In the prophet's other oracles the crimes were, for the most part, against the covenantal people. Amos understands that an aspect of God's law transcends Israel. He affirms a moral law that extends to noncovenantal nations, a law that will surely bring punishment if violated. As S. Paul, 72, puts it: "This is the best proof that the oracles of Amos against the foreign nations are intended to denounce the barbaric act of inhumanity itself, no matter by whom or against whom it was perpetrated. Such a crime is a direct offense against the Lord, whose moral laws operate and are binding within the international community of nations."

7. The Oracle against Judah (2:4–5)

⁴This is what the LORD says:

"For three sins of Judah,
　　even for four, I will not turn back ⌐my wrath⌐.

> Because they have rejected the law of the LORD
>   and have not kept his decrees,
> because they have been led astray by false gods,
>   the gods their ancestors followed,
> ⁵I will send fire upon Judah
>   that will consume the fortresses of Jerusalem."

COMMENTARY

4–5 Having pronounced judgment on various pagan nations, Amos next turns to Judah. God plays no favorites and cannot condone the sins of his people. While both Israel and Judah had a common religious heritage, the cleavage of the two kingdoms after the death of Solomon left wounds that never healed. Deep-rooted antipathies existed between the two kingdoms. Amos's denunciation of Judah would fall on sympathetic ears in Israel.

Judah is condemned for rejecting the "law of the LORD" (*tôrat yhwh*; v.4). Here is the first occurrence of this expression in these oracles, and its significance is obvious. This is an oracle against those who stand in relationship to the covenant. Hence they are judged on the basis of the light they possess—not on the basis of a common moral consciousness, but on the statutes of Yahweh himself.

The word translated "led astray" (*tāʿâ*) means basically "to wander around." It is used of straying animals and intoxicated persons, as well as moral aberration. Judah had been led astray by "false gods" (*kāzāb*, "lies"). The Hebrew expression "walked after them" ("followed," NIV) frequently relates to following false gods. The use of "lie" in conjunction with this expression shows that for Amos these deities are false in their essence. The sin of idolatry has caused Judah to violate the law of Yahweh. Like their fathers of old, they continue to bow down to the false gods of the pagans and spurn the Creator of heaven and earth.

Judah's punishment will be similar to that of the other nations—destruction by the fire of war (v.5). This was inflicted when Jerusalem fell to the Babylonians.

B. Oracles of Judgment against Israel (2:6–6:14)

1. A Lesson from History (2:6–16)

OVERVIEW

Though the Israelites may have rejoiced in the denunciation of their brothers in Judah, they themselves are to feel the lash of Amos's words. The

same formula that introduces the condemnation of their pagan enemies begins this powerful oracle. Again the numerical parallelism communicates that there are many crimes, only a few of which will be described. This oracle is the most extensive of all the oracles. Verses 6−8 set forth Israel's crimes, vv.9−11 appeal to God's past activity in their behalf, and vv.12−16 conclude the oracle with a vivid portrayal of their punishment.

⁶This is what the Lord says:
"For three sins of Israel,
    even for four, I will not turn back ⌐my wrath⌐.
They sell the righteous for silver,
    and the needy for a pair of sandals.
⁷They trample on the heads of the poor
    as upon the dust of the ground
    and deny justice to the oppressed.
Father and son use the same girl
    and so profane my holy name.
⁸They lie down beside every altar
    on garments taken in pledge.
In the house of their god
    they drink wine taken as fines.

⁹"I destroyed the Amorite before them,
    though he was tall as the cedars
    and strong as the oaks.
I destroyed his fruit above
    and his roots below.

¹⁰"I brought you up out of Egypt,
    and I led you forty years in the desert
    to give you the land of the Amorites.
¹¹I also raised up prophets from among your sons
    and Nazirites from among your young men.
Is this not true, people of Israel?"

                              declares the Lord.

¹²"But you made the Nazirites drink wine
    and commanded the prophets not to prophesy.

¹³"Now then, I will crush you
    as a cart crushes when loaded with grain.
¹⁴The swift will not escape,
    the strong will not muster their strength,
    and the warrior will not save his life.

> ¹⁵ The archer will not stand his ground,
>   the fleet-footed soldier will not get away,
>   and the horseman will not save his life.
> ¹⁶ Even the bravest warriors
>   will flee naked on that day,"
>
>   declares the LORD.

6 The Israelites are accused of selling "the righteous for silver." The word "righteous" (*ṣaddîq*) is parallel to "needy" (*ʾebyôn*), thus establishing a connection between them. The word *ṣaddîq* connotes righteousness, not necessarily in the sense of blamelessness but rather in the basic sense of "rightness" or "justice." The needy are seen as being in the right or having a just cause. The word *ṣaddîq* is used in this sense in Exodus 23:7, where in a context of litigation it is coupled with "innocent" (*nāqî*). In Deuteronomy 25:1 *ṣaddîq* is the antithesis of "guilty" (*rāšāʿ*). On a number of occasions (e.g., Isa 32:7; Jer 5:28) the prophets spoke of the "needy" as being in litigious situations. This shows us something of the social conditions of that time, when the poor had to fight for their just rights, which were all-too-frequently ignored.

The pronoun "they" applies to the oppressing classes, especially the judges and creditors who "sell the righteous." These people of power and influence are guilty of accepting bribes of money and apparel. They regard the oppressed classes so lightly that they accept such paltry bribes as a pair of sandals. Amos characterized their corruption as "selling."

7 Amos further describes the oppression of the poor as trampling "on the heads of the poor." The meaning of the verb here "to trample" takes it as a biform of *šûp* (so Paul, 79–80). However, the word translated "trample" (*šāʾap*) may also mean "gasp" or "pant." Here the text presents certain difficulties;

but if one follows the MT literally, the most favorable rendering is, "who pant after the dust of the earth on the head of the poor," meaning either that the oppressing classes long to see the poor brought to extreme anguish, or the oppressors are so avaricious that they craved the dust with which the poor have covered their heads. In ancient Near Eastern culture, pouring dust on one's head signified sorrow (e.g., 2Sa 1:2; Job 2:12).

Israel's decadence is marked by sexual promiscuity. Whether or not it refers to ritual prostitution is not clear. The word for "girl" (*naʿărâ*) is a general one and has no specific connotations. It is possible that the act described here refers to misuse of a legal aspect of concubinage such as that described in Exodus 21:7–11. More likely, however, it relates to the ancient laws against incest, as indicated in the words "profane my holy name." These words also occur in Leviticus 22:32, where they culminate a lengthy section dealing with personal and social purity. Leviticus 18:6–18 and 20:17–21 specifically prohibit incest. In 18:7 intercourse with one's mother is forbidden, which reflects the fact that husband and wife are one flesh. Thus an incestuous relationship with one's mother also dishonored one's father. Similarly, sexual intercourse with one's stepmother incestuously dishonored one's father (18:8; 20:11), and intercourse with an aunt by marriage was incestuous because it "uncovered the nakedness" of one's uncle (18:14; 20:20).

While these laws do not specify that the prohibition extended to intercourse with women outside the family, the principle may still apply. The use of one girl by both a father and a son is tantamount to incest in that the son uncovers the nakedness of his father, and vice versa, through their union with the same girl.

Even though the particular practice Amos condemns is difficult to determine, v.7 provides an insight into the social conditions of the time. The marital purity and faithfulness expected in a godly father are lacking, as both father and son engage in deliberate acts of disobedience to God.

8 Amos also pictures members of his society as sleeping by the altars on "garments taken in pledge." Clothing was regarded as valid collateral for securing debts. Hebrew law, however, required that garments taken in pledge be restored to the owner each evening (Ex 22:26–27; Dt 24:12–12) as a covering during sleep. But many are obviously disregarding this law by sleeping in the garments of others.

The placing of this practice in the prevailing cultus ("every altar") emphasizes the great disparity between religion and practice in Israel. This situation is further illustrated by the people's drinking in the "house of their god" the wine paid as fines. As S. Paul, 87, points out, "the irony is that precisely at the very places of worship, they act in a way that is condemned by the God of Israel."

9 Amos next recounts God's gracious acts during Israel's past. "Amorite" is an OT term sometimes used for the preconquest population of Canaan (Ge 15:16). The prophet reminds the people of God's destruction of the Canaanites in the conquest. The great height and strength of the Canaanites reflect a tradition begun at the return of the spies from their reconnaissance of the Promised Land (Nu 13:22–33). It points to their apparent invincibility and contrasts it with the overwhelming might of the Lord. Amos's vivid metaphor of the fruit and the roots portrays the destruction of the Canaanites when the Israelites took the land.

10 Amos saw the exodus and the forty years of wandering in the desert solely as expressions of the gracious power of Yahweh. Thus there is no need for him to mention Israel's disobedience in the wilderness. He simply points out that the Lord gave them "the land of the Amorites."

11 The raising up of prophets and Nazirites was another of God's gracious acts. The parallel reference to these two groups does not imply that they are one and the same, or that one is derived from the other. They are simply two groups who ministered God's word to Israel and showed the Lord's care for their spiritual welfare.

12 The word "Nazirite" (*nāzîr*) means "separate." Thus it denotes the consecration to God practiced by this group. Nazirites could come from any tribe and be male or female; this allowed non-Levites to assume a special status of consecration before the Lord. The Nazirites took a special vow of separation (cf. Nu 6:1–12)—indeed, one more stringent than even that of the Levites. They completely abstained from partaking of any product of the vine and from all fermented drinks. They vowed neither to cut their hair nor to touch a dead body. In mentioning these groups Amos rounds out his brief reference to Israel's history.

Verse 12 tells how Israel has treated the Nazirites and the prophets. They forced the former to drink wine and violate their vows, and they muzzled the prophets—a more heinous crime than simply opposing these religious groups by being tantamount to rejecting the word of Yahweh and the dedication to Yahweh that found expression among them.

Israel's rejection of the God who acted in their behalf—from Egypt to the present—is implicit in v.12. This rejection leads to the statement of doom that follows (vv.13–16). The coming judgment is vividly expressed in a series of images rapidly moving from one familiar realm to another.

13–16 Now God describes how he will punish Israel. Stuart, 319, points out how these punishments reflect what he calls the "helplessness curses," such as the curses found in Leviticus 26:36–39. First, Amos pictures the nation as being crushed like an object under the wheels of a heavily laden cart (v.13). This picture, drawn from the agricultural world, reflects Amos's familiarity with that life. The other images include a swift runner, a strong man,

and a warrior (v.14). These figures depict Israel's inability to escape the impending destruction. The archer cannot stand (v.15); the brave warriors will flee empty-handed (v.16), their weapons and armor scattered behind as on a battlefield.

The Israelites had experienced Yahweh's leading in the exodus and through the wilderness, with his sword hewing the way for them to the Promised Land. Now that sword will be turned against them because they have spurned the Holy One of Israel. The oracle closes with an awesome note of finality—"declares the LORD."

NOTES

....

6 Several commentators understand the words "sell the righteous for silver" to refer to the Israelite practice of debt-slavery to aid those who were insolvent (Ex 21:7–8; Lev 25:39–55; 2Ki 4:1; Ne 5:8; Isa 50:1). It is not always easy to distinguish the types of slavery legislated in the OT. However, where debt-slavery is clearly in view, the debtor initiates his servitude or that of a member of his family. This self-initiated servitude is not the emphasis in Amos 2:6, unless one understands the wealthy classes to have created the conditions under which the poor must enter debt-slavery. But that understanding is not consonant with the active and direct involvement that Amos attributes to the oppressing classes. The point is, rather, that the innocent are being accused of crimes they have not committed. The magistrates are accepting paltry bribes to punish the innocent. These dishonest practices violate the law (Dt 16:18–20).

S. Paul, 77–78, suggests that the word rendered "pair of sandals" (naᶜᵃlîm) should be understood as a noun from the verb ᶜlm ("to hide"), and thus a reference to a "hidden bribe." However, though "pair of sandals" is nowhere else attested as meaning an insignificant amount, it makes perfectly clear sense in the context and is best understood in the traditional sense.

7 The word שָׁאַף (šāʾap, "trample") may also mean "gasp" or "pant." If understood as "trample," the בְּ (bᵉ, "with") prefix on רֹאשׁ (rōʾš, "head") is difficult to construe as a preposition. E. Hammershaimb (*The Book of Amos: A Commentary*, trans. J. Sturdy [New York: Schocken, 1970], 48) suggests that bᵉ serves to introduce an object; he observes the similar function of bᵉ with the verbs פָּגַע (pāgaᶜ) and פָּגַשׁ (pāgaš). But these verbs, meaning "to meet, encounter," may prefer bᵉ because the concept of motion or direction inherent in them is consonant with the basic meaning of that preposition. Thus the translation "those who trample to the dust of the earth, the head of the poor" is difficult. The translation that most accurately renders the MT is, "who pant after the dust of the earth on the head of the poor."

BDB cites two roots for שָׁאַף (šāʾap). One means to "crush, trample upon," and the other is a parallel form of שׁוּף (šûp, "to bruise"). It is under the latter that Amos 2:7 is placed, along with 8:4; Psalms 56:2–3;

57:4; Ezekiel 36:3. *HALOT* and GKC cite the latter references under *šāʾap* as "to pant" or "to snap at." The LXX reads "sandals, with which to tread on the dust of the earth, and they have smitten upon the heads of the poor." This reading attests a verb not present in the MT—"smitten." The question is difficult, but the MT makes sense as it stands and best fits with the charge of greed in v.6.

8 The so-called Yabneh-Yam letter records an incident that reflects the biblical law of Exodus 22:26–27[25–26] regarding seizure of a person's garment for nonpayment of a debt (cf. *ANET*, 568; F. Cross, "Epigraphic Notes on Hebrew Documents of the Eighth–Sixth Centuries BC, II. The Murabbaʿat Papyrus and the Letter Found Near Yabneh-Yam," *BASOR* 165 [February 1962]: 34–46).

11 The word נָזִיר (*nāzîr*, "Nazirite") is based on the root נָזַר (*nāzar*, "to separate"), which shows that the Nazirite was a separated or consecrated person. *Nāzîr* is translated "prince" in a number of English versions (Ge 49:26, NEB, NIV; Dt 33:16, RSV, NEB, NIV; La 4:7, RSV, NIV, NEB). However, this word is best understood as having a secondary meaning derived from *nēzer*, sometimes translated "crown." The long hair of a Nazirite was his "separation [*nēzer*] to God ... on his head" (Nu 6:7). The use of *nēzer* to connote the headgear of the priest (Ex 29:6) and a royal crown (2Sa 1:10) seems to denote that the headgear is a sign of consecration to one's office.

13 The meaning of מֵעִיק (*mēʿîq*, "crush") is uncertain. The verb occurs only here. However, the meaning "press down" is supported by the related root עָקָה (*ʿāqâ*), which connotes the idea of "pressure" in Psalm 55:4. The ambiguity of the Hebrew is reflected in various English versions: "I am weighted down beneath you," NASB; "I will press you down," RSV. While the Masoretic tradition is admittedly difficult, it need not be rejected out of hand. The Hebrew says literally, "Behold I am pressing down under you as a cart loaded with sheaves presses down." Gese suggests that the word עוּק (*ʿûq*) means "to cleave, furrow" (H. Gese, "Kleine Beiträge zum Verständnis des Amosbuches," *VT* 12 [1962]: 417–24). If this meaning is correct, the picture is that of God's cleaving the ground before Israel as the wheels of a heavily loaded cart dig into the ground. Israel is thus impeded in its attempt to flee from the impending doom.

2. A Lesson based on Cause and Effect (3:1–12)

[1]Hear this word the LORD has spoken against you, O people of Israel — against the whole family I brought up out of Egypt:

[2]"You only have I chosen
   of all the families of the earth;
therefore I will punish you
   for all your sins."

[3]Do two walk together
   unless they have agreed to do so?
[4]Does a lion roar in the thicket
   when he has no prey?

Does he growl in his den
    when he has caught nothing?
5 Does a bird fall into a trap on the ground
    where no snare has been set?
Does a trap spring up from the earth
    when there is nothing to catch?
6 When a trumpet sounds in a city,
    do not the people tremble?
When disaster comes to a city,
    has not the Lord caused it?

7 Surely the Sovereign Lord does nothing
    without revealing his plan
    to his servants the prophets.

8 The lion has roared—
    who will not fear?
The Sovereign Lord has spoken—
    who can but prophesy?
9 Proclaim to the fortresses of Ashdod
    and to the fortresses of Egypt:
"Assemble yourselves on the mountains of Samaria;
    see the great unrest within her
    and the oppression among her people."
10 "They do not know how to do right," declares the Lord,
    "who hoard plunder and loot in their fortresses."

11 Therefore this is what the Sovereign Lord says:

"An enemy will overrun the land;
    he will pull down your strongholds
    and plunder your fortresses."

12 This is what the Lord says:

"As a shepherd saves from the lion's mouth
    only two leg bones or a piece of an ear,
    so will the Israelites be saved,
those who sit in Samaria
    on the edge of their beds
    and in Damascus on their couches."

COMMENTARY

1 A summons to hear the "word of the LORD" introduces this oracle. The summons is directed against "the whole family I brought up out of Egypt" and thus seems to include Judah as well as Israel. It is certain that Amos does not have high hopes for Judah (2:5), and he would never exempt them from divine wrath for their disobedience. The pronouncement of judgment, addressed primarily to the northern kingdom, warns Judah and Israel that their election by Yahweh in itself is insufficient ground for thinking they are nationally secure; God demands personal obedience as well.

Indeed, the remembrance of the exodus is a none-too-subtle allusion to their covenantal obligations. The book of the covenant, including the Ten Commandments and the associated case law (Ex 20–24), is prefaced by "I am the LORD your God, who brought you out of Egypt, out of the land of slavery" (20:2). God had shown them his grace by freeing them from Egyptian bondage, and now they should show their gratitude by obeying the law that followed.

2 The statement "you only have I chosen [*yādaʿ*, 'known'] of all the families of the earth" establishes Israel's elective privilege. The word *yādaʿ* bears a special sense of intimacy. Jeremiah 1:5 uses *yādaʿ* in a similar way to describe God's knowing and consecrating of Jeremiah even before his birth. Thus the word connotes more than simple awareness or acknowledgment. It includes the idea of God's sovereign activity whereby the object of that knowledge is set apart or chosen for a divine purpose. Such is the case with Israel, whose special relationship with God goes back to his covenant with Abraham (Ge 12:1–3), the grounds on which he delivered the Hebrews from Egypt.

Israel's privilege, however, generates her punishment. Verse 2 sets forth a foundational principle of Amos's message and of Scripture in general: Elective privilege entails responsibility. The two stichs of this verse are connected by "therefore" (ʿal kēn), establishing a logical relationship between them. Because Israel has failed to live up to her holy calling, she is to be punished.

God's choice of Israel as the vehicle of his redemptive purposes is, from the human standpoint, strange. The people were slaves, possessing no homeland; and Israel was the weakest of the nations of the world (cf. Dt 7:7). The calling of Christians is similar, for Paul reminds us that God calls the weak so that human boasting may be excluded (1Co 1:26–29).

3–5 The pronouncement of the judgment predicted in v.2 does not appear till v.11. It is preceded by a series of seven questions that culminate in an affirmation of Amos's prophetic authority. Only then does he depict the desperate plight of the nation soon to be surrounded by an adversary.

The first question (v.3) asks whether two can walk together if they have not agreed to do so. In the Hebrew the word "walk" is in the imperfect tense, denoting incomplete action. The question is, "Is it customary for two to walk together without agreeing to do so?" Certainly two people walking side-by-side would not be doing so only by sheer coincidence.

Verse 4 notes that a lion does not roar when it is stalking its prey. When a bird is ensnared, it is because someone has set a trap (v.5); and a snare is not sprung unless something triggers it.

6 To this point each question has begun with the effect followed by the cause. Now the order is reversed. Amos's style is far from stereotyped.

His writing is marked by variety and vigor. The prophets do not follow the mechanical, poetic style of the Ugaritic epic material. By rejecting it, they bring an element into their words that disturbs their smug hearers. Here the cause is the blast of the trumpet and the effect is the fear it brings to the city dwellers. The sound of a trumpet from a city wall warned of invaders; a trumpet in the square heralded bad news. Ultimately the cause of the "disaster" coming to a city is "the LORD." We should not conclude, however, that "disaster" (*rā'â*) implies "evil" in the ethical sense here. The word has that meaning in Hebrew, but the emphasis here on the city warrants only the meaning "disaster."

It is not necessary to see the figures in these questions as representations of Israel or her enemies. They are simply vivid analogies from life intended to illustrate the forthcoming conclusion (v.8).

7 The relationship of the first clause of this verse to the preceding clause is uncertain. Because there is no apparent logical connection between the sections, it is difficult to understand the particle *kî* in the sense of "for." It seems best to understand *kî* as an asseverative ("surely"). But this causes v.7 to interrupt the sequence of thought in vv.2-8 and has led some interpreters to see it as an intrusive element, possibly coming from the hand of the posited "Deuteronomist."

But v.7 seems to be an essential part of the narrative because the word "prophets" refers to "prophesy" in v.8. The words "lion" and "fear" in v.8 refer to "lion" in v.4 and "tremble" (*ḥārad*) in v.6. Without v.7 the idea of prophecy in v.8 stands alone, with no logical relation to the preceding argument (cf. 6:11 for a similar sentence). See S. Paul, 113, for a similar defense of the authenticity of the verse.

Verse 7 is important for understanding Amos's concept of the prophetic office. "Plan" (*sôd*) has as its basic meaning the thought of "intimacy." This word has several shades of meaning. It may connote a close relationship (Ge 49:6; Job 29:4; Ps 111:1; Jer 6:11) or the scheming of those united against others (Pss 64:2[3]; 83:3[4]), as well as the positive counsel derived from a close relationship (Pr 15:22). It may refer to something as intimate as a secret (Pr 11:13; 25:9) or close fellowship with a friend (Ps 55:14[15]). When used of God, *sôd* refers to his secret council (Job 15:8). It also may denote the intimate relationship between the righteous and God in which he "makes his covenant known to them" (Ps 25:14) and takes them "into his confidence" (Pr 3:32). Jeremiah uses the word to describe the relationship of a prophet to God through which God imparts truth (Jer 23:18, 22); for the prophet stood in an intimate relationship to God, one by means of which he shared God's counsel and words for the people. As S. Paul, 113, correctly concludes: "This verse firmly establishes the credibility of the prophet per se."

8 "The lion has roared" sounds an alarm. There is indeed cause for fear, though not from any lion or blast of a trumpet; it is Yahweh's voice through his prophet that should strike fear in people's hearts. Yahweh is no longer stalking quietly (cf. v.4)—he has pounced! He has spoken, and no one can contravene his word. So Amos pronounces judgment on the people. For a possible connection with 1:2, see comments on 1:2.

9 Amos summons the Egyptians and the Philistines of Ashdod to witness the oppression going on within Samaria. Amos may have named these particular nations because of their past oppression of Israel. The Egyptian bondage and recurrent Philistine oppressions in Israel's early history were not forgotten. So now Amos summons these oppressors to witness the violence being perpetrated by the rich and powerful of Samaria against their own poor neighbors—a kind of oppression that would surprise even the pagan nations. Amos's rhetoric shows that Israel is as violent as they were.

The word "fortress" (ʾarmôn) generally connotes a fortified building, such as a citadel (Ps 48:3[4]; Isa 34:13) or the fortified section of a palace (1Ki 16:18; 2Ki 15:25). But it may also refer to large, residential houses (Jer 9:21). The emphasis in vv.9–11 seems to be on "fortress" rather than residence because of the parallelism of ʾarmôn with ʿōz ("stronghold") in v.11 and the military motifs in the passage. (Compare "oppression" and the reference to the two warlike peoples of Philistia and Egypt in v.9 and "plunder" and "loot" in v.10.)

10 The Israelites, however, are different from aggressors because they are plundering and looting in their *own* fortresses rather than in enemy territory. Through oppressing the poorer classes, they have been plundering their own people; and Ashdod and Egypt are called to witness this evil.

"They do not know how to do right," Amos declares of the Israelites. The word "right" (nᵉkōḥâ) has the basic meaning of "straightness." Their moral sense has become so warped that the concepts of right and wrong are totally blurred.

11 "Therefore" logically connects the judgment segment of the oracle with the accusation stated in v.10. The following section of doom is a warning for those who flagrantly violate the covenant by treating a holy God lightly. Though the enemy who will overrun the land is not identified here, historically it was Assyria. Niehaus, 384, rightly points to a connection with the covenantal curse in Deuteronomy 28:52: "They will lay siege to all the cities throughout your land until the high fortified walls in which you trust fall down."

12 Amos concludes the oracle with the analogy of a shepherd who retrieves the remains of an animal, representing God's people, from the mouth of a lion, representing God. This analogy reflects the Mosaic law, for a shepherd was required to produce the remains of an animal killed while in his care as proof that he did not steal it (Ex 22:13). The analogy gives powerful expression to the idea of the remnant: There will be only bits and pieces of Israel left after the judgment of God.

The remainder of the verse is textually problematic, and there have been various suggestions for its interpretation. The lack of cohesiveness within the lines may be an example of the way some prophets of great literary skill, such as Amos, depart from poetical symmetry in order to achieve a powerful effect.

The word dᵉmešeq may, by a slight alteration in the pointing of the MT, be read "Damascus," in keeping with the ancient versions. The lines would then describe *how* the Israelites will be "saved": "those who sit in Samaria, on the edge of their beds, and in Damascus on their couches." The broken nature of the line may have been intended to elicit images of the broken remains of Israel's wealth in the minds of Amos's hearers. As the remaining parts of the slaughtered animal attest to its destruction, so the broken remains of the wealth of Israel will be a pathetic witness to the complete destruction of that kingdom.

The reference to Damascus may seem anomalous to the passage because the oracle is specifically addressed to Israelites. Yet it is not impossible that an Israelite colony was in Damascus at this time; for, in all probability, that territory had been annexed by Israel during the reign of Jeroboam (2Ki 14:28). Both Damascus and Israel were ultimately crushed in their futile attempt to take a stand against the Assyrian king Tiglath-pileser III. In 1:3–5 Amos predicted the downfall of Syria.

NOTES

2 For a discussion of "know" as a covenantal term, see H. Huffman, "The Treaty Background of Hebrew *yādaʿ*," *BASOR* 181 (1966): 31–37.

7 The particle כִּי (*kî*) in Ugaritic functions as an element of emphasis, somewhat like the Hebrew asseverative. However, it always occurs in an intraclausal structure (*UT* 9.17).

9 The LXX reads "Assyria" for "Ashdod," but this reading probably does not represent the original. It is easy to see how the great nation of Assyria could be paired with Egypt. But Amos does not mention Assyria anywhere in his prophecy, and Assyrian oppression of Israel was yet to reach its zenith.

12 The Code of Hammurabi has a law similar to Exodus 22:13: "If a visitation of god has occurred in a sheepfold or a lion has made a kill, the shepherd shall prove himself innocent in the presence of god, but the owner of the sheepfold shall receive from him the animal stricken in the fold" (Law 266; see *ANET*, 177).

In Hebrew "Damascus" is דַּמֶּשֶׂק (*dammeśeq*), while the word in the text is spelled *dᵉmeśeq*; only slight alterations in the Masoretic pointing are necessary to render the reading "Damascus." The reading *damask*, suggested by a number of commentators, is based on the Arabic *dimaqs*. But this speculation requires changing radicals. The reading "Damascus" seems to be the simplest solution, but admittedly the passage is difficult.

3. An Oracle against the House of Jacob (3:13–15)

> [13]"Hear this and testify against the house of Jacob," declares the Lord, the LORD God Almighty.
>
> [14]"On the day I punish Israel for her sins,
>   I will destroy the altars of Bethel;
> the horns of the altar will be cut off
>   and fall to the ground.
> [15]I will tear down the winter house
>   along with the summer house;
> the houses adorned with ivory will be destroyed
>   and the mansions will be demolished,"
>
> declares the LORD.

COMMENTARY

13 The threat of the preceding oracle gains renewed solemnity from the declaration of the Lord that precedes the next section. The command to "hear" is not addressed to Israel, for the text goes on to say, "and testify against the house of Jacob." Instead it is best understood as a rhetorical statement, similar to 3:9 ("proclaim"), where Amos addresses imaginary witnesses either for dramatic effect or to establish a legal atmosphere with Yahweh and Israel as adversaries (Isa 1:2; cf. Dt 32:1).

"House of Jacob" recalls Israel's heritage, especially the promise to the patriarchs that established the ground on which the Lord would deal with his people. The covenant became the external structure of the eternal promise (Ge 15:12–20) by providing the vehicle for obedience. Obedience to the covenantal stipulations marked one's participation in the promise. Israel as a nation had betrayed the covenant and so had forfeited every right to its promised blessing.

14–15 As a result of Israel's disobedience, the "altars of Bethel" (v.14) as well as the expensive homes of the people (v.15) will be destroyed. Amos focuses here on the two major aspects of Israel's disobedience: false religion and misuse of wealth and power. According to Israelite law, a fugitive could find refuge at the altar by grasping its horns (1Ki 1:50), but even this last-ditch opportunity for refuge will be lost (v.14).

NOTES

14 Amos mentions the altars of Bethel because they have been the focal point of Israel's rebellion (cf. 1Ki 12:32; 13:2; 2Ki 23:15–16). While some question exists as to whether the calf image at Bethel represented Yahweh or a false god, in either case the altars at Bethel were prohibited by the law prescribing the centralization of Israel's religious practice (Dt 12).

15 The "winter house" and "summer house" are either separate houses or two dwelling places in the same building. Many houses had an upper story that would be cool in summer (cf. Jdg 3:20). Jeremiah 36:22 refers to a winter house that was heated by a brazier. Amos's reference is best understood to apply to separate houses because of his use of עַל (ʿal, "along with"). While this preposition may mean "on," Amos hardly uses it in this sense, for that would mean that the winter house will be struck down on top of the summer house—the reverse of what is expected. It is best to understand ʿal in the sense of "together with" (BDB, 755), thus indicating separate houses. The winter house will be destroyed along with the summer house. The inscription of *Barrākib* refers to summer and winter houses as separate buildings (H. Donner and W. Rollig, *Kanaanäische und aramäische Inschriften* [Weisbaden: Otto Harrassowitz, 1966], 40). The inscription states that the kings of Samʾal had only one palace, which served as quarters for winter and summer. Another house was built to remedy the situation.

The reference to the "houses adorned with ivory" underscores the affluence of Amos's audience. Similar decorations have been found at Assyrian sites (see K. Schoville, *Biblical Archaeology in Focus* [Grand Rapids: Baker, 1978], 468–69, and more recently "Samaria," in *The New Encyclopedia of Archaeological Excavations in the Holy Land* [New York: Simon & Schuster, 1993], 1304–6).

4. The Pampered Women of Samaria (4:1–3)

¹Hear this word, you cows of Bashan on Mount Samaria,
    you women who oppress the poor and crush the needy
    and say to your husbands, "Bring us some drinks!"

> ²The Sovereign Lord has sworn by his holiness:
> "The time will surely come
> when you will be taken away with hooks,
> the last of you with fishhooks.
> ³You will each go straight out
> through breaks in the wall,
> and you will be cast out toward Harmon,"
>
> declares the Lord.

COMMENTARY

1 Amos begins this new judgment oracle with a call to the upper class women of Israel to hear God's condemnation of their oppression. The region of Bashan (located in Transjordan on both sides of the Yarmuk River) was known for its well-fed cattle (Ps 22:12; Eze 39:18), and Amos sarcastically likens the women of Samaria to these plump cattle that grazed in the rich uplands of Bashan. Amos accuses these rich women of oppressing the poor, just as he accused the male leaders of society. These women may not have been directly involved in mistreating the poor, but their incessant demands for luxuries drove their husbands to greater injustices. Their demand "Bring us some drinks" creates a vivid picture of their indolence.

2–3 An oath in which Yahweh swears by his holiness introduces the judgment section of this oracle. The element in the oath formula by which one swears forms an external guarantee of the thing being affirmed (cf. Heb 6:16). When God takes an oath, that element usually relates to the nature of the thing sworn. For example, in Isaiah 62:8 the Lord swore by his right hand and his mighty arm—metaphors of his strength—that he would do what he had promised. In Jeremiah 44:26 it is said that the Lord swore by his great name. The "name" signifies his reputation achieved by his mighty deeds, demonstrating the power and authority by which the oath is guaranteed.

The holiness of God is not a transferable divine energy but the absolute separation of God from anything secular or profane. When God swears by his holiness in Psalm 89:35, it is a guarantee that he will not lie, because doing so would be a violation of holiness. When he swears by his holiness in Amos 4:2, he guarantees that the judgment will become a reality, because the holy God does not lie, nor can his holiness allow sin to go unpunished.

The Hebrew words used to describe Israel's judgment (v.2) are obscure. "Hooks" (*ṣinnôt*) is generally understood as being derived from *ṣēn*, which may mean "thorn," though this meaning is dubious. The word *ṣēn* occurs only in the masculine plural, whereas *ṣinnôt* is feminine plural.

"Fishhooks" is *sîr*, which means "thorn" but does not have an attested feminine plural. In the only other occurrence of *sîr* in the plural (Hos 2:8), it is masculine. Here in Amos it is feminine plural (*sîrôt*). The common element of "thorns" in these two words underlies the suggestion that they refer to some kind of hook (on this issue, see S. Paul, "Fishing Imagery in Amos 4:2," *JBL* 97 [1978]: 183–90).

The feminine plural *ṣinnôt*, however, is attested in Hebrew as meaning "shields." Thus it may picture these indolent women, who lie on beds of luxury, as being carried away on the enemies' shields. If *sîr* is taken in its more common meaning of "pot" or "receptacle," its association with "fish" (*dûgâ*) may mean a receptacle for carrying fish or a cauldron for boiling fish. At any rate, these women will be taken in humiliating fashion through the breached wall of Jerusalem.

The referent of "Harmon" is uncertain. If it is a place, as it certainly seems to be, its location remains unknown. As S. Paul, 136, points out, "Ingenious suggestions are not wanting; only a suitable solution is still wanted."

NOTE

2 The verb קָדַשׁ (*qādaš*, "holy") connotes that which is separate from the secular or common (Ex 29:21, 37; 30:29; Nu 16:38). Because God is holy, he is not subject to human imperfection and will thus be faithful to his word.

צִנּוֹת (*ṣinnôt*, "shields"), the feminine plural of צִנָּה (*ṣinnâ*), is attested in 2 Chronicles 11:12. סִירוֹת (*sîrôt*, "pots"), the feminine plural of סִיר (*sîr*), is attested in 1 Kings 7:45. A possible Akkadian cognate of *ṣinnâ* is *ṣinnatu*, meaning "halter," which is appropriate to the context. However, it occurs only once in textual materials and is associated with the word *ṣerretu* in the vocabularies. It is possible that *ṣinnatu* is a phonetic variant of *ṣerretu*, a musical instrument, in which case it would not offer a solution to the problem here (I. J. Gelb et al., eds., *The Assyrian Dictionary* [Chicago: Oriental Institute, 1968], 201).

5. Sinful Worship (4:4–5)

4 "Go to Bethel and sin;
    go to Gilgal and sin yet more.
Bring your sacrifices every morning,
    your tithes every three years.
5 Burn leavened bread as a thank offering
    and brag about your freewill offerings—
boast about them, you Israelites,
    for this is what you love to do,"
            declares the Sovereign LORD.

COMMENTARY

4 Amos taunts the inhabitants of the northern kingdom with this shocking command: "Go to Bethel and sin." Bethel was the chief religious sanc-tuary of the northern kingdom. In the premonarchic period, it once housed the ark of the covenant and was one of the locations in the circuit followed by

Samuel in his work as judge (1Sa 7:16). Shortly after the division into two kingdoms, Bethel was established as a sanctuary by Jeroboam I to provide an alternative center to Jerusalem (1Ki 12:25–13:34). In the time of Amos, Bethel was known as "the king's sanctuary" (Am 7:13). It thus may have been the scene of royal as well as religious pomp.

The cultic worship practiced at Bethel in Amos's time combined concepts common to Canaanite religion, thus resulting in a syncretistic Yahwism devoid of real allegiance to the covenant of the Lord. Certainly, elements of Yahwistic religion were observed there (4:4–5; 5:21–23), and they may even have thought that the calf stood for none other than Yahweh. But the idolatrous influences had left their mark: external allegiance to cultic requirements fulfilled one's obligation to God. Inner allegiance to God—the very life of Yahwism—had been destroyed; and the covenantal obligation of heartfelt response to God and caring love for one's fellow human beings were forgotten.

Gilgal was another Israelite sanctuary in Amos's time (5:5; cf. Hos 4:15; 9:15; 12:11). Lest the people think that Bethel, with its pagan heritage, should be the only sanctuary that bears an onus, the prophet includes Gilgal.

The word "sin" (*pešaᶜ*) connotes the basic concept of "rebellion." Little do these worshipers know that as they participate in the cult to maintain their relationship to Yahweh, they are in rebellion against him. The sacrifices are those offered with respect to (*lᵉ*) "the morning." The preposition *lᵉ* is distributive and implies "every morning." Symmetry favors a distributive function for *lᵉ* in the next clause also—namely, "every three years" (but cf. NIV note, "tithes of the third day"). The sacrifices are probably not the continual burnt offering presented each morning and evening (Ex 29:38–41; Lev 6:8–13; Nu 28:3–4), for they were offered daily at the door of the tabernacle, while the context of Amos 4:4–5 deals with the individual sacrifices of pilgrims to the cultic centers. The other aspects of worship mentioned—the tithe, the thank offering, the freewill offering—are also individual obligations.

The practice of bringing tithes every three days does not appear in the law; rather a tithe was to be brought every three years (Dt 14:28). The word *yāmîm* may mean "years" (cf. Notes).

5 It is possible that Amos here represents the current-day practices prescribed for pilgrimage to the cultic centers; but it is also possible that he is using hyperbole to show the futility of offering many sacrifices and tithes. This latter view seems to reflect the intent of the passage, because Amos says, "This is what you love to do." It is as though he is telling them that even if they sacrifice every morning and tithe every three days in order to have something to boast about, in the end they are only engaging in acts of rebellion against God.

NOTE

4 יָמִים (*yāmîm*, "days") may be used to refer to the full cycle of days in a given period of time, such as an entire year (Ex 13:10; Jdg 11:40; 1Sa 1:3). It also has an indefinite sense and may mean "a few days" (Ge 40:4) or "some time" (1Ki 17:7; 18:1). In Deuteronomy 14:28 the tithe was commanded to be given every three years, but the word used there is שָׁנִים (*šānîm*), not *yāmîm*. Since *yāmîm* may mean "years," it is possible that Amos uses it here with that meaning.

The view adopted in this commentary, however, is that Amos means "every three days," since he sarcastically encourages the sacrifices to be offered much more frequently than the law requires ("every morning"); thus Amos ironically calls for them to go beyond the demands of the law. So in this view the presentation of the tithe every three days is consonant with his sarcastic call for offerings every morning.

REFLECTION

Interestingly, this call for overindulgence in religiosity parallels the hedonistic overindulgence of Israelite society in general as epitomized at Samaria. Modern-day people of the *new* covenant do well to learn the lesson that excessive religious activity does not a Christian make. It is still our sincere obedience to God that he seeks—indeed, requires.

6. A Look to the Past (4:6–13)

OVERVIEW

This section expresses one of the most fundamental aspects of prophetic thought, the immanence of God in history. Amos relates from Israel's past a series of events that he interprets as God's intervention for her good. Terrible as these catastrophes were, they were designed by a loving God to alert Israel to her sin and to the certainty of judgment; yet the nation did not return to him (v.11). This section vividly illustrates the permissive will of God that brings suffering so that his people may be brought closer to him (Heb 12:6). Each of these punishments was forewarned by the covenantal curses in Leviticus 26 and Deuteronomy 27–28. Since God's people have not paid attention to his "warning shots," the oracle climaxes with his announcement of definitive judgment (vv.12–13).

> ⁶"I gave you empty stomachs in every city
>   and lack of bread in every town,
>   yet you have not returned to me,"
>
>   declares the LORD.
>
> ⁷"I also withheld rain from you
>   when the harvest was still three months away.
> I sent rain on one town,
>   but withheld it from another.
> One field had rain;
>   another had none and dried up.
> ⁸People staggered from town to town for water
>   but did not get enough to drink,
>   yet you have not returned to me,"
>
>   declares the LORD.

⁹"Many times I struck your gardens and vineyards,
   I struck them with blight and mildew.
Locusts devoured your fig and olive trees,
   yet you have not returned to me,"

                                          declares the LORD.

¹⁰"I sent plagues among you
   as I did to Egypt.
I killed your young men with the sword,
   along with your captured horses.
I filled your nostrils with the stench of your camps,
   yet you have not returned to me,"

                                          declares the LORD.

¹¹"I overthrew some of you
   as I overthrew Sodom and Gomorrah.
You were like a burning stick snatched from the fire,
   yet you have not returned to me,"

                                          declares the LORD.

¹²"Therefore this is what I will do to you, Israel,
   and because I will do this to you,
   prepare to meet your God, O Israel."
¹³He who forms the mountains,
   creates the wind,
   and reveals his thoughts to man,
he who turns dawn to darkness,
   and treads the high places of the earth —
   the LORD God Almighty is his name.

COMMENTARY

6 The Hebrew of this verse is literally "I gave you cleanness of teeth" (NIV note), an expression describing a complete lack of food. The catastrophes mentioned are difficult to identify historically. They were neither necessarily recent nor specific. They reflect God's continuing activity in history in Israel's behalf. They also reflect God's outworking of the forewarned punishments for Israel's breach of covenantal loyalty. Here the punishment is famine (e.g., Lev 26:26, 29; Dt 28:53–56).

7–8 The "withheld rain" (v.7) is the latter rain that was so important to the full development of the crops. That rain fell on some towns and not on others might show that God's hand was in the catastrophe. Such a punishment was anticipated in the covenantal curses found in Leviticus 26:19 and

Deuteronomy 28:23–24. Nevertheless, the suffering (v.8) that resulted did not lead to repentance.

9–10 Even the blighted gardens and dying trees did not remind the people of their spiritual responsibility (v.9); neither did God's judgment on individuals (v.10). The covenantal curse in Deuteronomy 28:22 specifically mentions "blight and mildew" (see also 1Ki 8:37; Hag 2:17). Locusts are cited in Deuteronomy 28:39–42. The reference to plague and sword recalls the national curse of Leviticus 26:25 and Deuteronomy 28:49–57 for pursuing a life of disobedience to God. The "sword" refers to war and is a reminder of the long period of warfare with Syria (2Ki 13:3). For the warning that God would visit the plagues of Egypt on a sinful people, see Deuteronomy 28:27, 60.

11 Here Amos compares the overthrow of certain Israelite cities to the fall of Sodom and Gomorrah. Some expositors suggest that Amos is referring to earthquakes that occurred in the past, because Sodom and Gomorrah were apparently destroyed by an earthquake (Ge 19). But Sodom and Gomorrah are used as analogies of destruction in a number of passages without reference to the means of destruction (Isa 1:9; 13:19; Jer 50:40; Zep 2:9). It is best, therefore, to see this verse as referring to violence suffered by certain Israelite cities during the Syrian incursions mentioned in 2 Kings 13:1–9. This account refers to a "deliverer" (13:5) who restored the conquered people to their homes. The analogy of the stick snatched from the fire aptly describes the conquered towns that might have been lost forever to Israel but were "snatched" from the fire of conflict and restored to their inhabitants because of the intervention of this unnamed "deliverer."

This section throws light on the chastisement of the Lord. Chastisement is that aspect of God's dealing with his children in which he uses punishment to bring them back to him (see Pr 3:11; cf.

Heb 12:5–11). Of course, suffering does not always have this divinely corrective purpose (cf. the book of Job), and there are many reasons why God disciplines his people.

The point of vv.6–11 is that the Israelites have become spiritually hardened. Because Amos does not want his hearers to forget this fact, he states five times, "Yet you have not returned to me" (vv.6, 8–11).

As we have seen, the preceding verses contain a number of connections with Deuteronomy 28–29 (including this verse in Dt 29:23), where Moses set forth the blessings for obedience and the curses for disobedience. Thus, Amos shows Israel that the catastrophes mentioned are evidence that God has chastised Israel in the past for her sins. The curses of Deuteronomy have been realized. Soon the ultimate curse will follow: "Then the LORD will scatter you among all nations, from one end of the earth to the other" (Dt 28:64).

12 Judgment is impending, but Amos does not specify what the judgment will be. It is difficult to see the intended judgment in the catastrophes of vv.6–11, for the word "this" (kōh) in v.12 normally refers to what follows. Also, the calamities cited in vv.6–11 are broader in scope than the captivity Amos elsewhere envisions as the impending judgment.

Some commentators assume a redactive intrusion here. Wolff, 220, for example, understands vv.6–13 as the work of an editor, who depicts the destruction of "the sanctuary of Bethel by King Josiah." Other scholars assume a corrupt text.

It is possible, however, to explain the passage on the basis of Amos's literary style. If the interpretation of the significance of the pronominal suffix nû ("his") on ᵃšîbennû ("turn back") in 1:3 is correct (see comments), there is precedent in the book for the similar phenomenon in 4:12. The veiled reference to judgment in 1:3 adds force to the prophetic statement because of its enigmatic quality. The same thing may be true here. The haunting uncertainty in Amos's words makes the threat of judgment even more ominous. As S. Paul, 149–50, states, "This is another example of how Amos heightens the awesome response of his audience by alluding to some enigmatic horror yet to come."

The yet unspecified judgment is to come when Israel meets her God, and she is told to prepare for that awful moment. The coming encounter will not happen in a face-to-face sense but in Israel's destruction at the hand of God. The Israelites have already experienced God's intervention (cf. vv.6–11), but the imperative "Prepare to meet your God, O Israel" has an aura of finality. When Israel meets her God, she will finally learn the nature of the coming judgment.

The command "prepare" should not be understood as a plea for the people to repent. The die has been cast. They did not turn to God when he chastised them (vv.6–11), and now Amos holds out no hope for their full-scale repentance. The words seem nothing more than an imperative for the people to fasten their seatbelts for the national calamity about to befall them.

13 A hymnic element, portraying some aspects of the nature of the God the Israelites are to face in judgment, closes this section. "For" (*kî*, untranslated in the NIV) connects v.13 to the preceding reference to God. The word "forms" (*yôṣēr*) refers to God's activity in creation and is paralleled by "creates" (*bōrē'*). In Hebrew these words are participles, which are typical of hymnic elements.

This phenomenon is often used as an argument for their lateness, for participial constructions may be found in other poetic celebrations of God's creative power, especially in "Second Isaiah" (Isa 40:22–23, 26–29; 42:5; 44:24; 45:7, 18). The phenomenon also occurs in Jeremiah (Jer 10:12–16; 51:15–19) and in certain psalms (Pss 94; 104).

While the passages in Jeremiah are considered late additions by some scholars, there is good reason to believe that both psalms cited are of preexilic origin (cf. M. Dahood, *Psalms II* and *Psalms III* [AB; New York: Doubleday, 1968, 1970]), thus placing the tradition much earlier than "Second Isaiah." The reason for the participial structure is difficult to determine. It may be that the Hebrew theology assumed a role for God both in creating and in sustaining his universe. It is also possible that the participial construction may be simply a stylistic device.

The word "form" (*yāṣar*) has as its basic emphasis the shaping of the object involved, whereas "create" (*bārā'*) emphasizes the initiation of the object. Not only does God form the mountains and create the wind, but he also reveals to humanity "his thoughts" (*śēḥ̂ô*). The word for "thoughts" is never used of God in Hebrew; and, in the light of 3:7, it is unlikely that Amos believes that God reveals his thoughts to all people. It is best to interpret the suffix *ô* ("his") as applying to man and understand the verse to speak of God's activity in searching the hearts of all humankind and revealing their thoughts and motives.

In describing God's treading the high places of the earth, the hymn takes on a theophanic tone. The Hebrew word for "high places" (*bāmâ*) basically means "height." It may refer to pagan religious sanctuaries (Jer 7:31), but in the cosmic atmosphere of this hymn, it must refer to the mountains and hills. In ancient times possession of the heights of enemy territory meant that the enemy was virtually brought into subjection (Dt 33:29; Eze 36:2). The majestic picture of God as striding over the hills and mountains shows his sovereignty over the earth. A similar theophany occurs at the beginning of Micah, where it precedes the description of God's judgment in Samaria and Jerusalem (Mic 1:3–7; 3:9–12). The theophany presages judgment, as God steps into history and treads the heights of the earth This theophanic language, depicting God's presence in the events of history and in natural phenomena, shows their belief in his immanence.

The awe this picture strikes is heightened by the last line: "the LORD God Almighty" (*yhwh ʾelōhê-ṣebāʾôt*, lit., "LORD God of Hosts"). The "hosts" are generally taken to be either the heavenly bodies or the armies of heaven. While the latter is probably the best alternative, *yhwh ʾelōhê-ṣebāʾôt* certainly connotes the vast power of the God of heaven and earth.

In one bold sweep, this hymn shows the sovereignty of God—from his creation of the world to his daily summoning of the dawn, from his intervention in history to his revelation of the thoughts of humankind. Every believer can take comfort in the fact that, while sometimes it seems that God is not active in human affairs, the world is never out of his control. His sovereignty extends to every aspect of human experience.

This brief but sublime hymn is so in keeping with Amos's preceding words and lends such a note of finality to his message that its authenticity should be given fairer consideration. It implies the right of the Creator to judge his people and points to the divine judgment that is so vital a part of Amos's prophecy.

NOTES

8 The Hebrew of the first clause says literally, "Two, three cities wandered to one city to drink water." The implication is that the citizens of cities suffering drought sought water in localities where it was available, but they could not get sufficient water for their needs. Hence the NIV's translation, "People staggered from town to town."

11 The metaphor of a stick snatched from the fire is also applied to Israel in Zechariah 3:2, where Joshua symbolizes the nation. The fact that Israel did not return to God even after he had punished her as a nation is reechoed in Isaiah 9:13; Jeremiah 5:3; and Hosea 7:10.

12 The adverb כֹּה (*kōh*, "therefore") usually refers to what follows and כֵן (*kēn*) to what precedes (BDB, 462).

7. A Lament for Fallen Israel (5:1–3)

¹Hear this word, O house of Israel, this lament I take up concerning you:

²"Fallen is Virgin Israel,
   never to rise again,
deserted in her own land,
   with no one to lift her up."

³This is what the Sovereign LORD says:

"The city that marches out a thousand strong for Israel
   will have only a hundred left;

> the town that marches out a hundred strong
>   will have only ten left."

COMMENTARY

1–2 Amos next takes up a "lament" (*qînâ*; v.1). The lament was a song or poem that mourned the death of a relative, friend, or national hero. In this one Amos mourns the fall of Israel (v.2). The main verbs are in the perfect tense, expressing completed action. It is as though Amos is so certain what he says will happen that he treats it as an accomplished fact. He sees Israel as a virgin whose life has been ended in the bloom of youth. He describes her hopelessness in the words "never to rise again" and her desolation in the words "deserted in her own land with no one to lift her up."

Israel's predicted fate stands in stark contrast to the promise God gave to Abraham, that Abraham's descendants would be as numerous as the "dust of the earth" and as the stars in the sky (cf. Ge 13:16; 15:5). But Amos says that Israel has been cut off as a virgin who had never borne children, and the enemy will soon to carry her off to his own land.

This passage illustrates the principle that the blessings of God's promise—which is irrevocable and eternal (Ge 13:15; 17:19; cf. Heb 6:13, 17–18)—are conditioned on the obedience of its recipients. Its eternality is guaranteed by God's sovereign activity in history and the existence of a believing remnant in Israel, whose obedience to the covenantal stipulations marks them as the vehicle through which God will keep the promises.

3 This verse depicts the finality of Israel's demise in a manner reminiscent of Deuteronomy 28:25–30. As the cities send out their defending armies to face the invader, they will be cut down. Only a handful of ragged, war-weary men will be left of Israel's proud army.

NOTE

2 "Never to rise again" need not mean that God has no future role for Israel in his redemptive program. This seems to be precluded by Zechariah 12:10. Amos is here suggesting that the northern kingdom will never be reestablished as a nation, but there will be a believing remnant through whom the promises will continue (9:9–12).

8. Seeking True Values (5:4–17)

> ⁴This is what the Lord says to the house of Israel:
>
> "Seek me and live;
> 5   do not seek Bethel,
> do not go to Gilgal,
>   do not journey to Beersheba.

For Gilgal will surely go into exile,
    and Bethel will be reduced to nothing."
[6] Seek the LORD and live,
    or he will sweep through the house of Joseph like a fire;
it will devour,
    and Bethel will have no one to quench it.

[7] You who turn justice into bitterness
    and cast righteousness to the ground
[8] (he who made the Pleiades and Orion,
    who turns blackness into dawn
    and darkens day into night,
who calls for the waters of the sea
    and pours them out over the face of the land —
    the LORD is his name —
[9] he flashes destruction on the stronghold
    and brings the fortified city to ruin),
[10] you hate the one who reproves in court
    and despise him who tells the truth.

[11] You trample on the poor
    and force him to give you grain.
Therefore, though you have built stone mansions,
    you will not live in them;
though you have planted lush vineyards,
    you will not drink their wine.
[12] For I know how many are your offenses
    and how great your sins.
You oppress the righteous and take bribes
    and you deprive the poor of justice in the courts.
[13] Therefore the prudent man keeps quiet in such times,
    for the times are evil.

[14] Seek good, not evil,
    that you may live.
Then the LORD God Almighty will be with you,
    just as you say he is.
[15] Hate evil, love good;
    maintain justice in the courts.
Perhaps the LORD God Almighty will have mercy
    on the remnant of Joseph.

> ¹⁶Therefore this is what the Lord, the LORD God Almighty, says:
>
> "There will be wailing in all the streets
>   and cries of anguish in every public square.
> The farmers will be summoned to weep
>   and the mourners to wail.
> ¹⁷There will be wailing in all the vineyards,
>   for I will pass through your midst,"
>   says the LORD.

COMMENTARY

4 The word "seek" (*dāraš*), when referring to the Lord, means to turn to him in trust and confidence (Pss 34:4[5]; 77:2[3]; Jer 10:21). The word "live" (*ḥāyâ*), like "seek," is imperative and is connected by *waw* ("and") with the preceding imperative. It shows the result of the condition implied in the first imperative. Though the concept of "life" in the OT often relates to spiritual life, that meaning does not seem to apply here, for Amos uses "live" (*ḥāyâ*) in a context of national collapse. Since he has spoken of Israel as a fallen nation, the meaning of national life or restoration for *ḥāyâ* seems appropriate. When a similar command is given in v.14, *ḥāyâ* apparently refers to national welfare.

In this light, it is hardly correct to say that Amos confronts the people only with doom. He holds out a gracious invitation to them, but he expects only calamity because he knows they will not repent. His invitation may be instrumental in leading some of the people to seek the Lord; thus it contributes to the establishment of the remnant.

5 The people are warned not to keep relying for help on the centers of cultic worship, which can offer none. For when the invader comes, the centers will fall just like all the cities of Israel. Bethel, Gilgal, and Beersheba are not the objects of God's favor but of his judgment.

Bethel, in Amos's time a center of religious externalism, is the place where Jacob met the Lord (Ge 28:10–15). It was there that God reiterated the promise to him. How the religious significance of Bethel has deteriorated! The promise, first made to Abraham, had a covenantal structure requiring an inner response to God. In Amos's day, however, Bethel stood for mere external religion that did not require a sincere, heartfelt attitude toward God. So Bethel no longer represents the true promise. The idolatry practiced there can only lead to continued separation from God and the ultimate destruction of the nation. So the promise of Bethel becomes a promise of doom. For both Bethel and Gilgal, see comments on 4:4.

The reference to Beersheba shows that Israelites continued to cross the border into the southern kingdom to worship at the sanctuary in Judah. As Stuart, 346, has pointed out, "Beersheba, associated with Abraham (Gen. 22:19), Isaac (26:23), and Jacob (46:1–5), was, in spite of its southern Judean location, a popular pilgrimage spot for northerners (cf. Am. 8:14; 2 Kgs. 23:8)."

6 The name "house of Joseph" stands for the northern kingdom and reflects the descent of its largest tribe, Ephraim, from Joseph. The fire Amos speaks of is reminiscent of the judgment in the oracles of 1:3–2:11 and symbolizes the coming captivity. The most offensive of the false worship sites—Bethel—is specifically singled out for special mention.

A clear alternative is offered to the people in the word "or" (*pen*). The choice is to "seek the LORD," with all the blessing and favor that doing so will bring, or experience ultimate doom. One wonders at the spiritual blindness that is leading the people to the second choice.

7 In vv.7–12 Amos sets forth the reason for the coming judgment. "Justice" (*mišpāṭ*) connotes the fair and impartial administration of the requirements of the law, which required active concern for others (Ex 23:4–5; Dt 24:17–22). Jeremiah defines "justice" as defending the rights of the poor (Jer 5:28). These concepts are being violated in Amos's day, for justice is being turned into "bitterness." The word translated "bitterness" (*laʿanâ*) is literally "wormwood," one of the bitterest of plants. Elsewhere the word is used metaphorically of bitter experiences (Jer 9:15; La 3:15, 19). The perversion of justice in Amos's day is causing deep bitterness for the wretched people whose causes are being subverted in the legal system of that time.

8–9 Some scholars have considered the hymnic element in v.8 to be intrusive, as has already been noted (cf. "Unity" in the introduction). But the logical sequence of 6:8–13 is also broken by vv.9–10. These breaks may simply reflect Amos's literary style. The content of the doxology is certainly appropriate here.

In sublime words Amos depicts Yahweh's creative power in making the constellations, establishing the succession of day and night, and summoning the vast oceans to cover so much of the land. But then he turns from the sovereignty of God in creation to his sovereignty in human history, as seen by his overthrowing military strongholds (v.9). This turn fits perfectly with the reference to judgment in v.6. Also, the use of the verb *hāpak* ("turns") in v.8 contrasts with its use in v.7.

10 The accusation continues with Amos's description of his contemporaries' hating the one who reproves in the "court" (*šaʿar*, lit., "gate"). It was at the city gate that legal proceedings took place (5:15; cf. Dt 21:19; Jos 20:4; Ru 4:1). The "one who reproves" (*môkîaḥ*) is any individual who protests the injustices of the courts. These "reprovers" are hated, as are those who speak the truth during the proceedings. The very fabric of justice is being destroyed.

11 Amos next speaks vividly of the oppressive measures that exploit the poor and make the rich richer. "Therefore" introduces the judgment. The grand homes, built at the expense of the needy, will one day stand empty; and the vineyards will go untended. These symbols of Israel's wealth and greed, her houses and lands, are to become the objects of God's wrath. A terrible calamity is to befall the nation. As yet, it has not been fully described; but each of Amos's allusions to it builds on the other until in ch. 9 it reaches its fullest elaboration.

12–13 All these judgments result from the people's many sins (v.12)—sins that entail rebellion and failure to live up to God's standards. In the light of the corruption of the times, the prudent man says nothing because anything he may have said avails nothing (v.13). Protest will only make the situation worse and bring greater woe. Amos, as a prophet, would hardly condemn protest. He understands, however, that the innocent cannot find justice in the corrupt court system; therefore, it is best to avoid any reproof that may lead to even greater injustices. The book of Proverbs talks positively about the "prudent" (see Pr 10:5; 14:35; 15:24; 16:20; 17:2). While none of these passages describes the prudent as silent before evil, the word is closely connected with the concept of wisdom in general, and the book of Proverbs does teach that wisdom often mandates silence in certain situations (Pr 11:12; 13:3; 15:4; 17:28).

14 Amos exhorts the people to "seek good [and] not evil" as the way to life. In the similar exhortation in v.4, he urged them to seek Yahweh as the *object* of their trust and confidence, as opposed to the pagan sanctuaries. Here he urges them to seek good as the *means* of receiving the Lord's help.

The practice of "good"—that is, the social ethic of the law—will not only establish the ground on which the Lord will be able to mediate the benefits of his promise to Israel but will also reverse the trend toward social disintegration that is tearing the nation's fabric. To seek "good" is the only way the nation can be restored to "life."

To "seek good, not evil," then, means to concern oneself with good, to practice good, and to reject evil. As a result the Lord of hosts (see comment on 4:13) will be with them. This expression "the LORD ... will be with you" connotes the Lord's presence, not only to dispense national and individual blessing, but also to defend and fight for his people (cf. Dt 31:8; Jdg 6:12).

Amos then makes the ironic observation that the people think the Lord is with them. They think their privilege as Yahweh's elect and their lip service to him guarantee protection by him.

15 The people are not only to stop seeking evil (v.14) but are also to "hate evil [and] love good." The imperatives in this section are progressive. The people are exhorted to seek the Lord (v.4), not just in external allegiance to him but also in ethical obedience that involves commitment to him (v.14). The will, along with the emotive powers, is to be devoted to the love of good and the hatred of evil. Only this kind of devotion will bring "life." If the people fulfill these conditions, it is possible that the

Lord will "have mercy on the remnant of Joseph" (see comment on v.6).

Because the term "remnant" (*še'ērît*) connotes a portion of something, several commentators have applied "the remnant of Joseph" to those Israelites who will survive the Assyrian decimations (K&D, Mays). Verse 3 certainly supports that interpretation. Yet if Amos's exhortation in v.14 holds open the possibility of the nation's restoration based on their repentance, it is difficult to see why the similar appeal in v.15 is thrust far into the future to find fulfillment only in the remnant who will survive the impending destruction. If Amos's appeal to the northern kingdom for repentance in v.6 carries with it the possibility of escape from God's judgment, it is likely that the appeal of v.15 does also.

God's people through whom the terms of the promise are guaranteed are hardly the "remnant," for the word "perhaps" implies that God's promise can be invalidated. If the term "remnant of Joseph" is understood as a surrogate for the northern kingdom, the appeals of vv.14–15 are consonant with each other.

One difficulty with this view is that Israel had extensive territorial holdings and was hardly a remnant. Also, "remnant" implies a part of something. Yet in spite of the fact that the northern kingdom was enjoying the glory of the "Silver Age," Amos sees it as small and weak. He intercedes for the kingdom in 7:2 thus: "How can Jacob survive? He is so small!" The prophet sees Israel as God sees it—not mighty and powerful, but vulnerable and on the verge of destruction. "Remnant" may connote Israel's insignificance in the world of her day. In answer to the objection that the word connotes a part of something, Micah 4:7 uses it to refer to the whole nation in the restoration. It is parallel to "strong nation" in that couplet.

If these appeals for repentance seem not to be in accord with Amos's pronouncements of inevitable doom elsewhere, it may be that while he sees no hope for the nation, he continues to hold out the gracious offer of deliverance, even though only a few will respond.

16–17 "Therefore" relates back to the accusation in vv.7–12 and introduces the judgment of the Lord. Amos pictures the people weeping as the Lord passes through their midst while judging the sin he has so severely condemned. The chapter then ends like it began (vv.1–3)—with a lament.

NOTES

5 The alliteration in this verse is impossible to duplicate in English. The words "Gilgal will surely go into exile" appear in Hebrew as הַגִּלְגָּל גָּלֹה יִגְלֶה (*haggilgāl galōh yigleh*).

The call to come to Bethel in 4:4 and the warning not to seek Bethel in 5:5 are not incompatible. In 5:5 Amos warns the people that Bethel, which is used as a surrogate for their false worship, will not give life. In 4:4 his summons was given in a spirit of irony.

8 The word צַלְמָוֶת (*ṣalmāwet*, "blackness") is sometimes regarded as a word compounded from the roots צֵל (*ṣēl*, "shadow") and מָוֶת (*māwet*, "death"). The likelihood of this possibility is diminished by the paucity of compounded words in Hebrew and the root *ṣlm* that is attested in Akkadian. The Akkadian root *ṣalmu* means "black" or "dark" (Gelb, *Assyrian Dictionary*, 77–78). The Hebrew word may be understood as a form of this root with the abstract ending וּת (*ût*), thus meaning "blackness" or "deep darkness."

The constellations that are specifically mentioned here in Hebrew mean something like "the Group" and "the Fool," but they have been identified as Pleiades (a star cluster in the "shoulder" of the Taurus constellation) and Orion, "the Hunter," one of the most conspicuous constellations in the sky. Both are also mentioned in Job 9:9 and 38:31.

11 A number of allusions to Deuteronomy 28–29 may be present in the lament of vv.1–11. Note the concept of "going out" (v.3; cf. Dt 28:6, 19). The small number remaining to Israel in the same verse may be reflective of Deuteronomy 28:62. The reference to building houses and not living in them (v.11) is paralleled in Deuteronomy 28:30. Planting vineyards but not enjoying them finds a parallel in Deuteronomy 28:30, 39.

The reference to "stone mansions" reflects the great wealth of the time. The houses of the wealthy were not made of the usual kiln-dried mud brick (cf. Isa 9:10).

9. The Day of the Lord (5:18–20)

¹⁸Woe to you who long
　　for the day of the LORD!
Why do you long for the day of the LORD?
　　That day will be darkness, not light.
¹⁹It will be as though a man fled from a lion
　　only to meet a bear,

> as though he entered his house
> and rested his hand on the wall
> only to have a snake bite him.
> 20 Will not the day of the LORD be darkness, not light —
> pitch-dark, without a ray of brightness?

COMMENTARY

18 This verse affords an insight into the popular theology in Amos's time. "The day of the LORD" is an important eschatological concept that runs through the prophetic writings. Amos is the first to mention it, and he assumes that it is already a well-known concept in his culture. The day of the Lord refers to the complex of events surrounding the coming of the Lord in judgment to conquer his foes and to establish his sovereign rule over the world. The people were looking forward to that day. Apparently they understood it as the time when Yahweh would act on their behalf to conquer their foes and establish Israel as his people forever. They regarded their election as the guarantee of the Lord's favor.

But their moral vision is blurred. They fail to see the day of the Lord as the time when God will judge all sin—even theirs. They name the name of Yahweh but do not obey his precepts. For these people, Amos says, that coming day will be one of darkness.

19–20 Amos uses two metaphors to show the error of the popular concept of the day of the Lord (v.19). A man flees from a lion only to meet a bear. Another enters his home, his place of security, but is bitten by a snake. The meaning is both clear and powerful. The Israelites see the day of the Lord as a comforting concept. It is to them their ultimate salvation. But like the false security of the one who thinks he has escaped the lion and the one who is falsely secure in his home, the faithless Israelites will find that day to be a time of judgment for them. As a matter of fact, there is no hope for them in that day, for the day of the Lord will bring not one ray of light (v.20).

10. Unacceptable Worship (5:21–27)

> 21 "I hate, I despise your religious feasts;
> I cannot stand your assemblies.
> 22 Even though you bring me burnt offerings and grain offerings,
> I will not accept them.
> Though you bring choice fellowship offerings,
> I will have no regard for them.
> 23 Away with the noise of your songs!
> I will not listen to the music of your harps.

24 But let justice roll on like a river,
    righteousness like a never-failing stream!

25 Did you bring me sacrifices and offerings
    forty years in the desert, O house of Israel?
26 You have lifted up the shrine of your king,
    the pedestal of your idols,
    the star of your god —
    which you made for yourselves.
27 Therefore I will send you into exile beyond Damascus,"
    says the LORD, whose name is God Almighty.

COMMENTARY

21 The shock felt by the people when Amos so vehemently attacks their comfortable eschatology is immediately followed by another shock. The prophet turns to their worship and in words of burning eloquence proclaims Yahweh's hatred of their religious observances. Amos uses the same word (śānē', "hate") earlier to describe the attitude Israel should have toward evil (v.15). He applies that word here to the very things they think please the Lord. The routine observance of the Levitical ritual is empty because the people lack the love, concern, and humble obedience to God that marks sincere profession of faith. Their religiosity is a mockery of true religion. Every aspect of their ritual is an act of disobedience because it ignores the heart of the Law—love for God and concern for others.

22–23 The people may, Amos says, continue to bring sacrifices, but the Lord will not accept them (v.22). The "burnt offering" ('ōlâ) is the offering that was entirely consumed and was the main atonement offering (Lev 1). The "grain offering" (minḥâ) was any offering given as a gift to the Lord. However, sometimes the term specifies only the grain offering (Lev 2). The "fellowship offering" (šelem) was offered in part to the Lord and the rest was shared with the

offerer and his family and friends (Lev 3). Even their songs are a source of revulsion to the Lord. God says they will be put away from him (mēʿālay; v.23).

24 The element that will transform the people's sterile worship into worship acceptable to God is "justice." The interpretation that this verse speaks of the Lord's judgment and righteousness that should fill the land is inadequate, for Amos addresses only the people. "Justice" and "righteousness" relate to the social order. Only when personal concern for the law is incorporated into their social structure and "rightness" characterizes their dealings with others will their worship be acceptable. Token practice of justice and righteousness will not do.

Like the full commitment to "good" called for in v.15, justice and righteousness are to "roll on like a river ... like a never-failing stream." This great OT metaphor is one that the church needs to ponder. An on-and-off flowing of justice and righteousness is insufficient; like a stream that does not dry up with the summer heat, these virtues are to characterize the social order consistently and perpetually.

25–27 Verses 25–26 are difficult. Many commentators hold that because the question of v.25 expects a negative answer, Amos is affirming that sacrifice was unknown until after the wilderness period, or that it was not regarded as necessary for a proper relationship with Yahweh, with obedience being the sole requirement. But this interpretation does not do justice to the continuity of vv.25–26 called for by the Hebrew particle *waw* (untranslated in the NIV), which begins v.26; nor does it adequately explain why a statement denying the efficacy of sacrifice was placed in the judgment section of the oracle.

The question (v.25) does indeed call for a negative answer: No, the Israelites did not sacrifice in the wilderness. Evidently that forty-year period was a time when obedience to the Levitical institutions declined (Jos 5:5–6). This period began with the defection of the Israelites to idolatry at Kadesh (Nu 14:33–34; cf. Jos 5:6). Such defection in the wilderness period is emphasized elsewhere in the prophetic tradition (Eze 20:10–26; Hos 9:10; 13:5–6).

Verse 26 begins with a *waw* that is best understood as adversative: "But you have lifted." Israel disobeyed God and by her neglect of sacrifice turned to idolatry.

The words "shrine" (*sikkût*) and "pedestal" (*kîyyûn*) need not be altered to read "Sakkut" and "Kaiwan," names of the god Saturn, though that view is attractive. (For a defense of this view, see Niehaus, 433–34.) It is not certain that Amos knew of this deity, and the MT makes sense as it stands. The verse refers to the implements of the idolatrous worship of an unknown astral deity. Seen in this way, v.26 fits the formal structure well, for Amos, like Ezekiel and Hosea, traces the disobedience of God's people far back into their history. Verse 24 calls for obedience; the judgment section in vv.25–27 affirms their disobedience and bases the predicted judgment (v.27) on their long history of unfaithfulness to God. Exile to a far-flung land reflects covenantal curses such as those in Deuteronomy 28:64–68; 30:4.

NOTES

25 For a discussion of the function of הֲ (*hᵃ*) in questions expecting a negative answer, see GKC, par. 150d.

26 The LXX renders the reference to the deities in this verse as τὴν σκηνὴν τοῦ Μολοχ, καὶ τὸ ἄστρον τοῦ θεοῦ ὑμῶν Ραιφαν (*tēn skēnēn tou Moloch, kai to astron tou theou hymōn Raiphan*, "the tabernacle of Moloch and the star of your god Raiphan"). This phrase is quoted somewhat similarly in Acts 7:43, but "Raiphan" appears in some English versions as "Rephan" and "Moloch" as "Molech." It is not known why the LXX reads "Raiphan" for the Hebrew כִּיּוּן (*kîyyûn*). Possibly it is a form of "Repa," name of the Egyptian deity of the planet Saturn.

11. A Warning to the Complacent (6:1–7)

OVERVIEW

Generically, this type of oracle is called a "woe oracle" (see the opening word, *hoy*, "Woe") and develops from the laments connected to funerals. However, its prophetic use does not relate to actual death; rather, it communicates that the addressee is "as good as dead."

¹Woe to you who are complacent in Zion,
    and to you who feel secure on Mount Samaria,
  you notable men of the foremost nation,
    to whom the people of Israel come!
²Go to Calneh and look at it;
    go from there to great Hamath,
    and then go down to Gath in Philistia.
  Are they better off than your two kingdoms?
    Is their land larger than yours?
³You put off the evil day
    and bring near a reign of terror.
⁴You lie on beds inlaid with ivory
    and lounge on your couches.
  You dine on choice lambs
    and fattened calves.
⁵You strum away on your harps like David
    and improvise on musical instruments.
⁶You drink wine by the bowlful
    and use the finest lotions,
    but you do not grieve over the ruin of Joseph.
⁷Therefore you will be among the first to go into exile;
    your feasting and lounging will end.

COMMENTARY

1–2 With masterly irony, Amos addresses the self-satisfied rich, secure in their affluence (v.1; cf. Lk 6:24–25; 12:13–21). It cannot be proven whether the cities he mentions in v.2 have by this time met their doom. Assuming they have not, Amos's question is meant sarcastically—"Go to [these cities] and look.... Are they better off than your two kingdoms [i.e., Judah and Israel]?"—as though to echo what the people of Israel are saying: "Look at the other countries: there is none greater than ours." This interpretation is supported by the words "notable men of the foremost nation" (v.1),

which also has a note of sarcasm. Evidently the people of Amos's day are boasting of their national security and power. The prophet proclaims woe to those who feel secure in the strength of their nation. His parroting of their affirmations of self-assurance and national pride underscores their complacency and places their false pride in stark contrast to the doom he predicts in the subsequent context.

3 The people are unwilling to hear of the "evil day," the day of their demise predicted by Amos. Yet they are all too willing to make the poor miserable.

4–7 Verses 4–6 describe the opulence of that society. To Amos their luxuries are symbols of the oppression by which they aggrandize themselves. So those who have amassed all this wealth will be the first to go into exile (v.7).

NOTES

1 רֵאשִׁית (rē'šît, "foremost," v.1; "finest," v.6) and רֹאשׁ (rō'š, "first," v.7) are from the same root. Their use in this section may be an intended wordplay. The leaders of the "first and foremost nation," with all its finery, will be the "first" to go into captivity.

2 The location of Calneh is uncertain. The name may appear in Genesis 10:10 in association with Shinar, but the consonants may also be read "all of them" (RSV). Other occurrences of the name favor a location in the north. It is associated with Carchemish in Isaiah 10:9. Ezekiel 27:23 speaks of Canneh (evidently Calneh with an assimilation of the *l*) in association with Haran and Eden, thus also pointing to a northern location (cf. Y. Aharoni and M. Avi-Yonah, *The Macmillan Bible Atlas* [New York: Macmillan, 1968], 93).

Hamath was a city in Syria north of Damascus. Besides Amos 6:14, Hamath is cited also in 1 Maccabees 12:25.

Gath was one of the Philistine cities, located in southern Palestine near the coast of the Mediterranean Sea.

7 "Feasting" (*marzēaḥ*) is a word that occurs only twice in the Hebrew Bible (see also Jer 16:5) but is found in Ugaritic and other extrabiblical literature and has occasioned extensive discussion (see M. Pope, *Song of Songs* [AB; New York: Doubleday, 1977], 216–21, for bibliography). It seems to be a pagan rite of mourning that asserted the forces of life in the face of death and included ritual eating, drinking, and sometimes sexual activity. The occurrence of this word here may indicate the depths to which Israel's religious traditions have been degraded. However, a number of commentators (see Stuart, 360) believe that in this context it simply means overindulgent dining.

12. Pride before a Fall (6:8–11)

⁸The Sovereign Lord has sworn by himself — the Lord God Almighty declares:

"I abhor the pride of Jacob
and detest his fortresses;
I will deliver up the city
and everything in it."

⁹If ten men are left in one house, they too will die. ¹⁰And if a relative who is to burn the bodies comes to carry them out of the house and asks anyone still hiding there, "Is

anyone with you?" and he says, "No," then he will say, "Hush! We must not mention the name of the Lord."

¹¹ For the Lord has given the command,
 and he will smash the great house into pieces
 and the small house into bits.

COMMENTARY

8 The Lord swears by himself in the preface to this oracle of doom. The guarantee of this oath is the trustworthiness of Yahweh himself, and it is secured by his holiness and power. The parallelism of the oracle indicates that the "pride of Jacob" has to do with Israel's vaunted "fortresses" (ʾarmᵉnôt). Here the word "fortress" is better rendered "palace" (see Jeremias, 115–16), a symbol of the Israelites' misguided affluence (cf. 3:10, 15). The "city," evidently Samaria, and all its wealth are to be delivered over to a conqueror.

9–11 The continuity of the passage is broken by vv.9–10, for v.11 is connected conceptually and syntactically by the word "for" (kî) to v.8. The judgment (v.8) is vividly illustrated in vv.9–10. If ten men are in a house or fortress, they will die (v.9). When a relative of one of the dead comes to burn the corpses, should he find one person still alive, that person will not permit his mentioning the name of the Lord for fear that the Lord will turn his wrath on him (v.10). The NIV's rendering makes the interchange between the survivor and the relative unclear. It is likely that the negative reply would have been followed by an oath: "No, by God." The NLT captures the sense well in the translation, "No, by ...," with the speaker's being interrupted by the person warning against uttering the name of the Lord.

Verses 9–10 reflect the responsibility of an individual for the burial of members of his family. Since cremation was not acceptable in ancient Israel, the reference is probably to the burning of corpses during a plague. Verse 11 is a powerful picture of the destruction that will surely fall on oppressing Israel.

NOTE

10 In this interpretation the word מְסָרְפוֹ (mᵉsārᵉpô) is understood as a participle of שָׂרַף (śārap, "burn"). In most instances in the OT, corpses were buried (Ge 25:9; 35:29; Jdg 16:31). The bodies of Saul and his son may have been burned because they had been badly mutilated (1Sa 31:12); but more likely it was necessary to dispose of the bodies in haste before the Philistines could mutilate them further (K&D).

13. A Grim Paradox (6:12–14)

¹² Do horses run on the rocky crags?
 Does one plow there with oxen?

> But you have turned justice into poison
>> and the fruit of righteousness into bitterness—
> [13] You who rejoice in the conquest of Lo Debar
>> and say, "Did we not take Karnaim by our own strength?"
>
> [14] For the LORD God Almighty declares,
>> "I will stir up a nation against you, O house of Israel,
> that will oppress you all the way
>> from Lebo Hamath to the valley of the Arabah."

12–13 By posing the patently absurd questions (v.12), Amos introduces the scathing rebuke that follows. One expects the courts to dispense justice, but the rich and powerful dispense poison instead of justice and make bitter the fruit of righteousness. Those who do so are described as rejoicing in "Lo Debar" and "Karnaim" (v.13)—evidently the sites of recent victories in Jeroboam's incursion into Aramean territory. But Amos pronounces Lo Debar so that it means "no thing" (see Note). In other words, the capturing of Lo Debar is insignificant. Through this biting sarcasm he proclaims the utter futility of their burgeoning national influence.

"Karnaim" means "horns" and, by extension, "strength." The people's proud self-confidence is reflected in their boast that they took Karnaim by their own strength. According to Jeremias, 118, Karnaim is to be identified with "modern Sheikh Sa'd, north of the Yarmuk, six kilometers south of Nawa."

14 This verse specifies the judgment that will overtake the Israelites; a nation, not identified here by Amos, will oppress them from their northern border "from the entrance to [$l^eb\hat{o}$ (NIV note), or 'Lebo'] Hamath" (cf. 2Ki 14:25) on their northern border all the way to their southern border at the Wadi Arabah.

NOTE

13 Lo Debar, spelled לוֹ דְבָר ($l\hat{o}$ $d^eb\bar{a}r$) in 2 Samuel 9:4 and לֹא דְבָר ($l\bar{o}^{\,\prime}$ $d^eb\bar{a}r$) in 2 Samuel 17:27, is probably the city of Debir. In the MT of Amos 6:13, the word is spelled לֹא דָבָר ($l\bar{o}^{\,\prime}$ $d\bar{a}b\bar{a}r$), which means "no thing."

IV. THE PROPHETIC VISIONS (7:1–9:15)

A. The Vision of the Locusts, Fire, and the Plumb Line (7:1–9)

[1] This is what the Sovereign LORD showed me: He was preparing swarms of locusts after the king's share had been harvested and just as the second crop was coming up. [2] When

they had stripped the land clean, I cried out, "Sovereign Lᴏʀᴅ, forgive! How can Jacob survive? He is so small!"

³So the Lᴏʀᴅ relented.

"This will not happen," the Lᴏʀᴅ said.

⁴This is what the Sovereign Lᴏʀᴅ showed me: The Sovereign Lᴏʀᴅ was calling for judgment by fire; it dried up the great deep and devoured the land. ⁵Then I cried out, "Sovereign Lᴏʀᴅ, I beg you, stop! How can Jacob survive? He is so small!"

⁶So the Lᴏʀᴅ relented.

"This will not happen either," the Sovereign Lᴏʀᴅ said.

⁷This is what he showed me: The Lᴏʀᴅ was standing by a wall that had been built true to plumb, with a plumb line in his hand. ⁸And the Lᴏʀᴅ asked me, "What do you see, Amos?"

"A plumb line," I replied.

Then the Lᴏʀᴅ said, "Look, I am setting a plumb line among my people Israel; I will spare them no longer.

⁹The high places of Isaac will be destroyed
　　and the sanctuaries of Israel will be ruined;
　　with my sword I will rise against the house of Jeroboam."

COMMENTARY

1 The first of the series of visions that largely occupy the rest of the book consists of three dramatic elements. The first is the threat of a locust invasion "as the second crop was coming." This notation places the event just before the dry season. If the threat materializes, the people will be left without food till the next harvest. Apparently the king enjoyed the privilege of claiming the first mowing. The needs of the government were great, and the large military establishment had to be supported.

2–3 When Amos sees in his vision that the locusts have finished the devastation, he prays that what he has seen will not happen, since Israel ("Jacob") will not be able to survive it, for "he is so small." This appeal seems strange in view of Israel's extensive territory and economic prosperity. But when compared to other nations, Israel was small

even when it was prosperous. Further and more importantly, Amos has seen an awesome display of Yahweh's might in this vision; and, in comparison to that, the nation seems small and helpless. Amos's prayer is answered. The Lord relents and the threat is revoked (v.3).

4–6 The second aspect of the vision involves the threat of fire (v.4) — an all-consuming fire, lapping up the sea and land. Again Amos's prayer is answered (v.5) and the Lord relents (v.6), as he had done in the first part of the vision.

7–9 The third aspect of the vision is climactic and contains the didactic element of the vision. The Lord is seen standing by a plumb wall with a plumb line in his hand (v.7). The word "standing" (*niṣṣāb* [Niphal reflexive], "station oneself") connotes a posture of firmness and determination, thus providing a contrast to the change of heart attributed to Yahweh in the first two parts of the vision.

A plumb line is a standard by which a wall's vertical trueness is tested. So the Lord is testing the people by a standard. In the first two visions, no standard was given; therefore, the threatened judgment could be withdrawn. But after the vision of the plumb line, the Lord cannot be accused of arbitrariness if he carries out the threats. The people have failed to live up to their privilege as Yahweh's

people. They have been called to be holy (Ex 19:6). But their repressive society has violated the very standards of holiness. They gave lip service to the covenant of Yahweh but ignored the social concerns woven into its fabric. When the test came, they have been found wanting. The plumb line shows that the Lord is not an arbitrary judge.

The coming judgment will fall on the pagan sanctuaries of Israel and on the dynasty of Jeroboam (v.9). Thus the two major influences in Israelite life will perish.

NOTE

7 The NIV translates *ă¹nak* as "plumb line" in this verse (and v.8). The word's literal meaning of "lead" or "tin," however, leads some interpreters in a different direction. Jeremias, 131–32, for instance, argues that God is standing by a "wall of tin" with "tin" in his hand and announces that "tin" will come into the midst of his people. He takes the latter two instances as references to weapons. The "wall of tin" is a strong metal, but God is standing on it and will destroy it. Williamson has argued effectively, based on the context, that the NIV's understanding of the verse is most likely correct ("The Prophet and the Plumb-line: A Redaction-Critical Study of Amos vii," *OTS* 26 [1990]: 105–25).

B. A Historical Interlude (7:10–17)

OVERVIEW

Amos's visions are momentarily interrupted by a passage that gives us important information about Amos himself. The material may have been placed here because the event it describes actually followed

Amos's public report of the preceding vision. At any rate, the consonance between the two sections is apparent (see "Unity" in the introduction).

> ¹⁰Then Amaziah the priest of Bethel sent a message to Jeroboam king of Israel: "Amos is raising a conspiracy against you in the very heart of Israel. The land cannot bear all his words. ¹¹For this is what Amos is saying:
>
> > 'Jeroboam will die by the sword,
> > and Israel will surely go into exile,
> > away from their native land.'"

¹²Then Amaziah said to Amos, "Get out, you seer! Go back to the land of Judah. Earn your bread there and do your prophesying there. ¹³Don't prophesy any more at Bethel, because this is the king's sanctuary and the temple of the kingdom."

¹⁴Amos answered Amaziah, "I was neither a prophet nor a prophet's son, but I was a shepherd, and I also took care of sycamore-fig trees. ¹⁵But the LORD took me from tending the flock and said to me, 'Go, prophesy to my people Israel.' ¹⁶Now then, hear the word of the LORD. You say,

'Do not prophesy against Israel,
    and stop preaching against the house of Isaac.'

¹⁷Therefore this is what the LORD says:

'Your wife will become a prostitute in the city,
    and your sons and daughters will fall by the sword.
Your land will be measured and divided up,
    and you yourself will die in a pagan country.
And Israel will certainly go into exile,
    away from their native land.'"

COMMENTARY

10–13 Amaziah, the priest of the sanctuary at Bethel (the leading pagan shrine in Israel (3:14; 4:4; 5:5–6, see 1Ki 12:25–33), accuses Amos of conspiracy (v.10). The words reported by Amaziah (v.11) seem based on the threat recorded in v.9. Jeroboam's reaction is not given, but most likely it is reflected in Amaziah's order to Amos (vv.12–13). That the word "seer" (*ḥōzeh*) is associated with "prophet" (*nābîʾ*) in 2 Kings 17:13 affirms the legitimacy of the seer. Amaziah did not use "seer" in a derogatory sense. Indeed, since Amos has just received a vision, the term is appropriate.

14–15 Amos's reply to Amaziah's order is not without its interpretive problems. Did Amos say, "I am not a prophet," or, "I was not a prophet"? Most commentators have opted for the former because Amos replies in a sequence of verbless clauses, which

connote most naturally the present tense. On the other hand, a number of commentators have followed the rendering of the RV: "I was no prophet."

If the tense is present, Amos may have been denying that he is a *nābîʾ* ("prophet") in the sense that Amaziah understands him to be—that is, a professional prophet ("Earn your bread there," v.12). There are, however, certain difficulties with the present-tense view. First, Amos used the term *nābîʾ* ("prophet") of true prophets in 3:7. To use it otherwise here would be unusual. Second, Amos claims the function of a *nābîʾ* in 7:15 (*hinnābēʾ*, "prophesy").

The view that understands the affirmation of Amos in the past tense ("I was no prophet") seems to have the fewest problems. It retains the meaning of *nābîʾ* inherent in the nominal form in 3:7

and the verbal form in 7:15. Also, that the Lord took Amos from being a shepherd (*mēʾaḥᵃrê haṣṣōʾn*, "from tending the flock"; v.15) may mean that the nominal clauses in v.14 describing his profession as a "shepherd" (*bôqēr*) and a "caretaker of sycamore-fig trees" (*bôlēs šiqmîm*) should be understood to describe his past status.

Regardless of one's understanding of Amos's denial, he certainly denies any connection with professional prophetism and affirms that he is a prophet by divine vocation. (For the occupations that Amos refers to here, see "Authorship" in the introduction.)

16–17 Amos's encounter with Amaziah ends with a prediction of dire judgment, despite his insistence that Amos desist in his preaching against Israel (v.16). The judgment Amos pronounces against Amaziah and his family is personal in nature. Amaziah's wife will be violated, perhaps by the invading soldiers, and his children killed. He will lose all he has and will die in a "pagan" (*tᵉmēʾâ*, "unclean") country. So the priest, whose task it was to maintain the purity of the cult, will die in a Gentile land. A similar type of personal judgment was leveled by Jeremiah against the false prophet Hananiah (Jer 28:15–17).

NOTES

10 Amaziah's report of Amos's threat, while essentially accurate, moves the emphasis from the house of Jeroboam to Jeroboam himself. This shift may have inflamed the situation and thus served Amaziah's cause. Jeroboam himself was not overthrown, but his dynasty fell a very short while after his death.

14 The question of tense cannot be decided by the fact that the verbless clauses are followed (v.15) by the imperfect with *waw* consecutive וַיִּקָּחֵנִי (*wayyiqqāḥēnî*, "[the Lord] took me"). This grammatical construction connotes the past tense here, but that connotation no more determines the tense of the verbless clauses than the imperfect with *waw* consecutive does in Exodus 6:2–3. There the verbless clause אֲנִי יהוה (*ᵃnî yhwh*) must be understood in the present tense—"I am the LORD"—even though it is followed by the imperfect with *waw* consecutive וָאֵרָא (*wāʾērāʾ*, "I appeared") in v.3.

Generally, the tense of a verbless clause describes a state contemporaneous with the principal action (cf. GKC, par. 141e); yet one may question whether a verbless clause that precedes a verb in the past tense is also past tense. In Zechariah 13:5, the verbless clause לֹא נָבִיא אָנֹכִי (*lōʾ nābîʾ ʾānōkî*, "I am not a prophet") precedes the verbless clause כִּי־אָדָם הִקְנַנִי (*kî-ʾādām hiqnanî*, "for the land has been my livelihood") and is clearly present in tense. The solution must be sought on other grounds.

Zevit translated Amos's denial as "No! I am not a *nābîʾ*, I am not even a *ben nābîʾ*" (Z. Zevit, "A Misunderstanding at Bethel, Amos VII 12–17," *VT* 25 [1975]: 783–90). Y. Hoffmann ("Did Amos Regard Himself as a *Nabi*?" *VT* 27 [1977]: 209–12) countered this translation in observing that the "absolute denial" was never expressed by לֹא (*lōʾ*, "not").

The LXX translates the words of Amos in the past tense, Οὐκ ἤμην προφήτης ἐγώ (*ouk ēmēn prophētēs egō*, "I was not a prophet), as does the Peshitta-Syriac version.

Amos's occupation, described here as a בוֹקֵר (*bôqēr*), may be that of a herdsman in general. The apparent linguistic connection with בָּקָר (*bāqār*, "cattle") does not demand the conclusion that Amos tended cattle. The LXX translates the term in the more general sense of αἰπόλος (*aipolos*, "goatherd"). There is no need to emend the word to נֹקֵד (*nōqēd*, "shepherd"; BH). Zaleman proposed the reading דּוֹקֵר (*dôqēr*, "piercer"): "But I am a piercer and tender of sycamore figs" (L. Zaleman, "Piercing the Darkness at *Bôqēr* [Amos VII 14]," *VT* 30 [1980]: 252–53).

C. The Vision of the Summer Fruit (8:1–14)

[1]This is what the Sovereign Lord showed me: a basket of ripe fruit. [2]"What do you see, Amos?" he asked.

"A basket of ripe fruit," I answered.

Then the Lord said to me, "The time is ripe for my people Israel; I will spare them no longer. [3]In that day," declares the Sovereign Lord, "the songs in the temple will turn to wailing. Many, many bodies — flung everywhere! Silence!"

[4]Hear this, you who trample the needy
    and do away with the poor of the land,

[5]saying,

"When will the New Moon be over
    that we may sell grain,
and the Sabbath be ended
    that we may market wheat?"—
skimping the measure,
    boosting the price
    and cheating with dishonest scales,
[6]buying the poor with silver
    and the needy for a pair of sandals,
    selling even the sweepings with the wheat.

[7]The Lord has sworn by the Pride of Jacob: "I will never forget anything they have done.

[8]"Will not the land tremble for this,
    and all who live in it mourn?
The whole land will rise like the Nile;
    it will be stirred up and then sink
    like the river of Egypt.

[9]"In that day," declares the Sovereign Lord,

"I will make the sun go down at noon
    and darken the earth in broad daylight.

¹⁰I will turn your religious feasts into mourning
    and all your singing into weeping.
I will make all of you wear sackcloth
    and shave your heads.
I will make that time like mourning for an only son
    and the end of it like a bitter day.

¹¹"The days are coming," declares the Sovereign Lord,
    "when I will send a famine through the land —
not a famine of food or a thirst for water,
    but a famine of hearing the words of the Lord.
¹²Men will stagger from sea to sea
    and wander from north to east,
searching for the word of the Lord,
    but they will not find it.

¹³In that day

the lovely young women and strong young men
    will faint because of thirst.
¹⁴They who swear by the shame of Samaria,
    or say, 'As surely as your god lives, O Dan,'
    or, 'As surely as the god of Beersheba lives' —
they will fall,
    never to rise again."

COMMENTARY

1–2 While it is possible that Amos sees an actual basket of fruit (v.1) and that the Lord uses it as a means of revelation, its mention in this section of the book makes it likely that he sees the basket in another vision. There is a striking wordplay here (v.2). The word for "summer fruit" is *qāyiṣ*, similar in sound to the word *qēṣ*, which means "end" and is used in the response of the Lord: "The end has come for my people" ("The time is ripe for my people," NIV). For a similar wordplay oracle, see Jeremiah 1:11–12.

The basket of summer fruit, ordinarily associated with the joys and provisions of the harvest, becomes a mockery. The pleasant memories of past harvest festivals that it might recall are shattered by the decisive words "the time is ripe" (*bāʾ haqqēṣ*, lit., "the end has come").

3 Just as the apparent promise of the summer fruit was turned into the assurance of Israel's destruction, so the joyous temple hymns (cf. 6:5) will give way to the wailing of the populace of Israel when the wrath of Yahweh falls on them.

The last clause of v.3, though somewhat desultory, is typical of the vivid staccato style Amos used earlier in describing calamity (3:12). The text may be translated, "Many are the corpses—they are flung everywhere—Silence!" The translation of *hišlîk* as "flung" understands it as an indefinite singular—"one flings," or "they are flung" (cf. Notes). The word "silence" calls for the reverence warranted by this appalling scene.

4–6 The scene is followed by a recital (v.4) of the crimes of those whose disobedience to the Lord is responsible for the carnage. The words of v.4 are reminiscent of 5:11. The merchants cannot wait for the end of the holy days so that they can increase their wealth by giving short measure and raising prices (v.5; see Pr 11:1; 16:11). They even sell the sweepings to increase the weight (v.6)! Yet these exploiters are careful to observe the Sabbath. Though the marketplace is deserted on the holy days, in the bustle of commerce their god is quite in evidence. Their god is mammon and their true religious credo, "Gain at any cost."

7–8 In the oath formula, the "Pride of Jacob" (v.7) is best understood as an appellation for God (cf. 4:2; 6:8; cf. also Hos 5:5; 7:10). "Glory" is used as a surrogate for God in Jeremiah 2:11. It is the pride of Jacob—that is, the Lord, Jacob's glory—that guarantees this oath. The judgment that follows (v.8) will surely come because God does not allow his glory to be sullied.

Verse 8 describes the convulsions the land will suffer. The Nile River flooded annually and then receded, leaving fertile soil behind. In the process, however, this flooding could bring much damage, which is what the imagery focuses on here (and in 9:5). While some scholars believe this picture is metaphoric of an earthquake (Jeremias, 149), that view is not clearly called for in the text.

9 "In that day" refers to the day of calamity and need not be understood as referring to the end of history. It introduces a section that continues to describe the impending judgment in metaphorical language. The setting of the sun at noon describes an interruption of the natural order that will cause terror and panic among the earth's inhabitants. The upheaval predicted by Amos will disrupt the national life on such a scale that the fear and dread in the hearts of the people will be similar to the terror that a celestial cataclysm would cause.

10–12 The destruction to come on Samaria will cause bitter mourning. Amos describes the event in terms of a funeral for an only son (v.10). He continues the use of metaphorical language as he depicts a coming famine. It will be no ordinary famine but one of the words of the Lord (v.11). He pictures people searching for the word as starving people seeking food or water (vv.12–13). But they receive no word from the Lord. Having rejected the word for not realizing its great value, they will lose it forever (cf. Pr 1:24–27; Lk 17:22; Jn 7:34). The church must realize the preciousness of God's Word. We must obey and honor it, because it points to the source of life.

13–14 Judgment will even cause the young and strong to grow weak. The word "shame" (*ʾašmâ*) has the primary meaning of "guilt." Sometimes it is used of the guilt incurred from idol worship (2Ch 24:18; 33:23). Dan was the site of the worship of the golden calf under Jeroboam, and the "way to Beersheba" (*derek bᵊʾer šābaʿ*, "god of Beersheba," NIV) apparently refers to the pilgrimage to that site (see comment on 5:5). The various shrines Amos refers to may indicate that a geographical split in the concept of Yahweh was taking place. A similar split related to the Canaanite god Baal. Thus, the worship of Yahweh was becoming idolatrous. Those whose confidence is in their distorted, pagan view of Yahweh will fall.

NOTE

3 For a discussion of the indefinite singular, see GKC, par. 144d.

D. The Vision of the Lord Standing by the Altar (9:1–15)

1. The Destruction of the Temple (9:1–6)

¹I saw the Lord standing by the altar, and he said:

"Strike the tops of the pillars
    so that the thresholds shake.
Bring them down on the heads of all the people;
    those who are left I will kill with the sword.
Not one will get away,
    none will escape.
²Though they dig down to the depths of the grave,
    from there my hand will take them.
Though they climb up to the heavens,
    from there I will bring them down.
³Though they hide themselves on the top of Carmel,
    there I will hunt them down and seize them.
Though they hide from me at the bottom of the sea,
    there I will command the serpent to bite them.
⁴Though they are driven into exile by their enemies,
    there I will command the sword to slay them.
I will fix my eyes upon them
    for evil and not for good."

⁵The Lord, the LORD Almighty,
    he who touches the earth and it melts,
    and all who live in it mourn—
the whole land rises like the Nile,
    then sinks like the river of Egypt—
⁶he who builds his lofty palace in the heavens
    and sets its foundation on the earth,
who calls for the waters of the sea
    and pours them out over the face of the land—
    the LORD is his name.

COMMENTARY

1–4 In a vision Amos sees the Lord standing by the temple altar (v.1a). The Lord commands the temple to crumble, and it collapses on the people, thus destroying the whole nation (vv.1b–4). The temple in mind is almost certainly the holy place at Bethel, whose destruction occurred in 622 BC at the hands of the pious Judean king Josiah (2Ki 23:15–16).

Yet the oracle has more in mind than just this literal temple, for the collapse of such a building will affect only a few. Instead, the visionary temple represents the religion of the northern kingdom, which, in the end, will bring about the destruction of its adherents. The decay of the social structure that results from their cold externalism can lead only to national ruin. The gross sin of idolatry can lead only to judgment. The god of "greed" is no respecter of persons and often turns his voraciousness on those who are his own. Amos allows no escape for the nation.

5–6 The hymnic element is appropriate to the context, for it sets forth the power of the Lord to carry out his threat. This hymn contains several elements common to other prophetic hymns, such as the reference to the heavens and the calling forth of the waters (5:8). Observe also the parallel between 9:5b and 8:8.

2. Israel and the Other Nations (9:7)

⁷"Are not you Israelites
the same to me as the Cushites?"

declares the Lord.

"Did I not bring Israel up from Egypt,
the Philistines from Caphtor
and the Arameans from Kir?"

COMMENTARY

7 Cush was a territory roughly corresponding to Ethiopia and Nubia. It is infrequently mentioned in the OT. This country seems to have been chosen because of its great distance from Israel. It lay at the outer extremities of the important nations of the ancient Near East. At the time of Amos, it was probably considered an insignificant region. Thus it would be shocking to the Israelites, who boasted of their election, to hear that in the eyes of the Lord they are no better than those obscure Cushites.

Similarly, Israel is no different from the Philistines or Arameans in that the Lord governed the migrations of these people just as he led the Israelites from Egypt (for Kir, see comment on 1:5). The exodus had led the Israelites to assume that the Lord was unalterably committed to their welfare as a nation and that no other nation counted as far as he was concerned. But here Amos destroys that false assumption by affirming the sovereignty of Yahweh over all the nations. The exodus did not give them license to presume on the holiness and mercy of God.

3. The Restoration of the Davidic Kingdom (9:8–12)

8 "Surely the eyes of the Sovereign Lord
   are on the sinful kingdom.
I will destroy it
   from the face of the earth —
yet I will not totally destroy
   the house of Jacob,"

                                        declares the Lord.

9 "For I will give the command,
   and I will shake the house of Israel
   among all the nations
as grain is shaken in a sieve,
   and not a pebble will reach to the ground.
10 All the sinners among my people
   will die by the sword,
all those who say,
   'Disaster will not overtake or meet us.'

11 In that day I will restore
   David's fallen tent.
I will repair its broken places,
   restore its ruins,
   and build it as it used to be,
12 so that they may possess the remnant of Edom
   and all the nations that bear my name,"

                                        declares the Lord,
                              who will do these things.

COMMENTARY

8–10 The nation is to be destroyed, but not totally (v.8). Thus an element of hope is introduced at this point. Many scholars deny the words of vv.8–15 to Amos because the message of hope is not consonant with the gloomy message of total destruction presented to this point. But it is precisely this element of hope that places Amos in the mainstream of classical eighth-century prophetism. The concept of hope in these verses is quite unlike the eschatological hope of the postexilic period, and the eighth-century prophets placed their hope for the future in a kingdom portrayed with obvious Davidic motifs (Isa 9:7; Mic 5:2).

It is true that Amos holds out no hope for the nation of Israel. But saying so does not mean that he holds out no hope for a preserved remnant. One of the important elements of Amos's message is that the nation is not to be equated with the remnant; it is precisely that false hope that he attacks. The sifting process (v.9) will produce a true remnant from Israel (v.10; cf. Jer 30:11; for a study of the remnant in the OT, see G. Hasel, *The Remnant* [Berrien Springs, Mich.: Andrews Univ. Press, 1972]).

Amos's denial of the popular belief that the nation was automatically the remnant raises serious questions. Does he deny the concept of the remnant altogether? Does he see no continuation of the promise to Abraham? It is difficult to answer such questions in the affirmative, for to do so excludes Amos from the current of OT thought. Without the remnant passage of vv.9–15, the book of Amos is incomplete. Amos is not a prophet who pronounces only doom. There are rays of hope not only here but even in undisputed passages such as 5:4, 6, 15.

Some commentators deny that the figure of "sifting" in v.9 implies a process of separation. They see the "pebbles" as representing the wicked, who are not allowed to escape and who are destined for judgment. But v.9 is logically connected to v.8 by the word "for" (*kî*), where a separation between the destroyed kingdom and the remnant is implicit in the statement affirming that the nation will not be totally destroyed. Verse 9 thus explains v.8 by analogy.

The concept of separation is inherent in the figure of sifting. Failure to see separation in the sieve motif leaves unexplained the shaking of Israel "among all the nations" (v.9). Amos decreed that the nation was doomed to exile (7:17). The consonance of

this pronouncement with the "shaking" of v.9 is apparent. The process of winnowing, whereby the grain falls to the ground and the unedible refuse remains in the sieve, thus representing the sinners, is not necessarily in view here. The word "grain" does not appear in the Hebrew; it reads simply, "as one shakes with a sieve."

The word "pebble" (*ṣᵉrôr*) in v.9 need not be understood as "grain." It connotes any substance that is compacted and refers to anything that will not pass through a sieve. In 2 Samuel 17:13 ("a piece," NIV) and Proverbs 26:8, *ṣᵉrôr* is used of a pebble but never specifically of grain. There is no need to see a reference to good or evil in the word *ṣᵉrôr*. Amos simply states that while the smaller pebbles pass through, the larger ones remain in the sieve. This remaining material is analogous to the remnant.

11 "In that day" refers to a future but indefinite time. As it turns out, this divine work of restoration takes place initially in the postexilic period with the return of the exiles to Jerusalem but continues into the NT period, when it finds its ultimate fulfillment in the work of Jesus Christ, the Son of David (see below). The prophets viewed the time from the exile to the coming of the Messiah as a single period (see Note).

The word "tent" (*sukkâ*) refers to a rude shelter (a "hut") and pictures the "house" (dynasty) of David, which was becoming a dilapidated shack. [In Amos's time] the Davidic dynasty has fallen so low that it can no longer be called a "house."

The continuation of the Davidic dynasty is envisioned in prophecy as continuing in the Messiah, who is often referred to in Davidic motifs (Isa 9:6–7; Jer 33:15, 17; Mic 5:2). Amos thus affirms what other prophets affirm: the perpetuity of the Davidic "house." The national upheaval that ultimately led to the fall of Judah and Israel and the overthrow of the Judahite monarchy cannot vitiate God's promise.

The royal offspring will yet come. David's dynasty will be perpetuated in David's greater Son. He will uphold God's gracious promise.

The promise to David in 2 Samuel 7 also carries with it the promise of an eternal kingdom (vv.12–13). While the Davidic dynasty is most prominent in Amos's prophecy, it is difficult to separate that concept from the concept of regnal authority or kingdom. Both are probably in view.

The word *nōpelet*, an active participle, may be translated "fallen"; but there is no reason why it may not be given a continuing sense—viz., "is falling." The dynasty has not yet collapsed in Amos's time, but the seeds of its dissolution are present.

The Lord declares that he will restore that "tent." He will restore "their" (feminine plural) broken places. The plural pronoun apparently refers to the divided kingdom. He will restore "his" (masculine singular)—that is, David's—ruins and rebuild "it" (feminine singular), referring to "the tent" (*sukkâ* [feminine]). The Davidic dynasty, represented by the tent, will be restored.

12 Here the NT follows the LXX by reading "that the remnant of men may seek the Lord" (Acts 15:17) instead of "possess the remnant of Edom." The word "Edom" (*ᵉdôm*) is almost identical to "man" in Hebrew (*ᵓādām*). The subject of Acts 15:12–21, where this passage is quoted, is Gentile inclusion in the early church. James quoted this Amos passage to support the rightness of Gentile inclusion in the church. The textual question cited does not invalidate James's use of the passage, for the phrase "that bear my name" (*ᵃšer niqrāᵓ šᵉmî ᶜᵃlêhem*) always connotes that which is God's peculiar possession (Dt 28:10; 2Ch 7:14; Jer 14:9; 15:16). This is precisely James's argument. He saw Gentile inclusion in the redemptive program of God as having been predicted in Amos 9:11–12.

NOTE

11 With regard to the suggestion that the OT prophets saw the period of exile as continuing to the coming of Messiah, note Hosea 3:1–5, where the period of estrangement continues until the people seek "David their king." See also Isaiah 11:11; Micah 5:2–6; Zechariah 10:10, where Assyria, the nation that initiated the exile, functions as a surrogate of the oppressing nations in end-time events.

The NT (Ac 15:16) paraphrases בַּיּוֹם הַהוּא (*bayyôm hahûᵓ*, "in that day") in the words μετὰ ταῦτα (*meta tauta*, "after these things"). This translation is not that of the LXX, which reads ἐν τῇ ἡμέρᾳ ἐκείνῃ (*en tē hēmera ekeinē*, "in that day"). James may have been interpreting "in that day" in a way that better communicated the fact that the prophecy of Amos did not find its fulfillment in the Babylonian captivity. In doing so, James supports the suggestion that the captivity was understood as continuing throughout history.

סֻכָּה (*sukkâ*, "tent, shelter") connotes a "shelter" for animals (Ge 33:17), a "shelter" from the sun (Jnh 4:5), and the "booths" the Israelites occupied in observance of the wilderness experience (Lev 23:42).

REFLECTION

Since the inclusion of Gentiles takes place, according to Amos, in the kingdom of the scion of David, one may assume that that kingdom has been established in some way. It is invisible now but will appear in glorious power when Christ, David's greater Son, returns. If this passage in Amos predicted only a future inclusion of Gentiles in the millennial kingdom, it is difficult to understand why James would have appealed to it for support of Gentile admission to the first-century church. It seems clearly relevant to the issues facing the early church. If so, then James understood the restored Davidic monarchy to be represented, at least in its invisible sense, in the church in his time.

The inclusion of Gentiles in the divine promise is a concept attributed to the Servant in Isaiah (Isa 49:6). Amos echoes the same truth. The ancient promise that Gentiles as well as Jews (Ge 12:3) will experience divine blessing is fulfilled in the Offspring of David.

4. The Blessings of the Restored Kingdom (9:13–15)

¹³"The days are coming," declares the LORD,

"when the reaper will be overtaken by the plowman
    and the planter by the one treading grapes.
New wine will drip from the mountains
    and flow from all the hills.
¹⁴I will bring back my exiled people Israel;
    they will rebuild the ruined cities and live in them.
They will plant vineyards and drink their wine;
    they will make gardens and eat their fruit.
¹⁵I will plant Israel in their own land,
    never again to be uprooted
    from the land I have given them,"
        says the LORD your God.

COMMENTARY

13 A time is coming when there will be a superabundance of agricultural produce and wine (v.13). In this time Israel will be restored to the land forever (v.15).

The fact that the reaper will be overtaken by the plowman in this time implies a great abundance of the produce of the field. Scarcely can the grapevines be planted than the grapes are ready for pressing. The great amount of wine in this time is pictured in the metaphor of new wine flowing from the hills.

Amos sees here a radical reversal of Israel's fortunes. He depicts a time when God's blessing will be poured out in unimaginable abundance. Deuteronomy 28:4 and 30.9 both promise agricultural bounty for covenantal obedience.

14–15 The period when this abundance will be manifested will witness the restoration of Israel to her land. Ruined cities will be rebuilt (v.14), and Israel will again flourish as a nation. Amos sees this restoration as being permanent. He says that Israel will be planted in her own land "never again to be uprooted" (v.15). It is difficult to understand his words as finding fulfillment in the postexilic period, though the return to Jerusalem is an anticipation of a greater fulfillment to come.

Other OT prophets used somewhat similar language to describe this period. Like Amos, they associated the abundance of blessing with the Davidic King (Isa 9:2-7; 11:1-9; Mic 4:1-5; 5:2-5).

REFLECTION

The hope of Amos is not an isolated one that finds expression only in his book. Nor is it a purely prophetic tradition without relation to other OT traditions. It is an expression of one of the most important themes of OT theology: the promise. This promise, given to Abraham, reiterated to the patriarchs, reaffirmed to David, and expressed throughout the OT, affirms that God will mediate his redemptive blessings to Jews and Gentiles in a promised offspring or "seed." In the prophets, this offspring is clearly the Davidic Messiah, who in the NT is Christ. Amos affirms that God's promise has not been cancelled. In spite of the internal turmoil in the kingdom of Amos's day, God will establish the Davidic monarchy; and through that monarchy God's blessing will come to "all peoples on earth" (Ge 12:3).

OBADIAH

CARL E. ARMERDING

Introduction

1. BACKGROUND

Edom, established in the region around Mount Seir (see "Geography") as far back as patriarchal times (cf. Ge 36), was one of the small kingdoms that inhabited the Transjordanian highlands throughout the entire monarchical period. From the exodus and wandering narratives, as well as from Egyptian records, we know that by the thirteenth century BC Edom was well established in the area south and east of the Dead Sea. In the period of the monarchy, it was David's lot to bring Edom under subjection; and relations were often hostile from then on.

The full history of the country may be found in a variety of sources.[1] Of particular interest in the context of Obadiah's work are two questions relating to Edom: (1) When might the hostility between Edom and Judah have produced the kind of Edomite perfidy expressed in vv.10–14? (2) When in Edom's history were Obadiah's words fulfilled? The first question will be dealt with in the commentary at v.14, while the latter question is addressed here.

Despite periods of subjugation to Judah, there is clear evidence that Edom still constituted an independent monarchy about 594–593 BC (cf. Jer 27:3), and it provided at least partial refuge to Judah's fugitives then (cf. Jer 40:11). Although Ammon and Moab, like Judah, were subsequently subjugated by Nebuchadnezzar (ca. 582; Josephus, *Ant.* 10.180–82 [9.7]; cf. Eze 21:18–20, 28), no reference is made to Edom, which may therefore have followed Jeremiah's counsel to submit (Jer 27:6–7).

Edom's continued existence in the sixth century is also attested by excavations at Ezion Geber (Tell el-Kheleifeh). In particular, a seal dating from around 600–550 BC and bearing a typical Edomite name

---

1. Cf. J. R. Bartlett, "Edom," *ABD*, 2:287–95; B. Macdonald, "Archaeology of Edom," *ABD*, 2:287–95; B. Macdonald, "Edom," *ISBE*, 2:18–21; D. J. Wiseman, ed., *Peoples of Old Testament Times* (Oxford: Oxford Univ. Press, 1973), 229–58.

("belonging to *Qwsnl* servant of the king")[2] was discovered there, and an ostracon from the latter half of the sixth century BC lists four names of similar Edomite origin.[3] Edom also figures in OT writings from the exile, which bear witness to its continued existence, albeit guilty and threatened (e.g., La 4:21–22; Eze 25:12–14; 35; Da 11:41).

By 312 BC, however, it is certain that Petra was occupied by the Nabataeans (e.g., *Diodorus Siculus* 19. 95.2, 98.1), a nomadic Arabic tribe that had infiltrated the land. There is evidence that this transition to Arabic influence was already established in the fifth century. Ammon and Moab are cited as enemies of Judah's interests in the time of Nehemiah (ca. 444–432; Ne 2:10, 19; 4:3, 7; 6:1–15; 13:1–2, 23); Edom, however, is not named among Judah's traditional opponents, being replaced by the Arabs, who played a dominant role under Geshem (Ne 2:19; 4:7; 6:1–2; cf. 2Ch 17:11; 21:16; 22:1; 26:7). A similar transition is evident at Ezion Geber, where Arabic names replace Edomite names at the fifth-century site, which was controlled by the Arabs during the Persian period (late sixth to the fourth centuries).[4]

The destruction of Edom may therefore be located tentatively in the latter half of the sixth century, though recent scholarship suggests a gradual changeover from Edomite to Nabatean in place of the traditional view of an Arab invasion. This shift is corroborated by Malachi, who described as past history the reduction of Esau's "mountains into a wasteland" and "his inheritance to the desert jackals" (ca. 450; Mal 1:3–4; cf. Eze 32:29), though the prophet envisaged a continuing identity and national striving by Edom even in exile (Mal 1:4–5).

Bartlett[5] and others have suggested that Nabonidus (556–539 BC), the last of the Babylonian rulers, may have been responsible for a major destruction at both Bozrah (modern Buseira) and Tel el-Kheleifah (N. Glueck's Ezion-geber, an identification now disputed),[6] thus paving the way for Edom's eventual displacement into the Negev. He campaigned in southern Transjordan in 552 BC in the interest of policing the major trade routes of western Arabia, a task to which he devoted the greater part of his reign. Such a campaign could explain the overthrow of traditional Edomite control of the caravan routes leading to Egypt and the Mediterranean. It would also have provided incentive for the Nabataeans to abandon their brigandry along the trade routes, now protected by Nabonidus's military colonies, and to adopt a more settled existence in the land of the crippled Edomites.[7]

This reconstruction is still regarded as conjectural. Martin Noth concurs with the opinion of Bartlett in writing, "The final fate of the Edomite kingdom remains completely shrouded in darkness."[8] It is certain, however, that Edom's mountains were the scene of some measure of invasion and destruction in the sixth century, leading to the end of Edom as a monarchy and as a stable culture, though it would later emerge in new forms (Idumea) in the south of Judah.

---

2. Cf. Leslie C. Allen, *The Books of Joel, Obadiah, Jonah, and Micah* (NICOT; Grand Rapids: Eerdmans, 1976), 131; John R. Bartlett, "From Edomites to Nabataeans: A Study in Continuity," *PEQ* 111 (January-June 1979): 53.

3. Allen, *The Books of Joel, Obadiah, Jonah, and Micah*, 131.

4. Cf. Wiseman, *Peoples of Old Testament Times*, 229–58.

5. Bartlett, "Edom," *ABD*, 2:293.

6. G. Pratico, "Kheleifeh, Tell El-," *ABD*, 4:33.

7. J. Lindsay, "Babylonian Kings and Edom, 605–550," *PEQ* 108 (1976): 23–39.

8. Martin, Noth, *History of Israel* (London: Black, 1959), 294.

2. UNITY

The book of Obadiah is structured around two interrelated themes: the destruction of "Edom" (vv.1, 8), referred to also as "Esau" (vv.6, 8−9, 18 [2x], 19, 21), and "Teman" (v.9); and the vindication of "Judah" (v.12), referred to by the names "Jacob" (vv.10, 17−18), "Jerusalem" (vv.11, 20), and "Mount Zion" (vv.17, 21; cf. v.16), within the broader context of Israel as a whole (cf. vv.18−20). The prophecy abounds with these geographical and ethnic terms, which is one of the unifying factors of the book.

These terms also vividly express the dynamics of these few, intense verses. The juxtaposition of "Jacob" and "Esau," in particular, draws attention to the blood relationship uniting the two nations—it is defined explicitly at the center of the book (cf. "your brother"; vv.10, 12); and it is the violation of these ties that occasions both Obadiah's denunciation of Edom and the necessity for Judah's restoration. The book is similarly unified by the related concept of the "day" (*yôm*) of God's judgment (vv.8, 11 [2x], 12 [4x], 13 [3x], 14, 15) and by the principle of reversal that informs that judgment, stated throughout but most clearly in vv.15−16.

3. AUTHORSHIP

Nothing is known of the author of Obadiah. The name, which means "servant of Yahweh," is given to at least twelve other OT characters, none of whom seem obviously to be the author named in the book. Most attempts at correlation founder on the inability of scholars to date the book with certainty (see next section).

4. DATE AND OCCASION

The date and occasion for the book of Obadiah continue to be much debated. The prophecy is clearly a response to a time when Jerusalem was overrun by foreign armies, a sacking in which the Edomites were understood to have in some way collaborated (see comments on v.15). If, as argued below, it was the 586 BC destruction under Nebuchadnezzar, and if Edom itself came under Nabataean control by the fifth century BC, the date of the book is best left to sometime after the 586 invasion of Zion (cf. Barton, who limits these criteria to vv. 1−14 and admits that the remainder of the book could come from a later date).[9] A variation on this date is given by H. W. Wolff, who understands Obadiah to be a cultic prophet and probably an eyewitness to the destruction of Jerusalem but whose lament oracles, unlike those of Lamentations, are actually addressed to Edom and incorporate both preexilic sayings and original oracles.[10] The suggested *Sitz im Leben* is the temple ceremony of lament, as cited in Zechariah 7:3, 5; 8:19. In passing, it is worth noting the close parallel between the circumstances reflected in Obadiah 10−14 and those of Ezekiel 35:5−9, which would seem to present a strong case for the post−586 setting.

9. John Barton, *Joel and Obadiah* (OTL; Louisville: Westminster John Knox, 2001), 120−23.
10. H. W. Wolff, *Obadiah and Jonah: A Commentary* (BKAT; Minneapolis: Augsburg, 1986 [1977 German orig.]), 42−44; see also idem, "Obadja: ein Kultprophet als interpret," *EvT* 37 (1977): 273−84, for fuller argument.

In addition to commentators who have maintained a preexilic date, sometimes in conformity to Obadiah's place within the Minor Prophets,[11] others question whether any specific historical setting is intended, preferring to see Edom as the representative and archetypical enemy of Israel.[12] Still others shift the focus away from a specific author or historical setting to a community (or communities) for which the book was composed, thus featuring the reader(s) rather than the author(s).[13]

5. LITERARY FORM

The prophecy is composed of three major sections—vv.1–9, 10–14, 15–21—which portray the contrasting relations of Jacob, Esau, and the nations in past and future history. Verses 1–9 anticipate a "day" (v.8) of the "LORD" (vv.1, 4, 8) in which "Esau" (vv.6, 8–9) will be "cut down" in battle (v.9) by the "nations" (vv.1–2).

Verses 10–14 recollect a corresponding "day" of calamity (vv.11–14) in which "Jacob" (v.10) has been "cut down" (kārat; v.14) by Esau ("you," "your"; vv.11–14) in collaboration with "foreigners" (v.11).

This reversal of roles is completed in vv.15–21, which correspond closely to vv.10–14, as does that section to vv.1–9. A day (v.15) of the "LORD" (vv.15, 18, 21) is coming in which the house of "Jacob" (vv.17–18) will "possess" its inheritance (vv.17, 19–20), consuming the house of "Esau" (vv.18–19, 21) along with the "nations" (v.15; cf. vv.19–20).

This tripartite structure revolves around the book's central section, vv.10–14, to which both vv.1–9 and vv.15–21 correspond closely in different ways: vv.1–9 substitute Esau for Jacob in a fate that is outwardly identical, and vv.15–21 completely reverse the roles pictured in vv.10–14. Thus, there are two distinct facets to the theology of judgment set forth in Obadiah: the aggressor will reap what he has sown (vv.1–14; cf. vv.15–16), and the innocent victim will be exalted over his aggressors (vv.10–12).

No theory of justice can be complete without this two-edge principle, which ensures both punishment and restoration (cf. Ro 13:3–4). Verses 10–14 thus state the evidence from which the sentences are derived in vv.1–9, 15–21. Their centrality is stressed conspicuously by the absence of any reference to the Lord. The adjacent sections are framed and punctuated symmetrically by the sovereign decree of the Lord (vv.1, 4, 8, and vv.15, 18, 21); but the events of vv.10–14 find no origin or ratification in his will. In this context the destruction of Jerusalem is not envisaged as a visitation from God, and Edom cannot claim exoneration as an instrument of such judgment (cf. Isa 10:5–15; Jer 49:12; Zec 1:15).

The question of cultic prophecy has been introduced above; here we note that, in contrast to the typical preexilic prophecy against the nations, vv.2–9, vv.10–14, and the beginning of vv.15–21 are addressed directly to Edom in the second person (singular and plural alternate). If the purpose of earlier oracles was the comfort and encouragement of Israel, these direct-speech oracles, though like older forms undoubtedly used with an Israelite audience, call for a different setting and appear to confirm the argument for a

---

11. See, e.g, Jeffrey Niehaus, "Obadiah," in *The Minor Prophets*, ed T. E. McComiskey (Grand Rapids: Baker, 1993), 496–502; the full range of possibilities is explored in the comments on v.14; cf. Paul R. Raabe, *Obadiah: A New Translation with Introduction and Commentary* (AB; New York: Doubleday, 1997), 47–56.

12. John R. Bartlett, "Edom and the Fall of Jerusalem, 587 BC," *PEQ* 114 (January-June 1982): 21.

13. See, e.g., Ehud Ben Zvi, *A Historical-Critical Study of the Book of Obadiah* (BZAW; Berlin: de Gruyter, 1996).

liturgical or cultic *Sitz in Leben*.[14] Whether, as in Jonah's mission to Nineveh, any attempt was made to take the message to Edom itself must remain a matter of speculation.

6. GEOGRAPHY

The land of Edom lay adjacent to Judah, on its southeastern boundaries (Nu 34:3; Jos 15:1, 21; cf. Jos 11:17; 12:7; 15:10). It extended for about a hundred miles southward, from the Dead Sea to Elath on the Gulf of Aqaba (Nu 21:4). It was bounded by desert to the east and by the Arabah to the west; to the north the Zered Valley at the southern end of the Dead Sea formed a natural boundary with Moab (Nu 21:12; Dt 2:12–13). The main center of Edomite population comprised an area extending some seventy miles south from the Zered River, a narrow strip of mountainous country averaging no more than fifteen miles across, in which were located the main Edomite cities, such as Bozrah (cf. vv.3, 9).

The regions to the south and particularly those west of the Arabah were controlled loosely by Edom in periods of national strength (cf. Nu 20:14).[15] Edom was known as the land of Seir, Seir having been the ancestor of the Horites, who occupied Edom before being displaced and assimilated by the Edomites (cf. Ge 32:3; 36:20–30; Dt 2:4–5, 8, 12, 22, 29.

The name "Edom" (*pᵉdôm*) is associated with the adjective "red" (*ʾādōm*), being derived from the color of the pottage Esau sold his birthright for (Ge 25:30). The same color characterized Esau himself at birth (25:25); it is also evident in the varied hues of Edom's sandstone cliffs.

7. SPECIAL PROBLEMS

A striking similarity exists between Obadiah and one or more of Jeremiah's oracles against Edom in ch. 49. Specifically, Obadiah 1b–5 and Jeremiah 49:9, 14–16 exhibit such clear parallels that we are forced to conclude either a dependence of one on the other or a mutual dependence on a common source. Since the prophetic activity of Jeremiah is unambiguously datable to the late seventh and early sixth centuries BC (prior to or immediately following the fall of Jerusalem), and since we have placed Obadiah sometime after that destruction, it should follow that Obadiah drew from Jeremiah.

Many scholars contend, however, that textual comparisons argue not for simple copying (the common materials contain identical phraseology as well as less-exact parallels) but instead for a common source. For this reason it is often claimed that Jeremiah's material was secondary,[16] though that conclusion hardly seems necessary. Admittedly, the question is a complicated one. Differences will be treated in the body of the commentary, but in general one may concur with Watts, who quoted with approval T. H. Robinson's 1916 judgment that "the material is more original in Obadiah, but better preserved in Jeremiah."[17]

In addition to the obvious parallel in Jeremiah 49, interpreters have long wrestled with the specific role of Edom in OT prophecy. Raabe has examined the key passages (Isa 21:11–12; 34; 63:1–6; Jer 9:25–26 [24–25]; 25:21; 27; 49:7–22; Eze 25:12–14; 32:29; 35–36; Joel 3:19 [4:19]; Am 1; 9:12; Mal 1; and we

---

14. See Wolff, "Obadja: ein Kultprophet als interpret."
15. See *IDB* 2:24ff.
16. See the useful summary in Allen, *The Books of Joel, Obadiah, Jonah, and Micah*, 131–32.
17. John D. W. Watts, *Obadiah: A Critical Exegetical Commentary* (Grand Rapids: Eerdmans, 1969), 33.

might add Da 11:4) and concludes that Edom sometimes stands as a cypher or symbol of evil in all the nations around Israel, while on other occasions Edom is specifically singled out for condemnation (or continued existence, usually under Israel's aegis) because of a particular historical, literary, or geographical association.[18] If we are correct in identifying Obadiah's provenance with Edomite perfidy in connection with the destruction of Jerusalem in 586 BC, this provides both a specific historical rationale for Edom's prominent place in later prophetic utterances and may also point to one reason why, in some instances,[19] Edom is chosen as the exemplar of Israel's enemies as a whole.

However, as Raabe and others agree, Edom is more often seen as a specific nation with a special relationship to Israel and a unique prophetic history. The prophetic attitude toward Edom seems shaped by Edom's close geographical and historical associations during Israel's time in the land. Never far from the surface (e.g. Jer 49; Am 1; Mal 1), and dominant in Obadiah, are the ancient identification of Edom with Esau and the resulting expected fraternal relationship with Jacob, a relationship especially poignant in the breach. This may explain not only the unique condemnation of Edom but also the prominence given to its restoration as part of a renewed Israel (see esp. Am 9:12; Ob 19–21).

8. THEOLOGY

Obadiah has attracted more than its share of detractors, often connected to the claim that its theology is sub-Christian. Yahweh is seen as vindictive, and the feelings encouraged among his followers fall far short of Jesus' Sermon on the Mount. Happily, more recent commentators have seen Obadiah in its ancient prophetic context, with the resulting conclusion that the book stands squarely within the tradition of Israelite prophecy. Let me illustrate.

Prominence must be given to the question of Yahweh's wrath. Obadiah is no different from his colleagues in concluding that Israel's God is far from indifferent to good and evil and that there are consequences for choosing either. Edom, on the day when Jerusalem fell to its enemies, chose to ignore its obligations of brotherhood, stood idly by, and even profited from Israel's trouble. No tradition of Israelite prophecy would expect this inaction to go unpunished. What is unique in Israel's prophets is that Yahweh, their God, is equally sensitive to the misdeeds of his own people; truly "judgment begins at the house of God."

Second, Obadiah illustrates the working of retribution. The *lex talionis*, or law of retribution, informs the entire prophecy, as illustrated in vv.15–16. At one level this is nothing more than the wisdom principle, affirmed by Jesus, that if we judge others, we ourselves will be judged, or if we live by violence, we will die in the same way. But there is more: Yahweh has not simply set in motion natural principles of retribution but is also personally committed to equity in human affairs and personally ensures that judgment comes. In Edom's case, the perfidy is exacerbated by the special responsibilities of a covenant of brotherhood. What might be reprehensible in any setting is doubly condemned when brother rises against brother. Again, the question is whether we would prefer a God who is indifferent to good and evil or one whose standards of fairness cannot be compromised.

---

18. Raabe, *Obadiah*, 33–47.
19. Raabe (ibid., 45) suggests Isaiah 34; 63; Ezekiel 35–36; Amos 9; Obadiah.

Finally, Obadiah stands within orthodox prophetic circles by his confident assertion that evil is not the end of the matter, either for Israel or Edom. Mount Zion has been destroyed, but it will be delivered; Israel has lost its divine inheritance, but it will again take possession. Even Edom's mountains will be justly governed "in that day." From other prophetic Scriptures we can safely conclude that whatever remnant of Edom may survive the intense fire of judgment will share the glories of that final day when "the kingdom will be the LORD's" (v.21). Zion theology becomes universal theology, and Yahweh's dominion is eternal.

9. BIBLIOGRAPHY

Allen, Leslie C. *The Books of Joel, Obadiah, Jonah and Micah*. New International Commentary on the Old Testament. Grand Rapids: Eerdmans, 1976.

Baly, Denis. *The Geography of the Bible*. New York: Harper & Row, 1974.

Raabe, Paul R. *Obadiah: A New Translation with Introduction and Commentary*. Anchor Bible. New York: Doubleday, 1997.

Watts, John D. W. *Obadiah: A Critical Exegetical Commentary*. Grand Rapids: Eerdmans, 1969.

10. OUTLINE

Text and Exposition

I. THE MESSAGE FROM THE LORD (1)

OVERVIEW

Verse 1 summarizes the intent of vv.1–9 by announcing the Lord's decree against "Edom," which is to be overthrown in "battle" by the "nations." This is reiterated and amplified in vv.2–9: the Lord decrees (vv.4, 8) that "Edom/Esau" (vv.6, 8–9) will be humbled, plundered, and devastated in battle (vv.2–9) by the nations (v.7; cf. v.2). Verses 2–9 are divided into three interdependent sections (vv.2–4,

5–7, 8–9) by the repeated phrase "declares the LORD" (*neum yhwh*; vv.4, 8). Each section describes the abasement of Esau and the deception that precipitates his downfall. As in the prophecy as a whole, there is no reference to the Lord in the central section (cf. vv.5–7 and 11–14), which describes the human agencies of treachery and greed by which this abasement is accomplished.

---

¹The vision of Obadiah.

This is what the Sovereign LORD says about Edom—

We have heard a message from the LORD:
   An envoy was sent to the nations to say,
"Rise, and let us go against her for battle"—

COMMENTARY

1 Obadiah's prophecy opens with the formal announcement of a message from the Lord "about" or "against" (*le*; cf. Ps 137:7) Edom, a pattern repeated in the following lines. Although the verse constitutes an unusual opening to a prophecy, through the sudden change of speaker, the passage is unified by the parallelism noted above. Watts, 44, and others (e.g., H. W. Wolff, "Obadja: ein Kultprophet als interpret" *EvT* 37 [1977]: 273–84) deal with the apparent change of speaker by making the messenger formula, "Thus says …," an introduction to the direct address in v.2, though the same mixing of elements in Jeremiah 49:12–14 leads to caution about easy emendation.

"Edom" represents an alternative name for "Esau," the brother of Jacob (Ge 36:1, 8, 43; cf. Ob 6, 8–9, 18–19, 21). It also denotes the descendants of Esau (Ge 36:9, 16–17; cf. 36:31, 43), whose blood relationship with Israel is invoked repeatedly in the OT (Nu 20:14; Dt 23:7; Am 1:11; Mal 1:2; cf. Ob 10, 12); and it describes the land inhabited by them (Nu 20:23; 21:4; 34:3; cf. Ob 18–21).

The "message" (*šemûʿâ*; GK 9019; cf. Isa 28:9, 19; 53:1) is evidently a supernatural revelation, being "from the LORD," as in the preceding line—a conclusion corroborated by the prophecy's description as a "vision" (*ḥāzôn*; cf. Hab 1:1; 2:2–3). Such revelation was mediated primarily through the prophets, and the plural "we" (cf. Jer 49:14—"I" in an otherwise identical expression) might indicate a prophetic group; by extension it certainly includes the believing community to which the revelation is to be mediated. Suggestions of Obadiah's use in a liturgical context provide another possible context.

The intent of this message is encapsulated in the following lines, which define the measures initiated by the Lord against Edom. An "envoy" (*ṣîr*) is normally a human ambassador, "sent" (*šālaḥ*) to represent the authority of those he served. Verse 1 even more than its parallel in Jeremiah 49:14 points to an envoy who represents one of the combatants ("let us").

The dual thrust of v.1 indicates two levels at which human history moves. The Lord is the ultimate mover, but there is also an international political alliance motivated only by callous self-seeking (cf. vv.5–7). Even nations raised up by such base motives serve the overriding purposes of a God who sovereignly shapes human affairs through countless envoys of his own (cf. Ps 104:4). The "nations" are deaf to this realm, in which they serve unconsciously (cf. Isa 45:4–7); but it is the privilege and responsibility of Israel to walk in the knowledge of what it hears from the courts of the Great King.

II. THE ABASEMENT OF EDOM (2–9)

A. Edom's Character (2–4)

1. Edom's Future Smallness (2)

> 2 "See, I will make you small among the nations;
>   you will be utterly despised.

COMMENTARY

2 Verse 2 introduces the central motif of vv.2–9, anticipating Edom's abasement. This is stressed by the introductory exclamation "See" and by the parallel adjectives "small" and "despised," which both stand emphatically at the beginning of their clauses in the MT. The second adjective defines the first: Edom's smallness is qualitative, corresponding to its despicable and debased character.

2. Edom's Present Pride (3–4)

> 3 The pride of your heart has deceived you,
>   you who live in the clefts of the rocks
>   and make your home on the heights,
> you who say to yourself,
>   'Who can bring me down to the ground?'

⁴"Though you soar like the eagle
    and make your nest among the stars,
    from there I will bring you down,"

                 declares the LORD.

COMMENTARY

3–4 These verses reiterate the sentence of abasement in the final, climactic line ("I will bring you down"), analyzing its causes in terms of pride and deception, the concomitant of pride. "Pride" (*zādôn*; GK 2295; cf. *zēd*, "proud") is derived from a verb meaning "to boil up, seethe" (*zîd*; cf. Ge 25:29; Ps 124:5). A cognate noun denotes food that has been boiled (*nāzîd*); the root occurs three times in the account of Esau's squandered birthright. In its literal usage, the root thus describes food or water that boils up under pressure, from which the figurative application of inflated self-exaltation logically follows. The essence of this "pride" is insubordination, rooted in an inordinate self-estimation: the proud man rejects authority, whether from God or humans, and arrogates it to himself. Pride seems to have arisen naturally among both the Moabites (see Jer 48:29; Isa 16:6) and Edomites.

Edom's pride is grounded in its geographical location "on the heights," from which it draws its sense of security and self-sufficiency; it can flaunt external control, having the physical resources to evade it. Indeed, Edom's natural defenses were imposing. Its main centers of civilization were situated in a narrow ridge of mountainous land southeast of the Dead Sea (cf. v.1). This ridge exceeded a height of 4,000 feet throughout its northern sector, and it rose in places to 5,700 feet in the south. Its height was rendered more inaccessible by the gorges radiating from it toward the Arabah on the west and the desert eastward. Baly, 235, describes travel along this ridge, the route of the ancient King's Highway:

"The road, of course, keeps to the more level ridge land, but from time to time it approaches the rim and the traveler peers dizzily down into a bizarre world of dark, gigantic cliffs and deep, terrifying gorges. Here is a region altogether apart, forbidding, and inaccessible, the home still of the leopard and such other animals as man in his ferocity has not yet succeeded in destroying" (cf. Nu 20:17).

The frontiers of this lofty plateau were formed on the west by the Arabah, to which the land dropped over 4,000 within the space of a few miles. The northern border was similarly defended by the deep canyon of the Wadi Zered, and to the south the precipitous walls of the Wadi Hismeh mark the abrupt descent of the tableland to the desert. In addition to these natural fortifications, Edom was strongly defended by a series of Iron Age fortresses, particularly on the eastern frontier, where the land descended more gradually to the desert.

Such was Edom's refuge "in the clefts of the rocks" (*beḥagwê-selaʿ*, cf. SS 2:14; Jer 49:16), whose austere environment might well foster thoughts of invulnerability. The term "rocks" (*selaʿ*) is used of large rock strata, and here it describes the sandstone and granite cliffs from which Edom drew its security. "Sela" is also the name of an Edomite settlement captured by Amaziah (ca. 800–783; 2Ki 14:7). It is commonly associated with the subsequent Nabataean capital, Petra, whose name also signifies "rock" (cf. LXX of Ob 3; Mt 16:18), an identification now disputed on the basis of excavations at the site (*IDBSup*, 800). It is in any case preferable to follow the NIV of v.3 in omitting the geographical allusion from the text.

Edom's sense of security has "deceived" it (*nāšā*; GK 5958; cf. Jer 49:16). Although virtually impregnable to human forces, Edom is still utterly vulnerable before the wisdom and power of God. Edom's deceived pride has been expressed in the confident question, "Who can bring me down?" It is echoed in the unanticipated answer; "I will bring you down" (both from *yārad*)—a blunt reminder to all the proud of the earth and a word that indeed embodies the heart of the prophecy. All that follows develops and amplifies the reversal of conditions heralded in this message from the Lord (cf. Jer 49:21).

B. Edom's Calamity (5–9)

1. Edom's Ransacking (5–6)

⁵ "If thieves came to you,
    if robbers in the night—
Oh, what a disaster awaits you—
    would they not steal only as much as they wanted?
If grape pickers came to you,
    would they not leave a few grapes?
⁶ But how Esau will be ransacked,
    his hidden treasures pillaged!

COMMENTARY

5–6 Verse 5 picks up and repeats the Hebrew clause of v.4 (*ʾim …ʾim*, lit., "If … if "; cf. NIV's "Though … and") and its consequence (*hᵃlôʾ*, "would they not") contrasted abruptly with the impending fate of Esau (*ʾêk*, "Oh, what"). The same pattern is repeated in a slightly revised order (cf. Note) in the following lines of vv.5–6: conditional clause (*ʾim*, "If"), consequence (*hᵃlôʾ*, "would they not"), contrast (*ʾêk*, "But how"). The first contrast ("Oh, what …") is thus an integral part of the two verses; its insertion between the condition and its apodosis effectively communicates the intent of the analogy and the urgency that motivates it. The structural features that unify these verses also integrate them into the adjacent sections: v.4 is similarly constructed as a double conditional sentence (*ʾim …ʾim*, "though … and"); and v.8 opens with the words "will I not" (*hᵃlôʾ*), echoing both the consequences of vv.5–6 and the initial rhetorical question of v.3 that it counters.

As "thieves" plunder a household, so "grape pickers" strip a vineyard. Yet in both cases they "leave" at least a pittance that escapes detection and despoliation. By contrast Esau will be "ransacked" with a terrible thoroughness that leaves nothing (cf. vv.8–9; Jer 49:9–10). This will be the work not of thieves who come furtively and in haste "in the night," nor of vintagers who are restricted by law or by the urgency of their own greed from removing all the grapes (cf. Lev 19:9–10; Dt 24:19–21; Isa 17:6; Jer 6:9); instead, it will represent the Lord's own judgment, from which nothing can remain "hidden." The repeated exclamation "what … how" (*ʾêk*) is characteristic of mourning in the presence of death, and it anticipates Edom's decease. Whereas the Lord consistently promised to "leave" a remnant for Jacob, no such promise is extended to Edom (but cf. Am 9:12).

NOTE

5 Most commentators maintain that a transposition of lines has occurred here. For example, Allen would move אֵיךְ נִדְמֵיתָה (ʾêk nidmêtâ, "what a disaster awaits you") to follow דַּיָּם (dayyām, "only as much as they wanted"), thereby creating structure parallel to v.5b. Watts takes his cue from Jeremiah 49:9 and reverses the order of lines 1 and 2. However, the present order, as followed in the NIV and NASB, makes reasonable sense and is retained here.

2. Edom's Entrapment (7)

> [7] All your allies will force you to the border;
>   your friends will deceive and overpower you;
>   those who eat your bread will set a trap for you,
>   but you will not detect it.

COMMENTARY

7 The second line of this verse is relatively clear-cut in its meaning, and it forms a basis from which the adjacent lines may be understood (RSV and NRSV transpose lines 1 and 2). It threatens Edom with deception by its "friends"; the noun "friends" translates a phrase implying not merely coexistence but communal commitment (lit., "the men of your peace" [ʾanšê šᵉlōmekā]; so Ps 41:9[10]; Jer 20:10; 38:22). This deception is the expression of calculated hostility, as indicated by the verb "overpower" (yākōl lᵉ). The keynote of the line is the verb "deceived" (hiššîʾûkā, from nāšāʾ [GK 5958]); it epitomizes the treachery evoked by its juxtaposition to the subject, "friends," and it gains emphasis from v.3, where it is foreshadowed by almost the same form (hiššîʾekā). Thus, Edom's self-deception is now accompanied by deception from allies, belying its vaunted claim to independence.

The first line is clearly parallel to the second. The noun "friends" is echoed by "allies," in which the existence of covenantal loyalty is explicitly presupposed (ʾanšê bᵉrîtekā; lit., "the men of your covenant"). It follows that the verbs are parallel also. When followed by a personal object, the form "force" or "send away" (šillaḥ) is almost always used of authoritative dismissal away from the subject's point of reference (NRSV's "driven" captures the sense). The "border" will therefore be viewed from the perspective of anonymous "allies" and will represent their own national boundaries to whose limits (ʿad) the Edomites are expelled (but cf. Jer 49:19–20). Moreover, Edom is pictured as being rejected and betrayed by those allies when seeking help or refuge with them. Edom's fate in vv.1–9 is proportioned exactly to that of Judah in vv.10–14 (see Overview to v.1); it is therefore appropriate that Edom should be denied help and refuge as it had done to its brother Jacob's "survivors" (vv.10, 12, 14).

The third line is obscure in Hebrew, but this obscurity is mitigated by its parallelism with the preceding couplet (cf. Note).

NOTE

7 Line three is rendered obscure by its opening word לַחְמְךָ (*laḥmᵉkā*, "your bread"), translated in the NIV as "those who eat your bread," and by the noun מָזוֹר (*māzôr*, "a trap"), which does not occur elsewhere in the OT with this meaning. As it stands the singular noun "your bread" represents a second object to the plural verb יָשִׂימוּ (*yāśîmû*, "they will set, place"), thus suggesting the meaning "they will make your bread a trap." It yields good sense if "your bread" is interpreted as a synecdoche (i.e., a part for the whole): they make the friendship, expressed and ratified when they ate your bread, a trap (since their commitment was illusory). A similar meaning is suggested by the structure of the verse:

B	A
כֹּל אַנְשֵׁי בְרִיתֶךָ	עַד־הַגְּבוּל שִׁלְּחוּךָ
אַנְשֵׁי שְׁלֹמֶךָ	הִשִּׁיאוּךָ יָכְלוּ לְךָ
יָשִׂימוּ מָזוֹר תַּחְתֶּיךָ	לַחְמְךָ
kōl ʾanšê bᵉrîteka	*ʿad-haggᵉbûl šillᵉḥûka*
ʾanšê šᵉlōmeka	*hiššîʾûka yākᵉlû lᵉka*
yāśîmû māzôr taḥteyka	*laḥmᵉka*

This verse may be translated literally:

"To the borders they will force you" (A)—"all the men in covenant with you" (B).

"They will deceive you and overpower you" (A)—"the men at peace with you" (B).

"[The men of] your bread" (B)—"they will make a trap under you" (A).

The predicate (A) and subject (B) of the first line both end with the second masculine singular pronominal form ךָ (*kā*, "you"). The predicate (A) and subject (B) of the second line also end with this suffix; this correspondence between the two lines is strengthened by the repeated noun אַנְשֵׁי (*ʾanšê*, "men") and by the shared theme of commitment-treachery. The third line is similarly divided into two sections by the same suffix. The second section forms an unambiguous predicate (A), which further corresponds to its predecessors in reiterating the motif of treachery (see further below). It follows that the initial word לַחְמְךָ (*laḥmᵉka*, "your bread") corresponds to the preceding subjects. This parallelism is corroborated by the consonance of "bread" with the covenantal associations of the preceding subjects, and particularly by its correlation with the phrase אִישׁ שְׁלוֹמִי (*ʾîš šᵉlômî*, lit., "the man at peace with me"; "my close friend," NIV) in Psalm 41:9[10].

In view of these correspondences, *laḥmᵉkā* will function as subject (B) of the following clause: like the preceding forms with which it rhymes, it will be a genitive dependent on the noun *ʾanšê*, repeated in the first two lines and implied in the third by the plural verb. Although this is an unusual example of incomplete parallelism, it is well established by its context. A similar understanding is shown by the LXX, Symmachus, the Vulgate, and the Targums, which appear to read it as a participial form: לֹחֲמֶיךָ (lōḥªmêkā, "those who eat [with] you"). In view of the conspicuous parallelism established by the pronominal suffixes, laḥmºkā should therefore be regarded as an elliptical subject rather than as a second object. This yields a chiastic pattern that defines a self-contained unit of thought (ABABBA); it is summarized in the fourth line, which forms a transition to v.8: תְּבוּנָה (tºbûnâ, "detect," v.7; "understanding," v.8).

The noun מָזוֹר (māzôr, "trap") has the meaning "sore, wound" in Jeremiah 30:13 and Hosea 5:13. This translation is appropriate to the overall context of unexpected aggression, but not to the following prepositional form תַּחְתֶּיךָ (taḥteykā, lit., "under you"; "for you" [NIV], but cf. Jer 49:17). It may also be derived from the root מזר (mzr), meaning "to twist, weave, cover with a web" in postbiblical Hebrew (M. Jastrow, *A Dictionary of the Targumim, the Talmud Babli and Yerushalmi, and the Midrashic Literature* [London: Pardes, 1950], 756) and "to stretch out" in a cognate root in Syriac (*HALOT*, 510; cf. also Arabic and Old Babylonian). As such it would denote a "trap," "snare," or "net" spread out stealthily by a hunter, and therefore a recurrent symbol of deception. A similar interpretation is evidenced in the early versions (LXX, Syr., Vul. ["ambush"]; Targ. ["stumbling block"]; Theod. ["bond, fetter"]).

3. God's Initiative (8–9)

8 "In that day," declares the Lord,
"will I not destroy the wise men of Edom,
men of understanding in the mountains of Esau?
9 Your warriors, O Teman, will be terrified,
and everyone in Esau's mountains
will be cut down in the slaughter.

COMMENTARY

8–9 "Declares the Lord" marks the opening of a new section (vv.8–9) as it closes vv.2–4, thereby reverting to the perspective of God's initiative in the impending destruction of Edom. The oracle signaled by this formula commences with the words "in that day." The expression, familiar in the prophetic literature, frequently looks forward to a specific time appointed by God in his sovereignty when he will intervene in human history in judgment and salvation.

The parallel lines of v.8 are dominated by the references to Edom's noted "wise men" and their "understanding" (NIV's "men of understanding" interpolates from the previous line), both of which the Lord will destroy. Verse 8 thus echoes the intent of v.7, to which it is related explicitly by the noun "understanding" (tºbûnâ; so "detect," v.7). Verse 8 emphasizes the failure of Edom's traditional wisdom (cf. 1Ki 4:30; Job 1:1; 2:11; 4:1; Jer 49:7; La 4:21; Bar 3:22–23), thereby amplifying further the theme of deception. Ultimately, Edom will be deceived because the Lord gives it up to deception, and v.8 anticipates the violent slaughter that will accompany this failure.

Verses 8–9 are further related by their geographical references. The phrase "mountains of Esau" (har ʿēśāw; v.8; so vv.9, 19, 21; cf. Eze 35:2) constitutes a further correspondence to vv.2–4, where Edom's mountainous terrain is first described (cf. v.3).

The term "Teman" is generally taken to describe a region in the northern sector of Edom,

though it is identified by some scholars as a city on the site of modern Tawilan, near Petra (cf. Hab 3:3; Allen, 153; Baly, 235). In the present context the term clearly speaks of the population of "Edom" as a whole, with which it is correlated in vv.8–9.

As noted in v.7, no certainty exists regarding the historical outcome of this prophecy concerning Edom's demise at the hands of the "nations" (cf. "Background" in the introduction).

III. THE CHARGE AGAINST EDOM (10-14)

OVERVIEW

Verse 10 forms a brief statement of the charges against Edom, as v.1 summarizes the sentence developed in vv.2–9. This charge is defined as one of "violence" against "your brother Jacob" (cf. Joel 3:19); it is reiterated in detail in vv.11–14, where Edom is accused of participating in the "destruction" of "your brother" (v.12).

A. The Reason for the Charge (10)

¹⁰Because of the violence against your brother Jacob,
    you will be covered with shame;
    you will be destroyed forever.

COMMENTARY

10 The noun "violence" (ḥāmās; GK 2805) denotes both moral wrong and overt physical brutality (cf. Hab 1:2), both of which had characterized the course of Edom's relations with Israel. The OT traces this pattern to the very origins of the two nations, in the hatred of Esau for his brother Jacob (Ge 27:40–41). This hatred emerged again in

Edom's hostility to Israel after the exodus (Ex 15:15; Nu 20:14–21; Dt 2:4; Jdg 11:17–18), and Edom is numbered among Israel's "enemies ... who had plundered them" before they were defeated by Saul (1Sa 14:47–48). It is against this background of aggression that David's later campaigns are also to be understood (2Sa 8:13–14; 1Ki 11:15–16; 1Ch 18:11–13;

Ps 60). All this culminated in Edom's exultation over the destruction of Jerusalem (Ps 137:7; La 4:21–22; Eze 25:12; 35:5, 15; 36:5; Joel 3:19).

Verse 10 also summarizes the content of vv.2–9, resuming the key concepts with which that section opens and ends; it thus forms a pivotal verse within the prophecy in its terse juxtaposition of crime ("violence") and corresponding punishment ("destroyed"). It defines the principle of retaliation by which the judgments in both vv.1–9 and vv.15–21 are balanced against the wrong in vv.10–14 (cf. Overview to v.1).

B. The Explanation of the Charge (11–14)

OVERVIEW

Like vv.2–9, this passage consists of two sections—a precise definition of the charge (v.11; cf. v.2) and the reiteration and amplification of its main details in vv.12–14 (cf. vv.3–9). It is framed by the word "day," with which it opens and closes and which reverberates with tragic insistence throughout vv.12–14. Edom's action (vv.12–14) is precisely equated with that of the invading foreigners (v.11) and is therefore liable to the same judgment.

1. The Charge Defined (11)

11 On the day you stood aloof
    while strangers carried off his wealth
and foreigners entered his gates
    and cast lots for Jerusalem,
    you were like one of them.

COMMENTARY

11 The equating of Edom with the "foreigners" is intimated in the first two lines, which are structurally parallel. In the Hebrew text, both open with the phrase "on that day" ($b^e y \hat{o}m \dots b^e y \hat{o}m$; "On the day … while," NIV; cf. NASB, NRSV), which is followed in each case by an infinitive, a subject, and an adverbial qualification. The equation becomes explicit in the final line ("you were like one of them"). Edom has no easy excuse ("We were only bystanders!"); to fail to act, or to approve an evil act (Ro 1:32), is morally equivalent to perpetrating the crime itself.

The correlation of these subjects in the opening lines involves a definite contrast, based on the word "aloof." It is derived from a substantive used as an adverb or preposition with the meaning "in front of, opposite to, in the sight of" (*neged*); such usage normally implies the juxtaposition of one entity to another. In the specific prepositional phrase represented here (*minneged*; lit., *min-neged*, "from in front of"), this idea of juxtaposition signifies a definite detachment in virtually all of its occurrences, as suggested by the preposition "from" (Ge 21:16; 2Ki

2:7, 15; et al.). The intent of this phrase is therefore well represented by the NIV's "aloof" (so RSV, NASB; NRSV reads "stood aside"), which thereby differentiates sharply between the actual conduct of Edom and that of the rapacious "strangers"; the latter actually "entered" Jerusalem and cast "lots" for its conquered property and probably for its citizens (cf. Joel 3:3; Na 3:10).

It should be noted that most commentators perceive a progression in v.11 from detachment (line 1) to active involvement on the side of the enemy (line 5). The main weakness of such an interpretation is its failure to give sufficient weight to the opening contrast in v.11: Edom is specifically dissociated from the factual account of invasion and looting, which are then attributed to it in v.13 only in terms of prohibitions that do not necessarily purport to describe actual events (cf. v.13). However, the same point emerges with compelling clarity from both interpretations of v.11; in the sight of God, who looks not on the outward appearance but on the heart (1Sa 16:7), there is little distinction in moral accountability between overt sin and an inner bias toward sin that permits it to go unchecked (cf. Mt 5:21–32).

2. The Charge Repeated and Amplified (12–14)

OVERVIEW

This passage is united by a remarkable series of eight negatives (ʾal, "You should not ... nor ..."; see Note), corresponding to eight descriptions of a "day" of Judah's calamity (yôm; the NIV omits the first reference, before "your brother"; v.12; cf. RSV). It consists of two distinct subsections, v.12 and vv.13–14. Verse 12 is unified by its three clauses describing Edom's malicious exultation. Its opening and closing words recur near the beginning and end of vv.13–14 (ʾal-tēreʾ, "do not look [down]"; vv.12–13; bᵉyôm ṣārâ, "in the day of their trouble"; vv.12, 14), thereby framing the two sections and defining their limits. Both v.13 and v.14, in turn, form individual units within vv.13–14; v.13 is unified by the refrain "in the day of their disaster" (bᵉyôm ʾedām/ʾêdô; v.13 [3x]); the couplet in v.14 describes Edom's treatment of Judah's "fugitives/survivors."

These repetitions suggest that v.12 is the focal verse, being amplified in vv.13–14. Its emphasis on Edom's cruel role as a spectator lies at the heart of v.13 ("look down"); and it is repeated in the verb "wait" of v.14, which corresponds to the indictment in v.11 that Edom "stood" aloof. As in v.11, therefore, the main emphasis of these verses is on Edom's hostile attitudes rather than on its physical violence at Jerusalem.

> ¹²You should not look down on your brother
>   in the day of his misfortune,
>   nor rejoice over the people of Judah
>   in the day of their destruction,
>   nor boast so much
>   in the day of their trouble.

> ¹³ You should not march through the gates of my people
> in the day of their disaster,
> nor look down on them in their calamity
> in the day of their disaster,
> nor seize their wealth
> in the day of their disaster.
> ¹⁴ You should not wait at the crossroads
> to cut down their fugitives,
> nor hand over their survivors
> in the day of their trouble.

COMMENTARY

12 The initial Hebrew verb is the common root *rʾh*, meaning to "look on" or "see." Its connotations are varied, and either the sense of contempt ("look down on," NIV) or exultation ("gloat," NRSV) is drawn from the context and parallel verbs. The following verbs betray the perverted and reprehensible values of this typical enemy of Israel (e.g., "rejoice," *śāmaḥ*; "boast," lit., "enlarge your mouth"), for whom covenantal loyalty to a brother meant nothing.

13 Verse 13 echoes the description of the "foreigners" in v.11 by attributing their conduct directly to Edom (see below). However, v.11 has identified Edom with the foreigners in intent but not explicitly in action; and it is at the level of intent that Edom is accused of active participation in the sacking of Jerusalem. Even in these verses any inferences about Edom's conduct must be qualified both by the jussive forms of prohibition and by the preceding narrative on which they are based; while moving closer to participant status, Edom's historical role was still primarily an attitudinal one ("look down").

14 The distinction between action and intent is virtually obliterated in v.14, since the verb "wait" echoes the one action predicated clearly of Edom in v.11—"stood" (*ʿāmad*). This verse describes Edom's treatment of Judah's "survivors." It thereby corrobo-

rates the impression of detachment from the main scene of action, since the "fugitives" would be fleeing from the city. However, it also qualifies this detachment sharply, for it is shown to be accompanied by outright aggression, whose venom is in keeping with Edom's gloating over its fallen adversary.

The verb "cut down" (*kārat*) echoes its usage in vv.9–10 ("cut down, destroyed"): Edom's fate is in no way arbitrary but corresponds to the measure it has itself used (cf. Lk 6:37–38). The word "destruction" (*ʾābad*; v.12; so "destroy" in v.8) implies a similar application of the *lex talionis*, which is defined clearly in vv.15–16.

The central concern of these verses is with the "day" that befell the people of Judah. This is portrayed as a major tragedy by the foreboding epithets that are applied to it and repeated with the crushing weight of a death knell (cf. Zep 1:14–16). The nouns "distress" (*ṣārâ*; vv.12, 14) and "destruction" (*ʾābad*; v.12) both point to a national catastrophe of major proportion. It remains to ask whether this catastrophe can be identified with a specific historical occasion. That occasion will be characterized by the invasion of Jerusalem, wholesale plundering of its property, and probably enslavement of its people; by widespread slaughter both within Jerusalem and in the outlying regions; and by the participation of Edom in this disaster as a mocking bystander and as a collaborator with the foreign invaders, so betraying an existing bond of loyalty with Judah. Six periods in the history of Jerusalem and Judah present themselves for consideration, of which the last corresponds to these criteria most closely.

(1) Jerusalem surrendered to Shishak in the fifth year of Rehoboam (931–913 BC) after her fortified cities had fallen to the Egyptian ruler with his allied foreign troops. He then exacted heavy tribute, and his conquest was attributed to the Lord's judgment (1Ki 14:25–28; 2Ch 12:2–10). Moreover, Edom is identified explicitly as an adversary in this era after its incomplete suppression by David; and Edom's hereditary ruler is represented as a protégé of Egypt in the time of Solomon (cf. 1Ki 11:14–22). However, Rehoboam's submission to Shishak averted the enslavement, devastation, and flight described by Obadiah; this incident, therefore, does not provide a suitable background for Obadiah's prophecy.

(2) The next-recorded invasion of Jerusalem occurred in the reign of Jehoram (853–841 BC), when a coalition of Arabs and Philistines invaded Judah and carried off both the property and family of the king, which would have been located in Jerusalem (2Ch 21:16–17; 22:1). This occurred at a time of sharp conflict with Edom (2Ki 8:20–22; 2Ch 21:8–10; cf. 20:1–2; 22:23); however, this judgment was aimed specifically at the king, who experienced the main impact of the invasion (2Ch 21:14, 17). It is also unlikely that help would be anticipated from Edom in view of its aggression against Jehoshaphat, culminating in open rebellion during Jehoram's own reign.

(3) A third invasion of Judah is implied during the reign of Joash (835–796 BC). The Syrians caused widespread destruction among Judah's leaders, taking considerable spoil and defeating a large Judean army as a consequence of the Lord's

judgment on the king (2Ch 24:23–24). Edom's continued hostility is evidenced in the following reign of Amaziah, whose drastic measures against the Edomites may be associated with his reprisals for the murder of his father, Joash (2Ki 14:5–7; 2Ch 25:1–12). The account's reconstruction, however, is largely inferential, particularly with regard to Edom's role; in addition, it is unlikely that the Syrians' small expeditionary force would have crushed Jerusalem so completely as intimated by Obadiah (cf. 2Ch 24:24).

(4) Jerusalem was clearly captured in the time of Amaziah (796–767 BC), with seizure of its treasure and hostages at a period of open conflict with Edom (2Ki 14:7–14). This incident is scarcely consistent with Obadiah's prophecy, however, since the invaders were not foreigners but Israelites.

(5) The eighth century provides further evidence of Edomite aggression at a time when Judah was increasingly threatened by foreign powers, most notably during the reign of Ahaz (735–715 BC). As a consequence of his faithlessness to the Lord, this king suffered the catastrophic depredations of Syria, Israel, the Philistines, Assyria, and Edom itself (2Ch 28:17): Judah and Jerusalem became "an object of dread and horror and scorn," experiencing widespread bloodshed and captivity (2Ch 29:8–9; cf. 2Ki 16:1–20). The city was similarly threatened by Assyria in the following reign of Hezekiah (ca. 701 BC; 2Ki 18–19; 2Ch 32). It was in this century, moreover, that the first clear notes of judgment and conquest were sounded against Edom by Israel's prophets (Isa 11:14; 21:11; 34:5–15; 63:1–6; Am 1:6, 9, 11; cf. Nu 24:18; Joel 3:19). However, no record exists of Jerusalem's actually being captured. Again, therefore, no conclusive association can be made between Obadiah and this era.

(6) The final invasion of Jerusalem during Edom's existence as an independent nation took place when the city fell to the Babylonians in 586

BC, following Jehoiachin's previous capitulation to Nebuchadnezzar in 597. On both occasions the city suffered seizure of its "wealth" and wholesale deportation of its population (2Ki 24:13–16; 25:4–17; 2Ch 36:18, 20). In 586 the city, including the temple, was virtually burned to the ground (2Ki 25:9–10; 2Ch 36:19), and many of its inhabitants were massacred (2Ki 25:8–21; 2Ch 36:17; cf. Jer 6:1–9:22; Eze 4:1–7:27). There is specific reference to unsuccessful "fugitives" in the account of the king's escape with his retinue (2Ki 25:4–5).

Of particular significance are the accounts of Edom's conduct at this time. There is evidence for its participation as an ally in a coalition of Palestinian states against Nebuchadnezzar (Jer 27:3; 40:11); yet it was later accused of taking vengeance on Judah (Eze 25:12) and of delivering the Israelites "over to the sword at the time of their calamity, the time their punishment reached its climax" (Eze 35:5–6; cf. La 1:17). Edom was equally guilty at this time of rejoicing in Jerusalem's destruction (Ps 137:7; La 2:15–17; 4:21; Eze 35:11–15; 36:2–6); and it is therefore at this time that the prophetic announcements of Edom's annihilation reached a climax (Jer 9:26; 25:21; La 4:21–22; Eze 25:13; 32:29; 35:3–4; 7–9, 11, 14–15; 36:7). Specific correlations include numerous points of contact in Jeremiah 49:7–22 and in Ezekiel 35–36.

The balance of evidence, therefore, suggests that Obadiah is looking back to the fall of Jerusalem in 586 BC, in which Edom is clearly implicated. This conclusion falls short of proven certainty. In particular, it assumes that the position of Obadiah and Joel among the Minor Prophets is not of chronological significance; and it does not necessarily account for Obadiah's relationship to Jeremiah 49 (though Jer 49:14–22, dated ca. 600 BC, would clearly corroborate this argument), Ezekiel 35, and Joel. In the absence of other, compelling evidence against this interpretation, however, it provides a satisfactory context for Obadiah unmatched by any other period of Judah's political and religious history.

NOTE

12–14 The actual form of the eight parallel verbs ([w^e]$^\jmath al$ plus an imperfect) naturally favors translating them as prohibitions of a specific nature ("Do not gloat …"). Some (e.g., John R. Bartlett, "Edom and the Fall of Jerusalem, 587 BC," *PEQ* 114 [January-June 1982]: 21) have proposed that in place of an "eyewitness" account of Edom's role in the destruction of Jerusalem, these "prohibitions" represent the prophetic imagination—and an imagined charge to Edom. Most scholars, though recognizing the grammatical difficulty, allow the syntax of the passage to determine a meaning something like that reflected in the NIV ("you should not …") or NRSV ("you should not have …").

IV. THE DAY OF THE LORD (15–21)

OVERVIEW

The concluding oracular formula in v.18 ("The Lord has spoken") divides this passage into two main sections: vv.15–18 and vv.19–21. The first section (vv.15–18) is framed by its references to the Lord as the initiator of word and event ("day of the Lord … The Lord has spoken"). The sequence of themes follows the now-familiar reversal of roles—with destruction and deliverance, survivors and no survivors, possessors and dispossessed, and Joseph-Jacob and Esau juxtaposed in a stark antithesis.

This sequence is repeated in vv.19–21, amplifying the central concept of "possession" (*yāraš*; so "occupy, possess," or "dispossess"; cf. vv.19–20).

As in v.18, "Esau" is singled out from among the nations as the object of conquest, the passage being framed by the phrase "mountains of Esau" (vv.19, 21); this phrase is also contrasted with the role of "Mount" Zion, as the "house" of Jacob is opposed to the "house" of Esau in v.18. The prophecy concludes with the ringing affirmation: "The kingdom will be the LORD's" (v.21).

A. The Judgment of Esau (15–18)

> [15] "The day of the LORD is near
>   for all nations.
> As you have done, it will be done to you;
>   your deeds will return upon your own head.
> [16] Just as you drank on my holy hill,
>   so all the nations will drink continually;
> they will drink and drink
>   and be as if they had never been.
> [17] But on Mount Zion will be deliverance;
>   it will be holy,
> and the house of Jacob
>   will possess its inheritance.
> [18] The house of Jacob will be a fire
>   and the house of Joseph a flame;
> the house of Esau will be stubble,
>   and they will set it on fire and consume it.
> There will be no survivors
>   from the house of Esau."
>   The LORD has spoken.

COMMENTARY

15–16 These verses are both introduced by the conjunction "for" (*kî*; cf. NRSV, RSV), and they are parallel in structure. They exhibit a complex, alternating, thematic arrangement that is typical of Obadiah's style and that revolves around the central concept of retaliation that shapes this prophecy as it

does the entire OT view of moral order in a world ruled by God's justice.

"The day of the LORD" is a theme of great significance in Israel's eschatology (cf. *ZPEB*, 2:46–47), and it gives final definition to the preceding references to a "day" in Obadiah: Edom's and Judah's downfall both constitute elements in the pattern of this "great and dreadful day of the LORD" (Joel 2:31). It signals the climactic establishment of God's rule in human history and, as such, brings judgment on all those enemies who oppose his dominion. Such a judgment engulfed apostate and rebellious Israel, most notably in the fall of Samaria and of Jerusalem—so confounding the popular theology of the eighth and seventh centuries—and descended subsequently on "the Gentiles," those foreign nations not bowing to God's sovereignty.

This "day," then, with its eschatological overtones, defines the destiny of Edom and the nations in both vv.1−9 and vv.15−21. After the nations have had their "day" on the Lord's holy mountain, his "day" will come in power and great glory, with none to oppose its thrust. This "day" is, in the first instance, promised in terms that admit a preliminary fulfillment within history for the faithful remnant of Israel, and it is from this hope of restoration and blessing for a "holy" people that Obadiah derives his promise of "deliverance" and conquest for the "house of Jacob" (vv.17−21). Above all it is purged and restored Israel, whether in historical or eschatological terms, that serves as the instrument by which the Lord introduces and establishes his reign.

The opening line of v.15, therefore, constitutes the core of Obadiah's prophecy. It provides a theological framework for the preceding verses, in that the localized disasters befalling Edom and Jerusalem are not merely isolated incidents in a remote and insignificant theater of war, for they mark the footsteps of the Lord himself as he approaches to set up a "kingdom that will never be destroyed" (Da 2:44). The following verses are essentially a commentary on the implications of that impending "day."

Verse 15 accordingly sets forth its guiding principle of retaliation: "As you have done, it will be done to you." The actions perpetrated by the nation addressed will correspond precisely to those perpetrated on her, as indicated by the repetition of the same verb (ʿāśâ, "done") with different subjects; the final line reiterates the consequences of this law, thus emphasizing the certainty of its application.

Verse 16 demonstrates the same equivalence of past and future action ("drank," "drink," both from šātâ); Edom "drank" (i.e., executed judgment) on Judah's mountain; in the future the nations (cf. vv.1−2) "will drink and drink" on the mountains of Edom. The certainty of this equivalence is again emphasized by repetition of the consequences in the final lines. Drinking as judgment is a metaphorical parallel to the more literal "doing of deeds" repeated in both clauses of v.15. Now, however, with the coming of the day of the Lord, Judah's suffering is about to end; by contrast, Edom's is still, at the time of writing, future. God's messenger has summoned "the nations" (vv.1−2); they have been called to battle, and it is only a matter of time before they drink at Edom's wells.

Edom's transition from being the active agent of judgment to becoming the passive recipient is made more vivid by the use of second person verbs and pronominal forms. In v.15, and generally throughout, the second person forms are singular. Edom/Esau is the brother of Jacob (vv.10, 12); in Obadiah, more often than not the collective "Edom" is replaced by the singular "Esau." It is, at the end as at the beginning, a matter of faithfulness to the covenant of brotherhood.

The metaphor of drinking is commonly used of the experience of judgment and humiliation (cf. Hab 2:15−16). It recurs in the parallel passage of Jeremiah, which again alludes to Judah as the prior victim of such judgment (Jer 49:12−13; cf. 25:17−18, 28−29). Drinking may also be a sign of carousing and debauchery (e.g., Ex 32:6; 1Sa 30:16), and some commentators (e.g., Watts) attribute this meaning to the first reference in v.16. By an ironic twist, those who "drank" in celebration of their conquest over

God's "holy hill" will subsequently "drink" a very different cup. These implications are somewhat muted by the structural relations of vv.15—16 (cf. above).

17—18 The scene changes. God's "holy hill" (v.16) has been desecrated; now its true character is again manifested. "Mount Zion," the place of God's rule in Jerusalem, is rendered "holy" by his presence, localized in the temple (e.g., Pss 5:7; 11:4; 74:2; Joel 3:17, 21); and it demands of its inhabitants a corresponding holiness. The holiness of Yahweh, dwelling on Zion, stands as a guarantee of justice to God's people, but equally of judgment on all the nations that live in violence and pride. Powerful metaphors describe the divine holiness on Zion: at one moment God is a fire and Zion the furnace of the Lord (Isa 31:9); at another he is a roaring lion, consuming all before him (Joel 3:16; Am 1:2—2:16). But Zion is also a place of deliverance for those who seek refuge in the God of Zion (Pss 20:2; 53:6), with "salvation" equally a part of the biblical Zion traditions. Obadiah's announcement of salvation in v.17 belongs to this tradition.

The root underlying "deliverance" (*plṭ*; GK 7117 [vb.]; 7119 [noun]) implies escape from danger and widespread destruction, being used, for instance, of fugitives from military disasters (e.g., Ge 14:13; Jdg 12:4—5; Ob 14). It is applied most consistently to God's gracious preservation and purification of a remnant in Israel, particularly after the fall of Jerusalem (cf. Ezr 9:8—13; Isa 4:2; 10:20; 37:31—32; Jer 50:28; 51:50; Eze 6:8—9; 7:16; 14:22; 24:26—27; 33:21—22). The promise given here is repeated in similar terms in Joel 2:32, and both verses correspond closely to Isaiah 4:2—3; 37:31—32.

The final line expresses the outworking of this restoration. The verb "possess" (*yāraš*) and its cognate noun "possessions" are associated preeminently with Israel's conquest of the Promised Land, to which they are applied over one hundred times (e.g., Ex 6:8; Dt 3:8; 4:1, 22; cf. *TWOT*, 1:420ff.).

Israel succeeded in this conquest because it obeyed the Lord, who entered the battle on behalf of his people and dispossessed the enemy before them. When obedience turns to disobedience, Israel's "possession" of its enemies is reversed; now the enemies "possess" Israel and her land. The prophets, however, hold out to the nation the hope of repossessing the land on the basis of a return to Yahweh in repentance and obedience, the same condition of an obedient and militant faith (e.g., Isa 54:3; 57:13; 60:21; 61:7; Eze 36:12; Am 9:12; cf. Gal 3:29; 1Pe 1:4); and it is to this hope that Obadiah, together with the other prophets, appeals.

In keeping with the military associations of v.17, the "house of Jacob" (v.18) is to annihilate the "house of Esau," as the Israelites were to wipe out the Canaanites, whom they displaced. The destructiveness of "fire" consuming "stubble" forms a repeated image of the relentless judgment predicted here (e.g., Ex 15:7; Isa 10:17; Joel 2:5; Mal 4:1). This prophecy will revive an earlier subjugation of Edom under Saul, David, and their successors, a yoke Edom later threw off. Edom's final submission is, therefore, still anticipated by the prophets, in accordance with the oracle pronounced by Balaam (Nu 24:18; Isa 11:14; Eze 25:13—14; Am 9:12); as in Isaiah 11:13—14, it will be accomplished by a reunited Israel, intimated by the parallel terms "Jacob" and "Joseph" (cf. Pss 77:15; 80:1; 81:4—5; Jer 3:18). Unlike the house of Jacob, the house of Esau can expect no "deliverance," no remnant; as the Edomites had thought to plunder and possess the land of Israel, cutting off its "survivors," so it will happen to them.

A progression in the judgment of Edom is marked by v.18. The Lord had enlisted the heathen nations to eradicate Edom from its homeland in "the mountains of Esau" (cf. vv.8—9); now, however, his own people are to cooperate with him in destroying the "house of Esau" altogether. Historical events support this progression. Edom was displaced from its country east of the Arabah in the sixth and fifth centuries, in a period of Judah's weakness; this was therefore executed by foreigners, culminating in Nabataean possession of that territory. In the same period the surviving Edomites were settling west of the Arabah, in the Negev—a process reflected in the charges of Ezekiel (Eze 35:10, 12; 36:2, 5).

Thus the postexilic region of Judah extended no farther south than Beth-zur, north of Hebron. Hebron itself and the neighboring towns were all occupied by Edomite populations (cf. 1 Esd 4:50; 1 Macc 4:61; 5:65; *Jub* 38:8–9; Josephus, *Ant.* 13.257–58 [9.1], 13.395–96 [15.4]; *J.W.* 1. 62–63 [2.6]). By the end of the fourth century their territory had acquired the Hellenistic name for Edom: Idumaea (i.e., Edom-aea). However, the fortunes of Judah were revived under the Maccabees, or Hasmoneans (ca. 168–63 BC; *ZPEB*, 4:2–8), and this era saw a resurgence of Jewish aspirations to possess its former lands.

The Idumaeans were defeated in 166 BC by Judas Maccabaeus (d. 160 BC), who recovered the cities of southern Palestine ceded to them (cf. 1 Macc 5:3, 65). Under John Hyrcanus (135–104 BC) this conquest of the Idumaeans was completed (ca. 125 BC), and they were compelled to submit to circumcision and full observance of the Jewish law. They continued to haunt the Jews, however, for the family of Herod the Great was of Idumaean descent; but after the second century AD they had virtually been consumed by the house of Jacob, to which they lost their national identity and autonomy.

B. The Occupation of Edom (19–21)

> [19] People from the Negev will occupy
>   the mountains of Esau,
> and people from the foothills will possess
>   the land of the Philistines.
> They will occupy the fields of Ephraim and Samaria,
>   and Benjamin will possess Gilead.
> [20] This company of Israelite exiles who are in Canaan
>   will possess the land as far as Zarephath;
> the exiles from Jerusalem who are in Sepharad
>   will possess the towns of the Negev.
> [21] Deliverers will go up on Mount Zion
>   to govern the mountains of Esau.
> And the kingdom will be the LORD's.

COMMENTARY

19–20 Verses 19–20 form a distinct section after the concluding oracular formula in v.18, being unified by the keyword "possess, occupy" (*yāraš*; vv.19 [2x], 20; cf. v.17). These verses are written in an elliptical style, containing considerable difficulties in syntax and vocabulary; however, the MT is clearly reflected in the early versions (Targum, LXX, Symmachus, Theodotian, Aquinas, Vulgate), and the NIV's adherence to it is therefore to be followed. In particular, both occurrences of the verb "possess" in v.19 and the first in v.20 are absent from the MT; but they are clearly implied by the structure of the adjacent clauses and by the centrality of that verb in vv.17–20.

Not only the term "possess," but also the ethnic and geographical references resonate with the recollection of Israel's conquest of Canaan (cf. below). These references are virtually all specified or implied in the commission given to Israel in Deuteronomy 1:7. The "Negev" was not always to be the home of the Edomites, dispossessed as they were from their own "portion," the "mountains of Esau" (cf. Dt 2:4–5); rather, the reverse will be true. The "foothills" (*šᵉpēlâ*; lit., "Shephelah"), the low-lying region separating the Judean hills from Philistia, will extend itself westward. Even the northern territories of Ephraim and Samaria, lost to Assyria during the preexilic period, will again be part of Israel. Benjamin, the small tribe virtually absorbed by Judah in historic times, will move east and north into Transjordan and possess the lush highlands of Gilead, while exiles in Canaan (v.20; or "who are Canaanites"; note the antiquated name with its exodus and conquest overtones) and from Jerusalem will expand north to the Lebanese coast at Zarephath and south to the Negev.

"Sepharad" (v.20) is not definitely identified but may refer to Sardis in distant Lydia (near modern Izmir, Turkey); if so, it reflects an early colony of Jewish exiles (*ZPEB*, 5:342) who, with more local refugees, are expected to inherit portions of the Holy Land. (Medieval Jewry mistakenly identified Sepharad as Spain; cf. ibid.) In short, the land seen by Obadiah as promised to a reunited Israel in "the day of the LORD" is the land originally given to the twelve tribes. It was the inalienable bequest

of the Lord to Abraham and his descendants (Ge 13:14–17;26:2–5;28:13–15), and neither Edomite treachery nor Assyrian-Babylonian dispersion can keep God's promises from their fulfillment.

Reference to "exiles" (*gālût*) in v.20 further corroborates the historical background discussed earlier (see comments on v.14). The term is applied predominantly to the deported population of Judah after 586 BC (e.g., 2Ki 25:27; Isa 45:13; et al.). Such an application is clearly appropriate to the qualification "from Jerusalem"; no other major deportation from that city is known, and that background is most suitable to the events described in vv.10–14. The "Israelite exiles" will therefore be the survivors from the northern kingdom of Israel, from which they were deported after the fall of Samaria (cf. 2Ki 17:6, 18, 20, 23; 18:11). On this evidence, not only Israel but also Judah had been destroyed as an independent nation, and Obadiah's prophecy is proclaimed with heroic faith to "the poorest people of the land" (2Ki 24:14; 25:12, 22–24; Jer 40–44) during an era of destitution and weakness in the exilic or postexilic period.

21 Verse 21 corresponds to vv.19–20, which it summarizes with special reference to Edom, the three verses being framed by the phrase "mountains of Esau" (vv.19, 21). It reiterates the theme of conquest, expressed in the verb "govern" or "judge" (*šāpaṭ*). The noun "deliverers" (from *yāšaʿ*, GK 3828) has similar connotations of military victory (cf. Hab 1:2; 3:13, 18); significantly, the name "Joshua" (*yᵉhôšûaʿ*) is derived from the same root (*yšʿ*), as is that of Jesus, whose conquest procured a better inheritance "that can never perish, spoil or fade" (1Pe 1:4).

As in vv.19–20, this conquest finds its source in Judah and specifically in its capital, "Mount Zion." The ultimate goal of the conquest had been to unite Israel with centralized worship in the temple (Dt 12:1–28) and centralized rule in a dynastic monarchy (Dt 17:14–20; 2Sa 7). These were not to have autonomous functions, for they were the visible institutions of the theocracy through which the Lord himself was to rule as "king over Jeshurun" (Dt 33:5). Obadiah's vision of Mount Zion restored to its destined leadership of nations is grounded in these promises. It presupposes the existence of a nation obedient to its theocratic calling, which will "serve him without fear, in holiness and righteousness before him" (Lk 1:74–75; cf. v.17). And it finds its consummation in the true realization of that theocracy.

The Lord is indeed Israel's "king from of old" (Ps 74:12). He is in reality "the living God, the eternal King" (Jer 10:10), "the great King over all the earth" (Ps 47:2, cf. 47:7). But the day is coming when that kingdom will be acknowledged universally, when every knee will bow. It will be said to Zion, "The LORD, the King of Israel, is with you" (Zep 3:15; cf. Isa 24:23; 33:20–22; 40:9–10; 62:3; Mic 4:7–8; Zec 9:9); and they will say among the nations, "The LORD reigns" (Ps 96:10). Edom will be set aside, with "every pretension that sets itself up against the knowledge of God" (2Co 10:5); "and the kingdom will be the LORD's" (Ob 21; cf. 1Co 15:24–28; Rev 11:15; 12:10; 22:1–5).

JONAH

JOHN H. WALTON

Introduction

Much of the book of Jonah is subject to controversy, but a few facts may stand uncontested. Outside the book, Jonah is referred to only once in the OT (2Ki 14:25). This reference connects him with the reign of Jeroboam II, king of Israel, who reigned from 793–753 BC, thus placing Jonah in the generation after Elisha and immediately prior to the beginning of the great era of prophecy that began with Amos, Hosea, and Isaiah.

1. HISTORICAL BACKGROUND

Prophets and Eighth Century Israel

Prior to the time of Jonah there lived those familiar prophets such as Elijah and Elisha, and earlier still, Nathan and Samuel. Immediately subsequent to the time of Jonah, we enter the period of "classical prophecy" (identified with the writing prophets, beginning with Hosea and Amos in the middle of the eighth century BC). Several distinctions can be made between classical and preclassical prophecy. Most important is that the preclassical prophets addressed their messages to the king, while classical prophets addressed the people as well as the king.[1] Jonah's role in the book of Kings identifies him as fitting the preclassical mold.

The reign of Jeroboam II achieved unparalleled prosperity for the northern kingdom of Israel. Assyria was in a stage of weakness and was preoccupied with internal security, and Egypt continued in decline. Jeroboam was therefore free to expand his borders, with the Arameans as the only hindrance. This background is important because it shows that Israel at this time was near the top, not the bottom, in the realm of international politics. The book of Jonah, however, speaks little of Israel, for Jonah's mission was to Nineveh.

---

1. For discussion, see J. Holladay, "Assyrian Statecraft and the Prophets of Israel," *HTR* 63 (1970): 29–51.

Assyria in the Eighth Century

A century earlier, the Assyrian Empire under Shalmaneser III had extended its control into the west and gained authority over Syria, Israel, Judah, and many others areas. The end of Shalmaneser's reign, however, saw revolt by several Assyrian centers, including Nineveh. His son, Shamshi-Adad V, managed to subdue the rebellion, but during his reign control over the west weakened considerably.

Shamshi-Adad V died about 811 BC and left as heir to the throne his young son, Adad-Nirari III. Until the boy came of age the country was ruled by Shamshi-Adad's widow, Sammuramat, who seems to have retained extensive control until her death. Adad-Nirari reigned from his city of residence and capital, Kalhu, until 783 BC. He was succeeded by three sons—Shalmaneser IV, Assur-Dan III, and Assur-Nirari V—but their successive reigns marked a period of Assyrian weakness that could be characterized as practical anarchy. Particularly notable is the series of rebellions between 763 and 758 BC led by disaffected officials, who seem to have usurped royal prerogatives.[2] In such a political climate, a prophecy proclaiming the imminent fall of Nineveh would be taken quite seriously.

This trend was reversed in 745 BC with the accession of Tiglath-pileser III, who, though he claimed kinship to Adad-Nirari III, began a new dynasty that established Assyrian supremacy for a century. Tiglath-pileser was succeeded by Sargon II, Shalmaneser V, and finally Sennacherib, who was responsible for the enlargement of Nineveh. It was during his time that Nineveh became the capital of the Assyrian Empire.

2. Date

On the late end, the book of Jonah must have been written prior to the second century BC, since two apocryphal books from that time refer to the book of Jonah. Tobit 14:4 in some manuscripts mentions Jonah's exploits, while the Wisdom of Ben Sirach 49:10 speaks of "the twelve," showing that the canonical development of the twelve Minor Prophets had already been completed. On the early end, the book of Jonah cannot extend beyond the time in which the prophet lived, i.e., the first half of the eighth century BC.

Two major objections have been raised to dating the book near the beginning of this six-hundred-year range. First, it is claimed that the picture given of Nineveh in this book is legendary and unrealistic. Second, the account is considered to be replete with "Aramaisms" and examples of late biblical Hebrew. We will briefly explore these claims.

The Picture of Nineveh

There are two points in the claim that Jonah's description of Nineveh has become exaggerated with the passage of time. First, critics maintain that the size of the city is out of proportion ("a city of three-days'

---

2. P. Garelli, "The Achievement of Tiglath-pileser III: Novelty or Continuity," in *Ah Assyria … Studies in Assyrian History and Ancient Near Eastern Historiography Presented to Hayim Tadmor*, ed. M. Cogan and I. Eph'al (ScrHier 33; Jerusalem: Magnes, 1991), 47–51; A. K. Grayson, "The Struggle for Power in Assyria: Challenge to Absolute Monarchy in the Ninth and Eighth Centuries B.C.," in *Priests and Officials in the Ancient Near East*, ed. K. Watanabe (Heidelberg: Universitatsverlag C. Winter, 1999), 253–70.

journey," 3:3). Second, they point out that the use of the title "king of Nineveh" (3:6) shows authorial ignorance of the fact that neither biblical nor Assyrian sources ever refer to the king of Assyria as the king of Nineveh.

Size of the city. Two possible explanations can remove the impression of Jonah's exaggeration of the city's size. First, the use of the Hebrew word translated "journey" (3:3) indicates that it refers to the time the project will take rather than the size of the city (see comments on 3:3). Second, at this time Nineveh was the name of a province as well as a city, and the province could easily be what the author had in mind. D. J. Wiseman has suggested that the administrative district may have included Assur, Kalah, and Dur-Sharruken. The circuit of these cities would have comprised about fifty-five miles — a long three days of walking.[3] P. Ferguson makes the case that Assyrian scribes used the same determinative to designate the city as they did to designate the province, especially when the two shared the same name.[4] These points are treated in greater detail in the commentary.

"King of Nineveh." The most serious problem with the king of Assyria's being called the "king of Nineveh" is that during Jonah's time the king of Assyria did not reside in Nineveh. Though Nineveh may have been a large and important city, it was not a royal city. Jonah would not have encountered the king of Assyria on his throne in Nineveh, for the king of Assyria did not *have* a throne in Nineveh.

If the "king of Nineveh" is not the king of Assyria, however, this person could have been a governor or noble who was ruling the city/province. We noted above that during the lifetime of Jonah the Assyrian Empire was in a state of practical anarchy. The kings of Assyria during this period reigned through an oligarchy of four powerful officials.[5] The inscriptional evidence from various provincial governors during this time shows that the governors of the western provinces displayed a tendency toward independence during and after the reign of Adad-Nirari III. With Urartu growing strong, infiltrating contiguous countries, and disrupting Assyria's trade routes,[6] the king was sustaining military defeats and thus encouraged his governors to take political initiative. Adad-Nirari gave large tracts of land as well as privileges and prerogatives to various nobles.[7] Specifics regarding Nineveh are not clear since this period in Assyrian history is so poorly attested, but all of these factors would favor the possibility that administrative districts such as Nineveh could have operated somewhat independently.

Concerning terminology, the Hebrew word translated "king" in Jonah (*melek*), though used throughout the OT for kings, does not pose an insuperable problem if an Assyrian official is being described. The normal Akkadian (Assyrian) word for king is *šarru*, but the bilingual inscription from Tell Fekheriye translates the Akkadian *šaknu* ("governor") with the Aramaic *mlk*,[8] thus suggesting that West Semitic languages (Aramaic and Hebrew) sometimes used "king" to refer to local ruling governors or nobles. Furthermore,

---

3. D. J. Wiseman, "Jonah's Nineveh," *TynBul* 30 (1979): 38–39.
4. P. Ferguson, "Who Was the 'King of Nineveh' in Jonah 3:6?" *TynBul* 47 (1996): 301–14, esp. 305–7.
5. Grayson, "The Struggle for Power," 268.
6. S. Page, "The Stela of Adad-Nirari III and Nergal-Eres from Tell al-Rimah," *Iraq* 30 (1968): 151.
7. Ibid.
8. Y. Ikeda, "Looking from Til Barsip on the Euphrates: Assyria and the West in the Ninth and Eighth Centuries B.C.," in *Priests and Officials in the Ancient Near East*, ed. K. Watanabe (Heidelberg: Universitatsverlag C. Winter, 1999), 271–302, esp. 286; Ferguson, "Who Was the 'King of Nineveh' in Jonah 3:6?" 303.

the governor (*šaknu/mlk*) could have ruled over the city of Nineveh or the province of Nineveh. In fact, in the *limmu* list of Assyrian notables (which identifies each year by the name of an honored official), the designated official for the year 761 BC was Nabu-mukin-ahi, governor of the *region* of Nineveh.[9]

In summary, then, neither of the allegations charging that Jonah portrays a legendary or exaggerated picture of Nineveh can be maintained as a sound basis for objecting to an early dating of the book. The reference to a governor ("king") of the province of Nineveh would be appropriate to the historical period, and walking the province of Nineveh could easily have required three days.

Aramaisms

The term "Aramaism" refers to characteristically Aramaic elements (usually vocabulary) used in the Hebrew text after having been assimilated into Hebrew usage. Traditionally, these elements have been considered indications of a late text—a consideration reflecting the presupposition that the elements were assimilated because of the status of Aramaic as the lingua franca (standard international trade language) of the ancient Near East. Supposedly, Aramaic did not achieve that status until the later periods, well after the time of Jonah.

A more detailed discussion of this development cannot be conducted here, but let it suffice to say that the nature of linguistic evidence and the ever-expanding understanding of Northwest Semitic linguistic interchange warn against making conclusive chronological judgments based on that sort of evidence.[10] The incident in which the Rab-shakeh (an Assyrian officer) is urged to use Aramaic in conversing with the inhabitants of Jerusalem in 701 BC (2Ki 18:26) indicates that already at that time the use of Aramaic was dominant. There is, therefore, little basis for denying the possibility of Aramaic influence even in the time of Jonah, though it might be expected that there would be more Aramaic influence closer to the sixth and fifth centuries BC.

In addition to Aramaisms, the claim is made that the book also shows examples of late biblical Hebrew. Simon offers seven examples from vocabulary, three from grammar and syntax, four from idioms, and one from orthography.[11] These citations are worthy of discussion, but most of them can be considered arguable.[12] The book of Jonah has been associated with a largely unknown northern dialect of Hebrew that was under greater influence of Aramaic, a factor that could account for many of the uses observed by Simon.

While these objections, then, do not disprove a preexilic date for the book, neither does a refutation of them constitute proof *for* a preexilic date. It can be demonstrated that the book accurately preserves the tensions that existed in the eighth century BC and that its roots in historical time are not betrayed by its

---

9. The Akkadian text does not designate him by any official title, but the nature of the list of names around him and the nature of the other sections of the *limmu* list indicate that these are governors (cf. A. R. Millard, *The Eponyms of the Assyrian Empire, 910–612 BC* [SAAS II; Helsinki: Univ. of Helsinki Press 1994], 7–11).

10. For some additional discussion of the Aramaisms, see Leslie Allen, *The Books of Joel, Obadiah, Jonah and Micah* (Grand Rapids: Eerdmans, 1976), 187.

11. U. Simon, *Jonah* (Philadelphia: Jewish Publication Society, 1999), xxxix–xli.

12. Cf. G. Landes, "Linguistic Criteria and the Date of the Book of Jonah," *ErIsr* 16 (1982): 147–70.

linguistic features or by a fanciful or legendary portrayal of the background. These considerations leave open the entire range of possibilities indicated at the beginning of this section.

3. PURPOSE

According to my interpretation of Jonah, its purpose focuses on the issues inherent in classical prophecy. The book uses the example of Nineveh to educate both Israel and its prophets regarding what might be called the "ground rules" of this period (whether in its preexilic or postexilic segment). The classical prophets bore the task of warning Israel and Judah of coming judgment. Their warnings came in the form of prophetic pronouncement—usually deemed irrevocable. The book of Jonah tells them that repentance was a proper and acceptable response and could even counteract the prophetic pronouncement (cf. Eze 18:21). It had worked even for Nineveh, a naïve, wicked, pagan city.

When such warnings came to Israel (beginning just after the time of Jonah, according to 2 Kings 14:27), Nineveh's sparing served as the example that even though doom had been pronounced, repentance could bring mercy, and judgment could be postponed.[13] Aspects of this message include the concept that small steps in the right direction motivate (though they do not earn) God's compassion. After all, a smaller step than the one taken by the Ninevites could hardly be imagined, yet God's response was overwhelmingly merciful.

The identification of the above purpose does not imply that no other lessons are taught in the book. I do, however, reject the current interpretation that the book of Jonah was written to scold Jewish exclusivists in the postexilic period. Such a view assumes that Jonah was asked to preach repentance and does so. I find no evidence for such an assumption in the book.[14]

Likewise, it is unnecessary to explain Jonah's negative attitude as patriotism or concern for his prophetic reputation. The former position argues that Jonah would have been anxious for Assyrians to be destroyed on political grounds. At the time of Jonah, however, Assyria was not an oppressor of Israel. On the contrary, Assyria frequently tended to aid Israel indirectly by keeping the Aramaeans occupied. Concerning Jonah's prophetic reputation, he may have been concerned that something he had prophesied was not coming to pass, but it is difficult to derive from that concern a purpose for the book that is consistent with the object lesson of ch. 4. Jonah's reluctance to go will be addressed when we get to that chapter.

Jonah the Missionary?

Popular misconceptions about prophets sometimes lead people to think of them as missionaries. If the main objective of the prophets is understood in terms of leading people to repentance and delivering a message of hope, it would be easy to compare them to missionaries spreading the gospel message. Based on what we know about the prophets, however, this equation becomes problematic. Missionary functions fit into the prophetic categories of proclaiming instruction (repentance) and aftermath (hope).

---

13. See R. E. Clements, "The Purpose of the Book of Jonah," *Congress Volume: Edinburgh 1974* (VTSup 28; Leiden: Brill, 1975), 16–28.

14. For discussion of the weakness of this interpretation and others, see ibid.

These are the two least frequent types of oracles among the prophets, who, in contrast, often emphasize indictment and judgment. Moreover, it was not unusual for the prophets to omit instruction and/or hope altogether—something no missionary of the gospel would do.

The contrast becomes more striking when we consider specifically the example of Jonah who, oddly enough, is the one most frequently associated with missionary work. The differences are obvious:

- Jonah does not want to go—so intensely that he flees in the opposite direction.
- The only message Jonah preaches in the book is coming destruction—no call to repentance, no hope for deliverance, no instruction about God. In fact, God is not even mentioned in Jonah's proclamation.
- Jonah is disappointed and angry when the people of Nineveh respond favorably.

In short, Jonah does not have a missionary's attitude, a missionary's message, or a missionary's objective. It is not enough to say that he was delivering a message of God cross-culturally—so was Moses when he warned of the plagues. Likewise, it is not enough to classify Jonah as a missionary based on the result elicited by his message, i.e., the repentance of the Ninevites. That result was a panicked response to a threat, not an acknowledgment of the claims of God on their lives or an acceptance of Yahweh's lordship. The only "salvation" they experienced was that the destruction of their city was delayed. There was no blood of Christ to claim, and no indication is given that they intended to become people of the covenant, accept Yahweh as their God, and throw away their idols.

4. GENRE

Y. Sherwood has eloquently documented the history of interpretation of the book of Jonah as it provides, in her words, a "Cultural Hologram"[15] mirroring the angst of society throughout the ages. The discussion of the genre of the book in recent times has blended with the discussions of the book's purpose to take its place in this long history. Especially relevant is the ongoing debate concerning whether the book portrays historical events.

The evangelical *commitment* is to take the text at face value while resisting our culture's post-Enlightenment inclination toward skepticism. God must remain free to act in our world in improbable ways. The evangelical *task* is to assess accurately, with literary and theological sensitivity, what the face value of the text is, even if the result departs from traditional assessments. God must remain free to reveal himself by means of whatever genre he deems appropriate, and, when it comes to literary sophistication, an author must be given the benefit of the doubt. If the details of a book can be proven to be fanciful rather than factual, the reader is obliged to embrace some level of fictionality. Alternatively, however, even when details can be defended as authentic, as in the case of Jonah, one cannot necessarily label the work as journalistic history. Minimally, all that such authenticity proves is the quality of the author's sources or research, with the genre of the resulting work remaining to be determined. To put it succinctly, plausibility is not the same as historical authenticity. As J. Sasson observes, "plausibility and verisimilitude are also goals for imaginative

---

15. Y. Sherwood, *A Biblical Text and Its Afterlives: The Survival of Jonah in Western Culture* (Cambridge: Cambridge Univ. Press, 2000), 71.

writing, resulting in 'historical fiction' (in which historical personalities are placed within nonhistorical texts) or 'fictional history' (in which fictitious happenings are set within a historical event)."[16]

The problem is to discern what the author expects us to believe, on the one hand, and what he expects us to recognize as transparent literary devices, on the other. We should be willing to read through the eyes of faith, yet not be naïve readers, insensitive to the author's literary artistry and sophistication. The situation is worsened when potentially rhetorical devices involve the activity of deity. The reader must then decide whether the account features miraculous works or literary sophistication. The fact that most literary readings have been proposed by skeptical critics unwilling even to consider the miraculous has made it much more difficult for evangelicals to give such proposals a fair hearing. Both sides encounter the obstacles of being firmly entrenched in polemics and at times restricted by simplistic or modern categories of genre.

Adopting the worldview of faith that includes the possibility of miracles, our task becomes a literary one, for we must determine whether the author intended to claim that miracles *did* occur. The discussion is now no longer philosophical or theological, but literary. Granted that God can direct a large fish to swallow a man and drop him off three days later, we must ask whether the author is actually claiming that God *did* do that to Jonah, or whether he wants to make a point by creating a literary scenario that he never intended us to accept as a historical event. This question, then, is one of genre. Various genres for Jonah have been championed and critiqued through centuries of scholarly literature. The following selection is representative of some of the familiar categories proposed.

- *(Journalistic) history*: an account of events as they were experienced or witnessed
- *Epic*: a glamorized story recounting noteworthy events
- *Heroic/anti-heroic*: a story honoring or vilifying individual deeds
- *Satire*: a story ridiculing folly, vice, or incompetence
- *Legend*: a fanciful story about a historical character
- *Midrash*: an expansive, paradigmatic story
- *Parable*: a teaching story
- *Allegory*: a symbolic story
- *Parody*: a comical imitation of a serious work
- *Farce*: a story of comical exaggeration

To these, many other categories could be added.[17] But if we move beyond the categories, all pregnant with presuppositions, we could perhaps go back and start again from outside our conventional terms of classification. Z. Zevit has observed that we are still lacking and are woefully in need of a poetics of what he terms "truth-telling literature."[18] This epithet could be appropriately applied in some measure to the first half of the above list. Setting aside for the moment the man-swallowing fish and the subsequent vomiting

---

16. J. Sasson, *Jonah* (AB; New York: Doubleday, 1990), 327.
17. This list is rather random and the definitions always debatable. The intention here is simply to give a representative sampling.
18. Indicated in his *Religions of Ancient Israel* (New York: Continuum, 2001), 78–79, to which much of the following discussion is indebted.

onto the shore, we can explore some of the other issues in the book as a means of evaluating what form its truth-telling takes.

If we focus on three particular scenes—the sailors' vows, the prayer inside the fish, and the hilltop experience—it will be noticed that there are only three possible sources for the information:

(1) The Parties—the author interviewed the principal parties about their experiences (author as journalist)[19]

(2) Deity—the author was specifically informed by God in the process of inspiration (author as mystic)

(3) The Author—the inspired author had some license to be creative (author as artist and teacher)

Any of these options could result in truth-telling literature. Zevit has observed that biblical historiography employs devices used by some writers of fiction. He therefore concludes that a study is needed to compare poetic devices commonly used in narrative fiction and in truth-telling literature to develop a "scale of fictionality" in order to do sensitive genre analysis. He labels self-consciously truth-telling genres as "factographic." In such genres where the presentation is realistic and plausible with regard to the relationship between facts, the relationship between facts and background, and the relationship between facts, background, and the reader's perception of the world, he suggests that the major test applied to the literature should be deniability. "Whatever is not effectively denied or disproved is to be regarded as true."[20]

In Tennyson and Longfellow we see truth-telling emerging in poetic form as epic ("Charge of the Light Brigade") and heroic tale ("The Midnight Ride of Paul Revere"), respectively. These genres are far from journalism, but they intend to capture truth in ways that require poetry and its devices to achieve what journalism can never achieve. We would not be inclined to investigate the plausibility and historical reliability of each line in order to affirm the truthfulness of these literary works. We know better.

This perspective leads to a reevaluation of how skepticism may be wielded as a historical hermeneutic. In the early 1900s it was popular to interpret Jonah as an allegory. The word "Jonah" means "dove," and it was claimed that the dove was a symbol of Israel; therefore, Jonah was seen to represent Israel, while the fish supposedly represented Babylon, who "swallowed" Israel (in the captivity) as a punishment for her refusal to carry out her missionary mandate to the Gentile world (Nineveh). Some even went so far as to identify the vine of ch. 4 with Zerubbabel.

T. D. Alexander does a good job of demonstrating the weaknesses of categories such as allegory, midrash, and parable that have traditionally been popular among skeptical critics.[21] These genres are didactic but not truth-telling in the sense that they do not expect the reader to conclude that any of the events in the story actually took place in any form. Nevertheless, J. Sasson, a modern critic, adds his observations to substantiate the same general conclusion at which Alexander arrives.

---

19. Even if the author is Jonah (whose authorship the book does not suggest and which position would have many points against it), he would have to have found some of the sailors and have interviewed them to ascertain what happened after he was thrown in.

20. Zevit, *Religions of Ancient Israel*, 78.

21. T. Desmond Alexander, "Jonah and Genre," *TynBul* 36 (1985): 35–40.

If Jonah were a parable or a fable, I assume it would have duplicated the form of either composition: an anecdote followed by its own explanation. Although Jonah is beyond the size usual for a Hebrew parable or fable, the main obstacle in treating it as such is that its concluding verses (4:10–11) do not function as interpretive keys in the way that other conclusions to parables normally do; for nothing in these verses suggests that the narrator is shifting into another sphere of comprehension: the plant remains a plant in v 10 and the Ninevites remain Ninevites in v 11.[22]

In current trends within critical scholarship, genres such as parody[23] or satire[24] have become more popular. The former typically lampoons a piece of literature, while the latter targets people (specific or stereotyped categories) or events, as Jonah does. Satire can be either an enactment or a written composition in which vice, folly, or incompetence is held up for ridicule. The closer to reality a satire can be, the more effective it is. By definition it targets real people and tries to use the mannerisms and words that they use. Satire exaggerates reality but by its nature is based on reality.

Satire and parody are both known in the ancient world and the Bible. The examples of parody in the ancient Near East also target entities considered to be historical and from which historical information may be deduced.[25] In the realm of satire, the Babylonian Dialogue of Pessimism[26] targets a wide variety of cultural institutions. The biblical prophets at times satirize the people of their audience, as when Amos refers to the women of society as "cows of Bashan" (Am 4:1) and when Isaiah satirizes the manufacturers and worshipers of idols (Isa 44). In the NT, Jesus satirizes the scribes and Pharisees. Most interpreters would agree that in similar ways the book of Jonah wants us to laugh at the prophet's incongruity and senselessness[27] even as we are appalled by his behavior and attitude.

Simon offers numerous examples of the ironic humor in the book, though he considers the prophet to be serious about himself and therefore a pathetic figure.[28] As a result, he concludes that the book is not an ironic satire.[29] Yet Ackerman claims, "Only satire permits such a blend of wild improbabilities with ironic incongruities."[30] Clearly, even the literary critics read the indicators differently. I favor a position of compromise that would see the author as using satire to some extent without viewing the entire work as satirical.

---

22. Sasson, *Jonah*, 335–36.

23. J. A. Miles, "Laughing at the Bible: Jonah as Parody," *JQR* 65 (1975): 168–81; M. Orth, "Genre in Jonah: The Effects of Parody in the Book of Jonah," in *The Bible in the Light of Cuneiform Literature, Scripture in Context III*, ed. W. W. Hallo, B. W. Jones, and G. L. Mattingly (Lewiston, N.Y.: Mellen, 1990), 257–82.

24. J. Ackerman, "Satire and Symbolism in the Song of Jonah," in *Traditions in Transformation*, ed. B. Halpern and J. D. Levenson (Winona Lake, Ind.: Eisenbrauns, 1981), 213–46.

25. A. Livingstone, *Court Poetry and Literary Miscellanea* (SAA III; Helsinki: Univ. of Helsinki Press, 1989), 64–66; P. Michalowski, "Commemoration, Writing, and Genre in Ancient Mesopotamia," in *The Limits of Historiography*, ed. C. S. Kraus (Leiden: Brill, 1999), 84–86.

26. *COS*, 1.155: 495–96.

27. Note Hosea's indication that Ephraim is like a silly dove (cf. Jonah's name meaning "dove") in Hosea 7:11.

28. Simon, *Jonah*, xxi.

29. Ibid., xxii.

30. Ackerman, "Satire and Symbolism in the Song of Jonah," 227.

If this were so, what would be the intended object of the satire? Possibilities range from Jonah himself, to the prophetic institution that he serves, to the Israelite people of whom he is a part. Most people who consider the book of Jonah a satire would consider either Israelite attitudes or the prophetic office to be the reality that is satirized, but alternatively it would be possible that a real prophet and his mission were being satirized.[31] Though satire must be intentional, it need not be the main point. Satire may at times be the didactic objective, but it may also be a tool in the hands of the author as other points are made. I favor adopting a theological perspective in which the book could be seen to satirize the sort of theological distortion and narrowness that puts limits on God's freedom to respond compassionately to small steps in the right direction. Theological hubris and presumption become the objects of satire, and the prophet Jonah is their representative. The author's literary art recreates how this sort of theological creature might react and by what means God might use him despite himself—and maybe even bring him to his senses.

Satire operates in the matrix between realism and exaggeration. It depends on both and assumes that the audience may be able to recognize each extreme but at the same time be unable to find the line where one turns into the other. In other words, by its very nature satire intends to blur the lines between reality and hyperbole. Its artistic exaggeration is intended to use some truth to expose concealed truth. It is a truth-telling genre. "Overall satire is a subversive form that questions the status quo, unsettles people's thinking, assaults the deep structure of conventional thought patterns and aims to make people uncomfortable."[32]

Dante's *Inferno*, both poetic and didactic, is also widely recognized for its use of satire in the characterization of those he wants to expose as pathetic figures. He uses respected historical figures, even popes, identified transparently, and weaves them into his literary context to expose the truth of what they really are like and the truth about the institutions and systems they serve. This is truth-telling that moves beyond journalistic record to a certain style of characterization. Readers know that the characters Dante encounters are historical and are portrayed realistically. They also know that the inferno, though real, is here used as Dante's literary construct. The truth lies between the two poles as it is presented by the author and must be discerned by the reader. Confirming the truth of Dante's work would not entail exploring the authenticity of Dante's details of the inferno or what he portrays as taking place there. Truth-telling genres are not always to be confirmed through journalistic inquiry; but what genre indicators can we rely on to help us discern face-value truth?

Alexander explores what some people have considered to be genre indicators that betray the literary creativity of the author of Jonah. These indicators include historical improbability, the elements of exaggeration and surprise, dependence on other works, symmetrical structure, and the didactic nature of the book as a whole. Alexander finds each indicator insufficient to determine that Jonah should be moved toward the fictional end of the literary scale.[33] He argues that the historical setting, the opening of the book (which is similar to the openings of many prophetic books), and its traditional understanding all suggest that the genre indicators used by the author favor the position that at face value the book should be deemed didactic historical narrative.[34]

---

31. E. Dyck, "Jonah among the Prophets: A Study in Canonical Context," *JETS* 33 (1990): 63–73.
32. "Satire," *Dictionary of Biblical Imagery*, ed. Leland Ryken et al. (Downers Grove, Ill.: InterVarsity Press, 1998), 762.
33. Alexander, "Jonah and Genre," 44–55.
34. Ibid., 55–59.

It is important and true that what seems improbable to moderns may not have seemed at all so to ancients. Thus it is difficult for us to assess the face value of Jonah's text. Would the Israelites of OT times (or NT times, for that matter) have actually believed that Jonah spent three days and nights in the fish, or would they have viewed this information as artificial literary edifice? Alexander points out that the earliest known interpreters treated the story as factual, but those sources are already several centuries and cultures removed from the original context.

It may be more productive to probe the worldview of the ancient Near East. Did the Babylonians believe that Gilgamesh actually fought the Bull of Heaven—a divinely appointed creature sent as a response to the hubris of Gilgamesh and Enkidu? The fact that *we* might dismiss the Epic of Gilgamesh as mythological is irrelevant. It is likely that to the Babylonians the epic would have fallen into the category that Zevit called "factographic." They would not have doubted its reality, but neither would they go hunting for such a creature to display in their zoos.

So, back to Jonah—what would the observer have seen or the journalist recorded? These are the wrong questions to ask of a nonjournalistic account. But journalistic record is not the only form truth-telling can take. Could events really have happened the way the text presents them? Plausibly, but does the author want his readers to take the role of investigative reporters to determine the authenticity of the facts? Or does he want us as readers to accept the task of theological introspection by probing our attitudes and our perception of God in order to determine the truth? Probably the latter, but we cannot dodge the questions that tradition urges upon us. If, Dante-like, there is some combination of historical realia and literary creativity, where can/should we draw the line?

The unsatisfying answer is that the more refined the author's skill, the more doubtful is our ability to tell—and this author is very good. Our commitment remains unswerving in our acceptance of the face value of the text. Whatever must be believed to retain the authority of the text should be believed. To consider factual something that was intended to be fictional is not of greater merit than considering something fictional that was intended to be factual. Either fault entails a distortion of authoritative text. The book of Jonah should not be thought of as journalistic history, but it is a truth-telling genre; and it is likely that the Israelite audience would have considered the narrative a reflection of reality. I would therefore adopt the same position.

The above discussion has been based on the evidence available in the book itself. Many would claim that we also must be guided by the information afforded by the NT's references to the book of Jonah (Mt 12:39–41; 16:4; Lk 11:29–32). Do Jesus' references to the narrative of Jonah clarify how we should read it? The difficulty here is that Jesus gives an allegorical interpretation to Jonah's stay in the fish, yet few interpreters would claim that the author of Jonah intended his book to be an allegory of Jesus' death. This means that Jesus is exercising his freedom to reclassify the genre of the book in his use of it. The fact that Jesus uses it as an allegory does not demand that we understand the original intention of the author as allegorical, so that Jesus' use of Jonah cannot serve as a guide to determining its genre category.

5. NARRATIVE ART

Extensive analysis has been done on the narrative art of the book of Jonah and cannot be repeated here. There are varying proposals for the structure of the book that offer differing views regarding the number of sections and the relationship between them. Simon has summarized these proposals well in his commentary.[35] Despite differences of opinion regarding the book's structure, all are agreed on its extensive use of literary and rhetorical devices, such as inclusio, chiasm, concentric structures, key words, growing phrases, and wordplay.

6. JONAH AND THE BOOK OF THE TWELVE

Much recent discussion has addressed the role of Jonah among the Minor Prophets, canonically, the Book of the Twelve.[36] The order of these books is not entirely chronological, but the last seven (those after Jonah) do appear in chronological order. Assuming those last seven would not likely have been arranged by some other criteria that coincidentally ordered them chronologically, it is logical to view them as intentionally so ordered and turn our attention to the first five to investigate how they function in the collection. Jonah falls at the conclusion of this first sequence and may conceivably be seen as providing a transition between the two sections.

When we focus on the first four, Hosea and Amos are dated to the first half of the eighth century BC and addressed to northern kingdom of Israel, while Joel and Obadiah are typically dated to the postexilic period. If Jonah is the transition between the two halves and Hosea and Amos are to be classed together as the prototypical classical prophets, we might inquire as to whether Joel and Obadiah might be juxtaposed respectively to Hosea and Amos for a particular purpose.

I would therefore pose the question in the following terms: What common relationship could exist between Joel and Hosea on the one hand, and Obadiah and Amos on the other hand, that would find its synthesis in Jonah and introduce the chronological presentation of the remaining seven books? One obvious possibility would be "response and consequence." Without going into extensive detail, I propose the following perspective.

Hosea proclaims the impending judgment that grain, new wine, and oil will be taken away (Hos 2:9). Joel shows a repentant response to a prophet in whose time this same sort of threat is realized in a plague of locusts. As a result of the people's positive response, God restores those commodities (Joel 2:19). The juxtaposition of these two books shows the positive result of appropriate response by God's errant people. In contrast, Amos pronounces coming judgment on the nations. Edom is not only included in the initial list (Am 1:11–12), but is also targeted at the end (Am 9:12). It is logical, then, that Obadiah should follow Amos to illustrate the result of nonresponse found in the destruction of Edom. Thus, Joel and Obadiah serve as postexilic illustrations of the ongoing relevance of preexilic prophetic messages. In the process, they exemplify the deliverance that comes when people do respond and the judgment that comes when they do not.

With these two examples juxtaposed for the audience, the book of Jonah provides a synthesis. Nineveh, even the most pagan of cities showing the most uninformed response, experiences mercy at the hands of God. The appropriate response to the prophetic oracles of indictment and judgment is to begin taking steps in the right direction. As Jonah synthesizes the fruits of the juxtaposition of the two previous

---

35. Simon, *Jonah*, xxiii–xxxii.
36. See Ben Sira 49:10, second century BC.

pairings of books, it also provides a transition to the chronological sequence of prophetic collections. This sequence is concluded and synthesized by Malachi, which summarizes the call for response by its postexilic audience.

The role of the book of Jonah, then, is literally pivotal as it draws out the potential of repentant response to stimulate the divine compassion that postpones announced judgment. The chronological sequence of the next six books establishes this pattern in three segments. Micah shows the indictment and the positive results connected to the Assyrian crisis and the response represented in Hezekiah's reform. Nahum through Zephaniah evidence judgment against the empires (Nahum—Assyria; Habakkuk—Babylonia; Zephaniah—the whole earth) alongside the causes for hope by Judah represented in Zephaniah's relationship to Josiah's reform. Haggai and Zechariah show the response of building the temple and consequently offer their hope for the future. Malachi's summary, however, shows that the restoration has stalled and further response and purification are necessary. It also concludes with the rejoicing of those who fear the Lord (3:16–4:2) and the facing of the day of the Lord by those who reject him (4:3–6). Like Jonah, Malachi highlights the importance of response as the key to forgiveness.[37]

7. THE SIGN OF JONAH

Three passages comprise the references of Christ to the "sign of Jonah": Matthew 12:39–41; 16:4; and Luke 11:29–32. The context of the sayings is the request of the Pharisees for a "sign," presumably to authenticate Christ's message. In response to this request, the Pharisees are told they will get no sign but the sign of Jonah. In Matthew 12 Christ proceeds to make the analogy that as Jonah was three days in the belly of the great fish, so the Son of Man will be three days in the earth. In the ancient world it was believed that it took three days to travel to or from the netherworld—where Jonah was traveling from and to which Jesus is going. In both Matthew 12 and Luke 11, Christ comments that the Ninevites will stand up at the judgment and condemn the Pharisees for their unbelief.

Neither the analogy of Matthew 12 nor the future act of the Ninevites is positively identified as the "sign of Jonah" that was mentioned. Luke 11:30 gives the only positive clue: "For just as Jonah became a sign to the Ninevites, so shall the Son of Man be to this generation" (NASB). We must ask, then, how Jonah "became a sign to the Ninevites." While it is possible that Jonah's experience with the fish was used by him as a sign to the Ninevites, the text of Jonah makes no such connection. If this connection is not made in the text, we cannot expect that Jesus would assume that his questioners would know what he meant by the sign of Jonah. There is nothing in the rabbinic traditions to indicate an interpretation that Jonah used the incident with the fish to authenticate his message.

I believe it is best to understand the words for exactly what they say: Jonah himself becomes the sign. The Pharisees are asking for a sign so that they may have confirmation of the message Jesus is giving. The Ninevites would have sought in the omens similar confirmation of Jonah's message, or perhaps they would have found confirmation in the events that had been unfolding. In this case, Jonah would have become a sign to the Ninevites by the timing of his visit. Support can be found in Matthew 16:1–4, where the

---

37. I am grateful to Paul House for suggesting this summary role of Malachi in the second sequence and for input on this section as a whole.

mention of the sign of Jonah comes in the context of Jesus' criticism that the Pharisees can discern the signs of the weather but "cannot discern the signs of the times" (NASB). The time is ripe for the Messiah. Jesus' appearance and message give specificity to the signs of the times.

8. BIBLIOGRAPHY

Ackerman, James S. "Satire and Symbolism in the Song of Jonah." Pages 213–46 in *Traditions in Transformation*. Edited by B. Halpern and J. D. Levenson. Winona Lake, Ind.: Eisenbrauns, 1981.

Allen, Leslie. *The Books of Joel, Obadiah, Jonah and Micah*. New International Commentary on the Old Testament. Grand Rapids: Eerdmans, 1976.

Sasson, Jack M. *Jonah*. Anchor Bible. New York: Doubleday, 1990.

Wiseman, D. J. "Jonah's Nineveh." *Tyndale Bulletin* 30 (1979): 29–51.

9. OUTLINE

I. Jonah's Flight (1:1–17)
  A. Jonah's Call (1:1–3)
  B. The Ship, the Storm, and the Sailors (1:4–16)
  C. The Great Fish (1:17)
II. Jonah's Prayer and Deliverance (2:1–10)
III. In Nineveh (3:1–10)
  A. The City of Nineveh (3:1–3)
  B. The Message of Jonah (3:4)
  C. The Response of the Ninevites (3:5–9)
  D. God's Mercy (3:10)
IV. Jonah's Lesson (4:1–11)
  A. Jonah's Complaint (4:1–4)
  B. The Object Lesson: the Vine and the Parasite (4:5–8)
  C. The Application (4:9–11)

Text and Exposition

I. JONAH'S FLIGHT (1:1–17)

A. Jonah's Call (1:1–3)

¹The word of the LORD came to Jonah son of Amittai: ²"Go to the great city of Nineveh and preach against it, because its wickedness has come up before me."

³But Jonah ran away from the LORD and headed for Tarshish. He went down to Joppa, where he found a ship bound for that port. After paying the fare, he went aboard and sailed for Tarshish to flee from the LORD.

COMMENTARY

1 The first phrase of the book could be rendered "the instructions of the LORD" rather than the more common "the word of the LORD" to differentiate between the phrase used here (cf. also Jer 1:4 and Hos 1:2) and the phrase that is similar and used to introduce the majority of the prophetic books (Hos 1:1; Joel 1:1; Mic 1:1; Zep 1:1; Hag 1:1; Zec 1:1; Mal 1:1). In the latter, the "word of the LORD" refers to the message the prophet was presenting to his audience in the name of the Lord. Jonah 1:1 and the rest of this type, however, present instructions given by the Lord to his prophet (cf. also 1Sa 15:10; 2Sa 7:4; 1Ki 6:11; 16:1; 17:2, 8; 21:17, 28; Isa 38:4; and many instances in Jeremiah and Ezekiel).

2–3 Jonah is commissioned because the wickedness of Nineveh has come to the Lord's attention. This development does not imply that the Lord was previously unaware of that great city's depravity; rather, the situation there so degenerated that his patience has become overshadowed by the mandate of justice. In this way, the case of Nineveh is similar to that of Sodom and Gomorrah (Ge 18–19).

Jonah does not want to obey the instructions given to him, so he takes steps to avoid another audience. Someone given instructions in an official audience had a task to perform and would do so as the personal representative of the royal individual giving the commission (cf. Ge 41:46; 2Ki 6:32). Thus, it is such a commission (which was given in divine audience) from which Jonah is fleeing. Jonah does not necessarily think that distance will put him out of range of the Lord's reach (if he accepted the theology of Ps 139:7–12); he may have thought his flight will simply result in the Lord's finding someone else for the job. The Lord's tenacity, however, is soon to be demonstrated.

Jonah proceeds to Joppa and boards a ship bound for Tarshish, whose location is unknown. The most common identification has been Tartessus, on the southern coast of Spain. There is little evidence, however, to support this conclusion. The phrase "ships of Tarshish" (1Ki 10:22; Isa 23:1; etc.) refers to merchant ships, so it must have been a trading port. Tarshish could just be the farthest port imaginable. In English we might say that he headed for Timbuktu.

The Phoenicians were responsible for most of the sea traffic in the Mediterranean during the first half of the first millennium BC. It was they who pioneered exploration and trade by sea. It is therefore altogether likely that Jonah finds himself on board a Phoenician vessel. Commentators continue to debate whether Jonah pays the fare for himself only or hires the entire vessel. (Sasson, 83–84, favors the former, while U. Simon [*Jonah* [Philadelphia: Jewish Publication Society, 1999], 6, opts for the latter.) In either case, this is an expensive undertaking.

B. The Ship, the Storm, and the Sailors (1:4–16)

⁴Then the Lᴏʀᴅ sent a great wind on the sea, and such a violent storm arose that the ship threatened to break up. ⁵All the sailors were afraid and each cried out to his own god. And they threw the cargo into the sea to lighten the ship.

But Jonah had gone below deck, where he lay down and fell into a deep sleep. ⁶The captain went to him and said, "How can you sleep? Get up and call on your god! Maybe he will take notice of us, and we will not perish."

⁷Then the sailors said to each other, "Come, let us cast lots to find out who is responsible for this calamity." They cast lots and the lot fell on Jonah.

⁸So they asked him, "Tell us, who is responsible for making all this trouble for us? What do you do? Where do you come from? What is your country? From what people are you?"

⁹He answered, "I am a Hebrew and I worship the Lᴏʀᴅ, the God of heaven, who made the sea and the land."

¹⁰This terrified them and they asked, "What have you done?" (They knew he was running away from the Lᴏʀᴅ, because he had already told them so.)

¹¹The sea was getting rougher and rougher. So they asked him, "What should we do to you to make the sea calm down for us?"

¹²"Pick me up and throw me into the sea," he replied, "and it will become calm. I know that it is my fault that this great storm has come upon you."

¹³Instead, the men did their best to row back to land. But they could not, for the sea grew even wilder than before. ¹⁴Then they cried to the Lᴏʀᴅ, "O Lᴏʀᴅ, please do not let us die for taking this man's life. Do not hold us accountable for killing an innocent man, for you, O Lᴏʀᴅ, have done as you pleased." ¹⁵Then they took Jonah and threw him overboard, and the raging sea grew calm. ¹⁶At this the men greatly feared the Lᴏʀᴅ, and they offered a sacrifice to the Lᴏʀᴅ and made vows to him.

COMMENTARY

4–5 Once out to sea, the vessel encounters such a ferocious storm that even the seasoned seamen quail with fear. The initial response of every man is to cry out to his god. Each individual on board would have had his own family and city gods. In addition there was an entire hierarchy of protecting spirits, patron deities, lower echelon gods and goddesses, and senior members of the pantheon. An individual worshiper would not necessarily feel confident in approaching main or cosmic deities directly; he would go through divine channels. The statement, then, that each call on his own god may not only refer to the fact that those present worshiped various gods, but may also suggest that they are to invoke their patron or family-level deities, who will in turn petition their divine superiors and eventually influence the god responsible for the storm or who has been offended. Finally, we are informed that Jonah has gone below deck and has fallen asleep, apparently before the storm began.

6 Jonah is roused out by one technically designated "captain of the linesmen" ("linesmen" probably designating the entire crew). The ironic twist of this pagan seaman's telling an Israelite prophet that he ought to be praying has not escaped the notice of commentators. Furthermore, the exhortation that Jonah should "call on" his God repeats the verb found in his original commission from God (though using the preposition that occurs in 3:1).

The strategy of the sailors is clear. They figure that the more gods they can make contact with, the better chance they have of getting through to one who can do something about their plight. After all, they do not know which god is responsible for the storm. They seek a god who will take their case into the court of the gods and present a defense on their behalf—a god who will "take notice of" them.

7 The sailors decide to cast lots to discover "who is responsible" for the storm. What role would lots have in determining who is at fault? The natural inclination and the common suggestion of commentators has been that the lot will fall on the

guilty party. The difficulty is that in v.8, after the lot falls on Jonah, the sailors turn to him and ask, "Who is responsible for making all this trouble for us?" Commentators circumvent this problem by suggesting that the sailors want (or need) Jonah to confirm the outcome of the lots. But that suggestion is only one alternative.

8 The repeated question, "Who is responsible?" could indicate that the lots were expected to help them to determine: (1) who should first report the sin he may have committed that would incur the wrath of his god; or (2) which deity is responsible for the storm (George Landes, "Textual 'Information Gaps' and 'Dissonances' in the Interpretation of the Book of Jonah," *Ki Baruch Hu*, ed. R. Chazan, W. W. Hallo, and L. H. Schiffman [Winona Lake, Ind.: Eisenbrauns, 1999], 279). The fact that lots were not always used to pick one out of a group but were frequently used to determine order within the group could support the first option. When the temple duties were assigned, the lots were cast not to pick who would perform them but to determine which tribes would serve during which months. It established an order (Ne 10:34). Against this option is the fact that in Canaanite and Mesopotamian religions the individual was usually unaware of what his particular offense may have been. That an offense had occurred would be inferred from the circumstances, but a divining priest would generally be needed to isolate the offense.

Supporting the second option is the fact that the first answer Jonah gives identifies his God. Against this option is the wording inquiring about responsibility for the storm. Are they asking about guilt or cause? The language favors the former, thus ruling out the possibility that they expect a god to be identified. Furthermore, though Jonah answers by naming his God, that question is not among those pressed upon him by the sailors. It would have been a simple matter for them to ask which god he served if that were the information they sought. Finally, the identity of the god would do them no good if they had no knowledge of the nature of the offense, because they would not know what to do to appease the deity.

Perhaps the best solution is to understand the nature of the information given by the lots as direct but nonspecific (D. Stuart, *Hosea–Jonah* [WBC; Dallas: Word, 1987], 460). In this scenario, the casting of the lot tells them that Jonah is to be the source of the answer to their question. It is left to Jonah to clarify, in the best way he knows how, what his involvement might be. That is why the sailors' questions range far and wide.

Finally, it is worth noting that their first question, "What is your work/mission" ("What do you do?" NIV) is just as striking as the captain's calling on him to pray. What is his mission? He is a prophet called to go to Nineveh. Their question confronts him with the painful reality of his disobedience and betrayal of his vocation (Sasson, 126).

9 Jonah's response is short and to the point. He first identifies himself as a Hebrew. This comment answers several of their questions, but for Jonah it serves as an introduction to what follows. "I worship the LORD, the God of heaven, who made the sea and the land." Now the sailors become fearful. Their method has been more effective than they ever dreamed. Jonah serves a cosmic deity with direct jurisdiction over the sea—precisely the type of god who would be responsible for their plight!

Jonah's "fear" ("worship," NIV) of the Lord is in itself ironic, since he obviously did not fear enough to obey, and it stands in stark contrast to the sailors' fear, which leads them to be sensitive to any possible offense they might commit against this powerful deity (1:13–16).

10 The way the text presents the fact that the sailors know Jonah is fleeing from his God is unusual. When had Jonah told them? If he told them in his

speech in v.9, the text could have quoted another line of Jonah's speech to include that telling. Two alternatives may be considered. (1) The note of their knowing may be the narrator's way of indicating that Jonah proceeded to tell them the whole, long, sorry story (Sasson, 126). (2) A second possibility is that Jonah mentioned this detail in passing before the storm. The fact that Jonah is fleeing from an audience with his god would generally not have been cause for alarm. But now the sailors are overwhelmed by its significance: "You didn't tell us that this god *made the sea*!" They would have had no reason to think that Jonah's personal deity was a cosmic deity. That he is such gives them just cause for fear. The result of the lots, the cosmic nature of Jonah's deity, and an obvious offense against him make the case quite compelling. Their question, "What have you done?" is typical once guilt has been established.

11–13 When the sailors ask, "What should we do to you?" what answer do they expect? From v.13 it seems they expect Jonah to tell them to take him back, for this is what they attempt. Jonah's instructions raise several questions. How does he arrive at the conclusion that throwing him overboard is the proper course of action? Furthermore, why do the sailors need to throw him in? Why doesn't he just jump? It is possible that he is resigned to his fate and is ready to accept judgment. Alternatively, he may view himself in heroic/tragic terms, as one preferring to die than compromise his principles. In either case, the sailors' involvement will exonerate them.

14 The sailors decide they must take Jonah's advice, but they still seem either unconvinced of his guilt or unconvinced that his offense warrants such drastic punishment, for their action constitutes what is, in effect, human sacrifice. Offended gods could usually be placated by additional sacrifices or libations, or perhaps by a larger donation of grain to the priests. Human sacrifice was not a normal practice in the ancient Near East. It seems to have been resorted to occasionally but was, for the most part, abhorrent. The sailors therefore insist that the Lord has coerced them into this course of action by the events he has engineered. The phrase also recognizes that God's ways are unfathomable (cf. Pss 115:3; 135:6).

15–16 Having attached this disclaimer to their action, the sailors proceed to carry out Jonah's instructions. In v.4, the wind was "hurled" (NASB; "sent," NIV) into the sea by the Lord. In v.5, the cargo was "hurled" into the sea by the crew. In v.15, Jonah is "hurled" ("threw him," NIV) into the sea as well.

The effect is stunning—the sea stops its raging. The beginning of v.16 is identical in Hebrew to the beginning of v.10, but this time the direct object "the LORD" is attached. In v.10 the sailors were terrified. Jonah's revelation had them "scared stiff." The word translated "terrified" in v.10 is the same word that is used to describe awe or worship of a god. It is the same word used by Jonah in v.9. In v.16, then, the fear of the sailors has become a great, reverential awe of the Lord. They sacrifice to him (apparently after they return to shore) and make vows. What sort of vows would they have made? Most likely they are of a cultic nature. That is, they would promise additional sacrifices, or the like.

Both Canaanite and Mesopotamian religions understood the demands of the gods primarily in ritual terms. The performance of sacrifices and libations and the care of the temple were the primary religious responsibilities of the people. Even though the Lord was not like their gods, we would expect that they were not fully aware at this point of how much of a difference there was. While it is obvious that the calming of the sea would have had a lifelong effect on the sailors, the text gives no indication that it was a life-changing effect. No repentance is mentioned, and there is certainly no indication that they renounce their other gods or convert to a monotheistic faith in Yahweh. Anyone who comes in contact with the power of the Lord cannot help but be awed by him, but such awe does not necessarily produce a relationship with him.

Meanwhile, Jonah finds himself in an unusual, if not unique, situation.

NOTE

3 An examination of the Hebrew phrase *millipnê* shows that it was used when a person came out of an official audience with the king. For example, Joseph went out "from the presence of" Pharaoh into the entire land of Egypt (Ge 41:46), and a messenger came "from the presence of" the king of Israel to take Elisha prisoner (2Ki 6:32). There are also examples of official audiences with a prophet (2Ki 5:27) and with the Lord (e.g., Cain; Ge 4:16). Items such as the altar and the ark of the covenant are said to be in "the presence of" the Lord (Lev 10:2; 16:12; Nu 16:46; 17:9; 20:9). The Hebrew phrase as it is used in Jonah cannot merely signify that Jonah is running away from the Lord, for were that the case a different Hebrew term (*mipp⁀nê*) would have been used (Ge 16:6, 8; 35:1, 7; Ex 2:15; Jdg 11:3; 1Sa 21:10[11]; 1Ki 2:7; 12:2).

C. The Great Fish (1:17)

¹⁷But the LORD provided a great fish to swallow Jonah, and Jonah was inside the fish three days and three nights.

COMMENTARY

17 In a way, it is a shame that this most familiar part of the book has attracted so much attention, for such attention detracts from the purpose and message of the book. The use of the verb "provided" suggests the role of the fish should be viewed no differently from that of the sprouting vine (4:6), the action of the parasite that devours the vine (4:7), and the east wind that torments Jonah (4:8)—for they are all similarly "provided" by God (see Note).

The first section has shown Jonah's unwillingness to participate in the mission the Lord assigned to him. It was made apparent, however, that as a prophet of the Lord he had little choice in the matter. Other prophets were unwilling (e.g., Jeremiah, Moses), but none required the extent of coercion Jonah does.

NOTE

17 The verb describing God's role has been translated several different ways ("prepared," KJV; "appointed," NASB; "provided," NIV). Other uses of the word in this form occur in Job 7:3; Psalm 61:7; and Daniel 1:5, 10. The references from Job and Psalms are more useful for determining the meaning, for God is the subject there as he is in Jonah. "Ordain" is a preferred translation. Besides fitting the contexts, it places the emphasis squarely on the sovereignty of God, the key issue behind the events.

II. JONAH'S PRAYER AND DELIVERANCE (2:1–10)

¹From inside the fish Jonah prayed to the Lᴏʀᴅ his God. ²He said:

"In my distress I called to the Lᴏʀᴅ,
 and he answered me.
From the depths of the grave I called for help,
 and you listened to my cry.
³You hurled me into the deep,
 into the very heart of the seas,
 and the currents swirled about me;
all your waves and breakers
 swept over me.
⁴I said, 'I have been banished
 from your sight;
yet I will look again
 toward your holy temple.'

⁵The engulfing waters threatened me,
    the deep surrounded me;
      seaweed was wrapped around my head.
⁶To the roots of the mountains I sank down;
    the earth beneath barred me in forever.
But you brought my life up from the pit,
    O Lᴏʀᴅ my God.

⁷"When my life was ebbing away,
    I remembered you, Lᴏʀᴅ,
and my prayer rose to you,
    to your holy temple.
⁸"Those who cling to worthless idols
    forfeit the grace that could be theirs.
⁹But I, with a song of thanksgiving,
    will sacrifice to you.
What I have vowed I will make good.
    Salvation comes from the Lᴏʀᴅ."

¹⁰And the Lᴏʀᴅ commanded the fish, and it vomited Jonah onto dry land.

COMMENTARY

1 Most of the lines of Jonah's prayer can be identified as standard poetic phraseology recognized from other psalms (e.g., Pss 18:6; 42:7; 69:1–2, 14; 120:1). Furthermore, generically it is a song of thanksgiving for deliverance. No distress about having been swallowed by a fish is evident, nor are there questions about his fate. He does not pray for deliverance from the fish. He did cry out for deliverance (from watery Sheol) and God answered (by sending the fish) (v.2).

Yet something is amiss. Songs of thanksgiving generally work on the presumption of innocence — that the psalmist is suffering undeserved treatment (Rare exceptions such as Ps 31 do not alter the profile.) Jonah may be self-righteous enough to presume his innocence, but the audience is not

fooled. As we look at the phrases in the prayer, we can notice some striking incongruities. (For this approach to the prayer, see Ackerman.) How strange that it should start with "calling out" to the Lord — already established as a catchword in the book. He has refused to "call out" to Nineveh, and when the captain implored him to "call out" to his God during the storm, there is no suggestion that Jonah actually does so. Only as he approaches the depths of Sheol is he inclined to "call out." Then he assumes that the Lord heard his cry — as though he has somehow won God's favor.

Moreover, Jonah speaks of being "banished" from God's sight (v.4), though it will be recalled that he "fled" from God's presence. Toward the end he belittles those who cling to idols and observes that they forfeit the grace that could be theirs (v.8). Though this observation represents sound theology, it has a hollow ring in the context since the sailors, presumably among those who forfeit grace by clinging to idols, have proved by their response more worthy of grace than this recalcitrant prophet (Sasson, 195).

These and other observations, coupled with the total absence of remorse, repentance, or submission on the part of Jonah, have led Ackerman to suggest that the prayer is part of the satire as it parodies the elements of true prayer. He illustrates the concept by citing the prayer by the self-contented materialist in A. MacLeish's Pulitzer-prize-winning play on the book of Job, *J.B.*: "Our Father which art in Heaven, Give us this day our daily bread." Here it is the selection of what is said and what is not said that reveals the parody (Ackerman, 218–20). He cites a biblical example in the prayer of the Israelites recorded in Hosea 6:1–3, where the prophet's response shows that the prayer itself is a caricature.

2 Jonah describes himself as being in the "belly of Sheol" ("depths of the grave," NIV), thus drawing an interesting illustration: from the belly of Sheol to the belly of the fish. The term "Sheol" can be used in several different ways. In Israelite thought the term referred to a place to which the dead went (Isa 14:9). Sheol can be used as an expression for being close to death or can be synonymous with the grave, since the grave was seen as the portal to the netherworld (Ge 37:35; 42:38; 44:29, 31; Pss 18:5[6]; 30:3; 49:14; 116:3; Isa 28:15, 18). Jonah uses the term figuratively to describe the fact that he is at the brink of death.

3 The Lord is described as the one who cast Jonah into the sea. The waves are also described as belonging to the Lord, thus acknowledging that the sovereignty of God is in operation at every point of his ordeal. Yet at the same time, the wording suggests that the events represent a tragic sequence

of inexplicable disasters—far from the truth in Jonah's case.

4 The term "banished" appears to claim some nobility for his cause (cf. the same verb in 1Sa 26:19). The prayer anticipates full restoration, yet there has been no indication of a change of heart on Jonah's part. His words make it sound as though he expects vindication rather than forgiveness. A further question concerns which temple he is talking about. He is from the northern kingdom of Israel. Are we to believe that he has remained faithful to the temple in Jerusalem? If not, the parody grows in that this prophet does not even know where the presence of the Lord is to be found.

5 Both the KJV and NASB translate v.5 similarly by speaking of water as encompassing Jonah "to the very soul." The word used for "soul," however, has the physiological meaning of "throat" (Isa 5:14; 29:8; 58:11; Pr 3:22, parallel to "neck"), which would seem more appropriate in this context. The NIV captures the meaning well with "the engulfing waters threatened me."

6 The figure of "the underworld (earth) with its bars" ("the earth beneath barred me in," NIV) is used only here in the OT. The sentence is difficult because it has no verb. The sense, however, seems clear. The bars spoken of are the bolts on the gate to the underworld. Most city gates utilized bars for locking them. Akkadian literature attests the idea that the underworld has gates, specifically in the work called The Descent of Ishtar.

7 Jonah views himself as having remained loyal to the Lord to the very end (despite his disobedience), since he has not turned to other gods. Again the wording shows that he sees himself in noble and pious terms while at the same time raising the question about which temple his prayer rose to.

8–9 Jonah vows to offer a sacrifice of thanksgiving for the Lord's rescue of him. An important issue in this chapter is the question of whether or not this psalm implies that Jonah has repented and is now a willing prophet. Upon examination of the psalm, I do not find a single line that suggests Jonah has recognized the error of his ways and is anxious to pack his bags and head for Nineveh. In fact, he sees his destination as the temple.

Furthermore, the attitude he demonstrates in ch. 4 suggests the contrary is true. The lesson Jonah seems to have learned is not that it is wrong to disobey the Lord and try to escape one's commission, but rather that it is fruitless. Jonah, I would suggest, is not repentant but resigned to the facts: He is going to Nineveh one way or the other. The Lord will not even allow Jonah's death to interfere with this mission. So while Jonah is clearly thankful that his life has been saved, the fact that no repentance is mentioned in ch. 2 and the persistence of his bad attitude in ch. 4 suggest that this is the same Jonah who fled for Tarshish. He has simply been shown that this is one assignment he cannot shirk.

The concluding statement, "Salvation comes from the LORD," is important to the book's continuing development of its theme. Though the line reflects on Jonah's experience, it also describes the experience of the sailors and, more importantly, the outcome of the mission to Nineveh.

10 Even the fish cannot stomach this self-righteous, false piety, and in its divinely ordained regurgitation of Jonah it perhaps expresses God's opinion of Jonah's prayer. The text does not state where Jonah is "dropped off" by the fish; the logical implication, however, is that Jonah is right back near Joppa where he started. Reluctant obedience has instructive value, and Jonah now has the opportunity to demonstrate that he has learned at least this part of the lesson. So off he goes to Nineveh.

NOTES

6 The word used to refer to the underworld in this verse is rendered in the KJV, NASB, and NIV as "earth" and is the normal word for earth or land. Related terms in both Akkadian and Ugaritic are used for "earth" as well as "underworld" (Heb. ʾereṣ; Akkad. ʾerṣᵉtu; Ugar. arṣ; cf. N. Tromp, *Primitive Conceptions of Death and the Nether World in the Old Testament* [Rome: Pontifical Biblical Institute, 1963], 23ff.). The latter meaning may also be present in OT passages such as Exodus 15:12; 1 Samuel 28:13; Job 10:21–22; Ecclesiastes 3:21; and Isaiah 26:19. (For further discussion see Sasson, 188–89.) This meaning, however, seems strongest here in Jonah where the parallel is the "roots of the mountains."

8 The word translated "vanities" (KJV), "vain idols" (NASB), and "worthless idols" (NIV) is used elsewhere to refer to the worship of other gods (cf. 2Ki 17:15; Jer 2:5; 10:3, 8, 15).

III. IN NINEVEH (3:1–10)

A. The City of Nineveh (3:1–3)

¹Then the word of the LORD came to Jonah a second time: ²"Go to the great city of Nineveh and proclaim to it the message I give you."

> [3]Jonah obeyed the word of the Lᴏʀᴅ and went to Nineveh. Now Nineveh was a very important city — a visit required three days.

COMMENTARY

1–2 The wording of the call is slightly different this time (see Notes), and Jonah's response is markedly different, yet we are still not told the message that Jonah is to give.

3 The trip between Joppa and Nineveh would have been between five hundred and six hundred miles, depending on the route taken. By camel or donkey caravan, it would have taken just under one month to traverse the distance. By foot it may have taken up to five weeks.

The parenthetical section of v.3 gives us information about the task before Jonah. The city of Nineveh is described as "a great city to God" (see Notes regarding this translation). By context I suggest that this phrase means "in God's estimation."

The city is further described as "a visit required three days" ("a three days' walk," NASB). It is difficult to determine exactly what this "three days" refers to. The city of Nineveh's most famous benefactor was the Assyrian king Sennacherib (704–681), who reigned several decades after the historical Jonah. In his own description of his building projects (D. D. Luckenbill, "A Palace without Rival," *The Annals of Sennacherib* [repr. Eugene, Ore.: Wipf & Stock, 2005; orig. 1924], 111, col. 7 ll. 58–64), Sennacherib wrote that he enlarged the circumference of the city of Nineveh from 9,300 cubits (about 2.66 miles) to 21,815 cubits (about 6.25 miles). This latter circumference is supported by archaeologists, who have measured the site at about 12 kilometers (T. Madhloum, "Excavations at Nineveh," *Sumer* 23 [1967]: 77). Neither the circumlocution of the walls nor a path through the diameter of the city

(as surveyed by D. J. Wiseman) would constitute a walk of three days; therefore, several alternative solutions have been offered.

The NIV hints at another possibility when it translates the phrase as "a visit required three days." The city gate was frequently the location of business transactions as well as of public proclamations or decrees. Sennacherib's Nineveh had more than a dozen gates around the city. Jonah's itinerary would have included many if not all these gates, plus perhaps the palace, the temple courtyards, or other public places. Further support of this interpretation of the "three days" is found in Nehemiah 2:6, where the king was trying to find out more about Nehemiah's proposed leave of absence. Concerning this passage Wiseman, 36, notes: "Artaxerxes would well know the distance and length of time needed to travel from Babylon to Palestine, a route, at least via Samaria, customarily taken by the mounted Persian postal courier service. His question concerned the length of Nehemiah's absence from his duties."

In addition, as discussed above, the text could be referring to the province of Nineveh rather than just the city (see "Date" in the introduction).

In the case of Jonah, I interpret the comment not as a reference to the length of the journey or the size of the city, but rather as a comment on the temporal scope of the project. The task set before Jonah was expected to take him three days to complete. (One final consideration in this interpretation is that when Hebrew describes a journey of three days, a different phrase is used [cf. Ge 30:36; Ex 3:18; 5:3; Nu 10:33].)

NOTES

2 This verse calls for a different translation from that in 1:2. There, "denounce" best represents the Hebrew phrase that approximates "call out against" ("preach against," NIV). Here the Hebrew merely uses a different preposition with the same verb: "call out to," best rendered as "preach" or "proclaim" (so NIV).

3 The description of Nineveh is represented differently in various translations ("an exceeding great city," KJV; "an exceedingly great city," NASB; "a very important city," NIV). They have rendered the word most often translated "God" (*ʾĕlōhîm*; GK 466) as an adjective meaning "mighty" or some other superlative. Other verses that treat this word in this way include Genesis 23:6 and 30:8. But however legitimate such a rendering is in those passages, Jonah 3:3 differs from them in that its Hebrew has a preposition before *ʾĕlōhîm*, thus putting the word in a completely different category. This construction has something of a parallel in Genesis 13:13, where the men of Sodom are described as (lit.) "wicked men and sinners to the LORD." But there, "Yahweh" (God's personal name) follows the preposition rather than *ʾĕlōhîm* ("God") and cannot possibly be an adjective or adverb, though the preposition and syntax are similar to those in Jonah 3:3. It is unfortunate that finding an example of parallel syntax does not always clarify the meaning of a sentence.

B. The Message of Jonah (3:4)

⁴On the first day, Jonah started into the city. He proclaimed: "Forty more days and Nineveh will be overturned."

COMMENTARY

4 This remains the only record we have of Jonah's message to the Ninevites. Is this all he has to say? If he said more, why is only this line recorded? It seems unusual that the one proclamation that did not come to pass is the only one recorded. Would not the Ninevites have asked why this destruction was coming on them? Would not Jonah explain their wickedness and lead the way to repentance? To answer these questions, we must examine some aspects of religious belief in Nineveh and also take a closer look at Jonah's attitude.

(1) Ninevite beliefs. If someone were to come to your city and tell you that very shortly it would be destroyed, you would be full of questions. Who is going to do it? How? Why? What can be done to avoid it? How does the forecaster of doom know? The reaction of the ancient Ninevites was quite different. The primary source of difference lies in how the Assyrians viewed their gods and understood their deities' demands. They could rarely identify what they may have done to offend. Certainly every god desired sacrifice, so failure to offer sacrifice to some god would constitute one possible offense. The requirements of the gods were primarily in the realm of ritual: sacrifices, libations, temple donations, and various cultic duties. Thus in their wisdom literature we find sections such as the following:

Every day worship your god.
Sacrifice and benediction are the proper accompaniment of incense.
Present your free-will offering to your god,
For this is proper toward the gods.
Prayer, supplication and prostration
Offer him daily, and *you will* get your reward.
Then you will have full communion with your god.
In your wisdom study the tablet.
Reverence begets favor,
Sacrifice prolongs life,
And prayer atones for guilt.

> (W. G. Lambert, "Counsels of Wisdom," *Babylonian Wisdom Literature* [Oxford: Oxford Univ. Press, 1960], 105, lines 135–47)

Even of Shamash, the god of justice, it is said:
You observe, Shamash, prayer, supplication and benediction,
Obeisance, kneeling, ritual murmurs, and prostration.

> (Lambert, "The Shamash Hymn," ibid., 135, lines 130–31)

So it is not uncommon to find in the literature that the individual feels he is being punished by the gods but does not know why. A good example can be found in the interlinear (Sumerian/Akkadian) text titled "A Prayer to Every God," found in the library of Ashurbanipal, in which the individual claims ignorance of any offense and pleads that whatever deity is offended be appeased. He concludes with an observation showing frustration and the absence of knowledge or revelation that would clarify human relationships with the gods.

Man is dumb; he knows nothing;
Mankind, everyone that exists,—what does he know?
Whether he is committing sin or doing good, he does not even know.

> (*ANET*, 392)

The Assyrians' gods were capricious and unpredictable, so the Ninevites would not necessarily have asked why they were going to be destroyed. Who could know the mind of the gods? One Babylonian penned the following:

I wish I knew that these things were pleasing to one's god!
What is proper to oneself is an offense to one's god,
What in one's own heart seems despicable is proper to one's god.
Who knows the will of the gods in heaven?

Who understands the plans of the underworld gods?
Where have mortals learnt the way of a god?

(Lambert, "The Poem of the Righteous Sufferer,"
Babylonian Wisdom Literature, 41, lines 33–38)

Furthermore, even if the reason could be known, the Ninevites would not necessarily think that Jonah knew it. In Mesopotamia, prophets were given messages of imminent doom in dreams (for the most part), and the reasons were not always given. Sometimes there was no reason. In the Lamentation over the Fall of the City of Ur, Sin, the patron deity of the city asks why it was overthrown. The answer is given by Enlil, the head of the pantheon:

The judgment of the assembly cannot be turned back,
The word of An and Enlil knows no overturning,
Ur was indeed given kingship (but) it was not given an eternal reign.
From time immemorial, since the land was founded, until the population multiplied
Who has ever seen a reign of kingship that would take precedence (forever)?
The reign of its kingship had been long indeed but had to exhaust itself.

(P. Michalowski, *The Lamentation over the Destruction of Sumer and Ur* [Winona Lake, Ind.: Eisenbrauns, 1989], 59, ll. 364–69)

Pronouncements of destruction could be made not only by prophets but also those who practiced divination by reading omens. It is likely that Jonah's pronouncement would have been verified by the omens before it was so totally accepted. Omens were read from the movement of the heavenly bodies, the actions of animals, the flight of birds, and configurations of the entrails of sacrificed animals.

All of the above deal with matters of paganism: omens and divination, capricious gods, and cultic rituals. The reader might object that though we are dealing with pagan Assyrians, Jonah has come to Nineveh to represent the one God of Israel, who is consistent and who requires moral behavior. Quite true. Yet Jonah has not been sent, as far as we can tell, to preach the Israelite monotheistic religion to the Ninevites. I would contend, further, that Jonah has not even been sent to preach repentance and that 3:4 does, after all, represent the full content of his message.

This position can be supported by several factors. (1) We would expect that if only part of the message is recorded, it would be the most important part; therefore, if Jonah preached repentance, we would expect that message to be preserved. While arguing that he did not preach repentance could be an argument from silence, arguing that he did so lacks supporting evidence. The actual repentance of the Ninevites is not evidence because, as we learn in 3:9, they do not know whether repentance will help or not.

(2) Jonah's attitude. Another factor leading us to doubt that Jonah preached repentance is Jonah's prevailing attitude. In the discussion of ch. 2, I suggested that while Jonah was thankful that his life had been spared, he was not necessarily contrite over his stubbornness. Chapter 4 confirms that Jonah's attitude is still not what it should have been. Though we have

not yet determined why Jonah was unwilling to go to Nineveh or why he did not want Nineveh to repent, we can assume that this attitude would make him reticent to preach repentance if he didn't have to. The last thing he wants is for the Ninevites to escape their well-deserved doom.

(3) Perspective. In answer to our opening questions, then, I suggest the following. (a) Jonah's message is one of approaching destruction—nothing else. It is possible that his oracle is a more detailed proclamation of judgment, but since the stated oracle concerns only judgment, any speculation concerning indictment, instruction, or hope oracles must be set aside.

(b) The Ninevites would not necessarily have pressed Jonah for more information, for in their culture they would not automatically assume that the prognosticator had further information and, furthermore, would not necessarily believe that reasons for the coming doom *could* be known. They would assume that his knowledge has come from some sort of omen, and omens give knowledge, not reasons.

(c) Jonah's attitude is such that he certainly will not offer more information than he is required to give.

It follows, and is born out in the text, that the Ninevites are not told that it is specifically Yahweh, the God of Israel, who is going to bring this judgment on them, nor do they specify at any point that they place their belief in Yahweh.

C. The Response of Nineveh (3:5-9)

[5]The Ninevites believed God. They declared a fast, and all of them, from the greatest to the least, put on sackcloth.

[6]When the news reached the king of Nineveh, he rose from his throne, took off his royal robes, covered himself with sackcloth and sat down in the dust. [7]Then he issued a proclamation in Nineveh:

"By the decree of the king and his nobles:

Do not let any man or beast, herd or flock, taste anything; do not let them eat or drink. [8]But let man and beast be covered with sackcloth. Let everyone call urgently on God. Let them give up their evil ways and their violence. [9]Who knows? God may yet relent and with compassion turn from his fierce anger so that we will not perish."

COMMENTARY

5 Before we discuss the response itself, we might ask why these proud Ninevites would believe any Israelite. First, when delegations moved from country to country to conduct diplomatic affairs, it was not unusual for diviners or prognosticators to be part of the delegation to give confirmation that the negotiations had the favor of the gods of the visiting delegation (Wiseman, 42–43). Kings were often interested in collecting all the advice available in a given situation, as exemplified in the Bible when Jehoshaphat asked to hear the advice of Ahab's prophets as they considered a joint military endeavor (1Ki 22:2–7). This desire for advice from any quarter was especially true when something happened that required interpretation. Good examples can be found in the stories of both Joseph and Daniel, who gave interpretations that had been revealed to them by God but which were received by the foreign king in the same way the king received the interpretations of any divination expert.

It is not impossible that Jonah's message was an interpretation of something that had recently occurred in Nineveh. Suggestions have ranged from eclipse to earthquake to invasion, but it need not have been anything that catastrophic. The time period of Ashur-Dan III (772–755 BC) is known to have suffered under a serious bout of plague and numerous revolts (Y. Ikeda, "Looking from Til Barsip on the Euphrates: Assyria and the West in the Ninth and Eighth Centuries B.C.," in *Priests and Officials in the Ancient Near East*, ed. K. Watanabe [Heidelberg: Universitatsverlag C. Winter, 1999], 271–302, esp. 287). But threatening omens could take various forms, such as the alignment of planets or stars in the sky, animate or inanimate terrestrial occurrences, the configuration of the liver or kidneys of sacrificial animals, or the birth of malformed animals.

Even if Jonah's prediction were not the interpretation of omens that had been read prior to his arrival, it would be normal for the Assyrians to react to his message by checking the omens to see whether they agreed. It is therefore not difficult to accept the idea that the Ninevites would readily respond to Jonah's preaching. His status as a foreigner would be no obstacle, and his prognostication would have been double-checked. Jonah has not asked them to change religions, nor has he sought to dethrone their national god.

The response of Nineveh is first stated under the rubric, they "believed God" (see Notes). There is no indication in the book of Jonah that the Ninevites turned from their other gods or made any sort of commitment to Israel's God, or that they even knew the name "Yahweh." The text only states that the message Jonah had brought from God was accepted as true (cf. R. E. Clements, "The Purpose of the Book of Jonah," *Congress Volume: Edinburgh 1974* [VTSup 28; Leiden: Brill, 1975], 18).

6–7 The first steps taken by the Ninevites on hearing and accepting Jonah's message include the declaration of a fast and the donning of sackcloth. Was this the normal way the Assyrians went about repenting? When faced with bad omens, misfortune, or other signals that a god had been offended, incantations were frequently resorted to in order to avoid or counteract the foretold consequences. Seeking forgiveness from one's god or goddess for wrongs or offenses (though unknown) would be another approach. The idea of repentance per se is difficult to pin down in Mesopotamian literature. When seeking the favor of a deity whose disfavor had become evident, however, sacrifices, libations, supplication, and prostration were common actions. In a prayer to the moon-god Sin after an eclipse, one worshiper recorded the following:

I have spread out for thee a pure incense-offering of the night;
I have poured out for thee the best sweet drink.
I am kneeling; I tarry (thus); I seek after thee.
Bring upon me wishes for well-being and justice.
May my god and my goddess, who for many days have been angry with me,
In truth and justice be favorable to me;
May my road be propitious; may my path be straight.

After he has sent Zaqar, the god of dreams,
During the night may I hear the undoing of my sins;
Let my guilt be poured out.

(*ANET*, 386; cf. also "A Prayer to Every God" quoted above)

This approach is consistent with the rest of Mesopotamian literature, which reflects little inclination toward fasting or sackcloth (see Notes). While fasting is not detectable in religious rituals, mourning rites, or for repentance in Mesopotamia (S. Parpola, *Letters from Assyrian Scholars to the Kings Esarhaddon and Assurbanipal* II [Neukirchen-Vluyn: Butzon & Bercker Kevelaer, 1983]: 58–59), individuals did occasionally refrain from eating and drinking. For example, there were special instructions for certain days throughout the Babylonian year (S. Langdon, *Babylonian Menologies and Semitic Calendars* [Oxford: Oxford Univ. Press, 1935]). Other occasions on which the Mesopotamians did not eat or drink seem to be similar to the situation recorded in Acts 23:12, when a group of men vowed not to eat or drink until they had killed the apostle Paul (*CAD*, L, 126). While these deprivations may be called fasting, there are no obvious spiritual or cultic connections to the act.

The most understandable element of the king's decree calls for the people to turn from the violence of their ways—exactly what we would expect from the Assyrians. The gods demanded order in society and civilized behavior. Justice was a key requirement of their gods. There is no suggestion in the text that Ninevites are being converted to Torah, Yahwism, or even monotheism. A turning from wickedness is entirely understandable on its own without assuming a major theological paradigm shift.

8 Like the captain of the ship in ch. 1, who exhorted Jonah to call to his God, the king of Nineveh exhorts his people to call out to God, thus continuing the thematic emphasis on this activity. It has been considered strange that the animals are included in the order to don sackcloth. The nearest parallel to Jonah in ancient literature occurs in the apocryphal book of Judith (4:10–14), in which animals were dressed in sackcloth as part of a day of repentance. It is possible, however, that this example derived from imitation of the book of Jonah. That even beasts should be adorned with the signs of repentance is not outlandish. Even today funeral directors use black hearses to transport the dead, and horses in funeral processions are outfitted with black accessories.

9 It is important to note that in v.9 the Ninevites are uncertain as to whether or not their actions will cause God to set aside judgment—another indication that they are not receiving instructions from Jonah and that repentance is not part of Jonah's message. If the message coming from the Lord specified repentance as an option, they would have had no doubt that their actions were sufficient to assure their safety.

NOTES

5 The NASB translates "believed *in* God," but in doing so a nuance is added that is not expressed in the Hebrew. If we compare Numbers 20:12, which uses the same Hebrew construction, it shows us that the phrase need not entail any more than believing what God had said (NIV). Even though the Hebrew does include the preposition that is often translated "in," two factors mitigate against translating it that way. First, the preposition b^e can, and here does, simply introduce the direct object of the verb. Second, "believe in" has an idiomatic value in English that the verb-preposition combination does not carry in Hebrew.

6 The Akkadian term for sackcloth is *bašamu*. The most relevant usage of the term is in an inscription of Esarhaddon in which he is said to have "wrapped his body in sackcloth befitting a penitent sinner" (quoted in *CAD*, B:137 from R. Borger's publication of Esarhaddon's inscriptions, 102.II.i.3). Note also the Adad-Guppi Autobiography in which the mother of Nabonidus says: "In order to appease the heart of my god and my goddess, I did not put on a garment of excellent wool, silver, gold, a fresh garment; I did not allow perfumes (or) fresh oil to touch my body. I was clothed in a torn garment. My fabric was sackcloth" (*COS*, 1.147: 478). The Amarna letters include a good example of fasting while mourning a death: "When I heard what was reported, nothing was allowed to be cooked in a pot. On that day I myself wept.... On that day I took neither food nor water" (29.57).

D. God's Mercy (3:10)

> [10] When God saw what they did and how they turned from their evil ways, he had compassion and did not bring upon them the destruction he had threatened.

COMMENTARY

10 The final result is stated here — God saw their actions and decided not to bring the judgment to pass. This response by God was not on the basis of any moral standard or for any faith; it was not due to any righteousness the Ninevites possessed. They simply humbled themselves before God.

IV. JONAH'S LESSON (4:1–11)

A. Jonah's Complaint (4:1–4)

> [1] But Jonah was greatly displeased and became angry. [2] He prayed to the Lord, "O Lord, is this not what I said when I was still at home? That is why I was so quick to flee to Tarshish. I knew that you are a gracious and compassionate God, slow to anger and abounding in love, a God who relents from sending calamity. [3] Now, O Lord, take away my life, for it is better for me to die than to live."
> [4] But the Lord replied, "Have you any right to be angry?"

COMMENTARY

1–4 One common interpretation of Jonah's anger is that he is mad at God for having spared the city. The difficulty of this suggestion is that judging from 4:5 Jonah does not yet know that the Lord has relented. The statement in 3:10 was not made to Jonah but is made for the reader's benefit. Furthermore, Jonah does not resent the fact that the Lord is characterized by the attributes stated in v.2. Knowing of these attributes, however, Jonah recognizes that the response of the Lord will be in keeping with his character. The Ninevites have repented, so Jonah has no doubt that the Lord will relent.

Is Jonah angry, then, that Ninevites have repented? Many have suggested that as a good Israelite Jonah would have been delighted if Nineveh were destroyed. At the time of Jonah, however, Nineveh was not yet the capital city of Assyria, and Assyria was not yet the world power that fifty years later would tyrannize Israel. Furthermore, their repentance would have been patently logical, given the message Jonah preached. Once doom had been pronounced and then confirmed by other means, the Ninevites would naturally seek to avert their destruction. Once Jonah has presented his message, the remaining sequence of events was practically inevitable: the people would repent, and the Lord would relent. Jonah could not be distressed or even surprised that they repented, for repenting was their only logical course of action.

What instigates Jonah's anger is the entire chain of events. I have pointed out that it is all totally logical, and Jonah has foreseen it all from the moment of his call. This is the reason why Jonah fled, and he tells us as much. For Jonah, it has been a no-win proposition from the start. He realized that if he went to Nineveh and pronounced its doom, the people would certainly make some attempt to appease the angry deity. But what did they know about the Lord and his demands? Their spiritual perception was extremely naïve, thus making it impossible that they could have any understanding of what they were doing. Yet Jonah knew that God, because of his attributes, would accept their shallow repentance anyway (cf. M. Burrows, "The Literary Category of the Book of Jonah," in *Translating and Understanding the Old Testament*, ed. H. Frank and W. Reed [Nashville: Abingdon, 1970], 99, n.19).

Jonah is angry that the whole process is taking place. He will not be able to convert the Assyrians to a monotheistic belief in the Lord and has not been instructed to do so. But why should they be spared for such a superficial ritual, and for that matter, why should they even be warned?

B. The Object Lesson: the Vine and the Parasite (4:5–8)

⁵Jonah went out and sat down at a place east of the city. There he made himself a shelter, sat in its shade and waited to see what would happen to the city. ⁶Then the Lᴏʀᴅ God provided a vine and made it grow up over Jonah to give shade for his head to ease his discomfort, and Jonah was very happy about the vine. ⁷But at dawn the next day God provided a worm, which chewed the vine so that it withered. ⁸When the sun rose, God provided a scorching east wind, and the sun blazed on Jonah's head so that he grew faint. He wanted to die, and said, "It would be better for me to die than to live."

COMMENTARY

5−8 The object lesson is the key to the interpretation of the book. The first observation from the object lesson is that the word translated "destruction" in 3:10 is precisely the same noun that in 4:6 is translated "discomfort." It is by this similarity that we can make the correspondence, which in turn clarifies the importance of the object lesson: Jonah = Nineveh. To extend the comparison, the people of Nineveh have attempted to protect themselves from their "calamity" by their humble response, while Jonah has attempted to protect himself from his "discomfort" by constructing his hut. Both attempts are inadequate and require an act of compassion by God to accomplish the objective.

The second observation is that a subtle switch takes place in this section. Consistently throughout the book, Jonah spoke to, and was spoken to, by Yahweh, while the Ninevites referred only to ʾĕlōhîm. This is what we would expect, for the Ninevites were threatened by "deity," whereas Jonah is in specific relation to his God, Yahweh. In v.6, at the beginning of the object lesson, the text states that "the LORD God [yhwh ʾĕlōhîm] provided a vine" and then proceeds, through v.9, to use only the word ʾĕlōhîm, though God is dealing with Jonah—a second indication that the object lesson is intended somehow to parallel the events at Nineveh. Just as it was ʾĕlōhîm (as opposed to using Yahweh) who was interacting with the Ninevites, so it is ʾĕlōhîm who has ordained the object lesson. Verse 6 uses both designations, perhaps to draw attention to the switch.

The importance of these two observations is that they show that in the object lesson Jonah is being put in Nineveh's shoes. Both have an impending calamity and both take steps to protect themselves. God's compassionate mercy supplements the actions of each to bring effective relief. (For Nineveh, he relents; for Jonah, he supplies the plant.) The lesson to Jonah is driven home when God *does* to Jonah what Jonah *wanted him to do* to Nineveh—abandon him to his own devices. Jonah finds that without the plant (provided by God's mercy) he has no relief at all. In this same way he wanted God to withhold his mercy from the Ninevites, in which case they would discover how feeble their response had been. (For a more detailed discussion see J. Walton, "The Object Lesson of Jonah 4:5−7 and the Purpose of the Book of Jonah," *BBR* 2 [1992]: 47−57.)

Aside from giving us the meaningful equation Jonah = Nineveh, the object lesson of the plant also helps us to recognize a point that has often been overlooked: Nineveh's response, far from being a grand conversion, is naïve and barely registers. It is paralleled by Jonah's hut and in and of itself brings no relief from the impending doom. It is specifically the smallness of their response that drives home the message to Israel: even the smallest of responses by the most wicked and naïve people imaginable motivates God's compassion; how much more will informed responses by God's chosen people motivate God's compassion in their behalf?

Once we recognize this pattern in the comparison between Jonah and Nineveh, we realize that the book has been working along these lines from the beginning. In chs. 1−2 the impending disaster, the storm, was a result of Jonah's conscious disobedience. His response was one of resignation ("throw me in"), but mercy was evident in the fish that spared his life. We find, however, that God's mercy did not motivate human response—Jonah did not repent. In ch. 3 the impending disaster was the result of ignorant wickedness, and the response was repentance in an attempt at self-protection and characterized by resignation ("perhaps"; 3:10). God's mercy is represented in the postponed judgment. Here the human response motivated divine mercy. In ch. 4 the impending disaster was the result of existing conditions (heat), and Jonah's response, like the Ninevites', was his attempt at self-protection (hut). The initial mercy (the plant) was removed.

C. The Application (4:9–11)

OVERVIEW

In this application of the object lesson we find, as we would expect, God's answer to Jonah's complaint. In 4:4 God's question to Jonah about why he was angry went unanswered. Verse 5 led into the object lesson that was designed by God to help Jonah discover a different perspective (God's) on Nineveh's repentance and in so doing provides us with an answer to the question of 4:4. In regard to the event at Nineveh, Jonah was angry about the repentance of the Ninevites—not *that* they repented (for that was inevitable), or that God should exercise his mercy (equally to be expected), but that such repentance (Jonah would hesitate even to call it that) should qualify for God's mercy. It just seemed unfair.

In the object lesson, the shoe is on the other foot. It is now Jonah who is the recipient (as Nineveh had been) of undeserved grace. As in 4:4, Jonah's anger in 4:9 focuses on the mechanism by which mercy is granted: here the vine, there the repentance. With Nineveh, however, Jonah was angry because the mechanism (repentance) motivated God's compassion, despite their ignorance about God. In the object lesson, Jonah is angry because the mechanism (the vine) fails to provide lasting results, though he likewise has no understanding of it.

⁹But God said to Jonah, "Do you have a right to be angry about the vine?"

"I do," he said. "I am angry enough to die."

¹⁰But the Lord said, "You have been concerned about this vine, though you did not tend it or make it grow. It sprang up overnight and died overnight. ¹¹But Nineveh has more than a hundred and twenty thousand people who cannot tell their right hand from their left, and many cattle as well. Should I not be concerned about that great city?"

COMMENTARY

9 When God questions Jonah's anger the prophet is quick to defend his right this time, and he responds sharply with what may well have been a Hebrew expletive. Comparing the two situations, we find that Jonah's anger is inconsistent. The mechanisms (repentance and the vine) function equally by the sovereign grace and mercy of God. Nevertheless, Jonah is angry that the mechanism in Nineveh's case worked, yet for him, put in Nineveh's place, it did not work. By this lesson Jonah is shown that his anger about Nineveh has no real theological or philosophical base—rather, it is purely selfish. God has demonstrated that his mercy and grace do not function on the basis of merit but are instead ordained by his sovereignty.

10–11 Now it is Yahweh (as opposed to "God") who again speaks. He points out that Jonah is concerned about the vine, of which he has no understanding, and so defends his divine right in v.11 to be concerned about Nineveh. His mercy is motivated by compassion, not merit. The Ninevites' response did not merit postponed judgment, but it did stimulate his compassion. God's final statement turns on the verb translated "be concerned about" ("pity" or "spare," KJV; "have compassion on," NASB; see Notes). Jonah feels nothing for the plant itself, but he regrets that it is no longer available for his benefit. The actual object of pity is himself.

The force, then, of vv.10–11 is that just as Jonah regrets the failure of the plant and has pity on himself, so the Lord can defend his pity as a response toward the (feeble) repentance of the people of Nineveh. So again, Jonah = Nineveh. Nineveh was the object of the Lord's pity because of its people's repentance, and Jonah was the object of his own pity because of the withered vine.

Finally, the parallel is confirmed by the words the Lord speaks in vv.10–11. He notes that Jonah had no causal relationship to the vine at all. Jonah did not work for it, nor could he claim responsibility for it in any way. Parallel to this relationship between Jonah and the vine, the Lord characterized Nineveh as a city of 120,000 people who did not know their right hand from their left. In this context this characterization should be understood as a reference to the moral naïveté of the Ninevites. This is not an exaggeration of the size of Nineveh, for which estimates support a population in excess of 300,000 within the city walls for the period after Sennacherib's expansion (as assessed by S. Parpola; personal correspondence quoted in Sasson, 312). Just as Jonah was shielded by the vine, of which he had no understanding and which he in no way deserved, likewise the Ninevites were shielded by a repentance that they neither understood nor deserved credit for. Jonah therefore was shown that he had no basis on which to begrudge the grace of God.

NOTES

10–11 The verb *ḥws* (GK 2571) is used to characterize Jonah's attitude toward the vine and the Lord's attitude toward Nineveh. Though the same verb is used in both instances, it would probably be more accurate to translate it in different ways in that the object of Jonah's concern is inanimate. One does not have pity or compassion on a plant. The same verb is used with inanimate objects in Genesis 45:20, where Joseph instructs his brothers not to feel regret about leaving their possessions behind in Canaan. Obviously, they would not pity their possessions ("poor things have to stay in Canaan"), but rather might regret that they no longer have the use of them. Thus the use of this verb with inanimate objects turns the attention on the subject. When the verb is used with a person as the object, "pity" is a legitimate translation, but it must be understood to refer to pity that is demonstrated by action on behalf of the one pitied; therefore, by extension, "to spare" would be acceptable, for that is how God puts his pity into action. The verb is used opposite "destroy" in Ezekiel 20:17; 24:14.

REFLECTION

It has often been noted that the book of Jonah teaches obedience to the command of the Lord. That is certainly true, but we should not stop there. Jonah learns the hard way that in some matters the choice is not whether to obey or disobey; rather, it is whether we yield to God's command or leave him no choice but to drag us to obedience. There are times when God will not be denied—we can go willingly, grudgingly, or by pure force, but *go* we will.

Another lesson learned by Jonah is that nice and neat theological categories do not confine God. God is not limited to our perception or understanding of him. This is not to say that there are no theological absolutes. Jonah finds out, however, that there are fewer than he thought.

Finally, in connection with both of the above lessons, we see in Jonah a spiritual pride that we should all strive to avoid. Jonah feels that he knows best how God works, and he even disregards God's attempts to lead him out of his misconceived presuppositions. Our job is to follow, not to understand, the directions of God as he guides our lives and ministries.

So what became of Jonah? As we have seen, the book is not about him in the end, it is about God, so the text never tells us how his story ends. We may get a hint, however, from an unexpected source. In the introduction we noted that Jonah shows up again in 2 Kings 14:25. If I had to hazard a guess, I would say that the Kings incident comes after the book of Jonah, for in Kings we find Jonah giving a message of God's compassion on an undeserving people. The explanation given by the narrator of Kings even sounds a bit like God's assessment of Nineveh at the end of Jonah: "The Lord had seen how bitterly everyone in Israel, whether slave or free, was suffering; there was no one to help them. And since the Lord had not said he would blot out the name of Israel from under heaven, he saved them by the hand of Jeroboam son of Jehoash" (2Ki 14:26–27). Perhaps Jonah learned the lesson of God's compassion after all and spread the news to the northern kingdom, Israel.

MICAH

THOMAS E. MCCOMISKEY AND TREMPER LONGMAN III

Introduction

1. BACKGROUND

The superscription to the book of Micah situates its oracles during the reigns of three Judean kings: Jotham (750–735 BC [including a coregency with Uzziah]), Ahaz (735–715 BC), and Hezekiah (715–686 BC). In the period just prior to these years Israel and Judah had risen to heights of economic affluence but had fallen to depths of spiritual decadence. Under the able leadership of Jeroboam II of Israel (786–746) and Uzziah of Judah (783–742), the territories of both kingdoms became almost as extensive as they were during the reign of Solomon. It was a time of great economic prosperity, fostered for a time by the absence of international crises and by the mutual cooperation of both kingdoms. Excavations at the site of the ancient city of Samaria have yielded ivory inlays that attest to the accuracy of Amos's description of the luxurious life enjoyed by the prosperous citizens of this city (Am 6:4).

While Israel and Judah appeared to be strong externally, an internal decay was sapping their strength and threatening to destroy the social fabric of these two kingdoms. A burgeoning wealthy class was becoming richer at the expense of the poorer classes. The prophets saw this situation as a violation of the covenantal requirements and thus a hindrance to God's blessing and a guarantee of the dissolution of the nation.

But the internal sickness of Israel involved more than social wrongs. Canaanite religion also had extended its influence among some of the people. While Micah attacked the idolatry that accompanied the acceptance of Canaanite worship, it was not this aspect of Israel's condition that he emphasized most. It was rather the social injustices of the ruling classes to which Micah gave the greatest attention. (The extent of the intrusion of Canaanite influence at this time may be seen in the Samaria Ostraca, which contain many Hebrew names compounded with the name "Baal," a Canaanite fertility god.)

The halcyon days of peace were destined to come to an end, and they did during the time period that Micah functioned as a prophet. In the first place, Assyria arose from a state of quiescence to occupy a threatening posture on the national scene. Under Tiglath-pileser III (745–727), Assyria experienced a remarkable resurgence of power. At the same time Israel was being torn by internal strife and dissension.

Finally, under the leadership of Shalmaneser V, Assyria occupied Israel, the northern kingdom; and several years later the city of Samaria fell to Sargon II (722 BC).

Under Ahaz's leadership, Judah refused to enter an anti-Assyrian alliance with Israel (under King Pekah) and Syria (under King Rezin). As a result, Syria and Israel went to war against Judah in order to depose Ahaz and put a more amenable king on the throne. This war, commonly called the Syro-Ephraimite war, lasted from 734–732 BC. While the prophet Isaiah made it clear that it was God's will for Ahaz to resist these kings' overture (see Isa 7), Ahaz should not have appealed to Tiglath-pileser to intervene. His pro-Assyrian policies made Judah little more than a satellite of Assyria. Not until Hezekiah came to the throne (715 BC) were sweeping religious—and most probably social—reforms instituted. Assyria continued to threaten Judah under Hezekiah's reign, but an attempt by Sennacherib to take Jerusalem was frustrated (2Ki 19:32–36; 2Ch 32:21; Isa 37:33–37). Not until about a century after the death of Hezekiah did Jerusalem finally fall to the Babylonians.

2. UNITY

Ewald first questioned the unity of Micah in 1867 when he suggested that chs. 4 and 5 might have been written by someone other than Micah, possibly a contemporary of the prophet. He also suggested that chs. 6 and 7 were written in the reign of Manasseh. In 1871, Oort alleged that Micah 4:1–7, 11–13 were inserted by a later prophet who disagreed with Micah's ideology.[1] Kuenen promptly challenged Oort's view and defended Micah's authorship of the disputed verses.[2] Jeppesen, who has written a helpful history of research of Micah, also identifies the work of B. Stade as influential in the development of the modern critical study of the book.[3]

Chapters 4–7 are the most seriously questioned chapters of Micah. The literary-historical school, under the influence of Wellhausen, generally assigned portions of these chapters to post-Micah dates. Renaud (but see below for Renaud's more recent approach) and Robinson are more recent representatives of a similar approach.[4]

The form-critical approach, developed by Gunkel, sought to establish the compass of each pericope and place it in its historical situation in the life (*Sitz im Leben*) of Israel. Lindblom failed to find a literary coherence in the book but did affirm Micah's authorship of several pericopes, including portions of chs. 6 and 7.[5] Weiser revised the form-critical approach to Micah by assigning many of the pericopes to a cultic *Sitz im Leben*.[6] Supporting the latter method, Kapelrud, like Weiser, nonetheless affirmed the authenticity of the eschatological sections of the book.[7]

---

1. H. Oort, "Het Beth Efraat van Micha V:I," *ThT* 5 (1871): 501–11.
2. A. Kuenen, "De Koning uit Beth-Ephrath," *ThT* 6 (1872): 45–66.
3. K. Jeppesen, "New Aspects of Micah Research." *JSOT* 8 (1978): 3–32.
4. B. Renaud, *Structure et attaches littéraires de Michée IV–V* (Paris: J. Gabalda et Cie, 1964), 82–88, 111; T. H. Robinson, *Die zwölf Kleinen Propheten* (Tübingen: J. C. B. Mohr, 1964), 127.
5. J. Lindblom, *Micha literarisch untersucht* (Åbo: Åbo Akademi, 1929), 6–9, 67, 124, 136, 149, 153.
6. A. Weiser, *Das Buch der zwölf Kleinen Propheten* (Göttingen: Vandenhoeck & Ruprecht, 1963), 236–89.
7. A. S. Kapelrud, "Eschatology in the Book of Micah," *VT* 11 (1961): 392–405.

A more thorough discussion of the process of development of the book maybe found in Andersen and Freedman,[8] though most modern commentaries, including the one of Andersen and Freedman, are more interested in the final form of the text than speculation about its history of composition.

Central to the problem of the unity of Micah is an alleged lack of coherence in the book, a factor that leads some to see certain portions as later insertions. This problem can be resolved only on exegetical grounds. It will be considered thoroughly in the commentary.

It seems difficult, however, to assign Micah 4:1–4, which is also found in Isaiah 2:2–4, to a date after Micah's time since it is rooted in the eighth-century tradition. The reference to Babylon in Micah 4:10 may well be a figure of speech for the world powers. The predictive material in the immediate context is consonant with predictions in Isaiah 1–39.

Mays regards Micah 4–5 as a complex consisting of independent oracles "assembled to form the counterpart of the prophecies of judgment in chaps. 1–3."[9] For example, 5:2, 4, the promise of a king from Bethlehem, he regards as "an independent unit, juxtaposed to 5:1 to fill out the pattern"; he concludes that "5:1–4 is not an original unit of speech" but it was probably added in "exilic times."[10] This conclusion is based in part on the similar beginning of 5:1 with 4:8 (wᵉʿattâ), also considered late because it assumes the demise of Israel's king. The setting of 5:1 is the siege of Jerusalem by the Babylonians and is similar to Jeremiah's language and style.

However, it is not certain that 4:8 assumes the loss of the realm of which Jerusalem was the capital. It is certain that it predicts a Deliverer-King. In this regard it is no different from Isaiah 9:6–7[5–6], which belongs to a generally undisputed portion of Isaiah and which predicts a future Davidic kingdom. The Davidic theology did not emerge as full-blown in the eighth century. Its roots go back to 2 Samuel 7. Chapters 1–3 of Micah are generally considered to be authentic; yet there we can find statements of Jerusalem's demise (1:9, 12; 3:12) that do not demand the assumption that they were written later than the time of Micah. Also, comparisons of brief sayings with the language of other literary works are a tenuous procedure since they utilize such a limited body of material. Micah's charge in 6:1–8 and the theology of ch. 7 are in keeping with other eighth-century prophets.

The book exhibits an internal coherence in its basic structure. Three distinct sections may be discerned (1:1–2:13; 3:1–5:15; 6:1–7:20). Each begins with a summons to hear, is followed by an oracle of doom, and ends with a statement of hope. While this strikingly symmetrical pattern may have come about as the speeches of Micah were arranged after his death, the inner coherence, the logical sequence of argument, and the general prophetic propensity for symmetrical arrangement of thought support the originality of the literary pattern.

The first oracle anticipates the fall of Samaria and thus may have been written sometime before 721 BC. The second oracle does not mention Samaria—an indication that it may have been written after the fall of that city. Jeremiah 26:18–19 places a portion of this oracle (3:12) in the time of Hezekiah (715–686 BC). If the oracles are regarded as independent literary units, the whole oracle may be placed sometime in

---

8. F. I. Andersen and D. N. Freedman, *Micah* (AB; Garden City, N.Y.: Doubleday, 2000), 17–20.

9. J. Mays, *Micah: A Commentary* (OTL; Philadelphia: Westminster, 1976), 26.

10. Ibid., 27, 113.

the reign of Hezekiah. The third oracle is difficult to place chronologically. The social wrongs cited in the second oracle were also prevalent when the third was written, thus perhaps indicating that the second and third oracles were written in the same general period of time.

Recent efforts have been expended toward the discovery of the redactional history of the book's development. These scholars have concluded that the book came into being over a long period of time and that it was not completed until the postexilic period. However, while agreeing in principle, they have come up with rather divergent pictures of the composition of the book.[11]

3. AUTHORSHIP

The superscription to the prophecy (1:1) asserts the authorship of Micah, a short form of the name "Micaiah," which means "Who is like Yahweh?" The prophet who bore that name was from Moresheth (probably Moresheth Gath) in Judah, situated about twenty-five miles southwest of Jerusalem. The village was located on the edge of the rolling hills of the Shephelah near the coastal plain. This town lay in the general proximity of Isaiah's home, a factor that may explain certain similarities between the prophecies of both men. Waltke speculates, "Micah's identification as a Moreshite implies that he was an outsider to the capitals."[12]

Little is known about Micah apart from what may be inferred from his prophecy. The book eloquently affirms his sensitivity to the social and religious wrongs of his time. Outside of the book of Micah, the prophet is only mentioned in Jeremiah 26:17–19, where some of the elders at the time of Jeremiah remind the authorities of the prophecies of Micah in order to save the later prophet from punishment for his oracles of judgment.

4. DATE

The superscription (1:1) places Micah in the eighth century BC. The reference to the destruction of Samaria (v.6) places the beginning of his prophetic career sometime before the capture of that city (722/721 BC); and this chronology agrees with the superscription, which fixes the beginning of his ministry in the reign of Jotham (750–731 BC). The prophetic indictments of social and religious corruption fit well the time of Ahaz (735–715 BC) and could even be appropriate to the prereformation period of Hezekiah, who reigned from 715–686 BC. The reference to Micah's prophecy in Jeremiah 26:18–19 fixes at least a portion of Micah's message in the time of Hezekiah. The lament in 1:8–16 mentions cities in an order that may well coincide with the military expedition of Sennacherib's army in 701 BC, also during Hezekiah's reign. There is no convincing reason for rejecting the period of time delineated in the superscription.

5. LITERARY FORM

The book of Micah, like most of the other prophetic writings, is written in the style of Hebrew poetry and is thus marked by a characteristic parallelism of expression, terseness, and striking imagery. While his

---

11. See J. Jeremias, "Die Bedeutung der Gerichtsworte Michas in der Exiliszeit," *ZAW* 83 (1971): 330–53; Renaud, *Structure et attaches littéraires de Michée IV–V*; for a critique, consult B. Childs, *Introduction to the Old Testament as Scripture* (Philadelphia: Fortress, 1979), 431–34.

12. B. Waltke, *A Commentary on Micah* (Grand Rapids: Eerdmans, 2007), 3.

style does not attain to that of Isaiah, Micah's use of wordplay and contrast imparts a distinctive vividness to the book. As for the somewhat free form of the book, it need not indicate the hand of a later redactor; on the contrary, it may reflect the author's purpose to use a variety of literary devices to stir the emotions of the reader in accordance with the message of the oracles.

6. THEOLOGICAL VALUES

Crystallizing the theology of the OT prophets is a difficult task, since they did not set out to write systematic theologies. Micah's prophecy, for example, is a collection of oracles of judgment and hope that came about as a result of his deep emotional involvement in his nation's desperate plight. In Micah's case we have a collection of oracles that, in themselves, do not appear to present a consistent, unified development of theological themes. As a matter of fact, the prophet appears to jump from one theme to another, often without apparent connection (2:6–11; cf. 12–13; 3:5–8; cf. 9–12).

While Micah may not have written a theology, he certainly bases his pleas to the people on a consistent theology of God. The episodic nature of the oracles helps us understand Micah's concept of God. Each appeal to the nature of God, each application of the word of God by Micah to his people, gives us greater insight into the theology that lies at his heart—a theology he made known in colorful phraseology, urgent pleas, and formal oracles.

The first theological emphasis we meet in the book of Micah is the sovereignty of God (1:2). More to Micah than a mere tribal deity, the Lord God has acted within the sphere of the nations to effect their destiny as well as the destiny of his own people. The divine intervention of God in history is not limited by Micah to the eschaton, for he understands the destruction of Samaria and Jerusalem to be the result of the Lord's punishing these centers of wickedness for their rebellion against him. However, it will be in the eschaton that God's activity regarding the nations reaches its climax. Then the ultimate triumph and vindication of God's people will take place (4:11–13), and the nations will become subject to the rule of the Lord.

Another theological emphasis of Micah is the self-consistency of the Lord. He is immutably committed to his covenantal obligations. It is this theme, coupled with that of divine sovereignty, that gives such urgency to Micah's words. The Lord's consistency with the revelation of his will in the Mosaic covenant is not set forth in absolute terms by Micah but is seen in the Lord's condemnation of idolatry (1:5–7) and the social crimes of Micah's day (2:2; 3:1–3; 9–12; 6:8)—a prominent subject in the covenant (Ex 20:3–6; 23:1–9; et al.). While the word "covenant" (bᵉrît) is not mentioned by Micah, the terms of the covenant ratified at Sinai are unmistakably present.

That God seems austere and unbending is only a partial picture of his self-consistency. He is consistent also with his nature, and that nature is to forgive. We must not forget the statement of 7:18–20, which is at once a theological statement and a heartfelt response. God will not give up his people altogether; he will forgive the sins of the believing remnant.

Micah's doctrine of the remnant is unique among the prophets and is perhaps his most significant contribution to the prophetic theology of hope. The remnant is a force in the world, not simply a residue of people, as the word "remnant" (šᵉʾērît) may seem to imply. It is a force that will ultimately conquer the world (4:11–13). This triumph, while presented in apparently militaristic terminology (4:13; 5:5–6), is actually accomplished by other than physical force. By removing everything that robs his people of complete trust in him (5:10–15), the Ruler from Bethlehem will effect the deliverance of his people. The source of power for God's people in the world is their absolute trust in him and his resources.

The messianic King in Micah is not a redemptive figure as is Isaiah's Servant. We are not told by Micah how God can be consistent with his law and at the same time be consistent with his forgiving nature. The basis of the divine redemptive activity lies within the nature of God, according to Micah. We must look to Isaiah (Isa 53:4–6) to see that these dual aspects of the divine nature meet in the vicarious suffering of the Servant. The absence of a vicarious role in the redemptive work of the messianic King in Micah underscores the prophet's theological perspective, which is to assure us of the future exaltation and glory of the remnant; and he does so against the background of the humiliation the nation would soon endure.

We may state this aspect of Micah's theology thus: The nation will suffer the shame of defeat and exile. But that future is not the end, for certain triumph and glory lies ahead, not for the whole nation, but only for the remnant. The people of God will be delivered from affliction and exile by their King and will return with him, secure in his power. Thus Micah's focus is on the kingdom of the Lord and its manifestation in the world.

According to Micah, the kingdom is an expression of divine power and sovereignty within the sphere of the nations. The messianic King is depicted in close association with the Lord and embodies his might and authority. Micah presents the work of the messianic King almost entirely in terms of power. Even the tender act of caring for his own as a shepherd cares for his sheep is done in the strength of the Lord (5:4).

Micah speaks to a people whose disobedience has led them to ignominy and ruin. But he reminds them—and us—that the Lord is almighty; and because he is consistent with his Word and with his nature, God's people will not fail to receive all he has promised to them. Though now we suffer shame, glory and vindication lie ahead because the Lord will "be true to Jacob, and show mercy to Abraham" (7:20).

7. MICAH IN THE NEW TESTAMENT

The authors of the NT recognized that Micah's message transcended his immediate future and was relevant to the coming of Jesus Christ. As an example, the gospel of Matthew cites Micah 5:2 in reference to Jesus' birth in Bethlehem (see Mt 2:5). The reference from Micah looks forward to a future Davidic ruler, and Jesus Christ, a descendant of David, was appropriately born in Bethlehem.

8. BIBLIOGRAPHY

Allen, L. C. *The Books of Joel, Obadiah, Jonah and Micah*. New International Commentary on the Old Testament. Grand Rapids: Eerdmans, 1976.

Mays, J. *Micah: A Commentary*. Philadelphia: Westminster, 1976.

Waltke, B. "Micah." In *The Minor Prophets: An Exegetical and Expository Commentary*. Vol. 2. Edited by T. McComiskey. Grand Rapids: Baker, 1993.

———. *A Commentary on Micah*. Grand Rapids: Eerdmans, 2007.

9. OUTLINE

I. The Superscription (1:1)

II. The First Oracle: Israel's Impending Judgment and Her Future Restoration (1:2–2:13)

    A. The Impending Judgment (1:2–7)

    B. The Prophet's Reaction to the Pronouncement of Judgment (1:8–9a)

    C. The Prophet's Warning and Summons to the People (1:9b–16)

    D. The Prophet's Indictment of the Oppressing Classes (2:1–5)

    E. The True Prophet versus the False Prophets (2:6–11)

    F. The Prophet's Statement of Hope (2:12–13)

III. The Second Oracle: The Prophet's Indictment of the Leaders of the House of Israel and Israel's Future Hope (3:1–5:15)

    A. The Prophet's Indictment of the Rulers of Israel (3:1–4)

    B. The Prophet's Indictment of the Religious Leaders of Israel (3:5–8)

    C. The Result of the Leaders' Corruption on the Nation (3:9–12)

    D. The Future Exaltation of Zion (4:1–8)

    E. The Future Might of Zion (4:9–13)

    F. The Future King of Zion (5:1–4[4:14–5:3])

    G. The Future Peace of Zion (5:5–6[4–5])

    H. The Future Vindication of Zion (5:7–9[6–8])

    I. The Future Purification of Zion (5:10–15[9–14])

IV. The Third Oracle: God's Lawsuit against Israel and the Ultimate Triumph of the Kingdom of God (6:1–7:20)

    A. God's Accusations against His People (6:1–8)

    B. The Sentence of Judgment (6:9–16)

    C. The Prophet's Lament over the Lack of Godly Fellowship (7:1–2)

    D. The Prophet's Lament over the Corruption in His Society (7:3–6)

    E. The Godly Man's Attitude in the Midst of Discouragement (7:7–10)

    F. The Assurance of Victory for the Kingdom of God (7:11–20)

        1. Victory Described in Terms of the Extension of the Kingdom (7:11–13)

        2. Victory Assured because of God's Leadership (7:14–15)

        3. Victory Assured over the Nations (7:16–17)

        4. Victory Assured because of God's Nature (7:18–20)

Text and Exposition

I. THE SUPERSCRIPTION (1:1)

¹The word of the LORD that came to Micah of Moresheth during the reigns of Jotham, Ahaz and Hezekiah, kings of Judah — the vision he saw concerning Samaria and Jerusalem.

COMMENTARY

1 According to the superscription, the prophetic activity of Micah spanned the reigns of three kings of Judah in the second half of the eighth century BC and into the seventh century. This period was one of great spiritual decline especially for the northern kingdom; and the messages of Micah and the other eighth-century prophets, with their emphases on social justice and obedience to the obligations of the Mosaic covenant, were like a refreshing breeze in the arid climate of spiritual ignorance and disobedience.

Many scholars hold that the superscription may not have been written by Micah but may rather have been appended to the prophecy by a later editor. Similar superscriptions preface the works of other prophets (e.g., Isaiah, Hosea, Amos, and Zephaniah). The fact that these superscriptions are not rigid formulas may reflect the individuality of the various prophets involved.

Typically, a prophetic superscription will name the parentage of the prophet. We might speculate that the lack of mention of Micah's parents may be because they were undistinguished.

The prophecy of Micah is directed primarily toward Samaria and Jerusalem, the capital cities of the northern and southern kingdoms (Israel and Judah). While Micah's message is applicable to all the inhabitants of these kingdoms, he singles out the capitals because the leaders of these centers of influence are largely responsible for the social ills of that time (1:5–7; 3:9–12). In particular he singles out Jerusalem, not only because of the corruption of its leaders, but also because of its future glory — a central motif in the prophetic theology of hope.

The superscription identifies the form of the following message as a "word of the LORD" and as a "vision." The first characterization emphasizes that, though Micah is the intermediary, ultimately the message comes from God and carries his full authority. "Vision" can have a broad or a narrow meaning. In the broad sense, all the activity of a prophet was visionary (Eze 7:26), but in a more restricted sense, "vision" can denote a certain type of prophecy, one in which the prophet describes future events as though they are unfolding before his eyes.

II. THE FIRST ORACLE: ISRAEL'S IMPENDING JUDGMENT AND HER FUTURE RESTORATION (1:2–2:13)

A. The Impending Judgment (1:2–7)

²Hear, O peoples, all of you,
   listen, O earth and all who are in it,
that the Sovereign LORD may witness against you,
   the Lord from his holy temple.
³Look! The LORD is coming from his dwelling place;
   he comes down and treads the high places of the earth.
⁴The mountains melt beneath him
   and the valleys split apart,
like wax before the fire,
   like water rushing down a slope.
⁵All this is because of Jacob's transgression,
   because of the sins of the house of Israel.
What is Jacob's transgression?
   Is it not Samaria?
What is Judah's high place?
   Is it not Jerusalem?

⁶"Therefore I will make Samaria a heap of rubble,
   a place for planting vineyards.
I will pour her stones into the valley
   and lay bare her foundations.
⁷All her idols will be broken to pieces;
   all her temple gifts will be burned with fire;
   I will destroy all her images.
Since she gathered her gifts from the wages of prostitutes,
   as the wages of prostitutes they will again be used."

COMMENTARY

2 The opening statement of the prophecy consists in a summons to the nations to attend to the cosmic judgment scene so vividly described by the prophet in the subsequent verses. That the summons is directed to the nations and not only to Israel and Judah is clear from the parallel expression "earth and all who are in it."

In this anthropomorphic representation Micah pictures God as coming from his dwelling place to witness against the nations. The concept of witness is connected to the idea of covenant. In the ancient Near Eastern treaties that form the conceptual background of the covenantal form in the OT, the witness attested to the agreement made between the two parties, the suzerain and the vassal. In this case the vassal, the people of God, have promised to obey the law given to them by the suzerain, God. If, as has happened now, the vassals break the law, they become vulnerable to the curses of the covenant. It is the role of the witness to indicate the fairness of this judgment. Here God himself plays the role of witness to the breaking of the covenant.

The phrase "witness against" seems to be used here in the same sense as in Deuteronomy 31:19-21, 26, where the Song of Moses and the Book of the Law were to function as witnesses against the people. This ongoing witness served as a reminder of future punishment should the terms of the covenant to which they witnessed be violated. It is in this sense that God's judgment of his own people was to be a witness against the nations. It is a guarantee that ultimately they will be judged for their sin; for if God does not fail to judge his own people, he will certainly judge those who do not belong to him.

Micah, like Isaiah, sees the destiny of the nations as integrally related to the destiny of God's people. He deftly develops this theme throughout the prophecy. In 4:11-13 he states that the nations, while looking with pleasure on the misfortune of God's people, are blind to the fact that this suffering is the precursor to their own disaster. In 7:8-10 he affirms that though God's people will be punished for their sin, they have a God who forgives sin. The nations that do not know God will not know deliverance from his judgment.

The burning timbers and ruined houses of Samaria and Jerusalem will be an eloquent sermon

to the people of the world. From this destruction they will learn that God does not allow sin to go unpunished—even in the case of his own people. As the Song of Moses and the Book of the Law testified of the sin of the Israelites and pledged future punishment for it, so God's destruction of Samaria and Jerusalem will be a witness against the nations in that it will demonstrate God's hatred of sin and be the harbinger of their own eventual destruction.

3-4 The act by which God witnesses and executes judgment against the nations is depicted in a vivid anthropomorphic scene (vv.3-4) in which God comes forth from heaven to tread the high places of the earth and to bring about the destruction of Samaria and Jerusalem (1:6; 3:12). In this metaphorical representation, the prophet asserts one of the most basic concepts of OT theology, namely, that God is not only transcendent above the world but also immanent in it, and that he intervenes in history to effect his will.

The term "high places" (*bāmôt*; v.3; GK 1195) connotes several concepts. Aside from the basic meaning of "height" or "summit," it was used of pagan religious sanctuaries (Jer 7:31; Eze 20:29), the place of security and protection (Dt 32:13; Hab 3:19), and the place of military advantage, with its companion idea that the one who possessed the heights of the enemy's territory has brought the enemy into subjection (Dt 33:29; Eze 36:2).

Whether Micah intends "high places" to be understood as the heights of the earth or the pagan shrines of the land is difficult to determine. The cosmic scope of this context and the reference to mountains in v.4 seem to favor the former; yet he does predict the destruction of the centers of idol worship as represented by Samaria and Jerusalem (1:5-7). It seems best, therefore, to see in this phrase a double reference in which Micah envisions God as the majestic Sovereign who steps from heaven into the course of human events. Samaria and Jerusalem cannot stand before the might and power of the Conqueror who strides across the heights of the earth and before whom the pagan sanctuaries crumble as the mountains melt. The motif of double reference is not uncommon in the prophecy of Micah (cf. vv.10–16).

The cataclysm that accompanies God's intervention in history is described in terms of a violent storm or earthquake (v.4). The language is metaphorical and describes the intensity of the destruction of Samaria and Jerusalem. All creation shakes at the coming of the God of judgment. Similar language may be found in other judgment texts (Pss 46:6; 68:2; 97:5; Am 9:5; Na 1:5)

5 With telling force the prophet asserts that the national upheaval will be caused by the sins of the people of Israel. Verse 5 is built on the structure of two couplets, each with parallel cola. The reader is led to expect the first couplet's "transgression" and "sins" to be repeated in the second. In these rhetorical questions, however, only the word "transgression" is repeated; and the second question in the Hebrew is, "What are the high places [*bāmôt*] of Judah?" Many scholars emend the text on the basis of the LXX to read "sins" in the second colon, in keeping with the parallelism of the first couplet. But the most difficult reading should be seriously considered. Also, we should remember that poetic style was often enhanced by such unexpected variation. Indeed, as has been recently understood, a parallel line in Hebrew may be understood as one of progression of thought (A, what's more B) rather than strict symmetry (A equals B).

The word "transgression" in the first question assumes a previous referent and points back to the occurrence of that word in the first couplet. So, too, the second rhetorical question demands a previous referent because these questions clarify and lend continuity to the argument. Instead of utilizing the word the reader expects, the text departs from the

usual parallel structure and repeats the word *bāmôt* ("high places") used in v.3, thus giving to the term a specific connotation of idolatry. This feature lends support to the view that a double reference obtains in the use of this word in v.2. The rules governing parallelism are not, however, really broken by the writer; for *bāmôt* is a suitable word for use in parallelism with "transgression" because it occurs in apposition with "sin" (*ḥaṭṭāʾt*) in Hosea 10:8. Indeed, parallelism operates under the principle that the second colon does not simply repeat the thought of the first but actually sharpens it in some way. In this case, the second colon defines the nature of the transgression by false worship at the *bāmôt*.

This dramatic departure from the strict literary norm has the effect of identifying Samaria and Jerusalem as the chief objects of God's destructive activity described in v.3. Also, the close association between "high places" and "sin" in the mind of the prophet makes it clear that to him the incursion of non-Yahwistic religious practices is at the heart of the crisis in the house of Israel. Because of the influence of Canaanite religion, Israel is giving only lip service to Yahweh; and the ethical demands of the law, with their resultant benign effect on the social structure of the nation, are being disregarded. This sin is the one that leads to estrangement from God and will result in eventual captivity.

Literally the Hebrew says, "*Who* is Jacob's transgression?" The prophet personifies the cities of Samaria and Jerusalem, possibly because he wishes to depict them as harlots, as he does in the subsequent context, or because the Hebrew word *mî* ("who") was used when the writer has persons in mind (cf. Notes).

6–7 Samaria is to become a ruin, a place with vineyards planted on her sloping sides amid the stones of her ruined buildings. The expression "lay bare her foundations" (v.6) may echo the use of the word *gālâ* ("lay bare") for uncovering one's nakedness

(Lev 20:11, 17–18, 20–21), a term used in the OT of prostitution (Eze 16:36; 23:18) and lewdness (2Sa 6:20; Hos 2:10). The imagery of the harlot appears in v.7, according to which the wages Samaria has received from the practice of prostitution will be burned. The prostitution referred to is idolatry, which the OT consistently regards as spiritual fornication (Ex 34:15; Jdg 2:17; Eze 23:30; et al.).

The word translated "temple gifts" ('etnanneyhā, v.7) seems out of place in a sequence describing the destruction of idols and may reflect a Semitic root meaning "resemble"; hence it may refer to an image or idol (cf. Notes). But the same word in Hebrew also connotes payment to a harlot, and Micah uses it in that sense in the latter part of this verse. Here we may have another example of Micah's use of the pun, by which in this case he deftly identifies the idolatry of Samaria as spiritual harlotry.

The wealth that accrues to Samaria from her idolatry will be taken away from her to be used again for the wages of prostitution—i.e., the invading Assyrians will transfer the wealth of Samaria to their own temples, where it will again be used for idolatrous worship. Deuteronomy 23:17–18 prohibits religious prostitution and the use of prostitutes' wages for gifts to the temple.

NOTES

2 The major difficulty inherent in the interpretation of the phrase עֵד בְּ ('ēd bᵉ, "witness against") is that the burden of the prophecy is directed against Israel and Judah and not the nations (1:5–7; 3:12). It is difficult to see how the prophecy may be a witness against the nations when God proceeds to condemn his people alone. Aside from explanations that posit the influence of a redactor or that advocate transposition or deletion of verses, the difficulty is sometimes met by translating the preposition בְּ (bᵉ) in a locative sense, i.e., "witness among." For a full survey of the interpretation of the preposition, see J. T. Willis, "Some Suggestions on the Interpretation of Micah I 2," *VT* 18 (1968): 372–79.

It is suggested that the LXX so understands the expression ἔσται κύριος ἐν ὑμῖν εἰς μαρτύριον (*estai kyrios en hymin eis martyrion*, "the Lord will be among you for a witness"). The Greek phrase is used in the LXX, however, to translate the Hebrew expression in instances where it seems clearly to mean "witness against" (Jer 49:5); and Ignatius used the same Greek phrase to mean "witness against" (Willis, 376). That 'ēd bᵉ means "witness against" in many cases in the Hebrew is particularly clear from Deuteronomy 31:26 and Jeremiah 42:5, where the Hebrew word order is identical with that of Micah 1:2.

The translation "witness among" would make the nations simply the sphere of God's judgmental activity and would curtail any directly didactic element in it as far as the nations are concerned. Micah clearly asserts, however, that God's devastation of Samaria and Jerusalem has a direct bearing on the destiny of the nations; for the destruction of these cities is part of a plan that involves the ultimate subjugation of the nations (4:11–13; 7:3–10).

3 John Gray's suggestion (*The Legacy of Canaan: The Ras Shamra Texts and Their Relevance to the Old Testament* [VTSup 5; Leiden: Brill, 1965], 189) that בָּמֹות (*bāmôt*, "high places"; GK 1195) in Deuteronomy 33:29 should be translated "backs," in keeping with its meaning in Ugaritic, deserves consideration. Deuteronomy 33:29 would then indicate that Israel would tread on the backs of her enemies, and *bāmôt* would not in that case connote the heights of the enemy territory.

5 The word פֶּשַׁע (peša', "transgression"; GK 7322), like many Hebrew words of theological significance, was used in a secular sense as well. (See its use of the rebellion of Israel in 1 Kings 12:19 and the rebellion of Moab in 2 Kings 3:7.) In an ethical sense it may connote rebellion against God. The word חַטָּאת (ḥaṭṭā²t; GK 2633) comes from a root that means basically "to miss." It is used of warriors adept at using the sling (Jdg 20:16). Ethically it pictures sin as failure to meet God's standards. Both words cover the positive and negative aspects of sin.

Samaria was built by Omri and his son Ahab (1Ki 16:24), a pair known for their sympathy with the Baal cult in the north. Jerusalem, the city chosen by God for his earthly dwelling place, was time and time again perverted with the worship of false gods.

The suggestion that the reading בָּמוֹת (bāmôt, "high places") be retained because precise verbal parallelism is unnecessary to prophetic speech is supported by the fact that while "Israel" is the poetic complement to "Jacob" in line 1, the poetic complement to "Jacob" in line 3 is "Judah" in line 5.

For a full discussion of the use of מִי (mî, "who") when the writer had persons in mind, see GKC, par. 137.

7 The Arabic root *tnn* means "to resemble" and hence may witness to a Semitic root meaning "image" (B. Halper, "The Root TNN," *AJSL* 24 [1907–1908]: 366–69).

Note that using earnings from prostitution as gifts to the temple is specifically prohibited in Deuteronomy 23:17–18.

B. The Prophet's Reaction to the Pronouncement of Judgment (1:8–9a)

> [8] Because of this I will weep and wail;
> I will go about barefoot and naked.
> I will howl like a jackal
> and moan like an owl.
> [9] For her wound is incurable;
> it has come to Judah.

COMMENTARY

8–9 The prophet next laments the destruction of the great metropolis of Samaria by representing himself as wailing and going about unclothed as a sign of mourning (v.8; cf. 2Sa 15:30). The jackal and the owl were animals of the wilderness and are often found in judgment oracles according to which a city or civilized region was about to be desolated (Isa 13:21; 34:13; Jer 50:38). The judgment to come on Samaria is like an incurable wound, that is, it is irreversible (v.9). But in its malignant course it has come to Jerusalem as well. The motif of God's judgment as producing an incurable wound is not rare in prophetic literature (Jer 8:22; 10:19; 30:12; 46:11; Na 3:19).

C. The Prophet's Warning and Summons to the People (1:9b−16)

It has reached the very gate of my people,
  even to Jerusalem itself.
[10] Tell it not in Gath;
  weep not at all.
In Beth Ophrah
  roll in the dust.
[11] Pass on in nakedness and shame,
  you who live in Shaphir.
Those who live in Zaanan
  will not come out.
Beth Ezel is in mourning;
  its protection is taken from you.
[12] Those who live in Maroth writhe in pain,
  waiting for relief,
because disaster has come from the LORD,
  even to the gate of Jerusalem.
[13] You who live in Lachish,
  harness the team to the chariot.
You were the beginning of sin
  to the Daughter of Zion,
for the transgressions of Israel
  were found in you.
[14] Therefore you will give parting gifts
  to Moresheth Gath.
The town of Aczib will prove deceptive
  to the kings of Israel.
[15] I will bring a conqueror against you
  who live in Mareshah.
He who is the glory of Israel
  will come to Adullam.
[16] Shave your heads in mourning
  for the children in whom you delight;
make yourselves as bald as the vulture,
  for they will go from you into exile.

COMMENTARY

10 Micah intensifies the prediction of Samaria's desperate plight in a poem in which his masterly use of the pun is again evident. In historical retrospect, we can see that these cities are chosen because they are likely the ones subdued by the Assyrian king Sennacherib during his campaign in Palestine in 701 BC as he worked his way toward Jerusalem. They are located in the southern foothills (Shephelah) as one moves from the coast toward Jerusalem. The prophet employs wordplay between the names of the cities and their reactions in order to make his point (see notes in NIV text).

The play on words begins in v.10 with Gath (*gat*), which is somewhat similar in sound to the Hebrew word "tell" (*nāgad*). The Hebrew of the second clause reads "do not weep at all." It is tempting to read "do not weep in Acco" (NIV note), for the word "weep" in Hebrew is similar in formation to "in Acco"; but doing so requires assuming the dropping, or elision, of the *ayin* (ᶜ). The dropping is speculative and the elision is unattested in this way. If "in Acco" is accepted, this line would be the only one in which two towns are introduced in such narrow compass; and the Hebrew makes good sense as it stands. Since these towns appear to be clustered in the Shephelah (Y. Aharoni, *The Land of the Bible* [Philadelphia: Westminster, 1967], 339), the inclusion of Acco would also be geographically anomalous.

The phrase "Tell it not in Gath" is reflective of David's lament at Saul's death (2Sa 1:20). It warns the people not to weep lest the inhabitants of Gath, a Philistine city, learn of their impending destruction. In Beth Ophrah ("house of dust") the inhabitants are to roll in the dust as a sign of mourning (Jos 7:6; Job 16:15; Isa 47:1).

11–12 The people of Shaphir ("beautiful, fair, pleasant") are to experience something quite the opposite of what the name of their town means;

they will be reduced to shame and dishonor. Those who live in Zaanan ("come out") will not be able to come out from their city.

Beth Ezel (*bêt hāʾēṣel*) is unknown to us. The word *ʾēṣel* means "beside, contiguous to" (BDB, 69). It is difficult to be certain what Micah intends in this wordplay, but it is likely that we have a clue in *ᶜemdātô* ("standing place"). We may paraphrase the name "Beth Ezel" as "nearby house." Perhaps the town was in close proximity to Jerusalem. That its "standing place" is to be taken away may indicate that this town standing nearby will cease to exist. Thus a buffer ("standing place") between Jerusalem and the invading armies will be removed. The wailing will signify the destruction of the town as its citizens mourn their fate. In the MT "Beth Ezel" is followed by the causative particle *kî*. The reason Beth Ezel will do so is "because" Maroth ("bitter") will also endure God's punishment (v.12). The causal particle is again used. All this will happen because God will punish his people, including Jerusalem.

13–14 The inhabitants of Lachish (v.13) are to harness the team to the chariot. Assonance is achieved by pairing Lachish with *rekeš* ("steed"; "team," NIV). The citizens of Lachish are to flee the coming destruction like steeds.

The significance of Moresheth is difficult to determine. Its name is somewhat similar in sound to *mᵉʾōrāśâ* ("betrothed"), and since "parting gifts" were given to brides as dowries (1Ki 9:16), it is possible that the designation is intended to convey that the town of Moresheth Gath is soon to be parted from Judah as a bride parts from her family.

Aczib ("deception") will prove to be a deception (*ʾakzāb*) to Judah. The word is used of a stream that has dried up (Jer 15:18), so this city will cease to exist.

15–16 The name "Mareshah" (v.15) is somewhat similar to nominal forms based on the root *yāraš* ("to possess"). The wordplay is achieved by pairing this name with *yōrēš* (a participial form of *yāraš*), which occurs in the first part of the clause. The word *yōrēš* denotes a possessor or conqueror (Jer 8:10). Thus this town, whose name may have engendered associations with the word "conqueror," will be conquered. The glory of Israel, that is, the people (cf. Hos 9:11–13), will be forced to flee as David did to Adullam. This thought continues in v.16, where the people are to mourn because of the depopulation of the country.

This section (vv.10–16) begins with words that recall David's lament at the death of Saul and ends with the name of the cave where David hid from Saul. These dark moments in David's life form a gloomy backdrop to the description of the fall of the towns Micah speaks of. Though he is never directly mentioned, the figure of David appears hauntingly in the tapestry of destruction—not a David standing tall in triumph, but a David bowed down by humiliation. It is as though Micah sees in the fall of each town and the eventual captivity of the two kingdoms the dissolution of the Davidic monarchy. Like David's glory, that of Israel will come to Adullam.

NOTES

10 Note the similarity of the consonantal sounds in אַל־תַּגִּידוּ (*ʾal-taggîdû*, "Tell it not") to גַּת (*gat*, "Gath").

11 The name "Zaanan" is somewhat similar in sound to the word יָצָא (*yāṣāʾ*, "come out").

D. The Prophet's Indictment of the Oppressing Classes (2:1–5)

¹Woe to those who plan iniquity,
   to those who plot evil on their beds!
At morning's light they carry it out
   because it is in their power to do it.
²They covet fields and seize them,
   and houses, and take them.
They defraud a man of his home,
   a fellowman of his inheritance.

³Therefore, the LORD says:

"I am planning disaster against this people,
   from which you cannot save yourselves.
You will no longer walk proudly,
   for it will be a time of calamity.
⁴In that day men will ridicule you;
   they will taunt you with this mournful song:

'We are utterly ruined;
  my people's possession is divided up.
He takes it from me!
  He assigns our fields to traitors.'"
⁵Therefore you will have no one in the assembly of the LORD
  to divide the land by lot.

COMMENTARY

1–2 The oracle continues with a denunciation of the corrupt practices of the affluent and influential classes, whose hold on the structure of society was so strong in Micah's day. The oracle as a whole (1:2–2:13) reflects a distinct pattern. There is the summons to hear (1:2)—an element in each of the oracles—the announcement of doom (1:3–7), the prophet's reaction to the announcement (1:8–9), the warning summons (1:10–16), and the basis for the judgment culminating in the statement of hope (2:1–13). Generically, this type of oracle is called a "woe oracle" and develops from the laments connected to funerals. However, in the prophetic use there is no true mourning. It is a way of saying that the addressee is "as good as dead."

It is in 2:1–5 that the prophet establishes the basis for the national crisis and the future collapse of the nation. It is not the imperialism of Assyria or the fortunes of blind destiny that are bringing the house of Israel to this critical stage. It is her disobedience to her God. The prophets frequently recalled the terms of the Mosaic covenant, which promised blessing for the people should they respond ethically to the terms of the covenant and cursing if they should not (Dt 27–28). The covenant demanded that God's people show social concern (Ex 22:26; 23:4–9). Failure to do so would not only weaken the nation by affecting the social fabric but also, and even more importantly, would seriously affect the nation's relationship to God. It

would mean that the people had taken themselves away from the ground of the covenant that was the vehicle for national blessing.

The events of the eighth century produced two main classes of people: a burgeoning affluent group and a poor class that suffered at the hands of the rich. Micah turns to the powerful ruling classes and vividly pictures the intensity with which they seek to defraud the poor and become richer at the expense of the less fortunate. He pictures them as lying awake at night devising ($h\bar{a}\check{s}ab$) their plans (v.1). At first light of day, they proceed to put their schemes into action. They can do so because "it is in their power." They control the structures of society and have a free hand to perpetrate their deeds with impunity (cf. 7:3). They covet the houses and lands of those who cannot adequately defend themselves in this oppressive society (v.2). The story of Naboth and Ahab (1Ki 21) provides a good historical example of this type of sin.

3 Micah refers to the nation as a "people" ($mi\check{s}p\bar{a}h\hat{a}$; "family," KJV, RSV). Amos (Am 3:1) used the same expression to refer to the whole nation (Israel and Judah). Verse 3 begins with the word "therefore" ($l\bar{a}k\bar{e}n$), thus establishing the preceding catalog of wrongs as the basis for the disaster that Micah predicts in this verse. He pictures the disaster as a burden from which the people will be unable "to remove their necks" (lit. trans.). The Hebrew word ($m\hat{u}\check{s}$) that Micah uses here means "to remove" ("save," NIV). He has seen the captivity as certain (1:9), and they will not be able to avoid it. The prospect of the captivity is like a galling yoke or a heavy burden from which they cannot remove their necks. Because of the national humiliation, they will be unable to hold their heads high among the nations.

4 This verse contains a lament song that is characteristic of the way the people will mourn the desolation of the land. Their punishment will be tit for tat. They stole the land of others, now their land will be taken from them.

The clauses that precede the lament are governed by verbs in the impersonal third person singular. The first verbal clause (*yiśśā'ᶜᵃlêkem māšāl*) may be translated "one will take up a *māšāl*" ("lament song, proverbial song") or "a *māšāl* will be taken up" ("men will ridicule you," NIV). The preposition *ᶜal* may be understood in the sense of "concerning," and the whole phrase may be taken as introducing the lament song recorded in this verse. Because it is entirely in the first person, the lament song is clearly uttered by the house of Israel and not by someone else.

The word *māšāl* is used of figurative prophetic accounts (e.g., Isa 14:4). In general, however, it is a "descriptive saying," "byword," or "proverb" that has popular appeal or significance.

The second clause ("they will taunt you with this mournful song") is a remarkable example of alliteration in the Hebrew (*wᵉnāhâ nᵉhî nihyâ*). Again the verb (*nāhâ*) is in the impersonal third person singular and can hardly refer to an enemy of Israel, for it means "to lament." Literally the clause reads, "one will lament with great lamentation." Then follows a third verb (*'amar*, "saying"; untranslated in NIV) in the impersonal third person.

The lamentation concerns the fact that the land allotted (*ḥēleq*) to the people has changed hands (*mûr*). The land that was Israel's exclusive possession has become the property of her enemies, as is amplified in the next phrase where God is pictured as reassigning the land. The land is to be assigned to "traitors" or, better, "to a rebel." The singular substantive *šôbeb* may be a collective for the people of the enemy who will occupy the land, or it may refer to the Assyrian king himself. At any rate, Micah describes the enemy as a rebel—a description not out of keeping with Micah's view of the nations in their relationship to God; for Micah later describes them as "nations that have not obeyed" (5:15), thus imputing to them a rebellious nature.

5 As a result of the calamity, there will be "none to cast the line by lot in the assembly of the LORD" (RSV). This reference brings to mind the method by which Joshua apportioned the land to the tribes (Jos 14:1–5). The word "assembly" (*qāhāl*) may mean a "multitude" in general; but when used with an adjunctive word (in this case "LORD"), the phrase containing it takes on distinct limitations. It connotes the assembly of people that is distinctly the Lord's, i.e., the covenantal community (Dt 23). Because of their blatant disregard for the obligations of the covenant, the oppressors have removed themselves from any inheritance in the congregation. The prophet is saying that the corrupt people of his day will have no further participation in the covenantal community.

NOTES

4 For a discussion of the impersonal third person, see A. B. Davidson, *Hebrew Syntax* (Edinburgh: T&T Clark, 1901), 153–55.

Many scholars understand the preposition עַל (*ᶜal*) to mean "against" in the expression יִשָּׂא עֲלֵיכֶם מָשָׁל (*yiśśā'ᶜᵃlêkem māšāl*, "take up a proverb") and hence see the phrase as indicating that Israel is to be taunted by others in her misfortune. This interpretation presents some difficulty in that the two other verbs in this sequence of three cannot refer to Israel's enemies; for one verb means "to lament" (נָהָה, *nāhâ*), and the other, "to speak" (אָמַר, *ʾāmar*), introduces the lament that is spoken in the first person. The preposition ʿal need not mean "against" here any more than it does in Ezekiel 18:2, where it occurs with *māšāl* (GK 5442) in the sense of "concerning." It was the Hebrews themselves who uttered the *māšāl* concerning their own land in Ezekiel 18:2; and the use of this expression in Micah 2:4 may indicate that the proverbial saying will be current among the house of Israel after the captivity has become a reality. Those who understand *māšāl* to mean "a taunt song" must regard it as uttered by someone other than an Israelite. Allen, 285, understands it as taken up on behalf of Israel, while Mays, 65, sees it as a dirge sung by "professional mourners." *Māšāl* is understood too narrowly when translated "taunt song." As Mays, 65, observes, "*Māšāl* is a term applied to the broadest variety of sayings and songs."

The last word of the phrase וְנָהָה נְהִי נִהְיָה (*wᵉnāhâ nᵉhî nihyâ*) has been understood by some as a Niphal form of הָיָה (*hāyâ*, "it is all over"; KD). Others see it as dittography. The Dead Sea Scrolls, however, witness to the meaning "lamentation" (J. Carmignac, "Précisions apportées au vocabulaire de l'Hébreu biblique par la guerre des fils de lumière contre les fils de ténèbres," *VT* 5 [1955]: 351). It seems best to translate the phrase thus: "They shall lament with great lamentation."

The translation of שׁוֹבֵב (*šôbēb*; GK 8745) as "captors" (RSV) is attractive in view of the Hebrew root שָׁבָה (*šbh*, "take captive"). The same root (*šby*) is attested in Ugaritic (*UT* 68:29–30). This translation requires a textual emendation that has, however, little supportive evidence. The MT's form of the word requires that it be derived from שׁוּב (*šûb*, "turn back"). In its feminine form the word is used of a faithless or rebellious daughter (Jer 31:22; 49:4). The connotation "rebellious" for the Assyrian king will not be inappropriate (see comments above).

E. The True Prophet versus the False Prophets (2:6–11)

⁶ "Do not prophesy," their prophets say.
  "Do not prophesy about these things;
    disgrace will not overtake us."
⁷ Should it be said, O house of Jacob:
  "Is the Spirit of the LORD angry?
  Does he do such things?"

  "Do not my words do good
    to him whose ways are upright?
⁸ Lately my people have risen up
    like an enemy.
  You strip off the rich robe
    from those who pass by without a care,
    like men returning from battle.

> [9]You drive the women of my people
>   from their pleasant homes.
> You take away my blessing
>   from their children forever.
> [10]Get up, go away!
>   For this is not your resting place,
> because it is defiled,
>   it is ruined, beyond all remedy.
> [11]If a liar and deceiver comes and says,
>   'I will prophesy for you plenty of wine and beer,'
>   he would be just the prophet for this people!"

COMMENTARY

6 Micah quotes the false prophets of his day. "Do not prophesy," they say. The word translated "prophesy" (*nāṭap*; GK 5752) means primarily "to drip," a figure for words issuing from the lips. Though used of ordinary speech (Job 29:22), it predominantly describes prophetic speech (cf. Am 7:16). The prohibition against prophesying is immediately followed by another form of *nāṭap* ("they prophesy"; "their prophets say," NIV), indicating that the injunction to discontinue prophesying is in itself uttered by prophets—evidently the false, self-serving prophets of Micah's time. In the MT the command is in the plural, thus including along with Micah those who share his convictions.

The somewhat desultory character of v.6 reflects the emotion of the moment and creates a difficult problem for the interpreter. The first of the two negative clauses following the initial prohibition is governed by the Hebrew negative *lōʾ* and seems logically to carry through the prohibition: "They must [will] not prophesy about these things." The change of persons from second to third is not uncommon in the OT and occurs in the prophecy of Micah (1:2). The third clause is also governed

by *lōʾ* but cannot be a clause expressing command. It seems best to understand it as a clause connoting result: "disgrace will not leave us." The word translated "leave" is the Hebrew *sûg*, which never means "to overtake" but always "to leave" (but cf. BDB, 690–91). Thus the prophets who oppose Micah appear to be saying: "Do not prophesy. They must not prophesy of these things; for as long as they do, disgrace will not leave us."

The true prophets are apparently considered troublemakers whose powerful sermons disgrace the privileged classes and embarrass the false prophets. As long as their prophetic protest continues, so will continue the humiliation these corrupt leaders feel—thus the prohibition "Do not prophesy." This interpretation gains support from the subsequent verses.

7 Micah asks, "Should it be said, O house of Jacob?" (referring to the preceding statement of v.6). The sense of v.7 indicates that one should not blame the continuing disgrace on the prophetic pronouncements of Micah. The subsequent questions—"Is the Spirit of the LORD angry? Does he do such things?"—imply that it is not the nature of God only to punish or reproach, for the prophet continues, "my words [i.e., the words of the Lord through the prophet] do good to him whose ways are upright." If the ungodly people of his day would live according to the covenantal standards of the Lord, Micah's words will have a benign effect on their lives as well as on the life of the nation; and the reproach and disgrace they feel as he prophesies to them will become a means of blessing.

8 But the people are not living according to the standards of the Lord, for Micah says, "Lately my people have risen up like an enemy." This statement does not indicate against whom the people have risen up, but the subsequent context shows that their hostile acts are directed against the less fortunate. By their blatant disregard for the social concern demanded by the covenant, however, they are really rebelling against the Lord and evoking his anger (Ex 22:21–24; Dt 21:19; Mt 25:31–46).

The acts of unbelievable hostility Micah cites describe the ways in which the poor are treated like an enemy. The people forcibly strip off the outer garments of those who unsuspectingly pass by. Perhaps the reference is to debtors whose garments are confiscated in lieu of payment (Ex 22:26; Am 2:8; but cf. Notes). The word "strip" (*pāšaṭ*) frequently has the sense of a "raid" that a marauding party makes against an enemy (Jdg 9:33; 1Sa 23:27), and it is used also of stripping for spoil (Hos 7:1). This word, with its military connotations, seems to be deliberately chosen by Micah to illustrate how the poor are treated like enemies. In 3:5 Micah uses a similar motif as he pictures the avaricious prophets declaring war against those who cannot pay them.

The poor who are treated so cruelly are described as being averse (*šûb*) to war (cf. Ps 120:7). The peaceful and unsuspecting are suddenly bereft of some necessity of life by those who care nothing for their victims' security or comfort.

9–10 The money-hungry people even treat the women cruelly. That only women are mentioned implies that they are probably widows forced from their homes (cf. 2Ki 4:1–7). The children, too, are affected, for the Lord's blessing (*hādār*; GK 2077) is taken from them forever. The word *hādār* when used of God refers specifically to his glory or majesty. In Psalm 90:16 where the writer asks God to work in behalf of the people, *hādār* occurs in parallel with God's acts. In Psalm 149:9 the glory of God's faithful ones is the work of God in their behalf.

Because of the sin of the leaders of Micah's day, a whole generation will never see the glorious works of God but will live out their days in a strange land. Micah emphasizes this warning as the intensity of his language rises to a sharp command (v.10). The people are to be banished because the land has been irrevocably defiled. This statement echoes the pronouncement of doom spoken in this first oracle (1:2–7). Here, however, the desolation of the land is a result of sin primarily against the regulations of the covenant and not the sin of idolatry that was so central to that earlier denunciatory message. The prophet intertwines in this oracle the two basic manifestations of Israel's internal sickness: her idolatry, which has turned her from the purity of historic Yahwism to the worship of pagan deities, and her violation of the covenantal stipulations.

11 The people of this time have an intense desire for the fruits of their affluent society, expressed in the terms "wine" and "beer." So if someone were to preach to them of greater affluence and prosperity, they will listen to him; and he will readily find acceptance among them. The implication is that Micah's message of doom is unacceptable to those who are basking in the affluence of the eighth century.

NOTES

8 In each of its occurrences outside Micah (Isa 44:26; 58:12; 61:4), יְקוֹמֵם (*yᵉqômēm*, "rise up"; GK 7756) has the causative sense of the Polel and means "to set up." Several commentators have followed the lead of Ewald in translating the clause as "they" (i.e., the oppressors) have "set up" or "treated" my people as an enemy (cited in KD). That the verb is in the singular, however, presents a major difficulty. The verb may be regarded simply as an intensive conjugation of the ע״ו verb and need not have any causative connotation of the Polel. The translation "rise up" is acceptable grammatically (cf. GKC, par. 55c). Allen (292–93, n.46) emends the text to read קָמִים ... וְאַתֶּם לְעַמִּי (*wᵉʾattem lᵉʿammî ... qāmîm*, "you attack my people"). The emendation is adopted because עַמִּי (*ʿammî*, "my people") is the object of oppression in v.9, and the subsequent verbs have a second plural subject. However, *ʿammî* is used flexibly by Micah to refer to the oppressed classes (3:3) as well as the nation as a whole (1:9; 2:4; 3:5; 6:3, 5). The abrupt change of persons is typical of Micah's style (1:2; 2:3, 12; 3:9–10; cf. v.11 et al.). Particularly notable in this regard is 2:4, where the person changes from the first plural to third singular to first singular in the scope of three consecutive clauses. There is no versional evidence for the suggested emendation. Micah could easily have referred to the oppressors in his society as "my people," for the same term is used in 6:3, where he appeals to the rebellious to return to God.

The precise meaning of Micah's words in the second line of v.8 is difficult to understand. מִמּוּל שַׂלְמָה אֶדֶר תַּפְשִׁטוּן (*mimmûl śalmâ ʾeder tapšiṭûn*) is literally, "from the front of the garment you strip off the mantle [or 'glory']." The word *ʾeder* (GK 159) is unattested elsewhere in the OT as "mantle"; but it may be related to the feminine אַדֶּרֶת (*ʾadderet*), which has that meaning. Since Micah is describing the manner in which the people are being treated like enemies, it is possible that he imagines the oppressors brazenly standing before the less fortunate and spoiling them of their outer garments. There may be a wordplay in the use of *ʾeder* signifying that as the garments (*ʾeder*) are taken from the poor, they are also being stripped of their honor (*ʾeder*) because of the indignity they are forced to endure. The last line of the indictment (v.9) also speaks of the loss of honor or dignity: "You take away my blessing from their children forever." For a consideration of the options in the interpretation of this passage, see Allen, 296–97.

11 A typical Hebrew play on words is evident in Micah's use of שֶׁקֶר (*šeqer*, "lie") and שֵׁכָר (*šēkār*, "beer").

F. The Prophet's Statement of Hope (2:12–13)

> 12 "I will surely gather all of you, O Jacob;
>   I will surely bring together the remnant of Israel.
> I will bring them together like sheep in a pen,
>   like a flock in its pasture;
>   the place will throng with people.
> 13 One who breaks open the way will go up before them;
>   they will break through the gate and go out.

> Their king will pass through before them,
>   the LORD at their head."

COMMENTARY

12–13 The prophet turns abruptly to the statement of hope that ends the first oracle. In it he announces Israel's future restoration (v.12). The abruptness of the transition serves to place his message of hope in stark contrast to the message of the hypothetical preacher of v.11, who has falsely preached of continuing bright prospects for Israel. Micah's hope is not centered in his generation but in a remnant that will be led by their king from captivity to deliverance.

If studied in isolation from the total context of the prophecy, the passage may be understood simply as a prediction of the return from captivity. But this explanation is inadequate in view of the broader background of Micah's concept of the future. Micah envisions a kingdom of eternal duration with Yahweh as King (4:7). The Deliverer-King of 5:2–4 seems to be identical with the king of the present passage (v.13); he plays an important role in the restoration of God's people (2:13; cf. 5:3). In both passages the motif of the "flock" is prominent (2:12; cf. 5:4). The fulfillment of the great prophecy in 5:2–4 requires a ruler whose birthplace is Bethlehem and who will extend his influence to the ends of the earth and bring security to God's people. Micah's perspective of hope extends beyond a mere restoration from captivity to the messianic kingdom. It is then that Israel's hope will be finally and consummately realized.

Micah uses vivid pictorial language to depict the restoration of the remnant. He likens them to a flock of sheep penned up in an enclosure (v.12).

In the next clause the figurative depiction of sheep gives way to the picture of a vast throng of people. The word translated "throng" (*tᵉhîmenâ*) means "to murmur" (the root *hûm* being onomatopoetic). It depicts the murmuring of the members of a community (Ru 1:19) and the resonating sound of the earth echoing to the noise of a loud shout (1Sa 4:5; 1Ki 1:45).

The subject of *tᵉhîmenâ* is difficult to determine. One is tempted to regard *ṣōʾn* ("sheep") as the subject because it is feminine, but the parallel word *ʿēder* ("flock") is masculine. It is true that rules of agreement are not precise in Hebrew, but we would do well to look for another possibility. Although Micah depicts the remnant as a flock, which is feminine in Hebrew, he uses a masculine suffix to refer to the remnant in line 2. This use of the masculine makes it somewhat difficult to construe the remnant as the subject of the verb "murmur" since the verb is feminine. More likely the subject is to be found in the two feminine nouns *ṣārâ* ("pen") and *dōber* ("pasture"). If so, he may have used personification to picture the fenced pasturelands as murmuring, or perhaps the word is used as it is in 1 Samuel 4:5 and 1 Kings 1:45 to depict the pastureland as echoing the sound of the vast multitude.

We might expect Micah to sustain the metaphor by using another word for sheep when he speaks of the cacophony of sound that emanates from the enclosure, but he does not; he depicts them as people. Literally, he says that the pasture murmurs "because of [*min*, 'from'] the men" ("with people"

[NIV], i.e., because of the multitude of people). The prophet is not concerned with absolute precision in his use of figures of speech. Throughout his extended use of metaphorical language and his complex applications of gender, he does not lose sight of the fact that he is describing the destiny of people.

Suddenly a figure, called "the Breaker" (happōreṣ, "one who breaks open the way" [NIV]), appears in the narrative with no introduction (v.13). He is described as going up before the multitude. Where can they go? After all, they are confined. But their confinement is why his activity is described as "breaking." Led by the Breaker, the people burst through the gate of the enclosure to form a procession with their King at their head.

Micah envisions a time when the kingdom of God will burst forth into sudden reality and God's people will be manifested. Micah's theology of the kingdom is thus similar to that of Christ's, who in the parable of the wheat and the weeds (Mt 13:24–30) affirms that the true people of God will be manifested and gathered to him at the time of the harvest (v.30), an evident reference to the eschaton. Micah affirms that the strictures that now prevent the visible realization of the power and glory of God's kingdom and that blur the identity of God's people in the world will be shattered and the Breaker will lead his people to glory.

The Breaker will "go up before them." Then, according to the clausal structure, the multitude will burst through the gate. The Breaker must be one of the throng, because he goes before them to lead them out. His work is not done from outside the enclosure. Together they go forward with their King before them. The parallelism of the last clause establishes a close relationship between the work of the Breaker and the King of 5:2–4. Both arise from the people (5:2) and bring deliverance to the people (5:4); the people they lead are likened to a flock (5:4); and both are intimately associated with Yahweh (5:4). We may thus understand the Breaker to be Israel's King.

The last line of v.13 establishes a close connection between the Lord and the King. It is the Lord whose strength and power are manifested in the reign of the King. The King in v.13 reflects the strength and majesty of the Lord, as does the figure of 5:4. The remnant will receive its final glory and vindication only through the Messiah. He will arise from his people and lead them into the security of God's kingdom. This passage anticipates a later passage (4:7) in which Micah envisions the remnant as a "strong nation" over which Yahweh reigns.

NOTES

12 בָּצְרָה (bosrâ) need not be understood to mean "Bozrah," the Edomite city (so KD). The Hebrew root bṣr means "to make inaccessible" (BDB, 130–31). בִּצָּרוֹן (biṣārôn, "stronghold") comes from this root, as does מִבְצָר (mibṣār, "fortification"). While the meaning "pen" or "enclosure" is not attested for bosrâ, its parallelism with דֹּבֶר (dōber, "pasture") supports an affinity with bṣr.

13 The MT clearly identifies הַפֹּרֵץ (happōreṣ, "the Breaker") as one who arises from the people. It literally reads, "The Breaker will go up before them; they will break through and pass on." The people do not break through until the Breaker, who goes before them, has broken through. The people break out of the enclosure as they follow the one who makes the breach.

III. THE SECOND ORACLE: THE PROPHET'S INDICTMENT OF THE LEADERS OF THE HOUSE OF ISRAEL AND ISRAEL'S FUTURE HOPE (3:1–5:15)

A. The Prophet's Indictment of the Rulers of Israel (3:1–4)

¹Then I said,

"Listen, you leaders of Jacob,
  you rulers of the house of Israel.
Should you not know justice,
² you who hate good and love evil;
who tear the skin from my people
  and the flesh from their bones;
³who eat my people's flesh,
  strip off their skin
  and break their bones in pieces;
who chop them up like meat for the pan,
  like flesh for the pot?"
⁴Then they will cry out to the LORD,
  but he will not answer them.
At that time he will hide his face from them
  because of the evil they have done.

COMMENTARY

1 The second oracle begins, like the first, with a summons to hear the prophet's message. The summons is directed in this instance to the rulers of Judah and Israel. Micah begins this oracle with a devastating question: "Should you not know justice?" If any should know the meaning of justice, it is those who have the awesome responsibility of leadership. Here "justice" is used in the sense of fairness and equity in governmental administration.

2–3 The leaders mentioned in v.1 have everything upside down. They should "seek good, not evil" (Am 5:14), but instead they hate good and love evil.

The language of the prophet becomes vividly emotive as he describes the harsh treatment directed against the poor. He pictures the civil leaders as treating the exploited classes like animals being butchered and prepared for eating. The skin (ʿôr, a word frequently used for the hide of animals) is torn from them and their flesh butchered.

4 Because they have so treated the poor, these merciless authorities will not be heard when they cry to the Lord. Those who violate the stipulations of God's covenant cannot expect him to maintain the blessings of the covenant. It is disobedience that takes the people from the ground of the covenant and mars their relationship to God (cf. Ps 18:41; Pr 1:28; cf. note at 6:8).

NOTE

1 The words "Then I said" (*wā'ōmar*) remind us that Micah is being used by God to bring his judgment against the people. It also indicates that what follows in ch. 3 is a continuation of what came before, and indeed we find the same hard-hitting judgment brought against powerful oppressors that we saw in the earlier chapters.

B. The Prophet's Indictment of the Religious Leaders of Israel (3:5–8)

⁵This is what the LORD says:

"As for the prophets
   who lead my people astray,
if one feeds them,
   they proclaim 'peace';
if he does not,
   they prepare to wage war against him.
⁶Therefore night will come over you, without visions,
   and darkness, without divination.
The sun will set for the prophets,
   and the day will go dark for them.
⁷The seers will be ashamed
   and the diviners disgraced.
They will cover their faces
   because there is no answer from God."

⁸But as for me, I am filled with power,
   with the Spirit of the LORD,
   and with justice and might,
to declare to Jacob his transgression,
   to Israel his sin.

COMMENTARY

5 Micah addresses another group of leaders in Israel, the false prophets of the time. The Hebrew of v.5 is crisp and powerful: (lit.) "Who bite with their teeth and cry 'Peace!'" The word "bite" (*nāšak*; GK 5966) is always used in the OT for the bite of a serpent — except where the root reflects the secondary connotation of paying interest on loaned money. Its primary use of the serpent's bite has led some to interpret the phrase as describing the harm inflicted on the people by the lying prophets—prophets whose false message of peace is as harmful as a serpent's bite.

The evident antitheses in this verse seem, however, to warrant a different interpretation (e.g., NIV). The Hebrew says, literally, "Who bite with their teeth and cry 'Peace'; and if one does not put something into their mouths, they declare war against him." In this structure "bite" is paralleled by "not put into their mouths," and "peace" by "war." The parallelism thus determines that the word "bite" (nāšak) has to do with the action of putting something into the mouth. While nāšak is never used for "eating" in the OT, there is no reason why Micah cannot have used this forceful figure to express the voracity with which these greedy prophets accept the bribes given to them for the performance of their prophetic activity. The rudeness of the figure is appropriate to the language of the context (vv.2–3). The two connotations of nāšak—namely, "bite" and "exact, pay interest"—may be reflected here as a kind of pun.

The professional prophets continually cry "peace." They predict a bright future for Israel, while Micah predicts doom (cf. 1Ti 4:3).

6–7 The end will come for these religious hucksters (v.6). They sin with the gift of prophecy, so that gift will now be removed from them. There will be no visions and no divination, only darkness. No answers will be forthcoming from God.

While they then bask in the sunlight of power and affluence, the sun will go down on their prophesying and the resultant night will be devoid of vision or divination. It will be a time in which false predictions of peace (v.5) will be discredited by the reality of the captivity. These prophets will "cover their faces" (lit., "cover the beard"), an expression connoting deep mourning (v.7; cf. Lev 13:45; Eze 24:17, 22).

8 A strong adversative (wᵉʾûlām, "But"; "But as for me," NIV) introduces the affirmation in which Micah contrasts his prophetic activity with that of the false prophets. He asserts that he is filled with power "with [the help of] the Spirit." The implication is that the false prophets are not empowered by the Spirit but, as the preceding context has shown, are motivated by greed.

The word "justice" (mišpāṭ; GK 5477) is used frequently in the OT prophetic books in the sense of true religion—i.e., the crystallization of the ethic of the law (cf. Notes). Because Micah is not violating the covenantal standards, he stands in sharp contrast to the religious leaders who participate in and encourage the social exploitation of their time.

The word "might" is from the root gābar, from which the word geber ("man") derives. Here appears the feminine form gᵉbûrâ, a word connoting "might," "valor," or "manly courage." Because Micah is guiltless of his compatriots' crimes against their fellowmen, he can stand before his adversaries with the power of moral courage and a clear conscience. Thus he can fearlessly cry out against the sin of the house of Israel.

NOTES

8 The Hebrew particle אֵת (ʾet) in the expression אֶת־רוּחַ יְהוָה (ʾet-rûaḥ yhwh, "the Spirit of the LORD") may refer to the concept of assistance or direct agency (cf. Ge 4:1; Jdg 8:7; Est 9:29; Job 26:4; R. J. Williams, *Hebrew Syntax: An Outline* [Toronto: Univ. of Toronto Press, 1967], 61).

The word מִשְׁפָּט (*mišpāṭ*, "justice"; GK 5477) covers a wide range of meanings. It is used in legal contexts in the sense of "law" or "regulation" (Ex 24:3; Lev 5:10) and of the process of litigation (Nu 27:5; 35:12). The word also means "manner" or "custom," a connotation that may have derived from its use in legal contexts for a legal requirement (it occurs with this meaning in Ge 40:13; 1Ki 18:28). Frequently the word has a distinctly religious and ethical usage that is never entirely divorced from the Mosaic law. The prophets, in particular, use it in this sense. The law required the expression of concern for others (Ex 23:4–5; Dt 24:17–22). To the prophets *mišpāṭ* was the fulfillment of God's will as expressed in the law and hence had definite ethical significance. Jeremiah defined *mišpāṭ* as caring for the needy (Jer 5:28; 7:5), and Isaiah gave a classic definition of the term in Isaiah 1:17. James defined true religion in the traditional prophetic sense (Jas 1:26–27).

C. The Result of the Leaders' Corruption on the Nation (3:9–12)

⁹Hear this, you leaders of the house of Jacob,
　　you rulers of the house of Israel,
　who despise justice
　　and distort all that is right;
¹⁰who build Zion with bloodshed,
　　and Jerusalem with wickedness.
¹¹Her leaders judge for a bribe,
　　her priests teach for a price,
　　and her prophets tell fortunes for money.
　Yet they lean upon the LORD and say,
　　"Is not the LORD among us?
　　No disaster will come upon us."
¹²Therefore because of you,
　　Zion will be plowed like a field,
　Jerusalem will become a heap of rubble,
　　the temple hill a mound overgrown with thickets.

COMMENTARY

9 The address to the leaders of the house of Jacob continues with a biting portrayal of their sins (vv.9–12). Micah accuses them of despising justice (v.9). The Hebrew word *tā‘ab* ("despise") is a strong one that means utter abhorrence of something. It is used of the disgust for Job that he saw in his detractors (Job 30:10) and of the psalmist's disgust for lying (Ps 119:163). Amos used it in a way similar to Micah (Am 5:10).

10–11 As the leaders discharge their duties, they do so with bloodshed and greed (v.10), motivated by their desire for personal gain. Characterized by avarice and violence, their whole system of government inevitably is leading to corruption.

521

These leaders maintain a form of external religion based to some extent on the covenantal relationship. "Is not the LORD among us?" they ask (v.11). But they have lost sight of the ethical requirements of the covenant and, maintaining a mere shell of true worship of Yahweh, feel that their historical relationship to the Lord will prevent the onslaught of misfortune. Yet a clear body of prophetic tradition precedes this time and makes clear that God desires obedience, not allegiance to externals (1Sa 15:22; Ps 51:17). This optimistic but unfounded trust in Yahweh displayed by the leaders is described as "leaning on the LORD" (cf. v.11). It is a kind of trust, but one devoid of the fruits of real faith in obedience and ethical response to God (cf. Ro 6:1–4; Gal 5:16–26; Jas 2:18–26).

12 Because of the actions of the corrupt religious and civil leaders, the predicted doom will become a reality. The prediction begins with "therefore" (lākēn), establishing, as Micah has already done, that the cause of the captivity is the disobedience of the people.

One wonders whether the words of Micah were ever in the minds of these leaders as they walked the bustling streets of Jerusalem and passed Solomon's magnificent temple: "Because of you, Zion will be plowed like a field." What a telling illustration of the corporate effect of individual disobedience!

While the name "Zion" originally referred to the Jebusite stronghold captured by David (2Sa 5:7), which in Solomon's time was distinct from the site where the temple was actually built (1Ki 8:1), it became a synonym for the city of Jerusalem in the prophetic and poetic literature (Ps 149:2; Isa 4:3; 40:9; Am 6:1). That this later usage is its sense here in Micah 3:12 is clear, both from its forming a poetic complement to Jerusalem in the parallel structure and from its use in Jeremiah 26:18, where Jeremiah quoted Micah's words as analogous to his prediction of the destruction of Jerusalem (cf. Jer 26:11–12).

But like Jeremiah, Micah also includes the destruction of the temple in his prophecy. He pictures a wooded height, starkly bare. The temple, the visible sign of God's presence, is to be destroyed. As it did for their forefathers at Shiloh (1Sa 4:3–11), the symbol of the people's empty religion will perish.

D. The Future Exaltation of Zion (4:1–8)

OVERVIEW

The chapter division should not obscure the fact that Micah continues to speak of Jerusalem. However, there is an abrupt mood change from gloom to sublime hope as Micah portrays the future glory of the city. The temple mount, soon to become a shrub-grown hill (3:12), will be exalted in the latter days; and the city of Jerusalem will become the center of God's gracious activity to the peoples of the earth.

This oracle forms the basis of a similar expression of hope in the prophecy of Isaiah (Isa 2:1–4), where it occurs with some variations. It is difficult to determine its origin. While it is possible that it was an independent oracle used by both Micah and Isaiah, it seems likely that Micah is the original author. It is an integral part of his entire prophecy and follows logically from the preceding description of Jerusalem's doom. That the oracle is longer in the prophecy of Micah than in Isaiah may indicate that Isaiah has adapted it for his own purposes. The superscription to the oracle in Isaiah (Isa 2:1) may simply indicate that Isaiah is conscious of the controlling influence of the Holy Spirit in using the prophecy.

¹In the last days

the mountain of the Lord's temple will be established
  as chief among the mountains;
it will be raised above the hills,
  and peoples will stream to it.
²Many nations will come and say,
 "Come, let us go up to the mountain of the Lord,
  to the house of the God of Jacob.
He will teach us his ways,
  so that we may walk in his paths."
The law will go out from Zion,
  the word of the Lord from Jerusalem.
³He will judge between many peoples
  and will settle disputes for strong nations far and wide.
They will beat their swords into plowshares
  and their spears into pruning hooks.
Nation will not take up sword against nation,
  nor will they train for war anymore.
⁴Every man will sit under his own vine
  and under his own fig tree,
and no one will make them afraid,
  for the Lord Almighty has spoken.
⁵All the nations may walk
  in the name of their gods;
we will walk in the name of the Lord
  our God for ever and ever.

⁶"In that day," declares the Lord,

"I will gather the lame;
  I will assemble the exiles
  and those I have brought to grief.
⁷I will make the lame a remnant,
  those driven away a strong nation.
The Lord will rule over them in Mount Zion
  from that day and forever.
⁸As for you, O watchtower of the flock,
  O stronghold of the Daughter of Zion,
the former dominion will be restored to you;
  kingship will come to the Daughter of Jerusalem."

COMMENTARY

1 While in the near future Zion will be made desolate (3:12), that will not be the end of the story. Zion will be great again. Its greatness has nothing to do with its present physical features (it is, after all, a relatively small mountain), but rather with God's choice of it as his place of earthly dwelling. When Zion is so exalted, it will be like a magnet for the nations. There will be a constant flow of people going to Jerusalem in order to learn God's law.

When will these things happen? "In the last days" (*b⁺ah⁺rît hayyāmîm*) always denotes a period of time that, from the writer's perspective, is in the indefinite future. Indeed, the prophecy began to be fulfilled with the rebuilding of the second temple. Nevertheless, complete fulfillment awaits the ushering of the kingdom of God in its fullness (Rev 21–22).

2 The object of the people's attraction to Jerusalem is to be their desire for God's word, which emanates from the city. Micah sees a change in the hearts of all peoples at this time, when the law of the Lord will be received universally rather than by Israel and Judah alone.

3 The result of God's rule in this time will be that the nations of the world will experience peace. While the people of God, who are the church, have experienced peace in their hearts, it is difficult to limit this prediction only to Christians. The prophecy is national and even universal in scope and looks forward to a time when the nations will come so fully under the kindly influence of God's Word that war will be no more.

There can be no war when it is Yahweh himself who arbitrates disputes among the nations and whose authority determines the resolutions to their problems. So weapons of war will be fashioned into agricultural implements. The pastoral motif reflects the peace Micah sees as the ruling element of the messianic kingdom, a concept used also by other prophets to symbolize the tranquility of that time (Isa 11:6–10; Hos 2:15[17]; Am 9:13–15). The close identification between the Lord and the messianic King is evident in this prophecy of Micah. In the present passage Yahweh's rule is dominant, but in 5:2 that authority is vested in a king who, in certain ways, is distinct from God (v.4).

4 The peacefulness of this era is further described in pastoral imagery. It reflects the description of Solomon's kingdom in 1 Kings 4:25 and later became a description of conditions in the final days (Zec 3:10). The verse goes on to assert that the people will dwell in peace and safety, not because of their own strength but because of the Lord of hosts, by whose word this state of blessing will be effected. The certainty of this event is established in Micah's mind not because of groundless optimism or a naive trust in human nature, but because God has sovereignly declared that it will happen: "The LORD Almighty has spoken."

5 The reason for the people's safety and security is that they will walk in the name of the Lord forever. To "walk in the name" means more than simply adhering to the religious requirements associated with the deity in question. It means to live in reliance on the strength of that deity. In the case of Yahweh, it involves reliance on the might of his power, by which his attributes are manifested (cf. Notes).

The implication is that the nations have been walking in the strength of their gods, but that situation will not persist. The placing of the word "forever" at the end of the line in the

Hebrew text indicates its emphatic nature. Unlike the nations, God's people will enjoy his strength forever. It will be otherwise with the nations, for the dominion of their gods will come to an end when the people of the world submit to the rule of Yahweh and recognize the vanity of their false deities.

6–7 "In that day" (v.6) refers back to the era of Jerusalem's exaltation introduced in 4:1. The future regathering of Israel in the time of Zion's exaltation is described differently from the way Micah described it earlier (2:12–13). Here Micah depicts those who are regathered as lame, referring to their weakness as a result of God's afflicting them; he further describes them as exiles, connoting the shame of expulsion from one's homeland. The emphasis is on the misery and helplessness of the exiles and forms a striking contrast to the "strong nation" (v.7) they are to become as a result of God's intervention in their behalf.

The returning people do not automatically comprise the remnant, according to Micah, but are to be made into a remnant. The idiom *śîm leʿ* means "to make into" and is used similarly in 1:6. To Micah the remnant is more than simply a residue of people. It is the repository of God's grace and promise as well as the force that will ultimately conquer the godless nations at the end time (5:8–15). It is thus an act of grace that forms these poor exiles into a remnant and bestows on them the blessings of the messianic age (cf. Ro 11:1–6).

This distinct and profoundly theological use of the term "remnant" is developed further in the poetic structure where its corresponding member in the parallelism is "strong nation." Since the remnant is the beneficiary of God's promise, it cannot fail to experience ultimate vindication and glory. To Micah, therefore, the remnant is synonymous with power and might; and, in keeping with his

understanding, it forms an apt synonym to "strong nation" in the couplet.

The nation into which the remnant is transformed will have the Lord as its King forever (Isa 24:23; 52:7; et al.). The center of God's rule will be restored and exalted Zion.

8 The climax of this representation of Jerusalem's future glory is described in terms of its restoration as the seat of the "former dominion." The dominion soon to be lost in the dark time just ahead will be restored.

The phrase "watchtower of the flock" stands in apposition with "stronghold [ʿōpel] ... of Zion" and is synonymous with it. The ʿōpel was a fortified section of Jerusalem on the eastern side in the immediate area of the temple mount and the Kidron Valley. It was probably the same general geographical area known earlier as "Zion" or the "City of David"; for later books, such as 1 and 2 Chronicles and Nehemiah, rarely use the name "Zion" and apply the name ʿōpel to what might properly be termed "Zion." From 2 Chronicles 33:14 it is clear that ʿōpel was located in the immediate environs of the City of David. Micah seems to have used the term in the same fashion, for "watchtower of David" applies fittingly to the City of David. Nehemiah 3:25–27 places the ʿōpel and the king's house closely together as well. The appositional structure of the terms "watchtower" and "Zion" seems to negate the possibility that the "watchtower of the flock" was a tower in the vicinity of Bethlehem (Ge 35:19–21).

Since the expressions used by Micah have such close ties with the location of David's dominion, the words "former dominion" can mean little else than that the Davidic kingdom will in some sense be restored to Jerusalem. By asserting so, Micah stands firmly in the tradition of the preexilic prophets (Isa 9:7; Hos 3:5; Am 9:11).

NOTES

1 That בְּאַחֲרִית הַיָּמִים (*bᵉʾaḥᵃrît hayyāmîm*, "in the last days") does not always have an eschatological perspective may be seen in Genesis 49:1 and Deuteronomy 31:29, where it denotes an indefinite period in Israel's future.

5 For the concept of "strength" inherent in the expression "walk in the name," see Zechariah 10:12, where the phrase is parallel to "strengthen them." It is expressed also in 1 Samuel 17:45 (cf. 1Ch 14:11; Pss 33:22; 118:10–13; Pr 18:10). The word שֵׁם (*šēm*, "name") covers the nature, attributes, and even reputation of God. To "walk in the name" is to enjoy the strength expressed in God's attributes. See comment at 5:4.

E. The Future Might of Zion (4:9–13)

⁹Why do you now cry aloud —
    have you no king?
Has your counselor perished,
    that pain seizes you like that of a woman in labor?
¹⁰Writhe in agony, O Daughter of Zion,
    like a woman in labor,
for now you must leave the city
    to camp in the open field.
You will go to Babylon;
    there you will be rescued.
There the Lord will redeem you
    out of the hand of your enemies.

¹¹But now many nations
    are gathered against you.
They say, "Let her be defiled,
    let our eyes gloat over Zion!"
¹²But they do not know
    the thoughts of the Lord;
they do not understand his plan,
    he who gathers them like sheaves to the threshing floor.

¹³"Rise and thresh, O Daughter of Zion,
    for I will give you horns of iron;
I will give you hoofs of bronze
    and you will break to pieces many nations."

You will devote their ill-gotten gains to the Lord,
    their wealth to the Lord of all the earth.

COMMENTARY

9 The reader's attention is abruptly shifted from the graphic description of the future glory of Jerusalem to the realities of the current crisis. The section begins with the Hebrew word "now" (ʿattâ), a word that frequently bears a chronological connotation (i.e., "at this time"). From the heights of the previous pronouncement, Micah descends to the present dismal situation; his hearers are not to develop a false sense of security. The rhetorical questions are intended as affirmations. Israel will have no king. She will be left without a counselor.

The loss of the king not only means the dissolution of the government; in the context of Israel's theocratic structure, it means much more than it would to other nations. The king is the Lord's anointed and stands as his vicegerent, mediating God's law to the people. The loss of Israel's ruler will lead many to question the veracity of God's promises as they relate to the future of the nation and to the Messiah, who is to come from Israel. One can hardly imagine a harder blow, for it signifies that God has vented his wrath against his people. The extreme anguish the nation is to endure through losing its national sovereignty is pictured as that of a woman in childbirth (Isa 13:8; Jer 6:24; Hos 13:13).

10 Micah's use of contrast is again evident, for in the scope of one verse he both affirms Israel's doom and predicts her deliverance. A bright future and a glorious destiny may await her, but that future does not diminish Israel's present responsibility for her disobedience.

The prophet sees the captivity as taking place in three stages: leaving the city, sojourning in the stretches of the open country, and arriving at the land of captivity. The use of "Babylon" is not necessarily an indication that the verse is a later interpolation. "Babylon" may simply be a metonymy for Meso-potamia; or it may have been used in a pejorative sense of the world powers, whose hostility to Israel is exhibited in so many ways and will continue to be shown until the time of Israel's restoration. The use of "Babylon" in this sense may go back to Genesis 10:10 and 11:4-9, where Babylon's function as the center of godless world power is established.

That the plural "enemies" is used (v.10) and that the subsequent verses (vv.11-13) speak of "many nations" seem to indicate that "Babylon" has for Micah a broader significance than the empire that will soon replace Assyria as the dominant world power. On the contrary, he seems to be saying that God's people are to come under the dominion of godless nations, a dominion that will endure till the "Daughter of Zion," by the plan of God, will conquer the nations (v.13).

Any argument for a late date for this section must be based on more than simply the occurrence of the name "Babylon." The future tenses used in v.10, the correspondence of the dissolution of the monarchy of Judah to the events of the captivity (vv.9-10), and the accord that exists between this prophecy of the impending captivity and similar passages in the early chapters of Isaiah all support the placing of this passage in the period before the captivity, when the great eighth-century prophets carried on their ministries. Micah may have used "Assyria" in a similar fashion (cf. comment on 5:5).

A positive unity pervades the entire chapter. The statement of hope that opened the chapter is reiterated and complemented by the truth that it is not a hope to be realized by an unrepentant people who have not paid for their sins. They are to suffer for their disobedience; but beyond that night of despair is the bright morning of Zion's glory, when God's people will be redeemed from the hand of their enemies. For those who accept the validity of biblical prophecy, the picture of present crisis and future hope finds an adequate situation in the critical days in which Micah ministers.

11-13 The nations that exhibit hostility (v.11; cf. Ps 2:2; Zec 14:2) do so in ignorance (v.12); for as they gather to gloat over the misfortune of God's people, the nations do not know their part in God's plan for his people. The prophet pictures the nations as sheaves brought to the threshing floor; only too late do they recognize that they are to be threshed and broken by Israel herself (v.13). While the atmosphere of this passage is different from the placid mood of 4:1-4, there is no more need to see a different author reflecting a more militant ideology here than there is in Isaiah 9:2-7, where the peace that is predicted follows the conquest of Israel's oppressors.

The horn (v.13) symbolizes strength (cf. Dt 33:17; 1Sa 2:1). The wealth of the world is to be devoted to God, and all its might is to be under his dominion.

F. The Future King of Zion (5:1-4[4:14-5:3])

> ¹ Marshal your troops, O city of troops,
> for a siege is laid against us.
> They will strike Israel's ruler
> on the cheek with a rod.
>
> ² "But you, Bethlehem Ephrathah,
> though you are small among the clans of Judah,
> out of you will come for me
> one who will be ruler over Israel,
> whose origins are from of old,
> from ancient times."
>
> ³ Therefore Israel will be abandoned
> until the time when she who is in labor gives birth
> and the rest of his brothers return
> to join the Israelites.
> ⁴ He will stand and shepherd his flock
> in the strength of the LORD,
> in the majesty of the name of the LORD his God.
> And they will live securely, for then his greatness
> will reach to the ends of the earth.

COMMENTARY

1[4:14] Micah 5:1 is 4:14 in the MT and is thus understood to continue the preceding discussion (the versification of the MT of ch. 5 differs by one). But Micah's characteristic pattern of doom followed by hope suggests a typical use of contrast to emphasize his message. It thus forms an apt introduction to the section dealing with the Deliverer-King.

"Marshal your troops" is a summons to the soon-to-be beleaguered city of Jerusalem to gather troops for her defense against the siege. The enemy in mind is likely the Assyrian king Sennacherib and his army who attacked Judah in 701 BC (Waltke, "Micah," 702). The word "troops" (*gᵉdûd*) in the phrase "city of troops" is a nominal form derived from the verb *gādad* and is used always in a military sense. The expression "daughter of troops" (lit. Heb.) forms a Hebrew grammatical function denoting character and depicts Jerusalem as a warlike city. Here perhaps is an echo of the social crimes so vividly described in warlike terminology elsewhere in Micah (2:8; 3:2–3, 9–10; 7:2–6). The implication of this expression is then that Jerusalem, so renowned for its hostility toward the less fortunate, will suffer siege because of its wrongdoing.

Striking a king on his cheek represents the most extreme of insults and marks the victory of Israel's enemies over her (1Ki 22:24; Job 16:10; Ps 3:7[8]). The king is called "judge" (*šōpēṭ*; "ruler," NIV), depicting the judicial aspect of his office. This word may have been chosen to form a play with the word for "rod" (*šēbeṭ*).

2[5:1] The statement of doom is followed by one of hope, as the preceding picture of Jerusalem's fate and the ignominy of her king is followed by the prediction of a king who will bring lasting security to Israel and whose influence will extend to the ends of the earth.

Jerusalem is in trouble; hope is associated with the small town of Bethlehem Ephrathah. Ephrathah is the ancient name of Bethlehem (Ge 35:16, 19; 48:7; Ru 4:11; cf. Jos 15:59 LXX) and distinguishes it from other towns named "Bethlehem," such as the one in Zebulun (Jos 19:15). The use of "Ephrathah" identifies Bethlehem as the town

in which David was born (1Sa 17:12), thus establishing a connection between the messianic King and David. That the deliverance will come from Bethlehem Ephrathah is a surprise! God uses the small and the weak of the world to accomplish his mighty purpose.

The ruler is to come forth "to/for me" (*lî*), according to the Hebrew text. Yahweh is represented as speaking here, and the close identification of the king with the purposes of God is thus implied. Some commentators apply the phrase "from ancient times" to the remote beginnings of the monarchy, but this view is unsatisfactory. The term applies grammatically to the ruler. It is he whose activities stem from the distant past, yet whose coming is still future.

The words "whose origins" translates the Hebrew word *môṣāʾōtāyw* (lit., "his goings forth"). The expression "to go forth" means primarily "to conduct one's activities" (cf. 2Ki 19:27). Beyond that the phrase has a military connotation referring to the departure of an army for battle (2Sa 3:25; cf. 3:22; 5:2; 10:16; Nu 27:17; Isa 43:17) and may speak of the kingly activities of the Messiah in terms of his might and power—a fitting contrast to the weakness and subjugation of the Israelite monarchy pictured in the preceding verse.

The terms "old" (*qedem*; GK 7710) and "ancient times" (*mîmê ʿôlām*) may denote "great antiquity" as well as "eternity" in the strictest sense. The context must determine the expanse of time indicated by the expressions. In Micah 7:14, for example, *mîmê ʿôlām* is used of Israel's earliest history. But the word *qedem* is used of God himself on occasion in the OT (Dt 33:27; Hab 1:12), of God's purposes (Isa 37:26; La 2:17), of God's declarations (Isa 45:21; 46:10), of the heavens (Ps 68:33[34]), and of the time before creation (Pr 8:22–23). At any rate the word *qedem* can indicate only great antiquity, and its application to a future ruler—one yet to appear on the scene of Israel's history—is strong evidence that Micah expects a supernatural figure, in keeping with the expectation of Isaiah in 9:6[5], where the future King is called *'ēl* ("God"), an appellation used only of God by Isaiah. This understanding is also in keeping with the common prophetic tradition of God's eventual rule over the house of Israel (Isa 24:23; Mic 4:7; et al.). Only in Christ does this prophecy find fulfillment.

3[2] This verse begins with the word "therefore" (*lākēn*), which introduces the logical result of the emergence of Israel's ruler. Because a ruler will eventually come to deliver Israel, God will give her up only temporarily. That is, Israel will enter a period of absolute abandonment by God because of her sin (1:5–6; 2:1–5; 3:4, 9–12; 4:10; 6:9–16), but a ruler will come who will end the period of Israel's estrangement; therefore, Israel will be given up only until that time. Hosea also spoke of a period when Israel would not be God's people (*lō'-'ammî*) and saw the state of separation from God as continuing until the exiles returned and sought the Lord and the messianic King, who is called "David" (Hos 1:9; 3:4–5).

Micah sees the period of abandonment continuing until "she who is in labor gives birth." Several Protestant interpreters have seen Mary the mother of Jesus in this prediction. But this interpretation requires that the word "she" refer to a figure not previously cited in the context, thus introducing into the text an abruptness and a syntactical harshness that are unnecessary. Micah earlier (4:9–10) used the metaphor of a woman's giving birth in reference to Jerusalem, which by metonymy may represent the whole nation. It is best to maintain the same meaning of the figure here and to understand it as speaking of the bringing forth of the Messiah by Bethlehem in Judah. Up to this point the theme of Jerusalem's suffering has been central to Micah's message, and the

application of the figure in this way seems most natural.

The end of the period of Israel's estrangement from God is marked not only by the bringing forth of the ruler but also by the return to Israel of "the rest of his brothers." The pronoun "his" finds its nearest grammatical referent in the ruler of v.2. The brothers are those who share a common national heritage with him (cf. 2Sa 19:13) and are thus under his regnal authority and protection. We observed a similar relationship of the King to his people in 2:13, where the Breaker-King is one with them and emerges from them. The word "return" (*šûb*) implies an original identification with Israel. The need for their return indicates they have been dispersed. Micah has already spoken of them in his account of the remnant in 4:6–7. There the "exiles" (v.6), "those driven away" (v.7), will be assembled and brought under the Lord's rule.

The gathering of those who comprise the remnant is an essential element in Micah's theology (see 2:12–13; 4:6–7). The depiction of the future gathering of the remnant in 5:3 is presented in a captivity motif: the brothers have been dispersed—they are in exile. This depiction is not unusual in the prophets. Zechariah (Zec 10:10) said that God's people will return from Assyria, a nation that brought Israel into captivity but long since disappeared from the world scene. Isaiah (Isa 11:11–12) pictured the remnant as outcasts whom the Lord will gather from the lands of their dispersion. The future deliverance of God's people is presented in this way because the prophets saw the captivity as continuing, in a sense, until the coming of the messianic King (see comments on 5:5–6). Micah envisions a time when the national solidarity that characterized the Davidic kingdom will be realized again.

4[3] The kindly effect of the kingly reign of Messiah is described in pastoral terminology. While the image of king as shepherd has deep roots in the ancient Near East, in the Bible the image of the shepherd has its origins in David, who was literally a shepherd (2Sa 5:2; 7:7). Ezekiel 34:23–24 also develops the idea that the future ideal ruler will be a shepherd in the tradition of David. "As a shepherd he leads, defends, and cares for his wards" (Waltke, "Micah," 707). Israel will be lovingly cared for by the messianic King, who will carry out his duties in the strength of God. In effect Yahweh will reign over the people—but in the person of the King.

The expression "in the name of" is parallel to "in the strength of," thus establishing a connection between the two concepts (see Note on 4:5). The Deliverer will be the embodiment of the strength and might of God, communicate that attribute to the people under his authority, and thereby establish their security eternally. The gracious benefits of his reign will extend beyond national limitations, for the authority of the King will be universal in scope because his greatness will extend "to the ends of the earth." This description of his power goes perfectly with the description of universal peace seen earlier (4:1–4) and complements it by affirming that the peace described there will be effected by the Ruler born in the insignificant town of Bethlehem. Isaiah called him the "Prince of Peace" (9:6).

NOTES

1[4:14] The NIV takes the opening words of this verse (*titgōdᵉdî bat-gᵉdûd*) from a verbal root *gdd* II (GK 1518), "to band together." Hypothetically, the verb could be from *gdd* I, "to cut oneself," and thus the phrase could be translated, "Now gash yourself, daughter of a raider," but this view seems unlikely, for it would attribute a pagan mourning ritual to the people of God, who are evaluated positively in the context. Many versions go a third way, as represented by the NRSV: "Now you are walled around with a wall." This interpretation, too, takes the verb from *gdd* I, but with the idea of cutting stones.

Both בַּת (*bat*, "daughter") and בֵּן (*bēn*, "son") may be used with an adjunct to connote character or quality. Thus בַּת־גְּדוּד (*bat-gᵉdûd*, "daughter of troops") means "warlike city." Note also בַּת־בְּלִיָּעַל (*bat-bᵉlîyāᶜal*, "daughter of Belial") in 1 Samuel 1:16, which means "a worthless woman." Other words as well occur in this construct relationship to express character or quality.

3[2] Mays, 117, cites Deuteronomy 15:12 and 17:15 to show that אָח (*ʾāḥ*, "brother") means "member of the people." The eventual union of the northern and southern tribes was predicted by Ezekiel (Eze 37:15–23).

G. The Future Peace of Zion (5:5–6[4–5])

⁵   And he will be their peace.

When the Assyrian invades our land
    and marches through our fortresses,
  we will raise against him seven shepherds,
    even eight leaders of men.

> 6 They will rule the land of Assyria with the sword,
>   the land of Nimrod with drawn sword.
> He will deliver us from the Assyrian
>   when he invades our land
>   and marches into our borders.

COMMENTARY

5–6[4–5] The first line ("and he will be their peace") continues the thought of the previous unit, with its reference to a Davidic deliverer. He will bring them peace. This reference is reminiscent of the "Prince of Peace" mentioned in Isaiah 9:6. Then the placid picture vanishes for a moment, and the tramping boots of the invader are heard (v.5). The events described here are difficult to locate historically. Those who place this pericope in the context of the conquests of Antiochus III (who ruled from 283–187 BC) have great difficulty with the term "Assyrian"; yet if the passage is understood to describe a coalition of leaders who will successfully withstand the Assyrian invasion in the eighth century, the difficulties remain, for the Israelites offered no successful resistance at that time.

If, however, "Assyria" is a figure of speech for all the world powers that oppress Israel, both present and future, the problem disappears; then we may understand the passage as a prophecy of Israel's ultimate victory over her foes. Such a concept is in keeping with the total scope of Micah's message, for he saw "many nations" as oppressing Israel, not just Assyria (4:11–13; 7:16–17).

The prophet used the word "Assyria" typically in 7:12 (see comment), where in the restoration people come to Israel from Assyria. Hosea saw the period of oppression as existing until the Israelites would unite under the Messiah (Hos 3:1–5). Isaiah used the term "Assyria" in similar fashion in Isaiah 11:11, where the messianic age is described (cf. 11:10). He saw the eschatological restoration as being from "Assyria," "Egypt," and beyond.

Zechariah also used "Assyria" and "Egypt" (Zec 10:10) to refer to the nations from which God's people will be gathered when the kingdom is to be established. That the prophecy of Zechariah was written long after the fall of the Assyrian Empire is significant because it indicates that, in the mind of Zechariah, Assyria (no longer a nation in his time) represented more than the empire that brought down the northern kingdom.

The "seven shepherds" and "eight leaders" are to be understood as an indefinite but substantial number of leaders. The figure stresses the abundance of manpower Israel will enjoy when God accomplishes the work of gathering his people from the godless nations.

NOTES

5[4] The sequence of "seven … eight" is used also in Ecclesiastes 11:2. The progression "three … four" is used in Proverbs 30:15, 18, 21, 29 and Amos 1:3, 6, 9, 11, 13; 2:1, 4, 6. The former numerical sequence occurs frequently in Ugaritic, however (cf. *UT* 128:II:23–24; 8:2–3; 52:19–20, 66–67; et al.). The same sequence occurs in the Arslan Tash incantation text.

wšb *srty*, "and his seven concubines"
wšmnh *ʿšt* *bʿl*, "and the eight wives of Baal"

(W. F. Albright, "An Aramaean Magical Text in Hebrew from the Seventh Century BC," *BASOR* 76 [1939]: 5–11)

In most instances the numerical sequence is clearly not to be understood literally but may indicate an indefinite and probably much larger number.

H. The Future Vindication of Zion (5:7–9[6–8])

⁷The remnant of Jacob will be
     in the midst of many peoples
like dew from the LORD,
     like showers on the grass,
which do not wait for man
     or linger for mankind.
⁸The remnant of Jacob will be among the nations,
     in the midst of many peoples,
like a lion among the beasts of the forest,
     like a young lion among flocks of sheep,
which mauls and mangles as it goes,
     and no one can rescue.
⁹Your hand will be lifted up in triumph over your enemies,
     and all your foes will be destroyed.

COMMENTARY

7[6] The remnant, that group of believers trusting in the promises of God and surviving God's judgment, is to be transformed from an insignificant group (see 4:6–7, where they are described as "lame") to one of absolute dominance in the world (vv.7–9). It is in this way that the faith and ideals of this believing community will be disseminated throughout the earth.

While the remnant is specifically faithful Israel, there is a sense in which the church forms a part of the remnant by its grafting into the "olive tree" (Ro 11:17–24). The church, the body of true believers, also awaits the appearance of Christ and the conquest of her enemies.

That the remnant is likened to "dew" does not necessarily indicate that Micah has in mind the beneficial results of that natural phenomenon. The word "dew" is not always used in a good sense. Hosea, for example, used it of Israel's ephemeral love (6:4). The simile is explained in the next phrase, where Micah states that the dew and showers "do not wait for man." They come from the Lord and not at human behest. So the remnant will not be lifted to its place of sovereignty by the nations of the world or by the will of humankind but solely by the power of God. Waltke (*Micah*, 307–8) takes the image of the dew and the rain positively based on the fact that the almost exclusive use of these images is positive in other parts of Scripture. Thus, he believes they indicate that Israel is a blessing to the nations that come from heaven. But this interpretation is difficult to reconcile with the following two verses.

If v.7 is so understood, vv.7–8 need not have come from different authors. If we understand the "dew" and "showers" of v.7 to refer to fecundity and, hence, the calming effect of the remnant in the world, there is a sharp contrast between that concept and the militant description of the remnant in v.8. That description has led many to see an intrusion by a later author who was more "militaristic" than the "pacifistic" author of v.7. Such a view, however, is not demanded by the text.

8–9[7–8] Micah next uses metaphorical language picturing the remnant as a lion overcoming its prey. Thus he describes the inexorable way the remnant will achieve victory over the godless forces that oppose it. One should, of course, be careful to avoid pressing every detail of a metaphor. The vivid description of the stalking lion does not mean that the victory of the remnant will be achieved by bloodthirsty, militaristic conquest. Micah rather pictures the relentless force with which a lion captures its prey—"and no one can rescue." In v.7 the prophet indicated that the exaltation of the remnant will not be by the power of the nations. Now in v.8 he states that the nations will not be able to withstand the burgeoning power of the remnant in the end time. Both metaphors depict the inexorable progress of the remnant toward its ultimate triumph in the world.

The theme of the destruction of Israel's foes (v.9) is prominent in the OT. In it many writers have seen the course of history as a struggle in which the forces of evil oppose "the Lord and ... his Anointed One" (Ps 2:2). Only when the world is conquered by the Prince of Peace and the human will is subject to its Creator will there be lasting peace (Isa 63:1–6; Rev 19:11–16). Christ is called both the "Lamb of God" (Jn 1:29) and the "Lion of the tribe of Judah" (Rev 5:5).

NOTE

7–8[6–7] For a discussion of the alleged ideological differences between the metaphors of these verses, see R. E. Wolfe and H. A. Bosley, "The Book of Micah," *IB*, 6:934.

I. The Future Purification of Zion (5:10–15[9–14])

> [10]"In that day," declares the Lord,
>
> "I will destroy your horses from among you
>   and demolish your chariots.

¹¹I will destroy the cities of your land
and tear down all your strongholds.
¹²I will destroy your witchcraft
and you will no longer cast spells.
¹³I will destroy your carved images
and your sacred stones from among you;
you will no longer bow down
to the work of your hands.
¹⁴I will uproot from among you your Asherah poles
and demolish your cities.
¹⁵I will take vengeance in anger and wrath
upon the nations that have not obeyed me."

COMMENTARY

10–13[9–12] This section begins with the phrase "in that day" (*bayyôm hahû*), a phrase that indicates an indefinite future date. If the referent of this phrase is the period described in the previous context, in which the remnant will achieve victory over the nations (vv.7–9), then the prophet conceives of God as destroying the weaponry of the remnant and expunging their idolatrous practices after the conquest has been achieved, thus possibly implying that the conquest is accomplished by military force.

The phrase "in that day" may find, however, its referent in the description of Zion's exaltation in 4:1–4. In this case the purification of the remnant will take place in the initial stages of the era of peace (4:1–4); and the present passage (5:10–15) indicates that the inexorable conquest will not be accomplished by the sword but by the remnant's total dedication to God, brought about as God removes everything that would interfere with their total trust in him.

The phrase need not refer to the immediately preceding context but may refer to what follows and so is parallel to the structure of the pericope that begins at 4:6, where an identical phrase roots

that section in the era of peace introduced in 4:1. Even though 5:10 begins with the word *hāyâ* ("it shall be") and follows a succession of occurrences of the same word (vv.5, 7–8), it does not necessarily follow that the *hāyâ* of v.10 is in sequence with them and that the purification of vv.10–15 is subsequent to the conquest by the remnant described in vv.7–9. In each of the preceding occurrences of *hāyâ*, the word has a definite subject. But the subject of *hāyâ* at v.10 is indefinite, denoting a general condition: "It shall be in that day that...." There is a definite break in the verbal sequence and hence a logical interruption of the thought.

That the purification of the remnant takes place in the initial stages of the era of peace seems to be clear from v.15, where the expression of God's wrath against the nations—an event contemporaneous with the purification of the remnant—will be anomalous in a period characterized by absolute peace. It is hardly conceivable that an eighth-century prophet would envision the remnant as being exalted by God and made the vehicle of God's activity in the world while guilty of trusting in their own strength (vv.10–11) and still practicing idolatry (vv.13–14). It is for these reasons that eighth-century prophets proclaim Israel's eventual downfall.

The implication of vv.10–15 is that the instruments of war and the elements of idolatrous worship are wrong; so God removes them from the remnant. If the remnant is to use these means of achieving the ultimate goal of conquest, an inconsistency is introduced into the message of Micah; for it is Israel's idolatry and oppressive practices that he specifically condemns.

If the phrase "in that day" relates to the era of peace (4:1–4), then the prophet is to be understood as indicating that the remnant's rise to dominance over the nations is not to be by military might but rather by their total dedication to God. Spiritual renewal is to be the source of the remnant's power. It is comforting to know that the world will eventually be conquered, not by its own corrosive corruption or false or subversive ideologies, but by the gospel. The prophet foresees the eventual vindication and triumph of the people of faith.

Horses and chariots will be removed from Israel (v.10). These components of war will not only be anomalous during the reign of peace but will tend to undermine Israel's complete trust in God (Dt 17:16; Isa 2:7; Zec 9:10). The cities and defenses are to be destroyed (v.11), as well as the elements of false religion (vv.12–13). Witchcraft denotes the ways in which primitive people sought control of natural forces or power over individuals. The MT literally reads "witchcrafts of your hand," possibly referring to the acts of divination performed by hand. The phrase "cast spells" is a translation of the Hebrew word ʿānan, the root of which is dubious. It connotes a type of sorcery and is always condemned in the OT (Dt 18:10; 2Ki 21:6). The foretelling of the future is an aspect of this type of divination as it is of the "witchcraft" that Micah cited first (Jer 27:9).

Israel's images are also to be destroyed (v.13). The word "image" (*pesel*) refers to idols carved from some material. The root *psl* denotes a "sculptor" in Ugaritic and "craftsman" in a broader sense. The "sacred stones" (*maṣṣēbôt*) were standing pillars, usually of stone, that represented pagan deities. The word generally refers to anything that is piled up or set up, such as the monument erected by Joshua (Jos 4:9). Both terms used in this verse require manual structuring or fashioning; hence Micah says, "You will no longer bow down to the work of your hands."

14–15[13–14] Asherah (v.14) was a Canaanite goddess called in the mythological texts from Ugarit the "Creatrix of the gods." She was associated with all aspects of sexual life and thus with fertility in general. She was also a goddess of war. Sacred prostitution was an integral part of her cult, which is associated with poles probably representing the tree, a symbol of life and fertility. These poles were strictly forbidden, and Pentateuchal texts demanded their eradication from the land (Ex 34:13; Dt 7:5; 12:3; 16:21).

Verse 14b unexpectedly contains a reference to "cities" (cf. v.11) rather than a continuing condemnation of idolatry. The nearly symmetrical arrangement of parallel elements has been deliberate and exact throughout this section. But the structure here is characteristic of the modified parallelism noted in 1:5. To Micah cities are the centers of pagan worship, particularly the cities of Samaria and Jerusalem, though others are not exempted (1:13). "Cities" make a fitting parallel to "Asherim" in view of Micah's understanding of the idolatrous practices carried on in the cities. The repetition of "cities" throws into bold relief the fact of the inevitable captivity of the cities that are about to perish. It is also possible, however, that v.14 functions as a summary for the catalog of destruction in vv.10–13, in which case there is no synonymous parallelism here.

The nations that do not yield to God will be subjugated (v.15) so that the peace promised in 4:1–4 will never be threatened. This understanding supports the translation "witness against" in 1:2.

NOTES

10[9] Waltke (*Micah*, 320–21) points out that the verb "destroy," repeated in the next three verses, is a Hiphil of *krt* (GK 4162; lit., "to cut off"). It is a verb used in Leviticus for those who have offended the laws of purification and thus must be removed from the camp or even exterminated (Lev 17:10; 20:3, 5–6).

10[9] C. F. Keil (*The Twelve Minor Prophets* [Grand Rapids: Eerdmans, repr. 1949], 490) argues, "Only when the people of God shall have gained the supremacy over all their enemies, will the time have arrived for all the instruments of war to be destroyed." This view is at variance with the one taken here and is based, in part, on the fact that וְהָיָה בַיּוֹם־הַהוּא (*wᵉhāyâ bayyôm-hahûʾ*, "and it will be in that day") in v.10, "when compared with *hāyâ* in verses 5[4] and 7[6] shows at once that these verses are intended to depict the last and greatest effect produced by the coming of the Prince of peace" (ibid.). But the *hāyâ* in vv.5 and 7 is not the same idiom as that in v.10. Each has a stated subject ("this" in v.5 ["he," NIV] and "remnant" in v.7), whereas *hāyâ* in v.10 is used in the idiomatic expression "it will be in that day." This expression finds its counterpart in the somewhat similar expression in 4:1 rather than the two preceding occurrences of *hāyâ*.

IV. THE THIRD ORACLE: GOD'S LAWSUIT AGAINST ISRAEL AND THE ULTIMATE TRIUMPH OF THE KINGDOM OF GOD (6:1–7:20)

A. God's Accusations against His People (6:1–8)

¹Listen to what the LORD says:

"Stand up, plead your case before the mountains;
　let the hills hear what you have to say.
²Hear, O mountains, the LORD's accusation;
　listen, you everlasting foundations of the earth.
For the LORD has a case against his people;
　he is lodging a charge against Israel.

³"My people, what have I done to you?
　How have I burdened you? Answer me.
⁴I brought you up out of Egypt
　and redeemed you from the land of slavery.
I sent Moses to lead you,
　also Aaron and Miriam.

> [5] My people, remember
>   what Balak king of Moab counseled
>   and what Balaam son of Beor answered.
>   Remember your journey from Shittim to Gilgal,
>   that you may know the righteous acts of the LORD."
>
> [6] With what shall I come before the LORD
>   and bow down before the exalted God?
>   Shall I come before him with burnt offerings,
>   with calves a year old?
> [7] Will the LORD be pleased with thousands of rams,
>   with ten thousand rivers of oil?
>   Shall I offer my firstborn for my transgression,
>   the fruit of my body for the sin of my soul?
> [8] He has showed you, O man, what is good.
>   And what does the LORD require of you?
>   To act justly and to love mercy
>   and to walk humbly with your God.

COMMENTARY

1–2 The third oracle begins in the format of a legal controversy (v.1). God calls on the prophet (so Waltke, *Micah*, 344) to get up and present his case (representing God) to the mountains. The mountains are called as witnesses in the litigation (v.2). Micah uses the motif of other writers of the OT who called on inanimate objects to function as witnesses in a legal context (Dt 32:1; Isa 1:2). The enduring hills have mutely observed Israel's history from its very beginning; hence they are called "everlasting foundations" (v.2). If they could speak, they would witness to the truthfulness of the Creator's claims. The appeal to the mountains should be understood simply as an entreaty to witnesses that have been there throughout Israel's history.

The background to this language is the covenant, which has the form of a treaty. Witnesses were an integral part of a treaty relationship since a covenant was a legal document. They may be found in biblical covenantal texts (Dt 30:19; Jos 24:22–23, 27) as well as ancient Near Eastern treaties (i.e., *ANET*, 205). The function of the witnesses was to testify in the event that the members of either party failed to uphold their end of the agreement.

3 Micah places the classic disputation form of the prophets in a legal context as he pictures God's pleading with his people. The mood of the passage is at first foreboding as the opening words summon God to arise and state his case against Israel. But the passage takes on an atmosphere of pathos by picturing God as asking his people in what way he has wearied them. The Creator of those mountains seeks the cause of Israel's estrangement from him.

The verb "to burden" (*lāʾâ*, "to be weary"), when used in the causative stem (Hiphil) as here, signifies to wear down (Job 16:7), to cause someone to become impatient (Isa 7:13), or to become physically tired (Jer 12:5). The Lord's question emphasizes the second nuance and asks how he has caused them to become so weary of him that they have ceased to obey him. Their impatience with God cannot be due to inactivity on his part, for he has done so much for them. The recital of events from Israel's past is intended to challenge the objection that Israel's estrangement from God is the result of his failure to act for his people throughout their history.

4 Not only has God done nothing to harm Israel; he has done everything to bless them. The deliverance from Egypt is frequently cited in the prophets and represents one of the first acts of redemption in which God demonstrated his saving love for the people. That deliverance is an important aspect of the prophetic "theology of history."

The prophet cites Moses, Aaron, and Miriam as reminders to the people of the great leadership God provided them with. Moses was God's great prophet, the prototype of the line of prophets yet to come (Dt 18:15–22). Miriam was a prophetess (Ex 15:20); and Aaron, the progenitor of the Aaronic priesthood, was the representative of the people before God.

5 Micah also cites the failure of Balaam to curse the people (Nu 22–24) as evidence of God's activity among them. Besides the failure of Balak to frustrate the progress of the people, the journey from Shittim to Gilgal witnessed the defeat of Midian, the crossing of the Jordan, and the conquest of Jericho carried out from the base at Gilgal. The recital of events stops abruptly, as though the intent is to depict in one great sweep the progress of the nation from slavery in a foreign land to settlement in its own country.

The word translated "righteous acts" (ṣidqôt; GK 7407) is a plural form of the Hebrew word for "righteous." The word "righteous" means basically "rightness" and can apply to secular as well as religious spheres of life. Judges were to be "righteous" in a

legal sense (Lev 19:15). In reference to God's activities, however, the word underlines God's faithfulness to his standard, the covenantal obligations. God's great acts in behalf of Israel are seen as more than simply God's coming to the aid of his people. They are seen as manifestations of his righteousness as he maintains his faithfulness to the covenantal promises.

6–7 The recital of Israel's history suddenly ends, and the prophet is heard speaking in terse, abrupt words that somehow create a feeling of rapid movement and tension. Micah speaks, but it is as though he speaks on behalf of the people as they ask what their responsibility is in the light of God's faithfulness to the covenant. There is irony here; the section is meant to contrast external religion (to which they have been clinging) with true religion.

The prophet asks how one may come before "the exalted God." The word "exalted" represents the Hebrew word mārôm, which means "height." The expression is literally "God of the height" and speaks of God in his dwelling place in heaven (2Sa 22:17; Isa 33:5). How can this high God be reached in the far-off heavens? What is the proper way to worship him? With burnt offerings and calves a year old? Yearling calves are specifically cited on various occasions in the Pentateuchal legislation (Lev 9:2–3; cf. Ex 12:5) and seem to have been regarded as the choicest sacrifices.

"Thousands of rams" (v.7) suggests the large quantity of animals that one might offer to curry God's favor. Micah implies that God is interested neither in the choicest animals nor in the number of them offered—both factors belonging to a religion of works and externals. Even great quantities of oil will not bring the worshiper into fellowship with God. Oil was an important part of certain sacrifices, such as the cereal offering (Lev 2:1–16).

The list reached a shocking climax in the mention of the firstborn. Child sacrifice was a Canaanite practice sometimes carried out by certain Israelites

(2Ki 3:27; 16:3; Isa 57:5). In keeping with the preceding catalog, the firstborn represents the most precious thing one could give to God. Again the implication is that sacrificing one's firstborn is not what God wants.

8 Micah now asks and answers the question, "What does the LORD require of you?" He does so in a verse justly regarded as one of the memorable and timeless expressions of OT ethical religion (cf. Jas 1:27). It is a heart's response to God demonstrated in the basic elements of true religion, as shown to Israel in the social concerns reflected in the Mosaic legislation.

God has told his people what is good. The Mosaic law differentiates between good and bad and reflects God's will in many areas of their religious and social lives. It indicates what God requires (*dāraš*, "seeks") of them. They are to act justly (lit., "do justice," *mišpāṭ*). The word "justly" here has the sense of "true religion," that is, the ethical response to God that has a manifestation in social concerns as well (cf. Note on 3:8). "To love mercy" is freely and willingly to show kindness to others (cf. Notes below). The expression "to walk humbly with your God" means to live in conscious fellowship with God by exercising a spirit of humility before him. These great words recall similar words of our Lord in Matthew 23:23.

The prophet is not suggesting that sacrifice is completely ineffectual and that simply a proper attitude of heart toward God will suffice. In the preceding verse he painted a caricature—a purposefully exaggerated picture—of the sacrificial system to indicate that God has no interest in the multiplication of empty religious acts. Jeremiah 7:22–23 is often appealed to as evidence that the prophets rejected the Levitical system; yet Jeremiah promised that the offerings would be acceptable if the people were obedient (Jer 17:24–26). A similar attitude toward sacrifice is expressed in Psalm 51:16–17, but the succeeding verses show the author to be indicating that the Levitical sacrifices are acceptable to God only when accompanied by a proper attitude of heart toward him (51:18–19).

The ethical requirements of v.8 do not comprise the way of salvation. Forgiveness of sin was received through the sacrifices. The standards of this verse are for those who are members of the covenantal community and delineate the areas of ethical response that God wants to see in those who share the covenantal obligations.

NOTES

2 For a discussion of the characteristic רִיב (*rîb*, "disputation"; "case," NIV) form of the prophets, see W. Westermann, *Basic Forms of Prophetic Speech,* trans. H. C. White (Philadelphia: Westminster, 1967); G. E. Wright, "The Lawsuit of God: A Form-Critical Study of Deuteronomy 32," in *Israel's Prophetic Heritage,* ed. B. W. Anderson and W. Harrelson (London: SCM, 1962), 26–67; G. W. Ramsay, "Speech Forms in Hebrew Law and Prophetic Oracles," *JBL* 96 (1977): 45–58; and G. Gemser, "The *Rib* or Controversy Pattern in Hebrew Mentality," in *Wisdom in Israel and in the Ancient Near East: Presented to Professor Harold Henry Rowley by the Society for Old Testament Study in Association with the Editorial Board of Vetus Testamentum in Celebration of His Sixty-Fifth Birthday, 24 March 1955* (VTSup 3; Leiden: Brill, 1955), 120–37.

8 חֶסֶד (*ḥesed*; "mercy," NIV; GK 2876) has the basic meaning of "kindness" (Ge 19:19; 40:14; Ru 3:10). On occasion it contains an element of reciprocity, for the recipient of kindness was expected to show kindness in return (Ge 21:22–24; Jos 2:12–14). Kindness was expected between partners in certain previously existing relationships, such as marriage (Ge 20:13) and friendship (1Sa 20:8). *Ḥesed* is also an attribute of God and is basic to his acts of redemption; he demonstrates it to establish a relationship of *ḥesed* in which he expects an ethical response from humans as their reciprocal responsibility. The ethical aspects of *ḥesed* are peculiarly evident in the prophetic writings. They make clear that failure to show *ḥesed* breaks the terms of the covenant; and since the covenant is the vehicle for obtaining God's *ḥesed*, the covenant breaker has forfeited the right to obtain it. This principle applies on a broader scale to nations as well.

REFLECTION

The standards of ethical behavior discussed in v.8 (notably *mišpāṭ* and *ḥesed*) have not been abrogated for Christians, for the NT affirms their continuing validity. We are still called to the exercise of true religion, to kindness, and to humility (1Co 13:4; 2Co 6:6; Col 3:12; Jas 1:27; 1Pe 1:2; 5:5). Christians are in a covenantal relationship with God in which the law (*tôrâ*) has been placed within their hearts (Jer 31:33; cf. Heb 10:14–17), not abrogated. But obedience for Christians is to the indwelling Holy Spirit, not to the letter of the law (2Co 3:6).

B. The Sentence of Judgment (6:9–16)

⁹Listen! The Lᴏʀᴅ is calling to the city —
   and to fear your name is wisdom —
   "Heed the rod and the One who appointed it.
¹⁰Am I still to forget, O wicked house,
   your ill-gotten treasures
   and the short ephah, which is accursed?
¹¹Shall I acquit a man with dishonest scales,
   with a bag of false weights?
¹²Her rich men are violent;
   her people are liars
   and their tongues speak deceitfully.
¹³Therefore, I have begun to destroy you,
   to ruin you because of your sins.
¹⁴You will eat but not be satisfied;
   your stomach will still be empty.
  You will store up but save nothing,
   because what you save I will give to the sword.
¹⁵You will plant but not harvest;
   you will press olives but not use the oil on yourselves,
   you will crush grapes but not drink the wine.

> ¹⁶ You have observed the statutes of Omri
>   and all the practices of Ahab's house,
>   and you have followed their traditions.
> Therefore I will give you over to ruin
>   and your people to derision;
>   you will bear the scorn of the nations."

COMMENTARY

9 Another dramatic element is introduced. The voice of Yahweh is suddenly heard. The phrase "calling to the city" signifies the cry of alarm that is heard when disaster threatens a city. Micah adds the observation that it is wise to fear God's name. The word "fear" is spelled with the same consonants as the word "see" in Hebrew, and in the MT the word is vocalized so as to read "see." It is best to follow the versions in reading "fear," however, since the expression "see the name" is somewhat anomalous and the identical phrase "fear the name" occurs in Psalm 86:11.

Although several modern versions (NASB, NEB, RSV et al.) have emended the text of the last clause of v.9, the NIV follows the Hebrew, which makes good sense as it stands. The "rod" (*maṭṭeh*; GK 4751) is the punishment that Israel will endure, and she is told to "heed" it.

Isaiah uses the word *maṭṭeh* ("club") of the Assyrians (Isa 10:5, 24). In Isaiah 10:5 the nation of Assyria is pictured as the instrument of God's wrath. If Micah uses *maṭṭeh* in the same way here, there is then a logical connection with the cry of alarm in v.9. That alarm will herald the coming of the Assyrians, and the one who "appointed" the rod is God himself. The people are to "heed," i.e., attend to the fact that the invasion will come and that it was God who will effect it through the instrumentality of the Assyrians.

One cannot miss echoes of Hebrew wisdom literature in this verse and in the verses that follow. Of course, the motto of the book of Proverbs is that "the fear of the LORD is the beginning of knowledge" (Pr 1:7, with variant "beginning of wisdom" in 9:10). The book of Proverbs also uses the term "rod" as a means for correction of foolish behavior (though in Proverbs the near synonym *šēbeṭ* is used rather than *maṭṭeh*).

10–13 The MT begins v.10 with the word *ʿôd* ("yet"). It is in the place of emphasis in the clause. The Hebrew says, literally, "Are there yet in the house of the wicked treasures of wickedness and the short measure that is cursed?" The question, of course, is rhetorical and affirms that the oppressing classes are still getting gain from their mistreatment of the poor and that the oppression has not ended. Hence the punishment is deserved and now imminent.

Micah has emphasized social sins more than sins of idolatry, though ultimately they are closely intertwined in his thinking. In the brief catalog of Israel's sins that follows (vv.11–13), God continues to present his case and defend the sentence he is pronouncing. The response to the question of v.11 is, of course, a resounding "No!"

The society of Micah's time is characterized not only by violence but also by lying and deceit (v.12). False promises are being uttered and claims are made that are not fulfilled. In any society in which leaders of government deceive the people by making promises that are not kept, the will of the people is silenced and ignored and the structure of government weakened.

The Hebrew of v.13 states, literally, "I have made sick your smiting," that is, "I have struck you severely." It is because of the people's sin that God will bring ruin on them. It is not simply for the fortunes of history. The word "sick" in Hebrew is close in formation to the word "begin" (NIV, RSV); which meaning should be read here is uncertain. The use of "sick" (NASB) in the idiom is acceptable; the past tense may have been intended to imply the certainty of the event.

As in the previous verse, so here a connection with Proverbs can be seen. Proverbs often inveighs against the use of fraudulent scales (e.g., Pr 11:1; 16:11; 20:23; see also Lev 19:35–36; Dt 25:13–16; Eze 45:10). In addition, Proverbs also condemns ill-gotten gain and speaks about the negative consequences of such wealth (Pr 11:3, 18; 13:11).

14–15 The land is to fall under the devastation of the sword and be totally unproductive. The greed that motivates the rich in that day will no longer be satisfied because of the desolation of the land.

16 The prophet departs from the social sins of his society and turns to the pagan religious practices of the people. They are no better than the generation of Omri, the notorious king who headed the dynasty that produced Ahab, the husband of Jezebel, and allowed Baal worship to gain a strong foothold in Israel. Other crimes of that time included the persecution of Elijah and the murder of Naboth. Even in Micah's day the spirit of Omri lives on.

The second line of v.16 begins with the word *lᵉmaᶜan* ("to the end that"; "therefore," NIV). The meaning is that Israel's disobedience to God has brought the punishment the prophet is about to describe. Three calamities are to fall on Israel. First, she will become a "ruin." The word translated "ruin" is a nominal form of the verb *šāmam*, which means both "to be desolated" and "to be appalled." It frequently signifies the reaction of people appalled at God's judgment (Lev 26:32; Job 17:8; Eze 26:16); thus the nominal form may connote that which is an object of horror. This meaning seems best in view of the nature of the two other descriptive terms, for they are also to become an object of hissing ("derision," NIV) and "the scorn of other nations."

NOTES

9 In the OT יָרֵא (*yārē'*, "fear"; GK 3707) is a complex concept. It involves reverent awe (Job 37:23–24; Ps 33:8), knowledge of God (Pr 9:10), turning from evil (Job 28:28; Pr 8:13), humble obedience (Jer 26:19), genuine piety (Ge 22:12; Ps 34:11–15), and "fear" in the strict sense of the word (Ex 20:20). It is an attitude toward God that involves worshipful submission to him as well as a turning from evil. In short, it is similar to the conversion experience. The word for "wisdom" is not the typical one (*ḥokmâ*) but rather a close synonym, *tûšîyâ*, which appears in Proverbs 2:7; 3:21; 8:14.

10 While עוֹד (*ᶜôd*, "yet") appears before the interrogative particle הֵ (*h*), a somewhat rare grammatical function, it need not be understood as being connected with the preceding clause (see Ge 19:12 for another example).

13 The MT's הֶחֱלֵיתִי (*heḥᵉlêtî*, "I have made sick") is sometimes revocalized to read הַחִלּוֹתִי (*haḥillôtî*, "I have begun"), following the LXX, Theodotion, the Syriac, and the Vulgate. The statement "I have made sick your smiting" seems anomalous and may have led to the emendation. However, this function of the Hiphil is idiomatic (cf. GKC, par. 114n), and the association of the two words in Jeremiah 30:12—נַחְלָה מַכָּתֵךְ (*naḥlâ makkātēk*, "your wound is incurable")—confirms the validity of the expression.

C. The Prophet's Lament over the Lack of Godly Fellowship (7:1–2)

OVERVIEW

Like a day that begins with a dark, foreboding sky but ends in golden sunlight, this chapter begins in an atmosphere of gloom and ends in one of the greatest statements of hope in the entire OT. Clouds of gloom have rolled in on the horizon of the prophet's life because of the disobedience of the people and the somber fate that awaits his nation. But rays of hope—such as the affirmations in v.7—shine through the gloom. It is in the great affirmation of faith concluding the book (vv.18–20) that the darkness is completely dissipated. One may wonder why the prophet does not succumb to utter pessimism in view of the conditions of his day. The answer is in this chapter. It is because of the triumph of faith.

The developing optimism of this chapter is not due to the prophet's lack of concern for the poor. If any were concerned for the oppressed classes, it was the eighth-century prophets. Nor is it due to an optimistic humanism (vv.5–7). In the midst of a crumbling society, Micah can look beyond to a hope secure in the promises of God. Micah can be optimistic because he can see the hand of God working even in the midst of ruin and despair.

The prophet speaks here as a representative of the godly remnant. While most of the chapter is written in the first person, v.8 begins a corporate concept that cannot be limited to the prophet alone.

¹What misery is mine!
  I am like one who gathers summer fruit
  at the gleaning of the vineyard;
  there is no cluster of grapes to eat,
    none of the early figs that I crave.
²The godly have been swept from the land;
  not one upright man remains.
All men lie in wait to shed blood;
  each hunts his brother with a net.

COMMENTARY

1 This section begins with a lament as the prophet mourns the lack of godly fellowship in his time. The Hebrew reads, literally, "I have become like the fruit gathering." The metaphor pictures the remnant as seeking grapes and choice figs to satisfy its hunger but failing to find any, as though it were the time of harvest after these fruits have been picked. The

prophet is probably to be pictured as trying to glean following the harvest—a right of the poor specified in the law (Lev 19:9–10; 23:22; Dt 24:19–22).

2 The fruit described in the metaphor represents godly persons. The feeling of utter disappointment that would be felt by someone seeking food but finding none is meant to communicate the feelings of the godly as they observe the nation and its glaring lack of individuals who remain faithful to God. This passage is a vivid representation of the believer's need for fellowship with others of like faith. By severing fellowship with other believers, a person feels robbed of something precious. The language of v.2b does not describe actual murder but rather the excesses that characterize the treatment of the "have-nots" by the "haves." The description of violence among brothers reminds one of the warning of the father to his son to avoid those who seek to ambush innocents to shed their blood (Pr 1:8–20, esp. v.11).

D. The Prophet's Lament over the Corruption in His Society (7:3–6)

³Both hands are skilled in doing evil;
  the ruler demands gifts,
 the judge accepts bribes,
  the powerful dictate what they desire—
  they all conspire together.
⁴The best of them is like a brier,
  the most upright worse than a thorn hedge.
 The day of your watchmen has come,
  the day God visits you.
  Now is the time of their confusion.
⁵Do not trust a neighbor;
  put no confidence in a friend.
 Even with her who lies in your embrace
  be careful of your words.
⁶For a son dishonors his father,
  a daughter rises up against her mother,
 a daughter-in-law against her mother-in-law—
  a man's enemies are the members of his own household.

COMMENTARY

3 The situation in Micah's day is desperate. The result of the dearth of upright people (vv.1–2) is that there are no ethical rulers. The prophet describes the strong grip that those in responsible positions have on the throat of society. "The ruler demands gifts" means that the ruler insists on the distortion of justice for his gain (Ex 23:8; Dt 10:17; 16:19; 27:25; Pr 17:23; 28:21). Or perhaps he does so under the misguided notion that the distortion will ultimately benefit the nation. Power can corrupt if not guarded by the law of a higher Sovereign. The judicial system has been corrupted by the lust for bribes. The controlling classes (i.e., the rich) simply dictate their desires; and the implication here is that they receive them.

The Hebrew of the last line of v.3 is literally, "and so they weave it all together." This expression describes the conspiracy of the ruling classes just cited by Micah. The ruler seeks, perhaps, for the indictment of an innocent person; the judge carries it out for a bribe; and the rich man is involved in the conspiracy by speaking "the desire of his soul" (*hawwat napšô*; "what they desire," NIV). The word "desire" (*hawwâ*; GK 2094) is always used in a bad sense and may mean "evil desire" but more commonly "calamity" or "destruction." The word occurs in a similar context in Psalm 38:12[13], where it refers to the speech of those who seek the psalmist's life. It thus denotes the harm or injury the rich man desires to see carried out. This wicked scheme enjoys the cooperation of those who occupy positions of responsibility in society.

4 As Micah continues to characterize the society he lives in, he describes the best of the people as briers. "The best they can manage is to obstruct justice. These legal sharks have so conspired together that no one can negotiate the tangle of laws and rulings, and to attempt it will result only in painful injury. What a contrast to the sweet grapes and figs they should have been!" (Waltke, *Micah*, 427). If one should seek to find mercy or sympathy from

any of them, even those who appear to be upright and respectable, they will prove to be hard and piercing.

This description of Micah's contemporaries is suddenly interrupted. In keeping with his use of sudden, almost jarring contrasts, the prophet points to the coming judgment: "The day of your watchmen has come." The watchmen are the prophets (cf. Jer 6:17; Eze 3:17). They watch the course of their nation, see its internal decay and decline, and, like watchmen who guarded the cities of ancient times, warn of the danger inherent in the wrongs of the people. The day of the watchmen is the day of punishment predicted by the prophets, that is, the captivity.

5–6 Micah returns to the description of the wrongs of his society as he depicts the disruption in the family unit, normally the most intimate of human relationships. A man cannot trust his friends (v.5) or even his wife, and respect for one's parents has evaporated (v.6). This situation contrasts with Malachi's vision of the future, when the prophet Elijah returns: "He will turn the hearts of the fathers to their children, and the hearts of the children to their fathers; or else I will come and strike the land with a curse" (Mal 4:6).

E. The Godly Person's Attitude in the Midst of Discouragement (7:7–10)

⁷But as for me, I watch in hope for the LORD.
  I wait for God my Savior;
  my God will hear me.

⁸Do not gloat over me, my enemy!
  Though I have fallen, I will rise.
  Though I sit in darkness,
    the LORD will be my light.
⁹Because I have sinned against him,
  I will bear the LORD's wrath,

> until he pleads my case
> and establishes my right.
> He will bring me out into the light;
> I will see his righteousness.
> ¹⁰Then my enemy will see it
> and will be covered with shame,
> she who said to me,
> "Where is the LORD your God?"
> My eyes will see her downfall;
> even now she will be trampled underfoot
> like mire in the streets.

COMMENTARY

7 While family and friends cannot be trusted (vv.5–6), God certainly can be; this fact produces confidence in the heart of the godly. The clouds of gloom begin to separate as the prophet, speaking as the representative of the remnant, describes the attitude of the godly person amid such difficult circumstances. Micah does not succumb to despair or lethargy but rather says, "I watch in hope for the LORD." The word "watch" (*ṣāpâ*) means to "look" or "wait expectantly." It is used of blind Eli, who waited for the news of battle (1Sa 4:13; cf. v.15). It is the same word used for "watchmen" earlier in this chapter (v.4). The godly will look expectantly for God. As a watchman observes every shadow and listens to every night sound, so the godly look for evidence of God's working. To close one's eyes to the working of God, no matter how small the evidence may be, is to open the door to despair.

Micah also waits for God to act in his own time. By thus acquiescing to God's holy will, Micah finds peace in the knowledge of God's sovereign activity in the world. But Micah also expresses confidence that God will answer prayer. One can well understand how the societal wrongs of Micah's day might lead one to doubt the wise economy of God. But it is faith in God that keeps the prophet from utter despair. That faith is ultimately confirmed by the realization of the captivity, an event that is at once a national catastrophe and an evidence of God's justice and holiness in dealing with a corrupt society.

8 Not only does Micah trust God to act and to answer prayer, he also trusts God to vindicate the faithful (vv.8–10). The remnant is speaking in v.8. Though the faithful are subjected to difficult experiences, they will one day rise to receive their heritage. There is vivid contrast between God's people sitting in darkness and the gladdening effect of the light of God that will shine among them. The remnant of believers in any age can be confident of God's help and their eventual triumph (Mt 16:18).

In this verse Micah uses language similar to that in the psalms. Lament psalms call on God not to let an enemy gloat over the sad situation of the psalmist (Pss 35:19, 24, 26; 38:16), and thanksgiving psalms praise God for quieting the gloating of the enemy (Ps 30:1). Here Micah, speaking on behalf of the remnant in the confidence that God will quiet the enemy if necessary, tells them to stop gloating.

The enemy Micah has in mind here is certainly the Assyrian Empire.

9 With a return to the legal atmosphere of ch. 6, the remnant affirms their determination to wait until God pleads their cause and decides in their favor. They freely confess their sin in the awareness that the coming temporal punishment is a just punishment for their disobedience. This punishment is only for a time, however, for the remnant will be vindicated as they see God's righteousness. They can be confident of God's favorable action in their behalf; for they, unlike their guilty compatriots, stand on the ground of the covenant. Their sensitivity to sin, as illustrated in the opening line of this verse, and their allegiance to the covenantal stipulations mark them as those who participate in the promises that are such a vital element of the covenant between Israel and her God.

10 Ultimately the remnant will be exalted and the hostile nations of the world covered with shame and trampled like mud. This latter figure is used by Isaiah (Isa 10:6) of the invading Assyrians. Micah uses it of the conquest of the hostile powers in the day of Israel's exaltation.

F. The Assurance of Victory for the Kingdom of God (7:11–20)

1. Victory Described in Terms of the Extension of the Kingdom (7:11–13)

¹¹The day for building your walls will come,
    the day for extending your boundaries.
¹²In that day people will come to you
    from Assyria and the cities of Egypt,
  even from Egypt to the Euphrates
    and from sea to sea
    and from mountain to mountain.
¹³The earth will become desolate because of its inhabitants,
    as the result of their deeds.

COMMENTARY

11–12 The clouds of gloom have completely gone, and the remainder of the chapter is an exultant description of the eventual triumph of the remnant. The prophet envisions a great extension of the remnant's influence as he sees a future day when the nation will grow in area and numbers. In this terminology the prophet pictures the then-despised and persecuted remnant as occupying a position of broadest influence in the future.

The future nation, cleansed of her sin and ruled by the King born in Bethlehem, will be greatly increased in population by an influx of people from Gentile nations, symbolized by Assyria and Egypt, though another view believes that the people returning from these nations are actually Judean exiles. This latter view complements the message of 4:1–4 in that it gives to the revived nation of Israel a prominent role in the era of universal peace.

That the Gentiles are to become partakers of the promise through faith is a cardinal doctrine of both OT and NT (Ge 12:3; Am 9:11–12; Ro 9:30; Gal 3:6–9). The passage is similar to Amos 9:11–12, where the inclusion of Gentiles in the promise is rooted in the era of peace, when Israel's fortunes will be restored (Am 9:13–15).

At the same time that God's people prosper, however, the judgment of God will fall on the sinful world, for "the earth will become desolate." Like Isaiah (Isa 34–35), Micah sees a future judgment on the earth. Out of the decay of a crumbling society, Micah perceives the emergence of the kingdom of God. The prophet can be optimistic, for he knows that his lot is not with the impermanent society in which he lives but with the kingdom of God.

2. Victory Assured because of God's Leadership (7:14–15)

¹⁴Shepherd your people with your staff,
    the flock of your inheritance,
which lives by itself in a forest,
    in fertile pasturelands.
Let them feed in Bashan and Gilead
    as in days long ago.

¹⁵"As in the days when you came out of Egypt,
    I will show them my wonders."

COMMENTARY

14 Micah here speaks on behalf of the remnant. The remnant will triumph because of their relationship to God. This section is the remnant's prayer for restoration to the former days when their leaders brought them into the land. The remnant is pictured as dwelling alone, apart from the nations in a forest "in the middle of Carmel" (NIV note). Bashan and Gilead were agricultural areas of great fertility that became symbols of plenty (Ps 22:12; Jer 50:19; Eze 39:18). Reference to them here is symbolic. It is a request that Israel's former years of blessing be restored by her good Shepherd. Similar petitions may be seen in Psalms 28:9; 74:1; 80:1.

15 The answer that comes from God is a promise of the restoration of the days when he led the people from bondage to their inheritance in Canaan. The exodus was the central event in the prophetic theology of history. It was an event that could be repeated, because to the prophets history was continually being fulfilled. The exodus would occur again—but in a new and even greater way. To the prophets, the exodus was an event of more than historical interest. It revealed such attributes of God as his might, his sovereignty over the nations, and his love for his own.

Because God is unchanging and his attributes timeless, his people can expect his acts to be repeated again and again in history. For this reason Hosea viewed the impending captivity as a repetition of the Egyptian bondage (Hos 9:3; 11:5) and the exodus as a pattern of their release from the impending captivity (11:11; cf. 12:9). (For a discussion of the repetition of the acts of God and its implications, see F. Foulkes, *The Acts of God* [London: Tyndale, 1955].)

3. Victory Assured over the Nations (7:16–17)

> [16] Nations will see and be ashamed,
>   deprived of all their power.
> They will lay their hands on their mouths
>   and their ears will become deaf.
> [17] They will lick dust like a snake,
>   like creatures that crawl on the ground.
> They will come trembling out of their dens;
>   they will turn in fear to the LORD our God
>   and will be afraid of you.

16 As a result of God's intervention on behalf of Israel, the nations will be humbled before God and his remnant. The might of the nations, which brought Israel into captivity, will be as nothing before the great power of God. To lay the hand on the mouth is to indicate reverence and awe (Job 29:9–10; Isa 52:15). It indicates that they have been put in their place by a greater power, as Job was when God appeared to him (Job 40:4). The deafness of the nations may be caused by the thunderous events God brings about (Job 26:14).

17 The vindication of God and his remnant in the world is pictured in descriptive terms. The nations are depicted as animals crawling from their dens and trembling before the Lord. Indeed, the analogy with the snake licking the dust evokes memory of the punishment levied against the serpent in Genesis 3. The Assyrians and others often likened themselves to lions; here they are not courageous and bold and dangerous, but fearful and "trembling."

4. Victory Assured because of God's Nature (7:18–20)

OVERVIEW

The remnant of God's people can be optimistic, not only because of the future hope that is theirs, but also because of the nature of God. Here is the great resource on which the remnant can draw. According to Waltke (*Micah*, 463), in this concluding section "the prophet sees behind his saving acts to a greater superiority: his ability to forgive out of his very nature in order to keep his covenant obligations to the patriarchs."

> ¹⁸Who is a God like you,
>   who pardons sin and forgives the transgression
>   of the remnant of his inheritance?
> You do not stay angry forever
>   but delight to show mercy.
> ¹⁹You will again have compassion on us;
>   you will tread our sins underfoot
>   and hurl all our iniquities into the depths of the sea.
> ²⁰You will be true to Jacob,
>   and show mercy to Abraham,
>   as you pledged on oath to our fathers
>   in days long ago.

COMMENTARY

18 The question "Who is a God like you?" points to the uniqueness of Yahweh. The name "Micah" means "who is like the LORD?" Whether we have here another characteristic play on words is hard to say. The words "sin" and "transgression" recall the affirmation of Exodus 34:6–7, wherein the Lord proclaimed an essential aspect of his nature to be his willingness to forgive sin.

19–20 Because God's anger does not continue forever, the believing remnant can know that an end will come to their humiliation. God will not simply ignore his people's sin and its punishment, but he will take the sin, destroy it, and get rid of it. Israel's sin is like an enemy that God defeats and disposes of. The sea in the ancient Near East represented the forces of chaos; thus the sea is where Israel's sins belonged.

After the great statement of forgiveness of v.19, the prophet recalls the promise given to Abraham and reaffirmed to Jacob (v.20). The remnant's optimism is rooted in the promise sworn to Abraham and "our fathers" ("our ancestors," NRSV, TNIV).

REFLECTION

God's promise is eternal (Ge 13:15; 17:7–8, 13, 19; 48:4); and its elements are still applicable to Christians—though reinterpreted by the new covenant—because they are a spiritual people (1Pe 2:5), not a national entity as were the Israelites. We hear the same promises ringing in the NT: the Lord's being God to his people (Ge 17:7; cf. 2Co 6:16; Heb 8:10; Rev 21:3, 7), the concept of a royal people (Ge 17:6, 16; cf. 1Pe 2:9; Rev 1:6; 5:10), the land or place of rest (Ro 4:13; Heb 4:1–10), to name only a few. The promise is a continuum that guarantees an inheritance to all God's people. The church thus shares the same heritage and hope as God's people in the OT. We, too, expect to reign with the King from Bethlehem (5:2), our sins having been trodden underfoot (7:19). We, too, know the loving care of the Shepherd who feeds his flock in the strength of the Lord. Micah's concept of the remnant encompasses believers today.

NAHUM

CARL E. ARMERDING

Introduction

1. BACKGROUND

Nahum's prophecy is rooted in the Lord's revelation of himself at Sinai as a God of judgment and mercy, characteristics that apply to his dealings with both his own people Israel and the various nations he uses to accomplish his purposes. The notable self-portrait of this God Yahweh, in what has been called a Hymn to the Divine Warrior (Na 1:2–8; cf. commentary), provides the basis for increasingly specific application of God's judgment and mercy in the remaining verses of the book. Nahum thus stands firmly in Israel's prophetic tradition as one inspired to interpret the complexities of the present and future in the light of the past. While general truths about Yahweh's covenant and law belonged to every member of the covenant (Dt 29:29), the details of its outworking in history were understood only by those called to stand in the Lord's council (Jer 23:18, 22; Am 3:7).

The setting of the prophecy of Nahum is the long and painful oppression of Israel by Assyria—"Although I have afflicted you" (1:12)—and the prospect of its end—"I will afflict you no more" (ibid.). Although God is the ultimate author of Israel's affliction, Assyria, the rod of God's anger, is the agent of his wrath; and the cup in the Lord's right hand is now coming around to her. In its specificity, this prophecy focuses on one particular pagan agent of divine "affliction" and God's judgment of that nation, with Israel's ultimate vindication a collateral, but vital, theme.

Assyria had long been a significant participant in Israel's history, a situation that, from at least the eighth century on, was a focus of prophetic commentary (e.g., Hos 5:13; 7:11; 8:9; 9:3; 10:6; 11:5; 12:1; 14:3; clearly in the background of Amos). We know from contemporary records that as early as the ninth century, Shalmaneser III (858–824 BC) exacted tribute from Jehu in one of his western campaigns (ca. 824): "The tribute of Jehu [*Ia-ú-a*], son of Omri [*Ḫu-um-ri*]; I received from him silver, gold, a golden *saplu*-bowl, a golden vase with pointed bottom, golden tumblers, golden buckets, tin, a staff for a king."[1]

Adad-nirari III (810–782 BC) similarly claimed the submission of Israel ("Omri-land") among his Palestinian vassals.[2] However, Tiglath-pileser III (745–727) represents the first major scourge of Israel with the eighth century revival of imperial Assyria. Called "Pul" in 2 Kings 15:19 and 1 Chronicles 5:26, he invaded the northern kingdom during the reigns of Menahem and Pekah (ca. 752–732 [chronology is uncertain]; cf. 2Ki 15:19–20, 29; 1Ch 5:6, 26). Tiglath-pileser recorded this campaign: "Israel [lit.: "Omriland," *Bit Ḫumria*] … all its inhabitants [and] their possessions I led to Assyria. They overthrew their king Pekah [*Pa-qa-ha*] and I placed Hoshea [*A-ú-si-ʾ*] as king over them. I received from them 10 talents of gold, 1,000 [?] talents of silver as their [trib]ute and brought them to Assyria."[3]

Tiglath-pileser III extended his authority into Judah, where Ahaz (735–715 BC) pursued a policy of submission to Assyria ("[I received] the tribute of … Jehoahaz [*Ia-ú-ha-zi*] of Judah").[4] Ahaz thereby incurred the opposition of both Pekah, king of Israel (overthrown ca. 732), who followed the anti-Assyrian policy of his predecessor Ahab, and Isaiah, who denounced Ahaz's faithlessness in abandoning Yahweh's protection for that of Assyria when faced with Pekah's aggression (2Ki 16:5–18; 2Ch 28:16–25; Isa 7:1–25; 8:6–8; cf. Jer 2:36). During the reign of Ahaz, therefore, Judah was faced with the issue of submission or resistance to Assyria—an issue that confronted the nation for over a century and to which it responded in faith or fear according to its relationship to the Lord. Pekah was murdered by the puppet-king Hoshea (732–722), who adopted a vacillating pro-Assyrian policy. His fickle decision to turn to Egypt and repudiate his allegiance to Assyria provoked the invasion of Shalmaneser V (727–722).

Samaria fell after a long siege by Shalmaneser's successor, Sargon II (721–705 BC); the northern kingdom was destroyed and its population deported (2Ki 17:3–6; cf. 18:20–21; Isa 7:8; 8:4; 10:11; 36:20; Hos 9:3; 10:6, 14; 11:5). This catastrophe is explicitly attributed to the Lord's affliction of Israel for her sin (2Ki 17:20; cf. 17:7–19, 21–23; 18:9–12; see also 1Ch 5:26; 2Ch 30:7, Ne 9:30), as were the misfortunes of Ahaz in the same era (2Ch 28:19–20).

Palestine experienced further depredations under Sargon II (Isa 20:1–6) before facing the full brunt of Assyria's hostility in the reign of Sennacherib (704–681 BC). When Hezekiah (728–687) succeeded Ahaz and, at least partly from godly motives, abandoned his father's pro-Assyrian policy (2Ki 18:7–8, 19–20), Sennacherib invaded Judah (701), conquering its fortified cities and threatening Jerusalem before the decimation of his army by "a wasting disease upon his sturdy warriors" (Isa 10:16; cf. 2Ki 18:13–19:37; 2Ch 32:1–31, Isa 36:1–37:38; see comments on Na 1:11).[5] Again, the terrible distress preceding this deliverance was specifically attributed to the Lord as he chastened his unfaithful yet beloved people (cf. Isa 5:26; 7:17–18, 20; 8:7; 10:5–6, 11–12, 24–25; 29:1–4, 31:4, 8).

---

1. *ANET*, 281.
2. Ibid.
3. Ibid., 284.
4. Ibid., 282.
5. Cf. ibid., 287–88.

In the following century, although the biblical reports of earlier times are lacking, both Esarhaddon (681–669 BC) and his son Ashurbanipal (669–633) exercised dominion over Judah, to which Esarhaddon referred explicitly in a building inscription: "I called up … Manasseh [*Me-na-si-i*] king of Judah."[6] This may correspond to the biblical incident of Manasseh's bondage, a further instance of the Lord's affliction mediated by the Assyrians (2Ch 33:1–11).

Coming closer to the probable time of Nahum's prophecy, the stability of Ashurbanipal's long reign was followed by dynastic instability, his sons Ashur-etil-ilani and Sinshumlishir (?) being succeeded after brief reigns by the former's son, Sin-shar-ishkun (621–612 BC). During this period Nabopolassar established himself securely as king of Babylon (625–605), attacking and successively capturing the pro-Assyrian cities of Babylonia and achieving complete independence from Assyria by 616. In 614 Ashur was seized amid brutal massacre by the Medes under Cyaxares; and after this major Assyrian loss, an alliance was concluded between Nabopolassar and Cyaxares against Assyria. The siege and destruction of Nineveh, completed in 612, were the outcome of this alliance and of Assyria's failure to maintain its hold on the disparate and deeply hostile elements of its empire. Indeed, after 639 Assyria could scarcely be regarded as unscathed.

The final years of Ashurbanipal's reign (ca. 638–633 BC) are marked by obscurity, being largely devoid of historical records; uncharacteristically, during this period no great conquests are attributed to the Assyrian monarch, who had apparently withdrawn to Haran, abandoning the government of the empire to his successors. These implications of growing weakness are substantiated by Judah's history under Josiah (640–609); religious reforms expressed his repudiation of Judah's subordination to Assyrian rule and even extended his influence into the neighboring Assyrian province to the north (2Ki 23:15–20).

This evidence for the slackening of Assyria's grip on the west is confirmed also by the resurgence of Egypt as an independent power, for under Psammetik I (664–609 BC) it successfully challenged Assyria's control of the Palestinian coastal plain, capturing Gerar, Ashkelon, Ashdod, and other cities.[7] The condition of Assyria at the time of Nahum's prophecy, therefore, suggests a date prior to 640 and gives considerable weight to the authority of that prophecy. The downfall of the Assyrian colossus has been characterized as one of the greatest riddles of world history. In a similar vein, K. L. Oppenheim writes: "A strong period of silence blacks out the last twenty years of the reign of Ashurbanipal. From the prosperity and the apogee of Assyrian power and prestige — two topics on which the scribes of Ashurbanipal do not tire of elaborating in glowing terms — the country seems to have fallen with appalling suddenness into obscurity."[8]

The subjugation of Israel and Judah had involved political servitude, accompanied by severe demands for tribute or indemnities (cf. 2Ki 15:19–20; 16:8; 17:3; 18:14–16; Hos 10:6). Beyond the social disintegration brought about by foreign occupation, Assyria's policy of partial or full deportation, already imposed on the northern kingdom (2Ki 15:29; 17:6; 18:11; Hos 9:3; 10:6; 11:5), threatened to engulf Judah as well (2Ch 30:6, 10; Isa 36:16–17). Most significantly, it disrupted the nation's worship, since Assyrian political hegemony was accompanied by the cult of its gods and promoted the intrusion of a debilitating religious

---

6. Ibid., 291.

7. See *ZPEB*, 2:231; *ISBE*, 2:45.

8. Quoted in Walter A. Maier, *The Book of Nahum* (Grand Rapids: Baker, 1959), 108.

syncretism, first in the north, and then followed all too willingly by such Judean monarchs as Ahaz and Manasseh (2Ki 16:10–18; 17:24–41; 21:1–18; 2Ch 28:23–25; 33:1–11; cf. Ezr 4:2).

For this reason Judah's willing dependence on foreign powers was castigated as spiritual adultery constituting an abandonment of true allegiance to the Lord and of dependence on him (e.g., 2Ch 28:16–25; Jer 2:18, 36; Eze 16:28; 23:5–12; Hos 5:13; 7:11; 8:9; 12:1; 14:3). For the same reason political independence was a necessary corollary of religious reform (e.g., 2Ki 18:1–18; 22:1–23:30; 2Ch 29:3–32:1).

2. UNITY

Thematic

The two sections—Nahum 1 and 2–3—are unified thematically by key words: "fire" (*ʾēš*; 1:6; 2:4[2:5]; 3:13, 15); "consume, devour" (*ʾākal*; 1:10; 2:13[14]; 3:12 ["eater," NIV], 13, 15[2x]); and "destroy, cut down" (*kārat*, 1:14–15; 2:13[14; "leave no," NIV]; 3:15)—a fitting anticipation of the conflagration and slaughter attending Nineveh's end. These motifs illustrate the most prominent thematic strands uniting the three chapters, namely, destruction by fire (1:6, 10; 2:3–4, 13[2:4–5, 14]; 3:13, 15) and military disaster (1:12, 14–15[2:1]; 2:1, 3–5, 13[2:2, 4–6, 14]; 3:2–3, 8–11, 12–15, 19). Other principal strands are:

(1) Nineveh's wicked opposition to the Lord and his people (1:8–9, 11, 13, 15), expressing its universal cruelty and rapacity (2:11–3:1[2:12–3:1]; 3:4, 19)

(2) the Lord's corresponding opposition to Nineveh (1:2–6, 8–9, 14; 2:13[2:14]; 3:5)

(3) its decadence typified by self-indulgent merchants, unreliable defenders, and chronic drunkenness (1:10; 3:12–13, 15–18; cf. 3:11)

(4) its helplessness in the face of disaster (1:10; 2:9–10[2:10–11]; 3:11, 13)

(5) its exposure to the shame and spectacle of utter destruction (1:14; 3:5–7)

(6) its false dependence on water defenses and their subsequent betrayal (1:8; 2:6, 8[2:7, 9]; cf. 3:8)

(7) the destruction of the dynasty and of the idolatrous religion undergirding it (1:14; 2:6[2:7], 11–13; 3:18–19)

(8) the dispersal of the population (1:8; 2:1, 7–8[2:2, 8–9]; 3:7, 10–11)

(9) Nineveh's extinction (1:8–9, 12, 14–15[2:1]; 2:13[2:14]; 3:7, 19)

(10) the vindication of Judah (1:3, 7, 12–13, 15[2:1]; 2:2[2:3])

The prophecy is structured around these intricately interwoven elements, which set forth the causes (nos. 1–3, 10) and manner (nos. 4–9) of Nineveh's downfall. The close-knit composition of the book firmly unites its two main sections, and no rigid division can be made between them. They may, however, be roughly characterized as representing the judicial decree against Nineveh (ch. 1) and its precise execution (chs. 2–3). This execution corresponds in remarkable detail to the actual course of events, corroborated by historical and archaeological evidence, and represents an outstanding example of fulfilled prophecy (a major contribution of Nahum to the OT, perhaps neglected or depreciated precisely because it is now so obvious). It is therefore appropriate to deal with details of its fulfillment in chs. 2–3, at the most appropriate point of reference (e.g., flood, 2:6[2:7]; fire, 3:15); only where such a clear reference point is lacking are such details advanced to ch. 1 (e.g., idolatry, 1:14).

Stylistic

Stylistically, Nahum is unified by its vivid imagery (e.g., 1:3–8, 10; 2:3–4, 8, 11–13[2:4–5, 9, 12–14]; 3:2–3, 4–6, 12–13, 15–17) and the rapid switches of speaker and perspective (e.g., 1:7–8, 11–2:3[2:4]; 2:8–11[2:9–12], 2:13[14]–3:1; 3:4–8, 11, 18–19). These features contribute powerfully to the dramatic quality of the prophecy in its portrayal of a violent and fateful crossroads in history. This contrast of interlocked, conflicting destinies brilliantly illustrates this tumultuous time in political and social history, events of which are attested by ancient Near Eastern records. It is constructed, however, on a clear-cut dialectic of "good," identified with the Lord and his works (1:7; cf. vv.3, 12–13, 15[2:1]; 2:2[3]) and "evil," seen here as the enemies of the Lord and his people, typified by Nineveh, the very seat of wickedness (1:11; cf. vv.3–6, 8–11, 12, 14–15[2:1]; 2:1–10[2:2–11]), whose simple polarity orders and interprets that succession of events as moral history. And it is based on the concept of God's sovereign justice, whose working in salvation history eludes the sociologist and philosopher and is perceived by prophetic eyes alone. Thus, Nahum's prophecy moves at many levels. Its structure reflects this complexity.

3. AUTHORSHIP

Little is known of the author, Nahum (see 1:1). He is identified as "the Elkoshite" (*hāʾelqōšî*). Since the sixteenth century, an Arab tradition has identified Elkosh with Al Qosh, a village fifty kilometers north of modern Mosul in Iraq. Ancient writers—including Jerome and Eusebius—however, understood the prophet's home to be somewhere in Galilee. Many have speculated that NT Capernaum ("Town of Nahum") was his home, but there is no proof of this, or indeed any specific place. The name could equally relate to Nahum's ancestry.

4. DATE

From internal data it is possible to date the major blocks of material in Nahum, though critics continue to debate small pericopes. As a message of judgment, the book makes no sense if it was proclaimed following the collapse of the Assyrian empire in 612 BC. But references to the destruction of Thebes (No Amon) by the Nile (3:8) demand that the prophecy postdate that city's fall to Ashurbanipal in 664/3 BC. Further consideration of the still formidable state of Assyrian power reflected in the book itself requires that we date the prophecy prior to the decline of that kingdom after about 626 BC (cf. comment at 3:8). P. A. Verhoef believes that the prophecy was written sometime before 645 BC, which would be consistent with Assyria's power as reflected in the book.[9]

5. LITERARY FORM

The prophecy of Nahum is in two main sections—ch. 1 and chs. 2–3, which correspond to each other as outlined below.

---

9. See Verhoef's article on "Nahum, Book of" in *ZPEB*, 4:357.

Chapter 1, in a personal description, describes God's character as judge (or "divine warrior");[10] his judgment in relation to Nineveh (vv.2–11) and the sentence underlying that judgment (vv.12–14), incorporating its proclamation; the implications for both Assyria and Judah; and finally the response it elicits (v.15[2:1]). This chapter is dominated by its prediction of a total end for Nineveh and the dispersion of its inhabitants (vv.3, 8–9, 12, 14–15[2:1]).

Chapters 2–3 repeat this pattern, with detailed and explicit application to "Nineveh" (2:8[9]; 3:7); the two chapters echo ch. 1 in a number of corresponding subsections.

Overview of Structure

	Chapter 1	Chapters 2–3
	Judgment (A)	**Judgment (A')**
Executed on evil	1:11 (*rāʿâ*)	3:19 (*rāʿâ*)
By flood	1:8 (*šetep*)	2:6, 8[7, 9] (gates opened)
By fire	1:6 (*ʾēš*)	2:3[4]; 3:13, 15 (*ʾēš*)
That consumes	1:10 (*ʾākal*)	3:13, 15 (twice) (*ʾākal*)
By drunkenness	1:10 (*sābāʾ*)	3:11 (*tiškerî*)
Exception	1:7 (those who trust)	2:2[3] (Jacob/Israel)
	Sentence (B)	**Sentence (B')**
Messenger formula	1:12 ("This is what the LORD says")	2:13[14]; 3:5 ("declares the LORD Almighty")
Against	1:14 (*ʿāleykā*)	2:13[14]; 3:5 (*ʾēlayik*)
Result: Cut off	1:14–15 (*kārat*)	2:13[14]; 3:15 (*kārat*)
No more	1:14–15 (*lōʾ ʿôd*)	2:13[14] (*lōʾ ʿôd*)
End: vileness, shame	1:14 (*qālal*)	3:5 (*qālôn*)
	Response (C)	**Response (C')**
On the mountains	1:15[2:1] (*ʿal-hehārîm*)	3:18 (*ʿal-hehārîm*)
Proclaim	1:15[2:1] (*mašmîaʿ*)	2:13[14]; 3:19(2x) (*šāmaʿ*)

6. LITERARY PARALLEL

Nahum's prophecy has many affinities with the book of Isaiah. These affinities are signaled most clearly by the words in 1:15[2:1]: "on the mountains the feet of one who brings good news, who proclaims peace" (*ʿal-hehārîm, raglê mebaśśēr mašmîaʿ šālôm*), which recur verbatim in Isaiah 52:7 and are without close parallel

---

10. Cf. Kevin J. Cathcart, "The Divine Warrior and the War of Yahweh in Nahum," in *Biblical Studies in Contemporary Thought: The Tenth Anniversary Commemorative Volume of the Trinity College Biblical Institute 1966–1975*, ed. Miriam Ward (Somerville, Mass.: Greeno, Hadden, 1975), 68–76; Tremper Longman III, "The Divine Warrior: The New Testament Use of an Old Testament Motif," *WTJ* 44 (1982): 290–307.

elsewhere in the OT. A further clear correspondence is between Nahum 1:15[2.1]—"No more will the wicked invade you"—and Isaiah 52:1—"The uncircumcised ... will not enter you again." The reversal promised in both clauses is heralded by the refrain "no more, not again" (lōʾ ʿôd); this phrase is a keynote of Nahum 1:12–15[2:1] (cf. vv.12, 15) and occurs also in Isaiah 51:17–23 (cf. v.22), which anticipates the content of Isaiah 52. Similarly, the verb "invade" (ʿābar, Na 1:15[2:1]; in a touch of irony, the same verb describes Assyria as "passing away" in v.12) is used in the same context of invasion in Isaiah 51:23, where it is twice translated "walk over."

These evidences of literary dependence are reinforced by a common context. Both passages promise liberation (Na 1:12–15[2:1]; Isa 51:22; 52:1–5), specifically from "shackles" or "chains" (môsēr, Na 1:13; Isa 52:2) and from being "afflicted" (ʿānâ, Na 1:12; Isa 51:21; cf. also mākar, "enslaved," Na 3:4; "sold," Isa 52:3). This promise is addressed to "Judah" and to "Zion," its capital (Na 1:15[2:1]; Isa 52:1, 2, 7), in the wake of Assyrian oppression (Na 1:12–15[2:1]; Isa 52:4); and it is introduced in the same terms by the messenger formula ("This is what the LORD says," Na 1:12; Isa 52:3) and by the phrase "(and) now" (weʿattâ, Na 1:13; Isa 52:5), announcing a transitional moment in history. Thus the language and imagery of redemption in Nahum 1:12–15[2:1] corresponds with remarkable exactitude to that of Isaiah 51:21–52:7.

Moreover, the correlation between the book of Nahum and Isaiah 51–52 extends to the second theme of judgment on the oppressor. In Isaiah 51:22–23 the Lord promises to Zion's enemies the judgment she herself has suffered, and the same reversal of fortunes pervades Nahum (cf. 1:12–2:2, 11–13[1:12–2:3, 12–14]; 3:4–7, 16–17). In particular Nineveh will become "drunk" (šākar, Na 3:11; Isa 51:21); her leaders will prove inadequate ("lie down" [šākan], Na 3:18; cf. vv.16–17; "lie" [šākab], Isa 51:20; cf. v.18); she will experience the fate ascribed to Zion in Isaiah 51:19: "ruin" (šōd; cf. šaddedâ, "is in ruins," Na 3:7) and "destruction" (šeber, "wound," Na 3:19), "famine" (cf. the results of "locusts," Na 3:15–17) and "sword" (ḥereb, Na 2:13[14]; 3:3, 15). She will, in fact, experience the same "wrath" of God (ḥēmâ, Na 1:2, 6; Isa 51:17, 20, 22).

Considered individually these correlations are not uniformly distinctive, though the recurrence of Isaiah 51:19 in Nahum 3 is striking. They gain significance collectively in view of the established relation between Nahum and Isaiah 51–52. And they receive added corroboration from a further distinctive correspondence linking Isaiah 51:19 and Nahum 3:7. The clause "who can comfort you?" (mî yānûd lāk, Isa 51:19) is echoed in Nahum 3:7: "Who will mourn for her?" (mî yānûd lâ) and elsewhere only in Jeremiah 15:5. The following compressed question—"Who can console you?" (mî ʾanaḥamēk, Isa 51:19; lit., "How can I console you?")—is expanded in Nahum 3:7: "Where can I find anyone to comfort you?" (mēʾayin ʾabaqqēš menaḥamîm lāk), with one approximate parallel in Lamentations 2:13.

In view of the precision, uniqueness, and frequency of these correspondences, it seems evident, then, that Nahum's relationship to Isaiah 51–52 extends beyond participation in a common stock of prophetic imagery and motif to one of specific literary interdependence. This conclusion is confirmed by further extensive points of contact between the two books. First, in the opening couplet of Nahum 1:4, the image of God's drying the sea is preeminently Isaianic. Thus the terms "rebuke" (gāʿar), "sea" (yām), "rivers" (nehārôt), and "dry" (ḥārēb) all recur in Isaiah 50:2.

Additionally, the second couplet of Nahum 1:4 also finds an important parallel in Isaiah 33:9: the terms "Lebanon ... Bashan ... Carmel" do not recur together in a single verse or passage outside those two locations; and they are used in the same context of drought and desolation, expressed by the somewhat rare (sixteen times in the OT) shared verb "fade ... wither, wastes away" (ʾumlal).

The third motif shared conspicuously by Nahum and Isaiah is the Lord's anger. This is obviously a common theme throughout the OT; however, it is expressed distinctively in these books—particularly in terms of fire and other natural imagery and with explicit reference to Assyria.

The evidence for literary interdependence between Isaiah and Nahum is thus founded on unique, multiple verbal repetitions linking specific passages (e.g., Na 1:2 and Isa 59:17–19; Na 1:3–6 and Isa 29:6; Na 1:4 and Isa 33:9; 50:2; Na 1:4–5 and Isa 42:15; Na 1:15[2:1] and Isa 52:1, 7; Na 2:9–10[10–11] and Isa 24:1, 3; Na 2:10[11] and Isa 21:3–4; Na 3:5–7 and Isa 47:2–3; Na 3:7 and Isa 51:19). It is reinforced by the extensive continuity of imagery in other related passages (e.g., drought, earthquake, fire, stubble, burial, lions). And it is corroborated to the point of virtual certainty by the shared pattern of oppression, deliverance, and judgment experienced specifically in relation to Assyria (cf. Isa 5:26–30; 7:17–20; 8:4–8; 10:5–34; 11:11, 15–16; 14:24–27; 19:23–25; 20:1–6; 27:13; 30:27–33; 31:8–9; 36:1–37:38; 38:6; 51:17–52:7). There are forty-four references to Assyria in Isaiah, exceeded only by 2 Kings (forty-nine); no other OT book approaches this preoccupation with Assyrian history apart from Nahum and, to a lesser extent, Hosea and Jonah.

Evidently these correlations are of considerable significance for the literary criticism of Isaiah. They cannot be pursued in detail here, but several points are readily apparent.

The cycle of Isaianic prophecies regarding Assyria are usually attributed without dispute to Isaiah ben Amoz, who prophesied in Jerusalem in the eighth century; this would include most, if not all, of Isaiah 5–11; 14:24–27; 19:23–25; 20:1–6; 27:13–30:33.[11] It follows that Nahum is dependent on Isaiah in his allusions to Isaiah 5:24–30; 10:5–27; 29:6; 30:27–33, since Nahum is to be dated after 663 BC. Such dependency on previous witnesses is characteristic of the prophetic tradition, and it is logical in this case, in view of Nahum's preoccupation with the same issues as Isaiah.

This leaves numerous correspondences unexplained (particularly, Na 1:2 and Isa 59:17–18; Na 1:4 and Isa 33:9; 50:2; Na 1:4–5 and Isa 42:15; Na 1:3, 6 and Isa 66:15–16; Na 1:15[2:1] and Isa 52:1, 7; Na 2:9–10[10–11] and Isa 24:1, 3; Na 2:10[11] and Isa 21:3–4; Na 3:5–7 and Isa 47:2–3; Na 3:7 and Isa 51:19). It is conceivable that a "Second Isaiah," prophesying in the sixth century, would have drawn on Nahum in this way; the fall of Nineveh would then provide a suitable analogy for that of Babylon. However, it is remarkable that so original a prophet as the author(s) of Isaiah 40–66 should draw this heavily on a work of such restricted scope as Nahum.

Alternatively, Nahum was drawing on Isaiah 1–66 in its entirety. This explains the continuity of Nahum's imagery (e.g., fire, vengeance, drought) with passages distributed throughout Isaiah.[12] It also explains Nahum's application of prophecies concerning Babylon (Isa 13–14, 47) to Assyria, since he prophesied before the emergence of Babylon from its status as an Assyrian vassal. Although it is appropriate to the clear-cut evidence, which reveals Nahum as drawing on Isaiah, it must also be acknowledged that the "First Isaiah" oracles (Isa 13–14) have often been related to Babylonian-led rebellion against

---

11. Cf. A. Weiser, *The Old Testament: Its Formation and Development* (New York: Association, 1961), 187–93.
12. Cf. *ISBE*, 2:896.

Assyria by the eighth century Merodach-Baladan.[13] Other contemporary redactional theories propose the existence of "secondary" material in "First Isaiah," such as chs. 13–14, which are woven into the total "Isaiah" book through a rich redactional history in which God's purposes with Assyria merge into his later use of Babylon (e.g., Isa 47).[14] Under such circumstances, Nahum's use of Isaiah, as well as his own contribution in the late seventh century, becomes part of a developing tradition, fully realized in the canonical "Isaiah."

Finally, this provides a suitable interpretation of the outstanding correlation between Nahum 1:15[2:1] and Isaiah 52:7, where the concept of "peace"—an integral element of Isaiah's message (*šālôm*; cf. Isa 9:6–7; 26:3, 12; 27:5; 32:17–18; 39:8; 45:7; 48:18, 22; 53:5; 54:10, 13; 55:12; 57:2, 19, 21; 59:8; 60:17; 66:12)—appears as an undeveloped theme in Nahum more organically connected with the content of Isaiah, from which it is most likely to have been transposed. This appears more plausible than that a "Second Isaiah" appropriated and largely developed a peripheral motif of Nahum.

These interrelationships indicate that in Nahum we have an outstanding example of prophetic interpretation and application within the OT itself. They also hold out the possibility that this "minor" prophecy holds a key to the authentication of its great forerunner. "The eye cannot say to the hand, 'I don't need you!' And the head cannot say to the feet, 'I don't need you!' On the contrary, those parts of the body that seem to be weaker are indispensable" (1Co 12:21–22).

7. THEOLOGICAL VALUES

Theologically, Nahum stands as an eloquent testimony to the particularity of God's justice and salvation. To the suffering remnant, there was little question that God would and did punish his own covenantal people; but whether he was equally able and willing to impart justice to the powerful heathen nations surrounding Israel was untested, at least since Israel became a national entity. Among those nations, none had so dominated world affairs in the second millenium BC as had imperial Assyria. Arrogant, self-sufficient, cruel, and assertive, the Assyrians had dominated every small nation in the region at one time or another from the days of the first Tiglath-pileser (1115–1076 BC) onward. The righteous Israelite might well have asked, as did Habakkuk (Hab 1:2):

> How long, O Lord, must I call for help,
>   but you do not listen?
> Or cry out to you, "Violence!"
>   but you do not save?

The severity and kindness of God were both under scrutiny: the former as to whether it applied only selectively to his own people, and the latter in the context of God's ability and desire to bring about ultimate salvation for those who were faithful to him.

Between the divine plan for salvation history and the wretched condition of his oppressed people stood the power of a particular, powerful human foe—Assyria. Over four hundred years of Middle Eastern

---

13. John D. W. Watts, *Isaiah 1–33* (WBC 24; Waco, Tex.: Word, 1985), 185.
14. Cf. C. R. Seitz, "Isaiah, Book of First Isaiah," *ABD*, 3:487–88.

history pointed in the same direction: Assyria and her gods were in control, if there was in fact any control over universal, historical direction. Back in Jerusalem each brief fling at independence by a petty monarch ended in disaster. The temple on Zion had survived over the years, but the shadow of destruction already lay over it. The worship of Yahweh in the mid-seventh century had already disappeared in the north and was threatened by syncretistic forces in the south. Nineveh stood, with her gods, as the capital of the most powerful kingdom the world had ever seen. "Where, then, is your God?" the skeptic might rightly ask. "And if he exists, what kind of God is he?"

Into this situation comes the word of the Lord: "The LORD is a jealous and avenging God ... slow to anger and great in power; the LORD will not leave the guilty unpunished" (Na 1:2–3). Nineveh's day will come to an end; no power on earth can long endure when it sets itself against the Lord and his Anointed One in Zion (cf. Ps 2). The vivid imagery of Nahum's pictured demise of Nineveh is eloquent testimony to the power of a God whose strength is never simply an abstraction. A theology of divine sovereignty and justice, applauded by all the nations, emerges from the specifics of Assyria's fall.

It is not merely divine retribution, however, that emerges from the picture. There is also good news to proclaim. "Look, there on the mountains, the feet of one who brings good news, who proclaims peace!" (1:15[2:1]). Judah is called to celebrate, as God's people inevitably are, when the day of Yahweh's wrath is fully understood and the remnant are prepared in righteousness. The corollary to the severity of God is his kindness (ḥesed; GK 2876), a mercy that includes covenant-keeping and justice. Here is the theme of every prayer of every true remnant through the years as they cry out, "How long, O Lord, how long?" "Thy will be done, on earth as it is in heaven" is the natural concomitant of the cry, "Thy kingdom come!"

To the Christian longing for the day of good tidings, the message is clearly set forth in the new covenant. Paul, in Romans 10:15, extolled the preaching of the gospel of salvation with a quotation from this ancient book of judgment: "As it is written, 'How beautiful are the feet of those who bring good news!'" In this age it is the preaching of the gospel that will ensure the ultimate triumph of God, even as Romans 10:18 points out: "Their words [will go forth] to the ends of the world." This promise, not the Assyrian or even the Roman dominion, will be the final word on history.

When the forces opposing God are so firmly ensconced and the flickering lamp of God's people is at the point of extinction, however, it is easy for the remnant to forget. Nahum reminds us, as do the ruins of ancient Nineveh, that God himself is the ultimate Ruler. He will have the final word. There is good news for God's people. Just as years later the aged Simeon could pray in confidence (Lk 2:29–32):

> "Sovereign Lord, as you have promised,
> 　you now dismiss your servant in peace.
> For my eyes have seen your salvation,
> 　which you have prepared in the sight of all people,
> a light for revelation to the Gentiles
> 　and for glory to your people Israel,"

so the waiting supplicant in Nahum's day could look ahead to such a day. It was then—and continues today—to be the hope of the people of God: our eyes will see the salvation of the Lord.

8. CANONICITY AND TEXT

The canonicity and text of Nahum have never been seriously challenged. Most scholarly discussion of the date has turned on critical theories of the purpose of Nahum, with various scholars suggesting the book was composed not as a predictive prophetic word but as a liturgy utilized in temple worship at various junctures in Israel's history.[15] Studies of the so-called "divine warrior" passage in ch. 1, together with the reference to Judah's "festivals" in 1:15 [2:1], have fueled most theories.

Of particular interest has been the acrostic poem in ch. 1, with its disputed partial acrostic dominating studies of the entire poem in Nahum 1:2–10. The form and order of these verses have often been rearranged in the interest of restoring the acrostic, a proposal evoked by v.2, which opens with the first letter of the Hebrew alphabet, and by the presence of some of the subsequent letters at or near the beginning of succeeding lines. However, since only three letters occur in their expected position (vv.2a, 3b, 4), grounds for seeking an acrostic here, let alone for rearranging the text to conform to one, must be seen as tenuous but are sufficiently tantalizing to ensure continued speculation.

Canonicity has never been seriously questioned, as Nahum appears in all subsequent lists of Israelite prophets. Attempts to rework the text have centered on the acrostic in ch. 1, or words not well understood, some of which have in recent years been given further illumination from studies in Babylonian or Northwest Semitic lexicography.[16]

9. BIBLIOGRAPHY

Allen, Leslie C. *The Books of Joel, Obadiah, Jonah and Micah*. New International Commentary on the Old Testament. Grand Rapids: Eerdmans, 1976.

Bruckner, James K. *Jonah, Nahum, Habakkuk, Zephaniah*. NIV Application Commentary. Grand Rapids: Zondervan, 2004.

Longman, Tremper, III. "*Nahum.*" In *The Minor Prophets*. Vol. 2. Edited by T. McComisky. Grand Rapids: Baker, 1993.

Maier, Walter A. *The Book of Nahum*. Grand Rapids: Baker, 1959.

Patterson, Richard D. *Nahum, Habakkuk, Zephaniah*. Wycliffe Exegetical Commentary. Chicago: Moody Press, 1991.

Smith, Ralph L. *Micah–Malachi*. Word Biblical Commentary. Waco, Tex.: Word, 1984.

Thomas, D. Winton, ed. *Documents From Old Testament Times*. Oxford: Oxford University Press, 1958.

Yadin, Yigael. *The Art of Warfare in Biblical Lands*. New York: McGraw, 1963.

---

15. Ralph Smith, *Micah–Malachi* (WBC 32; Waco, Tex.: Word, 1984), 65–67.
16. See Kevin J. Cathcart, *Nahum in the Light of Northwest Semitica* (BibOr 26; Rome: Pontifical Biblical Institute, 1973), et al.

10. OUTLINE

I. The Anger of the Lord (1:1–15[2:1])

   A. The Judgment of the Lord (1:1–11)

      1. Awesome in Power (1:1–6)

      2. Just in Execution (1:7–11)

   B. The Sentence of the Lord (1:12–14)

   C. The Purpose of the Lord (1:15[2:1])

II. The Fall of Nineveh (2:1[2]–3:19)

   A. Warning and Promise (2:1–2[2–3])

   B. Nineveh's Destruction Detailed (2:3[4]–3:19)

      1. First Description of Nineveh's Destruction (2:3[4]–3:1)

         a. Onslaught (2:3–5[4–6])

         b. Failing defenses (2:6–10[7–11])

         c. An interpretive analogy (2:11–12[12–13])

         d. Judgment from the Lord (2:13[14])

         e. The verdict announced (3:1)

      2. Second Description of Nineveh's Destruction (3:2–7)

         a. Onslaught and failing defenses (3:2–3)

         b. An interpretive analogy (3:4)

         c. Judgment from the Lord (3:5–6)

         d. The verdict announced (3:7)

      3. Third Description of Nineveh's Destruction (3:8–11)

      4. Fourth Description of Nineveh's Destruction (3:12–19)

         a. Onslaught and failing defenses (3:12–14)

         b. Interpretive analogy and judgment from the Lord (3:15–17)

         c. The verdict announced (3:18–19)

Text and Exposition

I. THE ANGER OF THE LORD (1:1–15[2:1])

OVERVIEW

This chapter is structured as three units (cf. "Literary Form" in the introduction): the judgment of God (vv.1–11), the sentence to follow (vv.12–14), and the response elicited (v.15[2:1]), each of which involves a counterpoint of contrast between the goodness and severity of God. Within the first section, vv.2–6 form a general statement of the Lord's patience (v.3) and of his devastating judgment of his enemies (v.2). Verses 7–11 echo these contrasts in the reference to his goodness (v.7), defined further as being extended to those who "trust" and as affording protection from "trouble." These verses similarly picture the complete "end" (vv.8–11) of those who in their "wickedness" plot against the Lord.

Within this section a type of hymn has been detected, similar in form to various psalms (Victory Hymns [e.g., Pss 24; 68; 96; 97; 98; 114; 124–125; Longman, 769], or General Hymns [e.g., Ps 113; so R. Smith, 72, following C. Westermann, *Praise of God in the Psalms* (Richmond: John Knox, 1965), 122]). In the hymn, the Lord appears as the divine warrior (see also K. J. Cathcart, "The Divine Warrior and the War of Yahweh in Nahum," in *Biblical Studies in Contemporary Thought: The Tenth Anniversary Commemorative Volume of the Trinity College Biblical Institute 1966–1975*, ed. Miriam Ward [Somerville, Mass.: Greeno, Hadden, 1975], 68–76) who brings both judgment (vv.2–6) and salvation (vv.7–8). Verses 9–11 return to the general theme of judgment by focusing on the plots of an enemy, not specifically named but assumed to be Nineveh, as inserted in the NIV text.

Verses 12–14 (possibly including v.15[2:1]) introduce the judicial sentence on the enemy (again see the NIV's insertion of "Nineveh" in v.14) and comfort to the afflicted (the NIV inserts "Judah" in v.12) and embody the sovereign decree of God, based on the preceding evidence and amplifying it further. His protection brings deliverance from the "yoke" of oppression (v.13; cf. vv.12, 15[2:1]); it is promised to "Judah," whose trust as his covenantal people is expressed in true religious service (v.15[2:1]). Conversely, his judgment overthrows the oppressive military, political, and dynastic power of his enemies (vv.12–15[2:1]), whose wickedness is expressed in idolatry (v.14). Verse 15[2:1], whether as part of the preceding section or isolated, continues the counterpoint effect, in which the central theme of judgment is intertwined and contrasted with that of mercy.

The entire chapter is unified and dominated by its revelation of the character and activity of the Lord (the "divine warrior"), being punctuated repeatedly by explicit mention of his name (passim). It thereby sets forth the intricate yet coherent complexity of God's dealings with his creation: his ways in judgment and mercy are as varied as those of the nations he governs, his ways as profound as the sovereign purpose of his own heart.

The antiphonal character of ch. 1 extends to chs. 2 and 3: the enemy, hitherto anonymous (see comments on 1:8, 11, 14; 2:1[2]), is finally identified as "Nineveh" and its "king" (2:8[9]; 3:7, 18). The major structural break noted between 1:15[2:1] and 2:1[2] must therefore be qualified in the light

567

of the concurrent pattern, by which Nahum 2–3 merely extends the progressive specification of God's vengeance and mercy, initiated in the first chapter.

A. The Judgment of the Lord (1:1–11)

OVERVIEW

The opening verses of Nahum form a prologue dominated by the revelation of God's eternal power and divine nature in creation (cf. Ro 1:20). As in Romans 1:18–32, this revelation is characterized preeminently by God's justice, expressed in retribution (v.2) and wrath (vv.2–3, 6) that shake the entire creation (vv.3–6). The mercy of God, for all its reality, is in this oracle a fleeting counterpart to the awesome display of majesty.

The passage, framed by the word "wrath" (ḥēmâ; vv.2, 6), consists of a forceful enunciation of the "vengeance" accomplished by God's "wrath" (vv.2–3), manifested in nature (vv.3–5) and in society (v.5). These three elements are repeated in a summary section (v.6).

This dramatic representation has numerous echoes of the exodus and Sinai: in the representation of God's character (vv.2–3; cf. v.7) and in the natural imagery—"storm" and "clouds" (v.3),

the "sea" rebuked (v.4), and earthquake and "fire" (vv.5–6; cf. Hab 3). It also echoes the language of Isaiah (esp. v.2; cf. "Literary Parallel" in the introduction), whose work draws heavily on the historical analogies formed by the events of the exodus.

Also, this prologue is reminiscent of Elijah's ministry in its evocation of storm (v.3; cf. 1Ki 18:41–45) and drought (v.4; cf. 1Ki 17:1–7); of wind, earthquake, and fire (vv.3, 5–6; cf. 1Ki 18:38; 19:11–12; 2Ki 1:10–14). As such it forms a fitting prelude to the ensuing prophecy; as he judged Baal's spurious power over nature by natural means, so the Lord will judge Assyria's spurious military power by military defeat. However, the present passage has no clearly unified background. As in Isaiah, past history and natural phenomena form an analogy for the future, revealing the measure of God's power as it will be exercised in a new context of deliverance and judgment.

1. Awesome in Power (1:1–6)

¹An oracle concerning Nineveh. The book of the vision of Nahum the Elkoshite.

²The Lᴏʀᴅ is a jealous and avenging God;
    the Lᴏʀᴅ takes vengeance and is filled with wrath.
The Lᴏʀᴅ takes vengeance on his foes
    and maintains his wrath against his enemies.
³The Lᴏʀᴅ is slow to anger and great in power;
    the Lᴏʀᴅ will not leave the guilty unpunished.

His way is in the whirlwind and the storm,
  and clouds are the dust of his feet.
⁴He rebukes the sea and dries it up;
  he makes all the rivers run dry.
Bashan and Carmel wither
  and the blossoms of Lebanon fade.
⁵The mountains quake before him
  and the hills melt away.
The earth trembles at his presence,
  the world and all who live in it.
⁶Who can withstand his indignation?
  Who can endure his fierce anger?
His wrath is poured out like fire;
  the rocks are shattered before him.

COMMENTARY

1–2 On the prophet Nahum, see "Authorship" in the introduction. The adjective "jealous" (*qannô*; cf. also *qannā*; *TWOT*, 2:802–3; *NIDOTTE*, 3:937–40, where the translation "zealous" is preferred) is used solely of God, primarily in his self-revelation at Sinai (Ex 20:5; 34:14). Against this covenantal background it denotes the Lord's deep, indeed fiercely protective commitment to his people and his exclusive claim to their obedience and reciprocal commitment (cf. Dt 4:24; 5:9). Where this relationship of mutual commitment is threatened, either by Israel's unfaithfulness or by foreign oppression, the inevitable expressions of such jealousy are "vengeance" and "wrath," directed to restoring that relationship (e.g., Nu 25:11; Heb 10:27).

"Avenging" and "vengeance" (both *nōqēm*; cf. *TWOT*, 2:598–99) are judicial in nature, expressing judgment and requital for infractions of law and morality—primarily those committed with presumption and impenitence. Such infractions are defined in this case by the terms of the covenant they threaten to disrupt (cf. Lev 26:25; Dt 32:35, 41, 43). As a judicial function vengeance belongs supremely to God, the Judge of the whole earth (e.g., Dt 32:35), and to the ordained representatives of his authority (e.g., Ex 21:20–21; Nu 31:2–3; Jos 10:13; Est 8:13). Consequently, humans are forbidden to take the law into their own hands or to exercise their own vengeance on enemies. Nineveh—despite God's use of her violence—has done just that. Now, as she has devastated cities and populations, so it will happen to her: military invasion (2:1–10[2–11]), siege (3:14), slaughter (3:3), destruction by fire (1:10; 2:13; 3:13, 15), humiliation (3:5–7), captivity (3:10), exile (2:7[8]; 3:10–11), and utter devastation (2:10[11]). She has sown the wind and in her impenitence will surely reap the whirlwind.

Like jealousy, "wrath" (*ḥēmâ*; *TWOT*, 1:374–75; *NIDOTTE*, 2:170–71) denotes intense and passionate feeling; as noted above, it represents here the outworking of jealousy, which moves to eradicate every obstacle to its commitment. Utterly different, like the preceding terms, from the sinful self-will of humanity (cf. Jas 1:20), "wrath" constitutes a divine characteristic that must be faced whenever the proper limits of our relationship with God are broken; to deny God's "wrath" is to deny the reality of judgment and the necessity of atonement.

Verse 2 lays a foundation for the entire prophecy; all that follows is rooted in this revelation of the justice and burning zeal of the Lord exercised in behalf of his people. To wrest the following chapters from the context, seeing only the historical details of carnage and destruction, is to miss their significance as a demonstration of the terrible wrath and power of God (cf. Rev 6:16-17).

3 The Lord's anger is balanced by his forbearance ("slow to anger," a further attribute associated preeminently with Sinai (Ex 34:6; Nu 14:18; cf. Ne 9:17). It represents a restraint born of meekness and not of weakness—as evidenced by the contrast with his great "power"; it is not to be misunderstood as passivity (cf. Isa 65:2-5; Ac 17:30; Ro 2:3-5; 2Pe 3:9; Rev 2:21). Nor is it exercised indefinitely, for his "power" assures that he "will not leave the guilty unpunished," which translates the verb *niqqâ* (Piel, "to acquit, pronounce innocent"; cf. *TWOT*, 2:596-98.). This verb, therefore,

extends the forensic connotations of "vengeance" (*nāqam*), which it also echoes phonetically; and in fact the subsequent prophecy unfolds with the formal solemnity of a judicial procedure. This characteristic of divine justice is equally a facet of the Lord's self-revelation to Moses at Sinai (Ex 20:7; 34:7; Nu 14:18; Dt 5:11), asserting his maintenance of moral distinctions and accountability.

The theophany at Sinai forms the basis of Nahum's proclamation against Nineveh, as it did for Jonah (cf. Ex 34:6; Jnh 4:2), to which Nahum may well have been alluding. The forbearance of God had been extended to Nineveh a century earlier in response to her repentance (Jnh 3:10); but it was forfeited by her subsequent history of ruthless evil, making way for God's judgment instead.

Though without any complete analogy, the power and majesty of God are evidenced most dramatically in the forces of nature. "Whirlwind" (*sûpâ*) and "storm" (*šᵉʿārâ*) are often expressions of his judgment, the two terms recurring together in Psalm 83:15 and Isaiah 29:6; "clouds" also extend the preceding associations with Sinai (cf. Ex 19:9, 16). For all their grandeur, however, these mighty forces are dwarfed in the presence of the Lord, whom the highest heavens cannot contain; the tempest is but the disturbance caused as he marches by, and the dark storm clouds are merely dust stirred up by his feet (cf. 1Ki 19:11-13; cf. Hab 3:8).

> O tell of His might, O sing of his grace,
>> Whose robe is the light, whose canopy space;
> His chariots of wrath the deep thunderclouds form,
>> And dark is His path on the wings of the storm.

(Robert Grant, "O Worship the King")

4 The preceding description of the Lord's power is extended in the image of drought, consuming the fertile highlands of Palestine and their sources of water. The language of the first couplet is reminiscent of references to the exodus (cf. Ps 106:9; Isa 42:15; 44:27; 50:2), but as in Habakkuk 3:8 it is expanded by the following geographical terms to represent a scene of widespread desolation. "Bashan" in Transjordan, "Carmel" in northern Israel, and the "Lebanon" range on Israel's northern boundary are frequently represented together as the choicest forest and pasture regions of the Promised Land (cf. *TWOT*, 1:137, 455–56, 468). Nevertheless, all are revealed as vulnerable; like the pride and strength of humanity, they are devastated and "wither" before the burning anger of the Lord (cf. Isa 33:9; Joel 1:10–12; Am 1:2; Zec 11:1–2). The drought depicted here is abnormally severe in its catastrophic effects on the "sea" and "rivers"; it is more evocative of the drought commanded by Elijah, directed against the northern kingdom, within whose borders the devastated landscapes of this verse lie (cf. 1Ki 17:1–18:46).

5 An earthquake forms a third, and common, biblical manifestation of the Lord's power, causing the hills to "melt away" (*mûg*). Such melting may be brought on by intense heat (cf. Ps 97:3–5; Mic 1:3–4), a phenomenon associated with the earthquake at Sinai to which vv.2–3 allude. However, the verb "melt away" may also be applied to the effect of flooding (cf. comment on 2:6).

6 This verse summarizes vv.2–5, emphatically recapitulating the concept of anger by repeating the noun meaning "wrath." The kindred terms "indignation" (*zāʿam*) and "fierce [lit., "burning"] anger" (*ḥᵃrôn ʾappô*; cf. *TWOT*, 1:736) further

stress the concept, with the latter expression always describing divine anger (cf. to a similar but different construction for "human indignation"; *NIDOTTE*, 2:265–68, *ḥārôn*); once again, they describe the irresistible manifestation of this anger, before which the entire created world is subdued.

The simile of "wrath" being poured out "like fire" occurs elsewhere (2Ch 34:25; Jer 7:20; 44:6; La 2:4; cf. 2Ch 12:7; 34:21; Jer 10:25; La 4:11; Eze 14:19; 22:22; 30:15), fire being a common expression of the Lord's judgment. The verb "pour out" (*nātak*) is used literally of poured (Ex 9:33; 2Sa 21:10) or molten (Eze 22:20) liquid. More common is the figurative sense of divine wrath "poured out," as here.

The section concluding with v.6 is deeply imbued with the recollection of God's covenant with Israel, also sharing with numerous poetic passages their various images of divine judgment and power (cf. Pss 11:6; 18:7–15; 29:3–9; 50:3; 83:13–15; 97:2–5; Jer 23:29; Eze 38:19–22; Joel 2:1–11; Mic 1:4). However, the marked recurrence of all these features in the work of Isaiah suggests again that Nahum stands as an heir if not a disciple of Isaiah by interpreting God's covenant with Israel to his own time (cf. Isa 8:16).

2. Just in Execution (1:7–11)

OVERVIEW

This passage also portrays "the kindness and sternness of God" (Ro 11:22). Its continuity with vv.2–6, which it amplifies, is marked by a corresponding emphasis on the Lord as the prime mover in all that ensues (cf. vv.7, 9) and by the increasing definition of his adversaries (cf. *ʾōyᵉbāyw*, "his enemies," vv.2, 8; *ṣārayw*, "his foes," v.2; *ṣārâ*, "trouble," vv.7, 9). The passages are linked also by their

continuity of imagery: "flood" and "darkness" (v.8; cf. "storm," v.3); drought (*yābēš*, "dry"; vv.4, 10); and the consequent burning of "stubble" (v.10; cf. "fire," v.6).

As in vv.2–6, the redemptive work of God is juxtaposed to and overshadowed by his irrevocable judgment. This is set forth in vv.8–11, composed of three corresponding sections. Verse 8 describes the

Lord's foes and their annihilation (*kālâ ʿāśâ*, "make an end"; v.8) in two parallel clauses that resume the natural imagery of vv.2–6 (see above). Verses 9–10 define these foes more precisely as those who "plot" (*ḥāšab*; v.9) against the Lord; their fate is reaffirmed in identical terms (*kālâ ʿōśeh*, "bring to an end"; v.9) and in similar metaphorical language (v.10). Verse 11 resumes the charge of plotting (*ḥāšab*), which it applies more precisely to "one" individual; his fate is clearly implied by the pattern of the preceding verses. Verses 7–11 are thus unified by repetitions of vocabulary in vv.8–11 and by the conjunction ("but") that relates and contrasts v.7 to vv.8–11. They are distinguished from vv.2–6 and vv.12–15[2:1] by the inclusio framing vv.2–6 ("wrath") and by the introductory formula in v.12.

These verses have the menacing ring of a judicial indictment, citing the evidence against the accused. It reveals a conspiracy against the Judge himself, the Lord whose justice and supreme authority have been announced in the preliminary proceedings of vv.2–6. The outcome of the trial is therefore in no doubt, and the sentence is already anticipated in the charge developed here.

> ⁷The LORD is good,
>   a refuge in times of trouble.
>   He cares for those who trust in him,
> ⁸   but with an overwhelming flood
>   he will make an end of ˻Nineveh˼;
>   he will pursue his foes into darkness.
>
> ⁹Whatever they plot against the LORD
>   he will bring to an end;
>   trouble will not come a second time.
> ¹⁰They will be entangled among thorns
>   and drunk from their wine;
>   they will be consumed like dry stubble.
> ¹¹From you, ˻O Nineveh˼ has one come forth
>   who plots evil against the LORD
>   and counsels wickedness.

COMMENTARY

7 The goodness of God forms a basic tenet of Israel's faith, particularly celebrated in the psalmic literature whose language is prominent throughout v.7 (e.g., 2Ch 5:13; Pss 25:7–8; 69:16; 118:1, 29; 135:3; 136:1; 145:7–9; Jer 33:11). Also as here, it repeatedly forms the basis for the response of faith, expressed in trusting obedience (e.g., Ezr 8:18, 22; Pss 34:8; 73:1; 100:4–5, 106:1–3; 107:1–2; 109:21, La 3:25). Where the goodness of God is successfully impugned, faith soon crumbles (e.g., Ge 3:1–7; Nu 14:3, 27).

In this context, as an expression of covenantal commitment to defend his people, the Lord himself is a "refuge" or stronghold of protection (*māʿôz*, "strength"; cf. Ne 8:10; Pss 27:1; 31:2, 4; 37:39; Pr 10:29; Isa 25:4; Jer 16:19). He "cares for" (*yādaʿ*, lit., "knows"; e.g., Ex 33:12; Pss 31:7; 91:14; Jer 1:5; 12:3) the faithful, acknowledging their relationship to him and the claim on his goodness, which is inherent in that relationship. The "trouble" from which he gives protection is graphically illustrated in Judah's sufferings at the hands of Assyria. It demands a "trust" that is too often missing or misplaced, but it affords one of Scripture's most dramatic testimonies to the Lord as a "refuge" for those who indeed put their hope in him (Isa 33:2–4; 37:3, 6–7, 29–38; cf. Isa 12:2; 26:3–4). The note of grace sounded here, highlighted by its juxtaposition to the surrounding verses, is already implicit in v.3, and it foreshadows the theme of Judah's vindication in the following sections (vv.12–13, 14; 2:2[3]).

8 The goodness of God, like his patience, does not obviate his judgment. As in Psalms, his judgment is directed against those who refuse to submit to his rule and who are therefore both "his foes" (*ʾōyᵉbāyw*) and the oppressors of his loyal people; as long as evil exists, his judgment is an inevitable expression of his goodness in behalf of the victims of evil. The specific form of judgment expressed here is a "flood," recalling the previous description of storm in v.3 (cf. 2:6[7]). In a slight change of the metaphor, it banishes the enemy into "darkness" (i.e., death; cf. 1Sa 2:9; Job 15:23–30; Ps 88:12; Ecc 6:4).

These drastic measures are directed against a shadowy antagonist specified by "her place" (cf. NASB note). Both the feminine suffix and the noun denoting a locality confirm the NIV's interpretation ("⌐Nineveh⌐," cities being feminine in Hebrew; cf. 2:1[2], 7[8], 10[11], 13[14]; 3:5–8, 11–17; the NRSV's "his adversaries" parallels "enemies" in the last line but obscures the feminine suffix); but the prophecy effectively withholds the adversary's

identity until she is fully engulfed by the destruction that is still impending here (cf. 2:8[9]; 3:7).

9 The utter finality of this sentence is stressed by the phrase "bring to an end," repeated from v.8. It is reinforced by the terse ambiguity of the final line: "trouble" (*ṣārâ*; cf. v.7; *TWOT*, 2:778–79) will not arise again for God's people, for it will descend on those who trouble Israel (cf. *ʾōyᵉbāyw*, "his foes"; 1:8) in so conclusive a way that it need not arise again. The crime of these enemies, who are addressed directly in the Hebrew text (cf. NIV note, RSV, NRSV), is identified here as settled, premeditated antagonism: they do not stumble into sin but actively "plot" (*ḥāšab*) against the Lord (cf. *TWOT*, 1:330).

The abrupt switch of subject evident in the Hebrew of this verse is typical of Nahum's prophecy (cf. vv.11–12, 15[2:1]; 2:8[9], 9–10[10–11], 12–13[13–14]; note changes at 3:1, 5, 9, 11); this stylistic feature effectively evokes the violent crosscurrents of history that intersect in the fate of Nineveh. In proclaiming a complete "end" to Nineveh, this verse identifies the central theme of the book, to which all others are related as either cause or effect (cf. vv.8, 12, 14–15[2:1]; 2:13[14]; 3:7, 19).

10 As in v.8, the means of judgment are portrayed here in metaphorical language. The syntax of the first two lines is highly compressed and therefore somewhat obscure (cf. NIV note). The individual words, however, make good sense. They are clearly syntactically unified by a striking alliterative pattern involving repetition of the consonants *s, b, k, ʾ, m*; and the two lines are linked by complete assonance in their concluding participial forms (*kî ʿad-sîrîm sᵉbukîm, ûkᵉsobʾām sᵉbûʾîm*; cf. Ecc 7:5–6). The verse should therefore be interpreted as it stands, without recourse to textual emendation; though virtually impossible to reproduce fully, its effect is rendered partially by the translation, "Torn among thorns, drunk from their drinking."

"Thorns" (*sîrîm*) is one of many terms describing the spiny or prickly vegetation that proliferated in the semi-arid climate of Palestine (cf. *ZPEB*, 5:736). They often grew as a tangled, impenetrable mass (Hos 2:6); as such as they were good for little more than burning (Ecc 7:6). The Assyrians are portrayed as being "entangled" (*sābak*; cf. Ge 22:13) "among" or "like" (*ʿad*) such thorns, to which they correspond both in their worthless character and in their merited destruction.

The following, related image of drunkenness reiterates these varied associations: a drunkard is good for nothing useful, and drunkenness is both a cause and consequence of judgment. The keynote of both lines, however, is helplessness. Like Abraham's ram entangled in the thorns (Ge 22:13), a drunkard is incapacitated (cf. 1Sa 25:36; Isa 28:7); like drunkards the Assyrians will be helpless before the wrath of God.

These ideas are resumed in the concluding line: like thorns, stubble is without intrinsic value and is subject to be burnt; being "dry," it is easy prey for the flames by which it is "consumed." The concomitant themes are similarly expressive. Nineveh's destruction by fire is rooted in her helplessness to avert the disaster (cf. 2:9–10; 3:11–13); and this in turn is due to her decadence, characterized both as, and by, drunkenness.

11 The enemy is again defined as one who "plots" (*ḥāšab*) against the Lord, being specified further as a distinct individual from whom the rebellion emanates.

Such an individual is identified clearly in 3:18 as the "king of Assyria." The ruler envisaged here emerged from Nineveh in his opposition to the Lord ("from you" [feminine singular]), an opposition—unlike that of Assyrian kings prior to the destruction of Samaria in 722 BC—now directed against Jerusalem and the Davidic monarchy (cf. Ps 2).

Sennacherib, perhaps more than any of his dynasty, is notable for his aggression against Judah in campaigns that figure prominently in both his own records and the biblical text. According to the Assyrian annals describing his Judean campaign (ca. 701), he cruelly devastated forty-seven fortified cities, including Lachish, whose siege is graphically recorded in a series of reliefs discovered in his palace at Nineveh (cf. 2Ki 18:13; 19:8; cf. *ANEP*, 371–74). That Nahum is probably referring to Sennacherib's invasion is supported by his repeated reminiscences of Isaiah's prophecies relating to that era (see above); in particular, the verb "plots" recalls its description of Assyrian arrogance in Isaiah 10:7 (*ḥāšab*, "has in mind").

The intent of this plotting is "wickedness" (*bᵉlîyaʿal*; GK 1175; cf. also v.15[2:1]), a noun often translated as "worthlessness" ("Belial," KJV) and implying a total lack of moral fiber and principle (e.g., Dt 13:13, et al.; cf. *TWOT*, 1:111). This term is translated as "adversary" in the LXX and as such became in the intertestamental period a fitting title for Satan, the father of lies and lawlessness (i.e., Belial; cf. Jn 8:44; 2Co 6:15; 2Th 2:3; 1Jn 3:4–12).

B. The Sentence of the Lord (1:12–14)

OVERVIEW

The judicial sentence anticipated in the preceding unit is announced more formally in the introductory formulas of vv.12 and 14, which distinguish vv.12–13, v.14, and v.15[2:1] as corresponding subunits. This sentence decrees a complete reversal in the destiny of the opposing parties: Assyria's political and military *power* will be shattered (v.12), whereas Judah's political and military *bondage* will be shattered (vv.12–13). Assyria's religious system and monarchy will be *terminated* (v.14), while Judah's religion will be *revitalized* (v.15[2:1]). This pattern of reversal unites vv.12–15[2:1] and distinguishes them from 2:1[2], whose language links

it closely to 2:3–13[4–14] and 3:12, 14. Nahum 1:15[2:1] is therefore associated with vv.12–14 in this analysis, though separated from them in the MT. Although Assyria has destroyed and mutilated countless nations, including the schismatic northern kingdom, its fate is determined by its treatment of Judah and Zion.

---

¹²This is what the LORD says:

"Although they have allies and are numerous,
 they will be cut off and pass away.
Although I have afflicted you, ⌞O Judah⌟,
 I will afflict you no more.

¹³Now I will break their yoke from your neck
 and tear your shackles away."
¹⁴The LORD has given a command concerning you, ⌞Nineveh⌟:
 "You will have no descendants to bear your name.
I will destroy the carved images and cast idols
 that are in the temple of your gods.
I will prepare your grave,
 for you are vile."

COMMENTARY

12 The opening clause is typical of the formula by which a messenger received or transmitted a message from his lord. It occurs countless times—often augmented to include a more complete title of God—to introduce a message from the Lord (e.g., Ex 4:22, et al.) and is especially characteristic of the prophets, who transmitted the decrees of the Lord, the great King, to his obedient or disobedient subjects (e.g., Isa 10:24). The present decree is addressed to Judah ("you," with Judah implied, as in the NIV) and is essentially an oracle of salvation; it incorporates an announcement of judgment addressed directly to Assyria in v.14.

The decree reverses the fortunes of the Assyrians. Although they had "allies" (*šᵉlēmîm*; cf. D. J. Wiseman, "'Is It Peace'—Covenant and Diplomacy," *VT* 32 [1982]: 311–26, for a discussion of this translation; the RSV and NRSV retain "strong" or "at full strength"; see R. Smith, 77 note; Longman, 798, building on the root *šlm*, "to be complete, healthy," favors "intact" or "strong"), they will be "cut off" (*gāzaz*, normally used of shearing sheep; cf. Isa 53:7). Although "numerous," the Assyrians will "pass away" (*ʿābar*, "dwindle, perish"), as waters that dry up or as chaff driven before the wind (cf. Job 6:15; 30:15; Jer 13:24; Zep 2:2).

A similar reversal is decreed for Judah, whose penalty is remitted as that of Assyria is pronounced (cf. Isa 40:2; 51:22–23). To be "afflicted" (*ʿānâ*) is to be humbled and oppressed. As in this case, such affliction is repeatedly the agent of God's chastisement (e.g., Dt 8:2–3, 16; Pss 90:15; 119:71, 75), frequently being administered to his own people at the hands of foreign nations (cf. Hab 1:5–11). Though Nahum's attention is directed primarily to Assyria's guilt, it is clear from this reference that Judah, when unfaithful to the covenant, was equally subject to the jealous wrath of God. The brief statement "I have afflicted you" is therefore pregnant with the suffering of centuries, though expressed in a single Hebrew word.

Only against such a background can one appreciate the profound implications of what follows: the phrase "no more" (*lōʾ ʿôd*), which punctuates vv.12–15[2:1], truly means "life from the dead" (Ro 11:15). As noted previously, the phrase also characterizes Isaiah 51:22–52:1, whose promise of reversal and liberation from affliction is reproduced in this passage; and it balances the menacing refrain "still" (*ʿôd*) in the earlier chapters of Isaiah (Isa 5:25; 9:12[11], 17[16], 21[20]; 10:4; cf. 10:20).

13 The continuing existence of such servitude in Nahum's day is implied by the emphatic "now" and by the future orientation of the promised deliverance from the "yoke" and the "shackles." This further supports dating Nahum's prophecy before Josiah's reign, when Assyria ceased to be a threat to Judah. Unlike its earlier counterpart in Samaria, the southern kingdom would still experience political and religious revival in the reign of Josiah, which could, in the Lord's hands, have led to the breaking of Assyrian shackles; the surprising element is the lack of connection between Judah's religious revival and the predicted end to affliction.

What is revealed here seems to have resulted from Babylonia's rise to power rather than from Judah's reformation. In time Judah will go into exile, despite the brief interlude of revival, but significantly, this did not occur at Assyrian hands, as may well have been expected in the middle of the seventh century. The breaking of Assyria's yoke is strikingly affirmed by Nabopolassar, who, like the Assyrians themselves and Cyrus in later times, was an unwitting instrument of the Lord's purposes (cf. Isa 45:4–5): "As for the Assyrians, who since distant days had ruled over all the people and with heavy yoke had brought misery to the people of the land, from the land of Akkad I banished their feet and cast off their yoke" (The Babylonian Chronicle, quoted by Maier, 111).

14 The Lord's decree of judgment and salvation is again introduced by a formal pronouncement, "The LORD has given a command," followed by the preposition translated "concerning" (NIV) and the object "you." Apart from a shift in the object from feminine singular (vv.12–13) to masculine singular (v.14), we should have expected the same person to be addressed in all three verses. It is only the context—with v.14's shift from salvation to condemnation and reference to idolatrous objects (carved and cast images) to be destroyed—that leads to the NIV's correct assumption that the subject of the vocative has shifted from Judah to Nineveh. The continued contrast between the respective fates of these two nations, characteristic of Nahum's prophecy, continues with little need to name the one addressed.

The "name" of a population represented its living identity, perpetuated in its "descendants"; to be destitute of descendants, therefore, represented obliteration of identity and life itself (cf. Dt 7:24; 9:14; 1Sa 24:21; et al.). The root underlying "descendants" (*zrʿ*, "to seed, sow" [GK 2445]; Niphal; "be sown, fructified"; lit., "your name shall no longer be sown"; cf. NRSV, "be perpetuated") is associated with both physical and particularly dynastic succession. Cutting off the name implies the eradication of Nineveh's dynastic rule, therefore, and of the nation whose cohesion derived from the Neo-Assyrian monarchy now centered at Nineveh. A similar sentence is passed on Babylon and its king in Isaiah 14:4, 20–23. Nineveh's consignment to the grave reiterates the certainty of this extinction and also appears to allude to the imagery of Isaiah 14 (cf. vv. 9–11, 15–20). This judgment is rooted in the charge that the city, for all its regal and religious grandeur, is "vile" or "contemptible," "of no account" (*qālal*) — a charge echoing the intent of 1:10 and further developed in 3:5–6.

The Assyrian kings claimed to rule by the favor and authority of their "gods," whom they honored accordingly. Ashurbanipal, on a single cylinder, paid profuse homage to seventeen of the principal gods of the Assyrian pantheon. Two gods receive special reverence: Ashur, as "the great god who begat me," is honored seventy-nine times on this cylinder, with Ishtar, "The Mistress, Lady of Ladies," "Goddess of War," "Queen of the Gods," honored ninety-five times (Maier, 107; cf. also *ANET*, 289, 297).

The judgment of Nineveh's king, therefore, demands the destruction of the idolatrous religion on which his authority was founded. This cult was centralized in the "temple," which housed the "carved images" and "cast idols" within which its particular deity resided. These idols were normally made of precious wood plated with gold or of molten metal such as gold that had been poured into a mold. They were shaped in human form, even in the likeness of the reigning king, such as Sennacherib (*IDB*, 1:299). An elaborate ritual was required to endow them with life, sight, and purity, after which they were clothed in sumptuous garments and placed on a pedestal in their inner sanctuary, or cella. In keeping with their human likeness, they were fed three times a day, and their clothes were changed periodically (*IDB*, 1:298–99).

The utter inefficacy of such "gods," against which Israel's prophets sustained a vehement polemic, will thus be exposed in the destruction of their place of residence, an event they are powerless to prevent. The sentence was duly fulfilled (cf. also 3:7). The temple of Nabu, a major deity at Nineveh, was razed to the ground and buried with ash from the blaze. The statue of Ishtar was discovered, prostrate and headless, amid the ruins of her temple, which had stood at Nineveh for almost fifteen centuries.

C. The Purpose of the Lord (1:15[2:1])

> [15] Look, there on the mountains,
> the feet of one who brings good news,
> who proclaims peace!
> Celebrate your festivals, O Judah,
> and fulfill your vows.
> No more will the wicked invade you;
> they will be completely destroyed.

COMMENTARY

15[2:1] The message heralded in vv. 12–14 is concluded with a further messenger formula, already proclaiming the predicted "good news" of salvation (cf. "Theological Values" in the introduction) and disaster; the second section, 2:1[2]–3:19, concludes on the same note (cf. 3:19). The proclamation of "peace" (šālôm; GK 8934) is replete with the promise of God's redemption and, as noted previously, constitutes the most precise correlation of Nahum with Isaiah (e.g., Isa 9:6–7; 32:17; 53:5; 54:10, 13; 55:12; 57:19). The picture is one of joyous and complete restoration of the Lord's people and their legitimate worship.

The reversal of fortunes apparent in vv.12–13 is thus completed in vv.14–15[2:1]. As Nineveh's flourishing religion will be buried, so the worship of oppressed Judah will be resurrected. By implication it is still suppressed, as a corollary of the existing political subjection to Assyria. Such suppression of Yahwistic worship was entirely characteristic of the long reign of Manasseh, who abandoned the piety of his father, Hezekiah (cf. 2Ki 21; 2Ch 33), and his short-lived but evil son Amon; this provides further evidence for dating Nahum's prophecy toward the middle of the seventh century BC. The anticipated renewal of vital worship was accomplished in the reign of Amon's successor, Josiah, after about 631, in the eighth year of his reign, when he began to seek the Lord (2Ch 34:3; cf. 2Ki 22:3–23:27; 2Ch 34–35).

As in Hezekiah's reign, this assertion of religious independence demanded that the "wicked" (belîyaʿal; cf. 1:11) who opposed it be "destroyed." The verb "destroy" (kārat; GK 4162) is commonly used of cutting down an enemy in battle or of "cutting off" the name of the rebellious; it recurs with both of these connotations in 1:14; 2:13[14] ("leave ... no"; the NRSV in both verses renders it "cut off"); and 3:15 ("cut ... down"). It is also echoed in 1:12 (gāzaz, "cut off"). The verb "invade" (ʿābar) is similarly used of warfare, as indicated by the NIV's translation. It repeats, as a further irony or reversal, the verb translated "pass away" in 1:12: the invader will be swept away, the destroyer destroyed.

II. THE FALL OF NINEVEH (2:1[2]–3:19)

OVERVIEW

The judgment of God is not merely an abstract principle or rhetorical threat, as evidenced already in the natural phenomena that display his power. The judgment decreed in ch. 1 is now worked out with terrifying actuality.

Nahum 2:1–2[2–3] is transitional. On the one hand, it extends the dual perspective of judgment (v.1[2]) and mercy (v.2[3]) evident in 1:2–15[2:1]; and v.2[3] is clearly a development of 1:7, 12–13, and particularly of 1:15[2:1] ("Judah"–"Jacob ... Israel"). On the other hand, the military language and urgent imperatives of v.1[2] clearly anticipate the following description of battle in 2:3–10[4–11]; 3:2–3, 10–13; and particularly in 3:14.

Thereafter, the prophecy is devoted exclusively to Nineveh, expanding the emphasis of 2:1[2] on the "attacker" as the instrument of divine vengeance; and on Nineveh's vain attempts at self-defense. Nahum 2:3[4]–3:19 consists of three major sections—2:3[4]–3:7 (itself broken into two balanced subunits: 2:3[4]–3:1 and 3:2–7), 3:8–11, and 3:12–19—which reiterate the emphases shown below in the chart. The three sections coincide in describing (A) the savage onslaught awaiting Nineveh, which (B) she will be impotent to resist. This remarkable collapse of her defenses is then explained (C) by an array of interpretive analogies drawing on nature and history to reinforce the graphic descriptions of Nineveh's demise. Ultimately, however, (D) the judgment is from the Lord's hands, stated with terse finality in the focal points of the two chapters (2:13[14]; 3:5).

As in 1:2–15[2:1], this sentence and its execution have the ring of a judicial procedure; and its major sections are concluded by the promulgation of the verdict to both the accused and the victims.

Nahum 2–3

	2:3[4]–3:1	3:2–7	3:8–11	3:12–19
A. Attack and onslaught	2:3–5[4–6]	3:2–3a	3:10–11	3:12–13
B. Mocking of failing defenses	2:6–10[7–11]	3:3b	3:8–11	3:12–14
C. Interpretive analogy	2:11–12[12–13]	3:4	3:8–10	3:15–17
D. The Lord's verdict	2:13[14]–3:1	3:5–7	3:11	3:15–19

The above chart illustrates the structure, building on the pattern set forth in 2:1[2]. In the nature of the poetry, particularly in 3:12–19, various aspects of Nineveh's impending fate overlap, making a tidy division impossible. The chart sets forth the various elements; the poet's skill weaves them together into some of the most graphic verse in the Hebrew Bible.

The entire poem is rich with stylized vocabulary and varied grammatical forms, making it one of the most exalted examples of the Hebrew poet's art. Not infrequently, the repetition of words or forms provides the stylistic link to support the linkages in content set out above. Examples abound. A series of short, sharp imperatives in 2:1[2]; 2:9[10]; 3:14; 3:15 bring the reader into the center of the action. Several nouns describe the attackers (2:1[2]), including "soldiers" (*gibbōrê*; 2:3[4]); "warriors" (*ʾanšê-ḥayil*; 2:3[4]), and "picked troops" (*ʾaddîr*; 2:5[6]). Features of the city and its defenses are employed, e.g., "fortress" (*mᵉṣurâ*; 2:1[2]), "streets" (*ḥuṣôt*; 2:4[5], 3:10); "wall" (*ḥômâ*; 2:5[6]; 3:8); "gates" (*šaᶜᵃrê*; 2:6[7];

3:13); and many associated with water, e.g., "river" (*nᵉhārôt*; 2:6[7]), "river" or "waters" (*yām*; 3:8[2x]), and water (*mayim*; 2:8[9]; 3:8, cf. Notes).

Warfare's human products are also featured, such as the experience of being an exile or captive (*gālâ*; 2:7[8]; 3:10). Graphic military expressions lend color: chariot metal flashes like fire (*ʾēš*; 2:3[4]); the sword (*ḥereb*; 2:13[14]) and fire (*ʾēš*; 3:15) "devour" (*tōʾkal*; 2:13[14]; 3:15), thus "cutting off" (*kārat*; 2:13[14]; 3:15; see commentary) their prey. Hearts melt, knees give way, bodies tremble, and faces grow pale (2:10[11]); "plunder" (2:9–10[10–11]) and "pillaging" (2:10[11]) dominate the scene. Infants are dashed into pieces (3:10), lots are cast for the nobles, who are marched off in chains (3:10); people are scattered (3:18), and general destruction prevails. In all of it, both God and the nations celebrate the curse (*hôy*, "Woe"; 3:1) on the stricken oppressor, whose fatal wound evokes joy (3:19). In the end, there is simply no one to "mourn" (*yānûd*; 3:7) the spectacular collapse of the mightiest city in the Near East.

A. Warning and Promise (2:1–2[2–3])

¹An attacker advances against you, ⌐Nineveh⌐.
  Guard the fortress,
  watch the road,
  brace yourselves,
  marshal all your strength!

²The LORD will restore the splendor of Jacob
  like the splendor of Israel,
  though destroyers have laid them waste
  and have ruined their vines.

COMMENTARY

1[2] Nineveh's "attacker" (*pûṣ*; cf. Ps 68:1; Isa 24:1; Jer 52:8) is more literally a "scatterer," a common figure used for a victorious king; the verb *pûṣ* also describes the scattering of sheep, anticipating the final scene of 3:18 (with a different verb, *pûš*).

In fulfillment of this prophecy, Nineveh was attacked in 614 BC by Cyaxares, king of the Medes (c. 625–585 BC; *IDB*, 3:320). A sector of the suburbs was captured, but the city was not taken, for the Medes diverted their energies to the overthrow of Ashur. However, a subsequent alliance of Cyaxares with the Babylonian Nabopolassar led to their concerted attack on Nineveh in 612, apparently accompanied by the Scythians (Umman Manda?), a battle recorded in detail in the Babylonian Chronicle (see Thomas, 76; *ANET*, 304–5).

The Assyrians are mockingly called to action in military language reminiscent of Isaiah's exhortation to another doomed city (Isa 21:5). The city had in fact been well equipped to withstand both siege (cf. 3:14) and invasion. Sennacherib had spent no fewer than six years building his armory, which occupied a terraced area of forty acres. It was enlarged further by Esarhaddon and contained all the weaponry required for the extension and maintenance of the Assyrian empire: bows, arrows, quivers, chariots, wagons, armor, horses, mules, and equipment (cf. Eze 23:24; 39:9). The royal "road" had been enlarged by Sennacherib to a breadth of seventy-eight feet, thus facilitating the movement of troops. However, these material resources are of little use if the "strength" of the defenders cannot be marshaled; and by the end of the seventh century it was dissipated beyond retrieval.

2[3] This verse introduces the final reference to the salvation of God's people, whose "splendor" he will "restore." The noun "splendor" (*gāʾôn*; GK 1454) implies elevation or exaltation (cf. Job 8:11; Eze 47:5; *TWOT*, 1:143–44); it is used with negative connotations of pride or with positive associations of majesty expressed in power and dominion. Both usages are applied to Jacob, the latter being clearly intended here. In the poetic parallelism, "Jacob" and "Israel" represent the same entity (Ge 32:28; cf. 1Ch 16:17; Ps 105:23; Hos 12:12), denoting the full twelve tribes descended from Jacob. After the division of the kingdom, usage varies. Both names are more commonly applied to the northern kingdom alone, though following the destruction of Samaria, the southern prophets reclaimed these names

(Isa 14:1–4 et al.), perhaps in connection with attempts by Judean monarchs to restore Yahweh's influence in the old tribal lands (e.g., 2Ch 30).

In any case, given the context, "Judah" is envisaged here (cf. 1:12–13, 15[2:1]), though it is possible that the resurrection of Israel as a whole is promised (cf. Isa 9:1–8; 11:10–16; et al.). The verse concludes its picture of restoration with a reminder that "destroyers" (lit., "wasters" [participle of *bāqaq*])

had "laid waste" (*bāqaq*) the "vines" (presumably the third masculine plural verbal suffix "them" points to the parallel "vines")—a mainstay of Judah's economy (cf. Hab 3:17; Isa 5:1–7; 24:7–15). Whether the specific reference is to earlier agricultural decimation of the northern kingdom (Israel) or to results of Sennacherib's 701 BC invasion, it is clear that any restoration of the nation would require a renewal of its viticulture.

NOTES

1 The forms of the final three verbs, translated as imperatives in the NIV, are ambiguous in the MT. נָצוֹר (*nāṣôr*, "guard"), the first, is clearly an infinitive absolute functioning with imperatival force (cf. GKC, par. 113bb). The following two forms—צַפֵּה (*ṣappēh*, "watch") and חַזֵּק (*ḥazzēq*, "brace")—appear to be Piel imperatives with masculine singular subjects; on this understanding, they cannot be addressed to Nineveh, which is consistently treated as feminine (cf. עַל־פָּנַיִךְ, *ʿal-pānayik*, "against you"), and so they are addressed instead to the masculine singular מֵפִיץ (*mēpîṣ*, "attacker"). This is plausible since the verbs can all be understood from the perspective of those beleaguering the city, thus restricting movement to and from it; for instance, the verb נָצַר (*nāṣar*, "guard") is applied to Jerusalem as a city "under siege" (Isa 1:8).

However, the last three verbs also represent the more common form of the Piel infinitive absolute, corresponding to that of the Piel infinite construct (GKC, par. 52o); on this reading the subject of all four verbs must be determined from the context. The verb *ḥazzēq* recurs in 3:14—חַזְּקִי (*ḥazzᵉqî*, "strengthen")—in a similar context of five urgent commands. In that location they are clearly spoken to Nineveh, both because they call for defensive measures and because they are uniformly second feminine singular imperatives. In view of the precise correspondence of 2:1[2] to 3:14, it is clearly preferable to interpret 2:1 with reference to Nineveh too. This conclusion is also favored by the ensuing tactics of the "attacker," depicted as an active onslaught on the city rather than as preliminary siege warfare.

B. Nineveh's Destruction Derailed (2:3[4]–3:7)

OVERVIEW

Nahum 2:3[4]–3:7 forms the heart of 2:1[2]–3:19, describing the details of Nineveh's defeat and the express purpose of the Lord that motivates it. The onslaught that menaced Nineveh in 1:2–15[2:1] and overshadowed it in 2:1[2] now breaks with fury on the condemned city. The centrality of this section is marked by the precisely balanced structure that links its two units (2:3[4]–3:1; 3:2–7) and that defines the outlines of the following sections.

The attack is described in terms common to both 2:3[4]–10 and 3:2–3: "chariots" (*rekeb*, 2:3–4[4–5]; *merkābâ*, 3:2); "lightning" (2:4[5]) and "glittering" (3:3;

both *bārāq*); spears (*bᵉrōšîm*, 2:3[4]; *ḥᵃnît*, 3:3); "stumble" (*kāšal*, 2:5[6]; 3:3); "endless" (2:9[10]) and "without number" (3:3; both *ʾên qēṣeh*); "wealth" (*kābôd*, 2:9[10]); and "piles" (*kōbed*, 3:3). In addition both accounts are characterized by wild movement (2:3–5[4–6]; 3:2–3); the image of fire (*ʾēš*, "flashes, 2:3[4]; *lappîdîm*, "flaming torches," 2:4[5]; *lahab*, "flashing," 3:3), and the description of weaponry ("shields," 2:3[4]; "protective shield," 2:5[6]; "whips," "wheels," "horses," 3:2; "swords," 3:3) and troops (2:3[4], 5[6]; 3:3).

The close correlation of 2:9[10] and 3:3 evidences further irony: the "endless ... wealth" has been stolen at the cost of life itself, being transmuted into "piles [of dead] ... without number." In both passages details of the attack are followed by a metaphor (2:11–12[12–13]; 3:4), which is developed in the following indictment: the lions will be cut down (2:13[14]), and the harlot will be stripped (3:5–6). The indictments are concluded in identical terms, unparalleled in Nahum ("'I am against you,' declares the LORD Almighty," 2:13[14]; 3:5). They produce corresponding penalties, reversing the condition of the offenders in keeping with the law of retaliation: the beast of prey becomes a prey, the mistress of allurement an object of revulsion.

The exclamation "Woe" (3:1) is closely related to the preceding verses 2:11–13[12–14] by its reference to "victims" or "prey" (*terep* [root *ṭrp*]; cf.

2:12[13] [*terep*], 13[14]), of which it is full (*mālēʾ*; cf. 2:12[13]), and also by the association of "plunder" and "blood" with the preceding image of ravening animals. As such it corresponds well to 3:7, which is similarly linked to 3:5–6 by a key word: "see" (*rāʾâ*; cf. "show," 3:5; "spectacle," 3:6). Both passages (2:11–13[12–14] and 3:1) are addressed to the condemned party, specifically the "city" (3:1) of "Nineveh" (3:7), by anonymous witnesses (except 2:13[14], a saying of the Lord) to the proceedings; the final section of the prophecy concludes on a similar note (3:18–19). Nahum 2:11–13[12–14] and 3:1, taken together, are also distinguished from what follows. The abrupt description of the attacker in 3:2 corresponds to 2:3[4], which marks the beginning of a new unit; by implication 3:2 does so likewise.

The transition from 3:7 to 3:8 is less apparent, since vv.8 and 11 extend the direct speech of v.7; however, v.7 perceives Nineveh as already in ruins, thus differing from the perspective of vv.8–11, which still anticipate the debacle. For these reasons it appears preferable to associate 3:1 with 2:3–13[4–14]. The MT, however, separates 3:1 from 2:13[14] in its paragraph marking (cf. 1:15[2:1]), as does the NIV—a decision favored by the common function of the word "woe" to introduce a new accusation. It is therefore plausible that 3:1 is a transitional verse, like 2:1–2[2–3] (but see comment at 3:1).

1. First Description of Nineveh's Destruction (2:3[4]–3:1)

a. Onslaught (2:3–5[4–6])

> ³ The shields of his soldiers are red;
>   the warriors are clad in scarlet.
> The metal on the chariots flashes
>   on the day they are made ready;
>   the spears of pine are brandished.
> ⁴ The chariots storm through the streets,
>   rushing back and forth through the squares.

> They look like flaming torches;
>   they dart about like lightning.
>
> ⁵He summons his picked troops,
>   yet they stumble on their way.
> They dash to the city wall;
>   the protective shield is put in place.

COMMENTARY

3–4[4–5] The antecedent of "his" (v.3[4]) appears to be the "attacker" of 2:1[2], in view of the military language common to both verses. It is possible that "the LORD" (v.2[3]) is also intended, summoning an enemy against Nineveh as he had summoned the Assyrians against Judah (Isa 5:26–30; 10:5–6, 15; cf. 13:2–5). The attack is led by the invader's chariot forces, the most formidable wing of an army fighting in open terrain (cf. Jos 17:16, 18; Jdg 1:19). The Neo-Assyrian "chariots" were built of various types of wood, for lightness and speed, with fittings of leather and of "metal" that flashed with reflected light (v.3). The chariots were fitted with a pole and yoke for the horses, normally a team of two, and with spoked wheels and a single axle, which permitted a high degree of maneuverability. Under Ashurbanipal as many as four members comprised a chariot crew: the driver, equipped with a long spear and round shield, an archer, and two shield bearers for protection of their fellow crew-members.

The Assyrian shields were either round or rectangular in shape, the latter being designed to cover most of the body, particularly to defend archers or spearmen in siege warfare. The shields were made of wood or wickerwork covered with leather, which could have been dyed "red" (cf. Ex 25:5). Doubtless the enemy's chariots were similar in design, and they could account for all the features described in vv.3–4[4–5] (cf. "shields," "soldiers," "spears").

However, it is evident from the parallel passage in 3:2–3 that cavalry accompanied the chariots, a typical feature of Assyrian warfare; and both "shields" and "spears" might also be carried by the infantry who penetrated the defenses in 2:5–6[6–7] (cf. Yadin, 4–5, 294–95, 297ff., 452).

The conflict is located in the "streets" (*ḥûṣôt*), or its parallel "squares" (*reḥōbôt*; v.4[5]) of Nineveh, denoting its suburbs outside the inner defensive "wall" that has not yet been reached (cf. v.5[6]). (The primary sense of *ḥûṣ* is "outside"; streets are seen as outside the houses, or inner city.) According to the fragmentary information of the Babylonian Chronicle, three battles may have been fought during the three months of intense siege before the city fell (*ANET*, 303ff.; Maier, 112–13). Indeed, the historian Diodorus Siculus (ca. 20 BC), quoting earlier sources of varying authenticity, claims that the Assyrians were victorious in the early stages of the conflict; as a result they became overconfident and were decisively defeated while their soldiers were feasting and drinking (cf. Na 1:10; Da 5) (Maier, 109–10, 192).

5[6] Literally, the verse opens with "he remembers" (*zākar*) his nobles, or "picked troops." The context points to some kind of muster of troops ("summons," NIV; "calls," NRSV). The antecedent of "he" is rendered ambiguous by the verb translated "stumble" (*kāšal*) in the second clause, suggesting the weakness of the defenders rather than the ferocity of the attackers depicted in vv.3–4[4–5]. Such an interpretation would indicate that the reference is to the king of Assyria (cf. 3:18), whose troops are summoned to defend the "city walls." However, the final couplet is more appropriate to the rapid movement of the enemy ("dash"; cf. vv.3–4[4–5]), and the unusual term "protective shield" (sōkēk, lit., "covering"; cf. Ex 25:20; Eze 28:14, 16) appears to be used as a technical term describing the besiegers' defensive equipment (see below). It is therefore preferable to view v.5[6] as a further stage in the enemy's advance, as in v.6[7].

On this understanding the "picked troops" represent the shock troops directed to breach the "wall." The "protective covering" describes the screen set up to protect the troops engaged in undermining and penetrating the wall (Yadin, 316). The verb "stumble" retains an enigmatic ring. It is perhaps best explained in 3:3: the stumbling of the "picked troops" is due not to their weakness but to the "corpses" of their victims, which obstruct their advance; the conjunction "yet," which appears to conflict with this interpretation, is not present in the Hebrew.

b. Failing defenses (2:6–10[7–11])

⁶The river gates are thrown open
    and the palace collapses.
⁷It is decreed that ⌊the city⌋
    be exiled and carried away.
Its slave girls moan like doves
    and beat upon their breasts.
⁸Nineveh is like a pool,
    and its water is draining away.
"Stop! Stop!" they cry,
    but no one turns back.
⁹Plunder the silver!
    Plunder the gold!
The supply is endless,
    the wealth from all its treasures!
¹⁰She is pillaged, plundered, stripped!
    Hearts melt, knees give way,
    bodies tremble, every face grows pale.

COMMENTARY

6[7] This brief verse (five Hebrew words) marks a decisive turning point in the campaign, as the main line of defense is broken and the heart of the city destroyed. The noun "river" is plural in Hebrew, and in fact Nineveh lay at the confluence of three rivers. The Tigris flowed close to its walls, and two tributaries, the Khosr and the Tebiltu, passed through the city itself. Virtually all of Nineveh's fifteen gates gave access also to one of these rivers or to a canal derived from them, thus being designated "gates of the rivers." Alternatively, the "gates" are those controlling the flow of the rivers rather than those giving access to the city. All three rivers were capable of rising to flood proportions when swollen by rain, and the inscriptions of Sennacherib repeatedly describe both the undermining effects of flood on the walls and buildings and the extensive damage or sluicing operations required to correct the problems.

It is possible, therefore, that the "river gates" envisaged are those regulating the flow of water through one or more of these dams; indeed, the Akkadian term "gate of the river" (bab-nari) was applied to a canal gate by Sennacherib. When "thrown open" by the enemy, who already controlled the suburbs where they were situated, the gates would release a deluge of water, as a result of which the palace "collapses." The Assyrians flooded other cities themselves; it is fitting that their own city, corrupt and full of violence, should perish in the same manner. The verb mûg means "to melt" ("collapses," NIV). Its literal usage is primarily of dissolution by water, providing further corroboration for the preceding interpretation.

Nineveh's principal palaces in the seventh century included Sennacherib's residence, the alleged "Palace with No Rival." Adorned with cedar and cypress wood, bronze lions (cf. vv.11–13[12–14]), bull colossi of white marble, and many sculptured reliefs, the palace's main hall alone measured 40 by 150 feet. It was built in the place of a smaller structure, whose foundations had been eroded by flooding of the Tebiltu. Now the same fate threatens its successors, and fire sweeps away everything that survives the flood. The term "palace" (hêkāl) can also be translated "temple"; the major temples of Ishtar

and Nabu, restored by Ashurbanipal, were also ravaged in the fall of Nineveh. The judgment decreed for the idolatrous monarchy is fully accomplished.

7–8[8–9] These verses delineate (with some notorious translation difficulties; cf. Notes) the aftermath of this decisive turning point in v.6. Exactly who or what is referred to by the opening word (root nāṣab, to "stand, take a stand"; GK 5893) has been the subject of much debate. Following K. J. Cathcart (*Nahum in the Light of Northwest Semitica* [BibOr 26; Rome: Pontifical Biblical Institute, 1973]), many accept an emendation to weḥaṣṣebi, a name for Ishtar, the goddess of the city. In this case, the scene (v.7[8]) portrays the exile of the city goddess, not "the city" (NIV, NRSV). In that case, the verb gālal, which normally refers to going into exile, with a Pual perfect can be translated "is stripped" (see RSV, with "its mistress" as subject; cf. also Longman, 806, "The Beauty is stripped").

The picture, then, is of a desecrated goddess being led into exile amid the mourning of the "slave girls." The admittedly more common image of vast numbers of exiles being led into captivity (cf. Eze 7:16)—a recurrent feature of ancient Near Eastern literature (cf. the Curse of Agade, *ANET-Sup*, 650)—is also attractive, and a not uncommon scene in Assyrian wall carvings depicting the agonies of their captives. This interpretation, however, leaves us with no satisfactory translation of weḥuṣṣab in the opening of the verse.

The image of water (v.8[9]) depicts Nineveh's fate with vivid irony. Nineveh was a place of watered parks and orchards. As at the flood, however, "water" becomes a source of death, overflowing its boundaries and bringing chaos to the inundated city. Unlike the flood, this "pool" promises no respite as its waters "drain away" ("flee", cf. Notes). Although the first stich of the verse is difficult (cf. NASB and Notes), the second line is clear; like water ebbing quickly away when the dams are breached, the defenders of Nineveh heed no cry to remain at their posts.

9[10] The exaction of plunder characterized the Neo-Assyrian Empire throughout its history. From the days of the first Tiglath-pileser (1115–1076 BC) down to the destruction of the empire, Assyrian monarchs boasted of the booty taken in war (cf. *ANET*, 274–301), an activity especially prominent in the list of Ashurnasirpal II and Sennacherib. Those who submitted to them were drained of their resources more methodically by the exaction of tribute, a fate suffered by Israel and Judah at various times (cf. *ANET*, 281, 283, 288 for tribute recorded as sent from Jehu, Menahem, and Hezekiah). Thus in the seventh century Nineveh became the richest city throughout the ancient Near East as the seat of the Sargonide Dynasty, to which its kings returned with their prey.

Now it will suffer the same fate: its own people will be led away (cf. 2:7[8], but see comments; 3:10–11), and its "wealth" in "gold," "silver," and valuables will be seized. The fulfillment of this sentence is confirmed by the Babylonian Chronicle, which states that "they carried off much spoil from the city and the temple-area" (James H. Gailey, *The Layman's Bible Commentary* [Atlanta: John Knox, 1977], 15:1000).

Nahum's emphatic phrase *ʾên qēṣeh* ("no end") recurs in 3:3 ("without number," NIV), 3:9 ("boundless," NIV), and elsewhere only twice in Isaiah 2:7.

10[11] The defeat of the city is summarized forcefully in the initial line, expressed by the rhyme and alliteration joining its first three words (*bûqâ ûmᵉbûqâ ûmᵉbullāqâ*). The NIV's terse phrases capture the mood (cf. also NRSV's "devastation, desolation and destruction"). The inhabitants have failed to "brace" themselves (*ḥazzēq motnayim*, lit., "strengthen the loins"; v.1), and instead "bodies tremble" (*ḥalḥālâ bᵉkol-motnayim*, lit., "writhing in loins"). The verb underlying "tremble" (*ḥîl*; GK 2655) is often applied to labor pains and may foreshadow the charge of effeminacy in 3:13. It recurs in an identical context of disabling fear in Isaiah 13:8 and the nominal form is used in Isaiah 21:3. The expression of psychological states in terms of their physical manifestations is a common and vivid characteristic of Hebrew, particularly in poetry.

NOTES

7–8[8–9] These verses contain several difficult expressions, particularly "it is decreed" (v.7) and "its water" (v.8). The first translates a Hophal form derived from the verb נָצַב (*nāṣab*, "to stand") and literally means "it is caused to stand." A Hophal participle is clearly used in Genesis 28:12, describing the stairway "set up, erected," from earth to heaven (cf. Jdg 9:6 MT). No extant parallel to Nahum's nonliteral usage of this form occurs in the OT. However, a similar verb, קוּם (*qûm*, "to arise, stand"), is often used of establishing a covenant or decree (e.g., Ge 6:18; 9:11, 17; Nu 30:14; et al.). Another verb, כּוּן (*kûn*, "to stand, be firm"), is similarly used of establishing a throne or matter (e.g., 1Sa 20:31; 2Sa 7:13; 1Ki 2:12, 46). The same connotation of establishing a matter is evident in 1 Chronicles 18:3, and particularly in the use of the Niphal participle referring to "officers," i.e., those appointed to stand in an office, in 1 Kings 4:5, 7, 27; 5:16; 9:23; 22:47. The present usage, therefore, has adequate support and may be taken to express the certainty of Nineveh's exile, with undertones of the divine purpose that establishes it.

The initial couplet of v.8[9] appears to read in the MT as follows: "Nineveh (is) as a pool of water, since the days of it (existing), and/but they are fleeing." The NIV reads מִימֵי הִיא (*mîmê hîʾ*, "since the days of it") as *mêmê hî* or *mêmeyhā* ("its water"), which it transposes into the second clause after the conjunction

ו (wᵉ, "and/but"), in place of the pronoun הֵמָּה (hēmmâ, "they"). The MT's reading is admittedly obscure; in particular, it provides an awkward antecedent for the following clause, "they are fleeing." Alternatively, the form mîmê can be interpreted as the construct plural of מַיִם (māyîm, "water"), if read with sere (ê) in place of hireq (î) as its initial vowel (mêmê).

The use of an independent genitive pronoun is not attested by grammarians of biblical Hebrew (i.e., הִיא [hîᵓ, "of it"]; cf. GKC, par. 130d, n. 3); but it is found in Ugaritic (UT, 6:4). It yields the approximate translation: "Nineveh, its waters are like a pool," i.e., Nineveh is like a pool with all of its water. Such a reading of the noun is supported by the LXX and Vulgate and is well suited to the context (cf. 1:8; 2:6). In addition, the reading provides a suitable antecedent for the following clause, "they are fleeing, draining away" (נָסִים, nāsîm; cf. Dt 34:7; Ps 114:3, 5, where waters or moisture "flee"), extending the compressed ambivalence of the image. The waters that entered like a flood drain away like the very lifeblood of the city as its inhabitants forsake it. By contrast, the reading "from the days of it" is unquestionably more difficult but makes too little sense to be accepted here.

c. An interpretive analogy (2:11–12[12–13])

> ¹¹Where now is the lions' den,
>   the place where they fed their young,
> where the lion and lioness went,
>   and the cubs, with nothing to fear?
> ¹²The lion killed enough for his cubs
>   and strangled the prey for his mate,
> filling his lairs with the kill
>   and his dens with the prey.

COMMENTARY

11[12] The mocking rhetorical question introduces an extended metaphor that interprets the horror of the preceding verses. The NRSV follows a popular emendation, transposing two letters (i.e., mᵉᶜārâ ["cave"] in place of the MT's mirᶜeh ["place where they feed"]), though such a change is not demanded by the context. Nineveh had ravaged Mesopotamia like a savage beast of prey and must be judged accordingly.

This metaphor is particularly appropriate as a designation of Nineveh. Its kings compared themselves to lions in their terrible power (e.g., Sennacherib: "Like a lion I raged"), and its game parks sheltered such lions. Like a pride of rampaging lions, Nineveh had felt free to terrorize the land "with nothing to fear." The lion is a typical image of destruction in the OT, as in Assyrian literature, and Assyria had been represented in these terms as an agent of the Lord's judgment on Judah (Isa 5:29–30; Jer 50:17; et al.). Now, however, an accounting is due for the ruthless spirit in which that judgment is executed (cf. Isa 10:5–19).

12[13] The intent of the metaphor emerges clearly here. The verse is dominated by the root "killed" (*trp*, "torn," NRSV; GK 3271), recurring in the nouns "kill" (*terep*) and "prey" (*ṭᵉrēpâ*). The NRSV's "prey" and "torn flesh" are closer to the root concept, which, in its various forms, is normally used of wild beasts that hunt and tear open their prey. The verb "strangle" is equally apt to the image, and lions are represented as killing their prey in this manner in ancient Near Eastern art. Assyrian brutality matched and surpassed such displays of violence; and it is extensively chronicled, with sickening detail, with references to the flaying, walling up, and impaling of captives (cf. *ANET*, 285; *ANEP*, 373, Lachish Relief). The goal of the lion's violence is to obtain prey "for his cubs"; as the lion fills its "lairs with the kill," so Nineveh has been filled with foreign plunder, recounted in numerous military reports (cf. 2:9[10]).

d. Judgment from the Lord (2:13[14])

> ¹³"I am against you,"
>   declares the Lᴏʀᴅ Almighty.
> "I will burn up your chariots in smoke,
>   and the sword will devour your young lions.
> I will leave you no prey on the earth.
> The voices of your messengers
>   will no longer be heard."

COMMENTARY

13[14] The climax is announced in the verdict of condemnation passed on this seemingly unrestricted tyranny; it is introduced by a common phrase reserved exclusively for utterances of the Lord and repeated in 3:5 (cf. Jer 21:13; 50:31). The condemnation ("against you") begins with a literal scene of Assyrian chariots (see comment on chariots at 2:3–4[4–5]) burning up, before resuming the "lion" metaphor of vv. 11–12[12–13]. Here the "young lions" (cf. *kᵉpîr*, v.11[12]) are cut off by the sword (obviously referring to human, not animal, slaughter) and the "prey" (*ṭᵉrēpâ*; cf. v.12[13]) is cut off by the Lord himself. The threat of leaving "no prey" (lit., "I will cut off your prey," NRSV) is a metonymy of effect: the taking of prey will be cut off with the extermination of the predator.

These clauses are framed chiastically by a corresponding sentence against Assyria's "chariots" and "messengers": the predator is identified unambiguously as Nineveh, whose military power and political control over its empire are to be eradicated. The reference both to "chariots" and to "messengers" (the final *â* appended to the Hebrew of "your messengers" apparently being a dittography from the opening of 3:1; cf. Longman, 810) again recalls Sennacherib's "evil" plotted against the Lord (cf. Isa 37:9, 14, 24; cf. Na 1:11).

This verse draws together the major motifs and vocabulary of Nahum's prophecy: the Lord's inexorable opposition to Nineveh; the destruction of its military resources; the role of "sword" and "fire" that "consume" the enemy; the cutting off of

Nineveh and its "prey"; the termination of its cruelty, symbolized by the death of its "young lions"; and the reversal of fortunes that awaits Assyria and Judah, exemplified in the fate of the "heralds."

e. The verdict announced (3:1)

> ¹Woe to the city of blood,
>   full of lies,
>   full of plunder,
>   never without victims!

COMMENTARY

1 The relation of this verse to its context is rendered uncertain by the interjection "Woe" (*hôy*; cf. *TWOT*, 1:212; see the Overview to 2:3[4]–3:7 for the verse's relationship to the context of what precedes and follows). As noted there, normally what is commonly called a "woe oracle" (a set speech beginning with "woe" [Heb. *hôy*] and associated with a funeral procession) introduces a new section, suggesting here that v.1 belongs with 3:2–7; however, 3:1 is related thematically to 2:11–13[12–14] much more closely than to 3:4.

In addition, the introductory function of the expression "Woe" is by no means clear here. It is usually linked explicitly to what follows when introducing a new section, whereas no clear transition is apparent between vv.1 and 2. Nor in other passages is it consistently employed to begin or end an extended section. Thus, for example, it may occur in virtual isolation (Isa 33:1) or in close dependence on what precedes or follows (cf. Isa 1:4; 5:8–23; Zep 2:5; 3:1; Zec 2:6–7). At other times it brings a passage to conclusion (cf. Jer 30:7; 47:6; 50:27). The latter function predominates in contexts of mourning, and the following parallel section concludes on precisely this note (v.7). Thus the proposed association of 3:1 with 2:11–13[12–14] is validated by OT usage; moreover, it completes the distinctive parallel structure uniting 2:3[4]–3:1 and 3:2–7 (cf. introduction to 2:3[4]–3:7): both open abruptly with a battle scene (2:3–5[4–6]; 3:2–3), and both close with the decease and "mourning" of the condemned criminal. As such 3:1 summarizes Nahum 2:3[4]–13, linking cause (2.11–13[12–14]) to effect (3:3–10), crime to punishment.

2. Second Description of Nineveh's Destruction (3:2–7)

a. Onslaught and failing defenses (3:2–3)

> ²The crack of whips,
>   the clatter of wheels,

> galloping horses
>   and jolting chariots!
> ³Charging cavalry,
>   flashing swords
>   and glittering spears!
> Many casualties,
>   piles of dead,
> bodies without number,
>   people stumbling over the corpses —

COMMENTARY

2–3 These verses resume the battle scene of 2:3–5[4–6], evoking the rapid movement and particularly the sound of the onslaught led by the chariots. This evocation is enhanced through the guttural consonants by which it is expressed, especially in the alliteration of the final phrase (*merkābâ meraqqēdâ*, "jolting chariots"). The visual element of this imagery is developed in v.3 in terms of light and fire, as in 2:3–4[4–5] (cf. "flashing," lit., "flame"; "glittering," lit., "lightning"). The term "cavalry" may denote the mounted horsemen, as are depicted accompanying chariots in Assyrian reliefs, or it may refer to the horses of the chariot corps (cf. *TWOT*, 2:740: *pārāš*). "Swords" were characteristic weapons of foot soldiers, being used in hand-to-hand combat; they did not form part of the regular equipment of horsemen or chariot crews, at least among the Assyrians (Yadin, 294). The "spears" also formed an integral part of the infantry's weapons, without being restricted to them.

As in 2:3–10[4–11], the defenders are annihilated by the attack: four times—using three different words—the verse refers to the corpses left in the wake of the invading army. Possibly the "people stumbling" are the fugitives; but in view of the repetition of this verb (*kāšal*) in 2:5[6], they are more likely to be the victors, impeded by the sheer mass of dead bodies.

The allusions to 2:3[4]–3:1 reveal a grotesque irony in the catastrophe: in place of "wealth [*kābôd*; 2:9(10)] from all its treasures," Nineveh shall possess "piles" [*kōbed*; 3:3] of "dead"; "bodies without number" (*weʾên qēṣeh laggewîyâ*; 3:3) are the consequence of its "endless" supply (*weʾên qēṣeh lattekûnâ*; 2:9[10]). So terrible was the slaughter that even the Babylonian Chronicle refers to the evil manner in which a suburb of Nineveh was butchered.

b. An interpretive analogy (3:4)

> ⁴all because of the wanton lust of a harlot,
>   alluring, the mistress of sorceries,

who enslaved nations by her prostitution
and peoples by her witchcraft.

COMMENTARY

4 The defeat of Nineveh is again followed by a metaphor, whose interpretive function is here made explicit ("all because of," Heb. causal *min*; cf. 2:11–12[12–13]). The root underlying the word "harlot" (*znh*; GK 2390) occurs three times in this verse (cf."wanton lust, prostitution"), thus providing definition for this section, just as 2:11–12[12–13] is dominated by the figure of the lions. The biblical references to "prostitution" have varied connotations. They imply treachery and infidelity (Jdg 2:17; 8:33–34), pollution (Lev 20:3–5; Jer 13:27), and lust (Eze 23:5–21). All are appropriate to this city, which sacrificed any semblance of morality to personal interest.

Of primary significance in this context, however, is the prostitute's motive of personal gain and the ominous attraction she exercises to attain it, with fatal consequences for the victims (cf. Pr 7:5–27; though the "adulteress" is not offering her favors for hire, the result is the same). Nineveh's attraction is specified by the word "alluring" (NRSV's "gracefully alluring" capturing the sense of the two words employed), for her iniquity is overlaid with the splendor of her wealth and power. As formerly Ahaz was lured into unholy relations with Assyria (cf. 2Ki 16:7–18), so Nineveh has drained the life of those enticed by her smooth ways (cf. Isa 36:16–17). Both her quest for personal gain and the fate of the one attracted are evoked by the word "enslaved" (*mākar*, lit. "sold"; cf. KJV, NASB).

The harlot's practice of allurement and manipulation is abetted by the second major metaphorical characteristic of v.4: "sorceries,… witchcraft" (*kešāpîm*; GK 4176). Both sorcery and harlotry suggest control that is exercised by illicit, surreptitious, yet deadly means, and they occur together elsewhere (2Ki 9:22; Isa 57:3; Gal 5:19–20; Rev 21:8; 22:15). They correspond to the stealth of the hunting lion and, though less overt in their bloodshed, are equally destructive. Nineveh is here seen as using both immoral attractions (the city being a center of the cult of Ishtar—herself represented as a harlot) and sorcery (Assyrian society being dominated by magical arts; *IDB*, 1:283–87) as a means to enslave others. The metaphor is close to the reality.

c. Judgment from the Lord (3:5–6)

⁵ "I am against you," declares the LORD Almighty.
   "I will lift your skirts over your face.
 I will show the nations your nakedness
   and the kingdoms your shame.
⁶ I will pelt you with filth,
   I will treat you with contempt
   and make you a spectacle.

COMMENTARY

5–6 As the Lord's condemnation overthrows the city's brutality (2:13[14]), so it annuls the demonic power that promotes that brutality. The preceding metaphor is extended in vv.5–6, which portray the humiliation and disgrace of the woman indicted in v.4 (cf. 2:11–13[12–14]); the second person pronominal forms throughout vv.5–7 are feminine, as suggested by the removal of her "skirts." The same principle of reversal is effected: violence has been requited with violence (2:13[14]); Nineveh's hidden arts are destroyed by exposure; as she enslaved "nations," so will she be bared to the "nations." Such exposure is emphasized by the repeated root "to see" (*rʾh*, "show," v.5; "spectacle," v.6; cf. "see," v.7). Exposure of harlotry's shame is a recurring theme in both OT and NT (Jer 13:26–27; Eze 16:37–41; Hos 2:3–5; Rev 17:15–16).

d. The verdict announced (3:7)

> [7] All who see you will flee from you and say,
> 'Nineveh is in ruins — who will mourn for her?'
> Where can I find anyone to comfort you?"

COMMENTARY

7 This section returns to the theme of mourning in response to the Lord's verdict on the prostitution and sorcery of the metaphorical harlot. Given Assyria's prominence, mourning should have been expected from the world's merchants, cheated of their markets (cf. 3:16), and from Assyria's neighbors, who observed the destruction firsthand. But no mourners will be found; such was Nineveh's reputation for debauchery and violence. Despite the metaphor, v.7 is not about merely humiliating Nineveh; rather, it portends her imminent, total destruction. What mourners there may have been "flee away" (*nādad*; cf. NRSV, "shrink from you"), abandoning the city in her hour of trial, though not before stopping to applaud her demise (cf. 3:19).

The "ruins" of Nineveh reflect the Lord's determination to make a full "end" of it (1:8–9), and the fulfillment of this purpose is amply attested both inscriptionally and archaeologically. The Babylonian Chronicle merely summarizes a variety of contemporary records in its comment concerning the sacking of Nineveh: "They ... turned the city into a ruin mound and a heap of debris" (Thomas, 76).

The debacle is still regarded as one of the greatest riddles of world history. Within a span of eighty years, Nineveh, which had been raised to unrivaled prominence by Sennacherib and his successors, was obliterated from living memory. Sennacherib had boasted of his city: "Nineveh, the noble metropolis, the city beloved of Ishtar, wherein are all the meeting-places of gods and goddesses; the everlasting substructure, the eternal foundation; whose plan had been designed from of old, and whose structure had been made beautiful along with the firmament of heaven" (Maier, 318). But the Lord had purposed

Nineveh's end, and the imperial city was never rebuilt. What trouble Judah later experienced did not come "a second time" from that quarter.

For the next three hundred years at least, there is no evidence that the site of Nineveh was even occupied. Xenophon passed the ruins without recognizing them (ca. 400 BC; Maier, 135). Lucian stated: "Nineveh has perished, and there is no trace left where it once was" (ibid.). Layard, one of Nineveh's excavators, wrote as follows:

> We have been fortunate enough to acquire the most convincing and lasting evidence of that magnificence and power, which made Nineveh the wonder of the ancient world, and her fall the theme of the prophets, as the most signal instance of divine vengeance. Without the evidence that these monuments afford, we might also have doubted that the great Nineveh ever existed, so completely has she become "a desolation and a waste." (ibid., 135–36)

According to the Cambridge Ancient History (3:130–31), "no other land seems to have been sacked and pillaged so completely as was Assyria."

The references to "mourning" and "comfort" are parallel to those in Isaiah 51:19 regarding Jerusalem, and the humiliation of Nineveh corresponds to that of Babylon in Isaiah 47 (cf. vv.2–3, 9, 12). The other major prophecy regarding Nineveh—that in Zephaniah—shows similar affinities with Isaiah's oracles against Babylon and Edom in its prediction of utter desolation (Zep 2:13–15; cf. Isa 13:19–22; 14:22–23; 34:10–17; 47:8, 10; Rev 18:2, 7). Thus ends the life of imperial Assyria, unmourned and virtually forgotten!

3. Third Description of Nineveh's Destruction (3:8–11)

OVERVIEW

The clear structure uniting 2:3[4]–3:7 is abandoned after 3:7. Nahum 3:8–11 is linked to both 3:5–7 and 3:12–17 by the second singular pronominal forms ("you," "your") and may be considered an extension of the Lord's indictment of the harlot. Though the characteristic imagery of 3:5–7 is abandoned in these verses, which are distinguished by a different analogy in the comparison to Thebes, correspondences with the earlier analogies (the lion and the harlot) include being introduced by a rhetorical question, as in 2:11[12] (cf. 3:7). It is followed by an implicit sentence of judgment (3:11), corresponding to those in 2:13[14]; 3:5–6; and the direct address that frames this section (vv.8, 11) is also distinctive in the preceding judicial verdicts (cf. 1:9, 11, 14; 2:1[2]). In addition, 3:8–11 repeats from 2:3[4]–3:7 the central themes of Nineveh's defense and defeat signaled by specific repetitions of vocabulary (see Overview on 2:1[2]–3:19). It is therefore treated as a complex and abbreviated correspondent to the previous sections, on which it depends for its structural and thematic identity.

8 Are you better than Thebes,
   situated on the Nile,
   with water around her?

> The river was her defense,
>> the waters her wall.
> ⁹Cush and Egypt were her boundless strength;
>> Put and Libya were among her allies.
> ¹⁰Yet she was taken captive
>> and went into exile.
> Her infants were dashed to pieces
>> at the head of every street.
> Lots were cast for her nobles,
>> and all her great men were put in chains.
> ¹¹You too will become drunk;
>> you will go into hiding
>> and seek refuge from the enemy.

COMMENTARY

8 Thebes is the Greek name for the Hebrew "No Amon," or "the city of Amon" (cf. MT, NIV note; Jer 46:25; Eze 30:14–16). "Amon" was the chief god of the Theban pantheon and one of the principal deities of Egypt since the New Kingdom (ca. 1580–1090 BC); the term "No" is derived from Egyptian "city" (*nwt*; cf. Akkadian *nɔu*). Thebes, which lay on the Nile about four hundred miles south of modern Cairo, constituted the chief city of Upper, or southern, Egypt and was a leading center of Egyptian civilization. A place of temples, obelisks, sphinxes, and palaces, it has been described as the "world's first great monumental city" (*IDB*, 4:616). It was dominated by the mighty temples of Amon at Luxor and Karnak (both districts of Thebes) on the east bank of the Nile, opposite the funerary temples of the kings to the west. Its temples and palaces are said to have found no equal in antiquity, and they are still regarded by some as the mightiest ruins of ancient civilization to be found anywhere in the world.

As intimated above, the city lay on both banks of the Nile. The river was divided into the principal channels by the islands that interrupted its flow. There is also evidence of an embankment, built by Amenhotep III, to retain the waters of an artificial lake a mile long and one thousand feet wide (*ZPEB*, 2:231). Thebes could truly be described, therefore, as a city "with water around her." The term "river" (*yām*) is normally translated "sea" (cf. NRSV); it is applied elsewhere to the Nile (Isa 18:2; 19:5; cf. Jer 51:36), and indeed the Nile is known as "the sea" (*al-baḥr*) to this day. The strategic location of Thebes made the river its natural or "outer" wall, a normal meaning of the noun *ḥêl* (here translated "defense"). In addition, it enjoyed the protection of a main, inner "wall" (*ḥômâ*), visualized again here as constituted by the surrounding waters or extending from them (cf. Notes). It is thus equated with Nineveh, similarly defended by a "wall" and by water through its location on a great river (2:5–6[6–7], 8[9]).

9 Thebes had intermittent periods of great glory either as the political or religious capital of Egypt from Middle Kingdom times (ca. 2160–1580 BC) onward, reigning especially supreme in the Eighteenth to Twentieth dynasties of the New Kingdom (ca. 1580–1090) and in the Twenty-First Dynasty as well (ca. 1085–950). After some indifferent periods, the establishment of an Ethiopian dynasty (biblical "Cush") in the seventh century assured a continuing place for Thebes, with access to the strength of both Egypt and Ethiopia, supplemented by alliances with Libya and Put. The adjective "boundless" corresponds to "endless" (ʾên qēṣeh; 2:9[10]), evoking the vast resources shared by the two cities and foreshadowing the "bodies without number" (v.3) they were destined also to share.

"Libya" (lûbîm) lay to the west of Egypt, with which it possessed similar ties: the long-lived Twenty-Second Dynasty had originated from Libya (ca. 950–730 BC), exemplified in the ruler Sheshonk I (Shishak; cf. 1Ki 14:25–26). "Put," a name first appearing in the so-called "Table of Nations" (Ge 10) as a descendent of Ham, is also to be located in North Africa on the basis of biblical references that associate it with Egypt and Ethiopia (cf. Ge 10:6; 1Ch 1:8; Jer 46:9 et al.). It is now commonly identified with the same area as Libya on the basis of Old Persian inscriptions referring to Libya as Putaya (IDB, 3:971), and here it may be a second reference to Libya by virtue of an explicative function of the Hebrew conjunction waw (ABD, 5:560). Like Nineveh, Thebes was surrounded not only by natural defenses but also by the confederate resources of a vast and ancient empire.

10–11 For all of her strength, Thebes fell to the Assyrians (ca. 664/663 BC). The Ethiopian kings of the Twenty-Fifth Dynasty had provoked this attack by their policy of intrigue in Palestine. Rather than confront Assyria directly, they tended to incite the minor states to rebel against their Assyrian overlords, with a view to reestablishing Palestine as an Egyptian sphere of influence (cf. Isa 30:1–7; 31:1–3; 36:6; 37:9). As a result of such intrigue by Tirhaka

(689–664 BC; cf. Isa 37:9; ABD, 6: 573) with the prince of Tyre, Egypt was invaded by Esarhaddon in 675/674; the campaign was launched in earnest in 671, when the Egyptians were routed before the Assyrians, who captured Memphis. Upper Egypt, including Thebes, surrendered; Tirhaka fled south to Ethiopia, and his rule was abrogated in Lower Egypt, which Esarhaddon fragmented under the rule of minor princes.

Esarhaddon died in 669 BC as he was marching to suppress further insurrection in Egypt, and Tirhaka immediately moved north into Egypt again. Thebes resumed its traditional allegiance to him, Memphis was seized, and Lower Egypt was again overrun. In 667 Ashurbanipal was in a position to take Egypt in hand, reversing the previous sequence of events. Memphis fell to his troops, Thebes surrendered with the rest of Egypt, and Tirhaka again fled south to Napata, where he died. He was succeeded as king of Ethiopia by Tanutamon, who renewed the attempt to control Egypt. Again, Thebes reversed its allegiance, receiving him with acclaim. Memphis was taken, its Assyrian representatives were slaughtered, and Tanutamon gained temporary sovereignty over Egypt.

The Egyptians were no match for the Assyrian army, which returned under Ashurbanipal in 664/663. Tanutamon fled south like his predecessors, the Delta was reconquered, and Thebes fell. Both Ashurbanipal and Esarhaddon had exercised restraint in their Egyptian foreign policy as a means of securing loyalty in a distant country they could only with difficulty garrison effectively. Now, however, Ashurbanipal's patience was exhausted. Thebes was razed to the ground, in vengeance on its vacillating allegiance to Ethiopia, even as Samaria had earlier been punished for its vacillating approaches to Egypt (cf. 2Ki 17:3–6). His enraged and vehement attack on the city—and on "Egypt" and "Ethiopia" (Kusi), on which it relied—is documented in his annals (cf. CAH, 3:285), a report corroborated by the subsequent history of Thebes. From that time on it has been a place of monuments to a glory and dominance now long departed. Both the Egyptian and the Assyrian sources, therefore, validate Nahum's description of a city scattered to the winds, its posterity cut off, its trained "nobles" plundered, and its leaders fleeing for refuge.

Verse 10 abounds with echoes of the judgments on Nineveh in the prophecy to this point. Common vocabulary includes: the threat of "exile" (*gālâ*; cf. 2:7[8]); destruction in the "streets" (*ḥûṣôt*, 2:4[5]); and human resources represented by its "nobles" (*nikbādîm*) suffering the same fate as

Nineveh's "wealth" (*kābôd*, 2:9[10]; cf. 3:3). In v.11 this correlation is made explicit. Its first and third lines open with the emphatic "You too ... you too" (*gam-ʾat*), echoing the same adverb repeated twice in v.10 ("Yet she," *gam-hîʾ*; "[also] her infants," *gam ʿōlāleyhā* [cf. NRSV "even her infants"]). Nineveh was equated with Thebes in its defenses (v.8); it will surely be equated with Thebes in its downfall. The finality of this sentence is sealed by its further correspondence to 1:2−15[2:1]. Like Thebes, Nineveh will be "drunk," as decreed by the Lord (1:10). Like Thebes, she will seek "refuge" in vain (*māʿôz*; so 1:7), for she trusted in carved images and idols.

NOTES

8 The NIV appears to point מִיָּם, *mîyām* ("from the sea, river") as *mayim* ("waters"), in which it is supported by the LXX, Syriac, Vulgate, and NRSV. The MT is fully intelligible as it stands and may be translated either "her wall (consisted) of the river" or "her wall (extended) from the river." The repetition of a word within a verse is characteristic of Nahum's style, thus giving grounds for the MT's reading (e.g., 1:2, 4; 2:2, 8, 9, 11; 3:2, 3, 4[2x], 15[3x]; cf. many other repetitions between verses). It also serves to explain the variants, introduced by translators who found the repetition awkward or who overlooked it in reading the consonants *mym* for the common noun "water." Of the two options noted for the MT, the first is preferable, in view of the parallelism "river" = "defense"; "river" = "wall," and of the strong emphasis on the role of water in v.8. That Thebes is also protected by a conventional wall is attested by Homer, however, who wrote of its hundred gates (Maier, 315).

4. Fourth Description of Nineveh's Destruction (3:12−19)

OVERVIEW

Verses 12−19 are related to vv.8−11 by the direct address that extends from v.12 to the end of the chapter. However, the analogy of Thebes gives way to the image of Nineveh's being "consumed." The verb "to eat" (*ʾākal*) occurs four times ("eater," v.12; "consumed," v.13; "devour, consume," v.15; cf. 1:10; 2:13[14]). This motif pervades the section,

first in the reality of devouring "fire" (3:13, 15), and second in the vivid and repeated simile of the voracious "locusts" (vv.15, 16, 17[2x]; cf. "grasshoppers," v.15[2x]; "strip," v.16). But now, at the end of the prophecy, we discover that Nineveh and her "fortresses" are being "consumed" from two different directions: from without by "fire" (and "sword"; v 15), like fig trees stripped of their fruit (vv.12–15); but equally from within by her own officials, who like parasitical "locusts" strip her bare (vv.15b–18).

This imagery is developed with great artistry in a pattern echoing previous sections. Verse 15 corresponds closely to 2:13[14] in pronouncing the sentence on Nineveh. The two verses share the words "fire," "devour," "sword," "leave no ...," and "cut down." Verse 14 likewise corresponds closely to the call to defense in 2:1[2]; the series of five taunting imperatives echoes the four admonitions in 2:1[2], lacking other parallels in Nahum, with both directed to Nineveh's fortifications.

Although the focus is now predominantly on Nineveh's destruction and no longer on the external agents of that destruction (cf. 2:1[2]; 3–5[4–6]; 3:2–3), the failure of the defenses and the impotence of her own "troops" are a recurring feature (vv.12–13; cf. 2:6–10[7–11]; 3:3, 8–11). As with the metaphors in 2:11–12[12–13] (the lion) and 3:4–7 (the harlot-sorceress), this section is characterized by a vivid metaphor—the swarm of locusts (vv.16–17), whose work of consuming the city before abandoning it to its fate is developed in the accompanying sentence (v.15; cf. 2:13[14]; 3:5–6, 11). Finally, the section concludes with a response to this judgment addressed directly to its victim (vv.18–19; cf. v.7).

a. Onslaught and failing defenses (3:12–14)

¹²All your fortresses are like fig trees
    with their first ripe fruit;
when they are shaken,
    the figs fall into the mouth of the eater.
¹³Look at your troops—
    they are all women!
The gates of your land
    are wide open to your enemies;
    fire has consumed their bars.
¹⁴Draw water for the siege,
    strengthen your defenses!
Work the clay,
    tread the mortar,
    repair the brickwork!

COMMENTARY

12–13 For Nineveh no "refuge" (cf. *māʿôz*; v.11) will be forthcoming. Her "fortresses" (*mibṣār*, v.12; cf. Nu 32:17; 2Ki 3:19; et al.), probably walled cities guarding the approaches to Nineveh (much as Judah's walled cities, taken earlier by Sennacherib, guarded the way to Jerusalem; cf. "Background" in the introduction), are ripe for destruction, being dislodged with as little effort as "figs" ready for harvesting. As the "gates" (v.13) guarding entrance to the land, they are "open" to the enemy like those of Nineveh herself (cf. 2:6[7]).

In the cause-and-effect of the poetry of v.13 (a "taunt"), the gates are open because the "troops" (lit., "your people") are "women," clearly in the thinking of ancient society a metaphor for weakness (cf. Isa 19:16; Jer 50:37). Verses 16–18 further describe the situation with regard to Nineveh's (presumably male) leaders. Not only "troops," but also all the leading citizens ("merchants," "guards," "officials," "shepherds," "nobles," "people," NIV) have either abandoned the defenses or simply fallen asleep to the impending collapse. For Nahum's audience, the city's "people," by abandoning their role as leaders and defenders, have "become women." The prospects for so spineless a society are dim indeed.

14 For comments on the series of imperatives, which together continue the "taunt," see the Overview to 3:12–19. The opening call to "draw water for the siege" is a graphic reminder of one of the nightmares faced by a besieged city: that the water will run out. An enemy regularly cut off all external sources provided by the rivers flowing into the city (cf. 2:6[7]), and in the case of Nineveh the attackers will try to divert the aqueducts constructed by

Sennacherib to bring water into the city for gardening purposes. From about the thirteenth century BC, stone cisterns plastered with lime were the means used to store water for siege, and presumably Nineveh had such technology, though the sheer size of the city demanded an ongoing supply. The Babylonian Chronicle corroborates this anticipation of siege, referring to a campaign that lasted three months (Thomas, 76; *ZPEB*, 1:688, 690). It also intimates that operations against the city began in 614 under Cyaxeres (cf. 2:1), so that Nineveh was subject to intermittent siege for more than two years.

For "defenses" (*mibṣār*), see the comment on v.12. The word can also mean "fortifications" or walls of the city. "Clay" was the principal building material of Mesopotamia, which lacked adequate resources in stone (cf. Ge 11:3). The walls of Nineveh, which were built of such "worked clay" bricks or a massive earth embankment (*IDB*, 1:465–66; cf. also *BEB*, 1:192–95), averaged fifty feet in breadth, extending to over one hundred feet at the fifteen gates; they therefore demanded an enormous effort for their maintenance, as indicated here by the urgent and repeated references to the processes involved. Evidence of the Ninevites' ill-fated attempts at self-defense is still apparent in the rubble of a counter wall erected hastily within the city after the main fortifications were breached (Maier, 116–17, 340–41).

b. Interpretive analogy and judgment from the Lord (3:15–17)

> ¹⁵There the fire will devour you;
>   the sword will cut you down
>   and, like grasshoppers, consume you.
> Multiply like grasshoppers,
>   multiply like locusts!
> ¹⁶You have increased the number of your merchants
>   till they are more than the stars of the sky,

> but like locusts they strip the land
> and then fly away.
> ¹⁷Your guards are like locusts,
> your officials like swarms of locusts
> that settle in the walls on a cold day —
> but when the sun appears they fly away,
> and no one knows where.

COMMENTARY

15 Nineveh's conquest by fire together with sword is amply revealed in the ruins. Maier, 125–26, quoting A. H. Layard, writes: "The palace (Sennacherib's) had been destroyed by fire. The alabaster slabs were almost reduced to lime, and many of them fell to pieces as soon as uncovered. The palaces, which others had occupied, could only be traced by a thin white deposit, like a coat of plaster, left by the burnt alabaster upon the wall of sun-dried bricks." Greek tradition, in fact, records that the king himself set fire to his palace, perishing by his own hand in its flames (Maier, 109–10).

The devouring (ʾākal) fire evokes the destruction inflicted by "grasshoppers" or locusts, which similarly "consume" (ʾākal) everything that lies in their path. Verses 15–17 develop this image of "locusts" with intricate detail, which may be schematized as follows:

3:15	fire	devour		
	locusts	consume	multiply	
3:16	merchants, like locusts	strip	increased	fly away
3:17	guards, like locusts	(settle)	swarms	fly away

The NIV normally translates the noun "grasshopper" (yeleq) as "locust" (cf. Jer 51:14, 27; Joel 1:4; 2:25), which is preferable. The term is used in Psalm 105:34 with reference to the Egyptian plague that was clearly the work of locusts (cf. Ex 10:4–15; Ps 105:34, "grasshoppers," NIV); and the initial emphasis of v.15 is on their omnivorous behavior, typical of locusts rather than of grasshoppers.

The following word for "locusts" (ʾarbeh) denotes a different species or stage of development in the same type of insect (ZPEB, 3:948–50). This word is related phonetically, and possibly etymologically, to the Hebrew rābâ ("to increase, be many"; cf. NASB, "swarming locust"; BDB, 916). The association determines another abrupt transition in the repeated verb "multiply," becoming explicit in the following statement: "you have increased" (hirbêt). The ability of the locust to proliferate in vast numbers underlies its menace to vegetation, and this characteristic is also reflected in the OT (cf. Ex 10:5–6, 14–15; Jdg 6:5; 7:12; Jer 46:23; 51:14).

16 The significance of the startling comparison emerges in this verse: like locusts, Nineveh's "merchants" have proliferated beyond measure; and they likewise "strip" (*pāšaṭ*) the land. The comparison to locusts is extended with a series of graphic verbal images. Locusts "consume" and "multiply" (v.15); they "increase" and "strip" (v.16); they "swarm" (a noun) and "settle" (v.17). But, in a further element to the analogy, these "locusts"—Nineveh's "merchants" and "guards"—also "fly away," unconcerned for the region they have exploited.

17 This verse repeats the preceding comparison with emphasis on this final element: Nineveh's "guards" (*minnᵉzār*, from the root *nzr*, meaning "consecrate"; cf. "Nazirite") and "officials" (or "scribes" [NRSV], *ṭipsār*, possibly an Assyrian loanword; cf. BDB, 381), like her "merchants," are multitudinous

as "swarms of locusts"; they "settle" within her boundaries for shelter and food, but they abandon her and "fly away" when tribulation comes.

With remarkable artistry and use of word association, Nahum transforms the perspective of the prophecy. The sentence of judgment is now executed from within, by those claiming to serve Nineveh's interests as they flock to her (v.15), and her fall is explained in terms of the disloyalty of her own people (vv.16–17). The Assyrians based their empire on expediency and self-interest, multiplying for their own gratification power, wealth, and personnel like locusts. Now their empire will fall prey to the self-interest it has promoted—eaten away from within no less than it will be devoured by the sword from without.

c. The verdict announced (3:18–19)

¹⁸O king of Assyria, your shepherds slumber;
     your nobles lie down to rest.
Your people are scattered on the mountains
     with no one to gather them.
¹⁹Nothing can heal your wound;
     your injury is fatal.
Everyone who hears the news about you
     claps his hands at your fall,
for who has not felt
     your endless cruelty?

COMMENTARY

18–19 The collapse of effective loyalty penetrates even the aristocracy of Assyria, represented by its "nobles" and "shepherds," or "rulers" (*rōᶜeh*, v.18; cf. Isa 44:28; Jer 23:1, Eze 34:2–23; 37:24). Their destiny is expressed with the ironic

ambiguity typical of Nahum; although the vocabulary is unusual, their "slumber" (*nûm*) and "rest" (*yiškᵉnû*—many scholars follow the LXX, which reflects *yāšnû* [from *yšn*, "their sleep, death"] for *šākan* ["rest"], as a better parallel to *nûm*; cf. J. J. M.

Roberts, *Nahum, Habakkuk, and Zephaniah* [OTL; Louisville: Westminster John Knox, 1991], 76) foreshadow both their death (Jer 51:39) and the inertia that occasions it (Isa 56:10).

The corollary of this failure is the scattering of the people "with no one to gather them," a thought expressed frequently about sheep without "shepherds" (Isa 13:14; cf. Isa 40:11; Jer 23:3; 31:10; Eze 34:13; 37:21; Mic 2:12). Such scattering will duly accompany Nineveh's end (cf. 2:8[9]), on which the following comment has been made:

> The disappearance of the Assyrian people will always remain a unique and striking phenomenon in ancient history. Other, similar, kingdoms and empires have indeed passed away, but the people have lived on. Recent discoveries have shown that poverty-stricken communities did for many centuries perpetuate the old Assyrian names and various places, e.g., on the ruined site of Ashur, but the essential truth remains the same. A nation which had existed two thousand years and had ruled a

wide area, lost its independent character. (CAH, 3:130)

The "king of Assyria" is addressed directly throughout vv. 18–19, and ultimately it is his fatal injury that accounts for his breakdown in authoritative government and military leadership. As anticipated by Nahum, the dynasty falls with the city. The "wound" (v. 19) cannot be healed; the brief attempt by Ashur-uballit to keep the dynasty alive in Haran fails two years later. The injury is indeed fatal.

The book closes (cf. 1:15[2:1] with the response of witnesses who hear of these events (*šōmᶜê* ... *šēmaᶜ*, "hears ... news," v. 19; *mašmîaᶜ*, "proclaims," 1:15[2:1]); the "endless cruelty" (*rāᶜâ*, so "evil," 1:11) is ended! For the countless victims of Nineveh's cruelty, that is "good news." *Sic transit gloria mundi.*

For his anger lasts only a moment,
  but his favor lasts a lifetime;
weeping may remain for a night,
  but rejoicing comes in the morning. (Ps 30:5)

HABAKKUK

CARL E. ARMERDING

Introduction

1. HISTORICAL BACKGROUND AND DATE

Habakkuk's prophecy is set against a background of the decline and fall of the Judean kingdom (ca. 626–586 BC). Although nothing is known of the prophet himself apart from the book bearing his name—the book is not dated in the usual manner (cf. Am 1:1; Zep 1:1; etc.)—the general background of Habakkuk is clear from the internal data. Habakkuk 1:5–11 represents a period before 612 BC, when the Babylonians destroyed the Assyrian capital, Nineveh. More probably, the section predates 605, the year the Babylonians (the Chaldeans [*kaśdîm*]; 1:6) through Nebuchadnezzar extended their power into Syria-Palestine (2Ki 24:1–7; see Hab 1:5: "you would not believe, even if you were told"). By contrast it is sometimes argued that 1:12–17 and 2:6–20 must reflect a later period when the power and rapacity of the Babylonians had become common knowledge to the prophet. Various solutions have been proposed, but the best seems to be found in taking the sections of the dialogue as broadly representative of Habakkuk's spiritual struggles over a long period of time, possibly beginning as early as 626 and continuing as late as 590 or after.

During this period Judah enjoyed its last bit of prosperity under Josiah (d. 609 BC), and Assyria's wound was revealed as fatal with the ultimate fall of Nineveh. By 605, the short-lived Babylonian Empire had established its dominance over Palestine, with Judah's later kings either in vassalage to the Babylonians or in revolt against that status, usually by engaging in treachery with Egypt (2Ki 24–25). In 586 BC Jerusalem was destroyed and its people taken into exile. Conditions during the life of the prophet would have progressed from excellent—with considerable material prosperity and even promise of spiritual revival in the days of Josiah—to the height of desperation as the net was drawn closer and closer around the hapless capital. There is no direct evidence from the book that Habakkuk lived past the destruction of Jerusalem, though some find such evidence in 3:16–19 (cf. commentary).

2. UNITY

The major challenge to unity comes with ch. 3, the psalm. Stylistic shifts from the narrative portions and the older critical tendency to date psalmic material in the postexilic period have combined to call the authenticity of ch. 3 into question. The failure of the Qumran "commentary" to include an exposition of the psalm has, for some scholars, added weight to the denial of Habakkuk's authorship. Against this is the clear note of continuity of theme in all three chapters and, in general, the lack of any compelling reasons not to accept the book's attribution of the psalm to Habakkuk.

3. AUTHORSHIP

Nothing is known of Habakkuk except his name, which does not lend itself to attempts at finding a Hebrew meaning (contra Luther et al.). Of his temperament and personal situation, we know only what may be inferred from the book. Literary dependences and early canonical reception leave no doubt that Habakkuk's work was circulated and accepted early, but the details remain lost.

4. OCCASION AND PURPOSE

Prophecy is a result of revelation given to a person who then proclaims the inspired message to the people. Often such revelation and inspiration are occasioned by conditions in the nation (with the exception of Jonah and Jeremiah 27, prophecy is always proclaimed to Israel, even when about other nations) about which the prophet has been burdened.

Habakkuk is unique among the prophets because he does not speak for God to the people but rather to God about his people and nation. The similarity with the other prophets is in the setting: the people of God, covenantally bound to him since the days of the exodus, have sharply fallen away from those covenantal standards (1:2–4). Violence and law-breaking (covenantal violations) abound, and the wicked seem at least superficially to triumph. According to all that Habakkuk knows about God's holiness and covenant (cf. Dt 26–33, on which Habakkuk seems dependent), Yahweh should have arisen to correct the situation, particularly in response to believing prayer for change by such a one as Habakkuk.

But such correction has not been forthcoming, and the prayers of the righteous and the struggle for justice in the land seem in vain, with the result that God's program of redemptive history is threatened. In light of this context, it seems more appropriate, from a form-critical standpoint, to think of Habakkuk 1–2 not as a "lament," but more analogous to the "complaint" literature represented by Job, Jeremiah, and some of the psalms (e.g., Pss 12; 73:1–14).

The early part of the prophecy of Habakkuk is a dialogue in which the prophet's questions receive divine answers. Externally, the Assyrians would naturally have been a threat to Judah; and apart from the problem of the future of God's covenantal promises, the prophet would have expected Assyria to be "the rod of God's anger" (Isa 10:5–6). The new element is the introduction of Babylonian power, with such awful potential consequences and with no clear vision of when and how Yahweh will continue his commitments to the chosen line. But initially Habakkuk is more concerned with internal injustices and Yahweh's apparent complacency toward the evil generation. It is God's reply (1:5–11) that catapults the prophecy onto the international and eschatological level.

Larger questions quickly engulf the local concerns, and chs. 2–3 carry us well beyond the last days of Judah to the future. Habakkuk himself is never told when or exactly how it will end, but 2:14, 20 assure him of the ultimate triumph of Yahweh; the psalm in ch. 3 then shows that Habakkuk learns to live in the light of this fact.

5. STRUCTURE

Habakkuk 1:1–2:5 clearly is a dialogue between God and the prophet in which two stylized complaints are answered by two penetrating replies. The opening complaint (1:2–4) has to do with Judah's moral and spiritual decline and the apparent unwillingness of Yahweh to intervene. The first reply (1:5–11) sets forth the coming destruction by Babylon as Yahweh's discipline for errant Judah. For the patriotic and nationalistic covenantal Israelite, this is hardly a solution; thus, 1:12–17 complains that such a solution will only aggravate the problem of God's working in history and the apparent compounding of injustice. Habakkuk 2:1 leaves the prophet sitting on his spiritual tower awaiting an answer; while 2:2–5, the central message of the prophecy, foresees ultimate justice for the arrogant Chaldeans and calls for the righteous man, in the intervening years, to live by his faith (or "faithfulness," NIV note).

Habakkuk 2:6–20 is a taunt or mocking song put in the mouths of the nations that have suffered at the hand of Babylon. It consists of five "woes," punctuated by a vision of the universal knowledge of God's glory (v.14) and climaxed by a call for reverent submission to the Lord of history, who through all the vicissitudes of history remains seated in his holy temple (v.20). In typical prophetic form the taunt moves from the third to the second person, and the subject matter—with the exception of the fifth woe, which opposes idolatry—deals with a nation arrogantly building its own power at the expense of its less able neighbors.

Habakkuk 3:1–19 is a psalm, replete with musical directions (v.1: *šigyōnōt*, "shigionoth"; cf. Ps 7:1, and v.19: *negînôt*, "stringed instruments"). Because of its unique features, we have left fuller discussion to the commentary.

6. THEOLOGICAL VALUES

Habakkuk's message, the core of which is found in 2:4, is applied to a basic point in three NT books. Paul, in Romans 1:17, introduces his gospel as one of salvation by faith, not works, and cites Habakkuk 2:4, "the righteous will live by his faith," as OT support for his argument. Galatians 3:11–12 sees faith as the antithesis of law or legal salvation, and again Habakkuk 2:4 serves as proof. Finally, in an intriguing passage from Hebrews 10:37–38, Habakkuk 2:3–4 is again quoted; but the context focuses on the pending arrival of the fulfillment of the vision and the identification of the Hebrews with those who have faith and thus persevere under pressure.

The theological value of Habakkuk, however, cannot be limited to a few, though crucial, NT quotations. The prophet asks some of the most penetrating questions in all literature, and the answers he receives are basic to a proper view of God and his relation to history. If God's initial response sounds the death knell for any strictly nationalistic covenantal theology of Judah, his second reply outlines in a positive sense the fact that all history is hastening to a conclusion that is as certain as it is satisfying.

In the interim, while history is still awaiting its conclusion (and Habakkuk is not told when the end will come, apparently for him prefigured by Babylon's destruction), the righteous ones are to live by faith. The prescribed faith—or "faithfulness," as many have argued that *ʾemûnâ* should be translated (cf. NIV note on 2:4)—is still called for as a basic response to the unanswered questions in today's universe; and it is this, a theology for life both then and now, that stands as Habakkuk's most basic contribution.

7. CANONICITY

Habakkuk was early grouped with the other so-called Minor Prophets in the Book of the Twelve (attested as such in Sir 49:10 [ca. 190 BC]), the acceptance of which has never been questioned in either Jewish or Christian circles. Questions of the unity of the book do not seem to have affected its acceptance, and in fact there is no ancient record of a dispute over ch. 3.

8. BIBLIOGRAPHY

Andersen, Francis. *Habakkuk: A New Translation with Introduction and Commentary*. Anchor Bible 25. New York: Doubleday, 2001.

Baker, David W. *Nahum, Habakkuk and Zephaniah*. Tyndale Old Testament Commentaries. Downers Grove, Ill.: InterVarsity Press, 1988.

Bruckner, James K. *Jonah, Nahum, Habakkuk, Zephaniah*. NIV Application Commentary. Grand Rapids: Zondervan, 2004.

Roberts, J. J. M. *Nahum, Habakkuk, and Zephaniah*. Old Testament Library. Louisville: Westminster John Knox, 1991.

Robertson, O. Palmer. *The Books of Nahum, Habakkuk, and Zephaniah*. New International Commentary on the Old Testament. Grand Rapids: Eerdmans, 1994.

Yadin, Yigael. *The Art of Warfare in Biblical Lands in Light of Archaeological Discoveries*. New York: McGraw Hill, 1963.

9. OUTLINE

I. Habakkuk's Initial Complaint (1:1−4)

II. God's First Response (1:5−11)

III. Habakkuk's Second Complaint (1:12−2:1)

IV. God's Second Response (2:2−20)

    A. Prologue (2:2−3)

    B. Indictment (2:4−5)

    C. Sentence (2:6−20)

V. The Prayer of Habakkuk (3:1−19)

    A. Prologue (3:1)

    B. Invocation (3:2)

    C. Theophany (3:3−15)

    D. Response (3:16−19a)

    E. Epilogue (3:19b)

Text and Exposition

I. HABAKKUK'S INITIAL COMPLAINT (1:1–4)

OVERVIEW

These verses correspond closely to the psalms of lament, or a "complaint" section in a lament; prominent features of this form in vv.2–4 include the questions addressed to the Lord, the urgent description of dire need, and the sustained petition for deliverance (cf. Pss 10:1–13; 13:1–4; 22:1–21; 74:1–11; 80; 88). Habakkuk's prophecy is thus located clearly within the community of faith, exposed to many tribulations, yet oriented to the Lord as its help in trouble.

The structure of the passage is defined by prominent repetitions within it. Repeatedly Habakkuk emphasizes the opposing principles of evil and justice, thereby revealing his dominant concern: not only is the lawlessness of "violence" rampant, but it has also mastered the very mechanisms of law by which it should be curbed. In such circumstances it is clear that only divine intervention can correct the imbalance (cf. "save," v.2); when this intervention is not forthcoming, faith is stretched beyond its limits.

Habakkuk personally confronts the situation he describes; it is "before" him, he has to "look at" (v.3) it, and the wicked are at close quarters, hemming in the righteous (v.4). It is also evident that this has occurred in Palestine among God's people, which is the proper sphere of the "law" and the social justice flowing from its observance (see below; cf. Dt 4:8; Isa 2:3; Am 2:4). The "wicked" themselves are not defined precisely, however, and they have been identified either as fellow Judeans or as members of a foreign nation. Normally where "justice" and social "violence" are opposed in the OT, the "wicked" are Israelites unless clearly identified in other terms (e.g., Ex 23:1–9; Isa 5:7–15). Here, in a similar context and in accord with this pattern, they may be assumed to be Judeans.

¹The oracle that Habakkuk the prophet received.

²How long, O Lord, must I call for help,
   but you do not listen?
Or cry out to you, "Violence!"
   but you do not save?
³Why do you make me look at injustice?
   Why do you tolerate wrong?
Destruction and violence are before me;
   there is strife, and conflict abounds.
⁴Therefore the law is paralyzed,
   and justice never prevails.

> The wicked hem in the righteous,
> so that justice is perverted.

COMMENTARY

1 For comments on the prophet, see "Authorship" in the introduction.

2 The question "How long?" (v.2) is typical of a lament or complaint (Ps 13:1-2; cf. Pss 6:3; 80:4; 89:46; Jer 12:4; Zec 1:12). It implies a situation of crisis from which the speaker seeks deliverance, as is suggested in the following verb (*šiwwaʿ*, "call for help"). The verb "listen" (*šāmaʿ*; GK 9048) normally carries connotations of an active response to what is heard (e.g., Jdg 13:9; Ps 4:1; Eze 8:18); where that response is lacking, the righteousness of either the petitioner or the one addressed is called in question (cf. Job 19:7; 30:20; Ps 18:41). The crisis in which Habakkuk calls for help is "violence"; the response expected from the Lord, assuming that he "hears," is that he should "save."

"Violence" (*ḥāmās*; GK 2805) denotes flagrant violation of moral law by which a person injures primarily a fellow human (e.g., Ge 6:11). Its underlying meaning is one of ethical wrong, of which physical brutality is only one possible expression (e.g., Jdg 9:24; cf. *TWOT*, 1:297). *Ḥāmās* occurs six times in Habakkuk (1:2, 3, 9, 2:8, 17[2x]), a frequency exceeded only in the longer book of Psalms (14x) and Proverbs (7x); it is therefore a key word in this prophecy.

To "save" (*yāšaʿ*; GK 3828) means to deliver from what oppresses or restricts. Such salvation is to be found ultimately only in the Lord by those who are righteous toward him (e.g., Pss 18:27, 41; 33:16-19; Isa 59:1-2). This opening verse of Habakkuk's dialogue with the Lord sets the tone of ch. 1, which is fraught with the tension of unanswered prayer. The

faith underlying it will be only partially vindicated in ch. 2; it is affirmed more fully in ch. 3 (3:17-19), where it is vindicated by repeated assurances of the Lord's "salvation" (3:18; cf. vv.8, 13).

3 Like the "how long" in v.2, the interrogative "why" is even more typical of the complaint element in psalms that are often categorized as lament (e.g., Pss 10:1; 44:23-24; 74:1, 11; 80:12; 88:14, where the question is probably more rhetorical than here; see Andersen, 21). Three word pairs follow. The concepts of "injustice" (*ʾāwen*; GK 224) and "wrong" (*ʿāmāl*; GK 6662) are correlated in ten other verses; the NIV usually translates them as "evil" and "trouble." This word pair is also used predominantly in contexts of perverted justice and social oppression (cf. Job 15:35; Ps 7:14[15]). "Destruction" (*šōd*) and "violence" (*ḥāmās*; cf. comment at v.2) are similarly correlated repeatedly in Scripture, being associated with unjust oppression of the weaker members within a community (Jer 6:7; 20:8; Eze 45:9; Am 3:10).

The clause employing *ʾāwen* and *ʿāmāl*, especially in Hebrew, recalls Numbers 23:21, where the same verbs and objects occur with the same subject, Yahweh (cf. RSV; at least one commentator [Andersen, 114-15] argues that both passages point to Israel's unrelieved misery, observed by Yahweh, rather than her perfidy). In this allusion to God's blessing in old times, as in the preceding question, the prophet's sense of a chasm between past revelation and present reality (cf. 3:2) emerges. A third word pair, "strife" (*rîb*) and "conflict" (*mādôn*), evokes the anger and dissension born of conflicting and uncompromising wills (cf. Pr 15:18; 17:14; 26:20–21; Jer 15:10).

4 The disintegration of a society into such factions is bound up with its rejection of the forces that bring it unity—"law" and "justice." The "law" (*tôrâ*; GK 9368) may refer to any form of authoritative "teaching" (e.g., Pr 3:1; 4:2); in Scripture almost invariably it refers to God's "law," by which he reveals his will and directs the life of his people. When used in the singular without clear definition, as here, *tôrâ* signifies God's covenantal code established with Israel, given through Moses and set forth particularly in the book of Deuteronomy (e.g., Dt 1:5; 4:8; 17:18–19; 31:9; 33:4; Jos 8:31–32).

The "law" was mediated primarily through the Levitical priesthood (e.g., Lev 10:11; Dt 33:10), in close conjunction with the king or other governing authorities (e.g., Dt 17:8–11). Its effectiveness has therefore been "paralyzed" most extensively by corruption of the religious and civil leadership of the nation—a condition appropriate to the oppression described in v.3. Such a paralysis is seldom attributed to foreign powers, who in the OT function instead as God's instruments of judgment.

"Justice" (*mišpāṭ*; GK 5477) has broad and varied connotations in the OT, implying the exercise not merely of legal processes but of all the functions of government. It is through "justice" and the act of "judging" (*šāpaṭ*) that law and order are represented, legislated, interpreted, and enforced (cf. *TWOT*, 2:947–49). Within Israel this order is based on *tôrâ* ("law"), of which "justice" is the application (e.g., Nu 15:16; Dt 33:10).

NOTES

3 "Abounds" translates נָשָׂא (*nāśā'*, "to lift up"). The verb appears to be used intransitively here, thus requiring an unusual reflexive translation: "it lifts up (itself)" (cf. Ps 89:9[10]; Hos 13:1; Na 1:5). This reading is corroborated by the LXX's λαμβάνει (*lambanei*, "he takes"), used absolutely, and its difficulty explains the variants in certain other versions. It should therefore be retained, despite the unfamiliar grammatical usage. The verb may also be interpreted as having an impersonal subject, i.e., "one raises, exalts conflict" (cf. GKC, par. 144d; Isa 8:4).

II. GOD'S FIRST RESPONSE (1:5–11)

OVERVIEW

This passage is distinguished from vv.2–4 by a transition to the Lord as speaker. In form these verses resemble an oracle, yet scarcely the oracle of salvation that forms the turning point, explicitly or otherwise, in certain other laments/complaints (e.g., Pss 12:5; 13:5–6; 22:23–24; 28:6–7; 31:21–22). They correspond more closely to an expanded announcement of judgment on God's people, the prophet's complaint serving now as the accusation on which this is based.

This announcement is structured first as an introductory reference to the "nations" (*gôyîm*), who will be the source of the impending judgment (v.5; cf. Dt 28:65); second as a portrayal of the Babylonians, the specific "people" (*gôy*) from whom it will arise (vv.6–11a; cf. Dt 28:49–57); and finally as a brief but pungent verdict on this instrument of judgment (v.11b). Within the second section v.6 sets forth the character of the Babylonians ("ruthless"), their conduct ("who sweep"), and their motivation ("to seize"), each element being elaborated in vv.7–11.

These seven verses echo focal concepts from vv.2–4 in the references to "violence" (*ḥāmās*; v.9; cf. vv.2–3) and to the "law" (*mišpāṭ*; v.7; cf. vv.3–4). This balance between the two passages is signaled in v.5, where the verbs "look at" and "watch" correspond to "look at" (*rāʾâ*) and "tolerate" (*hibbîṭ*) in v.3, and in Numbers 23:21 (cf. comment on v.3). In effect the Lord's answer to "violence" is "violence," as stipulated in the "law," whose paralysis with regard to injustice is only temporary (cf. Isa 55:11; 2Ti 2:9).

The same principle (*lex talionis*) is applied subsequently to the Babylonians themselves (2:6–19). The Lord's sovereignty over the Babylonians, whom he has raised up, is thus implied for the corresponding situation in Judah (vv.2–4). Evil and calamity do not exist independently of the sovereign rule and redemptive purposes of God (cf. Am 3:6); but this truth is apprehended only by faith in God as he reveals himself (cf. Pss 37; 73; Ecc 8:11–13; Isa 51:12–16; Hab 2:4; 3:1–19). The truth applies equally to Judah or Babylon: the Lord's judgment of sin in his own people is thus extended to the same sin among the Babylonians, which is made explicit in v.11b and amplified in 2:6–19. The sovereignty of God does not eliminate human accountability; the time of the accounting merely varies (cf. Ro 2:4–11; 9:11–24; 1Ti 5:24).

---

⁵"Look at the nations and watch—
 and be utterly amazed.
For I am going to do something in your days
 that you would not believe,
 even if you were told.
⁶I am raising up the Babylonians,
 that ruthless and impetuous people,
who sweep across the whole earth
 to seize dwelling places not their own.
⁷They are a feared and dreaded people;
 they are a law to themselves
 and promote their own honor.
⁸Their horses are swifter than leopards,
 fiercer than wolves at dusk.
Their cavalry gallops headlong;
 their horsemen come from afar.
They fly like a vulture swooping to devour;
⁹ they all come bent on violence.
Their hordes advance like a desert wind
 and gather prisoners like sand.

> ¹⁰They deride kings
>   and scoff at rulers.
> They laugh at all fortified cities;
>   they build earthen ramps and capture them.
> ¹¹Then they sweep past like the wind and go on —
>   guilty men, whose own strength is their god."

COMMENTARY

5 This verse is addressed to a plural audience. The hearers, by implication Judeans, are treated as distinct from the "nations" (or Gentiles), at whom they are to "look." To be "amazed" is humanity's response to an event (lit., "a work that I am working," "a deed that I am doing") that utterly confounds all previous expectations (cf. Ge 43:33; Ps 48:5; Isa 13:8; 29:9; Jer 4:9); it runs counter to what the listeners "believe." The destruction of Jerusalem is such an event, creating both a national crisis and a theological crisis among God's people.

6 This verse, linked to v.5 by the repeated conjunction "for" (*kî* [untr. in NIV]; but cf. NRSV), identifies both the speaker and the amazing "work" introduced in v.5. The work entails Babylonia's rise to power; and the speaker is evidently the Lord, who alone rules the destiny of nations as described here. Conceivably the mere fact of Babylon's dramatic resurgence under Nabopolassar and Nebuchadnezzar is seen as the source of amazement. More likely, however, Babylon's impending domination of Judah is implied. This runs counter to popular theology (cf. Jer 5:12; 6:14; 7:1–34; 8:11; La 4:12; Am 6) but is fully in accord with the Lord's chastisement of his sinning people (cf. Dt 28:49–50; 1Ki 11:14. 23; Jer 4; 5:14–17; 6:22–30; Am 6:14), and it is clearly anticipated in 3:16.

The description of the Babylonians as "ruthless and impetuous" provides a faint echo of the rhyming word pair in Hebrew (*hammar wehannimhār*). Character produces conduct, and this Babylonian character is expressed by unprincipled rapacity. The phrase "the whole earth" suggests unrestricted scope for such behavior, which by implication will engulf Palestine also. However, the verse concludes with a wordplay — *lō'-lô* ("not their own"), whose sound and meaning undermine the imposing threat of the Babylonians: their conduct has no moral basis, so their achievements are without substance.

7 Verses 7–11 develop the description of the oppressors. Their character is rooted in a self-sufficiency that acknowledges no superior authority and no dependency, an attitude tantamount to self-deification (cf. v.11). Thus they are "feared" (*'āyōm*) and "dreaded" (*nôrā'*), usurping the place of God. If God's people refuse to fear him, they will ultimately be compelled to fear those less worthy of fear (cf. Dt 28:47–48; 58–68; Jer 5:15–22). In the final sentence the source of Babylonian law (*mišpāṭ*, "justice"; cf. vv.3–4) and "honor" ("dignity," NRSV) is exposed — it is self-generated. Contrast the true God-fearer, whose dignity derives from the Lord.

8 The Babylonian "cavalry" are compared to three predators whose speed and power bring violent death to their prey. The "leopard" and the "wolf" recur together with the lion in Jeremiah 5:6 as symbols of divine judgment on Judah (cf. Hos

13:7–8). "Vulture" translates the Hebrew word for eagle (*nešer*), a bird whose swift pursuit is frequently compared to a rapacious army on the move (2Sa 1:23; Jer 4:13; 49:22; La 4:19) and which, from a distance, can easily be mistaken for a vulture (cf. *BEB*, 1:350). The vulture is primarily a scavenger, feeding off carrion, whereas the eagle hunts and kills its prey. The imagery of the hunter better fits the historical context; in any case the reference constitutes a clear allusion to Deuteronomy 28:49–50.

9 As "law" (*mišpāṭ*) recurs in v.7 from vv.3–4, so "violence" (*ḥāmās*) recurs from vv.2–3: those who live by violence shall die by the violence of others (e.g., Ps 7:16; Pr 1:18–19; cf. Ge 9:6; Lev 24:20; Mt 7:2; Rev 16:5–6). The NIV's final two lines embody a doubtful parallelism. "Like a desert wind," describing the Babylonian advance, pictures the hot, scorching wind from the eastern desert; but the translation rests more on the parallel passage in Jeremiah 4:11–13 than on the Hebrew text. The NRSV preserves a more traditional reading. The parallel in line three—"like sand" (cf. Ge 22:17; Isa 10:22)—modifies the object "prisoners" (lit. "captives"), creating a vivid portrait of numberless prisoners helplessly collected for deportation.

10 The corollary of Babylonian autonomy (v.7) is contempt for all other authority, which is evaluated in purely military terms. The Babylonians "deride kings" and "scoff at rulers," since they can "laugh" at their defenses. The "ramps," constructed primarily of earth, were a graded incline along which the cumbersome battering rams could be moved in breaking through city walls (Yadin, 1963: 17, 20, 315; cf. 2Sa 20:15; Eze 4:2; 21:22; 26:8–9). The "wicked" who "hem in" the "righteous" (v.4) will themselves be hemmed in by the horrors of siege (cf. Dt 28:52–57; Jer 39:1).

11 The onrushing cavalry (vv.8–9) is checked by the siege warfare, in which it would not have participated (v.10; cf. Yadin, 1963: 297). As the fortified cities fall and resistance crumbles, the cavalry's pent-up energy is released and its progress resumes.

In an abrupt shift, the final words of v.11 entirely undermine the dramatic account of the Babylonians, developed at length at vv.5–11a. "Sweep past" they may, but the final verdict is already in, though the perplexed prophet may indeed have been forgiven for wondering how it would make any difference. "Guilty men" (lit., "and [so] he is guilty"; cf. NRSV, "they transgress and become guilty," taking Heb. *ʿābar* ["and go on"] in its figurative sense) is followed immediately by the reason for the guilt: "[his] strength is his god." As in the verses above, the Babylonian horde is personified in the singular forms; and ruthless arrogance is rightly epitomized as a form of self-deification. Such people acknowledge no accountability, seek no repentance, and offer no reparations, while violating the most fundamental order of created life. For such the verdict of "guilty" can mean only the sentence of radical destruction (cf. 2:6–20; 3:13–16).

NOTES

A number of textual variants occur in this passage that will not be handled in detail here. For a more extended treatment of these and subsequent variants, see the relevant passages in W. H. Brownlee, *The Text of Habakkuk in the Ancient Commentary from Qumran* (SBLMS 11; Philadelphia: Society of Biblical Literature, 1959) and *The Midrash Pesher of Habakkuk* (Missoula, Mont.: Scholars, 1979).

5 The DSS (lQpHab), LXX, and Syriac all imply the reading בֹּגְדִים (*bōgedîm*, "treacherous") for בַּגּוֹיִם (*baggôyim*, "among the nations"); the variant is also supported by Acts 13:41, quoting this verse according to the LXX tradition. The two readings involve the confusion of a single letter: ו (*w*) for ד (*d*). Both words are suitable to their context and recur repeatedly in Habakkuk. In the absence of decisive evidence favoring one reading, the MT should be followed, despite the strength of the variant tradition.

8 1QpHab, supported by the LXX, omits the verb יָבֹאוּ (*yābōʾû*, "come"). These two texts also differ from the MT and from each other in their vocalization of the repeated words פָּרָשָׁיו וּפָרָשָׁיו (*pārāšayw ûpārāšayw*, "their cavalry ... their horsemen"; the NIV renders the same Hebrew word by two English words). The LXX treats the second noun as a verb, whereas lQpHab treats the first as a verb. The LXX suggests an attractive alternative to the MT by embodying an extended wordplay in the sequence וּפָשׁוּ פָרָשָׁו וּפָרְשׁוּ (*ûpāšû pārāšāw ûpārešû*, lit., "their cavalry careers and cavaliers"), reminiscent of v.6: הַמַּר וְהַנִּמְהָר (*hammar wehannimhār*, "ruthless and impetuous"). However, the MT makes good sense as it stands, and this repetition of vocabulary has numerous parallels within Habakkuk (e.g., *mišpāṭ*, 1:4).

9 The noun מְגַמַּת (*megammat*; "hordes," NIV) is without parallel in the OT. The NIV and many commentators derive it from גָּמַם (*gāmam*), whose Arabic cognates denote "abundance." A less plausible derivation is from גָּמָא (*gāmāʾ*, "to swallow"; cf. Ge 24:17; Job 39:24). "Desert wind" translates the Hebrew קָדִימָה (*qādîmâ*), which occurs twenty times in Ezekiel with the meaning "east" or "eastward" (e.g., Eze 11:1; 40:6; 45:7; 48:10). The "east wind" or "desert wind" is normally represented by רוּחַ קָדִים (*rûaḥ qādîm*) or simply *qādîm*, without the suffix ה (-*â*). However, *qādîm* and *qādîmâ* are used interchangeably in Ezekiel with the meanings "east" and "eastward" (e.g., 40:6, 10; 47:1, 18; 48:8). It is therefore not impossible that they also share the meaning "east wind," possessed by *qādîm* in Genesis 41:6, 23, 27; Job 15:2; 27:21; 38:24; Psalm 78:26; Isaiah 27:8; and Hosea 12:1[2] (cf. Eze 17:10; 19:12; 27:26).

This interpretation is supported by the readings in 1QpHab, the Targums, Symmachus, Theodotion, the Vulgate, and the Palestinian Recension of the LXX. It also has some claim to grammatical validity in that the directive *â* may have a separative sense, i.e., "from the east" (cf. R. J. Williams, *Hebrew Syntax: An Outline* [Toronto: Univ. of Toronto Press, 1967], 16).

III. HABAKKUK'S SECOND COMPLAINT (1:12–2:1)

OVERVIEW

This section has characteristics of a second complaint, though it moves in the direction of lament, having many points of contact with 1:2–4. These include the invocation of the Lord's name (vv.2, 12); the urgent questions addressed to him (vv.13, 17); the description of the wicked's oppressing of the righteous (vv.13–17); and the issue of unrequited injustice that this raises, expressed in vocabulary echoing that of vv.2–4 (e.g., "righteous," "wicked," "tolerate," "look," "wrong"; v.13). The note of confidence expressed in v.12 is also typical of most laments—an attitude implicit in vv.2–4 in the prophet's perseverance and insistence that his answers come from the Lord. As in many of the Psalms, the difficult issues of God's goodness are set in a context not of philosophical speculation or cynical debate but of reverent worship and communion.

This section (1:12 – 2:1) is structured on an A-B-A pattern: (A) a statement of faith in the Lord's covenantal justice (v. 12); (B) an extended question on the existence of injustice (vv. 13 – 17); and (A) a concluding statement of faith (2:1), in expectation of the Lord's answer to this dilemma. The dilemma is a classical biblical one. In section A the Lord's universal justice is affirmed as the source of this specific exercise of judgment; in contrast, section B questions that justice because of God's use of the wicked Babylonians. The corresponding section A calls for the answer — a further divine revelation to give faith its proper response to the apparent moral contradiction. The entire passage represents the prophet's response to a divine revelation of the future (cf. vv. 5 – 6); and it follows that his response has the same futuristic orientation. The justice of God will be seen in a further revelation of what he will do beyond the present circumstances.

^{12}O LORD, are you not from everlasting?
My God, my Holy One, we will not die.
O LORD, you have appointed them to execute judgment;
O Rock, you have ordained them to punish.
^{13}Your eyes are too pure to look on evil;
you cannot tolerate wrong.
Why then do you tolerate the treacherous?
Why are you silent while the wicked
swallow up those more righteous than themselves?
^{14}You have made men like fish in the sea,
like sea creatures that have no ruler.
^{15}The wicked foe pulls all of them up with hooks,
he catches them in his net,
he gathers them up in his dragnet;
and so he rejoices and is glad.
^{16}Therefore he sacrifices to his net
and burns incense to his dragnet,
for by his net he lives in luxury
and enjoys the choicest food.
^{17}Is he to keep on emptying his net,
destroying nations without mercy?

$^{2:1}$I will stand at my watch
and station myself on the ramparts;
I will look to see what he will say to me,
and what answer I am to give to this complaint.

COMMENTARY

12 This verse offers a typical example of the intricate parallelism in Habakkuk. Line one is paralleled by line two; similarly, line four parallels line three; and finally, lines three and four parallel lines one and two, a parallelism both preserved and heightened in the NIV.

The first line is addressed to the "LORD" by his covenantal name (Ex 6:2–8), with reference to his involvement in covenantal history. Although the word "everlasting" (*qedem*; GK 7710) may refer to eternity (e.g., Dt 33:27; Ps 55:19), it more often denotes an unspecified point in past history (Isa 46:10; cf. Isa 37:26; La 2:17); and it is applied repeatedly to God's former preservation of Israel, supremely in the nation's deliverance from Egypt and settlement in the land (Pss 44:1; 77:5, 11; et al.). When used with the preposition "from" (*min*), as here, this word normally carries these historical connotations (cf. NRSV, "from of old"). Such a recollection of Yahweh's role in covenantal history is borne out by the remainder of the verse and by the prophecy as a whole (e.g., 1:6–8; 3:2).

The second line reiterates and personalizes the content of the first. The address to God is repeated in covenantal terms, evidenced by the adjective "my" (cf. Ps 71:22). The holiness of God is associated with his transcendent sovereignty and power, manifested in the past redemption of his people (3:3–15; cf. Ps 71:22–23; *TWOT*, 2:788); and Habakkuk's confidence of survival ("we will not die") reflects his knowledge of God's future commitment to his people in salvation history (Hab 3:13, cf. Lev 26:44–45; Dt 4:29–31).

The third and fourth lines are similarly parallel. The name "Rock" evokes the strength and reliability of the "LORD" as Israel's God (*TWOT*, 2:762), and the concepts of "judgment" and "punishment" are correlated repeatedly (cf. Isa 11:3–4

for the same roots). The verb "punish" (*yākaḥ*; GK 3519) has a varied usage, with the underlying judicial meaning of "establishing what is just or right." Frequently it signifies correction, verbal or otherwise, of an offender (e.g., Lev 19:17; Job 5:17; Ps 6:1).

In these contexts "punish" generally implies a chastening that is redemptive rather than destructive (cf. NLT, "to correct us, to punish us"); and the same overtones are appropriate to the present clause, with its address of confidence to Israel's "Rock." The same nuance is therefore inherent in the parallel noun "judgment" (*mišpāṭ*), previously translated "justice" (1:4[2x]) and "law" (1:7); in keeping with its broad definition in v.4, it here implies the restoration of rule and authority through removal of the causes of disorder. As intimated already in vv.7–8, the Israelites' rejection of God's authority mediated through the law has merely exposed them to the harsher experience of his authority mediated through an alien people. We may determine by our conduct how we will encounter God's sovereignty, but we cannot escape it!

13 The verbs "look on" (*rāʾâ*) and "tolerate" (*hibbîṭ*) are repeated from vv.3 and 5 (where *habbîṭ* is translated "watch"), marking a further development in this dialogue on justice. To "look" at a matter can imply that it is viewed with acceptance (cf. Pss 66:18; 138:6). That the Lord, unlike most ancient Near Eastern gods, refuses to countenance "evil" (*rāʿ*) and "wrong" (*ʿāmāl*; cf. v.3) is a basic tenet of Israel's faith (e.g.; Pss 5:4; 34:16, 21).

As in v.3, the violent discrepancy between this premise and the prophet's perception of reality provokes the question "why?"—a question founded, nevertheless, on the obedient faith expressed in v.12. The evil apparently tolerated is that of the "treacherous" (*bōgedîm*; GK 953), namely, those who are unreliable and break faith in relationship (cf. Jer 3:8, 11; Hos 5:7); the term is applied again to the Babylonians in Isaiah 21:2 (cf. Isa 39). The Lord's tolerance is implied because he has been "silent" or uninvolved (cf. Ps 50:21; Isa 42:14); the treachery is typically that of the wicked, who "swallow up" (cf. Ex 7:12; Pss 35:25; 124:3; La 2:16) the righteous as a wolf devours its prey.

The identity of the "wicked" has been disputed. Evidently they correspond to the fisherman in vv.15−17. The NIV's transition between vv.12−13 and vv.15−17 from a plural to a singular third-person subject is not present in the MT, where singular third-person forms predominate throughout. These verses are also linked by a continuity of theme, the image of devouring food pervading the passage. In turn, vv.12−17 show extensive continuity with vv.5−11. The image of fishing corresponds to that of hunting (v.8; cf. Jer 16:16). The express purpose is to consume the prey (vv.8, 16; the root *ʼkl* ["eat"] occurs in each verse). This is motivated by a boundless greed, gratified without principle and pursued by means of a far-flung, international aggression (vv.6−10, 13−17; the root *ʼsp* ["gather"] occurs in vv.9, 15, and the noun *gôyîm* ["nations"] in vv.5, 17). This greed entails the overthrow of all opposing human authority (vv.10, 14) and the deification of the aggressor's own power (vv.7, 11, 16). Both passages attribute this tyrannical imperialism to God's initiative in judgment (vv.5−6, 12, 14), yet without condoning it (vv.11, 13).

In view of these detailed correlations, it may be concluded that the "wicked" in v.13 correspond to the Babylonians in v.6. They are thus distinct from the "wicked" in v.4, just as the "violence" and perverted justice in vv.7 and 9 differ from that in vv.2−4; and they represent a further dramatic embodiment of the *lex talionis*, the "wicked" being judged through the "wicked" (cf. Eze 7:23−24).

As the "wicked" in v.13 correspond to the fisherman in vv.15−17, so the "righteous" correspond to the "nations," likened to fish (vv.14−17), as their respective prey. The designation therefore includes Judah, whose sin has caused her to be numbered among the nations of vv.14−17 in judgment (cf. Lev 26:33, 38; Dt 28:64−65; Jer 9:16; Eze 4:13, in all of which Israel is "scattered among" the nations, while ultimately being kept separate). Habakkuk's concern is, of course, his own people, both as the perpetrators and victims of injustice; and the dramatic exchange of vv.5−17 serves primarily to set his initial local concern in an international context of God's unfolding patterns of justice. For the prophet this only heightens the dilemma.

14 As in v.13, the presence of calamity and evil in the world is related without hesitation to God's sovereign control of human destiny (cf. Isa 45:7; La 3:37−38; Am 3:6; Ro 9−11). The comparison to "fish" implies a condition that is subhuman and vulnerable (cf. Ge 1:26, 28; 9:2; Ps 8:8; Ecc 9:12). The "sea creatures" (*remeś*, "creeping things") in the second line are seen as equally helpless, lacking the organization or leadership normally expected in human society. "Moving creature" (*rmś*; GK 8254), as either noun or verb, appears often with a qualifier, "on the earth" (e.g., Ge 1:26); Genesis 1:21 extends its usage to include "water swarmers." Parallelism has led to the NIV's preference for "sea creatures."

15 The NIV's rendering "the wicked foe" is not present in the MT, but it signals the continuity of vv.15−17 with the "wicked" in v.13. The "hook" (*ḥakkâ*) and line was an ancient, widely used device for fishing (cf. Isa 19:8; Mt 17:27). The "net" (*ḥērem*; GK 3052) was used for hunting and fishing and so had a diversity of application. It recurs figuratively as a symbol of aggression (Ecc 7:26; Mic 7:2) and divine judgment (Ecc 7:26; Eze 32:3), as here. The "dragnet" (*mikmeret*) is mentioned again as a fishing implement in Isaiah 19:8. The precise identification of these nets is not certain, owing to their infrequent occurrence and their varied, overlapping functions. However, they appear to correspond to the two main types of net, the throw net and the seine, used in NT times and still today in Palestine (cf. also *ISBE*, 3:523–24; *ANEP*, 33–34).

The verbs "rejoice" (*śāmaḥ*; GK 8523) and "be glad" (*gîl*; GK 1635) are used with great frequency in religious contexts of worship and praise (cf. 3:18), and almost uniformly so when they are parallel, as here (cf. 1Ch 16:31; Pss 14:7; 16:9; Joel 2:21, 23; Zec 10:7). They thus indicate not merely pleasure or merriment but a response affirming what is valued and honored. As in v.11, the Babylonians are here exposed as exalting the images of their own power and dominance; their system of values is utterly self-promoting.

16 The undertones of worship in v.15 become explicit in v.16, the two verses being linked also by the repeated adverb "therefore" (*ʿal-kēn*; cf. KJV, NRSV). The verb "sacrifice" (*zābaḥ*; GK 2284) denotes the slaughter of living creatures, usually in a context of worship and service offered to deity. The form of the verb occurring here normally has connotations of false, idolatrous worship (i.e., *zibbēaḥ*; e.g., 2Ch 28:4; 33:22; Ps 106:38; Hos 4:13–14; 11:2). To "burn incense" (*qāṭar*; GK 7787) has the broad meaning of "burning, causing a sacrifice to smoke." The verb is used with various animal sacrifices (e.g., Ex 29:13, 18, 25; Lev 1:9, 13, 15, 17) and specifically with incense as its direct object (e.g., Ex 30:7; Nu 16:40). More frequently it is used without an object, as here. Like the preceding verb, *qāṭar* occurs here in a form usually applied to illegitimate worship (i.e., *qiṭṭēr*; e.g., 2Ki 17:11; 23:8; Isa 65:7; Jer 19:13; 32:29; 44:21). Together the two verbs always have these connotations (cf. 1Ki 22:43[44]; 2Ki 12:3[4]; 14:4; 15:4, 35; 16:4; 2Ch 28:4). The prophet is complaining that

the Babylonians are clearly guilty of attributing to their own power the honor and strength due to God alone (cf. v.11).

The "hook" present in v.15 here recedes from view. The Babylonians' full-blown delusion of greatness is depicted better by the swift violence of the "net" and the unyielding, wholesale spoliation of the dragnet (cf. vv.8–11). The second reference in v.16 to "his net" translates the pronoun "them," referring to both nets mentioned in the verse. The vast catch they have procured has the one purpose of providing "food" for the Babylonian lifestyle. The adjectives underlying "luxury" (*šāmēn*) and "choicest" (*beriʾâ*) both have the meaning of "fat," suggesting prosperity (well rendered in the NIV). The root *šmn* (GK 9045) is associated elsewhere with the prosperity of the wicked, whose well-being makes them immune to any feeling of dependency or accountability (Dt 32:15; Ne 9:25 [rendered "fertile"]; Jer 5:28; cf. Dt 8:10–17; Mt 19:23–24). The same associations are present here, where the metaphorical language barely veils the fact that the food consumed by the Babylonians consists of nations and individual lives (cf. v.13).

17 This verse reverts to the question posed in v.13: Can injustice, now defined more vividly by the intervening verses, be tolerated indefinitely by a God of justice? The phrase "empty his net" is virtually identical with "draw his sword" (cf. Notes). Possibly a double entendre is intended here, since the sword symbolizes the military power of which the net has been the image in vv.15–16, and since this anticipates the transition from metaphor to literal counterpart, completed in the following clause. This transition reverses and balances that in v.14, bringing the extended metaphor back to the ugly reality it portrays.

A further double entendre is implicit in the phrase "without mercy." The verb underlying this translation (*ḥāmal*) has the basic meaning of sparing, removing from a situation (cf. *TWOT*, 1:296). It is used of holding back or refraining from an action, and commonly of pity as the attitude that causes one to hold back or remove from harm. Both ideas are appropriate here. As in vv.6–7, the Babylonians' unrestrained self-will has produced in them a hard insensitivity, making them a pitiless threat to other nations (cf. Dt 28:50; Jer 6:23).

2:1 The noun "watch" (*mišmeret*; GK 5466) has a varied meaning, denoting either the duty or act of watching, or a place of observation where such a responsibility is fulfilled. The vocabulary of the verse corresponds closely to Isaiah 21:8, where the roots *šmr* (watch/watchtower), *ʿmd* (stand, stay), *yṣb/nṣb* (station oneself), and *ṣph* (look/watchtower) occur. Habakkuk's "watch" is evidently portrayed as being on the city walls, as indicated by the parallel notice "ramparts" (*māṣôr*).

We do not know Habakkuk's home, but Mizpah represents a typical fortified city of this preexilic period. Yadin describes it as having had a solid wall six hundred yards long, four yards thick on average, and perhaps twelve yards high, thus posing a considerable obstacle to both battering rams and attackers scaling it (cf. Hab 1:10). It was built of stone with salients and recesses, being buttressed at its weak points with a total of ten towers; and it would have been crowned by a balcony with a crenelated parapet. The gate was also guarded by two towers, being carefully designed and fortified in keeping with its strategic function (Yadin, 18–23, 323–24, 378–79, 391, 398; cf. 1Ki 15:22; 2Ch 26:15).

It is therefore at some point on such defenses as these that Habakkuk sees himself on duty (cf. Ne 11:19; 13:19–22; Ps 127:1; Isa 62:6). This setting is corroborated by the following verb, "look" (*ṣāpâ*; GK 7595), used literally of keeping watch for some event. It is applied particularly to sentries

or watchmen on city walls (2Sa 18:24–27; 2Ki 9:17–18, 20), who were to warn the citizens of danger or other happenings outside (Isa 21:6; 52:8; Eze 33:2–6). The verb is applied figuratively to the prophets, who as Israel's watchmen are to see the Lord's purposes and communicate them to their people (Hos 9:8; cf. Isa 56:10–11; Jer 6:17; Eze 3:17; Mic 7:4, 7)—a fitting title for those called to be seers and visionaries.

Such figurative usage undergirds the imagery of this verse, where Habakkuk the prophet (1:1; 3:1) looks to God for revelation concerning the nations (cf. 2:2–3). His "ramparts" and "watch" are the place of responsibility assigned to him, to stand in the council of the Lord and to see his word (cf. Nu 12:6–8; 1Ki 22:14–23; Jer 23:18, 22; Am 3:7)—a role discharged in attentive, reverent prayer by the same conscientious watchfulness and persistence demanded of the literal watchman.

The final line has spawned a variety of translations with varied nuances of meaning. The literal reading might be something like, "and how I shall respond concerning my complaint," but many commentators (e.g., Roberts) and several modern translations (NLT, NRSV) prefer to see Yahweh as the subject in both lines three and four—i.e., "what he will answer...," a reading with little support in the versions (only Syriac). The traditional reading, followed by the NIV, is more difficult but can make sense.

The noun "complaint" (*tôkaḥat*; GK 9350; cf. *yākaḥ* ["punish"], 1:12) denotes an argument by which one seeks to establish what is right (Job 13:6; 23:4) and a rebuke or correction by which right is restored (e.g., Ps 39:11; Pr 1:23, 25, 30; 3:11; Eze 5:15). It occurs here with the possessive suffix "my" (cf. NRSV), indicating either the agent of the noun, meaning "the argument that I have offered" (so Job 13:6), or its object, meaning the correction that I receive (so Ps 73:14).

Both interpretations are apposite here, since Habakkuk is expecting a reply to his argument concerning God's justice (1:12–17), and since that argument has been precipitated by the announcement of a judgment that will overtake him with his nation (1:5–17). The second option—a rebuke or correction by which right is restored—is preferable, since it balances the use of the same verbal root (*ykh*; GK 3519) in v.12, so completing the concentric structure of 1:12–2:1: judgment (1:12), injustice (1:13), developed image of injustice (1:14–17), response to judgment (2:1; cf. introduction to 1:12–2:1).

Underlying both interpretations is Habakkuk's need to know how to respond to God's ways, both in his assessment of injustice and in his conduct amid the consequences of injustice. He reveals a mature wisdom in his determination that this response be shaped by what God himself would say. It is a wise man who takes his questions *about* God *to* God for the answers.

NOTES

12 The reading "we will not die" represents one of eighteen alleged scribal emendations, the *tiqqûnê sôperîm* (cf. E. Würthwein, *The Text of the Old Testament* [Oxford: Basil Blackwell, 1957], 14–15), the original reading supposedly being "you will not die." The intent of these emendations was to guard the divine name and character from unworthy associations—in this case, from the mention of death. The origin and value of these alterations is, however, doubtful; and since the MT is supported here by the LXX and Symmachus and implicitly by 1QpHab, there are no good grounds for abandoning its reading.

17 Several textual variants occur in this verse. The question, indicated by a single consonant הַ (*h*) is lacking in 1QpHab, the LXX, and the Syriac; but it is supported by the Talmud and the Palestinian Recension of the LXX. Since both readings are explicable and make sense, the MT's may be retained, particularly as the question it attests balances that in 1:13 and provides a suitable basis for 2:1.

חֶרְמוֹ (*hermô*, "his net") is supported by the LXX; 1QpHab and the Palestinian Recension read חַרְבּוֹ (*harbô*, "his sword"). The differences result from confusing מ (*m*) and ב (*b*). Both words are appropriate to their immediate context, since both imply the slaughter of nations, and since חֶרֶב (*hereb*, "sword") recurs repeatedly with the present verb רִיק (*rîq*, "to empty"; cf. Ex 15:9; Lev 26:33; Eze 5:2, 12; 12:14; 28:7; 30:11). The MT is preferable here, since it offers the more unusual reading while being more appropriate to its context; the transition from the imagery of fishing to that of the victimized nations in v.17 corresponds to that in v.14 and is consistent with the metaphor developed in vv.15–16.

"Keep on" translates the force of both the imperfect tense of יָרִיק (*yārîq*, "he empties") and the noun וְתָמִיד (*wᵉtāmîd*, "and continually"). The conjunction וְ (*wᵉ*, "and") is omitted by 1QpHab, the Talmud, and the Syriac but is retained in the LXX and Vulgate. Either reading may be derived from the other, and both make sense. The MT is to be retained as the more difficult reading, since it appears to associate *wᵉtāmîd* with the following clause (cf. the MT's accentuation), thus disturbing the obvious balance between them. The NIV in fact relates *wᵉtāmîd* to the preceding clause, but the syntax of the MT is preferable here. It serves to coordinate more closely the two clauses, both as questions and as continuous actions; and it heightens the emphasis on the first question, ending at חֶרְמוֹ (*hermô*, "his net").

IV. GOD'S SECOND RESPONSE (2:2–20)

OVERVIEW

Verses 2–20 have often been regarded as containing a number of disjointed passages, a judgment applied particularly to vv.2–6. However, there is much in the form and content of these verses to show that they constitute a unity, and they are treated as such here. Verses 2–3 form a prologue, establishing the context as a "revelation" (or "vision") concerning the Babylonian oppressor; vv.4–5 likewise refer to the Babylonians and form a summary of the preceding indictments (1:5–17); while vv.6–20 amplify those indictments, embodying them in an emphatic sentence of judgment on the tyrant. It is evident, then, that the content of the "revelation" of v.2 is given in vv.4–20—a conclusion supported by the clear break at 3:1 and by the length of this unified passage, which makes it suitable for preservation on a number of "tablets." In their form, vv.2–20 are cast as a judicial procedure ("Woe" oracles), the alternation between accusation and announcement of judgment being most apparent in vv.6–20 (cf. Isa 5:1–30; Mic 2:1–5).

A. Prologue (2:2–3)

²Then the LORD replied:

"Write down the revelation
  and make it plain on tablets
  so that a herald may run with it.
³For the revelation awaits an appointed time;
  it speaks of the end
  and will not prove false.
Though it linger, wait for it;
  it will certainly come and will not delay.

COMMENTARY

2 The noun "revelation" (*ḥāzôn*; GK 2606) denotes vision that is almost invariably supersensory in nature, as do the cognate words derived from the same root (*ḥzh*; cf. NRSV, *TWOT*, 1:274–75), and it is attributed especially to the prophets (e.g., 1Ch 17:15; 2Ch 32:32; Isa 1:1; Eze 7:26; Ob 1; Na 1:1). The cognate verb (*ḥāzâ*) is used to introduce Habakkuk's prophecy (i.e., "received," 1:1); in echoing 1:1, the present verse therefore serves to announce the central content of what he "receives," or sees, as the outcome of his disciplined watchfulness (2:1).

The "revelation" is to be written down to preserve it for the future (cf. Ex 17:14; Ps 102:18; Jer 30:2; 36:2), a motif explained in v.3. "Make plain" (*bā'ēr*; GK 930) may refer to clarity either in form—e.g., by engraving the words (Dt 27:8)—or in content (Dt 1:5). The reference to the writing material and consequent similarity to Deuteronomy 27:1–8 slightly favors the former. Like the Lord's revelation to Moses, this prophecy has a lasting relevance and must be guarded accordingly. The "tablets" may have been composed of stone, clay, or even metal (cf. *ABD*, 6:1001–4); for "tablets" the more perishable materials (parchment, papyrus) would not be expected. A similar means for preserving prophetic revelation occurs in Isaiah 30:8.

The purpose of this procedure is given in the final clause. "Herald" (*qôrē'*) is literally "the one who proclaims," including the sense of one "reading" a proclamation, as reflected in the KJV, RSV, and NRSV. Such reading might plausibly be done by a herald, whose role would then be to "run" with the message (cf. 1Sa 4:12; 2Sa 18:19–27; Est 3:13, 15; 8:10, 14; Jer 51:31). Alternatively, the idiom "run with" may refer specially to prophetic activity (Jer 23:21). The context is concerned in any case with preservation of the revelation as a source of encouragement, or warning, for the future (cf. v.3), rather than with its geographical proclamation.

3 The reasons underlying the directive of v.2 are made clear in v.3. Because the revelation "awaits" a future fulfillment, at "the end," and its impact extends beyond the present, it must therefore be transmitted and preserved in a permanent form. A further amplification of the important role of the "vision" has come through the discovery that what has been construed as a verb, "it speaks" (*wᵉyāpēaḥ*) or "hastens" (RSV), is analogous to a Ugaritic noun (*yph*) meaning "testifier" (*NIDOTTE*, 2:496–97). With the further possible emendation of "awaits" (Heb. adverb *ʿôd*, "yet") to "witness" (Heb. *ʿēd*), in parallel with "testifier," we arrive at "for the witness of the vision is for an appointed time; it/he is a tes-

tifier to the end, which will not prove false/he will not lie" (cf. Andersen, 198ff.; Roberts, 105ff.).

As in 1:2–4, the "vision" may confound human timing or any expected denouement, as indeed often the Lord's timetable and agenda differ from that of humans (cf. 1Sa 13:8–15; Isa 55:8–9; Jn 11:5–21; 2Pe 3:1–10). However, what may appear slow is nonetheless sure, all based on the certainty of the divine "vision." Biblical "hope" is not wishful thinking, but instead a perspective based on revelation (Ro 4:18).

"The end" (*qēṣ*; GK 7891) referred to is definite in Hebrew, but it is not clearly specified; its usage implies the termination of a certain object, activity, or period of time (cf. La 4:18; Eze 7:2–3; 21:25, 29). The immediate context of the "revelation" is the end of the Babylonian oppression (vv.4–20; cf. Jer 51:13), for which the prophet must "wait" (cf. 3:16). The noun "end" recurs frequently in Daniel (Da 8:17, 19; 9:26; 11:6, 13, 27, 35, 40, 45; 12:4, 6, 9, 13), closely associated with the term "appointed time" (*môʿēd*; Da 8:19; 11:27, 29, 35; 12:7], as here. In Daniel, however, the time of the end refers to the eschatological termination of Israel's oppression by wickedness (i.e., chs. 7–12).

Second, the purpose of v.2—that the reader, or "herald" (NIV) may "run"—is based on the certainty of the "revelation." There is an "appointed time" for its fulfillment as determined by Yahweh and revealed in Habakkuk's vision; it will not "prove false" or disappoint (cf. Isa 58:11) but "will certainly come." In consequence of this assurance, the herald may run with confidence and perseverance the race marked out for him (cf. 1Co 15:58; Heb 11:1; 12:1). The eschatological vision is further personalized by the LXX, which reads "(the) coming one will come" (*erchomenos hēxei*), in place of the MT's "he/it will certainly come" (cf. Mal 3:1; Mt 11:3; Heb 10:37). The logical outcome of this "revelation" is that one should "wait" (cf.

Pss 33:20; 106:13; Isa 8:17; 30:18; 64:4; Da 12:12; Zep 3:8).

Verses 2–3 thus provide a suggestive and compressed view of salvation history. Its future development is perfectly determined by God, who allows human beings to glimpse this future as a basis for faith and hope (cf. Ro 8:18–25; 1Co 15:51–58).

However, humans never see the entire pattern of salvation, so that events may seem delayed and disappointing. For this reason believers must lay hold of the future that God has revealed, waiting for it with eager faith and hope that surpass the apparent obstacles to its realization (3:17–19; cf. Ro 4:16–23; Heb 6:11–12, 18–19; 10:32–11:1; 12:1–29).

B. Indictment (2:4–5)

> 4 "See, he is puffed up;
>   his desires are not upright—
>   but the righteous will live by his faith—
> 5 indeed, wine betrays him;
>   he is arrogant and never at rest.
> Because he is as greedy as the grave
>   and like death is never satisfied,
> he gathers to himself all the nations
>   and takes captive all the peoples.

**COMMENTARY

4 The verb "puffed up" (ʿāpal; GK 6752) carries the basic meaning of "swelling." The same root occurs in Numbers 14:44, where the idea of arrogance and presumption is again evident. "His desires" translates napšô (nepeš, "soul, life"; GK 5883; cf. KJV, RSV), whose meaning includes also the idea of desire or appetite (e.g., Ge 23:8, "willing"; cf. TWOT, 2:587–91). The suffix "his" evidently refers to the Babylonians in continuity with 1:2–2:1; the present verse introduces the Lord's answer to Habakkuk's lament concerning the devouring Babylonians. The verb "to be upright" (yāšar) denotes what is literally straight (e.g., 1Sa 6:12; cf. Eze 1:7) or figuratively level (e.g., Pss 32:11; 33:1).

As in 1:4, the "righteous" (there haṣṣaddîq) may be defined by their commitment to the demands of tôrâ ("law"); as in 1:13 (also ṣaddîq), though in its application to pagan nations, the context of "law" is broader than the specific commandments given to the Hebrews. The noun "faith" (ʾemûnâ; GK 575) implies fairness, stability, certainty, and permanence, as do its numerous cognate terms (e.g., Ex 17:12, "steady"; Isa 33:6, "sure foundation"; cf. TWOT, 1:51–53). Hence it is commonly used of fairness applied to personal character and conduct, which is evidenced especially as reliability; thus in Deuteronomy 32:4 God's reliability ("faithfulness") is parallel to his name "Rock," with its connotations of stability and security as a basis for reliance (cf. Hab 1:12).

The nature of this reliability is defined by the context. In the present one, this quality of reliability and stability is predicated of the "righteous," the only plausible antecedent of "his." ("Their faith" in modern, gender-inclusive versions does not alter the sense.) It signifies that "his" commitment to righteousness is genuine and steadfast, the concepts of "faith" and righteousness often being coordinated in this way (e.g., 1Sa 26:23; Pss 33:4-5; 40:10; 96:13; 119:75, 138; 143:1). The clause thus expresses the Lord's demand for a righteousness that is pursued steadfastly from the heart, without vacillation, double-mindedness, or hypocrisy—its outcome being life (cf. Dt 6:1-25; 8:1-20; Eze 18:1-32; 33:12-20; Heb 6:9-12; Rev 2:10; 14:12). Such a meaning is conveyed more precisely by the noun "faithfulness," as the NIV normally translates ʾemûnâ (e.g., Dt 32:4; 1Sa 26:23; Ps 33:4; Hab 2:4 note; cf. Gordon Wenham, "Faith in the Old Testament," *Theological Students' Fellowship Annual* [1975-76]: 11-17). The NIV's rendering here reflects that of the LXX (i.e., "faith,") and of Romans 1:17, Galatians 3:11, and Hebrews 10:38, which are quoted from this verse.

The discrepancy between "faith" and "faithfulness" is more apparent than real, however. For a person to be faithful in righteousness entails dependent trust in relation to God (e.g., 1Sa 26:23-24); such an attitude is clearly demanded in the present context of waiting for deliverance (2:3; 3:16-19). And "faith" (*pistis*; GK *4411*) implies obedient commitment no less than trust (e.g., Ro 1:5; 10:3, 16-17; 15:18-19; 16:26; Heb 3:18-19; cf. *TDNT*, 6:174ff.). This brief clause of three Hebrew words thus epitomizes the response of steadfast commitment demanded in vv.2-3; and it thereby answers Habakkuk's concern for the righteous in Judah, imperiled by the judgment intended for the wicked (cf. 1:13). Contrary to appearances, God's judgment is selective and awe-inspiring in its precision; in the midst of disaster, his

grace overshadows the righteous and causes them to "live" (Ps 91). Both Paul and a later rabbinic tradition found in this pregnant statement a summary of the OT way of salvation; they diverged radically, however, in their beliefs concerning the attainment of such a saving righteousness.

5 "Betrays" translates the same verb (*bôgēd*) as "treacherous" in 1:13. "Wine," like the Babylonians, is deceptive and unreliable; although drunk to enhance one's life, wine can also impoverish, confuse, and destroy (cf. Pr 20:1; 23:20-21, 29-35; Isa 28:7). The reference to "wine" is unexpected, and several modern translations, notably the NRSV, follow 1QpHab (cf. Notes) by reading "wealth is treacherous." However, "wine" is an appropriate subject in the present verse, being associated with arrogance, unfulfilled greed, and social injustice elsewhere in the OT (e.g., 1Sa 30:16; 1Ki 20:12, 16; Pr 31:4-7; Isa 5:11-12, 22-23; Am 6:6). Isaiah 5:8-30—with its six woes directed against human drunkenness, greed, rapacity, and pride—offers a close parallel to Habakkuk 2:4-20.

The object of this betrayal is implicit in v.5, the pronoun "him" being absent in the Hebrew. His identity is clarified by the references to arrogance (*yāhîr*; cf. Pr 21:24) and restless ambition, clearly referring to the Babylonians (cf. 1:6-11, 13), as do the following clauses of this verse. And, indeed, the Babylonian regime was to be overthrown in just the circumstances of drunken pride portrayed here (cf. Da 5:1-31), such drunkenness being attested among ancient historians as characteristic of the Babylonians.

Napšô (translated "he"; lit., "soul," GK 5883) is also translated "his desire, throat, appetite" (cf. v.4; NRSV, NLT, NEB; *TWOT*, 2:587-91). A "throat" opening wide, in place of the literal "soul," or the figurative "he is greedy," is drawn in part from parallelism with the succeeding line. The following figures develop the image further, describing the extent of this greed: it is insatiable (cf. Pr 27:20; 30:15–16; Isa 5:14), as demonstrated already in 1:5–17. "Grave" (šeʾôl, "Sheol") is perhaps better translated "underworld," "hell," or "netherworld" (NAB; cf. KJV, NRSV), a place depicted repeatedly as devouring its prey (Nu 16:30–34; Pr 1:12).

The concluding couplet of v.5 describes in figurative terms the expression of this insatiable greed: political conquest. The verb "gathers" is repeated from 1:9, 15. The dominant metaphor, however, relates to the treachery of an addiction to wine, which, like political and military ambition, is an addiction that knows no limit of fulfillment and to which all other interests are sacrificed.

Verses 4–5 thus recapitulate the preceding account of the Babylonians' character, in which pride, greed, and naked aggression prosper and overshadow the moral consequences of their conduct. In the following five woes (vv.6–19), however, those consequences break with fury on their unstable edifice, and it is overthrown. The repeated intimations of Babylonian guilt and arrogance (1:7, 11, 13, 17; 2:4–5) are more potent in their implications than the entire grandiose achievement by which they are incurred (cf. Ps 37:1–2, 7, 9–10, 35–36; Ecc 10:1). All this, of course, stands in sharp contrast to the "faith/faithfulness" by which the "righteous one shall live" (v.4).

NOTES

4 The etymology of עֻפְּלָה (ʿuppʿlâ, "puffed up") is not entirely certain. It is cognate with either the Arabic ʿaflun ("a tumor") or gāfala ("be heedless, neglectful"); some philologists derive both OT occurrences of the roots עפל (ʿpl) from the second alternative (cf. TWOT, 2:686–87). Both derivations are appropriate to the sinfulness exposed in vv.4–19. The versions differ widely from the MT in their reading of this verb. The LXX, Aquilla, the Palestinian Recension, and the Vulgate all refer to some form of timidity or unbelief and apparently read עלף (ʿlp), with the derived meaning "to faint" (cf. Isa 51:20; Am 8:13; Jnh 4:8); this reading is attested in two Hebrew MSS and is quoted from the LXX in Hebrews 10:38. The Targum and Syriac both refer to wickedness and would have read עַוָּל (ʿawwāl, "wicked") or עַוְלָה (ʿawlâ, "wickedness").

The MT remains the preferable reading here. The difficulty of its rare verbal form and the lack of clear parallelism with v.4b explain the variants, whose renderings are suggested by the interchange of a single root consonant. In addition, the MT is corroborated by the same reading in lQpHab, and it is well suited to the preceding and ensuing descriptions of the Babylonians. (For a more detailed treatment of the text of vv.4–5, see J. A. Emerton, "Textual and Linguistic Problems of Habakkuk 2:4–5," *JTS* 28 [1977]: 1–18.)

5 The reading הַיַּיִן (hayyayin, "wine") is represented by the MT, Targum, and Vulgate. 1QpHab reads הוֹן (hôn, "wealth"). The Syriac, LXX, and Old Latin all refer to some form of arrogance and may have read *hawwān* or הַיָּן (hayyān, "arrogant one"); the root *hwn* ("to be easy") is applied to the Israelites' presumption in Deuteronomy 1:41. The LXX text edited by Rahlfs reads κατοινωμένος (katoinōmenos, "drunk with wine"), but this corroboration of the MT is based on a conjectural emendation. The variants thus involve dittography or haplography of the consonant י (y), with confusion of י/ו (y/w).

Of these readings the MT presents the greatest difficulty, in its sudden switch to "wine" as the subject. The alternatives are best explained as easier, more "appropriate" readings, facilitated by their similarity to the consonantal form of the MT and suggested by the moral terminology in 2:4 and by the Babylonian rapacity described in 1:5–17; 2:6–14. The Masoretic reading is suitable to its context, however, since it accords with the imagery of 1:8, 14–17; 2:4–5 (cf. comments on 2:5); and it foreshadows the references to drunkenness in 2:15–16. Its reading may therefore be followed, particularly as it is well supported by the versions.

"At rest" translates the verb יִנְוֶה (yinweh), which has no precise parallel in the OT. It is commonly treated as a denominative verb derived from נָוֶה (nāweh, "an abode, habitation"; e.g., Ex 15:13; 2Sa 7:8; Job 5:3; Pr 21:20; Isa 27:10; 65:10; Jer 23:3). From this derivation it would acquire the meaning "to be at home," i.e., "be settled, at rest" (cf. BDB, 627)—a meaning followed by the NIV and appropriate to the Babylonians' character (cf. 1:6, 8–11, 17). It also appears to underlie the interpretation in 1QpHab that applies it to apostasy, as forsaking the fold of the Lord (cf. Jer 50:7). Alternatively, the verb may signify "to aim at, attain a goal," i.e., "to succeed," since the Arabic root cognate with *nwh* has this meaning (cf. *HALOT*, 601). This translation is supported by the LXX's περάνη (*peranē*, "he completes, effects his purpose") and possibly by the Targum. It is also suitable to the following woes introduced by v.5 and to the judgment implied in 1:11–12; 2:4. Underlying these two main options is the idea of instability and failure (cf. Dt 29:28; 1Ki 14:15; Ps 37:10–11, 28–29; Pr 2:21–22; 10:30; Isa 13:20; Jer 1:10; 12:15–17). This forms a suitable parallel to בּוֹגֵד (*bôgēd*, "betrays"), in keeping with the more developed parallelism of the following two couplets: for the Babylonian, his pursuit of conquest portends his exile as the victim of conquest.

C. Sentence (2:6–20)

⁶"Will not all of them taunt him with ridicule and scorn, saying,

"'Woe to him who piles up stolen goods
    and makes himself wealthy by extortion!
    How long must this go on?'
⁷Will not your debtors suddenly arise?
    Will they not wake up and make you tremble?
    Then you will become their victim.
⁸Because you have plundered many nations,
    the peoples who are left will plunder you.
For you have shed man's blood;
    you have destroyed lands and cities and everyone in them.
⁹"Woe to him who builds his realm by unjust gain
    to set his nest on high,
    to escape the clutches of ruin!
¹⁰You have plotted the ruin of many peoples,
    shaming your own house and forfeiting your life.
¹¹The stones of the wall will cry out,
    and the beams of the woodwork will echo it.

¹²"Woe to him who builds a city with bloodshed
and establishes a town by crime!
¹³Has not the LORD Almighty determined
that the people's labor is only fuel for the fire,
that the nations exhaust themselves for nothing?
¹⁴For the earth will be filled with the knowledge of the glory of the LORD,
as the waters cover the sea.

¹⁵"Woe to him who gives drink to his neighbors,
pouring it from the wineskin till they are drunk,
so that he can gaze on their naked bodies.
¹⁶You will be filled with shame instead of glory.
Now it is your turn! Drink and be exposed!
The cup from the LORD's right hand is coming around to you,
and disgrace will cover your glory.
¹⁷The violence you have done to Lebanon will overwhelm you,
and your destruction of animals will terrify you.
For you have shed man's blood;
you have destroyed lands and cities and everyone in them.

¹⁸"Of what value is an idol, since a man has carved it?
Or an image that teaches lies?
For he who makes it trusts in his own creation;
he makes idols that cannot speak.
¹⁹Woe to him who says to wood, 'Come to life!'
Or to lifeless stone, 'Wake up!'
Can it give guidance?
It is covered with gold and silver;
there is no breath in it.
²⁰But the LORD is in his holy temple;
let all the earth be silent before him."

OVERVIEW

The sentence of judgment implicit in 2:4–5 and 1:5–17 is stated with absolute finality in these verses, which form five sections structured around the accusatory cry "Woe." Their structure may be illustrated by the refrain linking 2:8, 17; by the pattern "woe"—retribution—"because/for" informing 2:6–17 (cf. KJV, RSV, NRSV); and in the symmetrical juxtaposition of crime and punishment that pervades each of the five "woes."

COMMENTARY

6a The opening line introduces the oracle of woe (vv.6–20), characterized by three technical terms: (1) a type of proverb, translated by the verb "taunt" (*māšāl*; GK 5442; cf. Nu 23:7; 1Ki 4:32; Pr 1:1; Eze 24:3; *TWOT*, 1:533–34); (2) an ambiguous, allusive saying that requires interpretation and is translated "ridicule" (*mᵉlîṣâ*; GK 4886; cf. Pr 1:6; *TWOT* 1:479); and (3) similarly, a riddle or enigmatic saying, translated "scorn" (*ḥîdôt*; GK 2648; cf. Nu 12:8; Jdg 14:12–18; 1Ki 10:1; *TWOT*, 1:267). The first two terms have certain limited associations with mockery, but none are attested for the third. Moreover, all three terms occur together in Proverbs 1:6 without these overtones, as do *māšāl* and *ḥîdâ* elsewhere (Pss 49:4[5]; 78:2; Eze 17:2).

The dominant function in these and other usages of the noun is not to ridicule but to teach, as here v.6a introduces an oration exposing the Babylonians as an object lesson (*māšāl*) by means of compressed and allusive speech (*mᵉlîṣâ ḥîdôt*). Inasmuch as both the Assyrians and the Babylonians utilized the didactic function of wisdom sayings, there is a certain appropriateness in introducing these woes as wisdom, e.g., "Will not all of them raise over him a proverb, with mocking riddles ..." (cf. NRSV).

6b–8 Verses 6–8 represent an extended oracle or judgment, signaled by the opening declamation of "woe"—an interjection commonly used in prophetic literature to introduce a judicial indictment (Isa 5:8, 11, 18, 20–22; Jer 22:13; 23:1; Am 5:18; 6:1). Although it would be futile to try to identify each oracle with a specific incident, the charges are unambiguous: first, unjust acquisition of wealth, achieved by "extortion" (v.6b) and plunder (v.8), and second, more seriously, the wholesale destruction of a society and its environment in the pursuit of this wealth (v.8). The noun "extortion" (*ʿabṭîṭ*; GK 6294) denotes the accumulation of pledges

taken as security by a creditor (cf. Dt 24:10–13; cf. also *IDB*, 1:809–10; *ZPEB*, 1:79ff., 3:295; *ABD*, 2:114–15); such a procedure often accompanied the exploitation and even enslavement of the poor (cf. 2Ki 4:1–7; Ne 5:1–13).

The noun *ʿabṭîṭ* can also be read as a phrase, meaning literally "a cloud of dirt" (*ʿab ṭîṭ*; cf. KJV). This use of double entendre has numerous parallels in vv.6–20 and signals the allusive quality of the oration introduced as a *mᵉlîṣâ* and as *ḥîdôt*. In this instance the double meaning evokes the defilement accompanying such a path to wealth. The judgments announced in response to these accusations correspond precisely to the crimes, according to the law of retaliation that pervades the book. The word "debtors" (*nōšᵉkîm*, v.7; also "creditors," NIV note) is a verbal form derived from a noun signifying monetary interest. These "creditors" are defined as "the peoples who are left" (v.8), that is, the survivors within the conquered nations; and the sentence announced here was indeed executed by former victims of Babylon, the Medes and Persians (cf. Jer 25:25; 49:34–39; Eze 32:24–25; Isa 13:17–22; 21:2–10; Jer 51:11, 28; Da 5:28). Verse 8 closes with a refrain, repeated in v.17, emphasizing the bloodshed and violence that has characterized Babylonian society.

9–11 Verses 9–10 are each structured in three parallel cola, introduced by "woe" (*hôy*). The first tricolon sets out what the Babylonians attempted: to build a house with unjust gain, to set a nest on high, and to escape the impending doom. Verse 10's three lines present the stark disaster that such actions have produced. The entire passage echoes the preceding charges of rapacity (cf. vv.6, 8) and bloodshed (cf. v.8); the participle and accompanying accusative "gain by (unjust) gain" (*bāṣaʿ / beṣaʿ*; v.9) is generally associated with rapacity and wrongdoing (cf. 1Sa 8:3; Pr 1:19; *TWOT*, 1:122–23), associations that are stressed by the adjective "unjust" (*rāʿ*, "evil"), while the verb translated as "plotted the ruin" (*qāṣâ*; v.10) implies the cutting off of life.

The present section amplifies these accusations by exposing the self-interested purposes underlying such violence, namely, establishment of the Babylonian "realm" (v.9, NIV) or dynastic house (*bayit*; cf. ASV and RSV, but curiously obscured in the NRSV's "your houses"; *TWOT*, 1:105–6), by elevating it to the invulnerable security depicted by an eagle's "nest" (*qēn*; Nu 24:21; Jer 49:16; Ob 4). However, this exercise of evil to escape "ruin" (*rāʿ*, "evil") is futile, for people reap what they sow (cf. Ecc 8:8). As in vv.6–8, the sentence of judgment balances the crime: shame for self-exaltation, loss of life for destruction of life, a divided and discordant house (v.11) for a secure house. And, indeed, despite all of its impregnable defenses, Babylon will fall in precisely such circumstances of division and deluded pride (see Da 5:1–30; *IDB*, 1:270–71, 335ff.; *ZPEB*, 1:440ff.; *BEB*, 1:248).

The two lines of v.11 are, in Hebrew, preceded by "for" (*kî*; cf. RSV) and perfectly parallel one another. The pathetic cries of the nonverbal creation at the horrors they must witness provides an antecedent for our Lord's allusion to "stones crying out" (Lk 19:40).

12–14 The third "woe" reiterates from vv.6–11 the indictment of ruthless self-aggrandizement achieved by "bloodshed" (v.12; cf. v.8), applying it to the construction of the Babylonian capital, as it had been applied previously to Jerusalem (Mic 3:10). The judgment pronounced on such an enterprise is inevitable: any civilization built up by the destruction of other civilizations or by the unjust conscription of labor for its own ends becomes subject to the divine principle of retribution (v.13; cf. Jer 22:13–14; 51:58).

The divine origin of the judgments on the Babylonians becomes explicit in v.13. The main-

spring of human history is to be found not in its events themselves but in the revealed purposes of the Lord, who directs it. The title "LORD Almighty" may be translated more literally "LORD of armies" (*yhwh ṣebāʾôt* [GK 7372]; cf. NRSV, NIV Preface, *TWOT*, 2:750–51). It expresses the Lord's sovereign rule as king and commander over every created force, but primarily over Israel. It is associated repeatedly, as here, with his militant judgment of all that opposes his rule.

This new emphasis on the Lord himself is developed further in v.14, revealing the underlying purpose on which the preceding indictments are based. God's abiding intent is that his "glory" should fill the whole earth, as it has filled his house (cf. Ex 40:34–35; Nu 14:21; 1Ki 8:11; Pss 57:5, 11; 72:19), and that humankind should know it fully—a "knowledge" (*daʿat*; cf. *TWOT*, 1:336–37) that will be as the "sea" in its length, breadth, and depth. This entails the removal of all that rejects such "knowledge," of which the Babylonian character and aspirations are the very epitome.

The phrase "glory of the LORD" (*kᵉbôd* [GK 3883] *yhwh*; cf. *IDB*, 2:401ff.; *TWOT*, 1:426ff.; *ZPEB*, 2:730–35) is used of the visible presence of God, by which the preeminent value of his character and actions are revealed to humankind. It is associated most prominently with the tabernacle and temple, and especially with the cherubim above which the Lord is enthroned in ruling over Israel (e.g., Ex 29:43; Eze 9:3; 10:4, 18–19), his sovereign majesty being of the essence of his "glory." To know the Lord in such "glory" is, therefore, to abandon the Babylonians' proud autonomy and to honor him as Lord in submission and obedience, worship and praise (e.g., Lev 9:23–24; 2Ch 7:3; Pss 72:19; 102:15; Isa 42:8; 59.19).

15–17 The fourth "woe" introduces a new accusation, expressed by the image of inducing drunkenness with its consequences of incapacitation, humiliation, and utter vulnerability. Although Babylon is seen as the one dispensing this cup to Israel (Jer 51:7), the cup of wrath is ultimately the Lord's to dispense—when, to whom, and through whom he will (Job 21:20; Ps 75:8; Isa 19:14; 29:9–10; Jer 25:15–25). As he does, those forced to drink, whether Israelites or others, fall prostrate—confused and utterly humiliated in their presumptuous claim to self-determination. Because the Babylonian motives in such judgment are entirely self-interested—and because they seek their own "glory" (*kābôd*, v.16; cf. v.14) through their malicious humiliation of their "neighbors," with no acknowledgment of God's sovereign determination—they will succumb to the same drunken humiliation that they have administered to others, a judgment now attributed explicitly to the Lord (v.16; cf. vv.13–14). In the divine order of things, the cup always comes around.

The preceding crime is defined more literally as "destruction" and "violence" wrought on "Lebanon" (v.17). Often associated with the territory of Israel (e.g., 1Ki 9:19; 2Ki 14:9; Isa 33:9; Na 1:4), Lebanon, or probably the mountainous area bordering Israel, was part of Israel's divine allotment (e.g., Dt 1:7–8; Jos 1:4). In an especially poignant image, Lebanon's cedars are a symbol of Israel's beauty (SS 4:8; 7:4; Isa 35:2), making it the more tragic when the cedar is "broken" or its habitat decimated, whether by the Babylonians or others (cf. Jer 22:6–7, 23; Eze 17:3). In keeping with these connotations, the Babylonians' "violence" (*ḥāmās*) and "destruction" (*šōd*) refer to their rape and despoliation of the region of Israel—an injustice requiting Israel's own "destruction and violence"

(cf. 1:3, 9). Even the animals are not spared in the scorched-earth policies pursued by these violent invaders, who remain oblivious to their own impending doom. The final accusation of v.17 repeats the refrain of v.8, surely appropriate here.

18–20 A break in the pattern of the preceding accusations marks this concluding section of vv.6–20, the expression "woe" being transposed to the second verse (v.19) and there being no announcement of a specific judgment. The dominant motif of v.18 is its denunciation of "idols" as artifacts made by humans, from the beginning a denial of reality. Little wonder that their only capacity is to "teach" (*yārâ*) lies. A common biblical polemic against idols follows. Despite a widespread human tendency to "trust" in what we can create ourselves, the stark truth is that the created object (wood, stone, metal) remains dumb, lifeless, and impotent. It can be "trusted" only to deceive the one who has created it.

This argument is stated in each couplet of v.18. It gains further emphasis by its development in the following "woe" (v.19), whose function as an accusation may be inferred from vv.6, 9, 12, and 15. The reason these artifacts of "wood" and "stone" are unable to "give guidance" (*yôreh*) is because they are without "breath." It is therefore reprehensible folly for humans to call on them (cf. 1Ki 18:22–29).

By contrast the Lord is in his holy "temple," or "palace" (*hêkāl*, v.20; cf. *TWOT*, 1:214–15), ruling and judging in sovereign power (cf. Pss 11:4; 29:9–10; Isa 6:1–4; 66:1; Mic 1:2). Such a God is utterly worthy of complete and reverent trust (Zep 1:7; Zec 2:13).

NOTES

15–17 חֲמָתְךָ (*ḥᵃmātᵉkā*), translated in the NIV as "the wineskin," has in the MT a second masculine singular suffix ("your"; cf. KJV, ASV, RSV margin), a difficult reading replaced by a third masculine singular pronominal form in 1QpHab, Symmachus, and the Vulgate but corroborated by Aquilla, Theodotion, and

Quinta. The LXX, Syriac, and Targum omit the suffix entirely, which may reflect their evasion of the MT's difficult reading or their omission of the consonant ו (*w*, "his") by haplography before the following word, וְאַף (*wᵉʾap*, "even till"). The MT presents a most unexpected reading, the variants being easily explained as accommodations to the prevalent third singular forms following other "woes" in 2:6, 9, 12, 19. Moreover, such second singular forms are common in vv.6–20; indeed, they predominate in vv.16–17, whose direct address can be anticipated intelligibly by this reading (the pronoun "he," absent in the Hebrew of v.15, is supplied by the NIV). In view of the additional evidence in favor of the MT among the Greek versions, its reading should be retained; such a break in a prevailing pattern is paralleled elsewhere in vv.6–20, particularly in the position of the final "woe" (cf. v.19).

Ḥᵉmātᵉkā, the noun involved in this variant, is derived by the NIV from the unusual noun חֵמֶת (*ḥemet*), construct form *ḥēmat* ("a waterskin"; cf. Ge 21:14–15, 19). This interpretation is followed also by the KJV and certain Jewish commentators. The noun may be derived more readily from חֵמָה (*ḥēmâ*), which means "heat, venom, wrath," all of which are appropriate here. "Heat" is associated with drunkenness in Hosea 7:5–6; "venom" is associated with wine in Deuteronomy 32:33, and its destructive effects correspond to those of the "drink" given by the Babylonians (cf. Pss 58:4[5]; 140:3). "Wrath" is represented repeatedly as being "poured out" (e.g., 2Ch 12:7; 34:21; Ps 79:6; Jer 7:20; 42:18; Eze 7:8; 9:8), and it is again related to the image of the "cup" in Isaiah 51:17, 22 and Jeremiah 25:15; and the following word (*wᵉʾap*) can be interpreted as a parallel noun in the accusative case meaning "and (with) anger." It appears certain that these associations of *ḥēmâ* are intended here (cf. ASV, RSV); in view of Habakkuk's use of wordplay, particularly in vv.6–20, an allusion to a "wineskin" may also be implied.

Other examples of allusive double entendre in vv.15–17 include the imperative הֵעָרֵל (*hēʿārēl*, "be exposed"), which evokes הֵרָעֵל (*hērāʿēl*, "stagger"; cf. NIV note); and קִיקָלוֹן (*qîqālôn*, "disgrace"), which echoes קָלוֹן (*qālôn*, "shame") and evokes the phrase קִיא קָלוֹן (*qîʾ qālôn*, "shameful vomit"; cf. KJV, ASV).

REFLECTION

Habakkuk's polemic against every form of idol (*pesel*) is typical of OT religion. The insidious futility of idols is contrasted repeatedly with the living God's faithfulness and power, the basis of his unique claim to trust and obedience (e.g., Ex 20:4; Lev 26:1). As elsewhere, their futility is exposed in ironic terms, as in the phrase "idols that cannot speak"; phonetically it evokes a nonsensical babble (*ʾᵉlîlîm ʾillᵉmîm*; cf. Isa 28:10, NIV note), while the noun "idols" (*ʾᵉlîlîm*) is regularly applied to what is worthless and good for nothing (cf. *TWOT*, 1:46).

Their insidiousness is suggested by their ability to usurp the place of God in people's lives, claim-ing a "trust" (*bāṭaḥ*) that belongs to him alone and offering "guidance" (*môreh*) that can come from him alone (e.g., Ex 24:12; Ps 25:8, 12; Isa 2:3; cf. also the cognate *tôrâ*, "law"). In view of the Lord's implacable opposition to all such usurpers, the mere reference to his presence in v.20 constitutes an intimation of judgment—a judgment duly executed on Babylon (e.g., Isa 21:9; Jer 50:2, 38; 51:17, 47, 52) and still operative against all forms of contemporary idolatry (e.g., Ro 1:21–25; 1Co 5:11; 6:9; 10:7, 14; Gal 5:20; Eph 5:5; Col 3:5; 1Jn 5:21; Rev 9:20–21; 21:8; 22:15).

V. THE PRAYER OF HABAKKUK (3:1–19)

OVERVIEW

In its form and language, ch. 3 is closely related to the Psalms. The term "*Selah*" (cf. vv. 3, 9, 13) occurs only in the Psalms, as does the musical subscript "On ... stringed instruments" (v. 19b), while the phrase "For the director of music" (v. 19b) is seldom found elsewhere; all three elements occur together in Psalms 4, 54, 55, 61, 67, and 76. Similarly, Habakkuk's recollection of Israel's past history (Hab 3:2, 3, 7, 8–15) is typical of the praises, instruction, and supplications in the Psalms (e.g., Pss 42, 44, 68, 74, 78, 80, 83, 89, 105–106, 135–136).

More specifically the passage resembles the psalms of lament. Its entitlement as a "prayer" related to "*shigionoth*" is found elsewhere in lament form (cf. *šiggāyôn*; Ps 7:1), as are the ensuing supplication for "mercy" in the midst of distress (Hab 3:2; cf. 1:2) and the subsequent statement of confidence and joy (3:18–19). It shows particular affinities with Psalm 18, an acknowledgment of deliverance in response to David's lament (Ps 18:3–6). Conspicuous points of contact include the dramatic theophany (Ps 18:7–15; cf. Hab 3:3–15), the deliverance from affliction (e.g., Ps 18:2–3, 17–18, 46–50; cf. Hab 3:8, 13–14), and the assertion of praise and confidence in God (e.g., Ps 18:1–33, 46–50; cf. Hab 3:18–19).

An even closer relationship is apparent between Habakkuk 3 and the lament in Psalm 77. The two prayers demonstrate the same pervasive orientation to the past (Ps 77:3–12; cf. Hab 3:2–15), specifically to the exodus from Egypt (Ps 77:11–20; cf. Hab 3:8–15). Numerous words and motifs are common to these passages, including the language and imagery of earthquake and lightning. In keeping with these associations, Habakkuk's "prayer"

extends the note of lament introduced in ch. 1, a lament that is now transformed by acknowledgment of the Lord's anticipated intervention (cf. Hab 2:1–20). In its final form it belongs in the setting of temple worship that characterizes the Psalms; but its origin is to be found in the inspiration of the individual "prophet," as with many of the Psalms. Beyond that, the original setting remains a matter of conjecture.

The remarkable power and enigmatic intensity of the "prayer" are due in part to the depth of allusion that informs it: its few, compressed verses draw on the entire spectrum of salvation history, from creation and exodus to the final revelation of God's rule and judgment still awaiting its fulfillment. This allusive quality is focused on certain primary passages, which form a background for the chapter and which, in turn, evoke the great "salvation history" events of Israel. First, as noted above, Habakkuk 3 is closely dependent on Psalm 77, which has particular affinities to Exodus 15 (cf. Ps 77:10–20); for instance, both passages, like Habakkuk 3, stress the redemptive power of God in a context of sea and water, using the common vocabulary of redemptive praise literature. It is the memory of God's past faithfulness and salvation as illuminated by his Spirit that provides a basis for faith in analogous circumstances.

Second, Habakkuk 3 draws on the language and imagery of Psalm 18, which evokes the exodus in similar terms (cf. Ps 18:4–19). Unlike Psalm 77, Psalm 18 explicitly recalls the exodus as God's mighty victory over the enemy, foreshadowing Israel's subsequent conquests; and Habakkuk echoes the recollection of this psalm (cf. Hab 3:8–11,

18–19). However, Psalm 18 fuses this revelation of God's power with a subsequent theophany, that at Sinai (Ps 18:7–14; cf. Ex 19:9–19; Dt 5:22–27). As at Sinai, God's revelation is characterized by clouds and darkness (Ps 18:8–9, 11–12); by fire, thunder, and lightning (Ps 18:8, 12–14); and by devastating earthquake (Ps 18:7), as harbingers of the Lord's presence (cf. "came down," *yārad*; Ps 18:9[10]; Ex 19:11, 18, 20). The background of Sinai may be similarly implicit in Psalm 77 (cf. esp. vv.3–7). The Lord's intervention both at the Red Sea and in later times is grounded in Sinaitic covenantal history, by which he revealed his sovereign majesty and committed himself to Israel as his treasured possession; and this, rather than mere memory, was the anchor of Habakkuk's hope.

Third, the passage shows a conspicuous dependence on Deuteronomy 33, particularly 33:2 (cf. Hab 3:3–4). Deuteronomy 33, like Psalm 18, perceives Sinai as the "deposit" of God's covenantal commitment, guaranteeing Israel's future dominion (Dt 33:7, 11, 17, 21, 26–29; cf. Eph 1:14)—a conviction at least echoed in Habakkuk 3.

Finally, Psalm 68 expresses a broad retrospective on Israel's prehistory and history and shows repeated points of contact with Habakkuk 3. As Psalms 18, 68, and 77 draw on the poetic traditions and historical backgrounds to Exodus 15 and Deuteronomy 32–33, so the hymnic passages of Habakkuk 3 echo earlier stages in Israel's history, most notably the parting of the Red Sea, which evokes both the creation, when God divided the waters and imposed his will on them, and the flood, when he again brought life and order out of chaos and destruction. In the exodus, as in the beginning, God destroyed the powers of chaos and anarchy that threatened to engulf his creation; the cosmic battle portrayed in Habakkuk 3:8–15 draws on this background.

This retrospective orientation of Habakkuk pervades the literature of Israel, for whom God's past dealings, both in the arena of the natural world and the historical process, constitute the seedbed of future revelation and the promise of subsequent dealings (e.g., Ne 9:6–38; Pss 77–78; 83; 105–106; 114; Isa 51:1–16; 63:1–64:12). All God's mighty acts, from dividing the waters at creation, to redeeming his people in the exodus and through the Red Sea, to the theophany at Sinai exist as prototypes for later revelations of God's power, culminating in the eschatological manifestation of his reign (e.g., Jdg 5:4–31; Pss 18; 68; 97; Isa 64:1–4; Hag 2:6). These patterns culminate in the NT—in the institution of a new covenant on another mountain, amid darkness and earthquake, judgment and grace (cf. Mt 26:28; 27:45–51; Lk 9:28–36; Gal 4:24; Heb 10:16–31; 12:18–29); in the inauguration of another exodus, through blood, water, and the wind of God's Spirit (cf. Lk 9:31; 1Co 10:2; 1Pe 3:21); and in a new creation (cf. Jn 3:3–8; 2Co 5:17; Gal 6:15). The vision of Habakkuk stands in a noble tradition.

The chapter is arranged chiastically: prologue, v.1 (A); invocation, v.2 (B); theophany, vv.3–15 (C); response, vv.16–19a (B'); epilogue, v.19b (A'). It is framed by the corresponding musical notations in v.1 and in v.19b, which represent editorial comment on the intervening "prayer."

Verse 2, the invocation, is characterized by its first-person pronominal forms ("I," "our") and articulates the contrast between the past, awe-inspiring event in its power ("I have heard," *šāmaʿtî*; and "I stand in awe," or "I fear," *yārēʾtî*), and the present distress ("wrath," *rōgez*). Verses 16–19, the response, echo this prayer. Again the first-person forms ("I," "my") predominate, while the Lord is again the focus of Habakkuk's attention (vv.18–19). His orientation to the past is signaled by the same introductory vocabulary ("I heard," *šāmaʿtî*) and accompanied by the same awe and experience of present distress, amplified to portray its impact on the prophet himself ("quivered," *ṣālal*; "pounded ... trembled," *rāgaz*; cf. v.2) and on his society (vv.16–17). However, this correspondence of vv.2 and 16–19 contains a dramatic contrast. What Habakkuk hears in vv.16–19 is no longer derived from the remote past (cf. v.2) but from an overwhelming sense that God's power has invaded the present (v.16; cf. vv.3–15). As in the case of Job (Job 42:5), the new note of personal devastation mixed with faith is born of this revelation.

Verses 3–15, the theophany, consisting of two sections (vv.3–7, 8–15), constitutes the focal point of the chapter. The theophany is closely linked to v.2 as the answer to Habakkuk's petition for a revelation of God's deeds (vv.3–7) and in its direct address to "the LORD" (i.e., "you," "your"; vv.8–15). It is also linked to vv.16–19, God's "deeds" (vv.3–7) and their interpretation (vv.8–15) serving as the basis for Habakkuk's response. Mixed with the direct address of vv.8–15 are references to God in the third person (vv.3–7, 18–19). The three sections are further linked by the root *rgz* (v.2, "in *wrath*"; v.7, "in *distress*"; v.16, "my heart *pounded*"). The "wrath" of God (v.2) leads to the "distress" of Cushan and ultimately to the pounding of the prophet's heart.

Verses 3–7 and 8–15 each have their own internal structure, with the former unified by poetic associations with Sinai as the place of divinely wrought upheaval (cf. Ex 15:13–18; 19:9–19; Jdg 5:4–5; Ps 68:7–10). Verses 8–15 embody a consistent imagery of water, storm, and warfare and are further unified by the introduction of direct speech in the transitional question of v.8 ("you," "your"), answered in the second-person affirmation of vv.13–14. Both use inclusios (in vv.3 and 7, rhymed pairs of proper names — *Teman/Paran* and *Cushan/Midian* — having a common geographical association, while vv.8 and 15 both speak of the "sea" [*yām*] and "your horses" [*sûseykā*]). Both

focus on a primary event in salvation-history (Sinai and exodus/conquest) with a common vocabulary associated with that event.

Verses 13–14 serve as the climax of vv.3–15, not only answering the question of v.8 but also solving the theological dilemma posed by Habakkuk's initial cry. Although manifested in nature, the "wrath" of God is never random; "he" personally comes out to effect the judgment and salvation of his people. Verses 3–7 and 8–15 are thus defined as distinct units, with differing historical orientations but leading to the same conclusion. Sinai and exodus are not merely events from the past; they demonstrate for all ages God's sovereign control over both nature and history, all on behalf of his anointed (*māšîaḥ*). His kingdom comes amid the shaking of all things (cf. Hag 2:6, 21–22; Mt 7:24–27; 24:1–8, 27–31; Heb 12:26–29).

The structure relating ch. 3 to chs. 1–2 cannot be fully elaborated here, but there are numerous parallels. Common features include their headings (1:1; 3:1); the lament form underlying their prayers (1:2–4; 1:12–2:1; 3:1–2); the preoccupation with salvation, triumphantly vindicated in the final chapter (*yāšaʿ*; 1:2; 3:8, 13[2x], 18); the judgment on domestic sin through a foreign nation (1:2–11; 3:2, 14), the "wicked" (*rāšāʿ*; 1:13; 3:13) and their intent to "devour" (*ʾākal*; 1:8; 3:14); the concomitant disruption of the "nations" (1:5–17; 2:5–17; cf. 3:6–7, 12); the "revelation" that forms the turning point in the prophet's intercession (2:2–3; 3:3–15); the resultant promise of judgment ensuing on that nation (2:3–20; 3:12–16), as on a "house" destined to be razed to its foundations (*bayit*; 2:9–10; 3:13 [lit., "house of wickedness"]); the transformation effected by this promise, promoting both faith and patience (2:2–4; 3:16–19); the anticipation of God's universal reign (2:14; 3:3); and the common basis on the covenant, particularly Deuteronomy 28–32, that shapes the pattern outlined above.

Habakkuk 1–2 appears to emphasize the human agents in the outworking of this pattern; ch. 3 reveals its inward dynamics in the sovereign agency of God, who implements the covenant through whatever earthly means he chooses. Together they form a compelling and tightly meshed testimony to the ways of God in judgment and in grace.

A. Prologue (3:1)

¹A prayer of Habakkuk the prophet. *On shigionoth.*

COMMENTARY

1 The reference to "Habakkuk the prophet" marks a new section, distinct from chs. 1 and 2, which are similarly introduced (cf. 1:1). The following verses are characterized as a "prayer" (*tepillâ*; GK 9525; cf. *TWOT*, 2:725–26), a title attributed elsewhere to five psalms of lament (Pss 17, 86, 90, 102, 142) and also to an early collection of Davidic psalms (cf. Ps 72:20); in the Psalms, the term occurs most commonly in laments, where intercession is made for divine intervention and vindication against oppression or injustice (e.g., Pss 4:1; 6:9; 17:1; 35:13; 54:2; 55:1; 69:13; 86:6; 88:2, 13; 102:1, 17[2x]; 109:4, 7; cf. 1Ki 8:28–54).

These associations with the psalmic literature are reinforced by the phrase "On *shigionoth*"; the corresponding "*shiggaion*" appears as the title of another lament (Ps 7); and the preposition "on," or "according to" (*ʿal*), is used in musical directions at the head of numerous psalms (e.g., Pss 6, 8, 12, 22, 45–46; cf. Hab 3:19). The precise etymology and meaning of the phrase are uncertain, but it may be related to an Akkadian verb meaning "to howl, lament" (cf. *šāgag/šāgâ*; *TWOT*, 2:903ff.; *HALOT*, 948); its characteristics in Psalm 7 suggest that as a musical genre it constitutes a vehement cry for justice against sin. It is evident, then, that the heading that distinguishes ch. 3 also relates it to the preceding chapters, where a similar cry for justice is expressed in the same genre of a lament.

B. Invocation (3:2)

²Lord, I have heard of your fame;
    I stand in awe of your deeds, O Lord.
Renew them in our day,
    in our time make them known;
    in wrath remember mercy.

COMMENTARY

2 Habakkuk's "prayer" is oriented to the past as the basis for his appeal for present help (cf. Ex 32:13; Ps 77:11; Ac 4:25–28). The noun "fame" (*šēmaʿ*; GK 9051) is normally used of secondhand information (e.g., Job 28:22; Na 3:19), suggesting a remoteness from the hearer's own experience to the persons or events referred to (cf. Job 42:5). The Lord's "deeds" (*pōʿal*) envisaged here corroborate this sense of remoteness, being associated with his sovereign power and preeminently with his "work" at the exodus—a primary anchor of Israel's recollection, faith, and hope (e.g., Nu 23:23; Pss 44:1; 68:28; 77:12; 90:16; 95:9; 111:3), as is the cross to the Christian.

Habakkuk's appeal for "mercy" (*rāḥam*) is thus grounded in God's covenantal commitment to Israel, displayed in the events of the exodus as a whole and sealed at Sinai (cf. Dt 4:31); it is no wishful or manipulative plea for help grounded merely in the desperation of the moment. However, it is also an admission of how far Israel has fallen away from the revelation of God's character and ways, made "known" at the exodus. Not only do the "deeds" of that epoch represent secondhand knowledge, but the need to "renew" (*ḥîyâ*) them implies that their impact is facing extinction. Moreover, the imminence of "wrath" (or "turmoil," *rōgez*; cf. v.7), betrays the presence of sin, which the Lord is committed to judge in his people—a judgment rooted in the covenant no less than "mercy" (e.g., Ex 32:10–12; Dt 6:15; 29:20–28; 31:17; 32:22). This appeal for God's covenanted "mercy" in the face of present distress and judgment echoes Psalm 77:9, with which this chapter has much in common (see Overview).

C. Theophany (3:3–15)

³ God came from Teman,
    the Holy One from Mount Paran.
               Selah

  His glory covered the heavens
    and his praise filled the earth.
⁴ His splendor was like the sunrise;
    rays flashed from his hand,
    where his power was hidden.
⁵ Plague went before him;
    pestilence followed his steps.
⁶ He stood, and shook the earth;
    he looked, and made the nations tremble.
  The ancient mountains crumbled
    and the age-old hills collapsed.
  His ways are eternal.

⁷I saw the tents of Cushan in distress,
　　the dwellings of Midian in anguish.

⁸Were you angry with the rivers, O Lᴏʀᴅ?
　　Was your wrath against the streams?
　Did you rage against the sea
　　when you rode with your horses
　　and your victorious chariots?
⁹You uncovered your bow,
　　you called for many arrows.

　　　　　　　　　　　　　　　Selah

　You split the earth with rivers;
¹⁰　　the mountains saw you and writhed.
　Torrents of water swept by;
　　the deep roared
　　and lifted its waves on high.
¹¹Sun and moon stood still in the heavens
　　at the glint of your flying arrows,
　　at the lightning of your flashing spear.
¹²In wrath you strode through the earth
　　and in anger you threshed the nations.
¹³You came out to deliver your people,
　　to save your anointed one.
　You crushed the leader of the land of wickedness,
　　you stripped him from head to foot.

　　　　　　　　　　　　　　　Selah

¹⁴With his own spear you pierced his head
　　when his warriors stormed out to scatter us,
　gloating as though about to devour
　　the wretched who were in hiding.
¹⁵You trampled the sea with your horses,
　　churning the great waters.

COMMENTARY

3 The opening lines, "God came from Teman ... Mount Paran," establish the context for interpreting the theophany. "Teman," a word meaning "south," at times (cf. Ob 9) served as a name for Edom, or Seir, the land south and east of the Dead Sea traditionally occupied by the descendants of Esau, but could also refer to a region or tribe within Edom (*ABD*, 6:347; *ZPEB*, 5:624; cf. Ge 25:25, 30; 32:3;

36:1–9, 34; Jer 49:7, 20; Eze 25:13; Am 1:11–12; Ob 8–9). The wilderness of Paran was a large, relatively diffuse area lying between Kadesh Barnea to the north and Mount Sinai to the south (cf. Nu 10:11–12, 12:16, 13:3, 26) and bounded by Edom to the northeast and Egypt to the southwest (cf. Ge 14:6; 21:21; 1Ki 11:18). "Mount Paran" is mentioned only here and in Deuteronomy 33:2, which together with Judges 5:4–5 evokes the revelation of God's law at Sinai, thus fortifying the centrality of the Sinai imagery.

The noun "glory" (*hôd*; GK 2086) is used primarily of kingly authority (e.g., Nu 27:20; 1Ch 29:25; Ps 45:3; Zec 6:13), revealed preeminently in the Lord's sovereignty over creation and history (cf. 1Ch 16:27; 29:11–12; Job 40:10). The verb "covered" (*kissâ*) is used of extension over a surface either to permeate or conceal, with the precise meaning here indicated by the parallel verb "filled" and by the allusion to 2:14 (see below). Thus God's "glory" covers "the heavens" in permeating them, being revealed in them as an expression of his majesty (e.g., Job 37:22; Pss 8:1; 104:1; 148:13; cf. Dt 33:26, 29; Ps 68:34).

This thought is echoed in the following line; God's "praise" (*tehillâ*; GK 9335) is a metonymy denoting the power of his character and works, for which he is to be praised (cf. Ex 15:11 [ASV]; Ps 78:4) and which similarly pervades his creation. This couplet clearly evokes the eschatological proclamation in 2:14 (cf. "glory" [*kābôd*], "earth," "filled," "cover"). Like the preceding couplet in v.3, it looks forward to a new and universal manifestation of God's rule, grounding it in his past breaking into history at Sinai—a brief moment in history embodying repercussions for the whole of history, a remote event in the earth destined to fill the whole earth (cf. Eph 4:10; Php 2:7–11).

4 God's "glory" is manifested as light, interpreted by the NIV as a comparison with "the sunrise." The noun "splendor" (*nôgah*) denotes the shining of various sources of light, including the sun (2Sa 23:4; Pr 4:18), while "sunrise" translates the common noun "light" (*ʾôr*), often used of dawn and sunlight (e.g., Jdg 16:2; 1Sa 14:36). The noun "rays" (*qarnayim*) normally means "horns," with the derived meaning of "projections," such as beams or rays of light; an equivalent word is applied to the rays of the rising sun in Arabic poetry (Carl F. Keil, *The Twelve Minor Prophets*, vol. 2 [Grand Rapids: Eerdmans, 1949], 99). These associations may validate the NIV's rendering of v.4; certainly the sun does form a fitting biblical symbol of God's "splendor." However, the similarities in both theme and vocabulary from v.3 onward point to a different context.

As noted above, "splendor" is used of light sources other than the sun. In particular, it describes the radiance of God's presence in contexts that recall his theophanies at Sinai and in the wilderness (Ps 18:12; Isa 4:5; 60:1; Eze 1:4, 13, 27–28; 10:4); as at Sinai, this radiance is generally manifested as intense fire shrouded in clouds and darkness (e.g., Ex 19:16–19; Ps 18:8–12)—an image remote from that of the rising sun. In keeping with these associations, the noun "sunrise" is used of lightning (Job 36:32; 37:3, 11, 15), a prominent characteristic of Sinai and later theophanies (e.g., Ex 19:16; 20:18). On this understanding, the Lord is perceived as illuminating the world, not with the delicate light of sunrise but with the awe-inspiring radiance that characterized his descent on Mount Sinai—a light as brilliant as the lightning that accompanied that event, incandescent with his glory.

This interpretation is confirmed first by the close connection of vv.3–4 with Sinai, to which the image of a sunrise is most inappropriate (cf. Ex 19:9–19; Dt 5:22–26; Jdg 5:4–5; Ps 68:7–8). Second, this passage alludes specifically to Deuteronomy 33:2, in which God's glory is similarly portrayed. Third, the imagery of sunshine is equally remote from the ensuing vision. Instead, it is dominated by volcanic earthquake, storm, and specifically by lightning (Hab 3:11; cf. v.9), which again are consistent with Sinai. Finally, in a passage that corresponds closely to vv.3–7 (cf. Overview to ch. 3), the two nouns for "splendor" and "sunrise" recur together in v.11—translated as "lightning" and "glint," respectively—in the unambiguous context of a lightning storm (cf. Ps 77:17–18).

The final lines of v.4 are to be interpreted against this background. The "rays" (lit., "twin-rays," i.e., forked lightning) are flashes of light manifested at the Lord's presence. The "hand" is repeatedly a symbol of the Lord's power (e.g., Ex 13:14, 16; 14:31; Dt 3:24; 4:34; 32:41), to which the following line refers explicitly—a "power" manifested conspicuously in the forces of nature (e.g., Pss 68:33–35; 74:13; 77:14; 78:26; 150:1), which are "hidden" in his storehouses (cf. Dt 28:12; Job 38:22; Ps 135:7; Jer 10:13; 51:16; Sir 43:14). This imagery is clarified in the corresponding content of vv.9 and 11, where "lightning" serves the Lord as the "arrows" and "spear" in his hand (cf. Dt 33:2, "flaming fire at his right hand," RSV).

5 God's "power" is here revealed in judgment: "plague" (*deber*) and "pestilence" (*rešep*) are almost invariably attributed to the sovereign agency and judgment of God. Accompanying him in the context of Sinai, they probably refer to the plagues that devastated Egypt (Ex 9:3, 15; Ps 78:50) and attended Israel's disobedience to the covenant given at Sinai (Ex 5:3; Lev 26:25; Nu 14:12; Dt 28:21; 32:24; cf. 2Sa 24:13, 15; 1Ki 8:37; Jer 29:17–19; 34:12–20; Eze 5:12, 17; 6:11–12; Am 4:10).

6–7 The scope of this judgment embraces the "earth" as a whole (v.6; cf. v.3), which is convulsed by earthquake and volcanic upheaval. The verb "shook" (*yᵉmōded*; GK 4571) is derived either from a root cognate with the Arabic "to be convulsed" (*mûd*; *HALOT*, 501; cf. LXX, Targum, NRSV) or

from the Hebrew "to measure" (*mādad*; cf. Vulgate, KJV, RSV). The first etymology emphasizes the effects of God's action, whereas the second stresses the motive of judgment underlying it (cf. Isa 65:7; Da 5:25–28). There seems to be little basis for choosing between them. The repercussions of such judgment and physical upheaval are reflected among the "nations," the verb "tremble" (*nātar*; GK 6001) implying both emotional turmoil (cf. Job 37:1) and abrupt physical dislocation (e.g., "release," Ps 105:20; "sets free," Ps 146:7). This shaking of all things is specified more precisely in the following two couplets of vv.6–7. The "mountains" and "hills" are symbols of grandeur, permanence, and security in the "earth" (e.g., Ge 49:26; Dt 33:15); yet they too are revealed as frail and impermanent. Before God's might they are shattered and prostrated (cf. Job 9:5; Ps 97:5; Na 1:5).

The "nations," in turn, are exemplified more specifically by the tribes of "Cushan" and "Midian" (v.7). The Midianites were localized in Transjordan, ranging southward from the regions of Moab and Edom (cf. Nu 31:1–12; Jos 13:21; cf. *ISBE*, 3:349–51) and making incursions farther west (cf. Ge 37:28; Ex 2:15; 3:1; Jdg 6:8). The word "dwellings" (*yerîᶜôt*, lit., "curtains"; cf. Ps 104:2; SS 1:5; Isa 54:2; Jer 4:20; 10:20; 49:29; ASV, RSV) typifies their nomadic existence. The phrase "in anguish" translates the verb "to be agitated, quake" (*ragaz*; *TWOT*, 2:830–31; cf. *rōgez*, v.2); thus it echoes the verb "tremble" (v.6) in portraying the impact of God's "wrath" (v.8). The identity of "Cushan" is uncertain, but evidently it also denotes a nomadic group (cf. "tents") in similar "distress." This close parallelism suggests that "Cushan" was a nation related or even identical to "Midian"—an inference corroborated by the identification of Moses' wife as both Midianite and Cushite (Ex 2:18–22; 18:1–5; Nu 12:1).

The imagery of vv.6–7 again recalls the earthquake and volcanic upheaval at Mount Sinai (e.g., Ex 19:18; Jdg 5:4–5), thus echoing v.3 in its clear allusion to Sinai and so framing the intervening verses and providing a specific context for their interpretation. This inclusio defining vv.3–7 as a unit is signaled more precisely by the names in vv.3, 7, which correspond to one another in their common geographical association with Sinai and in the rhyme linking their final syllables (i.e., ān).

8 The inclusio uniting vv.3–7 marks this verse as the introduction to a new section. This is corroborated by the emphatic switch to direct address, extending to v.15 and unparalleled in vv.3–7, and also by the prominence of vocabulary denoting water and military conflict, similarly absent from vv.3–7. The Lord's "wrath" receives dramatic emphasis, being echoed by the words "angry" (ʾap) and "rage" (ʿebrâ). It is directed against the "rivers" (nehārîm) and the "sea" (yām). Here, although a precise identification eludes us, the passage can easily evoke Yahweh's display of power at the Red Sea, a focal point in Israel's memory (e.g., Ex 14:2–15:22; Dt 11:4).

The correlation of this verse with that event is substantiated by the reference to "chariots" and "horses" (cf. Ex 14:6–15:19; Dt 11:4; Jos 24:6), though here both belong to Yahweh, not the Egyptians, and to the Lord's victory, or salvation (yešûʿâ; cf. Ex 14:13, 30; 15:2; Ps 106:8–10). It is also substantiated by the context. It is appropriate, first, to vv.3–7, Israel's deliverance at the Red Sea being the precondition for the covenant at Sinai. Second, the verse corresponds in content to vv.12–15 (cf. Overview to ch. 3; cf. "anger," v.12; "deliver," "save," v.13; "sea," "your horses," v.15), where the deliverance from the Egyptian enemy is echoed even more clearly (cf. vv.13–14).

The opening parallel lines of v.8 refer to the "rivers" and "streams" (both nehārîm; cf. RSV, NRSV)

as witnessing the anger of the Lord. The waters of the Jordan may be envisaged (cf. Jos 3:13, 17; 4:7, 21–24; 5:1; Ps 114:3, 5), but more likely the word "rivers" (normally plural, as here) is equivalent to "sea." In addition to appearing in the Ugaritic Baal epic as parallel to "sea," "river" admits the meaning "currents" or "water mass," and is not restricted to inland rivers. The Lord's dramatic conflict with the "sea" echoes his dominion over the waters of creation and the flood (cf. Overview and vv.9–11), a complex of events that pervades Israel's literature as a pattern of future salvation and judgment (e.g., Pss 18:4, 15–16; 29:1–11; 65:7; 93:3–4; Isa 10:26; 11:15; 17:12–13; 43:16; 50:2; 51:10, 15; 63:11–12; Zec 10:11). The exodus and Sinai alike are the incarnation of events with universal significance.

God's "horses" and "chariots" evidence his power as the Lord of hosts" or armies ("Lord Almighty," NIV, e.g., in 2:13), and the martial imagery of v.8 permeates and unifies the following verses (vv.9–15). Elsewhere both clouds and winged cherubim serve as his chariot or throne (Ps 104:3; cf. Ps 18:10–12; Isa 19:1), drawn by the wind and resplendent with the brightness of lightning. Thus the Lord's chariotry represents the power of both wind and storm, driving back the sea and churning it up (cf. vv.9–11, 15; Ge 1:2; 8:1; Ex 14:21; 15:8, 10), with the cherubim and angelic hosts serving as executors of his will through the forces of nature (e.g., Ge 3:24; Dt 33:2; Ps 68:17; Rev 5:11; 7:1–2; 8:5–9:15).

9 All three Hebrew words in the second line of this verse are obscure, and they must be interpreted against the background of the first line. The noun "arrows" (maṭṭôt; GK 4751) normally means "rods," "staffs," or "tribes" (cf. TWOT, 2:574), but the first of these meanings can be applied to the shaft of a weapon (e.g., Isa 9:4; 10:5, 24; 14:5; 30:32; e.g., "bows," or by parallelism, "arrows"; cf. the same noun in v.14 translated "spear," or "arrows,"

NRSV). "Many" (šebūʿôt; GK 8651; cf. TWOT 2:899ff.) translates a form derived from either the noun "heptad/group of seven" (šābûaʿ), or the verb "to swear" (šābaʿ; cf. KJV, ASV). The NIV follows the first alternative, its rendering apparently suggested in the sevenfold volleys of arrows used in Israelite warfare (Yigael Yadin, *The Scroll of the War* [New York: McGraw, 1961], 131–32, 140; cf. J. H. Eaton, "The Origen and Meaning of Habakkuk 3," *ZAW* 76 [1964]: 152). By adhering to a more traditional rendering for both šebūʿôt and maṭṭôt, the KJV and ASV come up with a translation focused on the "word" (ʾōmer), i.e., "the oaths to the tribes were a *sure* word" (ASV). In the light of the obscurity of both alternatives, the NIV has the advantage of parallelism.

The reference in the final line is also obscure. The noun "rivers" (neʿhārôt) echoes the form repeated in v.8 (nehārîm), suggesting that it has the same associations with the exodus. These are reinforced by the verb "split" (bāqaʿ), often applied to the division of the Red Sea (cf. Ex 14:16, 21; Ne 9:11; Ps 78:13; Isa 63:12), which allowed God's people to walk securely on the dry "earth." However, the vision of the earth "split" by floods of water is equally appropriate to the following verses, with their undertones of creation and flood (cf. Ge 7:11; Ps 74:15; Pr 3:20).

10 The reference to "water" again evokes God's might revealed first in creation and later the flood. Echoes of driving back the Red Sea may also be heard in the nouns "deep" (tehôm; GK 9333; cf. Ex 15:5, 8; Pss 77:16; 106:9; Isa 51:10; 63:13) and "torrents" (zerem; GK 2443; cf. Ps 77:17). This verse in particular draws on the language of Psalm 77, where the exodus is the explicit focus of recollection (cf. Overview to ch. 3; e.g., 77:15, 20). Correspondences to Psalm 77 are also evident in the words "saw you" (rāʾûkā, 77:16[17, 2x]); "writhed" (yāḥîlû, 77:16[17]); and "roared" (nātan qôlô; cf. "resounded," 77:17[18]). However, both passages envision that event in cos-

mic terms as convulsing the "mountains" and the whole of nature (cf. Hab 3:6). They thereby portray the deliverance at the Red Sea as a reenactment of the flood, itself a reversal and renewal of creation when the Lord brought life and order out of the waters of the deep (tehôm; Ge 1:2).

These precursors of the exodus exhibit the same central imagery of sea and water, dominated by the Lord; and the upheaval of the mountains evokes the turmoil at the flood (Ge 7:11, 19–20), as does the reference to "torrents" (zerem), which denotes both a downpour of rain and the resultant flooding (TWOT, 1:252; cf. Ge 7:12; 8:2). It is this awe-inspiring power of God, the Creator and Judge of all the earth, that is manifested in retribution and salvation at the Red Sea. As at the cross, a universal cataclysm is compressed into a single, localized event in Israel's history; as at the cross, that event is destined to shake the universe.

11 The "sun" and "moon" are prominent symbols of God's created order, and particularly of its permanence (cf. Pss 8:3; 72:5, 7; 89:37), though note that the NRSV separates the "sun" from the "moon" and makes it the subject of the last clause in the previous verse ("the sun raised high its hands"). Their inactivity (ʿāmad, "stood") indicates the interruption of that order (cf. Jos 10:12–13; Isa 38:8). Here the picture may reflect the celestial phenomena at Gibeon (Jos 10:12–13) but may also point to an eclipse—sun and moon stay in their place and cease to give light. The noun "heavens" denotes an exalted dwelling place (zebulâ; cf. 1Ki 8:13; Ps 49:14, where "Sheol" is the opposite, cf. NIV's "princely mansions"); here sun and moon remain hidden or stationary in their heavenly abode.

The picture is not, however, focused on the absence of light or on the interrupted movement of sun and moon, as in Joshua 10. The last two lines, featuring "flying" or "burning arrows" and "gleaming" or "flashing spear" evoke a picture of lightning (cf. "glint" in Hab 3:4; Ps 77:18[19], and "arrows" in Pss 18:14; 77:17–18[18–19]; 144:6; Zec 9:14) in the wider context of a storm. At that point the darkness is that of a storm, as in vv.9–11, a figure evocative of divine judgment (cf. Ex 10:21–22; 14:20; Ecc 12:2; Isa 13:10; 24:23; Jer 4:23, 28; Lk 23:45), and ultimately is a harbinger of the eschatological day of the Lord (Joel 2:2, 10, 31; 3:15; Am 5:18–20; 8:9; Zep 1:15; Mt 24:29; Rev 6:12; 8:12; 9:2; 22:5). The correspondence to the Sinai imagery in vv.3–7 is clear.

12 This verse recapitulates the motif of God's wrath, the noun "anger" (ʾap) being identical to the NIV's "wrath" in v.8. The verbs "strode" in v.12 and "came out" in v.13 carry on the military imagery of vv.8–11 in a forceful recapitulation of the power of the Lord when he marches to battle against the "nations" (cf. Overview to ch. 3; cf. also Dt 33:2; Jdg 5:4–5; Ps 68:7). The words "strode" (ṣāʿad; cf. 2Sa 5:24; 6:13) and "came out" (yāṣāʾ; cf. Jdg 2:15; 4:14; 1Sa 17:20; 2Sa 5:24; Ps 108:11[12]) are reinforced by "threshed" (dûš), a vivid metaphor of harsh treatment by a conqueror (cf. Jdg 8:7; 2Ki 13:7; Am 1:3) and especially graphic when picturing the "strange work" (Isa 28:21) of the Lord in destroying the enemies of his people, paving the way for justice on the earth (cf. Isa 25:10; 28:27–28; Mic 4:13). The common metaphor of threshing, which implies violent shaking and crushing, calls to mind the Lord's action against the natural world (Hab 3:3–11) but is more commonly used, as here, to describe his action against hostile nations.

Habakkuk's vision, along with the common vision of the OT, embraces the conquest of the "nations" as an integral part of the exodus and of Israel's subsequent destiny (cf. Ge 24:60; 26:3–4; Ex 15:14–16; 34:24; Nu 24:8; Dt 4:38; 7:1, 17–26; 32:43; 33:17, 29; 1Ch 14:17; Pss 2; 9:5, 15–20; 18:43; 46:10; Isa 34:1–3; 54:3; 60:12–14). The Lord may appoint the Babylonians to curse Israel, but unless in their conquest they turn and "bless" Israel, they will surely inherit a curse themselves (cf. Ge 12:2–3; 27:29; Nu 24:9; Dt 28; Ps 105:12–15).

13 The military associations of "came out" have been noted above. They are reiterated in the words "deliver" and "save" (both from yāšaʿ; GK 3828), derived from the same root as "victorious" (v.8) and "save" (1:2) and forming a part of names such as "Joshua," "Isaiah," and "Jesus." This deliverance expresses the Lord's covenantal commitment to his "people" (ʿam; cf. Ex 3:7, 10, 12 et al.; Pss 68:7[8]; 35[36]; 77:15, 20[16, 21]) and to his "anointed one" (māšîaḥ, "Messiah"; GK 5431). The meaning of "people" is clear, but whether "anointed one" is merely a synonym for Israel is less so. The underlying root (mšḥ) is applied almost invariably to an individual; only in one doubtful instance might it refer to the people as a whole (Ps 28:8–9), though with significant resemblance to the present text. Most commonly it designates a king (e.g., 1Sa 2:10; 2Sa 23:1; Pss 18:50; 89:38, 51); but it may also denote other individuals appointed to leadership, such as the high priest (e.g., Ex 40:13, 15; Lev 4:3; 6:22) and the patriarchs (1Ch 16:22; Ps 105:15). In the present exodus context it appears to refer to Moses, who like King David combined in himself the messianic functions of shepherd (e.g., Nu 27:17; Ps 77:20), prophet (e.g., Dt 18:15; 34:10), and servant of God (e.g., Ex 14:31; Nu 12:7–8).

The context of the exodus also throws light on the identity of the "leader" (or "head," rōʾš; cf. *TWOT*, 2:825–26). Egypt represents an archetypal land of "wickedness" (rāšaʿ; cf. Ex 9:27), and the pharaoh of the exodus figured prominently as an agent of Israel's oppression. This is suggested also by the verb "crushed" (or "pierced," māḥaṣ), which is applied to the destruction of Rahab at creation (Job 26:12; cf. Ps 74:13–14)—Rahab is identified elsewhere with Egypt and specifically with the exodus (cf. Ps 87:4; Isa 30:7; 51:9). This understanding is reinforced by the associations of the noun "land," normally translated "house" (*bayit*; cf. below), since Egypt is characterized as Israel's "house of bondage" ("land of slavery," NIV; cf. Ex 13:3, 14; Dt 5:6; Jos 24:17).

However, this verse provides further evidence of the double perspective of the chapter: the oppression in Egypt foreshadows subsequent oppression, and the deliverance at the Red Sea embodies the promise of subsequent deliverance. The term "anointed one" also lends itself more readily to later usage, both with reference to the preexilic kings and in anticipation of the eschatological Messiah (e.g., Da 9:25-26; cf. 2Sa 7:11-16; Isa 9:6-7; 11:1-5; Jer 23:5-6; Eze 34:23-24; 37:22-25; Mic 5:2-5; Zec 6:9-14, 9:9-10). In the present chapter, set against the background of imminent danger preceding the exile (vv.2, 16-17; cf. 1:5-11) and also fraught with eschatological undertones of judgment and salvation, the "anointed" will therefore represent both the king in Habakkuk's own time and the Christ, whose sufferings and glory the prophets predicted (1Pe 1:10-12). In the same way, the oppressive "leader" must be identified in terms of Israel's history both before and after the exodus, as evidenced particularly by words such as "crushed" and "leader"—vocabulary consistently applied to Israel's conquests from earlier times to the eschaton (Nu 24:8, 17-19; Dt 33:11; Pss 18:38; 68:21, 23; 110:5-6; cf. Jdg 5:26).

Despite the exodus overtones in the chapter and the obvious contextual reference to Babylon (already identified in 1:13 as "wicked"), the "adversary" here cannot be limited historically any more than the one he opposes. The destruction of this enemy is specified in the final line by a complex metaphor based on the image of a house razed to its "foundations"—this being the usual translation of "foot" (*yᵉsôd*; cf. Ex 29:12; 2Ch 23:5; Job 4:19, La 4:11; Eze 13:14; 30:4; Mic 1:6)—anticipated already in the preceding noun "land," or "house." The metaphor establishes further associations with Babylon as with Egypt as the wicked house (cf. 2:9-13). The past devastation of Egypt and future destruction of Babylon foreshadow that of Israel's final enemies.

14 This devastation is elaborated further here, the verb "pierced" echoing a meaning of "crushed" and the noun "head" being identical to "leader." It is accomplished by turning the enemy's "spear," or "weapons," against himself (*maṭṭāyw*; cf. v.9). This is reminiscent of the overthrowing of Pharaoh's horses and chariots (cf. Ex 14:24-25), and it also represents a fitting judgment on the Babylonians. Indeed, Babylon fell to Cyrus without opposition, its "leader" being betrayed by factions among his own subjects (*IDB*, 1:335; 2:494-95; cf. Da 5).

The scene described in the following lines is similarly evocative of the exodus in the Egyptians' pursuit of the slaves they had afflicted (e.g., Ex 14:3-10). It also recalls the description of the Babylonians' rapacity in the preceding chapters (e.g., "stormed," 1:9, 11; "gloating," 1:15-16; "devour," 1:8, 13-17; 2:5). This victory is wrought on behalf of the "wretched" (or "humble, afflicted"; *ʿānî*; GK 6714; cf. *TWOT*, 2:682ff.). The noun denotes a condition of material or spiritual poverty; such affliction is caused predominantly by unjust oppression, but the cognate verb (*ʿānâ*) is also associated with chastening for sin. Both associations—of oppression and sin—are appropriate to the Israel of Habakkuk's time (cf. 1:2-4, 12-17; 2:4-5). The salvation promised by the covenant presupposes the judgment demanded by the covenant (Dt 28-32), and both will be worked out in the furnace of "affliction" (Isa 48:10).

15 Verse 15 reverts again to the language of v.8 (i.e., "sea," "your horses"), thereby defining vv.8-15 as a unit and establishing the historical context of the intervening verses. The phrase "great waters" represents a further allusion to the exodus from Egypt (*mayim rabbîm*; cf. Ps 77:19[20]; cf. Ex 15:10, *mayim ʿaddîrîm*, "majestic waters").

D. Response (3:16–19a)

> ¹⁶I heard and my heart pounded,
>   my lips quivered at the sound;
> decay crept into my bones,
>   and my legs trembled.
> Yet I will wait patiently for the day of calamity
>   to come on the nation invading us.
> ¹⁷Though the fig tree does not bud
>   and there are no grapes on the vines,
> though the olive crop fails
>   and the fields produce no food,
> though there are no sheep in the pen
>   and no cattle in the stalls,
> ¹⁸yet I will rejoice in the Lord,
>   I will be joyful in God my Savior.
>
> ¹⁹The Sovereign Lord is my strength;
>   he makes my feet like the feet of a deer,
>   he enables me to go on the heights.

COMMENTARY

16 As noted in the Overview to ch. 3, this verse corresponds closely to v.2. The term "heart" (*beṭen*; GK 1061) is applied in literal usage to the lower abdomen, particularly the womb or belly (e.g., Ge 25:23–24; Nu 5:21–22, 27; Jdg 3:21–22; Hos 12:3); as the seat of conception, it is used figuratively of the innermost thoughts and motives of human beings (e.g., Job 15:2, 35; 32:18–19; Pr 18:8; 20:27, 30; 22:18). As evidenced by the additional anatomical terms, the prophet is shaken and disabled throughout his being—he personally experiences the turmoil that pervades and characterizes the chapter.

The verb "pounded" echoes the same root in vv.2 and 7 (*rgz*), and it occurs again in the following line ("trembled"). The conspicuous repetitions of this root indicate the cause of Habakkuk's inward upheaval; it is occasioned by the imminence of God's "wrath" on Israel (v.2) and, more acutely, by the uncertainty of any time frame that accompanies the subsequent judgment on the enemy. This is corroborated by the final, explanatory lines, whose introductory words might be translated more plausibly, "because I must wait" (so NASB). These lines anticipate a "nation invading us" as instruments of that "wrath" (cf. Dt 32:15–33), "a ruthless and impetuous people ... bent on violence" (1:6, 9), with fearful consequences for Israel (cf. 1:5–11).

These lines also anticipate for that nation its own "day of calamity" (cf. Dt 32:34–43), though the closing phrase is not entirely clear as to the immediate object of the prophet's "waiting." The

NASB, like the KJV and ASV before it, leaves room for Habakkuk to await the coming invader's wrath on his own people rather than the more distant divine wrath on Babylon. In either case, the phrase implies great pressure and distress from which only the living God can give effective deliverance; for Babylon, whose own strength was its god (1:11), no such deliverance will be forthcoming (cf. Ps 18:41). For Habakkuk to see such things is to experience distress (cf. 1:5). To see beyond them to the Holy One who has appointed them is to demonstrate the greatness of faith and to find strength to "wait patiently" (cf. 1:12; 2:2–4; 3:18–19).

17 Divine judgment strikes the basic sources of Israel's agricultural economy. From the beginning, her prosperity was dependent on obedience to the covenant and on the Lord's consequent blessing (Lev 26:3–5, 10; Dt 28:2–14). Conversely, when Israel's corporate life was marked by disobedience and disloyalty to the covenant, the Lord's chastening followed, normally through natural and military disasters (Lev 26:14–33; Dt 28:16–17, 22–24, 30–31, 38–42; cf. Dt 11:16–17; Isa 7:23–25; Hos 2:12; Joel 1:7–12; Am 4:6–9; Hag 1:6–11; 2:16–19). In this graphic vision of a devastated economy, Habakkuk acknowledges his nation's apostasy and sets himself to face the inevitability of judgment (cf. 1:2, 4, 12; 3:2, 16). In an agricultural society, the devastation described will be total.

18 The patient faith demonstrated in v.16 reaches full expression in this verse. The parallel verbs affirming Habakkuk's joy (ʿālaz, "rejoice"; gîl, "be joyful") are frequently used in the Psalter to reveal the psalmists' confidence, often in the face of adversity (e.g., Pss 13:5; 16:8–10; 21:1, 6–7; 31:6–7; 32:10–11; cf. Isa 25:9; Joel 2:21, 23). For Habakkuk as for the psalmists, it is "God" himself and his intervention as "Savior" (yēšaʿ) that motivate his longing and his joyful attaining. The Babylonians, by contrast, "gloat" (ʿālaṣ [v.14], pos-

sibly an alternative spelling of ʿālaz) to "devour the wretched" (v.14) and "rejoice" (gîl, 1:15) over their prey. Their god is, in truth, their stomach, and their destiny is destruction (cf. Php 3:19).

The basis of Habakkuk's faith, as of Paul's, is first God himself as revealed in his covenantal promises. The covenant that promised the invasion and devastation of vv.16–17 also gives assurance of restoration to God's favor and presence (cf. Dt 30:1–10; 32:34–43); it is for this joy set before him that Habakkuk can set his face to confront and endure even the most devastating affliction.

19a This verse is clearly dependent on Psalm 18 in its affirmation of God-given "strength" (ḥayil; cf. Ps 18:32[33]) and most notably in the following two lines (cf. 18:33[34]). The image of "the feet of a deer ... on the heights" is found only in these two passages and in 2 Samuel 22:34, which is parallel to Psalm 18. However, the phrase "go on the heights" (dārak ʿal bāmôt or rākab ʿal bāmôt) is anticipated in Deuteronomy 33:29, which itself echoes Deuteronomy 32:13 (cf. Isa 58:14; Am 4:13; Mic 1:3). The "rider" or "trampler" may be God himself (Am 4:13; Mic 1:3) or Israel (Dt 32:13; 33:29; Isa 58:14), and the "heights" may be pagan "high places" (Dt 33:29, NIV), the "heights" of the Promised Land (Isa 58:14; cf. parallelism), or, in a general or even cosmic sense, merely "the heights."

While the language in its most exalted form transcends any particular event, in view of the extensive correlations in theme and language of Habakkuk 3 and Psalm 18 with Deuteronomy 32–33 (cf. Overview to ch. 3), Israel's "inheritance" is probably the "heights" envisaged here. Similarly, the reference to "strength" echoes the Song of Moses underlying this chapter (ʿōz; Ex 15:2, 13). Like the "deer" in its resilience, grace, and vigor, that faith draws its strength from God's providence; like the armies of Israel on the "high places" or "heights" (bāmôt), it lives only by its connection to the ultimate source of strength, the Lord himself, who "rides on the heights." This chapter is thus framed by the same initial and concluding emphases as Deuteronomy 33 (cf. Hab 3:3; also Dt 33:2). It thereby constitutes a remarkable statement of faith in God's "blessing" (Dt 33:1) in the very midst of disaster. Habakkuk himself stands as a noble example of the prophetic witness to God and the strength gained from that relationship in times of complete disaster.

E. Epilogue (3:19b)

For the director of music. On my stringed instruments.

COMMENTARY

19b The final line of the prophecy forms an editorial conclusion to ch. 3 expressed in the language of the Psalms. The Piel verb *nṣḥ*, from which "director of music" (*menaṣṣēaḥ*; cf. *TWOT*, 2:593) comes, is associated with supervisory authority, particularly of the Levites in relation to the music of the temple service (1Ch 15:21; 23:4; 2Ch 2:2, 18[2:1,17]; 34:12; Ezr 3:8–9). It is therefore translated in these terms in the Psalms, where it predominates (fifty-five times; e.g., Pss 4–6; 8–9; 11–14; 18–22; 39–42; 44–47; 49; 51–62; 64–70).

These musical connotations are reinforced by the following noun, "stringed instruments" (*negînôt*), which is translated "song" or "music" in common usage (cf. Job 30:9; Pss 69:12; 77:6; La 3:14; 5:14). The phrase recurs as a technical term, with minor variations, in the title of Psalms 4, 6, 54–55, 61, 67, and 76, and it resembles similar notations in the Psalms introduced by the preposition "on" (*ʿal*; cf. 3:1).

ZEPHANIAH

LARRY L. WALKER

Introduction

1. AUTHOR

As far back as the early church fathers, the etymology of Zephaniah's name was disputed. One explanation understood the name to contain the root ṣāpan ("to hide, shelter"). This etymology plus the common theophoric suffix yâ (for Yahweh) gives the meaning "Yah(weh) has hidden." This proposal may be supported by the fact that the root is also linked with the theophoric element El ("God") in Elizaphan (Nu 34:25) and Elzaphan (Ex 6:22; Lev 10:4). Berlin notes the presence of this root in extrabiblical names, including the name ṣpnyhw on a seal impression from early sixth-century Lachish.[1]

Another suggestion derives the name "Zephaniah" from the root ṣāpâ ("to watch") plus the common theophoric suffix yâ; thus the name signifies something like "Watchman for the LORD." In this case the Hebrew letter nun (n) is explained as a paragogic nun, such as in the name "Samson" (šimšôn), from šemeš ("sun").

Eight of the prophets have no family history recorded, six of the prophets have only the names of their fathers recorded, and Zechariah is identified by reference to his father and grandfather.[2] Only Zephaniah among the prophetic books exhibits a lengthy genealogy, tracing his ancestry back four generations to Hezekiah.

This genealogical note (four generations, instead of three) has been commonly accepted to refer to the famous Judean king Hezekiah. However, this presumption is not at all certain, and we have no other proof of any royal status for Zephaniah, despite the unusual mention of his great-great-grandfather. Some suggest that since the words "king of Judah" are not added to Hezekiah's name, the reference is not to King Hezekiah. Others explain this omission on the ground that "king of Judah" follows immediately

---

1. Adele Berlin, *Zephaniah* (AB; New York: Doubleday, 1994), 64–65.
2. O. Palmer Robertson, *Nahum, Habakkuk, and Zephaniah* (NICOT; Grand Rapids: Eerdmans, 1990), 252.

after Josiah's name. We simply lack conclusive evidence to this interesting question, but since only one of the sixteen prophetic books contains this unique variant, it appears to be more deliberate than accidental.

Three other men bore the name Zephaniah in the OT: a Levite descended from Kohath (1Ch 6:36–38), the second priest under the high priest Seraiah during the reign of King Zedekiah (2Ki 25:18–21; Jer 52:24–27), and the father of Josiah, an exile who returned from Babylon (Zec 6:10, 14).

2. DATE

The opening statement of the book notes that Zephaniah prophesied "during the reign of Josiah son of Amon king of Judah" (640–609 BC), the famous king who assumed the throne at the age of eight and later died in battle against Pharaoh Neco of Egypt. Since Zephaniah predicted the destruction of Nineveh (2:13–15), which took place in 612 BC, the only question open for discussion concerns the time of his ministry within these parameters. Because of references to the pagan elements still found within society (cf. 1:4–5, 8–9) as well as the other sinful and unreformed elements still present (3:1, 3, 7), some commentators suppose that Zephaniah wrote at a time prior to any reformation attempted by Josiah. However, others assume that only the predominance of idolatry had been broken by the time of Zephaniah's ministry, which came after the initiation of Josiah's reformation.

The reference to the "remnant of Baal" (1:4) is a key passage for commentators in dating the book. Some assume this statement reflects a time after Baalism had already been generally destroyed and only a "remnant" yet remained. Others respond that this is assuming too much; they believe that the point the prophet is making is only that eventually all Baalism will be exterminated and that this reference has nothing to do with the extent of Baal worship during Zephaniah's ministry.

Another reference that has been used to argue for the later date is 1:12: "those who are complacent, who are like wine left on its dregs." Some believe this comment indicates disappointment in the reformation of Josiah. The people who had endeavored to live up to the demands of the reforms had seen their dream of a reunited state crushed. But this interpretation is by no means certain.

Those who argue for a prereformation date point out references to astral worship (from Assyria?) and vestiges of Canaanite worship (1:4–5), foreign dress (1:8), false prophets and priests (3:4), and widespread injustice and violence among the civic leaders (3:2–3). But it is possible that Josiah's reforms were more superficial than we realize, and perhaps much idolatry remained. Moreover, Zephaniah seems to represent the condition of the people as a final one—doomed to judgment.

Another line of reasoning finds frequent allusions to Deuteronomy (Zep 1:13, 15, 17; 2:2, 5, 7, 11; 3:5, 19–20),[3] which, it is argued, could take place only after the rediscovery of the book of the law in 621 BC. This law, since it was violated by the priests, seems to have come already into public use (3:4). Zephaniah apparently makes no explicit reference to Josiah's reforms, and we can only make certain assumptions concerning his relationship to the reforms of Josiah.

---

3. Robertson (ibid., 254–55) gives a list of nine expressions and phrases in Zephaniah that have parallels in Deuteronomy.

3. POLITICAL BACKGROUND

After the wicked reigns of Manasseh (695–642 BC) and Amon (642–640 BC), the reforming king Josiah (640–609 BC) ascended the throne. During the reigns of his predecessors, apostate conditions had prevailed for more than half a century. It was during Josiah's reign that Zephaniah began warning the people of impending judgment. The fall of Samaria in 722 BC was a solemn reminder of God's justice and power.

Manasseh and Amon had remained loyal vassals to Assyria, but under Josiah the people experienced independence, for about this time Assyrian policy was changing as at home Assyria faced problems with Babylon and was no longer able to retain effective control in the west. Presumably, Josiah took advantage of the opportunity to launch sweeping reforms and moved to take possession of the provinces into which Assyria had divided the territory of northern Israel.

Although Zephaniah envisions an imminent invasion bringing about the downfall of Jerusalem (1:4, 10–13; 2:1; 3:1–4), the enemy is not identified. The general assumption understands the reference as being to Assyria. However, by the year 627 BC Assyrian ascendancy had been broken and therefore possibly posed little threat to Judah.[4] Another possibility for the reference is the Scythian incursions toward the end of the seventh century BC. Distinctive Scythian-style arrowheads from that era have been found in excavations at sites such as Lachish and Samaria, but the evidence remains indecisive. Although Babylon was only beginning its rise to power at the time of Josiah's death (609 BC), 2 Kings 22:15–20 seems to reflect anticipation of a coming invasion by Babylon.

4. RELIGIOUS BACKGROUND

The message of Zephaniah, along with the early discourses of Jeremiah and the history recorded in 2 Kings 21–23, reflects the social, moral, and religious conditions in Judah at that time. Manasseh and Amon had been godless kings, but Josiah was a God-fearing ruler (2 Kings 22 and 23). But any reform under Josiah does not appear to have influenced Zephaniah's audience much—his condemnation of the people gives the impression that he is addressing the majority of them. He does not mention Josiah's reforms, and the people are ripe for judgment.

The reforms of Josiah involved purging his nation of foreign cults and practices, and, since Assyrian power was slipping, no doubt heading the list for destruction were Assyrian religious practices. Various astral deities and old Canaanite practices were eradicated (2Ki 23:4–25). Cult personnel—including prostitutes of both sexes—were done away with. The shrines of the north and their personnel—especially the rival temple of Bethel—were destroyed. The message of the prophet reveals that all strata of society were involved in these aberrant practices, and the picture depicted is one of pervasive idolatry resulting in an immoral and corrupt society. There were priests, but they were idolatrous and were leading in the worship of false gods (Zep 1:4). Probably Josiah's most noteworthy reform, however, was the centralization of worship in Jerusalem—a move that was to have a great impact on generations to come.

---

4. Raymond B. Dillard and Tremper Longman III, *An Introduction to the Old Testament* (Grand Rapids: Zondervan, 1994), 417.

The precise relationship of Zephaniah to the reforms of Josiah has challenged commentators and students of this era. If Zephaniah preached after the reforms of Josiah, it appears that these reforms did not change society completely, for social injustice was widespread (3:1, 3, 7), and the rich enjoyed luxury at the cost of exploiting and oppressing the poor and disadvantaged (1:8–9). Religious remnants of Baalism were still present, and high places continued to flourish (1:4–5). Duplicity and syncretism were reflected in the recognition of both the Lord and Molech (1:5).

5. THEOLOGY AND MESSAGE

The prophetic message of Zephaniah was the first to be heard in Judah since the ministry of Isaiah and Micah, and the message he brought was awesome in nature and universal in scope (1:2). The book of Zephaniah serves as a compendium of the oracles of the prophets. In many ways Zephaniah links his prophecy to those of the earlier prophets, both in subject matter and expression. King has listed the extensive parallels between Zephaniah and his eighth-century predecessors, Amos, Hosea, Isaiah, and Micah.[5] In repeating and summarizing much of the judgment and salvation material common to all the prophets, Zephaniah does not hesitate to employ distinctive expressions used by them. "Be silent before the Sovereign Lord" (1:7) is found in Habakkuk 2:20; "the day of the Lord is near" (1:7) is found in Joel 1:15; and "the Lord has prepared a sacrifice" (1:7) appears in Isaiah 34:6.[6] In the tradition of the eighth-century Judahite prophets Isaiah and Micah (cf. Zep 3:1–3 with Isa 1:21–23 and Zep 3:3–5 with Mic 3:1–12), Zephaniah also shares features with his contemporary Jeremiah and with the sixth-century prophet Ezekiel.[7]

The focal point of Zephaniah's message is the "day of the Lord," a phrase that appears twenty-three times in Zephaniah and an expression used more by him than by any other prophet. Although other prophets (cf. Isa 2; Jer 46–51; Eze 7; Joel 2) do include this theme, in Zephaniah it ties the entire book together. For Zephaniah the day "is near" (1:7, 14); it is a day of "wrath,... distress and anguish ... trouble and ruin ... darkness and gloom ... clouds and blackness ... and battle cry" (1:15–16). The day of the Lord is a day of doom! The prophet declares this message because the people "have sinned against the Lord" (1:17).[8]

Up to the time of the writing prophets, the day of the Lord carried more positive content.[9] It was a welcome time of the Lord's presence reflected in liberating and sustaining his people and associated with the defeat of their enemies. But a change took place when Amos (Am 5:18–20) described that day in the language of inescapable judgment for the sinful people who transgressed God's covenant with them. Isaiah (Isa 2:12–21; 13:6–13; 34:1–8) also spoke of that day as a time of God's wrath on his own people. With the advent of these prophets, the Lord is presented as no longer fighting for his people but against

---

5. Greg A. King, "The Message of Zephaniah: An Urgent Echo," *AUSS* 34 (1996): 211–22.

6. For additional examples, compare Zephaniah 2:14 with Isaiah 13:21; 34:11, and Zephaniah 2:15 with Isaiah 47:8.

7. Many of these parallels are listed by Berlin, *Zephaniah*, 15–16.

8. Robertson (*Nahum, Habakkuk, and Zephaniah*, 267) notes that the concept of the "Day of Yahweh" is not limited to that exact phrase but also includes such expressions as "on the day of the sacrifice of Yahweh" (1:8); "in that day" (vv.9–10); "at that time" (v.12); and "the great Day of Yahweh" (v.14).

9. Maria Eszenyei Szeles, *Wrath and Mercy: A Commentary on the Books of Habakkuk and Zephaniah* (ITC; Grand Rapids: Eerdmans, 1987), 66.

them. However, Zephaniah also holds out a promise of shelter and safety for those who seek the Lord (Zep 2:3).

Achtemeier notes that modern ecclesiastical use of the "day of the LORD" is reflected in some lectionaries in which Zephaniah 1:7, 12–18 are coupled with 1 Thessalonians 5:1–10 or 1 Thessalonians 4:13–18, and with Matthew 24:14–15, 19–29 or Matthew 25:1–13.[10] The coupling equates Zephaniah's day of the Lord with the parousia, the resurrection from the dead, and the last judgment. This OT use of the day of the Lord has also been used in the realized eschatology of the NT; for example, the darkness of that day is found at the crucifixion of Jesus (from the sixth to the ninth hour).[11] Zephaniah's "day of the LORD," first manifested in the Babylonian conquest and exile, was only a harbinger of that ultimate cosmic and eschatological day of the Lord, which Paul often mentions (Ro 2:16; 1Co 1:8; Php 1:6, 10; 2:16; 2Ti 4:8).

The immediate application of Zephaniah's message was for the rebellious and defiled people who would not listen to their God or accept his instructions. Behind their facade of religious obedience were found deadly sins provoking the wrath of a holy God. The officials and rulers, the very ones responsible for leading the people, presumed upon their positions of authority and degraded and profaned their office (3:3–4). In graphic language the prophet describes the severe judgment on the godless: "Their blood will be poured out like dust and their entrails like filth" (1:17). That is, their priceless lifeblood is treated as mere dust and their very "entrails" ($l^e\hat{h}\hat{u}m$) like stinking human waste ($g\bar{a}l\bar{a}l$).

Despite such ominous, impending judgment, Zephaniah admonishes the "humble of the land" to "seek the LORD" and "seek righteousness" and "seek humility" and then "perhaps you will be sheltered on the day of the LORD's anger" (2:3). The "humble of the land" refers to those who humble themselves before the authority of their covenantal God. To "seek righteousness" means to seek the standards of the Lord of righteousness, the perfect God. The word "perhaps" does not express indecision but instead is a reminder that the final result lies in the hands of God and his sovereign grace. The message is addressed to those who had put their trust in such things as "fortified" cities (1:16) and silver and gold (1:18), things unable to save them in the end. Finally, along with a message of universal judgment is a message of universal salvation, when all the peoples "may call on the name of the LORD and serve him shoulder to shoulder" (3:9).

An important theological concept in Zephaniah is that of the remnant: "the remnant of the house of Judah" (2:7), "the remnant of my people" (2:9), and "the remnant of Israel" (3:13). This remnant eventually becomes the new "chosen people, a royal priesthood, a holy nation, a people belonging to God" (1Pe 2:9).[12]

Although the book of Zephaniah is brief, its possible intertextuality with Genesis and Deuteronomy has been noted. Berlin[13] observes that themes from the early chapters of Genesis appear in all three chapters of Zephaniah. Chapter 1 contains a description that is a reversal of the created order (see

---

10. Elizabeth Achtemeier, *Nahum–Malachi* (Interpretation; Atlanta: John Knox, 1986), 73.
11. Robertson (*Nahum, Habakkuk, and Zephaniah*, 272–73), after listing variations of the phrase "day of the LORD" in the OT, lists the various phrases in the NT that he believes carry the same referent.
12. For more on the concept of remnant in Zephaniah, see George W. Anderson, "The Idea of the Remnant in the Book of Zephaniah," *ASTI* 11 (1977/78): 11–14.
13. Berlin, *Zephaniah*, 13–14.

commentary), and the phrase "everything from the face of the earth" (1:2−3) may be compared with Genesis 2:6; 4:14; 6:1, 7; 7:4, 23; 8:8. Berlin believes this fact "reinforces the association with the stories of creation, expulsion from Eden, and the Flood." Zephaniah 2 echoes Genesis 10 with the expression "nations on every shore" (ʾîyê haggôyîm), found only in Zephaniah 2:11 and Genesis 10:5.[14] Zephaniah 3 may echo Genesis 11 with its phrase "purify the lips of the peoples" (3:9) and its reference to pure and correct speech (3:13).

But much more certain are the echoes and allusions connected with the book of Deuteronomy (and deuteronomic history, especially 2 Kings). The judgments listed in Zephaniah 1 recall the curses of Deuteronomy 28:29−49. The deuteronomic phrase "restore your fortunes" is found in Zephaniah 2:7 and 3:20. For more on intertextuality and echoes in Zephaniah of earlier material, see King, who has suggested and collected numerous possible examples.[15]

Zephaniah, along with other prophets, anticipates a time when all peoples will turn to and worship Israel's God (3:9−10). This new people will include both Jews and Gentiles (Gal 3:8−9, 14, 26−29). Possible messianic references (of one kind or another) have been suggested in 3:8−20.[16] Though Zephaniah may not speak of a personal royal Messiah, like the other prophets before him he speaks of a new messianic future with blessed results. By inference and implication, the messianic age, with its ingathering of the Gentiles, is found in Zephaniah.

6. FORMAT AND STYLE

The brief, fifty-three-verse book of Zephaniah was divided into three chapters in the Middle Ages, and earlier Masoretic notes divided the book into several divisions called *pisqot* (which always agree).[17] The brief Murabbaʿat text from Qumran also shows new sections beginning at 2:5 and 3:14.[18]

As in other prophetic books, the announcement of imminent judgment in the first part of Zephaniah is countered with the promise of coming restoration in the last part. Further division suggests for the book a tripartite structure, which basically assigns the material as (1) threats against Jerusalem and Judah (1:2−2:3); (2) threats against the nations (2:4−3:8); and (3) promises to both Jerusalem/Judah and the nations (3:9−20).[19]

The entire book of Zephaniah may be viewed as a chiasm designed to emphasize the character and certainty of the judgment about to fall on Judah and Jerusalem. The central and most emphatic portion of the book is the call for repentance (2:1−3), and the promise of salvation concludes the chiastic structure of the book (3:9−20). House believes that Nahum, Habakkuk, and Zephaniah are all from the same era,

---

14. For further possible parallels of Zephaniah 2 in Genesis 10, see ibid., 111−12.

15. King, "The Message of Zephaniah," 211−22.

16. For a survey and summary, see Gerard Van Groningen, *Messianic Revelation in the Old Testament* (Grand Rapids: Baker, 1990), 670−75.

17. These have been collected and presented in tables by Berlin, *Zephaniah*, 18.

18. Ibid., 18.

19. Brevard Childs, *Introduction to the Old Testament as Scripture* (Philadelphia: Fortress, 1979), 458; O. Kaiser, *Introduction to the Old Testament: A Presentation of its Results and Problems* (Minneapolis: Augsburg, 1977), 230.

share a strong interest in judgment, are linked in the canonical ordering of the Minor Prophets, and so are useful for noting how literary features may link adjoining books.[20]

The book is generally divided into seven or eight parts. Dorsey notes that S. R. Driver identified eight constituent units and R. L. Smith found seven (following closely the earlier analysis of Eissfeldt).[21] The following chiasm in Zephaniah as found by Dorsey is based on a seven-part symmetry that highlights the focal point of the book in the call to repentance (2:1–3).

A Coming judgment on the wicked of Jerusalem (1:2–6)
- They are idolatrous, follow Baal, swear by Molech, and do not seek Yahweh or inquire of him

  B Coming judgment on corrupt leaders (*śārîm*) and the rich of Jerusalem (1:7–13)
  - Their greed, violence (*ḥāmās*), and corruption
  - The view held by these people: Yahweh will do no good, nor will he do ill

    C Yahweh's judgment on all the nations: the great and terrible day of Yahweh (1:14–18)
   - Against all the earth and all the inhabitants (*yōšᵉbîm*) of the earth

      D CENTER: Call to repentance (2:1–3)

    C' Yahweh's judgment on all nations: oracles against the nations (2:4–15)
   - Yahweh will be against all the gods of the earth and against the inhabitants (*yōšᵉbîm*) of the seacoast, etc.

  B' Coming judgment of corrupt political leaders (including *śārîm*) and religious leaders of Jerusalem (3:1–7)
  - Their greed, violence (*ḥāmās*) against the law, and corruption
  - But Yahweh is righteous; he does no wrong

A' Coming restoration of Jerusalem and its fortunes (3:8–20)
- They seek refuge in Yahweh, call on his name, and serve him (not idols) with one accord
- Yahweh will purify the (idolatrous) speech of his people

The language of Zephaniah, though not as majestic as Isaiah's, is graphic. The verses sometimes form a series of vivid sketches, as in ch. 1, where the peculiarities of Canaanite ritual are sharply delineated. As in Isaiah, the judgments of the Lord are sometimes presented in vivid anthropomorphic imagery, as when Zephaniah describes him as searching the city with lamps (1:12).

Zephaniah's style is chiefly characterized by an overall energy and unity of composition. Rapid and effective alternations of threats and promises also characterize his style. As noted above, there are stylistic similarities between Zephaniah and other prophets; but we cannot be certain whether these are cases of borrowing or cases of coincidence because of common expressions or perhaps proverbial language. The

---

20. Paul R. House, "Dramatic Coherence in Nahum, Habakkuk, and Zephaniah," pp. 195–208 in *Forming Prophetic Literature: Essays on Isaiah and the Twelve in Honor of John D. W. Watts*, ed. Paul R. House and James W. Watts (JSOTSup; Sheffield: Sheffield Academic Press, 1996). Similar observations are found in Richard Patterson, "A Literary Look at Nahum, Habakkuk, and Zephaniah," *GTJ* 11 (1990): 17–27.

21. David A. Dorsey, *The Literary Structure of the Old Testament* (Grand Rapids: Baker, 1999), 310.

prophets had much in common, including the notable Hebrew parallelisms that can often be traced to Canaanite religious writings.

Zephaniah makes use of a variety of rhetorical figures of language: metaphor and simile (1:7, 11–12; 2:1–2, 4–7, 9; 3:3, 8, 16), literary/historical allusions (1:3; 2:4, 9; 3:9–10, 18), personification (1:14; 3:14–16), anthropopoeia (1:4, 12–13; 3:7, 8, 15), irony (1:11; 2:12), merismus (1:12), synecdoche (1:16; 2:11, 13–14; 3:6), enallage (3:7), hendiadys (3:7, 19), chiasmus (3:19), alliteration and paronomasia (1:2, 15, 17; 2:1, 4, 7), enjambment (1:9–12; 2:2–3, 14; 3:3, 7–9, 11–12, 18–20), and repetition and refrain (1:2–3, 14–16, 18; 2:2–3; 3:14–15).[22] Berlin calls attention to examples of wordplay in 2:4, where the names of cities echo their attributes, and to anaphora in 1:3, 5–6, 15; 2:2–3; 3:2.[23]

Several key words are repeated throughout this small book: *yôm*, "day" (21x); *qārôb*, "near" (10x); *ʾāsap*, "gather," *ʾereṣ*, "earth," and *šēm*, "name" (5x each); *šāpaṭ*, "judge" (4x); and *pāqad*, "punish/visit," and *qābaṣ*, "assemble" (3x each).

Zephaniah features frequent shifts of voice, from first person address spoken by God to the third person perspective of the prophet. Some have suggested this phenomenon reflects editorial work or different sources. Paul House understands the shifts as indicating the basic structure of the book, which he understands as a dramatic presentation. Certainly they are too numerous to be textual variants or "accidents" but instead are intentional for effect. Berlin accepts them "as a normal aspect of prophetic writing, since they occur in other prophetic books, too."[24] Perhaps this shifting is merely a striking way of identifying the words of the prophets with the message from God.

7. THE TEXT AND CRITICISM

Criticism of the short book of Zephaniah is limited and of little weight. Some interpreters assume it was assembled piecemeal from various periods. Eissfeldt denied to Zephaniah certain alleged exilic or postexilic additions.[25] For example, some critics claim the oracle against Moab and Ammon (2:9–11) is late because its language reflects conditions of the exile. Some take the account of the fall of Nineveh (2:15) as being added after the event had taken place. But such negative assessments are largely subjective and speculative. Berlin says, "The book as it stands ... presents itself rhetorically and structurally as a unified work ... and in its canonical form it was apparently intended to be interpreted as such."[26]

Hyatt places Zephaniah's activity under Jehoiakim (609–597 BC).[27] Smith and Lacheman explain the whole book as a pseudepigraphon compiled about 200 BC![28] Generally speaking, however, critics have not labored over the authenticity and genuineness of the book.

---

22. These examples were collected by Richard D. Patterson, *Nahum, Habakkuk, Zephaniah* (Chicago: Moody Press, 1991), 285.
23. Berlin, *Zephaniah*, 12.
24. Ibid., 12.
25. Otto Eissfeldt, *The Old Testament: An Introduction*, trans. P. R. Ackroyd (New York: Harper & Row, 1965), 425.
26. Berlin, *Zephaniah*, 20.
27. J. P. Hyatt, "The Date and Background of Zephaniah," *JNES* 7 (1948): 25–29.
28. L. P. Smith and E. L. Lacheman, "The Authorship of the Book," *JNES* 9 (1950): 137–42.

Despite some claims that the book of Zephaniah is not well preserved, the text is in relatively good condition, and further textual data are now available from the Dead Sea Scrolls: two fragmentary *pesharim* (commentaries) on Zephaniah from Qumran Cave 1 (1QpZep 1:18–2:2) and Cave 4 (4QpZep 1:12–13), and a scroll of the Minor Prophets from Muraba'at, dating from about AD 100, containing most of Zephaniah (1:1; 1:11–3:6; 3:8–20) in a textual tradition close to that of the MT.[29]

The Septuagint (LXX) of Zephaniah exhibits about the same general features as found with some of the other minor prophetic books. The book's septuagintal form has been studied exhaustively by Gerleman, who found few significant variants between its tradition and that of the MT.[30] A Greek translation of the twelve Minor Prophets from the first century AD was discovered at Naḥal Ḥever (8 Ḥev XII gr) and contains a few fragments of Zephaniah (1:1–4, 13–17; 2:9–10; 3:6–7).

The study by Ball[31] argues, on the basis of rhetorical analysis, for the integrity of the MT, as do the works by House[32] and Dorsey.[33] The general structural unity of the book, especially as related to the theological framework of the covenant, is also supported by Sheehan.[34]

8. BIBLIOGRAPHY

Achtemeier, Elizabeth. *Nahum–Malachi*. Interpretation: A Bible Commentary for Teaching and Preaching. Edited by James Luther Mays. Atlanta: John Knox, 1986.

Kapelrud, Arvid S. *The Message of the Prophet Zephaniah*. Oslo: Universitetsforlaget, 1975.

Keil, C. F. *The Twelve Minor Prophets*. Vol. 2 of *Biblical Commentary on the Old Testament*. Edited by C. F. Keil and F. Delitzsch. Grand Rapids: Eerdmans, 1949.

Patterson, Richard D. *Nahum, Habakkuk, Zephaniah*. The Wycliffe Exegetical Commentary. Chicago: Moody Press, 1991.

Robertson, O. Palmer. *Nahum, Habakkuk, and Zephaniah*. The New International Commentary on the Old Testament. Grand Rapids: Eerdmans, 1990.

Sabottka, Lindger. *Zephania*. Rome: Pontifical Biblical Institute, 1972.

Smith, J. M. Powis, and Charles B. Fagnani. *A Critical and Exegetical Commentary on Micah, Zephaniah, Nahum, Habakkuk, Obadiah and Joel*. International Critical Commentary. Edited by S. R. Driver and C. A. Briggs. Edinburgh: T & T Clark, 1965.

---

29. J. S. Kselman, "Zephaniah (Book of)," *ABD*, 6:1078.

30. G. Gerleman, *Zephania textkritisch und literaisch untersucht* (Lund: Gleerup, 1942).

31. Ivan Ball, "A Rhetorical Study of Zephaniah" (Ph.D. diss.; Ann Arbor: University Microfilms, 1972).

32. Paul House, *Zephaniah. A Prophetic Drama* (Sheffield: Almond, 1988).

33. Dorsey, *Literary Structure of the Old Testament*.

34. Clint Sheehan, "Kingdom through Covenant: The Structure and Theology of Zephaniah," *Baptist Review of Theology* 6 (1996): 7–21.

9. OUTLINE

In the first chapter Zephaniah centers his word of judgment on Judah; in the second chapter, after an exhortation to repentance, he predicts and pronounces judgment on Philistia, Moab, Ammon, Cush, and Assyria—neighbors of Judah; in the last chapter, after a word concerning judgment on Jerusalem, he promises future glory for Israel's remnant.

Text and Exposition

I. INTRODUCTION (1:1)

¹The word of the LORD that came to Zephaniah son of Cushi, the son of Gedaliah, the son of Amariah, the son of Hezekiah, during the reign of Josiah son of Amon king of Judah:

COMMENTARY

1 For the meaning of the prophet's name, see "Author" in the introduction. This author, in tracing his pedigree back four generations, gives us more information about his ancestry than does any other prophet. Perhaps he did so because the good king Hezekiah was his great-great-grandfather. The time of the prophecy took place during the reign of Josiah, king of Judah (see "Date" in the introduction). Under some of the other kings, the evildoers could have blamed the king's bad example, but Josiah would have been a good role model for them. However, they seemed to prefer Josiah's father, wicked Amon, as their role model.

The message in this book does not originate from Zephaniah; on the contrary, it is "the word of the LORD that came to Zephaniah," who is just one more messenger in a long chain of servants of the Lord who spoke his message to the people. Robertson, 251, summarizes, "Inspired of God so that their words were identical with God's words, these instruments of divine revelation mediated a confrontation with God too terrible for the people to endure on their own (cf. Deut. 18:15–17)."

II. DAY OF JUDGMENT (1:2–3:8)

OVERVIEW

Like other prophetic books, the book of Zephaniah begins with words of judgment and concludes with words of hope and salvation. The first part of the book (1:2–3:8) is characterized by words of retribution and a description of desolation; the last part (3:9–20) contains the promise of redemption and a description of deliverance.

For Zephaniah, "the day of the LORD" is in fact the day of judgment, and he uses the expression more than any other prophet.

A. Against Judah (1:2–2:3)

OVERVIEW

The subject of this passage is generally Judah but with a focus on Jerusalem. The fortunes (or misfortunes) of Jerusalem, the influential capital, greatly affected the larger and immediately surrounding areas.

1. General Warning (1:2–3)

OVERVIEW

Before Zephaniah focuses his attention on Judah, he issues a general warning of coming destruction in broad terminology. The inclusion of nature is a reminder that human sin affects nature itself (cf. Ge 3:17; Jer 12:4; Ro 8:20–21).

Destruction of "both men and animals," "birds of the air," "fish of the sea" is the same series of life forms as found in Genesis 1:20–26—but in reverse order. (Genesis orders the list as fish, birds, animals, and humans.) The inversion in Zephaniah is prob-

ably meant to describe God's act of judgment as an act of "anti-creation" (cf. Hos 4:1–3; Jer 4:23–26). (For more on the reversal-of-creation idea, see Michael De Roche, "Zephaniah 1:2–3: The 'Sweeping' of Creation," *VT* 30 [1980]: 104–9.)

God is judge of the whole world—but especially of his sinful and rebellious covenantal people, Judah. These privileged people of God are especially accountable for their conduct.

> 2 "I will sweep away everything
>   from the face of the earth,"
>
>   declares the LORD.
>
> 3 "I will sweep away both men and animals;
>   I will sweep away the birds of the air
>   and the fish of the sea.
>   The wicked will have only heaps of rubble
>   when I cut off man from the face of the earth,"
>
>   declares the LORD.

COMMENTARY

2 The expression "face of the earth" (*pᵉnê hāʾᵃdāmâ*), used of the great deluge of Noah's time (Ge 6:7; 7:4), refers to more than just a local land unless a specific limitation is added. Here it is used in the context of an all encompassing judgment scene.

3 Language that pairs humans and animals (the sixth day of creation) and birds and fish (the fifth day of creation) and prefaces each with "sweep away" vividly sets forth the totality and intensity of destruction. "The wicked will have only heaps of rubble" is variously rendered: "the stumbling blocks with the wicked" (KJV) and "overthrow the wicked" (RSV and NAB; cf. Notes). The general thrust of the passage, indicating thorough destruction, is clear enough.

NOTES

2 "Sweep away" translates אָסֹף אָסֵף (ʾāsōp ʾāsēp). Instead of the expected first person אֶאֱסֹף (ʾeʾĕsōp) after the preceding infinitive absolute ʾāsōp for emphasis, the author wrote אָסֵף (ʾāsēp), which has generally been understood as a Hiphil form of סוּף (sûp), a root signifying "cease, come to an end" (cf. KD, BDB). Keil argued that the different roots are sufficiently similar in meaning so as to be used this way. (Compare the LXX's ἐκλείψει ἐκλιπέτω, ekleipsei eklipetō, and the Vulgate's congregans congregabo, and observe that both versions use cognate roots.) Others have suggested various emendations to the text (cf. Sabottka, 5–7). The general meaning is clear, and the translation "sweep" echoes the sound of the Hebrew consonants. The versions have "utterly consume" (KJV), "destroy" (REB), "sweep away" (NRSV, TNK), and "put an end to" (GWT).

3 The NIV renders this verse: "The wicked will have only heaps of rubble," which translates וְהַמַּכְשֵׁלֹות אֶת־הָרְשָׁעִים (weHammakšēlôt ʾet-hārešāʿîm). This rendering understood the traditional consonantal text as a Hiphil participle, "the things that cause to stumble"; (cf. Patterson, 302). The NIV understood hammakšēlôt to refer to that which has been brought down ("heaps of rubble") and ʾet as the preposition "with." The KJV, taking this entire phrase as the object of the verb "consume," translates, "the stumbling blocks with the wicked." The KJV understands the participle to mean that which causes downfall ("stumbling blocks") and ʾet as the sign of the accusative. The NIV's marginal note reflects the uncertainty of this phrase. The LXX omits it. The other versions have: "I will make the wicked stumble" (TNK); "the stumbling blocks along with the wicked" (NKJV); "will make the wicked stumble" (NRSV); and "the ruins along with the wicked" (NASB).

2. Judgment for Judah (1:4–13)

OVERVIEW

After the opening, universal depiction of judgment, the prophet narrows his message to the small but special kingdom of Judah. Jerusalem and Judah had been recipients of the special revelation of God; now they will be recipients of his special judgment. The sins of idolatry, religious syncretism, indifference, and rebellion against God are especially noted.

⁴"I will stretch out my hand against Judah
    and against all who live in Jerusalem.
I will cut off from this place every remnant of Baal,
    the names of the pagan and the idolatrous priests—
⁵those who bow down on the roofs
    to worship the starry host,
those who bow down and swear by the Lord
    and who also swear by Molech,
⁶those who turn back from following the Lord
    and neither seek the Lord nor inquire of him.
⁷Be silent before the Sovereign Lord,
    for the day of the Lord is near.
The Lord has prepared a sacrifice;
    he has consecrated those he has invited.
⁸On the day of the Lord's sacrifice
    I will punish the princes
    and the king's sons
and all those clad
    in foreign clothes.
⁹On that day I will punish
    all who avoid stepping on the threshold,
who fill the temple of their gods
    with violence and deceit.

¹⁰"On that day," declares the Lord,
    "a cry will go up from the Fish Gate,
    wailing from the New Quarter,
    and a loud crash from the hills.
¹¹Wail, you who live in the market district;
    all your merchants will be wiped out,
    all who trade with silver will be ruined.
¹²At that time I will search Jerusalem with lamps
    and punish those who are complacent,
    who are like wine left on its dregs,
who think, 'The Lord will do nothing,
    either good or bad.'
¹³Their wealth will be plundered,
    their houses demolished.

> They will build houses
>   but not live in them;
> they will plant vineyards
>   but not drink the wine.

COMMENTARY

4 When the Lord says he will "stretch out [his] hand against," he is indicating a special work of punishment (cf. Isa 5:25; 9:12, 17, 21). If we assume that Josiah's reforms have already had some effect at this time, the reference to the "remnant of Baal" would be to the forms of Baal worship still left in the land from Manasseh's detestable institution of it (2Ki 21:3, 5, 7; 2Ch 33:3, 7). Assuming Josiah destroyed much but not all in this pagan cult (2Ch 34:4), the pockets of Baalism that still exist necessitate judgment and eradication. Baalism had been a seductive force faced by God's people from their early days in Canaan and had deep roots.

"The pagan and the idolatrous priests" reflects the traces of idolatrous worship that yet remain despite official action against the cult. God intends a judgment that will totally eliminate Baalism. This judgment will be fulfilled in Judah by the Babylonian invasion. The expression "the pagan and the idolatrous priests" translates Hebrew *hakkᵉmārîm ᶜim-hakkōhᵃnîm* ("the Chemarims with the priests," KJV; however, the same term is translated by the KJV as "idolatrous priests" in 2 Kings 23:5).

The choice is between Baal and the Lord. Which one is truly God? The choice is between the cyclical worldview of Canaanite Baalism or a sovereign God who governs all according to his sovereign purposes.

5–6 These verses delineate and describe the persons involved in this pagan worship. "Roofs" (i.e., "housetops") were flat (cf. 2Ki 23:5–6, 12; Jer 19:13; 32:29) and thus were convenient places for worship and viewing the sky. Astrology and the worship of heavenly bodies was one of the most ancient forms of idolatry, and even in modern western culture many believe their destiny is controlled by the stars. Early on, Moses had given warnings against worshiping the starry host (Dt 4:19), but Manasseh and his successors rebelled against such prohibitions (2Ki 21:3, 5; 23:5–6; Jer 7:17–18; 8:2; 44:17–19, 25). Josiah acted against this evil practice (2Ki 23:5), but (depending on the date of Zephaniah) the reference here suggests that it persists.

The last part of v.5 reflects the confused and compromising attitude of God's covenantal people who do "bow down and swear by the LORD" but who "also swear by Molech." The precise identification of the Hebrew reference is uncertain, as reflected in the rendering by the English versions: Milcom (NKJV, NASB, NRSV, NAB, GWT, CEV, ESV), Molech (NLT, NCV, TEV), Malcam (TNK), and Malcham (KJV). Whatever the exact reference, the point is that such "inclusive" idolatry is just as offensive to the Lord as exclusive idolatry. The deity called "Molech" is referred to in 1 Kings 11:33 and possibly in Amos 5:26 (cf. NIV note; "Moloch," KJV).

Finally listed are those simply and summarily described as the faithless and indifferent, those who "turn back" and "neither seek the LORD nor inquire of him" (v.6). Verses 5–6 class together those guilty of straightforward and outright idolatry, those guilty of spiritual compromise, and those guilty of plain indifference—all three are repugnant to the holy God, who redeemed this people to be his own special people and a light to the nations. They have violated the heart of the Decalogue, "You shall have no other gods before me" (Ex 20:3).

7 In view of the doom facing them, the prophet calls for silent attention before the Lord (cf. Hab 2:20). The reason: "The day of the Lord is near." Zephaniah's message is not merely ominous in its description but is also declared to be imminent and inevitable. The "day of the Lord" in view here is the day of reckoning; it is a term used of God's judgment. Obadiah (Ob 15) says it is a time when "your deeds will return upon your own head."

"The Lord has prepared [his] sacrifice"—the people of Judah (cf. Isa 34:6; Jer 46:10; Eze 39:17). "He has consecrated" (*hiqdîš*) the despised and dreaded Babylonians as his priests to slay this sacrifice. Isaiah (Isa 13:3) also called the Babylonians consecrated or "holy ones" (*m^equddāšāy*) summoned by the Lord. Jeremiah (Jer 46:10) and Ezekiel (Eze 39:17) similarly referred to the Lord's offering sacrifice in his judgment. When sinners will not repent and offer themselves as living sacrifices, then they become the sacrifices and victims of their own sins.

8 Robertson, 275, believes the alternation between third person ("the Lord's sacrifice") and first person ("I will punish") in this verse and elsewhere is a deliberate literary device for "vivifying the Lord's own involvement," not a reflection of "secondary origin of the materials."

The royal leaders ("the princes [*śārîm*; "officials," TNIV] and the king's sons"), who bore chief responsibility, are singled out for special notice. They should lead the people in righteousness, but instead they are ringleaders of evil; therefore, the Lord will punish the "king's sons" and "princes" but

not God-fearing Josiah himself. Indeed the reigns of the kings who succeed Josiah end in misery.

Though some commentators limit the expression "foreign clothes" to clothing worn by the idolaters when they worship, or even to the prohibition of men's wearing women's clothing (Dt 22:5), or vice versa, "foreign clothes" in this context probably simply refers to dress that imitates or reflects the foreign Egyptian or Babylonian styles and thus indicates a general inclination of the heart for things foreign. The Lord earlier issued some stipulations about Israelite dress (Nu 15:38; Dt 22:11–12), apparently to keep the people mindful that they are his special people (Nu 15:39–40) and belong solely to him. Any departure is viewed as disobedience and sin, evidencing a wayward attitude. But the sinful and confused people think they have to adjust to reality: "Assyria ruled the day; and if one is wise, one will be pleasant and as accommodating as possible to those who hold the reins of power" (Achtemeier, 69).

9 "Avoid stepping on the threshold" may reflect a cultic practice referred to in 1 Samuel 5:5, where we are told that the pagan priests avoided stepping on a defiled or sacrosanct threshold. This practice probably arose when the head and hands of the Philistine idol Dagon broke off and lay on its temple's threshold. However, it seems likely that this custom would probably only be observed in temples of Dagon and it is doubtful that such a practice would be transferred to Israelite worship.

Another interpretation understands this passage to refer to theft and plunder and thus fits nicely with the following couplet: "fill the temple of their gods with [the results of] violence and deceit." According to this interpretation, the verb should be translated "leap on" (KJV, NASB) or "over" (NKJV, NRSV, GWT, NAB, TNK) the threshold. Some modern versions resort to paraphrase to communicate their understanding of this enigmatic expression: "dance on the temple terrace" (REB); "worship Dagon" (NCV); "worshippers of pagan gods" (CEV); "participate in pagan worship ceremonies" (NLT); and "worship like pagans" (TEV).

10 "That day" refers to the day of the Lord, the time of great wailing and outcry from the various sections of the city. The Fish Gate, in Jerusalem's north wall, was probably near the present Damascus Gate and was the main gate to the north of the city (cf. Ne 3:3; 12:39; 2Ch 33:14). This is the direction the enemy would come from.

The Second Quarter (NIV, "New Quarter," but cf. 2Ki 22:14 [2Ch 34:22]; Neh 11:9) was probably near the Fish Gate and the temple. As its name implies, the area was probably a more recent addition. According to 2 Kings 22:14, Huldah the prophetess lived there.

"The hills" probably refers to those within Jerusalem (Zion, Ophel, Moriah), not to the surrounding hills. The "loud crash" vividly depicts the city as crashing down on the heads of its inhabitants.

11 "Market district" (*maktēš*; GK 4847) translates a Hebrew word that remains obscure. (The KJV and NKJV simply transliterate "Maktesh.") Though it is not clear whether the term should be understood as a common noun or a proper noun, in view of the context, it seems to represent the area where merchants gathered. Most commentators identify the site somewhere in the depression of the Tyropean Valley. The fact that the Hebrew word may mean "mortar" is especially appropriate since God is about to pound his people like grain in a mortar. In fact, some versions actually translate "Mortar" (NASB, GWT, NAB, ESV). However, the term probably simply designates an area well known to the people at that time, so the NIV and other translations (NLT, NCV) treat it as a common noun referring to an area or district.

12 As one on a raid and searching with lights, the Lord seeks those who displease him in order to punish them. The KJV, which translated the Hebrew term for "lamps" (*nērôt*) as "candles," inserted an anachronism into our text, since candles were not used until a much later period in history. These "lamps" were clay oil lamps commonly used at that time. (Their use for careful searching is also found in Luke 15:8, where again the use of "candle" in Roman times would still be anachronistic.)

The vivid imagery of "wine left on its dregs" (see Note), also used by Jeremiah (Jer 48:11), was proverbial for indifference and callousness, as shown by the parallel, "who are complacent." In making the best wine, the liquid is poured from vessel to vessel, separating the wine from its dregs or "lees" (the sediment of the grapes). If allowed to remain too long on its lees, the wine becomes thick and syrupy and subject to mold. So evil people are resting complacently on evil influences and are securely settled in their wicked society. The effect of wealth on evildoers at ease hardens the heart and leads to a false sense of security (cf. Am 6:1).

In this condition the rebels express their true inward conclusion that the Lord will do "nothing either good or bad." That is, they deny God's providence, as though he has brought about neither blessing nor judgment. For all practical purposes God is considered nonexistent and at least certainly is not thought to govern the world. These people end up trying to make themselves their own gods—the ultimate idolatry (cf. Ge 3:5). This prophetic indictment of complacency is also found in Isaiah 32:9; Ezekiel 30:9; and Amos 6:1. Unfortunately, complacency and apathy have all too often been treated lightly by God's people, with resulting tragedy.

13 The complacent and apathetic people are in a pathetic condition, wrapped up in and blinded by their riches. They will now realize how foolish they have been as they experience punishment that deprives them of the very means by which they gained their status (cf. Am 5:11; Mic 6:13–15).

Their wealth will become booty enjoyed by their enemy (Dt 28:30, 39).

The last four lines of v.13 are made up of the covenantal curses found in Deuteronomy 28:30, 39. Because of the people's complacency and impudence, God will bring on them the curses of the covenant, and they will not enjoy their wealth, homes, or vineyards (cf. Lev 26:32–33; Dt 28:30, 39; Am 5:11; Mic 6:15). The Lord will indeed demonstrate his activity and agency in the world. He will fulfill his promises to his people—for good or bad.

NOTES

4 "Chemarim" is the KJV transliteration of the Hebrew כְּמָרִים (kᵉmārîm; GK 4024), a term also found in 2 Kings 23:5 ("idolatrous priests," KJV; "pagan priests," NIV) and in Hosea 10:5 ("idolatrous priests," NIV, KJV). Some lexicons and commentators have suggested the term comes from a root for "black" (from the garments priests wore) or from a root for "zealous" (for their fanaticism), but the precise meaning remains uncertain. *HALOT*, 1:482, gives the meaning "priest." Usage in the Bible suggests the reference is to priests of foreign deities. The root may be preserved for us in some Canaanite personal names (Sabottka, 189). Some suggest that the use of כֹּהֵן (kōhēn), the other word for "priest" here, is a gloss to explain the enigmatic kᵉmārîm (Kapelrud, 22; Smith and Fagnani, 187) and is only a guess resulting from frustration over the precise nuance of kᵉmārîm. But the context indicates that here apostate or pagan priests are in view.

5 "Molech" or "Milcom," representing מַלְכָּם (malkām), may refer to a Canaanite deity mentioned in various Semitic texts, but the situation is complicated by the fact that מֶלֶךְ (melek, "king") is used as an epithet of other deities. Hence "their king" (as our text can be translated) may refer to Baal (cf. Sabottka, 24), whom the Canaanites viewed as their (divine) king. The Lucianic version of the LXX, the Syriac, and the Vulgate support the reading "Milkom," the detestable god of the Ammonites (1Ki 11:5, 33; 2Ki 23:13).

7 "Be silent" translates הַס (has), which is onomatopoetic for "hush!" Less graphic is the KJV "hold thy peace." This vivid interjection with imperatival force is used only seven times in the OT and always in noteworthy contexts (e.g., Am 8:3).

8 The expression "king's sons" may be inclusive of members of the king's household and not limited to sons of the reigning king. The LXX translates "house of the king" (cf. "royal house," NEB). The TNK translates "king's sons" but has a footnote: "apparently brothers of King Amon, who exercised influence during the minority of King Josiah (2 Kings 22:1)." Robertson, 275–76, believes the reference is to Jehoahaz and Jehoiakim and observes that "if the prophet was of the royal line himself, being the son of Hezekiah (1:1), he may have had special awareness of the situation prevailing in the royal palace."

9 The ancient versions do not help much with the difficult expression "stepping on the threshold." The Greek translators seem as much confused as modern translators. The NEB tries to capture the idea with its quaint rendering of this passage as, "all who ape outlandish fashions" and "all who dance on the temple terrace." The Targum's "all those who walk in the laws of the Philistines" may tie in with the practice reflected in 1 Samuel 5:5 (cf. Smith and Fagnani, 208).

The NIV's rendering of אֲדֹנֵיהֶם (ᵃdōnêhem) as "their gods" breaks with the traditional rendering of "their masters" (KJV, RSV). The traditional understanding takes the context and terminology to indicate the royal palace, not the temple. The NIV understands the context as a continuing reference to pagan temples. The term אָדוֹן (ʾādôn, "lord, master") is frequently used in Semitic inscriptions for deity (Sabottka, 43). The LXX has κυρίου τοῦ θεοῦ αὐτῶν (kyriou tou theou autōn, "the Lord their God"), but with several variants in the MS witness.

10 "New Quarter" translates מִשְׁנֶה (mišneh, lit., "second" [KJV]). According to Richard Hess, the name is mentioned only from the late seventh century onward and is identified by Mazar with the expansion of the city onto the hill west of the City of David (*NIDOTTE*, 2:1139).

11 "Market district" translates מַכְתֵּשׁ (maktēš). The versions vary: the LXX has τὴν κατακεκομμένην (tēn katakekommenēn, "cut down"); Vulgate, pilae; Targum, "by the brook Kidron." Aquila, Symmachus, and Theodotion have various translations (cf. Smith and Fagnani, 209). An educated guess would consider this area as some depression in the geography of Jerusalem, possibly an area noted for commerce. The NIV presents the option of a proper noun ("the Mortar") in its marginal note.

12 הַקֹּפְאִים עַל־שִׁמְרֵיהֶם (haqqōpᵊʾîm ʿal-šimrêhem) is literally, "the ones settled/congealed on their dregs [lees]," which is basically the way it is handled in the KJV, "the men that are settled on their lees." The RSV's "[the men] who are thickening upon their lees" does not communicate much, and the NLT's "those who sit complacent in their sins" captures the idea but misses the imagery. The ESV simply has "who are complacent," thus also missing the imagery of the Hebrew. The TNK has "rest untroubled on their lees." The NIV tries to capture the best of both approaches with its somewhat expanded translation. The root קָפָא (qāpāʾ) means "to thicken, congeal, coagulate" and is used of cheese in Job 10:10. The Hebrew שְׁמָרִים (šᵊmārîm) is used of lees also in Psalm 75:8[9]; Isaiah 25:6; and Jeremiah 48:11. Its etymology and ancient near eastern background is uncertain (*NIDOTTE*, 4:184).

Smith and Fagnani's suggested reading הַשַּׁאֲנַנִּים (haššaʾᵃnannîm, "the ones at ease"; 209), from the root שׁאן (šʾn), is presumptive and lacks textual support.

3. Description of That Day (1:14–2:3)

OVERVIEW

In striking poetic language Zephaniah describes the cataclysmic "great day of the LORD" (1:14), also called "the day of the LORD's wrath" (2:2) and "the day of the LORD's anger" (2:3). The prophet indicates the imminence of that day: "near — near and coming quickly" (1:14). It is much nearer than the people realize as it speeds toward full realization, and the prophet depicts in horrific detail that overwhelming day (cf. Am 5:18–20).

> ¹⁴ "The great day of the LORD is near —
>   near and coming quickly.
> Listen! The cry on the day of the LORD will be bitter,
>   the shouting of the warrior there.

¹⁵ That day will be a day of wrath,
   a day of distress and anguish,
a day of trouble and ruin,
   a day of darkness and gloom,
   a day of clouds and blackness,
¹⁶ a day of trumpet and battle cry
   against the fortified cities
   and against the corner towers.
¹⁷ I will bring distress on the people
   and they will walk like blind men,
   because they have sinned against the Lord.
Their blood will be poured out like dust
   and their entrails like filth.
¹⁸ Neither their silver nor their gold
   will be able to save them
   on the day of the Lord's wrath.
In the fire of his jealousy
   the whole world will be consumed,
for he will make a sudden end
   of all who live in the earth."

^{2:1} Gather together, gather together,
   O shameful nation,
² before the appointed time arrives
   and that day sweeps on like chaff,
before the fierce anger of the Lord comes upon you,
   before the day of the Lord's wrath comes upon you.
³ Seek the Lord, all you humble of the land,
   you who do what he commands.
Seek righteousness, seek humility;
   perhaps you will be sheltered
   on the day of the Lord's anger.

COMMENTARY

14 The day of the Lord is called "great," as it is also described in Joel 2:11 ("the day of the Lord is great"). It is probably called "great" because of its ominous threat and its awesome effects. It hangs over the people like the famous sword of Damocles; it is right at hand, certain, and hastening to its goal.

15 The "day" of judgment is mentioned seven times in this verse and the next, thus depicting the fullness of God's wrath being poured out. The repetitive "stacking" of vividly descriptive lines is designed to drive home the dreadful character of the great "day of wrath" of the Lord, the time when vent is given to the pent-up, divine holy anger. First, its stressful conditions are reflected in the words "distress," "anguish," "trouble," and "ruin." The Hebrew behind "trouble" (*šō'â*) and "ruin" (*mᵉšô'â*), with its dreary, monotonous similarity of sounds, reflects the pathetic situation.

Moreover, the ominous character of that terrible day is reflected by the use of such words as "darkness," "gloom," "clouds," and "blackness." The phenomena accompanying the theophany at Sinai are strikingly similar—all cosmic manifestations of the presence of God (cf. Ex 20:18). At Sinai it was God's covenantal love bringing them into his fellowship through the gracious giving of the law, but here it is his holy wrath revealed in fury against the obstinate sinners.

Luther mentioned that this passage was often chanted by Roman Catholic priests at funeral masses. The words from the Vulgate's version of this verse (*dies irae dies illa*) inspired the opening words of the thirteenth-century hymn by Thomas Celano on the last judgment, the day of God's wrath (though Achtemeier, 71, notes that this tradition has been questioned). At any rate, there are not fewer than 160 English and 90 German translations of this influential ancient Latin hymn (Patterson, 288–89).

16 The stark description continues so vividly that one feels personally present at the battle and able to hear the trumpet blasts from the attacking invaders (cf. Am 2:2). The trumpet and the battle cry represent warfare and battle and signal the people to get ready (cf. Jdg 3:27). Although the primary reference is to the mighty Babylonian army, ultimately it is the Lord himself behind the scene ruling the series of events. The concept of holy war is reversed here as the holy God fights through the

enemy against his own people instead of fighting their enemies through them for their benefit.

17 The prophet again brings in his cause-and-effect observation: this deep distress is "because they have sinned against the LORD." The judgment the people experience will cause them to stagger and stumble like blind men (cf. Dt 28:29), unable to find a way of escape from their calamity. In addition, their blood will be spilled out like "dust" (*ʿāpār*) and their entrails (*lᵉḥûm*) like "filth" (*gālāl*) trampled underfoot by their enemy. Their very life's blood (Lev 17:11) will be considered as cheap and common as dust (cf. 2Ki 13:7; Zec 9:3). God is against them. (The TNIV changes the earlier NIV "filth" [*gālāl*] back to the traditional "dung.")

18 To emphasize their desperate plight, the prophet warns the people that they cannot buy their way out. Neither silver nor gold will protect them from the wrath of the Lord (cf. Pr 11:4). The reference to silver and gold probably refers to their accumulated wealth, but it may also refer to their powerless idols, which were often covered with such metals (cf. Isa 30:22; Eze 7:19–20).

The "fire of his jealousy" graphically depicts his burning and zealous anger against his sinful people. W. Bailey (*Zephaniah* [NAC; Nashville: Broadman & Holman, 1999], 443) observes, "God is not jealous in the modern sense of being envious of that which rightfully belongs to someone else, but he is jealous in the Hebrew sense, earnestly desiring the honor that rightfully belongs to him."

This section started with comprehensive language, "everything from the face of the earth" (v.3), and it closes with the universal, "all who live in the earth."

2:1 This verse opens with the invitation to "gather together" (emphasized by the double use of the verb *qāšaš*) and includes the derogatory note, "shameful nation." (The TNIV changes second "gather" to "gather yourselves together.") The verb *qāšaš* is used elsewhere for the gathering of stubble or sticks for burning (cf. 1Ki 17:10, 12). The evil people are to gather themselves together like so much worthless straw (cf. Ex 5:7, 12) waiting for God's judgment.

The nation is called "shameful" (*lō³ niksāp*) because of their sin, which makes them dead to shame. The Hebrew is unusual and literally means "not desired" (KJV; see Note), but the point is not so much that they are not desired as that they have no shame (cf. *HALOT*, 1:490).

2 The threefold use of "before" (*bᵉṭerem*) emphasizes the urgency of the situation. The "appointed time" refers to the day of the Lord, the time of his giving vent to his holy wrath. The expression "the fierce anger" is parallel here to "the LORD's wrath" and should also be compared to "the fire of his jealousy" in 1:18. The prophet is again stacking terms to portray that indescribably horrible time when God unleashes his wrath in judgment on his people.

The gathering together (in repentance) must take place before the judgment if it is to be averted. The reference to "chaff" indicates that the wicked nation will be scattered before the fierce anger of the Lord, as chaff is scattered before the wind.

3 Three times the prophet urges the rebellious covenantal people to "seek" (*biqqēš*). To "seek the LORD" means that genuine repentance must be manifested in action. In contrast to those people who "neither seek the LORD nor inquire of him" (1:6), the prophet admonishes the "humble of the land" to "seek the LORD" and to "seek righteousness" and "humility."

In 2:1 the "shameful nation" was admonished to "gather together" (in repentance), and here the "humble" are encouraged to "seek the LORD," which is defined here as seeking righteousness and humility. The "humble" among God's people refers to those meek in spirit or attitude (cf. 3:12; Mt 5:5). The expression "humble of the land" (*ʿanwê hāʾāreṣ*) is also found in Job 24:4; Psalm 76:9[10]; Isaiah 11:4; and Amos 8:4, though the phrase is translated in a variety of ways in the NIV.

Seeking the Lord is essential to escaping judgment; even so, the prophet only holds out the *possibility* of escape: "perhaps [*ʾûlay*] you will be sheltered" (cf. Isa 26:20). The "perhaps" reminds us of God's sovereignty and warns against a cheap view of grace, the idea of sinning with impunity (Ro 6:1).

NOTES

15 יוֹם שֹׁאָה וּמְשׁוֹאָה (*yôm šōʾâ ûmᵉšôʾâ*, "a day of trouble and ruin") is an example of assonance in Hebrew (cf. the same combination in Job 38:27).

16 "Corner towers" translates הַפִּנּוֹת הַגְּבֹהוֹת (*happinnôt haggᵉbōhôt*). The KJV's "high towers" and RSV's "lofty battlements" understand *happinnôt* as a general word for a fortified and strategic tower. Though the first word literally means "corner," it probably referred to towers at various "angles" or "corners" in the wall.

17 "People" ("men," KJV) for אָדָם (*ʾādām*) is not an unusual translation for this word, which often means "humankind." "Entrails" for לְחֻם (*lᵉḥum*) is uncertain. In other contexts the word refers to "body" or "flesh." The parallel lines in this couplet support the NIV and TNIV translation. גְּלָלִים (*gᵉlālîm*, "filth") is the common Hebrew term for "dung" (cf. KJV).

2:1 הִתְקוֹשְׁשׁוּ וָקוֹשּׁוּ (*hitqôšᵉšû wāqôššû*) is appropriately rendered "Gather together, gather together," even though two different stems are used. The repetition of the root is probably for emphasis. "Shameful," a translation of לֹא נִכְסָף (*lōʾ niksāp*), is an old *crux interpretum*. The ancient versions reflect confusion about the meaning:"undisciplined" (LXX, Syr.), "unlovable" (Vul.), "that does not desire to be connected to the law" (Targ.; cf. Smith and Fagnani, 212). The KJV has "not desired," which was changed to "undesirable" in the NKJV. The NASB has "without shame," and the RSV, NRSV, NLT, TEV, and GWT have "shameless."

2 "Before the appointed time arrives" translates בְּטֶרֶם לֶדֶת חֹק (bᵉterem ledet ḥōq); the KJV renders "before the decree bring forth," but the RSV follows the Syriac: "before you are driven away." The MT reads literally "before a decree is born," which means "before that which has been decreed takes place."

לֹא (lōʾ) as a strengthening particle was already noted as early as the time of Keil, 139; Ugaritic used a prefixed לְ (l) with the imperfect for emphasis. אַף (ʾap, "anger") is found twice in this couplet, as reflected in the KJV. For stylistic reasons, apparently, the NIV translates it once as "anger" (when modified by "fierce") and once as "wrath."

3 Hebrew אוּלַי (ʾûlāy) can carry various nuances of meaning (cf. Ge 16:2; Ex 32:30; 1Ki 18:5; 2Ki 19:4; Job 1:5). The LXX here uses ὅπως (hopōs), which means "in order that." Modern English versions seem to favor "perhaps" here, though the GWT has "maybe."

B. Against Gentiles (2:4–15)

OVERVIEW

Representative nations from the four points of the compass are selected for indictment: Philistia (west), Moab and Ammon (east), Cush (south), and Assyria (north). Though no specific reasons are given for the inclusion of these nations, the inclusion of Cush (Egypt) and Assyria marks the two large international powers of the ancient Near East, and Moab and Ammon, along with Philistia, denote perennial local enemies of Israel. Unlike the prophecies of Amos against the surrounding nations, here Zephaniah does not give reasons for judgments on the particular targets of his prophecies—perhaps because Amos has already given the reasons. For some suggestions on the possible date, provenance, and purpose of these oracles, see Duane L. Christensen, "Zephaniah 2:4–15: A Theological Basis for Josiah's Program of Political Expansion," *CBQ* 46 (1984): 669–82. David Dorsey (*The Literary Structure of the Old Testament* [Grand Rapids: Baker, 1999], 312) notes that "the lines of these oracles follow almost without exception the 3 + 2 rhythm of the *qinah* (dirge) pattern conveying the feeling of a eulogy."

1. Philistia (2:4–7)

OVERVIEW

The land of Philistia consisted of five city-states: Gaza, Ashkelon, Ashdod, Ekron, and Gath. The absence of Gath here may indicate that it has already been destroyed. The origins of the Philistines are often located in Caphtor, modern Crete (Dt 2:23; Jer 47:4; Am 9:7). They were part of a migration of sea peoples who came to the coast of Israel from the Aegean, probably after being repulsed from Egypt.

> [4] Gaza will be abandoned
>   and Ashkelon left in ruins.
> At midday Ashdod will be emptied
>   and Ekron uprooted.
> [5] Woe to you who live by the sea,
>   O Kerethite people;
> the word of the LORD is against you,
>   O Canaan, land of the Philistines.
>
> "I will destroy you,
>   and none will be left."
>
> [6] The land by the sea, where the Kerethites dwell,
>   will be a place for shepherds and sheep pens.
> [7] It will belong to the remnant of the house of Judah;
>   there they will find pasture.
> In the evening they will lie down
>   in the houses of Ashkelon.
> The LORD their God will care for them;
>   he will restore their fortunes.

COMMENTARY

4 Of the four cities of Philistia mentioned in this verse, the first and the last involve wordplay. Lawrence Zalcman ("Ambiguity and Assonance at Zephaniah ii.4," *VT* 36 [1986]: 365–71) believes more than simple paronomasia is involved in this passage. He suggests the cities of Philistia are personified as women and consigned to four of the bitterest fates a woman could endure: abandonment, singleness, divorce, and barrenness. (See the response by Robert Gordis, "A Rising Tide of Misery: A Note on a Note on Zephaniah 2:4 [reply to L. Zalcman, 36:365–371, 1986]," *VT* 37 [1987]: 487–90, to Zalcman's suggestions.)

The Hebrew behind "Gaza will be abandoned" (*ʿazzāʿᵃzûbâ*) involves wordplay on similar-sounding terms. The four cities—Gaza, Ashkelon, Ashdod, and Ekron—represent the entire area of Philistia. The fourth city is described in the similar-sounding words "and Ekron uprooted" (*wᵉ ʿeqrôn tē ʿāqēr*). The fifth city in the pentapolis, Gath, is omitted here, as elsewhere (cf. Jer 25:20; Am 1:6–8; Zec 9:5–6), perhaps because Gath had been subjugated by David (1Ch 18:1) and had intermittently remained under Judahite control (2Ch 26:6; 2Ki 18:8).

Gaza and Ashkelon are summarily dismissed in judgment by a typical Hebrew synonymous couplet. By the time of Acts 8:26 Gaza had become a wasteland. Ashdod and Ekron are to be uprooted and emptied at midday—an unusual time for action since this hottest time is often used for siesta in the Middle East (cf. 2Sa 4:5; Jer 6:4). Undoubtedly the point being made is that judgment will fall on them as a surprise attack, or possibly that the battle will be decided in half a day. Robertson, 298, refers to the words of the Assyrian king Esarhaddon, who boasted of his half-day victory, "Memphis, his royal city, in a half day ... I captured, I destroyed, I devastated." Also, such a sudden collapse of the city would stand in striking contrast to the twenty-nine years in which Psammetichus I of Egypt besieged this same city of Ashdod—640 to 611 BC, dates that could possibly put this event during the time of Zephaniah's prophecy.

5 This first "woe" (*hôy*) oracle is addressed to the nations, beginning with the Philistines, moving on to the Moabites and Ammonites, and then to Assyria. These nations will be destroyed and the sites of their cities turned into grazing lands for others, or left empty. The next "woe" oracle begins at 3:1.

Kerethite ("Cretan"; cf. NAB, GWT) is a term used of the pre- or early Philistines, or perhaps originally of one branch of them (cf. Eze 25:16). David's bodyguard was made up of Kerethites and Pelethites (2Sa 8:18). They are mentioned several times in the OT (1Sa 30:14; 2Sa 8:18; 15:18; 20:7, 23; 1Ki 1:38, 44; 1Ch 18:17; Eze 25:16). Their traditional place of origin apparently was the region of Crete ("Caphtor" in Jer 47:4; Am 9:7). Zephaniah declares that their coastland will be emptied and become a wasteland (cf. Isa 14:28–32; Jer 25:20; 47:1–4; Eze 25:15–16).

6–7 The once heavily settled seacoast of the Philistines will become a desolate place for shepherds and sheep pens (v.6). The lowly shepherd will be able to find a place for his sheep to graze where there is no sowing or reaping and where no civilization flourishes. Eventually, however, it will be enjoyed and inhabited by "the remnant of the house of Judah," a group who will return after the exile. (The TNIV makes a significant change here from the NIV's "where the Kerethites dwell, will be a place" to "will become pastures having wells"; see Notes.)

A note of hope for Judah is sounded: "The LORD their God will care for them; he will restore their fortunes" (v.7). The verb behind "care for" (*pāqad*; GK 7212) is literally "visit," which can be used either in a negative way ("visit in judgment") or a positive way ("visit in blessing"); in this context it is obviously used in the positive sense. The remnant will occupy the sites of their former enemy the Philistines. (The alternative reading is "will bring back their captives" [NIV note].)

For the first time the concept of the remnant appears in this book, a concept whose meaning depends on the context. At times the focus is on the negative fact that a judgment is so severe and thorough that barely a remnant will survive (cf. Ge 7:23; Isa 17:6), but at other times the focus is on the positive fact that indeed a remnant is preserved for a future. The concept reflects both God's holy justice and his loving grace. In this place hope is extended in the promise that the tables will be turned when a remnant of God's people plunder their enemies. (For more on the concept of the remnant as a synthesis of punishment and hope, see George W. Anderson, "The Idea of the Remnant in the Book of Zephaniah" *ASTI* 11 [1977/78]: 11–14.)

NOTES

4 Paronomasia, a play on words, is involved with the threat against two cities of Philistia: עַזָּה עֲזוּבָה (*ʿazzâ ʿazûbâ*, "Gaza will be abandoned") and וְעֶקְרוֹן תֵּעָקֵר (*weʿeqrôn tēʿāqer*, "and Ekron uprooted").

5 חֶבֶל הַיָּם (*ḥebel hayyām*, "by the sea") occurs again in v.6, where the NIV translates "land by the sea." The word *ḥebel* originally denoted a "cord" or "measure," then was later applied to the tract of land measured out, or just a tract of land in general.

6 כְּרֹת (*keʿrōt*) is rendered "cottages" by the KJV and "Kerethites" by the NIV but "pastures" in the TNIV. The versions vary on their renderings: "pasture(s)" (TNIV, NASB, NLT, NRSV, ESV), "pasture-land" (GWT), "Cretans" (NAB), "Kerethites" (REB), and the TNK simply has "Cheroth." Keil, 141, suggested the term referred to the excavations made by shepherds as they "dig themselves huts under the ground as a protection from the sun." This has been a view popular with many commentators and is based on the root *krt*, meaning "to dig." Others prefer to find here another example of כַּר (*kar*), a word for "pasture" (cf. Isa 30:23, "broad meadow"), but its plural form in Psalms 37:20 and 65:13 is כָּרִים (*kārîm*) rather than כְּרֹת (*keʿrōt*). The RSV understands "meadows"; the KJV "cottages" is unwarranted. The NIV rendering of "Kerethites" is based on the general context, including the occurrence of this word in the preceding verse and the fact that the LXX has the term in both verses. But this approach leaves the question of why the term is masculine plural in v.5 but feminine plural in v.6—hence the NIV's marginal note admitting uncertainty, a fact reflected in the TNIV's change to "pastures." No meaning is suggested in *HALOT*, 1:501.

7 חֶבֶל (*hebel*) is reflected in the NIV "it"; the TNIV renders the term "that land." (The NIV sometimes represents a noun—more often a proper noun—with a pronoun.) וְשָׁב שְׁבוּתָם (*weʾšāb šeʾbiwtām*, "will restore their fortunes") is an expression in the NIV that normally has the margin giving the alternative reading: "will bring back their captives" (cf. Jer 29:14; Eze 39:25; Am 9:14).

2. Moab and Ammon (2:8–11)

OVERVIEW

These two nations are probably put together because they were ethnically related to Israel through Abraham's nephew Lot (Ge 19:36–38). Both were also hostile to the passage of the Israelites through their areas as the Hebrews made their way to the Promised Land (Nu 22–25). Only here are both nations addressed in the same oracle; elsewhere they are treated in separate oracles (Isa 15–16; Jer 48:1–49:6; Am 1:13–2:3). In later years frequent wars took place between Israel and these neighbors.

⁸"I have heard the insults of Moab
  and the taunts of the Ammonites,
 who insulted my people
  and made threats against their land.
⁹Therefore, as surely as I live,"
  declares the Lᴏʀᴅ Almighty, the God of Israel,
 "surely Moab will become like Sodom,
  the Ammonites like Gomorrah—

a place of weeds and salt pits,
    a wasteland forever.
The remnant of my people will plunder them;
    the survivors of my nation will inherit their land."

¹⁰This is what they will get in return for their pride,
    for insulting and mocking the people of the LORD Almighty.
¹¹The LORD will be awesome to them
    when he destroys all the gods of the land.
The nations on every shore will worship him,
    every one in its own land.

COMMENTARY

8 This oracle begins in the first person as the Lord himself announces the judgment that will fall on Moab and Ammon. Much of the language in this verse and the next echoes the destruction of the area, where Lot, the father of the Moabites and Ammonites, once lived. At the time of Zephaniah both nations were located near this area of God's fiery judgment consuming Sodom and Gomorrah and the other cities of the plain.

The encounter with Philistines (cf. vv.4–7) dates back to the time of the patriarchs (Ge 20–21; 26). The confrontation with Moab goes back to the time of Moses (Nu 22–25), followed by later conflicts (Jdg 3:12–30; 1Sa 12:9; 2Ki 3:5–27; 13:20). Conflicts with Ammon appear in Judges 10:6–11:33; 2 Samuel 10:1–11:1; and Nehemiah 2:10, 19; 4:3, 7. Moab and Ammon are mentioned together in conflict with Israel in Judges 3:13, and 2 Chronicles 24:26 mentions a conspiracy against King David that included an Ammonite and a Moabite.

Later, because of the fall of the northern kingdom and the decline of the southern kingdom, the pride of the nations east of Israel increased greatly. The Hebrew reads literally, "magnified themselves against," and refers to the haughty and arrogant invasion of the territory of Judah (cf. Jer 48:29; 49:1), as they showed their enmity toward God's people at every opportunity. Both Isaiah and Jeremiah also make note of the infamous conceit of Moab (Isa 16:6; Jer 48:29–30).

9 The comparison of Moab and Ammon to Sodom and Gomorrah is not surprising in view of their origin: Moab and Ammon were the offspring of the incestuous relations of Lot's daughters with their drunken father after he fled the destruction of Sodom and Gomorrah (Ge 19:30–38).

"Weeds" and "salt pits" reflect desolation and sterility. To this day many rock-strewn ruins of ancient villages in the regions of ancient Moab and Ammon bear silent testimony to the truth of the prophet's words: "a wasteland forever." This description may also echo the situation of ancient Sodom and Gomorrah after God "rained down burning sulfur" on them and "overthrew those cities and the entire plain, including all those living in the cities—and also the vegetation in the land" (Ge 19:24–25). Originally, Moab and Ammon became nations of survivors and refugees from God's judgment, but now they will come *under* his judgment.

Only a "remnant" of God's people will be needed to plunder these ancient enemies. It is ironic that the "survivors" of Israel will inherit the ancient sites of Moab and Ammon, for it is this general area that Abraham surrendered to his nephew Lot, who quickly selected this choice land; but now it will eventually pass to the descendants of Abraham, the man of faith. Apart from the sovereign grace of God, the fate of the covenantal people would be no different from the fate of Moab and Ammon (cf. Isa 1:9).

10 At this point the oracle shifts to the third person as the prophet speaks about the Lord and his response to the pride of Moab and Ammon, who have insulted and mocked "the people of the LORD Almighty." Zephaniah has "heard" (v.8) of the well-known pride of Moab, also referred to by Isaiah (Isa 16:6) and Jeremiah (Jer 48:29). Apparently Moab had an international reputation for an arrogant attitude. Earlier, Isaiah warned Moab of the consequences of its arrogance (Isa 16:13–14).

11 The Lord will be "awesome" (*nôrāʾ*) to his enemies when he destroys the "gods of the lands" by destroying the nations that depend on these gods, for these deities have no real existence apart from the people who first created them and then served them (1Co 8:4–6). There is irony in the expression "gods of the land/earth" (*ʾereṣ*), as those deities contrast with the God of heaven. By revealing the earthy and unreal nature of these gods, the God of heaven brings the nations to acknowledge him as the one true God. When he reveals himself in this way, the manifestation of his true nature can only produce fear and awe.

"Destroys all the gods" is literally "famish" or "make lean" [*rāzâ*; GK 8135] those gods (KJV), which expression probably refers to their being deprived of sustenance, worship, and perhaps even the sacrifices that supposedly fed them. The versions use a variety of translations to bring out the intrinsic meaning of this verb: "famish" (KJV, ESV), "shrivel" (NRSV, TNK), "starve" (NASB), "waste away" (GWT), "reduce to beggary" (REB), "shrink to nothing" (CEV), and "reduce to nothing" (TEV).

Not only those in the holy city and in the holy land will serve him, but also those on "every shore" and everyone's own land (cf. Ps 68:29, 30; Mal 1:11; Jn 4:21; 1Co 1:2; 1Ti 2:8). After the "gods of the land" are destroyed, the Lord alone remains to be worshiped by the "nations of every shore" and "every one in his own land," in addition to his remnant, who will then possess the territory of the nations (cf. vv.7, 9). Earlier, Isaiah foresaw the flow of the nations to Zion and the day in which there would be "an altar to the LORD in the heart of Egypt" (Isa 19:19) and a time when the "Egyptians and Assyrians will worship together" (19:23). Later, Malachi describes a time when the Lord's "name will be great among the nations" (Mal 1:11).

NOTES

8 וַיַּגְדִּ֫ילוּ (*wayyagdîlû*), "enlarged (themselves)" (cf. the KJV's "magnified themselves"), is one of those graphic expressions in Hebrew. The NIV "made threats" captures the idea.

9 "A place of weeds" translates מִמְשַׁק חָרוּל (*mimšaq ḥārûl*). *Ḥārûl* ("weeds") is attested also in Job 30:7 and Proverbs 24:31, but *mimšaq* (GK 4940) is found only here. The precise meaning remains elusive; some, out of desperation, attempt to find some help from מֶשֶׁק (*mešeq*) in Genesis 15:2, but it also is found only once and is uncertain.

3. Cush (2:12)

OVERVIEW

Even within the short book of Zephaniah the brevity of this oracle stands out. Also, we would expect the prophet, as a representative to the south, to use the old formidable foe, Egypt.

Cush was the area south of Egypt, that is Nubia or northern Sudan, later known generally as the area of Ethiopia. Kitchen describes it as originally "somewhere between the second and third cataracts of the Nile" (*NBD*, 256). However, Cush in this context probably stands for Egypt, perhaps because of Egypt's subjection to Cushite dynasties or simply because of the close connection of the two in times of war (Jer 46:2–9; Eze 30:5–9). For a period during the late

eighth and early seventh centuries BC, Egypt was ruled by the Cushite Twenty-Fifth Dynasty.

The abrupt change in the Hebrew from second person ("you") to third person ("they") is awkward. The NIV and TNIV (also the KJV) harmonizes both to second person for modern ease of reading, but the original is literally "you Cushites ... slain by my sword are they." Other versions paraphrase the reading in various ways. The original, though awkward for modern readers, is probably intentional as a literary device (see Note). This prophecy may have been fulfilled when Nebuchadnezzar conquered Egypt in 568 BC.

> 12 "You too, O Cushites,
>   will be slain by my sword."

COMMENTARY

12 Having foretold God's judgment on nations east and west of Judah, Zephaniah next directs attention to nations south and north: Cush and Assyria. The "too" (*gam*) indicates that the Lord will also bring Cush to an end just as he will Moab and Ammon.

Cush was located in the southern (upper) Nile region (cf. NIV note). The use of the term "Ethiopia" (KJV) is somewhat misleading because the boundaries of the two countries were not the same. It seems best, therefore, to transliterate the Hebrew *kûš* to designate this ancient area. (Translators face the same kind of issue with the terms Syria/Aram.) Since Egypt had been under the rule of Cushite kings

for years, the prophet's words undoubtedly include Egypt as well. Egypt and Cush were often closely related in history (cf. Jer 46:2–9; Eze 30:5–9).

Nebuchadnezzar served as the Lord's sword in slaying the Cushites: "I will strengthen the arms of the king of Babylon and put my sword in his hand" (Eze 30:24–25). Similarly, Isaiah 10:5 speaks of Assyria as the rod and club of God's anger and wrath. Also note the vivid portrayal of the Lord and his sword in Deuteronomy 32:40–42. In the book of Revelation, the One whose name is the Word of God strikes the nations with a sharp double-edged sword (Rev 1:16; 2:12, 16; 19:15, 21; cf. also Heb 4:12).

NOTE

12 The verse starts in the second person plural but ends with a pronoun in the third person plural, probably to express the people's estrangement from God. They are addressed in judgment in the second person with the result that they will end up as aliens from God.

4. Assyria (2:13–15)

OVERVIEW

The prophecies against surrounding nations climax with the word against Assyria, the strongest political factor and the most northerly nation of that time. Assyria, with its capital at Nineveh, was a cruel and fearsome power that had held its neighboring lands in its grip for decades. Though weakened by this time, Assyria was still a threat to Judah. Later, Nineveh was destroyed (612 BC) by the combined forces of the Babylonians and others. So it was to Babylon, rather than to the armies of Assyria, that Jerusalem fell in 587 BC.

The prophecies of Nahum address the Assyrian capital of Nineveh exclusively and condemn its idolatry (Na 1:14), violence (3:1–3), and sorceries (3:4). Zephaniah condemns its arrogance as expressed in its claim, "I am, and there is none besides me" (Zep 2:15). It is incredible that this once proud and threatening city is described in such terms of desolation. For centuries it became virtually lost to the rest of the world. Xenophon passed the site in about 401 BC and reported that he found not a trace of its existence in the desert sands of the area (Robertson, 312). Zephaniah predicts the desolation of the site of Assyria in language similar to that used earlier by Isaiah about Babylon (Isa 13:20–22).

¹³He will stretch out his hand against the north
    and destroy Assyria,
  leaving Nineveh utterly desolate
    and dry as the desert.
¹⁴Flocks and herds will lie down there,
    creatures of every kind.
  The desert owl and the screech owl
    will roost on her columns.
  Their calls will echo through the windows,
    rubble will be in the doorways,
      the beams of cedar will be exposed.
¹⁵This is the carefree city
    that lived in safety.

> She said to herself,
>   "I am, and there is none besides me."
> What a ruin she has become,
>   a lair for wild beasts!
> All who pass by her scoff
>   and shake their fists.

COMMENTARY

13 The prediction of Nineveh's utter desolation even while that Assyrian capital ruled the world testifies to the divine origin of Zephaniah's message. The prediction that God will leave Nineveh "dry as the desert" is remarkable in view of the fame of the city's great irrigation system. In the past God had used Assyria as the rod of his anger (Isa 10:5) against Israel; now he stretches out his hand against Assyria itself. Both of these great Mesopotamian powers are often treated similarly in Scripture.

14 Instead of foreseeing a scene of marching armies along with a prosperous population, the prophet predicts that all kinds of creatures will be found at Nineveh (cf. v.6). The site once inhabited by braggarts will become a site occupied by beasts, and the once-renowned city will become fit only for animals, some of which are difficult to identify with certainty. (For more details on these terms, see David J. Clark, "Of Birds and Beasts: Zephaniah 2:14," *BT* 34 [1982]: 243–46.) The "desert owl" (*qā'at*) and the "screech owl" (*qippōd*) represent scenes of desolation (cf. Isa 34:11; Ps 102:6[7]). Nineveh's formerly magnificent buildings, tumbled to debris, will become dwelling places for creatures of the night, and only doleful sounds will emerge from the doorways. The empty "windows" and "doorways" are signs of desertion and desolation. "Beams of cedar" are evidence of a prosperity, as reflected in the cedar palaces of David and Solomon (2Sa 7:2, 7; 1Ki 5:6, 8), but Nineveh's cedar work will lie exposed in the city's ruins.

15 Though complacent and carefree at the time of Zephaniah's prediction, the former glorious city will become a lair for wild animals and an object of contempt for every passerby. Nineveh had boasted in self-sufficiency, "I am, and there is none besides me" (cf. Isa 47:8), but the inspired prophet predicts that it will become a ruin and a habitat for the creatures of the fields—a most unlikely scene, as considered by the people of that age. This same claim of self-sufficiency is found in reference to Babylon (Isa 47:8) and Laodicea (Rev 3:17).

The expressions "scoff" (*šāraq*) and "shake their fists" (*nûa' yād*) have been rendered in various ways: "hiss and wag his hand" (KJV); "hiss ... wave his hand in contempt" (NASB); "hiss and make an obscene gesture" (GWT); "hisses ... shakes his fist" (NAB); "laugh in derision or shake a defiant fist" (NLT); "hisses and gestures with his hand" (TNK); "make fun and shake their fists" (NCV); "shrink back in horror" (TEV); "jeer and gesture" (REB); and "sneers and makes vulgar signs" (CEV). From this sampling it is obvious that translators do not know exactly what kind of gesture and attitude the Hebrew signifies; it could imply scorn, defiance, horror, or some other sense, but certainly a negative one.

NOTES

14 "Creatures of every kind" translates כָּל־חַיְתוֹ־גוֹי (*kol-ḥaytô-gôy*). The KJV translates the phrase as "all the beasts of the nations." The RSV ("all the beasts of the field") is based on the LXX, as the marginal note indicates. In Joel 1:6 *gôy* is used of a swarm of locusts, a similar usage to what we have here, where *gôy* is used of a swarm, pack, or crowd of creatures. (For other suggestions, see Sabottka, 95–96.)

The obvious uncertainty about קָאַת קִפֹּד (*qāʾat ... qippōd*, "desert owl and screech owl," NIV, NAB; "cormorant and bittern," KJV; "pelicans and hedgehogs," Keil, 146; "vulture and hedgehog," RSV; "pelican and heron," JB) is reflected in both the ancient and modern traditions, but the latest information suggests that they were terms for owls (cf. Sabottka, 96–97).

15 אֵיךְ (*ʾêk*) is translated in the NIV "What...!" This particle is used to indicate reproach (Jdg 16:15), amazement (Isa 14:4), and horror (Ps 73:19; cf. *TWOT*, 35). יָנִיעַ יָדוֹ (*yānîaʿ yādô*) is translated in various ways: "shake their fists" (NIV, JB; cf. NAB), "wag his hand" (KJV), "swing his hand" (Keil, 146). It is difficult to know exactly which emotion is reflected in this gesture. Keil, 149, suggests the idea "away with her, she has richly deserved her fate." Nahum 3:19 expresses another hand gesture at the fall of Nineveh: תָּקְעוּ כַף עָלֶיךָ (*tāqʿû kap ʿāleykā*, "claps his hands").

C. Against Jerusalem (3:1–8)

OVERVIEW

Finally, after a series of judgments against various surrounding nations predicted in ch. 2, the prophet focuses on Jerusalem and Judah—a powerful rhetorical device used also by Amos (Am 1:3–2:16). In the middle of this oracle (v.6), the prophet recalls the judgments he has inflicted on other nations surrounding Judah. This coming day of judgment for Judah includes both destruction for the unrepentant sinners and also purification of the remnant (vv.9–13), which produces mutual rejoicing for God and his people (vv.14–20).

The "city" (v.1) is not specified by name in this section, but its identity is revealed by the expression "the Lord within her" in v.5. In the following verses, reference is made back to the city (*hāʿîr*) by a series of verbs and personal pronouns in the feminine singular (vv.2–5, 7). In vv.1–5 the prophet speaks about the city, followed in vv.6–8 by the Lord's addressing it directly.

¹Woe to the city of oppressors,
    rebellious and defiled!
²She obeys no one,
    she accepts no correction.
She does not trust in the Lord,
    she does not draw near to her God.

³Her officials are roaring lions,
    her rulers are evening wolves,
    who leave nothing for the morning.
⁴Her prophets are arrogant;
    they are treacherous men.
 Her priests profane the sanctuary
    and do violence to the law.
⁵The Lord within her is righteous;
    he does no wrong.
Morning by morning he dispenses his justice,
    and every new day he does not fail,
    yet the unrighteous know no shame.

⁶"I have cut off nations;
    their strongholds are demolished.
I have left their streets deserted,
    with no one passing through.
Their cities are destroyed;
    no one will be left—no one at all.
⁷I said to the city,
    'Surely you will fear me
    and accept correction!'
Then her dwelling would not be cut off,
    nor all my punishments come upon her.
But they were still eager
    to act corruptly in all they did.
⁸Therefore wait for me," declares the Lord,
    "for the day I will stand up to testify.
I have decided to assemble the nations,
    to gather the kingdoms
and to pour out my wrath on them—
    all my fierce anger.
The whole world will be consumed
    by the fire of my jealous anger.

COMMENTARY

1 This second "woe" oracle is addressed to the defiled and polluted city (understood as Jerusalem), which is condemned for many reasons, including the misuse of office by her various leaders.

The guilty city harbors "oppressors" (those who disregard the rights of the poor, orphans, and widows)—"rebellious" (those who refuse submission to God's will) and "defiled" (*nigʾālâ*) people (those who are polluted by sinful conduct). Because of Israel's experience in history, they were commanded never to oppress a stranger (Ex 22:21[20]; Lev 19:33). For Israel, oppressive treatment of others was condemned (Lev 25:14; Dt 23:16[17]), but now the people are guilty of cruelty to and oppression of others.

The defiled or polluted people often wash themselves with water and observe other ceremonies of external sanctity so as outwardly to appear pure, but actually their whole life is defiled. After the exile, certain individuals were marked as "defiled" and excluded from the priesthood (Ezr 2:62; Ne 7:64), but here Zephaniah labels the entire group of rebels as disqualified from service to God. The pollution in this case is not that kind of ceremonial defilement designed as a teaching aid but an actual moral pollution associated with evil conduct.

2 The continuing indictment of Jerusalem contains three specific charges: (1) she obeys no one—not even the Lord; (2) she does not trust in the Lord; and (3) she does not draw near to her God, who is the one who can provide direction and guidance for her.

"She obeys no one" translates Hebrew *lōʾ šāmeʿâ beqôl* (lit., "she did not hearken to the voice"). Robertson, 318, notes, "ten times in the wilderness, the people would not hearken to God's voice ... so the Lord swore that none of them would ever see the land he had promised on oath to their fathers." No other city was privileged to "hear the voice [of God]"—not Nineveh or any of the other places mentioned above. Now God pronounces a "woe" (v.1) on the city of defiled rebels.

In the OT the expression "draw near" (*qārab*) is used about 158 times in the sense of draw near in worship. The evil people are guilty of neglect in this area of their lives, which should include praise, petition—and, of course, faith.

3–4 After the indictment against the city's population as a whole, four classes of leaders are singled out as representative of the total leadership of the people. Zephaniah deals first with the civil officials (v.3) and then follows with his treatment of the religious leaders.

(1) "Officials" (*śārîm*; "princes," KJV) probably represent the royal leaders who should be characterized by justice and equity rather than greed and avarice. They are described as "roaring lions" out for prey (cf. Pr 28:15; Eze 22:27; Am 3:4; Mic 2:2). Rather than being shepherds to protect their sheep from the wild animals, these individuals themselves have become lions that harm the people under their care and responsibility.

(2) "Rulers" (*šōpeṭîm*; "judges," KJV) also represent those in places of leadership, probably civil magistrates, who should be setting an example for the rest of the people; instead, they are tagged "evening wolves, who leave nothing for the morning," a label suggesting predatory and ravenous beasts (cf. Jer 5:6; Hab 1:8). Rather than saving some of the kill till morning, they greedily and viciously devour it without hesitation.

(3) "Prophets" (*nebîʾîm*), who should communicate God's message to his people, are described as arrogant and treacherous. They are called "treacherous" (unfaithful) because they are unfaithful to the one they claim to represent (cf. Jer 23:32; Eze 22:28). They use their office as a means of achieving their own ends. The tension and conflict between the true and false prophets seem to increase as the people face their end in the land. Robertson, 320, suggests this is reflected in "Jeremiah's use of the term *prophet* approximately ninety times, while in Isaiah the term occurs only seven times."

(4) "Priests" (*kōhanîm*) represent the other religious leaders; they are profaning the sanctuary and

violating the law. Their ordained function was to interpret the law and officiate at the sanctuary with reverence, but they have done just the opposite. Apparently at times the priests sat as chief justices in the land and worked in conjunction with the common court system (cf. Dt 17:8–12). The priests were expected to keep before the people the distinction between the common and the holy (cf. Lev 10:10), a distinction that helped the people recognize the difference between the Creator and the created order.

5 In contrast to the misleading leaders "within her" (*b^eqirbâ*, mentioned in v.3 but not translated in the NIV), the Lord in Israel's midst (*b^eqirbâ*) is a righteous standard ("he does no wrong") against which the people are measured. His holy and righteous presence demands judgment for sin and corruption (cf. Lev 19:2). Since he never does wrong, he is never implicated with iniquity.

The Lord continuously ("morning by morning") manifests his justice and righteousness before the people (contrast the evening wolves of v.3) in his treatment of both Israel and the surrounding nations. The morning, before the height of the day's heat, was the time for business, including legal proceedings. But the point here seems more to concern consistency. "Morning by morning" is used of the regular collection of the manna in the wilderness (Ex 16:21) and of the freewill offerings brought for the construction of the tabernacle (Ex 36:3). As the Lord faithfully provided daily manna for his people during their trial in the wilderness, so he will in the last days of Jerusalem display his righteousness. Despite these reminders, the people are so calloused, their hearts and minds so spiritually numb, that they recognize no sin and feel no shame for what they are doing.

6 Now the Lord himself speaks in the first person as he describes what he has done to other nations. They have been "cut off" or "destroyed" (TNIV)

and their strongholds demolished; their streets are left deserted and their cities destroyed. Cities that once buzzed with activity now lie desolate.

The nations referred to are not specified, so commentators disagree on their identity. Keil, 152, says the reference concerns "neither those nations who are threatened with ruin, ch. ii. 4–15, nor the Canaanites, who have been exterminated by Israel, but nations generally, which have succumbed to the judgments of God, without any more precise definition."

7 In view of the judgments mentioned in v.6, the Lord speaks imploringly to his people, "Surely you will fear me and accept correction!" He declares that judgment and punishment could have been averted and avoided; but the people, trapped in the grip of sin, "were still eager to act corruptly" (cf. Jer 7:13, 25–26). The expression "eager to act" (*hiškîmû*; the same verb used in Ge 19:2, from *škm*, GK 8899) can be understood literally as "rose early [to act]" (KJV; cf. above comment on "morning by morning").

8 We expect the "therefore" (in view of the preceding!) to be followed by a promise to pour out deserved judgment on those wicked people. Instead, the punishment is veiled (and sarcastic) as they are admonished to "wait for me … for the day I will stand up to testify." "To testify" refers to the bringing of accusations against the people (cf. Ps 50:7).

This verse also promises a purging and purifying action: The Lord promises "to pour out [his] wrath on them [the assembled nations]—all [his] fierce anger." He continues using strong language: "The whole world will be consumed by the fire of my jealous anger." This is the kind of universal judgment found in 1:2–3.

The last part of v.8 contains graphic words that portray a scene of great prophetic significance. The Lord has determined to gather the nations and kingdoms to pour out on them in great judgment his "wrath" and "fierce anger" and to consume them with "the fire of [his] jealous anger." Robertson, 325, understands the destruction of Jerusalem in 586 BC as well as the destruction of the city in AD 70 to anticipate the final devastation of the nations.

NOTES

1 The position of the indeterminate predicates מֹרְאָה (mōrᵉʾâ, "rebellious") and נִגְאָלָה (nigʾālâ, "defiled") before the subject ("oppressing city") gives them emphasis (according to Keil, 149). For stylistic reasons the NIV, TNIV, and NEB reverse the order. The analysis of mōrᵉʾâ is uncertain (cf. Sabottka, 102–3). The root מָרָא (mārāʾ; GK 5286) seems to refer to "fatness" of grazing. The root מָרַר (mārar; GK 5352) is used of "bitterness" or "despair," a meaning that could fit in this context. The NIV ("rebellious") takes this as an example of a final -ה root treated as a final-א root (cf. GKC, par. 75rr). The LXX's ἐπιφανής (epiphanēs, "glorious") shows an apparent understanding of the form as a Hophal of the root רָאָה (rāʾâ, "to see"). The KJV translates the word "filthy," but most modern versions translate it "rebellious." The other two words describing the unnamed city are also participles that describe the ongoing condition and nature of the people.

3 Israel's leaders are called "lions" also by Ezekiel (Eze 19:1–7), who in another place called them "wolves" (22:27). The KJV's "they gnaw not the bones till the morrow" for לֹא גָרְמוּ לַבֹּקֶר (lōʾ gārᵉmû labbōqēr) is misleading by suggesting not ravenous wolves but patient wolves, waiting till the next morning to gnaw! This translation also assumes that the verb גָּרַם (gāram) is from the noun gerem ("bone") and therefore means to "gnaw" or "break" bones (Nu 24:8). The JB's "they have had nothing to gnaw that morning" follows the same meaning for the verb but also expresses the ravenous character surely intended in this context, a meaning brought out in the NIV. The ancient versions already reflect difficulty with this passage (cf. Smith and Fagnani, 244–45). Recent research has not produced any new light that is decisive (cf. Kapelrud, 35). The GWT renders "they leave nothing to gnaw on for the morning," and the TNK has "they leave no bone for morning."

4 The NIV's "arrogant" translates פֹּחֲזִים (pōḥᵃzîm; GK 7069), whereas the TNIV translates as "unprincipled." The KJV's "light" presumably understands the verb in the sense of "wanton" (RSV). C. Rabin (Studies in the Bible [ScrHier 8; Jerusalem: Magnes, 1961], 398) distinguishes פחז (pḥz) I ("to boast"; Jdg 9:4 and this passage) from pḥz II ("to scatter"; Ge 49:4; "turbulent," NIV). The idea of boasting or arrogance is probably to be found in the cognate פַּחֲזוּת (paḥᵃzût) in Jeremiah 23:32, though the NIV translates it "reckless lies"; the NAB's "empty boasting" captures both ideas. The NIV is based on the meaning of pḥz I.

"Treacherous," from the root בגד (bgd), is used often to express the idea of unfaithfulness or faithlessness (TWOT, 1:89).

5 "Dispenses" translates מִשְׁפָּט יִתֵּן לָאוֹר (mišpāṭ yittēn lāʾôr). The KJV's "bring his judgment to light" is a more literal translation (cf. NASB, GWT). Other versions have "render judgment" (NRSV, NAB); "his judgment is more evident" (NLT; later revision, "hands down justice"); "brings justice to" (TEV); "brings about justice" (CEV); "governs fairly" (NCV); "shows forth his justice" (ESV); and "issues judgment" (TNK).

6 The verb כרת (*krt*) is literally "cut off" (NIV), but it is a common Semitic expression for "destroyed" (cf. TNIV) or "laid waste." "Strongholds" translates פִּנּוֹת (*pinnôt*), a word with a basic meaning of "corner" but with a wide range of meanings. Zephaniah 1:16 uses it of the tower strongholds.

"Destroyed" translates the Hebrew verb צדה (*ṣdh*)(II), which is found only here and listed by *HALOT* as probably an Aramaic loanword for "destroy." Also the parallel of כרת (*krt*), שמם (*šmm*), and הרב (*hrb*) suggest this idea.

7 מְעוֹנָה (*mᵉʿônāh*, "her dwelling") was read by the LXX as ἐξ ὀφθαλμῶν (*ex ophthalmōn*, "out of sight"), apparently reading the Hebrew as מֵעֵינֶיהָ (*mēʿêneyhā*). This reading is repeated in the Syriac and the NAB ("she should not fail to see") and the JB ("[she cannot] lose sight"); but the MT makes sense in this context, and there is no reason to depart from it.

אָכֵן (*ʾākēn*, "therefore"; NIV, "but") is sometimes used in a strongly contrastive sense, as here. Also, the eagerness to sin is vividly portrayed in הִשְׁכִּימוּ (*hiškîmû*, "they were still eager"), which the KJV renders literally: "they rose early." הִשְׁחִית (*hišḥît*, "to act corruptly") is intensified by the addition of עֲלִילוֹתָם (*ʿᵃlîlôtām*, "they did"), which when used of the action of humans usually refers to evil deeds (cf. *TWOT*, 2:671).

8 The Masoretes vocalized עד (*ʿd*) as *ʿad* ("plunder"); but the LXX, followed by the Syriac, read *ʿēd* ("witness"). Most of the recent versions (NRSV, NAB, NEB, JB, NCV, GWT) follow the LXX. The NIV note renders the MT. The KJV has "prey," changed in the NKJV to "plunder."

"I have decided" translates מִשְׁפָּטִי (*mišpāṭî*). The KJV's "my determination" is the idea expressed in most new translations (cf. NAB, NEB, RSV, JB). But this expression is understood by some (e.g., Keil, 154) to mean "my justice" (cf. v.5); it is God's justice that is reflected in his treatment of the nations. Notice in this verse the stacking of terms for God's holy justice and wrath: "wrath" (זַעַם, *zaʿam*); "fierce anger" (אַף חָרוֹן, *ḥārôn ʾap*); "jealous anger" (קִנְאָה, *qinʾâ*). The Masoretes noted that this is the only verse in the OT that contains all the letters of the Hebrew alphabet (except for שׂ [*ś*]), even including final forms.

III. DAY OF JOY (3:9–20)

OVERVIEW

"Then," after the judgment thus described, the Lord will turn to himself a people of "purified lips" (NASB) and united heart ("shoulder to shoulder"). The following verses describe in glowing terms the promises of blessing and restoration for God's people and the nations. This restored remnant will consist not only of a purged and forgiven group from Israel (cf. 3:11–13); the converted from the nations will also join with his people in the worship of the one true God (3:9–10). This will be a new community of holy people.

Verses 9–13 reveal a three-stage development: (1) vv.9–11a speak of the purifying of the nations and the return of the scattered; (2) vv.11b–12 speak of the purging of Jerusalem to leave only the "meek and humble, who trust in the name of the LORD"; (3) v.13 is a summary statement concerning the purified "remnant of Israel." Verses 14–20 then conclude this prophecy with the rejoicing of the saved people.

A. Return of a Scattered People (3:9–10)

OVERVIEW

"Then" (*kî 'āz*; v.9) refers to a time after the judgment just mentioned. These verses describe the scattered people who will return (v.10) and be purified so that they may worship and serve the Lord. The prophet does not explain the tensions in his message between worldwide destruction (which sounds like obliteration) and the promise of the conversion of the nations, as well as the renewed remnant of Israel. Robertson, 327, says of this mixed message that the prophet "does not explain how cosmic judgment and far-reaching salvation coordinate, but he faithfully proclaims both elements."

⁹"Then will I purify the lips of the peoples,
　　that all of them may call on the name of the Lord
　　and serve him shoulder to shoulder.
¹⁰From beyond the rivers of Cush
　　my worshipers, my scattered people,
　　will bring me offerings.

COMMENTARY

9 Before the scattering of the people at the tower of Babel, the world was unified by one language; but it was a world of rebellious people. In contrast, a new purified language will characterize a responsive people (cf. Ro 15:6). The lips or language that had become impure through use in idol worship will become purified so that all may in unison call on the name of the Lord. The reference to lips, the organ of speech, includes the heart behind the language; as Keil, 156, notes, "Purity of the lips involves or presupposes the purification of the heart." The outpouring of the Holy Spirit on the day of Pentecost brought about purification and renewal of heart and lips resulting in a widespread calling on the name of the Lord (Ac 2:21).

To "call on [*qārā'*] the name of the Lord" is to turn to the Lord out of a sense of need (*TWOT*, 2:810). Again, this kind of language may refer back to the preflood period (cf. Ge 4:26). The original unity of speech lost at Babel (11:1–9) will ultimately be restored so that all creation may worship God. Those of purified speech are enabled to serve "shoulder to shoulder" (lit., "one shoulder"; cf. Jer 32:39). In a similar vein, the expression "one mouth" is used to indicate unanimity in 1 Kings 22:13.

10 Cush, on the upper (southern) Nile, represented the southern extremity of the known world (see comments at 2:12.) "The rivers" presumably indicates the Blue and the White branches of the Nile.

Keil, 155, translates the latter part of this verse "will they bring my worshippers, the daughter of my dispersed ones, as a meat-offering to me," thus suggesting that the converted Gentiles will attempt to convert and bring wayward Israel as an offering to the Lord. But this idea seems strained (see Notes).

"My scattered people" translates Hebrew *bat-pûṣay* (lit., "daughter of my dispersed"; KJV; cf. Notes). God had warned his people through Moses (Dt 4:27; 28:64; 30:3) that they would experience dispersion (*pûṣ*) for disobedience. J. Alec Motyer (*An Exegetical and Expository Commentary on the Minor Prophets*, vol. 3, ed. Thomas E. McComiskey [Grand Rapids: Baker, 1998], 952) links the expression in Zephaniah with the use of *pûṣ* in the Babel account of dispersion in Genesis 11:4, but it seems strange to refer to those people as "my scattered [people]."

Earlier, Isaiah had described Cush as a land divided by rivers (Isa 18:2, 7) that sent envoys by sea in boats over the water (18:2). Isaiah also described a remnant returning from such distant places as Cush and Egypt (11:11; 27:13); he depicted these peoples as bringing gifts to the Lord (Isa 18:7).

NOTES

9 "Purify the lips" translates שָׂפָה בְרוּרָה (*śāpâ bᵉrûrâ*; lit., something like "purified lip," with "lip" representing speech or language). The passive participle *bᵉrûrâ* suggests something that has become purified and thus rules out Luther's interpretation of applying this to God's pure speech. The use of the singular form of the word for lip (שָׂפָה) often refers to language (Ge 11:1, 6–7, 9; Ps 81:5[6]; Isa 19:18; Eze 3:5–6). The rendering of the LB as "pure Hebrew" reflects an understanding that the reference is to the restoration of modern Hebrew in the new nation of Israel; this rendering was changed in the revision, the NLT, to "purify the speech."

"Shoulder to shoulder" translates שְׁכֶם אֶחָד (*śᵉkem ʾeḥād*, "one shoulder"). Supposedly, this expression is derived from the idea of bearers who carry a load with even shoulders. Though this figure does not appear elsewhere in Hebrew, it is attested in Syriac (cf. Smith and Fagnani, 248). The LXX, followed by the Syriac, translated *śᵉkem* as "yoke," a translation repeated in the JB. A similar expression—"one mouth"—is used to indicate unanimity in 1 Kings 22:13.

10 "My worshipers" represents עֲתָרַי (*ʿᵃtāray*), which the KJV rendered as "my suppliants" (also in the NRSV) but the NKJV changed to "worshipers" (also in the NASB and other later versions). The root עתר (*ʿtr*) is a rare word for prayer or worship probably related to an Arabic cognate meaning "to sacrifice" (cf. *TWOT*, 2:708).

"My scattered people" translates בַּת־פּוּצַי (*bat-pûṣay*, lit., "daughter of my dispersed"), a typical Hebraism meaning "my scattered [people]." Of greater question is the syntax of the sentence. The NIV (also KJV, RSV, NEB, JB) takes these two expressions ("my worshipers, my scattered people") as subjects of the verb; others (e.g., Keil, 157) take them as objects of the verb and understand the passage to say that the remote heathen will eventually worship the Lord and be used to convert the scattered Jews (cf. Keil, 157).

B. Restoration of a Sinful People (3:11–13)

OVERVIEW

Verses 11–13 describe the future restoration of God's people. God's program of restoration includes removal of the proud and haughty from the city (v.11), the presence of the "meek and humble" (v.12), and the promise that "no one will make them afraid" (v.13). This passage goes beyond the promise of return to the promise of glorious restoration. No more will shame, pride, or fear be in their midst. No more will deceit or lies be among them.

> ¹¹On that day you will not be put to shame
>   for all the wrongs you have done to me,
> because I will remove from this city
>   those who rejoice in their pride.
> Never again will you be haughty
>   on my holy hill.
> ¹²But I will leave within you
>   the meek and humble,
>   who trust in the name of the LORD.
> ¹³The remnant of Israel will do no wrong;
>   they will speak no lies,
>   nor will deceit be found in their mouths.
> They will eat and lie down
>   and no one will make them afraid."

COMMENTARY

11 "That day" refers to the day fulfilling vv.9–10, the time when Israel will be gathered together from the dispersion as the Daughter of Zion (cf. v.14). They will "not be put to shame" because the very source of pride and haughtiness will be abolished—the intolerable attitudes on "God's holy hill." This is the same city that earlier had been rebuked because it was not aware of its shame and guilt (3:5; cf. 2:1). Mount Zion will be made holy by the presence of God.

12 Instead of the haughty, there will be the "meek" (ʿānî) and "humble" (dāl), those "who trust in the name of the LORD." Their confidence and strength are derived from God himself.

13 Further description of this remnant of Israel presents them as free from all deception, duplicity, and deceit. They "will do no wrong" (lōʾ-yaʿăśû ʿawlâ) because the Lord "does no wrong" (lōʾ yaʿăśeh ʿawlâ, 3:5). "The moral character of the remnant conforms to the nature of the Lord who has delivered them" (Robertson, 331).

In such a spiritual condition they are fit to experience physical prosperity. The two lines of this verse shift to pastoral imagery depicting a flock at ease in a pasture. This picture is enhanced by the expression "no one will make them afraid," language identical to that used by both Jeremiah (Jer 30:10; 46:27) and Ezekiel (Eze 34:28; 39:26). The scene is one where God's ancient covenantal people join with people from widely scattered locations and call on the Lord with speech purified by the Holy Spirit.

NOTES

11 "Wrongs" translates עֲלִילוֹת (ᶜᵃlîlôt), a word usually appearing in the plural and applied to both humans and God. The deeds of God are good and right, but the ᶜᵃlîlôt of people are wicked (cf. *TWOT*, 2:671). In addition to this observation, it should be noted that our text uses the verb פָּשַׁע (pāšaᶜ, "to rebel, sin") with the noun "wrongs." The RSV captures the idea: "the deeds by which you have rebelled against me."

12 עָנִי וְדָל (ᶜānî wādāl, "meek and humble") are paired elsewhere (Job 34:28; Isa 26:6) and suggest those who are oppressed or in need. However, here they imply words denoting the opposite of proud and haughty (cf. v.11) and therefore should be understood more in a moral sense than in a social one (Robertson, 331). Donald B. Sharp ("The Remnant of Zephaniah: Identifying a 'People Humble and Lowly,'" *IBS* 18 [1996]: 2–15) suggests that this group may refer to Levites who fled south after the fall of Samaria, but the evidence is not decisive.

13 עַוְלָה (ᶜawlâ, "wrong") is often used with verbs of action, as here, and indicates the opposite of צֶדֶק/צְדָקָה (ṣedeq/ṣᵉdāqâ, "right"; cf. *TWOT*, 2:653). רָעָה (rāᶜâ, "eat") and רָבַץ, (rābaṣ, "lie down") are pastoral terms used because of the comparison of Israel to a flock.

C. Rejoicing of a Saved People (3:14–20)

OVERVIEW

The opening verses of Zephaniah contained some of the most vivid and graphic language of judgment found anywhere in Scripture. The entire universe is depicted as being overturned in judgment. In contrast, these closing verses contain some of the most moving descriptions of the love of God for his people found anywhere in Scripture. The Lord "will take great delight" (v.17) in his people, and they in turn are told to "sing ... shout aloud ... be glad and rejoice" (v.14).

This glorious picture of the future is described as a time of great joy; the Lord will be in the midst of his people. Fear and sorrow will be removed, and the Lord will restore their fortunes. It will be a time for singing and rejoicing (v.14). The time of punishment is past, and the Lord will have turned back their enemy (v.15). Fear and apprehension will be gone (v.16). God's people will rest in his love as he takes great delight in them (v.17).

Because they cannot celebrate their holy feasts in exile, the Lord's people are burdened with sorrows (v.18); but he will remove this reproach and deal with those who have oppressed his people (v.19). The concluding verse (v.20) reiterates the Lord's promise to gather and bring his people home, where their fortunes will be restored and they will enjoy honor and praise from "all the peoples of the earth."

¹⁴Sing, O Daughter of Zion;
 shout aloud, O Israel!
Be glad and rejoice with all your heart,
 O Daughter of Jerusalem!
¹⁵The Lord has taken away your punishment,
 he has turned back your enemy.
The Lord, the King of Israel, is with you;
 never again will you fear any harm.
¹⁶On that day they will say to Jerusalem,
 "Do not fear, O Zion;
 do not let your hands hang limp.
¹⁷The Lord your God is with you,
 he is mighty to save.
He will take great delight in you,
 he will quiet you with his love,
 he will rejoice over you with singing."

¹⁸"The sorrows for the appointed feasts
 I will remove from you;
 they are a burden and a reproach to you.
¹⁹At that time I will deal
 with all who oppressed you;
I will rescue the lame
 and gather those who have been scattered.
I will give them praise and honor
 in every land where they were put to shame.
²⁰At that time I will gather you;
 at that time I will bring you home.
I will give you honor and praise
 among all the peoples of the earth
when I restore your fortunes
 before your very eyes,"
     says the Lord.

COMMENTARY

14 An exhortation to sing and rejoice begins this conclusion to the prophet's message. "Daughter of Zion" (or better, "Daughter Zion," as in TNIV) refers here to the reassembled remnant of Israel, and "Daughter of Jerusalem" is a parallel expression to "Daughter of Zion" (cf. Isa 37:22); also note the parallel of Jerusalem to Zion in v.16.

The expression "shout aloud" (*hārî'û*) was often associated with warfare. When Israel entered battle, the sounding of the ram's horn was accompanied with a "shout" (Nu 10:9). Even the Lord shouts in victory at his enemy (Ps 108:9[10]).

15 In typical hymnic style the prophet follows the call to praise with the cause for praise: "The LORD has taken away your punishment ... turned back your enemy ... [he] is with you; never again will you fear any harm." The people are safe and secure because "the LORD, the King of Israel" is with them.

The fact that the Lord "is with" his people is stated also in vv.5 and 17. Balaam recognized of ancient Israel that "the LORD their God is with them; the shout of the King is among them" (Nu 23:21), and much later Zechariah calls the "daughter of Zion" to rejoice because her king comes to her (Zec 9:9–10; cf. Mt 21:4–5).

16 In that wonderfully glorious day, the remnant's hands will not hang limp, because there will be no despair for slack hands to symbolize (cf. 2Ch 15:7; Isa 13:7; Jer 6:24; Eze 7:17). Slack or fallen hands are a symbol of despair, but with the Lord in their midst and with nothing to fear, the people may now lift up their slack hands (cf. Heb 12:12).

17 Since the Lord "is with" (*bᵉqereb*, "in the midst of") his people, they need no longer fear; he is able to save them. "Mighty to save" (*gibbôr yôšîaᶜ*; cf. Jer 14:9) is an expression in Hebrew that

can be understood in an active verbal sense—"a warrior who will keep you safe" (REB); "a warrior who gives victory" (NRSV); "a warrior who brings triumph" (TNK); "a hero who saves" (GWT); "his power gives you victory" (TEV)—or as a noun with a modifier—"victorious warrior" (NASB, JB); "mighty savior" (NAB, NLT). Isaiah 10:21 mentions the remnant that will return to the "mighty God." The word *gibbôr* often refers to a warrior who is going out against the enemy (Isa 42:13).

The last half of this verse is a love poem of three parallel lines, each expressing the great love of God for his people. Robertson, 340, observes "that the Holy One should experience ecstasy over the sinner is incomprehensible." Other passages that speak of God's rejoicing in the love of his people include Isaiah 62:4–5; 65:19; and Jeremiah 32:40–41.

The Hebrew behind "he will quiet you with his love" was translated by the KJV, "he will rest in his love." The reading of the text has been understood and interpreted in various ways: (1) because of his love, the Lord will keep silent regarding his people's sins; (2) the Lord's love will be so strong and deep as to hush motion or speech—there will be silent ecstasy; and (3) the Lord's silence is due to his planning of good deeds toward Israel (see Notes).

Some commentators and versions (NAB, NEB, RSV, JB), however, read the Hebrew form from the root *ḥdš* ("to renew") instead of *ḥrš* ("to quiet"), thus yielding various ideas: (1) he will do new things; (2) he will renew his love; (3) he will renew himself in his love, (4) he will renew Israel through new life; and (5) he will show you his love. Luther perhaps caught the sense when he explained, "He will cause you to be silent so that you may have in the secret places of your heart a very quiet peace and a peaceful silence."

The prophet continues his description of this saving God as one who "will take great delight in you" and "rejoice over you with singing" (cf. Isa 62:5).

18 At this point the text shifts to the first person form of address as the Lord speaks directly to his people. The scattering of the people in judgment brought on sorrows as they yearned for the old assembly experiences at the appointed feasts, the festive meetings (cf. La 2:6). The Hebrew *mô'ēd* is not restricted to a particular "feast" but may be understood as relating to various feasts to which pilgrimages were made. Jack Lewis (*TWOT*, 1:389) correctly says, "Appearing at times (Hos 9:5) with *ḥag* (which designates the three great annual festivals), *mô'ēd* must be thought of in a wide usage for all religious assemblies." This experience of the people was realized during the exile of the nation, when the people were isolated from the meaningful celebrations that reminded them of God's activity in their past history of salvation.

19 Repeatedly in this verse the Lord continues to speak in the first person (see Notes). He is the one who initiates action in behalf of his people. He is the one who "deals with" their enemies and helps them meet their needs.

The Lord promises "at that time" to deal with all who have oppressed Israel (cf. Isa 60:14). The restoration of God's people is regularly represented in connection with the destruction of those nations that are hostile to God's purpose (59:17-21; 66:15-16). They will enjoy receiving praise (cf. 62:7) and honor—even from the lands where they were put to shame.

The pathetic condition of God's people is reflected in the references to the "lame" (cf. Mic 4:7) and "scattered," language using the imagery

of a flock (cf. Eze 34:4-6, 16). The last two lines (a chiasm) contain language reflecting the law of Deuteronomy, which threatened exile for disobedience but also promised ultimate restoration (Dt 30:1, 4). Robertson, 345, observes that the combination of "praise" (*tᵉhillâ*) and "honor" (*šēm*) is found outside Zephaniah only in Deuteronomy 26:19 and Jeremiah 13:11 and suggests the possibility that the two prophets found a common source in the book of Deuteronomy.

20 With a slight change in wording, the Lord repeats the promise just made, thus giving emphasis to it. (Note the reversed order of "honor and praise" in the two verses.) Additional emphasis is made by the repeated use of the personal pronoun "I" throughout vv.18-20: "I will remove ... I will deal ... I will rescue ... I will give them praise ... I will gather ... I will bring ... I will give you honor ... when I restore." The work of redemption is the work of the Lord. He had scattered them and now he will restore them. The expression "among all the peoples of the earth" includes a worldwide recognition of their glory that exceeds the original localities of the exile.

This closing verse is also supplemented with the addition of the temporal clause "when I restore your fortunes [cf. 2:7] before your very eyes." The work of redemption, as well as judgment, belongs to the Lord. He will accomplish his purposes with his people. This promise is the basis of their hope and joy.

Though some of this promise found fulfillment in the restoration of the people after their seventy years of captivity (note the "before your very eyes" in the last line), much of this promise remains for a yet future, more inclusive restoration. The book opened with a judgment of cosmic proportion; now the book closes with a worldwide scene of restoration.

NOTES

14 Emphasis is made by the stacking of Hebrew words with similar meaning: רָנַן (rānan, "sing"), רוּעַ (rûaʿ, "shout aloud"), שָׂמַח (śāmaḥ, "be glad"), and עָלַז (ʿālaz, "rejoice").

15 The form תִּירְאִי (tîrʾî) was understood to involve the root רָאה (rʾh, "see") by the KJV translators, but most translations (RSV, NEB, NAB, JB) understand the form to contain the root ירא (yrʾ, "fear"), though Kittel's note says two Hebrew MSS read תִּרְאִי (tirʾî), which reflects the root rʾh. Internal evidence also supports the term for fear here (cf. Sabottka, 128).

17 גִּבּוֹר (gibbôr, "mighty") probably is to be understood as the subject of the verb "save"; hence the RSV's "a warrior who gives victory." This term is often used of the heroes and mighty men of Israel. "He will take great delight in you" is rendered more literally by the KJV as "he will rejoice over thee with joy" and parallels the last line: "he will rejoice over you with singing."

"Quiet you" follows the MT's חָרַשׁ (ḥāraš) and is similar to other versions: "he will be quiet in his love" (NASB); "quiet you with his love" (NKJV); "with his love he will calm all your fears" (NLT); "you will rest in his love" (NCV); "soothe with his love" (TNK). But some versions emend the text to read חָדַשׁ (ḥādaš, "renew"): "renew you in his love" (NRSV); "renews you with his love" (GWT); "in his love he will give you new life" (TEV); "refresh your life with his love" (CEV); "renew you in his love" (NAB). This emendation involves the change of one letter and changing the vowels to read a Piel form. The LXX and Syriac reflect "renew," but the MT makes sense here and need not be emended.

18 The NIV takes "sorrows" to be the subject of "they are a burden and a reproach to you"; the TNIV understands "your appointed festivals" to be what is "a burden and reproach for you." The NIV text note offers a third option, understanding "reproach" to be the "burden" the people bear. The MT's accentuation is unexpected here; we expect the *atnah* to be on the preceding word, מִמֵּךְ (mimmēk, "from you"). Attempts to reflect the MT's accentuation in translation are awkward (cf. KJV, "who are of thee"; Keil, "they are of thee").

19 Four times the Lord speaks in the first person, once in the form of a first person singular suffix with a participle ("I will deal"), and three times in the form of finite verbs ("rescue ... gather ... give them").

"Will deal" translates עֹשֶׂה (ʿōśeh), the common verb that means "to do" whatever is called for by context (so also NEB, NAB; cf. "take action," JB). For more examples of this use of the verb, see Jeremiah 18:23; 21:2 and Ezekiel 22:14; 23:25, 29.

"Honor" translates שֵׁם (šēm; GK 9005), the Hebrew word for "name," which is often used in the sense of "fame" (so the KJV) and of defeat of enemies (cf. Isa 63:12; Jer 32:20; Ne 9:10). The NIV translates the word "renown" in Isaiah 63:12 and Jeremiah 32:20.

20 The infinitive קַבְּצִי (qabbᵉṣî, "to bring, gather") may be unexpected here, but it is not necessary to adopt the suggested emendation אֲקַבֵּץ (ᵃqabbēṣ, "I will bring"). Perhaps the temporal use of the infinitive is intended here, as the RSV reflects: "At that time I will bring you home, at the time *when* I gather you together" (emphasis mine). ("Home" is supplied by the NIV, TNIV, and the RSV; the NIV supplies it with the second line and the RSV with the first line.)

HAGGAI

EUGENE H. MERRILL

Introduction

1. BACKGROUND

The precise chronological information provided in the book (see Date, below) makes possible a clear identification of the times in which the prophet Haggai ministers to his community. In general, the setting is Jerusalem in the postexilic period, a time when the struggling returnees are preoccupied with the reestablishment of their homeland within the larger context of the Persian Empire.[1] More specifically, the principal task at hand is the building of a Jewish temple on the ruins of the glorious house of worship erected by Solomon 430 years earlier and razed to the ground by the Babylonian armies just sixty-six years prior to Haggai's time.

The Babylonian Empire, mighty as it was, enjoyed only a brief period of Near Eastern hegemony. Initiated by its crushing of the Neo-Assyrian state in 605 BC, its first and only truly great ruler, Nebuchadnezzar II, moved quickly not only to incorporate the Assyrian domains but also to add to them. A target of importance to readers of the OT was the tiny state of Judah, a nation which, though under at least some Assyrian control from time to time, had remained relatively independent. Nebuchadnezzar changed all that. At first content to take some choice Jewish captives (including Daniel; Da 1:1–7) in 605, he followed up with a major deportation in 598 in which young King Jehoiachin was taken prisoner; then, following rebellion against Babylon by Jehoiachin's successor, Zedekiah, Nebuchadnezzar sent his armies against Jerusalem in 586, this time leveling the city, destroying the temple, and carrying off the cream of Judean society.

---

1. For a brief but helpful overview, see Peter R. Ackroyd, *Israel under Babylon and Persia* (Oxford: Oxford Univ. Press, 1986), 13–19.

Meanwhile, another powerful force was emerging to the east of Babylon, namely, the nascent elements of what would become the Persian Empire. Its founder, Cyrus II (the Great), by sheer will and brilliant strategy had by 550 BC merged the Medes and Persians into a fearsome political and military machine bent on the conquest of the whole region. Nebuchadnezzar's death in 562 had greatly weakened the Babylonian Empire, and the rulers who succeeded him could do little or nothing to prevent the slide to certain doom.

Following the ephemeral reigns of Evil-Merodach (562–560 BC), Neriglissar (560–556), and Labashi-Marduk (556), Nabonidus (555–539) came to power—the last ruler before Babylonia was defeated by the Persians. Nabonidus was not a native Babylonian nor was he a devotee of Marduk and the other Babylonian deities. Needless to say, these traits gained him no popularity, so for much of his reign he ruled in absentia through his son Belshazzar.[2] It was this unfortunate surrogate who saw the handwriting on the wall and lost his life on the very night of the Persian sacking of his city (Da 5).

Cyrus, having conquered Babylon and thus the Neo-Babylonian (or Chaldean) Empire in 539 BC, continued his reign until 530. His most important act from a biblical standpoint was his decree in 538 that the Jews of Babylon could return to their homeland, a region by then known as Yehud, part of the vast province of Abar Nahara ("across the [Euphrates] river"). His successors were Cambyses II (530–522), Gaumata (522), Darius Hystaspes (522–486), Xerxes (486–465), Artaxerxes I (464–424), Darius II (423–404), and Artaxerxes II (404–358). Hystaspes is the Darius referred to in Haggai and Zechariah. Xerxes was the husband of Queen Esther, his OT name appearing as Ahasuerus. Ezra and Nehemiah led returns from Persia under the auspices of Artaxerxes I, a ruler who, like Cyrus, granted unusual favors to the Jewish Diaspora.

Little can be known about the nonexiled Jews who remained in their homeland. For them life went on, but almost certainly with no sense of national or even religious cohesion, at best in conditions of economic ruin, and with little, if any, political leadership worthy to be called such. The absence of any literature from the period between 586 and 539 BC, biblical or otherwise, attests to the social and cultural vacuum left in the wake of the catastrophic demolition of the Jewish state at Babylonian hands.[3]

Ironically, much more is known of the Jews of the Diaspora, largely because of biblical texts. Ezekiel, himself a captive, speaks of Jewish communities in Persia that appear to have had some measure of independence. Daniel, among the earliest of the deportees, provides glimpses into Jewish life in and around Babylon during both the Babylonian and Persian periods. On the whole, life there was bearable except for intermittent times of persecution occasioned by the Jews' refusal to submit to pagan idolatry.

The same spirit pervades Ezra's recapitulation of Jewish history in the decades between Cyrus's liberation decree and his own time (ca. 540–440 BC). Again and again the rulers of Persia unbegrudgingly acceded to the requests of the Jews to return to their homeland. Frequently their permission was accompanied by promises of protection as well as generous outlays of material provision. Such beneficence

---

2. The so-called Verse Account of Nabonidus provides the link between himself and his son Belshazzar. See James B. Pritchard, ed., *Ancient Near Eastern Texts Relating to the Old Testament*, 3rd ed. (Princeton: Princeton Univ. Press, 1969), 312–15; P.-A. Beaulieu, *The Reign of Nabonidus, King of Babylon 556–539 B.C.* (YNER 10; New Haven, Conn.: Yale Univ. Press, 1989), 188–97.

3. Archaeological data provide virtually all that can be known from this period. See Ephraim Stern, *Archaeology of the Land of the Bible*; Vol. II, *The Assyrian, Babylonian, and Persian Periods 732–332 B.C.E.* (New York: Doubleday, 2001), 428–38.

continued through the remainder of the biblical period (ca. 400 BC). At the same time, of course, the Persians were attending to their own self-interest, for a strong Jewish state would provide a buffer between them and the hostile and increasingly powerful nations of Greece and Egypt.

As for the immediate setting of Haggai, the book reflects the brief time from Cyrus's decree to 520 BC — only eighteen years. The initial contingent, under the leadership of Sheshbazzar and Zerubbabel, commenced its return in 538 with the full blessing and support of the Persian government (Ezr 1–2). Among the objectives was rebuilding the temple, a goal endorsed by Cyrus himself (2Ch 36:22–23; Ezr 1:1–4). Having gathered materials for the project, Zerubbabel (by now the governor of the jurisdiction) and Jeshua (the chief priest) oversaw the laying of the temple's foundations, a project of profound joy (Ezr 3:8–13).

By this time, however, resistance began to set in — resistance led by certain unnamed adversaries who no doubt were jealous of the favors being shown to the Jewish newcomers (Ezr 4:1–2). Despite their claim to be worshiping the same God as the Jews did, their demands to participate in the building had been soundly rebuffed (v.3). They therefore attempted to turn the Persian kings against the Jews but apparently without success (vv.4–5). At the same time, the project ground to a halt, not to be resumed until the second year of King Darius Hystaspes, that is, 520 BC. It was under the aegis of this good king that Haggai and Zechariah took heart and initiated their ministry of temple completion (Ezr 4:5; Hag 1:1; Zec 1:1). There may indeed have been external forces that dampened the initial enthusiasm for the project, but the overall impression left by Haggai is that the work lagged because of the torpid indifference of the Jews themselves. It is this indifference that the prophet confronts and that provides the centerpiece of his message.

2. AUTHORSHIP

The prophet Haggai is the only individual in the OT to bear that name. With this fact, coupled with the name's meaning "festival" or the like, some scholars propose that the author is anonymous and that the name is a nom de plume appropriate to the theme of festivity connected to building of the temple. Thus the name is akin to that associated with the name Malachi, more a title than a personal name (cf. commentary of Malachi).

This proposal, however, founders on the fact that most prophetic names are "message-bearing," some even more so than Haggai. Furthermore, Haggai is mentioned in Ezra 5:1 as a prophet who, with Zechariah, delivered exhortations to the returnees to build the temple (cf. Ezr 6:14). Unless the name Zechariah is also a pseudonym, one must suppose that a prophet named Haggai actually existed.

Zechariah is identified as "the son of Berekiah, the son of Iddo" (Zec 1:1), whereas Haggai is silent as to his ancestry. However, the same can be said of Amos, Obadiah, Micah, Nahum, and Habakkuk, none of whose prophetic credentials or nomenclature is in jeopardy. In short, there is no reason to doubt that the book of Haggai was authored by a man of that name.

Granting this assumption, what more can be said of Haggai? First, one is struck by the brevity of his ministry, at least within the confines of his book. All his activities described there take place in fewer than four months. After that, nothing more is heard of him. Does he retire from public ministry? Does he cease to write as a canonical spokesman? Does he die, perhaps of old age?[4]

---

4. Hans Walter Wolff, *Haggai: A Commentary* (Minneapolis: Augsburg, 1988), 17.

None of these questions finds an answer in the biblical text. Some suggest the last as a reasonable hypothesis, but the suggestion can be no more than mere inference. For example, Haggai appears to identify himself with the old people who had seen the temple of Solomon in all of its glory some sixty-six years earlier (Hag 2:3; cf. Ezr 3:12). But there is no explicit testimony on his part that he had seen it with his own eyes. Moreover, so the argument goes, Haggai was a public figure — a well-established and well-recognized prophet — eighteen years earlier (Ezr 5:1). Yet even if one should grant for the sake of argument that a prophet normally must have been at least thirty years old before he functioned in that capacity (cf. Eze 1:1), Haggai would still not need to be more than in his early fifties at the time of his book's setting.

In the final analysis, such speculation bears little fruit and has little or nothing to do with the credentials of the prophet or the meaning and efficacy of his ministry, including that of the composition of his book.

3. DATE AND PLACE OF ORIGIN

A major characteristic of postexilic biblical writings is their strict attention to chronological matters. Ezekiel dates his ministry and oracles with precision (Eze 1:1–2; 8:1; 20:1; 24:1; 26:1), as do Daniel (Da 1:1; 2:1; 7:1; 8:1; 9:1; 10:1), Ezra (Ezr 3:1, 8; 7:8–9; 8:31; 10:16), Nehemiah (Ne 1:1; 2:1; 5:14; 8:2; 9:1; 13:6), Esther (Est 2:16; 3:7; 8:9; 9:1, 17–19), and Zechariah (Zec 1:1, 7; 7:1). This feature falls in line with the general trend in the secular historiography of the day, a trend toward an annalistic style employed to document the accomplishments of kingdoms and their rulers. The most famous of these documents are the so-called "chronicles" of the Neo-Babylonian kings, beginning with Nebuchadnezzar's father, Nabopolassar.[5] These chronicles are particularly helpful because they make reference to events also recorded in biblical history, thus permitting the events of the latter to achieve firm historical and chronological precision.

Nowhere is this benefit more clear than in the dating of events in Haggai. By correlating biblical data with those of ancient Babylonia and Persia and then modern calendars with ancient ones, it is possible to determine, for example, that the first day of the sixth month of the second year of Darius (Hag 1:1) is August 29, 520 BC. The last date in the book, the twenty-fourth day of the ninth month of Darius's second year (2:10, 18), is December 18, 520.[6]

The place of origin of the book of Haggai is also indisputable. The prophet locates himself in Jerusalem, in particular in the vicinity of the temple. It is there that he delivers his message, presumably first in oral form, and it is likely that he subsequently composes it there as well. Of a more specific setting nothing is said.

4. DESTINATION

The immediate audience to which Haggai addresses his oracles is the postexilic Jewish community in and near Jerusalem. There can be little doubt, however, that the written text soon circulates throughout Yehud and eventually beyond, among the Diaspora. This circulation would include the thousands of Jews who remain in Babylonia and Persia.

---

5. D. J. Wiseman, *Chronicles of Chaldaean Kings (626–556 B.C.) in the British Museum* (London: The Trustees of the British Museum, 1961).

6. Richard A. Parker and Waldo H. Dubberstein, *Babylonian Chronology: 626 B.C.–A.D. 75* (Providence, R.I.: Brown Univ. Press), 1956.

As Scripture, of course, the destination of the book is the whole people of God, Jew and Gentile alike. Its teachings, though not directed to the specific situation of the modern world and church, find application and relevance to believers of every generation. The book's recognition as a canonical work guarantees this relevance.

5. OCCASION AND PURPOSE

Few books are as clear as Haggai in establishing the matters of occasion and purpose. The situation is that the second temple, having been started, is far from completion (Hag 1:2−4; 2:3, 18−19). Such scandalous neglect of this crucial step in reestablishing the postexilic community is displeasing to the Lord (1:9−11; 2:16−19). The prophet thus is summoned by God to call the people to repentance (1:7; 2:14−15) and to lead them in the task of rebuilding (1:8, 14; 2:4a)—a task that will come to successful fruition because of the Lord's presence and power (1:13; 2:4b; 2:19).

6. LITERARY FORM

The book of Haggai presents itself as a series of prophetic oracles separated by chronological notations (1:1−11, 12−15; 2:1−9, 10−19, 20−23). The first four oracles address the immediate situation, that is, the ruinous state of the temple and the need to resume its construction, whereas the last oracle is eschatological with clear apocalyptic overtones. Such overtones occur elsewhere as well, especially in the promise of the Lord to fill a future temple with the wealth of the nations and with his own glorious presence (2:6−9).

Haggai also exhibits traces of narrative, a feature tied to its chronological data. The word of God comes to the prophet at a given point (1:1), he delivers it (1:2−11), and he with his audience then undertake the work of rebuilding (1:14−15). The word comes again (2:1, 10), prompting Haggai to enter into dialogue with certain priests (2:12). Action is certainly limited, but there is nevertheless a sense of directed motion, one leading to a historical conclusion.

More specifically, according to some scholars the book consists largely of poetic material, the prose being mainly the narrative interludes already described. Though Hebrew prose and poetry are not always easy to distinguish from each other, the following analysis, based on the BHS, enjoys some consensus:[7]

Prose	Poetry
1:1−2	1:3−11
1:12−15a	1:15b
2:1−2	2:3−9
2:10−13	2:14−19
	2:20−23

---

7. None of the major modern English versions formats the book in this manner, but see S. R. Driver, *An Introduction to the Literature of the Old Testament* (Edinburgh: T. & T. Clark, 1913), 344; Duane L. Christensen, "Impulse and Design in the Book of Haggai," *JETS* 35 (1992): 445. For a good discussion of the matter pro and con, see Richard A. Taylor and E. Ray Clendenen, *Haggai, Malachi* (NAC 21A; Nashville: Broadman & Holman, 2004), 71−73.

Far from being bereft of poetic quality and other features of *belles lettres*, Haggai exhibits a number of devices that reveal a work of thoughtful, artistic expression. The book displays the use of metric rhythm (1:3–6, 8; 2:4–5, 21–23),[8] chiastic structure (1:4, 9, 10; 2:23), a dialogic paraenesis (1:4, 5, 9; 2:11–13; cf. a similar feature in Malachi), and at least one example of paronomasia (1:4 [*ḥārēb*, "ruin"]; 1:11 [*ḥōreb*, "drought"]). Dorsey proposes a couple of examples of internal chiastic structures.[9] These will receive attention in the exposition below.

7. THEOLOGICAL VALUES

The most socially, politically, and theologically devastating event in Judah's long history of 345 years was the destruction of Solomon's temple, the place where the Lord had said he would "cause his name to dwell" (Dt 12:5 et passim). In a real sense the disappearance of this center of Judah's cultus reflected the removal of the Lord himself from among his people. Just as they went into Babylonian exile, so did the Lord, his departure having been viewed in a vision by Ezekiel as a rising up of his glory from the midst of Jerusalem to a place of at least temporary residence on the Mount of Olives (Eze 11:22–23).

The Jews who made up the Diaspora and those who remained in Judah shared alike a sense of abandonment by God. Through good times and bad they had depended on the covenantal faithfulness of the Lord to preserve them. Despite their incessant disobedience he had done so, even restoring them to spiritual vitality and political stability time and time again. In 586 BC all that came to an end. The kingdom was dismantled and its rulers slain or deported. Zion, the city of the Lord, was reduced to ashes, its population decimated or exiled, and, most tragic of all, the temple razed. All the rest might be somehow overcome, but the ruin of God's house marked the ruin of their very identity as the people of the Lord. It seemed as if he had abrogated his covenant with David and had at last turned his back forever on the unfaithful nation.

The decree of Cyrus half a century later revived their forlorn spirits, however, for that decree included permission and provision for the Jewish exiles to return to Jerusalem and to rebuild their sacred temple. With unbounded joy and resolve they did so, seeing in this new building a new opportunity to live out covenantal obedience. Surely God was not finished with them yet, and the second temple would make that conviction plain for all to see.

But the initial enthusiasm for the project soon waned under the pressure of outside hostility and a creeping spirit of self-centeredness that gave the reestablishment of the socioeconomic community priority over the renewal of the theocracy. A crisis of faith hung heavy over the issue of the importance of the temple. Was it worth the effort to rebuild it, especially since it could never match the glory and grandeur of the earlier one? Were it ever to be built, was there any guarantee that the Lord would be pleased with it? More than that, would he indeed remember his ancient promises and restore the remnant nation and its rulers to their redemptive function?

Into this crisis steps the prophet Haggai. His is a daunting task, indeed—to redirect the nation's focus, to lead his people to a different set of priorities, and to assure them that God is with them. More important,

---

8. Thus, with some reservation, David L. Petersen, *Haggai and Zechariah 1–8* (Philadelphia: Westminster, 1984), 32.

9. David A. Dorsey, *The Literary Structure of the Old Testament* (Grand Rapids: Baker, 1999), 316.

God will be glorified in this temple in an unprecedented way, and through Zerubbabel, the scion of David, he will usher in a golden age of salvation and peace.

8. CANONICITY

Every extant ancient canon includes Haggai, always as a part of the "Book of the Twelve," the so-called Minor Prophets. The lengthy discussions of the rabbis as to canonical criteria—found primarily in the Talmud—never refer to Haggai as a disputed writing. Finally, allusions to or citations of Haggai in the New Testament make certain that the early church regarded Haggai as fully canonical, inspired Scripture (see Hag 1:1; cf. Mt 1:12; Hag 2: 6, 21; cf. Mt 24:29 and Heb 12:26–27; Hag 2:23b; cf. Mt 12:18).

9. SPECIAL PROBLEMS

On the whole, Haggai attests few problems of a textual, literary, or historical nature. Those that pose particular difficulty will receive attention in the exposition to follow. The Septuagint (LXX) offers several additions to the Masoretic Text, most of them being explanatory glosses that need not presuppose a different Hebrew tradition. As for longer expansions (notably 2:9, 14, 17, 21), since these are attested to only by the LXX, it could well be that they are idiosyncratic readings designed to be commentaries on the Hebrew Vorlage. In any case, they are awkward and disruptive of the otherwise smooth reading of the texts.

The major structural issue is whether 1:15 is part of 1:12–15 or 1:15–2:9. Since Haggai routinely introduces his oracles with chronological notations (cf. 1:1; 2:1; 2:10; 2:20), it is strange that 1:12–15 ends with such a notation. Many scholars therefore divide 1:15 in two, assigning v.15b to 2:1 and v.15a to 2:5–19, where it serves as a chronological introduction to what they consider to be still another oracle.[10] Moreover, since 2:15–19 seems to address the same matters as 1:1–11, these scholars would move 2:15–19 to a position prior to 2:1. While ingenious, such a resort is unnecessary and lacks support from ancient manuscripts and versions. The exposition will demonstrate the propriety of leaving the structure well enough alone.

10. BIBLIOGRAPHY

Baldwin, Joyce G. *Haggai, Zechariah, Malachi*. Tyndale Old Testament Commentaries. London: Tyndale, 1972.

Merrill, Eugene H. *Haggai, Zechariah, Malachi: An Exegetical Commentary*. Chicago: Moody Press, 1994.

Meyers, Carol L., and Eric M. Meyers. *Haggai, Zechariah 1–8*. Anchor Bible 25B. Garden City, N.Y.: Doubleday, 1987.

Motyer, J. Alec. "Haggai." Pages 963–1002 in *The Minor Prophets*. Ed. Thomas Edward McComiskey. Grand Rapids: Baker, 1998.

Smith, Ralph L. *Micah–Malachi*. Word Biblical Commentary 32. Waco, Tex.: Word, 1984.

Taylor, Richard A., and E. Ray Clendenen. *Haggai, Malachi*. New American Commentary 21A. Nashville: Broadman & Holman, 2004.

Verhoef, Pieter A. *The Books of Haggai and Malachi*. New International Commentary on the Old Testament. Grand Rapids: Eerdmans, 1987.

---

10. Thus, e.g., Carroll Stuhlmueller, *Rebuilding with Hope: A Commentary on the Books of Haggai and Zechariah* (ITC; Grand Rapids: Eerdmans, 1988), 15.

11. OUTLINE

Text and Exposition

I. REBUILDING THE TEMPLE (1:1–15)

A. Introduction and Setting (1:1)

¹In the second year of King Darius, on the first day of the sixth month, the word of the LORD came through the prophet Haggai to Zerubbabel son of Shealtiel, governor of Judah, and to Joshua son of Jehozadak, the high priest.

COMMENTARY

1 King Darius Hystaspes, a usurper of the Persian throne, came to power in 522 BC and reigned until 486. In a short time he reasserted Persia's dominion over the whole Middle Eastern world following the mysterious death of Cyrus's son Cambyses and the assassination of his would-be successor, Gaumata, the latter at the hands of Darius himself. The stability that ensued provided an environment in which such domestic matters as temple building could be undertaken without resistance. No doubt such a turn of events encouraged Haggai and Zechariah to exhort their Jewish countrymen to get on with that very task (cf. Ezr 4:1–5).

Thanks to the recovery of ancient chronological and astronomical data it is possible to assign precise dates to events in postexilic Judah (see "Date" in the introduction). The sixth month, Elul, corresponds to August–September in modern calendars, and the first day of the month in the year 520 was August 29.

Exactly on that day, Haggai says, he communicated to Zerubbabel and Joshua a divine revelation concerning the rebuilding of the temple (cf. v.8). An otherwise unknown prophet (except in Ezr 5:1 and 6:14; see the introduction), Haggai must have held a status and reputation such that he had ready and sympathetic access to Judah's most powerful leaders, Zerubbabel and Joshua. Zerubbabel, whose name (derived from *zēr bābili*, "seed of Babylon") reflects his Babylonian upbringing, was a grandson of King Jehoiachin (1Ch 3:17–19) and his successor in the line of Davidic-covenant rulers. His office in the postexilic state was that of governor (Heb. *pehâ*), a title applied in the Persian period to both Jewish (Mal 1:8; Ne 5:14, 18; 12:26) and non-Jewish (Ezr 8:36; Ne 2:7; 3:7; Est 3:12) officials.

Because the Chronicler identifies Zerubbabel as the son of Pedaiah (1Ch 3:19) and nephew of Shealtiel (3:17), it is likely that Zerubbabel had become Shealtiel's foster son, perhaps by virtue of the levirate tradition whereby a brother assumed parental responsibility on behalf of his deceased sibling (Dt 25:5–10). As for Sheshbazzar, identified in Ezra as the "prince of Judah" (Ezr 1:8) and then governor (5:14), he is perhaps the same as Zerubbabel or, more likely, Zerubbabel's immediate predecessor, a brother or uncle who, before he himself could carry out the task of building the temple, gave place to Zerubbabel (Ezr 5:16; cf. 3:8, 10; Meyers and Meyers, 11).

Joshua son of Jehozadak sprang directly from Aaron, as the genealogy of 1 Chronicles 6:1–15 makes clear (cf. Ezr 3:2, 8; 5:2; 10:18; Ne 12:26; Zec 6:11). His credentials and qualifications to function as high priest are therefore beyond dispute.

B. The Exhortation to Rebuild (1:2–11)

²This is what the Lord Almighty says:"These people say,'The time has not yet come for the Lord's house to be built.'"

³Then the word of the Lord came through the prophet Haggai: ⁴"Is it a time for you yourselves to be living in your paneled houses, while this house remains a ruin?"

⁵Now this is what the Lord Almighty says:"Give careful thought to your ways. ⁶You have planted much, but have harvested little. You eat, but never have enough. You drink, but never have your fill. You put on clothes, but are not warm. You earn wages, only to put them in a purse with holes in it."

⁷This is what the Lord Almighty says:"Give careful thought to your ways. ⁸Go up into the mountains and bring down timber and build the house, so that I may take pleasure in it and be honored," says the Lord. ⁹"You expected much, but see, it turned out to be little. What you brought home, I blew away. Why?" declares the Lord Almighty. "Because of my house, which remains a ruin, while each of you is busy with his own house. ¹⁰Therefore, because of you the heavens have withheld their dew and the earth its crops. ¹¹I called for a drought on the fields and the mountains, on the grain, the new wine, the oil and whatever the ground produces, on men and cattle, and on the labor of your hands."

COMMENTARY

2 The introduction of the Lord by the epithet "the Lord of hosts" (v.2, NASB; NIV has "the Lord Almighty") is instructive because (1) the task of temple construction is beyond human capacity; and (2) the imperium of the world's great powers, including Persia, must be recognized by the Jews as being subject to the Sovereign of the universe, their own God. In fact, this term occurs more times proportionately in the postexilic prophets (fourteen times in Haggai; fifty-three times in Zechariah; twenty-four times in Malachi) than anywhere else in the OT. The God who rules over all creation is able to meet every need of the disheartened community.

The people's problem is immediately pointed out to them by the Lord:The time for temple building has not come—or so they are saying. But this seems inconsistent with the readiness with which they began the project eighteen years earlier. Within two years of their return from exile they laid the foundations of the temple with great joy and fanfare (Ezr 3:8–11). Even then, however, the celebration was tinged with sadness as the elderly among them reflected with nostalgia on the meagerness of this second temple compared to the glorious temple of Solomon they had seen with their own eyes (Ezr 3:12–13; cf. Hag 2:3). It seems that this dampening of enthusiasm won the day, for nearly two decades later little if anything more was accomplished.

One must also take into consideration the opposition to the project by the Jews' enemies, who came to see the return of the Jews to the land and the reestablishment of their state as a threat to their own territorial claims (Ezr 4:1–2, 4; 5:3–5). Such pressure was bound to undermine Jewish morale. Thus, Haggai's contemporaries are insisting that the time for rebuilding the temple "is not coming" (thus the participle). The word for "time" here (ʿēt; GK 6961) has the idea of a set or appointed time, the appropriate moment for something to be done (*NIDOTTE*, 3:565). That time has not arrived, nor does it seem to be imminent.

3–4 Whatever the people's rationale, the Lord challenges it by throwing back at them their own words. In a rhetorical question he asks them how it can be the time (haʿēt) for them to build their own houses and yet not the time to build his house (v.4). There seems to be no comparison between their preexilic homes and those they now have built. Nor has external opposition appeared to slow them down in that task. What, then, explains the success of the one project and the failure of the other?

The answer lies in their misplaced priorities. In an ironic twist the Lord describes the houses they have built in terms of certain features of the old Solomonic temple. So lavish are the interiors of their dwellings that they are paneled (sᵉpûnîm) like that glorious house of the Lord (see 1Ki 6:9; 7:3, 7). Though unable to raise the dwelling place of the

Lord from its ruins, the people have still found time, energy, and resources to squander on themselves.

5–6 The displeasure of the Lord is immediately apparent in the terse but unmistakable warning: "Give careful thought" to what you are doing (v.5). Such wrong-headedness can no longer go unchallenged and uncorrected. In fact, the corrective hand of God has already become apparent to those with eyes to see. In a series of strong adversatives the folly of having misplaced priorities finds graphic expression. The community has apparently suffered agricultural losses and general economic malaise, conditions that may well have been attributed by them to the chaotic social and political times or to plain bad luck. To forestall any such erroneous conclusions, the Lord lays the blame for all these circumstances squarely at the feet of those responsible—the returnees, who having begun so well have defected from the will of God in their own self-interest.

The signs of God's disfavor are plain for all to see, if only the people will open their hearts to the realities around them. (1) They have sowed much but reaped little. (2) What little they have managed to harvest is insufficient to feed them to satisfaction (lit., "eating without satisfaction"). (3) They have drunk, but not enough to become intoxicated, so short is the supply (see Notes). (4) They have clothed themselves, but so inadequate or scarce are their garments that they can never get warm. (5) The one who hires himself out (so the Hebrew) does indeed earn wages, but to no avail. The cost of living is such that he may as well put his money in a bag full of holes, for it is not nearly enough to provide for himself and his family.

This list of disasters is not random. Long before the destruction of the temple and the exile, the Lord threatened some of these very judgments for covenantal disobedience. The "curse" section of Deuteronomy threatens drought and famine

(Dt 28:16, 18, 38), lack of wine (28:39), and pervasive poverty and want (28:19, 23–24, 44). Their disobedience had resulted in the exile to begin with (2Ki 17:19–23; 2Ch 36:14–17), and now their self-centered disloyalty to the Lord is bringing further covenantal curses on them.

7–11 There was only one remedy—they must give sober thought to what they are doing (lit., "set your heart upon your ways"; cf. v.5) and make amends. The first step is practical, indeed. The people are to go up to the hill country (lit., "mountain"), a reference no doubt to the forest lands that surrounded Jerusalem in ancient times (v.8). Some scholars suggest this designation refers to Lebanon, the source of the famous cedars used in the construction of Solomon's temple (1Ki 5:6). But this case is highly unlikely given the poverty of the people, the great distances involved in transporting such timbers, and the lack of any reference here to cedar wood. Indeed, the lack of such prized building material may well have contributed to the dismay of the old men who compared this temple so unfavorably with the former one (Hag 2:3).

The commands come thick and fast—"go up ... bring down ... build" (v.8). No matter the people's misgivings, the Lord promises that he will take pleasure in the temple and be glorified through it.

The size and splendor of the project matters little. What do matter are obedience and a reordering of priorities. The Lord's glory will be seen in two ways—in the completion of the temple itself and in his filling it with his presence (2:7).

In an interesting chiastic structure, the promise of pleasure and glory (v.8) forms the central point of matching descriptions of the people's situation leading to the prophet's exhortation to build (see David A. Dorsey, *The Literary Structure of the Old Testament* [Grand Rapids: Baker, 1999], 316). Though they live in richly decorated houses, their economy has deteriorated thanks to poor crops and inflation (vv.4–6). In reverse order, the cause of inflation in v.9 is attributed to divine intervention. Whatever profit was gained through agriculture has been "blown away," made valueless. When it reached their houses, it came to naught because God's house (the temple) was neglected (ḥārēb) in the process. At the same time, the crops were failing because of drought (ḥōreb; v.11), brought about by lack even of dew on the ground (v.10).

This disaster, which has affected field, vineyard, and orchard crops, thus wreaking havoc on human and animal alike, is no fluke of nature. God called for drought, and like an obedient servant drought has come. The heavens and earth, i.e., all nature, cooperate in this work of divine judgment (v.10).

NOTES

6 "They have drunk, but not enough to become intoxicated" is a literal rendering of the Hebrew: שָׁתוֹ וְאֵין־לְשָׁכְרָה (šātô wᵉʾên-lᵉšākᵉrâ). The NIV renders the sentence, "You drink, but never have your fill"; the NLT, "You drink but are still thirsty"; the NAB, "you have drunk, but have not been exhilarated." The cognate noun šēkar ("strong drink, beer"; thus *HALOT*, 972) favors the idea of inebriation (cf. Meyers and Meyers, 26).

9 The Hebrew הִנֵּה (hinnēh), translated here "but see," is read by the LXX, Syriac, and Targum as הָיָה (hāyâ), "it was"; thus, "you expected much, but it turned out to be little," dropping the particle. The meaning is unaffected, but the more difficult MT is to be preferred by reason of its likely originality.

C. The Response of God's People (1:12–15)

¹²Then Zerubbabel son of Shealtiel, Joshua son of Jehozadak, the high priest, and the whole remnant of the people obeyed the voice of the LORD their God and the message of the prophet Haggai, because the LORD their God had sent him. And the people feared the LORD.

¹³Then Haggai, the LORD's messenger, gave this message of the LORD to the people: "I am with you," declares the LORD. ¹⁴So the LORD stirred up the spirit of Zerubbabel son of Shealtiel, governor of Judah, and the spirit of Joshua son of Jehozadak, the high priest, and the spirit of the whole remnant of the people. They came and began to work on the house of the LORD Almighty, their God, ¹⁵on the twenty-fourth day of the sixth month in the second year of King Darius.

COMMENTARY

12 So powerful and persuasive are Haggai's words that Zerubbabel and Joshua, together with the rest (or remnant) of the people of Jerusalem, set about the task of temple building, an endeavor that had been dormant for about eighteen years (from the second year and second month [April/May] following Cyrus's decree in 538 BC [Ezr 3:8] to the second year and sixth month of the reign of Darius Hystaspes, i.e., 520 BC [Hag 1:15]). Within three weeks, it seems, the prophet's convicting message has fallen on fertile soil (1:1; cf. v.15) and now springs up in determined action. They recognize clearly that the voice of the prophet is no less than the voice of God himself (v.12). Having heard the word of the Lord, they "fear"—that is, they recognize his awesome sovereignty—a cause and effect attested elsewhere in sacred history (see esp. Dt 4:10; 5:29; 13:11; 17:13; 19:20; 20:3; 21:21; 31:12–13).

13 The close connection between the message of the prophet and the message of the Lord finds emphatic expression again in v.13, this time in the unusual construction *maPak yhwh bᵉmaPᵃkût yhwh* (lit., "the messenger of the LORD in the message

of the LORD"). Haggai's message, then, cannot be separated from its divine source and inspiration. When Haggai speaks, it is God who speaks, at least in these revelatory contexts. Thus Haggai says, "I am with you," words attributed to the Lord at the same time. Any reticence about the fearsome prospects of temple building should be allayed by this promise of God's association with it.

14 Evidence of this presence of the Lord is immediately apparent in the reaction of Zerubbabel, Joshua, and all the people, whose spirits are aroused to action on their hearing the pledge of divine participation. The verbal stem makes clear that the urge to take up the challenge does not originate with the people but with the Lord himself (v.14). But they are, at the same time, obedient to God's prompting and with enthusiasm put their hands to the task (v.14b).

15 The introduction (see "Special Problems") dealt with the question as to whether v.15 concludes the section 1:1–15 or introduces 1:15–2:9. In addition to the comments there, it should be pointed out that despite the fact that prophetic messages of this kind do indeed usually commence with a chronological notation (cf. Hag 1:1, 2:1, 10, 20; Zec 1:1, 7; 7:1), there is no compelling reason to insist this must always be the case. In the present instance, in fact, the weight of evidence supports the traditional view that the chronological data belong exactly where they are. First, v.15 provides the ending frame of a pericope that begins with virtually identical information, but in a chiastic order. This can be graphed as follows:

Verse 1	Verse 15
second year of Darius	twenty-fourth day of the month
sixth month	sixth month
first day	second year

The need for v.15 to conclude the pattern is obvious.

Second, the notation in 2:1 is incomplete in that it lacks reference to a year. That information is supplied by 1:15, thus making the year the pivotal point of a structure that binds 1:15 and 2:1 together and in that order:

1:15a day
   1:15b month
      1:15c year
   2:1a month
2:1b day

When these factors are taken together, the placement of the chronological note of 1:15 is not only reasonable but also necessary. By the modern calendar the initial message to build came on August 29, 520 BC, and by September 21 the work had commenced. The point is clear: When God's faithful messengers proclaim his word with power and conviction, inevitably the Lord will move the hearts of people to obedience.

NOTE

12 For the MT's אֱלֹהֵיהֶם, *ʾĕlōhêhem*, "their God," the LXX presupposes אֲלֵיהֶם, *ʾălêhem*, "to them," a reading supported also by the Syriac, Targum, and Vulgate. The frequency of the epithet "the LORD their God" in Haggai argues favorably for the MT's reading.

II. THE GLORY TO COME (2:1–9)

A. A Reminder of the Past (2:1–3)

²:¹On the twenty-first day of the seventh month, the word of the LORD came through the prophet Haggai: ²"Speak to Zerubbabel son of Shealtiel, governor of Judah, to Joshua son of Jehozadak, the high priest, and to the remnant of the people. Ask them, ³'Who of you is left who saw this house in its former glory? How does it look to you now? Does it not seem to you like nothing?'"

COMMENTARY

1–3 Less than a month after the work on the temple began again (1:14–15), Haggai receives another revelation from Yahweh, this time to encourage the community to continue the project despite its less-than-impressive beginnings. The date of this vision—the twenty-first day of Tishri—is significant, and the vision is communicated by Yahweh on that very day because of its significance. It marked the seventh day of the Feast of Sukkoth (or Tabernacles), exactly 440 years after Solomon had completed and dedicated the first temple (1Ki 6:38; 8:2). Moreover, the Feast of Sukkoth was also the time of covenantal renewal, when the people of Israel recommitted themselves to fulfill the terms of their special relationship with Yahweh (Dt 31:9–13; cf. Ne 7:73–8:1, 18). The disheartened people need to remember that the God who has called them into covenant can and will crown their devoted efforts with success.

Having sensed their frustration, the prophet asks the remnant community how they have remembered the former temple, as compared to what was promised by the foundations of the new one. Only the elderly among them could respond as eyewitnesses, of course, because the Solomonic structure had been razed to the ground sixty-six years earlier—long before most of Haggai's audience had been born. He knows already that they view it as though it were nothing (Heb. *kᵉᶜayin*), for sixteen years earlier, when the project first got underway, the old men had wept when they saw how disappointing the prospects were for recovering the glory of the Solomonic past (Ezr 3:12). At that time the pessimism of the elders apparently so affected the morale of the people as a whole that in this day of Haggai's vision virtually everyone is despondent and in need of a word of encouragement.

B. The Presence of the Lord (2:4–5)

⁴"'But now be strong, O Zerubbabel,' declares the Lᴏʀᴅ. 'Be strong, O Joshua son of Jehozadak, the high priest. Be strong, all you people of the land,' declares the Lᴏʀᴅ, 'and work. For I am with you,' declares the Lᴏʀᴅ Almighty. ⁵'This is what I covenanted with you when you came out of Egypt. And my Spirit remains among you. Do not fear.'"

COMMENTARY

4–5 With a strong adversative (*wᵉᶜattâ*) the prophet does not wait for a response to his questions but instead quickly introduces the solution to the people's profound sense of dismay, namely, the presence of Yahweh. He agrees with them that the temple that is underway suffers badly by comparison

with the other, but success and glory are not to be measured in terms of size and splendor.

Three times Haggai uses the verb *ḥazaq* (in the imperative; GK 2616)—once to Zerubbabel, once to Joshua, and once to all the people of the land. The basic meaning of the verb is to be strong, but in the context here the idea clearly is that of taking courage. The same verb occurs four times in Joshua 1 (Jos 1:6, 7, 9, 18) in a similar situation. Moses, the great liberator and leader, is dead, and Joshua, seeing himself woefully inadequate by comparison, needs to be encouraged by the Lord, who promises to be with him (Jos 1:5, 9).

Likewise, says Haggai, Yahweh will also be with his people. In fact, he will be with them as Yahweh of hosts, an epithet with strong associations of success and conquest (*NIDOTTE*, 3:733−35). His presence will assure them of victory over their pessimism and over any other obstacles that may stand in the way of their accomplishing the goal of rebuilding God's house.

The object of their fear is not the formidable task of building that confronts them, nor even the hostility of their enemies, who seek to frustrate their efforts; rather, it is the fear that God has abandoned them, their return from Babylonian exile notwithstanding. Thus they must know that he is present with them (v.4) and, more important, that he has not annulled his covenant with them. Just as the exodus had been followed by the Sinaitic covenant, so their second exodus—the return to the land—is attended by God's covenantal oath that he is their God and they are his people.

NOTE

5 The awkward Hebrew (lit., "the thing I covenanted with you") in the first line (lacking in the LXX) requires some such addition as: "This is what I covenanted with you" (NIV), "just as I promised" (NLT), or perhaps "In light of the word that I covenanted with you ... do not fear." The grammar is best satisfied by viewing "do not fear" as an apodosis preceded by the entire first part of the verse as a protasis. That is, in view of God's ancient promises and the present ministry of his Spirit among them, the Jews have nothing to fear.

C. Outlook for the Future (2:6−9)

⁶"This is what the LORD Almighty says: 'In a little while I will once more shake the heavens and the earth, the sea and the dry land. ⁷I will shake all nations, and the desired of all nations will come, and I will fill this house with glory,' says the LORD Almighty. ⁸'The silver is mine and the gold is mine,' declares the LORD Almighty. ⁹'The glory of this present house will be greater than the glory of the former house,' says the LORD Almighty. 'And in this place I will grant peace,' declares the LORD Almighty."

COMMENTARY

6−9 What Yahweh has done in the past he will do again—and in just a little while. The past that is implicit here is the past described in vv.4−5, that is, the events surrounding the exodus, the revelation at Sinai, the conquest, and the history of Israel up to the time of the first temple. The "little while" may suggest something imminent, perhaps to be associated with the temple then under construction, but the language and tone of the passage as a whole is clearly eschatological. The "shaking" (*rᶜš*), the universal dimension ("the heavens and the earth" and "all nations"), and "the glory of this present house" (*kᵉbōd habbayit hazzeh hāʾaḥᵃrôn*) all speak of a cataclysmic and radical age that will far transcend what Israel has experienced in the past.

Not to be overlooked is the heavy emphasis on God's sovereign initiative. *He* will shake the heavens and earth, *he* will shake the nations, *he* will fill the house with glory, *he* will bring peace. Such an emphasis is in line with the title ascribed to him four times in the passage—the "LORD of hosts" (NASB). As many scholars have noted, the atmosphere here is one of holy war. Such war—designed by Yahweh, led by him, and accompanied by terror and shaking on the part of the enemy—results in Yahweh's appropriation of the spoils, and brings ultimate peace.

Yahweh had prosecuted holy war against Egypt, especially in the exodus deliverance. Exodus 15, the poetic account of that miraculous intervention, employs many of the motifs picked up here by Haggai. The sea was under Yahweh's dominion (Ex 15:5, 8, 10), the earth was rent (15:12), and there was the promise of peace under his gracious reign in the ages to come (15:17–18).

The conquest under Joshua also resonates with holy war themes echoed in Haggai. Yahweh took the initiative by promising to be with his people (Jos 1:9, 17) and by leading the way in the form of the ark of the covenant (3:1–17; 6:1–14). The displays of his power brought terror on the nations (2:9–11; 5:1) and were manifest in his control of natural elements, such as displayed in the Hebrews' miraculous crossing of the Jordan (3:14–17; 4:6–7, 23–24) and the destruction of Jericho's impregnable fortifications by a mighty earthquake (6:20–21). With this done, the treasures of the city became the property of Yahweh, the spoils of war that were the fruit of conquest (6:24; 7:10–13). When Achan stole some of the goods devoted to Yahweh, Joshua rebuked him severely and demanded that he give glory to Yahweh (7:19). The whole enterprise of exodus and conquest was designed to do this very thing.

The prophets share this view of the future. Jeremiah knows of a day when the heavens and earth will be so disturbed as to resemble the primordial creation before it achieved order (Jer 4:23–26). In that day the nations will tremble with terror (Isa 64:2; Eze 38:20; Mic 7:16–17) and, in submission to Yahweh as King, will render to him their praise and homage (Zec 14:9, 16–21). This latter response is in view in Haggai's rather enigmatic statement that "the desired of all nations will come" (Hag 2:7), a phrase referring to the treasures to be brought to the eschatological temple (cf. Isa 60:4–9).

Despite this display of material splendor, true glory will not be found in it but in Yahweh's presence in the temple and among his people. After all, the silver and gold belong to him anyway (v.8), so they can hardly add anything to him or to his majesty. The glory that will fill the temple will far outshine anything that decorated Solomon's magnificent edifice, for it will consist of the unveiled radiance of God's visitation. The struggling postexilic remnant has no cause for regret or lament as they consider the paltry beginnings of their temple project. From this nucleus God will undertake a building program that will eclipse anything that has preceded it.

NOTE

7 The term for "desired" (*ḥemdat*) is singular, but the predicate is plural (*bāʾû*). The subject should be understood, then, either as a collective (with the MT) or revocalized (with the LXX) as a plural (*ḥᵃmudōt*).

III. THE PROMISED BLESSING (2:10–19)

A. Present Ceremonial Defilement (2:10–14)

¹⁰On the twenty-fourth day of the ninth month, in the second year of Darius, the word of the LORD came to the prophet Haggai: ¹¹"This is what the LORD Almighty says: 'Ask the priests what the law says: ¹²If a person carries consecrated meat in the fold of his garment, and that fold touches some bread or stew, some wine, oil or other food, does it become consecrated?'"

The priests answered, "No."

¹³Then Haggai said, "If a person defiled by contact with a dead body touches one of these things, does it become defiled?"

"Yes," the priests replied, "it becomes defiled."

¹⁴Then Haggai said, "'So it is with this people and this nation in my sight,' declares the LORD. 'Whatever they do and whatever they offer there is defiled.'"

COMMENTARY

10–14 The twenty-fourth day of the ninth month (Kislev)—December 18 according to the modern calendar—follows the date of the previous pericope by almost two months. The work of temple reconstruction is presumably well underway by now, but this is not the end of the issues with which the prophet must contend. While the temple structure and all of its physical and material accoutrements are essential to Jewish worship, it is after all only the arena in which these cultic activities take place. And these activities, it seems, are far from being conducted in a proper way or with a proper spirit. "Whatever they do and whatever they offer there is defiled" is the Lord's assessment of the people's religious activity (v.14).

To address this deplorable situation the Lord once more speaks through Haggai, again confronting the community with a series of questions (a dialogical method common in the postexilic literature;

cf. Mal 1:2, 6–9). The first question is whether it is possible for holiness to be communicated from one object to another by mere physical contact (v.12). The second is the converse: Is unholiness contracted by means of a person who, having touched a dead body, touches food or drink (v.13)?

Though these questions may have had practical relevance to some situation in the practice of the temple cultus, their deeper purpose is to address the spiritual condition of the people themselves. Can they become holy merely by undertaking religious exercise? Can their ungodliness be best explained by their having succumbed to the moral and spiritual pollution around them?

These questions are to be directed to the priests, because among their other responsibilities is their commission to be teachers of the law (Dt 17:8–11; cf. Mal 2:7). Their interpretation of relevant texts will provide ultimate authority as to their meaning and implementation. The first question inquires about meat that has been consecrated for sacrifice. By virtue of the holiness attached to this consecration, can it impart holiness to other food and drink that has not been set apart for sacrifice?

The answer is an unequivocal "No" (v.12). The priestly appeal is most likely to Leviticus 6:27[20], which teaches that a consecrated offering renders any food it touches consecrated also. However, the person carrying consecrated meat in a garment is not thereby consecrated, nor can he consecrate food by coming in contact with it. Moreover, the garment itself cannot communicate holiness, thus the negative reply. Presumably, if the holy meat touches other food directly, it will sanctify it (J. Milgrom, *Leviticus 1–16* [AB 3; New York: Doubleday, 1991], 449–50).

The answer to the second question is less complicated and ambiguous, for the law is clear that corpses are ritually impure, and anyone or anything that comes in contact with them is automatically defiled (Lev 7:19; 22:4–6; Nu 19:11–13, 22). The principle that derives from these laws is apparent: Holiness is not communicable, but defilement is.

Verse 14 reveals the intent of these hypothetical questions. By analogy or perhaps by a fortiori argument (the so-called *qal wa-ḥomer* of Jewish exegesis), the argument is that if in relatively inconsequential matters of the law uncleanness is contracted, how much more so in heavier, more serious issues? The Lord first discloses the condition of the people to be impure (Heb. *ṭāmēʾ*) so that everything they do and everything they offer to Yahweh is unclean (v.14). He then implies that it is because they themselves have been corrupted by improper association with uncleanness that whatever they attempt to do is tainted. Exactly what that association is cannot be known with certainty, but it may have to do with the corrupting influence of the people with whom the Jews had dealings upon their return from exile (see Ezr 6:6–15; cf. Hag 1:9).

B. Present Judgment and Discipline (2:15–19)

¹⁵"'Now give careful thought to this from this day on — consider how things were before one stone was laid on another in the Lord's temple. ¹⁶When anyone came to a heap of twenty measures, there were only ten. When anyone went to a wine vat to draw fifty measures, there were only twenty. ¹⁷I struck all the work of your hands with blight, mildew and hail, yet you did not turn to me,' declares the Lord. ¹⁸'From this day on, from this twenty-fourth day of the ninth month, give careful thought to the day when the foundation of the Lord's temple was laid. Give careful thought: ¹⁹Is there yet any seed left in the barn? Until now, the vine and the fig tree, the pomegranate and the olive tree have not borne fruit.

"'From this day on I will bless you.'"

COMMENTARY

15–19a Having forcefully pointed out to the people their moral and spiritual deficiencies, Haggai proceeds to show them the evidence of God's displeasure with their failings. This is primarily manifested in drought and disease, which has stunted their crops and brought them to a position of near starvation.

The question is how long this situation has prevailed. It was clearly in effect four months earlier when Haggai first appealed to the people to rebuild the temple (Hag 1:1). They have failed to do so since the day the foundations of the building were laid in 536, sixteen years earlier, and consequently the Lord sent drought and dearth as punishment (1:9–11).

But did these adverse agricultural calamities afflict them all that time? The answer lies largely with the meaning of the phrase "from this day on" (v.15). The Hebrew adverb *māᶜᵉlâ* (translated "on" in the NIV) is best rendered "onward" when speaking of time, but is it time yet to come, or time already past? Are they to think from this day forward about the meaning of their plight, or are they to reflect from the present day back to the beginning of these disasters? If the latter, how far back?

The answer lies in the parallelism between "consider from this day onward" (v.15a) and "before one stone was laid on another in the Lord's temple" (v.15b). "Onward" clearly refers here to a backward glance, one that extends to the day the foundations were first laid. Their obstinate disobedience—whatever form it may have taken—resulted in sixteen long years of divine displeasure. Greatly reduced harvests, storms and agricultural disease, and insufficient seed for plantings yet to come (vv.16–19) all testify to the utter failure of life lived apart from submission to the will of God.

19b There is hope nonetheless, a hope expressed in jarring contradiction to the note of pessimism that is sounded in vv.15–19a. "From this day on I will bless you" (v.19b). The two previous occurrences of *hayyôm hazzeh* ("this day"; vv.15, 18) included also the term *māᶜᵉlâ*, indicating a view to the past, "this day and onward [or 'backward']." The adverb is lacking here, and that absence plus the imperfect form of the verb "bless" puts beyond doubt that the situation from then on will be radically different.

The only explanation for this turn of events is a turning back to God in repentance and renewal, a set of conditions not explicitly asserted in the text at this point. The most obvious solution to this apparent silence regarding such reformation is the proposal that the message of the pericope bracketed by the identical chronological references (vv.10, 18) has had its intended (if unspoken) effect. The message has been heard, accepted, and acted on. Just as the appeal to rebuild was obeyed three months earlier, thus permitting the Spirit of Yahweh to empower them for the work (1:12–15), so now the exhortation of the prophet has landed on fertile soil, thus giving that same Spirit freedom to bless from this time forward.

IV. ZERUBBABEL THE CHOSEN ONE (2:20–23)

²⁰The word of the Lord came to Haggai a second time on the twenty-fourth day of the month: ²¹"Tell Zerubbabel governor of Judah that I will shake the heavens and the earth. ²²I will overturn royal thrones and shatter the power of the foreign kingdoms. I will

overthrow chariots and their drivers; horses and their riders will fall, each by the sword of his brother.

²³"'On that day,' declares the Lᴏʀᴅ Almighty, 'I will take you, my servant Zerubbabel son of Shealtiel,' declares the Lᴏʀᴅ, 'and I will make you like my signet ring, for I have chosen you,' declares the Lᴏʀᴅ Almighty."

COMMENTARY

20–23 The name "Zerubbabel" occurs seven times in Haggai (1:1, 12, 14; 2:2, 4, 21, 23), five times as the recipient or intended recipient of divine revelation (1:1, 2:2, 4, 21, 23). Only in this last section is he described as something other than the governor of Judah, namely, as Yahweh's servant (v.23). The implications of this, particularly in a context freighted with apocalyptic language, are most significant.

Following his rebuke of the nation for its moral and spiritual lapses and the consequent economic disasters that ensued, Haggai had disclosed the totally unexpected promise that from that day forward God would bless them (2:19). That blessing, it turns out, will have special fulfillment in an eschatological age in which Zerubbabel somehow will play a major role.

The connection between the promised blessing and Zerubbabel is clear from the chronological datum that the word of Yahweh came to him on the twenty-fourth day of Kislev, the same day on which the promise was made (v.20; cf. vv.10, 18). Moreover, the revelation was delivered to him alone and not to the population at large, a sign that he will be the conduit through which God's favor will be displayed. But in what sense will Zerubbabel be the divine agent? Despite his Davidic ancestry, are the times propitious for this governor of a tiny

state to bring to pass the cumulative hopes of all the prophets?

The scenes of cataclysmic upheaval and destruction that portray the collapse of all human kingdoms and the establishment of that of Yahweh are enough to put beyond doubt that Zerubbabel is a type or foreshadowing of a greater one to come, a ruler not just with Davidic lineage but with independent Davidic authority. He will be like Yahweh's signet ring, one chosen to rule on Yahweh's behalf (v.23). In terms identical to those of vv.6–9, Yahweh says he is about to shake (thus the participial form of $r^cš$) the heavens and the earth, a reversal of his work of creation when he brought the heavens and the earth into existence (Ge 1:1; cf. Jer 4:24). Beyond this act, he will overthrow royal thrones, along with the military might of the nations that rely on them (v.22).

The scene here is somewhat different from that in v.7, in which it is said only that the nations will be shaken ($r^cš$) but not destroyed. The sequence is that the nations will first acknowledge the sovereignty of Yahweh and pay tribute to him but then will suffer total defeat by internecine war. The messianic Psalms 2 and 110 are particularly pertinent here in this context of a coming Davidic ruler. Psalm 2, speaking of Yahweh's adopted son, declares that he will be the heir to the nations of the earth (Ps 2:8), the claim to which can be actualized only in the destruction of those nations (2:9). Psalm 110 describes the nations as the Messiah's footstool (Ps 110:1) over which he will reign (110:2), having brought them to submission by God's mighty power (110:5-6).

The NT is not silent on the matter. In Revelation, John describes the coming of Jesus in the eschaton as a warrior who, with the heavenly hosts, will defeat the nations of the earth and rule over them with an iron scepter. His name will be "King of kings and Lord of lords" (Rev 19:11-16). The connection between Zerubbabel and the NT Messiah is inescapable, at least in terms of Christian hermeneutical tradition.

The characteristically eschatological phrase "on that day" (v.23) further sets the scene for the identification of Zerubbabel. He is a figure of the last days, one to be called "servant" and "signet." The former epithet immediately calls to mind those texts that feature a coming one who will carry out the will of God by proclaiming the message of reconciliation to the nations both by his words and his atoning death. Isaiah 41:8 speaks of him as "Israel"—one, like Zerubbabel, who is chosen (Isa 41:9). This same combination of servant and chosen occurs in Isaiah 42:1 to describe the servant who will establish justice in the earth (42:4).

The reference to the future Zerubbabel as a signet ring is especially instructive in the light of its only other occurrence in this sense, in Jeremiah 22:24. In that passage Yahweh, addressing Jehoiachin by the name "Coniah," says that even if he were the signet ring on Yahweh's right hand, Yahweh would pull him off and deliver him over the Babylonians (22:25). Jehoiachin was, of course, Zerubbabel's grandfather (see comment on 1:1), so the connection here is especially noteworthy. But Jeremiah went on to say of Jehoiachin that no descendant of his would ever sit on David's throne—thus, it seems, disqualifying Zerubbabel from rulership (Jer 22:30). And since Jesus was also descended from Jehoiachin (Mt 1:11), is he also not precluded form that royal privilege?

The answer is twofold: (1) Zerubbabel is never explicitly told that he will be king, and (2) the royal lineage of Jesus came to be traced not through Joseph, the descendant of David through Solomon and thus Jehoiachin, but through David's son Nathan (Lk 3:23-38). Historical Zerubbabel thus gives way to eschatological Zerubbabel, the chosen signet ring of Yahweh. It is he who will fulfill the regal purposes of God in the ages to come.

ZECHARIAH

KENNETH L. BARKER

Introduction

1. HISTORICAL BACKGROUND

Zechariah's prophetic ministry takes place in the time of Israel's restoration from Babylonian captivity, that is, in the postexilic period. Approximately seventy-five years have elapsed since Habakkuk and Jeremiah predicted the invasion of Judah by the Neo-Babylonian army of King Nebuchadnezzar. When their "hard service" (Isa 40:2) in Babylonia was completed, God influenced Cyrus, the Persian king, to allow the Jews to return to their homeland and rebuild their temple (Isa 44:28).

The historical circumstances and conditions under which Zechariah ministered are, in general, those of Haggai's time, since their labors were contemporary (cf. 1:1 with Hag 1:1). In 520 BC Haggai preached four sermons in four months. Zechariah began his ministry two months after Haggai began his. Thus the immediate historical background for Zechariah's ministry began with Cyrus's capture of Babylon and included the completion of the restoration, or second, temple.

Babylon fell to Cyrus in 539 BC.[1] Cyrus then signed the edict that permitted Israel to return and rebuild her temple (2Ch 36:21–23; Ezr 1:1–4; 6:3, 5). According to Ezra 2, a large group (about fifty thousand) did return in 538–537 BC under the civil leadership of Zerubbabel (the governor) and the religious leadership of Joshua (the high priest). This group completed the foundation of the temple early in 536 BC (Ezr 3:8–13). But several obstacles arose that slowed and finally halted the construction (4:1–5, 24).

---

1. See *ANET*, 306, for the account of Babylon's fall according to the so-called Nabonidus Chronicle; also 314–16 for other historical accounts, including one by Cyrus.

During the years of inactivity, Cyrus died in battle (530 BC), and his son Cambyses II, who was coregent with Cyrus for one year, reigned (530–522 BC).

Political rebellion ultimately brought Darius Hystaspes to the throne in 522 BC. (The Behistun Inscription pictures him putting down an insurrection.) His wise administration and religious toleration created a favorable climate for the Jews to complete the rebuilding of their temple. He confirmed the decree of Cyrus and authorized resumption of the work (Ezr 6:6–12; Hag 1:1–2), which began in 520 BC. The reconstruction of the temple was completed in 516 BC. For additional events in the history of the period, see the historical background of Ezra, Daniel, and Haggai.

2. UNITY

One of the first to question the unity and authenticity of the book of Zechariah was Joseph Mede in 1653. Because Matthew (Mt 27:9) apparently attributed Zechariah 11:12–13 to Jeremiah, Mede felt that Zechariah 9–11 should be designated to the preexilic period and assigned to Jeremiah. (For possible solutions to this problem, see comments at Zechariah 11:12–13.) In 1700, Richard Kidder maintained that chs. 12–14 were also written by Jeremiah. In 1785, William Newcome advanced the view that chs. 9–11 were written before the fall of Samaria and chs. 12–14 at a later date but before Nebuchadnezzar's destruction of Jerusalem. This preexilic hypothesis was followed in general by Hitzig, Knobel, Ewald, Bleek, von Orelli, and Schultz.

In 1792, however, Corrodi reasoned that chs. 9–14 (the co-called "Deutero-Zechariah") were composed in about the third century BC, long after the time of Zechariah. Corrodi was followed, with modifications, by Paulus, Eichhorn, Stade, Cornill, Wellhausen, Eckardt, Cheyne, Kirkpatrick, Driver, Kraeling, Heller, and others.

The arguments against Zechariah's authorship of chs. 9–14 include (1) differences in style and other compositional features and (2) historical and chronological references that allegedly require a later date. To such objections there are satisfactory answers. For example, the differences in style may be adequately accounted for by the change in subject matter; the variation in literary form in the two major divisions of the book (see below); and the possibility that chs. 9–14, which are not dated, were written at a considerably later period in Zechariah's life, perhaps just before his death. Besides, as George L. Robinson has observed, there is "no mode of reasoning so treacherous as that from language and style."[2]

---

2. *ISBE*, 5:3139 (1939 ed.). For a comprehensive list of vocabulary differences between the two parts of the book, see the commentary by Hinckley G. Mitchell, "Haggai and Zechariah," in *A Critical and Exegetical Commentary on Haggai, Zechariah, Malachi and Jonah* (ICC; Edinburgh: T. & T. Clark, 1912), 236. One could just as easily draw up a list of the vocabulary that both parts share, thus offsetting the argument based on differences. Nothing determinative or conclusive is gained by such exercises; however, to demonstrate that my counterclaim is valid, it may be useful to present the following partial but suggestive list of words and expressions common to both major parts of the book: (1) "that no one could come or go" (7:14) and "*against marauding forces*" (9:8, emphasis mine), the Hebrew idiom being the same in both verses (and meaning, lit., "from crossing and returning"), and the phrase occurring nowhere else in the MT; (2) "declares the LORD" (appearing thirteen times in Part 1 of the book, and also in 10:12; 11:6; 12:1, 4; 13:2, 7–8); (3) "the LORD Almighty" (1:6, 12; 2:9; 9:15; 10:3; 12:5); and (4) "will be" (2:4), "were at rest" and "were settled" (7:7), "will remain intact" (12:6), and "remain" (14:10), the Hebrew verb (lit., "be inhabited, dwell") being the same in each instance. One

An example of a historical and chronological reference that purportedly calls for a post-Zecharian date is the mention in 9:13 of Greece rather than Persia as the dominant power. But besides the fact that Greece was a considerable power even in Zechariah's time, to this objection it may be answered that 9:13 is prophecy (probably of the conflict between the Maccabees and the Seleucids), not a description of the current situation. The verse constitutes a problem only for those who cannot accept prediction as a legitimate prophetic function. After observing that where the chronological note is important the dates are given (Zec 1:1, 7; 7:1), but that the headings in 9:1 and 12:1 contain no date, Baldwin asks, "May it not be that the author intends us to see that in what follows [chs. 9–14] he is no longer tied to historical time but is rather expressing theological truths related to God's future purpose?" She goes on to write:

> Moreover there is progression as the book moves from the establishment of the postexilic community, with its rebuilt temple and recommissioned leader and its understanding of the role of God's people among the nations (chapters 1–8), to the more eschatological perspective of chapters 9–14. Here the prophet rings the changes on the themes of jubilation, rebuke, mourning for a suffering shepherd and cataclysmic judgment, but according to the recognizable pattern which occurs in its simplest form in part one. The final note, the universal kingship of the Lord of Hosts (14:16–21), picks up the same theme from 6:15, 8:22 and 14:9, bringing it to a climax by laying stress on the removal of every obstacle to wholehearted worship of the Lord as King over all. Thus the book is a unity that progresses from historic time to end time, from the local to the universal.[3]

It is not unreasonable, then, to conclude that the book of Zechariah, from beginning to end, is the work of the author whose name it bears.[4] Further substantiation of this position is given in the section on structure and in works by Baldwin, Bullock, Dillard and Longman, and Perowne.[5] For some cautions in using statistical analysis alone to determine the book's unity, see Portnoy and Petersen.[6]

---

could also mention certain similarities of ideas: (1) joy because of the coming of the King (2:10; 9:9); (2) the necessity for repentance and cleansing (1:4; 3:4, 9; 9:7; 12:10; 13:1, 9); (3) the return and restoration of the theocratic nation (2:6; 8:7–8; 9:12; 10:6–10); (4) the exaltation of Jerusalem (1:16–17; 2:11–12; 12:6; 14:10–11); (5) the subjection and/or conversion of Israel's enemies (1:21; 2:11; 12:3–9; 14:12–19); and (6) the picture of the Messiah as the true and ideal King of Israel (6:12–13; 9:9). For additional themes common to parts 1 and 2, see Brevard S. Childs, *Introduction to the Old Testament as Scripture* (Philadelphia: Fortress, 1979), 482–83. Finally, it "is inevitable, and even desirable, that in ordering and developing complex ideas a writer will draw upon a number of rhetorical modes and devices" (C. Shrodes, C. Josephson, and J. R. Wilson, *Reading for Rhetoric* [New York: Macmillan, 1967], vi).

3. Joyce G. Baldwin, "Is There Pseudonymity in the Old Testament?" *Themelios* 4 (September 1978): 9.

4. For additional data supporting the literary unity of Zechariah, see James A. Hartle, "The Literary Unity of Zechariah," *JETS* 35 (June 1992): 145–57.

5. Joyce G. Baldwin, *Haggai, Zechariah, Malachi: An Introduction and Commentary* (TOTC; Downers Grove, Ill.: InterVarsity Press, 1972); Hassell Bullock, *An Introduction to the Old Testament Prophetic Books* (Chicago: Moody Press, 1986); Raymond B. Dillard and Tremper Longman III, *An Introduction to the Old Testament* (Grand Rapids: Zondervan, 1994); T. T. Perowne, *The Books of Haggai and Zechariah* (Cambridge: Cambridge Univ. Press, 1886).

6. Stephen L. Portnoy and David L. Petersen, "Biblical Texts and Statistical Analysis: Zechariah and Beyond," *JBL* 103 (March 1984): 11–21.

3. AUTHOR

An attempt has already been made to demonstrate the reasonableness of attributing all fourteen chapters to Zechariah (cf. 1:1, 7; 7:1). More may be added at this point about the prophet personally. Like Jeremiah and Ezekiel, Zechariah is not only a prophet but also a member of a priestly family. He was born in Babylonia and was among those who returned to Judah in 538–537 BC under the leadership of Zerubbabel and Joshua (cf. Iddo, Ne 12:4).

At a later time, when Joiakim was high priest, Zechariah apparently succeeded his grandfather Iddo (Zec 1:1, 7) as head of that priestly family (Ne 12:10–16). Since it was the grandson (Zechariah) who in this instance succeeded the grandfather (Iddo), it has been conjectured that the father (Berekiah, Zec 1:1, 7) died at an early age, before he could succeed to family headship.

Though a contemporary of Haggai, Zechariah continued his ministry long after him (cf. Zec 1:1 and 7:1 with Hag 1:1; see also Ne 12:10–16). Considering his youth in the early period of his ministry (Zec 2:4, "young man"), it is possible that Zechariah continued ministering into the reign of Artaxerxes I (465–424 BC).

4. DATE

The dates of Zechariah's recorded messages may be correlated with those of Haggai and with other historical events as follows:

(1) Haggai's first message (Hag 1:1–11; Ezr 5:1): August 29, 520 BC

(2) Resumption of the building of the temple (Hag 1:12–15; Ezr 5:2): September 21, 520 (The rebuilding seems to have been hindered from 536 to about 530 [Ezr 4:1–5], and the work ceased altogether from about 530 to 520 [Ezr 4:24].)

(3) Haggai's second message (Hag 2:1–9): October 17, 520

(4) Beginning of Zechariah's preaching (Zec 1:1–6): October/November 520

(5) Haggai's third message (Hag 2:10–19): December 18, 520

(6) Haggai's fourth message (Hag 2:20–23): December 18, 520

(7) Tattenai's letter to Darius concerning the rebuilding of the temple (Ezr 5:3–6:14): 519–518 (There must have been a lapse of time between the resumption of the building and Tattenai's appearance.)

(8) Zechariah's eight night visions (Zec 1:7–6:8): February 15, 519

(9) Joshua's crowning (Zec 6:9–15): February 16(?), 519

(10) Urging of repentance, promise of blessings (Zec 7–8): December 7, 518

(11) Dedication of the temple (Ezr 6:15–18): March 12, 516

(12) Zechariah's final prophecy (Zec 9–14): after 480(?)[7]

---

7. On the reason for the question mark, see the discussion on unity (above). For the system of dating, see Baldwin, *Haggai, Zechariah, Malachi*, 29; also Richard A. Parker and Waldo H. Dubberstein, *Babylonian Chronology 626 B.C.–A.D. 75* (Providence, R.I.: Brown Univ. Press, 1956), 30.

5. PLACE OF COMPOSITION

At the time of his prophesying and writing, Zechariah is clearly back in Judah; he ministers to the returned exiles (Zec 4:8–10; 6:10, 14; 7:2–3, 9; Ne 12:1, 12, 16).

6. OCCASION AND PURPOSE

The occasion is the same as that of the book of Haggai. Approximately fifty thousand former exiles arrived in Jerusalem and the nearby towns in 538–537 BC with high hopes of resettling the land and rebuilding the temple (Ezr 2). Their original zeal was evident; immediately they set up the altar of burnt offering (Ezr 3:1–6). They resumed worship and restored the sacrificial ritual suspended during the seventy years of exile in Babylonia. The people then laid the foundation of the temple in the second month of the second year (April/May 536 BC) of their return (Ezr 3:8–13). But their fervor and activity soon met with opposition in various forms (Ezr 4:1–5; Hag 1:6–11), so the reconstruction of the temple ground to a halt and did not resume until 520 BC (Ezr 4:24).

The chief purpose of Zechariah and Haggai is to rebuke, motivate, and encourage the people to complete the rebuilding of the temple (Zec 4:9–10; cf. Hag 1–2), though these prophets are clearly interested in spiritual renewal as well. Also, the purpose of the eight night visions is explained in Zechariah 1:3, 5–6, where the Lord asks Israel to return to him; then he will return to them, and his word will continue to be fulfilled.

7. THEOLOGICAL VALUES

George L. Robinson calls Zechariah "the most Messianic, the most truly apocalyptic and eschatological, of all the writings of the OT."[8] As for the messianic aspect, Zechariah "prophesies" Christ's first coming in lowliness (6:12), his humanity (6:12), his rejection and betrayal for thirty pieces of silver (11:12–13), his being struck by the sword of the Lord (13:7), his deity (3:4; 13:7), his priesthood (6:13), his kingship (6:13; 9:9; 14:9, 16), his second coming in glory (14:4), his building of the Lord's temple (6:12–13), his reign (9:10; 14), and his establishment of enduring peace and prosperity (3:10; 9:9–10). These messianic passages give added significance to Jesus' words in Luke 24:25–27, 44. Zechariah 9:9; 11:13; 12:10; 13:7 are quoted in the NT and applied to the Messiah or the gospel story (Mt 21:5; 26:31; 27:9–10; Mk 14:27; Jn 12:15; 19:37; Rev 1:7). Dillard and Longman conclude:

> Christian readers of this prophet cannot but notice that the coming age of full redemption is inaugurated by a messianic king who makes a humble appearance, bringing righteousness and salvation to Jerusalem while riding on a donkey (9:9; Matt. 21:5). He is the shepherd king, but a smitten shepherd (13:7; Matt. 26:31), pierced and betrayed (11:12–13; 12:10; Matt. 26:15; 27:9–10; John 19:34, 37). But it is this King who will subdue the nations (12:8–9) and establish his kingdom among men (14:3–9).[9]

Since I agree with many scholars that messianic hopes and expectations accelerated during the exilic and postexilic periods, I make no apology for the rather strong messianic emphasis of this commentary. But, of course, passages can be messianic in different ways (see comments at 2:10).

---

8. *ISBE*, 5:3139 (1939 ed.).

9. Dillard and Longman, *Introduction to the Old*, 436.

As for the apocalyptic and eschatological aspect, Zechariah predicts the final siege of Jerusalem (12:1–3; 14:1–2), the initial victory of Israel's enemies (14:2), the Lord's defense of Jerusalem (14:3–4), the judgment on the nations (12:9; 14:3), the topographical changes in Israel (14:4–5), the celebration of the Festival of Tabernacles in the messianic kingdom age (14:16–19), and the ultimate holiness of Jerusalem and her people (14:20–21). Bullock declares, "What Ezekiel was to the late pre-exilic and exilic eras, Zechariah was to the postexilic age. Not only did he outline the program of restoration, the heart of which was the Temple and priesthood, but he, like Ezekiel, filled in much detail about the eschatological age that lay ahead."[10]

The prophet's name itself has theological significance. It means "the Lord [Yahweh] remembers." "The Lord," the personal, covenantal name of God, is a perpetual testimony to his faithfulness to his promises. He "remembers" his covenantal promises and acts to fulfill them. In Zechariah, God's promised deliverance from Babylonian captivity—including a restored theocratic community and a functioning temple, the earthly seat of divine sovereignty—leads into even grander pictures of the salvation and restoration to come through the Messiah (see comments at 3:8–9; 4:3, 14; 6:9–15; 9:9–10; 10:2, 4; 11:4–14; 12:10–13:1; 13:7; 14:4–9).

Finally, the book as a whole teaches the sovereignty of God in history over people and nations—past, present, and future (see 1:10–11; 2:13; 4:10, 14; 6:5, 7; 8:20–23; 9:10, 13–14; 10:11; 12:1–5; 14:9, 16–19). See also the next two sections for further theological teaching of the book.

8. LITERARY FORMS AND HERMENEUTICS

The book of Zechariah is primarily a mixture of exhortation (call to repentance, 1:2–6), prophetic visions (1:7–6:8), a prophetic oracle of instruction or exhortation involving a symbolic coronation scene (6:9–15), hortatory messages (mainly of rebuke and hope) prompted by a question about fasting (chs. 7–8), and judgment and salvation oracles (chs. 9–14). The prophetic visions (or dream visions) of 1:7–6:8 are apocalyptic ("revelatory") literature, which may be defined as "symbolic visionary prophetic literature, composed during oppressive conditions, consisting of visions whose events are recorded exactly as they were seen by the author and explained through a divine interpreter, and whose theological content is primarily eschatological."[11] Bullock notes that "George Eldon Ladd's term 'prophetic-apocalyptic' is an appropriate one for Zechariah."[12]

Apocalyptic literature is basically meant to encourage God's people. When the apocalyptic section of Zechariah is added to the salvation oracles in chs. 9–14, it becomes clear that the dominant emphasis of the book is encouragement to God's people in light of the glorious future.

A special problem created by the apocalyptic visions (1:7–6:8) and by the judgment and deliverance oracles (chs. 9–14) is how they are to be handled hermeneutically. As will become clear in the exposition,

---

10. Bullock, *Introduction to the Old Testament Prophetic Books*, 310.
11. Ralph Holland Alexander, "Hermeneutics of Old Testament Apocalyptic Literature" (Th.D. diss., Dallas Theological Seminary, 1968), 45.
12. Bullock, *Introduction to the Old Testament Prophetic Books*, 312; cf. also John N. Oswalt, "Recent Studies in Old Testament Eschatology and Apocalyptic," *JETS* 24 (1981): 289–301.

my own approach is essentially that of Alexander.[13] A rather accurate and complete descriptive label of the approach would be the grammatical-literary-historical-theological method. Among other implications, this label basically means that even in prophetic literature one should interpret literally unless the context of the book itself or of the Bible elsewhere clearly suggests doing otherwise. Obviously, since certain literary genres — such as apocalyptic literature and poetry in general — abound in types, symbols, and other figures of speech, much in these types of literature must be interpreted typologically, symbolically, and figuratively. Fortunately, in most instances the text itself or the biblical context (the analogy of faith) furnishes the interpretation of such language.

Hermeneutically, I am also in basic agreement with Eugene Merrill who, in discussing the quotation of 9:9 in Matthew 21:5, well says:

> The Christian exegete must do his work against the backdrop of the entire revelation of God, OT and NT alike. All judgments about the OT text must be suspended until the fullness of the biblical witness is brought to bear. Then and only then can one be said to be doing biblical exegesis in the proper sense of the term, for exegetical method must embrace a hermeneutic of the whole and must recognize the indispensable contribution of a synthetic, comprehensive biblical theology. The passage in question (and any other in fact) must seek its fullest meaning in subsequent revelation, particularly when that revelation takes pains (as in this case) to cite an antecedent passage and offer its own interpretation.
>
> This does not relieve the exegete of the task of viewing the passage in its own historical, cultural, and literary context, however.[14]

Such an approach is sometimes referred to as "canonical exegesis," which I endorse.[15]

9. STRUCTURE AND THEMES

Structure

While Zechariah may be divided into two parts (chs. 1–8 and chs. 9–14), it likewise falls rather naturally into five major divisions:

(1) 1:1–6, introduction and call to repentance
(2) 1:7–6:8, eight night visions
(3) 6:9–15, the symbolic crowning of Joshua the high priest
(4) chs. 7–8, the question about fasting
(5) chs. 9–14, two prophetic oracles (9–11 and 12–14).

---

13. See Alexander, "Hermeneutics of Old Testament Apocalyptic Literature"; see also A. Berkeley Mickelsen, *Interpreting the Bible* (Grand Rapids: Eerdmans, 1963), 265–305; Bernard Ramm, *Protestant Biblical Interpretation* (Boston: Wilde, 1956), 220–53; the more theological discussion in S. Lewis Johnson, *The Old Testament in the New* (Grand Rapids: Zondervan, 1980), 55–57, 69–71, 78–79, 93–94; and Kenneth L. Barker, "Micah," in *Micah, Nahum, Habakkuk, Zephaniah* (NAC 20; Nashville: Broadman & Holman, 1999), 41.

14. Eugene H. Merrill, *An Exegetical Commentary: Haggai, Zechariah, Malachi* (Chicago: Moody Press, 1994), 251.

15. For more on this, see Barker, "Micah," 41.

The chiastic structure of Zechariah's eight visions in one night has been recognized since at least 1898.[16] One possible presentation of this structure (different from Bullinger's) may be seen in the *NIV Study Bible*:[17]

a The Lord controls the events of history (1:7–17)
   b Nations that devastated Israel will in turn be devastated (1:18–21)
   b Israel will be fully restored (ch. 2)
      c Israel will be restored as a priestly nation (ch. 3)
      c' Israel will be restored under royal and priestly leadership (ch. 4)
   b' Lawbreakers will be purged from Israel (5:1–4)
   b' The whole sinful system will be removed from the land (5:5–11)
a' The Lord controls the events of history (6:1–8).

Other versions of this structure may be found in Bullock,[18] Hill and Walton,[19] and Webb.[20]

For an excellent visual representation of the unified, chiastic plan of chs. 9–14 based on Lamarche, see Baldwin,[21] though Lamarche's chiastic structure of chs. 9–14 is not quite as clear or convincing (at least to me) as that delineated above for 1:7–6:8. Baldwin then goes on to delineate a similar chiastic arrangement in chs. 1–8, thus arguing on structural grounds for the unity of the entire book. Elsewhere she concludes, "So closely knit is the fabric of the book that one mind must be responsible for its construction, and the simplest explanation is that the prophet Zechariah himself is the author of the total work that bears his name."[22]

Themes

The central theme of Zechariah is encouragement—primarily encouragement to complete the rebuilding of the temple. In fact, Laetsch calls Zechariah "the prophet of hope and encouragement in troublous times."[23] Various means are used to accomplish this end, and these means function as subthemes. For example, great stress is laid on the coming of the Messiah and his overthrow of all anti-kingdom forces

---

16. E. W. Bullinger, *Figures of Speech Used in the Bible* (Grand Rapids: Baker, repr., 1968), 376.
17. See Kenneth Barker, "Introduction to Zechariah: Literary Forms and Themes," *NIV Study Bible: Fully Revised*, ed. Kenneth Barker (Grand Rapids: Zondervan, 2002), 1431.
18. Bullock, *Introduction to the Old Testament Prophetic Books*, 313–14.
19. Andrew E. Hill and John H. Walton, *A Survey of the Old Testament* (Grand Rapids: Zondervan, 2000), 538.
20. Barry G. Webb, *The Message of Zechariah* (BST; Downers Grove, Ill.: InterVarsity Press, 2003), 106. For a somewhat different approach to the book's structure, see Meredith G. Kline, "The Structure of the Book of Zechariah," *JETS* 34 (June 1991): 179–93; David J. Clark and Howard A. Hatton, *A Handbook on Haggai, Zechariah, and Malachi* (New York: United Bible Societies, 2002), 66–67.
21. Baldwin, *Haggai, Zechariah, Malachi*, 78–79.
22. Baldwin, "Is There Pseudonymity in the Old Testament?" 9–10.
23. Theodore Laetsch, *The Minor Prophets* (St. Louis, Mo.: Concordia, 1956), 403.

so that the theocracy can be finally and fully established on earth. The consideration of the then-current local scene thus becomes the basis for contemplating the eschatological, universal picture.

10. CANONICITY AND TEXT

Canonicity

The second division of the Hebrew canon (the Prophets) closes with the Book of the Twelve (i.e., the Minor Prophets), and Zechariah is placed next-to-last in the list. Neither Jew nor Christian has ever seriously challenged its right to be in the canon. Its value as Scripture is demonstrated by the frequency with which the NT quotes and alludes to the book.

Text

Text-critical problems in Zechariah are comparatively few. They are discussed in the "Notes" sections of this commentary.

11. BIBLIOGRAPHY

Baldwin, Joyce G. *Haggai, Zechariah, Malachi: An Introduction and Commentary*. Tyndale Old Testament Commentaries. Downers Grove, Ill.: InterVarsity Press, 1972.

Barker, Kenneth L. "False Dichotomies between the Testaments." *Journal of the Evangelical Theological Society* 25 (1982): 3–16.

———. "Micah." Pages 1–136 in *Micah, Nahum, Habakkuk, Zephaniah*. By Kenneth L. Barker and Waylon Bailey. Vol. 20 of New American Commentary. Nashville: Broadman & Holman, 1999.

———, ed. *The NIV Study Bible (Fully Revised)*. Grand Rapids: Zondervan, 2002.

———. "The Scope and Center of Old and New Testament Theology and Hope." Pages 293–328 in *Dispensationalism, Israel and the Church*. Edited by Craig A. Blaising and Darrell L. Bock. Grand Rapids: Zondervan, 1992.

———. "The Value of Ugaritic for Old Testament Studies." *Bibliotheca Sacra* 133 (1976): 119–29.

Baron, David. *The Visions and Prophecies of Zechariah*. Grand Rapids: Kregel, repr. 1972.

Boice, James Montgomery. *The Minor Prophets*. Grand Rapids: Kregel, repr. 1996.

Bullinger, E. W. *Figures of Speech Used in the Bible*. Grand Rapids: Baker, repr. 1968.

Cashdan, Eli. "Zechariah." Pages 266–332 in *The Twelve Prophets*. Edited by A. Cohen. London: Soncino, 1948.

Cathcart, Kevin J., and Robert P. Gordon. *The Targum of the Minor Prophets*. Wilmington, Del.: Michael Glazier, 1989.

Chambers, T. W. "Zechariah." In volume 14 of *Commentary on the Holy Scriptures*, by J. P. Lange, translated by Philip Schaff. New York: Scribner & Co., 1867–1884.

Clark, David J., and Howard A. Hatton. *A Handbook on Haggai, Zechariah, and Malachi*. New York: United Bible Societies, 2002.

Davidson, A. B. *Hebrew Syntax*. 3rd ed. Edinburgh: T. & T. Clark, 1901.

De Vaux, Roland. *Ancient Israel: Its Life and Institutions*. Translated by John McHugh. London: Darton, Longman & Todd, 1961.

Eichrodt, Walther. *Theology of the Old Testament*. Translated by J. A. Baker. 2 vols. Philadelphia: Westminster, 1961, 1967.

Ellis, David J. "Zechariah." Pages 1025–50 in *The New Layman's Bible Commentary*. Edited by G. C. D. Howley et al. Grand Rapids: Zondervan, 1979.

Feinberg, Charles L. *God Remembers: A Study of the Book of Zechariah*. New York: American Board of Missions to the Jews, 1965.

Fohrer, G. "Twofold Aspects of Hebrew Words." Pages 95–103 in *Words and Meanings*. Edited by P. R. Ackroyd and B. Lindars. Cambridge: Cambridge University Press, 1968.

Gundry, Robert H. *The Use of the Old Testament in St. Matthew's Gospel.* Leiden: Brill, 1967.

Holladay, W. L. *A Concise Hebrew and Aramaic Lexicon of the Old Testament.* Grand Rapids: Eerdmans, 1971.

The Illustrated Family Encyclopedia of the Living Bible. 14 vols. Chicago: San Francisco Publications, 1967.

Johnson, S. Lewis. "The Triumphal Entry of Christ." *Bibliotheca Sacra* 124 (1967): 218–29.

Klein, George L. *Zechariah.* New American Commentary 21B. Nashville: Broadman & Holman, 2008. (Unfortunately, this excellent work appeared too late for use in this revised commentary.)

Laetsch, Theodore. *The Minor Prophets.* St. Louis: Concordia, 1956.

Leupold, H. C. *Exposition of Zechariah.* Grand Rapids: Baker, 1965.

McComiskey, Thomas E. "Zechariah." Vol. 3 of *The Minor Prophets.* Edited by T. E. McComiskey. Grand Rapids: Baker, 1998.

Merrill, Eugene H. *An Exegetical Commentary: Haggai, Zechariah, Malachi.* Chicago: Moody Press, 1994.

Meyers, Carol L., and Eric M. Meyers. *Haggai, Zechariah 1–8.* Anchor Bible. New York: Doubleday, 1987.

———. *Zechariah 9–14.* Anchor Bible. New York: Doubleday, 1993.

Perowne, T. T. *The Books of Haggai and Zechariah.* Cambridge: Cambridge University Press, 1886.

Petersen, David L. *Haggai and Zechariah 1–8.* Old Testament Library. Philadelphia: Westminster, 1984.

———. *Zechariah 9–14 and Malachi.* Old Testament Library. Louisville: Westminster John Knox, 1995.

Pusey, E. B. *The Minor Prophets.* 2 vols. Grand Rapids: Baker, repr. 1950.

Snaith, Norman H. *The Distinctive Ideas of the Old Testament.* New York: Schocken, 1964.

Unger, Merrill F. *Zechariah.* Grand Rapids: Zondervan, 1962.

Webb, Barry G. *The Message of Zechariah.* The Bible Speaks Today. Downers Grove, Ill.: InterVarsity Press, 2003.

12. OUTLINE

Part I (chs. 1−8)

I. Introduction to the Entire Book (1:1−6)
   A. The Date and the Author's Name (1:1)
   B. A Call to Repentance (1:2−6)

II. A Series of Eight Night Visions (1:7−6:8)
   A. The First Vision: The Horseman among the Myrtle Trees (1:7−17)
   B. The Second Vision: The Four Horns and the Four Craftsmen (1:18−21 [2:1−4])
   C. The Third Vision: The Surveyor (2:1−13 [2:5−17])
   D. The Fourth Vision: The Cleansing and Restoration of Israel (3:1−10)
   E. The Fifth Vision: The Gold Lampstand and the Two Olive Trees (4:1−14)
   F. The Sixth Vision: The Flying Scroll (5:1−4)
   G. The Seventh Vision: The Woman in a Basket (5:5−11)
   H. The Eighth Vision: The Four Chariots (6:1−8)

III. The Symbolic Crowning of Joshua the High Priest (6:9−15)

IV. The Problem of Fasting and the Promise of the Future (7:1−8:23)
   A. The Question by the Delegation from Bethel (7:1−3)
   B. The Rebuke by the Lord (7:4−7)
   C. The Command to Repent (7:8−14)
   D. The Restoration of Israel to God's Favor (8:1−17)
   E. Kingdom Joy and Jewish Favor (8:18−23)

Part II (chs. 9−14)

V. Two Prophetic Oracles: The Great Messianic Future and the Full Realization of the Theocracy (9:1−14:21)
   A. The First Oracle: The Advent and Rejection of the Messiah (9:1−11:17)
      1. The Advent of the Messianic King (9:1−10:12)
         a. The destruction of surrounding nations but the preservation of Zion (9:1−8)
         b. The advent of Zion's king (9:9−10)
         c. The deliverance and blessing of Zion's people (9:11−10:1)
         d. The leaders warned and the people encouraged (10:2−4)
         e. Israel's victory over her enemies (10:5−7)
         f. Israel's complete deliverance and restoration (10:8−12)
      2. The Rejection of the Messianic Shepherd-King (11:1−17)
         a. The prologue (11:1−3)
         b. The prophecy of the rejection of the good shepherd (11:4−14)
         c. The rise and fall of the worthless shepherd (11:15−17)
   B. The Second Oracle: The Advent and Reception of the Messiah (12:1−14:21)
      1. The Deliverance and Conversion of Israel (12:1−13:9)
         a. The siege of Jerusalem (12:1−3)

Text and Exposition

PART I (CHS. 1–8)

I. INTRODUCTION TO THE ENTIRE BOOK (1:1–6)

A. The Date and the Author's Name (1:1)

¹In the eighth month of the second year of Darius, the word of the LORD came to the prophet Zechariah son of Berekiah, the son of Iddo.

COMMENTARY

1 The eighth month of Darius's second year was October/November 520 BC. According to Haggai 1:1, Haggai also began his prophetic ministry in the second year of King Darius, on the first day of the sixth month (i.e., on August 29, 520 BC). (For a synchronization of the old lunar calendar with Julian-Gregorian calendar dates, see Baldwin, 29; also Richard A. Parker and Waldo H. Dubberstein, *Babylonian Chronology 626 B.C.–A.D. 75* [Providence, R.I.: Brown Univ. Press, 1956], 30.) Zechariah was therefore a contemporary of Haggai. While it is clear that one of their purposes was to encourage the Israelites to rebuild the temple, it is equally clear that these prophets were vitally interested in spiritual renewal as well (see, e.g., vv.2–6).

At the time of Israel's return from the Babylonian exile, the Jews had no king of their own by whose reign to date events. So Zechariah's prophecy—as well as Haggai's—had to be dated by the reign of Darius, king of Persia and suzerain of Judah. (See in the introduction "Historical Background" on Darius and the Behistun Inscription, which greatly advanced the deciphering of Akkadian, the language of ancient Babylonia and Assyria.) Thus the

dating by a pagan king indicates that this period occurs in "the times of the Gentiles" (Lk 21:24).

"The word of the LORD" is a "technical term for the prophetic word of revelation" (*TDOT*, 3:111). That the word of the Lord "came" to Zechariah is indicative of the vitality of the divine word in the OT. This so-called word-event formula occurs approximately thirty times in Jeremiah and fifty times in Ezekiel (ibid., 3:113, n. 182). When the Hebrew refers to the coming of the word of the Lord, it denotes the historical character of that word—its character as an event. But elsewhere God's word not only "comes," it also "comes true" or is fulfilled (v.6; cf. Isa 55:8–11).

In the ancient Near East, the word of a god was thought to possess inherent power, guaranteeing its effect. The Akkadian epic *Enuma Elish* (4:19–28) illustrates this idea (cf. *ANET*, 66). In this passage the destructive and creative or restorative power of the Babylonian god Marduk's word is related to his right to rule above all others. Similarly, the Lord's efficacious word, which can both destroy and deliver or restore, suggests his right to absolute sovereignty. He alone is the Great King, and he reigns supreme. One of the ways he demonstrates his sovereignty and superiority, then, is by speaking and fulfilling his dynamic word. The power of God's word, of course, resides in his will, not in magic. (For a discussion of the signification of "the LORD" as the personal name of God, see K. L. Barker, *WBE*, 2:1047–49.)

The recipient of the divine revelation is identified as "the prophet" Zechariah. A possible definition of the Hebrew *nābî'* ("prophet"), based on both etymology and usage, is "one called by God to be his spokesman," thus giving at least one reason the prophets spoke with such authority (cf. v.3). The recipient is further identified as "son of Berekiah, the son of Iddo." The three names in the complete patronymic formula ("Zechariah," "Berekiah," "Iddo") mean "the LORD remembers," "the LORD blesses," and "timely [?]." Feinberg, 17, combining the three names, believes they signify that "the LORD remembers," and "the LORD will bless" at "the set time," which, in a sense, is the theme of the book.

Iddo was among the priests who returned to Jerusalem with Zerubbabel and Joshua (or "Jeshua"; Ne 12:4, 16). Zechariah, who was born in exile, would have been quite young at the time of the return. Since Berekiah was his father, the NIV correctly identifies Zechariah as a "descendant" (i.e., "grandson," not "son") of Iddo in Ezra 5:1 and 6:14. Semitic words for "son" can mean "grandson" or "descendant." Like Jeremiah and Ezekiel, then, Zechariah was a member of a priestly family when God called him to the prophetic office and ministry.

NOTES

1 The definition of נָבִיא (*nābî'*, "prophet") is based partly on an assumed etymological relationship to the Akkadian verb *nabû* ("to call"). Such an etymology was proposed originally by W. F. Albright (*From the Stone Age to Christianity*, 2nd ed. [Baltimore: Johns Hopkins Univ. Press, 1957], 303). The Hebrew substantive is either a verbal adjective or the alternative form of the Qal passive participle, thus giving the word a stative or passive sense. On prophets and prophecy in the ancient Near East, see, most recently, K. A. Kitchen, *On the Reliability of the Old Testament* (Grand Rapids: Eerdmans, 2003), 373–420, 581–91.

A possible reference in Matthew 23:35 and Luke 11:51 to the prophet Zechariah has created a problem. In the Matthean account Jesus used the expression "from the blood of righteous Abel to the blood of Zechariah son of Berekiah." It is possible that the prophet was martyred, though there is no independent record of this happening. Probably the reference is to the martyrdom of another Zechariah, the son of Jehoiada the priest, around 800 BC (2Ch 24:20–22; see note on Mt 23:35 by D. A. Carson, "Matthew," *EBC*, 8:485).

Regarding the problem of Jehoiada versus Berekiah, the *New Scofield Reference Bible* (1032–33, n.3) explains: "This [Berekiah] was probably the actual father of this martyr, Zechariah, who is designated in 2 Chronicles as son of his famous grandfather, Jehoiada, who had died at the advanced age of 130 before Zechariah began his ministry. Cp. 2 Chr. 24:15, 20–22; 36:16; Lk. 11:51." In this case the term "son" is being used in the sense of "grandson" or "descendant" in the Chronicles passage (see above). If this explanation correctly resolves the difficulty, our Lord is saying, in effect, "from the first murder in the Bible [Ge 4:8] to the last [2Ch 24:20–21]," for the last book in the Hebrew canon is Chronicles, not Malachi.

B. A Call to Repentance (1:2-6)

²"The Lord was very angry with your forefathers. ³Therefore tell the people: This is what the Lord Almighty says: 'Return to me,' declares the Lord Almighty, 'and I will return to you,' says the Lord Almighty. ⁴Do not be like your forefathers, to whom the earlier prophets proclaimed: This is what the Lord Almighty says: 'Turn from your evil ways and your evil practices.' But they would not listen or pay attention to me, declares the Lord. ⁵Where are your forefathers now? And the prophets, do they live forever? ⁶But did not my words and my decrees, which I commanded my servants the prophets, overtake your forefathers?

"Then they repented and said, 'The Lord Almighty has done to us what our ways and practices deserve, just as he determined to do.'"

COMMENTARY

2–3 Because a holy and just God must deal with sin, Zechariah begins his message by reminding his people of how angry their faithful, covenantal God had been with the covenant-breaking sins of their unfaithful, preexilic forefathers (v.2). This reminder should have made a tremendous impact on Zechariah's hearers; they well knew that the exile they recently returned from was the direct result of God's wrath against their ancestors, and that the temple they are now rebuilding was destroyed because of the sins of their forefathers (2Ch 36:16). "Forefathers" is more literally "fathers"; but Semitic words for "father" can mean "grandfather," "forefather," or "ancestor."

The divine wrath (v.2) is followed by the availability of divine grace (v.3). Verse 3 contains the main statement of the contemporary call to repentance, one of the conditions for the personal experience of God's full blessing. It begins with the inferential, or consequential, use of the Hebrew conjunction *waw* ("therefore"), as quite frequently with the *waw* consecutive perfect (BDB, 254, par. 4). The point may be stated thus: "Therefore, since the Lord was very angry with your forefathers because

they refused to repent, do not make the same mistake they did; rather, return to me." Three times in v.3 for emphasis the words of the call to repentance are said to be the authoritative declaration of "the Lord Almighty." The introductory clause, "This is what the Lord Almighty says" (NIV), or "Thus says the Lord of hosts" (NASB), contains the messenger formula *kōh ʾāmar* ("Thus says").

The literature of the ancient Near East contains references to messengers who carried a god's or a king's words to a king or a people (cf. J. F. Ross, "The Prophet as Yahweh's Messenger," in *Israel's Prophetic Heritage*, ed. B. W. Anderson and W. Harrelson [New York: Harper & Brothers, 1962], 100–101). The messenger bore the authority of the one who sent him and appeared on the scene to deliver, not his own word, but the word of his sender. The messenger was the mediator of a word. The OT prophet is to be understood as the faithful conveyer of a message (cf. *TDOT*, 1:339–40).

Zechariah, then, comes with the message and authority of Israel's divine King, who is "the Lord Almighty." The NIV's preface explains the sense of this phrase as "he who is sovereign over all the 'hosts' (powers) in heaven and on earth, especially over the 'hosts' (armies) of Israel." Similarly, Eichrodt (1:193–94) concludes that "ṣᵉbāʾōt does not refer to any particular 'hosts,' but to all bodies, multitudes, masses in general, the content of all that exists in heaven and in earth ... [a] name expressive of the divine sovereignty." As "the LORD Almighty," Yahweh is the controller of history, who musters all the powers of heaven and earth to accomplish his will (see further Barker, ed., NIVSB at 1Sa 1:3 n.). Patrick D. Miller Jr. (*The Divine Warrior in Early Israel* [Cambridge, Mass.: Harvard Univ. Press, 1973], 154–65) considers this epithet as part of the OT's Divine Warrior motif. He isolates the activities of the Divine Warrior as salvation, judgment, and kingship (ibid., 170–75). The messianic King will also be a divine warrior or strong ruler ("Mighty God" in Isa 9:6[5]; cf. Isa 10:21).

The content of the Lord Almighty's word through his prophetic messenger is, in brief, "Return to me ... and I will return to you" (cf. Mal 3:7). If the people of Zechariah's day will only return to the Lord or repent, i.e., change their course and go in the opposite direction from that of their forefathers, the Lord will return to them with a blessing instead of a curse. The Hebrew verb *šûb* ("return") can mean "repent" (as in v.6). One might expect, "Return to my law, word, or covenant"; instead, the appeal is to "return to *me*, your covenantal God and King." The emphasis is on personal relationship and allegiance.

4–6 The opening appeal (v.3) for repentance (change of mind and life) is elaborated with a lesson from the past. History is replete with warnings, but unfortunately people do not often learn from the mistakes or successes of the past. "Forefathers" (v.4) refers to the preexilic ancestors (v.2); and "earlier prophets" refers to the preexilic prophets, who had warned of the approaching Babylonian exile—prophets such as Isaiah, Habakkuk, and Jeremiah. Note that the oracles of the latter

are already regarded as "canonical" by Zechariah. The following words in v.4 are not intended as a direct quotation from any particular prophet but as a general summary of the message of the preexilic prophets to God's erring people (but cf. Jer 35:15).

"Evil ways" and "evil practices" form a hendiadys stressing the forefathers' wicked behavior in God's sight. In their failure to respond to the prophets, the people had not responded to God ("me"), for he is the one who had sent the prophets (cf. Jer 7:25–26). Instead of responding with repentance, faith, and obedience, the people "mocked God's messengers, despised his words and scoffed at his prophets until the wrath of the LORD was aroused against his people and there was no remedy" (2Ch 36:16). Such brazen refusal to respond properly was the principal reason for the fall of Jerusalem and the Babylonian exile (2Ch 36:15–21).

Defiance of God and disobedience to his word are always dangerous. The result for Judah, as well as for the northern kingdom of Israel earlier, was disaster. The nature of that disaster is stated in vv.5–6. The answer to the rhetorical questions of v.5 is obvious: Both the forefathers and the prophets who warned them are dead. And some of those prophets died without seeing their predictions fulfilled. They have gone "the way of all the earth" (1Ki 2:2).

Verse 6 reminds us that though the messengers may be gone, God's words live on to be fulfilled (cf. Isa 40:6–8; 55:10–11). These words are further defined as "decrees"—the specific requirements of the law, including the threats and curses for breaking those requirements. Although God's words were uttered by his servants the prophets, they are still his words ("my words"), for his Spirit inspired them (2Pe 1:21).

The designation of the prophets as "my servants" is not a demeaning title but an honorific one, for it is a rare privilege to serve the Lord, who is both Israel's King and the Sovereign of the universe.

Indeed, humans are exalted, not debased, in such service. As pointed out by W. Zimmerli (*TDNT*, 5:663–65), the meaning of this relationship is influenced by the usage of "servant" in the royal courts of the ancient Near East. In particular, Israel was Yahweh's kingdom, and the prophet was the messenger of the divine King's word. The office of messenger is also found in the secular royal courts. The messenger-servant-prophet belongs to King Yahweh's court and is assigned a specific, active mission to fulfill on earth.

In a bold personification, God's words and decrees—including threats and curses for disobedience—are pictured as "overtaking" the disobedient forefathers (v.6; for a similar personification see 5:3–4). The question, of course, anticipates an affirmative reply. God's curse did, in fact, pursue and catch up with the wrongdoers. "The exile, which involved the removal of leaders and the destruction of national institutions, was the death of the nation (Ezek 37:11)" (Baldwin, 91). This happened in direct fulfillment of the curse warnings in Deuteronomy 28:15, 45, where the same verb ("overtake") is used (cf. Jer 1:12 for the principle). According to Deuteronomy 28:2, blessings, too, can "overtake" ("accompany," NIV). The choice is up to the subjects of the kingdom.

The same situation obtained in Jesus' day. Destruction and dispersion again came because of the people's disobedience, unbelief, and rejection of him. The application is clear: Pay attention to God and his word, for even though his messengers die, his word lives on. Proof that it does is that its curses are fulfilled; they "overtake" the rebels.

God's word—whether promise or threat—always accomplishes his purpose (Isa 55:10–11).

"Then they repented" ("came to themselves" or "changed their minds") is apparently a reference to what happened to the preexilic ancestors and/or to their offspring during the exile and immediately afterward (cf. Ezr 9–10; Da 9:1–19). They acknowledged that they had brought the divine discipline of the exile on themselves because they had refused to "listen," or "pay attention," to the Lord and to his words of warning through his servants the prophets. They also acknowledged that the Lord is just and righteous in his judgment, for he had done to them what their ways and practices deserved, all in accord with what he had "determined to do" (cf. La 2:17). The end result was forgiveness and restoration, likewise in accord with his promise (cf. Dt 30:1–3; Isa 55:6–7; Jer 3:12; Joel 2:12–13).

"To sum up this introductory message, Zechariah is making a plea for a wholehearted response to the Lord's invitation to return to him.... On exactly the same terms as had been offered to their fathers, young and old alike are invited to return to God. If they will do so, the covenant relationship will be renewed, and spiritual restoration will accompany the material restoration of the Temple" (Baldwin, 92). Webb, 64, adds: "The sin of the people ... lay not so much in what they were doing as in what they were not doing. It wasn't the 'sin' of home improvement, or interior decorating—as though these things were wrong in themselves—it was the sin of immersing themselves in these things *while the Lord's house remained a ruin* (Hag. 1:4)." (See also Feinberg, 21, for more principles and applications.)

NOTES

2 קֶצֶף (*qeṣep*, "anger") following *qāṣap* ("he was angry") is an example of the cognate accusative, which stresses the verbal idea; hence the translation "was very angry" (cf. LXX; *IBHS*, 166–67; GKC, pars. 117 p, q; see also Davidson, par. 67b). Other examples of this syntactical phenomenon may be found in vv.14–15

and 7:9. Such anger on the part of God should not be classified as an anthropopathism. To deny real emotions to God is to deprive him of one of the clear marks of personality or personhood, which include intelligence, sensibility, and volition. The doctrine of impassibility—sometimes restricted in meaning to emotions, as though God had no emotions—in certain systematic theologies is without foundation in a truly biblical theology and so is unsound.

3 אֻם (nᵊ'um, "declares") is probably the Qal passive participle construct, meaning "is the utterance of [the LORD]."

4 The Kethiv and the Qere have different nominal forms for "practices," but there is no essential difference in meaning. The Qere overcomes a problem of gender in the Kethiv, but either reading is possible.

5 In Hebrew the first part of the verse, like the last part, features the *casus pendens* construction for emphasis (*IBHS*, 76–77; GKC, par. 143c): "Your forefathers, where are they?"

II. A SERIES OF EIGHT NIGHT VISIONS (1:7–6:8)

A. The First Vision: The Horseman among the Myrtle Trees (1:7–17)

⁷On the twenty-fourth day of the eleventh month, the month of Shebat, in the second year of Darius, the word of the LORD came to the prophet Zechariah son of Berekiah, the son of Iddo.

⁸During the night I had a vision—and there before me was a man riding a red horse! He was standing among the myrtle trees in a ravine. Behind him were red, brown and white horses.

⁹I asked, "What are these, my lord?"

The angel who was talking with me answered, "I will show you what they are."

¹⁰Then the man standing among the myrtle trees explained, "They are the ones the LORD has sent to go throughout the earth."

¹¹And they reported to the angel of the LORD, who was standing among the myrtle trees, "We have gone throughout the earth and found the whole world at rest and in peace."

¹²Then the angel of the LORD said, "LORD Almighty, how long will you withhold mercy from Jerusalem and from the towns of Judah, which you have been angry with these seventy years?" ¹³So the LORD spoke kind and comforting words to the angel who talked with me.

¹⁴Then the angel who was speaking to me said, "Proclaim this word: This is what the LORD Almighty says: 'I am very jealous for Jerusalem and Zion, ¹⁵but I am very angry with the nations that feel secure. I was only a little angry, but they added to the calamity.'

¹⁶"Therefore, this is what the LORD says: 'I will return to Jerusalem with mercy, and there my house will be rebuilt. And the measuring line will be stretched out over Jerusalem,' declares the LORD Almighty.

> [17]"Proclaim further: This is what the LORD Almighty says: 'My towns will again overflow with prosperity, and the LORD will again comfort Zion and choose Jerusalem.'"

COMMENTARY

7 In a series of eight apocalyptic visions on a single night, God reveals his purpose for the future of Israel—Judah and Jerusalem in particular, since Jerusalem was the seat of the Davidic dynasty and the location of the Lord's throne (i.e., the temple). The revelations usually follow this general pattern: (1) introductory words, (2) a depiction of what Zechariah sees, (3) the prophet's request for the meaning of the vision, and (4) the angel's explanation. An oracle accompanies four of the visions (1:14–17; 2:6–13; 4:6–10; 6:9–15; so Baldwin, 92–93), thus making their message more specific. Each vision "contributes to the total picture of the role of Israel in the new era about to dawn" (ibid., 93). Petersen, 112–13, maintains that "these visions of Zechariah entail not only a literary unity but also a progression." (Petersen, 116–19, also points out eight contrasts between Zechariah's visions and those in Ezekiel 40–48.) As an encouragement to the people to persevere in the work of rebuilding the temple, God discloses to them through his prophet his gracious purposes.

The setting is the time of Darius, and the date is February 15, 519 BC, about three months after Zechariah's call to repentance (cf. 1:1). On this same day five months earlier, the rebuilding of the temple had resumed (cf. Hag 1:14–15; see also 2:10, 18, 20). It was evidently a day in which God took special delight because of the obedience of his people. The last half of the verse is identical with the last half of 1:1.

8 The basic teaching of the first vision (vv.8–17, including the oracle in vv.14–17, if Baldwin's

analysis is correct) is that although God's covenantal people are troubled while the oppressing nations are at ease, God is "jealous" for his people and will restore them, their towns, and the temple. The vision comes during the night of the twenty-fourth day of the eleventh month (v.7). The Hebrew for "I had a vision" is simply "I saw," but the verb *rāʾâ* ("to see") here has the meaning reflected in the NIV (cf. Nu 12:6; Isa 30:10; Hab 1:3; see *NIDOTTE*, 3:1010–11). From this verb comes the participial noun "seer," another name for a prophet.

The vision portrays a man on a red horse standing among myrtle trees in a ravine. The "man" is identified in v.11 as "the angel of the LORD." In Revelation 6:4 the red horse (see also Zec 6:2) is associated with a sword, the instrument of war and death, which may also be the significance of the color here (cf. Isa 63:1–6). Archaeology tells us that "representations of horsemen are known in Iranian [Persian] art from the third millennium BC onwards; and the cavalry was the mainstay of the Persian army at all times" (*Illustrated Family Encyclopedia*, 8:90).

In Nehemiah 8:15 myrtle trees, which are evergreen, are associated with the Festival of Tabernacles for making booths; and in Isaiah 41:19 and 55:13 they are included in a description of messianic kingdom blessings. Perhaps, then, they speak of the hope and promise of the future, the restoration from Babylonian exile being but the initial stage in the progressive fulfillment of that promise. The trees are situated in a ravine. At the foot of the Mount of Olives are myrtle groves in the lowest part of the

Kidron Valley. The ravine may picture Judah's lowly condition at the time; but, as suggested above, there is a ray of light or hope for the future.

Behind the horseman are red, brown, and white horses—presumably with riders on them, since they report to the angel of the Lord in v.11. These other riders or horses apparently represent angelic messengers (cf. v.10). White horses are associated with vengeance and triumph (cf. Rev 19:11, 14).

9–11 After Zechariah respectfully ("my lord") inquires about the meaning of the vision, the interpreting angel (see also in vv.13–14, 19; 2:3; 4:1, 4–5 [cf. Heb.]; 5:10; 6:4) indicates that he will explain the meaning (v.9). It is, however, the horseman among the myrtle trees who does the explaining (v.10). The explanation is that the other horsemen are angelic messengers sent by the Lord on missions throughout the earth. "Like the Persian monarchs who used messengers on swift steeds to keep them informed on all matters concerning their empire, so the Lord knew all about the countries of the earth, including the great Persian state" (Baldwin, 95). Such angels are part of the Lord's "hosts" (see Barker, ed., NIVSB, at 1Sa 1:3 n.). The verb *šalaḥ* ("sent") seems to suggest that the horsemen are angelic messengers, for the Hebrew word for angel (*malʾāk*) means literally "sent one, one sent with a message, messenger." The root is *lʾk*, which occurs in Ugaritic as a verb meaning "to send" (cf. *UT*, 426).

In v.11 the horseman among the myrtle trees in v.8 is identified as "the angel of the Lord" (see *NIDOTTE*, 2:942; *TLOT*, 2:671; *TDOT*, 8:317–24; *TWOT*, 1:465). Here he serves mainly as the captain of the Lord's host (the other horsemen). Elsewhere the angel of the Lord is often identified with the Lord himself (cf. Ge 16:11, 13; 18:1–2, 13, 17, 22; 22:11–12, 15–18; 31:11, 13; Ex 3:2, 4; Jos 5:13; 6:2; Jdg 2:1–5; 6:11–12, 14; 13:3–23; Eze 43:6–7; Zec 3:1–2). The other horsemen report to him that the whole world is at rest and in peace.

Such a description of the Persian Empire is confirmed by the inscription and bas-relief that Darius had incised on a rock at Behistun (or Bisitun) 328 feet above the highway connecting Ecbatana and Babylon. The bas-relief portrays the surrender of those who had rebelled against the king, while the inscription tells in Persian, Elamite, and Babylonian the story of the political unrest in Persia during the first two years of Darius's reign and praises his feats of valor. Darius boasted that in nineteen battles he defeated nine rebel leaders and subdued all of his enemies. So the empire was again virtually quiet by 520 BC.

Copies of this Behistun Inscription were sent to all the nations of the empire in their own languages. A fragment of the Babylonian copy survived in Babylon, and a piece of the Aramaic text was found in the Jewish colony at Elephantine (Yeb) in Egypt (cf. *Illustrated Family Encyclopedia*, 8:91). While the Persian Empire as a whole was secure and at ease by this time, the Israelites in Judah were oppressed and, of course, still under foreign domination, as the next verse makes clear.

12 The angel of the Lord is moved to intercede for the people of Judah. He desires the completion of the process of restoration, which requires the reconstruction of the temple, Jerusalem (for information on Jerusalem see Barker, "Micah," 45), and the other towns of Judah. The report of the horsemen must have disappointed God's chosen people, for it tells of rest and peace among the nations, when they are expecting instead the "shaking of all nations" (Hag 2:6–9, 20–23) as the sign of returning favor and full blessing to Zion (cf. Perowne, 71).

Through intercession suggestive of our Lord's high priestly prayer as our Mediator (Jn 17), the angel of the Lord prays that in the mercy of God this situation will be rectified. The experience of God's disciplining anger for seventy years was first predicted by Jeremiah (Jer 25:11–12; 29:10; cf. also 2Ch 36:21; Ezr 1:1; Da 9:2). This period may be calculated from 605 BC (the time of the first deportation from the land) to about 536 or 535 (the time when the first returnees were settled back in the land), or from 586 (when the temple was destroyed) to 516 (when the temple was rebuilt). Either way, the point is that the people wonder why God is still angry with them when the appointed time of their punishment has expired (or is almost over; cf. Perowne, 71). The answer comes in the following verses.

13–15 Although it was the angel of the Lord who interceded in v.12, the Lord's answer comes directly to the interpreting angel and through him to Zechariah; or "the LORD" (v.13) may refer to the angel of the Lord, who will then be giving the reply he has received from the "LORD Almighty." The angel of the Lord is identified with the Lord elsewhere (see comment on v.11). The answer contains words that promise kindness (or "good things") and comfort (cf. Isa 40:1–2). The kind and comforting words (v.13) are those in the oracle of vv.14–17. In v.14 Zechariah is told to proclaim to the people that the Lord is "very jealous" for Jerusalem.

Attributing jealousy to the Lord poses no problem, for in OT usage jealousy is but the intolerance of rivalry or unfaithfulness. How one expresses that intolerance determines whether or not it is sin. When applied to the Lord, it usually concerns Israel and carries with it the notions of the marriage or covenantal relationship and the Lord's right to exclusive possession of Israel. In this context the key idea is that of God's vindicating Israel for the violations against her, as v.15 indicates. Actually, jealousy is part of the vocabulary of love; through such language the Lord shows his love for Israel (see Barker, ed., NIVSB at Ex 20:5 n.). Pusey, 2:344, paraphrases: "I ... *am jealous* ... with tender

love which allows not what it loves to be injured" (emphasis his). The holy hill of Zion is particularly singled out as the Lord's special object of electing love (Pss 78:68; 132:13–14; cf. Zec 8:1–8).

In contrast to the Lord's jealous love for his people, he is "very angry" with the nations that have treated them so harshly (v.15). The chiastic structure of v.15 (which in Hebrew begins with "great anger") in relation to v.14 (which in Hebrew ends with "great jealousy") emphasizes the Lord's anger; the participle *qōṣēp* ("angry") is probably intended to express the durative nature of that anger. The nations God has used to discipline his people include Assyria and Babylonia (cf. Isa 47:6, directed against the Babylonians; see also 52:4–5). They are characterized as "feeling secure" (cf. v.11). The sense is that the nations are arrogantly (or carelessly) at ease.

The reason for the divine displeasure is stated in the latter part of v.15. Since v.2 plainly says that the Lord is "very angry" with his sinning people, the clause "I was only a little angry" might be better rendered "I was angry only a little while." Such a nuance for *mᵉˤāṭ* ("little") is possible (Holladay, 206; see, e.g., Job 24:24). If this rendering is correct, then in v.2 the stress is on the intensity of the anger, whereas in v.15 it is on the duration of the anger. This view is indirectly supported by Isaiah 54:7–8. The full charge against the nations, then, is that "they added to the calamity" of the divine discipline, not only by going too far and trying to annihilate the Jews, but also by prolonging the calamity. There is an implicit warning here against anti-Semitism (cf. Ge 12:3).

16–17 The Lord next presents the more positive aspect of the "kind and comforting words" (v.13). The word "therefore" shows the force: Because God has a jealous love for Israel and a jealous anger against her enemies, the following promises will be fulfilled. In response to the intercession of v.12 the

Lord promises to return to Jerusalem with mercy (cf. Eze 43:1–5; 48:35, which seem to reach to the end times for the final stage of the progressive fulfillment). The assurance that the temple ("my house") will be rebuilt expresses the divine mercy.

The measuring line is that of those who are to reconstruct Jerusalem in a program of expansion (cf. 2:1–5). Baruch Halpern ("The Ritual Background of Zechariah's Temple Song," *CBQ* 40 [1978]: 178, n. 51), comparing Jeremiah 31:38–40, correctly notes that the measuring line is "a symbol of restoration." When one compares several other pertinent biblical references, it appears likely that the temple completed and dedicated in 516 BC (Ezr 6:15–16) is only the initial stage in the complete fulfillment (or in the "filling to the full") of vv.16–17 (note Isa 2:2–3; Jer 31:38–40; Eze 40–42; Ac 15:14–18).

Verse 17 anticipates a time when the towns of Judah (i.e., "my towns") will "overflow" (or "spread out") with prosperity. Thus the Lord will again comfort Zion and choose Jerusalem (cf. Isa 14:1). The temple as the Lord's house, and Jerusalem as the Lord's elect city in which his house and earthly throne are located, are inseparably linked in these verses. The "prosperity" in v.17 is to be connected with the "kind" words in v.13, and the "comfort" in v.17 with the "comforting" words in v.13, for the same Hebrew roots are involved in both places. Feinberg, 38, has an excellent summary of the teaching and application of the first vision:

The distinctive features of comfort for Israel in this first vision are: (1) the presence of the Angel of Jehovah in the midst of degraded and depressed Israel; (2) His loving and yearning intercession for them; (3) the promises of future blessings. We may say, then, that the import of the vision is this: although Israel is not yet in her promised position, God is mindful of her, providing the means of His judgment on the persecuting nations, and reserving glory and prosperity for Israel in the benevolent and beneficent reign of the Messiah.

The series of visions carry us through God's dealings with Israel from the time of their chastisement by God under the Gentile powers until they are restored to their land with their rebuilt city and temple under their Messiah King. The first vision gives the general theme of the whole series; the others add the details.... When the world was busy with its own affairs, God's eyes and the heart of the Messiah were upon the lowly estate of Israel and upon the temple in Jerusalem.

NOTES

10 Speiser (*Oriental and Biblical Studies: Collected Writings of E. A. Speiser*, ed. J. J. Finkelstein and M. Greenberg [Philadelphia: Univ. of Pennsylvania Press, 1967], 506–14) has argued for a durative Hithpael of הָלַךְ (*hālak*, "to go"), going back originally to a *tan* form, as in Akkadian. Such a sense would fit nicely in the context here: "They are the ones the Lord has sent to go continually throughout the earth."

11 עָנָה (*ʿānâ*; GK 6699) does not always mean "to answer, reply." Sometimes it means "to respond, testify, speak, ask, report," as here (NIV; see esp. BDB, 772–73). The same is true of the Ugaritic *ʿny*, which can mean simply "to say, speak up" (*UT*, 458). Other OT references that bear out this meaning are Job 3:2 and Daniel 2:26.

13 נִחֻמִים (*niḥumîm*, "comforting") is not an adjective but a noun, functioning syntactically as a case of nominal apposition, with the collocation of the thing and the attribute (GKC, par. 131c; Davidson, par. 29e).

14 קִנְאָה (*qinʾâ*, "jealousy") is the cognate accusative (see Note on v.2); so is קֶצֶף (*qeṣep*, "anger") in v.15.

15 אֲשֶׁר (ʾăšer) is here used in the sense of "for" (*HALOT*, 1:99; BDB, 83, par. 8c). The NIV lets the juxtaposition of the clauses carry the force. רָעָה (rāʿâ, "calamity"; GK 8288) can mean not only the "evil" that someone does but also the "disaster" encountered as a consequence (Fohrer, 102).

16 שַׁבְתִּי (šabtî, "I will return") is probably best construed as a prophetic perfect (*IBHS*, 490) in view of the future orientation of vv.16–17. רַחֲמִים (raḥămîm, "mercy, tender love, compassion") is usually classified as the intensive plural (e.g., GKC, par. 124e), though it can also be simply the abstract plural (ibid., par. 124a; *HALOT*, 3:1218).

B. The Second Vision: The Four Horns and the Four Craftsmen (1:18–21 [2:1–4])

> [18]Then I looked up — and there before me were four horns! [19]I asked the angel who was speaking to me, "What are these?"
>
> He answered me, "These are the horns that scattered Judah, Israel and Jerusalem."
> [20]Then the LORD showed me four craftsmen. [21]I asked, "What are these coming to do?"
>
> He answered, "These are the horns that scattered Judah so that no one could raise his head, but the craftsmen have come to terrify them and throw down these horns of the nations who lifted up their horns against the land of Judah to scatter its people."

COMMENTARY

18–19 [2:1–2] The second and third visions build on the concept of the comfort promised in vv.13 and 17, first by presenting the manner in which God will execute his great anger against the nations that have afflicted Israel (second vision), and second by guaranteeing the prosperity and expansion promised to Israel (third vision). The four horns (v.18) are identified as the nations (or their rulers) that attacked Judah, Israel, and Jerusalem to scatter their people (vv.19, 21). When used figuratively, "horn" usually symbolizes strength — either strength in general (Ps 18:2) or the strength of a country, i.e., its king (Ps 89:17; Da 7:24; 8:20–22; Rev 17:12), or the power of a nation in general (here?). The horns are presumably on the heads of animals, since they are capable of being terrified (v.21).

The Targum translates "four horns" as "four kingdoms" (so Cathcart and Gordon, 187; for the equation of "horns" and "kingdoms," see Da 8:22). The kingdoms in question are claimed by some scholars to be the four world empires of Daniel 2 and 7 (namely, Babylonia, Medo-Persia, Greece, and Rome). Others suggest Assyria, Egypt, Babylonia, and Medo-Persia (e.g., Charles C. Ryrie, *Ryrie Study Bible* [Chicago: Moody Press, 1995], Zec 1:18–21 n). Since the reference in vv.19 and 21 is to nations that have already "scattered" God's people (though the Heb. verb can also be translated "scatter" [present tense]), the latter view seems preferable. God's people are referred to under the all-inclusive designation "Judah, Israel and Jerusalem," i.e., the whole nation scattered in exile. Jerusalem is mentioned because it is the capital of the united kingdom of Israel.

20 [2:3] The craftsmen have been interpreted in at least two ways: (1) many of those who hold that the four horns symbolize the world empires of Daniel

2 and 7 (see previous comment) maintain that the craftsmen represent Medo-Persia, Greece, Rome, and the Messiah, since they are the destroyers of the preceding world empires (for the messianic role see Da 2:34–35, 44–45); (2) others believe that the craftsmen denote the peoples and nations God used to overthrow Israel's past enemies—nations such as Egypt, Babylonia, Persia, and Greece, or perhaps Persia alone. In any event, it is clear in Scripture that all Israel's enemies—past, present, and potential—will ultimately be defeated.

21 [2:4] The prophet's inquiry this time concerns not identity or meaning but function. The answer given (apparently by the interpreting angel) is that the horns came to scatter the people of Judah and render them helpless and powerless. This idea seems to be repeated from v.19 for emphasis. The horns that did these things to Israel, Judah, and Jerusalem (v.19) have, by the time of Zechariah's prophecy, already been conquered and absorbed into the Persian Empire. The craftsmen are to be identified, then, at the very least with the world empire of Persia—and possibly with a few other nations as well (see comments on v.20). Their function was to terrify and throw down the powers that, in arrogant defiance of God, went beyond all bounds in punishing and scattering God's covenantal people. In v.15 the nations "feel secure" (or "are at ease"); now they are to be terrified and overthrown.

NOTE

21 [2:4] לְהַחֲרִיד (lᵉhaḥᵃrîd, "to terrify") and לְיַדּוֹת (lᵉyaddôt, "to throw down") are good examples of the use of the infinitive construct with לְ (lᵉ, "to") to denote purpose (*IBHS*, 606–7; *GKC*, pars. 114f–g).

C. The Third Vision: The Surveyor (2:1–13 [2:5–17])

¹Then I looked up—and there before me was a man with a measuring line in his hand! ²I asked, "Where are you going?"

He answered me, "To measure Jerusalem, to find out how wide and how long it is."

³Then the angel who was speaking to me left, and another angel came to meet him ⁴and said to him: "Run, tell that young man, 'Jerusalem will be a city without walls because of the great number of men and livestock in it. ⁵And I myself will be a wall of fire around it,' declares the LORD, 'and I will be its glory within.'

⁶"Come! Come! Flee from the land of the north," declares the LORD, "for I have scattered you to the four winds of heaven," declares the LORD.

⁷"Come, O Zion! Escape, you who live in the Daughter of Babylon!" ⁸For this is what the LORD Almighty says: "After he has honored me and has sent me against the nations that have plundered you—for whoever touches you touches the apple of his eye—⁹I will surely raise my hand against them so that their slaves will plunder them. Then you will know that the LORD Almighty has sent me.

> [10]"Shout and be glad, O Daughter of Zion. For I am coming, and I will live among you," declares the LORD. [11]"Many nations will be joined with the LORD in that day and will become my people. I will live among you and you will know that the LORD Almighty has sent me to you. [12]The LORD will inherit Judah as his portion in the holy land and will again choose Jerusalem. [13]Be still before the LORD, all mankind, because he has roused himself from his holy dwelling."

COMMENTARY

1[5] The scope of the restoration and blessing promised in this vision is such that its fulfillment must extend beyond the historical restoration period to the messianic kingdom era. Perowne, 74, acknowledges: "The [second] vision which describes the destruction of her enemies is followed by another, in which the consequent growth and prosperity of Jerusalem are depicted, and which in the largeness of its predictions extends into the more distant future."

The persons connected with the introductory part of the vision are Zechariah, a surveyor, the interpreting angel, and an unidentified angel. Some have suggested that the surveyor ("a man") is the angel of the Lord (cf. 1:11; 6:12; Eze 40:2–3). The "measuring line" is a symbol of preparation for rebuilding and restoring Jerusalem and the temple, ultimately in the messianic kingdom, as the following verses make plain. The restoration of the people, the temple, and the city immediately after the Babylonian exile is only the first stage in the progressive fulfillment of the promises that follow (see also Eze 40:3, 5).

2–4a[6–8a] When Zechariah asks the surveyor where he is going, he replies that he is going to measure the width and length of Jerusalem, evidently to mark its boundaries. This will be the first step toward the restoration of the city and the realization of the promised blessing (cf. 1:16; Eze 40:5; Rev 11:1). At this point the interpreting angel starts to leave (cf. TNIV, "While the angel who was speaking to me was leaving, another angel came to meet him"); but as he does so, he is met by another angel and is instructed to convey the message of vv.4–13 to Zechariah, who, in turn, will naturally declare it to his people. While some interpreters believe that the "young man" is the surveyor, it seems best and simplest to identify him with Zechariah.

4b[8b] The measuring is done with expansion in view; now that purpose is to be achieved. The promise is given that Jerusalem will become so large and prosperous that it will expand beyond its walls. Indeed, it will overflow so much that it will be as though it has no walls. Evidently many of its people and animals will have to live in the surrounding unwalled villages (cf. Eze 38:11). Nothing like this has yet happened in the history of the city (certainly not in the time of Nehemiah, as is clear from Ne 7:4; 11:1–2). For this reason some commentators take the language of this verse and the following verses "spiritually" and apply it to the expansion of the church or the new (heavenly) Jerusalem. But Feinberg, 45, responds vigorously to such an approach:

> What baseless and unfounded hermeneutical alchemy is this which will take all the prophecies of judgment upon Israel at their face value, to be understood literally, but will transmute into

indistinctness any blessing or promise of future glory for the same people? It is a sad state when men cannot see how kingdom conditions can exist alongside of spirituality. To many minds the introduction of literalness in kingdom promises does away with spirituality. What is so unspiritual about the personal, visible reign of the Messiah of Israel? Does not the same Word that predicts it also state clearly that from that Jerusalem, the seat of the government of the righteous King, will go forth the law and the Word of Jehovah (Isa. 2:1–4)? Wherein is the law lacking in spirituality? Paul declares the law to be holy, righteous, and good (Rom. 7:12). Again, we must maintain that literalness and a material kingdom with material conditions of prosperity *in no wise* exclude or militate against spirituality. (emphasis his)

The realization of the full scope of this prophecy must therefore still be in a future earthly kingdom (cf. Barker, "Micah," 84–87; "Scope and Center," 302–4, 318–28).

5[9] "The primary purpose of the city walls was to prevent the enemy from breaking into the city, to deny him ... his advantage of mobility" (Yigael Yadin, *The Art of Warfare in Biblical Lands*, 2 vols. [New York: McGraw-Hill, 1963], 1:19). However, though Jerusalem will become so large and prosperous that many of its inhabitants will spill over beyond the walls into the "suburbs," they will still be secure because of the divine protection ("a wall of fire around it") and the divine presence ("its glory"). "I" is emphatic in the original, hence the NIV's "I myself." The "wall of fire" is reminiscent of the "pillar of fire" at the exodus (Ex 13:21). Both "fire" and "glory" are emblematic of God and his protection and guidance (Isa 4:5–6). In fact, both of these recall the exodus (Ex 13:22; 14:20; 40:34).

The future safety of Jerusalem and its people, including those living in the surrounding unwalled villages, is guaranteed. In addition, there is the promise of the Lord's glorious presence in regal holiness and majesty (cf. 1:16; Ps 24:7–10). The Lord's *kābôd* ("glory") is the "weight" of the impression of his self-manifestation. Here the manifestation is concerned with the final actualization of his rule. This anticipates the Lord's personal presence through the Messiah in his kingdom on earth (cf. 2:11–12; 14:9; Isa 60:19; Eze 43:1–5; 48:35). So then, the literal kingdom will be very spiritual.

6–7[10–11] According to Baldwin, 93, 107–8, vv.6–13 constitute another prophetic oracle, not part of the vision proper. The land of the north (v.6) is Babylon (v.7), north being the direction from which the Neo-Babylonian army had invaded Judah (cf. Jer 1:14; 4:6; 6:1; 20:4–6; 31:8; et al.). "You who live in Daughter Babylon" (TNIV) is a clearer rendering of the vocative at the end of v.7. The reference is to the Jews who did not return from Babylon in 538–537 BC but who chose to remain in Babylon. They are now being called to join the other returnees in Jerusalem, evidently to help them rebuild the temple and restore the city. The same Lord who scattered them desires that they be restored and repatriated.

The places of the Diaspora ("scattering") include not only Babylon ("the north") but also Assyria, Egypt, Persia, and the neighboring countries ("the four winds of heaven"; cf. Isa 43:5–6; 49:12). "Zion" (v.7) refers to the exiles from Zion in Babylon. "Flee" (v.6) and "escape" (v.7) imply that some imminent peril is coming on Babylon. Exactly what that peril is in the period immediately following 519 BC is historically uncertain. There is a similar exhortation to God's people to come out of the Babylon of Revelation 17–18 just prior to its final and complete destruction (cf. Rev 18:4–8).

8[12] The opening words of the quotation ("After he has honored me and has sent me") are difficult and have given rise to several different translations and interpretations. For some of the possibilities, see Baldwin, 109; she prefers (with Theophane Chary, *Aggée-Zacharie Malachie* [Paris: Sources bibliques, 1969], 70), "With insistence he sent me." The Hebrew has only, "After glory [or 'honor'; more lit., 'weight, heaviness'] he has sent me." Some understand this sentence to be saying, "he has sent me to manifest my own glory" in judging the oppressing nations. Others take it to mean, "he has sent me to glorify God [the Father]," on the argument that God's glory is inseparably linked with the fortunes of his people (cf. Isa 61:3; Jn 17:4). Still others construe "glory" as a surrogate for God and make it the subject (cf. TNIV, "After the Glorious One has sent me against the nations"; cf. also Meyers and Meyers, 165). The NIV supplies a first-person singular pronoun ("me") with the word for "glory" or "honor," thus yielding the sense contained in its rendering.

Another problem is the identity of the referent in the pronominal suffix "me" both here and in v.9. While many think "me" refers to Zechariah, others maintain that in the light of the language and the full scope of these verses, the pronoun looks toward the messianic Servant-Messenger, the Angel of the Lord (so, e.g., Baron, Feinberg, Leupold, Unger). If the latter view is correct, as seems likely, the speaker, identified as the Lord Almighty at the beginning of the verse, is the Messiah himself, the Angel of the Lord. The mission of this person is directed against the nations that have plundered God's chosen people. Such treatment of the Jews is condemned because harming them is like striking the "apple of [God's] eye," an obvious anthropomorphism (see Notes on v.8). "Apple" is literally "gate," that is, the pupil, an extremely sensitive and vital part of the eye that must be carefully protected. God is so closely identified with his people that they are precious to him, and he is zealous to protect them and take care of them (cf. Dt 32:10;

Ps 17:8; Mt 25:34–45; Ac 9:1, 4–5). Verse 9 gives proof of such care.

9[13] In a menacing gesture the Lord will raise his hand against Israel's enemies (cf. Isa 11:15; 19:16). The Hebrew for "raise" may also be rendered "wave." All it takes for God to punish his people's enemies is a wave of his hand, as it were—another evidence that the speaker here and in v.8 is deity (the Messiah or the Angel of the Lord). "My hand" refers to the display of divine omnipotence—God's infinite power. Here it is exerted in behalf of God's people and against their enemies.

God will bring about a reversal of the fortunes of his people; the tables will be turned. The Jews, who were slaves of the nations that plundered them (v.8), will now plunder those nations (cf. Isa 14:2). Such reversals are common; the destroyed are often self-destroyed. Haman was hanged "on the gallows he had prepared for Mordecai" (Est 7:10; cf. also Gal 6:7–8). When all these things happen, the people "will know that the LORD Almighty has sent" his messenger. The fulfillment will authenticate the message and ministry of the messianic Servant-Messenger (or the Angel of the Lord or, possibly, Zechariah). These words also stress the certainty of the fulfillment.

10[14] In fulfillment of the great OT covenants, particularly the Abrahamic covenant, this section anticipates full kingdom blessing in the messianic era. Then "many [Gentile] nations" (v.11) will become the people of God, but the Lord's special favor will continue to rest on "the holy land" (v.12). The section begins with a call to joy, followed by the reason for such jubilation (cf. 9:9). The reason given is the personal coming of God himself to live among his people in Jerusalem (Zion). This language is ultimately messianic—indirectly or by extension from God in general to the Messiah in particular.

One of the four major categories of messianic prophecy is indirect messianic prophecy (the other three being direct, typical, and typical-prophetical). Indirect messianic prophecy refers to passages that can be literally and fully realized only through the person and work of the Messiah—e.g., passages that speak of a personal coming of God to his people, as in v.10 and 9:9 (cf. also Isa 40:9–11; Mal 3:1). The same is true of references to the expression "the LORD reigns or will reign," characteristic of the so-called Enthronement Psalms (e.g., 93; 95–99). These "eschatologically Yahwistic" psalms are probably best labeled theocratic ("rule-of-God") psalms. The point is that all passages that speak of a future coming of the Lord to his people or to the earth, or that speak of a future rule of the Lord over Israel or over the whole earth, are ultimately messianic—indirectly or by extension; for to be fully and literally true, they require a future, literal messianic kingdom on the earth.

"The verb 'dwell' [NIV, 'live'] (*šākan* [GK 8905], from which is derived 'shekinah') recalls the making of the tabernacle (*miškān*) 'that I may dwell in their midst' (Ex. 25:8)" (Baldwin, 111). She continues: "This same purpose attached in turn to the Temple (1 Kings 6:13), and when Ezekiel looked forward to the new Temple he saw the coming of the glory of the Lord (43:2, 4) and His acceptance of the Temple as the place of His throne (verse 7) for ever (verse 9)." For further biblical development of the theological theme of God's dwelling or living among his people, see vv.11–13 and 8:3 (cf. also Jn 1:14; 2Co 6:16; Rev 21:3).

11–12[15–16] In the great messianic future, many nations "will be joined with the LORD" (v.11) or "will join themselves to the LORD" (the Hebrew can be rendered either way). Such an ingathering of the nations to the Lord echoes the promise in the Abrahamic covenant, "All peoples on earth will be blessed through you" (Ge 12:3; cf. 18:18; 22:18; see also Isa 2:2–4; 56:6–7; 60:3; Mic 4:1–4; Zec

8:20–23; 14:16–18). The result is that they, too, will become the people of God.

All these things will happen "in that day." "That day" is frequently an abbreviation for the "day of the LORD," which has both historical and eschatological applications and calls for special study. The context here concerns the eschatological fulfillment of the day. A few other key passages on the eschatological day of the Lord are Isaiah 2:12–21, dealing with judgment; Isaiah 24–27, concerned with both judgment and blessing; Joel 1:15, stressing judgment; 2:28–3:21, emphasizing both judgment and blessing; Amos 5:18–20 on judgment, but 9:11–15 on blessing; Zephaniah, the early part of which refers to judgment but the latter part to blessing—all in connection with the prophet's theme, the day of the Lord; and Zechariah 14, where reference is made at the beginning of the chapter to the coming invasion of Jerusalem by hostile nations and to the (second) coming of the Messiah (the Lord), followed by the blessing of the messianic kingdom—all under the heading of the "day of the LORD" (v.1). The Messiah's advent is the turning point between the judgment and the blessing aspects of "that day."

It seems clear, then, that the events of Daniel's seventieth "seven" (Da 9:27)—i.e., the entire tribulation period (Rev 6–18), which is the judgment aspect of the day of the Lord—the Messiah's second advent to the earth (Rev 19), and the messianic kingdom age (Rev 20), which is the blessing aspect of "that day," are all included in the scope of the day of the Lord. In the light of biblical usage, the eschatological day of the Lord may be defined as earth's final period of time. It commences with the judgment of Daniel's seventieth "week." It continues with the Messiah's (Christ's) return and reign on earth. And it extends to the appearance of the new heavens and the new earth (Rev 21:1), when the messianic kingdom will continue as (or, perhaps better, merge with) the eternal kingdom (1Co 15:24–28; Rev 21–22). Thus, many supernatural, momentous events fall within the time span of the day of the Lord.

Humans, so to speak, are having their day now; the Lord's day is yet to come. He will have his day at the time of the events of Daniel's seventieth "week" (the "time of trouble for Jacob," Jer 30:7) and of his own second coming and glorious reign on earth—a reign that will endure forever. Finally, since the text states that this conversion of many nations will take place "in that day" (the eschaton), the present ingathering (Ac 15:12–18) is but a stage in the complete fulfillment (cf. Mt 24:14; Rev 7:9; 21:24, 26).

If the person who said "I will live among you" (v.10) is also the speaker of the same words in v.11, as seems certain, then the "me" at the end of v.11 must refer to the messianic Servant-Messenger (or Angel of the Lord), for the speaker in v.10 is clearly deity.

The conversion of many nations to the Lord does not abrogate the promise and purpose of God for Israel, his chosen and special covenantal people (cf. Barker, "False Dichotomies," 10–16; "The Scope and Center," 302–4, 318–28; "Micah," 38–40, 82–87). In keeping with that promise, v.12 indicates that the Lord will inherit Judah (both land and people) and will again choose Jerusalem (cf. 1:17), for many decisive events will yet take place there (e.g., 14:4). There is a similar emphasis on both Gentile and Jewish blessing in Isaiah 19:24–25:"In that day Israel will be the third, along with Egypt and Assyria, a blessing on the earth. The LORD Almighty will bless them, saying, 'Blessed be Egypt my people, Assyria my handiwork, and Israel my inheritance.'" Saints in the church are also said to be part of the glorious inheritance of Christ (Eph 1:18; cf. Isa 52:15; 53:10–12).

The people of Judah are described as the Lord's portion in the "holy land" (v.12; cf. Ps 78:54). Similar epithets are "holy hill" (Pss 2:6; 15:1; cf. Zec 8:3),

"holy city" (Isa 48:2; Da 9:24; Mt 27:53; Rev 21:2), and "holy nation" (Ex 19:6; cf. 1Pe 2:9). The temple, as the place of God's earthly throne, was by definition "holy" (Ps 65:4; Jnh 2:4). But that holiness extended beyond the temple and beyond the holy city to the entire land (cf. also Zec 14:20–21, where common things become holy because they are used for God's service; cf. Baldwin, 112). The root idea of the Hebrew word for "holy" is "separate" or "set apart" (here, in v.12, for God's use and glory; cf. Snaith, 24–25 [full discussion in 21–50]; see also *TLOT*, 3:1103–18; *HALOT*, 3:1066–67, 1072–78). The land of Israel is rendered holy (i.e., sacred, not common or ordinary) chiefly because it is the site of the earthly throne and sanctuary of the holy God, who dwells there among his covenantal people.

In Isaiah 6:1–5 the ascription of "holiness" to the Lord begins with the Lord seated as King on a throne, high and exalted. Thus the Lord is "separated" spatially from his creation. Then, too, there is a close connection between the Lord's holiness and his kingship. Isaiah saw the Lord on his majestic throne in the year that Judah lost one of its better kings (Uzziah) after a long and prosperous reign (cf. 2Ch 26). Thus the Lord is "separated" from the frailties of human rulers. Isaiah 6:3 closely associates the Lord's regal glory (his manifested character) with his "holiness." After seeing the vision, Isaiah's first utterance declared the Lord to be King (6:5; note the emphatic word order in the original). So the concept of the root *qdš* ("holy"; GK 7731) in Isaiah 6 relates to the high, exalted, and "set apart" King of Israel.

It is instructive to note that the remnant is a "holy" ("separated") seed (Isa 6:13). The Lord, the holy and all-glorious King, will acquire a holy people, who are to display and declare his holiness and glory (cf. further Ex 19:6; Lev 11:44–45; 19:1; Pss 24:3–10; 29:1–2, 10; 96:9; cf. 1Pe 1:15–16; Rev 4:8). Finally, according to Zechariah 3:9; 13:1; 14:20–21 (cf. Isa 35:8; 62:12), a time is coming when the land and the people will be "holy" (or "holier") in their experience.

13[17] All humankind is exhorted to be still (in awe) before the Lord because, in a threatening gesture (cf. v.9), he has roused himself from his holy dwelling (probably in heaven) and will judge the enemies of his people (cf. Hab 2:20; Zep 1:7). He is about to break his apparent silence by acting in behalf of his elect (see, ultimately, 12:1–5; 14:1–5). With the opening of the scroll with seven seals in Revelation 5–6; 8, the present apparent silence of God will similarly be broken, unleashing the greatest judgments ever to strike the earth; yet once again his beleaguered people (or a remnant of them) will be delivered, restored, and blessed.

The first vision introduced the judgment (or curse) and blessing motif (1:15–17). That motif is then developed in the second and third visions in an alternating cycle: judgment for the nations (1:19–21) but blessing and glory for Israel (2:1–5); judgment for the nations (2:6–9) but blessing for Israel—and the nations (2:10–13).

NOTES

4a[8a] רוּץ (*ruṣ*, "run") here means "run as a messenger" or "run with the message" (as in Jer 23:21), and so is appropriate for an "angel-messenger."

4b[8b] פְּרָזוֹת (*pᵉrāzôt*, "without walls") is an adverbial accusative of condition or manner (GKC, pars. 118 m, q, r; Davidson, pars. 70a; 71, rem. 1); hence, more literally, "Jerusalem will be inhabited [or 'will dwell'] as unwalled villages."

6[10] GKC (par. 154b) explains the prefixed ו (*waw*) in וְנֻסוּ (*wᵉnusû*, "Flee") as the "waw copulativum" that joins a sentence apparently to what immediately precedes but, in reality, to a sentence that is suppressed. This is especially true when the *waw* is joined to an imperative. Sometimes the suppression of the protasis is due to passionate excitement or haste, which does not allow time for full expression, as in the instance before us.

7[11] בַּת (*bat*, "daughter") in phrases such as "Daughter of Babylon" and "Daughter of Zion" (v.10; 9:9) is a form of personification roughly equivalent to "city of ..." or sometimes "people of ..." (BDB, 123, par. 3).

8[12] עֵינוֹ (*ʿênô*, "his eye"), according to ancient Hebrew scribal tradition, is a *tiqqun sopherim* ("scribal emendation"). The Masorah informs us that the original reading was עֵינִי (*ʿênî*, "my eye"). The anthropomorphism was thought to be too bold; so the scribes changed "my" to "his," intending that the antecedent be understood as "whoever" instead of God. If the correct text is "my eye," as seems probable, the reading strengthens the case for a messianic (or at least "Angel of the Lord") interpretation of the passage, for then the speaker throughout the oracle is even more clearly deity. For a full discussion of the problem of scribal emendations, see C. D. Ginsburg, *Introduction to the Massoretico-critical Edition of the Hebrew Bible* (New York: Ktav, 1966), 347–63. The working principle for such textual changes was to alter all indecent, anthropomorphic, offensive expressions, particularly those that the scribes felt would detract from God in any way. The scribes were not consistent in the application of the principle, however, for some rather bold anthropomorphisms remain—even in the utterances of God himself.

9[13] "My hand" is not only an anthropomorphism but also a metonymy of the cause (hand) for the effect (power; Bullinger, 546–47). The suffix in לְעַבְדֵיהֶם (*lᵉʿabᵉdêhem*, "their slaves") is best taken as an objective genitive (cf. GKC, pars. 128h, 135m), whose meaning can be brought out clearly by translating the clause as "so that they will be plunder for those who served them."

10[14] בָּא (*bāʾ*, "coming") features the *futurum instans* or imminent action use of the participle (*IBHS*, 627–28; GKC, par. 116p). וְשָׁכַנְתִּי (*weśākantî*, "and I will live") is the *waw* consecutive perfect, as the accent on the ultima indicates; it continues the *futurum instans* idea of the participle.

12[16] עוֹד (*ʿôd*, "again"; perhaps better, "yet") "does not imply that God must choose Israel afresh, but that now, at long last, He will be able to manifest to the world the immutable character of His original choice and its practical outworking in renewed, restored, and resettled Israel" (Feinberg, 51).

13[17] הַס (*has*, "be still" or "be silent") is probably an example of onomatopoeia, in this instance reproducing the sound one might make to tell someone to be quiet, silent, or still. The similar word "hush" in English may also be onomatopoetic. נֵעוֹר (*nēʿôr*, "he has roused himself") is the Niphal form of the verb, here used reflexively rather than passively, though either is possible.

D. The Fourth Vision: The Cleansing and Restoration of Israel (3:1–10)

¹Then he showed me Joshua the high priest standing before the angel of the Lord, and Satan standing at his right side to accuse him. ²The Lord said to Satan, "The Lord rebuke you, Satan! The Lord, who has chosen Jerusalem, rebuke you! Is not this man a burning stick snatched from the fire?"

³Now Joshua was dressed in filthy clothes as he stood before the angel. ⁴The angel said to those who were standing before him, "Take off his filthy clothes."

Then he said to Joshua, "See, I have taken away your sin, and I will put rich garments on you."

⁵Then I said, "Put a clean turban on his head." So they put a clean turban on his head and clothed him, while the angel of the Lord stood by.

⁶The angel of the Lord gave this charge to Joshua: ⁷"This is what the Lord Almighty says: 'If you will walk in my ways and keep my requirements, then you will govern my house and have charge of my courts, and I will give you a place among these standing here.

⁸"'Listen, O high priest Joshua and your associates seated before you, who are men symbolic of things to come: I am going to bring my servant, the Branch. ⁹See, the stone I have set in front of Joshua! There are seven eyes on that one stone, and I will engrave an inscription on it,' says the Lord Almighty, 'and I will remove the sin of this land in a single day.

¹⁰"'In that day each of you will invite his neighbor to sit under his vine and fig tree,' declares the Lord Almighty."

COMMENTARY

1 The fourth vision is different from the three previous ones in that there are no questions from the prophet and no explanations by the interpreting angel. The reasons for these omissions are that the identity of Joshua is known from the beginning and the action is explained as the vision unfolds (cf. Baldwin, 113). As indicated in the NIV's note at v.1, Joshua is the same person as Jeshua in Ezra and Nehemiah. Both forms of the name mean "the LORD saves" (cf. NIV note at Mt 1:21).

This chapter presents the grand prophecy of Israel's restoration as a priestly nation. Regarding Israel's calling, Exodus 19:6 states, "You will be for me a kingdom of priests and a holy nation." Just as it was certain that there could be no failure in the restoration work on the temple, which the remnant had taken up anew, so it is assured that God's future program for Israel will be consummated at the return of the Messiah to the earth (Zec 14). In this apocalyptic vision the high priest Joshua represents the sinful nation of Israel (cf. comment on v.8). However, though Israel is presented in defilement, she is also cleansed and restored as a kingdom of priests for God—a condition that will be realized in the messianic age. This symbolic interpretation becomes progressively clearer as one moves through the chapter (see Clark and Hatton, 121). Basically, visions four and five "concern Judah's standing before God and her spiritual resources" (Baldwin, 113).

The revealer of the vision is either the interpreting angel or, more likely, God himself (cf. 1:20). As has been said, Joshua represents Israel in her priestly character. The scope of this passage demands that interpretation. Then, too, in v.8 Joshua and his colleagues are definitely said to be symbolic of the future. The Angel of the Lord must be deity, for in v.2 he is specifically called "the LORD." Thus he clearly represents God. "Standing before the ... LORD" is a technical designation for priestly ministry (metonymy of adjunct, Bullinger, 606; cf. Dt 10:8; 2Ch 29:11; Eze 44:15). Hence the scene is set in the temple.

Although the scene is not basically a legal one, Satan's accusation invests it with a judicial character. The position of standing at the right side was the place of accusation under the law (Ps 109:6). Satan knows the purposes of God concerning Israel and therefore has always accused the Jews and accuses them still. The tool of his nefarious opposition to Israel has primarily been the Gentile nations—a case that will be particularly true during the period of Daniel's seventieth "week."

Satan is the accuser—not only of Joshua (i.e., Israel) but also of all believers (Job 1–2; Rev 12:10). Undoubtedly the accusation here relates to the sin of Joshua (cf. vv.3–4) and is made in the hope that God will reject his people irrevocably. But this we know he will never do, as the following verses assert (cf. also Lev 26:40–45; Jer 31:36–37; 32:40; Ro 3:1–4; 11:1–2). Regarding $w^e ha\acute{s}\acute{s}\bar{a}t\bar{a}n \ldots l^e\acute{s}it^n\hat{o}$ ("and Satan ... to accuse him"), Chambers, 35, says, "The force of this antanaclasis can hardly be expressed in a version—the *opposer to oppose him* fails to convey the force of the proper name Satan" (emphasis his). Other scholars, however, do not take $\acute{s}\bar{a}t\bar{a}n$ (GK 8477) as a proper noun; they translate, "and the accuser ... to accuse him." One cannot be dogmatic about this issue, as it is sometimes difficult to determine when (or whether) a particular common noun also began to function as a personal name. With such nouns the presence or absence of the definite article does not settle the question. There is a similar problem with the Hebrew word for "man" and "Adam" in the early chapters of Genesis (cf. NIV note on Ge 2:7).

2 Israel's denunciation (v.1) is followed by her defense. The defender is none other than the Lord himself. Since here the speaker is clearly the Angel of the Lord (cf. v.1 and the quotation in v.2), this verse gives further evidence of the deity of the Angel of the Lord. That God has chosen Jerusalem further proves that Joshua portrays Israel as a nation. The quotation contains a double rebuke of Satan ("the accuser"). The words are repeated for emphasis, "and with the repetition the motive which led Jehovah to reject the accuser is added. Because Jehovah has chosen Jerusalem, and maintains His choice in its integrity" (K&D, 2:251–52; cf. 1:17; 2:12).

God's sovereign choice of Jerusalem in grace shows the unreasonableness of Satan's attack (cf. Ro 8:33). The reference to the burning stick snatched from the fire is an additional indication that Israel, not Joshua, is ultimately in view. Israel was retrieved to carry out God's future purpose for her (cf. Am 4:11). The "fire" refers to the Babylonian captivity. Metaphorically, Israel was snatched as a burning stick from that fire (cf. 1Co 3:15; Jude 23). However, this event may also look back to the deliverance from Egypt (cf. Dt 4:20; 7:7–8; Jer 11:4) and forward to the rescue from the coming period of tribulation (cf. Jer 30:7; Zec 13:8–9; Rev 12:13–17).

3 The reason for Satan's accusation is now given, namely, Israel's impurity. This verse raises the problem of how a holy God can bless a filthy nation such as Israel. The answer is that he can do so only by his grace through the work of the Messiah. The Hebrew word *ṣôʾîm* ("filthy"; GK 7364) is "the strongest expression in the Hebrew language for filth of the most vile and loathsome character" (Feinberg, 58; cf. *NIDOTTE*, 3:726). Petersen, 193, adds, "'filthy' may refer to human fecal contamination and to the lack of holiness ... it entails." So Joshua may have been covered with excrement—only in the vision, of course! Such clothes represent the pollution of sin (cf. Isa 64:6). To compound the problem, Joshua (i.e., Israel), contaminated by sin, is ministering in this filthy condition before the Angel of the Lord. Webb, 38–39, 43, summarizes:

> Joshua's filthy clothes represent, not only his own sin, but the sin of the whole land (v.9); that is, the whole community. None of them is clean in God's sight, and therefore qualified to worship and serve him. Nor can they do anything about it themselves; it is a problem that only God can

solve ..."I [God] will remove the sin of this land in a single day" (3:9). Joshua and his associates are told that they are "men symbolic of things to come"; the future reality is linked to the coming of someone whom God refers to as "my servant, the Branch" (3:8) ... its full development does not come until the second part of the book, in which Zechariah speaks of a day when God will open a fountain, to cleanse his people from sin and uncleanness (13:1). We can't grasp this fully without also considering Zechariah's teaching about the Messiah.... The people of God will finally be all who have come to the cleansing fountain.... In the end there will be only two kinds of people: those who acknowledge God's kingship and those who don't. And only the former can properly be called his people.

4 The NIV, probably correctly, identifies the unnamed (see MT) speaker as the "angel" of the Lord. The removal of the filthy clothes (apparently by angels—"those who were standing before him") may connote that Joshua is thereby deprived of priestly office. If so, he is reinstated in v.5. Theologically, however, there also seems to be a picture here of the negative aspect of what God does when he saves a person. Negatively, he takes away sin. Positively, he adds or imputes to the sinner saved by grace his own divine righteousness (cf. v.5). The act of causing Joshua's sin to pass from him (cf. Heb.) represents justification, not sanctification. It is forensic forgiveness that is in view, as seen from v.9, which interprets Joshua's cleansing by applying it to the land (i.e., the people)—another evidence that more than Joshua himself is in view here.

Next, Joshua is to be clothed with rich or fine garments—God's representative clothed in God's righteousness. God's servant goes from filthy clothes to festive garments. The "rich garments" (the Hebrew word is used only here and in Isa 3:22) speak of purity, joy, and glory; but their chief significance is that they symbolize the restoration of Israel to her original calling (Ex 19:6; Isa 61:6). There is a contrast here: Joshua in filthy garments, representing Israel as a priest but defiled and unclean, versus Joshua in festive garments, representing Israel's future glory in reconsecration to the priestly office.

"I have taken away" emphasizes the agent of the forgiveness. It is God who causes sin to be removed, ultimately on the basis of the messianic Servant's substitutionary death. But here it was actually the Angel of the Lord who forgives sin, thus identifying him with deity (cf. Mk 2:7, 10), or at least as God's representative.

5 As Zechariah contemplates the scene, he cannot help but ask that the work be completed—hence his request. Joshua is then crowned with a clean turban and clothed with rich garments, symbolic of divine righteousness. Previously Joshua was filthy; now he receives a clean turban. On the front of the turban are the words "HOLY TO THE LORD" (Ex 28:36; 39:30), which provide another preview of Israel's future purging and reinstatement to her priestly function. "While the angel of the LORD stood by" is a circumstantial clause. The thought is that he is on hand, approving and directing Joshua's purging, clothing, and crowning on the basis of the fact that God's righteousness and mercy are being bestowed.

6–7 Israel's originally intended position will finally be realized. The Angel of the Lord gives a charge to Joshua (v.6), in which two conditions are stated (v.7), with three results following. The protasis is indicated by *ʾim* ("if"), the conditional particle. The apodosis or result is marked by *wᵉgam*, with *wᵉ* being translated "then." "Walk in my ways" (the first condition) refers to the personal life and attitude toward the Lord ("walk in obedience to me," TNIV). Personal or practical righteousness is in view (cf. 1Th 4:1; 1Ti 4:16). "Keep my requirements" (the second condition) speaks of the

diligent and faithful fulfillment of official, divinely appointed, priestly duties. Official faithfulness is in view.

An analysis of the three results of meeting the two conditions reveals Israel's earthly calling and her glory and ministry in the messianic age. (1) Israel will govern the house of God. This function includes deciding disputed matters in connection with the sanctuary. Furthermore, from the temple the other nations will be ruled and judged by the Messiah of Israel, the head of the nations (cf. Jer 31:7).

(2) Israel will have charge of God's courts. This role implies guarding the temple courts from pollution and idolatry. The temple will then be a house of prayer for all nations (Isa 56:7). Jeremiah 31:22 may well anticipate such a role for Israel in the future: "The LORD will create a new thing on earth—a woman will surround a man." The last line of the verse is probably a proverbial statement that Jeremiah applied to Israel's relationship to God, the woman representing Israel and the man representing God in Jeremiah's usage. The TNIV translates the last line, "the woman will return to the man" (with a footnoted alternative: "protect" for "return to"). The meaning may be that Israel will at last protect God's interests rather than God protecting Israel.

(3) Israel will have free and ready access to God in the priestly function, just as the angels ("these standing here"; cf. v.4) have access to God. This circumstance may be regarded as a renewal of Israel's covenant of priesthood or as the reinstatement of the nation to her original calling, her priestly office and function (cf. Ex 19:6; Isa 61:6). Because of the work of Christ, Christians enjoy free access to the presence of God now (cf. Heb 4:16; 10:19–22).

8 The persons involved in this prediction are Joshua, his colleagues, and the Branch, the Servant of the Lord. They foreshadow greater events in the future. Joshua and his fellow priests represent coming events and persons. They are said to be men of *môpēt* ("divine sign, wonder," "prophetic significance," or "token of a future event"; cf. Isa 8:18). They symbolize future events for Israel, as the NIV correctly interprets. They excite wonder because they are types of Israel in close association with someone to come.

This coming one is called "my servant, the Branch"—two well-known OT appellations for the Messiah. As Servant, the Messiah comes into the world to do the will of the Father. Through his work, Israel will yet be redeemed and restored as a priestly nation, which Joshua and his priestly associates typify. (For a full development of the messianic Servant motif, see H. Blocher, *Songs of the Servant* [Downers Grove, Ill.: InterVarsity Press, 1975]; F. Duane Lindsey, *The Servant Songs* [Chicago: Moody Press, 1985]; and C. R. North, *The Suffering Servant in Deutero-Isaiah* [London: Oxford Univ. Press, 1956]; see also the comments at 1:6.)

As "the Branch," the Messiah is presented in the OT in four different aspects of his character (King, Servant, Man, and God). According to some interpreters, these aspects are developed in the NT in the four Gospels: (1) in Matthew as the Branch of David, i.e., as the Davidic messianic King (Isa 11:1; Jer 23:5; 33:15); (2) in Mark as the Lord's Servant, the Branch (Isa 42:1; 49:6; 50:10; 52:13; Eze 34:23–24; Zec 3:8); (3) in Luke as the Man whose name is the Branch (Zec 6:12); and (4) in John as the Branch of the Lord (Isa 4:2). The Aramaic *Targum Jonathan* interprets the Branch as the Messiah, the "anointed one" (so Cathcart and Gordon, 192).

9 Here is a revelation of what the Messiah will accomplish in behalf of Israel. Some interpret the "stone" as Israel. It seems best and more consistent with the context however, to take "stone" as another figure of the Messiah (cf. Bullinger, 896–97). To

the Jews at his first advent, the Messiah (Christ) was the stumbling stone and rock of offense (Isa 8:13–15; cf. Ps 118:22–23; Mt 21:42; 1Pe 2:7–8). But to those who trusted in him, he was a never-failing refuge (Isa 28:16; 1Pe 2:6). Moreover, he is to be the smiting stone to the nations (Da 2:35, 45). At present he is the foundation and chief cornerstone of the church (Eph 2:19–22). And to restored Israel in the messianic era, he will be the dependable rock of the trusting heart.

While some understand the stone as a precious gem with seven facets (lit., "eyes"), typical of the Messiah's glory, it is probably better to interpret the figure in the light of biblical usage—in keeping with the above passages. The seven eyes then speak of the fullness of the Holy Spirit or of the Godhead and are symbolic of infinite intelligence and omniscience (cf. 4:10; Isa 11:2; Col 2:3, 9; Rev 5:6).

The engraving on the stone is difficult to interpret but is explained by the early church fathers as follows: "Beautiful beyond all beauty must be those glorious scars with which He allowed His whole Body to be riven, that 'throughout the whole frame His love might be engraven'" (cited by Pusey, 2:359). Thus they refer these words to the wounds of Christ. The passage possibly connotes a sealing action by God, or perhaps a beautifying activity.

Next, the Lord (the Angel of the Lord?) purges and cleanses Israel from sin. The sin of that land—not of Joshua but of the people of the land of Israel is taken away in a single day, as symbolized by the removal of the filthy clothes in v.4. Prophetically, the one day is the once-for-all deliverance potentially provided at Calvary and to be actually and finally realized in Israel's experience at the second advent of her Messiah, when there will be cleansing and forgiveness for the nation as a whole (Zec 12:10–13:1; Ro 11:26–27). Then the benefits of the Day of Atonement and the provisions of the new covenant will be fully applied to Israel. In 2:12 Israel was called "the holy land." This appellation will be even more appropriate in the messianic age, after the action spoken of here in v.9. Thus the Messiah will accomplish the marvelous transformation of Israel from shame to glory. As Webb, 88–89, puts it:

> What Zechariah has just seen done symbolically for Joshua ... will one day be done actually for the whole *land* (the entire community) — in a single day, once and for all, when the Messiah comes.... One day, God would send his servant the Branch, and then the problem of uncleanness would be dealt with finally.... The solution is shown to be ... realized only in the person and ministry of the Messiah, the perfect servant of God. Joshua had the promise of his coming, and of the *day* when he would deal with sin; we have the fulfilment of it in the cross of Jesus Christ. His cry "It is finished!", uttered with his dying breath, was the triumphant announcement that the long-awaited "day" had finally come, and that the promised cleansing had been realized. (emphasis his)

10 The result of the action of vv.8–9 is peace and security for God's people. God's purpose for Israel will be realized in the theocratic kingdom, when Israel will enjoy contentment, peace, and prosperity — similar to the peaceful and prosperous days of King Solomon (1Ki 4:25). That day is the eschatological time of Israel's cleansing and restoration as a kingdom of priests — the messianic era (see comment on 2:11 and "the day of the LORD").

This closing verse pictures Israel's future condition under divine favor and blessing when there will be no more curse. The vine and the fig tree speak not only of spiritual blessing but also of the agricultural blessing of the land when the desert will blossom like the crocus and once again be fruitful (cf. Isa 11:1–9; 35; 65:17). There can be no such prosperity and peace for Israel until the messianic kingdom has fully come on earth, no such kingdom until Israel is restored, and no true restoration of Israel until the Lord returns to the earth with his saints (cf. Da 7:13–14, 27; Mic 4:1–4). Baron's summary (122) is illuminating:

> And thus, in the last verse of this chapter, a picture is given of a day ... when, on account of sin pardoned, free access to God's throne granted, and the Deliverer having come anointed with the plentitude of the Spirit and sealed by God the Father, each true Israelite would invite his friends as joyful guests to partake of festal cheer under his own vine and fig-tree. The days of peace once more are seen. The glorious era of the earthly Solomon has indeed returned in greater splendour under the reign of the Prince of Peace. "Paradise lost" has become "Paradise regained."

In this vision of the restoration of Israel as a kingdom of priests, Exodus 19:6 finds its fullest expression. The accomplishments of the Messiah in Israel's behalf are summarized in Romans 11:26–27, providing a fitting conclusion to this chapter:

> And so all Israel will be saved, as it is written:
>
> "The deliverer will come from Zion;
>   he will turn godlessness away from Jacob.
> And this is my covenant with them
>   when I take away their sins."

NOTES

1 "And Satan standing at his right side" is a circumstantial clause introduced by the simple *waw*. The definite article in הַשָּׂטָן (*haśśāṭān*, "Satan" or "the accuser") is used to elevate to distinctive prominence a particular individual of the class (so Davidson, par. 21c). לְ (*lᵉ*, "to") before the infinitive construct שִׂטְנוֹ (*śiṭnô*, "accuse him") expresses purpose (cf. *IBHS*, 606–7).

2 מֻצָּל (*muṣṣāl*, "snatched") is a Hophal participle from the root *nṣl*, here used with adjectival significance.

3 The verb הָיָה (*hāyâ*, "was") with the participle לָבֻשׁ (*lābuš*, "dressed") is a periphrastic construction, stressing habitual condition (cf. Davidson, par. 100, rem. 2). The nominal clause at the end of the verse describes a state contemporaneous with the preceding verb; the NIV therefore translates the conjunction "as" (cf. GKC, par. 141e).

4 וְהִלְבֵּשׁ (*wᵉhalbēš*, "and I will put [or 'clothe']") is a Hiphil infinitive absolute, taking the place and having the force of a finite verb (cf. GKC, par. 113z; Davidson, par. 88a, rem. 1). This analysis, which continues the first person of the preceding verb, is to be preferred over the LXX's reading ("and clothe him"), which changes the person of both the subject and the object.

5 The context dictates that יָשִׂימוּ (*yāśîmû*, "Let them put") be taken as a jussive (cf. GKC, par. 109a and n. 109k). The word for "turban" is צָנִיף (*ṣānîp*, from a verb meaning "to wind around").

8 הַכֹּהֵן הַגָּדוֹל (*hakkōhēn haggādôl*, "high priest") furnishes a good illustration of the vocative use of the definite article (GKC, par. 126e [e]; Davidson, pars. 21–22).

9 The correct etymology of מוּשׁ (*mûš*), the root behind the form rendered "and I will remove," is probably the Akkadian *mêšu*, "to forgive, disregard sins" (M. Civil et al., eds., *The Assyrian Dictionary*, 10/2 [Chicago: Oriental Institute, 1956–]: 41–42).

E. The Fifth Vision: The Gold Lampstand and the Two Olive Trees (4:1–14)

OVERVIEW

The main purposes of this vision are: (1) to encourage the two leaders, Joshua and Zerubbabel, in the work of rebuilding the temple by reminding them of their divine resources, and (2) to vindicate them in the eyes of the community (so Baldwin, 119). In this chapter the lampstand probably represents the idea of testimony (light bearing; cf. Mt 5:16; Rev 1:20; 2:5). Zerubbabel and Joshua (the two olive branches, vv.12–14) are testifying to God's power in completing the temple. The whole nation of Israel is also intended to serve as God's witness to the other nations of the world. In the coming tribulation period, two special witnesses for God will again appear on the scene (Rev 11:3–12). All effective testifying must be done in the power of God's Spirit (symbolized by the oil, v.12). By his Spirit, God provides the enablement to do his work—then and now (v.6).

¹Then the angel who talked with me returned and wakened me, as a man is wakened from his sleep. ²He asked me, "What do you see?"

I answered, "I see a solid gold lampstand with a bowl at the top and seven lights on it, with seven channels to the lights. ³Also there are two olive trees by it, one on the right of the bowl and the other on its left."

⁴I asked the angel who talked with me, "What are these, my lord?"

⁵He answered, "Do you not know what these are?"

"No, my lord," I replied.

⁶So he said to me, "This is the word of the LORD to Zerubbabel:'Not by might nor by power, but by my Spirit,' says the LORD Almighty.

⁷"What are you, O mighty mountain? Before Zerubbabel you will become level ground. Then he will bring out the capstone to shouts of 'God bless it! God bless it!'"

⁸Then the word of the LORD came to me: ⁹"The hands of Zerubbabel have laid the foundation of this temple; his hands will also complete it. Then you will know that the LORD Almighty has sent me to you.

¹⁰"Who despises the day of small things? Men will rejoice when they see the plumb line in the hand of Zerubbabel.

"(These seven are the eyes of the LORD, which range throughout the earth.)"

¹¹Then I asked the angel, "What are these two olive trees on the right and the left of the lampstand?"

¹²Again I asked him, "What are these two olive branches beside the two gold pipes that pour out golden oil?"

¹³He replied, "Do you not know what these are?"

"No, my lord," I said.

¹⁴So he said, "These are the two who are anointed to serve the Lord of all the earth."

COMMENTARY

1 In order to prepare Zechariah to receive the fifth vision, the interpreting angel awakened him from his ecstatic sleep of wonder and astonishment over the previous vision. The wakening obviously took place on the same night, thus further corroborating the view that Zechariah received all the visions during one night.

2 If the lampstand of Zechariah's vision corresponds to those known from archaeology, probably the most accurate reconstruction is that of K. Galling. It is described by Baldwin, 119–20: "Lamp pedestals excavated from Palestine ... were cylindrical in shape, hollow, and looked rather like a tree trunk.... Zechariah's lampstand (*menôrâ*) was probably just a cylindrical column, tapering slightly

towards the top, on which was *a bowl....* Zechariah's large bowl ... had *seven lamps on it, with seven lips on each of the lamps.* The picture is of seven small bowls, each with a place for seven wicks, arranged round the rim of the main bowl" (emphasis hers; see also the description and sketch in Clark and Hatton, 135). A drawing of Galling's reconstruction is reproduced in *IDB*, 3:66, and in Robert C. North's article ("Zechariah's Seven-Spout Lampstand," *Bib* 51 [1970]: 189). North differs slightly from Galling and believes that each of the seven lamps has only one light instead of seven (see North, 201, for his reconstruction). However, he essentially follows Galling in the lampstand's basic design and construction.

More important than how the lampstand looks is what it signifies, as has already been suggested in the Overview. The seven "channels" (or, more likely, "lips" or "spouts" for wicks; see the diagrams of Petersen, 220, 222) to each of the seven lamps (forty-nine spouts in all) would seem to stress the abundant supply of oil, which in turn symbolizes the fullness of God's power through his Spirit (seven being the number of fullness or completeness; cf. v.6).

3 Possibly the two olive trees stand for the priestly and royal offices in Israel. Undoubtedly the two olive branches (vv.12, 14) represent Joshua-Israel (ch. 3) and Zerubbabel (ch. 4; cf. v.14). According to v.12, each of the two olive trees has an olive branch beside a golden pipe that pours out golden oil. The olive oil is conducted directly from the trees to the bowl of oil at the top of the lampstand—without any human agency ("might" or "power"; v.6). Similarly, Zerubbabel and Joshua are to bear continual testimony for God's glory and are to do God's work—e.g., on the temple and in the lives of the people—in the power of his Spirit (v.6). This combination of the priestly and royal lines and functions is apparently intended to point ultimately to the messianic King-Priest and his offices and functions (cf. 6:13).

4–6 The purpose of the vision is to encourage Zerubbabel to complete the rebuilding of the temple and to assure him of his enablement by God's Spirit for the work. The answer to Zechariah's inquiry (v.4) is postponed (see vv.11–14) in order to emphasize the final verse of the chapter and, in the meantime, to focus attention on only one of the two olive branches, namely, Zerubbabel (v.6) and his special ministry. "These" (v.4) refers to the two olive trees of v.3, as v.11 makes clear.

Verse 6 interprets the symbolism of the oil ("by my Spirit"). Just as there is a constant and sufficient supply of oil without human agency, so Zerubbabel's

work on the temple and in the lives of the people is to be completed not by human might or power but by divine power—constant and sufficient. The work is dependent on God; he will provide the oil, the strength of his Spirit. Such enablement is sorely needed because of the opposition and apathy hindering the rebuilding (Hag 2:1–9). "Looked at from a human point of view the manpower available was inadequate for the task.... Only if His Spirit governs every detail can service be glorifying to Him" (Baldwin, 121). Verses 6–10 are perhaps best regarded as an oracle within this vision.

7 Faith in the power of God's Spirit can overcome mountainous obstacles—indeed, it can reduce them to "level ground." In a bold apostrophe ("you"; cf. Bullinger, 901–5), a defiant challenge is laid down against whatever would hinder the rebuilding of the temple. The figurative mountain may include opposition (Ezr 4:1–5, 24) and the people's unwillingness to persevere (Hag 1:14; 2:1–9; for a similar use of the word "mountain" see Isa 40:4; 41:15; 49:11; Mt 17:20; 21:21; Mk 11:23; 1Co 13:2). That the project will ultimately succeed is indicated by the assurance that Zerubbabel will experience the joy of helping put the capstone in place, thus marking the completion of the restoration temple. The shouts at the end of the verse can be understood as either an ejaculatory description of the finished structure ("How perfectly beautiful it is!"), or as a prayerful desire for God's gracious blessing to rest on it (NIV). The latter seems more likely in this context.

8–9 Verse 8 ("the word of the LORD came to me") appears to support the notion of taking this section as an oracle within the vision. In contrast to ch. 3, which focused on Joshua, v.9 again focuses on Zerubbabel. The laying of the temple's foundation refers back to what took place in 537–536 BC (Ezr 3:8–11; 5:16). The year is now 519, three years before the fulfillment of the prediction that

Zerubbabel will complete the superstructure (Ezr 6:14–18). So then, a delay in the execution of God's will need not end in ultimate defeat. Finally, the completely restored temple (in 516 BC) will prove the divine commission of the speaker.

On the difficulty of identifying the speaker in this formulaic expression, see the comment at 2:11. Here, as there, "me" apparently refers to the messianic Servant-Messenger (or the Angel of the Lord). Feinberg, 76–77, maintains that just as ch. 3 had an immediate application to Joshua and then went on to speak of the messianic Branch and Stone, so this chapter has an immediate reference to Zerubbabel and then beyond him to the Messiah (cf. 6:12–13).

10 The question here obviously implies that some of the people have a negative attitude toward the temple project and those involved in it. In the context "the day of small things" refers to the "day" of beginning the work on the temple and now continuing it. Some, forgetting that little is much when God is involved, think the project is insignificant (Ezr 3:12; Hag 2:3). But God is definitely in this rebuilding program; by his Spirit (v.6) he is enabling Zerubbabel to finish the work. Perhaps the "despisers," having forgotten that God's work is usually accomplished through a small, believing, righteous remnant, are also discouraged because the group of workers is relatively small. Yet their persevering faith and work will be rewarded when they joyfully see the "plumb line" (but see below) in the hand of Zerubbabel to complete the task.

The Hebrew for "plumb line" is difficult. The words may also be rendered "separated [i.e., chosen] stone," referring to the capstone of v.7. The parenthesis at the end of the verse is also difficult. The NIV understands this verse as a reminder to Zerubbabel and the people that God is omniscient ("seven eyes"). As such, he knows, sees, and governs all. Since he thus oversees the entire earth, he is in control of Israel's situation. So understood, "eyes" is an anthropomorphism for God's all-knowing ("seven") observation (cf. Bullinger, 875), and "range" is a personification of the eyes. (See also the comment on "seven eyes" at 3:9.) However, the Hebrew syntax reflected in the TNIV is probably to be preferred for this verse: "Who dares despise the day of small things, since the seven eyes of the LORD that range throughout the earth will rejoice when they see the chosen capstone in the hand of Zerubbabel?"

11–14 The question and response of vv.4–5 in the vision are now resumed after the intervening oracle of vv.6–10. In v.12, Zechariah repeats his question from v.11 in order to be more specific. He desires an explanation of what he has seen in vv.2–3. In v.12 the Hebrew for "golden oil" is literally "gold," but the NIV correctly represents the sense (the oil is being described by its color).

The answer to the prophet's inquiry comes in v.14, where the two olive branches are implicitly identified as Zerubbabel, a member of the line of David, and Joshua the high priest. In the light of the context (chs. 3–4), they must be "the two who are anointed to serve the Lord." In the Hebrew text they are designated as "sons of oil," but the NIV has accurately captured the sense ("anointed" as God's appointed leaders). Both priest and ruler have been anointed for service to the Lord and the covenantal community.

The oil takes us back again to v.6 ("by my Spirit"). It has already been suggested in the comment at v.3 that this combination of ruler and priest is evidently intended to point ultimately to the messianic King-Priest (cf. 6:13; Ps 110; Heb 7). In keeping with one of the key ideas of the chapter (i.e., bearing testimony), only the messianic King-Priest may be acknowledged as the perfectly "faithful and true witness" (Rev 3:14). Finally, since God is declared to be "the Lord of all the earth," he is master of all the circumstances in which Zerubbabel and the people find themselves.

NOTES

....

2 The Qere reading, וָאֹמַר (*wāʾōmar*, "I answered"), is to be preferred over the Kethiv, which has the third person. The Qere is supported by many Hebrew MSS and the ancient versions. The repetition in the construction שִׁבְעָה וְשִׁבְעָה (*šibʿâ wᵉšibʿâ*, lit., "seven and seven") is best understood distributively (cf. GKC, par. 134q; Davidson, par. 38, rem. 4). Thus the sense is "with seven channels [or 'spouts'] to *each* of the lights." The same syntactical idiom occurs in 2 Samuel 21:20 and 1 Chronicles 20:6.

6 The quotation at the end of the verse is unusually emphatic, with no subject or predicate.

7 Either אַתָּה הַר־הַגָּדוֹל (*ʾattâ har-haggādôl*, "you, O mighty mountain") is an instance in which the adjective is definite and the noun is anarthrous (Davidson, par. 32, rem. 2), or the first part of the expression is to be read אַתָּ הָהָר (*ʾattā hāhār*; so GKC, par. 126x). The repetition of חֵן (*ḥēn*) in חֵן חֵן לָהּ (*ḥēn ḥēn lāh*, "God bless it! God bless it!") is for emphasis: "May *all* [divine] favor rest on it!"

9 Baldwin, 52–53, maintains that the temple's foundation was not destroyed in 586 BC (2Ki 25:9); therefore, it would not have been necessary to lay the foundation again in 537. If she is correct, the first part of v.9 should be translated, "The hands of Zerubbabel have begun to rebuild [or restore] this temple." Such a meaning for יָסַד (*yāsad*) seems attested in 2 Chronicles 24:27. (Baldwin argues for this meaning in order to remove certain apparent contradictions elsewhere.) וְיָדַעְתָּ (*wᵉyādaʿtā*, "then you will know") is a *waw* consecutive perfect, as the accent on the ultima shows. Here it also introduces a temporal and/or logical consequence (cf. GKC, par 112p).

10 בַּז (*baz*, "despises") is probably a characteristic perfect, best rendered in English by the present tense. On the form itself see GKC, par. 72dd.

14 Based on Ugaritic etymological cognates, the meaning "lord, sovereign" for אָדוֹן (*ʾādôn*; GK 123) is apparently a semantic development from an original meaning of "father." There is also the form אֲדֹנָי (*ᵃdōnāy*), regarded by many as the plural of *ʾādôn* with the suffix "my"; hence "my lord" (this is the word the Masoretes read in place of the ineffable, sacred Tetragrammaton, *yhwh* [Yahweh]). But the most probable explanation of *ᵃdōnāy* is that it contains a nominal afformative, which strengthens the meaning of the simple form *ʾādôn*, so that the meaning "Lord" (referring to God) results. For the whole discussion see *TDOT*, 1:59–72; also Barker, "The Value of Ugaritic," 124–25.

F. The Sixth Vision: The Flying Scroll (5:1–4)

¹I looked again — and there before me was a flying scroll!

²He asked me, "What do you see?"

I answered, "I see a flying scroll, thirty feet long and fifteen feet wide."

³And he said to me, "This is the curse that is going out over the whole land; for according to what it says on one side, every thief will be banished, and according to what it says on the other, everyone who swears falsely will be banished. ⁴The Lᴏʀᴅ Almighty declares, 'I will send it out, and it will enter the house of the thief and the house of him who swears falsely by my name. It will remain in his house and destroy it, both its timbers and its stones.'"

COMMENTARY

1–2 The sixth and seventh visions are in harmony with one of Zechariah's concerns, namely, the promotion of spiritual renewal. In this vision, lawbreakers are condemned by the law they have broken; in the next one, the land is purged of wickedness. There is a movement here from promise (ch. 4) to threat. In v.1 the scroll is not rolled up but flying (i.e., unrolled for all to read). Significantly, in the postexilic (restoration) period there was a renewed interest in the study and teaching of God's law (Torah).

Not only is the scroll open for all to read, but it is also large for all to see (v.2). Its message of judgment is not concealed from anyone. Such a bold, clear pronouncement of punishment for sin should spur the people to repentance and righteousness. The dimensions of the scroll are calculated on the basis of a cubit's equaling eighteen inches (cf. NIV note and the Table of Weights and Measures at the end of an NIV Bible). "He" (v.2) refers to the interpreting angel (v.5; 4:11).

3 The message and meaning of the scroll are revealed. Those who persist in breaking the covenant (Ex 20) will experience the curse (punishment) for disobedience and unfaithfulness (Dt 27:26). Since the scroll is apparently inscribed on both sides, like the two tablets of the Law (Ex 32:15), one side must contain the curse against those who violate the third commandment of the law, while the other side contains the curse against those who break the eighth commandment. The thief has broken the eighth commandment, and whoever has sworn falsely has violated the third commandment; it becomes clear from v.4 that the third commandment is in view rather than the ninth.

We have here a form of synecdoche in which the species is put for the genus (cf. Bullinger, 625–29). In other words, these two representa-tive sins—perhaps perjury and theft were the most common ones at this time—stand for all kinds of sin. The point is that Israel is guilty of breaking the law in its entirety. As Petersen, 252, puts it, "These two cases are significant because they represent the two basic forms of infraction included in the Decalogue, crimes against Yahweh and crimes against humanity."

According to James 2:10, we break the whole law if we stumble "at just one point." Such lawbreakers are to be "banished." The precise meaning of the Hebrew verb so translated is difficult. Does it mean "cut off" (executed) or "banished"? Since both are lexically possible, one cannot answer dogmatically. Either way, it amounts to the more original etymological notion of "cleansing" or "purging" the land from chronic covenant breakers. With exegetical insight Baldwin, 127, observes, "*every one who steals* is a pithy way of saying 'every one who wrongs his neighbour,' and *every one who swears falsely* (invoking the divine name) sums up blatant disregard for God's holiness" (emphasis hers); for God has always required adherence not only to the letter of the law, but also to the spirit of the law (cf. Barker, "False Dichotomies," 5–6).

4 The pronoun "it" refers to the curse (v.3). There can be no hiding, no escape, from the judgment of that curse. God's word, whether promise or threat (as here), is efficacious (cf. Isa 55:10–11; see also comments on Zec 1:1, 6). "It" will enter and destroy the homes of the guilty. Even the privacy of their homes will afford them no refuge from divine judgment (cf. Nu 32:23). The word "thief" recalls Exodus 20:15, and "him who swears falsely by my name" is a clear echo of 20:7—though both commandments apply more broadly than to the particular infractions singled out here. On "it will remain," Pusey, 2:366, comments that the phrase is "lit., 'lodge for the night,' until it has accomplished that for which it was sent, its utter destruction." To judge from the materials used in the houses (cf. Hag 1:3–9), it is primarily the wealthy and those in power who are guilty of committing these sins.

NOTES

1 וְאָשׁוּב (wā'āšûb, "again") is explained in GKC, par. 120d: "The principal idea is introduced only by the second verb, while the first ... contains the definition of the manner of the action, e.g. Genesis 26:18 וַיָּשָׁב וַיַּחְפֹּר [wayyāšob wayyaḥpōr] and he returned and digged, i.e., he digged again" (emphasis theirs).

2 On בָּאַמָּה (bā'ammâ, lit., "by the cubit") see GKC, par. 134n.

3 מִזֶּה ... מִזֶּה (mizzeh ... mizzeh) means "on one side ... on the other side" (BDB, 262). The Niphal נִקָּה (niqqâ, "will be banished") is a prophetic perfect (cf. IBHS, 490; GKC, par. 106n).

4 הוֹצֵאתִיהָ (hôṣē'tîhā, "I will send it out") is also a prophetic perfect. וּבָאָה (ûbā'â, "and it will enter") is a waw consecutive perfect but with the same force as the preceding prophetic perfect, on which it depends for its syntactical function. The same applies to וְלָנֶה (welāneh, "it will remain"); on the slightly anomalous form, cf. GKC, par. 73d. וְכִלַּתּוּ (wekillattû, "and it will destroy it") stands for וְכִלְּתְהוּ (wekallithû; GKC, par. 75mm).

G. The Seventh Vision: The Woman in a Basket (5:5–11)

⁵Then the angel who was speaking to me came forward and said to me, "Look up and see what this is that is appearing."

⁶I asked, "What is it?"

He replied, "It is a measuring basket." And he added, "This is the iniquity of the people throughout the land."

⁷Then the cover of lead was raised, and there in the basket sat a woman! ⁸He said, "This is wickedness," and he pushed her back into the basket and pushed the lead cover down over its mouth.

⁹Then I looked up—and there before me were two women, with the wind in their wings! They had wings like those of a stork, and they lifted up the basket between heaven and earth.

¹⁰"Where are they taking the basket?" I asked the angel who was speaking to me.

¹¹He replied, "To the country of Babylonia to build a house for it. When it is ready, the basket will be set there in its place."

COMMENTARY

5–6 In 2:12 Israel was called "the holy land." In 3:9 a future day was anticipated when the sin of that land will be taken away. The sixth vision has just dealt with the purging of flagrant, persistent sinners from the land. Now, in the seventh vision, this motif continues to be developed as the removal of wickedness is vividly depicted. Not only sinners but also the whole sinful system must be removed—apparently to the place of its origin (Babylon).

What Zechariah sees this time is a measuring basket (v.6; lit., "an ephah"); here the measure stands for the container. An ephah is less than a bushel, so a normal ephah measuring basket (or barrel) would not be large enough to hold a person. This one is undoubtedly enlarged—like the flying scroll (v.2)—for the purpose of the vision. The end of v.6 indicates that the basket represents the people's iniquity or crookedness, which pervades the land.

7–8 The import of the measuring basket is now fully revealed: When the cover of lead is lifted from the basket, wickedness, personified by a woman (cf. Rev 17:3–5), is exposed. Like the basket itself (v.6), the woman in it represents the sin of the people in Judah, whose measure or cup of evil is full (cf. Ge 15:16). The whole evil system is to be destroyed.

In v.8 the Hebrew word for "wickedness" is feminine. This may explain why the wickedness of the people is personified as a woman. "Wickedness"—a general word denoting moral, religious, and civil evil—is frequently used as an antonym of "righteousness" (e.g., Pr 13:6; Eze 33:12). The woman (i.e., wickedness) "attempts to escape from captivity, but the angel with superior strength is able to confine her to the ephah, though the verbs indicate a struggle involved. The power of evil was to be taken seriously" (Baldwin, 129). For an analogous event see 2 Thessalonians 2:6–8.

9 The fate of the woman (wickedness) is portrayed: She is to be removed from the land. Although some regard the two women as agents of evil (partly because the stork is an unclean bird; see Lev 11:19), it seems preferable to regard them as divinely chosen agents. They, along with the wind

(also an instrument of God; see Ps 104:3–4), will thus demonstrate that the removal is the work of God alone. The simile "wings like those of a stork" is evidently intended to show that the winged women, carried along by the wind, are capable of supporting the woman in the basket over a great distance.

10–11 The destination of the women bearing the sin away is "Babylonia" (*šinʿār*, "Shinar"). As I have pointed out elsewhere, Shinar "in Genesis 10:10 apparently includes the area of both Sumer and Akkad" (*WBE*, 2:1631). It therefore roughly corresponds to ancient Babylonia (cf. also Ge 11:2; 14:1, 9). Ellis, 1034, notes: "Thus where Judah had been exiled was a fitting place for wickedness to be worshipped, but not in the land where God had placed *his* name. The idolatry of Babylon must once and for all be separated from the worship of the God of Israel" (emphasis his). Baldwin, 130, agreeing with Frey, suggests that if "the removal of Wickedness to Babylon is in preparation for the final onslaught between good and evil, the vision leaves no doubt about the outcome. God has evil in His power."

The evil will be put in a "house," perhaps referring to a temple or ziggurat. "Its place" may have in view a base or pedestal on which the basket and its contents are set up as an idol, "as Dagon or Ashtaroth, or Baal had their houses or temples, a great idol temple, in which the god of this world should be worshiped" (Pusey, 2:369). Feinberg, 93, concludes: "The two visions of our chapter thus bring before us God's twofold method of dealing with sin in His people. He pours out His wrath upon the transgressors who are impenitent, and then sees to the utter removal and banishment of sin from the land, that it may in truth be the holy land." Second Corinthians 7:1 provides an appropriate application for us: "Since we have these promises, dear friends, let us purify ourselves from everything that contaminates body and spirit, perfecting holiness out of reverence for God." (For possible eschatological connections or overtones of the "Babylon" motif, see Rev 17–18.)

NOTES

6 עֵינָם (ʿênām) presents a text-critical problem. As it stands, it means "their eye" (i.e., their appearance), which does not yield a good sense (cf. the parallel in v.8, where the woman in the basket is interpreted as wickedness personified). The NIV, probably correctly, follows one Hebrew MS, the LXX, and the Syriac in reading עֲוֹנָם (ʿᵃwōnām, "their iniquity"; cf. the use of this word in 3:4, 9). The pronominal suffix refers to the people, perhaps with special reference to the godless rich. The only significant variation between the two readings is the *waw* instead of the *yod*. Even here it should be borne in mind that in many ancient Hebrew MSS the only perceptible difference between the two letters is the length of the downward stroke. A long *yod* and a short *waw* are virtually indistinguishable. To support further the reading, "their iniquity [or 'perversity']," Baldwin, 128, adds:"The ephah, named by Amos in his invective on short measure given by the merchants (Am. 8:5), symbolized injustice *in all the land*. The life of the community was vitiated by iniquity that infected it in every part (cf. Hag. 2:14). The meanness that prompted the making of false measures was a symptom of an underlying perversity that was at the root of perverse actions and relationships" (emphasis hers).

9 Syntactically וְרוּחַ בְּכַנְפֵיהֶם (wᵉrûaḥ bᵉkanᵉpêhem, "with the wind in their wings") is a circumstantial clause (cf. GKC, pars. 156a, c).

10 On הֵמָּה (hēmmâ, "they") instead of the expected feminine הֵנָּה (hēnnâ), see GKC, par. 32n.

11 לָה (lāh, "for it") is sometimes written with *raphe* instead of *mappiq* (cf. GKC, pars. 23k, 103g). The feminine suffix refers to the measuring basket (or ephah). The subject of וְהוּכַן (wᵉhûkan, "when it is ready") is "house," and the subject of וְהֻנִּיחָה (wᵉhunnîḥâ, "it will be set") is "basket" (or "ephah"); this determination can be made by correlating the genders of the nouns with those of the verbal forms. For the latter verb the LXX supports an active form, wᵉhinnîḥuhā ("they will set it"), but there is no sound reason to repoint the MT.

H. The Eighth Vision: The Four Chariots (6:1–8)

¹I looked up again — and there before me were four chariots coming out from between two mountains — mountains of bronze! ²The first chariot had red horses, the second black, ³the third white, and the fourth dappled — all of them powerful. ⁴I asked the angel who was speaking to me, "What are these, my lord?"

⁵The angel answered me, "These are the four spirits of heaven, going out from standing in the presence of the Lord of the whole world. ⁶The one with the black horses is going toward the north country, the one with the white horses toward the west, and the one with the dappled horses toward the south."

> ⁷When the powerful horses went out, they were straining to go throughout the earth. And he said, "Go throughout the earth!" So they went throughout the earth.
> ⁸Then he called to me, "Look, those going toward the north country have given my Spirit rest in the land of the north."

COMMENTARY

1 This last vision obviously corresponds to the first one, though there are differences in details, such as in the order and colors of the horses. (Regarding the latter problem, see the extended note in Baldwin, 138–40.) In the words of Merrill, 181, "If ever a case could be made for matching complementary visions throughout the unfolding of the visions structure in Zechariah, it can be made here. This last of the eight shares so much in common with the first that the two … must be viewed as book ends enveloping the whole series."

As in the first vision, the Lord is again depicted as the one who controls the events of history. He will conquer the nations that oppress Israel. Since his war chariots claim victory in the north (v.8), total victory is certain. The chariots of v.1 serve basically the same symbolic function—they are vehicles of God's judgment on the nations. Such judgment is probably also the symbolic significance of the "bronze" mountains (cf. the bronze snake [Nu 21:9] and the bronze altar [Ex 27:2]). The two mountains most naturally refer to Mount Zion and the Mount of Olives (so K&D, Pusey, et al.), with the Kidron Valley between them. As I have pointed out elsewhere (*ZPEB*, 2:84):

> In Joel 3:14 this expression ["valley of decision"] refers to the valley of Jehoshaphat (Joel 3:2, 12). The latter in turn seems to be a symbolical name of a valley near Jerusalem which is to be the place of God's ultimate judgment on the nations gathered to attack Jerusalem. Significantly, Jehoshaphat had witnessed one of the Lord's historical victories over the nations (2 Chron 20). The valley has been traditionally identified with the Kidron, but the location remains a problem. Perhaps the solution is contained in Zechariah 14:4, which indicates that when the Lord returns to the Mount of Olives a great valley will be opened. Since Jehoshaphat's name means "The Lord judges," possibly this newly opened valley is so named because of the Lord's judgment there.

On the other hand, Merrill, 183, connects the two mountains with the creation of two mountains through the splitting of the Mount of Olives in 14:4 (see comments there).

2–3 The chariots seem to represent angelic spirits (cf. v.5), while the variegated horses evidently signify divine judgments on the earth (cf. v.8). Unger, 102–3, comparing Revelation 6:1–8, suggests that the red horses symbolize war and bloodshed; the black horses, famine and death; the white horses, victory and triumph; and the dappled horses, death by plagues and other judgments. White horses (cf. also 1:8) are clearly associated with vengeance and triumph in Revelation 19:11, 14. The fact that there are four chariots may indicate that the angelic spirits are ready to embark on universal judgments (cf. expressions such as "the four winds of heaven" [2:6; Jer 49:36; Eze 37:9], "the four quarters of the heavens" [Jer 49:36], and "the four corners of the earth" [Rev 7:1]).

4–6 "These" (v.4) refers to the chariots, with the horses harnessed to them. In v.5 the four chariots are identified as four spirits (i.e., angelic beings; cf. comment at 1:10). Although the same Hebrew word can also mean "winds" (cf. NIV note), angelic "spirits" as agents of divine judgment seems more appropriate, particularly since they stand before God here (but see Feinberg, 98, who argues for "winds"). For "the Lord of the whole world," see comment at 4:14.

In v.6 the chariot with the black horses hitched to it goes toward the north, primarily toward Babylonia, but also the direction from which most of Israel's formidable enemies invade her land. As the MT stands (cf. Notes and NIV note), the chariot with the black horses is followed northward by the one with the white horses. However, with a slight change in the Hebrew text (cf. Notes), the latter chariot goes toward the west (as in the NIV), i.e., toward the islands and coastlands of the Mediterranean area. The south (at the end of v.6) is principally Egypt but also the other main direction (in addition to the north) from which Israel's foes invade her country. As the text now stands, nothing is said of the east, possibly because the Arabian Desert lay in that direction. Similarly, nothing is said of the chariot with the red horses, but the latter are undoubtedly included among "the powerful horses" of v.7.

7–8 As in v.3, "powerful" (v.7) describes all the horses. All are eager to take the chariots (angelic spirits) on the mission of bringing divine judgment on the peoples of the earth. But the horses cannot begin until authorized to do so. "From first to last (cf. 1:10) the affairs of the nations are under God's direction, not man's" (Baldwin, 132). "Those going toward the north country" (v.8) designates either the black horses and their chariots or both the black horses and the white horses (see comment on v.6).

The interpretation of the last part of v.8 depends on how "my Spirit" is to be understood. Under any view the pronoun "my" indicates that the speaker is ultimately deity (i.e., God or the messianic Servant-Messenger, i.e., the Angel of the Lord). If the NIV ("Spirit") is correct, the meaning is that "recent events had been the work of God's Spirit, but now that work is finished, and the messengers to the north have set God's *Spirit at rest*. No more remains to be done" (Baldwin, 132, emphasis hers). If, however, the NIV note ("spirit") is correct, the meaning is that the angelic beings dispatched to the north have triumphed and thus have pacified or appeased God's spirit (i.e., his anger). This interpretation receives some support from 1:15, where God's displeasure was aroused against oppressive nations. Either way, since conquest is announced in the north, victory is assured over all enemies.

NOTES

1 On the syntactical function of וָאָשֻׁב (wāʾāšub, "again"), see the note at 5:1. נְחֹשֶׁת (nᵉḥōšet) means "bronze" (sometimes "copper"), not "brass" (an alloy unknown in the biblical period).

3 אֲמֻצִּים (ʾᵃmuṣṣîm, "powerful") probably describes all the horses (as in the NIV; cf. v.7 for support), not just the dappled ones (as in the KJV and NASB).

6 The NIV fills in the ellipsis at the beginning of this verse. "The one [i.e., 'the chariot'] with." As the text in the middle of the verse stands (MT), אַחֲרֵיהֶם (ʾaḥᵃrêhem, "after them," NIV note) means that the white horses followed the black ones to the north. A slight emendation, however, yields אַחֲרֵי הַיָּם (ʾaḥᵃrê hayyām, "after [or 'behind'] the sea," i.e., "toward the west," NIV). Another factor to consider is that the

MT itself may possibly mean "toward the west." After all, מֵאָחוֹר (mēʾāḥôr) means "from the west" in Isaiah 9:12[11], and אַחֲרֹנִים (ʾaḥărōnîm) means "men of the west" in Job 18:20. Perhaps, then, such a nuance should be allowed for ʾaḥărêhem; thus "after [or 'behind'] them" = "their west." With the preposition אֶל (ʾel, "toward") added, the complete phrase would mean "toward the west."

7 For the significance of the Hithpael in לְהִתְהַלֵּךְ (lᵉhithallēk, "to go"), see note at 1:10. The speaker in וַיֹּאמֶר (wayyōʾmer, "and he said") is either the interpreting angel or the Lord himself. Grammatically, the feminine gender of וַתִּתְהַלַּכְנָה (wattithallaknâ, "so they went") agrees with "chariots" instead of "horses."

III. THE SYMBOLIC CROWNING OF JOSHUA THE HIGH PRIEST (6:9–15)

---

⁹The word of the LORD came to me: ¹⁰"Take silver and gold from the exiles Heldai, Tobijah and Jedaiah, who have arrived from Babylon. Go the same day to the house of Josiah son of Zephaniah. ¹¹Take the silver and gold and make a crown, and set it on the head of the high priest, Joshua son of Jehozadak. ¹²Tell him this is what the LORD Almighty says: 'Here is the man whose name is the Branch, and he will branch out from his place and build the temple of the LORD. ¹³It is he who will build the temple of the LORD, and he will be clothed with majesty and will sit and rule on his throne. And he will be a priest on his throne. And there will be harmony between the two.' ¹⁴The crown will be given to Heldai, Tobijah, Jedaiah and Hen son of Zephaniah as a memorial in the temple of the LORD. ¹⁵Those who are far away will come and help to build the temple of the LORD, and you will know that the LORD Almighty has sent me to you. This will happen if you diligently obey the LORD your God."

COMMENTARY

9–10 The position of this actual ceremony after the eight visions is significant. The fourth and fifth visions, at the center of the series, were concerned with the high priest and the civil governor in the Davidic line. Zechariah here links the message of those two visions to the messianic King-Priest. In the fourth vision (ch. 3), Joshua was priest; here (6:13) the Branch is to officiate as priest. In the fifth vision (ch. 4), Zerubbabel was the governing civil official; here (6:13) the Branch is to rule the government. In 4:9 Zerubbabel was to complete the rebuilding of the temple; here (6:12) the Branch will build the temple. In 4:14 Zerubbabel and Joshua represented two separate offices; here the Branch is to hold both offices (6:13). Thus restored Israel is seen in the future under the glorious reign of the messianic King-Priest. The passage is typical-prophetical. Joshua serves as a type of the Messiah, but at certain points the language transcends the experience of the type and becomes more directly prophetic of the antitype.

Unger, 109–10, stresses the importance of the context:

Immediately following the overthrow of Gentile world power by the earth judgments symbolized by the horsed chariots (Zech. 6:1–8) occurs the manifestation of Christ in His kingdom glory (Zech. 6:9–15) typified by the crowning of Joshua the high priest. This is the usual prophetic order: first, the judgments of the day of the Lord; then full kingdom blessing (Ps. 2:5, cf. Ps. 2:6; Isa. 3:24–26, cf. 4:2–6; 10:33, 34, cf. 11:1–10; Rev. 19:19–21, cf. 20:4–6).

The eight night visions have ended, but the coronation of Joshua is closely connected with these revelations which extend in scope from Zechariah's day to the full establishment of Israel in blessing. The crowning of King-Priest Messiah is thus set forth symbolically by the coronation of Joshua, which is not a vision, but an actual historical act, which evidently took place the day following the night of visions.

The last thing the prophet saw was the horses galloping away with their war chariots. And in Jerusalem, what a sight meets his eyes, to demonstrate that the truth contained in his visions was already coming to pass!

Verse 9 introduces a prophetic oracle. (For the formula see also 1:1 and comment; 4:8; 7:4; 8:1, 18.) In the first part of v.10, representatives arrive from Babylon with gifts for the temple; and in the last part of the verse, Zechariah is told to meet them. The meeting takes place in the home of one Josiah, who is entertaining the returned exiles. In v.14 he is honored with the name "Hen" ("Gracious One").

11 In a coronation scene Zechariah is told to take the silver and gold brought from Babylon, to make a crown for royalty, and to put it on Joshua's head. The Hebrew word for "crown" is not *nēzer* (used for the high priest's crown or turban) but *ʿaṭārôt* (GK 6498), referring to an ornate crown

with many diadems—a plural of extension (cf. Rev 19:12). From the verses that follow, it becomes obvious that the royal crowning of the high priest is a type of the goal and consummation of prophecy—the crowning and reign of the messianic King-Priest; therefore Joshua, who was never a priest-king, is a type of the messianic Branch of v.12 (see comment at 3:8).

According to v.13, the Branch will be a priest on his throne. Thus the fulfillment in the Messiah transcends Joshua's status and experience (cf. Ps 110:4 [also part of a coronation scene]; Heb 7:1–3). It is in part to keep this hope alive that this crown is made for Joshua's symbolic crowning and then placed in the temple as a reminder of this hope. How appropriate, therefore, that both the type (Joshua) and the antitype (Jesus) have a name meaning "the LORD saves" (cf. NIV note at Mt 1:21)!

Some interpreters argue that the original reading at the end of the verse was "Zerubbabel son of Shealtiel" instead of "Joshua son of Jehozadak." But Eichrodt (2:343, n.1) correctly considers "that the interpretation of this passage in terms of Zerubbabel, which can only be secured at the cost of hazardous conjecture, is mistaken and that a reference to a hoped-for messianic ruler after Zerubbabel's disappearance is more in accordance with the evidence." Furthermore, no Hebrew manuscripts or ancient versions have the "Zerubbabel" reading.

12 This verse predicts that the messianic Branch will appear as Joshua's antitype and will build the temple. The Aramaic Targum Jonathan (as translated in Cathcart and Gordon, 192, 198), the Jerusalem Talmud, and the Midrash all regard the verse as messianic. The reference was also regarded as messianic by some early church fathers (e.g., Justin Martyr, *Dial.* 106, 121). The words are addressed to Joshua, yet it is clear that the language refers to the messianic Branch. John 19:5—"Here is the man!"—may well be intended by John as an allusion to the statement, "Here is the man whose name is the Branch." If so, Alan Richardson's comment (cited in Leon Morris, *The Gospel according to John* [NICNT; Grand Rapids: Eerdmans, 1971], 793, n. 10) is indirectly apropos:

> Adam ... was created by God to be a king over the whole created world; all creation was to be ruled by a son of man ... (Ps. 8 ...). In Christ, the Son of Man, God's original intention in the creation is fulfilled. He is the new Adam, the Messianic King. Thus, we have in Pilate's words a striking example of Johannine *double entendre*; whereas Pilate might merely have meant "Look, here is the fellow," his words contain the deepest truth about the person of Christ.

Indeed, Christ is pictured in Revelation 19:12 as the majestic Sovereign of the universe, wearing on his head "many crowns"—an ornate crown with many diadems (cf. Zec 6:11).

For the Branch as a messianic appellation, see comment at 3:8. As the "Branch," he will "branch out" from his place. (The NIV here reflects the wordplay in the Hebrew text.) "His place" (lit., "what is underneath") most likely refers to his humble and obscure origin, land, and people (cf. Isa 53:2; Mic 5:2).

Verse 12 closes with the prediction that the Branch will build the temple of the Lord. Since the rebuilding of the restoration temple is to be completed by Zerubbabel (4:9–10), it is difficult to see how this reference can apply to that temple. Instead, it must have in view the temple of the messianic age (cf. Isa 2:2–4; Eze 40–43; Hag 2:6–9).

13 Not only will the messianic Branch build the temple, but he will also have regal splendor, will take his seat on his throne and rule, and will perfectly combine the two offices of king and priest. The clause at the end of v.12 is repeated at the beginning of v.13 for emphasis, stressing the fact that "it is he" ("he" also being emphatic in the Hebrew; hence the NIV

rendering), namely the Branch, not Joshua, who will build the temple. The NIV has captured the sense of the idiom in the second clause of the verse, though "he will bear regal splendor" would be a more literal translation. As Perowne, 97, points out, the Branch will be clothed with "*royal* majesty, as the word is used [in] Dan. xi. 21; 1 Chron. xxix. 25" (emphasis his).

"Will sit" means "will sit enthroned" (cf. BDB, 442, 1.a). "His throne" refers to the promised Davidic throne (2Sa 7:16; Isa 9:7; Lk 1:32). As to the prediction that the Branch "will be a priest on his throne," Baldwin, 137, observes: "Nowhere else in the Old Testament is it made so plain that the coming Davidic king will also be a priest." One possible exception to her statement is Psalm 110.

The clause at the end of the verse means that the messianic Branch will combine the two offices of king and priest in full accord. As Ellis, 1035, puts it, the prophecy looks "forward to a time when kingly and priestly rule are combined in one." Apparently passages such as this one caused the priestly sect of Qumran to expect two messianic figures "at the end of the days": (1) the eschatological high priest-messiah of the line of Phinehas (cf. Nu 25:10–13) and (2) the eschatological son-of-David messiah (2Sa 7). Thus they were expecting a priestly messiah and a kingly messiah, with the priestly one ranked above the kingly one.

Since it seems clear that the sect at Qumran was priestly, it is not surprising that there the priestly messiah is elevated over the kingly messiah. Both messiahs are to be God's instruments in the end time, when the true priesthood and the legitimate monarchy are to be restored in accordance with God's promise. The community at Qumran also believed in the coming of an eschatological prophet, but there is some doubt as to whether they regarded him as messianic (cf. further *TDNT*, 9:511–20; F. F. Bruce, *Second Thoughts on the Dead Sea Scrolls* [Grand Rapids: Eerdmans, 1956], 80–89). Of course, the point of the biblical passages is that the two offices and functions will be united in the one person of the Messiah, the Davidic king (see Ps 110; Heb 5; 7). See the Reflection on 9:10, which deals with the office and functions of ancient kingship.

14 It is to keep the messianic hope alive that the crown is made for Joshua's symbolic crowning and then placed in the temple as a reminder of this hope. Historically, however, it is a memorial to the devotion of the emissaries who came all the way from Babylon with such rich gifts for the temple. They, in turn, are typical of the group in v.15. "Hen" (meaning "Gracious One") is doubtless another name, and an appropriate one, for Josiah, used on this occasion to honor him because he is so hospitable (v.10).

15 Gentiles will contribute materials for the construction of the messianic kingdom temple. When they do so, the people will know that the Lord has sent his messenger (Messenger?) to them. All these things will take place if the people render absolute obedience to the Lord's word. "Those who are far away" must refer to Gentiles and must parallel such passages as 2:11; 8:22; Isaiah 2:2–4; 56:6–7; 60:1–7. They will help build the temple by contributing their wealth (silver, gold, and other materials) to it, as was done for Solomon's temple and for the second temple (cf. the preceding verses). Isaiah 60:5–7 also predicts this occurrence.

For the identification of the messenger ("me"), see comments at 2:8–11; 4:9. Perowne, 98, gives the correct understanding of the conditional clause at the end of the verse: "The meaning is not, that the coming and work of Messiah, but that their share in it, depended on their obedience." The conditional element—obedience—relates, then, to the people's participation individually (cf. Dt 28:1–2, 15; 30:1–10). In the new covenant (Jer 31:33–34; Eze 36:26–27), God personally guarantees that the people will ultimately obey; his Spirit will enable them to do so.

NOTES

10 לָקוֹחַ (lāqôaḥ, "take"), an infinitive absolute, is used here as a finite verb, in this case as an imperative (Davidson, par. 88, rem. 2). In the ellipsis after the verb, the NIV correctly inserts the obvious object from v.11. הַגּוֹלָה (haggôlâ) is a metonymy of adjunct in which the abstract ("exile") is put for the concrete ("[returned] exiles"). וּבָאתָ (ûbāʾtā, "Go") is a *waw* consecutive perfect continuing the imperatival force of the preceding infinitive absolute, on which it depends for its syntactical function.

11 While there is some textual support for the singular עֲטֶרֶת (ʿăṭeret, "crown") instead of the plural עֲטָרוֹת (ʿăṭārôt), the preferred reading is given in the commentary. Note that the singular form of the verb in v.14 argues against KJV's "crowns." The purely conjectural emendation of "Joshua" to "Zerubbabel" has already been discussed and rejected.

12 צֶמַח שְׁמוֹ (ṣemaḥ šᵉmô, "whose name is the Branch") is explained in Davidson (par. 144, rem. 3) as a transposed descriptive sentence. Perhaps as a signal that a new and different temple is in view, הֵיכָל (hêkāl, "temple") is now used for the first time in the book, though it is used later of the second temple. Etymologically, the word is ultimately derived from Sumerian *é.gal* (lit., "great house"; cf. also Akkad. *ekallu*, "royal palace," in *The Assyrian Dictionary* [Chicago: Oriental Institute, 1956–1989] 4:52–61).

14 On the reason for the singular תִּהְיֶה (tihyeh, "will be") in spite of a plural subject, see Note and commentary on v.11. "Helem" (NIV note) is either another name for "Heldai" or represents an unintentional scribal corruption of that name.

15 The NIV has conveyed the nuance of the infinitive absolute, שָׁמוֹעַ (*šāmôaʿ*, "diligently"). The *nun* at the end of תִּשְׁמָעוּן (*tišmᵉʿûn*, "obey") is either an old indicative plural ending or the so-called paragogic *nun* (*IBHS*, 514–17). According to BDB (1034, 1.m), the idiom שָׁמַע בְּקוֹל (*šāmaʿ bᵉqôl*, "listen to the voice of") often means "obey"—hence the NIV translation.

IV. THE PROBLEM OF FASTING AND THE PROMISE OF THE FUTURE (7:1–8:23)

OVERVIEW

Perowne, 98, has a masterly synthesis of chs. 7 and 8:

After the lapse of nearly two years, Zechariah is again called to prophesy, the occasion of his doing so being the arrival at Jerusalem of a deputation, sent from Bethel to enquire whether they ought still to observe a national fast, which had been instituted in the time of the captivity, vii. 1–3. The answer of Almighty God by the prophet falls into four sections ... each of which is introduced by the same formula, vii. 4, 8; viii. 1, 18. The return in the last of these sections (viii. 19) to the question out of which the whole arose, shows that the prophecy is really one. In the first section the people are reminded that their fasting and feasting had alike been observances terminating upon themselves and devoid of religious motive and spiritual aim, and consequently unacceptable to God; in accordance with the teaching of the earlier prophets, in the times of Jerusalem's prosperity, vii. 4–7. In the next section the substance of this teaching, as insisting on moral reformation and not on outward observances, is given; and to the neglect of it are traced the rejection by God of His people, and the calamities that had come upon them in their captivity and dispersion, vii. 8–14. Passing now to a happier strain of hope and promise, the prophetic word tells of the bright days of holiness and prosperity in store for Jerusalem, in contrast with her earlier condition of distress and discord, and urges the people, on the strength of these promises, to holy obedience, viii. 1–17. The concluding section predicts that the question from Bethel shall be solved, by the transformation of the fasts of their captivity into joyful feasts, to which willing multitides shall throng from all parts of the land; heathen nations joining also in their celebration, and counting it an honour and protection to be associated with a Jew, viii. 18–23.

A. The Question by the Delegation from Bethel (7:1–3)

¹In the fourth year of King Darius, the word of the LORD came to Zechariah on the fourth day of the ninth month, the month of Kislev. ²The people of Bethel had sent Sharezer and Regem-Melech, together with their men, to entreat the LORD ³by asking the priests of the house of the LORD Almighty and the prophets, "Should I mourn and fast in the fifth month, as I have done for so many years?"

COMMENTARY

1 As early as 1:3–6 it was clear that Zechariah was interested in the spiritual renewal of the postexilic community. Here he deals further with this problem. The purpose of chs. 7 and 8 is to impress on the people their need to live righteously in response to their past judgment and future glory. E. Achtemeier (*Nahum–Malachi* [Interpretation; Atlanta: John Knox, 1986], 134) calls 7:1–14 a prophetic *torah*, using *torah* in the sense of "teaching, instruction." The date in v.1 is equivalent to December 7, 518 BC, not quite two years after the eight night visions (1:7; cf. "Date" in the introduction [pars. 8, 10]; cf. also the comment on 1:1).

2–3 The occasion of the oracle is now given. Unfortunately this occasion is somewhat obscure, for the Hebrew in v.2 is open to several different interpretations. The NIV translation is as defensible as any; indeed, according to Feinberg, 115–16, and Unger, 120–21, this translation is most preferable. For the various possibilities see the English versions and commentaries (esp. Baldwin, 141–43).

In the view adopted here, the occasion is a question about fasting raised by a delegation from Bethel (cf. Ezr 2:28; Ne 7:32; 11:31). To judge from the foreign names—"Sharezer" and "Regem-Melech"—the members of the delegation were probably born in Babylonia. They direct their question to the temple priests and the divinely appointed prophets—the latter includes Zechariah—at Jerusalem. Their inquiry is reasonable. The fasts had been observed in exile, but should they be continued in these better times back in the homeland? Now that the temple is nearly rebuilt, it would seem that they are no longer necessary.

Thus, the mission of these Jews concerns a fast day instituted by the Jews in exile in commemoration of the destruction of Jerusalem. (The OT itself required only one fast day—on Yom Kippur, the Day of Atonement; see Barker, ed., NIVSB, at Lev 16:29, 31.) In the beginning there was doubtless sincere participation in the observance of the day; now it is becoming a mere formality. According to 8:19, the question includes all the fasts commemorating major events related to the fall and destruction of Jerusalem and the temple, namely, the "fasts of the fourth, fifth, seventh and tenth months." Note the following comment (*Illustrated Family Encyclopedia*, 8:93):

> Counting the beginning of the year from the month of Nisan, the Jewish sages identified these dates as follows (in the Talmudical tractate *Rosh Hashanah* 18b): the fast of the fourth month fell on the ninth of Tammuz, the day when the city walls were breached (2 Kings 25:3–4; Jer. 39:2); the fast of the fifth month was on the ninth of Ab, when the house of God was destroyed by fire (2 Kings 25:8–10); the fast of the seventh month was on the third of Tishri, the anniversary of the assassination of Gedaliah the son of Ahikam (ibid. 25; Jer. 41:2); and the fast of the tenth month fell on the tenth of Tebeth, which was the day when the king of Babylon laid siege to Jerusalem (2 Kings 25:1, Eze. 24:2). In Zechariah's day, sixty-eight years after the destruction, when the rebuilding of the Temple was almost complete, the question naturally arose whether the time had not come to annul these fasts, since Jeremiah's prophecy about the duration of the exile might well be thought to have been fulfilled.

NOTES

2 וַיִּשְׁלַח (*wayyišlaḥ*, "had sent") is one of several instances in which the *waw* consecutive preterite functions as a pluperfect (see also Ge 12:1 and Davidson, par. 48, rem. 2; see further *IBHS*, 552, including n. 13).

"Bethel" is apparently a metonymy of the subject in which the city is put for its inhabitants (Bullinger, 579–80). פְּנֵי (*pᵉnê*, lit., "face of") is an anthropomorphism "used of the Divine presence in happiness and of Divine favour" (idem, 873). The notion "to seek the face [i.e., favor] of the LORD" is contained in the NIV, "to entreat the LORD."

3 The singular הַאֶבְכֶּה (*haʾebkeh*, "should I mourn") is used collectively for the people of Bethel, just as the whole nation of Israel is often construed in the OT as a corporate personality (or solidarity). The Niphal infinitive absolute הִנָּזֵר (*hinnāzēr*, "should I ... fast") in this context must mean, "Should I separate [or 'consecrate'] myself by fasting?" (cf. BDB, 634); hence the NIV translation.

"So many years" is interpreted in v.5 as "the past seventy years."

B. The Rebuke by the Lord (7:4–7)

> ⁴Then the word of the LORD Almighty came to me: ⁵"Ask all the people of the land and the priests, 'When you fasted and mourned in the fifth and seventh months for the past seventy years, was it really for me that you fasted? ⁶And when you were eating and drinking, were you not just feasting for yourselves? ⁷Are these not the words the LORD proclaimed through the earlier prophets when Jerusalem and its surrounding towns were at rest and prosperous, and the Negev and the western foothills were settled?'"

COMMENTARY

4–5 Through Zechariah the Lord strongly rebukes the attitude behind the question in v.3. Making an effective use of rhetorical questions, the Lord casts doubt on the people's sincerity when they previously observed the fasts. They had turned a time that should have convicted them of their past and present sins into a rote ritual devoid of its divinely intended purpose—e.g., prayer and repentance. They had turned it into a time of self-pity for their physical condition, a time devoid of genuine repentance and moral implications.

Since the question from the people of Bethel raised a larger issue touching the whole nation, the words of vv.5–7 are addressed not just to the people in Bethel but also to "all the people of the land [primarily Jews living in or near Jerusalem and Judah] and the priests." Priests must also listen to God's word that comes through the prophets. For the significance of the fasts mentioned in v.5, see comments at vv.2–3. Since these fasts commemorated events related to the destruction of Jerusalem and the temple in 586 BC, the "seventy years" are to be reckoned from that time. Strictly speaking, sixty-eight years have transpired; seventy is thus a rounded number.

"Me" (v.5) is set in obvious contrast with "yourselves" (v.6): Was it really for *me*? Was it not actually for *yourselves*? Their fasting had become a mere religious formality unsupported by obedience to the word of God (cf. Isa 1:11–17; 58:1–7).

6–7 Ellis, 1037, suggests, "there is the strong inference in the prophet's words (v.6) that just as feasting was enjoyed in self-interest, so fasting could similarly be undertaken for motives other than those for which self-denial was originally designed." The reference to "the earlier prophets" (v.7; cf. Isa 58) shows that the problem is not lack of knowledge but lack of obedience. Without obedience and personal application, religious observance is meaningless. The Lord is not pleased with any religious act that is practiced with selfish and insincere motives and purposes. "At rest" and "prosperous" point to the preexilic situation, when Jerusalem and the surrounding towns of Judah were bustling with life and the fields were being farmed—in contrast with their current condition resulting from disobedience, with only a partial restoration and without the full resumption of agriculture. The Negev (generally the area south of Beersheba down to the highlands of the Sinai Peninsula) and the western foothills (between the Judean hills and the Mediterranean coastal plain) were among the agricultural and grazing areas.

NOTES

5 וְסָפוֹד (wᵉsāpôd, "and mourned") is the infinitive absolute appearing as a substitute for the finite verb, in this case as a continuation of the preceding perfect (GKC, par. 113y–z). הֲצוֹם (hᵃṣôm, "really"), however, represents the emphatic use of the infinite absolute, stressing the idea in the accompanying finite verb (GKC, par. 113 l–n; *IBHS*, 585–87).

On the somewhat rare connecting vowel (to the pronominal suffix) in צַמְתֻּנִי (ṣamtunî, "Did you fast for me?"), see GKC, par. 59a (d). On the use of אָנִי (ʾānî, "me") following this form, see GKC, pars. 117x, 135e; on the indirect object use of the suffix, see Davidson, par. 73, rem. 4.

6 הֹאכְלוּ (tōʾkᵉlû, "you were eating") is either the customary imperfect or the "historical" imperfect, much like the Greek customary imperfect or historical present.

C. The Command to Repent (7:8–14)

⁸And the word of the Lᴏʀᴅ came again to Zechariah: ⁹"This is what the Lᴏʀᴅ Almighty says: 'Administer true justice; show mercy and compassion to one another. ¹⁰Do not oppress the widow or the fatherless, the alien or the poor. In your hearts do not think evil of each other.'

¹¹"But they refused to pay attention; stubbornly they turned their backs and stopped up their ears. ¹²They made their hearts as hard as flint and would not listen to the law or to the words that the Lᴏʀᴅ Almighty had sent by his Spirit through the earlier prophets. So the Lᴏʀᴅ Almighty was very angry.

¹³"When I called, they did not listen; so when they called, I would not listen,' says the Lᴏʀᴅ Almighty. ¹⁴I scattered them with a whirlwind among all the nations, where they were strangers. The land was left so desolate behind them that no one could come or go. This is how they made the pleasant land desolate.'"

COMMENTARY

8–9a With a solemn, authoritative message from God, the prophet focuses on the covenantal unfaithfulness, disobedience, and unrighteousness that first led to the Babylonian exile. He does so hoping that the restored community will perceive the moral implications of their fasting and allow their forefathers' disobedience and its consequences to serve as a warning to them. This section also explains why the people's fasting means nothing to God: They are guilty of legalism—external adherence to the letter of the law while disregarding the internal spirit, the true divine intent of the law (cf. Barker, "False Dichotomies," 5–6). In view of the past tense in v.11, v.9a should be rendered, "This is what the LORD Almighty *said*" (as in the TNIV).

9b–10 With a series of social, moral, and ethical commands, the Lord gave his people four tests of their spiritual reality.

(1) "Administer true justice." While the Hebrew word *mišpāṭ* (GK 5477) certainly includes the concept of "justice," Eichrodt, 1:241, correctly asserts:

> [This] is no abstract thing, but denotes the rights and duties of each party arising out of the particular relation of fellowship in which they find themselves. In this way everyone has his own special *mišpāṭ*: The king, the Deity, the priest, the firstborn son, the Israelites as a group, and so on. The task of righteousness is to render this justice, and the claims which it implies, effective in the proper way, so that the good of all those united in the one community of law may be safeguarded.

There is a sense in which, at the broadest level, *mišpāṭ* ultimately has in view "the proper ordering of all society." It would seem that this more comprehensive meaning is definitely called for in Isaiah 42:1, 4, where it is presented as the mission of the messianic Servant of the Lord: He will establish "a proper order" on earth. F. Duane Lindsey (*The Ser-*

vant Songs [Chicago: Moody Press, 1985], 44) maintains that "any translation less comprehensive than 'a right order' or a similar phrase fails to take account of the far-reaching accomplishments purposed for Yahweh's Servant. The Servant's task is to rectify within history all aspects and phases of human existence—moral, religious, spiritual, political, social, economic, and so forth." Again he notes that *mišpāṭ* "describes the totality of the just order that the Servant will cause to prevail on the earth" (ibid., 49). Perhaps it is not amiss to suggest that as the Lord's servants today, we too are to strive to help bring about such a proper and just ordering of all society (cf. Mic 6:6–8; see Barker, "Micah," 111–15).

(2) "Show mercy and compassion." While *ḥesed* (GK 2876) includes "mercy," it really has a stronger meaning. "Faithful love" is a better rendering. (Compare Hosea 10:12, where the same Heb. word is translated "unfailing love"; Hosea 12:6, where it is translated "love.") According to Snaith, 99, "the word represents a broad wedge of which the apex varies between 'love, mercy' at the one extreme, and 'loyalty, steadfastness, faithfulness' at the other." At the latter extreme it denotes "that attitude of loyalty and faithfulness which both parties to a covenant should observe towards each other" (ibid.; for covenantal love applied to God, see Barker, "False Dichotomies," 7–11). Since *raḥᵃmîm* ("compassion," GK 8171) is related to the Hebrew word for "womb," it may connote a tender, maternal kind of love. Faithful love and tender compassion are to govern all relationships among the covenantal people of God.

(3) "Do not oppress." Oppression is denounced so frequently in the OT that it is not necessary to multiply references to it (e.g., Am 2:6–8; 4:1; 5:11–12, 21–24; 8:4–6). The most common victims of oppression are listed here as "the widow ... the fatherless, the alien [or 'foreigner'] ... the poor." These people

were the weakest, the neediest, the most defenseless, and the most disadvantaged members of their society—and the ones with the fewest legal rights.

Related to the Hebrew word for widow (ʾalmānâ; GK 530) is the Akkadian *almattu*, which Chayim Cohen defines as "a once married woman who has no means of financial support and who is thus in need of special legal protection" ("The 'Widowed' City," *JANESCU* [The Gaster Festschrift] 5 [1973]: 76). He continues:

Finally, the statements made by Mesopotamian rulers to demonstrate their great concern with the plight of the *almattu* are best understood in the light of the above definition. Hammurabi's rationale for the writing of his laws is typical of such statements.... "In order that the mighty shall not wrong the weak, in order to provide justice for the homeless girl and the once married woman without financial support."

This concern is also seen in the Ugaritic text *2 Aqhat* 5:7–8: "He [Danel] judges the case of the 'widow,' he adjudicates the cause of the 'orphan'" (for the text see *UT*, 248; and for the biblical concern for such people see Dt 10:18; Isa 1:17, 23; Jer 5:28; Jas 1:27; cf. 1Jn 3:16–18).

Cohen goes on to suggest that the above definition for "widow" is "much more appropriate in [OT] contexts dealing with the protection of the rights of the socially disadvantaged classes in Israelite society.... Conversely such widows as Abigail and Bath-Sheba are never called ʾalmānâ because they probably did have some means of financial support" ("The 'Widowed' City," 77). Richard D. Patterson adds: "Throughout the Babylonian legal stipulations and wisdom literature the care of the widow, the orphan, and the poor is enjoined, since the ideal king, as the living representative of the god of justice, the sun god Shamash, is expected to care for the oppressed and needy elements of society" ("The Widow, the Orphan, and the Poor in the Old

Testament and the Extra-Biblical Literature," *BSac* 130 [July–September 1973]: 226; for a fuller treatment of these weak and helpless members of society, who were so easily victimized, see 223–34).

(4) "Do not think evil of each other." Light is shed on this last part of v.10 by the opening part of 8:17, where the almost identical Hebrew is translated "do not plot evil against your neighbor." (The TNIV correctly renders this imperatival clause the same in both verses.) This command certainly excludes a spirit of hatred, vindictiveness, and revenge that devises or plots wicked schemes to harm others (cf. Mic 2:1–2). "Here, then, is a concise yet comprehensive range of ethical teaching condensed into four pithy utterances. Without attention to their importance, any fasting becomes a mere parade of ritualism which, as the history of Judah had shown, can lead to moral and spiritual disaster" (Ellis, 1037). The clear inference is that the people of the restored community need to repent (change their way of thinking and living) and to begin practicing this ethical teaching; otherwise their fasting is mere formalism, legalism, and hypocrisy.

11–12a These verses stand in stark contrast to the previous ones: the Lord instructed the people to carry out the four commands of vv.9–10, but they refused ("they" referring to the preexilic ancestors, as the reference to "the earlier prophets" in v.12 shows). The lesson to the Jews of the restoration period is clear: Do not be like your unrepentant, unfaithful, disobedient, covenant-breaking ancestors, or you will suffer a similar fate. One indispensable ingredient of true spirituality is a dogged attentiveness to familiar truths, but they did not "pay attention." Deuteronomy 9:6, 13, 27 is echoed in "stubbornly they turned their backs," thus characterizing the Israelite ancestors as a stiff-necked and stubborn people. The fact that they "stopped up [or 'covered'] their ears" seems to reflect the disciplinary dulling of their ears in Isaiah 6:10 (cf. Ac 28:27).

In v.12 the people even "made their hearts [including their minds and wills] as hard as flint" (cf. Eze 3:8–9). The precise meaning of the Hebrew word for "flint" is disputed. The NIV preface states: "It should be noted that minerals, flora and fauna, architectural details, articles of clothing and jewelry, musical instruments and other articles cannot always be identified with precision. Also measures of capacity in the biblical period are particularly uncertain." In this instance the specific kind of mineral is uncertain.

Verses 11–12 involve the use of anabasis to stress the unseen cause of Israel's trouble: For the most part they were a recalcitrant, unresponsive, and obdurate people (cf. Bullinger, 431). Nor would they listen to the word of God in the law through the prophets (v.12). The latter were the secondary agents of divine revelation. The primary agent was the Spirit of God ("by his Spirit"). That is, the words of the prophets were inspired by God's Spirit. There are similar assertions in Nehemiah 9:20, 30 (cf. 2Pe 1:21). "It was the spirit which gave rise to the word of God uttered in times past and now of normative significance in the present, and which is at the same time the power-giving life to the community" (Eichrodt, 2:64, n. 2).

12b–13 The result of the forefathers' rejection of the command to change—i.e., to reform their ways and actions (Jer 7:3)—was the terrible experience of God's wrath manifested in the destruction of Jerusalem and the temple in 586 BC and in the ensuing exile to Babylonia. The motif of God's wrath is reminiscent of 1:2, 15. Dispersion was part of the curse for disobedience to the Old (Mosaic) covenant (cf. v.14). The chiastic arrangement of v.13 is used to express just retribution (so Baldwin, 148). Jeremiah had warned of precisely this consequence (Jer 11:11–14).

14 The scattering was one of the curses for covenantal disobedience (Dt 28:36–37, 64–68), as was the desolation of the land (28:41–42, 45–52). "The nations" refers primarily to Babylonia and Egypt, though "all" may at the same time anticipate a future, more widespread Diaspora—the principle of progressive fulfillment again. "Behind them" means "after they were removed from it." The Hebrew construction translated "that no one could come or go" occurs also in 9:8, where the NIV has "*against marauding* forces" (emphasis mine). Unger, 131, believes that the use of this "peculiar expression" in the second part of the book "is one of the internal evidences binding together the first part of the prophecy (chapters 1–8) with the last part (chapters 9–14)" (cf. "Unity" in the introduction).

"This is how" means "by their sins" (e.g., unbelief and disobedience). Because of such sins, "they made the pleasant land [Israel] desolate." How does all this relate to the question of fasting? Ellis, 1037–38, answers: "Thus, whilst Zechariah may well not have answered the original enquiry directly, he had nevertheless taken up the very essence of ritual in the heart of the worshiper, which was that the outward form of religious activity was useless and lifeless without an accompanying spirit of obedience, confession and repentance" (see 1:1–6).

NOTES

9 מִשְׁפָּט (*mišpaṭ*, "justice") is a cognate accusative, here expressing a concrete instance of the effect or product of the action of the verb (Davidson, par. 67b), and אֱמֶת (*ᵉmet*, "true") is an attributive, adjectival, or descriptive genitive (GKC, par. 128p).

11 "Stopped up their ears" is literally "made their ears heavy that they might not hear," thus revealing the privative sense of the preposition מִן (*min*) in מִשְּׁמוֹעַ (*miššᵉmôaᶜ*); cf. Davidson, par. 101, 1.c. (2). The same construction occurs in verse 12.

13 The use of קָרָא (qārāʾ [third person], "he called") instead of the expected קָרָאתִי (qārāʾtî [first person], "I called"), to agree with the following וְלֹא אֶשְׁמָע (weʾlōʾ ʾešmāʿ [first person], "I would not listen"), is explained in the NIV's preface: "And though the Hebrew writers often shifted back and forth between first, second and third personal pronouns without change of antecedent, this translation often makes them uniform [as here], in accordance with English style and without the use of footnotes."

יִקְרָאוּ (yiqrʾû, "they called"), אֶשְׁמָע (ʾešmāʿ, "I would listen"), וָאֶסְעָרֵם (weʾesāʿarēm, "I scattered them"; v.14), and לֹא יְדָעוּם (lōʾ yeʾdāʿûm, "they were strangers"; v.14) are either preterites without waw consecutive (as often in poetry) or are to be explained as with Baldwin, 148: "The prophet has been using the third person in the previous verses and he continues to do so until suddenly he finds himself using the very words of the Lord, so vivid is the message in his mind. This also explains the future tense.... When the judgment was formulated the situation was still future." This expositor inclines toward the first option (classifying the forms as preterites).

14 "The idea of universality is sometimes expressed by the use of ... contrasted expressions, as Zech. 7:14" (Davidson, par. 17, rem. 5): מֵעֹבֵר וּמִשָּׁב (mēʿōbēr ûmiššāb, "that no one could come or go"). The "contrasted expressions" are actually a form of merism, thus conveying the thought that "no one could go anywhere or do anything."

D. The Restoration of Israel to God's Favor (8:1–17)

¹Again the word of the Lord Almighty came to me. ²This is what the Lord Almighty says: "I am very jealous for Zion; I am burning with jealousy for her."

³This is what the Lord says: "I will return to Zion and dwell in Jerusalem. Then Jerusalem will be called the City of Truth, and the mountain of the Lord Almighty will be called the Holy Mountain."

⁴This is what the Lord Almighty says: "Once again men and women of ripe old age will sit in the streets of Jerusalem, each with cane in hand because of his age. ⁵The city streets will be filled with boys and girls playing there."

⁶This is what the Lord Almighty says: "It may seem marvelous to the remnant of this people at that time, but will it seem marvelous to me?" declares the Lord Almighty.

⁷This is what the Lord Almighty says: "I will save my people from the countries of the east and the west. ⁸I will bring them back to live in Jerusalem; they will be my people, and I will be faithful and righteous to them as their God."

⁹This is what the Lord Almighty says: "You who now hear these words spoken by the prophets who were there when the foundation was laid for the house of the Lord Almighty, let your hands be strong so that the temple may be built. ¹⁰Before that time there were no wages for man or beast. No one could go about his business safely because of his enemy, for I had turned every man against his neighbor. ¹¹But now I will not deal with the remnant of this people as I did in the past," declares the Lord Almighty.

¹²"The seed will grow well, the vine will yield its fruit, the ground will produce its crops, and the heavens will drop their dew. I will give all these things as an inheritance to the remnant of this people. ¹³As you have been an object of cursing among the nations, O Judah and Israel, so will I save you, and you will be a blessing. Do not be afraid, but let your hands be strong."

¹⁴This is what the LORD Almighty says: "Just as I had determined to bring disaster upon you and showed no pity when your fathers angered me," says the LORD Almighty, ¹⁵"so now I have determined to do good again to Jerusalem and Judah. Do not be afraid. ¹⁶These are the things you are to do: Speak the truth to each other, and render true and sound judgment in your courts; ¹⁷do not plot evil against your neighbor, and do not love to swear falsely. I hate all this," declares the LORD.

COMMENTARY

1–2 Zechariah next contrasts Israel's past judgment (ch. 7) with her future restoration (ch. 8). The purpose of both chapters is essentially the same: In ch. 7 Israel was to repent and live righteously after the punishment of her captivity; here she is to repent and live righteously because of the promise of her future restoration. Chapter 8 contains ten promises of blessing, each beginning with "This is what the LORD (Almighty) says" (vv.2, 3, 4, 6, 7, 9, 14, 19, 20, 23). "God's strange work is judgment. His delight is to bless His people" (Unger, 133).

This section is basically a salvation (or deliverance) oracle, the principal features of which are: (1) the self-predication of God (cf. v.2); (2) the message of salvation (vv.3–8); (3) the direct address (vv.9–17); and (4) the "do not be afraid" phrase (vv.13, 15). It is "the LORD Almighty" (see comment on 1:2–3) who stands behind this glorious prophecy. A more literal rendering of the chiastic structure of the quotation in v.2 reads thus: "I am jealous for Zion with great jealousy; with great burning, or ardor, I am jealous for her." For a resolution of the problem of God's jealousy, see comment on 1:14.

Here the divine jealousy is directed toward the restoration of Israel.

3a On the Lord's returning to Zion and dwelling in Jerusalem, see comments on 1:16 and 2:10.

3b The blessed results of the Lord's return are now delineated. The first result is a new character for Jerusalem, calling for new epithets. It is difficult to determine whether the first epithet should be translated "the City of Truth" or "the Faithful City" (cf. Isa 1:26). Either is possible, and both will be true. Verse 16, however, would seem to favor the former for this context. Furthermore, the temple mount will be called "the Holy Mountain" because of the Lord's holy presence there (cf. 14:20–21). "Jerusalem did not acquire this character in the period after the captivity in which, though not defiled by gross idolatry, as in the times before the captivity, it was polluted by other moral abominations no less than it had been before. Jerusalem becomes a faithful city for the first time through the Messiah, and it is through Him that the temple mountain first really becomes the holy mountain" (K&D, 2:312).

4–5 Other results of the Lord's return to dwell in Jerusalem are undisturbed tranquillity, long life, peace, prosperity, and security (similar to Isa 65:20–25). The weakest and most defenseless members of society will be able to live securely. About these verses Perowne, 102, says: "We read, as a fulfillment of this prophecy, that in the days of Simon, in the times of the Maccabees, 'the ancient men sat all in the streets communing together of good things' (1 Macc 14:9); while our Lord alludes to the games of children in the market-place, as a familiar incident in His own days. Matt. xi. 16, 17." Although it may be possible to regard these historical references as stages in the progressive fulfillment of the passage, they certainly do not completely fulfill the scope of this grand prophecy. The final stage awaits the second advent of the Messiah.

6 Such eventualities may seem too good to be true in the eyes of the Jewish remnant living "at that time," but the Lord Almighty does not so regard them. Nothing is too hard for him (see Ge 18:14; Jer 32:17, 27). Unger, 137, explains the thought of the verse thus: "If the remnant of the nation in that future day will scarcely be able to comprehend how such miraculous things just promised could become a reality, the divine reply is, 'Because they seem difficult to you, must they also seem hard to me?'" The answer is obvious.

7–8 Although God's action in v.7 is expressed in terms of saving, it is tantamount to regathering. "I will save my people" means "I will gather them from exile, bondage, and dispersion" (cf. Isa 11:11–12; 43:5–7; Jer 30:7–11; 31:7–8; cf. also *ZPEB*, 2:89). "The east" and "the west" are best understood as a merism (where opposites are used to express totality) meaning "wherever the people are." Thus the regathering here will be universal. Perowne, 103, observes: "The promise is larger than has yet been fulfilled." In v.8 Israel's predicted complete restoration to covenantal favor and blessing rests on nothing less than the faithfulness, veracity, and righteousness of God. "To live in Jerusalem"

need mean no more than "to go there frequently to worship."

"They will be my people, and I will be … their God" is covenantal terminology pertaining to intimate fellowship in a covenantal relationship (cf. Ge 17:7–8; Ex 6:7; 19:5–6; 29:45–46; Lev 11:45; 22:33; 25:38; 26:12, 44–45; Nu 15:41; Dt 4:20; 29:12–13; Jer 31:33; 32:38; Eze 37:27; 2Co 6:16; Rev 21:3). Though Israel may go through a Lo-Ammi ("Not My People") stage, she will be fully restored as Ammi ("My People"); so says God himself in Hosea 1:8–2:1; 2:23. It is true that Paul quoted Hosea in connection with Gentile salvation in Romans 9:25–26. But this is the application of a theological principle from the OT, the ultimate, complete, final fulfillment being yet future for Israel. The theological principle involved is that God is a saving, forgiving, delivering, restoring God—one who delights to take "Not My People" and make them "My People."

In the case of Gentiles, as in the church, he does so in his sovereign grace by grafting them into covenantal relationship and blessing (Ro 11; see Barker, "The Scope and Center," 322–23). Hans Walter Wolff (*Hosea* [Philadelphia: Fortress, 1974], 29) acknowledges as much: "Since the people outside Israel—who are Not-My-People and Without-Pity—are to become a part of the blessed people of God (Rom 9:24f.; 1 Pet 2:10), these words take on a meaning unforseen [sic] by the prophet. In this way the prophet's words are becoming fulfilled. But this is not yet completed with respect to Israel (Rom 10:1; 11:26) or the nations (Rev 7:9 ff.)." Israel's restoration depends on the dependable ("faithful and righteous") God.

9 The immediate purpose of all this encouragement is to motivate Zechariah's audience to complete the rebuilding of the temple. The people addressed are those who have been listening to the preaching first of Haggai (1:1) and then of Zechariah (1:1; cf. Ezr 5:1–2), since 520 BC. (It is now 518.) The laying of the temple foundation referred to in this verse is, accordingly, not the original one in 536. Rather, it is best understood as follows: "As a more precise definition of יוֹם יֻסַּד [yôm yussad, 'when the foundation was laid'] the word לְהִבָּנוֹת [lᵉhibbānôt, 'so that it may be built'] is added, to show that the time referred to is that in which the laying of the foundation of the temple in the time of Cyrus became an eventful fact through the continuation of the building" (K&D, 2:315). To recapitulate the historical situation, although the foundation was restored in 536, the actual building of the superstructure was hindered from 536 to 530, when it ground to a halt. In effect, then, the "founding" (almost in the sense of "building" or "rebuilding") of the temple did not begin in earnest until 520. "Let your hands be strong" is a way of saying "be encouraged" (Jdg 7:11).

10 "This verse presents a contrast of the present, when they had begun to obey the Word of God, with the past, when they did not" (Unger, 140). Its background appears to be the conditions described in Haggai 1:6–11; 2:15–19. "Before that time" refers to the period prior to 520 BC (at least 530–520 if not 536–520). "Before this work was started the commercial and civic situation was desperate" (Ellis, 1038). "No one could go about his business safely" is literally "No one could go out or come in safely." The NIV has captured the sense of the merism ("go out or come in") by "go about his business." The "enemy" (NIV) included the Samaritans (Ezr 4:1–5).

11–13 "But now" shows that the reasons for the people's discouragement have passed; God will now provide grounds for encouragement. Verse 12 stands in contrast to Haggai 1:10–11. In Haggai 2:19, God through his prophet predicted just such a reversal as we have here. On the one hand, the fecundity described is part of the covenantal

blessings for obedience promised in the Pentateuch (Lev 26:3–10; Dt 28:11–12) and in Ezekiel 34:25–27. On the other hand, Israel's being an object of cursing among the nations (v.13) is part of the covenantal curses for disobedience threatened in Deuteronomy 28:15–68 and predicted in Jeremiah 24:9; 25:18; 29:22. On the fact that both Judah and Israel are addressed in this message of salvation and blessing, Perowne, 105, comments: "Not only the two tribes but the ten. This has never yet been fulfilled" (see also Jer 31:1–31; Eze 37:11–28). "As" God's old covenantal people were an object of cursing, "so" God will save them (cf. vv.7–8), and they will be a blessing (cf. vv.20–23). Consequently, they are not to fear but to be encouraged (cf. v.9 and the comment there).

14–15 These verses specify God's part in the people's restoration to favor and blessing; vv.16–17 delineate their part. In the past God had to bring disaster on them as covenantal discipline (on God's determination [v.14], see Jer 4:28; 51:12). The Hebrew phrase lᵉhāraʿ here does not mean "to do evil" in a moral and ethical sense but "to bring disaster," just as rāʿâ "is the 'evil' which someone does and the 'disaster' which he encounters in consequence" (Fohrer, 102; cf. Isa 45:7). Strictly speaking, the Hebrew for "showed no pity" does not mean "repented not" (KJV), as though God could repent (cf. 1Sa 15:29; Ps 110:4); rather, it means something like what the NIV has (cf. Jer 20:16).

"So now" (v.15) answers to "just as" (v.14): "the very sorrows of the past became pledges for the hopes of the future" (Chambers, 14:64). As strong as was God's determination to bring disaster (v.14), so strong is his determination to do good (v.15). On the nature of this doing good, see vv.12–13. This is cause for not being afraid (repeated from v.13 because the fulfillment is certain).

16–17 Once again God's and Zechariah's interest in spiritual renewal comes to the fore (cf.

7:9–10). "The precepts that follow sum up the character of those who are in covenant relation with the Lord of hosts" (Baldwin, 153–54). After the announcement of God's gracious action (v.15) comes the stipulation of what he expects from his people in grateful response. Thus their obedience in the moral and ethical sphere has a gracious basis, just as did the law itself (cf. Barker, "False Dichotomies," 6–8). Jerusalem will indeed be "the City of Truth" (v.3) when its inhabitants are truthful and when true judgment is rendered in its courts. "Speak the truth to each other" is echoed in Ephesians 4:25. As the NIV indicates, the Hebrew *šālôm* ("sound") is probably best understood as descriptive of "judgment." The root idea of the word seems to be "wholeness, completeness, soundness," though it is used principally of a state of "well-being, health, harmony, peace, security, and prosperity" (see *NIDOTTE*, 4:131–33).

The Hebrew for "courts" is literally "gates." The gates of cities in ancient Israel often had built-in stone benches, where people could sit with friends, transact business, make legal contracts, hold "court," make public proclamations, and the like (Ru 4:1–2; 2Sa 18:24). At Tell en-Nasbeh (Mizpah), a gate has been found lined with stone benches that were seats for those conducting business there (*WBE*, 1:655–56).

The two positive injunctions (v.16) are balanced by two negative ones (v.17). On the first negative command, see comment on 7:10b. The second prohibition has to do with perjury (cf. comments on 5:3–4). "Do not love" perjury is another way of exhorting the people to hate it. The reason for these stipulations comes next: God hates perjury and wicked schemes to harm others. Proverbs 6:16–19 designates seven things the Lord hates. Three of them relate directly to vv.16–17 here: "a lying tongue," "a heart that devises wicked schemes," and "a false witness who pours out lies." One theological rationale for ethics, then, is awareness that God hates attitudes and actions contrary to his character. We must love what God loves and hate what he hates.

NOTES

2 קִנְאָה (*qinʾâ*, "jealousy") is a cognate accusative (GKC, par. 117p q). A synonym חֵמָה (*ḥēmâ*, "burning, ardor") is used in the parallel line instead of the expected cognate accusative; cf. Davidson, par. 67, rem. 2.

3a שַׁבְתִּי (*šabtî*, "I will return") is a prophetic perfect. וְשָׁכַנְתִּי (*wešākantî*, "and I will dwell"), however, is a *waw* consecutive perfect but with the same force as the preceding prophetic perfect, on which it depends for its syntactical function. (See Notes on 1:16; 2:10.)

5 "When an attribute qualifies several substantives of different genders, it agrees with the masculine, as being the *prior gender*" (GKC, par. 132d, emphasis theirs). This rule applies to מְשַׂחֲקִים (*mesaḥăqîm*, "playing").

6 "A question need not necessarily be introduced by a special interrogative pronoun or adverb. Frequently the natural emphasis upon the words is of itself sufficient to indicate an interrogative sentence as such" (GKC, par. 150a). This observation applies to גַּם־בְּעֵינַי יִפָּלֵא (*gam-beʿênay yippālēʾ*, "but will it seem marvelous to me?").

10 If וָאֲשַׁלַּח (*waʾăšallaḥ*, "for I had turned [lit., 'dispatched']") is not to be repointed *wāʾăšallaḥ*. The form is either a preterite without *waw* consecutive or a customary or historical imperfect (cf. the Greek customary imperfect and historical present; see Davidson, par. 51, rem. 6).

15 On the syntactical function of שַׁבְתִּי (*šabtî*, "again"), see Note at 5:1; cf. Davidson, par. 83 (c).

17 רֵעֵהוּ (rēʿēhû, "your [lit., 'his'] neighbor") is an objective genitive; thus, "evil of your neighbor" means "evil against your neighbor." "To the rule that אֵת is used only before def. obj. there are apparent exceptions" (Davidson, par. 72, rem. 4). Here ʾet "seems merely to give emphasis or demonstrative distinctness to the subj., particularly the emph. which … is natural in *resuming* things already spoken of" (ibid., emphasis his). A more literal rendering of the end of the verse, to reflect the syntax, is "'For all these things are what I hate,' declares the LORD."

E. Kingdom Joy and Jewish Favor (8:18–23)

> ¹⁸Again the word of the LORD Almighty came to me. ¹⁹This is what the LORD Almighty says: "The fasts of the fourth, fifth, seventh and tenth months will become joyful and glad occasions and happy festivals for Judah. Therefore love truth and peace."
> ²⁰This is what the LORD Almighty says: "Many peoples and the inhabitants of many cities will yet come, ²¹and the inhabitants of one city will go to another and say, 'Let us go at once to entreat the LORD and seek the LORD Almighty. I myself am going.' ²²And many peoples and powerful nations will come to Jerusalem to seek the LORD Almighty and to entreat him."
> ²³This is what the LORD Almighty says: "In those days ten men from all languages and nations will take firm hold of one Jew by the hem of his robe and say, 'Let us go with you, because we have heard that God is with you.'"

COMMENTARY

18–19 In this closing section of the chapter and of Part I of the book, the Jews are told that there will be a reversal of their mourning and their position in the world. Returning at last to the question about fasting, the Lord announces through his prophetic messenger (v.18) that there will come a time when fasting will cease. The people's mourning (expressed in fasting) will be turned into joy, for their low position among the nations will be changed. And they will be a source of blessing to Gentiles, for all the peoples of the earth will join them on pilgrimages to worship the Lord in Jerusalem.

"The prophet has dealt with major ethical and spiritual principles which underlie all outward observances. From what he has said, as well as the way he has said it, it is evident that his 'digression' from the specific question put to him (cf. 7:3) was for a good purpose. Now he turns to answer that question" (Ellis, 1038–39). He begins by announcing that a day is coming when their fasts and mourning will give way to festivals (cf. Isa 65:18–19; Jer 31:10–14). "The manifestation of the kingdom will be attended by such a fulness of salvation that Judah will forget to commemorate the former mournful events and will only have occasion to rejoice in the benefits of grace bestowed by God" (Unger, 148; the four fasts mentioned in v.19 have already been discussed at 7:2–3).

Verse 19 closes with an exhortation to Zechariah's contemporaries to "love truth and peace" (cf. vv. 16–17). "Apart from the two great commandments (Lv. 19:18, 34; Dt. 6:5, and repeated elsewhere in Dt.), only in Amos 5:15 is there a command to love [in the OT], though in Psalm 31:23 there is an exhortation to love the Lord. The frequency or infrequency with which a truth occurs in Scripture is no guide to its importance" (Baldwin, 155, n. 1). Such love "underlies the whole covenant relationship and therefore also the ethics set out under the covenant as the condition of blessing" (ibid., 155).

20–22 For similar predictions see 2:11; 14:16, Isaiah 2:1–5, and Micah 4:1–5. As v.22 indicates, the "peoples" of v.20 are Gentile nations. On the phrase "to entreat the LORD" (v.21), see the Note on 7:2. For another example of the use of the singular "I" (v.21) for the inhabitants of a city, see the Note on 7:3 (cf. 1Sa 5:10, where the first person plural pronouns are singular in Hebrew). In v.22 the "response is in inverse order to the invitation, so forming a chiasmus, and avoiding monotony of style" (Baldwin, 155). In view of the parallelism with "many peoples," "powerful nations" is perhaps better translated "numerous nations" (the Heb. for "powerful" is rendered "numerous" in Ex 1:9 and Isa 53:12 [NIV note]).

Numerous Gentiles will make a pilgrimage to Jerusalem. "Jerusalem is no longer viewed simply as the heart of Judaism but as the centre of God's dealings with all nations, and as a glorious realization of the ancient promise given to Abraham (cf. Gen. 12:3)" (Ellis, 1039). The purpose of the pilgrimage is to seek and entreat the Lord. "With the Davidic kingdom established, Israel will be a medium of blessing to the entire globe" (Unger, 148; see also Isa 55:5; 56:6–7; cf. Mk 11:17).

23 "In those days" is equivalent to "in that day" (see comment on 2:11). "Ten" is one way of indicating a large or complete number in Hebrew (e.g., Ge 31:7; Lev 26:26; Nu 14:22; 1Sa 1:8; Ne 4:12). Baldwin, 156, points out: "The word *Jew* ... occurs first in Jeremiah 34:9, and only for the second time here. It is frequent in Ezra-Nehemiah." Feinberg, 146, says, "The prophecy teaches, then, that Israel will be the means of drawing the nations of the earth to the Lord in the time of the Messiah's reign of righteousness upon earth."

The verse closes with the reason for the Gentiles' desire to accompany the Jews on pilgrimages to Jerusalem: "We have heard that God is with you." What better reason could there be? Ellis, 1039, puts it thus: "True spirituality is attractive to those who exercise genuine faith; but to others it may be a deterrent. The universalism with which the first part of the book ends is therefore not one of expediency, brought about by dialogue or conference. It is the work of God, initiated by him and mediated through his people." And Baldwin, 156, comments: "The renewed covenant of the postexilic period (8:13) includes the nations, who, as Ezekiel saw (36:23), would recognize the Lord as God when, through the renewed Israel, He vindicated His holiness. True godliness draws others to Him (1Co. 14:25), and is a factor used of God in completing the number of His people."

NOTES

21 The precise function of the infinitive absolute הָלוֹךְ (*hālôk*) is difficult to pinpoint. It may mean "at once" (NIV). However, since pilgrimages are involved, "regularly" may be the preferred nuance (cf. 14:16, cf. also GKC, par. 113u).

23 אֱלֹהִים עִמָּכֶם (*ᵉlōhîm ʿimmākem*, "God is with you") is an example of asyndeton. The כִּי (*kî*, "that") that usually introduces an object clause is sometimes omitted (Davidson, par 146, rem. 3; GKC, par. 157a).

PART II (9–14)

V. TWO PROPHETIC ORACLES: THE GREAT MESSIANIC FUTURE AND THE FULL REALIZATION OF THE THEOCRACY (9:1–14:21)

OVERVIEW

Part II of Zechariah contains two undated oracles, though they probably belong to the time of Zechariah's old age (shortly after 480 BC). More important than the date are the wide scope of the prophecies and their frequent emphasis on the eschaton, particularly the arrival of the great messianic era. In evaluating Lamarche's hypothesis on the unity of Zechariah 9–14, Petersen, 28, observes that the hypothesis is based on the notion that a messianic royal figure is central to the message of those chapters. He then claims: "Few scholars today hold this to be the case." But I suspect that the majority of evangelical scholars do hold it to be the case. While chs. 1–8 contain occasional glimpses of future events, chs. 9–14 are almost exclusively eschatological. The future orientation is rendered more certain by the eighteen occurrences of the phrase "on that day."

The theme of Part II centers on the judgment and blessing that accompany the appearance of the messianic King. The mood of the first oracle is characterized by change. In the midst of judgment (9:1–7), Israel finds deliverance (9:8). Yet in the midst of blessing (9:9–10:12), Israel experiences sorrow (11:1–17). And when the messianic King comes, he is rejected! The judgment with which the first oracle begins commences north of Judah and proceeds southward, down the west coast of Syro-Palestine (9:1–7). But Israel will be preserved for the advent of her Messiah (9:8). Thus this first section stands in sharp contrast to 1:11 and prepares the way for 9:9. Those interpreters are probably correct who understand 9:1–8 as a prophetic description of the Lord's march southward to Jerusalem, destroying, as Divine Warrior, the traditional enemies of Israel.

As history shows, the agent of the Lord's judgment was apparently Alexander the Great. After defeating the Persians (333 BC), Alexander moved swiftly toward Egypt. On his march he toppled the cities in the Aramean (Syrian) interior, as well as those on the Mediterranean coast. Yet on coming to Jerusalem he refused to destroy it. Verse 8 attributes this protection to the miraculous intervention of God. (For a different and less literal approach to 9:1–8, see Baldwin, 158.)

A. The First Oracle: The Advent and Rejection of the Messiah (9:1–11:17)

1. The Advent of the Messianic King (9:1–10:12)

a. The destruction of surrounding nations but the preservation of Zion (9:1–8)

An Oracle

¹The word of the Lord is against the land of Hadrach
    and will rest upon Damascus—

for the eyes of men and all the tribes of Israel
    are on the Lᴏʀᴅ—
[2] and upon Hamath too, which borders on it,
    and upon Tyre and Sidon, though they are very skillful.
[3] Tyre has built herself a stronghold;
    she has heaped up silver like dust,
    and gold like the dirt of the streets.
[4] But the Lord will take away her possessions
    and destroy her power on the sea,
    and she will be consumed by fire.
[5] Ashkelon will see it and fear;
    Gaza will writhe in agony,
    and Ekron too, for her hope will wither.
Gaza will lose her king
    and Ashkelon will be deserted.
[6] Foreigners will occupy Ashdod,
    and I will cut off the pride of the Philistines.
[7] I will take the blood from their mouths,
    the forbidden food from between their teeth.
Those who are left will belong to our God
    and become leaders in Judah,
    and Ekron will be like the Jebusites.
[8] But I will defend my house
    against marauding forces.
Never again will an oppressor overrun my people,
    for now I am keeping watch.

COMMENTARY

1–2a In v.1 syntactical and semantic problems are encountered immediately. First, how is *maśśāʾ* ("An Oracle"; "A prophecy," TNIV; GK 5363) syntactically related to what follows? Is it a heading, as the NIV translators and the editors of the Hebrew Bible (critical editions) have construed it? Or is it to be joined with the rest of the verse ("The burden of the word of the Lᴏʀᴅ is …"), as in the NASB? The matter is uncertain, so one cannot be dogmatic about the answer. Either view is possible.

Second, semantically or lexically, what is the meaning of *maśśāʾ*? Does it mean "oracle" (or "prophecy") or "burden" (as claimed by P. A. H. de Boer, *An Inquiry into the Meaning of the Term Maśśāʾ* [Leiden: Brill, 1948], and W. C. Kaiser [*TWOT*, 2:602])? Once again absolute certainty is not possible. Some interpreters, however, have insisted on the meaning "burden" and have consequently reached the hasty conclusion that chs. 9–14 consist of judgment oracles. But such a classification will not stand the test of literary analysis. When one examines the literary genres, or forms, in these chapters, it soon becomes evident that they contain not only judgment oracles but also salvation oracles and a mixed type (with both judgment and deliverance).

BDB, 672, defines *maśśā'* as meaning "utterance, oracle," and Holladay, 217, lists "pronouncement" as the definition. If the term derives from *nāśā'* ("to lift up"; GK 5951), as many lexicographers and exegetes believe, the derivation may shed some light on the meaning of *maśśā'* here. The verb *nāśā'* is used of lifting up or uttering a *māšāl* ("oracle") in Numbers 23:7, 18; 24:3, 15, 20–21, 23, and of lifting up the voice ("shouted," NIV) in Judges 9:7 ("voice" is omitted from the Hebrew idiom in Isa 3:7; 42:2). *Nāśā'*, then, means not only "to carry," hence the meaning "burden" for *maśśā'*, but also "to lift up" in a more general sense; therefore *maśśā'* could refer to the "lifting up" of the voice, i.e., to utter an oracle — hence the meaning "oracle" or "prophecy" (TNIV). The latter seems to fit the contents of these chapters better.

Zechariah 9:1; 12:1 and Malachi 1:1 all begin in the same manner in Hebrew. (The TNIV renders the beginnings of all three verses, "A prophecy: The word of the Lord.") Thus it is likely that Zechariah 9–14 and Malachi were written during the same general (postexilic) period.

On the dynamic activity of God's word in v.1, see comments on 1:1, 6. Hadrach is to be identified with Hatarikka, in the vicinity of Hamath (*ANET*, 282–83; see also Merrill F. Unger, *Israel and the Aramaeans of Damascus* [1957; Grand Rapids: Baker, repr. 1980], 85–89, and my updated bibliography in the Introduction of that work). Damascus was the leading city-state of the Arameans.

The last half of the verse may be rendered, "For the eye of the Lord is on all mankind, as well as on the tribes of Israel" (as in the NIV note). But the most natural translation of the Hebrew is that of the NIV. The only question is, what does it mean? Feinberg, 156, suggests that the picture is "one of terror at the visitation of God upon the then great world-powers." Unger, 153, however, declares: "What is meant is that when all civilized men at that time, as well as all the tribes of Israel, were fastening their gaze intently upon Alexander the Great and his phenomenal conquests, they were *actually fastening their eyes upon the Lord*. Alexander was simply God's servant of judgment and chastisement (cf. vs. 4 where the Lord Himself is said to have dispossessed Tyre, when Alexander is known to have done so)" (emphasis his). The parenthetical thought may also be that the eyes of people, *especially* all the tribes of Israel, are toward the Lord (for deliverance). Finally, in the Aramean sector, the judgment extends to Hamath (modern Hama), which Amos called "great Hamath" (Am 6:2).

2b–4 The Lord's word of judgment next came on the great Phoenician cities of Tyre and Sidon, particularly the former. The judgment of Tyre and Sidon is also foretold in greater detail in Ezekiel 26:3–14; 28:20–24. Ezekiel's prophecy against Tyre was remarkably fulfilled to the letter, first through Nebuchadnezzar, then through Alexander (see *ZPEB*, 5:832–35). By building a causeway out to this island bastion, Alexander accomplished what Nebuchadnezzar could not do in thirteen years.

The last clause of v.2 may be either concessive ("though they are very skillful"; cf. Eze 28:5) or causal ("because they think they are so wise"; cf. Eze 28:4). Either way, their skill or wisdom is explained in v.3, which describes Tyre's island fortress (Isa 23:4) and the great wealth the city acquired through commerce. There is a wordplay (paronomasia) between "Tyre" ("rock") and "stronghold" (or "rampart") in the Hebrew (ṣōr māṣôr). "Strong-hold" refers to the seemingly impregnable island defenses of offshore Tyre (New Tyre), which was surrounded by a wall 150 feet high. The similes in the rest of the verse underscore Tyre's prover-bial wealth. Despite her abundance and power, she will be destroyed (v.4). (For an account of Tyre's fall [332 BC] and of Alexander's role in it, see George Willis Botsford and Charles Alexander Robinson Jr., *Hellenic History* [4th ed.; New York: Macmillan, 1956], 314–20, and Albert A. Trever, *History of Ancient Civilization* [New York: Harcourt, Brace & World, 1936], 1:456–59.)

5–7 Verse 5 features two common stylistic devices. First, the names form a chiasm. Second, there is a wordplay between "see" and "fear" in the Hebrew (tēreʾ ... tîrāʾ). Four of the five cities of the Philistine pentapolis are mentioned in vv.5–6. Gath is omitted, evidently because it had lost all signifi-cance by this time. The Philistine cities are greatly alarmed at Alexander's inexorable advance. This is particularly true of Ekron, the northernmost city and the one that will suffer first; her "hope" that Tyre will stem the tide will meet with disappointment.

In the Hebrew there is no "her" with "king," nor is there a definite article. Perowne, 110, then, may well be correct in his judgment: "The predic-tion is, not that the then reigning monarch should perish, but that monarchical government should cease. Such tributary monarchies were abolished by Alexander." "Foreigners" ("a mongrel people," TNIV; v.6) probably refers to people of mixed nationality; they characterized the postexilic period (Ne 13:23–24). "In the middle of verse 6 there is a change from the third to the first person. Now the Lord explains what He will do. He is going to transform the Philistines by breaking down their stubborn pride, removing repulsive ritual, and making them part of the 'remnant' of His people" (Baldwin, 161).

The name "Palestine" is derived from the word "Philistines" (or "Philistia"). Their arrogance is mentioned at the end of v.6. The Philistines' "repulsive ritual" is described in the first half of v.7. The "blood" is that of idolatrous sacrifices, and "forbidden food" refers to polluted or ceremonially unclean foods. Obviously, other idolatrous practices are also included. Yet a Philistine remnant will belong to God and will become leaders in Judah. "Leaders" in the LXX is literally "chiliarch," i.e., "leader of a thousand"; the Hebrew word (ʾallup) occurs also in 12:5–6. Perowne, 111, asserts, "The meaning is that the Philistine, the nation personi-fied as before, shall take his place, ruler and people, as one of the divisions of the Jewish nation."

This interpretation is confirmed by the predic-tion that Ekron (probably a synecdoche of a part for the whole) will be like the Jebusites in a good sense. When David conquered Jerusalem, he did not destroy the Jebusites; instead, he absorbed them into Judah (e.g., Araunah in 2Sa 24:16; 1Ch 21:18). So it will be with a remnant of the Philistines (cf. TNIV "become a *clan* in Judah").

8 The verse begins with "But," setting it in con-trast with the preceding judgments on the sur-rounding nations. "I" signals the fact that it is God who is speaking through Zechariah. Just as God is to be a "wall of fire" around Jerusalem (2:5), so here he will "defend" his chosen people and land. "House" is probably a metonymy for the land and people of Israel, among whom the Lord has his earthly throne, so to speak, in the temple at Jeru-salem. The defense is against the marauding forces of Alexander. "Marauding" literally means "cross-ing and returning," and some have suggested that the reference is specifically to Alexander in going to and from Egypt. But the idiom is likely noth-ing more than a general way of describing Alex-ander's overrunning of that area (cf. 7:14, where the same Hebrew expression occurs with a slightly different nuance). A fascinating story of Jerusalem's marvelous preservation on this occasion is told by Josephus (*Ant.* 11.317–39 [8.3–5]). The story may well be based on a historical incident (and also appears in the Midrash). Boice, 193–94, summarizes the situation:

> When Alexander was besieging Tyre he sent a letter to the high priest, who lived in Jerusalem, requesting him to send him assistance and to supply his army with provisions. The priest declined to do this because ... he had sworn an oath of loyalty to King Darius.... This infuriated Alexander, and he determined to besiege and sack Jerusalem as soon as the coastal conquests were behind him. When the seven-month siege of Tyre and the two-month siege of Gaza were over, Alexander started for the Jewish capital. Jaddus, the high priest, was terrified, not imagining how he could meet the victorious forces of Alexander and fearing the worst for his people. He therefore ordered the Jews to make sacrifices to God and ask for deliverance from the advancing danger. That night ... God spoke to Jaddus in his sleep, telling him to take courage. He was to adorn the city with wreaths and then open the gates and go out to meet the invaders. The people were to be dressed in white garments and the priests in the robes prescribed by law. Josephus writes: "When Alexander while still far off saw the multitude in white garments, the priests at their head clothed in linen, and the high priest in a robe of hyacinth-blue and gold, wearing on his head the mitre with the golden plate on it on which was inscribed the name of God, he approached alone and prostrated himself before the Name and first greeted the high priest."

Alexander's men were astonished at this, and Parmenion, his second-in-command, asked why he had bowed down to the Jewish high priest. Alexander replied, "It was not before him that I prostrated myself but the God of whom he has the honor to be high priest, for it was he whom I saw in my sleep dressed as he is now, when I

was at Dium in Macedonia. As I was considering with myself how I might become master of Asia, he urged me not to hesitate but to cross over confidently, for he himself would lead my army and give over to me the empire of the Persians. Since, therefore, I have beheld no one else in such robes, and on seeing him now I am reminded of the vision and the exhortation, I believe that I have made this expedition under divine guidance and that I shall defeat Darius and destroy the power of the Persians."

Most scholars are skeptical of this account, but it is a fact that Jerusalem and the surrounding cities of the Jews were not destroyed by Alexander and most of the gentile cities were.

"Without denying that the story is in a legendary dress, we may admit the 'probability' of Alexander's visit to Jerusalem, and the certainty that the city was spared, and the people favoured by him, in accordance with the terms of Zechariah's prophecy" (Perowne, 113).

Petersen, 1, maintains that in spite of the mention of nations' and cities' names in vv.1–7, "there are no ... readily identifiable historical events that lie behind these texts." Yet I have attempted to show that there are. Similarly, Carl J. Laney (*Zechariah* [Chicago: Moody Press, 1984], 94, n. 2) follows Hanson's interpretation of ch. 9 as a "Divine Warrior Hymn" and claims that "no one historical setting really answers the situation described in the passage" and that the text "must be forced to serve one historical hypothesis or another" (Paul D. Hanson, *The Dawn of Apocalyptic* [Philadelphia: Fortress, 1975], 94). While I concur with this view in general, I am not totally convinced of all the details. Laney, 95, goes on to say categorically that the hymn "describes the march of a Divine Warrior ... who intervenes directly, apart from human agents." "Apart from human agents" is a dogmatic assertion that cannot be proved. Actions are often attributed to the Lord in Scripture, even in situations where we know human agents were involved. Exodus 23:30 indicates that God would drive out the Canaanites. Yet we know from the next verse (as well as from the book of Joshua) that he used the Israelites to do the actual driving out. Besides, Zechariah 9 itself speaks of "foreigners" (v.6), "marauding forces" (v.8), and "an oppressor" (v.8).

Above I have expounded 9:1–8 in the light of a particular historical setting—hopefully without "forcing." Specifically, I favor the view that in the Lord's march (as Divine Warrior) southward to Jerusalem, destroying Israel's traditional enemies while sparing Jerusalem, the agent of his judgment was Alexander the Great. This interpretation seems to be supported adequately by both history and Josephus. Significantly, Laney, 97, himself writes: "The complete overthrow of Tyre by Alexander the Great in 332 BC illustrates how even such a powerful city can be broken."

Compare the similar situation in Micah 1, where the Divine Warrior (Yahweh, "the Lord"; Mic 1:2–4) uses the Assyrians as his human agents to carry out his judgment against Samaria and Jerusalem: "The Divine Warrior's use of Assyria to carry out his judgment or conquest in this pericope [Mic 1:2–7] and the next one [Mic 1:8–16] is similar to his use of Babylonia in [Mic] 3:12;

4:9–10; 5:1 and of Alexander and Greece in Zech 9:1–8" (Barker, "Micah," 52). Note also what McComiskey, 3:1162, says when he maintains that certain "aspects of Zechariah's prophecy do not ... resonate in complete harmony with Alexander's conquests ... and the subsequent section (vv.8–10) affirms that these events will come to fruition in the kingdom of the Messiah." He further maintains that the "conquests of Alexander ... are but an earnest of the conquests of Christ's kingdom."

"Never again" (v.8) must anticipate the second advent of the Messiah for the final, complete fulfillment. "Oppressor" (*nōgēs*) is translated "slave driver" in Exodus 3:7 and elsewhere; thus it echoes the Egyptian bondage motif. On the divine providence at the end of the verse, see Exodus 3:7 and Psalms 32:8; 121. Unger, 160, put it well: "For their preservation at the time of Alexander and for their future deliverance from every oppressor, Israel is indebted to the providence of God which watched over them for good." Baldwin, 162, sums up 9:1–8: "The first section of this second part of the book establishes from the start two important facts: the Lord's victory is certain, and He intends to bring back to Himself peoples long alienated from Him. These truths underlie all that follows and culminate in the universal worship of the King, the Lord of hosts, in 14:16–19."

NOTES

1 Some commentators notwithstanding, the preposition בְּ (*beʿ*) probably here means "against" (BDB, 89, 11.4.a). The conjunction וְ (*weʿ*, "and") before Damascus apparently introduces a circumstantial clause, literally, "with Damascus as its resting place." As it stands, עֵין (*ʿên*, "eye[s]") is in the construct state; hence, "eyes of men."

Several exegetes propose reading "Aram" instead of "men," an emendation involving only a minor change of one letter in the Hebrew. Unfortunately, "Aram" is not attested in any Hebrew MSS or ancient versions; so there is no textual evidence to support the change. The conjunction וְ (*weʿ*, "and") prefixed to "all" may mean "especially" (BDB, 252, 1.a; GKC, par. 154, n. 1).

2a וְגַם (wᵉgam, "and ... too") resumes the thought prior to the dashes: The Lord's word will rest not only on Damascus but also on Hamath. גָּבַל (gābal, "to border") is a denominative verb, from גְּבוּל (gᵉbûl, "border").

2b חָכְמָה (ḥākᵉmâ, "they are skilled") is singular (in spite of the compound subject), most likely because Zechariah was thinking primarily of Tyre, as the next verse indicates. Some (e.g., Baldwin, 159) suggest that there should be a period after "Sidon" and that the following clause should begin a new sentence that continues into v.3: "Because she is very skillful [or wise], Tyre has...."

8 מִצָּבָה (miṣṣābâ, "forces, army") stands for מִצָּבָא (miṣṣābāʾ) and is another of the numerous examples of orthographic confusion between final ה (h) and final א (ʾ); see, e.g., GKC, par. 75nn-rr.

b. The advent of Zion's King (9:9-10)

> ⁹ Rejoice greatly, O Daughter of Zion!
>   Shout, Daughter of Jerusalem!
> See, your king comes to you,
>   righteous and having salvation,
>   gentle and riding on a donkey,
>   on a colt, the foal of a donkey.
> ¹⁰ I will take away the chariots from Ephraim
>   and the war-horses from Jerusalem,
>   and the battle bow will be broken.
> He will proclaim peace to the nations.
>   His rule will extend from sea to sea
>   and from the River to the ends of the earth.

COMMENTARY

9a As has been seen, vv.1-8 probably prophesied the military campaigns of Alexander the Great as he advanced on a warhorse southward from Aram (Syria) and subjugated city after city. The scene depicts intense battle and war, yet it is the implements of war that the messianic King is said in v.10 to remove from Israel. Verses 7-8 in particular form a transition to vv.9-10, which the Talmud and the Midrashim take as messianic. The approach here likewise classifies vv.9-10 as "direct" messianic prophecy, though some prefer the "typical" category.

The language in the opening part of v.9 is an echo of Zephaniah 3:14. Zechariah first calls on Jerusalem's people to rejoice. "Daughter of Zion" and "Daughter of Jerusalem" (poetic ways of speaking of Zion and Jerusalem; cf. Note at 2:7) involve several figures of speech: (1) personification ("Rejoice ... Shout"); (2) metonymy of the subject, in which the city is put for its inhabitants (Bullinger, 579-80); and (3) synecdoche of the part (Jerusalem) for the whole—the entire covenantal nation.

9b The prophet now gives the reasons for the rejoicing. The jubilation is over a new Sovereign.

The first reason for joy, then, is the coming of the messianic, Davidic (note "your") King (see Reflection below). Zechariah announces his coming in the opening line quoted above. "To you" may be alternatively rendered "for you," i.e., "for your benefit" (dative of advantage). After announcing the King's coming, the prophet describes the King's character: He is righteous and therefore saving; he is humble, or gentle, and therefore peaceful.

First, the King is righteous, thus conforming to the divine standard of morality and ethics, particularly as revealed in the Mosaic legislation (on this characteristic of the ideal king, see 2Sa 23:3–4; Ps 72:1–3; Isa 9:7; 11:4–5; 53:11). Second, he is saving. The Niphal *nôšā‘* (GK 3828) may be either passive or reflexive. If it is passive, the probable meaning is "having salvation" (NIV). If it is reflexive, the likely meaning is "showing himself a Savior-Deliverer." "Saving" attempts to reconcile the two major possibilities. Third, in contrast to most kings (such as Alexander), he is humble (TNIV "lowly") or gentle (cf. Isa 53:2–3, 7; Mt 11:29). Fourth, he is peaceful, for this is the meaning of his riding on a colt, the foal of a donkey. He does not come on a warhorse (v.10).

Although Jesus was acclaimed Messiah at his so-called triumphal entry into Jerusalem (Mt 21:1–9; Mk 11:1–10 [on a possible connection of Mk 11 with the Divine Warrior motif in Zec 14 and with Greco-Roman entry processions, see Paul D. Duff, "The March of the Divine Warrior and the Advent of the Greco-Roman King: Mark's Account of Jesus' Entry into Jerusalem," *JBL* 111 (Spring 1992): 55–71]; Lk 19:28–38; Jn 12:12–15), his own people nonetheless rejected him and his peace (cf. Lk 19:39–44 and, later, his crucifixion). Johnson, 228–29, captures the significance of the scene.

> Because they will not have Him at His first coming in peace, peace shall flee from them. Seeing the future discipline and chastening of the nation, He

wept. Walking headlong to ruin, they shall have to learn the sad lesson that the triumphal entry was not only the story of the nation's rejection of its King, but also of their King's rejection of them.

> Yet, all is not lost. The future holds a glorious hope. The promises, unconditioned in their ultimate fulfillment, shall be realized. Israel may deny Him, crucify Him, and attempt to forget Him; but His word is inviolable. Disobedience may thwart the enjoyment of the promises, but it cannot cancel title to them or the ultimate possession of them. The day is coming, as He Himself suggested a few days later, when Israel in full understanding shall shout the acclamation again, as they see Him coming the second time for deliverance: "Blessed is he that cometh in the name of the Lord" (cf. Mt. 23:37–39). Then shall take place the entry that is really triumphal (cf. Zech. 14:1–11). In the meantime, their house, as history has proved, is desolate.

10 The first reason for rejoicing is the coming of the King (v.9). The second reason is the establishment of his kingdom—a kingdom of universal peace in Israel and among the nations and of universal sovereignty. Again in contrast with Alexander's empire, which was founded on bloodshed, the messianic King will establish a universal kingdom of peace (but cf. Rev 19:11). A shift begins from the foundation for peace (v.9) to the fact of peace (v.10).

The progressive fulfillment of v.10 reaches to the Messiah's second advent, when weapons of warfare will be either removed or converted to peaceful pursuits (cf. Isa 2:4; 9:5–7; 11:1–10; Mic 5:10–15). The chariot is related to Ephraim because it was characteristic of the army of the northern kingdom of Israel. An impressive sidelight on the removal of warhorses from Jerusalem is Zechariah's statement that the messianic King will enter the city riding on a donkey, an animal symbolizing peace, not war (v.9).

The chariot, the warhorse, and the battle bow represent the whole arsenal used in ancient warfare, so the passage implies the destruction of this whole arsenal. Not only will there be disarmament and peace in Israel, but the messianic King will also proclaim "peace" (*šālôm*) to the nations—a fulfillment of the Abrahamic covenant (cf. 14:16; Ge 12:3; 18:18; 22:18; but cf. Rev 19:11–16, where the Messiah returns first as Divine Warrior).

"From sea to sea" has been variously explained as "from the Nile to the Euphrates" (cf. Ge 15:18; Ex 23:31), "from the Mediterranean to the Red Sea," and "from the Mediterranean to the Dead Sea."

The question is really not important because the context makes it clear that the expression is a merism indicating that the extent of the Messiah's rule is to be universal. The same is true of the phrase "from the River [Euphrates] to the ends of the earth" (cf. Ps 72:8–11; Isa 66:18). "The only realistic hopes of world peace still centre in this king" (Baldwin, 167). In fact, there can be no true, lasting peace—whether internal or external—apart from this "Prince of Peace" (Isa 9:6).

NOTES

9b As the NIV shows, the וְ (*wᵉ*) prefixed to עַל (*ʿal*, "on") is to be construed as epexegetical (GKC, par 154a, n. 1[b]). On the problem of two donkeys in Matthew, Johnson (222, n. 10) explains:

> Much ink has been spilt over the fact that Matthew mentions two animals while the other gospels mention only one. M'Neile, as others, feels that Matthew misunderstood the Hebrew synonymous parallelism of Zech. 9:9 and spoke 'mistakenly of two animals.' … The passage, then, becomes a shining example of a prophecy which, erroneously interpreted, creates a new and erroneous tradition. But this is not a necessary view at all, although many eminent interpreters have their names attached to it. It is more in accord with the context to have Matthew introduce the second animal to emphasize the fact that the colt was really unused, as the synoptics indicate. The mother animal was necessary since the unbroken young donkey would not have submitted to being ridden amid the tumultuous crowds unless she were along.

For a thorough treatment of this subject see D. A. Carson, "Matthew," *EBC*, 8:437–38. See also Gundry, 197–99.

The plural אֲתֹנוֹת (*ʾᵃtōnōt*, "donkey") here denotes an indefinite singular or a whole species (Davidson, par. 17, rem. 3; GKC, par. 124o; *IBHS*, 122).

10 The editors of *BHS* propose reading (with the LXX) the third person הִכְרִית (*hikrît*, "he will take away") instead of first person הִכְרַתִּי (*hikrattî*, "I will take away"). But such shifts in person are common enough in prophetic literature (e.g., 12:10: "They will look on me … and they will mourn for him").

REFLECTION

Kingship in the Ancient Near East

In synthesizing all the available historical data, we discover that ancient Near Eastern kingship had at least six major functions: (1) the king represented the gods before the people (his role as mediator-messenger-prophet-servant); (2) he represented the people before the gods (his role as priest); (3) he maintained justice (his role as judge); (4) he was commander-in-chief of the military (his role as warrior); (5) he "tended" his people, which included protection, provision, and guidance (his role as shepherd); and (6) he guaranteed *šālôm* (GK 8934)—well-being and harmony—in society and nature (one of his general roles as king).

Zechariah portrays the Messiah as the complete and perfect King by applying all six royal functions to him (see comments at the following verses): (1) mediating Servant (3:8); (2) Priest (6:13); (3) Judge (14:16–19); (4) Warrior (9:1–8; 10:4; 14:3–4); (5) Shepherd (11:8–9; 13:7); and (6) "Peace"-bringing King (3:10; 9:9–10).

The kingship of Yahweh. Some passages attributing kingship to Yahweh (the Lord) are 1 Samuel 12:12; Psalms 93; 95; 99 ("theocratic psalms"); Isaiah 33:22; 43:15; and Ezekiel 20:33. Regardless of mediatorial vice-regents, the Hebrew mind looked beyond the immediate mortal king to Yahweh's kingship (cf. Isa 6:1, 5). The divine *means* of rule was the theocracy, by which chosen agents represented Yahweh and carried out his divine will. The *basis* of Yahweh's kingship over Israel was their covenantal election and redemption; see Genesis 12:1–3, with the motifs of land (Dt 30:1–10), seed (2Sa 7:1–16), and blessing (Jer 31:31–40).

Kingship in Israel. The Davidic kings served as a reflection of Yahweh's kingship and were typical of the ideal messianic King to come. They were divinely chosen, not elected by the nation. The relationship between the king and Yahweh was based on a personal covenant made with David and his royal progeny (2Sa 7:12–16). The Davidic covenant established a Father-son relationship between God and the king (2Sa 7:14). This relationship was a kind of adoption, entailing discipline and direction. The "adoption" of David as "son" comes to the fore in Psalm 89:26–27.

Among David's descendants will be the messianic King, who will be the accepted "Son" and King above all kings (Ps 2:6–9). The messianic King in David's line will represent Yahweh perfectly, for he will be a wise Ruler ("Wonderful Counselor"), a strong Ruler or divine Warrior ("Mighty God"), a fatherly Ruler ("Everlasting Father"), and a peace-bringing Ruler ("Prince of Peace"). These designations are his "throne names" (Isa 9:6–7).

The king in Israel performed the same basic functions as ancient Near Eastern kings in general did, except that he did not serve as priest. This significant limitation of the Davidic kings, along with their failures even in the other functions, caused the people to look forward to one who would be the perfect, complete King and would establish the promised, ideal messianic kingdom. Significantly, the contemporary sepulcher inscription of King Tabnit of Sidon "is notable above all because of the priestly and royal titles given to the ruler of Sidon" (E. Lipinski, *Near Eastern Religious Texts Relating to the Old Testament*, ed. Walter Beyerlin [Philadelphia: Westminster, 1978], 245; see Zec 6:11–13).

The ideal king portrayed in Psalm 72 exhibited four features: (1) righteousness/justice, (2) salvation, (3) humility, and (4) *šālôm* ("well-being, harmony, completeness, balance, security, peace, prosperity," etc.; see also Zec. 9:9–10).

See further Barker, "The Scope and Center," 305–18.

c. The deliverance and blessing of Zion's people (9:11–10:1)

> [11] As for you, because of the blood of my covenant with you,
>   I will free your prisoners from the waterless pit.

¹²Return to your fortress, O prisoners of hope;
  even now I announce that I will restore twice as much to you.
¹³I will bend Judah as I bend my bow
  and fill it with Ephraim.
I will rouse your sons, O Zion,
  against your sons, O Greece,
  and make you like a warrior's sword.

¹⁴Then the Lord will appear over them;
  his arrow will flash like lightning.
The Sovereign Lord will sound the trumpet;
  he will march in the storms of the south,
¹⁵ and the Lord Almighty will shield them.
They will destroy
  and overcome with slingstones.
They will drink and roar as with wine;
  they will be full like a bowl
  used for sprinkling the corners of the altar.
¹⁶The Lord their God will save them on that day
  as the flock of his people.
They will sparkle in his land
  like jewels in a crown.
¹⁷How attractive and beautiful they will be!
  Grain will make the young men thrive,
  and new wine the young women.

¹⁰:¹Ask the Lord for rain in the springtime;
  it is the Lord who makes the storm clouds.
He gives showers of rain to men,
  and plants of the field to everyone.

COMMENTARY

11–13 Although the Messiah's mission is to establish his kingdom of "peace" (šālôm), he must first conquer all enemies and deliver his people. This he sets out to do (vv.11–16; cf. Ps 110). Before he can reign in peace, he must fully deliver and restore Israel. The passage is filled with battle terminology: prisoners (v.11), fortress (v.12), bow (v.13), sword (v.13), arrow (v.14), trumpet (v.14), and slingstones (v.15). Here the Messiah is depicted as a conquering King (the Divine Warrior motif again).

"You" (v.11) is emphatic and refers to Zion (v.9). The "blood of my covenant with you" probably has in view the Mosaic or Sinaitic covenant (Ex 24:3–8). "Prisoners" evidently refers to those still in the land of exile, Babylonia. The Lord will free them because he is bound to them by covenantal relationship. The "waterless pit" recalls Joseph's and Jeremiah's similar predicaments (Ge 37:24; Jer 38:6–9). In v.12 those outside the land who have hope in the future, delivering King (vv.9–10) are exhorted to return. While "fortress" may refer initially to Jerusalem (Zion) and Judah, the ultimate reference may well be to God himself, the only source of real security. "Twice as much" is a metonymy of the subject (Bullinger, 585), indicating full or complete restoration. (For the same figure but in a negative context indicative of full retribution, see Isaiah 40:2; 51:19; for a positive context, see Isa 61:7.)

The basis for the hope is given in v.13, of which Laetsch, 458, says, "In a bold metaphor the Lord compares Himself to a warrior using Judah as His bow, Ephraim as His arrow." The verse is progressively fulfilled. The initial, partial fulfillment is apparently to be found in the conflict between the Maccabees ("Zion") and the Seleucids ("Greece"). But the final, complete fulfillment awaits the outworking of chs. 12 and 14 and 9:16–17. The point of the verse is that God's people will gain the victory over their enemies.

14–16 Verse 14 contains the language of theophany or epiphany (cf. Ps 18:7–15; Hab 3:3–15; see further Claus Westermann, *The Psalms: Structure, Content and Message* [Minneapolis: Augsburg, 1980], 51–52). The language is also anthropomorphic ("will sound ... will march"). Here the sound of the trumpet is evidently a reference to thunder. The words are reminiscent of Exodus 19:16–19. God will come down to aid, protect, and deliver his covenantal people. The symbolism of v.14 "reminds one of Assur, the national god of Assyria, seen hovering protectingly over the embattled armies of his people, as appears on Assyrian reliefs" (Unger, 168). Perhaps the first stage in the progressive

fulfillment of v.15 is to be found in 1 Maccabees 3:16–24; 4:6–16; 7:40–50. The *Illustrated Family Encyclopedia*, 8:94, has this illuminating archaeological note on "slingstones":

When the Messianic age dawns, the Israelites, with the Lord fighting at their side, will wreak vengeance on their foes (cf. Zech. 10:3–7). The prophet's description of this apocalyptic war is realistic in detail, the various weapons mentioned by him being amongst the most important used by the armies of the ancient East: the sword, the bow and arrow (ibid. 9:13–14), and also "slingstones"—large pebbles or smooth stones from the bed of a watercourse (1 Sam 17:40) which were shaped to fit into the sling.... But all these will be of no avail against the Israelites.

The sling was a long-range weapon, like the bow. Hence, in battle the units of slingers and archers were generally positioned side by side. The Dead Sea Scroll of "The War of the Sons of Light Against The Sons of Darkness" also mentions "standards of slingers," each of the soldiers grouped beneath which was armed with seven slingstones (column 5, lines 1–2). The way in which the slinger operated his sling is well illustrated on the reliefs of Sennacherib (704–681 BC) portraying the capture of Lachish.... The artist has drawn the slingers in the act of hurling their slingstones, each with a pile of reserve ammunition at his feet. This weapon was a menace not only to the defenders who fought from the top of the wall of a besieged city, but also to the inhabitants inside, since its high trajectory made it possible for stones to be shot over the wall into the city's streets.

See also Yigael Yadin, *The Art of Warfare in Biblical Lands* (New York: McGraw-Hill, 1963), 2:296–97. In fact, Yadin's work on all the weapons of warfare mentioned in the book of Zechariah is helpful.

On the bowl used for sprinkling the corners of the altar, see Leviticus 4:7. Unger, 169, maintains that this is a simile of Israel's warriors streaming with the blood of their conquered foes (for a less military and less gory view, see Baldwin, 169–70). Verse 16 plainly declares the divine deliverance of Zion's people. "That day" is the time orientation "which always in chapters 9–14 embraces the final eschatological era of Israel's future reinstatement and deliverance" (Unger, 169).

"His people" is an appositional genitive; thus his people *are* the Lord's flock (cf. Ps 100:3). As for the rest of the verse, there is an apparent antithesis between the "slingstones" (v.15) used to subdue Israel's enemies and the precious stones or "jewels" (the saved, victorious remnant) that will sparkle in the Lord's land. "The figure is evidently of the reward of the faithful martyrs and valiant saints of Israel who enter the kingdom of Messiah" (Unger, 170).

The Hebrew for "crown" (*nēzer*) is often used of the crown of the high priest. How appropriate, then, for Israel, restored as a priestly nation (see ch. 3; also Ex 19:6; Isa 61:6)! Ellis, 1042, summarizes v.16: "Thus with a picture of the people restored and rejoicing without restraint in God's mighty deliverance, the prophet sees them as *jewels of a crown*, living emblems of all that the Lord has done for them" (emphasis his).

17 With Israel's deliverance comes blessing, including agricultural prosperity, because Israel's covenantal God controls the weather and the rain (10:1). The result is a land of peace, prosperity, and plenty. "They" is literally "he" (possibly the Lord), but the singular could be collective for the delivered remnant of the future; the context (v.16) seems to favor the collective understanding. "Grain" and "new wine" are signs of prosperity.

10:1 This verse probably contains a veiled polemic against Baal and Baalism (see also Jer 14:22; Am 5:8; cf. further Barker, "The Value of Ugaritic," 120–23). Yahweh, not Baal, is the one who controls the weather and the rain and gives life and fertility to the land; therefore, God's people are to pray to him and trust in him. Some scholars regard the spring rains as literal; others understand them as spiritual and typical. Perhaps both are in view, the literal rains being also typical of spiritual refreshment. Certainly in the grand consummation of the messianic era, both the physical and spiritual realms will flourish (cf. Isa 55:10–12; Hos 6:3; Joel 2:21–32).

NOTES

11 שִׁלַּחְתִּי (*šillaḥtî*, "I will free") is a prophetic perfect, as are the first two perfects in v.13.

12 "The *personal pronoun* which would be expected as the subject of a participial clause is frequently omitted" (GKC, par. 116s; emphasis theirs). This case applies to מַגִּיד (*maggîd*, "I announce").

13 אֶפְרַיִם (*'eprayim*, "with Ephraim") is an adverbial accusative. יָוָן (*yāwān*, "Greece") seems to be a transliteration of the Greek for "Ionia." Here, though, it refers primarily to the Seleucids, who sprang from Seleucus I Nicator—son of a Macedonian noble, one of Alexander's generals, and founder of the Seleucid Dynasty, which held certain eastern portions of Alexander's short-lived empire, including Syria.

14 תֵּימָן (*têmān*, "south") is literally "what is on the right [hand]," i.e., as one faces eastward; hence "south" (cf. יָמִין [*yāmîn*], "right hand").

16 מִתְנוֹסְסוֹת (*mitnôsᵉsôt*, "they will sparkle") is apparently a Hithpoel participle from נסס (*nss*); cf. BDB, 651.

17 יְנוֹבֵב (*yᵉnôbēb*, "will make thrive") is a Polel imperfect from נוב (*nwb*). The verb does double duty for both "grain" and "new wine."

d. The leaders warned and the people encouraged (10:2−4)

2 The idols speak deceit,
    diviners see visions that lie;
they tell dreams that are false,
    they give comfort in vain.
Therefore the people wander like sheep
    oppressed for lack of a shepherd.

3 "My anger burns against the shepherds,
    and I will punish the leaders;
for the LORD Almighty will care
    for his flock, the house of Judah,
    and make them like a proud horse in battle.
4 From Judah will come the cornerstone,
    from him the tent peg,
    from him the battle bow,
    from him every ruler.

COMMENTARY

2 Zechariah warns Israel's idolatrous leaders (vv.2−3a) but encourages the people (vv.3b−4). There is also a clear contrast between vv.1 and 2: Prayer to God brings blessing (v.1), but trust in idols (or the false gods they represent) produces disappointment and sorrow (v.2). The Hebrew for "idols" is *t^erāpîm* (GK 9572), a reference to household gods (see Ge 31:19; cf. Moshe Greenberg, "Another Look at Rachel's Theft of the Teraphim," *JBL* 81 [1962]: 239−48). They were used for divination during the period of the "judges" (Jdg 17:5; 18:5). "Diviners" were consulted to foretell the future. Since they "see visions" and "tell dreams," they are included among the false prophets ("deceit ...lie ...false ...in vain"; cf. Jer 23:30−32, 27:9−10). Resorting to diviners for information and guidance is specifically proscribed in Deuteronomy 18:9−14, for God provided true prophets (and ulti-

mately the messianic Prophet) for that purpose (Dt 13:1−5; 18:15−22; Isa 8:19−20; see Jn 4:25; 6:14; Ac 3:22−23; for an illuminating exposition of Dt 18, see Edward J. Young, *My Servants the Prophets* [Grand Rapids: Eerdmans, 1952], 20−37).

Because diviners are unreliable, "they give comfort in vain" (i.e., when they wrongly promise rain and fruitful seasons; cf. v.1; Jer 14:22). Similarly, because diviners speak lies, "therefore" the people are led astray like sheep without a shepherd. What the people need is spiritual leadership, but it is lacking (cf. Mk 6:34). "The physical victory described in the previous section must be accompanied by a deeper and more fundamental spiritual battle" (Ellis, 1042).

Although "shepherd" can refer to any leader, it is primarily a royal motif, whether referring to human kings (Isa 44:28; Jer 23:2−4), to the divine King

(Pss 23:1; 100:3), or to the messianic Davidic King (Eze 34:23–24). "Shepherd" was a familiar metaphor in the ancient Near Eastern world; e.g., in the prologue to the Code of Hammurabi, Hammurabi describes himself as "the shepherd, called by Enlil ... the one who makes affluence and plenty abound" (*ANET*, 164).

3–4 God threatens to judge the selfish, corrupt, unqualified leaders of the nation (cf. Eze 34:1–10). Since the earthly leaders do not take proper care of the "flock," the Lord promises to care for them himself and to make them like a proud horse triumphant in battle. "Those who in their submission to the Lord are like sheep become invincible as war-horses in His service" (Baldwin, 174). Verse 3 contains an interesting wordplay on the Hebrew *pāqad* (GK 7212): first "punish," then "care for." The word is susceptible of either negative or positive nuances (see BDB, 823, for references).

Verse 4 is variously interpreted. Those commentators are probably correct who, with the Targum (which renders "cornerstone" as "their king," referring to the Davidic king or Messiah, and "tent peg" as "their anointed One" or "Messiah"; so Cathcart and Gordon, 209), take it as messianic (the pronoun "him" referring to Judah, as in the NIV). So understood, the Messiah will come from Judah (cf. Ge 49:10; Jer 30:21). He is called (1) "the cornerstone" (cf. comment on 3:9; cf. also esp. Ps 118:22; Isa 28:16); (2) "the tent peg," a figure of a ruler as the support of the state (so BDB, 450; cf. Isa 22:23–24); and (3) "the battle bow," part of the Divine Warrior terminology (cf. Ps 45:5; Rev 19:11–16). From Judah will also come "every" divinely sanctioned king and ultimately the Messiah. Although the Hebrew *nôgēś* ("ruler") is used pejoratively in 9:8, it seems best to agree with BDB, 620, that here it is used in a good sense.

NOTES

2 Apparently, the ן (*n*) at the end of יְנַחֵמוּן (*yᵉnahēmûn*, "they give comfort") was originally an ending of the indicative mood (cf. W. L. Moran, "New Evidence on Canaanite *taqtulū(na)*," *JCS* 5 [1951]: 33–35). In this article Moran advances the theory that Amarna Canaanite forms ending in *ūna* are indicative, while those ending in *ū* are jussive or otherwise volitive (but see also *IBHS*, 514–17).

3 הָעַתּוּדִים (*hāʿattûdîm*, "the leaders") is literally "the he-goats," used figuratively of leaders (Isa 14:9; Eze 34:17).

4 יֵצֵא (*yēṣēʾ*, "will come") is probably intended to serve as the verb for "cornerstone," "tent peg," "battle bow," and "every ruler" (as the NIV renders it). As the alternative translation in the NIV note indicates, יַחְדָּו (*yaḥdāw*, "together") can be translated either at the end of v.4 or at the beginning of v.5.

e. Israel's victory over her enemies (10:5–7)

> [5]Together they will be like mighty men
>   trampling the muddy streets in battle.
> Because the Lord is with them,
>   they will fight and overthrow the horsemen.

6 "I will strengthen the house of Judah
    and save the house of Joseph.
I will restore them
    because I have compassion on them.
They will be as though
    I had not rejected them,
for I am the Lord their God
    and I will answer them.
7 The Ephraimites will become like mighty men,
    and their hearts will be glad as with wine.
Their children will see it and be joyful;
    their hearts will rejoice in the Lord.

COMMENTARY

5 The Lord promises to make Israel mighty and to reunite and restore the nation, thus causing the people to rejoice in him. Judah (v.4)—i.e., its people—is probably the antecedent of "they" (v.5). In the context "mighty men" has a military connotation: "valiant warriors." "Because" introduces the reason for their victory: supernatural help ("the Lord is with them"; cf. Jos 1:5; Jer 1:8). Because of divine aid the infantry overcomes the cavalry (a symbol of power). God's people win against superior odds. Though the final, complete fulfillment doubtless lies in the future, perhaps the first stage in the progressive fulfillment of the passage is to be found in the Maccabean victories (167–142 BC, by the end of which period the Jewish Hasmonean dynasty was established).

6–7 The opening part of v.6 is chiastically arranged. The Hebrew order is "I will strengthen the house of Judah, and the house of Joseph I will save." There will be a reunification of south (Judah) and north (Joseph). The reason for their restoration is given as God's tender compassion. The reason for their not continuing in a state of rejection is that the Lord (Yahweh) is their covenantal God, bound to his people in a covenantal relationship (cf. Ro 11). God's promise to answer them implies that they will pray to him for deliverance. Not only will Judah be like mighty men (v.5), but so also will Ephraim (v.7), thus resulting in great exuberance. For gladness associated with wine see also Psalm 104:15. But here the association is only a simile. The Lord is the secret, source, and sphere of this joy (as in Ps 32:11; Php 4:4).

NOTES

5 By analogy with בּוֹשִׁים (*bôšîm*), בּוֹסִים (*bôsîm*, "trampling") occurs here instead of the expected בָּסִים (*bāsîm*; cf. GKC, par. 72p).

6 וְהוֹשְׁבוֹתִים (*wᵉhôšᵉbôtîm*, "I will restore them") is anomalous. According to some scholars, the form should be וַהֲשִׁיבוֹתִים (*wahᵃšîbôtîm*), as in v.10, from שׁוּב (*šûb*; GK 8740); so GKC, par. 72x and the NIV.

Others propose וְהוֹשַׁבְתִּים (wᵉhôšabtîm, "I will cause them to dwell"), from יָשַׁב (yāšab; GK 3782), a reading supported by many Hebrew MSS and the LXX. Still others (including some Jewish writers of the past) suggest that the form is deliberately conflated in order to carry both ideas: "I will bring them back and cause them to dwell." This last proposal has also been made for the troublesome form וְשַׁבְתִּי (wᵉšabtî) in Psalm 23:6. So understood, the sense there would be "and I will return and dwell." Probably, though, in Psalm 23:6 the form is from yāšab, and the yā has been lost through aph(a)eresis. The NIV, probably correctly, assumes that the context of the Zechariah passage favors in this verse the same reading of the word as that in v.10 ("bring back" or "restore").

7 יָגֵל (yāgēl, "will rejoice") is a classic example of an apparently jussive form used as an ordinary imperfect (cf. GKC, par. 109k; Davidson, par. 65, rem. 6).

f. Israel's complete deliverance and restoration (10:8–12)

> ⁸I will signal for them
>   and gather them in.
> Surely I will redeem them;
>   they will be as numerous as before.
> ⁹Though I scatter them among the peoples,
>   yet in distant lands they will remember me.
> They and their children will survive,
>   and they will return.
> ¹⁰I will bring them back from Egypt
>   and gather them from Assyria.
> I will bring them to Gilead and Lebanon,
>   and there will not be room enough for them.
> ¹¹They will pass through the sea of trouble;
>   the surging sea will be subdued
>   and all the depths of the Nile will dry up.
> Assyria's pride will be brought down
>   and Egypt's scepter will pass away.
> ¹²I will strengthen them in the LORD
>   and in his name they will walk,"
>
>   declares the LORD.

COMMENTARY

8–9 The Lord promises to regather his people from distant lands. He will strengthen them, but the power of their ancient and traditional oppressors will wane. Verse 8 begins with an anthropomorphism,

"I will signal [lit., 'whistle'] for them," thus apparently continuing the shepherd metaphor (see Jdg 5:16). "Now, as true shepherd of his flock, he calls the sheep and gathers them home" (Ellis, 1043). The Hebrew for "redeem" is often used for ransoming from slavery or captivity (see Isa 35:10; Mic 6:4; cf. 1Pe 1:18-19). "Before" seems to recall the situation in Egypt (Ex 1:6-20).

Even in the Diaspora the Jews will remember the Lord (v.9). In keeping with the meaning of Zechariah's name, "The LORD [Yahweh] remembers" his covenantal people and promises. Now the prediction is made that they will remember him. And they will also survive and return to the Promised Land. "Though in far-off lands, the people of Israel will not forget their God, and generation after generation will survive along with the expectation of a final homecoming" (Ellis, 1044). Walter C. Kaiser Jr. (*Toward an Old Testament Theology* [Grand Rapids: Zondervan, 1978], 255) underscores and clarifies the significance of this promise (v.9):

> Yet even after Israel had been restored to the land after the Babylonian exile, the prospect of a regathered, reunified nation still appeared in Zechariah 10:9-12. The importance of this passage and its late postexilic date should not be lost by those who interpret the promise of the land spiritually or as a temporal blessing which has since been forfeited by a rebellious nation due to her failure to keep her part of the conditional (?) covenant. On the contrary, this hope burned brighter as Israel became more and more hopelessly scattered.

For additional data on Israel's future regathering and restoration, see also Walter C. Kaiser Jr., "Micah-Malachi," in *Mastering the Old Testament*, ed. Lloyd J. Ogilvie (Dallas: Word, 1992), 384-87.

10-12 In vv.10-11 the names "Egypt ... Assyria ... Assyria ... Egypt" form a chiasm. These two ancient oppressors of God's chosen people are probably intended to represent all the countries in which the Israelites have been dispersed. They evoke memories of slavery and exile. The promise of regathering (v.10) is similar to that in Isaiah 11:11-16 (note "a second time" in Isa 11:11; Eze 39:27-29). "Gilead" lies east of the Jordan and "Lebanon" west of the Jordan—both in the territory of the old northern kingdom. *The Illustrated Family Encyclopedia*, 8:95, has this to say about Lebanon and Gilead:

> At the end of the apocalyptic war, the Lord will gather in the widely scattered exiles of His people. The house of Judah and the house of Joseph will be united as of old and they will all be mighty warriors (Zech. 10:6-7; cf. Isa. 11:11-16). In the prosperity that follows, the rapidly multiplying population will spread till it reaches Lebanon and Gilead. Lebanon ... is referred to in the Old Testament as a symbol of strength, dignity and splendour (e.g., 2 Kings 19:23; Isa. 35:2), as are the mountains of Gilead. Hence the two are sometimes also mentioned together to denote power and pride ... (Jer. 22:6). In our verse too this combination may be intended to demonstrate the future power and glory of the Messianic kingdom of Israel. The territory of Gilead in Trans-Jordan, with its good soil and abundant crops, was accounted one of the most fertile regions of Palestine, together with the Carmel, Bashan and the hills of Ephraim (Jer. 50:19). North of the river Jabbok the soil of Gilead is of the type known as "terra rossa" which is very suitable for agriculture; while the land to the south of the river favours both cultivation and pasture alike (cf. Mic. 7:14; Song of Sol. 6:5).

On the statement that "there will not be room enough for them" (v.10), see v.8 and Isaiah 49:19-21; 54:2-3. Obstacles will be no barrier (v.11). The people "will pass through the sea of trouble" (v.11)—as at the Red Sea, or the Sea of Reeds. The "scepter" (i.e., "rule") of other great powers over them will cease. If the Ephraimites (northern kingdom) are still in view (see v.7), God is promising in v.12 to do the same for them as he did for Judah (v.6), namely, strengthen them. The source of the strength is the Lord himself ("in the LORD"). Walking "in his name" is probably here equivalent to serving "as his representatives or ambassadors," though it may also mean that they will live "in keeping with his revealed character"—by divine enablement, of course. The TNIV renders the clause, "and in his name they will live securely."

NOTES

8 אֶשְׁרְקָה (ʾešrᵉqâ, "I will signal") is a cohortative of resolve or determination, as in the NIV. On the emphatic use of כִּי (kî, "surely"), see BDB, 472, 1.e.; GKC, par. 159ee. The NIV, probably correctly for this context, construes פְּדִיתִים (pᵉdîtîm, "I will redeem them") as a prophetic perfect.

10 Something like "place" or "room" must be supplied in thought after יִמָּצֵא (yimmāṣēʾ, "there will [not] be found").

11 Although the subject of וְעָבַר (wᵉʿābar, "will pass") could be the Lord, it seems preferable to take it as a collective reference to Israel (so the NIV), echoing their "passing through" the Red Sea. וְהִכָּה (wᵉhikkâ, "will be subdued"; lit., "one will strike") is here used impersonally. יְאֹר (yᵉʾōr, "the Nile") is one of several Egyptian loanwords in Hebrew.

A rather clear case of assonance appears at the end of the verse: אַשּׁוּר (ʾaššûr, "Assyria") and יָסוּר (yāsûr, "will pass away").

12 On the probable significance of the Hithpael יִתְהַלָּכוּ (yithallākû, "they will walk"), see the Note on 1:10. Applied here, it would mean "they will walk continually."

2. The Rejection of the Messianic Shepherd–King (11:1–17)

a. The prologue (11:1–3)

> ¹Open your doors, O Lebanon,
>   so that fire may devour your cedars!
> ²Wail, O pine tree, for the cedar has fallen;
>   the stately trees are ruined!
> Wail, oaks of Bashan;
>   the dense forest has been cut down!
> ³Listen to the wail of the shepherds;
>   their rich pastures are destroyed!
> Listen to the roar of the lions;
>   the lush thicket of the Jordan is ruined!

COMMENTARY

1–3 This little poem is beset with problems. For example, is it the conclusion of the previous section, or a poetic introduction to the following section? Obviously the answer depends, in part at least, on one's interpretation. Some interpret it as a taunt song describing the lament over the destruction of the power and arrogance of the nations (ch. 10), represented by the cedar, the pine, and the oak (vv.1–2). Their kings are represented by the shepherds and the lions (v.3). So understood, this section provides the conclusion for the preceding one. Others, however, without denying the presence of figurative language, interpret the piece as a description of the devastation of Syro-Palestine because of their rejection of the Messiah and Good Shepherd (vv.4–14). Verses 1–3 then serve to introduce the next section.

The names in the text—Lebanon, Bashan, and Jordan—seem to favor this second approach. Part of the fulfillment would then be the destruction and further subjugation of that whole area by the Romans, including the fall of Jerusalem in AD 70 under Emperor Vespasian and General Titus, as well as the fall of Masada in 73. This action quelled one of several Jewish rebellions against Rome. Understood in this way, the passage stands in sharp contrast to what has just preceded in ch. 10, with its prediction of Israel's full deliverance and restoration to the covenantal land. Now the scene is one of desolation for the land (vv.1–3), followed by the threat of judgment and disaster for both land and people (vv.4–6).

The picture that now unfolds is vivid and graphic "in words arranged with great rhetorical power, full of poetic imagery and lively dramatic movement" (Chambers, 14:83). Unger, 188, says: "One can feel the severity of the judgment visited upon the land

(and inevitably upon the people also) which prepares the reader for the description of the heinous crime of Israel that provoked such severe visitation of wrath." Apostrophe (e.g., "Open," v.1) and personification (e.g., "Wail," v.2) are among the figures of speech used.

Lebanon (cf. 10:10) was famous for its cedars (v.1), but they will be consumed. In the Talmud the Jewish rabbis identified Lebanon here with the second temple, "which was built with cedars from Lebanon, towering aloft upon a strong summit—the spiritual glory and eminence of Jerusalem, as the Lebanon was of the whole country" (Baron, 378–79, esp. n. 2, where the reference in the Talmud is given). First Kings 6:15–18 and 2 Chronicles 2:8–9 may support such an interpretation of "Lebanon." The royal palace in Jerusalem is definitely referred to as "Lebanon" in Jeremiah 22:23 (see 1Ki 7:2). But whether literal or figurative, the passage announces a judgment that will embrace both people and land, including Jerusalem and the temple. The pines (or junipers) and the oaks are to wail (v.2); for if the cedars do not survive the coming destruction, neither will they.

Bashan lay east of the Jordan and north of Mount Gilead. The Israelites took it from the Amorite king Og at the time of the conquest of Canaan (Nu 21:32–35). It was allotted to the half-tribe of Manasseh (Nu 32:33; Jos 13:30; 17:5). Bashan was renowned for its rich pastures and abundance of choice cattle (Dt 32:14; Eze 39:18). The oaks of Bashan are to wail because the dense (or, perhaps better, "inaccessible") forest of Lebanon (vv.1–2a) has been felled. How, then, can these lesser and more accessible trees escape?

If v.3 is figurative, the shepherds and lions represent the rulers or leaders of the Jews (cf. v.5 and

10:3). The language is strikingly similar to Jeremiah 25:34−38. The Hebrew text is marked by an abbreviated literary style and elliptical construction (e.g., "Listen—the wail of the shepherds!"), as well as by the emphatic repetition of "listen" and "destroyed" (though the NIV has "ruined" for the second occurrence of the same Heb. word); note also the repetition of "wail" in v.2. The shepherds are wailing because the coming destruction will leave no pastureland for their flocks. Similarly, the lions are roaring because their lairs and food are gone, again because of the coming destruction.

For further defense of the position taken here on the functioning of 11:1−3 as the introduction to the rest of the chapter, see Charles H. H. Wright, *Zechariah and His Prophecies* (Minneapolis: Klock & Klock, repr. 1980), 299−303; Paul L. Redditt, *Haggai, Zechariah and Malachi* (NCBC; Grand Rapids: Eerdmans, 1995), 122−23; Frederick A. Tatford, *Prophet of the Myrtle Grove* (Eastbourne, Eng.: Prophetic Witness, 1974), 125−29; Feinberg, 197−200; Leupold, 204−6; Unger, 188−91; Boice, 200−201; Laetsch, 466−67; McComiskey, 1187−89; Merrill, 283−84; and Meyers and Meyers, 293.

NOTES

2 הֵילִילוּ (*hêlîlû*, "wail") is probably onomatopoeic by capturing the sound "of the wind wailing through the trees, fanning onward the fiery judgment sweeping over the land" (Unger, 189). For "dense" (or "inaccessible"), the Kethiv reads הַבָּצוּר (*habbāṣûr*, Qal passive participle), while the Qere reads הַבָּצִיר (*habbāṣîr*, verbal adjective or alternative form of the Qal passive participle). Actually, either is possible—without altering the meaning. On the word's lack of agreement in definiteness with "forest," see GKC, par. 126w; Davidson, par. 32, rem. 2.

3 קוֹל (*qôl*, "listen"), which usually means "voice, sound," is here used as an interjection (BDB, 877, 1.f; GKC, par. 146b). גְּאוֹן (*geʾôn*, "the lush thicket of") is literally "the pride [or 'majesty'] of"; but, as BDB notes (145, 1.c.), it here refers "to the green and shady banks, clothed with willows, tamarisks, and cane, in which the lions made their covert," hence the NIV reading. For a thorough study of the Jordan River and the Jordan Valley, see Elmer B. Smick, *Archaeology of the Jordan Valley* (Grand Rapids: Baker, 1973).

b. The prophecy of the rejection of the good shepherd (11:4−14)

⁴This is what the LORD my God says: "Pasture the flock marked for slaughter. ⁵Their buyers slaughter them and go unpunished. Those who sell them say, 'Praise the LORD, I am rich!' Their own shepherds do not spare them. ⁶For I will no longer have pity on the people of the land," declares the LORD. "I will hand everyone over to his neighbor and his king. They will oppress the land, and I will not rescue them from their hands."

⁷So I pastured the flock marked for slaughter, particularly the oppressed of the flock. Then I took two staffs and called one Favor and the other Union, and I pastured the flock. ⁸In one month I got rid of the three shepherds.

The flock detested me, and I grew weary of them ⁹and said, "I will not be your shepherd. Let the dying die, and the perishing perish. Let those who are left eat one another's flesh."

> ¹⁰Then I took my staff called Favor and broke it, revoking the covenant I had made with all the nations. ¹¹It was revoked on that day, and so the afflicted of the flock who were watching me knew it was the word of the LORD.
>
> ¹²I told them, "If you think it best, give me my pay; but if not, keep it." So they paid me thirty pieces of silver.
>
> ¹³And the LORD said to me, "Throw it to the potter"—the handsome price at which they priced me! So I took the thirty pieces of silver and threw them into the house of the LORD to the potter.
>
> ¹⁴Then I broke my second staff called Union, breaking the brotherhood between Judah and Israel.

COMMENTARY

4–5 The reason for the calamity in vv.1–3 is now given, namely, the people's rejection of the messianic Shepherd-King (vv.4–14). Just as the Servant in the Servant Songs (found basically in Isa 42; 49; 50; and 53) is rejected, so here the good Shepherd (a royal figure) is rejected. The same messianic King is ultimately in view in both instances. The purpose of this section, then, is to dramatize in a typological fashion the rejection of the coming messianic Shepherd-King and the resulting rejection of Israel, ending in her judgment. "My God" (v.4) indicates Zechariah's personal, intimate relationship with the Lord.

What follows is addressed to the prophet. Evidently, he is instructed to act out the role of a good shepherd for the flock, i.e., Israel (see comment on vv.7–8). With this interpretation Cashdan, 314, agrees: "The prophet is directed by God to act the role of a shepherd (ruler) to the flock (Israel), since the earlier shepherds neglected the flock and led them to the brink of disaster. He thereupon enacts the part of a good shepherd, tending his flock with gentleness and loving care, but his efforts are spurned and in despair he leaves them to their fate.... Kimchi regards the prophecy as

Messianic." The "slaughter" spoken of is explained in v.5, where the sheep (the Jews) are bought as slaves by outsiders. At least part of the fulfillment came in AD 70 and after. The sellers are their own shepherds—bad rulers or leaders.

6 "For" introduces the reason for the misery described in v.5, namely, the Lord's displeasure. The verse also interprets the parable of the flock. The "land" (not "earth") is Israel. While the fulfillment may have been partially realized during the intertestamental period, it also seems to reach to Roman times; so one example of "king" would perhaps be the Roman emperor (cf. Jn 19:15), and those who "oppress ['devastate,' TNIV] the land" would include the Romans.

7–8 Zechariah carries out his divine instructions (v.4). The fact that he says he actually does so supports the notion that he acts them out. Thus he becomes a type of the messianic Shepherd-King. He gives special attention and care to the oppressed (or "afflicted"; v.11) of the flock. (For a different interpretation of this phrase, see Thomas J. Finley, "The Sheep Merchants of Zechariah 11," *Grace Theological Journal* 3 [Spring 1982]: 51–65.) He also takes two staffs to ensure divine "favor" on the flock and to ensure its "unity." Such unity (cf. Eze 37:15–28) will be the result of the gracious leadership of the good Shepherd. (For the significance of the breaking of the two staffs, see vv.10 and 14.)

Since so many interpretations have been given of the first part of v.8 (forty, by one count), obviously no certainty is possible. "In one month" has been taken to refer to (1) a literal month, (2) a short period of time, and (3) a longer period of indefinite duration. One's conclusion on this matter will depend on one's identification of "the three shepherds." Four of the more popular identifications are: (1) Eleazar, John, and Simon (the leaders of the three Jewish factions during the siege of Jerusalem by Titus in AD 70; see Baron, 396, n. 1); (2) Seleucus IV, Heliodorus, and Demetrius Soter (three Seleucid kings; see H. G. Mitchell, "Haggai and Zechariah," in *A Critical and Exegetical Commentary on Haggai, Zechariah, Malachi and Jonah* [ICC; Edinburgh: T. & T. Clark, 1912], 307); (3) Jason, Menelaus, and Alcimus (high priests; see Ellis, 1045); and (4) three classes of leaders, such as prophet, priest, and king (or a lesser civil authority). This much is certain: The good Shepherd will dispose of unfit leaders. Baldwin, 183, raises an interesting question: "Is the number three used in that way [symbolically] here ... to signify completion? If so, the good shepherd would be removing from power all the unworthy leaders who frustrated his work."

8b–9 In spite of the ideal ministry of the good Shepherd, the flock as a whole detests him. Similarly, he grows weary of them. (See the analogous reaction of God in Isa 1:13–14: "I cannot bear your evil assemblies ... your appointed feasts my soul hates. They have become a burden to me; I am weary of bearing them." Here Zechariah continues to be a type of the messianic good Shepherd-King.) In v.9 the good Shepherd terminates his providen-

tial care of the sheep, so that they even "eat one another's flesh." According to Josephus, such cannibalizing actually happened during the Roman siege of Jerusalem in AD 70 (*J.W.* 6.193–213 [3.3–4]). Baldwin, 184, remarks: "By withholding his leadership the shepherd abandoned the people to the consequences of their rejection of him: death, and mutual destruction. He simply let things take their course."

10–11 A further consequence of the Shepherd's rejection is the cessation of his gracious favor. One indication of this is the revocation of his covenant of security and restraint, by which he had been apparently holding back the nations from his people (cf. Eze 34:25; Hos 2:18). Now, however, the nations (e.g., the Romans) will be permitted to overrun them. Ellis, 1045, is probably correct in identifying "the afflicted of the flock" (v.11) with "the faithful few who recognize the word of the Lord, who know true authority when they see it in action." See also v.7, where the same Hebrew phrase is rendered "the oppressed of the flock." (The TNIV renders it the same in both verses: "the oppressed of the flock.") The last "it" in v.11 evidently refers to Israel's affliction and oppression by the nations.

At least part of the fulfillment of these verses is to be found in Matthew 23 (note esp. vv.13, 23–24, 33–39). Faithful believers discern that what happened (e.g., the judgment on Jerusalem and the temple in AD 70) is a fulfillment of God's prophetic word—a result of such actions as those denounced in Matthew 23, which led to the rejection of the good Shepherd.

12–13 Now comes the final, outright rejection of the good Shepherd, including even "severance" pay (his death is predicted in 13:7). "Give me my pay" (v.12) speaks of the termination of the relationship; "keep it" is a more emphatic way of terminating the relationship. The "flock" (v.11) responds with thirty pieces of silver as remuneration for the Shepherd's services. This sum was not only the price of a slave among the Israelites in ancient times (Ex 21:32) but is also apparently a way of indicating "a trifling amount" (see Erica Reiner, "Thirty Pieces of Silver," *JAOS* 88 [January–March 1968]: 186–90, for this idea; also Petersen, 97).

Next (v.13) the Lord instructs Zechariah, "Throw it to the potter"—possibly a proverb. The NIV captures the irony and sarcasm in Zechariah's description of the thirty pieces as "the handsome price at which they priced ['valued,'TNIV] me!""So I took" indicates not only the prophet's obedience but also the fact that he is still "impersonating" the good Shepherd by acting out this "parable" or "report of a symbolic action" (Petersen, 89). On the silver being thrown in the temple to the potter, Unger, 200, says: "The fulfillment of this prophecy in Matthew 27:3–10 is proof enough that the money was flung down in the temple and immediately taken up by the priests to purchase a field *of a potter* for a burying ground for the poor" (emphasis his).

For the NT's use of vv.12–13 see Matthew 26:14–15; 27:3–10. For a list of the textual differences see Gundry, 126–27. The obvious textual differences are best accounted for by the fact that Matthew is apparently quoting Zechariah 11:12–13 and alluding to Jeremiah 19:1–13. William Hendriksen (*Exposition of the Gospel according to Matthew* [NTC; Grand Rapids: Baker, 1973], 946–48), who basically follows Gundry, has a helpful treatment of the whole complex of problems involved (see also Gleason L. Archer, *Encyclopedia of Bible Difficulties* [Grand Rapids: Zondervan, 1982], 345; D. A. Carson, "Matthew," *EBC*, 8:528, 560–66; Barker, ed., NIVSB at Mt 27:9n). Perowne, 127, has this summary:

Like the earlier prophecy of the King (ix. 9), the prophecy of the Shepherd is remarkable for its literal fulfillment. The "thirty pieces of silver" were

literally the "goodly price" paid for Him, "whom they of the children of Israel did value.""The potter" was literally the recipient of it, as the purchase money of his exhausted field for an unclean purpose (Matt. xxvii. 5–10).

14 The first staff, called "Favor," is already broken (v.10). Now the second one, called "Union," is broken as well. This signifies the destruction or dissolution of the covenantal nation, particularly of the unity between the south and the north. Chambers, 86, correctly says: "The breaking up of the nation into parties bitterly hostile to each other, was one of the most marked peculiarities of the later Jewish history, and greatly accelerated the ruin of the popular cause in the Roman war." Feinberg, 211, has this observation:

With real insight Dods notes the chronological sequence of the events: "It will be observed that the breaking of the first staff preceded, while the breaking of the second staff succeeded, the final and contemptuous rejection of the Shepherd by the people. This, too, is the historical order. The Jews had long been under foreign rule, Idumaean and Roman, before they were scattered and lost coherence as a nation." Now that we have concluded this section it will be all the more readily seen that the passage unquestionably speaks of the spiritual condition of Israel during the time of the Second Temple, and especially in the period of Christ's ministry, which eventuated in the catastrophic rejection by Israel of their Messiah and the subsequent breakup of the Jewish commonwealth. The Romans did come and take away both their place and nation. See John 11:48.

Yet even this new destruction and dispersion are not permanent; otherwise there would be no point in the promises of Israel's future deliverance, regathering, and restoration in the succeeding chapters.

NOTES

4 הַהֲרֵגָה (*hah⁴rēgâ*, "slaughter") is a genitive of purpose or intention (cf. GKC, par. 128q), hence "marked for" (NIV).

5 The singular יֹאמַר (*yō'mar*, "say") instead of the plural is explained in Davidson, par. 116, rem. 1: "General plurals are sometimes construed with sing. pred. from a tendency to individualize and distribute over every individual, or apply it to any individual supposed." Many examples are given in Davidson (q.v.). The same applies to יַחְמוֹל (*yaḥmôl*, "spare").

The Qere וַאעְשִׁר (*wa'śir*, "I am rich") is simply a reading of the Kethiv (*wā'a'śir*) with syncope of the *aleph* (GKC, par. 19k). In such cases the *aleph*, though quiescent, is still usually retained as a historical spelling (as here).

Apparently the reason for the change from the feminine pronominal suffix in קֹנֵיהֶן (*qōnêhen*, "their buyers"), agreeing with צֹאן (*ṣō'n*, "flock"), to the masculine one in וְרֹעֵיהֶם (*w⁴rō'êhem*, "their own shepherds") is that the focus is now on the עַם (*'am*, "people"), represented by the "flock."

6 The pronominal suffix "them" must be supplied in thought after אַצִּיל (*'aṣṣîl*, "I will ... rescue"). When the suffix to be supplied is obvious from the context, it is frequently omitted from verbs in Hebrew.

7 Probably most modern interpreters follow the LXX and emend לָכֵן עֲנִיֵּי (*lākēn 'aniyyê*, "particularly the oppressed of") to לִכְנַעֲנִיֵּי (*likna'aniyyê*, "for the traffickers of"), but the MT makes good sense (see also v.11).

10 For a reasonably reliable current study of בְּרִית (*b⁴rît*, "covenant"; GK 1382) see *TDOT*, 2:253–79, and the bibliography there; see also D. J. McCarthy, *Old Testament Covenant: A Survey of Current Opinions* (Richmond, Va.: John Knox, 1972); Moshe Weinfeld, *Deuteronomy and the Deuteronomic School* (London: Oxford Univ. Press, 1972), 75–81; idem, "The Covenant Grant in the Old Testament and in the Ancient Near East," *JAOS* 90 (1970): 184–203; *TLOT*, 1:256–66; *NIDOTTE*, 1:747–55.

11 On the text-critical problem in the Hebrew for "and so the afflicted of," see note on v.7.

13 As it stands, "into the house" is an adverbial accusative of place (locative accusative), but it should not be overlooked that the preposition בְּ (*b⁴*, "in, into") is frequently omitted before a word beginning with *b*, as here.

c. The rise and fall of the worthless shepherd (11:15–17)

¹⁵Then the LORD said to me, "Take again the equipment of a foolish shepherd. ¹⁶For I am going to raise up a shepherd over the land who will not care for the lost, or seek the young, or heal the injured, or feed the healthy, but will eat the meat of the choice sheep, tearing off their hoofs.

¹⁷"Woe to the worthless shepherd,
    who deserts the flock!

> May the sword strike his arm and his right eye!
> May his arm be completely withered,
> his right eye totally blinded!"

COMMENTARY

15–16 With the Shepherd of the Lord's choice removed from the scene, a foolish and worthless shepherd replaces him. Zechariah acts out the role of such a bad shepherd, thus signifying that a selfish, corrupt, and greedy leader will arise and oppress the flock—the people of Israel. So the first oracle of Part II of the book ends on a note of sorrow. "Again" (v.15) doubtless refers to v.7, where Zechariah took two shepherds' staffs as the equipment of the good Shepherd. The "equipment" also includes a bag for food, a pipe or reed for calling the sheep, a knife, and a case for setting and binding up broken bones. The bad shepherd is characterized as "foolish" here, a word denoting "one who is morally deficient" (cf. NIV note at Pr 1:7).

The reason for Zechariah's impersonation of a foolish (and "worthless"; v.17) shepherd is explained in v.16 ("For"): God is going to raise up a shepherd who will not do what a good shepherd should; instead he will destroy the sheep. Removing "not" from the sentence results in an enlightening description of a truly effective pastoral ministry in the church today: (1) "care for the lost [*hannikḥādôt*]," or, with BDB (470, 2), "care for those in the process of being ruined or destroyed"; (2) "seek the young [*naᶜar*]" (cf. Isa 40:11; however, if BDB, 654, is correct, the reference here is to "the scattered"); (3) "heal the injured"; and (4) "feed the healthy." The bad shepherd will do none of these things. Instead of feeding the sheep, he will feed *on* them and prey upon the unwary. He will even tear off their hooves—apparently, as Unger, 204, suggests, "in avaricious search for the last edible morsel."

17 This same sinister figure is now called "the worthless shepherd" because of his diabolical deeds, such as deserting the flock, in contrast to the actions of the good Shepherd (Jn 10:11–13). For this reason judgment is pronounced against him. While this counterfeit shepherd may have found a partial, historical fulfillment in such leaders as Simeon bar Kokhba (or Kosiba), who led the Jewish revolt against the Romans in AD 132–35 and was hailed as the messiah by Rabbi Akiba, it seems that the final stage in the progressive fulfillment of the complete prophecy awaits the rise of the eschatological Antichrist (cf. Eze 34:2–4; Da 11:36–39; Jn 5:43; 2Th 2:3–10; Rev 13:1–8).

The imprecation calls for his power ("arm") to be paralyzed ("completely withered") and his intelligence ("right eye") to be frustrated or nullified ("totally blinded"). For the fulfillment with respect to the Antichrist or "beast," see Revelation 19:19–21; 20:10. "With arm and right eye out of action the leader will be powerless to fight, or even to take aim, against his enemies" (Baldwin, 187). Feinberg, 213–14, concludes the first oracle and introduces the second: "The judgment here (vs. 17) brings to a close the cycle of prophecy which began with judgment (9:1). Judgment has gone from the circumference (the nations) to the center (Israel); Zechariah will yet reveal that in blessing the direction will be from the center (Israel) to the circumference (the nations) as in chapter 14."

NOTES

16 יְכַלְכֵּל (*yᵉkalkēl*, "feed, sustain, support, nourish") is a Pilpel imperfect from כּוּל (*kûl*, "to hold, measure").

17 רֹעִי (*rōʿî*, "shepherd") and עֹזְבִי (*ʿōzᵉbî*, "who deserts") feature the *Hireq compaginis* (GKC, par. 90 l–m), evidently owing its origin to an archaic ending of the construct state. This construct ending is found also in certain words in Akkadian. יָבוֹשׁ (*yābôš*, "completely") and כָּהֹה (*kāhōh*, "totally") are infinitives absolute, accentuating their respective verbal ideas. The accompanying finite verbs, in turn, are probably best construed as jussives (NIV).

B. The Second Oracle: The Advent and Reception of the Messiah (12:1–14:21)

OVERVIEW

Zechariah next encourages God's covenantal people by contrasting initial judgment on them with their ultimate deliverance, restoration, and blessing. That "in [or 'on'] that day" appears sixteen times in the second oracle places it, for the most part, in the eschaton. The oracle basically revolves around two scenes: the final siege of Jerusalem and the Messiah's return to defeat Israel's enemies and to establish his kingdom fully. Feinberg, 218, sets the stage for this last section of the book: "Says Dods, 'It is obvious that from the beginning of the twelfth chapter to the end of the book it is one period that is described.' In these chapters the city of Jerusalem holds a prominent place.... The Tetragrammaton is found with marked frequency.... The nations of the earth ... play a major role in the events set forth."

1. The Deliverance and Conversion of Israel (12:1–13:9)

a. The siege of Jerusalem (12:1–3)

> ¹This is the word of the LORD concerning Israel. The LORD, who stretches out the heavens, who lays the foundation of the earth, and who forms the spirit of man within him, declares: ²"I am going to make Jerusalem a cup that sends all the surrounding peoples reeling. Judah will be besieged as well as Jerusalem. ³On that day, when all the nations of the earth are gathered against her, I will make Jerusalem an immovable rock for all the nations. All who try to move it will injure themselves.

COMMENTARY

1 For "An Oracle" (v.1) see comment on 9:1. It is somewhat surprising to be informed that the oracle concerns "Israel" instead of "Judah and Jerusalem," but it is clear that in chs. 12–14 "Israel" means the whole nation, not just the northern kingdom. The oracle begins by describing the Lord's creative power in the heavens, on the earth, and in humanity (Ge 2:7). He is "able therefore to accomplish what He predicts" (Perowne, 128). Perhaps this description is also a means of strengthening the royal and sovereign authority of the message (see comment on "the word of the LORD came" at 1:1).

2–3 Jerusalem is pictured as a cup "round which all nations gather, eager to swallow down its inviting contents" (Perowne, 129). But as they drink from her, they become intoxicated and reel (see

Barker, ed., NIVSB at Isa 51:17n.). The end of v.2 indicates that the siege of Jerusalem will obviously affect Judah as well.

In v.3 Jerusalem is compared to a heavy, "immovable rock" that the nations attempt to move but in the process of doing so only hurt themselves. Their failure, of course, will be due to special divine intervention and protection (vv.4–5). On the invasion of Jerusalem (v.3), "when all the nations of the earth are gathered against her," see also 14:2; Joel 3:9–16; Revelation 16:16–21.

b. The divine deliverance (12:4–9)

> [4] "On that day I will strike every horse with panic and its rider with madness," declares the LORD. "I will keep a watchful eye over the house of Judah, but I will blind all the horses of the nations. [5] Then the leaders of Judah will say in their hearts, 'The people of Jerusalem are strong, because the LORD Almighty is their God.'
>
> [6] "On that day I will make the leaders of Judah like a firepot in a woodpile, like a flaming torch among sheaves. They will consume right and left all the surrounding peoples, but Jerusalem will remain intact in her place.
>
> [7] "The LORD will save the dwellings of Judah first, so that the honor of the house of David and of Jerusalem's inhabitants may not be greater than that of Judah. [8] On that day the LORD will shield those who live in Jerusalem, so that the feeblest among them will be like David, and the house of David will be like God, like the Angel of the LORD going before them. [9] On that day I will set out to destroy all the nations that attack Jerusalem.

COMMENTARY

4–6 In Deuteronomy 28:28, "panic [or 'confusion of mind']," "madness," and "blindness" (v.4) are listed among Israel's curses for disobeying the stipulations of the covenant. Now these curses are turned against Israel's enemies. Special emphasis is laid on the horses in order to exalt God's power. On God's "watchful eye" over his people see 9:8 and Psalms 32:8; 33:18; 121. Feinberg, 223, observes: "In

the same hour that God blinds the eyes of Israel's enemies [actually their horses], He will open His own upon the house of Judah in love and compassion to protect them."

For the literal meaning of the Hebrew for "leaders" (v.5), see comment on 9:7. These wise leaders discern that the source of the people's strength is their God, "the LORD Almighty." In v.6 these faithful leaders are compared to a fire that destroys wood and sheaves of grain; thus they will consume their enemies (cf. Jdg 15:3–5; Mic 5:5–6). By contrast Jerusalem and her people "will remain intact in her place."

7–9 In the coming deliverance there will be no superiority or inferiority complexes or ranking of some above others in honor. "The Lord will deliver the defenseless country before the fortified and well-defended capital, so that both may realize that the victory is of the Lord" (Feinberg, 225; for the principle of v.7 see Jer 9:23–24; 1Co 1:29, 31; 12:22–26; 2Co 10:17). Ultimately the Lord is the one who does the saving (v.7), the shielding or protecting (v.8), and the destroying of enemies (v.9). He will make the "feeblest" (lit., "the one who stumbles") among them like David (v.8), who was celebrated as a great warrior. And the members of the Davidic dynasty will be "like God," which, in turn, is explained as being "like the Angel of the LORD going before them." God will be with them,

will go before them, and will give them supernatural strength (cf. 4:6; for the "Angel" motif referred to here see Ex 14:19; 23:20; 32:34; 33:2, 14–15, 22).

Verse 9 is a summary of the previous verses. Perowne, 132, interacts with Wright's interpretation of the verse:

It is true, as Mr. Wright points out, that in the only other passage in which this phrase ["I will set out," lit., "I will seek"] is used of Almighty God, the intention, though "manifested clearly and distinctly," was abandoned (Ex. iv. 24). But it does not follow that "this passage is not an absolute promise of the utter destruction of the nations," but only a promise conditional upon the future conduct of the Jews. The passage as a whole is quite against such a supposition. The verse would be a strange anti-climax, if after such promises as are contained in ver. 2–8 it only asserted, "My aim shall be to do all this that I have promised in glowing terms; but all may be frustrated and come to nought through the unfaithfulness of man."

NOTES

5 According to Unger, 211, a "plausible and meritorious reading is *emtsah leyoshebhey....* This assumes a slight dittography." The resultant translation would be thus: "The strength of the people of Jerusalem is in the LORD Almighty, their God."

7 Conversely, יֹשֵׁב יְרוּשָׁלַם (*yōšēb yᵉrûšālaim*, "Jerusalem's inhabitants"), both here and in vv.8 and 10, may be due to haplography, so that the reading should be יֹשְׁבֵי (*yōšᵉbê ...*), as supported by some Hebrew MSS and the ancient versions.

8 The use of אֱלֹהִים (*ᵉlōhîm*, "God") here is similar to that in Exodus 4:16; 7:1.

c. Israel's complete deliverance from sin (12:10–13:9)

> ¹⁰"And I will pour out on the house of David and the inhabitants of Jerusalem a spirit of grace and supplication. They will look on me, the one they have pierced, and they will mourn for him as one mourns for an only child, and grieve bitterly for him as one grieves for a firstborn son. ¹¹On that day the weeping in Jerusalem will be great, like the weeping

of Hadad Rimmon in the plain of Megiddo. ¹²The land will mourn, each clan by itself, with their wives by themselves: the clan of the house of David and their wives, the clan of the house of Nathan and their wives, ¹³the clan of the house of Levi and their wives, the clan of Shimei and their wives, ¹⁴and all the rest of the clans and their wives.

¹³:¹"On that day a fountain will be opened to the house of David and the inhabitants of Jerusalem, to cleanse them from sin and impurity.

²"On that day, I will banish the names of the idols from the land, and they will be remembered no more," declares the LORD Almighty. "I will remove both the prophets and the spirit of impurity from the land. ³And if anyone still prophesies, his father and mother, to whom he was born, will say to him, 'You must die, because you have told lies in the LORD's name.' When he prophesies, his own parents will stab him.

⁴"On that day every prophet will be ashamed of his prophetic vision. He will not put on a prophet's garment of hair in order to deceive. ⁵He will say, 'I am not a prophet. I am a farmer; the land has been my livelihood since my youth.' ⁶If someone asks him, 'What are these wounds on your body?' he will answer, 'The wounds I was given at the house of my friends.'

⁷"Awake, O sword, against my shepherd,
    against the man who is close to me!"
    declares the LORD Almighty.
"Strike the shepherd,
    and the sheep will be scattered,
    and I will turn my hand against the little ones.
⁸In the whole land," declares the LORD,
    "two-thirds will be struck down and perish;
    yet one-third will be left in it.
⁹This third I will bring into the fire;
    I will refine them like silver
    and test them like gold.
They will call on my name
    and I will answer them;
I will say, 'They are my people,'
    and they will say, 'The LORD is our God.'"

COMMENTARY

10 Now there is movement from physical deliverance, just described, to spiritual deliverance (cf. the pattern of Dt 30:1–10). In anthropomorphic language the Lord promises an effusion of his Spirit on his covenantal people. The imagery is doubtless that of water as an emblem of the Holy Spirit.

The recipients are the royal leaders and people of Jerusalem, representative of the inhabitants of the whole land. The content of the effusion is "a spirit of grace and supplication," that is, "the Spirit which conveys grace and calls forth supplications" (Perowne, 132–33). While it is possible to construe "spirit" in the sense of "disposition," it seems preferable to follow the NIV note (and Perowne) and see here a reference to the Spirit of God. This approach is more in accord with what appear to be parallel passages (Isa 32:15; 44:3; 59:20–21; Jer 31:31, 33; Eze 36:26–27; 39:29; Joel 2:28–29). Because of the convicting work of God's Spirit, Israel will turn to the Messiah with mourning.

The most common meaning of the Hebrew preposition translated "on" is "to" (NIV note), and there is no good contextual reason to depart from it here. The emphasis, then, is not on looking "on" (or "at") the Messiah literally but on looking "to" the Messiah in faith (cf. Nu 21:9; Isa 45:22; Jn 3:14–15). According to some premillennialists, this will take place at the second coming of the Messiah (Christ) to the earth. According to others, it will happen just prior to his second advent.

The object of the people's look of faith is identified as "the one they have pierced" (cf. Isa 53:5; Jn 19:34; Rev 1:7). John 19:37, which quotes this part of the verse, is but a stage in the progressive fulfillment of the whole. The final, complete fulfillment is yet future for Israel (Ro 11:25–27). Evidently the prospect of a "pierced" Messiah was such a stumbling block to the Jews that, according to C. C. Torrey ("The Messiah Son of Ephraim," *JBL* 66 [1947]: 273), the Babylonian Talmud (*Sukkah* 52a) presents two Messiahs; the one here in v.10 is identified as the Messiah son of Joseph. The similes at the end of the verse accentuate the people's mourning (see Jer 6:26 on mourning "for an only child" and Ex 11:5–6 on mourning "for a firstborn son"). (For the Jewish interpretations of the verse

see Baron, 438–44, and Cashdan, 321–22.) R. L. Smith (*Micah–Malachi* [WBC; Waco, Tex.: Word, 1984], 278) notes:

> Both the Babylonian and Palestinian Talmuds take the reference to be the Messiah (cf. F. F. Bruce, *NT Development* 112). The fourth Gospel (Jn 19:33–37) and Rev 1:7 identify the pierced one with Jesus. Undoubtedly this passage in Zech. 12 is eschatological. It speaks of the "end-time" as far as the prophet was concerned.... Bruce is correct in saying that the prophet in Zech. 12:10 suggests something that is more than what appears on the surface.

11 The convicting work of the Spirit of God will produce national contrition or repentance, led by the civil (royal) and religious leaders. The future weeping ("on that day") in Jerusalem will be so great that it is compared with "the weeping of Hadad Rimmon in the plain of Megiddo." *The Illustrated Family Encyclopedia*, 8:96, summarizes the major interpretations of this simile:

> The sound of weeping and wailing that fills the streets of the city will rise to the intensity of the cries of grief uttered for Hadad-Rimmon in the plain of Megiddo. This comparison is sometimes explained as a reference to a public mourning for some notable dignitary. Such, for example, is the rendering of the Targum Jonathan in 2 Chron. 35:25. Hieronymus [Jerome] (5th cent. AD), on the other hand, interpreted Hadad-Rimmon as the name of "a city close to Jezreel which is today called Maximianupolis," and which modern scholars locate at el-Lajjun near Megiddo. The modern Arabic name is derived from the Latin noun "legio," since it was here that the Sixth Legion (*Legio Ferrata*, the "Iron" Legion) had its camp from the revolt of Bar-Kokhba onwards.... Situated on the "Sea Road," the place had great strategic importance as guarding the passage from the valley of Jezreel to the coastal plain. Still a

third interpretation would refer the words of our verse to Hadad-Rimmon the god of rain and fertility (perhaps to be identified with Baal, the Canaanite-Ugaritic god of fertility), whose death was annually bewailed at the end of the spring, with the coming of the summer's shriveling heat. A similar ritualistic lament was also uttered for Tammuz (Eze. 8:14). The fertile plain of Megiddo would indeed have made an appropriate setting for the mourning over Hadad-Rimmon, since in Palestine the success of the crops depends on an adequate seasonal rainfall.

Keith N. Schoville (*Biblical Archaeology in Focus* [Grand Rapids: Baker, 1978], 444) apparently agrees with the third view above, for he writes: "It is worth noting that a phenomenon common to all Israelite levels at Megiddo is an abundance of cult objects, especially ceramic figurines, along with objects for normal use bearing foreign cultic designs. The last reference in the Bible to Megiddo alludes to such religious syncretism (Zech. 12:11)." I, however, prefer to take Hadad-Rimmon as a place name (containing the names of ancient Semitic fertility gods) near Megiddo. So understood, the simile in v.11 refers to the people of this town mourning the death of King Josiah (2Ch 35:20–27; see v.22 there for the plain of Megiddo and vv.24–25 for the mourning).

12–14 The expressions "each clan by itself" and "their wives by themselves" (v.12) are doubtless intended to emphasize the sincerity of the mourning as true repentance. This is no purely emotional public spectacle. Nor are professional mourners involved. Individually and corporately, this is the experience of Leviticus 16 (the Day of Atonement) and Psalm 51 (a penitential psalm) on a national scale. As the colon in the NIV indicates, this general statement of the mourning (v.12a) is followed by the particulars (vv.12b–14). The mourning includes the royal house of David and the family of

his son Nathan (2Sa 5:14), also the house of Levi and the family of Shimei son of Gershon, the son of Levi (Nu 3:17–18, 21), as well as "all the rest" (v.14).

While the repentance is led by the civil (royal) and religious leaders, it extends to every clan in the nation. Isaiah 53:1–9 may well be their confession on that great occasion. Such true repentance, of course, "remains a gift of God's Spirit (verse 10)" (Baldwin, 194); and, in keeping with his covenantal promise, he will bestow that gift.

13:1 The repentance at the end of the previous chapter leads to what Perowne, 134, calls worthy fruits of repentance in vv.1–6. But v.1 also contains new-covenant terminology. In Jeremiah 31:33–34 God promised Israel these provisions: (1) enablement through his Spirit to obey his law (v.33a; cf. Eze 36:26–27); (2) an intimate personal relationship and fellowship (v.33b); (3) a saving knowledge of himself (v.34a; cf. Ro 11:26a); and (4) the forgiveness of sins (v.34b; cf. Eze 36:25; Zec 3:4, 9). It is clear from the NT (e.g., Lk 22:20; 1Co 11:25; Heb 8–10) that the church—Gentiles and the spiritual remnant of Israel (Ro 11:1–16)—is today the recipient of the benefits promised to Israel in the new covenant. The church's receipt of those benefits is made possible only by God's sovereign, gracious grafting of Gentiles into that place of blessing (Ro 11:17–24).

These blessings will yet be experienced by ethnic Israel at the second advent of their Messiah (Ro 11:25–29), thus preparing the priestly nation for the Lord's service (ch. 3). The cleansing referred to in v.1 is related particularly to the fourth provision of the new covenant (see above) and is ultimately made possible through the atoning death of the Pierced One (12:10).

2–3 Not only will there be personal internal cleansing—morally and spiritually—but also external cleansing, as the country is purged of idols and false prophets, both of which were such a constant snare and source of deception to Israel (10:2–3; Jer 23:30–32; 27:9–10; Eze 13:1–14:11). God himself ("I") declares that he will rid the land of the names (i.e., the influence, fame, and even the very existence) of the idols. That false prophecy was still a problem in the postexilic period is clear from Nehemiah 6:12–14.

That both idolatry and false prophecy will once again be a problem in the future is evident not only here but also in Matthew 24:4–5, 11, 15, 23–24; 2 Thessalonians 2:2–4; and Revelation 9:20; 13:4–15. The spirit of impurity that inspired the false prophets to lie will also be removed. In that future day, if anyone dares to utter false prophecies ("lies"; v.3), his own parents—in obedience to Deuteronomy 13:6–9—will take the lead in executing him. The Hebrew for "stab" is the same verb as "pierced" in 12:10, thus indicating that the feelings and actions shown in piercing the Messiah will be directed toward the false prophets.

4–6 Because of these stern measures, a false prophet will be reticent to identify himself as a prophet and will respond to questioning evasively. To help conceal his true identity, he will not wear "a prophet's garment of hair" (v.4), such as Elijah wore (2Ki 1:8). Instead, to avoid the death penalty (v.3), he will deny being a prophet and will claim to have been a farmer from his youth (v.5). And if some suspicious person notices marks on his body and inquires about them (v.6), he will claim that he received them in a scuffle with friends or as discipline from his parents during childhood. Apparently the accuser will suspect that the false prophet's wounds have been self-inflicted to arouse his prophetic ecstasy in idolatrous rites (as in 1Ki 18:28; cf. also Lev 19:28; 21:5; Dt 14:1; Jer 16:6; 41:5; 48:37).

A few expositors assign a messianic sense to v.6 (see Unger, 228–30, for the best defense of such a position, though most of his arguments are weak, forced, irrelevant, or debatable). The following observations, however, militate against any messianic import of the verse:

(1) it presupposes an unnatural break between vv.5 and 6, with a complete change in subject matter;

(2) in order to find a proper antecedent for "him," it reverts all the way back to 12:10, thus regarding 12:11–13:5 as parenthetical, which is neither obvious nor necessary;

(3) the most natural antecedent for "him" (v.6) is "he" (v.5), since $w^e\bar{a}mar$ ("if someone asks") at the beginning of v.6 certainly seems to be a response to $w^e\bar{a}mar$ ("he will say") at the beginning of v.5;

(4) there is a rather clear change in subject matter in v.7, thus indicating that the break is between vv.6 and 7, not between vv.5 and 6;

(5) there is a change of person in v.7, thus indicating the same break;

(6) the verb changes to the imperative mood in v.7, so also indicating that break;

(7) the literary form changes to poetry in v.7, thus further indicating a break between vv.6 and 7.

7 "This startling poem resumes the shepherd motif from chapter 11, though in chapters 12 and 13 the subject of leadership has never been far from the prophet's thoughts" (Baldwin, 197). Compared to the immediately preceding verses, the oracle now moves back to the time when Israel will be scattered because of her rejection of the true messianic Shepherd. Then, after the announcement of the dispersion, the oracle seems to advance to a future period when Israel will undergo a special, purifying discipline—a refining, likened to that of silver and gold (vv.8–9). The surviving remnant will be the Lord's people (v.9).

Verse 7 begins with an apostrophe to a personified instrument of violent death. According to Bullinger, 548, "sword" (*hereb*) is sometimes a metonymy of cause for effect—sword is put for slaughter. Similarly, Edwin Yamauchi (*TWOT*, 1:320) notes: "In Ps 22:20 [H 21] *hereb* is used as a metaphor for a violent end." Death is announced against one whom God calls "my shepherd," i.e., the royal good Shepherd—the true Shepherd of 11:4–14 in contrast to the foolish and worthless shepherd (11:15–17). God also identifies him as "the man who is close to me," on which Baldwin, 197–98, comments: "The expression 'who stands next to me' is used elsewhere only in Leviticus (*e.g.* 6:2; 18:20) to mean 'near neighbour'; similarly the shepherd is one who dwells side by side with the Lord, His equal." The expression eventually leads to John 10:30: "I and the Father are one," and to John 14:9: "Anyone who has seen me has seen the Father" (cf. Jn 1:1–2).

In 11:17 it was the worthless shepherd who was to be struck; now (v.7) it is the good Shepherd (cf. 12:10). Apparently the one who wields the "sword" is God himself. If so, this is perhaps the best explanation for the shift from the feminine gender of "awake" (agreeing with "sword," which is feminine) to the masculine gender of "strike" (agreeing with God ["Lord Almighty"]). In 12:10–14 the Messiah's death is presented as an act of Israel, but in 13:7 his death is the sovereign act of God (cf. Isa 53:10; Ac 2:23). In John 10:15, 17–18 it is Jesus himself who lays down his life. One could also mention the role of the Romans in crucifying Christ. Of course, all these passages are true. They are supplementary and complementary, not contradictory.

When the Shepherd is struck, the sheep (cf. 10:3, 9) are scattered, in fulfillment of the curses for covenantal disobedience (Dt 28:64; 29:24–25). Keil (K&D, 2:397–98) correctly maintains that the thought is that the Lord

will scatter Israel or His nation by smiting the shepherd; that is to say, He will give it up to the misery and destruction to which a flock without a shepherd is exposed.... The flock, which will be dispersed in consequence of the slaying of the shepherd, is the covenant nation, *i.e.* neither the human race nor the Christian church as such, but the flock which the shepherd in ch. xi 4 sqq. had to feed.

This part of v.7 is quoted by Jesus not long before his arrest (Mt 26:31; Mk 14:27) and applied to the scattering of the apostles (Mt 26:56; Mk 14:50), but the scattering is probably intended to serve as a type of the Diaspora, which occurred in AD 70 and following. Some interpreters take "I will turn my hand against [or 'on' or 'over']" in a negative sense, others in a positive way. Perowne, 140, strikes a balance: "For correction, but in mercy, ver. 8, 9. Comp. Is. i 25."

"The little ones" are the remnant (vv.8–9), "the oppressed" or "afflicted of the flock" (11:7, 11). Isaiah, too, spoke much of the remnant (e.g., Isa 6:13; 66:22–24).

8–9 These verses apparently precede vv.1–6 chronologically. They depict a refining process for Israel. While what happened in AD 70 at the hands of the Romans may have been an initial stage in the prophecy's progressive fulfillment, the final and complete stage is yet future, for Israel as a whole is not in the proper covenantal relationship with God described in v.9. The fact that a remnant will survive ("one-third"; v.8) reveals God's mercy in the midst of judgment. *The Illustrated Family Encyclopedia*, 8:97, elucidates the refining process mentioned in the first half of v.9:

The process of refining metals, especially precious metals such as silver and gold, serves the prophets of Israel as a metaphor of the nation's spiritual purification (cf. Isa. 1:25 ...). Thus, in our verse here, the remnant of Israel is compared to the small quantity of pure metal which is left after the smelting and refining: two thirds of the people will be cut off and perish, while the remaining third will be further reduced by being purified in the fire (Zech. 13:8–9). The method of extracting pure gold from the silver and other metals mixed with it by constantly repeated firing was known at an early period in human history, perhaps as early as the first half of the second millennium BC. A Greek author gives a detailed description of the way in which gold was refined in a porous clay vessel. The vessel, containing lead, salt and zinc in addition to the gold ore, was tightly sealed and then placed in a fired kiln for five days. During this time the dross stuck to the sides of the container, while the pure gold collected in its centre. From many passages in the Old Testament (e.g. Eze. 22:21–23; Ps. 12:6) it would seem that this method, or one similar to it, was also the one used in biblical times. The processes of metal-working employed in the classical world are illustrated by a bas-relief decoration on a Greek goblet of the Hellenistic period (4th cent. BC).... It shows the bearded smith-god, Hephaestos, seated in a smithy beside a kiln ... and holding in his hand the tools of his craft, a pair of tongs and a hammer.

The survivors (cf. Jer 30:7) are those of 12:10–13:1; they will constitute the Jewish nucleus of the messianic kingdom and will evidently include the 144,000 of Revelation 7:1–8 and 14:1–5. "The last four lines of the verse have an appropriate chiastic structure—*they, I, I, they*—reflecting that there are two sides to any relationship, even when it is between God and man" (Baldwin, 198, emphasis hers). The calling on the Lord's name includes the "supplication" of 12:10. The verse closes with the covenantal formula: "I will say, 'They are my people,' and they will say, 'The LORD is our God.'" Thus the new covenant will be fulfilled for Israel, and they will be restored to proper covenantal relationship with the Lord (cf. also Eze 20:30–44, esp. v.37 for their restoration to "the bond of the covenant").

Webb, 171–76, summarizes how the NT quotes or alludes to Zechariah 12–13 (and I would add to

his references the allusion to 14:4 in Acts 1:11–12) in such an effective manner that I quote from him at length (172–73):

In order to appreciate how the New Testament writers refer to Zechariah we need to understand two things. First, *all* the Old Testament promises about the coming kingdom of God find their fulfilment (ultimate meaning) in Jesus Christ. Furthermore, they are not fulfilled in some general way (i.e. the fulfilment is "somehow" related to Jesus Christ), but in the very specific *events* of his birth, life, death, resurrection, ascension and coming again. This means ... that the fulfilment does not come all at once, but in two major phases. As Jesus both has come and will come, so the kingdom of God has come and will come ... the same Jesus who told his disciples that the kingdom was already present, told them to pray for its coming. The key to understanding this apparent contradiction is to grasp the basic truth at the heart of it, namely the kingdom of God comes *in Jesus Christ*. In the New Testament the time of fulfilment that Zechariah spoke about as *that day* opens out into *the last days*—the whole period beginning with the first coming of Christ to make atonement for sin, and his second coming in glory to judge the world. This is the age we now live in!

The second major thing we must grasp is the landmark significance of the birth of Jesus Christ. In that momentous event God became incarnate; he entered our world *in the person of his Son*, Jesus Christ. In Zechariah God himself and the Messiah (the Branch, the king) are closely connected, but always distinguished from one another. In the New Testament, however, the two become one in the God-man, Jesus Christ. It is no longer merely a matter of intimate, close relationship; God *really is present* in Jesus Christ. This is why the New Testament writers can refer to passages in Zechariah that refer specifically to God and point to Jesus as the one in whom they are fulfilled. (emphasis his)

As a follow-up to Webb's last sentence just quoted, see my remarks at 2:10. Next, Webb quotes Revelation 1:7: "Look, he is coming with the clouds, / and every eye will see him, / even those who pierced him; / and all the peoples of the earth will mourn because of him." Then he comments (173–74):

> At his return, Jesus Christ will *again* be seen by "those who pierced him," and they will "mourn because of him." But this time it is not just Israel, but "all peoples of the earth" who are in view. The rejection of Jesus, God's Messiah, was not the sin of Israel alone, but of the whole human race, and all will face judgment for it on the last day unless they repent.... So in many ways the New Testament tells us that Zechariah's message about the coming of the kingdom of God finds its fulfilment in Jesus Christ. The first stage in the climactic battle to usher in the kingdom of God has already been fought in Jerusalem, in the death, resurrection and ascension of Jesus Christ. The final stage will be fought there also, when he returns.

We now consider that return in ch. 14.

NOTES

10 וְתַחֲנוּנִים (wᵉtaḥᵃnûnîm, "supplication") is either the plural of intensification or simply the abstract plural. The shift from first person in אֵלַי (ᵓēlay, "on me") to third person in עָלָיו (ᶜālāyw, "for him") is explained in the notes at 7:13 and 9:10.

The infinitive absolute וְהָמֵר (wᵉhāmēr, "and grieve bitterly") is here used as a substitute for the *waw* consecutive perfect (Davidson, par. 88, rem. 1).

12–14 Single words are sometimes repeated in order to express a distributive sense. This is true of לְבָד (lᵉbād, "by itself" or "by themselves") throughout these verses (GKC, par. 123d).

13:1 The preposition לְ (lᵉ, "to") in לְבֵית (lᵉbêt, "to the house of") could just as easily be rendered "for [the benefit of]" (*IBHS*, 207–8).

5 As the MT stands, the last clause of this verse should probably be rendered "a man sold me [as a slave] in my youth" (cf. NIV note). But many Hebrew specialists propose that אָדָם הִקְנַנִי (ᵓādām hiqnanî, "a man caused another to buy me," i.e., "sold me") be slightly altered to אֲדָמָה קִנְיָנִי (ᵓᵃdāmâ qinyānî, "the land has been my possession/ livelihood"), thus yielding the rendering in the main text of the NIV.

6 בֵּין יָדֶיךָ (bên yādeykā, lit., "between your hands"; cf. NIV note) is an idiom meaning "on your back/ chest," i.e., "on your body." The same idiom occurs in Ugaritic Text 68:14–15: *hlm ktp zbl ym bn ydm [tp]t nhr*, "Strike the shoulder [i.e., 'back'] of Prince Yamm, between the hands/arms [i.e., on the back] of Judge Nahar" (see *UT*, 180, for the text; *ANET*, 131, for Ginsberg's translation). Thus Ugaritic demonstrates that "between the hands" is parallel to "shoulder" or "back." Essentially the same idiom appears in 2 Kings 9:24, where the Hebrew has, literally, "between his arms" ("between the shoulders," NIV). Thus the Ugaritic and Hebrew expressions are basically the same, since "hand" in Hebrew can also mean "arm" (1Ki 10:19; Jer 38:12; Eze 13:18).

On the absence of the preposition בְּ (bᵉ, "in, at") before בֵית (bêt, "house"), see note on 11:13. "My friends" is literally "those who love me [objective genitive]" and so is open to either of the ideas suggested in the commentary above ("friends" or "parents").

9 On the construction of the similes see Davidson, par. 91, rems. 1, 3.

2. The Messiah's Return and His Kingdom (14:1–21)

a. The siege of Jerusalem (14:1–2)

¹A day of the LORD is coming when your plunder will be divided among you.
²I will gather all the nations to Jerusalem to fight against it; the city will be captured, the houses ransacked, and the women raped. Half of the city will go into exile, but the rest of the people will not be taken from the city.

COMMENTARY

1–2 The ultimate goal of all history is the Lord's personal appearance and reign. But prior to the literal and full manifestation of his kingdom, the earth must experience the throes of birth pangs. Verse 2 furthers the idea of refining, initiated in 13:8–9, as the nations gather at Jerusalem and ravish her. Baldwin, 199, describes the chiastic arrangement of the chapter:

The dramatic reversal from defeat to victory is well expressed in the chiastic structure of this section. Verses 1–6 begin with Jerusalem crushed in defeat. "The day of the Lord ... is darkness, and not light" (Am. 5:18), but, though awesome events continue to overtake the city, there is progression towards one particular day, known to the Lord (verse 7). This is the turning-point. From that day Jerusalem becomes the source of light and life. There the Lord sets up His world government, and whereas at the beginning Jerusalem was being despoiled, at the end all the nations are financing God's kingdom. Whereas at the beginning God's people suffer, at the end His enemies suffer and die. Unity in the Lord is the only unity that endures. His kingship is very greatly stressed, hence the fall of those who oppose Him.

Unger, 239–40, stresses the importance of normal, consistent hermeneutics in interpreting ch. 14.

The chapter begins with an invasion of Jerusalem similar to that in the opening part of ch. 12. Verse 1 is a general statement; v.2 provides the particulars. Although "a day of the LORD" is not the usual construction for "the day of the LORD," the expression doubtless bears the same meaning; "that day" occurs throughout the context (chs. 12–14; cf. Eze 30:3; Am 5:18–20; Joel 1:15). Perhaps this particular construction is used here to emphasize the fact that the "day" is distinctively the Lord's (cf. Isa 2:12). Humans are having their day now; the Lord's day is yet to come (see comment at 2:11). "Your" (v.1) refers to Jerusalem (v.2). Both "your" and "you" are an apostrophe in which Jerusalem is directly addressed.

"I" (v.2) is a reminder that the sovereign God is in complete control. As the Lord of history and nations, he is the Prime Mover. Ultimately the scene depicted here (i.e., of contingents from all nations gathered to fight against Jerusalem) is probably the same as the one in Revelation 16:16–21; 19:19–21 (Armageddon). This eschatological verse alone—with its statement that "the city will be captured"—is sufficient to refute the notion popular in certain circles that "the times of the Gentiles" (Lk 21:24) were fulfilled at the rebirth of the modern state of Israel in 1948. According to

Lukan theology, after "the times of the Gentiles are fulfilled," Jerusalem will be trampled on no more. Since Zechariah 14:2 clearly indicates that Jerusalem will be "trampled on" again in the future, the "times of the Gentiles" would seem to extend to the Messiah's second advent, when those "times" will be replaced by the final, universal, everlasting, messianic kingdom of Daniel 2:35, 44–45.

The rest of v.2 delineates some of the horrors that yet await Jerusalem and its people. Chambers, 110, correctly observes: "Only a part of the inhabitants are to be driven into exile, the rest remain.

It was different at the Chaldaean conquest of Jerusalem, for then the greater portion were carried away, and afterwards even 'the remnant that was left' (2Ki 25:11). The verse cannot therefore refer to that subjugation. Nor can it be applied to the overthrow of the holy city by Titus, who neither had all nations under his banner, nor left a half of the population in possession of their homes." The final, complete fulfillment, then, must lie in the future. At that time all these things will happen to fulfill the curses pronounced for covenantal disobedience (Dt 28:30).

NOTES

1 The pronominal suffix in שְׁלָלֵךְ (šᵉlālēk, "your plunder") is best taken as an objective genitive.

2 תִּשָּׁגַלְנָה (tiššāgalnâ, "will be raped") presents a Kethiv and Qere variation. The Masoretes apparently found the meaning of the Kethiv to be very obscene and proposed, instead, the euphemistic reading (in the margin of the Hebrew Bible) תִּשָּׁכַבְנָה (tiššākabnâ, "will be lain with").

b. The Messiah's return and its effects (14:3–8)

> ³Then the Lᴏʀᴅ will go out and fight against those nations, as he fights in the day of battle. ⁴On that day his feet will stand on the Mount of Olives, east of Jerusalem, and the Mount of Olives will be split in two from east to west, forming a great valley, with half of the mountain moving north and half moving south. ⁵You will flee by my mountain valley, for it will extend to Azel. You will flee as you fled from the earthquake in the days of Uzziah king of Judah. Then the Lᴏʀᴅ my God will come, and all the holy ones with him.
>
> ⁶On that day there will be no light, no cold or frost. ⁷It will be a unique day, without daytime or nighttime — a day known to the Lᴏʀᴅ. When evening comes, there will be light.
>
> ⁸On that day living water will flow out from Jerusalem, half to the eastern sea and half to the western sea, in summer and in winter.

COMMENTARY

3–5 Just when it seems that all hope is gone, "then the Lᴏʀᴅ" himself appears as Divine Warrior and delivers his beleaguered people. (On the Divine Warrior motif see comment on 1:3.) But who is this "Lᴏʀᴅ"? When one compares this scene, including v.4, with Acts 1:9–12 and Revelation

19:11–16, it would appear certain that "the LORD" here is ultimately the Messiah. The passage, then, is indirectly messianic (see comment on 2:10). "The day of battle" ("a day of battle," TNIV) is any occasion on which the Lord supernaturally intervenes to deliver his people, such as at the Red Sea (Ex 14:13–14). Acts 1:11–12 may well allude to the prophecy that "his feet will stand on the Mount of Olives" (v.4), which is situated "east of Jerusalem." *The Illustrated Family Encyclopedia*, 8:98, describes this mountain and its significance:

The Day of the Lord, the day when God will take vengeance on the nations that have done harm to Israel, is a conception that first occurs in the utterances of the prophets of the Assyrian and Babylonian periods (Isa. 25:6–9 ...), and is repeated in the visions of their post-destruction counterparts (Eze 38–39). On this day the Lord of Hosts will appear in His glory on the Mount of Olives, the mountain that rises high above Jerusalem, to war against the nations and mete out retribution to them. At this awe-inspiring theophany, the whole mountain will shake (cf. Jdg. 5:4) and be cloven asunder, as the earth was convulsed in the great earthquake that occurred in the reign of Uzziah, king of Judah.

The Mount of Olives—referred to by this name only here in the Old Testament (though a similar expression, "the Ascent of Olives," occurs in 2 Samuel 15:30)—is, in Ezekiel's words, "the mountain which is on the east side of the city" (Eze. 11:23). The aura of sanctity which had enveloped it from the early days of Israelite history was in no way diminished in later times. Thus, in the period of the Geonim (8th–11th cent. AD), prayers were regularly offered up on the Mount of Olives, which faced the Temple Mount, and the Scrolls of the Law were carried round in circuit there on the festival of Hoshana Rabba, while its slopes were dotted with the tombs of the pious. The mountain rises to a height of 2710 ft. above sea-level, thus being as much as 330 ft. higher than the Temple

Mount. Its soil—grey Rendzina—is well suited to the growth of olive trees which thrust their roots down into the brittle rock. Hence, in the Mishna and Talmud it is called the Mount of Anointing.

(See also Barker, ed., NIVSB, Zec 14:4 n.; Mk 11:1 n.)

In the eschaton, when the Lord will stand on this mountain, it will split in two (perhaps because of an earthquake, but not necessarily so), creating a great valley running east and west. Verse 5 states the purpose of the valley: to afford an easy means of rapid escape from the final anti-Semitic onslaught detailed in v.2; the Mount of Olives has always constituted a serious obstacle to such an escape to the east.

Although some scholars construe the Hebrew for Azel as a preposition ("beside") or a common noun ("side"), it seems best to understand it as the name of a place east of Jerusalem, thus marking the eastern end of the newly formed valley. Some relate it to the Wadi Yasul, a tributary of the Kidron (cf. "Azal" in *ISBE*, 1:374). The future escape of God's people is compared with the time when their ancestors "fled from the earthquake in the days of Uzziah king of Judah"—an earthquake so devastating and memorable that it is mentioned also in Amos 1:1 (see Barker, ed., NIVSB, Am 1:1n). Yohanan Aharoni (*The Land of the Bible*, trans. A. F. Rainey [London: Burns & Oates, 1966], 91) even suggests that it may have destroyed Level VI at Hazor around 760 BC.

In announcing the Lord's coming, Zechariah expresses his own personal faith in and relationship to God ("my God"). "All the holy ones" will be in the Lord's retinue when he comes. These apparently include both believers and unfallen angels (see Mt 25:31; Rev 19:14).

6–8 The precise meaning of these verses in Hebrew is admittedly uncertain, but the general picture is clear. The eschatological aspect of the day of the Lord described here will be characterized by cataclysmic phenomena, including cosmic signs (cf.

Isa 13:9–10; Joel 2:31; 3:15; Am 5:18; Mt 24:29–30; Rev 6:12–14; 8:8–12; 9:1–18; 14:14–20; 16:4,8–9). At the end of v.6 ("no cold or frost") the NIV follows the interpretation of the ancient versions. Feinberg, 254–55, however, probably correctly translates the verse this way (and then defends his translation):

"And it shall come to pass in that day, that there shall not be light; the bright ones [i.e., luminaries] will be congealed" (v.6). The first portion of the verse has caused no difficulty, and is abundantly set forth in other prophetic passages.... But the last two words have called forth various views and differing interpretations....

The difficulties are several: (1) the verb (if we take the *Kethibh*) is masculine while the subject is feminine; (2) the word used for the lights of heaven is found nowhere else in that meaning; (3) if the second word is taken as a noun (so the *Qere*), no such noun is found. It is probably best ... to understand that last clause as a reiteration in figurative language of that which is stated ... in the first clause. The LXX and Vulgate with others (reading *weqaruth weqippaʾon*) translate "cold and ice." But these are not opposites to light, as Keil has shown.... Gesenius-Robinson (1882) prefers the *Kethibh*, as does Keil. We have stated our preference in the translation above. Job 31:26 gives us a parallel use for the noun, while Exodus 15:8 and Job 10:10 furnish the same verb with the meaning of "curdle, contract, congeal." That day will be characterized by absence of light, for the luminaries of heaven will be congealed to give forth no brilliance.

Note the TNIV translation of vv.6–7: "On that day there will be no sunlight, no cold, frosty darkness. It will be a unique day—a day known only to

the LORD—with no distinction between day and night. When evening comes, there will be light."

Because of the topographical, cosmic and, indeed, even cataclysmic changes, that day will be "unique" (v.7). The situation will be such that it can be classified as neither day nor night—"a day known [only] to the LORD." But after the judgment and suffering (possibly the refining of 13:8–9) are past, "there will be light" again, possibly symbolizing the ushering in of the new order.

Is the "living water" (v.8) literal (physical) or figurative (spiritual)? Bullinger, 896, suggests that water can be emblematic of God, the gift of the Holy Spirit, or the blessings and merits of Christ. It is probably best to view the water as both literal and symbolic (cf. Pss 46:4; 65:9; Isa 8:6; Jer 2:13; Eze 47:1–12; Jn 4:10–14; 7:38; Rev 22:1–2). As indicated in the NIV note, "the eastern sea" is the Dead Sea and "the western sea" is the Mediterranean (hence the TNIV rendering). Roland de Vaux, 189–90, explains why spring and autumn are not mentioned along with summer and winter:

The year was divided into two seasons, the winter, *ḥoreph*, and summer, *qayṣ*, corresponding roughly to the cold and hot seasons, to seedtime and harvest (Gen. 8:22; cf. Ps 74:17; Is 18:6; Za 14:8).... This simple division corresponds to the climate of Palestine, where the hot, dry season and the cold, wet season succeed each other fairly quickly, leaving no distinct sensation of spring and autumn, as in more temperate countries.

Perhaps the main point here is that "living" (fresh or running) water will not dry up in the summer, as most Palestinian streams do in the "hot, dry season."

NOTES

4 גֵּיא (*gêʾ*, "valley"), in spite of the pointing, is probably in the absolute state (BDB, 161; GKC, par. 128w, n. 1).

5 The NIV note offers this alternative: "My mountain valley will be blocked and will extend to Azel. It will be blocked as it was blocked because of the earthquake." This reading presupposes repointing the verbs to נִסְתַּם (*nistam*), from סתם (*stm*), and receives support from the LXX, Targum, and Symmachus. The MT, however, has נַסְתֶּם (*nastem*), from נוס (*nws*), and is supported by the Vulgate and Peshitta. Since the MT makes good sense (see the exposition) and there is no convincing reason to change it, the MT is to be preferred (as reflected in the main text of the NIV).

The translation "by my mountain valley" is justified by analyzing גֵּיא (*gêʾ*, "valley") as an adverbial accusative of place (locative accusative) or perhaps as an adverbial accusative of manner. Apparently "mountain" is plural here (see Heb.) because it was "split in two" (v.4).

"With him" is literally "with you" (another direct address).

c. The establishment of the Messiah's kingdom (14:9–11)

⁹The Lord will be king over the whole earth. On that day there will be one Lord, and his name the only name.

¹⁰The whole land, from Geba to Rimmon, south of Jerusalem, will become like the Arabah. But Jerusalem will be raised up and remain in its place, from the Benjamin Gate to the site of the First Gate, to the Corner Gate, and from the Tower of Hananel to the royal winepresses. ¹¹It will be inhabited; never again will it be destroyed. Jerusalem will be secure.

COMMENTARY

9 Statements such as "the LORD will be king over the whole earth" stand at the very center of a truly biblical theology (cf. Barker, ed., "Scope and Center," 305–18; idem, ed., NIVSB, 780–87; Albert E. Glock, "Early Israel as the Kingdom of Yahweh: The Influence of Archaeological Evidence on the Reconstruction of Religion in Early Israel," *CTM* 41 [1970]: 558–605; Gary V. Smith, "The Concept of God/the Gods as King in the Ancient Near East and the Bible," *TJ* 3 [Spring 1982]: 1–38, esp. 33–38). When this comes true in the fullest sense, the prayer of Matthew 6:9–10 will be answered:

Our Father in heaven,
hallowed be your name,
your kingdom come,
your will be done,
on earth as it is in heaven.

While the Hebrew for "earth" can be rendered "land," Unger, 256, correctly argues for "earth" here: "*The translation 'land,'* while certainly in line with the context outside of verse 9 (i.e., vss. 1–8 and 10), *is not consonant with the larger context of the verse itself.* That *the Lord will be one and his name one* only in Palestine is unthinkable. The scope of verse 9 demands the larger meaning of the Hebrew word 'earth,' and strikes the note of universality in its wording and thought pattern" (emphasis his).

According to the remainder of v.9, the time is coming when there will be no more idolatry, polytheism, or even henotheism, but only high, ethical monotheism. This theological statement recalls the Jewish Shema (Dt 6:4). "God's name Yahweh [the LORD] expressed all He had ever been and ever would be (Ex. 3:13–17)" (Baldwin, 204).

10–11 The land around Jerusalem is to be leveled while Jerusalem is to be elevated (see v.4 for the cause of these topographical changes). Geba ("height") was located almost six miles north of Jerusalem at the northern boundary of the kingdom of Judah (2Ki 23:8). As the text indicates, the Rimmon mentioned here is the one situated "south of Jerusalem" (thus distinguishing it from other OT towns of the same name). It is usually identified with En Rimmon ("spring of the pomegranate tree," Ne 11:29; cf. Jos 15:32), modern "Khirbet Umm et-Ramamim, about thirty-five miles south-west of Jerusalem, where the hill country of Judah slopes away into the *Negeb* or south" (Baldwin, 204).

The term "Arabah" (primarily rendered "plain" in the KJV) "was applied specifically in part or wholly to the depression of the Jordan Valley, extending from Mt. Hermon, a 9100-ft. (2775-m.) elevation in the Anti-Lebanon Range, due S beyond the Sea of Chinnereth (Galilee), and including both sides of the river Jordan, the Dead Sea, and the region slightly to the southwest as far as the head of the Gulf of Aqabah" (*ISBE*, 1:218). That Jerusalem will thus be elevated (probably both physically and in prominence) is in agreement with Isaiah 2:2 and Micah 4:1 (see Barker, "Micah," 83–84). The Benjamin Gate, the First Gate, and the Tower of Hananel were all at the northeastern part of the city wall; the Corner Gate was at its northwestern corner; and the royal winepresses were just south of the city (cf. Jer 31:38). "Thus the naming of landmarks on the east, west, north and south walls emphasizes that the whole city is included" (Baldwin, 204).

Furthermore, the city will be densely populated ("inhabited," v.11; cf. 2:4), never again to be depopulated through destruction (as at the time of the exile to Babylonia, Isa 43:28). "In Zec. 14:11; Mal. 4:6 'curse' (Heb. *ḥērem*, RSV margin 'ban of utter destruction') refers to a ban which was sometimes placed on a captured city, which meant that everything in the city was consecrated to the deity and offered as a holocaust (cf. Josh. 6:17–19, 24)" (see "Curse," *ISBE*, 1:837; for further study of the Hebrew word translated "destroyed" [*ḥērem*], see *TWOT*, 1:324–25). Finally, "Jerusalem will be secure" (see Jer 31:40).

NOTE

10 The anomalous וְרָאֲמָה (*wᵉrāʾᵘmâ*, "will be raised up") is explained in GKC, par. 72p.

d. The punishment of Israel's enemies (14:12–15)

¹²This is the plague with which the LORD will strike all the nations that fought against Jerusalem: Their flesh will rot while they are still standing on their feet, their eyes will rot in their sockets, and their tongues will rot in their mouths. ¹³On that day men will

be stricken by the LORD with great panic. Each man will seize the hand of another, and they will attack each other. ¹⁴Judah too will fight at Jerusalem. The wealth of all the surrounding nations will be collected—great quantities of gold and silver and clothing. ¹⁵A similar plague will strike the horses and mules, the camels and donkeys, and all the animals in those camps.

COMMENTARY

12–15 The prophet next reveals how God will deal with the antikingdom forces of vv.1–3. (1) He will strike them with a "plague" (v.12), just as he did the Assyrian army of King Sennacherib in 701 BC (Isa 37:36). (2) The Lord will strike the enemies of himself and his people with "great panic" (v.13), causing them to "attack each other" (cf. Jdg 7:22; 1Sa 14:15–20; 2Ch 20:23). (3) The rest of the people of Judah will rally to defend the capital (v.14; cf. 12:2). The validity of this last point rests on the NIV's rendering "at Jerusalem," not "against Jerusalem" (RSV).

Verse 14 ends with the gathering of the plunder, or spoils of battle, by the Jews—a reversal of v.1. Verse 15 adds that a plague similar to that of vv.12–13 will strike the beasts of burden, thus preventing their use for escape.

NOTE

12 The infinitive absolute הָמֵק (hāmēq, "will rot") is here used as a substitute for the finite verb. Davidson (par. 88c) states that "where the action in itself, apart from its circumstances, is to be stated, the inf. abs. is sufficient." The singular pronominal suffix in בְּשָׂרוֹ (beśārô, "their flesh," lit., "his flesh") has the distributive or individualized use (Davidson, par. 116, rem. 1).

e. The universal worship of the King (14:16–19)

¹⁶Then the survivors from all the nations that have attacked Jerusalem will go up year after year to worship the King, the LORD Almighty, and to celebrate the Feast of Tabernacles. ¹⁷If any of the peoples of the earth do not go up to Jerusalem to worship the King, the LORD Almighty, they will have no rain. ¹⁸If the Egyptian people do not go up and take part, they will have no rain. The LORD will bring on them the plague he inflicts on the nations that do not go up to celebrate the Feast of Tabernacles. ¹⁹This will be the punishment of Egypt and the punishment of all the nations that do not go up to celebrate the Feast of Tabernacles.

COMMENTARY

16 In spite of the awful decimation predicted in vv.12−15, there will be "survivors"—a converted remnant from those nations—who will make an annual pilgrimage to Jerusalem "to worship the King" (see 8:20−23; Isa 2:2−4; Mic 4:1−5; also Eze 40−48 for more on the nature of that worship). Two other passages also combine "the King" with "the LORD Almighty" (Ps 24:10; Isa 6:5). The Festival of Tabernacles marked the final harvest of the year's crops (Lev 23:34−43). Perowne, 147, suggests that, of the three great pilgrimage festivals (Passover, Pentecost, and Tabernacles), the reason Tabernacles (or Booths) will be selected as the festival for representatives of the various Gentile nations is that "it was the last and greatest festival of the Jewish year, gathering up into itself, as it were, the year's worship."

The Festival of Tabernacles is to be a time of grateful rejoicing (Lev 23:40; Dt 16:14−15; Ne 8:17). The people are to live in "booths" as a reminder that their ancestors lived in booths when the Lord brought them out of Egypt (Lev 23:42−43). Beginning with the period of Ezra and Nehemiah, the reading (and perhaps teaching) of "the Book of the Law of God" became an integral part of the festivities (Ne 8:7−8, 12, 17−18; cf. Isa 2:3). The festival seems to speak of the final, joyful regathering and restoration of Israel in full kingdom blessing, as well as of the ingathering of the nations.

This festival may continue to have some significance (at least typically) in the eternal state (in the new Jerusalem on the new earth), since God will "tabernacle" ("live," NIV) with his people (Rev 21:3). Josephus (*Ant.* 8.100 [4.1]) says that Tabernacles was "especially sacred and important." For a more complete study of this festival, see De Vaux, 495−502, 506, who maintains that "the entire passage is devoted to the eschatological triumph, to that 'Day' when Yahweh will be king over the whole earth (v.9), and the feast of Tents is mentioned only because it was the main feast for pilgrimage to Jerusalem."

17−19 The prophet next unfolds what will happen to the recalcitrant nations that refuse to send delegations on this annual pilgrimage to worship the King in Jerusalem: The blessing of rain will be withheld from them (v.17; according to Dt 28:22−24, drought was one of the curses for covenantal disobedience). Baldwin, 206, relates v.17 to 9:11−10:1, "where an adequate rainfall is connected with the prosperity of the Messianic era." Unger, 268, observes: "In Ezekiel 34:26 the word ['rain'] is used figuratively of spiritual blessing, and Zechariah's usage, while literal, does not exclude the spiritual connotation." This principle is illustrated in v.18 with Egypt, but the Hebrew text may be read in different ways, as indicated in the NIV note.

Ellis, 1050, suggests that "perhaps the Heb. is a rhetorical question: 'shall not the plague come upon them?'" Accepting the reading in the NIV note, Baldwin, 207, points out that "Egypt was an exception among the nations because it depended for water not on rainfall but on the Nile. As Egypt had experienced plagues at the time of the Exodus, and through them had been brought to acknowledge God's sovereignty, so *plague* was a fitting symbol of disaster in the new era" (emphasis hers). Ultimately plague, too, may include the withholding of rain, for drought (v.17) will cause the Nile's inundation to fail. Thus will all be punished who do not make the annual pilgrimage to

Jerusalem to worship the King and to observe the thankful expressions associated with the Festival of Tabernacles (v.19), and thus will the King be universally worshiped.

NOTES

16 לְהִשְׁתַּחֲוֹת (lᵉhištaḥᵃwōt, "to worship") is not to be derived from שׁחה (šḥh) or שׁחח (šḥḥ), as once thought; rather, it is the Hishtaphel stem of the root חוה (ḥwh, from an original ḥwy; see Barker, 'The Value of Ugaritic," 125).

19 חַטָּאת (ḥaṭṭᵃʾt; GK 2633) affords an excellent example of the meaning "punishment" for this word, instead of "sin" or "guilt." Thus what Fohrer, 102–3, says of רָעָה (rāʿâ, "evil") and עָוֹן (ʿāwōn, "sin") is likewise true of ḥaṭṭᵃʾt.

f. "HOLY TO THE LORD" (14:20–21)

> ²⁰On that day HOLY TO THE LORD will be inscribed on the bells of the horses, and the cooking pots in the LORD's house will be like the sacred bowls in front of the altar. ²¹Every pot in Jerusalem and Judah will be holy to the LORD Almighty, and all who come to sacrifice will take some of the pots and cook in them. And on that day there will no longer be a Canaanite in the house of the LORD Almighty.

COMMENTARY

20–21 Here the nature of the messianic kingdom is depicted: It will be characterized by "holiness" (for the meaning of this word, see comment on 2:12). Perowne, 148, gives an overview of these verses:

> The ornaments of worldly pomp and warlike power shall be as truly consecrated as the very mitre of the High Priest, and every vessel used in the meanest service of the Temple as holy as the vessels of the altar itself, ver. 20. Nay, every common vessel throughout the city and the whole land shall be so holy as to be meet for the service of the sanctuary, and every profane person shall be for ever banished from the house of the Lord, ver. 21.

He adds (149): "All distinction between sacred and secular shall be at an end, because all shall now be alike holy."

The teaching of these verses may be summed up like this: There will be holiness in public life ("the bells of the horses"; v.20), in religious life ("the cooking pots in the LORD's house"; v.20), and in private life ("every pot in Jerusalem and Judah"; v.21). Even common things become holy when they are used for God's service. So it is with our lives.

"Holy to the Lord was engraved on the plate of gold worn on the turban of the high priest (Ex. 28:36) as an expression and reminder of his consecration,

but it was meant to be true of all Israel (Ex. 19:6; Jer. 2:3)" (Baldwin, 207). So God's original purpose for Israel (Ex 19:6) will be fulfilled. "Cook" (v.21) means "cook the sacrifices." While the Hebrew for "Canaanite" can also mean "merchant" (cf. NIV note)—possibly referring either to 11:5 or to the kind of activity condemned by Jesus in Matthew 21:12–13 (cf. Jn 2:13–16)—"Canaanite" seems the better translation for this context. (Merrill, 366, concurs, as do also Meyers and Meyers, 489–92, 506–7].) "Canaanite" then represents anyone who is morally or spiritually unclean—anyone who is not included among the chosen people of God (cf. Isa 35:8; Eze 43:7; 44:9; Rev 21:27).

The final scene of Zechariah anticipates Revelation 11:15, toward which all history is steadily moving—"the kingdom of the world has become the kingdom of our Lord and of his Christ, and he will reign for ever and ever"—and Revelation 19:16—"On his robe and on his thigh he has this name written: KING OF KINGS AND LORD OF LORDS." The only appropriate human response is to heed Robert Grant's hymnic exhortation:

O worship the King, all-glorious above,
And gratefully sing His power and His love;
Our Shield and Defender, the Ancient of days
Pavilioned in splendor and girded with praise.

MALACHI

EUGENE H. MERRILL

Introduction

1. **Background**
2. **Authorship**
3. **Date and Place of Origin**
4. **Destination**
5. **Occasion and Purpose**
6. **Literary Form**
7. **Theological Values**
8. **Canonicity**
9. **Special Problems**
10. **Bibliography**
11. **Outline**

1. BACKGROUND

Postexilic OT literature is marked by, among other things, abundant and precise chronological information that helps to establish its setting. A notable exception to this is the book of Malachi, which provides not a single chronological reference. All that is certain is that it was composed in the period following the return of the Jews from Babylon and Persia, that is, sometime after 538 BC. More precisely, it presupposes the construction of the second temple, since cultic abuses had already surfaced in the community and had to be addressed by the prophet. The terminus ad quem is also difficult to establish. The most that can be said with reasonable certainty is that Malachi was a product of the fifth century BC, more likely toward the beginning of that period (see "Date and Place of Origin").

Haggai and Zechariah had flourished under the reign of Darius I Hystaspes (522–486 BC), who, in the spirit of magnanimity of his Persian predecessors, not only permitted the Jews of the province of Yehud to rebuild the temple at Jerusalem but also generously assisted the project both in terms of protection and material assets (Ezr 4:5; Hag 1:1; Zec 1:1).[1] That project began in 520 BC and was completed by 515. After this time, the OT falls silent as to life in the Jewish community, whether at Jerusalem or elsewhere. The thread of the narrative does not appear again until the book of Esther picks it up with its account of the reign of King Xerxes and his Jewish queen, Esther.

Xerxes (known in the OT as Ahasuerus; Est 1:1) succeeded Darius I in 486 BC and reigned until 465. After undertaking major construction projects in the Persian cities of Susa and Persepolis, Xerxes turned

---

1. For a helpful survey of the period see Edwin M. Yamauchi, *Persia and the Bible* (Grand Rapids: Baker, 1990); Peter R. Ackroyd, *Israel under Babylon and Persia* (Oxford: Oxford Univ. Press, 1986), 162–279.

his attention to foreign affairs, dealing first (and successfully) with Egypt, which had broken its ties of subservience with Persia in Xerxes' first year. He then initiated a series of campaigns against the Greek states. Victorious over the Spartans at Thermopylae, Xerxes suffered ignominious defeat at the hands of a Greek coalition at Salamis, and after a second, more devastating setback at Mycale in 479 Xerxes returned to Susa for good. His life of dissipation and self-indulgence is well documented in the book of Esther (Est 1:1–22) as well as by the Greek historian Herodotus (*History* 9.109–13).

Though Esther provides insight into the life of the Jewish community of the Persian Diaspora, it says nothing about affairs in Yehud. This historical lacuna is redressed at least partially for the period of Xerxes' successor, Artaxerxes I Longimanus (464–424), under whose reign both Ezra and Nehemiah were authorized to return from Babylonia to Jerusalem. Ezra's return took place in 458 BC. This gifted priest and scribe had the full support of the king in carrying out any projects or reforms he felt necessary (Ezr 7:1–26).

Chief among Ezra's concerns for reform was the issue of the intermarriage of Jews with their heathen neighbors (Ezr 9:1–4), an issue resolved by his demand that those involved divorce their spouses—a step they no doubt took with some lack of enthusiasm (10:1–44). The implications of this measure for Malachi's statement that God hates divorce (Mal 2:16) and thus for the date of Malachi are clearly significant. Did Ezra countervail the revelation of the prophet concerning divorce, or did Malachi's word come in response to an impetuous act on Ezra's part (see "Date and Place of Origin")?

Nehemiah's trek to Jerusalem took place in 445 BC, thirteen years after Ezra's arrival. He had been a cupbearer in the court of Artaxerxes when, having heard of the deplorable state of affairs in his ancestral homeland, he requested permission of the king to go there to provide stability of leadership—a request readily granted (Ne 2:1–9). Artaxerxes displayed the same beneficence toward Nehemiah as he had toward Ezra; thus, Nehemiah was able to enjoy the king's protection against the Jews' enemies and also draw upon the royal resources for the reconstruction of the city that remained to be done.

In addition to the rebuilding of the walls of Jerusalem, Nehemiah, like Ezra, also had to deal with social issues, marriage and divorce figuring chief among them (Ne 13:23–31). His response to the problem was decidedly different, however, for he skirted the matter somewhat by permitting the status quo with regard to illicit marriages already made but solemnly warning the people against contracting such relationships in the future. Again the question must be raised: Did Nehemiah exhibit a "softness" toward marriage to pagans that Ezra subsequently had to address more firmly by commanding divorce, or did Nehemiah refrain from it because he had been influenced by Malachi's strictures? There is a third option: Did Malachi prohibit divorce because of Ezra's unwarranted endorsement of it and Nehemiah's apparent ambivalence toward it?

In any case, the books of Ezra and Nehemiah as well as Malachi reveal severe crises in the life of the postexilic community in regard to its lethargy about reconstituting the infrastructures of the state, indifference toward matters of cult and social propriety, and compromise with the insidious moral and spiritual inroads fostered by association with its pagan neighbors. As severe as hostility from the outside remained toward the Jews, the benign reigns of Artaxerxes and his successor, Darius II (423–404 BC), guaranteed the Jews sufficient freedom to accomplish the task of nation-building. The real problem was internal—a spiritual malaise reflected most clearly in Malachi and one he seeks to address as a spokesman of the Lord.

2. AUTHORSHIP

The book of Malachi opens with the formula (lit. trans.): "Oracle: the word of Yahweh unto Israel by the hand of Malachi" (1:1). The closest parallel in the other prophets is Haggai 1:1, which states (lit. trans.): "The word of Yahweh came by the hand of Haggai the prophet to Zerubbabel" (Hag 1:1). The identical "by the hand of" is offset by several differences that have caused many scholars to raise questions about the authorship of the book.[2] First is the use of the term "oracle" (*maśśāʾ*), which stands in the absolute form (thus, not "oracle of" or the like). All other uses appear to be in the construct, with the meaning "oracle of," or in a phrase, such as "this is the oracle" or "the oracle that came to X." The only exceptions are in Zechariah 9:1 ("Oracle: the word of the LORD against the land of Hadrach") and 12:1 ("Oracle: the word of the LORD against Israel," both lit. trans). Thus the opening of Malachi is identical to what scholars generally agree are the last two major blocks of material in Zechariah (i.e., chs. 9–11 and 12–14). Some have argued, therefore, that originally Malachi constituted the fourth major section of Zechariah.

This theory, coupled with the name "Malachi" itself, has led to the conclusion that the book is anonymous. The name consists of the common Hebrew noun *malʾāk*, "messenger," plus the first person pronominal suffix, thus "my messenger." Since this term occurs also in Malachi 3:1, where it clearly is to be rendered "my messenger," some conclude that it must be understood that way at the beginning of the book as well.

In response, three major points must be considered. First, there is no textual or traditional evidence that Malachi was ever anything but an independent work, one disconnected from Zechariah. Second, if the book is of unknown authorship, it would be the only example of such among the OT's canonical prophetic works; thus its incorporation into the canon would have been most unlikely. Third, all the names of the prophets have translational value. For example, both Hosea and Isaiah relate to the root *yšʿ*, which means "salvation"; Joel means "Yahweh is God"; Obadiah means "the servant of Yahweh"; and Zechariah, "Yahweh remembers." There is no more reason to question "Malachi" as a personal name than there is to question these others, none of which is thought to be anything other than a personal name.

In short, there is no basis for the claim that the book was authored by someone other than the prophet whose name it bears. The fact that Malachi has no patronym is irrelevant to this point since that is also true of many other prophets, such as Amos, Obadiah, Micah, Nahum, Habakkuk, and Haggai.

3. DATE AND PLACE OF ORIGIN

Malachi's frequent references to priests, sacrifices, and other matters pertinent to the temple make it clear that he lives in or near Jerusalem. *When* he ministers and writes his prophetic treatise is quite another matter. These very allusions to the temple service do, of course, presuppose the completion of the temple, and for the abuses he addresses to have become as serious as he depicts them to be, one would suppose that some considerable number of years have elapsed since the political and religious community were reconstituted.

---

2. A good overview of the issues involved may be found in Andrew E. Hill, *Malachi* (AB 25D; New York: Doubleday, 1998), 15–18. Hill argues for "Malachi" as a personal name.

Beyond these observations, it is impossible to determine precise dates.[3] The best that can be hoped for is to view the situation described by Malachi against the backdrop provided by Ezra and Nehemiah and in particular the one issue common to them all, namely, that of intermarriage and divorce. Ezra arrived to Jerusalem in 458 BC, and despite the turmoil of the community in certain respects, he seems to have found none of the cultic aberrations that so preoccupy Malachi. The same is true of Nehemiah a few years later. He had to contend with the hostility of some of the surrounding peoples (Ne 2:17–20; 4:1–20; 6:1–9); he led in the reconstruction of the city walls (3:1–32); and he dealt with the need to populate Jerusalem and the surrounding areas (11:1–36). It is true that Nehemiah confronted matters of covenantal law, such as usury (5:1–13), the profanation of the temple by allowing unbelievers to dwell in its chambers (13:4–9), neglect of the Levites (13:10–14), and violation of the Sabbath (13:10–22); but these violations are clearly different from and derivative of those addressed by Malachi.

The problem of intermarriage and divorce, then, is the point in common that may help determine, if not the date of Malachi, at least the prophet's position vis-à-vis Ezra and Nehemiah. There are three possibilities: (1) Malachi is last in the series, written therefore some time after the last date in Nehemiah, ca. 432 BC (Ne 13:6); (2) Malachi is contemporary with Ezra or Nehemiah or both (458–432); or (3) Malachi precedes the other two. The whole hinges largely on the books' respective attitudes and responses to the question of divorce.

The first option seems most unlikely, for Nehemiah appears to have dealt with the issue quite resolutely and finally, but without counseling divorce (Ne 13:23–25). Malachi's injunctions against divorce would be unnecessary if divorce was not part of Nehemiah's solution to the problem of intermarriage. As for Ezra's edict commanding divorce, it must be understood that the marriages being terminated were (as with the case in Nehemiah) between Jews and Gentiles and not (as in Malachi) between Jews alone. Though one might question Ezra's action on the grounds of a lack of biblical precedent, it is not appropriate to view that action as contradicting Malachi. However, it is difficult to imagine that the prophet is contemporary with either Ezra or Nehemiah and is unmentioned by them, or that they fail to share other concerns relative to social and religious life. Thus the second option is also most unlikely.

On balance, the best case can be made for the priority of Malachi (the third option). Malachi addresses the corruption of the priesthood and other issues that go unmentioned by Ezra and are of relatively little concern to Nehemiah. The prophet seems to have put them to rest. The nagging problem of intermarriage and divorce would not go away, however, and divorce, at least, is an issue common to all three books. As for intermarriage, the term is technically correct for only Ezra and Nehemiah since both books are referring to the marriage of Jews to pagans (Ezr 10:1–4; Ne 13:23–27). Malachi's unqualified statement that Yahweh "hates divorce" (Mal 2:16) comes in the context of marriage within the covenantal community. Otherwise, Malachi is silent about the measures taken by Ezra and Nehemiah relative to the dissolution of these improper relationships.

Neither Ezra nor Nehemiah addresses the matter of divorce in strictly Jewish marriages, thus perhaps suggesting that that abuse had already been resolved, likely by Malachi. Malachi's silence about the

---

3. For a number of options, see Clendenen in Richard A. Taylor and E. Ray Cendenen, *Haggai, Malachi* (NAC 21A; Nashville: Broadman & Holman, 2004), 204–7. Clendenen favors the early date argued for here.

marriages of concern to Ezra and Nehemiah provides at least implicit evidence that intercultural marriages have not yet begun to be a problem. This would more likely be the case early in the fifth century than in the latter part of the century. The priority of Malachi to the others seems best able to account for all the aspects of the problem. A date for Malachi at 480–470 BC is not at all unreasonable.[4]

4. DESTINATION

The message of Malachi is addressed to "Israel" (1:1), a politically anachronistic term inasmuch as the nation by that name had been overrun and taken into Assyrian exile 240 years before Malachi's day. The name expresses the eschatological hope of the small and struggling postexilic Jewish community that it will someday be reestablished to the glory of ancient Israel. In any event, it is to that nucleus of a nation that the prophet speaks, just as his prophetic predecessors Haggai and Zechariah had done. More narrowly, Malachi singles out the priests as special objects of condemnation (2:1–9). They have corrupted the worship of Yahweh and by their example opened the door to syncretistic worship (2:10–13) and to the breakdown of marriage and family relationships (2:14–17).

5. OCCASION AND PURPOSE

Within a few decades of the return of the Jews to Jerusalem and the rebuilding of the city and temple, a cynical spirit had overcome the tiny state of Yehud. The people began to forget their priorities and placed their own interests and needs above those of Yahweh (see Hag 1:2–6). Sadly, this truth characterized even their worship—while the people prospered, they offered to Yahweh the leftovers, as it were (Mal 1:6–10). In doing so they denigrated God and brought reproach on his name in the eyes of the world at large (1:11–14). The priests were the ringleaders in all these failures and set the tone for societal breakdown, especially in family life (2:1–16). In general, the milieu was one of relativism and the denial of absolutes (2:17).

The outcome lies ultimately in an eschatological day on which the messenger of Yahweh will announce judgment and cleansing (3:1–6). Meanwhile the community must repent of its sins and failures, especially in rendering to Yahweh the homage due him (3:7–12). Having noted a favorable response to this appeal by some (3:16), Malachi returns to the eschatological scene, one that portrays both hope and wrath (3:17–4:3). In a final note of exhortation, the prophet urges the people to repent in view of the return of Elijah, the prophet who will be Yahweh's instrument for both awesome retribution and gracious redemption (4:4–6).

In brief, the book is addressed to the postexilic Jewish community and constitutes an urgent appeal to repentance for cultic and social malfeasance, an appeal especially pertinent and important in the light of God's eschatological advent in judgment and salvation.

---

4. David L. Petersen, while not suggesting specific dates, proposes a setting "dated to the late sixth or early fifth century B.C.E." (*Zechariah 9–14 and Malachi* [Louisville: Westminster John Knox, 1995], 5–6).

6. LITERARY FORM

A major feature of the book is the use of a dialogical device in which the Lord through the prophet asks rhetorical questions of the audience, or, conversely, the audience addresses questions to the Lord.[5] This interchange is common to the wisdom tradition, in which information and/or truth is gained by interrogation. Malachi also displays the element of the *rîb* pattern, a legal setting and framework in which charges and counter-charges are leveled until the truth emerges and a verdict is rendered. The questions in Malachi deal primarily with such matters as whether or not the covenant is in effect (1:2–5); why the Jews, if they are indeed the people of Yahweh, do not obey and serve him (1:6–14); why they abuse one another though members of the same body (2:10–16); why they think they can rob God of what is his (3:7–12); and how it is that the wicked appear to prosper at the expense of the righteous (3:13–15).

As for style and genre, the work is fundamentally prose, though there are some snatches of poetry here and there (e.g., 1:6–8a; 4:4–6). In addition, literary devices exist such as rhythmical pattern (1:11; 3:1, 6–7), figures of speech (1:6, 9; 2:3, 6–7; 3:2; 4:1–2), and chiasm (1:2–3; 2:7a–b, 17a–b; 3:1c–d, 11; 4:6a). Most of these devices are common to elevated Hebrew prose and should not be construed as defining Malachi as a whole, or even major parts, as poetry.

7. THEOLOGICAL VALUES

The placement of Malachi not only at the end of the prophets, but also, in the Christian canon, at the end of the OT as a whole, is most fortuitous theologically, for though the book fails to bring Israel's hopes to satisfactory fruition in history, its eschatological thrust points to a time when a messenger will announce the coming of the Lord (3:1).[6] The "sun of righteousness" will also rise with healing in its wings for those who fear the Lord, and they in turn will tread the remains of the wicked beneath their feet (4:2–3). The messenger will be none other than Elijah, revived and preaching a message of repentance (4:4–6). The Gospels open with this theme, thus consciously carrying forward and bringing to completion the unrealized hopes of Israel (Mt 3:1–12; Mk 1:2–8; Lk 3:2–17; Jn 1:6–8, 19–28).

Other major theological themes include: (1) the sovereignty of God as displayed in his election of Israel to be a covenantal people (1:2) and in the insistence that he is the King who alone is worthy of worship and praise (1:14; cf. 1:11); (2) the responsibility of Israel to worship and serve the Lord sacrificially and with integrity (1:7, 10, 13; 2:8, 10–11, 17; 3:8, 14); (3) the gracious offer of forgiveness to those who repent from their sins and return to covenantal faithfulness (1:9; 3:7, 10–12, 16–18; 4:2–3); and (4) judgment on those who persist in their wicked rebellion (1:14; 2:2, 3–4, 9; 3:2–3, 5, 9; 4:1, 6).

The setting of the book, as is to be expected, gives rise to its theology. As is clear from the rest of the postexilic historical and prophetic material (i.e., Haggai, Zechariah, Esther, and Ezra–Nehemiah), the newly reestablished Jewish community struggled with many issues. They had returned to their land under the aegis and

---

5. Ernst Wendland, "Linear and Concentric Patterns in Malachi," *BT* 36 (1985): 108–21; E. Ray Clendenen, "The Structure of Malachi: A Textlinguistic Study," *CTR* 2 (1987): 3–17.
6. See Robert B. Chisholm Jr., "A Theology of the Minor Prophets," in *A Biblical Theology of the Old Testament*, ed. Roy B. Zuck (Chicago Moody Press, 1991), 418–33.

protection of the Persian government, but their initial euphoria at resuming their role as the covenantal nation was soon dissipated by hostility from without and a creeping, demoralizing cynicism from within. The poverty and weakness of the community led the people to despair over the prospects of success for the future.

Malachi addresses this cynicism by rebuking his audience for their lack of theological propriety and perspective and by exhorting them to repent from these attitudes and turn to the God who brought them back as a people and whose purposes for them are far from being at an end. The present situation may, indeed, seem bleak, but the future holds promise of a mighty working of God whereby Israel will resume her role as God's servant people and agent of his universal dominion. The Lord will surely come, and with him will come all the aspirations and visions of the prophets, including Malachi's.

8. CANONICITY

Every ancient canon, Hebrew and otherwise, includes Malachi among the undisputed books of Scripture and always as the last of the twelve Minor Prophets. The only question at all related to canonicity is whether Malachi is an independent book or part of a "Zecharianic" collection that consists of Zechariah 1–8; 9–11; 12–14, Malachi (see discussion above under "Authorship"). All that need be said here is that the mere presence of the term *maśśāʾ* ("oracle") at Zechariah 9:1 and 12:1 as well as at Malachi 1:1 proves nothing as to Malachi's original literary setting. As we have argued already, the absolute form of the noun in Malachi is enough to show a fundamental distinction. In addition, there exists no text or tradition that views Malachi as anything but independent. It is positioned at the end of the Minor Prophets no doubt for chronological reasons, since Malachi is clearly the latest of the books of the OT prophets (see "Date and Place of Origin").

9. SPECIAL PROBLEMS

Apart from some perceived difficulties of an historical, literary, or compositional nature (see sections 1–6 above), the book is relatively free of genuine problems. The textual traditions exhibit a remarkable uniformity of readings both among the Hebrew manuscripts and between them and the various versions. Most of the compositional difficulties are simply the inevitable and inherent result of all translational activity. One of the more celebrated examples of a versional deviation from the MT is the permutation by the Greek of 3:22–24 (Eng. 4:4–6). Whereas the Hebrew has verses 22, 23, 24, the LXX reads verses 23, 24, 22. Most scholars correctly construe this variation as a tendentious reading designed to permit the book to end on a much more positive note.

10. BIBLIOGRAPHY

Baldwin, Joyce G. *Haggai, Zechariah, Malachi*. Tyndale Old Testament Commentary. London: Tyndale, 1972.
Hill, Andrew E. *Malachi*. Anchor Bible 25D. New York: Doubleday, 1998.
Kaiser, Walter C., Jr. *Malachi: God's Unchanging Love*. Grand Rapids: Baker, 1984.
Merrill, Eugene H. *Haggai, Zechariah, Malachi*. Chicago: Moody Press, 1994.
Smith, Ralph L. *Micah–Malachi*. Word Biblical Commentary. Waco, Tex.: Word, 1984.
Taylor, Richard A., and E. Ray Clendenen. *Haggai, Malachi*. New American Commentary 21A. Nashville: Broadman & Holman, 2004.
Verhoef, Pieter A. *The Books of Haggai and Malachi*. New International Commentary on the Old Testament. Grand Rapids: Eerdmans, 1987.

11. OUTLINE

Text and Exposition

I. SUPERSCRIPTION

¹An oracle: The word of the LORD to Israel through Malachi.

COMMENTARY

1 The first word of the book is *maśśāʾ* ("oracle"; GK 5363), a nominal form derived from the verb *nśʾ*, "to bear, carry." Many versions translate the nominal as "burden" or the like, thus suggesting that the message of the Lord is sometimes heavy, not pleasant to deliver and less pleasant to hear. However, the term frequently occurs without this negative association, so "oracle" is appropriate as a less tendentious rendering.

Appositional to *maśśāʾ* is the common phrase "word of the LORD," which puts beyond doubt that the message about to be delivered is not that of the prophet but one that comes from God. Its intended historical audience is "Israel," a name that, though anachronistic in a postexilic setting, is appropriate in the light of the later reference to Jacob (v.2) and the eschatological perspective of the book, which understands the chosen nation to be regathered Israel and not just Judah (3:6; 4:4).

The combination "the word of the LORD" and "through" (lit., "by the hand of") occurs only here

and in Haggai 1:1, 3; 2:1 (cf. a similar formula in Jer 50:1). It is thus a late Hebrew idiom emphasizing the role of the prophet as the agent of divine revelation. The name of that prophet is Malachi, no doubt a hypocoristicon for a fuller name, such as Malachijah, "Yahweh is my messenger." Many scholars object to this interpretation, however, and prefer the view that the book's authorship is unknown and that the present name is lifted from 3:1, where the form *malʾāk* refers to God's messenger who will come in the future.

That the LXX reads "his messenger" in the superscription gives some support to these scholars' position. They argue that Malachi was once part of the Zecharianic corpus (Zec 1–8; 9–11; 12–14; Malachi) and thus lacked any name. Once it had become separated for some reason, "his messenger" became altered to "my messenger" (the meaning of "Malachi"). However, the Hebrew textual tradition is consistent in understanding *malʾākî* (GK 4858) as a personal name.

II. GOD'S ELECTION OF ISRAEL (1:2–5)

²"I have loved you," says the LORD.
"But you ask, 'How have you loved us?'

"Was not Esau Jacob's brother?" the LORD says. "Yet I have loved Jacob, [3]but Esau I have hated, and I have turned his mountains into a wasteland and left his inheritance to the desert jackals."

[4]Edom may say, "Though we have been crushed, we will rebuild the ruins."

But this is what the LORD Almighty says: "They may build, but I will demolish. They will be called the Wicked Land, a people always under the wrath of the LORD. [5]You will see it with your own eyes and say, 'Great is the LORD—even beyond the borders of Israel!'"

COMMENTARY

2–5 The first issue raised by the prophet concerns God's gracious selection of Israel as a special people and the inability or unwillingness of postexilic Judaism to understand or accept this great truth. The shattering experience of the exile has undermined their confidence in this relationship, so Malachi is compelled to trace its history back to its source.

He does so by recollecting the patriarchal period, when God chose (the meaning in covenantal contexts of the verb *ʾhb*, "to love"; GK 170) Jacob over Esau, a choice made while both twins were in their mother Rebekah's womb (Ge 25:23) and confirmed later by a number of explicit and implicit promises (27:27–29; 28:13–17; 35:9–15; cf. Dt 7:6–11). Inasmuch as love equals election, "hate" (*śnʾ*; GK 8533) obviously means nothing more than rejection. Paul makes this meaning clear in his elaboration of the doctrine of election in Romans 9:6–13.

Esau's rejection did, of course, have practical ramifications for his descendants, that is, the nation of Edom (vv.3–4). It is impossible (and unnecessary) to pinpoint the historical events alluded to here (see, e.g., 1Sa 14:47; 2Sa 8:12, 14; 1Ki 11:15; Jer 49:14–19; Ob 1, 8), for the whole history of Edom was one of struggle and disaster. In response to the question, then, "How have you loved us?" the Jews have only to reflect on Edom's miserable lot in life compared to their own. And their situation will never improve, for despite Edom's hopes for the future God has written them off. Israel, by contrast, will not only succeed but also prosper and be a source of blessing to the whole world (v.5). This promise to Abraham (Ge 12:3) finds expression in the church today (Gal 3:8) and in eschatological Israel in the ages to come (Ro 11:25–32).

III. THE SACRILEGE OF THE PRIESTS (1:6–2:9)

A. The Sacrilege of Priestly Service (1:6–14)

1. Their Unacceptable Sacrifices (1:6–10)

[6]"A son honors his father, and a servant his master. If I am a father, where is the honor due me? If I am a master, where is the respect due me?" says the LORD Almighty. "It is you, O priests, who show contempt for my name.

"But you ask, 'How have we shown contempt for your name?'

[7]"You place defiled food on my altar.

"But you ask, 'How have we defiled you?'

"By saying that the Lᴏʀᴅ's table is contemptible. [8]When you bring blind animals for sacrifice, is that not wrong? When you sacrifice crippled or diseased animals, is that not wrong? Try offering them to your governor! Would he be pleased with you? Would he accept you?" says the Lᴏʀᴅ Almighty.

[9]"Now implore God to be gracious to us. With such offerings from your hands, will he accept you?"—says the Lᴏʀᴅ Almighty.

[10]"Oh, that one of you would shut the temple doors, so that you would not light useless fires on my altar! I am not pleased with you," says the Lᴏʀᴅ Almighty, "and I will accept no offering from your hands."

COMMENTARY

6 The prophet makes a conceptual transition from describing Jacob as his elect people (his son) to the question that if this is so, why does he as the Father receive no honor from Israel, his son? It seems the height of ingratitude for one who has been made a son on the basis of nothing but grace to fail to respond with respect and obedience.

From the time of the exodus Israel had been known as the Lord's son. When he told Moses to return to Egypt to lead the people out, he instructed him to say to Pharaoh, "Israel is my firstborn son" and "Let my son go, that he may worship me" (Ex 4:22–23). But Israel was also the servant of the Lord. The Mosaic covenant had placed Israel in this relationship (Dt 10:12, 20; 28:47) so that Israel could serve a redemptive role in God's plan of reconciling the world to himself (Isa 41:8–9; 42:18–22; 43:10; 44:1–5, 21–23; Jer 30:10; 46:27–28). The terms "son" and "servant" (v.6) must surely have brought to the minds of Malachi's hearers the awesome privileges they enjoyed as those whom God loved in such a remarkable way.

As representatives of the people as a whole, the priests are here specifically addressed. It was they who were to intercede between the people and the Lord in sacrifice and worship and who were the teachers of Torah. For them to fail is to invite the inevitable failure of the covenantal nation in its responsibilities before God. Employing an a fortiori argument, the Lord asks why the priests, with their inestimable privileges, should fail to honor and serve him when ordinary sons and servants are expected to do so for human masters (v.6). In fact, he says, the priests have despised his name. That the verb *bwz* is in the participial form suggests they despise him on a regular basis—in effect, they are belittlers of God.

7–8 In mock horror the priests ask how they have despised him, and the answer is in the contempt with which they view the table of the Lord (v.7). The same verb *bwz* describes the attitude of the priests to the table. The word "table" (*šulḥan*), synonymously parallel to "altar" (*mizbēaḥ*), leads to another analogy from human life and relationship—that pertaining to the governor (v.8). In a sense the altar is the table of the Lord on which are placed the offerings of which he partakes as they are consumed in the flames.

But what kinds of offerings are the priests presenting on the people's behalf? They are described as "defiled food" (Heb. *leḥem mᵉgōʾāl*, lit., "desecrated bread") and livestock that is physically defective, a direct violation of ritual law (Dt 15:21). Not only are they bold enough to offer such contemptible and flagrantly illicit tokens of worship, but they also defend their practice by declaring, in effect, "there's nothing wrong with this" (thus *ʾên rāʿ* twice in v.8). Sin, when left unpunished, emboldens the sinner to persist in evil ways and even to justify them. Eventually, good becomes evil and evil becomes good (Isa 5:20; cf. Mic 3:2; Mal 2:17).

These same priests, says the Lord, would hardly dare to serve the governor of the province with such fare (v.8). Indeed, he will take no pleasure in the person who manifests such rudeness and insubordination, nor will he pay such a person even the slightest attention (thus the idiom *yiśśāʾ pāneykā*, "lift up your face"). If this is the case with a human ruler, how can one expect the infinitely transcendent God of the universe to do so?

This second comparison between the Lord and human figures (father and master in v.6; the governor in v.8) invites attention to an epithet of the Lord that occurs twenty-four times in this brief book, "LORD Almighty" (*yhwh ṣᵉbāʾôt*, "LORD of hosts"; GK 3378, 7372). Eleven of these occurrences appear in this passage (1:6–2:9), thus underscoring the vast difference between God and human persons and institutions. This underscoring is necessary first of all because the tiny province of Yehud is but an afterthought in comparison to the vast Persian Empire of which it is a part. The Jews need to know that as mighty as are Persia's kings, their God is mightier, for he is the Lord of heaven and earth.

But Malachi is also concerned to stress the idea that the insubordination of the people and priests of Yehud is not against some minor deity who can be trifled with but against "a great king" (1:14) who will call them to account. Thus as both a master and a governor he is Lord Almighty (vv.6, 8).

9–10 In the light of the failure of people and priests to acknowledge God's sovereignty and render proper respect, the prophet urges that they repent (cf. v.9a). The difficult Hebrew of v.9b is best understood as a protasis/apodosis construction to be rendered something like: "Since you have sacrificed in such a manner, do you expect God to look favorably upon you?" Clearly the answer is "No." In a note of despair, the Lord wishes that some priest will at least close the doors of the temple and put an end to the religious charade, since under the circumstances none of their hypocritical acts of worship is acceptable to him (v.10). The point is clear: Empty religious formalism does not impress the Lord, nor does it bring blessing or satisfaction to those who engage in it (cf. Ps 40:6–8; Isa 1:11; Jer 6:20; 7:22–23; Am 5:22; Mic 6:6–8).

NOTE

8 The LXX and Vulgate read, "will he be pleased with it" (*hayirṣēhû*), rather than the MT's "will he be pleased with you" (*hayirṣᵉkā*). Though the meaning is not greatly changed, the more difficult reading of the MT appears more likely to be original.

2. Their Rebellious Spirit (1:11–14)

[11]"My name will be great among the nations, from the rising to the setting of the sun. In every place incense and pure offerings will be brought to my name, because my name will be great among the nations," says the LORD Almighty.

[12]"But you profane it by saying of the Lord's table, 'It is defiled,' and of its food, 'It is contemptible.' [13]And you say, 'What a burden!' and you sniff at it contemptuously," says the LORD Almighty.

"When you bring injured, crippled or diseased animals and offer them as sacrifices, should I accept them from your hands?" says the LORD. [14]"Cursed is the cheat who has an acceptable male in his flock and vows to give it, but then sacrifices a blemished animal to the Lord. For I am a great king," says the LORD Almighty, "and my name is to be feared among the nations."

COMMENTARY

11–14 Hypocritical worship is a certain sign of the heart attitude of a person who is out of fellowship with God. This is true of the community addressed by Malachi despite the fact that God loves them and has elected them to be his special people (v.2). This is all the more amazing in view of the fact that someday in the future the despised nations of the earth that have not enjoyed God's elective grace will praise his name and offer up to him proper incense and sacrifice (v.11). The phrase "from the rising to the setting of the sun" frames the extent of this acknowledgment of the Lord — it will be universal. Someday these pagans — contrary to the practice of Malachi's generation — will show unrestrained zeal for and obedience to the things of God.

The sense, if not the language, of this promise is eschatological, since it is not true of Malachi's day. The day of universal worship of the Lord by the Gentiles awaits a future time, one already described by Malachi's prophetic predecessors (Isa 66:18–21; Jer 3:17; 4:2; 12:14–17; Zec 14:16–21). The church age has obviously inaugurated this worldwide recognition of Israel's God as the God of all nations (Ac 2:5–21; 13:44–48; 15:7), but the greater fulfillment awaits the day of Christ's coming again (Rev 5:9; 7:9–12; 11:9, 15–18).

The point here, however, is the contrast between these nations, which enjoy none of the benefits of covenantal relationship with God and yet who will worship him in sincerity and truth, and God's elect people Israel, who despite all these benefits have dishonored and disobeyed him. Once more the prophet argues a fortiori: How can a people be blessed if they fail to measure up to the performance of nations that know none of those blessings?

For God's name to be great (v.11) is, to employ a figure of speech, to elevate God himself. His name is his reputation, his standing in the community, as it were. When Israel approached the temple to offer their sacrifices, they went to the place where God had "caused his name to dwell" (Dt 12:5, 11), that is, to the place where he sat in regal splendor. By their denigration of the sacred altar (again "table," as in v.7) and its sacrifices (here lit., "fruit" or "produce," not "food" as in v.7), the people have profaned God's name—an egregious violation of the third commandment. They have "secularized" his name and reputation and drained it of its holiness by their attitude toward worship.

Even their pro forma performance of temple duties is a bother to these priests, who clearly would rather be doing something else. They consider their ministry to be a wearisome thing, its responsibilities something to brush off as hardly worth their time. They go through the motions because it is expected of them, but there is no joy or satisfaction in it. Rather than take the trouble to ensure that the work of the temple is carried out properly in every detail, the officiants at worship accept any kind of animal from the people, whether it be stolen (thus *gāzûl*, v.13; NIV "injured"), lame, or sick, all of which sorts of offerings are strictly forbidden in the law (Lev 22:17–25; Dt 15:21). No wonder the Lord asks, "Should I accept them from your hands?" Implicit in the question is whether not only the sacrifices but also the priests and their service are worthy of his approbation.

The answer is a decisively negative one. Anyone who attempts to foist off on the Lord that which is second rate is cursed in his eyes (v.14). This is especially the case when the offerer has in his possession a choice male animal (*zākār*), one whole and in its prime (Ex 12:5; 34:19; Lev 1:3, 10; 4:23; 22:19), but keeps it for himself rather than presenting it to the Lord as a votive offering. This is the height of hypocrisy because the individual has made a public show of promising his best to the Lord but then has secretly exchanged it for something inferior in the privacy of his sacrifice. He may fool other people by this sleight of hand, but the God who knows and sees all will hold him to account.

The sinfulness of the priests and people engaged in such hypocrisy is exacerbated by the fact that they perpetrate it not against a human being or even just any god, but against the "great king ... the LORD Almighty" (v.14b). Such treasonous and blasphemous behavior is hardly imaginable. The section ends as it began, with comparisons and contrasts between human beings and their roles on the one hand and the Lord God of heaven on the other. If mere humankind is worthy of love and respect, how much more their Creator? He whose name (i.e., reputation) is feared amongst the pagan nations surely ought to be revered among his own people, whom he has graciously brought into covenantal fellowship with himself.

B. The Sacrilege of the Priestly Message (2:1–9)

1. The Corrupted Vocation of the Priests (2:1–7)

[1]"And now this admonition is for you, O priests. [2]If you do not listen, and if you do not set your heart to honor my name," says the LORD Almighty, "I will send a curse upon you, and I will curse your blessings. Yes, I have already cursed them, because you have not set your heart to honor me.

³"Because of you I will rebuke your descendants; I will spread on your faces the offal from your festival sacrifices, and you will be carried off with it. ⁴And you will know that I have sent you this admonition so that my covenant with Levi may continue," says the LORD Almighty. ⁵"My covenant was with him, a covenant of life and peace, and I gave them to him; this called for reverence and he revered me and stood in awe of my name. ⁶True instruction was in his mouth and nothing false was found on his lips. He walked with me in peace and uprightness, and turned many from sin.

⁷"For the lips of a priest ought to preserve knowledge, and from his mouth men should seek instruction — because he is the messenger of the LORD Almighty."

COMMENTARY

1–2 Having uttered a curse against the deceiver who pawns off defective animals for sacrificially appropriate ones (1:14), the Lord again addresses the priests and sets forth a commandment (*miṣwâ*; GK 5184) to them. This technical term would be profoundly meaningful to them, for it is the most common term to describe the statutes of the Mosaic covenant. They are supposed to be implementing the covenant's obligations, particularly in the realm of worship and the cult. To fail in these obligations is to put the priests in the vulnerable position of experiencing God's judgment.

The charge is to give most careful heed ("listen and … set your heart") to giving glory to the name of the Lord (v.2), best done by discharging their priestly responsibilities in line with the Torah and with genuine devotion to the Lord. Failing this duty, they can expect the curse of God; indeed, rather than experiencing the blessings that attend obedience, they will encounter the opposite — God's retribution. The definite article on *mᵉʾērâ* ("curse") indicates that a particular curse is in view, namely, the one(s) associated with covenantal violation (cf. Lev 26:14–39; Dt 27:11–26; 28:15–57). But this warning is more than an idle threat, for the onset of the divine curse has already begun. This cau-

tion may be understood in the sense that the coming curse is as good as accomplished, since Malachi does not elaborate the nature of any punitive curse that has already occurred.

3 This understanding is strengthened by what follows in v.3. Here the curses are viewed as future events, of which two will come to pass: (1) the offspring of the priests will be cut off, and (2) the priests' faces will be smeared with the entrails of sacrificial animals.

The second of these curses contains imagery that, while repulsive to any sensitive person, is unimaginably so to priestly officiants, who must be pure of any kind of contamination in order to qualify for their ministry (Lev 21:1–24). The term describing the filth that will smear the faces of the priests is *pereš*, the undigested contents of the stomach and intestines of an animal. The law required that such refuse be carried outside the camp and burned, lest it render the community impure (Ex 29:14; Lev 4:11–12; 8:17; Nu 19:5–7). For a priest merely to touch such abhorrent waste meant automatic disqualification for ministry. To have it spread on his face was the height of scandal. In fact, just as such refuse must be eliminated from the community, so must the priest who is contaminated by it (v.3).

4-7 The purpose for this strong warning to the priests is to caution them against the perversion of their office that has already begun (v.4). The Lord made a covenant with Levi guaranteeing him life and well-being (thus Heb. šālôm), but only as he revered the Lord and served him faithfully (v.5). This duty is precisely what the postexilic priests are failing to fulfill; thus they are already in violation of the covenant and are in danger of being cut off from their sacred office, that of custodian and teacher of Torah (v.7).

The covenant referred to here no doubt pertains to the one made with Phinehas, a grandson of Aaron who at a crisis point in Israel's spiritual life showed himself mightily on behalf of the Lord. When the Hebrews encamped on the plains of Moab, they became enticed by the Baalism of the area, and some began to involve themselves in lascivious idolatry (Nu 25:1-5). Having witnessed one particularly egregious act of sexual immorality, Phinehas, with spear in hand, slew the guilty parties, an Israelite man and a Midianite woman (v.8). The Lord therefore held back the plague that was already underway and then singled out Phinehas for special recognition. God praised him and promised to make with him a covenant of everlasting priesthood characterized by well-being (šālôm; vv.10-13).

In the words of Malachi, Levi (i.e., Phinehas, his descendant) "stood in awe" at the name of the Lord and was known as one whose mouth uttered "true instruction" (lit., "a tôrâ of truth") and not falsehood. He walked in peace and uprightness and was responsible for the conversion of many to the Lord (v.6). This rich legacy could and would be forfeited if the priests addressed by Malachi do not repent of their corrupt ways and once more serve the Lord in integrity and truth.

NOTE

3 Some disagreement attends the first of these curses since the Hebrew for "rebuke your descendants" seems at first glance to make little sense. The LXX, followed by Aquila and the Vulgate, reads "shoulder" (Gr. ōmon) for "descendants," probably presupposing Hebrew z⁽rôaᶜ, "arm." This reading requires that gᶜr ("rebuke") also be altered since the notion of rebuking the arm makes even less sense. Again, the Greek has aphorizō ("separate"), depending perhaps on a Hebrew text reading gdᵏ ("cut off"). The sentence then reads "I will cut off your arm" rather than "I will rebuke your descendants." However, not a single manuscript or version attests gdᵏ (only a possible grᶜ, "withdraw"), so this supposition is pure conjecture. The difficult Hebrew is best left alone, the idea of descendants suffering for the sins of their fathers being a common enough biblical idea (Ex 20:5; Dt 28:18, 32, 41, 53, 55, 57).

2. Covenantal Violation by the Priests (2:8-9)

⁸"But you have turned from the way and by your teaching have caused many to stumble; you have violated the covenant with Levi," says the LORD Almighty. ⁹"So I have caused you to be despised and humiliated before all the people, because you have not followed my ways but have shown partiality in matters of the law."

COMMENTARY

8-9 The warning against the priests' violating their sacred vocation is not theoretical or in the abstract. They have already done so in two ways: (1) by turning aside from the way, that is, from the manner of life commensurate with their office, and (2) by causing many to stumble because of their false teaching. Literally, "they have made many stumble in the Torah" (v.8). Rather than discharging their responsibilities as the Lord's messengers in the spirit of truth and uprightness, as Phinehas had done (v.6), they have corrupted the covenant of Levi (i.e., Phinehas). The idea is that the priests, by prostituting their privileged position to their own advantage, use their good offices to wicked ends.

Their charade has already found them out, however, and the people of the community can see that their priests are despicable (the same verb used to speak of the priests' attitudes toward the Lord's

name in 1:6 and the temple altar in 1:7, 12) and humiliated. They have departed from the pathway of obedience and adherence to Torah and, in particular, have shown favoritism to persons of prestige in the community in clear violation of their office (Dt 1:17; cf. 10:17; 16:19; 24:17).

The harsh criticism leveled by the Lord against the priesthood should not be at all surprising given the catalog of infidelity, selfishness, and arrogance outlined here. But such behavior by a few or even by a generation of priests cannot annul the covenantal pledge of an everlasting priesthood guaranteed to Phinehas and his descendants (Nu 25:13). A sacred office must always be distinguished from unworthy (or even worthy) persons who occupy it, for the office in itself is divinely sanctioned and can withstand the misappropriation to which it is sometimes subject.

IV. THE REBELLION OF THE PEOPLE (2:10-16)

A. The Disruption of the Covenant (2:10-12)

[10]Have we not all one Father ? Did not one God create us? Why do we profane the covenant of our fathers by breaking faith with one another?
[11]Judah has broken faith. A detestable thing has been committed in Israel and in Jerusalem: Judah has desecrated the sanctuary the LORD loves, by marrying the daughter of a foreign god. [12]As for the man who does this, whoever he may be, may the LORD cut him off from the tents of Jacob — even though he brings offerings to the LORD Almighty.

COMMENTARY

10-12 Though the priests have been severely castigated by the Lord for their perfidious attitudes

and behavior, the lay people can scarcely find much comfort in the divine scolding, for they, too, are deserving of God's condemnation and judgment. Their sin is more a corporate one, a transgression of the covenantal standards the Lord expects them to meet in relation to their pagan neighbors and among themselves, within the covenantal community.

Turning to the latter point first, the prophet points out that the basis for proper relationships within the body is the recognition that all of its members have a common "Father," that is, God. This is no appeal to universalism, for the text goes on to identify the body as those who commonly embrace the "covenant of our fathers" (v.10). The epithet "Father" to describe God is not a common one in the OT (see Isa 1:2; 63:16; 64:8; Jer 3:4, 19; 31:9), but it is implicit in a great many texts in which Israel is called God's child (e.g., Ex 4:22–23). The fact that God is the Father of the nation obviously leads to the conclusion that his children are brothers and sisters. How, then, can they act so treacherously against each other?

The point being made is further strengthened by the argument that God is also the creator of the nation. This is not a statement of his work of creation in general or cosmically, for the context is one of covenant. He created Israel by calling Abraham out of paganism and through him eventually establishing a people who would serve him in the task of redeeming the world. This gracious act of making a nonpeople the elect and gifted servant of the Lord should also do away with any spirit of hostility of one toward the other.

But Judah has fallen short in this regard, especially in the realm of family life. As nations Israel and Judah have married "the daughter of a foreign god" (v.11), that is, have entered into illicit relationships with other nations by recognizing and even embracing their gods (2Ki 17:7–23). By doing so, they have, in effect, abandoned the Lord, their true lover, and have gone after gods (Eze 16:15–29; Hos 2:2–7). This treachery is abominable and nothing short of a profanation of all that is holy. The parallelism between "Judah has desecrated the sanctuary [lit., profaned the holy thing]" and "has marr[ied] the daughter of a foreign god" suggests that the "holy (thing)" is the covenant itself. By pursuing other gods Israel and Judah have cut the covenantal bond that tied them to the Lord. In effect, they have divorced him.

Malachi responds with the imprecation in 2:12, "May the LORD cut him off from the tents of Jacob." The verb *krt* ("cut off"; GK 4162) is a technical term for excommunication, removal from the covenantal community. Just as Judah has cut herself off from the Lord by her many infidelities, may the Lord cut himself off from all in her midst who persist in their rebellious ways. This includes (lit.) "him who awakens" and "him who answers," a figure of speech (a merism) that expresses totality, that is, the sleeping and the awake, or everyone. No one guilty of treachery against the Lord will be immune. Even those who go about their religious exercises will come under condemnation, for what they do is hypocritical. It does no good to pretend to be devoted to the Lord while at the same time doing violence to one's brother or sister (v.12b).

NOTE

12 The MT reads "him who is awake and him who answers" (ʿēr and ʿōneh). The LXX reads ʿēr as ʿad ("until") and construes ʿōneh as a participle for the homonym ʿānâ, "be humble," thus, "until he is humbled." The difficult Hebrew is preferred, reflecting perhaps a merism, a figure of speech suggesting the totality of the people.

B. The Illustration of the Covenant (2:13−16)

¹³Another thing you do: You flood the LORD's altar with tears. You weep and wail because he no longer pays attention to your offerings or accepts them with pleasure from your hands. ¹⁴You ask, "Why?" It is because the LORD is acting as the witness between you and the wife of your youth, because you have broken faith with her, though she is your partner, the wife of your marriage covenant.

¹⁵Has not ⌊the LORD⌋ made them one? In flesh and spirit they are his. And why one? Because he was seeking godly offspring. So guard yourself in your spirit, and do not break faith with the wife of your youth.

¹⁶"I hate divorce," says the LORD God of Israel, "and I hate a man's covering himself with violence as well as with his garment," says the LORD Almighty.

So guard yourself in your spirit, and do not break faith.

COMMENTARY

13−14 The action of a community is obviously the action of the sum total of its members. Judah's sin of spiritual infidelity (i.e., her going after other gods while abandoning her own) is a corporate expression of the individuals of the nation who historically became idolatrous and thus violated the covenant with the Lord to which they had subscribed. Though by the postexilic era there is no indication that the Jews any longer embraced idolatry, intermarriage with heathen peoples, which often led to idolatry and which symbolized a breakdown of covenantal separation, was a serious social and religious problem. Both Ezra and Nehemiah, with Malachi, had to address the issue, though they did so in quite different ways (Ezr 10:1−44; Ne 13:23−27; see the introduction).

Verse 13 clearly connects with v.12 in its reference to hypocritical worship. The Lord pays no attention to the offerings of those who participate in illicit spiritual relationships, nor will he give heed to those who, having entered into improper marriages, go through religious ritual no matter how intense and emotional it may be. Intermarriage of Hebrews with heathens was strictly forbidden in the law (Ex 34:15−16; Dt 7:3), and though the law prescribed no remedy for such relationships once entered, they clearly were taboo. Ezra, of course, commanded that they be terminated by divorce, whereas Nehemiah counseled that intermarriage should cease in the future.

The situation addressed by Malachi is greatly exacerbated by the fact that in order for Jewish men to marry neighboring heathen women, they had to divorce their Jewish wives. (Jewish women did not have the right to divorce their husbands.) This situation, in fact, is what clarifies the issue of marriage and divorce as raised by Malachi, Ezra, and Nehemiah. Their situations are different and must be dealt with differently. In the present passage it is clear that the men of Malachi's audience have betrayed their Jewish wives and begun to pursue others (v.14; cf. v.11). But they had married their Jewish wives according to the law and custom and with God as witness. Marriage was therefore a most serious undertaking, one that was to be indissoluble and everlasting.

A man's wife was his companion since his youth, and by covenantal oath the man promised to care for and be faithful to his wife alone. The reference to covenant in v.14 ties this kind of relationship to the one referred to earlier, in which the Lord and Judah were also covenantal partners in a marriage arrangement, so to speak (v.11). Just as Judah abandoned that marriage in order to engage in partnerships with pagan gods, so these Jewish men are divorcing their wives in order to marry heathen women.

15 To make his point, Malachi (in an extremely elliptical Hebrew construction) makes indirect reference to Abraham (v.15). First he points out that no one would behave as these Jewish men are behaving if he had in him even the least bit of the Spirit of God. What, then, did that "one" (i.e., Abraham) seek? He sought an offspring from God. In doing so, he bypassed his wife, Sarah, and had a son by his concubine, Hagar. Though clearly there was no divorce and remarriage in that case, the way Abraham handled the matter was tantamount to rejecting one wife and taking another. This example, Malachi says, is a poor one to set, one not to be emulated whatsoever. Watch yourselves, he warns, and do not betray your wife in like manner (v.15b).

16 The whole admonition is climaxed by the flat declaration, "I hate divorce, says the LORD" (v.16). This unequivocal condemnation also includes those who, having been guilty of divorce, try to hide from its awful consequences but cannot because of the violence to wife and family that divorce inevitably brings. In a striking figure of speech the prophet says that those who divorce wear violence as a garment for all to see. Underscoring the solemnity of his warning, Malachi urges once more that his audience pay heed to their inner spirit (or conscience) and remain faithful to their wives (v.16b; cf. v.15).

NOTE

16 The MT suggests a third person masculine singular subject, "he hates divorce," for the expected first person common singular, "I hate divorce." However, the construction could well constitute an elliptical clause to be rendered, "For (the LORD) says, 'I hate divorce'" (= "he hates divorce").

V. RESISTANCE TO THE LORD (2:17–4:3[3:21])

A. Resistance through Self-Deceit (2:17–3:5)

1. The Problem (2:17)

> ¹⁷You have wearied the LORD with your words.
> "How have we wearied him?" you ask.
> By saying, "All who do evil are good in the eyes of the LORD, and he is pleased with them"
> or "Where is the God of justice?"

COMMENTARY

17 The last major section of Malachi deals with three areas in which the Jewish community opposes the plans and purposes God has for them. The first of these betrays an abysmal self-delusion that causes the community to assume that because evil often seems to go unpunished, those who practice evil must, in fact, be righteous; otherwise, it must be that God is unconcerned about human behavior—as with the righteous, so with the wicked. Taken together, these perspectives fall under the theological rubric of theodicy: How can a just God permit evil, and why do the righteous suffer?

2. The Promise (3:1–5)

> ¹"See, I will send my messenger, who will prepare the way before me. Then suddenly the Lord you are seeking will come to his temple; the messenger of the covenant, whom you desire, will come," says the LORD Almighty.
>
> ²But who can endure the day of his coming? Who can stand when he appears? For he will be like a refiner's fire or a launderer's soap. ³He will sit as a refiner and purifier of silver; he will purify the Levites and refine them like gold and silver. Then the LORD will have men who will bring offerings in righteousness, ⁴and the offerings of Judah and Jerusalem will be acceptable to the LORD, as in days gone by, as in former years.
>
> ⁵"So I will come near to you for judgment. I will be quick to testify against sorcerers, adulterers and perjurers, against those who defraud laborers of their wages, who oppress the widows and the fatherless, and deprive aliens of justice, but do not fear me," says the LORD Almighty.

COMMENTARY

1 The answer to the problem of theodicy lies in the future, in the eschatological day, when the Lord will break into history to make all things right. He will introduce that age by sending "my messenger" (Heb. *mal'ākî*), a prophet like Malachi himself. That messenger will in turn prepare the way (see Isa 40:3 for the same idiom) for another figure, the Lord, who will come to his temple.

Christian scholarship is agreed that the messenger is John the Baptist (Mt 11:10; Mk 1:2) and that the Lord of whom he is the forerunner is Jesus the Messiah (Mt 3:1–3; 21:12–17; Lk 2:41–51).

Here he is called *'ādôn* and not Yahweh because it is Yahweh of hosts who is speaking. The passage does not address the issue of his deity or humanity, for to do so would be out of keeping with pre-NT revelation and raise insoluble problems for Malachi's hearers.

The major interpretive question centers on identifying the "messenger of the covenant" referred to in v.1b. Most scholars see him as the *'ādôn* just mentioned, but the double occurrence of "messenger" in the passage argues more persuasively for the title's being attributed to the same person and thus not to the *ʾādôn*. From the NT's viewpoint, then, John the Baptist is the messenger of the covenant as well as the messenger who prepares the way for the *ʾādôn*.

This interpretation finds support in 4:5, where Elijah the prophet also comes just before the great day of the Lord to bring reconciliation and harmony to the Lord's chosen people. In clarifying this promise, Jesus said that John the Baptist was Elijah, "if you are willing to accept it" (Mt 11:14; cf. Mk 9:11–13; Lk 1:17).

2–4 When the messenger of the covenant comes, he will proclaim a purifying and refining message, one especially directed to and effective among "the Levites," that is, the priests (vv.2–4). Though the gospel narratives do not provide much direct evidence for this happening (but see, e.g.,

Nicodemus [Jn 3:1; 19:39]; and many priests who later believed [Ac 6:7]), there is no question that John's ministry paved the way for the life-changing message of the gospel and the establishment of the church (Ac 19:1–7).

5 A more distant eschatological note is sounded in v.5, where the third-person pronouns referring to the messenger and the *ʾādôn* revert to the first person of v.1, the subject of which is the Lord. He will come in the last days in judgment and will right the wrongs perpetrated by those who violate the Torah. The list of these sins is merely representative of the Ten Commandments and the subsidiary stipulations of the covenant that apply them to specific cases. The question was asked, "Where is the God of justice?" (2:17). It is now answered: "I will come near to you for judgment" (v.5).

B. Resistance through Selfishness (3:6–12)

1. The Problem (3:6–9)

⁶"I the LORD do not change. So you, O descendants of Jacob, are not destroyed. ⁷Ever since the time of your forefathers you have turned away from my decrees and have not kept them. Return to me, and I will return to you," says the LORD Almighty.

"But you ask, 'How are we to return?'

⁸"Will a man rob God? Yet you rob me.

"But you ask, 'How do we rob you?'

"In tithes and offerings. ⁹You are under a curse — the whole nation of you — because you are robbing me."

COMMENTARY

6 The second issue of communal disobedience raised by Malachi lies in the area of stewardship. God has blessed them, but they have failed to reciprocate by returning to him what the law requires. The Lord rebukes them with more than a little hint of impa-

tience, but it is impatience generously leavened by grace (v.6). Without that grace he would long since have destroyed them for their lack of compliance.

7–9 The history of Israel was a history of covenantal violation. Over and over the people turned aside (*sûr*) from its stipulations (*ḥuqqîm*). They continued to do so even after the exile, but as always God now invites them to return (*šwb*) to him. If they do so, he will return (*šwb*) to them.

But in smug self-righteousness they challenge the Lord to show them in what respect they have defected (v.7). From a host of possibilities, the Lord singles out one—they have robbed him by withholding their "tithes and offerings" (v.8). This defect may perhaps be seen in the selfishness of the people fifty years earlier, when they took pains to provide for themselves while the temple of the Lord lay in ruins. Those matters concerning which Haggai addressed them (Hag 1:4-6) must be addressed all over again by Malachi.

The tithe was an ancient custom, one practiced notably by both Abraham (Ge 14:20) and Jacob

(Ge 28:22) and then mandated in the Mosaic law as an expression of covenantal fealty (Lev 27:30-32; Nu 18:21-32; Dt 12:5-19; 14:22-28; 26:12); therefore tithing was not optional, though certain offerings such as thank offerings and votive offerings were. The particular offering in view here (the *tᵉrûmâ*, the "offering" mentioned in Nu 18:24-28) was at times required since it was given as part of the tithe to support the priesthood. Such is probably the case here as well.

In any event, the failure of the people to adhere to this obligation has already subjected them to "a curse" (Heb. *mᵉʾērâ*), a clear reference to the Deuteronomic judgment that would fall on violators of the covenant (Dt 28:15-19). Verses 11-12 describe the nature of the curse, one affecting the agricultural produce of the land.

2. The Promise (3:10-12)

> ¹⁰Bring the whole tithe into the storehouse, that there may be food in my house. Test me in this," says the Lᴏʀᴅ Almighty, "and see if I will not throw open the floodgates of heaven and pour out so much blessing that you will not have room enough for it. ¹¹I will prevent pests from devouring your crops, and the vines in your fields will not cast their fruit," says the Lᴏʀᴅ Almighty. ¹²"Then all the nations will call you blessed, for yours will be a delightful land," says the Lᴏʀᴅ Almighty.

COMMENTARY

10-12 The remedy for the curse and for the disobedience that it has prompted is to comply with the Lord's will with regard to the tithe. "Bring the tithe," the Lord commands, and all will be well (v.10). The place to which it must be brought is, of course, the temple, here described as "the storehouse." This way of speaking of the temple and its storage facilities maintains the agricultural imagery already associated with the curse and clearly

articulated in v.11. The people have begun to suffer from agricultural deprivation because the Lord has first been denied the foodstuffs that should have come to him. This complaint in no way suggests that sacrifices to God are construed as divine nourishment—a common pagan idea but only that denial of what belongs to God will result in denial of what his people need should they withhold their tithes.

The Lord challenges the people to put him to the test: Undertake the tithe as they ought to do, and God will open heaven's windows and shower them with blessings beyond their capacity to absorb. No doubt rainfall is in view but also more—indeed, everything that well-watered soil can produce will be theirs. Everything that has caused famine and failure of crops (personified as "the destroyer," Heb. ʾōkēl) will be overcome (v.11), and once more Israel will be a delightful land, one recognized as such by all nations (v.12).

C. Resistance through Self-Sufficiency (3:13–4:3 [3:21])

1. The Problem (3:13–15)

¹³"You have said harsh things against me," says the LORD.
"Yet you ask, 'What have we said against you?'
¹⁴"You have said, 'It is futile to serve God. What did we gain by carrying out his requirements and going about like mourners before the LORD Almighty? ¹⁵But now we call the arrogant blessed. Certainly the evildoers prosper, and even those who challenge God escape.'"

COMMENTARY

13–15 The final cause for the prophet's rebuke is the attitude of the community that it is futile to serve God because those who do so appear to be no better off than those who do not. They profess to have faithfully discharged their responsibilities before the Lord but to no productive end. Indeed, the arrogant and wicked among them not only go unscathed but are actually happy in their wrongdoing and are even promoted to greater positions of prominence and well-being. Despite all the ways in which the wicked have tested God, they escape his judgment and apparently even his displeasure (v.15).

The central issue here is one of theodicy. How can it be fair and just for God to ignore the prideful arrogance and independence of his creatures while maintaining his character as the absolutely holy and righteous One? The Jews addressed here are petulantly reminding the Lord of his inconsistency in this respect and for spite are labeling blessed those who ought to be cursed and subject to God's wrath.

2. The Promise (3:16–4:3 [3:21])

¹⁶Then those who feared the LORD talked with each other, and the LORD listened and heard. A scroll of remembrance was written in his presence concerning those who feared the LORD and honored his name.

¹⁷"They will be mine," says the LORD Almighty, "in the day when I make up my treasured possession. I will spare them, just as in compassion a man spares his son who serves him. ¹⁸And you will again see the distinction between the righteous and the wicked, between those who serve God and those who do not.

⁴:¹"Surely the day is coming; it will burn like a furnace. All the arrogant and every evildoer will be stubble, and that day that is coming will set them on fire," says the LORD Almighty. "Not a root or a branch will be left to them. ²But for you who revere my name, the sun of righteousness will rise with healing in its wings. And you will go out and leap like calves released from the stall. ³Then you will trample down the wicked; they will be ashes under the soles of your feet on the day when I do these things," says the LORD Almighty.

COMMENTARY

3:16 Though it must have seemed to the prophet that all of his words of warning and calls to repentance have been to no avail, such, happily, is not the case. Some people do fear — that is, come to understand God for who he really is, and in the light of that understanding confess and repent of their sins (v.16). As a result, their names are inscribed on the Lord's memorial scroll, a record of all those who truly know him and walk in covenantal fidelity before him.

The concept of such a collection of names originated long before Malachi's time (cf. Ex 32:32; Isa 4:3; Da 12:1) and reappears in the NT as "the book of life" (Rev 20:12–15). It should not be understood as a literal written record but as the infallible retention of the names of the redeemed of all the ages in the omniscient mind of the Lord.

3:17–18 At the last day, when wrath is about to be poured out on the earth, the Lord will recollect those whose names he knows and he will spare them from judgment (v.17). They will be clearly identified as his own people, his special possession (Heb. *segullâ*; cf. Ex 19:5; Dt 7:6; 14:2; 26:18). No longer will it be impossible to distinguish between the righteous and

the wicked, as the Lord's critics are presently charging, for then all hypocrisy will be stripped away and what has been interpreted as divine indifference will be seen as patient longsuffering (v.18).

4:1–3 [3:19–21] Lest there be any doubt as to the reality of approaching judgment, the prophet describes it in most graphic and dramatic terms. It is imminent (thus the participle), he says, and devastating. The very reference to it as "the day" is evocative of its nature, for the term is commonly associated with eschatological destruction (see Zep 1:8, 15–16; cf. Eze 36:33; 39:8, 11, 13; Zec 14:7; Mal 3:2, 17; 4:3[3:21]). Like a furnace, the fury of the Lord will consume to nothingness all who stubbornly resist his gracious overtures. Then it will be clear that he is not at all indifferent to sin or sinners.

By contrast, those who fear him (cf. 3:16) will experience rejuvenating renewal as the healing beams of the rising sun radiate about them (4:2[3:20]). This beautiful metaphor describes the reversal of the curse of sin and mortality by which the human race has been held in bondage. The sun should not be identified here as a messianic figure per se, but clearly what the sun accomplishes is associated with messianic expectations. Isaiah speaks of the servant as one by whose "wounds we are healed" (Isa 53:5), and Zechariah, the father of John the Baptist, prophesies of his son that he will prepare the way for one who like "the rising sun will come to us from heaven to shine on those living in darkness" (Lk 1:78−79).

The freedom he will bring is like that of a young calf that, having been constricted in a narrow pen,

is released to run and jump and play for sheer joy. At the same time, the redeemed will display their sovereignty as the vice-regents of the Lord by placing their feet on the backs of their conquered foes, the irredeemable enemies of "the LORD Almighty" (v.3). The day of the liberation of God's chosen ones will, ironically, be the day when, with him, they resign those who have resisted his grace to the everlasting bondage of death.

VI. RESTORATION THROUGH THE LORD (4:4−6 [3:22−24])

4"Remember the law of my servant Moses, the decrees and laws I gave him at Horeb for all Israel.

5"See, I will send you the prophet Elijah before that great and dreadful day of the LORD comes. 6He will turn the hearts of the fathers to their children, and the hearts of the children to their fathers; or else I will come and strike the land with a curse."

COMMENTARY

4−6 [3:22−24] The prophet climaxes his book with a solemn exhortation by the Lord to remember the Torah with all of its statutes and ordinances (v.4[3:22]). The technical language here is clearly Deuteronomic, an appeal to that statement of the covenant composed by Moses on the occasion of the covenant's renewal in the plains of Moab (cf. Dt 4:23; 8:11, 19). To remember is not simply to recollect but also to obey, to live according to what has been taught.

One reason for the exhortation is the imminent dawning of the "day of the LORD" (v.5). This term, as noted in connection with 4:1, speaks of a coming time in which God will radically break into

history and human affairs, bringing salvation and peace to those who know him but judgment and destruction to those who do not. It is in light of such a cataclysmic event that God's people should remember and carefully observe the requirements of their covenantal commitment.

The herald proclaiming that day will be Elijah the prophet, identified in the NT as John the Baptist (see comments on 3:1−6). But the description of the day as "great and dreadful" moves the application beyond John and the first advent of Christ to the eschatological day of the final resolution of history. This Elijah will be the instrument of God to effect reconciliation among God's people and thus to deliver them from the awesome destruction of Yahweh the warrior (4:6). The epithet is implicit in the use of the term *ḥērem* ("curse" in v.6; GK 3051), a word characteristic of so-called "holy war" or "Yahweh war" texts. The Lord will indeed come in judgment, but those who know him and who are ready to receive him will be delivered from that awesome and final work of divine retribution.

Though it is doubtful that the literal OT prophet Elijah is in mind here (but see Mt 17:1–13), any more than that the returned Elijah is literally John the Baptist, there is no reason to doubt that a literal anti-type of Elijah will one day appear. That antitype is perhaps one of the unnamed witnesses of Revelation 11, the one who has the power "to shut up the sky so that it will not rain" (Rev 11:6). The other figure, it seems, is Moses, who has power "to turn the waters into blood and to strike the earth with every kind of plague" (11:6). The Moses and Elijah of Malachi 4 will appear again in the last days and embody both Torah and the Prophets, the whole Word of God, as a final witness to God's sovereign glory.

We want to hear from you. Please send your comments about this book to us in care of zreview@zondervan.com. Thank you.

ZONDERVAN®

ZONDERVAN.com/
AUTHORTRACKER
follow your favorite authors